INSIDE

3D STUDIO
MAX
VOLUMES II AND III
LIMITED EDITION

DAVE ESPINOSA-AGUILAR
JOSHUA R. ANDERSEN
STEVE BURKE
RALPH FRANTZ
JASON GRAY
JASON GREENE
ERIC GREENLEIF
WILLIAM HARBISON
JEREMY HUBBELL
PAUL KAKERT
SANFORD KENNEDY
RANDY KREITZMAN
BOB LAMB

GEORGE MAESTRI
JESSE K. MIGUEL, AIA
PHILLIP MILLER
LARRY MINTON
MICHAEL J. NEIL
DAN O'LEARY
ERIC C. PETERSON
MICHAEL TODD PETERSON
KEN ALLEN ROBERTSON
JAROD RUFFO
JONATHAN SAWYER
ADAM SILVERTHORNE
LEE STEEL
ANDREW VERNON

SERIES EDITOR: PHILLIP MILLER

New Riders

New Riders Publishing, Indianapolis, Indiana

Contributions from KINETIX , a Division of Autodesk

Inside 3D Studio MAX Volumes II and III, Limited Edition

By dave espinosa-aguilar, Joshua R. Andersen, Steve Burke, Ralph Frantz, Jason Gray, Jason Greene, Eric Greenleif, William Harbison, Jeremy Hubbell, Paul Kakert, Sanford Kennedy, Randy Kreitzman, Bob Lamb, George Maestri, Jesse K. Miguel, AIA, Phillip Miller, Larry Minton, Michael J. Neil, Dan O'Leary, Eric C. Peterson, Michael Todd Peterson, Ken Allen Robertson, Jarod Ruffo, Jonathan Sawyer, Adam Silverthorne, Lee Steel, Andrew Vernon

Published by:
New Riders Publishing
201 West 103rd Street
Indianapolis, IN 46290 USA

Printed in the United States of America 1 2 3 4 5 6 7 8 9 0

Library of Congress Cataloging-in-Publication Data

```
Inside 3D Studio MAX / Steve D. Elliott … [et al.].
       p.   cm.
   Includes index.
   ISBN 1-56205-699-9 (v. 3)
   1. Computer animation. 2. 3D Studio.
   1960-
   TR897.7.I56    1997                       96-
38753
       006.6-dc20                            CIP
```

Warning and Disclaimer

This book is designed to provide information about 3D Studio MAX. Every effort has been made to make this book as complete and as accurate as possible, but no warranty or fitness is implied.

The information is provided on an "as is" basis. The authors and New Riders Publishing shall have neither liability nor responsibility to any person or entity with respect to any loss or damages arising from the information contained in this book or from the use of the discs or programs that may accompany it.

Associate Publisher	David Dwyer
Marketing Manager	Mary Foote
Managing Editor	Carla Hall
Director of Development	Kezia Endsley

Product Director
Alicia Buckley

Development Editors
Laura Frey
Ed Metzler

Acquisitions Editor
Dustin Sullivan

Senior Editors
Sarah Kearns
Suzanne Snyder

Project Editors
Amy Bezek
Gina Brown
Gail S. Burlakoff
Matt Litten
Cliff Shubs
Karen Walsh

Copy Editors
Keith Cline, Wendy Garrison, Cricket Harrison, Michelle Warren, Molly Warnes

Technical Editors
Mark Gerhard, Larry Minton

Software Specialist
Steve Flatt

Assistant Marketing Manager
Gretchen Schlesinger

Acquisitions Coordinator
Stacey Beheler

Administrative Coordinator
Karen Opal

Manufacturing Coordinator
Brook Farling

Cover Designer
Karen Ruggles

Cover Production
Aren Howell

Book Designer
Anne Jones

Director of Production
Larry Klein

Production Team Supervisors
Laurie Casey
Joe Millay

Graphics Image Specialists
Wil Cruz, Brad Dixon, Tammy Graham

Production Analysts
Dan Harris, Erich J. Richter

Production Team
Kim Cofer, Rowena Rappaport, Elizabeth San Miguel, Scott Tullis

Indexer
Chris Barrick

About the Authors

dave espinosa-aguilar is a project manager, programmer, and animator for Toxic Frog Multimedia in Reno, Nevada. A graduate in electrical engineering and physics of Gonzaga University, dave has been training architects and engineers for 12 years on 3D modeling and visualization. dave served as President of the Autodesk User Group International in 1996, and has been a regular faculty member of AutoCAD, Animator Pro, Animator Studio, and 3D Studio DOS and MAX courses offered at Autodesk University, A/E/C Systems, MechanCAD, and other Multimedia/CAD conferences. In his spare time, dave also does product support for Autodesk on CompuServe's AMMEDIA, KINETIX, and ACAD forums.

Joshua R. Andersen is currently a 3D artist and animator at GlyphX, Inc. His previous experience in this field includes work as a graphics artist for a multimedia firm, and as a 3D modeler at Viewpoint Datalabs, Intl. He has used 3D Studio MAX since its early beta versions, and has experience with many other high-end 3D animation and modeling packages on Silicon Graphics workstations as well as on PCs.

Steve Burke is a graduate of the Business Entrepreneurship program at the University of Southern California. In addition to running his own business, Steve has worked as an artist in the game industry for six years. He is currently the Art Director at Strategic Simulations, Inc., makers of strategy, fantasy, and war games. Steve has a beautiful wife, a baby girl, a wacky brother, and a passion for creating happy, friendly artwork with a smattering of sarcasm.

Ralph Frantz is a successful freelance animator working out of Southern California. He keeps busy by working on a wide variety of 3D animation projects, including work on the film *Virtuosity*, as well as work for broadcast network television and local TV commercials. He has worked on game projects, commercial 3D screen savers, industrial videos, corporate presentations, and technical animation for a CD-ROM–based training program for Nissan sales and service personnel. He spent Siggraph 96 in the Kinetix plug-in partners booth giving demos of the softbody dynamics system plug-in HyperMatter by Second Nature Industries. He helps out with MAX demos at the local 3D users groups and is often called upon to supplement in-house animators at the local animation houses.

Jason Gray is a computer systems engineer who has used 3D Studio MAX since its beginning. He co-owns a CGA company called Genesis Creations which has done several commercial and private projects. His areas of expertise include composition, landscape generation, and animation. He currently resides in Hawaii and enjoys "fun in the sun" with his children. He also sits on the high council of Graphixzexpress, a professional 3D club. He can be reached at soft3d@gte.net.

Jason Greene is a multimedia animator and designer living in Boulder, CO. When he's not figuring out an artistic way to explain Internet technology or making corporate logos explode (at the request of clients), Jason heads to the hills to pursue mountain biking, snowboarding, and napping.

Eric Greenlief is co-owner of Image Production Company, of Salt Lake City, Utah, which specializes in architectural walk-throughs and product presentations using 3D Studio and 3D Studio MAX. Eric teaches and develops curriculum for Computer-Aided Industrial Design at ITT Technical Institute in Murray, UT. Other courses he has taught since 1992 include AutoCAD Modeling and AutoCAD Customization. He has a degree in CAD and a bachelor's degree in Industrial Design. Eric has been using 3D Studio since Release 1 and is an active participant in the 3D Studio mailing list on the Internet. He also has close ties with the film industry in Salt Lake City and Los Angeles.

William Harbison has been able to draw for as long as he can remember, but it wasn't until 1982 that he was first introduced to a computer. He prepared for his graphics career by plotting pictures on graph paper and entering the coordinates into his Sinclair ZX Spectrum 16K computer. In 1988, after some years of practice, he was offered a job by computer games developer Ocean Software on the strength of a few demonstration bitmaps that he had sent on an audio cassette. In his seven years there, he developed game for almost every popular game system on the market, most of which were film tie-ins—including "Jurassic Park" on the PC. He had been using 3D Studio at this point for about a year, but it wasn't until his last project, "Pitball" on the Sony Playstation, that he was given the chance to use it extensively in creating Full Motion Video for some of the game's many characters. He is currently working on a PC title for Ingames Interactive UK.

Jeremy Hubbell is a senior technical instructor for Kinetix. His primary responsibilities range from developing multimedia course curriculum to worldwide training and product development. His current project is the development of all training for 3D Studio MAX and the implementation of that training within the U.S., Canada, and Latin America. Since joining Autodesk in 1994, Jeremy has been involved in many projects—from the complete re-engineering of Kinetix training materials and curriculum to the development and publishing of all Autodesk training materials on an interactive CD.

Paul Kakert is founder and president of Forensic Media, an Iowa based corporation that specializes in producing animations for use in the courtroom. He has used 3D Studio since Release 1, and has published articles regarding the use of 3D Studio, MAX, and numerous plug-ins for *3D Artist* magazine. He has developed state bar-accredited seminars on forensic animation for attorneys, investigators, and reconstructionists. His animations have been used by attorneys throughout the U.S. and featured in TV specials and training videos for accident investigators and animators. He can be reached at 319-391-8289 or by e-mail at pk@forensicmedia.com.

Sanford Kennedy left a career as a Design Engineer working on guided missiles and communication satellites in the aerospace industry to work in special effects after he saw *Star Wars*. He met Special Effects Director John Dykstra, winner of the Academy Award for the visual effects on *Star Wars* and was hired to design and build computer motion controlled camera systems. He later established Sanford Kennedy Design in Los Angeles and over the next 20 years expanded into movie props, special makeup effects, and mechanical effects for commercials. He has worked on 48 motion pictures, ranging from *The Empire Strikes Back* to *Batman* and *Starship Troopers*. He began writing about computer graphics in 1988, and when 3D Studio came out, he added computer animation to his activities. He now works full time as an animator, writer, multimedia content producer, and beta tester. Sanford has three bachelors degrees in the fields of Fine Art, History, and Industrial Technology. Recently, he taught 3D Studio classes at the American Film Institute in Hollywood.

Randy Kreitzman is employed with Kinetix as a Quality Engineering Analyst, working exclusively with 3D Studio MAX. He has been animating since 1991, starting out with 3DS Release 1, working his way through Alias/Wavefront, and finally coming back to Kinetix to work with MAX. Randy lives in Northern California's Sonoma County with his loving partner, three sled dogs, and two horses. He wants to thank Kimberlie and the girls for their neverending inspiration and support, and the Yost Group for making some of the best software on the planet.

Bob Lamm is Manager at CYNC Corp., a video/multimedia equipment dealership that also sells Kinetix products. He graduated from MIT in 1978 and spent most of his career in facility design. He can be reached by phone at (617) 277-4317, or by e-mail at lamm@cync.com.

George Maestri is a Los Angeles-based writer and animator with experience in both traditional and computer animation. He has written for a number of animated shows, including the Cable Ace nominated series *Rocko's Modern Life*. George has developed original shows for several major networks, including Nickelodeon, FOX, ABC, Carlton UK, and Comedy Central. He also has written numerous articles on computer animation for magazines such as *Digital Video*, *Computer Graphics World*, *Publish*, *New Media*, and *Animation Magazine*. As a visual artist, he has animated and directed both traditional and computer animation for a number of major studios, including Nickelodeon, Film Roman, and MGM. George is the author of the best-selling *Digital Character Animation*, also from New Riders Publishing.

Jesse K. Miguel, AIA, is the 3D Design Visualization Manager for HNTB Corporation, an architectural/engineering/planning firm at their Kansas City, Missouri headquarters, where he will be directing the development of 3D computer graphics and animation at the HNTB Technology Group in their A/E/P Design Technology division. He has created computer animation for use in video and multimedia presentation used for public hearing, client presentations, and HNTB's web site. He also provides development support for 3D Computer Design for over 40 HNTB design offices throughout the country.

Mr. Miguel is a registered architect in Missouri and Massachusetts, and is a member of the American Institute of Architecture, the National Council of the Architectural Registration Boards, the Kansas City/AIA, the Kansas City 3D Studio User's Group, and the North American Autodesk User's Group. He has coauthored *3D Studio Architectural Rendering* by New Riders Publishing. His 3D computer models were featured in *Computer Graphics World* and *Computer Aided Engineering*. He holds advanced degrees in architecture from Washington University in St. Louis, and the Massachusetts Institute of Technology (M.I.T.) in Cambridge, Massachusetts.

Phillip Miller is the Product Manager for 3D Studio MAX at Kinetix. He is responsible for coordinating support for 3D Studio MAX from the Kinetix side, while working closely with the Yost Group to ensure that the best possible tool is created for the artists who use it. He previously managed Autodesk Multimedia's Developer Relations Program, and has also led Autodesk's 3D Studio training program. Phillip is a registered architect who, before joining Autodesk, was a project architect in the Midwest. He earned a Masters degree in architecture from the University of Illinois.

Phillip is the coauthor of Inside 3D Studio Release 3, Inside 3D Studio Release 4, and a contributor to 3D Studio Special Effects and Inside 3D Studio MAX Volumes I and II, all published by New Riders.

Larry Minton is the owner of Avguard Animations near Columbus, OH. He has been a 3D Studio hobbyist since 1991, but recently decided to turn his hobby into his career. Larry was a 3D Studio MAX beta tester, as well as the technical editor of New Riders' *3D Studio MAX Fundamentals*. Larry is an active participant in CompuServe's Kinetix and AMMEDIA forums. Larry is a contributor to *Inside 3D Studio MAX Volume I, II, and III*.

Michael J. Neil earned a degree in Political Science from Syracuse University. As Marketing Director at Mike Rosen & Associates, P.C., a national award-winning architecture, land planning, landscape architecture, and virtual reality development firm serving the commercial, industrial, and residential real estate development industries, he has garnered international media attention for the firm's work using virtual reality technology, and manages the firm's computer graphics and virtual reality development projects. Michael lives in Philadelphia, is active in the community, and sits on the boards of several philanthropic organizations.

Dan O'Leary is vice president of n-Space, Inc., of Orlando, FL, where he helps oversee product and concept development. He co-founded n-Space in November 1994 as a premiere developer of games for advanced console and PC platforms. Danny was a beta tester for 3D Studio MAX and remains an active member in CompuServe's Kinetix forum. He holds a bachelor's degree in Mechanical Engineering from Auburn University.

Eric C. Peterson is the owner of Sisyphus Graphics, which provides commercial, technical, and forensic animation contracting services. As Technical Director, Sisyphus Software, he developed algorithms for 3D Studio and 3D Studio MAX plug-ins. Eric concentrates on the algorithmic and interface design aspect, and his wife Audrey, a Software Engineer, is responsible for code design and construction. As a team, the two worked as consultants to Yost Group, assisting in the development of MAX 2.

Michael Todd Peterson is the owner of MTP graphics, a rendering and animation firm that specializes in architectural visualization and multimedia.

In addition to this book, Mr. Peterson has authored or coauthored *Inside AutoCAD for DOS, 3D Studio for Beginners, AutoCAD in 3D*, and *3D Studio MAX Fundamentals*.

Ken Allen Robertson holds an M.F.A. in acting and directing from the National Theatre Conservatory and has appeared in numerous stage and film productions. Since becoming involved with computer graphics, he has created 3D models and animations for Mattel and the 1996 Summer Olympics. For the past two years Ken has been working on next-generation real-time 3D game titles for PC and set-top gaming platforms, and prototype models and animations for interactive 3D Internet chat environments. He was a contributing author to *3D Studio Hollywood and Gaming Effects*. Ken teaches 3D Studio, MAX, and CGI special effects at the Computer Arts Institute in San Francisco, CA. He can be reached at aceallen@hooked.net.

Jonathan Sawyer earned a B.A. in architecture from Yale University and a Masters of Industrial Design from Pratt Institute, Brooklyn, NY. Soon after entering the building business, Sawyer started a small combined design and build firm, doing residential and light commercial projects. His continued work in architecture led to his current focus: the use of computers for imaging and presentation. A native Philadelphian, he lives there with his wife, Elizabeth.

Adam Silverthorne studied Electronic Visualization in the Department of Architecture at UC Berkeley. His education included 2D Drafting CAD/CAM, 3D Modeling, and Lighting Techniques. Adam has also studied traditional animation and sculpting, and he holds a degree in Twentieth Century Literature, with a focus on Narrative Fiction. Currently, Adam works in television, where he helps coordinate the production of an animated children's show. Adam also created and maintains the San Francisco 3D Studio MAX User's Group Web Page, and helps coordinate monthly meetings.

Lee Steel spends most of his time using 3D to do prototype visualization for the electro-mechanical design industry and site visualization for civil engineering firms in the Northeast. Since 3D Studio Release 1, he has spent much of his free time beta-testing IPAS routines for 3DS DOS and newer plug-ins for 3DS MAX. This activity led to a regular column in the now extinct *Planet Studio* magazine, and articles for *3D Design* and *3D Artist* magazines. Lee co-founded 3D Artists & Animators, a nationwide chain of 3D users groups that cater primarily to Kinetix multimedia product users but also diversify into other packages used with 3DS. He can be reached at betalab@megahits.com.

Andrew Vernon is a 3D artist and writer living in the Sierra Nevada foothills of California. He operates Moving Figure Animation & Multimedia in Oregon House. Andrew worked in Kinetix Technical Publications and was the online Help System writer for both 3D Studio MAX and Character Studio. He frequently writes articles on 3D graphics, animation, and multimedia for magazines such as *3D Design*. For information about Moving Figure, see http://www.jps.net/avernon.

Trademark Acknowledgments

All terms mentioned in this book that are known to be trademarks or service marks have been appropriately capitalized. New Riders Publishing cannot attest to the accuracy of this information. Use of a term in this book should not be regarded as affecting the validity of any trademark or service mark.

Acknowledgments

New Riders would like to thank everyone who gave up a little piece of his or her life for this book. Know that your efforts are sincerely appreciated.

Contents at a Glance

Table of Contents

Introduction

Inside 3D Studio MAX Volumes II and III, Limited Edition *combines* Volume II: Advanced Modeling and Materials *and* Volume III: Animation *into one convenient binding. It also includes five bonus chapters that aren't included in either of the previous volumes of* Inside 3D Studio MAX.

Organization of the Book

Inside 3D Studio MAX Volumes II and III, Limited Edition is organized into three major sections, with partitions in each section. These sections are as follows:

- ■ ***Inside 3D Studio MAX Volume II: Advanced Modeling and Materials***—A complete tutorial and reference on materials and modeling. It includes coverage of the many types of modeling done in the industry, from modeling for real-time games to modeling for engineering visualization. Also included is expert coverage of MAX's powerful Material Editor. Learn how to use the Material Editor alone and with plug-ins to make natural, man-made, special effects and animated materials.

- ■ ***Inside 3D Studio MAX Volume III: Animation***—A complete tutorial and reference on animation. It includes coverage of animation techniques used in the industry, from animating with transforms to character animation to animating the environment. Also included is expert coverage of MAX's powerful Video Post module. Learn how to use the Video Post module for compositing and editing animations as well as for creating special effects.

- ■ **Five Bonus Chapters**—Coverage on using Photoshop with MAX, troubleshooting MAX under Windows NT, landscape composition, architectural rendering, and using Amapi.

Volume II: Advanced Modeling and Materials

The first section of the *Limited Edition* is comprised of the complete text of *Volume II: Advanced Modeling and Materials*. This text is broken into the following four parts:

Part I is a survey of the modeling and mapping techniques available, and how you can make use of multiple techniques to accomplish your task. Later in this book, you will get plenty of specific examples and practice. Real-world images are dissected and discussed in terms of their structure and textures.

Part II covers advanced modeling techniques in MAX. The modeling tools are not explained; rather, the techniques that are best served by MAX's modeling tools and plug-ins are described. Advanced modeling tutorials take you through the steps needed to create low-polygon count models for the web, precise and highly defined models for engineering visualization, accurate models for architecture, and efficient, believable models for real-time games.

Part III takes you through the unique world of character modeling. From creating a character to modeling it with MAX tools and plug-ins, this section teaches the best methods of modeling for a variety of situations.

Part IV explores the world of MAX's Material Editor. These chapters cover the making and management of your material library. With just a few steps and the expert advice found in these chapters, you can have your own unique library of natural, man-made, special effect, and animated materials.

Volume III: Animation

The second section of the *Limited Edition* is comprised of the complete text of *Volume III: Animation*. This text is broken into the following five parts.

Part V is an overview of the computer animation industry. Learn the story behind the creation of MAX. Hear what major production houses have to say about MAX's power. Also learn how you can more effectively use MAX in your own productions.

Part VI covers animation techniques in MAX. The tools are not explained; rather the techniques that are best served by MAX's tools and plug-ins are described. Animation tutorials take you through the steps needed to animate with transforms, controllers, expressions, and multiple modifiers. Also covered is accurate animation for forensics.

Part VII takes you through the unique world of character animation. From creating a character to animating it with MAX tools and plug-ins, this section teaches the best methods of animating for a variety of situations.

Part VIII explores animating the environment. These chapters cover how to animate cameras, lights, and atmospheres to get just the feel you are looking for in your animations. Also covered is how to animate with particles and space warps to generate snow, confetti, a windtunnel effect, and more. The expert advice doesn't stop there—Hypermatter is also covered in this section.

Part IX covers the powerful Video Post module within MAX. This section extends your knowledge of Video Post by teaching you how to create special effects and how to compose and edit your animations within Video Post.

The Bonus CD chapters include information on how to market yourself and your animations. It tells the secrets of how to network, create a demo reel, and get your animations noticed! Also covered in the bonus CD chapters is animation rendering information.

The Five Bonus Chapters

Part X, the five bonus chapters, don't cover one theme such as animation or modeling. They are filled with additional techniques for working with other products such as Photoshop and Amapi, how to create realistic landscapes, and how to troubleshoot MAX on your NT system. Three bonus chapters are printed in this book, and two bonus chapters are on the accompanying CD.

Appendices

The accompanying CD-ROM contains extra information on integrating 3D Studio MAX with AutoCAD, how to market yourself and your animations—telling the secrets of how to network, create a demo reel, and get your animations noticed! Also covered in the CD chapters is animation rendering information.

How to Read the Exercises

Unlike most tutorials that you read, the exercises in this book do not rigidly dictate every step you perform to achieve the desired result. These exercises are designed to be flexible and to work with a wide range of situations. The benefits you receive from this approach include the following:

- A better understanding of the concepts because you must think through the example rather than blindly follow the minutiae of many steps

- A stronger ability to apply the examples to your own work

Most exercises begin with some explanatory text, as shown in the following sample exercise. The text tells you what the exercise should accomplish and sets the context for the exercise.

SAMPLE EXERCISE FORMAT

You may encounter text such as this at the beginning of or in the middle of an exercise when one or more actions require an extended explanation.

1. Numbered steps identify your actions to complete the exercise.

Indented text adds extra explanation about the previous step when it is needed.

The word *choose* in an example always indicates a menu selection. If the selection involves a pull-down menu, you will be told explicitly where to find the menu item. If the selection is from another part of the user interface, you will be told which component to click and the location of the interface. Setting the Hemisphere option for a Sphere object, for example, requires clicking the Hemisphere check box in the Creation Parameters rollout (you would have been told previously whether you were accessing the rollout from the Create panel or the Modify panel). The word *select* always refers to selecting one or more objects, elements, faces, or vertices. Select never refers to menus or other user interface components.

Because this book is designed for people who already have some experience with 3DS MAX, some exercise steps are implied rather than explicitly stated. You may, for example, find yourself instructed to "Create a smooth, 20-segment Sphere with a radius of 100 units," rather than reading all the steps required to create the sphere.

Exercises and the CD-ROM

Most of the examples and exercises use files that are either included on the accompanying CD-ROM or shipped with 3D Studio, or they show you how to create the necessary geometry. Example files are located on the accompanying CD-ROM. Instructions on how to use the CD-ROM files or how to install them on your hard drive are described in the following section.

Using the Inside 3D Studio MAX Limited Edition CD-ROM

Inside 3D Studio MAX Limited Edition comes with a CD-ROM packed with many megabytes of plug-ins, scenes, maps, and other sample software. The files can be used directly from the CD-ROM, so "installing" them is not necessary. You may want to copy files from the CD-ROM to your hard drive or another storage device. In that case, you can use the install routines found with some of the sample programs or copy the files directly to a directory on your hard disk.

Not all plug-ins used in this book were available to be put on the CD. Please contact the vendors of these plug-ins for more information.

Installing the Exercise Files

All exercise files not included with 3D Studio MAX are contained in a single subdirectory on the accompanying CD-ROM. You can access these files directly from the CD-ROM when you execute the examples, or you can create a directory called \I3DSMAX on your hard drive and copy the files there. Some of the example files require maps from the CD-ROM that ships with 3D Studio MAX. You will need to copy these files to a subdirectory that is referenced in the 3DS MAX Map-Paths parameter.

3D Studio MAX automatically looks for map files in the directory from which a scene file was loaded. If you copy the example files to your hard drive, make sure you keep the mesh files and map files together or at least put the map files in a directory where 3D Studio can find them at rendering time.

A number of sample scenes, animation files, and maps are provided on the CD for your use. These are licensed free for your use. You cannot, however, resell or otherwise distribute the files.

Registering Shareware

Most of the sample programs on the CD-ROM are either demonstration programs or shareware programs. Shareware programs are fully functioning products that you can try prior to purchasing—they are not free. If you find a shareware program useful, you must pay a registration fee to the program's author. Each shareware program provides information about how to contact the author and register the program.

Using CompuServe and the Web

The CompuServe Information Service is an online, interactive network that you can access with a modem and special access software. The most important feature of this service (at least as far as this book is concerned) is the KINETIX forum.

The KINETIX forum is an area of CompuServe that is maintained by Kinetix for the direct support of 3D Studio MAX and other Kinetix software. Hundreds of people from all over the world visit this forum daily to share ideas, ask and answer questions, and generally promote the use of 3D Studio MAX. If you ask a question on the forum, you are as likely to receive an answer from one of the original programmers as you are to receive an answer from any number of other 3D Studio MAX artists. Every question, from the most basic to the most mind-bending puzzler, receives the same quick and courteous treatment.

Kinetix also maintains a site on the World Wide Web where you can get the latest information about 3DS MAX, future software releases, and plug-in development. You can also send questions and feedback directly to Kinetix and download software. The Kinetix web site is www.ktx.com.

New Riders Publishing

The staff of New Riders Publishing is committed to bringing you the very best in computer reference material. Each New Riders book is the result of months of work by authors and staff who research and refine the information contained within its covers.

As part of this commitment to you, New Riders invites your input. Please let us know if you enjoy this book, if you have trouble with the information and examples presented, or if you have a suggestion for the next edition.

Please note, however: New Riders staff cannot serve as a technical resource for 3D Studio MAX or for questions about software- or hardware-related problems. Please refer to the documentation that accompanies your software or to the applications' Help systems.

If you have a question or comment about any New Riders book, you can contact New Riders Publishing in several ways. We will respond to as many readers as we can. Your name, address, or phone number will never become part of a mailing list or be used for any purpose other than to help us continue to bring you the best books possible.

You can write us at the following address:

New Riders Publishing
Attn: Alicia Buckley
201 W. 103rd Street
Indianapolis, IN 46290

If you prefer, you can fax New Riders Publishing at:

317-817-7448

You can also send electronic mail to New Riders at the following Internet address:

abuckley@newriders.mcp.com

New Riders Publishing is an imprint of Macmillan Computer Publishing. To obtain a catalog or information, or to purchase any Macmillan Computer Publishing book, call 800-428-5331 or visit our web site at http://www.mcp.com.

Thank you for selecting *Inside 3D Studio MAX Volumes II and III, Limited Edition*!

INSIDE

3D STUDIO

MAX

VOLUME II:
ADVANCED MODELING AND MATERIALS

Cover art by Steve Burke

DAVE ESPINOSA-AGUILAR

JOSHUA R. ANDERSEN

STEVE BURKE

PHILLIP MILLER

MICHAEL J. NEIL

ERIC C. PETERSON

MICHAEL TODD PETERSON

KEN ALLEN ROBERTSON

JONATHAN SAWYER

LEE STEEL

ANDREW VERNON

SERIES EDITOR:
PHILLIP MILLER

Part I

GETTING STARTED

IMAGE TAKEN BY TODD PETERSON

Chapter 1

by Todd Peterson

THE WORLD OF MODELING AND MATERIAL TECHNIQUES

Modeling and materials are two of the most difficult and challenging aspects of 3D work. The subject matter that you are trying to model will ultimately determine how difficult it will be to create the model. It is easier to model a house than an elephant, for example, but the materials can be more complex in the house than on the elephant.

To make matters even more complicated, when you model an object in 3D Studio MAX, you must choose from many different methods and approaches to modeling that object. Each method produces slightly different results and takes different amounts of time and effort to complete. You could model the elephant, for example, by using splines and lofts—but using splines is a slow and overly difficult task. Alternatively, you could model the elephant by using patch surfaces with modifiers. This method should be a little more effective and a little quicker. And in yet another method, you could use plug-ins (add-on software) for 3D Studio MAX and model the elephant quickly and efficiently by using metaballs or NURBS (non-uniform rational B-splines).

This chapter provides an overview of some of the methods you can use to model objects and create materials for them. The chapter surveys some of the techniques available and looks at how you can use multiple techniques to accomplish your task. Plenty of specific examples and practice exercises appear later in this book. This chapter, though, focuses on the following topics:

- The modeling process
- Materials in the modeling process
- Architectural modeling
- Biped modeling
- Complex character modeling
- Technical modeling
- Industrial modeling
- Plug-in overview
- Modeling plug-ins
- Material plug-ins

The Modeling Process

As a process, modeling has three main stages: conceptual sketching, rough models, and modeling techniques. Each stage helps you to define exactly how the object you are trying to model will look in the scene. The definitions that result from these different stages must be considered relative to, and in the context of, the type of use the object will have in the scene. A model of a space ship, for example, can be rather simplistic if it has good materials, whereas a model of a house or convention center needs a lot more detail in the modeling process.

The modeling process demands a full range of your skills and abilities. In the conceptual sketch stage, for example, your traditional art skills are at the forefront. In the rough model stage, however, your skills as a sculptor feature more prominently. Only in the modeling techniques stage do you use your computer skills to actually create the model.

At this point, you may be asking yourself why the first two stages of the process are necessary. The conceptual sketch and rough model stages are necessary to help you visualize the object that you are going to draw and create in MAX. Of course, not all stages are necessary for every type of object you might create. Modeling a house may require a few quick conceptual sketches, for example, but you rarely need to build a model of the house.

The following sections examine the specific stages of the modeling process in more detail.

Conceptual Sketches

Conceptual sketches are generally the first attempts to put ideas into some sort of visual form. Sketches can range from individual images drawn in pen and ink, pencil, or paint, to full-blown storyboards that illustrate modeling and animation intent. By sketching your model first, you can begin to refine the design of the object well before you actually begin modeling it. The more you know about how to build the model before you actually begin, the faster and more accurately you will be able to build the model.

Conceptual sketches are a traditional medium used time and time again to help convince clients, bosses, and others that a design vision merits the effort, before you invest a great deal of time and money in creating the CGI model.

Conceptual sketches can be created in a wide variety of formats or media. You can create conceptual sketches as pencil on paper, ink and film, paint and canvas, or even pen and napkin. Sketches also do not have to be perfect. You are trying to convey a general idea of what the object will look like, how it will move, and so on. This can be expressed through a series of quick sketches. If you need more detail, you may consider sketching a blow up of the area where you feel you may need more detail.

The conceptual sketching stage is the time to try different versions of the same object. You can quickly and easily sketch small or large changes and see the result well before you begin to model in MAX. The amount of sketching and the detail are solely up to you. Conceptual sketches enable you to explore difficult modeling and material tasks such as muscles, texture, hair, and so forth. Sketches help you to decide how much detail you need in your CGI model and how to create the model more efficiently by adding only the necessary detail. Remember, you always want to create the model with as little detail as possible. Sketching can help you decide where you can lose detail and where you cannot.

After you have finally refined your vision to your personal comfort and standards, you can move on to the next stage of the modeling process.

Rough Models

Rough models can be created in two ways: as physical models or as CGI models. Physical models are small, fairly detailed models of the object made out of a material such as clay or papier-maché. CGI models, on the other hand, are rough, low-detail, computer-generated models. Most of the time, CGI models suffice. But when a model is exceptionally complex (a dragon or a dinosaur, for example), a physical model yields more accurate results.

Physical models are made of clay or other pliable materials and are intended to be small-scale 3D representations of an object. When Draco from *Dragonheart* or the T-Rex from *Jurassic Park* were being designed, for example, several small models of each were built. These models were then used as the basis for creating the final CGI model.

For many projects, you do not need to create even a rough model. Architectural models, for example, are generally simple enough to never really need a rough model. When you create a character that you will eventually animate, however, rough models become a necessity. They not only give you a true sense of 3D scale that helps you create your model, they also give you a true representation of the actual creature.

From the CGI standpoint, building rough models is an excellent method for further refining your model. Essentially, the modeling process is one of refinement. You start with a rough model and refine any portion of that model until you have the final model you want. Best of all, you can save each revision and return to it at any time to start over or take a different approach.

Modeling Techniques

After you decide what your object will look like, you can begin the modeling process. You can use many different approaches and methods to create your model. The method you choose depends not only on how you like to model but ultimately on what you are modeling. In 3D Studio MAX, you can use any of the built-in modeling tools or a wide variety of plug-ins or other compatible software. All these options present several techniques that are quick and easy to use. These techniques include, but are not limited to, the following:

- Mesh modeling

- Spline modeling

- Patch modeling

- Solid modeling

- NURBS modeling

- Metaball modeling

Mesh Modeling

The objects used in mesh modeling comprise only 3D faces or mesh triangles. By joining many small 3D faces, you can quickly and easily create a mesh surface. Generally, mesh modeling is the most popular method. Even packages that enable you to model in a different technique eventually convert their surfaces to meshes for rendering.

In 3D Studio MAX, when you create a box, sphere, cone, or other primitive, you are creating a Mesh object. This object can then be modified into a wide variety of other, more complex objects. Mesh modeling is great for simple objects such as spheres, walls, and doors. Figure 1.1 shows two examples of mesh models.

FIGURE 1.1
Two examples of mesh models.

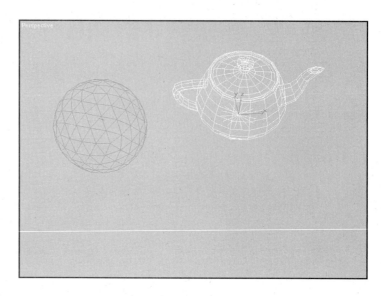

Spline Modeling

Spline modeling takes a slightly different approach to creating the object, but still produces a mesh model. A *spline* is a 3D line, arc, or circle. Spline modeling takes a spline, called a *shape*, and extrudes or lofts the shape along another spline, called the *path*. The shape can be modified as it travels along the path. Spline modeling makes creating objects such as glass bottles, wine glasses, and even bananas very easy. Spline modeling can be used also to create objects such as the walls in a house. Figure 1.2 shows an example of a spline model.

FIGURE 1.2
A spline model.

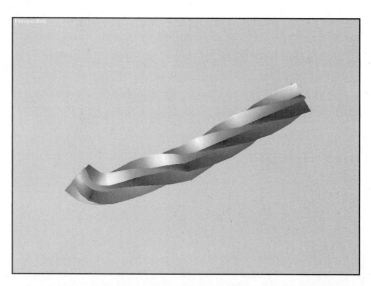

Patch Modeling

Patch modeling makes use of Bézier patches. When you work with patch modeling, you create a flat surface controlled by a lattice, or *grid*, of points. By modifying the position of the lattice points, you can create gentle curves in the surfaces. You can also create patches between splines by creating the flat surface and then adjusting the vertices of the patch to match the splines. You can use patches to quickly and easily model complex surfaces such as faces or bodies. Figure 1.3 shows an example of a patch model.

FIGURE 1.3

A patch model.

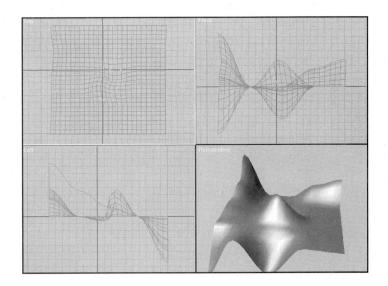

Solid Modeling

The solid modeling method also relies on mesh modeling. Unlike patch modeling, however, solid modeling creates objects by using Boolean logic to combine two or more objects. (You can subtract the volume of one object from the volume of another, for example.) Solid modeling can be used to create objects such as windows in a wall or a drill hole in a piece of wood (see fig. 1.4).

Mesh, spline, patch, and solid modeling can be implemented directly inside 3D Studio MAX. The next two methods, which require third-party plug-ins, are presented just to provide an example of how powerful third-party applications can be.

FIGURE 1.4
A solid model.

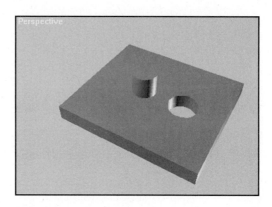

NURBS Modeling

Non-uniform rational B-spline (NURBS) modeling is similar to spline modeling but makes use of advanced mathematics to control the surfaces. Hence, NURBS surfaces are extremely accurate and precise. NURBS programs have the capability not only to create primitives and complex extruded surfaces, but also to create a blended surface between two other surfaces. This requires some work in other modeling systems. To give you an idea of how powerful NURBS modeling is, imagine trying to draw a spline directly on the curved surface of a sphere. You cannot do this in MAX, but you can with a NURBS program.

As a matter of fact, you can thank NURBS for all the slick aerodynamic cars on the road today. Car designers began using NURBS in the late '80s because the accurate surfaces could be quickly machined and created. NURBS tools are extremely powerful for modeling complex curved surfaces such as cars, faces, shoes, dinosaurs, and so on. To use NURBS with MAX, you need a third-party program such as Sculptor NT or Rhino. In either case, the files are brought into MAX as 3DS files and are converted to meshes at that point. Figure 1.5 shows an example of a NURBS model.

Metaball Modeling

The last method to mention at this point is metaball modeling, a relatively new modeling process that also requires the use of a plug-in. Metaball modeling produces a mesh surface by creating surface tension between a set of spheres. You can adjust the strength of a particular sphere to define how much it affects the surface. Metaball modeling can be used to model many complex objects such as liquid metal, faces, hands, bodies, and so forth. Figure 1.6 shows you an example of a model created with a metaball modeling program.

FIGURE 1.5
A NURBS model.

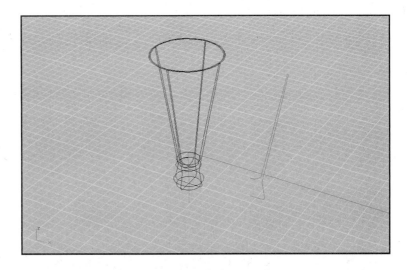

FIGURE 1.6
*A hand created using
Metaballs.*

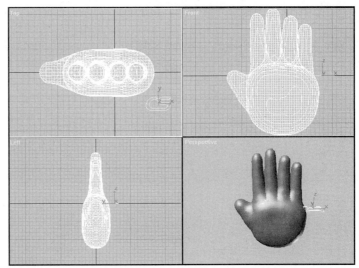

Of the many different approaches and methods for modeling, only a few are
mentioned here. Other methods are being developed all the time. Later in
this chapter, you explore specific examples that enable you to use one or more
of these techniques.

Materials in the Modeling Process

Up to this point, this chapter has focused only on modeling. Materials,
however, have a direct effect on how you model your object. Using a bump map

to create the appearance of depressions in a surface, for example, is much easier than actually trying to model those depressions. When you are creating objects, especially in the conceptual sketch and rough model phases, you should give serious thought to the way you are going to use materials. They will help dictate where you add detail to a model and where you do not.

You can create a brick wall out of a box, for example, by using a brick texture map in combination with a brick bump map. This works very well in the center of the object. When you look at the edges, however, you do not see the mortar joints you would see in real life. The only way around this is to actually model each brick in the scene. This process is time-consuming (in both modeling and rendering time) and, in many instances, people who view your scene probably won't even notice the edges of the brick!

Ultimately, knowing exactly when to create the *appearance* of geometry with materials and when to actually create the geometry comes with experience. As you progress through this chapter and this book, you will get a good sense of where and when to create more detail in your models and when to rely on trickery with your materials to achieve the same effect.

The Real World

When you are creating models and materials in a CGI environment such as 3D Studio MAX, the real world surrounding you serves as your best source of guidance. If you want to create a creature such as Draco from *Dragonheart*, for example, there is no real-world image, character, or object from which to draw. But don't despair. The real world does in fact offer many images and experiences (including movement) that can influence your modeling of Draco.

Draco is a dragon with wings and four legs. When Draco flies, you can base the motion as well as the modeling on something similar (a bat, for example). When the dragon walks, you can base the motion and modeling on a cat, a horse, or even a dog. You take only what you need from the various real-world examples and combine those characteristics into your final object.

Although motion is of secondary importance in this discussion of modeling, the way a creature moves depends directly on how the creature is built. A giraffe moves differently than a horse, for example, because the giraffe's legs and neck are longer, and the front part of its body is thicker and taller than those parts of a horse, resulting in a different movement. When you model the giraffe, you must take into account the way the shape of the giraffe affects its movement. In this way, you can determine where you need to add detail in the model.

The same types of observations can be applied to materials as well as to geometry. The real world is full of examples of a wide variety of materials you can use. You can even photograph many of these materials, scan them into your system, and use them in your scenes.

When you're basing objects on real-world examples, you must develop two key skills: observation and attention to detail. Without these skills, it will be difficult for you to create objects that, when animated, look correct.

Observation

Observation is the key to determining how things act, look, and work in the real world. One of the best ways to observe how things are put together in real life is to try to draw or sketch them by hand—a bit old-fashioned, but it requires focused attention and trains your eye to be patient and specific. These days, you can take a camera and photograph anything you want so that you have a copy of the object you are observing. Although a photograph provides an accurate picture of the object, the insight you gain by sketching will enable you to more thoroughly observe what the picture shows or doesn't show—a photograph is only two-dimensional after all.

Consider a lion, for example. You most certainly can photograph a lion and try to create a model of the lion based on the photograph. This works, to an extent. When you sketch or draw the lion by hand, however, you get a better sense of scale, texture, and spatial relationship. While you sketch you also pick up many of the lion's more subtle features, such as whiskers or underlying muscular structure, that you might miss by simple observation of a photograph. The underlying muscular structure is most evident when the lion is moving. You cannot get the information you need from a photograph in this case. These details give a model the greatest sense of realism in a CGI environment. Ideally, you will always have as much information as possible available to you when you are modeling. This includes sketches, photos, or even anatomy books.

Attention to Detail

Attention to detail goes hand-in-hand with observation. The more details you pick up from real-world examples, the easier it is to eventually model the object you want to create.

Again—consider the example of a dragon. To create the wings of a dragon, you might base them on the wings of a bat. When you look closely at a bat's wings you can see how they are put together, which gives you hints for creating them in the computer environment. You can also pick up many subtle (and not so subtle) hints about materials and how you need to create them for your model. As Mies Van de Rohe, a famous architect, once said, "God is in the details!" You should, therefore, pay attention to them.

How Much Detail Do You Need?

When you observe real-world examples on which to base your objects, always try to remember where to draw the line between putting too much detail in a model versus using advanced materials to create the effect.

When you create an animation, you should always strive to keep the polygon count as low as possible so that you use less memory and the animation renders faster. Never add unnecessary detail to the model. If you can get the look you want by working a little harder on the materials, go ahead and use the materials. Don't waste time and resources trying to model it.

Again, this is an experience issue. The temptation is great to create as much detail in the model as you can, partly because doing so on the computer is easy. Some people are also skeptical about being able to achieve the same results by using less geometry and better materials. The more experience you get modeling and creating materials, the easier it is to know when you have enough detail in the model and when to start creating more advanced materials.

Now that you have had a brief overview of the modeling process, it is time to look at specific examples and how you might model them. Later in the book you are given exact exercises. The examples in this first chapter are provided to help you think about the methodology behind creating the object and how much work it will take.

Architectural Modeling

Architectural modeling is one of the more popular uses of 3D Studio MAX. Architects create their models in AutoCAD and import them into MAX or create them wholly in MAX. Architectural models are generally planar in nature and are relatively easy to model. But because they also tend to have a great deal of detail and many different materials, they are more complex than other models you will see later in this chapter and in this book.

Architectural modeling encompasses everything from conceptual design work to office buildings to houses to churches to cathedrals. Architectural modeling can also be used by artists other than architects. Many games on the market today, for example, have architectural backdrops created by architects.

Chartres Cathedral in Chartres, France

The twelfth-century cathedral at Chartres, located about an hour from Paris, France, is one of the most spectacular examples of Gothic architecture and stained glass in the world (see fig. 1.7).

FIGURE 1.7
*The Chartres Cathedral
near Paris.*

Chartres Cathedral presents an interesting problem to the computer artist. First, it is a very complex building for an architectural model. The complexity is evident in the intricate detail of the stained-glass rose windows and the ornamentation on the outside of the cathedral. Second, the stained glass windows themselves present a challenge not only in modeling, but also in materials.

Modeling Techniques

Before you start looking at modeling techniques, you need to understand the scope of Chartres Cathedral and just how complex a modeling task it presents. Figures 1.8 through 1.11 show various views and details of the cathedral.

FIGURE 1.8
*The side facade of
Chartres Cathedral.*

FIGURE 1.9
The buttressing details.

FIGURE 1.10
A tower detail.

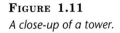

FIGURE 1.11

A close-up of a tower.

As the preceding set of figures shows, the overall form of the church is not particularly difficult, but the details are extremely intricate. The first thing to decide in the modeling process is how much intricate detail you want to show. The answer depends on how close you get to the building in your animation or still. If you are a fair distance away, you can use mapped materials to create the illusion of detail. But if you are fairly close, you probably will have to model most of the details to get an accurate view of the building.

Because this is such a complex building, you must use a variety of techniques to model it. Spline modeling, for example, should be used to create the detail on the flying buttresses (see fig. 1.9). A combination of spline modeling and solid modeling should be used to create the side facade (see fig. 1.8) and the towers (see figs. 1.10 and 1.11). The main nave of the cathedral can be modeled by using standard mesh modeling, because its geometry is fairly simple.

The exterior of Chartres Cathedral is covered with many figures inspired by religious texts. You do not necessarily have to model these, but if you decide to, model only five or six different figures and use them repetitively wherever you need them. If the figure is a decent distance from the camera, use materials to imitate it.

The figures themselves can be modeled using any technique discussed in this book. Just remember that they are small and repetitive, hence they will be extremely low resolution with very little detail. You could, for example, create a few metaballs and use them as the figures. Ultimately, a box mapped with a material that is a photograph of the figures will probably yield the best result.

This approach is just one of several you can take with this model. Some of the more exotic yet effective approaches include using the photographs to generate the model from within a photo modeling program. This approach results in a low-detail building, good for a backdrop only. Another option is to build a model of the cathedral (not an easy task) and laser scan the model in through a scanning service. This technique is highly accurate, but expensive and time consuming.

Your best approach is to model the overall form of the church and then go back and add detail until you are satisfied with the model. You will use many modeling techniques to complete the model, and will end up with a fairly large, complex model. Figures 1.12 and 1.13 show you two views of the completed model inside of 3D Studio MAX, before materials are applied.

FIGURE 1.12

An Isometric View of the cathedral.

FIGURE 1.13
*A Perspective View of
the cathedral.*

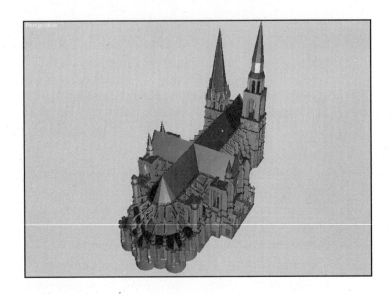

Material Techniques

As for materials, Chartres Cathedral is simple in most respects. The base material in the building is limestone. You can literally scan in a photograph of the limestone and create the material based on that. The roof of the cathedral is a standard green copper. The only difficult materials on this particular building are in the stained glass windows (see figs. 1.14 and 1.15).

As you can see from figure 1.15, the stained glass is quite complex. Scanning in a photograph of the material is about the only way to portray it accurately. You must use a photo that is not distorted by perspective so that your bitmap material will be somewhat accurate.

With a great deal of work and a little ingenuity, you can eventually model the cathedral.

Biped Characters

Biped characters are objects meant to be animated by using Kinetix's Character Studio software. Biped characters are modeled with enough detail that when they are animated, the mesh transforms smoothly. Too little detail results in a blocky, faceted mesh when animated. They are also modeled with the skin as a single mesh controlled by the underlying Biped skeleton. Other parts of the body, such as hair, fingernails, and so on, are linked to the skin and move when the skin is animated.

FIGURE 1.14
Stained glass.

FIGURE 1.15
Close-up of stained glass.

The Dancing Alien

In this example, you explore the dancing alien—a great example of a biped character—modeled by and available through Viewpoint DataLabs International, Inc. Figure 1.16 shows a wireframe of the alien.

FIGURE 1.16

The wireframe dancing alien. (3D models by Viewpoint DataLabs International, Inc.)

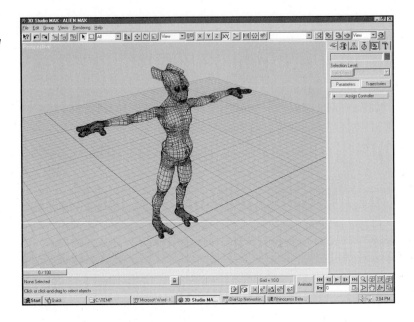

Modeling Techniques

When you are modeling a character for use with Biped, you need to model it in a specific pose. Biped characters work best when modeled with arms straight out to the sides and feet roughly shoulder width apart. This pose makes it easier to apply the skeleton and animate the model correctly. Figure 1.17 shows the correct pose for the alien.

FIGURE 1.17

The dancing alien, posed. (3D models by Viewpoint DataLabs International, Inc.)

Notice that the alien model does not have much detail and that the hands and feet have higher density meshes than the rest of the body (see fig. 1.16), which indicates that these parts of the body will be more heavily animated than the rest. There is relatively little detail in the head because facial animations generally are not applied to Biped characters. (More complex characters, discussed later in this chapter, do have facial animations.)

To model this character, you can take several different approaches. This character can easily be modeled by using metaballs. It can also be modeled with a little work by using patches. More than likely, this model was built as a clay model and laser scanned in, creating higher degrees of accuracy. Because this last approach is extremely expensive, you must rely on your own skills to create this character.

Another, more interesting, approach available in 3D Studio MAX is to create a rough outline of the character by modifying a Box object with Edit Mesh and Extrusions. Then apply the MeshSmooth modifier to smooth the object into a more natural form. A little more work beyond that, and you can quickly approximate this character.

The key thing to remember here is not to add too much detail where you don't need it. Study this model and how it is built. You can see exactly what the model is intended to be used for in an animation.

Material Techniques

The alien character presents a unique problem when it comes to materials. Because the skin is one object, the application of a material to the surface becomes much more of a problem than it would be if the skin were several objects. Also, mapping of materials is a problem because of the curved nature of the body.

One approach to this problem is to apply a bitmap, probably using the shrink-wrap mapping method, and keep adjusting the bitmap until it is correct. This works fairly well when the skin is all one material. Many characters in real life, however, have changing colors on their skin. A frog, for example, is mostly green on the backside and a very light green (almost yellow) on the underside.

Another method you might try is to use a plug-in, such as unwrap, which creates a bitmap with a diagram of the mapping layed out flat. You can then quickly and easily paint directly on the bitmap with your favorite paint program and apply it to the object.

The best method, arguably, requires the use of a plug-in such as 4D Paint or Fractal Design Detailer. These plug-ins enable you to paint directly on the 3D model, using any of a wide variety of brushes. You apply some mapping coordinates to the geometry, export it to the paint program, and then begin to literally paint your creature into life. This is the most powerful method for creating overly complex materials for objects such as this alien character. Figure 1.18 shows the alien character loaded in 4D Paint and with a little paint applied.

FIGURE 1.18

The alien being painted in 4D Paint. (3D models by Viewpoint DataLabs International, Inc.)

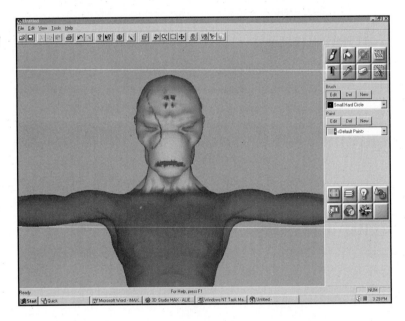

Three-dimensional object painting is extremely powerful for character models. If you are going to work much with these types of models in 3D Studio MAX, you should strongly consider picking up one of the many 3D paint programs available on the market.

Complex Character Models

A complex character model is similar to a Biped character, except that the complex model has much more detail. Complex models are generally fully animated from head to toe, including facial expressions, eyes, ears, wings, and even bulging muscles.

A Dragon

A dragon is a great example of a complex character model. A dragon has many interesting parts to model, such as wings, a tail, a body, and so on. In general, dragons have complex heads with horns, teeth, and other features. If you are going to animate the dragon blowing fire or talking, extra detail and attention to the head is necessary to model it correctly for animation. Figure 1.19 shows you a dragon that has already been modeled in 3D Studio MAX.

FIGURE 1.19

A dragon model. (3D models by Viewpoint DataLabs International, Inc.)

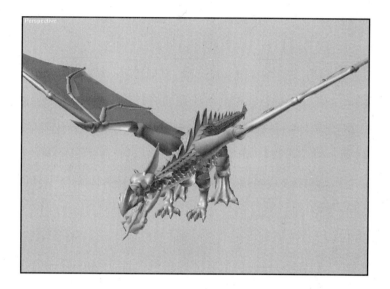

Modeling Techniques

As figure 1.19 shows, a dragon is an extremely complex and difficult character to model. This is an instance where the more time you invest in conceptual sketches and rough models, the better off you will be. Take the wings for instance. How many different ways do you think you could create the wings? Probably a lot. With sketching, you can explore these options before you spend the time trying to model them. This is especially true of other parts of the dragon, especially the head.

To model a dragon, you must use almost every modeling technique you can imagine. Because of the complexity of the shapes, a dragon really requires the use of a NURBS modeler. A dragon's head is an excellent example of a complex shape. NURBS modelers excel at creating complex surfaces and are even better at creating blends between such surfaces.

TIP

A good NURBS modeler to try is Rhino, from Robert McNeel and Associates. You can download a beta (at the time of this writing) from www.rhino3d.com. By the time this book is published, you may be able to download a demo of the final program.

The best approach to modeling a creature such as a dragon is to try and break the modeling into small tasks. You can model the wings as a separate object, for example, and then later attach them to the body. You can model the head and later attach it to the neck. This helps to keep your file sizes smaller and to make the modeling process go a little faster than if you were to model the entire creature in one fell swoop.

When you model a complex character such as this, keep in mind exactly which parts of the object will be animated more than others. You must provide enough detail in these areas so that the object can be animated smoothly. If you do your conceptual sketches correctly and create a storyboard of the character, you will know where and when to add the extra detail.

Also realize, however, that when you are working on a model as complex as a dragon, you must make a serious investment of time to complete the model. Newer modeling tools are constantly being developed and may eventually help to reduce the time involved.

Material Techniques

Dragons consist of very complex materials. Because the dragon is created as a single mesh, you are pretty much forced down the road of using a 3D paint program to correctly create a material for this type of character. Any other method will require so much trial and error in creating and placing the maps that it is worth your money to buy the appropriate program.

Other than that, pay attention to materials in nature when you create the materials for a creature such as a dragon. Base your materials on some known quantity, such as scales from a snake or wings from a bat. This makes the process of creating materials much, much easier.

Technical Modeling

A *technical model* is a model of an object that must be created precisely, to exact measurements. A space station or a car engine might be considered examples of technical models. Many technical models are created in other programs—such as AutoCAD, Mechanical Desktop, and even Pro Engineer—and brought into 3D Studio MAX for visualization purposes only.

A Space Station

A space station is a good example of a technical model. Even though only one space station exists, you have probably seen one of the many animations NASA has produced of the space shuttle docking with the International space station. Figures 1.20 and 1.21 show examples of a space station.

FIGURE 1.20

The international space station.

FIGURE 1.21

Another version of the international space station.

Modeling Techniques

Most of the forms in a technical model are fairly simple but accurate. Figure 1.21, for example, shows mostly planar or cylindrical elements. These can be modeled as simple objects and then modified to match the space station. Alternatively, the cylinders can be created as lofted splines.

Precision and detail are the keys here. Other than that, technical models should be fairly easy to create.

Material Techniques

Materials in a technical model are also fairly simple. Generally speaking, they are a collection of metallic or plastic materials that can easily be created in MAX. You might also see a set of logos that can be scanned in. Occasionally you will run into slightly more difficult materials, such as those on the solar panels of the space station, but even they can be created with just a little work in the MAX Material Editor.

Industry Modeling

Industry models are similar to technical models and are created to help sell a product. You can create models of cars, boats, jet-skis, and so on. These models should be as photorealistic as possible, to create the highest sales impact.

Modeling a Ferrari

A Ferrari is a good example of a technical model. It is a sleek, well-defined, popular car that can be easily modeled in MAX (see fig. 1.22).

Modeling Techniques

As mentioned earlier in this chapter, NURBS modelers are used to design most cars today. Hence, NURBS modelers make the most sense when you want to model this type of object. As a matter of fact, the original design models can be converted into 3D Studio MAX and rendered, if necessary.

Figure 1.22

*A Ferrari model. (3D
models by Viewpoint
DataLabs Interna-
tional, Inc.)*

NURBS make sense because most cars have precise curves and blends between curves. Unfortunately, because MAX does not use NURBS at this time, you have to resort to a plug-in or some other method of modeling. Of course, with a little work you can easily create a car by using patch modeling.

Like other slightly complex objects, many cars are built with plastic as physical models and then laser-scanned in. You probably have seen (or built) the many plastic car models available at any hobby store.

Material Techniques

Generally, industry models are easy to assign materials to. Most cars have one primary color, which can be either metallic or flat, and some secondary colors on the trim. Because of the fabrics or leathers on the interior, it may require a little more work to model correctly. For the most part, however, industry models are fairly straightforward and easy to create.

Regardless of the type of model you are trying to create in 3D Studio MAX, you must use one or more techniques to create the model. The following reminders are the keys to success:

- Plan before you build.
- Create sketches and rough models.
- Observe the real world for hints on modeling and materials.

- Add detail only where necessary.

- When modeling, always keep in mind the final objective.

Plug-In Overview

One of the true powers of a system such as 3D Studio MAX is the extensibility of the system—in other words, how easy it is to expand and enhance the program. You can enhance 3D Studio MAX by adding plug-ins (third-party software), adding functionality to the system without having to buy a whole new program.

Why Plug-Ins Are Important

Plug-ins are important because they give you additional ways to create objects that would be much more difficult to create with MAX alone. The fact is, you can create just about anything you want with the tools in MAX and a little work. Plug-ins just make your life easier.

Plug-ins in MAX are available in many different forms including Video Post, Bitmap I/O, File I/O, space warps, and so on. Most, however, come in the form of modeling and material plug-ins. The rest of this chapter explores some of the more popular plug-ins from these two categories.

Modeling Plug-Ins

Modeling plug-ins provide additional ways to create an object in MAX. Some of these methods are unusual; others are simply enhanced or advanced methods. You could purchase a modeling plug-in for any of a variety of reasons. Two reasons you might purchase a plug-in are: the plug-in provides you with functionality not present in MAX; or the plug-in reduces your modeling time and increases accuracy enough to justify its cost.

The next few sections cover several types of modeling methods. Specific plug-ins are mentioned for each type.

Metaballs

In *metaball modeling,* you use spheres as a modeling tool. By placing a set of spheres close to each other and assigning a tension value to them, you can create a surface based on those spheres. Figure 1.23 shows a series of spheres; figure 1.24 shows the resulting metaball surface.

FIGURE 1.23

A series of spheres.

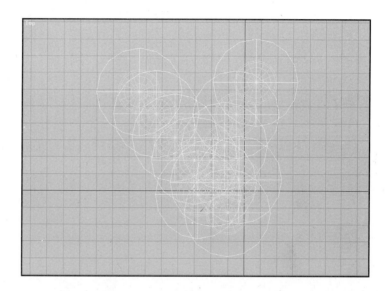

FIGURE 1.24

The metaball surface.

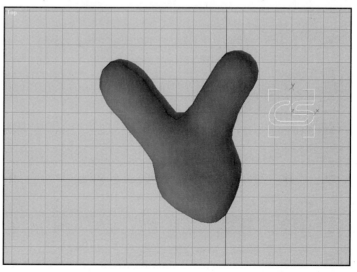

You can purchase two primary plug-ins to create metaballs: Clay Studio from Digimation, and Metareyes Metaballs from REM Infogracia. Both have a solid set of features and enable you to quickly and easily create a metaball model. Metareyes has one unique feature—metamuscle—that enables you to create creatures similar to the one shown in figure 1.25.

FIGURE 1.25
A metamuscle model and the resulting surface.

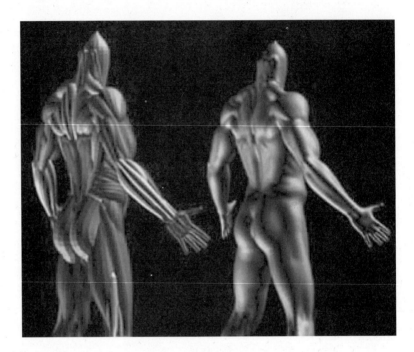

Plug-ins are integrated directly into the MAX interface. A grouping tool on the Clay Studio interface (see fig. 1.26) enables you to place metaballs next to each other without creating a surface between them and is helpful for hands and other such objects.

NURBS (Non-Uniform Rational B-Spline)

Currently, the only NURBS modelers available for use with 3D Studio MAX are stand-alone programs that export 3DS files that you can import into MAX. The best of these is Rhinoceros from Robert McNeel and associates. Figure 1.27 shows the interface for Rhino. Figure 1.28 shows a model created in Rhino and rendered in 3D Studio MAX.

Figure **1.26**
The Clay Studio interface showing some of the controls. Note the Group Workshop Button.

Figure **1.27**
The Rhino interface.

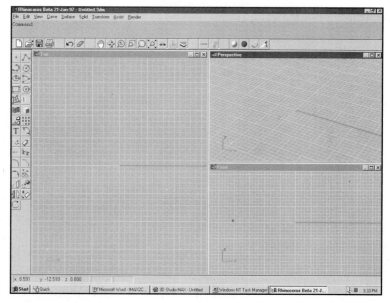

Rhino provides a complete set of NURBS tools with many, many different functions. The other NURBS modeler worth looking at is 4D Vision's Sculptor NT, another stand-alone product (see fig. 1.29). Like Rhino, it provides many NURBS modeling tools. The difference between the two lies in the way they're used, and which you should choose depends on your personality and how you like to model.

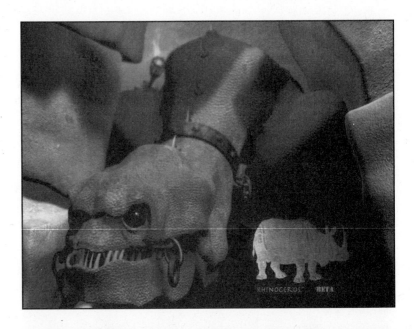

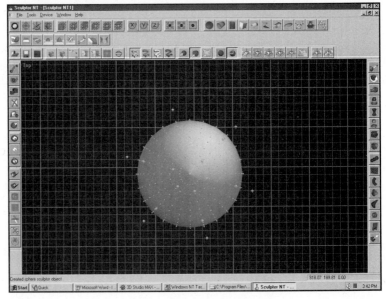

If you want to create an object with many different complex curved surfaces, one of these two products should do the trick. Yes, you can probably accomplish the same thing in MAX, but probably not as fast as with one of these programs.

Spline Tools

If you have used MAX for a while, you undoubtedly are familiar with the Lofting system in MAX for creating objects based on splines. Surface Tools, another plug-in from Digimation, makes spline modeling very easy. With Surface Tools, you can create 3D splines that approximate the contours of a surface. You can draw a spline to represent the line of a cheekbone, for example. Then, by applying Surface Tools, a surface of Bézier patches can be quickly and easily generated and manipulated. Figures 1.30 and 1.31 show examples of a set of splines and the resulting surface.

FIGURE 1.30

A set of splines.

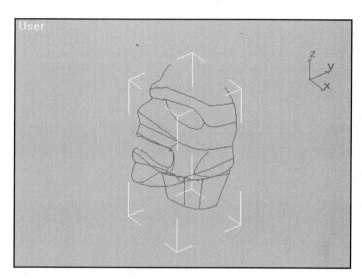

FIGURE 1.31

The resulting surface after applying Surface Tools.

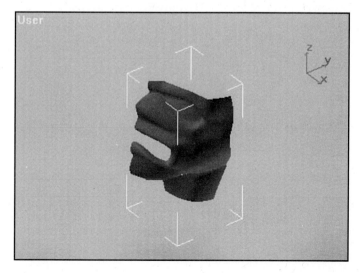

Powerful selling points for this plug-in are its ease of use and speed. With only a few hours of practice, you can begin modeling rather complex objects. As a matter of fact, with a little work, you could probably model the head of Draco from the movie *Dragonheart* in a day or two and get close to approximating the "real" head.

Using Other Plug-Ins as Modeling Tools

Through some inventive programming, developers have found ways to use other plug-ins and effects in MAX as modeling tools. If you purchase Bones Pro from Digimation, for example, you get a tool called SnapShot Plus. SnapShot enables you to use any space warp in MAX as a modeling tool. You could create a sphere and explode it with a space warp, for example. If you capture the mesh one or two frames after the explosion, you get a series of triangles that resemble leaves on a tree.

To take this a step further, other developers have produced shareware plug-ins that enable you to use particle systems as modeling tools. They work on a similar principle as SnapShot, converting the particle system over to an object at any given frame in the animation.

These are just two examples of MAX's inventive, powerful programming interface. Newer plug-ins, such as Atomizer from Digimation, enable you to create an object and do a one-to-one replacement of particles in a particle system with that object. If you use metaballs, you can create objects such as flowing water. Modeling plug-ins are exciting—and getting more so every week.

Material Plug-Ins

Material plug-ins provide additional functions to MAX's already powerful Material Editor. The two primary types of material plug-ins are paint programs and procedural textures.

3D Paint Programs

3D Paint programs are some of the most popular plug-ins for use with MAX. Some of the paint programs work with MAX; others are completely stand-alone. Of the available paint programs, 4D Vision's 4D Paint is probably the best. It works as a utility plug-in in MAX and enables you to export objects directly from MAX into 4D Paint, and vice versa. This type of integration makes it a powerful plug-in.

3D Paint programs work by enabling you to paint directly on the surface of an object. You can paint a variety of map types (such as diffuse, bump, and others) simultaneously or individually. In addition, you can create your own brushes, sprays, and so on. You can even create a brush that uses a bitmap as its paint. Figure 1.18 showed the 4D Paint interface.

3D Paint programs are the most flexible, powerful way to create complex materials for objects created as a single mesh, such as the Alien mentioned earlier in this chapter. 4D Vision has a demo of this plug-in on its web site at www.4dvision.com. Download it and give it a try. Direct experience provides the best way to gauge the power of this plug-in.

Procedural Materials

Procedural materials are generated through the use of mathematical algorithms and create some sort of real-world texture. One way to create a wood material is to use a photograph of wood. Alternatively, you can create a wood material by using a procedural noise that simulates the wood grains. Procedural materials are generally implemented as map types in Material Editor. You can apply the procedurals as diffuse maps, bump maps, or any other type of map in MAX.

A good example of a procedural plug-in is Texture Lab from Digimation. With this collection of six new material maps you can create everything from advanced noise maps to fire to electricity. The Texture Lab Fire map is loaded as a diffuse map in the MAX Material Editor.

Procedural materials are easy to use because they do not require UVW mapping coordinates. Instead, they rely on the world coordinate system to apply their textures. This means that when you cut a section out of the object to which you applied the material, the resulting object will still be mapped correctly. This is usually not the case when you use a standard bitmap-based material and UVW mapping coordinates.

Procedural materials also provide much greater control over the material's appearance. Mapped materials generally have only one look because editing the bitmap in MAX is not easy. Procedurals, however, are based on variables that can be quickly and easily manipulated to create some interesting effects. Figure 1.32 shows a rusted tin roof created with Texture Lab.

FIGURE 1.32
FIGURE 1.32
A rusted tin roof created through the use of a procedural material.

Image courtesy of Brandon Riza
Created using Texture Lab: Elemental Tools
available through Digimation
www.digimation.com

In Practice: The World of Modeling and Material Techniques

- **Visualize.** Always visualize the object as much as possible before modeling it.

- **Attention to Detail.** Pay attention to things that exist in the world. You can draw a great deal of inspiration from them.

- **Just the Right Amount of Detail.** The key is details and knowing when to add detail and when not to.

- **Sketching.** Work your ideas out with hand sketches before you begin modeling. This will save you time and frustration.

- **Modeling.** If the object you are working on is overly complex, consider building a clay model as a reference.

- **Modeling Techniques.** In 3D Studio MAX, especially with the use of plug-ins, there are literally dozens of methods for modeling the same object. Select the methods you like to use the most and stick with them. Remember, whatever method you choose, the underlying process is always the same.

Part II

ADVANCED MODELING IN 3D STUDIO MAX

IMAGE BY JONATHAN SAWYER

Chapter 2

by Jonathan Sawyer
with Michael Neil

ARCHITECTURAL MODELING AND RENDERING

The last 15 years have seen the shift from hand-drafting to CAD in most architecture offices. Rarely do you find, even in small offices, construction documents still drawn by hand with parallel rule and triangle; even red-lining and mark-up is moving to the computer in many offices. In much the same way, it is very likely that the current explosion in the use of, and interest in, 3D computer visualization will force the practices of hand-rendering and model-making further and further into the background. Architects, Industrial Designers, Interior Designers—anyone who makes esthetic decisions in three dimensions—will inevitably find that 3D computer visualization is a very effective way to communicate design ideas.

In this chapter, you will use some of the techniques that enable you to make 3DS MAX do what you want it to do as an architectural modeler. You will model and render a small building, from a basic wall layout all the way through to the details that add the realism you need for a convincing presentation. This chapter deals with certain ways to use the modeling tools in 3DS MAX that are specific to architectural modeling. Accuracy is important in this context. Some topics considered include:

- Establishing the basic walls from plans

- Controlling lofts to produce architectural moldings

- Easy ways to build roofs

- Miscellaneous trim and detail

Building a 3D Architectural Model

Building a 3D model on the computer often highlights design problems and can aid in the search for a solution. On the simplest level, the process of constructing a wireframe of a building often reveals construction problems: sections and elevations that conflict, roof slopes that may not work, components that won't fit. If it does not fit together on your screen, it won't work on the jobsite either. Similarly, on a stylistic and esthetic level, a computer rendering reveals a lot—animation enables an experience of a space much more like the real experience. Eventually, full immersion in the architecture, by means of virtual reality, will likely become an important presentation and design tool.

Before any of this can happen, however, you need to build a wireframe.

In the broadest sense, a wireframe can be any of a variety of 3D computer representations. For the purposes of this chapter, a wireframe is a collection of digital entities, including lines, vertices, and faces, that make up a computer model. This model is solid in the sense that it contains surfaces, represented by collections of triangles, that define the surfaces of the object being modeled, for example, a house. This is different from true "Solid Modeling," in which additional information about the object being modeled is part of the database, information such as weight, density, and so on. In this context, you are only building a collection of "skins" that will represent the walls and other components of the building.

3DS MAX is designed to serve many different modeling, rendering, and animating applications. It was not specifically designed to model buildings. Certain strategies can make it easier to use 3DS MAX's considerable power to produce good, clean architectural models.

The building that you will model is an ornate but symmetrical poolhouse or bathhouse, a structure that might be found at a country club or on a private estate, containing changing rooms. The detailing and massing of this outbuilding are formal and have sufficient richness to enable you to explore the details of modeling techniques, but the building overall is simple enough that you will be able to complete the modeling of the exterior.

Modeling the Structure

Modeling a building for architectural presentation and analysis has very different requirements than modeling cartoon characters, aliens from a distant planet, or morphing toothpaste tubes. It's not so clear what aliens look like, at least to most people, so the modeler enjoys a little more latitude in interpretation. Almost everyone knows what buildings look like, however, and those expectations must be met.

Meeting those expectations in the digital world means building an electronic structure in steps that are not unlike the steps involved in building a real building. The walls are located and laid out and are then erected in basic form; openings are sized and located, and details are added in layers until the building is complete. Coloring and texturing the computer model is roughly analogous to painting and wallpapering an actual building, although the appearance of some surfaces is dictated by the material itself, of course, as in the case of a brick wall. Nonetheless, the broad analogy holds, and the first stages of modeling a building on the computer involve the roughing in of the walls.

Starting Out

There are a few different approaches to the first step in architectural modeling—the basic layout of the walls and their various openings. Each way has advantages and disadvantages. Listed below are a few possible methods:

1. Extrude walls up from lines that you get from a floor plan, either an existing plan or one that you have drawn in a CAD program or in 3DS MAX specifically for the purpose.

2. Build the building the way real houses are actually framed—build the walls "lying down" and then stand them up and fit them together. This method may also be familiar because it is similar to the way architectural models have always been built, out of foam-core or chip board walls are cut out and then stood up and glued together.

3. Use Boolean Operations and other modifications to manipulate primitives, adding sections and cutting openings.

4. Use a wall section in its entirety as a shape and loft the entire wall of a building in one operation, along with all its various projections, cornices, and other linear details.

5. Hybrid methods where some of the initial modeling is done in a CAD program, and the result is then imported into 3DS MAX for the addition of details.

Extruding from Floor Plans

In many cases, a building to be modeled will already exist as plans. These plans can be imported into 3D Studio MAX and the walls built directly on top of them. This has the distinct advantage of ensuring that the walls will end up in the right place, assuming, of course, that the plans themselves are accurate. Plans can be drawn in 3D Studio MAX and extruded to form the walls, but in this scenario, in which all the dimensions need to be entered, it makes more sense to simply build primitives to the correct size and then modify them, which is essentially method number 3 mentioned above. The extra step of creating lines for a plan and then extruding or lofting them to form the walls hardly makes sense.

After importing the plans (a process covered elsewhere in this book), some alterations will be necessary. It is advisable to remove lines designating doors and windows, as well as most other things that do not represent the wall masses. Splines may need to be closed. Some thought will have to be given to how high to extrude or loft the various wall sections, which will in turn involve decisions about the interior modeling versus the exterior modeling, among other considerations. Other problems that will arise entail the openings, which are represented as breaks in the lines of a floor plan, and thus will become full-height, floor-to-ceiling openings when you extrude the walls, regardless of what they represent in the plan. A window, for example, will need to have wall sections added from its sill down to the floor (and to the ground, on the exterior), and above its header to the ceiling (or to the cornice, on the exterior). Keep in mind also that the various openings will need to be of a size that will allow clearance for the insertion of modeled jambs and trim in later steps. This may entail modifying the plans from which you are working before you extrude them.

If you are modeling a structure both inside and out, or one that has changes in the wall surfaces on the exterior, then polygons that span from the bottom of the wall section to the top will likely need to be redrawn and rearranged, if you want to assign different materials to different rooms. If you extrude a wall from the foundations to the top of the second floor, for example, which would be a quick and easy way to build a complete side of a house, then on the inside, all the wall surfaces will receive one material. The second floor bedroom and the family room below, for example, will share the same wall surface and hence the same material assignment. This could be rectified by erasing and redrawing faces, but that creates more steps.

One possible solution is to loft or extrude each floor separately and then stack them up. In this method, it is critical that they have the same footprint, so that they will join seamlessly. During this process, mapping coordinates can be added, saving some work down the road.

Building the Walls "Lying Down"

The second method mentioned involves drawing the walls as elevations, in the form of collections of lines and arcs, attaching the various parts to make one spline object, and then extruding it to the thickness of the wall. The window and door openings are just that—openings, sized to allow the insertion later of the miscellaneous trim pieces. The wall sections are then "stood up" and moved into place. This method is the cyber version of the way that houses are framed in the real life, in the standard stick-framing system. It has the advantage of being visually clear because you simply draw the wall the way that you want it to look in elevation. It suffers the same limitations as the previously described system, however—the need to separate wall planes for different interior rooms as well as exterior surfaces changes. It has the advantage of not having to be patched up with missing wall sections, as the previous system required. Again, size the openings to provide clearance for the trim that will be inserted later in the wall openings. In this respect, it is again analogous to the actual construction a building. Clearances are crucial.

After the walls are drawn with splines and extruded, they need to be rotated and moved into place, and the corners of the various walls need to be joined cleanly. Assuming that care and accuracy were used in the initial layout of the wall spline shapes, then joining the wall sections should be a simple matter of positioning the walls corner-to-corner and then attaching them as objects. Lastly, the vertices can be welded at the corners to complete the object.

This method may appeal to architects who are used to traditional model building methods, with the time-honored materials of foam-core, chip-board, and bass and balsa wood. You cut your openings in "sheet goods" and then glue the pieces together. Because architects are almost always at home visualizing buildings as elevations, then this method is comfortable.

Boolean Modeling of Walls

Boolean modeling is akin to carving your building out of blocks of solid material, which has an intuitive aspect of its own; architects are, in many ways, sculptors of three-dimensional space.

In this method, the building masses are defined with primitives, such as cubes. These primitives can either be built directly with the 3D Studio MAX Create Panel, which offers boxes and spheres and so on, or they can be built as lofts from shapes. Once a massing has been established, the inside can be hollowed out using Boolean Subtractions, leaving behind a shell that is the thickness of the walls. Openings are then cut in the appropriate locations by creating various solids and using Boolean Subtraction to cut holes in the walls. Always use a Hold before actually performing the Boolean operation, or do a Save. The Boolean engine in 3D Studio MAX is superior to the one in 3D Studio DOS, but it is by no means foolproof.

Here again, the mesh will probably need to be modified for the same reasons that were encountered in the other methods; different room surfaces will need to broken up, as well as separating the inside from the outside. Some of this can be accomplished by simple Multi/Sub Object mapping at the material application stage, but other problems will require rearranging the geometry.

Cross-Section Lofting to Form Walls

A possible method for making walls and some of the associated trim is to loft the entire cross-section of the wall in one operation. This method is very quick initially, but it requires the most clean-up and post-lofting manipulation of any of the methods.

In this scheme, an entire wall section is lofted around a path that follows the footprint of the wall. It will be seen that this allows the formation, in one operation, of cornices, stringcourses, crown moldings, overhangs, parapets—in short, any detail that runs parallel to the ground. After the lofting is accomplished, Boolean subtractions could be used to cut the various openings.

The strength of this method is also its weakness; it produces many elements in one operation, but often they will then need to be separated to receive their materials. Multi/Sub Object Mapping can solve much of the problem, but it does not solve the issue of what to do if it becomes necessary to edit some of the elements later—if, for example, you decide to delete a stringcourse or change its profile. In these cases, you have no choice but to edit the mesh and separate the elements. Also, this method results in a model with a greater number of polygons for the same result.

On the other hand, this method is so fast and easy for some building shapes that it might be the only choice. An example would be a curving wall with a balcony and continuous sunshade. There are some building shapes that could only be modeled, for all practical purposes, with some sort of lofting. Some examples of buildings that would be easy to loft and almost impossible to build otherwise include Wright's Guggenheim Museum in New York or the Opera House in Sydney, Australia.

Combinations with Other Programs

Another possibility is to perform initial 3D modeling in CAD to establish the basic wall volumes, and then import the model into 3D Studio MAX. Roughing in basic wall volumes in CAD in this way makes it possible to take advantage of the high degree of precision available in CAD packages. You can, therefore, start out in 3DS MAX with a perfectly accurate basic structure; each subsequent modeling operation in 3DS MAX adds small inaccuracies that have a tendency to accumulate. Thus, the more accurate your starting point, the better. 3DS MAX was never designed to match the accuracy of CAD programs.

This last method is the one that you will use in this chapter. Start by loading from the accompanying CD the file called WALLS.max. This basic model was built in AutoCAD, using a third-party parametric modeler that operates entirely inside AutoCAD. A few such front-ends are available. After importing into 3DS MAX, it is often necessary to correct some of the surface normals in the model. In the model that you are starting with, this has already been done. Also the units have already been set to U.S. Standard Fractional Inches, and the Home Grid increment set to 1", with major lines every 12".

Some Points About Lofting

In the scene, you will use a selection of shapes already made as profiles for lofting the various cornices, stringcourses, plinths, and other continuous, linear details. These shapes were created using 3DS MAX's spline creation and editing tools, described in the 3DS MAX documentation and also in *Inside 3D Studio MAX Volume I*. The shapes are next to each other on the ground plane in the middle of the main building shape and can easily be located by selecting them in the Select by Name dialog box and then looking for the axis tripod.

3DS MAX makes modeling linear architectural elements such as crown molding relatively painless, but there are certain demands placed on the lofting process in an architectural context. Specifically, the precision in the scaling and teetering of the shape along the length of the loft is crucial to correct lofting. In a precisely rectilinear path, such as the path followed by the baseboard, cornice, or door trim, a snag occurs when a profile that is the correct width on the straight runs of the path is pivoted by the lofter at the point where the path turns a corner. Because the profile width is unchanged, the lofted object tapers in at the corner in an undesirable fashion, unacceptable for architectural trimwork. Figure 2.1 shows such a situation exaggerated for clarity, with the corrected loft on the right where the shape has been scaled up at the corner points to compensate.

FIGURE 2.1

Uncorrected loft compresses at corners; loft with the scale-corrected shape at the corners yields uniform cross-section.

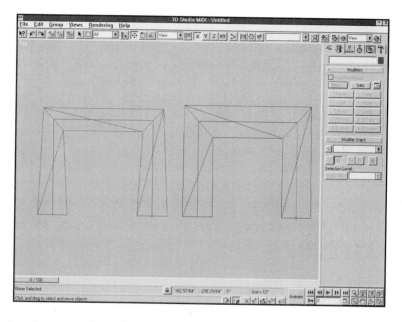

This discussion focuses primarily on the width of the shape as seen in what might be called a top view, where the path lies in a plane perpendicular to the reader's line of sight. When looking at the path from the side, which is to say edge-on, the dimension of the shape profile is constant. Such is the situation whenever the path of the loft lies entirely in one plane, as is the case with a run of door casing, or the baseboard in a room, or the crown molding that runs around a room where the ceiling is a constant height. But this scenario is not always the case in architecture; consider a run of baseboard that, for example, goes up a staircase, turns a corner at the top, goes down a hall, and then turns again and goes up more stairs. In this case, scale corrections would have to be made to both the width and the height of the shape, depending on the location and direction of the turn in the path, because the path of the loft does not lie in one plane.

Fortunately, simple formulae help to figure out how much to scale the shapes.

For a given angle θ, where θ is equal to the angle of rotation of the shape on the path (such that, one-half the angle of the change in direction of the path itself), the rotated shape must be larger than the starting shape by a factor given by

1/sineθ

This quantity is commonly expressed as

cosecantθ

and can be looked up in any table of trigonometric values or generated by a pocket calculator that has trigonometric functions. If your calculator lacks a cosecant function, take the inverse of the sine of the angle of the shape.

Multiply the original length of the shape by the quantity cosecantθ to arrive at the correct length for the shape at the point at which the angle θ occurs. In 3DS MAX, this is easy: Perform a non-uniform scale on your shape, in the desired axis, until reaching the percentage that corresponds to your factor. Table 2.1 gives some values for common angles.

TABLE 2.1

Scale Factors for Loft Shapes

Angle of Turn in Path (2θ)	Angle of Shape Rotation (θ)	Percentage Scale Factor for (cosecantθ)	Non-Uniform Scale
135°	67.5°	1.0824	108.24%
90°	45°	1.4142	141.38%
60°	30°	2.0000	200%
45°	22.5°	2.6131	261.31%

If the angle of the shape exceeds 90 degrees, look up the cosecant for that angle's acute complement.

LOFTING THE COLUMN BASECAPS

Start by making a simple loft to form the trim at the top of the bases that the columns will rest on. First, create a closed spline rectangle exactly the size of one of the cubes that make up the object Colbase. The object Colbase consists of eight identical boxes, part of the WALLS.max file. It does not matter which one you choose to use for the following steps.

1. Select the line tool in the Create panel, and set steps to 0 in the interpolation area of the roll-out.

2. Turn on the 3D snap tool, making certain that vertex is the #1 snap priority.

3. Snap four line segments, connecting the four top vertices of any one of the objects called Colbase (see fig. 2.2). Be sure to snap the lines in a counter-clockwise order, so that the face normals of the loft that will be made from this path will point outward.

4. Answer yes when 3DS MAX asks whether or not you want to close the spline.

5. Name the new spline **Colbasepath**, or something else that you can easily associate with this operation.

FIGURE 2.2

Rectangular spline snapped to the top vertices of one of the Colbase objects.

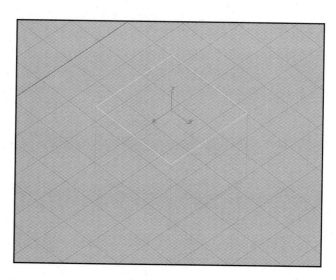

Now scale the shape, which for this loft is the shape called Stringshape. Because the corners of this loft are 90 degrees, and the shape rotation is 45 degrees, the shape needs to be scaled up by 141.38% (see table 2.1). With this particular loft, it should be scaled before being placed on the path because the path is a closed spline and the shape will be placed at a corner and thus rotated. If the path were an open spline, the shape would be placed at the first vertex, at one end of the path, and so would not be rotated. In that case, scaling for the corners would be accomplished after the shape had been placed on the path, by using the scale deformation controls. This method is used later in the chapter.

6. Select the object called Stringshape from the Select by Name button.

7. Zoom in on the shape in the top viewport and perform a Shift-clone on it, selecting Copy as the clone method. You want to keep an unscaled copy for future use. Rename the clone something like **Colbasetrim** to differentiate it from the original shape, which will be used again for another loft.

8. Apply an XForm modifier to the copy and select non-uniform scale from the transform toolbar. The axis constraint is irrelevant because you are going to use type-in. If there is a concern about this shape being instanced later, then this scaling operation should be performed on the shape after it has been assigned to the loft; in this case, however, this shape is already a copy and so will likely be used only in this loft. The original shape remains for other, later uses.

NOTE

The shape can be scaled by applying a non-uniform scale transform, rather than by applying the scale as an XForm modifier. If the scale is not applied as an XForm modifier, however, the loft ignores the scaling and uses the original, unscaled shape instead. Generally, it is a good idea to apply a scale transform as an XForm modifier, thus placing it in the stack like any other modifier, and thereby preserving your flexibility.

9. To pop up the Scale Transform Type-in dialog, right-click on the scale button in the transform toolbar.

10. In the X field of the Offset Screen column, type 141.42, and press Enter.

TIP

Use the Scale Transform Type-In dialog for accurate scaling, rather than dragging to scale. Even if you set the snap increment to less that 1", dragging the scale operation still only yields whole-inch read-outs on the status line. For greater accuracy, use the type-in method.

11. Close the dialog, turn off Sub-Object in the modify panel to deactivate the gizmo.

Now you are ready to place the shape on the path.

12. With the shape still selected, open the Hierarchy panel and select Affect Pivot Only from the Adjust Pivot roll-out.

13. Move the pivot point to the extreme lower right end of the shape. This ensures that the shape will be placed correctly on the path.

14. Select the path Colbasepath, select Loft Object from the Create panel, click on Get Shape, check Copy button below the Get Shape Button, and then click on the scaled shape. For this example, copy is chosen in case you want to use the shape again elsewhere; if not, you can always erase it at the end of the project (see fig. 2.3).

15. Open the Modify panel, expand the Skin Parameters roll-out, and check the Skin box under Display.

16. The loft appears. It bulges in the straight runs between corners because of the scale questions previously discussed. In this case, however, it's easy to fix. Set the path steps to 0 in the Skin Parameters roll-out, and the loft becomes uniform because there are no steps between corners where the shape can reside. The lofter lofts directly from corner to corner. Setting path steps to 0 also cuts the polygon count of the loft from 2,016 to 336, as you can tell by right-clicking on the object and then choosing Properties from the pop-up menu.

17. Rotate and examine the object in a shaded view. Its profile is smooth and quite acceptable. Quick render it to see how it will look. Now check the Optimize Shapes button, and re-render. There is no visible difference, but checking the polygon count reveals that it has dropped to 176. Optimize Shapes makes intelligent decisions for you—it eliminates the steps in the segments of the shape that are straight, where steps are unnecessary anyway, and preserves them in the parts of the shape that are curved, where you want the smoothness that the steps provide.

18. Now decrease the shape steps setting one step at a time, re-rendering between each change. It is difficult to see a difference in the smoothness of the loft until you get down to 2 steps; at 1 step, it is faceted, and at 0 steps, it is no longer acceptable. But the polygon counts drop nicely: at 2 steps, 104; at 1 step, 80; at 0 steps, 56. You be the judge of the results that you need, taking into account the proposed end-usage of the model. For this exercise, settle on 2 steps as a good compromise between modeling economy and detail (see fig. 2.4).

FIGURE 2.3
The shape placed on the loft.

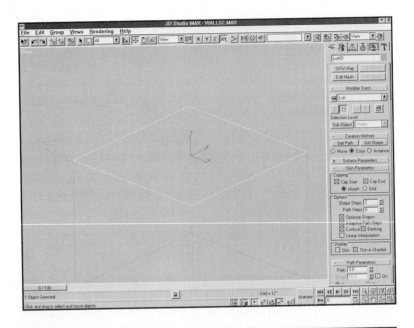

FIGURE 2.4
The loft skinned with optimize shapes checked and shape steps set to 2.

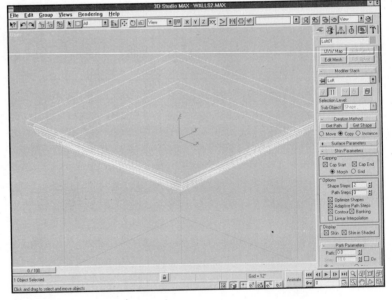

TIP

If you prefer, you can position the shape on the path by skipping the steps involving the repositioning of the pivot point, and move the shape by choosing Shape under the Sub-Object menu and moving it with the move tool, checking it in various viewports. If you were making a loft that had modifications of the same shape at different points on the path, or had many occurrences of a shape, it would be easier to set the pivot point one time and then place the shape.

The last step is to put a top on the basecap.

≈9. Apply an Edit Mesh modifier to the lofted object.

20. Choose Face from the Sub-Object menu, and click on Build Face in the Miscellaneous area of the roll-out.

21. Build two triangular faces by clicking on the top corner vertices of the lofted object, to make a solid top for your base. Check it in a shaded view (see fig. 2.5).

FIGURE 2.5

Drawing faces to close the top of the basecap.

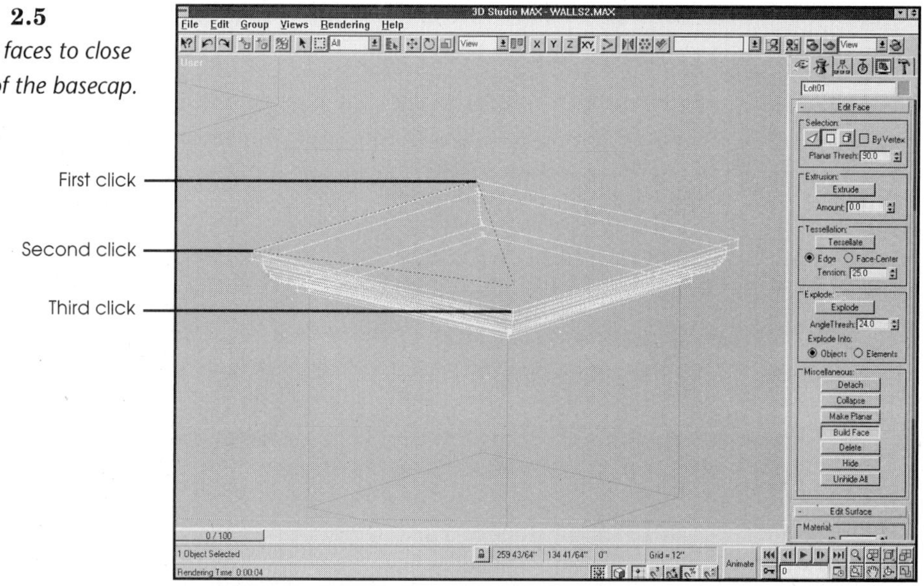

First click

Second click

Third click

NOTE

Remember that when using Build Face, the order in which you select the vertices is important. Select vertices in a counter-clockwise order if you want the surface normal of the resulting surface to face toward you (that is, be visible from your point of view). Select them in a clockwise order if you want them to be visible from the other side (that is, from a viewpoint opposite your own).

22. Finally, rename the lofted basecap something useful like **Colbasecap**, and copy it on to the tops of the other seven Colbase objects. Use Instance as the clone method, in case you want to change it later, and use snaps to position clones accurately on top of the other bases. This is probably easiest to accomplish in the top viewport. As a bookkeeping measure, it is a good idea to group all eight basecaps in a group called Colbasecap, to avoid cluttering up the object list.

LOFTING THE PLINTHS

Your next step is to make a base molding, or plinth, for these column bases. This example uses the path you have already created, in combination with another shape in your scene.

1. From the Select by Name dialog, select the object called Colbasepath.

2. Drag it down near the bottom of the Base object by using the appropriate transforms and constraints. Exactly where you put it is not important; you just need to be able to see it below the basecap. Alternatively, you can leave it where it is and simply hide the Basecap object.

3. Follow the same procedures that we used to make the Basecap object, but use the shape called XBaseshape. Copy the shape, scale it up 141.38%, move its pivot point, place it on the path called Colbasepath, and optimize it (see figs. 2.6 and 2.7).

4. Check the loft in a shaded view; the surface normals may need unifying.

5. When it's finished, rename it, move it down to the bottom of the Column Base object so it rests on the ground plane, and then copy it to the other seven Base objects.

6. Group them and name the group something like **Colbaseplinth**.

FIGURE 2.6
The shape for the plinth placed on the path.

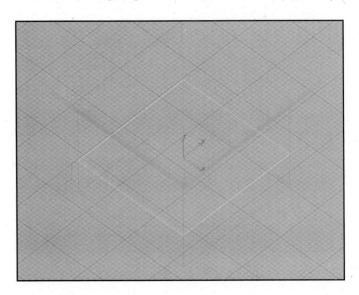

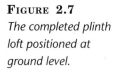

FIGURE 2.7

The completed plinth loft positioned at ground level.

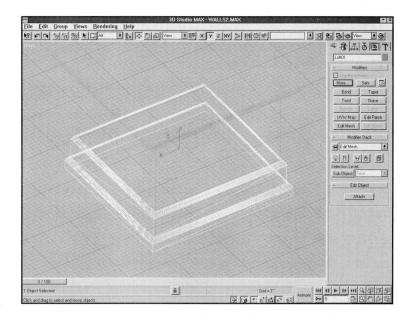

LOFTING THE STRINGCOURSE

This building has two volumes on either side of a central arcade or breezeway. On either side of this central arcade is a building mass, each containing changing rooms. Each side has two doors and a stringcourse that runs around the building about three feet above the ground; below this decorative ledge, the wall surface steps out by 3". The stringcourse that makes up this ledge is the next thing to be modeled.

First, the shape used for the previous loft needs to be slightly modified.

1. Select Stringshape from the Select by Shape dialog, and then zoom in on it in the top viewpoint. This is the original, unscaled shape from the previous exercise.

2. Turn on 2D snap and select the line tool from the Create panel. With Stringshape still selected, click on the checked box beside Start New Shape in the Object Type roll-out. This adds the line you are about to draw to Stringshape.

3. With the Home Grid on, draw a line from the upper left point of the shape to a point exactly nine inches to the right. Figure 2.8 shows the result.

4. Apply an Edit Spline Modifier, and then select the two vertices that lie at the point where you joined this new line to the existing shape. Weld them by clicking the Weld button in the Vertex Sub-Object roll-out.

5. Finally, as before, use Affect Pivot Only in the Hierarchy panel to move the pivot point to the lower right corner of the shape.

FIGURE 2.8
Stringshape modified with the addition of a line on top.

Weld these vertices ——

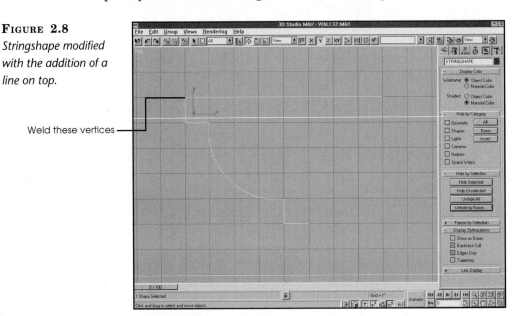

The next step is to create the path for this loft.

6. Select Basewall from the Select by Name dialog. This object contains four Wall objects, two of which are mirror opposites of the other two. To make it easier to see what you're doing, hide all the other objects in the scene.

7. Snap a line around the top of one of the long wall planes by using 3D snap and vertex as the #1 snap priority (see fig. 2.9). Snap the lines in a counter-clockwise order. Call it **Stringpath1**.

8. Use Stringpath1 and the new, modified version of Stringshape to create a loft, and in the Skin Parameters roll-out, set Shape Steps set to 2, Path Steps to 0 (because there are no curved sections on the path), and Contour On and Banking Off.

FIGURE 2.9
Path created on top of one of the Basewall sections.

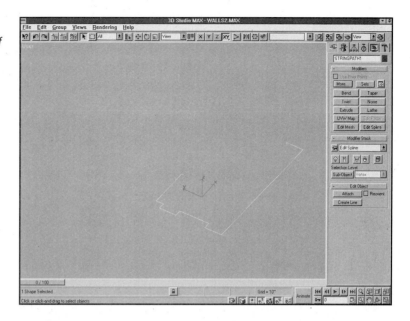

The resulting loft is distorted because the shape is both incorrectly teetered and incorrectly scaled at the vertices (see fig. 2.10).

FIGURE 2.10
Lofted shape with contour option on but shapes at the vertices unadjusted.

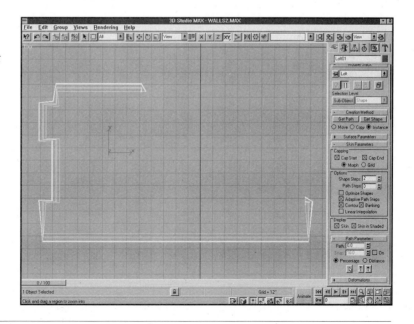

Teetering the Shape

Fixing the teetering problem will be accomplished first. For architectural moldings, you obviously want the shape profile at each vertex to lie precisely on a line that bisects the angle created by the change of direction in the path. This produces a symmetrical turn in the loft, mimicking the mitering that a carpenter would do with the actual molding. Two ways enable you to do this:

- Loft the shape and then use the Teeter Deformation controls in the Deformation roll-out at the bottom of the Modify panel to pivot the shape at the vertices to the correct angle.

- Manipulate the vertices of the path.

Both methods work well, but the second scenario is a little faster and more accurate. It takes advantage of 3DS MAX's capability to simultaneously display the lofted result while you adjust the vertices of the path generating the same loft.

MANIPULATING THE VERTICES TO TEETER THE LOFT

Following are the steps involved in correcting the vertices of the path to produce a correct loft.

1. Expand the top viewport. From the Select by Name dialog, select Stringpath1. Right-click on any vertex on the spline to display the pop-up menu, and choose Bézier from the menu, to change the vertex type. Zoom in as necessary.

   The Bézier handles will appear, and by dragging the handles, it is possible to interactively twist the tangent of the path spline at the vertex and thereby pivot the shape precisely at that vertex. Because the loft is still skinned, you get to see the result of the adjustments every time you release the handle after a drag operation. The only remaining question is how much to pivot the vertex; a reference line makes it easy. Creating one is quick with this particular loft, where the path aligns exactly with the X and Y axes.

2. Use the Home Grid and 2D snaps with grid intersections as the highest priority to draw a guide line at exactly a 45-degree angle to the path.

3. Mirror it by using the copy option with no offset, creating an X-shaped object. Use Edit Spline to attach the two together. Now you have two lines, one to use with each angle orientation. The object is visible in figure. 2.11 in position at a corner of the loft.

4. Move this X-shaped object so that the appropriate leg of the object passes exactly through the path vertex that is being adjusted. This can be accomplished by setting 2.5D or 3D snap with vertex point as top priority and dragging the intersection of the guide shape to the path vertex.

5. Reselect the path, select the vertex, and drag one of the Bézier handles until the shape at the vertex aligns with the guide line. The loft makes a symmetrical angle (see fig. 2.11).

FIGURE 2.11

Adjusting the vertex with the Bézier handles so that the corner of the loft lies on the guide line.

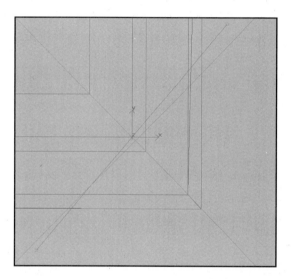

NOTE

As figure 2.11 shows, the handles do not necessarily lie precisely perpendicular to the loft angle when the shape has been correctly teetered. This results from the asymmetrical effect exerted on the vertex by the different length segments on either side of that vertex. If the segments on either side of the vertex are the same length, the handles are perpendicular to the shape at the vertex (that is, parallel to the other leg of the X-shaped Guide object).

6. Repeat the preceding steps for all the vertices on the path. Figure 2.12 shows the loft with the teetering corrected by the shapes still incorrectly scaled at the vertices. This is most evident at the ends of the loft.

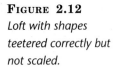

FIGURE 2.12
*Loft with shapes
teetered correctly but
not scaled.*

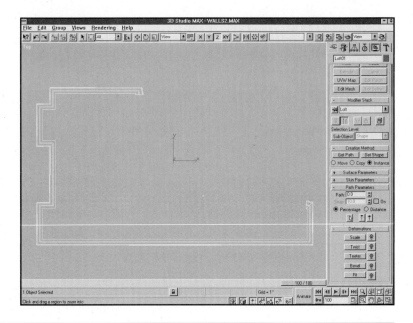

TIP

To provide more accuracy and sensitivity in the adjustment, it helps to stretch the Bézier handles out to the edges of the view that you have zoomed in on.

Creating guide lines for any angle is easy. Use vertex and edge snaps to draw a line segment that lies exactly on top of either of the path segments that meet the vertex you want to adjust. Then use the Rotate Transform dialog to enter a precise quantity to rotate the line one-half the angle that the path forms. Then move the line into place and proceed as outlined in the preceding exercise.

Using the Teeter Deformation Dialog

The first method previously mentioned to correct the shape teetering at the vertices involves using the Teeter Deformation dialog found under the Deformations roll-out at the bottom of the Modify panel. The use of this box is covered elsewhere, but a few things should be kept in mind when using this dialog to correct lofted architectural moldings and shapes.

■ Placing control points on the curve is inherently imprecise; the snaps do not have any effect, and placing the control points accurately at the vertex locations is a matter of repeated zooming in and moving. If this is not done with reasonable care, the teetering adjustment that you want to occur at the vertex of the path will be slightly off. This tuning process can be time-consuming.

■ If the Contour box is checked in the Skin Parameters roll-out, the shapes automatically teeter an amount that is difficult to measure, governed by the vertex and segment properties at each vertex. To teeter from this state to the precise angle that bisects the path angle necessitates guide lines, as used previously, and it then becomes easier to use the previous outlined method. Turning off Contour, however, produces a loft in which all the shapes at each vertex remain at zero rotation (see fig. 2.13). Then it is easy to use the Type-In option in the Teeter dialog to enter the correct rotation (45 degrees, 67.5 degrees, and so on, for example).

Figure 2.13

Loft with Contour unchecked and shape at each vertex at zero rotation.

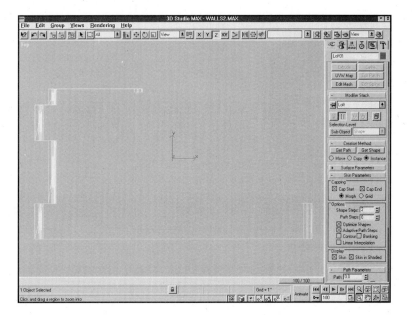

The scaling problem, fixed in the previous exercise by scaling the shape before placing it on the path, can be fixed in this case in either of two ways:

- Placing a scaled copy of the shape at the vertices (other than the end vertices, of course) by using the Path Parameters roll-out in the Modify Panel.

- Use the one, unscaled shape automatically placed at the end of the path, and then use the Scale dialog found under the Deformation roll-out to scale the shape up at the vertices.

Neither method is completely accurate.

Using Path Parameters to Place Scaled Shapes

The Path Parameters controls do not provide a way to place a shape exactly at a vertex; they only enable you to place a shape a certain distance down a path from the first vertex. Unless you know exactly what that distance is, it becomes a matter of repeated zooming in and moving. Also, you are limited by the precision of 3DS MAX and by the units that you have selected to work in, and so you may not be able to move the shape precisely the correct amount even if you know what that amount is. Fractional Inches, which you will likely be using for architectural work, is less accurate than Decimal units, but neither is useful unless you know the exact distance down the path to the vertex that you are trying to reach. It might be some nice, round number such as 3", in which case things are easier. Otherwise, you could try to determine it with the tape measure tool, but that entails the same limitations of precision.

Using the Scale Deformation Controls

The Scale Deformation dialog is the easier method, although it is still not perfect.

1. Insert control points on the Deformation Curve at each vertex location (the vertical lines in the Deformation Grid). Use the X-axis for loft paths that lie in the X/Y World plane, as this one does. Set symmetry off.

2. By zooming in and adjusting, position the control points as accurately as possible at the vertex locations. Snaps are not applicable here, so it's a matter of fine-tuning.

3. Move the control points up at the vertices using move axis constraints, by selecting them one by one and typing in the appropriate scale values (as discussed previously) in the right-hand field at the bottom of the dialog. It would be handy to be able to select all the control points that you want to move the same amount and move them together, but 3DS MAX only enables you to drag the control points when multiple are selected; type-in entry is disabled. A possible strategy here is to select all the points that require similar displacements and then drag them to the correct value, using zoom to get greater and greater levels of precision. If you want to be able to enter the exact amount, however, you must do it one point at a time.

4. With this loft, the scale deformation at all the vertices is 141.38%. Figure 2.14 shows the scale-corrected loft.

FIGURE 2.14
Scale-corrected loft and Scale Deformation dialog.

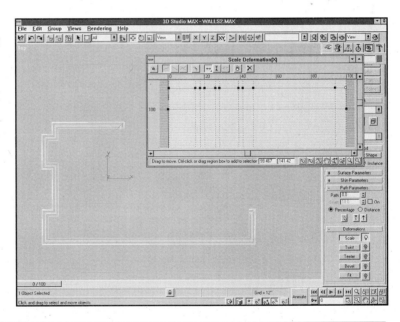

This section of Stringcourse is now lofted and corrected. The final steps follow:

1. Check surface normals and correct as necessary. Rename this loft **Stringcourse**.

2. Close the top of the ledge of this Stringcourse where the ledge bumps out and the columns are to rest (see fig. 2.15). This can be done in various ways:

■ Use Sub-Object, Vertex, Collapse to bring some of the top vertices together.

■ Use Sub-Object, Vertex, Weld, Target to join the vertices.

■ To fill in the wider ledge top that occurs right at the corner of the building, it is necessary to either move a vertex by using move constraints or add one to the edge of the loft. You probably want to create some guide lines or boxes to help move the vertices so that the edges at the top of the shape remain perpendicular. Figure 2.15 shows this operation in progress, and figure 2.16 shows a shaded view of the finished Stringcourse in place on the building with the widened ledge sections ready for the columns that will sit on them.

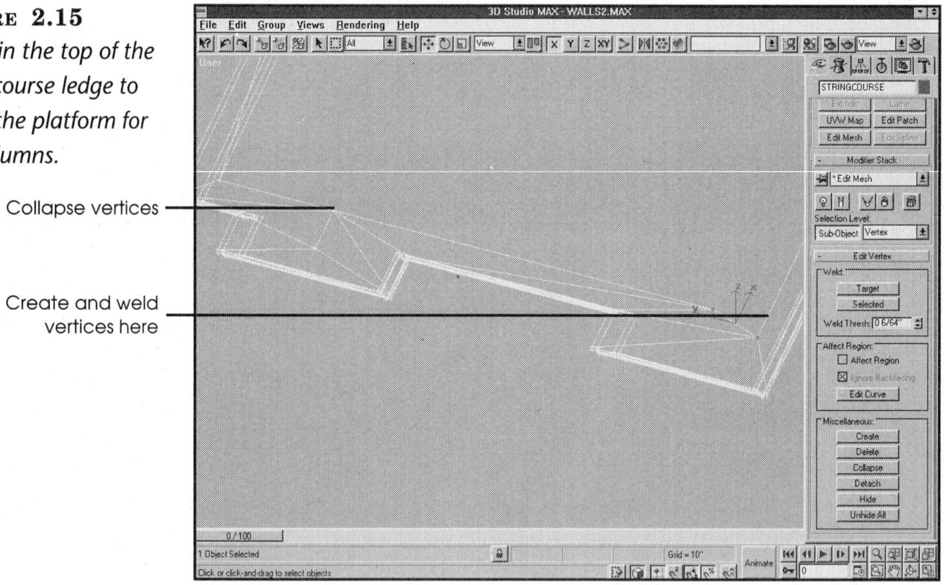

FIGURE 2.15

Filling in the top of the Stringcourse ledge to make the platform for the columns.

Collapse vertices

Create and weld vertices here

FIGURE 2.16
*The finished
Stringcourse in place
on the project to date.*

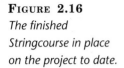

FIGURE 2.16
*The finished
Stringcourse in place
on the project to date.*

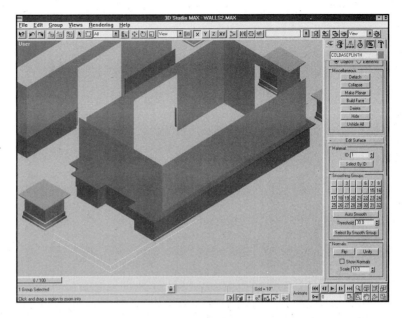

3. Use the outlined procedures to create lofts on the tops of the other three sections of Basewall, and then attach them to make one object called Stringcourse.

Making the Columns and Cornices

Forty columns surround this building. Columns are easy to make in 3DS MAX. Two methods in particular are worth mentioning:

■ Draw a spline outline for the column, and then apply a Lathe modifier to create a surface of revolution.

■ Draw a straight line and loft a circle by using the line as the path, and then create the profile of the column by manipulating the function curve in the Scale Deformation dialog.

It is also possible to build up a column shape out of primitives (cylinders, squashed spheres, and so on). This method will most likely leave you with unnecessary hidden faces, as well as being harder to modify later. Both of these mentioned methods enable you to draw the outline of the column by adjusting the Bézier handles of a spline, making it possible to tune the shape of your column quite closely. Figure 2.17 shows the base of a column lofted with a straight line and a circle, and then modified with the function curve in the Scale Deformation dialog.

FIGURE 2.17

Bottom of Column and Scale Deformation box with the function curve that generated the loft scaling.

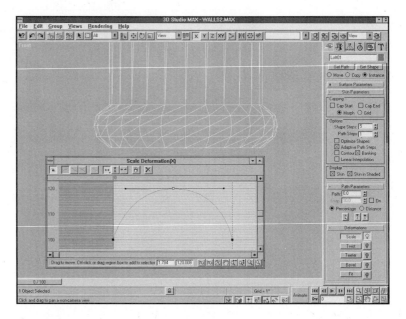

Here, the shape of the function curve is the same as the profile of the loft, a situation generally not the case in the Loft Deformation controls. Just as with a spline, you can achieve precise shaping of the curve by the use of the Bézier handles. The result here is the base of a Tuscan Order column, awaiting the addition of the abacus to complete it.

It is somewhat more difficult to control the polygon count with this method; forcing straight sections of the column to have no steps, and therefore fewer polygons, is easier to achieve with the spline-and-lathe method. If you want your columns to have entasis, they will contain no straight sections and will have much higher polygon counts. For this project, the columns are straight-sided. Follow these steps:

1. Draw a spline that outlines your column, or use the one called Columnspline supplied in the .Max file. This spline is the correct height, so if you decide to draw your own, make it the same length.

TIP

If you have straight sections in the columns, as the shape Columnspline does, it greatly reduces polygon counts. Remember to set steps to zero when drawing lines; set it higher when drawing arcs. If you use Attach to make the spline one shape, each section retains its steps. If you create a single spline by turning off the Start New Shape option, however, the results are less predictable. If you draw the line segment first with zero steps, and then uncheck Start New Shape and draw an arc with higher steps, for example, the arc is forced to have zero steps like the line segment. Maintaining control of these factors results in more efficient modeling.

2. Apply a Lathe modifier to the spline. The Direction area of the Parameters roll-out supplies options for X, Y, and Z. Pick the one that aligns the white axis line with the length of the spline. You end up with the curious object shown on the left in figure 2.18.

3. Turn on Sub-Object. Axis is the only option in the Sub-Object menu.

4. Drag the yellow axis line sideways, to generate a column similar to the one on the right in figure 2.18, the shaft of which is eight inches in diameter. If you prefer some other proportion, then drag to suit.

5. Create two boxes, at the top and bottom of the column, to form the abacuses and attach them to the column. Make them as wide and long as the decorative bulge in the column and 1-$\frac{1}{2}$ inches high, and the columns will be the correct height.

6. Copy the column to the locations shown in figure 2.19 —four on each of the Colbase objects, and two on the wide sections of the ledges that are part of the Stringcourse that was lofted in the previous exercise. Notice that the four outer Colbase objects do not have columns yet. The Columns that go there are taller and will be scaled later from a column already modeled.

FIGURE 2.18
Lathed column shape
before and after Lathe
Axis adjustment.

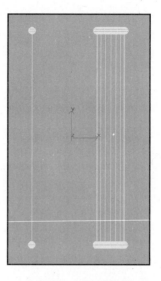

FIGURE 2.19
Columns placed on the
Colbases and on the
Stringcourse.

Columns on
stringcourse ledge

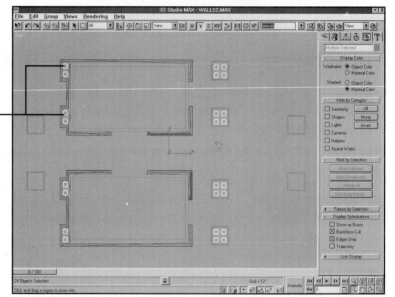

The Cornices

Two cornice lines are on this structure. One cornice line runs around the two
building masses that comprise the changing rooms, and the other cornice
line is higher and defines the central arcade through the building. All the

cornices have the same profile, a shape included in the .Max file called Corniceshape. It can be found lying on the construction plane beside the other shapes. A path called Cornicepath1 is also in the scene; it is the path to be used to loft the cornices that run around the tops of the changing rooms. Cornicepath2 can be used to loft the cornices that run the length of the central breezeway. They all have been modeled already, using the previously described techniques, and can be unhidden if you do not wish to model them. They are called Cornice1 and Cornice2 (for the sections that go around the changing rooms) and Cornice3 and Cornice4 (for the ones that flank the central arcade). Note that on the front and the back of the building, where the cornices project out from the walls, the undersides of the lofts have to be filled in to make ceilings for these porch-like overhangs; otherwise the loft yields a floating cornice with nothing inside it when you look up underneath. This is easily done by selecting the vertices at the bottom inside corners of the cornice lofts and dragging them until they meet the exterior wall surface, filling the gap (see fig. 2.20).

FIGURE 2.20

Filling in the underside of the cornice lofts.

Drag vertices —

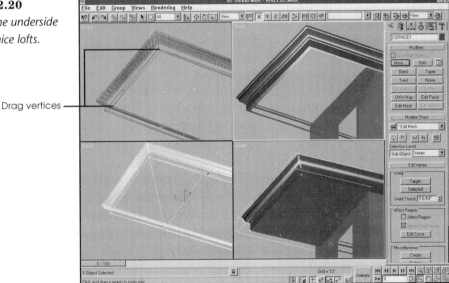

NOTE

In a fully detailed model, of course, the ceiling of these overhangs and porches would be a different material from the cornices themselves; there would also likely be a reveal where the bottom edge of the cornice projected down below the surface of this ceiling by an inch or two. The additional modeling that this involves is not central to the point of this chapter, but feel free to do it if you want.

More Columns

The next step is to place the remaining columns. The cornices that flank the arcade are supported by taller columns than the ones that surround the changing rooms. It is just a matter of copying and stretching an existing column.

1. In a side view, copy a group of four columns with Transform and X constraint (see fig. 2.21).

2. Select the top vertices, and stretch the columns up until they reach the underside of the arcade cornice (see fig. 2.21).

3. Position the columns on one of the unoccupied Colbase objects, and then copy them to the remaining Colbase objects under the arcade cornices (see fig. 2.22).

FIGURE 2.21

Columns copied and stretched to support the arcade cornices.

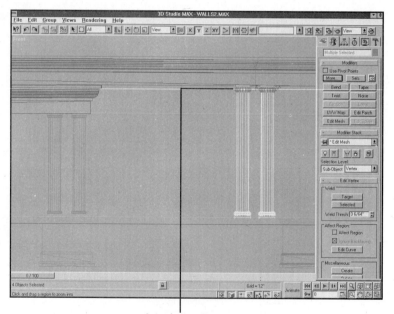

Select all vertices
at column tops

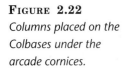

FIGURE 2.22
Columns placed on the Colbases under the arcade cornices.

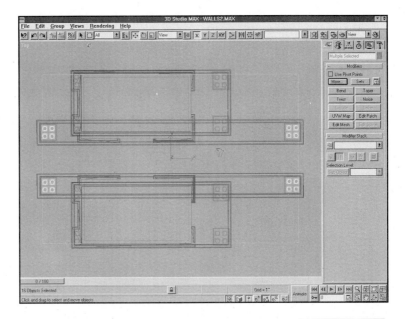

Adding Roofs

The simple hip and gable roofs on this bathhouse can be made quickly in 3DS MAX. In this model, it is not necessary to model the roofs inside and out, as would be required if the structure had cathedral ceilings, open trusswork, or a second floor with dormers. Situations like that require more complex modeling, but the basic techniques described in the following exercise will be of value in modeling any roof. For this building, you need only model primitives to achieve the shape needed, visible from the outside.

CHANGING ROOM ROOFS

The bathhouse has two hipped roofs that cover the changing rooms on either side and a gabled section that covers the central arcade. The first roofs to model are the hipped sections over the changing rooms.

1. Hide everything except either Cornice1 or Cornice2 (or whatever you called the cornices over the changing rooms, if you modeled them).

2. Create a box close to the size of the outside edge of the cornice. This can be done best in either the top viewport or in a user view. Snaps do not help you at this point; the box will be adjusted later to fit exactly. The height of the box is not important at this point. Call the box **Roof**.

3. In a side viewport, use edge snaps to move the box up or down until it rests precisely on the top edge of the cornice (see fig. 2.23).

4. In the top viewport, zoom to any corner and use edge snaps to move the box in both X and Y to align its corner exactly with the corner of the cornice.

5. Adjust the box by region-selecting vertices in the top viewport to move one entire side of the box, using the appropriate axis constraint (see fig. 2.24). Edge snap enables you to drag the sides of the box to align with the cornice edge. Do this on both sides of the box that need aligning (the other two sides having been aligned earlier when you zoomed in and aligned the corners).

FIGURE 2.23

Roof box resting on the top edge of the cornice.

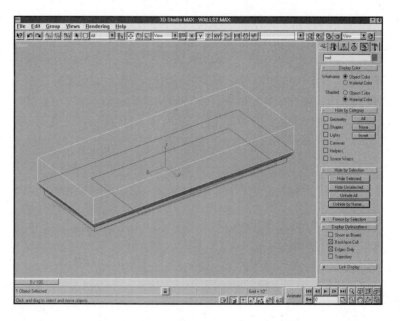

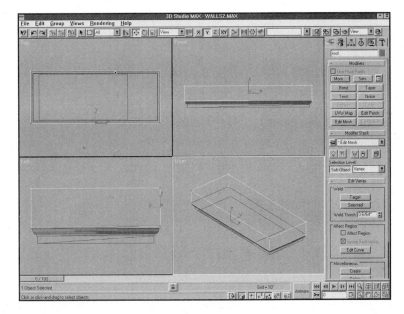

You now have a box that is exactly the length and width of the cornice. It would be more realistic, however, to have a drip-edge on the roof, a projection of an inch or two past the surface below.

6. Use the same method as before to expand the box all around by two inches. Region select vertices on one side of the box at a time and move the vertices out from the cornice by two inches. You can do this by zooming in and dragging, and watching the offset readout field in the status line. It is easier, faster, and more accurate, however, to right-click on the Move Transform button and type in your movement. You can do this without having to zoom in each time, and still achieve accuracy. Figure 2.25 shows the Move Transform Type-In dialog.

7. Select the bottom face of the roof and delete it. The roof is now a shell resting on the cornice.

NOTE

Because of this slight overhanging drip-edge, which adds a significant detail of realism with the shadow line that it casts, you must remember when assigning a material to the roof for rendering that the material should be made two-sided; otherwise, it will be possible to look up through the slight projecting edge of the roof and see the sky.

FIGURE 2.25

Using Move Transform Type-In to enlarge the roof box by two inches on all sides.

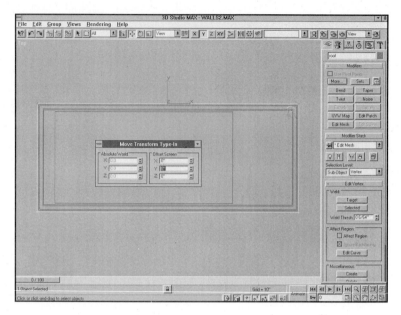

Setting the height of the ridge and pitch of the roof comes next. This building has roof pitches of 12-in-12, so the rise equals the run. The height of the ridge is therefore equal to one-half the total span of the roof. After these numbers are established, you can adjust the vertices to easily produce the roof form needed.

8. Determine the total span of the roof. This can be done by using the Tape Tool. It is, however, simpler and easier to go to the bottom of the Modifier Stack of the Roof object and read the dimension right out of the base parameters boxes.

9. While at the base parameters level, change the height of the box to equal half the box's width. The box is now precisely the height of the ridge for a 12-pitch roof.

10. Go back up to the top of the Modifier Stack and select two vertices at the top of the roof box and at one end, as shown on the left in figure 2.26.

11. Click on Collapse from the Miscellaneous section of the Edit Vertex rollout to weld the two selected vertices together at a point exactly mid-way between their original locations. The result is visible on the right in figure 2.26.

FIGURE 2.26

Using Collapse to bring together vertices to form the gable of the roof.

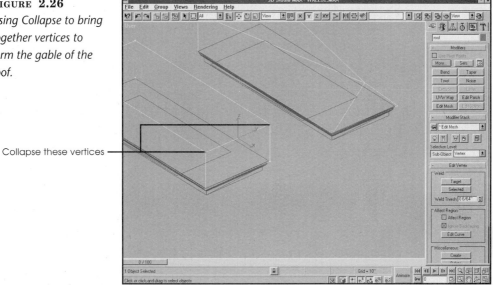

Collapse these vertices ──

12. Do the same for the rear set of vertices, and you have the basic shape of a 12-pitch gable roof with a two-inch drip-edge at the eaves.

These side roof sections are hips with equal pitches on all sides. You need to place a 12-in-12 pitch on what is now the front and rear gable surfaces of this roof.

13. Select the front ridge vertex, as shown on the left in figure 2.27, and use the Move Transform Type-In dialog box to move it towards the center of the roof by a distance equal to one-half the width of the roof (or the ridge height). The result is a hipped roof with 12-in-12 pitch all around, as shown on the right in figure 2.27.

14. Move the rear ridge vertex by the same method to complete the roof shape.

NOTE

These operations can also be accomplished by applying Taper modifiers, but it is more complicated and less accurate. Almost any symmetrical roof can be built with the preceding outlined steps. A roof with different pitches on all sides or different eave heights might require techniques such as Tapering, but generally this is not necessary.

FIGURE 2.27

The front and rear hips formed by moving the vertices by the type-in method.

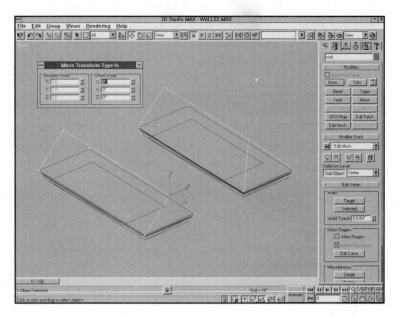

15. Use Move Transform Type-In to move the entire roof shape down one inch, to more closely represent the way the roof edge would meet the cornice.

16. Copy the roof shape to the other cornice on the other side of the building.

THE ARCADE ROOF

The central roof mass that covers the arcade can be built in the same way.

1. Hide everything except the two central cornices, called Cornice3 and Cornice4 (or whatever you named them, if you modeled them).

2. Use the same method to build a gable roof over these two cornices. This roof section is also 12-in-12 pitch but is not hipped. You should end up with a roof that looks like the one in figure 2.28.

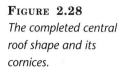

FIGURE 2.28
The completed central roof shape and its cornices.

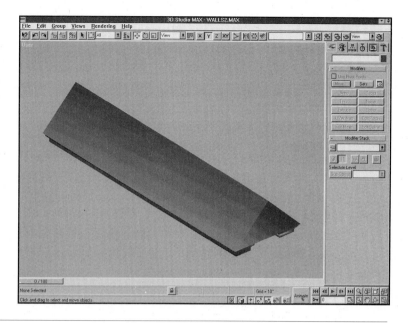

MAKING THE PEDIMENTS OVER THE ARCADE

The central arcade has a barrelvault ceiling and a Neo-Palladian style gable treatment at each end. Some Boolean Modeling and some lofting easily produce these details.

1. Hide everything except the central roof and its two cornices.

2. Create a cylinder the long axis of which lies parallel to the central roof, with a diameter approximately equal to the distance between the cornices. The diameter will be more closely adjusted later. The length of the cylinder should be greater than the length of the central roof (see fig. 2.29).

3. Use Align to center the cylinder on the middle of the bottom edge of the gable of the roof. Figure 2.29 shows the orientation.

FIGURE 2.29
The Cylinder shape in position.

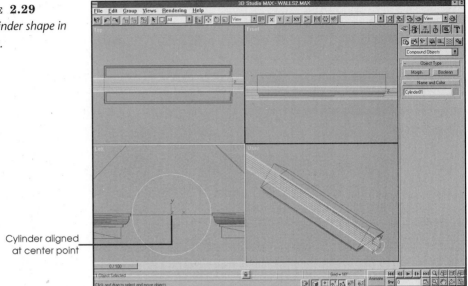

Cylinder aligned
at center point

4. Adjust the base parameters of the cylinder so that the diameter is six inches greater than the diameter of the barrelvault. Compensate for minor inaccuracies, if necessary, by shifting the cylinder sideways. Absolute precision is not essential here.

5. Perform a Boolean Subtraction, subtracting the cylinder from the central roof, using the Move option in the Pick Boolean roll-out to produce the shape seen in figure 2.30.

6. Hide the cornices. Apply an Edit Mesh modifier to the roof and select the faces that make up one of the gable-ends. This is seen on the right in figure 2.31.

7. Detach the selected faces and rename them **Tympanum**.

8. Move Tympanum back from the front of the roof to get it out of the way, as on the left in figure 2.31. It will be readjusted later. Perform the same operations on the other gable at the opposite end of the central roof.

FIGURE 2.30
The barrelvault cut through the roof shape by using a Boolean Subtraction.

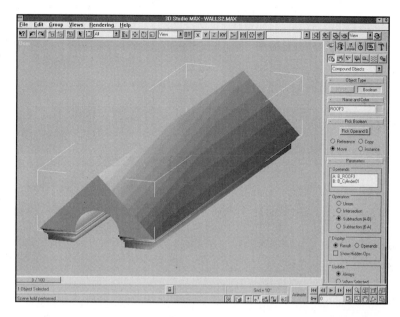

FIGURE 2.31
Creating and moving the object Tympanum.

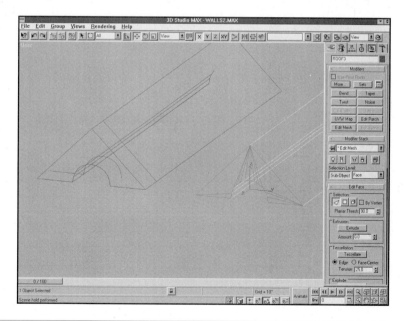

ADDING MOLDINGS TO THE PEDIMENT

To complete the pediments at each end of the central roof, various moldings are needed. The first one to model is the rake molding, the one that follows the pitch of the roof.

1. Make a copy of the shape called Stringshape, the original, unscaled shape from the first exercise. Call it **Rakeshape**.

2. Apply an XForm modifier to the copy of Rakeshape and Uniform Scale it up by 200%. Then Non-Uniform scale it on the Y-axis by a factor of 141.38%, to account for the fact that the loft path will be making 90-degree turns. This scaling is performed on the Y-axis and not the X-axis as in previous examples because of the vertical orientation of this loft path. Remember that this scaling must be accomplished by using an XForm modifier, not by directly applying the scaling; otherwise, the loft ignores the scaling and uses the unscaled version.

TIP

Don't forget that it is easy and accurate to apply these transforms by right-clicking on the Transform button and typing in the displacement.

3. In the Hierarchy, use Affect Pivot Only to move Rakeshape's pivot point to the topmost point of the shape. Figure 2.32 shows the resulting shape.

FIGURE 2.32
Rakeshape scaled up and the pivot point moved to the upper corner.

New point location ——

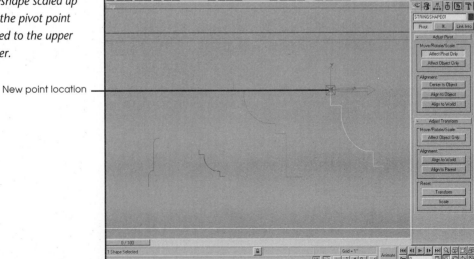

Now the path for this loft can be drawn:

4. Using 3D snap with Vertex Point as the highest priority, snap a line from one corner of the eave of the roof shape up to the ridge and down to the other corner, outlining the roof edges. Name the spline **Rakespline**.

5. Move the spline slightly inward from the roof to avoid the possibility of the edge of the lofted molding showing through the roof surface when you render. To do this, select the ridge vertex of Rakespline and using Move Transform Type-in, move it straight down $1/4$ or $1/2$ inch. Select each of the vertices at the eaves in turn and move them inward a small amount in the same way so that there is a slight gap between the spline and, the roof object.

6. Create the loft by using Rakespline as the path and Rakeshape as the shape. Set path steps to 0 and shape steps to 2, and then click on Optimize Shapes. The resulting loft can be seen on the right in figure 2.33. Rename the loft **Rake1**.

7. Open the Teeter Deformation box in the Deformations roll-out at the bottom of the Modify panel. Select the existing control points at the ends of the function curve in the Teeter box one at a time and move them vertically by typing in values in the field at the bottom of the box. The left-hand control point receives a teeter of –45 degrees, the right-hand one a teeter of 45 degrees. The corrected loft is visible on the left in figure 2.33.

FIGURE 2.33

Teeter-corrected loft and Teeter Deformation box showing displacement of the function curve.

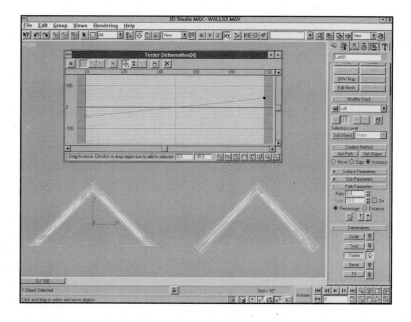

N O T E

The previous examples used vertex manipulation to teeter the shapes at the vertices of lofts; this case, however, presents a situation where it is easier to use the Teeter Deformation box. This is due to two things: First, the control points that you are adjusting are already exactly located at the vertices because they are at the ends of the path, and so the time-consuming and somewhat inaccurate process of placing control points at vertices can be skipped; Second, you know that the teeter required is exactly 45 degrees because the roof pitch is 45 degrees, being 12-in-12. Thus it is easy to type the displacement right in.

8. Correct Surface Normals as necessary.

9. Unhide the two central cornices, Cornice3 and Cornice4, and use edge snap to reposition the outermost surface of the rake molding that you just lofted to be flush with the outermost surface of the cornices.

THE BARRELVAULT MOLDING

The other molding that will be added to these pediments is a curved molding that outlines the barrelvault. First the path is generated.

1. Looking straight on at the pediment, draw a circle the diameter of which is approximately the width of the barrelvault.

2. Use Align to center the circle precisely in the middle of the barrelvault, in the same way that you aligned the cylinder to the roof shape. Use X-position and center/center in the Align dialog box.

3. Adjust the diameter of the circle to be close to the diameter of barrelvault. Absolute accuracy is unnecessary.

4. Draw a rectangle that overlaps the bottom half of the circle, the top of which aligns with the bottom edge of the barrelvault (see fig. 2.34).

5. Attach the circle and the rectangle and perform a Boolean Subtraction, leaving only the top half of the circle (see fig. 2.34).

6. Erase the bottom line segment of the circle, leaving only an arc that follows the curve of the barrelvault. This is visible on the right in figure 2.34. Rename the object **Barrelpath** and move it from the middle of the barrelvault to near the pediment. Final placement occurs after the loft is created.

FIGURE 2.34

Using Boolean operations to create the path for the molding to trim the barrelvault.

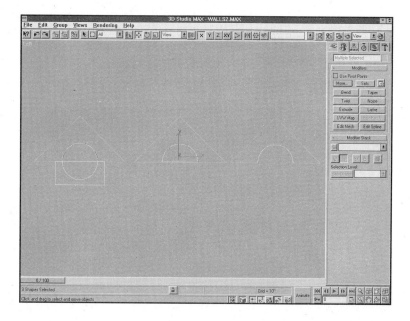

7. There is in the .max file a shape called Barrelshape; use it to create a loft with Barrelpath. It may be necessary to flip the shape as you are getting it by holding down Ctrl, and it may also be necessary to rotate the shape after it's placed on the path by using Sub-Object/Shape in the Modify panel. The correct orientation is shown in the upper left viewport of figure 2.35.

8. It will probably be necessary to set the path steps to 8 or higher to get a smooth shape; shape steps can be 2 or 3. The lower right viewport in figure 2.35 shows the loft with path steps of 10 and shape steps of 2. Polygon count is 616. Generally, it is difficult to produce good curved lofts without high face counts; when the shape also has curved sections, the problem is compounded. Rename the loft **Barrelmold**.

Now all that remains is to position the various components of the pediment and clean up some edges.

9. Use edge snap and the appropriate axis constraint to move Tympanum1 until it aligns with the inner edge of Rake1.

10. Now move Barrelmold until it wraps around the edge of the tympanum.

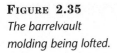

FIGURE 2.35
The barrelvault
molding being lofted.

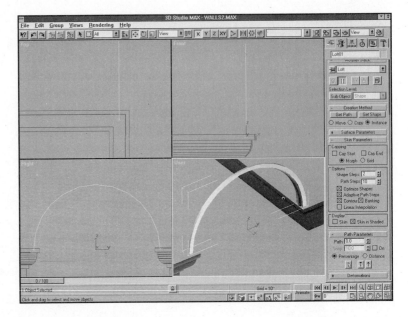

11. In the object Roof 3, the arcade roof, delete the two horizontal planes that make up the bottom of the shape on either side of the barrelvault, using Sub Object/Face to select them. This leaves only the roof planes and the actual surface of the barrelvault.

12. Select the faces that make up the barrelvault and detach them from the roof. Call the new object Barrelvault.

13. Select all the vertices at the end of the object Barrelvault, and drag them inward until the end of Barrelvault fits into Barrelmold.

14. Finally, shrink the object Tympanum slightly in the same way that you adjusted the Rakepath—select the ridge and eave vertices of Tympanum and move them slightly away from the Roof object by means of the Move Transform Type-In. This prevents the top edge of Tympanum from showing through the roof surface during rendering.

Figure 2.36 shows the finished pediment.

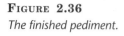

FIGURE 2.36
The finished pediment.

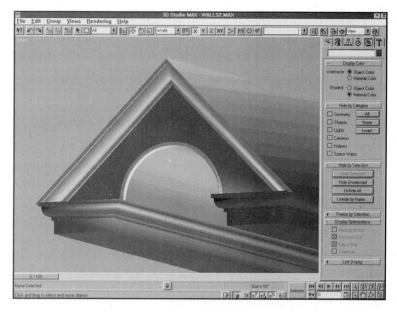

The preceding steps can now be duplicated on the other pediment at the opposite end of the building.

The Doorways

To complete the exterior of this building, you need only a few more details. The next thing to create is the door frames for the four doorways that lead in and out of the changing rooms.

1. Hide everything except the objects Wall-out and Wall-in. In the right viewport, zoom in on one of the doors.

2. Draw a box 48 inches wide, 6 inches long, and 10 inches high. Center the box on the doorway opening in the wall. The height is not important at this point.

3. Region-select the upper left vertices of this box, and using Move Trans-
    form Type-In, move the vertices two inches to the left. In the same way,
    move the upper right vertices two inches to the right.

4. Near the center of the box, create another box with a length of 10 inches,
    a width of 8 inches, and a height of 12 inches.

5. Use Align to center the second box on the first. Click on X, Y, and Z in the
    position options and center/center.

6. Region-select the lower left vertices of the center box object and use Move
    Transform Type-In to move the vertices one inch to the right. Move the
    lower right vertices of the same mass to the left one inch. The central box
    is now tapered in at the bottom.

7. Attach the two boxes and rename the resulting object **Lintel**.

8. In the top viewport, move the lintel to span equally across the Wall-in
    and the Wall-out objects, as seen in the top viewport of figure 2.37. The
    lower left viewport of figure 2.37 shows the finished lintel.

FIGURE 2.37

The finished lintel in position.

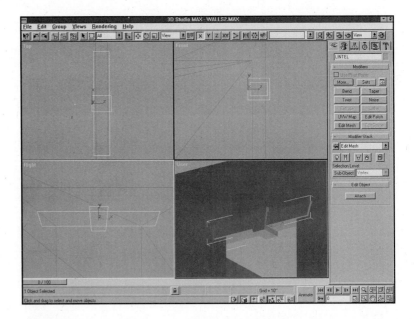

9. In the side viewport, use edge snap to move the lintel so that the bottom
    of the lintel aligns with the top of the doorway opening in the wall
    surface.

Now, create the door jambs.

10. Hide the lintel. Use 3D snap with vertex priority to draw a line around the doorway opening by snapping to the corners of the doorway. Call this line **Jambpath**.

11. Use the various loft techniques previously explored to loft a door jamb by using the shape called Jambshape included in the .Max file and the Jambpath created in the preceding step. It may be necessary to rotate Jambshape after placing it on the path so that the molded edge details face out into the doorway opening (see fig. 2.38). With the loft selected, use Sub-Object/Shape to rotate the shape. Scale and Teeter the loft as needed.

12. Center the jamb over the Wall-in and Wall-out surfaces so that it protrudes equally from each wall surface. Center it below the lintel. The finished opening should look like the one shown in figure 2.38.

FIGURE 2.38

The finished doorway in place in the wall.

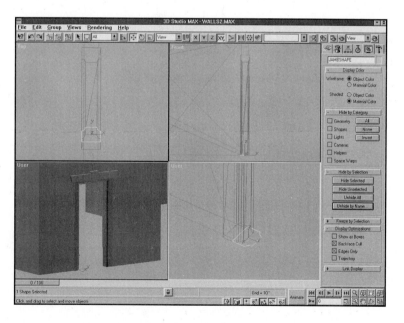

13. Copy the jamb and lintel to the other three doorways. It will be necessary to enlarge the jamb and lintel and reposition the keystone in the lintel to fit the larger doorways that face out into the arcade. Don't use a non-uniform scale for this; it stretches the width of the side jambs and the keystone in an undesirable way. Just select all the vertices on one side and pull them out to fit the doorway. Figure 2.39 shows the finished doorways.

14. Make final adjustments to the size of the jambs as necessary by unhiding the doors and doorknobs already modeled in the .Max file and resizing the jambs to just fit the doors. Alternatively, you could resize the doors to fit the jambs. In either case, this should be done by selecting and moving groups of vertices. Figure 2.40 shows the finished bathhouse.

FIGURE 2.39

The doorways and the doors and knobs.

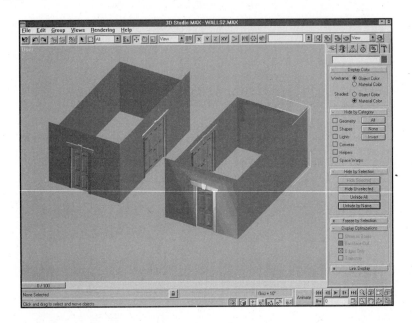

FIGURE 2.40

The finished Neo-Classical bathhouse.

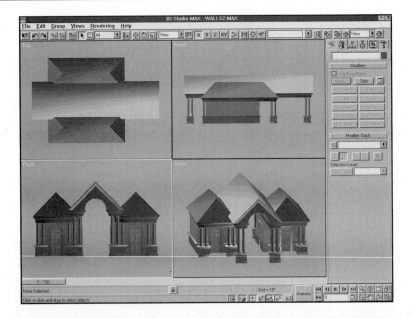

The exterior is now finished with a level of detail adequate for most views. Close-ups might require more detail, depending on what you're looking at. The interior could be modeled using these procedures—baseboards, doorways, crown moldings, and chair rails.

In Practice: Architectural Modeling and Rendering

- **The Basic Walls.** Working from existing CAD documents is likely to be the starting point for a lot of architectural modeling and rendering. There are advantages to roughing-out the basic walls in CAD and then importing them into 3DS MAX, but it is also useful to import just plans and extrude up from there. Be aware of how various entities import into 3DS MAX.

- **Lofting Moldings.** A lot of the details in architectural modeling are lofts. Scaling and Teetering the shape correctly at the vertices is the most important step for good architectural lofting.

- **Polygons.** Face counts climb quickly in architectural models. Always be economical in modeling, keeping in mind the fact that a lot of detail and accuracy may never be noticeable.

- **Instancing and Referencing.** Make use of 3DS MAX's capability to cross-reference parameters from one object to another; architectural models often have repetitive elements and instancing them can make later changes a simple matter.

- **Overlapping Planes.** Faces need not always meet perfectly, and it is a waste of time to make them do so when it's unnecessary. Door trim, for example, can overlap the wall plane next to it. That's what it does in a real building. Don't spend time where it's not needed.

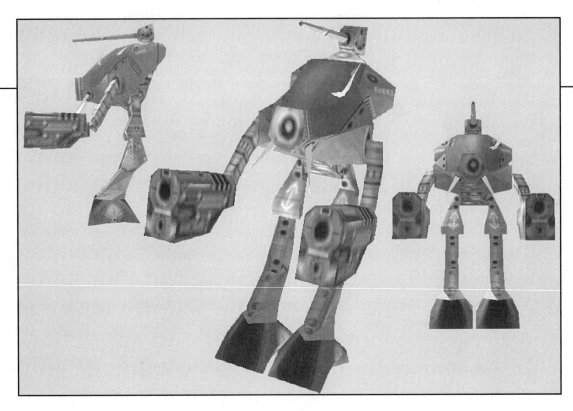

IMAGE USED WITH PERSMISSION OF GAMETEK

Chapter 3

by Ken Allen Robertson

MODELING FOR REAL-TIME 3D GAMES

No area of 3D graphics is garnering as much attention as real-time gaming—and no other area shows as much potential for massive growth in the next few years.

Real-time 3D is only in its infancy in the consumer market. Set-top gaming systems that support real-time are in their first generation. Many real-time graphics engines (as opposed to 2D sprite graphics) are only now beginning to be widely used by PC game developers. Renderware, Brender, and Microsoft's DirectDraw (a software engine for Windows 95 graphics) are among the real-time graphics engines gaining popularity. 2D sprite graphics, however, still dominate the PC gaming market.

The massive influx of Internet games is also fueling the drive to real-time 3D games (Quake currently is the most notable). With the advent of Java and VRML 2.0, the promise of real-time Internet 3D games that can be played from any type of machine is near. 3D *MUDs* (multi-user-dungeons)—ongoing role-play worlds on the Internet—are being developed by many companies around the world.

The skills of the real-time 3D artist are broad and varied. In addition to in-depth knowledge of the software used to generate source materials (3D meshes, texture maps, animations, and so on), a real-time artist must have a firm grasp of the programmatic principles that make real-time 3D possible. This does not mean that one should be a computer programmer—far from it, in fact. The excitement of real-time games lies in the artist's creations, generated on the spot and in instant response to the user's whims, with a life and personality of their own.

Modeling is the key issue and the most critical part of creating graphics for real-time games. The myriad issues and technical details that go into making a model efficient (low-polygon count), believable, aesthetically pleasing, and poised to behave and display properly in the real-time world are issues that face the real-time artist alone; real-time engines, after all, rely on only the most basic elements of 3D graphics to create their illusion.

Fortunately, 3D Studio MAX is a dream tool for creating real-time graphics. 3D Studio MAX not only provides excellent modeling tools to control every facet of creating a model, down to the face and vertex level, but also provides fast, efficient shaded and texture-mapped views of the model being created, enabling the user to accurately preview the "look" of the finished product in the game itself.

Although all real-time game engines vary slightly in structure, capabilities, and the paradigms used to create speed, the principles behind each engine remain the same.

This chapter covers the following topics:

- 2D versus real-time 3D graphics
- The basics of real-time 3D
- The differences between real-time and prerendered 3D graphics
- Principles and techniques for using 3D Studio MAX in modeling real-time objects
- The future of real-time 3D graphics

2D Versus Real-Time 3D Graphics

You may be wondering why real-time 3D didn't appear earlier. Actually, it did. Arcade games using 3D vector graphics, such as *Tempest* and *Star Wars*, appeared in the mid-'80s. Military simulations have been using real-time 3D on high-end machines for training for quite some time. Only recently, however, could these graphics be nicely shaded and texture-mapped at a speed that could match 2D animated graphics.

To fully appreciate the speed difficulty, you need to understand the difference between 2D and 3D animation at the computational level.

2D animation relies on the principles of traditional cel animation. A huge number of pictures are created, and then captured in sequence for playback in the chosen medium—in this case, a computer of some kind (including PCs, set-top gaming systems, custom-designed arcade systems, and so forth). The computer pulls the pictures from memory and displays them on-screen as fast as necessary to give the illusion of movement. The factors critical to 2D animation are data storage space (which accounts for the rise of the CD-ROM as the preferred gaming medium), the speed at which that data can be read, and how fast that data can be displayed. The computer does not have to do much "thinking" to display 2D animation.

3D graphics require much less storage than their 2D counterparts because the 3D pictures are not predrawn (with the exception of texture maps). The "recipe" for the 3D picture (meshes and animation) is stored as a mass of formulas and called up when needed. Because the pictures are being drawn on-screen by the program as they are being seen, and not before, the computer must "think" much more and much faster than it does with 2D images.

Imagine the difference between someone pulling nicely arranged pictures from a stack and someone else trying to accurately draw, at the same speed as the person who's pulling pictures, a collection of objects that yet *another* person is moving around. Imagining such a scenario should help you easily grasp the difference in what is demanded of a machine running a real-time application. Only the current high-speed processors are capable of meeting these extreme demands. Even then, the geometry being drawn must be simple and have a low polygon count to make the process fast enough to meet acceptable display speeds.

Real-Time 3D Basics

Modeling for real-time graphics is a delicate process. One must have an accurate picture of what the result will be after the object being modeled is exported into the real-time engine. The more you know about how the average real-time engine thinks, the better your initial efforts will be, and the more time and frustration you will save yourself.

Real-time 3D and high-end, prerendered 3D graphics have many elements in common. To achieve the speed necessary for presentable game play, however, real-time must use only the most necessary elements—namely, the geometry, the transform, and the surface properties of the mesh. Most of the time, these elements are created by the export program (a third-party application that converts the source model into a language the game engine can read) and put into some kind of text file (or a "c" file, before compilation into binary code) so that they can be manually edited, if necessary. Sometimes these elements can be parceled out to a number of separate files (one for geometry, one for surface properties, and one for the transform) that are combined when the file is compiled for the game engine. Currently, there are plug-ins that enable the user to export directly from 3DS MAX into Playstation, Sega Saturn, and DirectDraw formats. More plug-ins are under construction to support the myriad of real-time formats being used in gaming. Most premade, real-time 3D Application Programming Interfaces (APIs) provide a proprietary converter that works with the 3DS or DXF format. Freeware converters for exporting OBJ and VRML files are available from several web sites on the Internet, such as 3dcafe.com and max3d.com

The geometry is exactly what you would expect: a list of numbered vertex positions in 3D space, followed by a list of how to connect these vertices into coherent polygons. The normal (or visible solid) side of the polygon is determined either by the order in which the vertices that comprise the polygon are chosen, or by a separate list of vertex normals also attached to the polygon construction list.

Most real-time engines use triangular polygons, just as 3D Studio MAX does. Some systems use quadrilateral polygons. Still other systems let you define quads and other types of polygons, but break them down into triangles at rendering time. This can be a computationally expensive and unpredictable process. The best results seem to come from predefined triangular polygons. Although they require more storage than other polygons, predefined triangular polygons tend to render faster, and always display as intended. The 3DS MAX file format exports only triangles, which is why it is so widely supported among real-time engines.

A smooth export of the source model into the game engine always proves a bit tricky, and often requires a great deal of tweaking. High-powered modeling programs, such as 3DS MAX, often add unusable information to the relatively simplistic real-time game engine. Most of this information is *invisible* (it may or may not be apparent when you look at the model in 3DS MAX). This information can have drastic effects on the exported real-time model, causing it to be drawn in the wrong orientation or position, or to behave improperly when animated in the game engine. The biggest trouble areas for export are generally the transform and the surface properties.

The Transform

The *transform* is a numerical matrix that describes the orientation, position, and often the scale of an object in 3D space. This number is applied to every vertex in the object, and therefore acts as the object's center. In practice, imagine that every object you create is written as though it were centered at the global origin (0,0,0). To create this object farther off in 3D space, you could rewrite every vertex to the new location, or you could add to each vertex the distance (X, Y, and Z) the object must travel to reach the new position. Clearly, the latter method is the more efficient: Even though it takes two processes to achieve the new position, only one number is being created on the fly. The same process can be used to rotate or scale the object. This matrix may change syntax from program to program, but it will always be there because it is critical to controlling objects in 3D space.

When an object is moved in a 3D game, it is the transform that is actually affected. Prescripted animations, such as a character walking or the wheels of a car turning, are performed as if the object were standing still. To move the main object through space, the player's input is translated into a series of numbers that is combined with the transform to propel the object in the desired directions. In this way, a simple series of numbers can be generated from whatever input device is used (keyboard, joystick, and so on) to create fast, responsive action.

As mentioned earlier, the transform is usually an invisible number set in the modeling program and a numerical string in the data file(s) created by the export program. In 3DS MAX, however, the transform is also a visual tool that shows exactly how the physical geometry of the object is written.

When you select the object whose transform you want to see, and then select Reset Transform from the drop-down menu of the 3DS MAX Utilities panel, a bounding box that represents the object appears. When an object is created, it is automatically aligned to the orthographic viewports. If you rotate this object, scale it, or move it, the bounding box goes with and maintains its relative location and orientation. If, however, the object is reoriented away from its orthographic alignment, and then has its transform reset, the bounding box moves back into orthographic alignment. This effectively rewrites the object geometry and resets the axis of the object, causing the object to behave differently than expected. The results will be obvious when you animate the object in a real-time game.

Normally the transform is not something you have to worry about. When you work with primitives, 3DS MAX automatically generates them properly aligned. The only time a transform can get misaligned with primitives is when they are cloned or mirrored. When you perform these operations, always check the object's transform immediately after the modification. If a transform is off on an object that is part of a hierarchical model, to correct the transform you must detach the hierarchy, realign the object, and re-create the hierarchy. Figure 3.1 shows an object with a properly aligned transform. Figure 3.2 shows an object whose transform will cause problems when animation is applied to it.

FIGURE 3.1

An object with a correctly aligned transform.

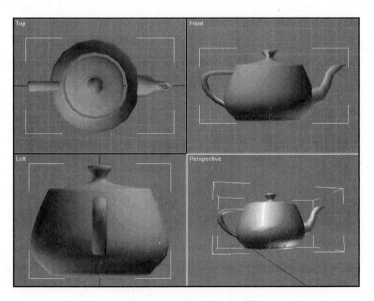

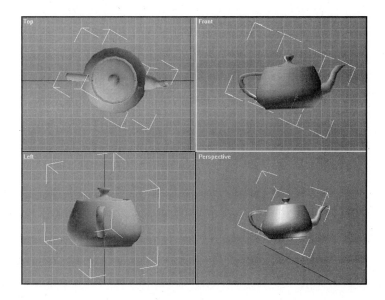

The only other time transforms can be generated differently than what you might want is when you are lofting objects that are naturally skewed. Remember that, by default, MAX automatically sets an object's local coordinates to align with those of the global coordinate system. If a Loft object is created askew to the global system, its local transform matrix will be misaligned. If an object must be created this way, manipulate it after it has been completed so that it comes as close as possible to orthographic alignment; then reset the transform and proceed with the rest of the model and animation.

You may be thinking that realigning the object center would accomplish the same thing as resetting the object's transform. That is correct when you are not exporting the object into a real-time engine. Unfortunately, most exporters are not able to use this bit of information, as it does not rewrite the actual geometry of the object as performing a "reset transform" does. In fact, to ensure that an object performs in the real-time engine in the same way it performs in MAX, make certain that the pivot point is aligned to the object. The pivot point dictates the origin of the object, but having its alignment correspond to the object ensures that rotational alignment and values will be the same in the game engine.

Surface Properties

Surface properties in a real-time engine are almost identical to those in MAX—namely, the smoothing algorithm (flat shading or Gouraud shading only for real time), the color of the polygon, the shininess, opacity, self-illumination, and the texture map applied to the polygon. These properties generally are defined after the vertex list but before the faces they apply to.

In addition, several real-time engines allow colors to be assigned to the vertices themselves, which can create the illusion of the object being lit, without direct lighting being applied to the model. Because most of the surface attributes are translated into numerical data, some strange translations can happen during the exporting process. Colors, for example, are translated from a 0 to 255 scale to a 0 to 1 scale. No hard and fast rules dictate how to minimize problems when exporting source materials from MAX. Generally, these materials must be manually adjusted in the real-time text file, unless a third-party visual exporting system is used (such as those used with most set-top gaming systems). The best approach here is to be aware that surface properties may be a trouble area during exporting, and to examine the final product closely.

Again, MAX proves to be an excellent real-time tool. It provides flat and Gouraud-shaded viewing options, enabling the artist to view an object (before the object is exported) in a manner that closely represents what the object will look like in a real-time gaming engine.

Differences Between Real-Time and Prerendered 3D

The way real-time games and prerendered 3D graphics are created differ in five major areas:

- Z-buffering
- Levels of detail (LODs)
- Shadows
- Texture map size (and color depth)
- Shading modes

The basic difference in these systems is a result of what they are intended to do: Prerendered graphics need to look as realistic as possible; Real-time needs to be as fast as possible.

Z-Buffering

Z-buffering is a computationally intensive process of determining which polygons are behind which (from the active viewpoint) so that a scene is drawn correctly with the proper depth. When you render a scene from MAX, visible portions of objects with correct mapping, shadows, and so on are produced for a near-photorealistic reproduction of the way the physical world is perceived. This process can be much too slow for real-time games. Most game engines do have the capability to perform modified Z-buffering (a faster but less accurate process than MAX). For fastest performance, however, *binary separation planes* (or BSPs) are created to give the processor a simple decision process as to what gets drawn in front of what. These planes divide concave (self-overdrawing) objects into convex pieces. These pieces, combined with the transform of the object, can be quickly evaluated by the computer to determine proper placement of objects.

Most real-time games also have a *far clipping plane*—a predetermined distance from the user's viewpoint, beyond which no objects are rendered, even though they are stored in memory. The far clipping plane can greatly increase the number of objects in a game world because the computer doesn't always have to draw everything simultaneously.

Often, far clipping planes are disguised by fog so that objects don't just "pop" into the universe, but appear to arrive out of a misty veil.

Levels of Detail

Levels of detail (LODs) also are critical in achieving the speed necessary to create an enjoyable game. In short, they are "stand-in" objects used to represent the real object at a greater distance from the user's viewpoint. When the object is close to the player, the highest-resolution model available is drawn. When the object takes up a small portion of the screen, a lower polygon count model is swapped in. Very often, at the greatest distances at which the object can still be seen, a colored box is used to represent the object. The increase in speed is dramatic because the processor does not have to calculate all the faces of the full object, but still draws the same number of pixels the object would take up on-screen. Figure 3.3 shows a model with its high, medium, and low LODs.

FIGURE 3.3
A model with high, medium, and low levels of detail (LODs).

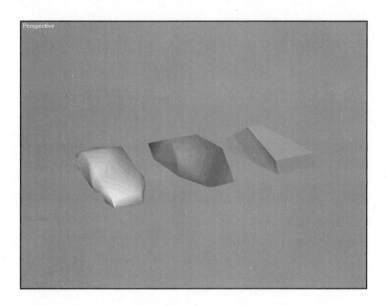

Complex objects (such as trees), which require a large number of polygons even to approximate, can be represented by an X-shaped arrangement of quads that can be mapped with a picture of a high-resolution object and an opacity map (or "cookie cutter" map) that makes everything outside the desired object invisible. This technique can also be used effectively with LODs or complex game *sprites* (2D animated objects). Figure 3.4 shows a tree model created with this cookie-cutter method for use in a real-time environment.

FIGURE 3.4
A real-time tree model.

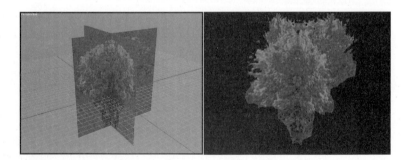

Shadows

Although shadows add a great deal of realism to any 3D scene, they require far too much calculation time to be feasible in a real-time engine. Instead, shadows are generally created by mapping a silhouette onto a semitransparent polygon positioned parallel to the ground plane of the game world. The same cookie-cutter technique mentioned earlier can be used for simulating shadows. Figure 3.5 shows an object with its real-time shadow plane attached.

FIGURE 3.5
An object with a shadow plane attached.

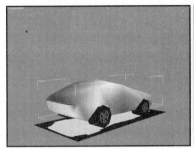

Map Size and Color Depth

Because of active memory limitations (RAM) and the processor demands of calculating TrueColor (24-bit) images, most real-time engines utilize smaller texture maps at a smaller color depth (usually 8-bit). Most systems use texture maps sized from 16-by-16 pixels up to 128-by-128 pixels. As a result, texture maps can be stored in RAM for quickest access whenever necessary (depending on the platform, up to 60 times a second).

Although some set-top gaming platforms can use 24-color maps, most systems use 8-bit color for texture maps. On many PCs, 8-bit color is the average display color depth. Because this is 3D, however, remember that light sampling is still calculated, in some form, and colors will vary. On systems that can display higher color modes, your 8-bit map can reach TrueColor levels when different lighting is applied.

Shading Modes

Real-time engines currently support only two shading modes: Flat shading (which makes an object look faceted) and Gouraud shading (which smoothes out most edges). Phong shading is too processor-intensive to be fast enough for real-time games.

Modeling for Real Time

With all the limitations of real-time games, modeling for real time involves a great deal of thought and precision. Real-time models must achieve the right balance of detail and low geometric complexity to make them fast, recognizable, and believable elements of the gaming experience.

Although modeling varies some from platform to platform, several basic principles should always be considered at the start of a gaming project:

- Put the detail in the map, not the mesh.

- Don't build what you don't need.

- Model convex whenever possible.

- High-res for low-res modeling.

Put the Detail in the Map, Not in the Mesh

Every polygon added to a real-time mesh takes a certain amount of time to render. Even if it is less than 1000th of a second, that time adds up and diminishes the possible frame rate during game play. To be effective, however, an object's texture maps must be able to fit into RAM. And the texture maps will be drawn much faster than the polygons needed to create the details that could be "painted" into the texture map. Therefore, any detail that can be effectively simulated by adding it to the texture map should be mapped, not modeled—as should any detail that is too mesh-intensive to be effective (such as the "cookie cutter" trees discussed earlier).

A great example of when to map instead of modeling is the muscle tone in a character. Nice, rounded muscle structure is far too polygon-intensive to accomplish in real-time. When muscles are added to a texture map, however, a similar effect can be achieved through careful use of simulated highlights and shadows, with almost no cost in frame rate.

A helpful process when you create real-time models is to create a fully detailed, high-face-count model first. Then construct the low-resolution model over the high-resolution model, using the latter as a template. You can then take individual orthographic renderings from the high-count model, tweak them in a paint program, and then use them as texture maps for the low-res model. This process is discussed in more detail in the "Dealing with Texture Limitations" section later in this chapter.

Another related process is to load two images (preferably scanned pictures) of the object you're creating, seen from the side and the front, as a texture map to be placed on a two-quad "tree" in MAX. This tree can then be displayed as a shaded template to be built over. This technique can be very handy as a reference for building real-time characters.

Don't Build What You Don't Need

This (the heading for this section) may seem obvious, but it should be a principle you return to often to ensure that your objects maintain the lowest possible polygon count.

Real-time game environments are more akin to Hollywood movie sets than they are to real-life environments. Like a movie set, they are seen only from limited viewpoints. Specific knowledge of where your objects and environments will and will not be seen by the player is critical to efficient modeling. Figure 3.6 shows a real-time environment from a top-down view (a view the player would never be able to see) that illustrates set-like construction.

FIGURE 3.6

"God's eye" view of a real-time set.

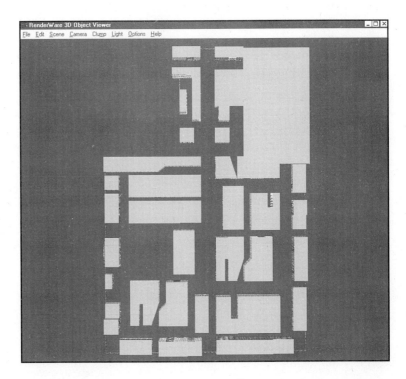

If you were building the cars for a racing game, for example, you would need to know whether the cars would ever flip over, exposing the undercarriage. If not, you could eliminate that part of the mesh and add detail (if necessary) to the parts of the vehicles that would be seen most often.

Segmented real-time characters offer another example. Normally the segments are modeled solid at the joints so that no holes appear in the mesh throughout a full range of motion. In a game setting, your model may not need a full range of motion, or different versions of the model may be swapped in depending on the action, damage to the character, and so forth. By eliminating the "capping" polygons inside the joints (which are never seen) you lower the total face count of the model, and make rendering more efficient.

Model Convex (Whenever Possible)

The differences between Z-buffering and using BSPs in real-time gaming systems were discussed earlier in this chapter. *BSPs* are a system by which game designers can "pre-make" decisions for the game hardware as to which objects (or parts of an object) will be drawn on-screen last (over the other screen objects) to create the illusion of depth. The use of BSPs creates a dramatic speed increase over Z-buffering, which not only has to keep the movement of the game going but also must determine object placement on-screen based on the position of every polygon in the scene.

For BSPs to be effective, they must divide objects into pieces that can be drawn correctly on their own, without any sort of depth information. This means that you must make convex pieces—where all the face normals of the object face away from the center of the object and do not point to each other. Convex pieces are absolutely critical to real-time game engines because they can be rendered at the maximum speed possible and still display correctly. Figure 3.7 shows a model with its BSPs visible. The data would be invisible in the real-time game engine.

The best test of convexity is to look at the object in a shaded, perspective view (smooth or faceted), hide the faces on opposing sides of the object (top and bottom, left and right, or front and back), and rotate the object in multiple directions. If you can see a solid face through an empty space in the model (where the normals are facing away, making the polygons invisible), the object is not convex and will need modifications (or more dividing) before it can be used effectively in a BSP sorting engine. Repeat the process for each opposing pair of sides. Figure 3.8 shows the visible differences between a convex and a concave object.

FIGURE 3.7
*A model with visible
BSPs inserted.*

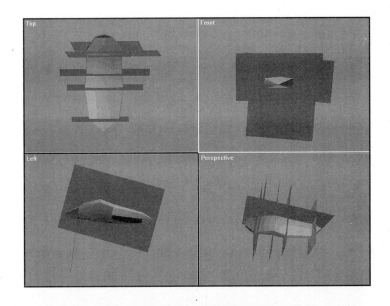

FIGURE 3.8
*A convex object section
and a concave object
section.*

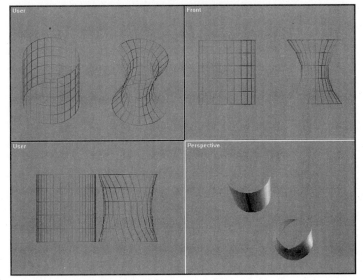

High-Res for Low-Res Modeling

When you're working with low polygon counts, it can be extremely difficult to see whether a proper level of detail has been accomplished to make the object clearly recognizable and distinguishable from other similar objects. It can be extremely helpful, therefore, to build a high poly-count "template" object, with as much detail modeled as possible, over which to construct a low-count model. This process clarifies where detail is needed in the low-count object, and where it can be omitted and placed in the texture map. And, as mentioned before, the high-detail model can be used to generate intricate texture maps for the low-count model later on.

Note that trying to use the Optimize modifier in MAX to lower the polygon count of the high-detail mesh to acceptable real-time levels is highly unadvisable. The Optimize modifier is an excellent tool for making a complex mesh more efficient, and even for using on a real-time model just to make certain that there are no unnecessary polygons, but it can easily create unpredictable losses in detail when you're trying to drastically reduce a high-count model. The Optimize modifier works by eliminating faces that are determined to be coplanar, based on the entered face and edge threshold angles. The Optimize modifier has no intelligence as to which details are important and which are not; it just uses a straight numerical algorithm. When a parameter high enough to bring drastic face count reductions is entered, the Optimize modifier also eliminates most of the nice smooth areas that have been created to round out certain edges.

Real-Time Modeling Techniques

The best way to ensure that your model has appropriate detail where it's needed and the lowest possible polygon count is to create the model with a low polygon count to begin with, and then to add detail and subtract faces only where necessary. The sub-object editing tools of the Edit Mesh modifier will become your best friends when you finalize a real-time model.

For object creation, however, the best options fall into the following two categories:

- "Conscious" lofting
- Modifying primitives

Conscious Lofting

Lofting Mesh objects has long been a mainstay for creating complex shapes in 3D Studio, and continues to be a critical MAX tool for the real-time artist. Lofting with deform-fit creates beautifully detailed meshes by adding interpolative steps between vertices on both the fit shapes and the shape(s) being lofted. Unfortunately, this can add a tremendous number of polygons very quickly. But by lofting with no added steps, and by using multiple shapes on the loft path, you can generate extremely detailed models with predictable face counts and detail. Also, lofting objects this way creates clean cross-sections that can then be divided by BSPs, if necessary.

The following exercise demonstrates this process by using a staple of real-time games—a car. Instead of a boxy NASCAR type of vehicle, however, you create something more organic and smooth—a high-tech sports car.

1. On the accompanying CD, open the file named CAR01.max. You will see a high-res sports car model, frozen, for use as a template. You will also see a spline outlining the top of the vehicle, a cross-section shape (derived from the most complex area of the vehicle—the hood, centered above the wheel wells), and a straight line to be used as a preliminary loft path. Figure 3.9 shows these objects.

FIGURE 3.9

The objects in the exercise file CAR01.MAX.

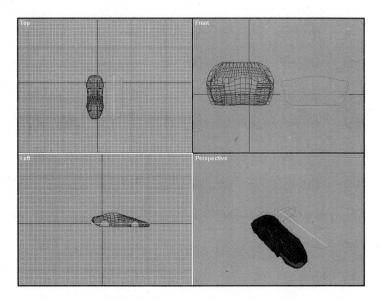

2. Select the top outline shape in the Front viewport, hold down the Shift key, and rotate the shape 90° around the viewport's Z axis, so that you create a new shape aligned to the side view of the frozen car. Name this new shape **side outline** (see fig. 3.10).

FIGURE 3.10

The car outline, rotated to align with the side of the model.

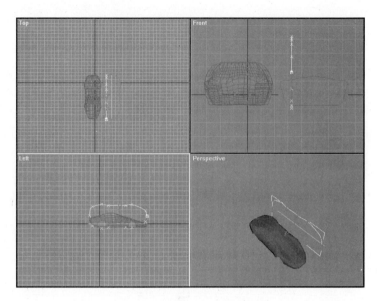

Deform fit creates a path that derives its shape from the vertices of the two fit shapes. Wherever a vertex is present, a path step will be inserted. If the two fit shapes share the same vertices in the same alignment, a minimum number of path steps will be created, therefore creating the minimum amount of geometry in the Loft object. To ensure the fit shapes contain the same vertex alignment, you just clone the more complex of the two shapes. In the next step you adjust the clone to match the profile of the car from the side, by using the vertices present in the top outline, keeping them in their original alignment.

3. Select the new spline, and go to the Modify panel. Click on the Edit Spline button, and turn on the Sub-Object button, and select Segment from the rollout menu. Select all the segments on the bottom half of the shape (in the Left viewport) and delete them.

4. Turn off the Sub-Object button, and move the entire spline close to the top of the car in the Left viewport.

5. Turn the Sub-Object button back on, but select the Vertex Sub-Object this time. Still in the Left viewport, start moving the vertices so that they form a tight outline of the top of the car. Be certain to move the vertices on the viewport's Y axis *only*. You can adjust the Bézier handles of the vertices by using both the X and Y viewport axes to make the outline tighter.

6. Mirror this spline across the Y axis, and make a copy. Attach the bottom spline to the top, and continue the outline process with the bottom vertices adhering to the same rules of vertex manipulation as in step 5. Both the front and back vertex pairs need to be welded together. Don't worry about modeling the wheel wells at this stage. You can also delete any vertices that you don't need for straight segments—but don't *add* any.

The final outline should look something like the one in figure 3.11.

FIGURE 3.11
The final modified side outline.

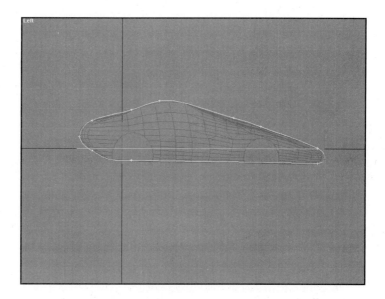

You now have all the elements you need to create the deform-fit loft.

NOTE

The loft will be created by lofting the general shape from the nose to the tail. You could also loft from one side of the car to the other, or from the top to the bottom, but this method gives you the simplest loft shape to work with and keeps the rounding on the sides of the vehicle. The other options would not give you the nice clean cross-sections you can use later for possible BSPs.

7. Select the cross-section shape, and click on the Create panel. Click on the Geometry button, and then select Loft Object from the drop-down menu.

8. Click on the Loft button, select Get Path as the creation method, and then click on the path01 line. This should give you a long loaf-of-bread-type

shape. Uncheck the Cap-Start and Cap-End options. Check both the Skin and Skin-in-Shaded options in the Skin Parameters area. For now, leave Shape Steps and Path Steps at the default setting of 5. Figure 3.12 shows the shape you should have just created.

9. Go to the Modify panel and, with the Loft object still selected, click on the Deformation rollout panel. Click on the Fit button. The Deformation Fit window pops up.

10. In the Deformation Fit window, uncheck the Make Symmetrical button (the first button on the upper-left side of the window). Then click on the Display X Axis button, immediately to the right.

11. Click on the Get Shape button (second to the last on the top menu bar), and then click on the Top-Outline shape. It should appear in the Deformation Fit window, and your loft should now become a strange blobby shape (don't worry about this for now). Repeat the process for getting the Y axis fit shape.

NOTE

3D Studio MAX depends on the alignment of the axes of all shapes, those being lofted and those being used for deformation. For this reason, if the axes on the shapes are not aligned properly, the first Loft object will appear blobby and not as you intended. This problem can be solved by reorienting the axes of the original shapes. Because the Deformation Fit window gives you options to manipulate the shapes, however, it is often more helpful to adjust the parameters there, so that you get immediate visual feedback when the object is correctly created. The mesh itself can then be oriented visually, after it is created, to match the Template object.

12. Click on the Display XY Axes button, and view both shapes in the Deformation Fit window.

13. Click on the Rotate 90° CCW button. The fit shapes will look squashed, but the object will be rendered correctly, only backward.

14. Rotate the new object 180° from the top view so that it lines up with the Template object.

15. In the Surface Parameters of the Loft rollout, set the Path and Shape Steps to zero. Figure 3.12 shows the final model.

FIGURE 3.12

The final low-res model.

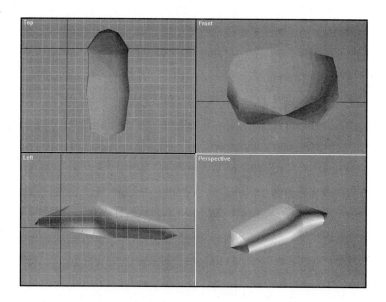

You now have a low-res car that closely approximates the original object. You could add modifications to the original loft shape and place them on your loft path to further enhance the detail of the vehicle without adding more faces. The level of detail can be taken as far as necessary, however, by manipulating the vertices of multiple cross-section shapes and placing them into the existing path steps.

The other primary way of creating an efficient real-time mesh, which usually creates lower face counts but is not as BSP-friendly, is to start with a primitive (preferably a multisegmented cylinder or box) and manipulate the individual vertices to match the Template object.

Modifying Primitives for Low-Resolution Models

The following exercise will demonstrate this modeling process. It uses the shareware plug-in Edit Mesh2, available on the Kinetix CompuServe forum.

1. Open the file CAR02.max on the accompanying CD. You should see only the car Template object from the preceding exercise.

2. Create an eight-sided cylinder, centered on top of the car template, and extend the cylinder's height to match the car's length. Leave the Height and Cap Segment settings at their default level for now. You should have something similar to the objects shown in figure 3.13.

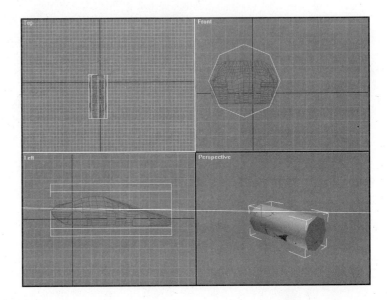

The car should now be almost completely concealed by the newly created cylinder. Next you need to set the segments of the cylinder to approximate the linear changes in the side and top profiles of your template.

3. Set the Height segments to 8 to approximate the number of linear changes in the side profile of the car. (Because the top profile should be quite a bit less, this number will create adequate geometry for you to work with and be accurate to all views of the car.)

4. Click on the Edit Mesh modifier, activate the Sub-Object menu, and select Vertex from the drop-down menu. In the Front viewport, begin selecting vertex groups down the length of the cylinder, moving them to line up with the front view of the template car. Figure 3.14 shows what the modified cylinder should look like now.

5. Go to the Left viewport and begin lining up the cross-section lines with the linear changes in the side view of the template car. Then begin moving vertices on the top and bottom of the cylinder to closely match the template profile (see fig. 3.14). You can also begin moving the vertices (in the middle of the cylinder's length) to line up with the wheel wells.

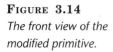

FIGURE 3.14

The front view of the modified primitive.

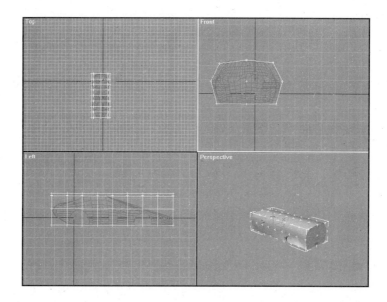

6. Now go to the Top viewport and continue the process with any vertices that are out of alignment with the template's profile. You may find that rotating small groups of closely placed vertices gives more rounded corners on the front and the back.

While modeling this way, it's always a good idea to keep a shaded Perspective viewport active, checking it often to make certain that a vertex has gone where you intended. If it did not, use the Undo feature until it reaches the place where the error occurred. (The more often you check, the less you have to undo in case of an error.)

You have almost completed this model. Clearly, you can add more detail by hiding selected faces and modeling more interior detail (such as the fenders or the hood cowling), but for the purposes of this example, you should move on to the last large bit of detail.

7. Switch to Face Sub-Object mode, and select the faces that were created earlier for the wheel-well area. Select only the wheel wells on one side of the car.

8. Click on the Extrude button, and extrude these faces –7.0 units. This creates the wheel-well inlets, and adds only six polygons per wheel well. Repeat the procedure with the other side. Go to the Display panel and click on Hide Unselected to hide the Template object and see the final real-time car.

As you can see, you have created a vehicle with as much detail as the preceding version, but saved over 80 polygons in the process. You can easily see by the cross-section alignment, however, that this would be a difficult model to separate with BSPs if you had to. The best way to make this model would depend entirely on the game engine being used.

Dealing with Texture Limitations

As you have already seen, quite a bit of detail can be accomplished with limited meshes. To get the most out of limited geometry, however, you must rely on texture maps. Maps have their own limitations—either limited size, limited color depth (usually 8-bit), or both. Fortunately, you can work around these limitations and still produce excellent results.

Dealing with Limited Colors

Opinions abound on the subject of how to create a real-time environment by using 256 colors. Many people favor starting with a limited palette (prepicking the colors that will be used) and making all texture maps from those colors. Others believe that better results derive from creating the maps with the full 16.7 million colors available, and then using another program to evaluate the texture maps and remap them into the 256 most-used colors.

Generally, however, when you create texture maps with 16.7 million colors, you don't use them all (or even a significant percentage of them). To achieve a happy medium between the two previously mentioned methods, first decide on a general scheme (based on the scene, time of day, mood, and so on), and then paint in 24-bit color, focusing on the selected color scheme. This method also provides a better distillation to 256 colors when you create the final game palette, while still keeping the scene focused toward the visual goals identified with the color scheme.

If you don't have access to a program capable of distilling a 256 palette from multiple images (and remapping the colors in those images to the new palette), your best choice is to start with a predetermined 8-bit palette.

Limited Map Size

All gaming platforms today use small texture maps, ranging from 16-by-16 pixels to 128-by-128. Although this may be intimidating for those whose smallest maps are 320-by-240 (one quarter the size of the average monitor display at low resolution), after a bit of practice you will discover how much detail you can achieve in a very small area. You may even find that texture mapping with small maps opens new techniques for creating larger maps when you're creating prerendered 3D images.

A great temptation is to create a texture map at a high resolution and then scale it down to the parameters of whatever real-time engine you are working with. This seldom works well. Scaling, in most paint programs, is done by a mathematical elimination of pixels based on the percentage of down-scaling. When you reach real-time limits, where every pixel counts, this process can make quite a mess of an originally great texture map— filling it with scattered, color-cycling pixels and making an otherwise smooth map look rocky or rough.

Your best bet for making certain that the exact detail you want (and nothing else) appears on-screen during game-play is to start with the same size texture map that will be in the game. This technique leaves no room for extraneous information, and enables you to be very precise as to what amounts of detail go where. And you can use multiple maps (or a large map carved into real-time sizes) on an object with very little impact on the speed of the game.

Adding "Impossible" Detail

As you might have gathered from everything discussed in this chapter so far, real-time is mostly a matter of creating the best illusion with what is technologically possible. Most of the model-creation process, so far, has been accomplished by using limited versions of what is already available in 3DS MAX, and using simple planning and efficiency to achieve results. Some things, however, cannot be done in real time. Certain mapping types (bump mapping, shininess, and specular mapping), specific lighting design, and many other techniques are beyond the limitations of real-time games at this point, because of the bare-bones shading limitations needed to create speed. These more complex maps require the computationally expensive Phong Shading mode, and must simply be "faked." Here again, a little planning can go a long way.

Faking a Bump Map

Bump maps, in prerendered 3D, are a way to create the illusion of limited surface relief on an object. Artists have been doing this in flat images for thousands of years by creating highlights and shadows in still images. The same techniques work very well for creating "fake" bump maps. Determine the angle of your light source (high and right always creates a believable, recognizable source), and paint in the highlights and shadows. The only difference is that your shadows will not move in response to the real-time light source, and the "bumps" will not be visible from the edge of the faces to which they are applied. Figure 3.15 shows a "faked" bump map.

FIGURE 3.15
A "faked" bump map.

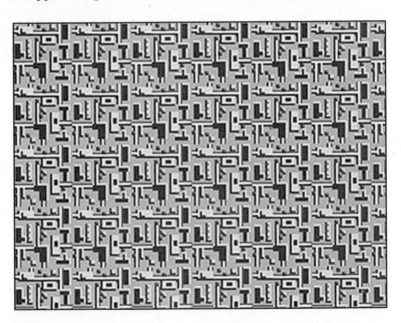

If creating bumps through painting seems a bit intimidating, you can create your bump-mapped material, apply it to a flat plane in 3DS MAX, add lighting, and render the image out to a file for use on your real-time mesh. But remember the earlier comment about map sizes: Render the image to the size it will be in the game, instead of rendering the image larger and scaling it down later.

Faking "Mood Lighting"

To create spot-light effects (such as under-lighting or light pooling), you can repeat the preceding "create it in MAX" technique or use the lighting filters available in many image-editing packages (such as Photoshop or Painter) to get similar results. Moving a MAX light around in 3D space can give you a much more specific effect than using a light fixed to a two-dimensional plane.

Curved Surfaces

Creating a curved surface with geometry is an almost impossible accomplishment in real time because curves require a high number of polygons.

Fortunately, creating the illusion of a curved surface in a texture map is not difficult. It can be painted into the map using a highlight for the highest point on the surface, and blending that into half-tone at the sides of the curve, with shadows reacting to the light source. Again, rendering a fully mapped, highly detailed curved surface in MAX and then using it as a texture map for the flat-surfaced real-time object yields great results.

The following exercise demonstrates most of the previously mentioned concerns when texture mapping. It uses the Edit Mesh2 plug-in, downloadable from the Kinetix CompuServe forum, and the Edit Spline2 plug-in on the CD-ROM.

REAL-TIME TEXTURE MAPPING

1. From the accompanying CD, open the file called Wheel01.max. This is a sporty mag-wheel (see fig. 3.16) that would add a nice bit of detail to your real-time sports car. It was modeled in high detail, and is obviously much too complex to be used in real-time, especially when you consider that it would have to be multiplied by four. The chrome reflection map on the spokes of the wheel would also be impossible in real-time, but renders very nicely in MAX.

FIGURE 3.16

The high-detail wheel mesh in MAX.

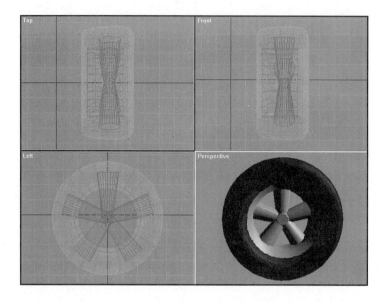

2.   Change the Left viewport display method to Bounding Box mode. With the Zoom Region tool, go into the Left viewport and scale the view very close to the wheel's bounding box, leaving a small space around the outside for cropping later (see fig. 3.17). In the Environment settings, set the background color to a bright yellow (red –255, green –255, blue –0). This makes cropping and manipulation in your paint package much easier later on.

FIGURE 3.17

The cropping area of the bounding-boxed wheel.

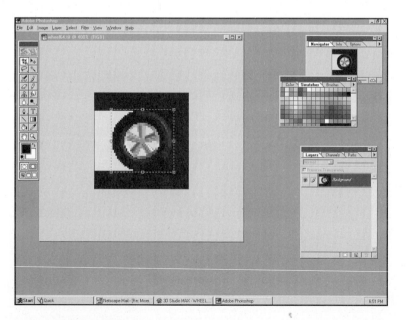

3. Render the Left viewport, at a size of 64 by 64 pixels (an average real-time texture map size), with anti-aliasing turned off. Save the file as a 32-bit Targa filecolor with alpha channel, and name it wheel_src.tga. This is the source file for your texture map.

4. In your favorite image editing program open wheel_src.tga.

5. First, crop the image down to only the pixels you want, leaving no border around the wheel. With the Cropping tool, create an outline that fits exactly to the outside edge of the tire. Crop the image. Resize the image back to 64 by 64 pixels.

6. Now, with the Magic Wand tool, select the yellow pixels that are left. If you are using Photoshop, select one of the yellow corners around the wheel, and then choose Similar under the Select drop-down menu. This should select all the yellow pixels, including the ones between the spokes of the wheel.

NOTE

Rendering the image from MAX with anti-aliasing turned off provides a clean edge around the wheel. By setting the background to an extremely bright color, not found anywhere else in the image, you can create a map in which you can easily replace the background color. Additionally, you can add other colors if your map does not easily fit exactly onto the real-time object (and might leave undesired edges). If you see strange edges when the map is applied, you can go back to the image and "tweak" it to make certain that you get a clean texture map.

7. Choose pure black as your foreground color, and fill the yellow area. If any partly yellow pixels remain at the selection line, stroke the selection line with a two-pixel line of black, centered on the selection line.

8. In the Channels panel, go to the alpha channel (channel 4 in Photoshop), select all the image, and cut it.

9. Go back to the RGB channel, and select Blur from the filters drop-down menu. This adds back the anti-aliasing you removed from the rendered image. Set Color mode to 8-bit (256), and save the image as wheel64.tga (see fig. 3.18). This is your color texture map.

FIGURE 3.18
The wheel64.tga
image.

10. Under the File menu, select New. The setting should automatically be 64 by 64 pixels because this was the size of the alpha channel you cut to the Clipboard. Paste the alpha channel into the new file, and set Color mode to grayscale. Select white as your foreground color. This time, fill in just the black corners around the edge of the wheel; this ensures that the edges of your wheel are solid all the way around. Save the image as wheel64o.tga (see fig. 3.19). This is your opacity map.

FIGURE 3.19
The wheel64o.tga
image.

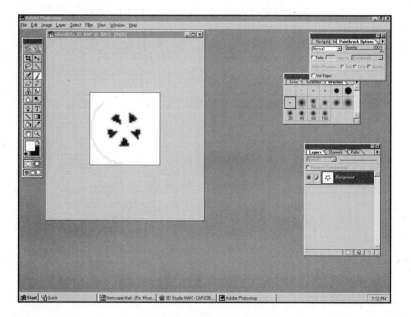

11. Go back into MAX, but this time open the file called CAR03.max (your real-time car from the last modeling exercise). At one of the wheel-wells create an eight-sided cylinder with one height segment, to be used as a

wheel for your car. Make the depth and radius roughly the appropriate size for your vehicle (see fig. 3.20). Keep the new Wheel object selected, and choose the UVW modifier from the Modify panel. Make certain that the mapping type is planar, that the top is aligned with the top of your newly created wheel, and then choose the Fit option to fit the mapping coordinates to the bounding box of your wheel.

FIGURE 3.20

The real-time car, with one wheel added.

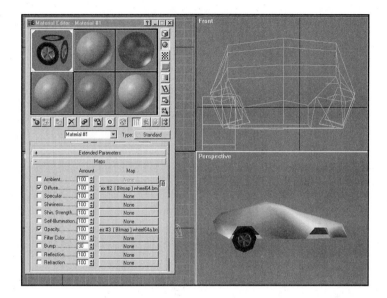

12. Open the Material Editor and create a new material that has constant shading, no shininess, and no shininess strength. Apply the material to the wheel.

13. In the maps area of the Material rollout, load wheel64.tga into the Diffuse channel, and wheel64o.tga into the Opacity channel. Change the material sample type from a sphere to a cube so that you can see exactly what the map looks like on the wheel. In the Alpha Source section of the Map Parameters panel, set the Alpha Source to none (opaque).

14. Render a clean view of the newly mapped wheel, and adjust it until it has a nice rounded feel on the edge of the tire and you can see through the spokes. Clone this object three times, and place the copies into the other wheel wells (see fig. 3.21).

Using Opacity for "Impossible Detail"

Sometimes an object is far too complex to be modeled convincingly in a low-polygon fashion. When you are using 3DS MAX to create models of objects with holes and complex edges—objects so detailed that you cannot make them recognizable—you can use a simple opacity map to create the effect.

Fortunately, almost all real-time systems have some capacity for using opacity maps—whether they are 8-bit grayscale maps or just 1-bit black-and-white, cookie-cutter type maps. This capability enables the model maker to add detail that would otherwise be impossible. The effect is not quite as clean as it would be in 3D Studio MAX, but the result is still quite effective. The following exercise shows how opacity can be used to create the illusion of hair on a real-time character.

1.   In the Chapter 3 directory on the accompanying CD, open the file called hair01.max. You will see the head of a real-time humanoid character.

2. Click on the Create panel, and create a box with three segments for height, length, and width. The specific size does not matter, just make certain that the top of the box is bigger than the top of the head.

3. With the box still selected, go into the Modify panel, select Edit Mesh, click on the Sub-Object button, and then select Face from the drop-down menu. Select all the faces except those on the top of the box, and delete them.

4. Open Material Editor, and click on the Get Material button. Click on the Material Library radio button on the top left of the editor, and load hair.max from the accompanying CD. This library has only two materials for this scene: the Phong skins material on the head (which should already be in place), and the hair material in the second material slot (which consists of a comic-book type hair map and a black-and-white opacity\shininess map). Click on the Hair window, and assign the material to the top plane of the box.

5. Minimize the Material Editor, go back to the Modify panel, and click on the UVW Map button. Click on the Sub-Object button, and rotate the mapping gizmo so that the top aligns with the top edge of the box-top in the Top view. Click on the Fit button.

If you have not already done so, configure one of your active viewports to display in Smooth with Highlights mode. You should be able to see the hair map on the Box object now, which makes the next few steps much easier.

6. Click on the Edit Mesh modifier again, and select the Sub-Object button, but select Vertex this time. Begin moving the vertices of the box top down around the head so that it starts to form a sort of shower cap shape, moving the hair where it should be on the head. Don't worry if the lines start to go through the top faces on the head. Render a view occasionally to see how the opacity mapping is making the complex shape of the hair look molded onto the head. Figure 3.22 shows the model after this step, and figure 3.23 shows the rendered version.

7. Click off the Sub-Object button, select the Head object. Select Edit Mesh, and choose the Vertex sub-object. Begin to move the vertices of the top of the head to "tuck" them under the hair. You may find it useful to alternate between editing the hair and the head vertices until you find the best combination.

FIGURE 3.22
The head with the hair molded around it.

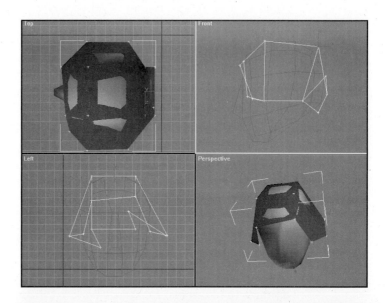

FIGURE 3.23
The rendered version of the head, with the hair molded around it.

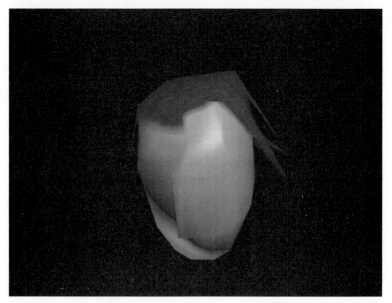

8. Now for the final step. Because this is a real-time model, you want to eliminate any geometry that will not be seen. Select the Head object, click on Edit Mesh, turn on the Sub-Object button, and select Face. Now delete from the head any faces that are completely covered by the Hair object, or that protrude slightly through the hair (do frequent renderings with this step to ensure that you haven't created any visible holes in the head).

The Future of Real-Time

With technology rapidly expanding, real-time 3D is certain to grow past its current limitations, but so will prerendered 3D graphics. Real-time 3D will always be the domain of those who use their imagination to create the illusion of reality, instead of relying only on the latest tools. 3DS MAX will always be a tremendous asset to the real-time artist, however, because of its vast (and continually expanding) tool set and its capability to use these at the most basic levels of a 3D object.

With the introduction of real-time 3D to a mass consumer market, 3D gaming is here to stay. When the technology becomes available, gamers will almost certainly be able to create their own personalized stand-in 3D representatives (or avatars) to take into battle, tackling international opponents across the Internet, or on their own in ever-expanding, increasingly detailed worlds. In the future, real-time gaming will almost certainly become less like a computer game and more like stepping into a new world, filled with personalities, characters, and adventure. The promise of virtual reality will finally be fulfilled.

In Practice: Modeling for Real-Time 3D Games

- Real-time 3D gaming relies on speed and must use only the bare basics of 3D to accommodate the extensive calculations necessary. These basics include limited geometry, limited texture map sizes and color depths, and often, the use of Binary Separation Planes (BSPs) rather than slower Z-buffering calculations for depth.

- Modeling is the most critical process in real-time 3D because everything depends on the alignment and efficiency of the object being created.

- Creating a 3D template over which to model is a useful procedure for creating real-time objects with enough detail in the right places.

- The basic procedures in creating a real-time model are "conscious lofting" and modifying primitives.

- Detail that cannot be accomplished with mesh can be created with texture maps, using opacity, "faked" bump maps, and rendered images of high-detail meshes manipulated for real-time use.

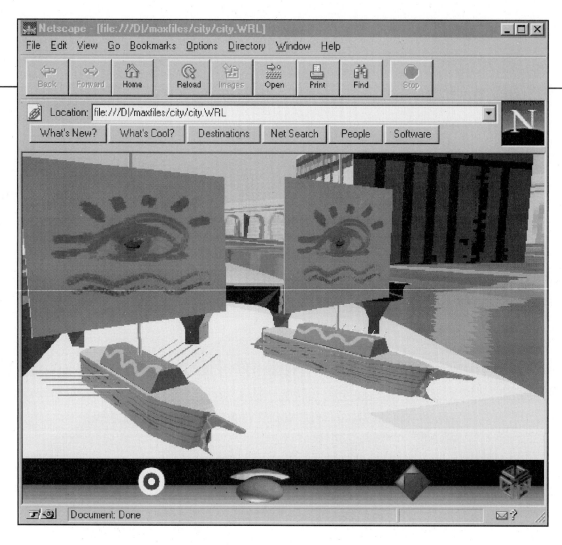

IMAGE BY ANDREW VERNON

Chapter 4

by Andrew Vernon

MODELING FOR VR AND THE WEB

The World Wide Web's unexpected emergence and hectic growth has been one of the phenomena of the '90s. Although exact figures are not available, it's generally believed that the number of people accessing the web will grow from about 20 million today to about 200 million by the year 2000. During this same time period, computer processing power is expected to continue to double every 18 months, coupled with an enormous expansion of line bandwidth and modem speed. Barring some disaster, the future of the web is very bright indeed. It's no wonder, therefore, that so much creative talent—and money—is being invested in it. Virtual Reality Markup Language (VRML, usually pronounced vermal) is one of the best ways that 3D artists and animators can take advantage of the tremendous opportunity presented by the web's growth.

VRML, as conceived by its creators, is much more than a method of displaying 3D models. It's a conceptual system that might ultimately enable you to navigate the web as one continuous 3D space, in the same way that HTML enables you to navigate the web as one giant hypertext document. This is the real potential of "cyberspace." In the future, web addresses will map to the interiors of personal or corporate 3D spaces within the context of a borderless virtual world. This world continuously will be extended but will always be coherent and consistently navigable because it is implemented in a common language—VRML.

This chapter helps you keep up with the fast-paced world of 3D on the web. It covers the following topics:

- Modeling tools and techniques

- Summary of what is and is not exported by VRMLOUT

- Creating a virtual world with 3DS MAX and VRMLOUT

- VRML browser reviews

- The best of the web

Note

If you want to find out more about the goals and potential of VRML, go to Mark Pesce's site at www.hyperreal.com/~mpesce/. The latest VRML specification is available at vrml.sgi.com/moving-worlds/spec/index.html. All the web addresses mentioned in this chapter are included in a bookmarks file (Ch4bkmk.htm) provided on the accompanying CD-ROM.

VRML is an *"open" standard*—a specification openly published that does not contain code owned by any corporation. VRML was created and is maintained by individuals who have a vision of 3D on the web and want to make it possible for anyone to use it freely. Naturally, the open philosophy of VRML is endangered in this age of megacorporations. If a company such as Microsoft, for example, were to develop a proprietary VRML specification—one that added Microsoft's own "extensions" to the VRML specification—many people would doubtless be tempted to use it. The result would be that models created by using this version of VRML would not display, or would not display properly, on browsers that support the original VRML specification, and vice-versa. This is not to suggest that Microsoft, or any other company, is about to do so. Rather, it is an illustration of the potential that exists in cyberspace, as in any other world, to descend from order and civilization into chaos and anarchy. Good citizens of cyberspace can, and should, remain aware of the freedom of speech issues involved in the maintenance of an open standard, and avoid using proprietary versions of the language (should any appear).

Having said that, the outlook today is very positive. The VRML Consortium, formed December 1996, has taken over responsibility for the development of the language from the VRML Architecture Group. Hopefully, all those companies that might otherwise have gone their separate ways will now come together and make VRML the single, solid standard it needs to be.

Modeling Tools and Techniques

As with all files destined for display on the World Wide Web, smaller is better with VRML. On a standard 28.8 kbs modem, with average network traffic, a VRML file of 150 KB downloads in about 120 seconds. To that time, you must add extra time for downloading any texture map files. Download performance, then, is the first issue: How long does it take to download the file from the web server and load it into memory? This is a function of file size. The only time file size might not be an issue is when you are creating VRML worlds for access over an intranet in a particular organization.

The second issue is navigation speed or performance after the file loads into memory, a function of model complexity. This relates to file size, of course, because the more complex the model and the more faces it has, the larger the file. The main bottleneck here, however, is in the video display: How many pixels does the video display card have to process and put out to the screen? When you navigate within a VRML world, the browser interprets the VRML code and passes it to your PC hardware, which actually renders it in real time.

NOTE

The term *browser,* as used here, refers to the VRML-viewer software that plugs into your web browser (Netscape or Internet Explorer). Available VRML browsers are reviewed later in the chapter.

Keep in mind that performance that depends on file size is a more subjective measure. What seems an unacceptably long download time to one person may seem quite acceptable to another. Download time is the lesser of the two limitations. Generally speaking, you won't want to miss out on the vitality that texture maps bring to your model for the sake of the extra time needed to download them. What you definitely want to avoid is creating models with so many faces that the computer gets bogged down trying to display them.

This section introduces tools and techniques you can use to work with both these limitations and produce VRML files optimized for download and navigation performance on the web.

Using Tools Built into 3DS MAX

You can reduce file size and speed performance in several ways, just by careful management of the objects you create. Before you begin modeling a scene for the web set a face (polygon) "budget" appropriate for the complexity of the scene and then roughly portion out the number of faces for the different objects. The Polygon Counter (a utility that comes with the VRMLOUT plug-in for 3DS MAX) helps you stay within your budget.

The sample world used throughout this chapter (City.wrl), for example, has about 2750 faces. Its file size is about 150 KB (the compressed size is less than 30 KB)—still a large file.

Reducing the Number of Segments

The simplest thing you can do to cut your face count is to reduce the number of segments in any primitive you create. The default segment settings for 3DS MAX primitives give you more faces than you want for a VRML world. When you create a primitive in a scene destined for export to VRML, therefore, go immediately to the Modify panel and use the spinners to reduce the number of segments.

Figure 4.1 shows two rows of primitives rendered in 3DS MAX. The upper row shows the primitives with the default number of segments. The lower row shows the same set of primitives after segment reduction. How much you reduce depends on how the primitive will be viewed in the scene. Objects that remain in the background can be reduced much more than objects intended to be viewed up close. This illustration shows how you can easily cut the face count in half (or more) without losing an enormous amount of quality. Table 4.1 summarizes the face savings between these two sets of primitives.

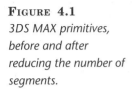

FIGURE 4.1
3DS MAX primitives, before and after reducing the number of segments.

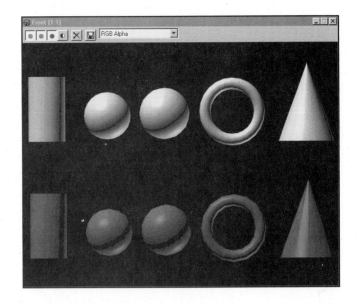

TABLE 4.1

Summary of Face Savings Earned by Segment Reduction

Primitive	Default Segments	Face Count	Reduced Segments	Face Count
Cylinder	24	96	12	48
Sphere	24	528	16	224
Geosphere	4	320	3	180
Torus	24/12 sides	576	16/6	192
Cone	24/5 height	288	12/1	48
TOTAL		1808		692

Deleting and Hiding Faces

Another very simple thing you can do is delete from the objects in your scene any faces that will never be visible. In the scene of an ancient city in this chapter, for example, deleting the faces on the underside of the landscape object cuts the number of faces from 1072 to 709 (see fig. 4.2). This particular object is a box with 14 segments each way, which was molded with the

Freeform Deformation modifier to create slopes and hills. If you were happy with a completely flat landscape, you could reduce the face count to 12 by using a simple box.

Actually, you don't have to use a base object to create an effect of the ground under your buildings. VRML 2.0 provides a Ground Color option for the Background helper, which enables you to set the color of the viewport below the horizon (this helper is described later in the chapter).

FIGURE 4.2
Hiding faces that will never be visible.

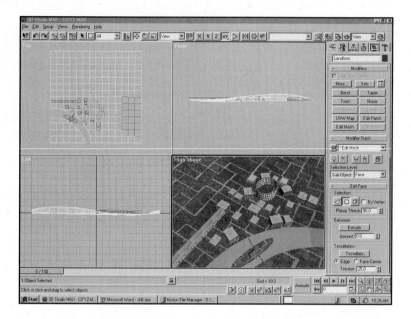

Another option is to hide the faces you don't want instead of deleting them. Because the VRMLOUT plug-in doesn't export hidden faces, those faces will not be part of the eventual download file size. 3DS MAX still counts the hidden faces, however, and you will not have a completely accurate face count during the modeling process. Whether you delete or hide faces is up to you. You may find it more convenient to delete them if your model is intended solely to be viewed in a VRML browser.

Using the Optimize Modifier

You're doubtless already familiar with the Optimize modifier; it's hardly necessary to point out its advantages for creating low-face-count models for VRML worlds. Perhaps the most useful thing at this point is to look at some examples of objects optimized with this modifier at different levels of severity. Figure 4.3 shows what happens to a palm-tree mesh with successive increases in the Face Threshold setting.

FIGURE 4.3

Different settings for the Optimize modifier.

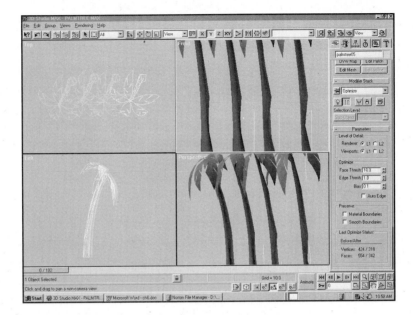

- The tree on the left is not optimized and has 554 faces.
- The second tree has the Face Threshold set to 8 and has 538 faces.
- The third tree has the Face Threshold set to 12 and has 420 faces.
- The fourth tree has the Face Threshold set to 18 and has 342 faces.

From experiments like this, you may conclude that you can turn up the Face Threshold to 12 and still get acceptable results for objects that stay in the middle distance, but that a setting of 18 distorts the mesh too much. Generally, the more complex the mesh, the more dramatic the savings you get by using the Optimize modifier. You need to experiment to find what works best for your scene.

Using Instances

An *instance* is an interdependent copy of a 3DS MAX object; when you make a change to any of the instances, all the other copies change also. Instances are useful in creating smaller-size files for the web; when you use an instance, the set of faces that make up the instance object has to be defined only once in the VRML code. Consequently, you can use the same piece of geometry many times without any increase in the download time for the file. Figure 4.4 shows an example of the use of instances in a VRML world. All the rectangular buildings in the scene are instances, derived from a single box primitive.

FIGURE 4.4

Using instances for multiple occurrences of the same geometry.

Texture Mapping Versus Geometry

Figure 4.4 also shows another easy way to reduce the amount of geometry that needs to be described in the VRML file—use texture mapping instead! The buildings in this scene are mostly plain boxes, as mentioned earlier. By applying different texture maps to the boxes, however, and changing the scale and orientation of the buildings, you make the scene look much more varied than it really is. Although texture maps increase the download time as well as the speed of screen redraws, the extra time incurred is a small price to pay compared to what it would cost to model the doors, windows, and columns of all the buildings.

When you upload texture maps, remember that the Unix system your web server is most likely running is case-sensitive, and will not find the map files unless the case is exact. If you specified a map called bridge.gif in the

Material Editor, for example, but the file you upload to the web server is called Bridge.gif, the map will not display.

Texture maps look strange but not unattractive when you zoom in close enough to see the pattern of the colored pixels. This is becoming part of the "style" of VRML models, as you'll see if you look at some of the web sites listed later in this chapter. One way to work with this limitation rather than against it is to design texture maps that make no attempt to look realistic, but look as though they were painted on, like stage scenery.

You might have noticed in figure 4.4 that the buildings appear to have different maps on their different sides. You can apply the same map to all sides of a box by using the Box option of the UVW Map modifier in 3DS MAX. To get different maps on different sides, however, you have to use different maps. The mapping in this scene was done using a feature of the 3D paint program, Fractal Design Detailer. This feature, called *implicit mapping,* enables you to use a single texture map to paint on all six sides of a box (see fig. 4.5). You can do the same thing without a 3D paint program by using a freeware plug-in for 3DS MAX called Unwrap (available on the accompanying CD-ROM).

FIGURE 4.5
Box-mapping technique in Fractal Design Detailer.

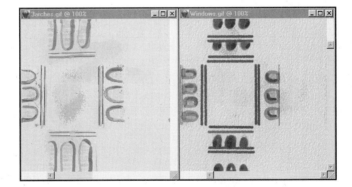

Creating Camera Views

Placing cameras in the scene is not, of course, a modeling technique per se, but it needs to be mentioned here because cameras are so useful in making a successful VRML world. The different cameras you create in your scene are listed by the VRML browser, usually in the menu that pops-up when you right-click in the browser's viewport. Users can navigate within the scene by selecting one camera view after another; be sure to provide plenty of them and name them descriptively. Even very large worlds that navigate painfully slowly in the browser can be viewed pleasurably from a series of camera views.

Use the cameras you create to show off the best views of the scene—to point out unusual perspectives or to provide close-ups of the parts of the scene over which you lavished the most care. If you leave it to the user to navigate through the scene, you have no control over what he or she will look at. With a good selection of camera views, on the other hand, you can control this to a large extent. Because selecting cameras is simpler than manually navigating with the mouse and because the browser makes an elegant transition from one camera to another, if you make an interesting and original sequence of camera views, they will be used.

Types of Animation

VRML 2.0 provides animation support for the VRML worlds you export from 3DS MAX. The following list identifies a fairly wide variety of animation methods that you can use:

- Simple transforms (move, rotate, and scale)

- Animated hierarchies and inverse kinematics

- Coordinate interpolation animation, such as animated modifiers (Bend, Taper, and so on)

- Morphing

- Character Studio animation

You can do any kind of animation that doesn't involve changing the number of vertices. If the animation requires use of the Modifier stack, you need to turn on the Coordinate Interpolation option when you export the scene.

It's easy to exceed your file-size budget quickly when you start using animation, especially with coordinate interpolation. With this last type of animation, the VRMLOUT exporter has to track the position of every vertex over time, requiring the generation of a lot of code in the VRML file. Simple transform animation, on the other hand, is not nearly so demanding. Use it whenever possible.

It's useful to think of animation as a moving accent in an otherwise-still VRML world; in the current climate of the web, a little goes a long way.

Some animation examples follow in the project section, "Creating a Virtual World with 3DS MAX and VRMLOUT."

Using Tools Provided by the VRMLOUT Plug-In

The VRMLOUT plug-in provides some special tools for managing your scene. These include the Polygon Counter, the Level of Detail helper, and the Export dialog box. The next sections discuss these tools in detail.

The Polygon Counter

The *Polygon Counter* is an excellent little gadget that keeps count of the number of faces in the scene as a whole, as well as in the selected object or objects. You can set a budget for the number of faces in the scene or for each object; the counter displays a colored "thermometer" when you approach the limit or go over the top. This utility is invaluable when modeling for VRML export. You soon get a sense of how many faces should be in various objects, according to their relative importance in the scene, and the Polygon Counter helps keep you on target. Use it in conjunction with the Optimize modifier for a real-time graphic display of the optimization process; as you change the modifier values by using the spinners, the Polygon Counter changes also. Figure 4.6 shows the Polygon Counter in use with the Optimize modifier.

FIGURE 4.6
Using the Polygon Counter utility.

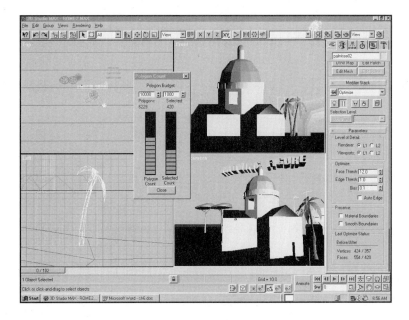

The Level of Detail Helper

The *Level of Detail* helper (LOD) is one of the VRML Helper objects you can place in your scene. It speeds up navigation in the viewport by displaying different objects, depending on their distance from the viewer. You can have the browser display a detailed version of a building, for example, when the viewer comes within 100 units. As soon as the viewer moves farther away, the browser can display a less detailed version of the same building, with fewer faces.

You don't have to use different versions of the same objects. By substituting completely different objects, you can do a kind of simple morphing.

LOD objects are covered in the project section of the chapter, "Creating a Virtual World with 3DS MAX and VRMLOUT."

Settings in the Export Dialog

The VRMLOUT plug-in's Export dialog has a number of settings that affect file size.

Always leave the Primitives option checked when primitives are in the scene. This parameter tells the exporter to convert 3DS MAX primitives to VRML primitives, which require less code in the VRML file. The 3DS MAX scene with the two rows of primitives shown in figure 4.1, for example, exported to 45 KB with this option checked but increased to 85 KB when it was unchecked.

If you never need to look at the VRML code generated by the exporter, you can uncheck the Indentation parameter. Indentation makes the VRML code easier to read. Unchecking this parameter reduced the 45 KB file just mentioned to 38 KB.

The Digits of Precision option controls the accuracy with which dimensions are calculated. Reducing the Digits of Precision from the default 4 to 3 is probably acceptable unless you have an architectural model or some other scene in which measurements need to be precise. Decrementing this parameter reduced the size of the test file to just under 36 KB.

It's probably not worth reducing the value of the Sample Rate parameter for transform animation. Doing so doesn't save you much in terms of file size, but it does rapidly start to make the animation play back less smoothly. You might want to experiment with the sample rates if you have coordinate-interpolation animation in the scene. Reducing the value in this case can make a significant difference in file size.

Other Techniques

You can use a couple of other techniques to speed things up: one to help control screen-update performance, and the other to help reduce download time.

The EMBED HTML Statement

The *EMBED statement* is a technique for constraining the size of the viewport occupied by the browser on the web page. By controlling the size of the browser, you can ensure, for example, that the user will not try to display the scene maximized on a 17-inch monitor or otherwise on such a large scale that the computer cannot properly process the number of pixels that must be rendered.

The HTML format for the statement follows:

```
<EMBED SRC=filename.WRL WIDTH=300 HEIGHT=200>
```

Figure 4.7 shows the Cosmo browser constrained to an area of the screen with the EMBED statement (from the Kinetix site at www.ktx.com).

FIGURE 4.7

Use of the EMBED HTML statement to constrain the size of the browser viewport.

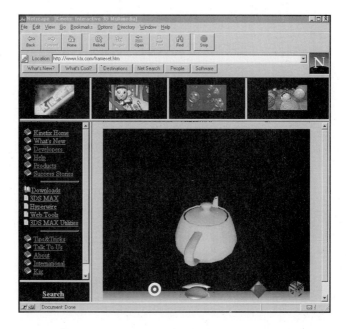

GZIP File Compression

The good news about file compression is that it works well, greatly reducing the size of the VRML (WRL) file. The bad news is that you probably have to use a Unix command to do it. If your web site is on a Unix web server, as most of them are, you are probably already familiar with the Telnet-type commands needed to create directories, set access rights, and so on. To compress a VRML file, change to the directory where the file resides and type:

gzip *filename*.wrl

This creates a gzipped (compressed) file with the name:

filename.wrl.gz

When you attempt to view a gzipped file from your web page, the message `Warning: Unrecognized encoding: x-gzip` appears. This is not a problem because when you click on OK, the file opens as usual. Browsers may some day be smart enough not to display pointless messages. Until then, the inconvenience is minor; don't let it stop you from compressing your files.

What VRMLOUT Can and Cannot Export

Before you create a scene for export to VRML, you should be aware that not everything you can model or animate in 3DS MAX is supported by the VRML 2.0 standard. Table 4.2 lists the elements of the 3DS MAX scene that can be exported to a VRML 2.0-format file, as well as some notable elements that cannot be. If you're not sure whether something will or will not export, you can always make a simple test scene, export it, and load it in your VRML browser.

TABLE 4.2

Summary of Exportable and Nonexportable Elements

Can Be Exported	Cannot Be Exported
Geometry	Smoothing groups
Hidden objects (Export option)	Hidden faces
Transform animation	
Coordinate interpolation animation	

Can Be Exported	Cannot Be Exported
Inverse kinematics	Inherit links
Animated cameras	
Light color	Volumetric lights
Standard materials and multi/sub-object materials (see the following indented list)	Other types of materials
Ambient, diffuse, and specular color	All other aspects of the material not listed in the first column
1 map (in diffuse channel)	
Shininess	
Opacity	
Wire frame	

Creating a Virtual World with 3DS MAX and VRMLOUT

This section explains how to create a virtual world for the web, using 3D Studio MAX and the VRMLOUT plug-in. You can access a web page that displays the completed sample world used in this chapter at www.jps.net/avernon/worlds.html. The page also contains instructions for viewing the various VRMLOUT features in the sample world. You should view this web page in your web browser, both to see what you will be doing if you work through the rest of this chapter and to get the real-world experience of the way a large VRML file actually performs.

If this is not possible, the same VRML file (CITY.WRL) is included on the accompanying CD-ROM. You can open it locally by using your web browser's Open File menu option. Whether you view the file live on the web or locally, you need to have a VRML 2.0 browser installed, and, as discussed in the Browser Review section of this chapter, Live3D 2.0 is recommended.

The CITY.WRL sample world is designed to demonstrate most of the helpers of the VRMLOUT plug-in (see the Kinetix web site, www.ktx.com, for updates). This section steps you through the process of adding each helper to a partially complete version of the sample scene (City.max). It describes the procedure used and indicates what you then need to do to see that helper in action in the browser (navigation, clicking on objects, and so on).

General Procedure for Using VRMLOUT

The following list summarizes the general procedure for adding the individual helpers. This should prove helpful before you begin because the procedure is the same or very similar for all of them.

1. Create your scene in the usual way with lighting, materials, and animation. Pay special attention to creating and naming cameras; they are listed in the VRML browser and are an important means of navigation. (In the 3DS MAX file you start with, the cameras are already defined.)

2. Go to the Create panel and choose Helpers. Then select the VRML option from the drop-down list. Select VRML 2.0 for all the features described in this section unless otherwise noted.

3. Click on the button for the helper you want (TimeSensor, for example), and then click and drag in the Top viewport to place the helper icon. (Figure 4.8 shows some of the helper icons used in the sample file.) Most of the helper icons can go anywhere in the scene. Some, such as the Level of Detail helper, must be placed next to the objects they affect.

4. Link the helper to the objects in the scene that it affects. You usually do this by picking the objects, as described in the procedure for each helper.

5. Export the file in WRL format. Select VRML 2.0 for all the features described in this section. If you have a static scene with no animation, you probably don't need VRML 2.0 export and can export the file in VRML 1.0 format instead. This means that your file will also be viewable in browsers not yet VRML 2.0 compliant. Check the VRMLOUT plug-in help file for a list of which features belong to VRML 2.0 and which are included in VRML 1.0.

FIGURE 4.8
VRMLOUT helpers in the 3DS MAX scene.

Anchor

NavInfo

Background

Sound

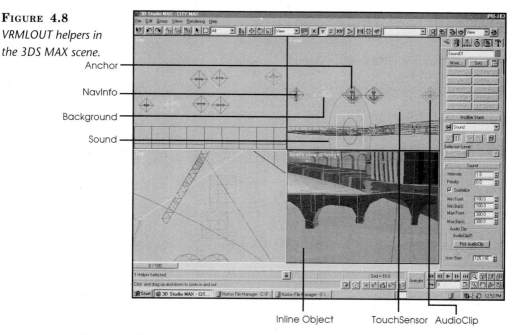

Inline Object   TouchSensor   AudioClip

6. Test the file in your VRML browser. To test the file, open it from your hard disk first to make sure that the helper works as expected. Then upload the file to the web server and test the world live on the web.

Adding the VRMLOUT Helpers to a Scene

You don't need to add the helpers to the sample scene in any particular order. There's no right order to placing them, although starting with the background seems logical.

This chapter does not attempt to describe all the many parameters for these helpers; that is done adequately in the VRMLOUT help file and elsewhere. Instead, this chapter focuses on the parameters you should be especially aware of and those that need to be changed from the default values.

Background

The *Background* helper defines the colors for a sky or ground backdrop to the world. This can be a plain color or a gradation made of two or three colors. If you define both sky and ground, you get a horizon line. The Background helper also provides options to set a bitmap image for the sky and ground (however, no browsers support this feature yet).

You should place a Background helper in your scene whenever you want to control the colors of the Browser viewport. In daylight scenes, for example, you want a sky-colored background. (Cosmo and Sony Community Place both display a black background by default.)

In this procedure, you use a Background helper to create a blue-sky backdrop for the scene:

1. Open the City.max file on the accompanying CD-ROM. This file requires the Free Form Deformation plug-in from the Kinetix web site.

2. Select the Background helper from the VRML 2.0 helpers in the 3DS MAX Create panel. No linking is required; just place the icon in the Top viewport and adjust the settings. Figure 4.9 shows the settings to use (the blue in the sample file has an RGB value of 40,140,220).

3. From the File menu, choose Export, and then choose VRML from the list of export formats.

4. In the Export dialog, select VRML 2.0 from the list. You can leave the other settings as they are.

5. Open the VRML file in your web browser (in Netscape, choose Open File from the File menu).

The colored-sky background should be visible as the file loads.

FIGURE 4.9

Settings for the Background helper.

NavInfo

The *NavInfo* helper enables you to control some of the characteristics of the browser display, such as navigation type and speed, whether a headlight is on, and so on. The default browser settings are generally acceptable, so a NavInfo helper is not essential. You may want to place one to increase the speed setting from 1.0 to about 5.0, however, if navigation seems slow when you test the file on the web.

In this procedure, you use a NavInfo helper to speed up the navigation slightly:

1.   Continue with the City.max file.

2.   Select the NavInfo helper under VRML 2.0 helpers in the 3DS MAX Create panel. No linking is required; just place the icon in the Top viewport and adjust the settings. Figure 4.10 shows the settings to use.

3.   From the File menu, choose Export, and then choose VRML from the list of export formats.

4.   In the Export dialog, select VRML 2.0 from the list. You can leave the other settings as they are.

5.   Open the VRML file in your web browser (in Netscape, choose Open File from the File menu).

The NavInfo settings take effect when you load the file.

FIGURE 4.10

Settings for the NavInfo helper.

TimeSensor

The *TimeSensor* helper controls animation settings such as Start and End Frames and Looping. By adding a number of TimeSensors to the objects in your scene, you can play segments of the scene's animation out of sequence— something you cannot do in 3DS MAX. Suppose, for example, that you have two boats rowing down the river with exactly the same animated stroke of the oars. By using a separate TimeSensor for each boat, and selecting a different range of frames, you can have the stroke of the oars different for each.

In this procedure, you place a TimeSensor to loop an animation and to start the animation when the file is loaded. Figure 4.11 shows the settings to use.

1. Open the Galley.max file. This file already has an animation for the movement of the oars.

2. Select the TimeSensor helper under VRML 2.0 helpers in the 3DS MAX Create panel.

3. Place the icon in the Top viewport.

4. Click on the Pick Objects button, and then click on each of the oars individually. Make certain that you select all the animated objects to be controlled by the TimeSensor.

5. Turn on the Loop and Start on World Load options.

6. Export and test the file.

FIGURE 4.11

Settings for the TimeSensor helper.

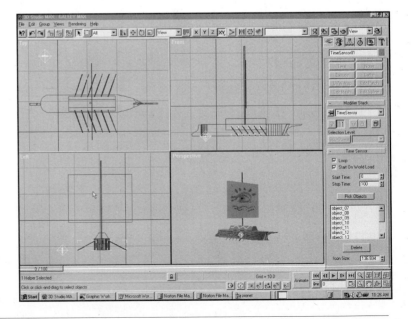

Inline Object

The *Inline Object* helper inserts another WRL file into the world in place of the Inline helper icon. This is useful for the following reasons.

- Because inline files start to load at the same time as the "host" file, the scene as a whole builds faster.

- By instancing one inline file, you can quickly insert more than one copy of an object.

- You can include objects created by someone else.

In this procedure, you place two Inline objects to insert two copies of the galley model into the scene.

1. Open the City.max file.

2. Select the Inline helper under VRML 1.0/2.0/VRBL helpers in the 3DS MAX Create panel.

3. Place the icon in the Top viewport at coordinates 480X, 430Y and enter Galley.wrl, the name of the WRL file to insert.

4. Hold down the Shift key and drag the Inline icon to create a second Inline object. Make it an instance of the first, and place it at coordinates 472X, 400Y.

5. Export and test the file.

When you use an Inline object, always make certain that the helper icon is positioned and rotated correctly relative to the other objects in the scene. The object or objects to be inserted must have been created at the same scale as the host scene. The inline file must be in the same folder as the host file.

Notes on viewing this feature in the browser: The two galleys (boats) on the river are the Inline objects (see fig. 4.12). The initial camera view's setting for the world gives the best view of these objects. Note that the two boats start loading almost immediately when you load the exported file (see fig. 4.13).

FIGURE 4.12

Inline objects as they appear in the 3DS MAX scene.

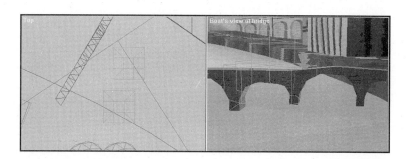

Level of Detail (LOD)

The *LOD* helper speeds redraw time by substituting different versions of an object. The more detailed, complex object is loaded when the viewer is close; the less detailed, less complex object is loaded as the viewer moves away.

FIGURE 4.13

Inline objects as they appear in the VRML world.

To add a LOD object to a scene, choose VRML 1.0/2.0/VRBL from the list in the Create panel to display the LOD helper. Follow the procedure in the VRMLOUT help file to create the LOD objects. Because you need to place the objects at the same coordinates, you cannot see them all simultaneously. The best way to handle them is to hide and unhide them as necessary. Figure 4.14 shows the settings used for the LOD objects in the sample file.

To see this feature in the sample file, open the Lodcity.wrl file in your browser. The initial camera view's setting for the world gives you a view of the LOD objects. Navigate forward in the viewport toward the building immediately in front of you. As you draw near, the plain texture-mapped-box building changes to a fully modeled version.

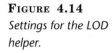

FIGURE 4.14
Settings for the LOD helper.

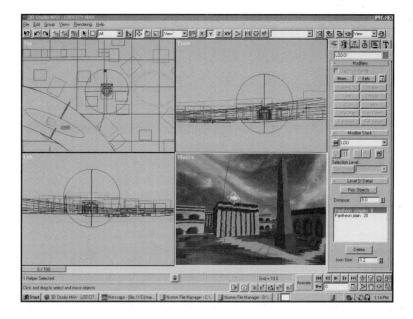

Anchor

The *Anchor* helper creates a link from an object in the VRML world to another URL (WRL or HTML file) or to another camera viewpoint in the same world.

In this procedure, you add several Anchor objects to set up jumps to different cameras in the scene. The viewer can then click on four objects to go to close-up camera views: the Colosseum, the Island, the Aqueduct, and the River.

1. Open the City.max file. The different camera views are already defined.

2. Select the Anchor helper under VRML 2.0 helpers in the 3DS MAX Create panel.

3. Place the icon in the Top viewport.

4. Click on the Pick Trigger Object button, and then click on the Colosseum Building object.

5. In the Description field, enter **Go to Colosseum camera**. Some browsers (such as Live3D 2.0, for example) display this text in the Browser viewport to guide the user.

6. Select Set Camera, and then choose the Colosseum camera from the list.

7. Repeat steps 3 through 6 to add three more Anchors to the scene. The trigger objects are the Island (**Go to Island view camera**), the Aqueduct Structure (**Go to Aqueduct camera**), and the River (**Go to Downriver camera**).

8. Export and test the file.

Notes on viewing this feature in the browser: Select the Map View with Anchors camera viewpoint from the list in the browser. You should then be able to click on the four objects—the Colosseum, the Island, the Aqueduct, and the River—to go to close-up camera views. In Cosmo, the pointer in the Browser viewport changes to a cross to indicate that you are over an object for which an anchor has been defined (see fig. 4.15).

FIGURE 4.15

Selecting an anchor link.

TouchSensor

The *TouchSensor* helper starts an animation or sound file when the user clicks on the linked object.

In this procedure, you add a TouchSensor helper to open the Colosseum door:

1. Continue with the City.max file.

2. Select the TouchSensor helper under VRML 2.0 helpers in the 3DS MAX Create panel.

3. Place the icon in the Top viewport.

4. Set one of the 3DS MAX viewports to show the Colosseum camera view.

5. Click on the Pick Trigger Object button, and then click on the right door (Door2) to the Colosseum. The name of the object appears in the Control panel.

6. Click on the Pick Action Objects button, and then on the left door (Door 1).

7. Export and test the file.

When you place a TouchSensor, first pick the *trigger object* (the object to be clicked on). Then pick the *target object* or objects (the object(s) animated or the Sound helper activated). Figure 4.16 shows the settings used in the sample file.

Notes on viewing this feature in the browser: Select the Colosseum camera viewpoint from the list in the browser, and click on the right door to open the door.

FIGURE 4.16

Settings for the TouchSensor helper.

AudioClip and Sound

The *AudioClip and Sound* helpers work together to provide 3D, spatialized sound in the world. *Spatialized sound* is sound that increases in volume as you approach its source.

In this procedure, you add an AudioClip helper and a Sound helper to create the 3D sound of oars splashing in the water:

1. Continue with the City.max file.

2. Select the AudioClip helper under VRML 2.0 helpers in the 3DS MAX Create panel.

3. Place the icon in the Top viewport.

4. For URL, enter **splash.wav**.

5. Add a text description (optional); this text does not appear in the browser).

6. Check the Loop box and the Start on World load box.

7. Select the Sound helper under VRML 2.0 helpers in the 3DS MAX Create panel.

8. Place the Sound helper in the Top viewport, close to the Inline objects on the river.

9. Click on the Pick AudioClip button, and then click on the AudioClip helper you just added. The name of the AudioClip appears in the Control panel.

10. Use the Min/Max spinners to adjust the blue and red ellipsoids. These two ellipsoids show the distances within which the sound is at full volume and still audible, respectively. Figure 4.17 shows the settings to use.

FIGURE 4.17
Settings for the Sound helper.

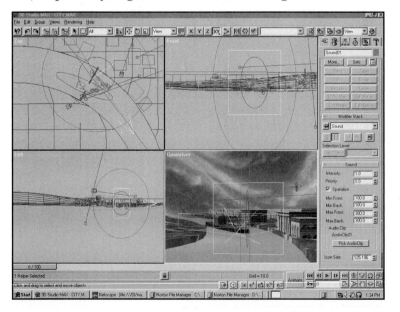

11. Export and test the file.

Notes on hearing this feature in the browser: Navigate toward the ships on the river. As you get closer, you should hear the oars splashing in the water. As you go farther away, the sound fades out.

This completes the construction of the ancient city world. If you've followed the steps in this section, you now know how to use all the helpers provided by the VRMLOUT plug-in, except for Fog and Billboard. Fog is not supported by any browsers yet, and Billboard doesn't seem to work as specified, so at this point you have all the tools you need to take your 3DS MAX scenes into the wonderful world of VRML and the web.

Browser Review

Several VRML browsers are available that do a fine job of implementing the VRML specification. As this book is being written, *VRML* means VRML 2.0. The VRML 2.0 spec was approved in mid-1996, and the best browsers already support it. Not all VRML 2.0 browsers are equal, however. This section looks at some of them, comparing them specifically in terms of how well they handle VRML files exported from 3DS MAX with the VRMLOUT plug-in.

A Note on VRML 1.0 Browsers

Things change very quickly on the web, and what is true today may not be true—or be only relatively true—tomorrow. Other browsers may appear that are superior to the ones discussed here. These browsers are the best available today, however; they are likely to continue to evolve along with the VRML specification itself.

On the other hand, some browsers have not evolved fast enough to be included in this review. The most notable of these is the Topper browser from Kinetix, which still supports only VRML 1.0. Topper adds some extra functionality (called *VRBL*) that is not in the VRML 1.0 specification, but these extra functions (which are for basic animation) have been superseded by the new functionality in VRML 2.0. Also, Topper does not seem to be maintained by anyone at Kinetix and is therefore not recommended.

NOTE

Changing VRML browsers is a simple task: Download the new browser and run the setup program. In most cases, this automatically installs the new browser over the old one. The next time you access a VRML world, the new browser should run (exceptions are noted in the following browser description sections).

World View, from Intervista

Intervista's World View is a handsome browser with excellent navigation tools—a genuine and very fast VRML 2.0-compliant browser. Intervista does not display the lights and texture maps of the MAX model very well, however, having obviously sacrificed some display quality to speed. Figure 4.18 shows the sample WRL file in the World View browser. Even in black and white, you should be able to see the pixelation of the textures and the absence of shadows (compare this with figs. 4.19 and 4.20, in the next two sections). World View is recommended as a primary browser only if navigation speed is much more important to you than appearance.

FIGURE 4.18

A sample VRML file in Intervista's World View.

TIP

World View has a Pointer tool that enables you to click on an object to zoom in on it. Another tool, Stand-Up Straight, puts you in an upright position relative to the horizon.

Download the browser at www.intervista.com. World View automatically installs itself over Live3D in Netscape without stopping to inform you that it has renamed the Live3D DLL. It has an uninstall program in case you want to get Live3D or another browser back again.

Community Place, from Sony

Community Place, a recently released browser from Sony in Japan, is promising but has some peculiarities. In particular, the navigation tools are difficult to use and don't seem to do what you expect (not easily zooming directly forward in the viewport, for example). This browser also has the odd characteristic of unexpectedly animating the model, moving it slowly upward in the vertical axis as soon as it has loaded. With collision detection on, it does provide a suitably unpleasant thudding sound effect when you walk into something. As for the display of lights and textures, Community Place generally is somewhat better than Intervista's browser (compare fig. 4.19 with fig. 4.18), and it (Community Place) loads and navigates a file almost as quickly as the Intervista browser. This browser rates third place (this author's view).

FIGURE 4.19

Sample VRML file in Sony's Community Place.

Download the browser from www.sony.com. Community Place does not install automatically over Live3D in Netscape. You must manually remove or rename the Live3D DLL file in the Netscape\Navigator\plug-ins folder after Community Place is installed. It has no uninstall program; if you want to get Live3D or another browser back again, you must manually restore what you removed or renamed.

Cosmo Player, from Silicon Graphics

The VRMLOUT plug-in was originally developed and tested with the Cosmo browser in mind. Cosmo's capability to display 3DS MAX lights and textures is much better than that of the other browsers reviewed here. The drawbacks to Cosmo are its speed—it can be extremely slow especially in file loading (5 to 10 times slower than Live 3D)—and its navigation tools, which are quite primitive compared to those that come with World View and Community Place. You must navigate by manipulating the navigation control in the dashboard rather than moving the mouse in the viewport itself. The display quality is so much more faithful to the original, however, that Cosmo receives a qualified number two recommendation from this author.

Download the browser at www.sgi.com. Cosmo automatically installs itself over Live3D in Netscape.

FIGURE 4.20

Sample VRML file in Silicon Graphics' Cosmo Player.

Live3D 2.0 from Netscape

As this book is being written, Netscape 3.0 still ships with Live3D 1.0, which is strictly a VRML 1.0 browser. In January 1997, however, you could download a new version—Live3D 2.0—that does support VRML 2.0. Future releases of Netscape will have Live3D 2.0 built in.

Live3D is a very attractive, very fast browser with good light- and texture-display capabilities (see fig. 4.21). This is really the browser to use for general-purpose web surfing, although you might want to try Cosmo to see whether you prefer it. This browser receives the number one recommendation from the author.

Download Live3D 2.0 at www.netscape.com.

FIGURE 4.21

Sample VRML file in Netscape's Live 3D 2.0.

The Best of the Web

What makes a great VRML world, given the limitations of today's technology? This section points you to some of today's best VRML web sites and discusses some general characteristics of these top-flight VRML implementations.

Oz Inc. (*www.oz.com*)

The Oz site worlds show what can be done with simple geometry and complex texture maps—a theme covered earlier in this chapter. Figure 4.22 shows the excellent use of lighting in one of the worlds from this site.

NOTE

The Oz site has the best VRML worlds the author has found so far.

FIGURE 4.22

Stage world from the Oz Inc. site.

Unfortunately, the Oz worlds were not modeled in 3DS MAX. They are exported for VRML 1.0 and are best viewed with Live3D. If you use Cosmo Player to open some of these worlds, an error results because of the incompatible sound systems.

The Genesis Project (*www.3d-design.com/livespace/ genesis*)

The Genesis Project, an ongoing demonstration site for VRML features, operates under the auspices of *3D Design* magazine. It provides a good example of a world created with 3DS MAX and VRMLOUT, showing simple but effective use of animation and texture mapping. At present, this world can only be browsed with Intervista's World View.

Intervista's VRML Circus (*www.intervista.com/products/worldview/demos/index.shtml*)

This site has some nice character animation, probably done with the Character Studio plug-in (see fig. 4.23).

FIGURE 4.23

Animated juggler from Intervista's site.

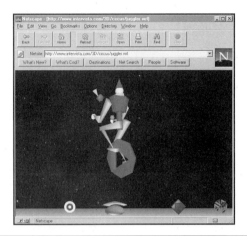

Steel Studio Landscape (*www.marketcentral.com/vrml/gallery.wrl*)

This world provides a great example of the use of scale. Try zooming back from the initial camera view (see fig. 4.24) to see the real extent of the objects that make up the scene.

FIGURE 4.24

The Steel Studio landscape.

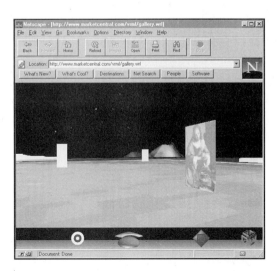

Construct's Stratus Gallery (*www.construct.net/stratus/*)

The Stratus gallery is an elegant way of displaying 2D artwork in a 3D world (see fig. 4.25). The gallery shows good use of many different camera viewpoints (one for each canvas hung in the gallery).

FIGURE 4.25

Artwork hanging in the Stratus gallery.

For a list of other notable VRML sites, refer to the Ch4bkmk.htm bookmarks file on the accompanying CD-ROM.

In Practice: Modeling for VR and the Web

- **VRML's bright future.** VRML is an open standard that provides an evolving framework for 3D artists. The combination of 3DS MAX, the VRMLOUT plug-in, and VRML 2.0 browsers such as Cosmo and Live3D makes it possible for you to create truly interactive environments you can share with others through the medium of the World Wide Web. If you are an architect, for example, you can point potential clients to models they can walk through. If you are a game designer, you can set up spaces where users can play against one another online. VRML has tremendous potential for many applications.

- **Modeling techniques.** You can use many simple techniques to keep down the size of your scenes so that when you export them to VRML format, they load quickly and perform well. These techniques include: reducing the number of segments in primitives, deleting unnecessary faces, optimizing objects, and using instances.

- **The VRMLOUT plug-in.** The VRMLOUT plug-in enables you to export VRML 2.0-compatible worlds from 3DS MAX scenes. It even supports some VRML 2.0 features not yet available in any browser. Adding the VRMLOUT helpers is a simple process, but you can create some powerful effects with them (multiple clickable trigger objects and 3D sound, for example).

- **Think VRML.** Creating scenes for display and interaction on the World Wide Web is essentially different from creating scenes for film and video or CD-ROM. You always have to think about the limitations of the medium and how to make the most of them. "Thinking VRML" also means trying to visualize how people will relate to the worlds you create, and how they will experience them and navigate through them, all of which implies cooperation and sharing—and that's what the Web is all about.

Please contact the author via his web site and let him know about the new VRML sites you have enjoyed exploring or, especially, those you have created yourself.

IMAGE BY ERIC C. PETERSON

Chapter 5

by Eric C. Peterson

TECHNICAL MODELING FOR ENGINEERING VISUALIZATION

What constitutes "technical" modeling? That question, presented to a dozen different animators, may well elicit a dozen different answers. In a general sense, technical modeling describes any number of animation and rendering disciplines more concerned with the quantitatively accurate representation or duplication of an event than with the artistic or interpretive elements.

Computer Aided Design (CAD) tools such as AutoCAD and Cadkey are designed as technical modeling packages. They also incorporate specialized tools—dimensioning engines, symbol libraries, and plotter drivers, for example—optimized for the technical drawing and illustration task. CAD tools, however, often don't provide the high-end rendering capabilities typical of dedicated rendering packages, and few provide the animation capabilities increasingly in demand in technical presentations and documentation.

Toward that end, the technical illustrator has two options: to use rendering and animation plug-ins or add-ons for the modeling and drafting software; or to use purpose-built rendering and animation software, separate and distinct from the design and drafting system. Because add-ons for the drafting software frequently cost as much as a purpose-built package by itself—and are often limited in capability as well—turning to tools designed specifically for the rendering and animation task often makes more sense.

3D Studio MAX for Windows NT is the successor to the four iterations of 3D Studio for DOS. MAX doesn't incorporate every last feature of 3D Studio Release 4, whose CAD-like interface presented a gentle learning curve to many engineers, architects, and drafters, but MAX still provides a formidable array of modeling tools that supports precision work. In conjunction with MAX's vast array of animation and rendering tools directed toward supporting the artist, it presents an environment with few equals (or none).

This chapter covers the following technical modeling topics, especially as they apply to 3D Studio MAX:

- Technical modeling characteristics
- Purposes of technical modeling
- Why the intended audience for technical animations is unique
- Why technical animation is unique
- Typical technical modeling products
- A large technical proposal animation illustration project revealed

Characteristics and Purposes of Technical Modeling

Some aspects of technical modeling, rendering, or animation chores are common to the different applications in the genre. That is, some identifiable characteristics are associated with all technical applications. Others may be present in some applications, but not all. These characteristics include the following:

- The presentation of events in a specific and rigorous time sequence

- The duplication of the appearances of objects or locations with high quantitative accuracy

- The retention or simulation of the precise relationship between events or objects

- The presentation of information in a manner to facilitate instruction

- The presentation of information in a manner to facilitate immediate recognition of a particular and specific object, event, location, or relationship

- The use of Computer Aided Design system-generated data at any point in the development of the animation

Clearly, some of these characteristics describe other, nontechnical applications as well, especially some advertising efforts. A better job must be done of defining applications and audience. The next sections go into these areas in more detail.

The next few paragraphs present some very specific groups of applications that exhibit the characteristics just listed.

Legal Animation

The term *legal animation* usually evokes images of automobile accident reconstructions prepared for courtroom presentation. Although common, this is only one application of legal animation. Auto accident animations fall into a larger class of legal animation products whose purpose is to present the conclusions of the "expert witness"—usually an accident reconstructionist or forensic scientist skilled in the simulation and reconstruction of events, based on evidence.

Some experienced animators at this point will wonder at this chapter's use of the term "legal animation," when the trades usually term it "forensic animation." The distinction is this: the latter category does not include patent law animation, which is almost a purely educational tool and rarely reconstructive or interpretive.

A common misconception on the part of animators and legal representatives who have never used legal animation is that the animator becomes the expert witness or that the animator performs the services of the forensic scientist or reconstructionist. This position is both dangerous and untenable, and the animator trying to enter this field is well advised to understand the relationship between the parties involved. In most cases, the animator works closely with the forensic scientist to implement the expert's opinion of just exactly how a specific sequence of events transpired. The degree to which the animation product accurately and precisely matches what the expert witness believes to have happened is a measure of the animation product's usefulness in the courtroom.

The animator, unless he or she is also the reconstructionist or forensic scientist, usually never sees the courtroom.

A second and growing application for legal animation is the use of animation products in patent litigation. Because the jury system cannot pick and choose members specifically suited for a particular trial, rarely is the jury chosen to sit in judgment for a complex technical patent litigation case well versed in the technical issues involved. In these cases, the expert witnesses for each side—usually engineers or scientists—may work closely with animators to construct graphic representations of processes or mechanisms to demonstrate in the simplest possible fashion why the processes at issue are alike or different. When the parties to the litigation present complex technical issues to the jury in this way, the jurors are able to reach an informed decision without necessarily understanding the intricacies of the underlying technology.

Technical Documentation

In the design and construction of complex equipment and systems, the creation of the documentation may precede the actual existence of the equipment by weeks, months, or even years. Particularly in the delivery of specialized equipment to the government, milestones for deliverable documentation products can be before any hardware has been built. Even in relatively small projects, for example, in which the total system cost barely reaches seven figures, the government may require preliminary technical documentation four to six months before the hardware is actually assembled. Today, animation and rendering products derived from the CAD design data frequently take the place of the photographs and hand-drawn line drawings of old.

Concurrent engineering describes a process in which all phases of a design effort—design, design for manufacturing, documentation, and tooling design—occur simultaneously. In support of these accelerated efforts, facilitated in part by advanced software design tools, other advanced software tools have appeared.

Syndesis Corporation, for example, publishes a range of products, collectively called Interchange, that translate modeling data formats. Many of the formats are CAD-based, and others support animation software. Newer products from other developers support very difficult translations, such as that between Parametric Technologies' Pro/Engineer and 3D Studio MAX. Given these tools, it is possible to isolate subassemblies of a product and proceed with documentation many months before tooling-up and manufacturing has even begun—by moving data from the design tool to the rendering tool. Given the quality of the output of modern rendering tools such as 3D Studio MAX, the result frequently costs even less than studio photography.

Technical Promotional Illustration

A related application of technical modeling involves rendering images of a product or piece of equipment for press release or advertisement even before a prototype exists. Marketing specialists may even recognize that a prototype may not be photogenic and may choose a rendering of the "production version" over costly construction of nonoperational stand-ins, once the standard for this sort of requirement.

NOTE

The author's experience is more closely aligned with one-off systems or systems destined for only a very limited production run. In such cases, the marketing effort is very highly directed and not truly comparable to that associated with a mass-market product. When industrial designers get involved, as is inevitable—and prudent—for products intended for larger production runs, the process is much more involved and more dependent on a cooperative effort between system designers, industrial designers, and marketers.

The computer model has the advantage of being much less costly than an actual nonworking prototype to modify as the design evolves. An additional advantage of computer models is that they are inherently easier—as digital products—to graft into artwork or advertising copy.

Technical Proposal Illustration

Perhaps the widest use of technical animation and rendering is in the document known as the *technical proposal*. Throughout the defense and government research complex, and through much of commercial industry, the allocation of resources in support of new and original capital equipment depends in large part on the success of technical proposals.

The process works like this: Organization A decides it needs a multimillion dollar SuperWidget to do a particular job. The job might be cleaning nuclear waste tanks, removing the paint from aircraft as a prelude to overhaul, applying sealant to the seams in automobile bodies on the assembly line, sorting documents, or assembling terminals and the connected wiring into wiring harnesses. Whether organization A is private or government, it probably will first survey potential suppliers, perhaps prequalify a subset of those, and finally solicit quotes from those it determines are qualified to bid.

The quoting process is much more than faxing a price figure to the solicitor. A primary component of the bidding process is to convince the solicitor that the bidding firm has the know-how and experience to design, build, test, and deliver a successful design. This process usually includes detailed cost estimates broken down to the level of major components in the equipment, preliminary designs, detailed designs of critical subassemblies, resumes of critical development and test personnel, development schedules, and quite possibly an animated portrayal of the equipment in operation.

Bidders quite often invest hundreds (or even thousands) of man-hours in a large technical proposal. Compared to that, the effort involved in generating a technical rendering or animation seems trivial.

Figures 5.1 through 5.4 depict illustrations prepared for or from technical proposal animations. Figure 5.1 represents a set of equipment modules selected to perform a testing operation. At the time this image was created, some of these components did not yet exist, and yet the potential client was interested in the appearance of them.

FIGURE 5.1

This is modular testing equipment, some of which does not yet exist.

Figure 5.2 depicts a modular testing system for automobile components. Note the safety covers in various positions, the storage position for the keyboard, and the detailed computer housing whose manufacturer is identifiable based on case characteristics alone. These features were essential because the soliciting firm for this system uses an approved vendor list and only a limited number of computer suppliers, and because the request for quotes specifically mandated some operational features.

FIGURE 5.2

FIGURE 5.2

This is a testing station for automotive electrical components.

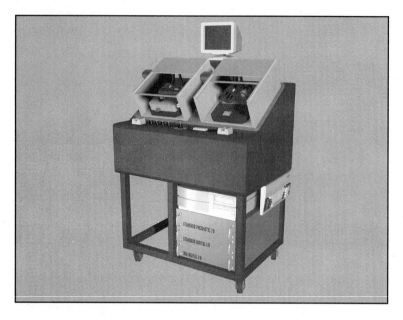

Figure 5.3 represents the final iteration of an avionics test set delivered to the United States Air Force. This illustration, also part of an animation, is actually the fourth iteration of the design—yet was still prepared months before the system was assembled. The system designers used earlier versions of this rendering prepared during the proposal phase to present control layouts and to address safety issues.

FIGURE 5.3

This is an avionics test set for fighter aircraft line replaceable units.

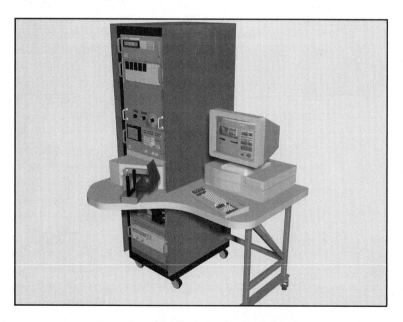

Figure 5.4 represents a lunar soil sampler, a concept for a study project that would have compared various approaches to this application.

FIGURE 5.4
A proposed deployable lunar soil sampler rests on a simulated lunar surface.

The Unique Audience for Technical Animations

The unusual thing about technical renderings is that the audience most likely contains experts who are more than happy to tear the work apart. Thus, the illustrations and animations must convey not only the appearance of a particular system, but also that the system is well thought-out and solidly designed. This also holds true for legal animation, in which opponent experts do everything possible to discredit your work—the manner in which it adheres to the reconstructionist's timing schedule, and the degree to which the vehicles or mechanisms resemble the real things.

When used as a documentation tool, the work is probably part of an evaluated deliverable that must satisfy the client in terms of accuracy, completeness, and ease-of-understanding. Often, a defense client evaluates an illustrated technical manual by providing the manual and the system described to a competent, but unprepared, technician. The efficiency with which the technician tears down, repairs, or reassembles the hardware is taken to be a measure of the completeness of your illustrations.

When used as a sales tool, the technical animation is reviewed by technical and management experts whose job is to compare your work with other work aimed at the same high-quality target. Any shortcoming or inconsistency stands out and could cost your employer millions of dollars.

This scrutiny differs completely from that faced by the entertainment industries that use computer animation. Not surprisingly, therefore, the ranks of technical illustrators derive in part from drafters and engineers rather than from artists and sculptors. Yet the tools used are the same and the end product, to the uninitiated, is similar. The purpose of this chapter is to describe some typical but advanced aspects to the construction of a technical model, providing an example to engineers and sculptors alike.

Why Technical Animation Is Unique

The foregoing discussions presented some qualitative, loosely example-driven reasons why technical animation is different from entertainment applications. Loose examples and general discussions are fine, but all the arm-waving in the world cannot adequately describe precisely the reasons that technical animation represents a separate discipline, unless it's possible to somehow classify and categorize the differences in techniques and applications. These differences fall into identifiable categories:

- Schedule requirements
- Precision
- Recognition
- Running in slow motion
- Typical technical modeling products

Schedule Requirements

Most animators would cringe at the requirement that a model have millimeter-level accuracy. Taken in the context of a large defense project, that is not a handicap. It isn't unusual for an animation or still image created in support of a multimillion dollar proposal to itself cost hundreds of man hours. Models frequently begin in CAD systems, and animators may actually have precise geometry they transform into renderable models.

A related consideration is that a technical animation may cost many, many times what a similar entertainment animation costs, not only because of the direct labor involved but also because of the labor spent defining and verifying requirements. Into this category also fall site surveys, library models laboriously digitized by service bureaus, and tedious conversion or construction of new models.

During the preliminary design of a nuclear reactor containment vessel refurbishment device, for example, one bidder devoted approximately 120 hours of engineering labor—at loaded rates approaching $100 an hour—converting one complex set of drawings into a single renderable model for use in proposal illustrations. A single illustration wound up in the proposal. Thus, the generation of one illustration from one complex model cost almost $12,000. In a gaming application, such expensive models may be crucial to gameplay, used over and over again in many scenes or used in vital plot-driven animations. For the purposes of one technical proposal, the single illustration presented a design—already laid out in detail in both text and schematic—so that the nontechnical evaluators would better understand the presentation.

Precision Counts

It isn't unusual for an accident reconstructionist to work not in frames not in fields, but in increments of tenths or even thousandths of a single second. No game animator ever set keys in increments of .001 second, but an accident reconstructionist who stands up in court and swears to this level of accuracy requires his animators to implement precisely the motion his calculations determine to be most likely.

NOTE

This is a vitally important point not only for animators who may not be closely familiar with MAX's advanced timekeeping features, but also for plug-in developers (or any potential plug-in developers) perusing this text. Plug-ins, especially plug-ins that can *ever* be used in forensic animation, absolutely must be subframe aware. That is, the plug-in must provide for those cases in which the animator attempts subframe keying with the plug-in. This isn't idle speculation. The author developed the algorithmic elements for Make Tracks for 3D Studio Release 4 and for MAXTrax for MAX. The original algorithm called for frame-specific keying, or for the creation of as many as 30 steps in the procedural trail per second. For applications using this

continues

plug-in, such as the electronics superstore gift-wrapping animation seen in the southwestern U.S. during the 1995 Christmas season, frame-keying is fine because no close-up, no slow-motion, and no subframe examination of the effect is ever important. A customer reported late in 1996 that MAXTrax would not satisfy his reconstructionist client, however, because a close-up of a skid mark generated with the utility failed to depict the marks accurately to the nearest .010 second. Because of the extremely high speeds involved in the accident, and because of the stakes involved in the lawsuit, the reconstructionist wanted to see skid marks accurate to the nearest four to six inches—a requirement at odds with the .033 second resolution of a plug-in designed to update only at integral field counts. The MAXTrax algorithm was modified to accommodate updates at nonintegral value keyframes.

One could argue that this makes MAX a better technical tool in one respect than 3D Studio Release 4 because no subframe keying was possible with the DOS versions—*and* the argument would be correct.

Recognition Counts

In a game animation, it is frequently important that an object resemble a class of objects, or that it implement an art director's vision of how a particular object must appear. In technical animation, each model must often be CAD-accurate so that no question whatsoever exists about accuracy or operation. A visual difference, no matter how slight, that interferes with apparent viability or causes the slightest doubt on the part of witnesses, can be fatal to the goal of the animation product.

Running in Slow Motion

Unlike entertainment products, in which a single frame with a glitch may be left in the final cut because no single viewer will catch it, a technical animation will be run in slow motion over and over and over again. And this will happen, repeatedly, in front of expert witnesses scouring your work for problems, usually on a projection big-screen television. Each field artifact has to be cleaned up. Each impulsive motion with no physical analog has to be smoothed. No transient visibility or smoothing artifacts are permitted— vastly different than the scrutiny directed at a product that might wind up as a 320-by-200 pixel lossy compressed AVI.

Typical Technical Modeling Products

Legal animation is almost always just that—technical modeling and precision keyframing in support of full animations. Technical proposal illustrations, on the other hand, are almost always still images and— if the project is large enough—animations as well. In support of consistency and the highest possible quality, the models used for both products are usually the same, resulting in uncharacteristically (for other genres) detailed animations. Still images, the animator may be certain, will be blown up by presenters into overhead transparencies, posters, report covers, and at the very least 8½-by-11 inch glossies. No detail remains hidden.

Modeling for a Technical Proposal

Figure 5.5 depicts the illustration effort accompanying a relatively large ($1,000,000 range) technical proposal effort. The rendered output of the models pictured was presented on everything from giveaway mousepads to overhead transparencies to 11-by-17 inch report covers. Additionally, a full animation of the robotic workcell using precise timing and actual motion programming was required by the solicitation, supplied in high-quality video format for distribution by the client within his organization.

NOTE

The term *workcell* may be a new term to some readers. It will not be a new term to the large percentage of programmers and developers, however, who derive in no small part from the ranks of roboticsts and animation engineers. The mathematics of 3D graphics are the same as the mathematics of robotic motion control. Workcell describes a frequently modular, or *cellular*, work space in which a robot and its closely related tooling is installed in a production environment.

Figure 5.5 depicts a complex robotic system whose function is to remanufacture fighter aircraft canopies. The system shown here is the basis for the technical portion of this chapter.

FIGURE 5.5
A canopy processing system consisting of industrial robot and custom-engineered components is shown as its designers intend that it be installed.

Unfortunately, for reasons of confidentiality, a discussion of the precise function of the workcell cannot be included here. The workcell facilitates the remanufacturing of fighter aircraft canopies damaged by any of a variety of events. Toward that end, equipment in the workcell moves the canopy around and the robot moves a tool over the components of the canopy. Fortunately, any additional information is irrelevant to the discussion of this scene's creation.

Purpose of the Model

Figure 5.5 depicts the third iteration of the model. A preliminary model, created during early discussions with the client, served as a reference point from which both the client and the designers could build. The need for safety equipment was the first to surface, and the preliminary model served as a base into which the safety features of the client's choice could be incorporated. Note the vertical optical interrupt towers at each corner of the equipment pit. Details, such as the collocated control station and operator chair, came later to provide a visual indication of the system's user-friendliness and of the relative comfort in which the (unionized) operator would work.

System design consultants also recommended placing the system in a pit to minimize the visual impact of the large, powerful central robot (in fact, quite a frightening piece of equipment). Interestingly enough, the elevation of the control and observation deck with respect to the machinery has significant psychological implications for management reviewers, not technically educated, who might have seen demonstrations of this same robot at another facility.

Note the lettering visible on the robot arm. This was vital to the system concept because research indicated that this brand name was favored by the client as an equipment supplier. It was also known that a competitor had advanced the use of a different robot arm less suited to the application and with logistical support requirements far less convenient to the end user. Thus, the detail visible in the rendering is a subtle indicator to the reviewers—even those cost and logistical support management types who would recognize the *name* of the equipment if not the *shape* of the model—that this supplier had done more and better planning in the preliminary design of the workcell.

The renderings, as they evolve in keeping with actual design changes, will likely be used in end-user training manuals and videos as well. Given the cost of such a system, using available computer simulations to provide training and orientation tools makes far more sense than taking downtime to present or film the actual hardware.

Components of the Scene

This is a complex robotic workcell. It accurately represents the actual design. It lacks, however, visually distracting but mechanically trivial features such as cable management hardware and pneumatic and hydraulic plumbing. Fortunately, these elements are as unnecessary as they are unsightly and tedious to model.

Robot

The robot is a large standard industrial unit typical of heavy-duty welding, lifting, and general-purpose process machines available in Europe and Japan. No U.S. firm manufactures comparable machines. The machine illustrated is a Staubli Automation RX-170L, the heaviest, largest unit offered by the firm that some years ago purchased Unimation from Westinghouse. Fortunately for the animators, this is a simple kinematic linkage with no closed four-bar structures that—until 3D Studio Releases 4 and MAX—were the bane of modelers and animators alike. Furthermore, the links of the machine are closed and solid, formed from relatively simple primitives and loft/surfrev shapes in combination. Note that detailed drawings of this machine were available to the modeler, but CAD models were not.

Its appearance was critical to the success of the renderings because technical evaluators for the customer would recognize it instantly. Thus, a large effort ensured the accuracy of both the dimensions and materials used in the construction of the robot model.

The robot model makes heavy use of primitives, extended primitives, and custom lofts.

Robot Tool

The tool wielded by the robot is an accurate representation of an existing tool employed by similar systems in the field. Its design features are significant to process operation and critically important to the quality of the presentation. The level of detail is sufficient to support close-ups that would lose much of the remainder of the scene. The robot tool employs mostly primitives and surfrevs.

Aircraft Canopy

Even more important than the robot, the aircraft canopy is unique because of its size. In fact, it was the size of this canopy that dictated the use of the Staubli RX-170L because no other industrial machine of comparable configuration would reach the entire canopy. Note that both the canopy glass and frame are present, and that *both* surfaces of the glass are required to support close-ups and particle special effects added to the animation.

Although detailed drawings of the canopy were not available, a very large high-quality plastic model of the entire aircraft yielded a canopy digitized at critical points to provide the required geometry.

The aircraft canopy is a complex mesh formed from custom loft planning, Boolean operations, and multiple extrusions and reorganizations.

Support Hardware

The framework holding the canopy is an element of the design proposed by the supplier. It needs to be accurate to the extent that it is practical to build, does not interfere with robot motion, and attaches to the canopy at the mounting points specified by the client. The support hardware represents components fabricated from simple welded steel stock.

The hardware below the mounting frame is an accurate portrayal of similar hardware that exists in similar systems. There are large semicustom linear drives, notable because the only visible drive hardware is the accordioned flexible cover over each linear shaft and screw. There are also large rotary table drives, notable because the orientation of the motor is critical to system clearances.

Environment

Various design considerations suggested that the system be mounted in a pit. For the concrete enclosure, aesthetics and practical considerations mandated chamfering the upper edge of the pit to reduce generation of debris and to facilitate sealing the concrete with a paint. The safety railing is more than simple welded pipe because similar systems have become showpieces for other end users, with visitors constantly moving through for demonstrations. The safety systems mandated by law and prudence are built into heavy structural supports designed to integrate visually with the appearance of the robot and canopy handler.

The desk and chair are library components from the Kinetix Commercial Props Compact Disk. Because these meshes are copyrighted, they are omitted from the scene file on the accompanying CD. The chair was not modified. The desk was heavily modified to improve smoothing group consistency and to eliminate unnecessary faces. The materials of the desk also were changed.

The computer and associated peripherals were created by the modeler for another project and are, in fact, the same components depicted in figures 5.2 and 5.3. Remember that the shape of the computer had special significance for figure 5.2; here, it is just another computer.

Robot Construction

The robot exists as a linkage of six objects, each of which has unique construction requirements and features. Each represents a separate exercise in technical modeling. These objects are—in order from the base to the tool—the Robot Base, Waist, Upper Arm, Lower Arm, Main Wrist Link, Wrist Pitch Link, and Tool/Roll Link.

Robot Base

One of the most recognizable elements of the robot, and therefore one of the most critical to the success of the model, is the base. Figure 5.6 shows the base in the MAX interactive display's viewports. Note that this project's default viewports are not the standard default viewports; they are more closely akin to a CAD configuration in which the three orthographic views align properly in the American style.

FIGURE 5.6

The robot base mesh looks like this in the interactive display.

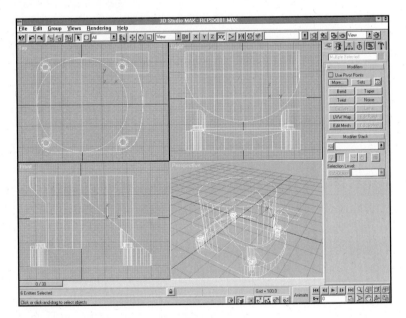

BUILDING THE ROBOT BASE

You build the base in several steps. Figure 5.7 shows the base shape imported from a CAD drawing.

NOTE

This robot, environment, and support system hardware has one common minimal dimension: five millimeters. Generally, five millimeters serves as a good basic value—a minimum resolution—for all the existing hardware and new design. Certainly the actual detailed design of the system employs a greater precision, but the value of five first came up because all the quoted robot dimensions were in multiples of five. From there, preliminary design of the support equipment moved along with the same resolution.

This is also a convenient unit because convenient snap grid sizes are in multiples of ten units.

Note that the projects do *not* redefine the basic units in the MAX setup to millimeters. There is no need to do this unless these meshes will be merged with other meshes built to scale later on. Changing MAX's system units setup is risky and something to be avoided. Using a *consistent* set of units is all that's necessary.

FIGURE 5.7

The robot base shapes look like this when the file loads.

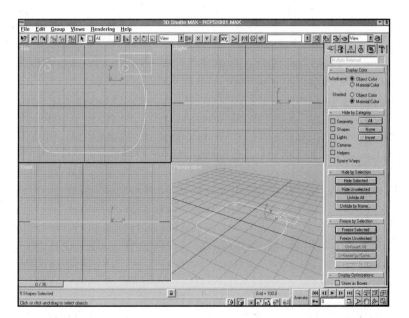

The robot base and source shapes are contained in the file RCPSX001.MAX on the accompanying CD. This is *not* the actual file taken from the complete scene, but rather a file built up specifically to illustrate the creation of the mesh from the component splines. Note that many of the modifiers applied will destroy the splines or incorporate them into a mesh. The sample file, as all other sample files in this chapter do, contains copies of the splines used and the finished object, frozen, so that you can follow along and use the complete object as a template.

1. Select the main shape only. Apply an Extrude modifier with a distance of 75 to the base cross section.

2. Apply an Optimize to the Extruded shape, with values of 10 for Face Threshold, 5 for Edge Threshold, and .25 for Bias. Turning on Auto Edge within the Optimize results in a faster regenerating base with no loss of resolution and is generally preferable, unless you want the edges delineating the sides of the base to remain visible. Figure 5.8 depicts the base at this point in its construction.

FIGURE 5.8

The robot base extrusion looks like this after step 2.

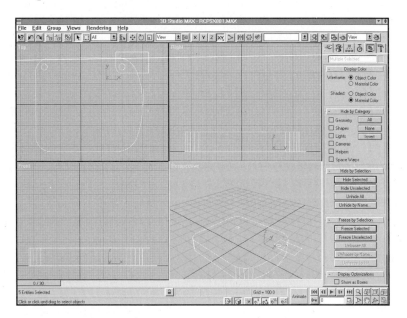

NOTE

Many regard what the exercise does next as unnecessary, undesirable, and poorly considered. MAX is a fantastic modeling tool and an even better animation tool. After the animator gets a shape in MAX to a point at which it is verifiably correct for a technical model, however, there is no reason to retain the history of the solid unless it is likely to be used elsewhere. Because subsequent operations include Edit Mesh steps and Booleans, a Collapse at this point loses little information but improves the stability of subsequent steps. You can use the Editable Mesh feature directly to bypass the overhead required by the use of Edit Mesh, but it *is* wise to retain all the history you might need until a part is complete and verifiably correct or until the part has passed a major milestone.

3. If you want, edit the object stack and do a Collapse All. Note that a Collapse All changes the object into an Editable Mesh type object. Editable Meshes give the animator full access to the tools formally available only under Edit Mesh, but without the overhead required by the Edit Mesh modifier.

4. Select the robot base object and use Display to turn off Edges Only.

5. Apply an Edit Mesh modifier to the robot base object, turn on Sub-Object, and select Edge. Then reconfigure the edges on the upper surface by using Divide and Turn until the result resembles figure 5.9. Some selections and the use of Visible and Invisible are also required. Note that the configuration of edges along the side is mirrored for the other side, which is not visible.

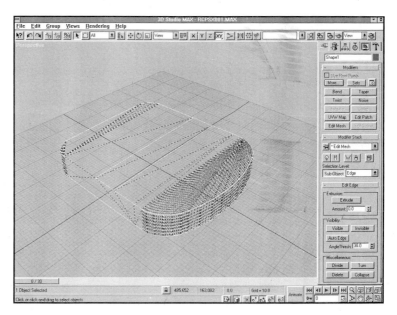

Figure 5.9

Edited robot base edges subsequent to step 5.

6. Select Sub-Object Vertex. From the Front view, use Selection Sets, Rotate, and Move to change the profile to that depicted in figure 5.10. Liberal use of Absolute Snap here on a grid of 10 units in each direction is very useful for placing the vertices correctly.

A Skew applied to the upper vertices of the rounded end, with a value of 117.5 at a direction of 0.0 along X, goes a long way toward shifting them properly. An Edit Stack here followed by a Collapse All speeds up evaluation somewhat, but be absolutely certain that the base is correct so far. Examine the Template object in the sample file for verification.

FIGURE 5.10

*Edited robot base
vertices after step 6.*

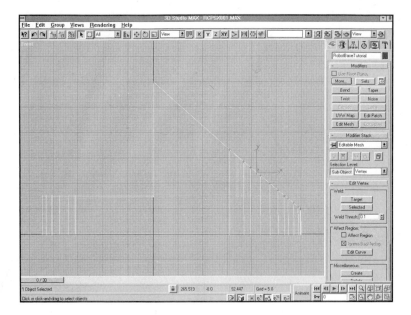

7. Use Absolute Snap to create a cylinder of radius 225 and height 305 with 36 sides, and place it over the frozen template. These dimensions are the same as those of the partial cylinder incorporated into the base. Note that you may have to create the cylinder and then modify it to get the exact dimensions. You may also have to rearrange your Snap priorities to get the cylinder to settle properly, or choose a particular edge when you move it. Using the top edge with High Snap Priority assigned to Grid works well and enables you to keep the 10-unit grid at this time.

8. Collapse the cylinder into an Editable Mesh and delete the faces of the bottom surface. They serve no useful purpose and consume unnecessary resources. A Cylinder does consume fewer resources than an Editable Mesh, but that point will soon be moot. The precise sequence here is, of course: Select, Modify, Edit Mesh, Sub-Object: Face, Crossing Off, Select Faces, Delete, Edit Stack, Collapse All.

9. Select the shape labeled BaseCutout and apply an Extrude modifier with a value of 400, using both end caps on and a single segment. Note that BaseCutout is a simple linear shape created by using Create Spline with a segmentation of 0. Move the resulting solid so that the midplane aligns approximately with the midplane of the base-in-progress. Use the Y-Axis Only button on the Move panel to move the cutout object in the Top viewport, thus preserving the precise relationship of the cutout to the cylinder.

NOTE

No, the cutout did *not* come from a CAD package. The cutout represents a cast-in feature of low precision. Because appearance and ease of construction are more important than precision for this particular feature, the cutout was constructed in MAX, using the base as a reference.

At this point, the interactive display should resemble figure 5.11.

FIGURE 5.11

This is the cutout in place after Step 9.

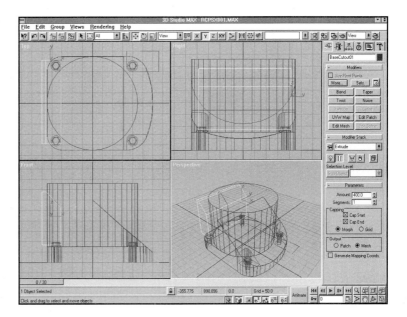

10. Select the cylinder. Use Create, Geometry, Compound Objects, Boolean to subtract the Cutout object from the cylinder. Then, having verified that the result is correct by comparing it against the template, use Modify, Edit Mesh, Edit Stack, Collapse All to reduce the Boolean to an Editable Mesh again. Note that in the absence of a template, you compare features to grid lines or use a ruler helper.

11. Most modelers skip this step or attempt to use a Boolean. A Boolean *fails*, however, because the bottom of the cylinder no longer exists. Use Modify, Editable Mesh, Sub-Object Edges to divide the edges of the cylinder coincident with the vertical edges of the wedge-shaped portion of the base object you've created so far. Move the two new vertices up in line with the top of the wedge, and then use Edge, Turn; Vertex, Move; or Vertex, Select; Skew; or Face, Delete to clean up the object so that it resembles figure 5.12. This is not necessarily the precise sequence required because the editing sequence can be iterative.

Generally speaking, the modeler needs to balance the complexity of the model with the prospect of having hidden portions of faces. Hidden faces—even partially hidden faces—increase rendering time. However, subdividing faces—either with the use of a Boolean operation or at the edge/vertex level—in order to reduce overlap and hidden surface area can overly complicate the mesh by creating a multiplicity of faces. In this case, move the edges of the cylinder up because it results in minimal increase in face count while reducing overlap. Modifying the faces of the sloped portion, however, is both unnecessary and undesirable because doing so only increases complexity while not reducing face overlap. Also, note that placing the cylinder vertices coincident with the back of the slope is critical for correct smoothing.

NOTE

Balancing face complexity with face overlap could be a quantitative problem, but the problem is far too complex to evaluate in a deterministic fashion in order to find the best solution to each modeling choice. Over time, the animator/modeler develops a "feeling" for what becomes worthwhile and for what isn't.

FIGURE 5.12

This is the modified cylinder Editable Mesh after step 11.

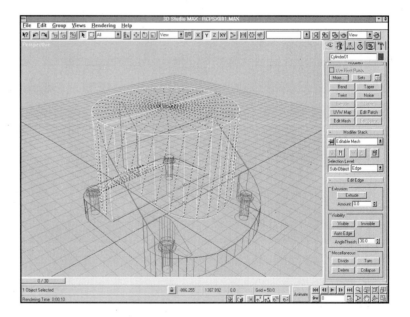

12. Attach the modified cylinder to the sloped base and select and weld the eight vertices—four from the cylinder, four from the wedge, at the four corners of the old upright, vertical surface of the wedge—by using a threshold of approximately .8 to 1. Select and delete the faces on the

back, vertical portion of the slope. Apply a Smooth modifier to the object with a default threshold, collapse the stack, hide the frozen template object, and do a sample render to verify the object so far. The important thing to look for is the lack of a visible break between the sides of the wedge and the cylinder. If breaks are visible in the curved forward lower edge of the base, make visible a few critical edges, and use Sub-Object: Face and MeshSmooth modifiers until the edge renders smoothly. This is also a good time to go over the mesh, using Vertex, Weld, Target to get rid of slivers of unnecessary geometry, and to clean up the object in general. Compare it to the template and collapse the stack.

At the two front corners of the sloped base are flats where installation bolts can tighten against a flat surface.

NOTE

There are two ways to install the hollows and the bolt holes that pierce the base. In the first method—the one used to create the template object—the animator must use Edge, Divide and Edge, Turn to split the model along the midplane. The Boolean operations necessary to form the holes and hollows are then performed on one half, and the finished half is mirrored to create a second finished half. The two finished halves are then attached and welded. This method results in a perfectly symmetrical model.

The other method is to mirror the smaller Boolean objects and to perform twice as many Boolean operations on the single whole object. This method is often faster than the first but has the following drawbacks:

- The model is not symmetrical.

- If the Boolean fails on one side, the animator must revert to the first method.

- If the Boolean doesn't fail, but generates unsightly mesh or smoothing artifacts, twice as many faces, edges, and vertices may need to be cleaned up manually.

The first drawback is often not truly a problem, but the more detail-minded may consider it a serious source of frustration if the mesh has to be modified later. Note that this tutorial could have instructed you (the animator) to split the robot base earlier in its construction if the first drawback were of paramount importance, but in most cases it's more a matter of preference than anything else.

13. Apply an Extrude modifier to the shape labeled NutPad. The value of 400, used for the last Extrude, serves here as well. Note that because this is another CAD-generated shape, substantial segmentation exists along the "straight" edges. This isn't a problem for now; read the following tips on Booleans to understand why.

TI P

Booleans fail for a number of reasons. The most serious problems associated with Boolean operations, or those that are most likely to cause failures, are as follows:

- Coincident, unwelded vertices

- Any edge belonging to only a single face that participates in the Boolean intersection

- Normals of adjacent, essentially parallel faces that are opposed in direction

- Multiple, re-entrant intersections (the intersection of a pincushion with the collection of all pins assembled into one object, for example)

Generally speaking, a Boolean operation between two objects—both well-constructed, with complete, enclosed volumes, uniform normal direction, and welded vertices, where the intersection between the surfaces of the two can be described as a single, closed curve—is least likely to cause a Boolean failure.

TI P

Generally speaking, welding all the vertices of the two operands prior to performing a Boolean considerably improves the chances that the Boolean will succeed.

TI P

The Boolean algorithm implemented in 3D Studio MAX has certain fundamental limitations. By planning ahead, however, you can avoid problems with these limitations. Ordinarily, subtracting a simple object from a complex object may cause an undesirable loss of mesh resolution at the intersection under certain circumstances. That is, cutting a box with no segmentation into a convoluted surface may distort the surface of the convoluted surface along the edges of the intersection with the box. The problem is very difficult to duplicate reliably and, interestingly, is generally not a problem with default objects like GSpheres. The problem seems more common when the surface of higher resolution is open (even though the open edges are not involved in the Boolean) or when the surface of higher resolution has substantially higher mesh segmentation in one direction than the other.

14. Move the extruded cutout into position in the Front viewport by using only the Y-Axis Only button. Note that, at this point, the template should be Frozen again to avoid selecting it unnecessarily.

15. In the Top viewport, make a mirrored copy of the extruded cutout symmetrically about the midplane of the base so that the second cutout aligns with the finished cutout on the other side of the template.

TIP

When you prepare shapes and splines specifically to be extruded into Boolean operands, use Snap liberally on the vertices that will have no part in the final operations. In the cutout just extruded, for example, the outer and forward edges are both well clear of the base geometry and are both aligned with the snap grid. Thus, placement of the cutout object prior to the Boolean is simplified because at least two of the edges align with the snap grid.

This is an important point: Boolean operations frequently remove temporary features. Any temporary feature can be built and placed to make the process as convenient as possible for the animator. Edges and bounding dimensions that need not appear in the final model can be placed as alignment tools.

16. Select the Robot Base object and Boolean it with the two cutout objects in succession, selecting "subtract" from the option roll-up in the compound object/Boolean menu. Collapse the final object into an Editable Mesh after you verify the dimensions and placement against the template master.

17. Note that the intersections of the cutouts with the base have created numerous vertices around the fillets in the cutout. Applying a MeshSmooth at Face level to eliminate hidden lines cleans up this excess resolution. Collapsing the object again after using Display to unhide the hidden lines, and examining the mesh minimizes the resulting overhead of the Base Mesh. Render a sample image after unfreezing and hiding the Template object. Some manual cleanup of edge visibility, coincident vertex welding, and edge orientation is probably unavoidable. Be prepared to spend a little time here cleaning up the mesh, especially around the two Booleaned cutouts.

18. Optional steps: If the robot will never appear without its mounting bolts, the mounting holes don't need to be cut into the base. Two circular splines, RobotHole1 and 2, are already in the sample file, ready to Extrude, Move, Mirror, and Boolean into the base. It's important to move the resulting cylinders below the plane of the bottom of the base and to make them long enough to pierce the base completely, but otherwise there should be few problems.

19. The bolts are simple lofts between hexagonal and circular curves of identical vertex counts. The washers are cylinders. A simple goldish metallic material duplicates the alodyned finish of very high-grade structural bolts.

Figure 5.13 depicts the finished robot base with mounting bolts. Note that you don't have to cut the mounting holes into the base because the bolt heads and washers, of course, cover the bolt holes.

FIGURE 5.13
This is the finished robot base.

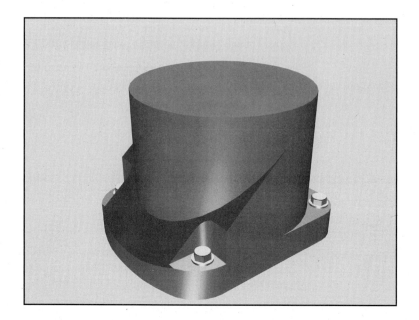

Canopy Construction

The aircraft canopy is one of the most difficult, complex technical models an animator might ever have to create. Not only is it essential that the canopy assembly flow in smooth curves, it must also resemble as closely as possible an actual canopy with precise dimensional constraints. Worse, because the object is mostly transparent, the detail of the inner surface shows through in many views. This object requires complex loft, deformation fit, Boolean, and vertex and edge-level manipulation.

1. Load the file RCPSX002.MAX from the accompanying CD. Note that this file follows the same format as the others: A frozen Template object resides in the file for reference, and all the necessary shapes are present as well. In the case of the canopy, the shapes derived from CAD data and moved from there to 3D Studio Release 4 via a DXF import for minor cleanup, and from there to 3D Studio MAX. Figure 5.14 shows the interactive display immediately after this file is loaded.

FIGURE 5.14

Canopy shapes in interactive display look like this.

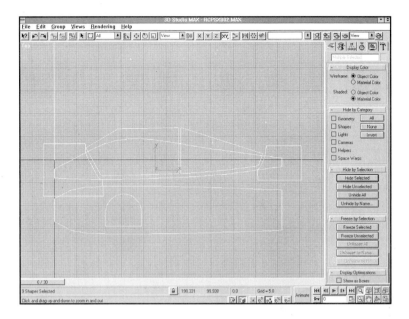

2. Use Select by Name in the toolbar to select CanopySideActual. This is the actual CAD-derived profile of the aircraft canopy assembly, the frame of the windscreen, and the transparent material together. Note the difficult fit shape inherent in this profile: the fillets at the bottom corners, the sharp edges at the upper corners. The requirements are further complicated by the need for a varying cross-section that, more than anything else, resembles sections taken from the same curve as it traverses the length of the canopy. Note most especially that the side profile is the only shape that represents the true profile of a required object in this file.

T I P

One of the biggest and most frequent mistakes a modeler can make is to try to build a complex or difficult shape in too few steps. MAX possesses incredible modeling features, but trying to use one or another to implement too many features in great, sweeping operations is predestined to fail. Trying to loft the canopy section shown within fit curves identical to true top and side profiles, for example, would squeeze the section at the ends into unnatural, contorted shapes. Laboriously building multiple sections gets better— but still not correct— results. *Never* be afraid to take three, four, five, or more steps to get a solid near a finished step. Plan for the operations ahead of time and they will not seem so great a burden.

One such plan-ahead operation is *overlofting*, or extending the Loft object on either end of the required geometry in preparation for later Booleans or editing. That technique is presented here in the second technical exercise of this chapter.

3. Select and examine the shape called CanopySideExtended. Note that this shape is derived from the true CAD-based side profile, with a few critical modifications. First, the fillets and sharp edges have been merged into smoothly flowing lines that terminate at either end at blunt segments with sharp corners, top and bottom. The precise dimensions of the blunt ends are unimportant. In fact, by creating the ends along grid lines and fixing the corners at grid intersections, the animator can move and reposition the shape easily, using the Snap system.

4. Select and examine the shape called CanopyTopExtended. Note that no "Actual" version exists in this file because it is unnecessary to the exercise. If the section and the cuts made later with Boolean operations are correct, there is no need for one because a comparison of the final solid and the actual side view is enough to verify a correct build. As with the extended side profile, the CanopyTopExtended spline derives from actual CAD data derived from the digitized model and extended into smoothly flowing lines beyond the actual top profile, terminating at blunt ends with sharp corners on either side. The CAD drawings of the top and side profiles began aligned. As the top profile was modified and as the revised side profile grew in length, the original segments of the splines remained unchanged, and hence, aligned. The CanopyTopExtended spline extends precisely the length of the CanopySideExtended spline, and the ends of each are aligned at the same grid lines.

5. Create a line segment as long as the extended profiles in a convenient position.

6. Select the CanopySection spline and use Create, Geometry, Loft Object. Use the Get Path button and select the line segment. Use the default options, but turn on Skin in the Display roll-up area so that the Loft object is visible.

7. Select Modify while the Loft object is selected and open the Deformations roll-up, an area available only in the Modify branch. Select Fit, turn Symmetry Off, unlock Aspect Ratio, and use Get Shape to select the extended top profile.

8. Switch deformation fit curves and use Get Shape to select the extended side profile.

9. Use the Generate Path button. At this point, you may want to switch to a Shaded viewport to preview the canopy. Your Loft object should look something like the one in figure 5.15.

FIGURE 5.15

This is how the preliminary canopy loft appears after step 9.

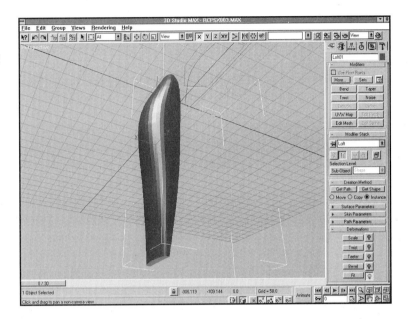

10. Much of the extra resolution in this object represents a carryover from the CAD-generated splines that imported as Bézier objects. Unfortunately, this Canopy object at this point is so complex that adding modifiers slows the evaluation pipeline to such a degree that the scene becomes unwieldy. Apply an Edit Mesh modifier after verifying that the loft matches the profiles from the CAD data, and Collapse the object by using Edit Stack. This may take a few minutes on slower machines.

11. Apply an Optimize modifier with values of 1, 1, and .1, and then a Smooth with a default value of 30 degrees and Auto Smooth checked. Collapse the mesh again when the Shaded viewport shows a good, clean mesh.

12. Notice that the mesh is asymmetrical. This is both a handicap and a blessing. It is a handicap because the animator should correct the asymmetry in this highly technical mesh, and a blessing in that subsequent Boolean operations will produce slightly different results on the two halves, enabling the modeler to pick and choose parts of the mesh based on their appearance and Boolean solutions.

13. Hide the deformation fit curves and the section; they are no longer necessary to the construction of the canopy. Leave the trim splines and the extended side view visible.

14. Numerous Booleans are required. First, use Edit, Clone to make a copy of the canopy object, select both the original and the copy, and move both into place in the Top view so that they are aligned with the CanopySideExtended spline. You must be creative with Snap priorities to align the solids with the deformation curve. Now deselect one copy and hide the other. From now on, always be sure to have two copies of the canopy, one of which is protected and unmodified. Booleans destroy the separable histories of meshes and are difficult to undo; always make backup objects before proceeding.

15. One after another, select and Extrude the two glass cutouts and the fore and aft trim splines. Select the set of four extrusions and move them into place in the Right view so that they straddle the canopy. One by one, use Edit Mesh and Edit Stack to collapse the four extrusions into Editable Meshes. At this point, the scene should look like that shown in figure 5.16.

FIGURE 5.16

Canopy solids are aligned with splines in this view of the display subsequent to step 15.

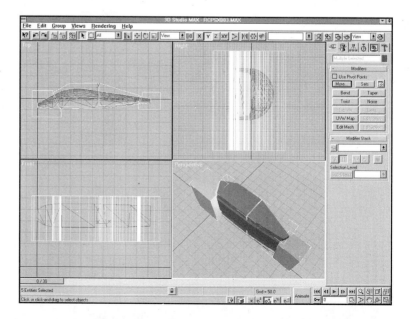

16. Although you could use creative mapping techniques to achieve the transparency of the canopy assembly over the two windows, by using Booleans you not only can achieve greater realism with simpler maps, but also have the glass and frame appear in the scene independent of one another. Begin the complex construction of the separate canopy glass areas by using Edit, Clone to make copies of the two glass cutout extrusions now collapsed into Editable Meshes. Hide the two copies. Hide also the extended side profile spline, which is no longer necessary for construction.

17. Use Boolean subtract to remove, one after another, the four cutouts visible from the canopy copy. The result will look something like figure 5.17. The operations may be more reliable if the mesh is collapsed after every Boolean.

FIGURE 5.17

The canopy appears here minus ends and glass.

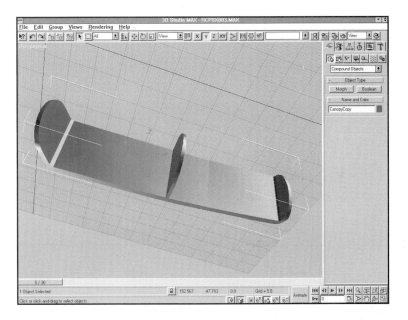

18. Apply a Smooth modifier and collapse the canopy mesh.

TIP

It is possible to use a Smooth modifier with Autosmooth on to locate the "bad" faces from a nonrobust Boolean operation. That is, when autosmoothed, a mesh with single reversed faces has unique smoothing groups assigned to the "bad" faces. Extra faces whose edges represent a discontinuity cause breaks in the smoothing groups and the assignment of additional groups.

TIP

Many modelers have difficulty isolating and remapping the sections of an object formed by a Boolean operation. If hundreds of windows are cut into the sides of a ship's hull by subtracting the cylinders from the hull loft, for example, it is very tedious to select the faces corresponding to the window glass, after the Booleans are complete, for retexturing. 3D Studio Release 4 provided an incredibly powerful tool for organizing Boolean result geometry by assigning materials to the operands *prior* to performing the operations. Then, Show Material would select the faces corresponding to the operands with the material specified. MAX unfortunately reassigns the material of one operand to the faces of both subsequent to Booleans, but the Face ID Numbers *are* unique for the geometry derived from the two operands. Thus, an Edit Mesh used to pick selection sets based on Face Material ID Number will isolate the faces corresponding to one operand or the other, even if the material itself is not retained.

Use the smoothing groups to locate reversed and extra faces. Select all vertices at the Sub-Object level, and weld them by using a threshold of .5 to 1 millimeter. Weld target vertices manually, as necessary. Expect to spend some time cleaning up the canopy mesh at this time. Be careful not to change the overall dimensions or appearance of the frame.

Use Edge, Turn; Vertex, Weld; and Autosmooth as necessary until an Autosmooth with a relatively small threshold—on the order of 10 degrees or less—reliably separates the cutouts, bottom, ends, and framework exterior into separate smoothing groups. There will be 10 smoothing groups when you achieve success: three for each window cutout, three for the outside bottom and ends of the canopy, and one for the surface of the "frame" corresponding to the outer skin. Select faces by smoothing groups to select only the bottom, ends, and two cutout areas. Delete these faces to leave only the exterior of the frame. At this point, the mesh should resemble figures 5.18 and 5.19.

19. Carefully compare the right and left sides of the exterior surface and find the side that is more precise or that has greater resolution and can be made more precise. Delete the faces of the discard half, mirror the remaining faces, attach the two objects, and re-weld. Collapse the mesh. The purpose of this operation is to restore symmetry and improve the predictable nature of the extrusions and scaling operations to follow.

Be certain during the face selection part of this operation that Select Face is in "single face" mode, probably with crossing Off.

FIGURE 5.18

The canopy frame exterior surface should look like this.

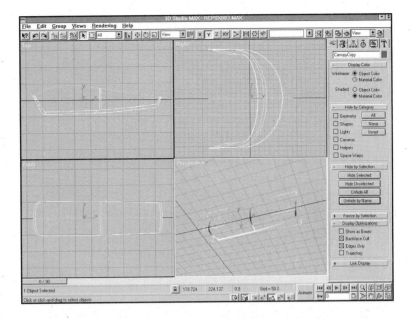

FIGURE 5.19

The canopy frame exterior surface should also look like this.

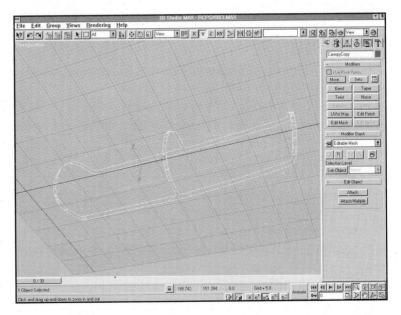

20. Use Edit, Clone to make a copy of the exterior surface of the canopy frame, and then hide it. Use Editable Mesh, Sub-Object: Face mode to select the entire frame, and then type a value of –5 in the Extrude section of the rollout.

WARNING ──

A bug exists in MAX 1.0 and 1.1 that may cause a failure or crash during the next step. It is advisable to Save or Hold your scene here.

21. *Without deselecting the extruded faces*, use scale and move transforms on the face selection set to produce a "lining" of faces with respect to the original exterior framework. Generally, this is possible in the Right or Left viewport in the following sequence:

■ Non-uniform scale in viewport Y, only until the framework thickness is approximately equal all around

■ Nonuniform scale in viewport X, only to shrink the thickness of the uppermost rib and to reduce the protrusion of the bottom edges below the outer surfaces

■ Motion of the selected faces in viewport X, only to restore the thickness of the uppermost web and to move the bottom inner edges even with the bottom outer edges

At this point, your incomplete, inside-out canopy frame missing an outer skin now will resemble the image of figure 5.20.

FIGURE 5.20

Make the canopy frame ribbing extrusion look like this.

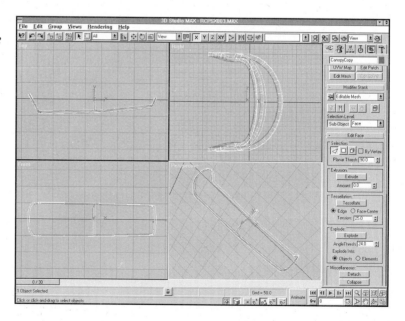

22. Note that, at this point, two problems exist with the ribbing surfaces. First, the normals are reversed because the extruded surfaces derived from faces directed outward with a negative extrusion value. Second, extruded surfaces have the same smoothing group as the parent faces. Thus, it is necessary to select all the faces of the ribbing, invert the normals, and then resmooth the ribbing with a Smooth modifier. Unhide the original exterior framework surface mesh and shade the viewport. Note that the two meshes represent a complete formed support frame with thickness and correct smoothing. Attach the two, weld all vertices, and resmooth to simplify the database. Then collapse the mesh (see fig. 5.21).

FIGURE 5.21

This is the finished canopy framework.

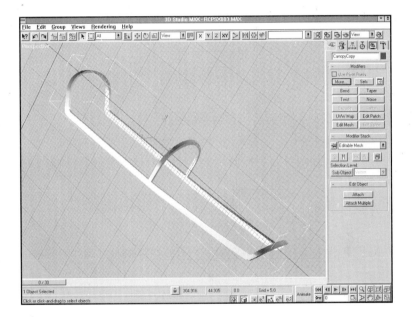

23. Hide the canopy framework.

24. Unhide the original copy of the canopy loft, collapsed into an Editable Mesh along with the two Glass cutout objects (see fig. 5.22).

25. Use Select and Edit, Clone to make another copy of the lofted Canopy object.

26. Use Boolean Intersections twice to create, in turn, the intersections of each glass cutout with one of the Canopy Loft Meshes each. Note that this is the last copy of the Canopy Loft Mesh if you follow instructions precisely. You may want to make another backup copy in case something goes wrong. The result is two collapsed meshes, each of which represents one segment of the transparent portion of the canopy (see fig. 5.23).

FIGURE 5.22

FIGURE 5.22

This is the scene prior to preparing to build the glass.

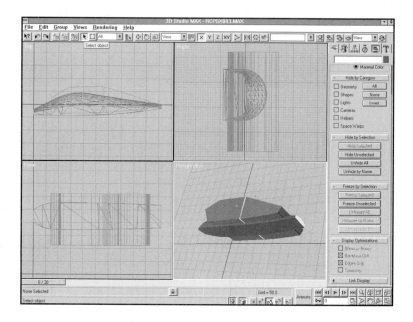

FIGURE 5.23

Preliminary canopy transparencies after Boolean intersections look solid, like these.

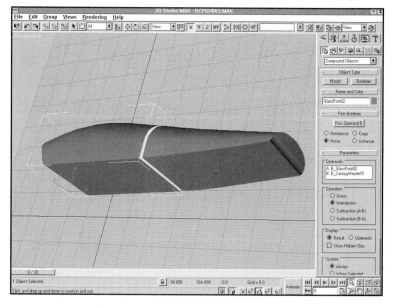

27. Edit the two Canopy Transparency objects, as follows:

   ■ Clean up the results of the Boolean operations, eliminating loose edges, loose vertices, jagged edges, and flipped normals.

■ Use Smooth modifiers and smoothing groups in the Sub-Object: Face branch of Editable Mesh to locate and eliminate any remaining flipped or loose faces.

■ Use Edge, Turn and Vertex, Weld, or Optimize modifiers to improve the appearance of the outer surfaces.

■ Use Smoothing modifiers and Selection sets to isolate and delete the inner and end surfaces.

■ Choose the side that has the fewest undesirable face artifacts and the best mesh resolution. Delete the other halves and then mirror, attach, and weld duplicates of the retained halves. Resmooth and collapse the finished surfaces.

Figure 5.24 shows the finished outer transparency surfaces.

FIGURE 5.24
These are finished canopy glass exterior surfaces.

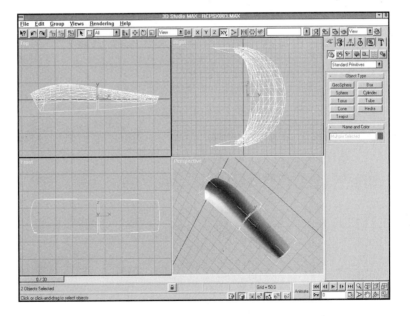

28. As with the framework, use Select, and Edit, Clone in turn to make copies of the outer glass surfaces. Hide both copies of one glass segment and one copy of the other.

29. In this order, do the following:

■ Editable Mesh, Sub-Object: Face, select all. Enter an extrude value of −3.5, and choose Extrude in the Face menu.

- In the Right viewport, without changing the Face Selection set, use a nonuniform scale in viewport Y only to reduce the overall dimension of the inner surface until the width of the extruded edges is nearly constant.

- Use a nonuniform scale with the Face Selection set in the viewport X-only direction, and then use an X-only move to reduce the overall span of the inner surface and to move it back up near the (now missing) outer surface. The bottom edges, both inner and outer, should be roughly even.

- Select all faces. Flip Normals.

- Unhide the corresponding outer surface and then attach, weld, resmooth, and collapse. Figure 5.25 shows the Aft canopy transparency at this point in the process.

- Repeat all steps for the Forward canopy transparency.

The result of this complex operation is roughly equivalent to a Pro/Engineer "shell" operation on the solid and selected outer surface. The result, if the steps are done correctly, is a solid object of near-constant thickness with square, separately smoothable edges. As noted previously, this is essential here because the glass needs to look as realistic as possible and because the glass and frame may be rendered separately in some applications of the model. Figure 5.25 shows the finished transparency meshes.

FIGURE 5.25

The finished transparency solids have two sides.

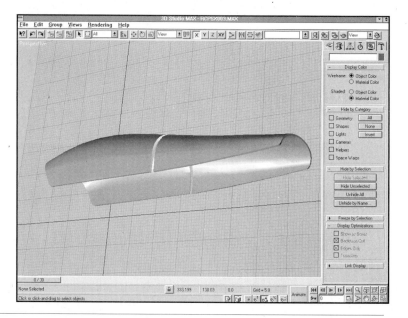

Construction of materials is omitted from this chapter; the reader is free to examine the finished sample file to analyze the materials used in the canopy frame and glass.

Robot Waist Construction

The robot waist is important because it represents a combination of Loft objects with primitives and because it uses detailed mesh elements in lieu of texture mapping to achieve extremely realistic and detailed specific appearances.

1. Load the file RCPSX003.MAX from the accompanying CD. Figure 5.26 depicts the contents of the file immediately after loading. Note that this file contains most of the source geometry as well as a finished version, currently frozen and usable as a reference template for the exercise.

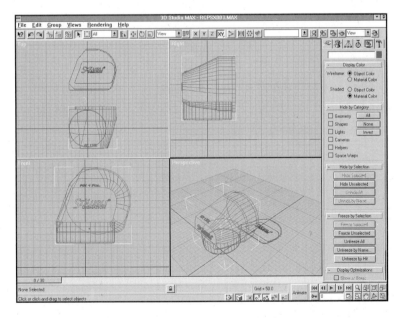

2. The file does not contain the loft path. Construct the loft path by using the frozen geometry as a reference in the Top viewport, building a path with vertices at the levels of the various cross sections. Ignore the geometry belonging to the lettering and shoulder hub at the back of the object.

3. Select the WaistEnd spline shape and then use Create, Geometry, Loft Objects, Loft. Click on the Get Path button and select the linear path created in step 2.

4. Using the Modify panel, change Path Steps to 0 and Shape Steps to zero. This is possible because the imported CAD splines have a great deal of detail that needs to be optimized out later or minimized now.

5. The first vertex occurs at 32.5 percent of path length. No additional shape is required here, however. Turn off Adaptive Path Steps.

6. The second vertex occurs at a distance of about 320 units along the path length. Move to that level on the path and use Get Shape to select the WaistMiddle spline.

7. Move to a level of 335 on the path and use Get Shape to Copy WaistLarge into the Loft. Do the same at a distance of 465, a percentage of 100. At this point, the Loft object should resemble the geometry of figure 5.27.

FIGURE 5.27

The preliminary waist object looks like this next to its template master.

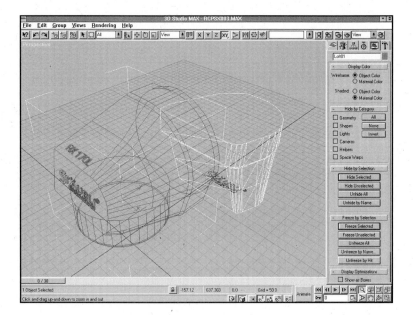

8. Optionally, collapse the mesh now.

9. Using Snap and grid lines, move the Loft object into a position where it corresponds with the frozen template. If this object were being built in conjunction with the other robot segments, the overall CAD layouts or

the completed modules would form similar references. Use combinations of Snap priorities with Absolute Snap to align the two objects to the 5 millimeter grid. You may need to do a mirror depending on the direction in which you drew your path.

10. Note that the objects don't match exactly. Use Edit Mesh or Editable Mesh in Sub-Object: Vertex mode with selection sets and Move to warp the Loft object into correspondence with the finished object. The finished object was aligned with a photograph in the Top view; because the photo cannot be distributed, the finished object will have to do here. The finished object should look like the one in figure 5.28.

FIGURE 5.28

The finished robot waist main housing was built against a photo reference.

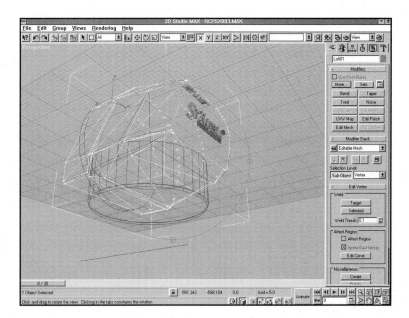

11. Note that the object, even after all the vertices have been moved around, does not correspond with the finished object. The object represents a casting. The casting possesses some complex transitions between sections that are difficult to duplicate by using the sections only. Use combinations of Sub-Object: Edge, and Divide and Turn to realign the lower-left edges with the finished transition. This level of editing is, in some cases, the only way to achieve the final result.

This step may require numerous jumps between selection sets and viewports. Be prepared to spend 10 minutes to an hour sculpting the surface into the desired profile. Most of the changes are concentrated along the one lower edge. Figure 5.29 depicts the edited object.

FIGURE 5.29

The completed robot waist main housing looks like this after sculpting is complete.

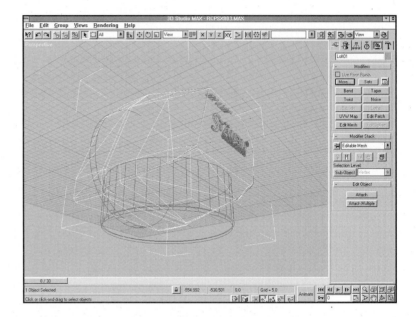

12. Smooth using Autosmooth with a threshold of around 20 degrees. It may be necessary to smooth the transition between the bulk of the object and the larger section manually to make the transition sharp.

13. Construct three cylinders to match the profiles of the three cylinders attached to the complete template. The larger cylinder at the bottom has parameters of radius, 225; height, 150; with 36 sides. The smaller bottom cylinder has parameters of 220, 10, and 36. The shoulder root has parameters of 250, 30, and 36. Because the waist root and shoulder root mate with circles of larger diameter or with other geometry, neither cylinder needs end caps. The larger cylinder below the Loft Mesh needs only the lower end cap.

14. Unhide the NameText spline—already collapsed into a single Bézier Spline—and apply an Extrude modifier with a distance of 5. Turn off the Start end cap and apply a Smooth modifier with Autosmooth. Collapse the mesh but do not attach it to the main casting object. Use Rotate and Move to align the new solid cast text with the text on the original object.

15. Use Create, Shapes, Text with an "Arial" font or near equivalent to create the text RX 170L. Using the Front viewport with a text size of 40 to 45 will get you closest to the final result with a minimum effort. Extrude five units with only the front end cap, then resmooth, skew, scale, and collapse this mesh to most closely match the text on the top of the casting. Attach this lettering to the top slanted portion of the casting, aligned approximately with the finished work.

16. Assign a safety orange plastic material to the casting and a gloss black to the loose lettering. Attach the two objects. Figure 5.30 shows a rendering of the finished mesh.

FIGURE 5.30
The finished robot waist mesh should resemble this after the lettering is positioned.

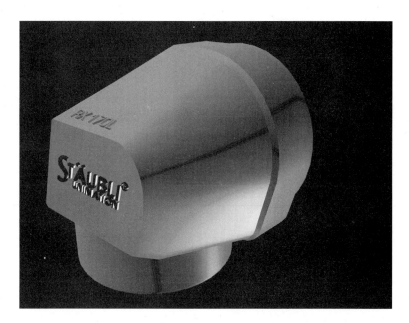

Note that the linkage and arrangement of the robot modules are straightforward applications of hierarchical linking and pivot-point control.

In Practice: Technical Modeling

■ **Technical Applications.** Technical Application Modeling is used in support of animation and rendering chores that require very high degrees of precision and accuracy. The degree to which accuracy and precision is required may be unfamiliar to entertainment animators.

- **Modeling Methods.** In creating a technical model, be prepared to spend a great deal of time integrating CAD data into the MAX environment, tweaking Snap priorities and settings, and editing objects at the edge and vertex level.

- **Object Oriented Mesh Building.** Although MAX supports an incredible array of history-sensitive, fully editable object stack operations, the demands of technical modeling, the number of steps involved in an object's construction, and the ease with which an object can be verified objectively against the source data call for a different mode of modeling where Collapse is far more popular than in general use.

- **Complex Object Creation.** Sometimes numerous steps contribute to the creation of a single complex part. Never try to accomplish too much in too few steps. Be creative in the application of Boolean, Extrude, and Edit Mesh operations and in their combinations.

Part III

CHARACTER MODELING

IMAGE BY KEN ALLEN ROBERTSON

Chapter 6

by Ken Allen Robertson

CHARACTER MODELING BASICS

Creating animated characters is a multifaceted and complex process. Traditionally, most attention has been focused on making characters move in an exciting and illuminating way. But animation is the last step in the process of character creation. This chapter—indeed, this book—does not delve into the technical process or evaluations involved in creating great character animation. Fortunately, the process of animation is well-covered in both Inside 3D Studio MAX Volume III, *and in George Maestri's wonderful book,* Digital Character Animation, *also published by New Riders. Rather than cover the animation process, this chapter focuses on the creation process necessary to facilitate the animation process.*

Before you begin to model the character, you must know how the character will look, behave, and move. You must also know what part the character plays in moving the story forward, and what tasks the character must perform within the context of the story you are telling. Without knowing at least this amount of information, you will likely reach an impasse at some point, in which the modeling of the character inhibits it from performing as it should. Defining your character, therefore, becomes the critical first step in creating the illusion of a living being.

Characters must look as though they belong to the world of the story. Otherwise, they will be ineffective storytellers. A perfectly still character that already conveys life, personality, and emotion can serve as a blueprint for that character's qualities of motion when the animation process begins. Your audience will immediately identify with such a character the moment it appears.

Before examining the technical software aspects that make it possible to create characters (aspects covered extensively in the next two chapters) and before you touch the keyboard, it is important to review some principles that will give your characters life before you ever create them:

- Introduction to characters

- The definition of character

- Developing the story

- Developing the character's personality

- Defining how the character needs to function

- Defining the visual design of the character

Introduction to Characters

When humankind first began communicating with pictures, characters instantly became a critical and popular part of storytelling. From Cro-Magnon cave paintings to the high-tech, computer-generated beings of today, images that mirror humanity intrigue and fascinate us. These images have become omnipresent in modern society. Characters are used to teach, sell, entertain, and enlighten.

Characters have gone through an extraordinary evolution from their humble beginnings. Every time a new medium is created and made available to the public, characters are among the first creations presented. They are pushed and pulled by their creators to test the strengths and weaknesses of the medium in which they find themselves. Computer-generated characters are no exception.

Computer-generated characters have come a long way in a very short time. From the stained-glass knight in 1985's *Young Sherlock Holmes* to the myriad personalities of 1995's *Toy Story*, computer artists have consistently pushed their equipment, software, and imagination to the very edge in an attempt to capture every aspect of life's endless possibilities. Fortunately, hardware and software companies have been willing to meet the challenge alongside the artists.

Until recently, truly astounding computer characters were relegated to high-end workstations running high-priced software. But as consumer-level PCs grow in speed and capability, "character power" is now becoming available to a wider group of artists. 3D Studio MAX has put the powerful tools formerly available only in high-priced animation packages, as well as tools unique in the software industry, into the hands of those artists.

Unfortunately, however, the millennia-old skills of story-telling have not been made as widely available to computer artists. Only in recent years have the principles of animated story-telling, tried and tested for more than 60 years, become available to the average computer artist. Many books on the subject of animation, which had gone out of print, are only now coming back on the retail market, most notably *The Illusion of Life* by Disney animators Ollie Johnston and Frank Thomas and *Cartoon Animation* by Preston Blair.

No amount of power or tools by themselves can create a character. It takes a creator who is part artist, part storyteller, part actor, part director—all under the guidance of a dreamer—to breathe life into an inanimate collection of computer data. Most artists, when first faced with having to create a character, may feel a bit like Dr. Frankenstein. The task of creating a living being can be daunting and overwhelming, and the need to see whether it *can* be done may easily exceed the need to design the way it *should* be done. The mysteries of giving the illusion of life to an object of your own creation are very rarely covered in software manuals.

Remember, a character is a device used to tell a story, and a story will vary a little with each medium in which it is told. 3D graphics have the capability to mimic two different mediums: live-action film and hand-drawn animation. For the first time, a medium can almost perfectly imitate reality—

albeit, a reality not bound by "real-world" physics. This is a critical distinction that makes 3D computer characters unique from their relatives in any other medium, and that can provide countless variations of style. Your characters, to accomplish their roles in their respective stories, must be responsive not only to the story itself but to the medium and to the style in which the story is being told. Hamlet would look terribly out of place in a shoot-em-up action film, and Daffy Duck would probably not be taken seriously as a pivotal part of an historical drama (even if he did not move or talk). Without a knowledge of your particular story, the style being used to tell the story, and the medium in which it will be told, you set up your characters to fail—from the start.

The Definition of Character

What distinguishes a character from any other object in a 3D world? Characters do have several properties: movement, voices, faces, and so on. But other objects that are not considered characters can have these properties also. For a definition to be of any use in the character-creation process, it must identify the bare minimum attributes that distinguish a character from a noncharacter.

In that light, the following definition should prove helpful:

> A *character* is any object to which a thought process, emotional life, and distinguishable personality may be attributed, and which "acts" of its own accord.

With this definition, you can easily distinguish a character from a noncharacter, whether the character is an animal, a humanoid, a robot, or a household item. As the preceding definition makes clear, character comprises four major attributes. These attributes create a blueprint of the questions that need to be answered before your character can begin to take on a life of its own.

Thought Process

What constitutes a thought process? Human beings are constantly thinking (see fig. 6.1). "About what?" you ask. The answer: "About events—those that have happened or are going to happen, whether imaginary, real, or perceived as imaginary or real." Almost every human thought chain begins with the recollection or awareness of some sort of event, and then expands into the interpretation of it. The basic thought string "If x happens, what will it mean?" is familiar to all. Likewise, as something is happening, the normal human thought process is to evaluate the event and determine our personal response to it (including no response). Notice that this is a precursor to the fourth character attribute—the ability to take action.

FIGURE 6.1
What constitutes a thought process?

Is your character a quick thinker or slow? Does the thought process flow easily through the character's brain, or is it as thick as molasses in winter? Does the character evaluate each event that happens for its niceness, its potential harm, its money-making potential, or its potential for a great practical joke?

Different characters will think differently, some sliding through enormous chains of evaluations with grace and speed—whereas for others, remembering their own name would bring on a hemorrhage. Considering how your character thinks is a great step toward making your character come to life, even if you never show the character just "thinking."

The thought process can be developed with the personality, by itself, or as a springboard from which you can jump back and forth between the personality and emotional life as well as the thought process. The important thing to remember is that thought process should be considered, at some point, a critical aspect in the "life" of the character.

Emotional Life

Emotions also can be a by-product of the thought process, or a result of the events that spark the thought process (see fig. 6.2). Emotions are the character's reaction to its interpretation of the events it is experiencing or has experienced.

FIGURE 6.2
Emotions can be the
result of an event that
sparks the thought
process.

Consider the difference between two characters being slapped in the face. One might react with outrage, viciously attacking the slapper. The other might take it as a sign of great affection and fall madly in love with the slapper. Imagine that the two characters are identical twins. Now notice the difference in the way you picture the two characters—the subtle differences in how they stand, the expression on their faces, and so forth—and you can easily see that having a clear idea of a character's emotional life benefits the design and modeling process.

Personality

Personality is most simply defined as a predisposition to certain patterns of emotion and thought. A character that always expects other characters to take advantage of him, for example, will always be grouchy, untrusting, and wary. Whenever another character appears to do something nice, the mistrusting character will examine that character's motives and actions for any sign of trickery.

Knowing a character's personality smoothes out many decisions about how the character will look and move. An exercise later in this chapter will help to simplify and enhance the process of defining a character's personality.

Beginning a New Character

The process of creating a character can begin in many places: with the character itself, that has inspired the story you are going to tell; with the story, in which the character plays a part in moving the story to its conclusion; or with the world of the story, from which the characters and the story are born. Whatever your starting point, all character design must go through the following steps:

- Developing the story

- Developing the character's personality

- Completing a definition of how the character needs to function (physically and as a story device)

- Visually designing the character

The first three steps are pretty much interchangeable and can be accomplished in any order. But the final step should always be the visual design of the character (from which the character will be modeled). Rough sketch ideas can certainly accompany any of the early steps, but final visual design should be done only after the story, personality, and character function have been completely fleshed out. Otherwise, the character will not be able to perform the tasks set for it.

As you read the following paragraphs, think about a character you are currently working on (even if you believe that character is almost totally complete) or begin to create a new character in your mind. Ask the questions being posed (and any others that might arise in the process) and begin to get an idea of the answers, keeping in mind that the answers are likely to modify themselves a bit as you consider each new aspect of your character's life.

Developing the Story

Besides being a simple linear narrative, a story must have four other elements to make it interesting, attractive, and alive: mood, stylization, setting, and multiple characters. Other elements may come into play, but these four must be present to bring the story to a life beyond mere words.

Mood

Every story has an overall mood or feel to it. That mood may be spooky, warm, cheerful, funny, frightening, somber, tragic, and so forth (see figs. 6.4 and 6.5). Stories, as they progress, go through many mood changes, but every story has a prevalent mood to which it returns again and again. This is the mood you want your audience to remember long after your story is over.

FIGURE 6.4
Compare the mood of this figure with figure 6.5.

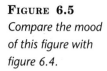

FIGURE 6.5
Compare the mood of this figure with figure 6.4.

A great tool for defining mood is the ever-popular, low-tech thesaurus. After you have approximated the overall mood you want to achieve, crack open your thesaurus and see whether other words mean approximately the same thing. Those other words might strike you as being juicier or more precise or appropriate to the story you wish to tell. Often, this can add an immediate spark of even greater life to your story, making obvious the little details you may have yet to discover.

When you know the overall mood of the story, ask how the particular character you are examining adds to that mood. Does the character drive the mood of other characters or strive against the mood you have set? The answer to this question will be a great beginning to your definition of the character's emotional.

Stylization

Stylization is the prevalent visual style you use to tell the story. A circus-like atmosphere of bright, saturated primary colors says something very different about your world and its characters than a shadowy, stark, film-noir style palette says.

Some stories automatically lend themselves to one style or another. Taking a story from its obvious stylization and forcing it into another will result in your story and characters being seen as a spoof on the new style. A Mother Goose fairy tale stylized to resemble a 1930s monster movie will most likely be perceived as a send-up of the material being presented. Characters, too, can be counter-stylized, but they will probably suffer the same fate.

With the current state of 3D graphics, "near-photoreality" is a frequent choice. Understand that this too is a choice, and that reality, when put under the microscope of a presentational medium, rarely looks real. Think about the visual differences between an action-adventure movie and the average man-on-the-street documentary. Both present pictures that have the appearance of reality, but the action-adventure film has been carefully tailored into a heightened and focused reality. Its limited focus and carefully placed lighting and camera angles create a reality that appears more real than reality itself, which is vital to the pulse-pounding, sweaty-palm mood it needs to be effective. Just choosing "reality" as the overall stylization is not enough. You must decide what kind of reality you want to present.

Clearly, stylization has a major impact on the visual presentation of your character.

Setting

What is the world of your story? Characters that inhabit a medieval kingdom of magic would look terribly uncomfortable in an urban ghetto, even though characters in both worlds might have similar personality traits. Remember, stories are devices of limited focus. Just as most planets in science fiction stories are dominated by one topographical setting (forests, deserts, ice, and so forth), a focused story takes place primarily in one world. That world can be psychological as well as physical, springing from the imagination of a child or an oppressive world of tyrannical overlords (see figs. 6.6 and 6.7).

Keep in mind your intended audience's view of the world. Will they see a child's imaginary world through the eyes of a child or those of a disapproving parent? Will the oppressiveness be seen from the overlord's point of view, or from that of the oppressed?

After you nail down the setting, examine your character. Is the character an outcropping of the world or a foreign element in it? From which viewpoint does the character see this world? Does the character share the viewpoint of the audience or have one completely contradictory to that of the audience? This provides a base for the thought process that goes on within this character.

FIGURE 6.6
Your story's world can spring from the imagination of a child.

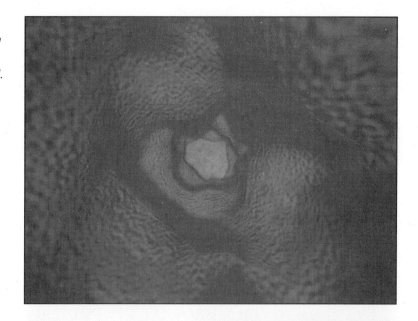

FIGURE 6.7
Your story's world can spring from an oppressive world of tyrannical overlords.

Multiple Characters

Stories grow out of the interaction between characters. Even if only one moving character is in the scene you are creating, everything that affects the character in such a way as to move the story forward should be treated as another character. This includes the audience itself, if your character breaks the fourth wall (the invisible barrier through which the character watches the story) and becomes aware of the audience through asides or direct reaction to the audience's presence.

By considering the character's reaction to all the other characters in the scene, you will gain a clear picture of the breadth of emotion a character must be able to express. You will also gain a clear picture of where the character model must accommodate these expressions by having the supporting geometrical construction with which to achieve them.

Developing the Character's Personality

The previous steps of clarifying the story and how it will be told should create a fairly complete blueprint of the character's personality in the context of the story. But what if the character has to go through multiple stories? If actions or events are added to the story, or you discover new events while you're animating, how will you determine how the character will react? What you have seen before will be a clue to the total personality of the character, but it will not be the complete picture. You need to make a conscious definition of the character's overall disposition toward the world. By doing this, you can create a physical posture, expression, and an idea of how the character moves that can make it more readily identifiable and easily accessible to your intended audience. The following exercise will provide an simple, effective, and reusable tool that will help you in nailing down a tight definition of your character's personality.

THE PERSONALITY PARAGRAPH

Write a paragraph (or two) describing your character's attitude toward its world. Avoid any physical description of the character, just focus on emotions and emotionally charged adjectives and adverbs (for example, he looks angrily on the playfulness of the little fuzzy creatures). When you have finished, go back to the trusty thesaurus, look up the adjectives and adverbs you have written down, and see whether any synonyms give you a better or more powerful idea of your character's overriding personality.

Does the character see the world as a great big playground? A massive opportunity for playing jokes? A world of ravenous predators, waiting and watching? The world's largest salad bar? Or a place filled with money that should belong to your character (but, unjustly, doesn't)?

What opportunity does each new day bring to your character? Does the character greet each day angrily, fearfully, cheerfully, greedily, or snidely? Adverbs make great catalysts to the discovery and refinement of personality. Use them often in your paragraph.

Defining How the Character Functions

Characters function in many ways, both physically within the story and as a plot device to move the story forward. By defining the tasks set out for your character in both areas you will gain a deeper understanding of the way the animated character must move, and what its physical structure must be to accomplish the movement.

Functioning as a Plot Device

Is your character the protagonist, whose actions drive the story forward? Is the character the hero that saves the day? Is the character the antagonist, determined to thwart the hero at all costs? Or is the character a representative of the world of the story, expressing the concerns and cares of the unseen masses? No matter who or what the character is, it will have some critical part to play in the telling of the story. Even crowds of nameless, faceless characters have a function—adding drama, ridiculing the main character, or helping to create the mood. Identifying this function will be of great benefit in identifying the physical appearance and personality of your character.

Physical Functions

Does your character need to run and jump to escape the villain (see fig. 6.8)? Lift impossibly heavy objects (see fig. 6.9)? Swallow dynamite and contain the explosion in its stomach? Or does your character collapse with exhaustion at the mere mention of physical labor?

FIGURE 6.8
*Does your character
need to run and jump
to escape the villain?*

FIGURE 6.9
*Does your character
need to lift impossibly
heavy objects?*

You must know what tasks await your character to know what sort of physical structure the character model must have. And if you know how the character responds to physical tasks, you have another part of the picture of the character's outward appearance.

Visual Design

If you have been reading with a particular character in mind, notice whether these suggestions have changed your ideas for the character's outward appearance. If you have been reading and mentally creating a prototype for a new character, how clear a picture do you have now of the character's outward appearance? You can see why visual design of a character is the last step—the outside of a character must express its inner life.

Now that the life of the character has been pretty much defined (but feel free to explore further), you can bring the character into a physical (computer-generated) existence.

Before you begin modeling, you should be aware of three elements that can be of tremendous help in the process:

- References

- Sketches

- Maquettes

Use one or all of these elements to finalize the visual design of the model before you begin modeling in the computer.

References

Almost all character creators, whether make-up artists, sculptors, actors, painters, or animators, have found quick and easy access to character references. These references can be videotapes, photographs, books, magazines, whatever. But having visual references can fill out the details that make a character unique.

What sort of references should you seek? Pictures that express the personality you have defined serve as excellent references. What profession or archetype would you classify your character as having? Find pictures of those professions or traditional representations of those archetypes. Find pictures of whatever is unique to your character, its nationality, time period, social status, and definable psychosis. These pictures will show what these attributes actually look like, or how they have been represented in the past.

Sketches

Even if you and pencils have maintained a mutually respectful distance for most of your life, rough sketches of a character further flesh out its outward appearance. The sketches do not have to be major works of art, and they don't have to be absolutely accurate. Instead, they serve as visual aids in focusing the direction of your model. You should strive to create at least a top, side, and front sketch of your character. With these in hand, you can more readily see where the character needs to go, what is lacking, and what is correct. And remember, nobody else ever has to see the sketches. Even a final sketch, however, does not preclude a last-minute change of mind (due to a flash of brilliant inspiration) when the modeling process begins.

Maquettes

Maquettes are sculpted models that give you a 3D representation of your character. Even with orthographic sketches of you character, you will not have a completely accurate picture of what the model will look like in 3D. Use whatever materials you have handy—clay, papier-maché, Sculpey, what-ever—but having a reference that you can pick up and rotate around is invaluable. And again, you don't need to be Michelangelo, and no one else needs to see the final product. As long as it helps your creation process, do it!

3D computer graphics are a relatively new medium. As such, new aesthetics will be tried, accepted, and rejected for a long time to come. New techniques and tools are being invented every day. But the ability to create an interesting story full of vibrant and passionate characters, and the skill to tell that story well, are talents that have been prized since the very dawn of mankind. Those talents will be treasured until the end of the human race; stories, and the characters that make them possible, help human beings to reflect, relax, learn, and dream. The characters you create today may be passed down from generation to generation to generation and medium to medium. Create them on strong foundations—they might be around for a while.

In Practice: Character Modeling Basics

- A character is any object that "acts" of its own accord, and to which a thought process, emotional life, and distinguishable personality may be attributed. Defining these aspects of your character will create a life for the character, a life that suggests patterns of movement, and therefore, construction techniques and requirements.

- Before creating the character, define the story in which it must act and define how that story will be told.

- Define the personality of the character, comprising the patterns of emotion and thought your character most often experiences and the disposition of the character toward the world.

- Define how the character functions in the story, both physically (accomplishing certain tasks) and as a plot device.

- The last step in creating a character (before modeling) is the visual design of the character.

IMAGE BY JOSHUA R. ANDERSON

Chapter 7

by Joshua R. Anderson

CHARACTER MODELING WITH PATCH TOOLS

Patch modeling is a fairly new feature to 3D Studio users, and few methods for creating models from patches have been developed or shared. The patch tools in 3D Studio MAX enable you to create simple patch models with relative ease. If you need more information on the basics of patch editing and modeling, Chapter 14 in Inside 3D Studio MAX Volume I *is an excellent reference. Complex surfaces require advanced techniques to achieve the look you want. This chapter not only demonstrates advanced patch modeling techniques, it also shows you many techniques used to model great looking characters by using MAX patches. This chapter has two major objectives: to show how to model complex* surface objects by using both the patch tools in MAX and plug-ins, and to show character modeling techniques by doing the following:

- Showing the benefits of patch surfaces over mesh objects in character modeling

- Describing in detail the limitations of patches so that you can decide whether they suit your project

- Teaching new techniques in patch modeling that use the tools provided with MAX

- Introducing plug-ins, which greatly expand the patch modeling potential of MAX

- Stepping through the process of creating a complex character

- Showing important techniques to use when modeling single-skinned characters for animation

Using Patches in MAX

Working with patches in MAX is different from most other programs. Although it is true that patches are controlled in much the same way as splines, the surface appears to be made of polygons (just like a mesh object). This can be confusing at first, but when you approach patches as a completely separate entity—a balanced mixture of both spline and polygonal geometry—you should begin to understand the power behind patch modeling. Patch modeling requires a different thought process than that required when working with mesh objects or splines. Although techniques for patch modeling vary, the planning of the model is crucial. The planning can dramatically affect both the quality of the model and the time it takes to create it. Many plug-ins, both free and commercial, exist to make patch modeling easier. Not all of the available plug-ins are used in this chapter, but they are listed here.

- Surface Tools

- Edit Spline 2

- Interpolate Spline

- Reverse Spline

- Edge2Spline

- Mesh2Spline

- Patch MatID and PatchOut

Patch Versus Mesh Considerations

When choosing between using a patch model or mesh model, remember the following important facts:

- Patches are parametric like primitives, meaning their resolution—or poly count—is dynamic.

- Patch surfaces are ideal for flexible, organic surfaces, but can run into trouble when hard edges are needed.

- Patch models generally have higher hardware requirements than mesh models of similar complexity.

- Patch models and mesh models work fine together in the same scene.

You may choose to use patch models for the organic objects in your scene and mesh models for architectural and mechanical objects. You may have some objects organic in some parts and mechanical in others. In any event, patch objects should not be left out of the planning process for a project.

When working with a large amount of splines and patches, the RAM requirements can greatly exceed those required by mesh objects. This problem can be reduced or eliminated altogether by collapsing the edit modifiers in the Modifier Stack and re-applying them as needed. This is because MAX stores the edits of each spline and patch vertex, and collapsing the modifier clears all of that storage. This can even reduce the file and RAM size to below that of a mesh object.

Modeling Issues

Creating good-looking patch models with only the tools provided with MAX can be a daunting task, although it is definitely possible. If you have the right tools and techniques, however, patch modeling can be the easiest way to create complex models, especially characters. The dragon shown at the opening of this chapter (and used in the tutorials later in this chapter) was modeled from scratch in about three working days. Your mileage may vary, but this gives you a reasonable idea of what you can expect after you become accustomed to patch modeling.

In reality, patch modeling is much more straightforward than mesh modeling. You deal more with the shape of the model than with its structure. This makes modeling easier to learn and more fun to do.

Animation Issues

Patch models carry several distinct advantages over mesh models when it comes time to animate them:

- The dynamic resolution of patch models ensures optimal rendering times and better detail and smoothing for close-up shots (see fig. 7.1).

FIGURE 7.1
Identical surfaces with different step values.

Patch steps set at 1

Patch steps set at 3

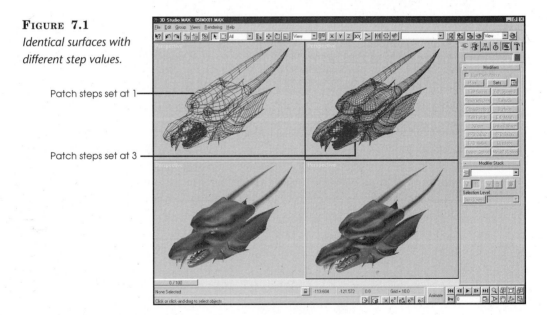

- Patch surfaces can be smoothly bent and stretched without the aid of a skin plug-in (see fig. 7.2).

FIGURE 7.2
An arm with Linked
Xform from the arm to
the bones.

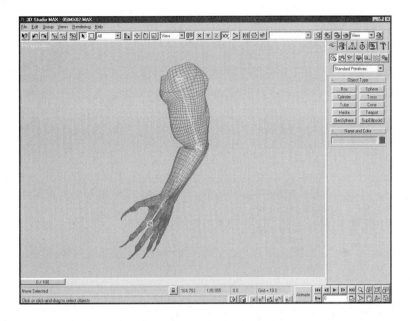

- If you are working with Morph Targets and using Surface Tools, you can easily pose the model by returning to the spline level in the Modifier Stack and setting its pose. The vertex count rémains the same, and the surfaces are smoothly transformed to their new pose (see fig. 7.3).

FIGURE 7.3
A head with mouth
open and closed.

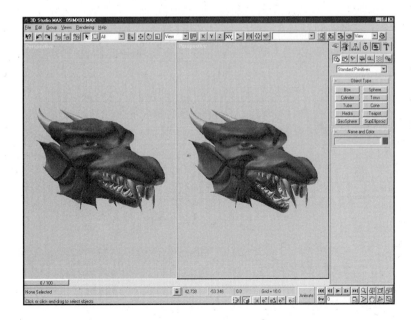

Animating patch models can be a great relief from rigid mesh models. Patch models' flexibility extends well beyond their easy bending and stretching—beyond even the dynamic resolution. The Modifier Stack enables you to go back and to easily make large or small changes to any part of your object and still have the surface come out looking just as good.

Patch Limitations in MAX

Although patch surfaces are versatile and easy to work with, it is important to know what you cannot do with them. Many of the seeming drawbacks of patches shown in this section should not actually be regarded as limitations, but rather as aspects of patch modeling that need to be known (just as the aspects of mesh modeling should be).

General Surface Control Problems

Patch surfaces, by nature, are rendered smoothly. They are not composed of faces, edges, and vertices as are mesh models, and they cannot be edited at that level. With this in mind, you can understand some of the problems you would face if you approached patch surfaces and thought you could use the same techniques as used on mesh models.

Smoothing groups do not exist where patch models are concerned. Because of this, creating a sharp edge in the middle of a patch surface requires the special technique shown in the section of this chapter entitled "Fine-Tuning the Surface."

Normals are another tricky problem with patches, as they are controlled by the direction of the splines used to create the patch. No *Flip Normals* feature for patches is built into MAX. You can, however, apply a two-sided map to the patch surface if needed or turn off Back Face Cull. Both sides are displayed in such a case.

TIP

You may want to assign a keyboard shortcut to toggle Back Face Cull on and off if you model with patches a lot.

Accuracy Issues

Although precise surface curvature is not generally required for the majority of the work done in MAX, for some projects it may be necessary. It is important to note that although it is easy to adjust the curves of the splines that control a patch surface, the patch surfaces themselves can be quite difficult to match with another. The difficulty arises because you are essentially dealing with what could be seen as a broad-tipped brush for laying out a surface. Even with Manual Interior turned on, you are moving a region of the surface rather than directly manipulating its structure. For this reason, you may want either to opt for mesh objects altogether for such a project, or to use patches to create the initial surface and then convert it to a mesh for more precise control.

Texture Mapping Issues

Of all the limitations of patch surfaces, texture mapping may be the most serious for one critical reason: Patch surfaces can hold only one material. If you attach two mesh objects they retain both their mapping coordinates and their assigned materials. If you attach two patch objects, they retain their mapping coordinates but inherit the material of the parent patch. If you are dealing with jointed characters, this is not a problem. If you plan to use Bones Pro or some other skin plug-in, however, you need to change your patch object into a mesh. This is not too drastic because the mesh object looks just like the patch object. You just can't adjust the topology steps any more, and you lose the patch lattice.

TIP

Physique in Character Studio seems to be the exception to this problem, because it can be applied to a selection of objects. Just select all the patch surfaces, then apply Physique to them.

A pair of free plug-ins is available that overcomes this problem altogether. Patch MatID and PatchOut enable you to use Multi/Sub-Object materials on patch objects. Another free plug-in, Face Map 2, enables you to use face maps on triangular patches and meshes. Peter Watje made all three of these, and they enhance other plug-ins he has made.

Basic Patch Modeling Overview

Patch models can be created from just about anything in MAX. Primitives provide a quick base if you are building a less complex patch object; extrusions and lathes can provide more complex starting points. (Primitives or extrusions do not need to be turned into patch objects unless you need the attributes of a patch to model the object.)

Applying the Edit Patch modifier affects primitives differently. Generally, it conforms optimally for the primitive to which you apply it. You should understand, however, the way in which MAX constructs its patches from mesh and primitive objects.

Overall, patch primitives are more limited in function than their mesh counterparts. Unless you need a specific feature that can be found only in patches, it is best to stick with standard primitives.

You will probably find creating patches from extruded splines to be the most useful of the basic patch creation methods. It gives the most control over patch layout and overall form. If you want a patch cylinder, for example, it is better to extrude a circle as a patch rather than to apply the Edit Patch modifier to a cylinder primitive (see fig. 7.4).

FIGURE 7.4

An example of a primitive patch and an extruded patch.

Primitive cylinder with Edit Patch applied

Extruded circle with Patch option selected

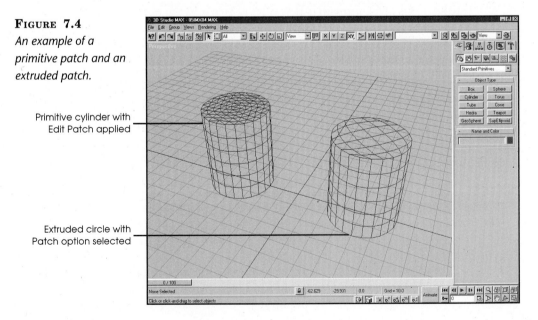

You have much more control over how many patches the cylinder will be composed of and how the patches are laid out. The patches on the extruded cylinder are divided by the control vertices on the circle used to create it and the number of segments. The patches on the primitive cylinder are always in the same arbitrary layout. You cannot add more patches to it without subdividing it or deleting a patch, selecting an edge, and adding a patch.

Modeling a Hand with the Patch Tools in MAX

The power that the splines give you in manipulating complex surfaces makes them an excellent tool for creating cars, characters, food, and designer furniture and architecture. Remember that the entire surface is controlled by splines, and that the Bézier splines give you full control over the surface curvature. Because of this, you can lay out a complete framework by using Bézier splines. You can then apply patches to the framework and align them to it by using the same methods used to create it. Not only do you have the patch modeling tools with which to work, but also some of the tools in MAX usually only associated with meshes. Booleans can add a great deal of functionality to patches, enabling you not only to trim surfaces but to add incredible detail.

Needed Resources

One of the most important aspects of patch modeling is source material use and management. Without quality source materials, professional results are difficult to achieve (if not impossible). Depending on the shape of the object you are creating, images of different views are required. For a hand, the most important views are of the top and bottom. Although you can get away without using a side view, it is highly recommended that you use one to achieve correct proportions. Access to a scanner is important, although not vital in many cases. A good image editor is almost always needed to make adjustments to the images and to create a wireframe template over them. Other things can make patch modeling easier as well, but they are not required. A digitizer to create a basic mesh to which to snap your splines can increase speed as well as improve accuracy. A vector-based drawing program that can export to DXF can make creating the initial 2D template a lot easier. In this exercise, sketches of a hand have been scanned and imported into Adobe Photoshop.

Creating a Template from an Image

When modeling a hand that will be animated, it is crucial to apply certain structural attributes. This is not only because the hand is a complex mechanical system, but because slip-ups in hand mechanics can cause this easily recognized appendage to appear fake and unprofessional. Joints must have more patch density than the areas between them. The point at which the fingers meet the base of the hand should be meticulously sculpted because of the multiple directions of stretching that occur there. The palm of the hand has defined lines along which folding of the skin occurs, and that wrinkle considerably when the hand closes even partially. Before attempting to model a hand, study your own closely. No anatomy books, videos, or images can compare with first-hand experience. It seems like a funny pun, but it's actually the best way to describe the process. Locate the points of rotation. Observe the overall structure. Hands are not static objects. Their internal bone structure enables the base of the hand to conform to a surface while still retaining a great deal of strength. The first thing you need is to have your source material in digital form so that it can be loaded into an image editor.

FIGURE 7.5

A sketch of the top view of a hand.

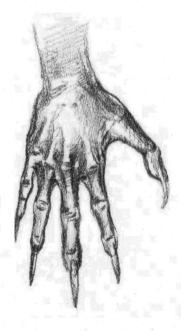

Figure 7.6

A spline layout derived from a sketch of the top view of a hand.

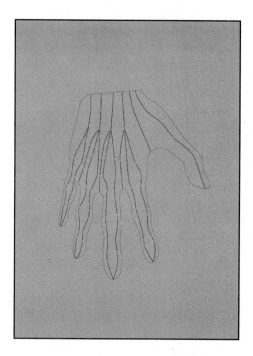

Draw the template on the image similar to the ones shown in figures 7.5 and 7.6. Afterward, if your image is on a white background, fill it in with gray. This makes working on it in MAX much easier.

TIP

In Photoshop, you can draw the lines on separate layers and place them on a gray layer after you are finished.

After you have a viable template of the top view on which to build your framework, make a template of the palm. The palm image should be exactly the same size. The lines for the palm need to be drawn to match the lines where the skin folds. The easiest way to start the palm template is to overlay the top-view template on the image of the palm. Use the same outline as the top image and continue the lines running the length of the hand around the palm. Be careful to line up the palm folds correctly. If your estimation of the end point locations of the palm folds is a little off, put the line where it should be on the palm and it can be fixed when the framework is made. If it is off by too much, you should fix it in the template. You may find it easier to start with the palm and then do the back of the hand.

If you choose to make a side view of the hand, it should consist only of an outline and a horizontal line representing the top outline as viewed from the side.

NOTE

You may be wondering why you need to go through this process. After all, you could load the image into MAX and draw the splines over the image. Creating a gridwork on the image is necessary, however, because it would be very difficult to lay out a proper spline framework without it. By laying out all the lines beforehand, you can see where every spline will intersect, which is where the control vertices must be placed.

Creating a Spline Framework

A spline framework is not the same as a wireframe; it does not represent the actual surface. A spline framework works at a different level, as more of a foundation supporting the surface. Remember that patch edges operate like splines. You will be using the framework to conform the patch edges to the shape you create with it.

TIP

Much of the work in this section can be accomplished more easily in a vector drawing program or an image editing package that can export paths in a format that MAX can read. In Photoshop, for instance, you can trace the template with paths and then export the paths in Adobe Illustrator format, which MAX can read in as Bézier splines. After importing, use the InterSpl plug-in to adjust the smoothness of the spline curves. Not only is this easier, it's also faster and usually more accurate.

1. Start MAX. Set the top template as the background image and make the background image visible in a Top viewport.

2. Using the Line tool in Create Shapes, trace the outline of the template first, placing a control vertex wherever it intersects another spline.

3. Turn off Start New Shape, and trace the lines that run the length of the hand, (again) placing control vertices at every intersection.

4. Clean up the trace, using the Edit Spline modifier. Use a combination of vertex types to create an accurate trace.

5. Freeze all the splines except for the outline.

6. Set the palm template as the background image and make the background image visible in a bottom view.

7. In the bottom view, trace the outline of the template.

8. Trace the lines running the length of the hand, (again) placing the control vertices at each intersection, and snapping the endpoints of the splines to the outline.

9. Lock axis movement so that you will only be moving vertices perpendicular to the grid. This varies depending on which reference coordinate system you use. (I recommend switching to the World coordinate system for this process and locking movement to the Z axis.)

10. Create a viewport layout so that you have one top view and one side view. This gives you the maximum viewable area.

11. Use the top view to select control vertices and the side view to move the vertices up and down.

12. Unfreeze the splines for the top of the hand and freeze the palm splines.

13. Perform the same procedure for the top of the hand (see fig. 7.7).

FIGURE 7.7

Lengthwise splines for the top of a hand after they've been raised.

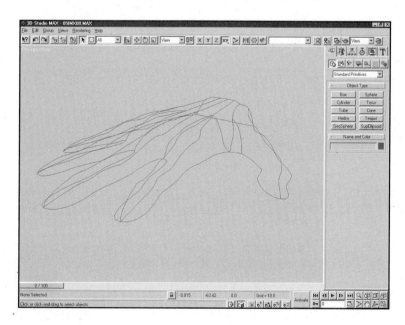

Inspect the layout of the splines closely. Use 3D snap to position the control vertices at intersecting splines on top of each other, and adjust any curves that are not aligned correctly. The result should be a fairly nice, yet simplified contour of the hand. The last process of creating the spline framework is fairly easy.

14. From the top view, with 3D Snap turned on and only Vertex Snap active, draw the lines that run the width of the hand. As you are drawing the new lines, make certain that the cursor is snapping to the vertices on the horizontal lines.

TIP

Notice the "V" shape of the splines on the knuckle joints. The extra spline gives the joint more faces so that when it bends and stretches, the surface remains smooth.

15. Lock axis movement to Y/Z.

16. In a User or Perspective viewport, adjust the curves of the vertical lines to match the curve of the hand as closely as possible.

17. With the Edit Spline modifier active, but not in SubObject mode, use the Attach command to attach all the splines together (see fig. 7.8).

FIGURE 7.8

Completed spline framework for the hand.

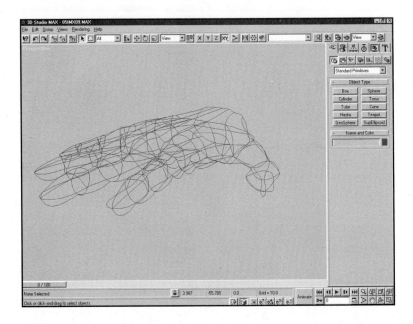

That's it. The spline framework is complete. You probably want to collapse the stack and re-apply Edit Spline at this point. This optimizes the stack. After you have done this, save the file and a copy of the splines; they can be used for other things later.

Building the Patch Surface

Creating a patch surface by hand in MAX can be a time-consuming process at first. After you gain some experience with patch placement and alignment, however, your modeling speed increases dramatically. The hard part is already done after you have a well-designed spline framework. A poorly constructed framework can make creating the patch surface take much longer, if it can be constructed at all.

1. Open the file 07imx09.max on the CD, hide the palm splines, and freeze the top splines.

2. Create a quad patch, move it to the base of the hand, and align it as closely as possible to a square along the bottom of the outline.

3. Apply Edit Patch and place the patch vertices on their respective spline vertices. Don't worry too much about accuracy for this model, just place them as closely as you can.

4. Go to the Edge sub-object level and select the top edge of the patch.

5. Click Add Quad Patch and align the new patch to the patch framework.

6. Repeat step 5 until you reach the top extent of the hand, replacing quad patches with tri patches if triangles are in the framework.

7. Add patches to the left edges of the patches you created. You can do this to multiple patches at a time. Just select all the edges that require quad patches, then click on Add Quad Patch, and then do the same for tri patches with Add Tri Patch.

8. Weld each new pair of patch vertices together and snap them to the framework.

9. Repeat steps 7 and 8 until the top of the hand is covered with patches (see fig. 7.9).

FIGURE 7.9

A hand with patches added to the top.

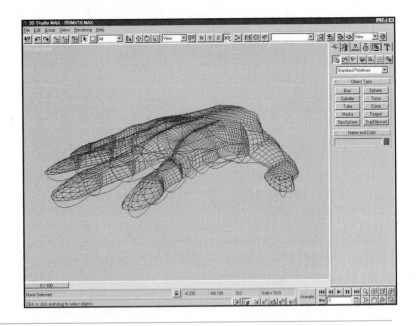

After this process is finished, perform a similar process for the palm. When the entire surface is created, examine it closely in both shaded and wireframe mode. Align the patch edges with the splines in the framework as closely as possible, and try to keep a smooth continuity to the surface (see fig. 7.10).

FIGURE 7.10

A completed hand shown both in wireframe and shaded mode.

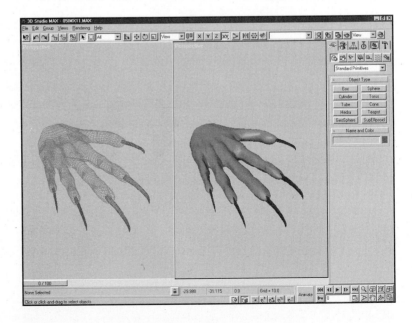

TIP

When working with patches, apply a two-sided material to them. This aids greatly when working in shaded mode because you can see the surface from both sides and catch surface problems very difficult to see from just one side.

When working with patch surfaces, it is important to remember that they are surfaces, not solid models. You can add detail much more easily by adding more surfaces rather than by trying to build the details into the existing surface.

Now the hand is finished, and should look like figure 7.10. The claws are very simple objects that can be added later.

Modeling a Torso from an Image

The subtle variations in curves and proportion make modeling a torso seem deceptively easy. All too often, however, these subtleties are missed. This is partially because most traditional modeling methods make it difficult to create a mesh structure that supports the complex curvature of the torso. The exercises in this section help take the guesswork out of modeling the torso. Although the torso could be modeled using methods similar to those used to create the hand, the Surface Tools plug-in is demonstrated to show how much faster it makes patch modeling.

The Surface Tools plug-in, created by Peter Watje and distributed by Digimation, removes a great deal of the work from creating patch models and can actually help make much better models as well. Combined with several free plug-ins also created by Peter Watje for patch and spline editing, patch modeling becomes an even more powerful method for creating many complex surface types.

Surface Tools is composed of two modifiers: Cross Section and Surface. Most of their basic usage is described in the manual that accompanies the product, so the following sections focus on actually creating a full character by using Surface Tools and combining the functionality given by the other plug-ins with it. In the following tutorials, several methods are used to generate the spline framework of different parts of the body. Note that the optimal methods for creating spline frameworks for different shapes and detail levels vary. You may find yourself mixing and matching the different methods based on your resources and the type of model you are building.

Needed Resources

Naturally, the more source material you have on the modeling subject the better; certain types work better for different objects. For a less detailed model, you may only need images of the side and top. For more accuracy, you may want to use photographs of a marked-up object. For optimal accuracy and detail, you should start with digitized data. For this first tutorial involving the creation of the dragon's body, only a pair of sketches were used: one of a top view, and one of a side view (see fig. 7.11). This is a fast way to create a spline framework, although not very accurate. The peaks and valleys of the surface are fairly well defined in the sketches, however, and this should make it easy to create something similar.

FIGURE 7.11
*A side view sketch
of a dragon.*

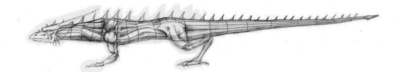

Creating a Template from an Image

The steps involved in creating a template from an image for a Surface Tools model are identical to those used in creating the template for the hand—with an emphasis on form, however, rather than on mechanics. Keep in mind that splines can do a lot of the work for you. Many times, you won't need a spline for both the peak and the valley because the spline control handles can be used to make a rounded peak fairly easily. This reduces the number of splines required and gives you a wider range of polygon count adjustment.

Creating a Spline Framework

Surface Tools gives you some leniency when creating the spline framework; it welds control vertices for you at a tolerance you specify. This can speed things up somewhat for some models, but on a model like this one—with such a large difference in patch sizes—it is best to use 3D Snap and be exact. Otherwise, it welds together vertices of multiple smaller patches. Other than that, create the spline framework for the dragon body by using the same steps used on the hand (see fig. 7.12).

FIGURE 7.12

A completed spline framework for half of the dragon's body.

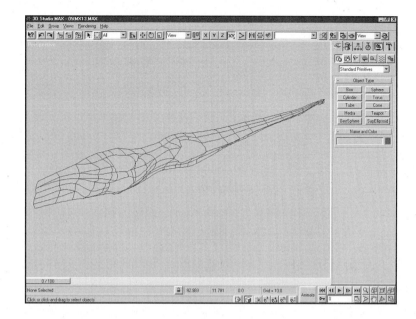

WARNING

Vertices of splines that have been attached to each other do not snap to each other. Leave all the splines unattached until you have finished creating the spline framework. If you have already attached them, you can select independent splines and segments and detach them. After you are finished modifying the splines, remember to reattach the splines.

Creating the Patch Surface

To create the patch surface, apply the Surface modifier to the spline framework. Because the spline control vertices rest on each other at the intersections, you can set the weld threshold very low. For this example, set the weld threshold to .01. The following symptoms indicate that your weld threshold is too high:

- Patches with edges that don't follow the spline framework
- Visible lines or seams on the back side of the patch surface
- Holes in the patch surface

Many times, the normals of the patches wind up reversed. If this is the case, choose the Reverse Normals option in the Surface modifier. On some occasions, some of the patches along the edge of the surface are flipped. This is because the starting points of the splines are mismatched. Try to keep all the starting points in the spline framework on the same end.

Another problem erupts when the spline framework has sections with more than four control vertices. Because five-sided patches do not exist, Surface Tools cannot fill these in. You must either weld two of the points together or add another spline inside the section. This can be a useful tool for adding holes to your surface as well.

The Surface modifier's steps operate like those for the Edit Patch modifier and translate directly over if you apply an Edit Patch modifier to the surface. Lowering the steps to 1 or 0 dramatically speeds up redraw times while you are working. Setting the steps up to 5 or higher gives you crisp, smooth detail for rendering output.

Fine-Tuning the Surface

Many times, after the patch surface is created, you get something close to what you want. Rarely, however, does it turn out exactly the way you want it. This is especially the case where tri patches are joined with quad patches. This often causes a variation in shading or puts small wrinkles on the surface. Most of the time, this only occurs in tight curves; try, therefore, to keep tri patches on broad, flat areas.

The internal layout of the patch surface is controlled not only by the position of the edges but by the length of the control handles as well. Normally, you will want to keep an even spread of patch density, but in some situations, you can sacrifice faces in one area and add them in another without adding more splines. The steps or faces of a patch will gather to where the control handles push or pull them.

Creating a Sharp Edge on a Patch Surface

A common problem associated with patches is the difficulty of getting a sharp edge along a surface. This is made even more difficult by the fact that patches do not have smoothing groups. The first thing to remember is that you should plan the sharp edges before you create the surface; it is really only possible to obtain one along the patch edges. That means you need to have a spline running along wherever you need a sharp edge. After your surface follows this guideline, follow these steps:

1. Make certain that the lattice is visible, and go to the Vertex sub-object level of the Edit Patch modifier.

2. Convert all the vertices that run the length of the intended sharp edge into Corner vertices, and adjust them to meet your angle requirements.

3. Select all the patches that run the length of the sharp edge on one side of it and detach them.

4. Get out of sub-object mode and reattach the patches (see fig. 7.13).

5. Re-weld the patch vertices along the areas you want to be smooth again.

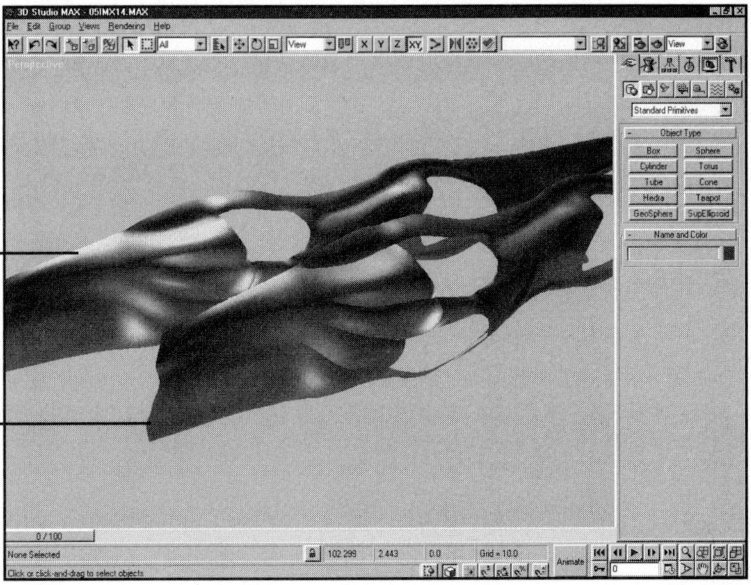

FIGURE 7.13

An example of the difference between smooth and sharp edges.

Torso with smooth muscles

Torso with sharp-edged muscles

This is currently the only way to create a controlled sharp edge along a patch surface. Some flaws exist with it, however. The vertices along the sharp edge are no longer welded. If you do weld them, it smooths the surface, and if you move them one at a time, it creates a break in the surface. When you need to adjust those vertices, always select both vertices.

Creating a Patch Head from a Mesh Object

The most accurate way to create a detailed patch object is to derive its splines from a mesh object. This can actually save a great deal of work both in preparation and in touchup—you can use a low-detail mesh to create the splines. The head created in this exercise was originally sculpted in clay, marked up with only the amount of lines required to get its surface detail, and then digitized. The process should be planned carefully to use as few triangles as possible. After you have the mesh object, you can use a free plug-in called Edge to Spline to create the splines.

Creating the Spline Framework with the Edge to Spline Plug-In

The process involved in creating a framework from a mesh is different, and in some ways, more involved than the previous methods shown in this chapter. These ways, however, almost always lead to a more accurate, detailed end product more quickly. The reason for this is that not only do you have exact locations for each vertex, but you also have the spline layout created by the mesh.

T I P

When selecting edges to convert to splines, selecting multiple sets of edges speeds things greatly. As you select them, make certain that none of them cross or attach to any of the other selected edges in any way.

1. Open file 07imx15.max from the CD. This is the mesh of the dragon's head.

2. Select a series of edges, following the contour of the object.

3. Select the Utilities command panel and then select Edge to Spline from the drop-down list.

4. Click on Pick Object and then click on the head (see fig. 7.14).

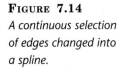

FIGURE 7.14

A continuous selection of edges changed into a spline.

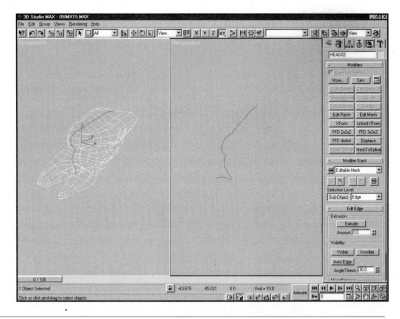

The edges selected in sub-object mode are converted into a spline. The spline's control vertices are left as corner vertices. It is useful to convert them into smooth or Bézier vertices as you go along; this separates their segments from the mesh slightly, enabling you to see what you have accomplished. Repeat the process until all the edges have been converted into splines, and then attach all of them together.

You probably need to edit the splines somewhat to get accurate curves across the object. Use the four types of control vertices as required. If the mesh object was planned out correctly, it should not require an excessive amount of editing.

Mirroring and Attaching Spline Frameworks

It is fairly standard practice to model half of a symmetrical object and then mirror it. This cuts modeling time in half and helps keep proportions accurate. The same holds true for patch modeling, but some differences exist when working with splines. Make certain that all the end-control vertices along the edge are exactly aligned along one axis at 0 in the World coordinate system. If they are not, apply a non-uniform scale on them along that axis.

WARNING

Do not scale vertices that are either Bézier, Bézier corner, or smooth. This scales their handles and curves as well, creating a nightmare of cleanup work. Change the end handles to Corner before scaling them. You can always change them back later.

After the object meets these parameters, follow these steps:

1. Open file 07imx16.max from the CD.

2. Detach the spline that runs along the edge on which the object will be mirrored.

3. Change the coordinate reference system to World, and the pivot point to Use Transform Coordinate Center.

4. Click Mirror, set Y as the Mirror Axis, select Copy, and then click on OK.

5. Exit Sub-object mode, attach the mirrored splines, and open Sub-object mode again.

6. Go to the Vertex sub-object level and weld all the vertices that run down the center.

7. Get out of sub-object level and reattach the center spline (see fig. 7.15).

FIGURE 7.15
Dragon head splines mirrored.

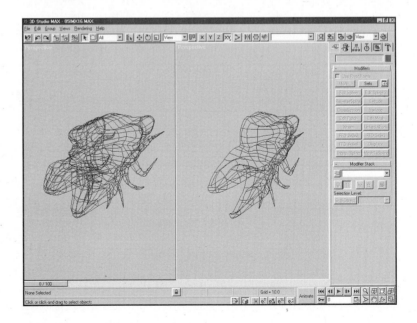

Inspect the mirrored edge, checking for any vertices that were not welded or which were welded improperly. Remember that you can only have three- and four-sided patches. You may need to adjust the curves of some of the center vertices to create a smooth transition.

After the framework is in order, apply the Surface modifier to it with a low-weld threshold, and then look over the object again. Check for surface irregularities and holes. If holes exist, it is usually the result of either a section with more than four vertices or a place where two vertices lie outside the weld threshold. You can fix the former problem by adding new splines to the sections and the latter problem by uniformly scaling the vertices together or raising the weld threshold slightly.

Modeling an Arm with Cross Sections

One of the easiest ways to model a narrow and fairly simple appendage is to just use cross sections. This enables you to keep the joint where arm and torso meet exact, while creating a consistent, flexible surface for the arm. This section shows how to create the cross sections to create the arm and introduces the Cross Section modifier. The Cross Section modifier creates for you all the lines that run the length of the cross sections.

Creating Splines for Cross Sections

The first thing to remember when creating cross sections is that left as they are, they offer limited control. Think of cross sections as a quick start for creating the base shape of your object. Keep that in mind as you plan the layout of the object and you usually wind up with much better models when finished. Notice that in the torso, holes were left where the arm, wing, and leg can extend from. These are used to create the initial cross section and are what the subsequent cross sections are based on.

1. Open file 07imx17.max from the CD. This file requires Surface Tools from Digimation.

2. Select the spline segments that make up the hole for the arm and detach them as a copy.

3. Apply an Edit Spline modifier to the new spline and weld the vertices to make it a single spline.

4. At the spline sub-object level, clone the spline by holding down the Shift key and moving it to the right.

5. Select all its vertices and then apply a non-uniform scale on them to 0 percent. This flattens the cross section, making it much easier to work with.

6. Now edit the vertices of the cross section, conforming it to the shape you need for the shoulder. Then rotate it and position it below and to the right of the first cross section (see fig. 7.16).

FIGURE 7.16

Arm cross section splines created by cloning the edges of the hole left in the torso framework.

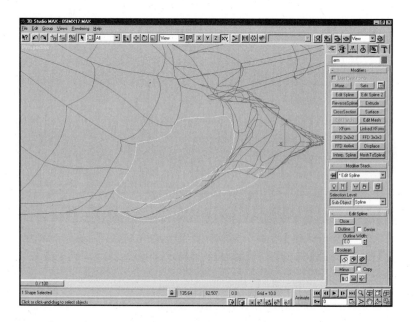

Repeat this process until you have all the cross sections needed for the arm. This step should not take too much effort because you won't have a good idea of what it will look like until the lengthwise splines are added. At that point, most of the modeling is done.

Editing the Cross Section Splines

After all the cross sections are complete, apply the Cross Section modifier with Smooth selected, and then apply an Edit Spline modifier to the entire new set of splines. To get a solid idea of what really needs to be done to it to make it look like an arm, apply the Surface modifier with a low-weld threshold to it.

Although the general shape of the arm is okay, leaving the framework as it is results in poor muscle arrangement. The vertices must be edited to get the proper shape of the arm. This is why the second Edit Spline modifier was applied.

1. Open file 07imx18.max from the CD. This file requires Surface Tools from Digimation.

2. Leave the Surface modifier in the stack, but go back to the second Edit Spline modifier.

3. Go to the Vertex sub-object level and then modify the vertices—both in placement and in curvature—until you have what you think is much closer to the actual arm.

4. Remaining in sub-object mode, click on and hold the Show End Result button (see fig. 7.17).

FIGURE 7.17
Seeing the effects of your editing.

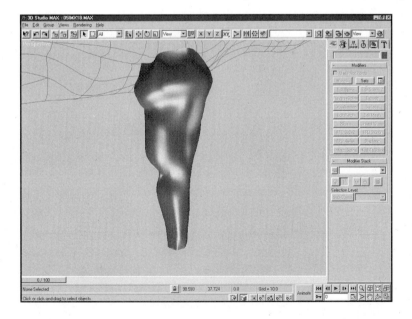

By using Show End Result, you can see the effects of your editing quickly, without ever leaving the Edit Spline modifier. This makes for faster modeling times and better models. Use the same procedure to model the leg and wing, the horns, and the ear bones.

In Practice: Character Modeling with Patch Tools

- **Patches versus meshes.** Patches lend themselves to creating complex surfaces much more easily than meshes. This makes them well-suited for modeling single-skinned characters.

- **Patch limitations.** Modifiers that require the mesh structure of faces, edges, and vertices convert a patch into a mesh. If there is no way to avoid using one of these modifiers, finish making any changes you need to the model in patches, save a copy, and then convert it to a mesh.

- **Basic patch models.** Creating patches from primitives or extruded or lathed splines can be a good starting point for simple patch objects. There is no need to convert a primitive into a patch object unless you need patch attributes to edit the primitive.

- **Planning for a patch character.** Planning out a model beforehand is much more important when creating a patch model. Good source materials and a sound knowledge of Bézier splines are vital assets to creating a good model.

- **Modeling with only the patch tools in MAX.** Creating complex patch models with only the patch tools in MAX is definitely possible. It just takes a lot more work than when plug-ins are used.

- **Spline frameworks.** The spline framework is the structure on which a good patch model is based. It provides an easily editable infrastructure and enables you to make large changes by just moving the spline vertices.

- **Plug-ins.** Several plug-ins are available that greatly enhance patch modeling in MAX. Most of them are free and add functionality ranging from spline editing to texture mapping.

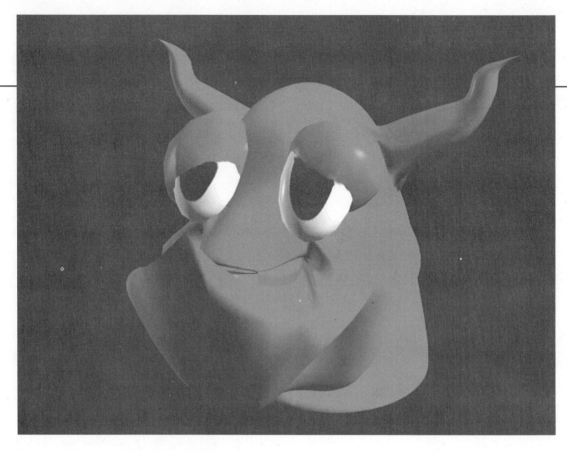

IMAGE BY KEN ALLEN ROBERTSON

Chapter 8

by Ken Allen Robertson

CHARACTER MODELING WITH PLUG-INS

To understand the paradigm inherent in the design of MAX, imagine that the program is like your closet. You have certain types of clothing, shirts, jeans, and shoes arranged to mix and match in any way you see fit. In addition, you have special pieces for special occasions—jackets, dress shirts, and ties. You can add to this collection at any time. The new pieces take their place alongside the others, no different than the others (only newer). You don't have to go to a different closet to get the newer pieces, or perform some special procedure to insert them into the closet in the first place. In addition, you can use these new pieces with the older pieces to create entirely new combinations (why not a tuxedo jacket with sneakers and jeans?).

MAX takes advantage of the latest thinking in object-oriented programs, providing a vast array of elementary (and not-so-elementary) 3D processes. By providing every user with the MAX Software Developer's Kit, Kinetix gives any user with the knowledge (or the desire to learn) access to almost all these functions—to be arranged in new combinations as the developer sees fit. As another benefit, development in the 32-bit Windows environment (either Windows 95 or NT) provides access to an even greater library of functions called the Microsoft Foundation Class library. This library consists of the most basic elements of windowed programming and graphics. MAX provides the developer with the world's greatest collection of building blocks to stack and arrange (and rearrange) to create new and exciting combinations with ease and stability.

Character modeling—an exacting and multifaceted process—will certainly reap the greatest rewards from this new paradigm. Already, amazing packages such as Surface Tools, Bones Pro, and Metareyes 4.0 are making incredible leaps, enabling artists to create characters recently possible to create only in 3D packages that cost at least three times what MAX costs. New plug-ins are also being generated almost daily, a number of them available for limited or no cost to the end user. With animation packages such as Morph Magic, Hypermatter, and Metacloth on the horizon, 3DS MAX has proved itself to be a world class professional tool for character creators.

This chapter covers the following topics:

- General principles for character modeling with plug-ins
- Seamless versus segmented modeling
- Using plug-ins for character modeling

General Principles for Character Modeling with Plug-Ins

Although every new plug-in will vary a little in how it utilizes the power of MAX, some general rules make character modeling a much simpler and effective process, no matter which techniques are used. The following general rules should be observed:

- Start simple and add detail.

- Have references constantly available.

- Work in halves.

- Know the tools for "tweaking"—one tool is never enough.

Start Simple and Add Detail

When you have a beautiful character design that just begs for an artist to build it, you can easily get caught up in the massive details involved in fully realizing a stunning model. You might focus on one part of the model until it is complete, and then move on to the other parts. Often, however, this method leads to creating detail that conflicts with parts of the model created later in the process. These conflicts can result in frustrating, tedious manipulations of the model to tweak it into a workable form.

You should instead try to envision the modeling process more along the lines of sculpting: Building the basic proportions of the model in a simplistic form, aligning them to their proper locations, and then adding detail as needed. All the current modeling tools lend themselves easily to this process, and the MAX modifier stack is an incredibly useful tool to go back over your steps if you take a wrong turn during the modeling process. This process also enables you to see where detail is (and is not) needed.

A helpful technique is to build a *mock-up*—a stand-in character made up of simple primitives, boxes, and spheres—as a prototype of your character, similar to figure 8.1. A mock-up provides you with a simple, proportionally accurate model that can be frozen and used in the background, and over which to sculpt the detailed model. If you are planning to use Bones Pro to animate the model, this framework can also serve as the beginnings of your skeleton. If you are using Character Studio for your animation, creating a biped for your mock-up proves quick and effective.

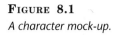

FIGURE 8.1

A character mock-up.

Have References Constantly Available

Characters can have their beginnings in any number of places—an idea sparked by a picture, a song, a story idea, or any combination of these are only a few examples. If you start the character-modeling process in the computer without a clear visual idea of what the final character should look like, however, you are bound to go through an exercise of trial and error that dramatically increases the time required to create the character. Before you start modeling, create visual references, such as sketches and *maquettes* (small sculptures). If you are building a previously created character, you should have multiple pictures of the character at hand.

If you have the time, it is highly recommended that you create a maquette for the character. Two-dimensional information available through sketches, even if extensive *turn-arounds* (various views of the character) are created, can be deceptive and misleading when translated into three dimensions. By having a three-dimensional reference available, however, you can easily focus on any part of the character with which you are having trouble. You can actually pick up the maquette and rotate it to get a clearer picture of the modeling requirements.

With your visual references for the character at hand, you have ready access to the essential blueprint of the character. Better yet, you can load your visual references for the character (whether preexisting or created for your current project) into MAX as a texture map on two crossing planes. You then have the critical information for the character on-screen, accessible without your having to divert your attention from the modeling process on your monitor. If you have created a maquette of your character, take pictures of the side and front views of the maquette, scan them, and use these as texture maps. Remember, though, to always keep the maquette nearby.

As you progressively add detail to your character, other available kinds of references come into play. Excellent resources for detailing a character include books on human anatomy and proportion, pictures of various types of animal anatomy, and pictures of humans and animals in motion. You should consult these resources when you add muscle tone, creases, folds, and bumps to characters. The detail you add will make a character look more alive.

Work in Halves

The look of all organic characters benefits from having some *asymmetry* (one side different than the other); the asymmetry makes them appear more "real." You can save a great deal of time, however, by initially creating only half the character. This "halving" also makes it easier for you to focus as you detail the model. To realize the benefits of halving, create half the model and add all the necessary detail. Then make a mirror clone of the model. Attach this mirrored clone to the piece you originally created. This results in an exact symmetry that you can then tweak to create the asymmetry discussed earlier.

One danger in creating half-models is the possibility of leaving a seam down the middle where the halves are joined. To avoid this problem, be certain to test the mirroring process often. To so test, create the mirror clone, take a look at how the halves match up, and then delete the clone and go back to working the original piece. After the model is completed and joined, use any of the smoothing tools available (Relax, MeshSmooth, or Bones Pro Smooth, for example). Make certain to use these tools on the vertices that run down (or very near) the seam *only*. In this way you can make the seam invisible.

Know the Tools for "Tweaking"—One Tool Is Never Enough

Character modeling is a process of finesse. As mentioned earlier, it is generally advisable to start with simpler forms and add detail as you progress. Fortunately, MAX provides a bevy of tools to do just that. You should familiarize yourself with these tools. They can, after all, be the difference between an average model and a spectacular character.

3DS MAX includes the following tools that enable you to add detail to characters as you progress through your modeling:

- Sub-object controls of the Edit Mesh Modifier (face, vertex, and edge editing)

- Relax

- MeshSmooth

- Free-form deformation

The following sections review the simple ways in which these tools can be applied to a model. For an explanation of the exact parameters of these tools, refer to *Inside 3D Studio MAX Volume I*.

Sub-Object Controls of the Edit Mesh Modifier

Being familiar and confident with sub-objects and their controls is critical to the process of finessing a model. The capability to access the model at its most basic level has always been an excellent part of 3D Studio, and MAX has pushed this capability even further.

Even if you are just selecting sub-objects within the Edit Mesh modifier, to be adjusted with other modifiers, you can save time and produce much greater results by knowing how to maneuver through the sub-object panels and also knowing which sub-objects to select for which modifiers.

Face Controls

The following face controls are those most often used in character modeling (in addition to selecting).

- Extrude
- Tessellate
- Build face

Extruding a face (or a group of faces) is critical to adding large features to the surface of a mesh. Extrude is, therefore, an extremely important tool. You can start modeling a head by modifying a sphere, stretching it longer, and sculpting the basic skull shape with free-form deformation. To add the nose to the model, you can create a separate nose model and perform a Boolean union to attach the two pieces. Boolean operations are often unpredictable, however, and can leave tiny gaps or odd smoothing and can drastically increase geometric intensity.

By selecting the polygons on the face that would correspond to the placement of the nose and then extruding them, your positioning can be exact. The geometry stays extremely close to its original density, and the face remains in one solid piece. The nose faces can then be manipulated into the desired position. Then, with MeshSmooth and Relax, a smooth and organic feature is created.

Tessellating and building go hand-in-hand with extruding faces. If you don't have the proper geometry to extrude a complete smooth feature, performing a simple tessellation of the desired faces can often provide the desired geometry. Generally, it is a good idea to also tessellate the faces around the ones you want to extrude. This gives you a cleaner base from which to perform the extrusion.

If adding faces is not the problem, or if the geometry is too dense to get a clean selection, building faces is often an excellent option. Delete the dense faces in the area from which you want to extrude, and then build new faces attached to the surrounding points in a way that makes the desired area for modification easier to see and better supports the extrusion process.

TIP

When creating faces, always be certain to select the vertices in a *counter-clockwise* order. Otherwise, the normal of the newly created face will face away from you and the polygon will appear to be invisible.

Vertex Controls

In addition to moving vertices to sculpt the model, the most helpful tool in the Vertex Sub-object panel is the Affect Region button. By adjusting the Falloff, Pinch, and Bubble settings, you make it a rather simple matter to pull small organic protrusions from the mesh objects. Used in this way, the vertex controls are the best tools for adding bump-like detail to a character; face controls are better suited for larger, flatter features.

Edge Controls

Two controls in the Edge Sub-object panel are often used for tweaking a character mesh. These controls—Dividing and Turning—enable you to use the vertex and face controls with great efficiency and precision.

Dividing an edge is an excellent way to add pinpoint detail to a mesh. By selecting an edge and dividing it, you provide another vertex for manipulation and create two more faces exactly where you need them for extrusion. Before you begin an edge division process, it is helpful to select all the edges near the area where you will be working and click on the Visible button in the Visibility section of the Edit Edge rollout menu. This will make all the edges in the proximity visible, so that you will get immediate feedback on your division operation.

Turning an edge is also highly useful, especially if the edge operations are going to support a vertex manipulation later. By turning an edge, you choose the way the polygons line up with existing geometry and where you will see the results of the final vertex\face operations. Again, it is helpful to make all edges in the proximity of your work area visible before turning an edge.

Relax

The Relax modifier is a dream tool for the character modeler. By selecting the desired faces or edges and applying a Relax modifier, you can turn hard edges into rounded, organic ones.

A particulary useful way to use Relax is after you model in simple forms and then use sub-object tools to add simple detail. By using the Relax modifier you can change sharp forms to organic ones.

Although you can get similar results by using the Relax settings in the MeshSmooth modifier, performing a separate relax operation before you use MeshSmooth is highly recommended—it leaves a very clear picture of what the precise relax results are and where the MeshSmooth modifier is required.

Relax can also be used with patch models without converting them into mesh objects (as many other modifiers, including MeshSmooth, will do).

MeshSmooth

If the Relax modifier is a dream tool, the MeshSmooth modifier is beyond dreams for the character modeler.

MeshSmooth combines a Relax control with a modifier that creates the geometry necessary to make a completely organic mesh from even the most hard-edged objects. This is an amazingly powerful feature.

By using a MeshSmooth modifier, you can model organic characters by starting with extremely simple figures, as shown in figure 8.2. Such simple features can provide clarity, proportion, and ease of manipulation. You can then move on to organic forms as a final step, without being bogged down with dense geometry during the initial creation process. In addition, MeshSmooth works on sub-objects (faces) with just as much accuracy, making it simple to add detail with sub-object tools and then smooth that detail into organic features at any point in the modeling process.

MeshSmooth should definitely be a major part of your character mesh-modeling process.

Free-Form Deformation

Free-form Deformation builds a simple lattice cage around an object or any selected group of sub-objects. By pushing and pulling the control points of the lattice, you can gently mold mesh surfaces into curved forms without the harshness of manipulating the sub-objects directly.

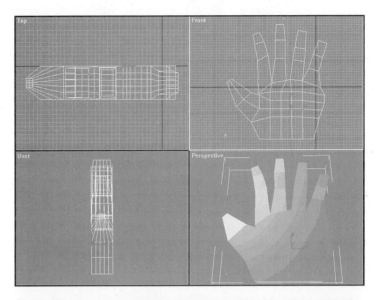

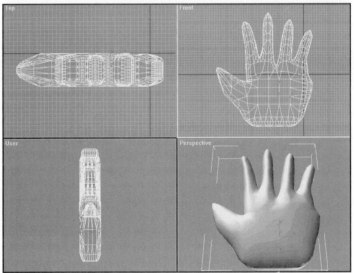

Free-form Deformation proves especially useful for adding finesse to a model. If you are creating a face, for example, it is fairly easy to select the polygons you want to make up the nose and extrude them from the face itself. By adding a Free-form Deformation modifier to the nose polygons, you can create a nose that would make a plastic surgeon proud. Certain tasks are very difficult to perform with simple sub-object tools, especially if you want to keep the modifications rounded and organic. These difficult tasks include adding the correct curvature on the tip of the nose, making the tip a bit back-tilted to give the illusion of snootiness, and stretching the nostrils to make them bulbous. With Free-form Deformation, however, the process becomes more like sculpting clay than dealing with stiff and unforgiving polygons.

In addition, Free-form Deformation serves as a wonderful alternative to modifying patch models with the vertices of the patch itself—all this without converting the model to polygons.

As a general rule, look to Free-form Deformation whenever you need to pull detail from the surface of a model or add a curve to the existing polygon surface.

Seamless Versus Segmented Modeling

In the not-too-distant past, seamless versus segmented modeling was not an issue. At first, if you were not using a high-end 3D package, you had little choice but to animate a segmented model and hide the seams as best you could. After skeletal deformation became an option for 3D Studio users, an animated segmented model looked clunky in comparison to the smooth-skinned animated models. Segmented models were almost abandoned in most circles. With the advent of real-time 3D, however, interest in creating effective segmented models has revived. (See Chapter 3, "Modeling for Real-Time 3D Games," for more about real-time 3D.)

Modeling segmented characters is not drastically different from creating seamless meshes. When you begin a model, you should know whether it will be animated with a skeletal deformation system (Character Studio or Bones Pro) or by rotating the various parts of the body itself. The method of animation and the amount of detail needed in the animation will determine whether the mesh can be created with patches or polygons alone. If you are creating a character that uses detailed facial expression (or is lip-synched with prerecorded speech), you probably want to use patches to get the smoothest animation from the finite details of the face without having to worry about hard polygonal lines appearing in the face during the animation. If you are creating a model that uses only bodily animation, even if you are creating tummy-wobbles or muscle bulges, it probably is in your best interest to use polygons because they are easier to control on a large scale (especially with skeletal animation systems) and have many more tools available for the mesh-modeling process than patches (at this time).

If you are dealing with patches, and especially if you are using Surface Tools, it is best to create the model in as few pieces as possible so that they can be easily "stitched" together.

If you are working in polygons that will later be joined (through Boolean operations and smoothing), try to create the largest segments possible. If you are creating a humanoid character, for example, create the arm in one piece (if possible) instead of creating a separate lower and upper arm. This will enable you to perform fewer joining operations, resulting in fewer areas to smooth over (a process that can be time-consuming). If you create half the body—welding only the arm, leg, and neck—and then mirror the model after the smoothing is completed, you save yourself six operations and realize an exact symmetry.

If you are working on a model to be animated by using the model's segments, the requirements of the animation determine the size of the segments. You should never, however, have multiple segments between the joints themselves.

Using Plug-Ins for Character Modeling

Three types of character-modeling plug-ins are:

- Patch modelers
- Metaballs modelers
- Skeletal systems

The only existing modeling paradigm not currently supported under MAX is the use of NURBS to model characters. It is highly probable, however, that this omission will be well-addressed in the near future. This section discusses the currently supported systems only.

Skeletal systems, although widely known for their animation capabilities, also have unique modeling properties. When used with a little foresight and cleverness, they can create quite stunning and unique effects.

Patch Modeling

As this book was being written, Surface Tools was the only plug-in available that aids in modeling with patches (discussed in great detail in the preceding chapter). Because patch modeling in general is very new to previous 3D

Studio users, however, and because patches are tremendously powerful tools for character creation and animation, other plug-ins are almost certain to surface in the not-so-distant future.

With that in mind, it is worth taking another brief foray into modeling with the Surface Tools plug-in. This discussion of Surface Tools is limited to examining a slightly different technique more applicable to creating animated cartoonesque characters than to the creation of realistic characters.

The following exercise does not detail the various supporting plug-ins that have been created for Surface Tools. It does, however, show a fast and effective procedure for modeling. For in-depth descriptions of the Surface Tools plug-ins, refer to Chapter 7, "Character Modeling with Patch Tools." For a technical look at the parameters of patches in general, refer to *Inside 3D Studio MAX Volume I*.

With plug-ins, you are never limited by one technique. You are limited only by your creativity and knowledge of the tools at hand.

NOTE

To perform the following exercise, you must have the Surface Tools plug-in installed. No other supporting plug-ins are required. The Edit Spline 2 and Edge-to-Spline plug-ins will be very useful, however, and are referred to in the exercise.

CREATING A CARTOON HEAD WITH SURFACE TOOLS

Because this is a cartoon character, exact precision to the line is less critical than the look and feel of the character in 3D space. Instead of tracing a sketch that has been loaded into a MAX background, therefore, you will just refer often to the sketch. This gives you the freedom to mold and sculpt the character—when you see the character actually realized in 3D space—as you see fit.

1. Go to the Create panel and click on Splines. Select the NGon object type and, in the Parameters rollout, set Sides to 12 and turn on Circular. In the Front viewport, create an n-gon.

2. Go to the Modify panel, and click on Edit Spline (or Edit Spline 2 if you have it installed). Click on the Sub-Objects button, and choose Spline from the drop-down menu.

3. Select the spline in the Left viewport. Hold down the Shift key and clone the spline by moving a new copy a little to the left of the original spline. The new spline will serve as the mouth of the character.

4. Choose the Uniform Scale transform from the top toolbar, and scale the original spline down very small so that it is only barely recognizable as a circle. This will be the back of the characters mouth, visible only when the character opens wide.

5. Select the new spline and perform another clone by holding down the Shift key and moving the copy to the right this time at a position roughly half-way between the back of the mouth and the mouth splines. Scale this spline a little bigger than the mouth so that it is easily visible and distinguishable from the mouth spline in the Front viewport.

6. Perform the clone operation six more times, moving the new copy to the right each time to a position easy to see (and select) from the Left viewport. Scale the new shape so that it is easily visible and selectable from the Front viewport. Scale the first two clones up and the last four down, so that the splines form a roughly ellipsoidal shape when seen from the Left viewport (see fig. 8.3).

FIGURE 8.3

The final spline objects before adding the Cross-section modifier.

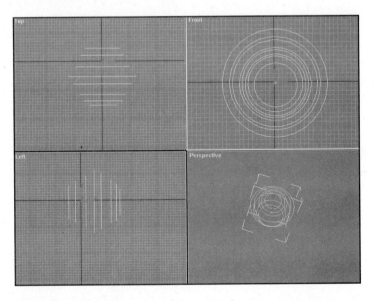

7. After all the splines are in place, deselect all the spline sub-objects and select the Cross-section modifier. Choose Bézier as the Spline Option parameter. This creates splines that turn our spline cross-sections into a single-piece 3D spline model.

8. Apply the Surface modifier to the cross-sectioned object. Make certain that none of the spline options are checked and that Threshold is set to 1.0. You should now have a smooth shape that looks similar to a vase tipped on its side (see fig. 8.4).

FIGURE 8.4

The surfaced spline object.

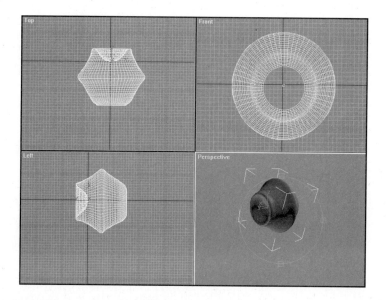

9. Go to the Modifier Stack rollout and click on the arrow to the right of the stack display window to drop-down the stack list. Click on the Cross-Section modifier to make it active. Then immediately click on the Edit Spline (or Edit Spline 2) button, adding a second spline editing operation. This enables you to use the splines created by the Cross-Section modifier. By clicking on the Show End Result toggle button, you can immediately see whether an operation has produced the desired results.

NOTE

If the Edit Spline modifier is grayed out after dropping down the modifier stack, go down one more level to the first Edit Spline and then back to the Cross-Section modifier. This re-identifies the object to MAX as a spline object.

10. You can now begin sculpting the shape of the character's head. Start by selecting the vertices on what should be the upper lip, pressing the spacebar to lock down the selection set. Move them forward, effectively "folding" the lip into place and then rotate this set into an alignment

more representative of the angle of the lip. Repeat this procedure with the vertices that should comprise the lower lip (see fig. 8.5).

FIGURE 8.5

The model with lips in place.

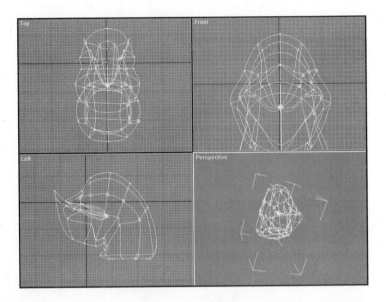

11. Now you will create the character's neck (which can later be "stitched" onto a spline body) by moving the last two splines you created. Select these splines with the Spline sub-object, move them down below the main part of the head, and then rotate them 90° (clockwise, in the Left viewport) from their original position.

12. Now you can begin to fully flesh out the character by pushing and pulling individual vertices, as though you were molding the character with clay. Continue sculpting until you have a three-dimensional representation of the spirit of the character in the sketch.

13. Now create the horns. Create a five-sided circular n-gon and move it close to the position where it will sit on the head. After the original spline is in position, you perform the same edit spline/clone procedure you used for the head. This time, however, you will create only three copies, each new copy scaling down to a tapered point for the horn. The copies should be rotated as shown in figure 8.6.

FIGURE 8.6
*The position of the
horn splines.*

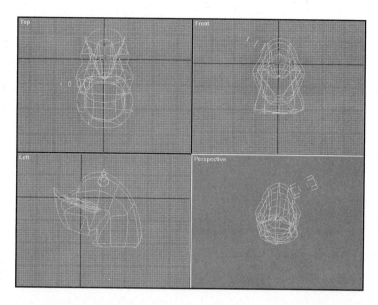

14. Add the Cross-Section modifier to the horn splines, and then add another Edit Spline modifier. Scale the vertices on the last horn spline down to a single point. Perform a Mirror transform on the horn, and make a copy of the object on the other side of the head. The copy will not be used in construction, but as a visual reference of what the result will be.

NOTE

MAX might ask if you want to weld co-incident endpoints when scaling a cross-sectioned model, or when moving vertices closer to other vertices, such as in the horn. This is because MAX does not currently support branching splines (splines that have more than one line passing through a single vertex). Surface Tools creates the illusion of branching splines by moving the vertices of non-branching splines virtually on top of the coinciding vertices of other non branching splines. Often, welding co-incident endpoints results in collapsing the "virtual" branching spline into a single spline, making it impossible for Surface Tools to add a patch to an area of the spline model. If you choose to weld co-incident end-points, immediately push the "display end-result" button in the Modifier Stack panel to ensure that no surface patches have been eliminated. If they have, undo the weld, then continue with the next step in creating your model.

15. Select the main Head object. In its modifier stack, go back to the last Edit Spline modifier, and make it active. Deactivate the Sub-Object button. Click on the Attach button in the Main panel, and select the horn on the left side of the head (as seen from the front).

At this point, you are going to attach the head and horn spline objects by "stitching" them together. If you have the Edit Spline 2 modifier, this is a fairly easy procedure. Be certain to set up your snap settings so that Vertex Snap receives first priority and all other geometry is turned off (see fig. 8.7). Set the snap strength to 20 and click on the 3D radio button.

NOTE

The Edit Spline 2 modifier is more helpful when using Surface Tools than the original Edit Spline modifier because it enables you to see the vertices of the spline object at all times in all the other sub-object modes.

FIGURE 8.7

The Snap Settings for the attachment procedure.

16. Now click on the Create Line button. Click on any of the vertices at the base of the horn, draw a line to the nearest corresponding vertex on the head, and click again. Finish the operation with a right-click. Continue the procedure until all the vertices at the base of the horn are stitched to the head. You most likely will have to rotate the view around the head to see clearly where to align the vertices on the horn side. Click on the Show end result toggle in the Modifier Stack panel to make certain that the process hasn't created any holes in the final surfaced model. If they have, try welding the new vertex groups (where the horn lines have been attached to the head) by selecting two corresponding vertices only and using a low weld threshold setting. Often this immediately solves the problem.

17. You are now ready for the final steps to complete the head. In the Modifier Stack, go to the Surface modifier and delete it. This reduces the head to a spline cage only. In the Edit Spline modifier (which should be at the top of the stack now), go to the segment Sub-Object level. Select all the segments on the side of the head opposite the one to which you just attached the horn. Delete these segments, leaving only half the head. Look carefully at the object and adjust any vertices that look out of place or that are not what you expected.

18. Deselect the Sub-Object button and mirror the head, creating a copy that lines up exactly with this half. Back in the Edit Spline modifier, click on the Attach button and select the unselected half. Apply a Surface modifier to the newly attached halves.

19. Go back to the last Edit Spline modifier, and then go the vertex Sub-Object level and select all the vertices down the middle of the object. Then deselect the small circle of vertices that make up the back of the throat. Weld the selected vertices at a low threshold (1.0 should do), and then press the Show End Result toggle button to check whether welding has created any holes. If any seams appear in the model, select the vertices along the seam and reweld them at a slightly higher threshold, repeating the process until the seam disappears. The final model should look something like figure 8.8.

FIGURE 8.8

The final rendering of the devil head.

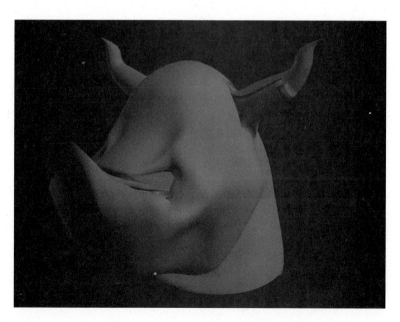

Metaballs Modeling

To create polygonal models, metaball modelers first create reference spheres. Each reference sphere is surrounded by a field that either attracts (positive) or repels (negative) other metaball geometry. This field also has a finite distance and a fall-off of intensity as the distance from the center of the sphere increases.

When two metaballs with attraction fields are placed close together, they suck together like drops of water in outer space. The closer together they are the more they are sucked into each other. When two metaballs with repelling fields are placed close together, they will not generate any surface. If a metaball with a repelling field is pushed *near* a sphere with an attraction field, the attracting sphere will generate a surface resembling a sphere with a dent in it. If a metaball with a repelling field is pushed *into* a sphere with an attraction field, the attracting sphere is split into two kidney shapes around the repelling field of the first sphere. This effect can only be seen when an *isosurface* (a mesh object that is generated based on these fields and the position of the metaballs) is created. Metaballs, however, can be animated in this stage to create convincing fluid effects, leaving the isosurface to be generated during the rendering process.

When several metaballs of varying positive and negative fields are grouped together, they result in an extremely smoothly curved surface. This technique is especially useful for creating characters because the modeler can use it to build rolling surfaces with great amounts of organic detail for muscle tone or facial features.

As with almost all plug-in technologies that were used with 3D Studio, metaballs modeling has taken a massive leap forward with its integration into MAX. This leap comes in the form of Metareyes 3.0 from InfoGrafica, a major developer of MAX plug-ins.

The latest paradigm leap involves not just metaballs, but *meta-muscles*— chains of metaballs along a spline curve that create a sausage-like surface. What once took several metaballs to create can now be done with a single meta-muscle. In addition, meta-muscles can be used in conjunction with other meta-muscles of varying positive and negative field intensities in the same ways that single metaballs could be used before. This paradigm creates a massive increase in the detail that can be achieved with metaballs modeling and a tremendous reduction in the amount of time necessary to complete a detailed model.

As if this weren't enough, meta-muscles come in two varieties: static and dynamic. Actually, all meta-muscles have dynamic properties, namely, contraction and oscillation levels, as well as some inertia control. This discussion so far has dealt with static metaballs modeling to create a mesh surface. Dynamic meta-muscles are created initially as sort of barbell shapes—two metaballs connected by a single straight spline. This shape is then generated into an object that bulges between the two initial spheres, like a biceps muscle, changing its thickness in reaction to the animation. The end spheres can now be linked to parent objects (most likely bones), and the bulging area between the two initial spheres will expand and contract almost exactly as a real muscle reacts to movement. This muscle also has a definable inertia level that will control how much the muscle wobbles in reaction to the movement of the parent objects. At long last, creating and animating jello arms is now possible!

This section, however, does not deal with dynamic meta-muscles (because they depend on animation). Instead, this section focuses on creating detailed organic surfaces from static meta-muscles. Note, however, that the modeling process of both dynamic and static meta-muscles is almost identical, with minor exceptions (such as the linking of the dynamic reference spheres).

For the following exercise, you must have Metareyes 3.0. If you have another metaballs modeler available, you can achieve similar results, but the meta-muscle structure is unique to Metareyes 3.0.

For reference material, any number of "Anatomy for the Artist" books contain excellent visual diagrams of muscles. In addition, any weight-lifting magazine has excellent pictures of arm structure and detail from many different viewpoints. Because this is a super-hero arm, you need to take liberties and use your imagination as you embellish the model.

CREATING A META-MUSCLE SUPER-HERO ARM

1. Go to the Create panel, click on the Systems tab, and click on the Bones button. Create a bone in the Front viewport, starting at the top of the viewport and dragging toward the bottom. Select the entire bone by drawing a rectangular fence around it. Hold down the Shift key and clone the bone by moving it directly beneath the first bone. Link the bottom bone to the topmost bone (bone01, unless you have chosen different names). Freeze both of these objects; they will serve as templates to

ensure that the scale and proportion of the upper arm and lower arm are accurate and as the link that holds the model together for the generation of the fusion surface at the end of the exercise.

2. To begin the meta-muscle structure, go back to the Geometry tab in the Create panel and click on the Metareyes button. Make certain that the muscle type is static and the fusion type is soft positive. Over the top bone in the Front viewport, create one meta-muscle that consists of three spheres—smaller spheres at the ends with a slightly bigger sphere in the middle. This meta-muscle will serve as a blank fusion surface, covering the little areas not covered by the major muscles.

3. Clone the first meta-muscle and move it over the bottom bone. You should now have something resembling two sausage shapes (see fig. 8.9).

FIGURE 8.9

The two meta-muscle blanks.

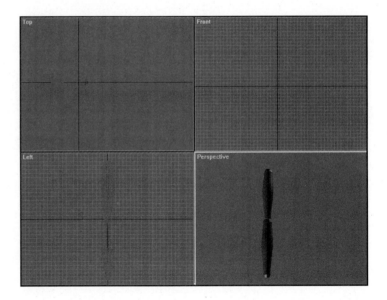

4. Now you can begin building the major muscle groups. Go back to the Create panel and click on the Metareyes button, leaving the muscle type as static. This time, however, change the fusion to medium hard positive (light green). The muscles will squish down less when you generate a fusion surface for the mesh, creating greater muscle definition. Begin by creating the deltoid (the shoulder cap). In the Left viewport, create a meta-muscle at the top of the arm, ending just above the halfway point of the upper arm. This meta-muscle should consist of two spheres—the first just

over twice the diameter of the arm blanks, and the last about half the diameter of the arm blank. This should result in a reverse pyramid shape (see fig. 8.10). In the Front viewport, move this object over to the right so that its left edge lines up closely with the left edge of the arm blank.

FIGURE 8.10

The deltoid shape.

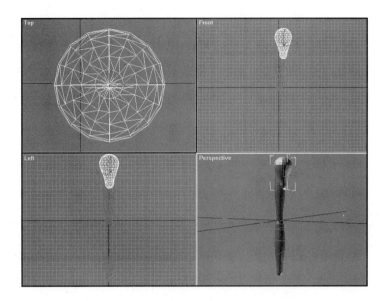

5. In the Left viewport, create the bicep by creating another three-sphere meta-muscle just to the right of the arm blank. This time, use a small sphere at the top of the arm (under the deltoid), a large sphere at about the middle of the arm—this is a super-hero's arm, don't be afraid to go for the big guns—and another small sphere at the base of the upper arm. The spline that links them together should curve out slightly from the arm blank.

6. For the triceps, select the biceps muscle in the Left viewport and make a mirror copy of it across the X axis, offsetting it about –30 units. In the Modify panel, choose Muscle Edit, click on the Sub-Object button, select Move, and move the middle and bottom muscles up (one at a time), aligning them just below the spaces between the spheres on the biceps muscle. The result should resemble figure 8.11. Scale down the middle sphere of the triceps to your liking, using the Muscle Edit modifier.

Now you can begin to create the major muscles of the forearm. You can also begin to see the advantage of meta-muscles over metaballs.

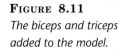

FIGURE 8.11

The biceps and triceps added to the model.

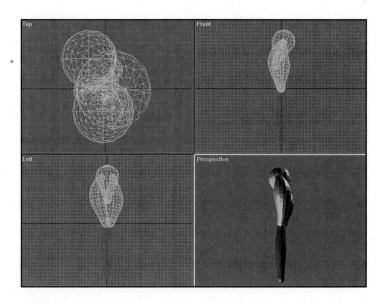

7. Create a four-sphere meta-muscle, starting at the base of the triceps with a small sphere, moving about one-third of the way down the lower arm, and creating a much larger sphere (which will be the major forearm muscle). Then move about another third of the way down, and create a slightly smaller sphere. Finally, at the base of the lower arm, create another small sphere (approximately the same size as the first sphere).

8. In the Modify panel, choose the Muscle Edit modifier. Click on the Sub-Object button and begin to move the lower three spheres of the last meta-muscle so that they wrap around the lower arm (see fig. 8.12). Make certain that the large sphere remains about halfway between the triceps and biceps muscles in the Left viewport, and only about a third of the way down the lower arm blank.

9. Now create the last muscle for the forearm—another three-sphere muscle, similar to the biceps but with a much smaller scale variation—along the side of the forearm opposite the major forearm muscle bulge.

10. The last thing you need to create is the elbow. Go into the Create panel and click on the Metareyes button. This time, switch the fusion to hard positive (light blue). Create a three-sphere meta-muscle, starting within the base of the triceps, close to the blank. The first muscle should be completely inside the triceps. Create the second muscle at the joint of the two blanks (scaled up a tiny bit), and create the third sphere inside the muscle at the back of the forearm, again—well inside and close to the

blank. Then create another single-sphere meta-muscle, just to the left of the muscle you last created. To finish it off and shape it more like an elbow, create two single-sphere meta-muscles with medium-hard negative fusion (emerald green) to the left and right of the elbow sphere. Move them just to the left of the elbow sphere in the Left viewport. You should end up with a complete mesh that resembles figure 8.13.

FIGURE 8.12
The arm with two forearm muscles added.

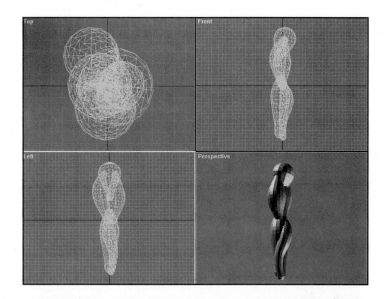

FIGURE 8.13
The finished meta-muscles.

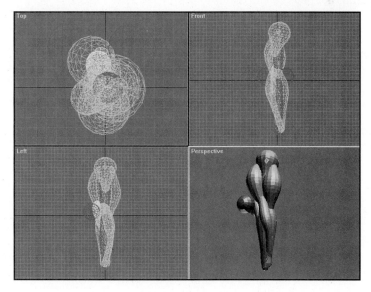

If you are not quite satisfied with the overall shape and placement of the muscles, now is the time to adjust them—before you generate the final surface. You have already seen how the Muscle Edit modifier works. To move, rotate, or otherwise transform entire meta-muscles, however, you must disable the dynamic properties of the muscle being worked on; otherwise the transform operation may not work at all, or may have results that affect the other meta-muscles in ways you did not intend. Remember that all meta-muscles have dynamic attributes, such as inertia levels, contraction, and oscillation, which react to animation. The specifics of these functions are beyond the scope of this discussion; they apply only when you are animating a meta-muscle model, not when you're modeling.

If you need to move, rotate, or scale an entire meta-muscle, go to the Utilities panel and select Metareyes from the drop-down menu. Select the specific muscle(s) on which you want to perform gross adjustments, go to the Tools rollout of the Metareyes panel (see fig. 8.14), and click on the button labeled Selected Din. No. This sets the dynamic status of the muscle to off and enables you to transform the selected muscles. After you complete the transform(s), go back to the Metareyes Utilities panel, select the adjusted meta-muscles, and click on the Selected Din. Yes button. This reactivates the dynamic status of the meta-muscles before you generate the fusion surface.

FIGURE 8.14

The Metareyes Utility
Tools panel.

Metareyes has very advanced features for generating a fusion surface for a complex model, such as an entire humanoid. The way in which these surfaces are generated depends on the hierarchy and grouping set up in the Metareyes utilities. For the purposes here, the arm, which belongs to one hierarchical chain, should be fused as one group, and the elbow as a separate group that shares only the elbow "muscle" as a common element. If you were working on a more complex chain, however, you could use the option of creating more groups based on the sub-hierarchies you have built into the model. Note, however, that although meta-muscles can be linked to each other, the fusion works much better when they are linked to separate objects such as bones or dummy objects.

11. Now you can generate the final fusion surface for the forearm. Unfreeze the bones and link all the meta-muscles to the top of the bone hierarchy. In the Utilities panel, choose Metareyes from the drop-down menu.

12. In the Metareyes Utilities panel, press the Select Model button, and select a meta-muscle (any one of them); they should all be selected now, if they have been properly linked to the bone chain.

13. In the dialog under the Make Groups panel, enter the name **arm**, and then select all the meta-muscles in the arm except the two negative spheres at the elbow and the elbow sphere itself. Press the Make Group button.

14. Now select the elbow muscle, the elbow sphere, and the two negative spheres. Enter the name **elbow** in the Groups dialog, and press the Make Group button.

   Your model should now have two fusion groups: the main muscles of the arm that will not be affected by the negative spheres; and the elbow group in which the negative spheres will interact to shape the elbow sphere and elbow muscle, with the common fusing muscle of both groups being the elbow muscle. This is a major advantage over standard metaballs modeling. With standard metaballs, all metaballs act on all other metaballs, without the capability to choose which groups are not affected by other groups, and still have them fuse together into a single mesh object.

   At this point, the model is technically complete. You could animate the bones you have created and the mesh object would appear in the rendering. If you want to create a mesh object that can be used with other mesh surfaces, and that you can see the final result of before rendering, however, you need to generate the mesh from the Metareyes Utilities panel.

15. In the Mesh Generation dialog, enter the name **arm** again, and then click on the Mesh Generation button. This produces the final fusion surface of the model (see fig. 8.15).

FIGURE 8.15
The final mesh arm.

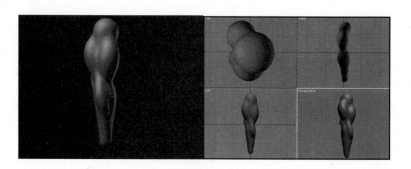

You could go on to add quite a bit of detail, creating very small muscle groups that would render as veins bulging on the surface of the arm, for example, or recreating some of the larger muscles (such as the deltoid) with smaller muscle segments, to add striation for an even more buffed look. The only limit is time and imagination.

Modeling with Skeletal Systems (Bones Pro MAX)

Although skeletal deformation systems are known primarily for their capability to animate seamless meshes for lifelike results, certain systems have tools that enable you to use them for modeling as well. Bones Pro MAX is one such system that provides tools for amazing results, especially when you're detailing a model.

You begin the process by creating a basic model (in this case, a head). Then you apply a specific set of bones to produce cosmetic results, bumps, or crevices in the mesh. In this way, the process closely resembles that of sculpting prosthetic makeup features on an actor. The same results can be achieved by using Displace modifiers or space warps. With Bones, however, you do not have to create the various sub-object selection sets necessary to creating the effects with displacement. With Bones, you also have an active visual tool that enables you to make modifications interactively, without having to adjust an external bitmap. The next exercise demonstrates this process by turning an average-looking head into a humanoid alien similar to those seen in many popular television shows.

You must have Bones Pro MAX installed for the next exercise.

DETAILING A HEAD WITH BONES PRO MAX

1. Open the file named Bonehead.max on the accompanying CD. This is a basic no-frills humanoid head mesh, which has been frozen for the first part of the exercise. This is the basic model to which you will add alien features. Select the head mesh and freeze it.

   The first bones you create will be the active detail bones. When you have an entire set of them, you will link them to a common object and then create the retaining bones—the bones that will hold the mesh in place while you use the detail bones to modify the face.

2. In the Create panel, select the Systems tab. Click on the Bones button. On the left half of the model, create three bone segments, which will actually be four bones, starting at the center and dragging to the left (see fig. 8.16).

FIGURE 8.16

The position of the first bone chain.

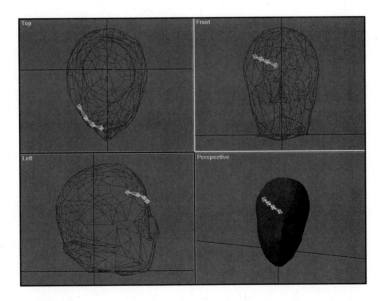

3. Clone this bone set three more times by rotating around the parent bone—two above the current set and one below. Do this by setting the transform center to the parent bone, holding down the Shift key, and rotating about the Y axis. This will be half the bone set for the forehead details.

4. Now create some bone for the nose detail. Create one bone, angle it so that it lines up with the nose, and align it on the nose bridge. Then hold down the Shift key and clone the bone by moving it down. Do this two times, until the entire bone set looks like that shown in figure 8.17.

FIGURE 8.17
The facial bone set.

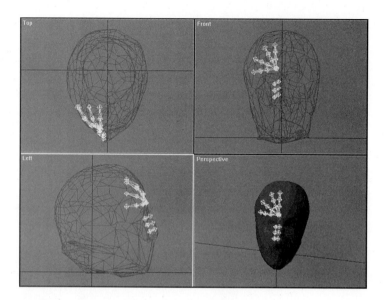

5. The last cosmetic bones you need to add are those for the cranial bumps. To do this, create a single bone, drawing from the bottom to the top, approximately the same length as the nose bones. Clone this bone five times to get a good dispersal of cranial bumps across the top of the skull.

6. Now select all the facial bones (all the bones except the ones created in the last step), and perform a mirror copy operation in the Front viewport to create symmetrical detail on the other side of the face. Offset the new bones about 2.8 units.

7. Select all the bones, and create a named selection set for these bones called **Cosmetic Bones**, in the Named Selection Set box in the top toolbar.

8. On the Hierarchy panel, with all the bones still selected, click on the Affect Pivot Only button in the Move/Rotate/Scale sub-panel, and click on the Align to World button in the Alignment sub-panel. Now freeze all the selected bones.

    Now you need to create the retaining bones that hold the geometry you don't want to modify.

9. Find the original forehead detail bones (the first set created), unfreeze them, hold down the Shift key, and move and clone these bones up in a space unoccupied by the cosmetic bones. Copy these bones in the same way that the cosmetic bones were created. These will be used to create negative or "retaining bones," for areas where the mesh should not change shape drastically.

10. Continue the copying operation by creating bone copies that go between all the original bones on the nose and on the cranium, unfreezing the desired sets of frozen cosmetic bones as needed. When you have finished, create the mirror copies of these bones as well. Name these bones **Negative Bones** in the Selection Set box, and realign their pivots with the world in the IK panel (just as you did with the cosmetic bones). Freeze this set also.

11. The last bones you need to create are the retaining bones at the sides of the head and the base of the cranium (at the back). Because simple large bones will do for this, create one bone at each side of the head (going bottom to top) and one lateral bone at the back of the head, below the last cranial ridge bone. Name this set **Retaining Bones**. Reset their pivots, and freeze them as well. You should now have something resembling the setup shown in figure 8.18.

FIGURE 8.18

The final bones setup.

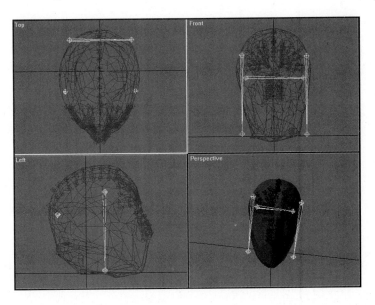

12. Unfreeze the head and all the bone sets. Then, on the Utilities panel, choose the Skeleton utility from the drop-down menu.

13. Select each of the named sets, starting with the Cosmetic Bones set. Click on the Generate Boxes button. In the dialog, enter **cos** in the Name prefix slot (see fig. 8.19). Leave the default Box width setting as it is. Repeat the procedure for the Negative Bone set (with the prefix **neg**) and the Retaining Bones set (with the prefix **ret**). Set the Box width of the retaining bones to 0.75.

FIGURE 8.19

The setup for generating the cosmetic bones.

14. Delete all the original Bones objects, and go to the Create panel. Select the Space Warps tab. Create the Bones warp icon, somewhere easy to select from the head. Bind the head to the space-warp by clicking on the Bind to Space Warp button in the top toolbar, clicking on the head and holding, and dragging over to the Bones Pro space warp icon you just created.

15. Select the Bones space-warp. Then, in the Modify panel's Bound Node sub-panel, click on the None button. Choose the head from the pop-up list.

16. In the Bones sub-panel, click on the Assign button and choose all the Bones objects (with the prefixes cos, neg, and ret).

17. In the main selection toolbar (on the top of the screen), click on Select by Name and select all the cos objects. Then click on the Animate button and advance to frame 1.

18. With the coordinate system set to local, and all the cos objects still selected, uniform scale all the objects until you can see large protrusions from the head object (see fig. 8.20).

19. Click on the Bones space-warp, and go back to the Modify panel. Click on the Influence Editor button. You should see all the Bones objects. Click on the Select bones from list button, and select all the cos objects. Then click on the Exclude unlinked bones from selected bones button.

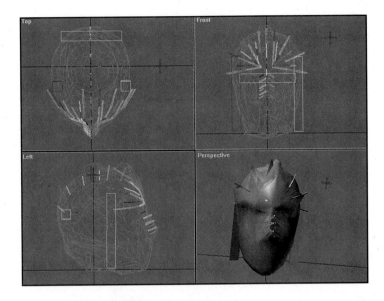

20. Click on the Invert bones' selection button in the Influence Editor, selecting all the neg and ret bones. Click on the Exclude unlinked from selected bones button. This ensures that the areas you don't want to move will not move.

21. Now close the Influence Editor, and begin to move the cosmetic bones around to make the model suit your taste. All aliens are different—feel free to customize this one a bit.

22. When you have completed your adjustments of the cosmetic bones, click on the Utilities panel, and find the Snapshot Plus utility.

23. Select the head mesh, and click on the Snapshot button. Make certain that your snapshot settings are for only one copy (see fig. 8.21).

24. Select everything except the new head mesh, and hide those pieces.

25. To finish, perform a MeshSmooth modifier operation on the new head, adjusting the settings until the model looks like a nice organic humanoid (see fig. 8.22).

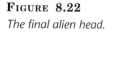

FIGURE 8.22

The final alien head.

With this process, you can perform multiple iterations on your snapshot models, stacking various levels of detail on top of previous details (again, very similar to adding prosthetic makeup to a character).

Using 3D Paint to Map a Model

3D paint packages are a relatively new invention in the world of 3D graphics, and even newer to the PC. These packages can be quite a benefit to texture mapping, especially if you are familiar with certain techniques used to paint traditional (plastic, polyvinyl, or resin) models.

3D paint packages do, however, have limitations. It is very difficult to create intricately detailed bitmaps of repeat minute detail (such as lizard skin or scratched metal). In principle, if you have an overall complex map that must be present on the model, create it in a traditional paint package (such as Photoshop), apply it to the model, and use the 3D paint package to add the details on top of the map.

Currently, three 3D paint packages are available, two of which support exported 3DS files, and one that works as a seamless plug-in with MAX.

The two packages that support exported 3DS files are Fractal Design's Detailer and 3D Paint.

Detailer has some excellent features, one of the best being its very affordable price. You have access to most of the natural media tools available in Fractal Design's Painter, including the *image hose* (a paint device that enables you to "pump" an image onto a selected area of a mesh). The only drawbacks to this program are its speed (quite slow, even on a very fast machine) and the fact that you have to convert any patch or meta-objects to mesh, export them through the 3DS format, and reimport them. Therefore, if you are creating anything besides a diffuse color map (opacity, specular, self-illumination), you will also have to reimport it into the objects material when you reload the mesh.

3D Paint has been the only 3D paint program available to 3D Studio users since 3D Paint became available on the PC. The new NT version is a good stand-alone product that, although it still suffers from the 3DS export problems mentioned earlier, is fairly fast and reliable.

The last package, and the only package that functions as a MAX plug-in, is 4D Paint. In addition to its capability to keep patch models as patches while painting, 4D Paint reads the MAX material in its entirety, and automatically creates layers for opacity, bump maps, self illumination, you name it—a feature that is not available in the other packages. The only MAX material function that 4D Paint does not currently support is sub-object materials.

Granted, you are definitely going to pay for this functionality (the current cost of 4D Paint is almost twice that of its closest competitor), but you are going to get quite a bit for your money.

The following exercise offers a brief foray into 3D painting, using 4D Paint.

You must have 4D Paint to do the following exercise. You may be able to achieve similar results with another 3D paint package, but the process and specific steps will vary.

Using 4D Paint to Texture-Map a Head

1. Open the file named Bonehead02.max on the accompanying CD. This file requires Edit Mesh 2 load correctly. This is the head mesh created in the last exercise, separated into two objects: the back of the head and the face. The face already has a texture applied to it—a grassy green alien skin, complete with a bump map (see fig. 8.23). Shrink-wrap mapping also has been applied to this mesh.

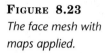

FIGURE 8.23

The face mesh with maps applied.

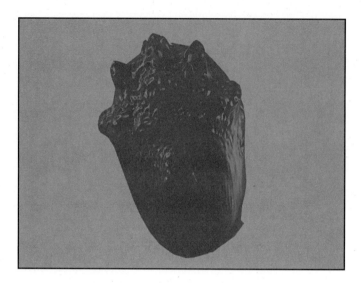

2. Select the Face object. Then on the Utilities panel, choose the 4D Paint utility from the drop-down menu. Click on the Paint! button; 4D Paint will start up and automatically load the maps that comprise the face material.

3. Click on the Layers Window button in the bottom-right corner of the 4D Paint window. Select Color Map from the tabs on the pop-up display. You will see a queue of color entries, including Color Base Layer and Renderer Layer. Click on the New button and create a new color layer, which will go into place at the top of the stack (see fig. 8.24). This is the layer you will modify, so as not to modify your original bitmap texture.

   To take full advantage of the capabilities of a 3D paint package and what it can do for a character, start by adding some subtle shadows and highlights to the face (like putting makeup on an actor). Then you will customize your lizard-skinned alien by adding stripe details and spots to make it look a little more tribal and unique.

4. Click on the Brush Tool button in the upper-right tool panel, and then click on the Brush drop-down list and highlight Default Brush. Right-click on the highlighted name, and the Edit options will appear. Choose Edit Brush. In the Brush Settings dialog, click on the General tab, and rename the brush **Shadow**, leaving the rest of the settings at their default levels. Click on the Brush Head tab, and create a long thin brush with a high fall-off that matches the settings in figure 8.25. When you finish, close the Brush Editor and say Yes to create a new brush.

The Color Layer dialog in 4D Paint.

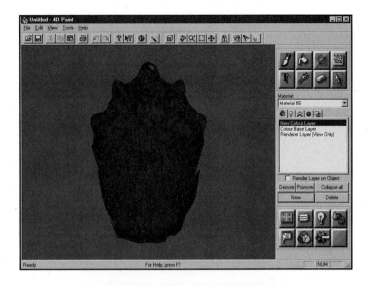

FIGURE 8.25
The Brush Settings for the first brush.

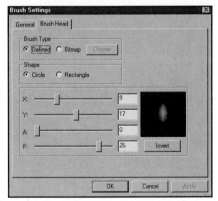

5. Click on the Color Picker button from the bottom-right panel, and select the Fore box. Create a darkish brown color that is about 50 percent transparent. This will be your shadow color. Minimize the Color Picker; you will use it quite a bit in this exercise.

6. Leave the paint choice at default for the moment, and begin painting in some shadows. These shadows should be subtle; they are more like makeup than a bump map or modeled detail. Punch in shadows around the forehead bones, under the chin and brow ridges, and even around the muzzle. Remember that Undo is available, and you can paint with a free hand. If something is not to your liking, you can undo it immediately, or go through a series of Undo operations, or use the eraser in the upper-right Tool panel to erase just a portion. Indulge yourself, but keep it subtle (see fig. 8.26).

FIGURE 8.26

The final shadow-painted face.

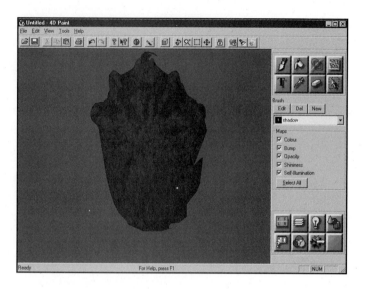

7. Now add some highlights. Go back and create a new color layer in the Layer Editor. Edit your brush so that it is only five pixels wide (X setting). This time, however, instead of using the default paint, go to the Paint drop-down list and choose Drybrush. With Drybrush selected, right-click on the Paint drop-down list and choose Edit Paint for the Editor menu. Set the Drybrush Paint settings to match those in figure 8.27. Rename this paint **Highlight**, and save it.

One of the great features in almost all 3D paint packages is the variety of paints available for creating different effects. 4D Paint, in keeping with the concepts used by plastic kit modelers, includes several unique paints whose effects vary according to information from the different maps that make up the material on an object. Drybrushing looks at the level of light in the bump map and applies more paint in areas that have a high luminosity value, creating a streaked, spotty, organic look that is excellent for subtle effects.

8. Open the color picker, lighten your paint to a medium amber color, and begin punching in the highlights. Again, the sky's the limit. Have fun but keep it subtle; that subtlety will pay off.

9. Now for the last bit of color detail. Create another color layer called **Stripes**. Add some war-paint type details in different colors (yellows and reds will probably work best on this green background) and with various brushes, using a default paint. You should end up with something resembling figure 8.28.

FIGURE 8.27
The Drybrush Paint Settings.

FIGURE 8.27
The Drybrush Paint Settings.

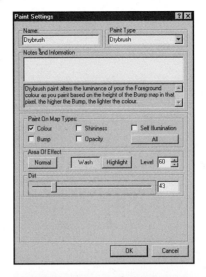

FIGURE 8.28
The final color maps.

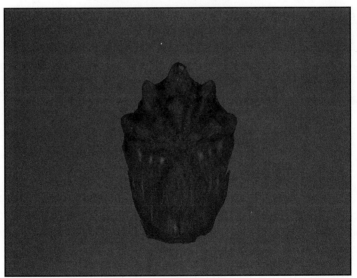

10. For the final bit of detail, go back to the Layers Window and create a new bump layer called **Added Bumps**. Finish the model by actively painting a bump map under the color layer. Create a 10-by-10 brush with no fall-off, name it **Added**, and save it. Click on the Paint drop-down list and select the Bump paint. With this option selected you will paint on the bump layers only, and will not add color variations to the diffuse maps. Open the Color Picker and slide the Bump Paint Slider all the way up. Create some raised detail dabs (these work very well under the

war-paint colors) and some long strokes, to add more detail to the bone forehead and all over the face. Finish by changing the bump paint to its lowest setting in the color-picker.

11. When you have completed the bump details, press the MAX Out button in the lower-right of the Tool panel. For the map export method, choose Generate New Bitmaps, enter **alien** as the prefix, and name the new files when 4D Paint asks you to. These new files will automatically replace the images you had as bump and diffuse maps in the Material Editor hot spot for the material applied to your character.

The final image should look something like that shown in figure 8.29. Compare this with the first alien image, figure 8.23. Notice how the subtle changes have made a drastic difference in creating the feeling of a living being.

FIGURE 8.29

The final texture mapped alien head.

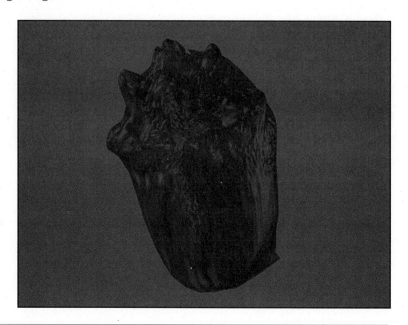

The technological leap in power and paradigm from 3D Studio release 4 to 3DS MAX has opened entire worlds of character power previously unavailable to the PC-based 3D artist and to plug-in developers. Plug-ins for MAX are becoming available at break-neck speed (including free, low-cost, and premier packages). The majority are either aimed directly at, or have tremendous benefit to, character creators. Keep you eyes and ears ever vigilant and your mind flexible. New techniques present themselves with every new addition to the ever-expanding power of MAX plug-ins.

In Practice: Character Modeling with Plug-Ins

- The object-oriented design of MAX makes plug-in integration seamless and easier to create.

- When creating a character model, start simple then add detail.

- Always have sketches, maquettes, or photographic references available when creating a character.

- Create the model in halves that can later be mirror-copied and tweaked to create a more natural asymmetry.

- One creation tool is never enough when building a character. Be very familiar with the Edit Mesh sub-object tools, Relax, MeshSmooth, and FFD modifiers.

- The process for creating seamless and segmented models is mostly identical. But you need to know how the model will be animated, how much detailed animation (such as facial expression) will be used, and if you need to use patches or polygons to suit the animation techniques and details.

- Plug-ins for character modeling currently extend from only three types of plug-ins: Patch modelers, Metaballs modelers, and Skeletal systems.

- Metaballs are reference spheres that have an attracting or repelling field around them, that are combined to create a very smooth, very organic "isosurface."

- Meta-muscles are a new paradigm in metaballs modeling that uses metaballs created along a spline path to construct sausage-like shapes that resemble muscles, and can be combined like metaballs to generate detailed isosurfaces that resemble musculature.

- Skeletal systems, such as Bones Pro Max, can be used in conjunction with a Snapshot tool to add organic detail to a model before animation.

- 3D paint packages are best used to detail general detail texture maps created in a 2D paint package, rather than creating entirely new surface textures from scratch.

Part IV

MATERIAL AND TEXTURE MAPPING

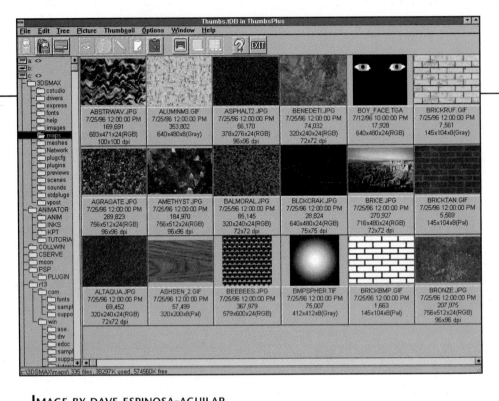

IMAGE BY DAVE ESPINOSA-AGUILAR

Chapter 9

by dave espinosa-aguilar

MATERIALS MANAGEMENT AND MANIPULATION

One of the more challenging aspects to becoming more productive and proficient with 3D Studio MAX is learning how to acquire, manage, manipulate, and align materials effectively. Very little information is available on the following: sources for material maps; how to organize a project's materials internally and externally so that they can easily be manipulated, referenced, imported into, or exported from any other project; how to manipulate complex materials within a scene; how to apply materials in an accurate and predictable manner onto any geometry;

and how to take advantage of materials previously generated in 3D Studio DOS R4. This chapter presents discussions on the following topics:

- Strategies for optimizing the design of materials

- Material acquisition

- Material alignment techniques

- Material management philosophies

- Material and bitmap navigation

- Importing material files from 3D Studio DOS

The Materials Lab

3DS MAX will never run faster on your machine than it does the moment you launch a new session. With no objects in your scene to calculate, every control, every dialog, and every viewport updates as fast as it ever will, unless you increase your system's resources. For this reason, many developers and designers of materials use fresh new sessions—*materials lab sessions* dedicated solely to constructing materials—to do their materials design, instead of trying to design within the scenes where the materials eventually will be used. Although there are numerous ways in 3DS MAX to disable the viewing of objects, to minimize the calculations of surfaces and speed up rendering times, nothing can compare to minimizing the size of your session. Put another way, MAX always runs faster working on nothing than it runs working on something.

Realistic scenes can get complicated very fast, and the use of many elaborate materials in a scene can get unwieldy if the materials are not designed and organized ahead of time. With the capability to save materials out to external files, it becomes practical to keep similar materials together in their own libraries, and to edit these materials separate from the scenes that will eventually use them. Another good reason for keeping your materials separate from scenes is that they can be used with any scene instead of being limited to the scene in which they were designed.

A materials lab also enables the designer to subject a material to a wide range of different geometries and lighting considerations without making any changes to the scene in which the material will eventually be used. Any object onto which a material will be applied can be imported individually into a fresh session. Its geometry can be varied to optimize the number of surfaces needed to accommodate the material being designed. Lights can be created from any angle to experiment with levels of brightness, shininess, and opacity in a material. Deformations and corruptions to the bitmaps themselves, used for the mapping channels, can be toyed with and applied for fast renders on objects. Changes in mapping models can also be experimented with. These things and more can all be done without affecting the final complicated scene. The perfected material can then be saved to a material category file, imported into complicated scenes, and applied to objects with a minimum of tweaking.

Following is a list of typical questions and concerns for any material being designed in a materials lab:

1. **Which essential bitmaps are needed for the material?**

   For the vast majority of man-made materials you will ever create, you need a bitmap (or series of bitmaps) of the actual material. Although paint packages can assist in creating helpful masks, patterns, and a variety of random imperfections for materials, realistic textures usually depend to a large degree on realistic images. You can acquire these images in numerous ways, not the least of which is to use a portable raster-image camera and literally take planar snapshots of the materials as they occur in the real world. The resolution of these bitmaps should vary with the level of detail in the material. Be certain that you have enough pixels to accommodate the smallest, narrowest features (such as a spider web). Keep in mind that the resolution and brightness of the bitmap itself has a profound impact on the appearance of the materials that use it.

2. What geometry will the material be applied to?

The number of surfaces an object has greatly determines the appearance of any material applied to it. If need be, import the object(s) from the complicated scenes that will use them so that their vertex counts can be optimized for the material to be applied. If further tessellation of faces is necessary to get a reasonable deformation or smoothness to the geometry, you can easily and quickly experiment with, and render values for, this process without any overhead from complicated scenes.

3. What lighting will the material receive, and from where?

The realism of a material is only as effective as the lighting it receives. Put another way, displayed in a room with no lighting, the most sophisticated material ever designed will appear black. It is recommended, therefore, that you create a "lighting studio" as part of your materials lab. In this way, you can design materials with whatever experimental lighting you need. Then you can see how materials hold up under any lighting conditions, without having to modify the existing lighting settings in the final scene and without having to render the final scene.

4. How far will the camera be from the objects with the material?

This is a crucial issue for any project. If an object is far enough away from the camera, with more complicated objects targeted in the foreground, the distant object may not require intense detail. It won't matter how much attention to detail you spend on an 8×4×4 inch brick if the brick is viewed from a mile away. By the same token, the closer you get to an object, the more important detail in a material becomes. If the resolution of the bitmaps used in a material is not high enough, pixels and "jaggies" may actually become visible as you near an object. Motion studies and storyboards can help tremendously with this phase of materials design. Have an idea ahead of time of where your camera will go and what it will target, before you start tweaking the objects and materials that will appear in front of it.

5. How long will the material actually be in view of the camera?

Trickiest of all is deciding how much attention to detail one should give, based on the amount of time an object will appear in front of the camera. Objects that are seen for only a few seconds, or are seen only as a blur for a second or two as a camera pans quickly past them, may not require intense detail. Make the time in front of your camera a consideration when you design these materials.

The considerations for creating impressive materials are certainly not limited to these five aspects of material design, but they do have a profound impact on anyone's productivity with 3DS MAX. One of the most common factors reducing MAX's productivity is ineffective time management with materials design.

No clear-cut formulae exist for this aspect of 3DS MAX. Every material you design must be based on the objects and scenes being created and the ways in which you decide to view them. For the most part, sweetspots are found through trial-and-error rendering, which is why having a dedicated materials lab session that optimizes editing refreshes and rendering-time calculations can be so helpful.

Materials Acquisition

This section treats sources for images that can be used to design materials, and how to use them to create seamless tileable materials. 3DS MAX comes with a large set of predefined default materials that can be used for production work or as examples of how to design your own materials. Where do the bitmaps for these materials come from, though? How were they edited to tile perfectly, and how can you acquire bitmaps of the same level of quality for specialized materials and create tileable materials from them?

The following sections discuss several examples of hardware and software in light of using them to acquire images for designing your own materials. Keep in mind that price of the solution should always be a consideration.

Scanners

For acquiring photorealistic colored or grayscaled images from old magazines, photographs, and practically anything you can roll a mouse over or set down on a glass surface, scanners can be well worth the investment if you plan to design many of your own materials. Depending on the types of images you work with, you may decide to look into hand-scanners, desktop scanners, or large-format scanners.

Key considerations in the purchase of any scanner include:

- What resolutions can the scanner provide (often referred to as the DPI or *dots per inch*)?

- At what color depths can it scan (monochrome, grayscale, 8-bit, TrueColor, and so on)?

- What file formats does it output, and are they compatible with your bitmap editing and conversion software?

- How large will the scanned images need to be?

- Does the scanner need to be portable or shared by other users?

- What kind of warranty does it come with? Is there local repair support for it if something breaks down?

- Are special drivers or software necessary to run it? Are the drivers and software compatible with the operating system and software you currently use?

- How much memory does the scanner require to accommodate the images and process them?

- How long has the scanner manufacturer been in business, and how often do they update their equipment and drivers? What is the typical longevity of their products and support for their products?

As an alternative to purchasing a scanner, you might want to use the scanning services available at many business office supply warehouses, copy/print houses, and reprographics and blueprinting companies. Such a service may be a far more economical way to get the raw bitmaps you need for your first few projects before you invest in your own equipment.

Preexisting Image Libraries

Many companies today provide CD-ROM libraries of textures and materials, complete with optimized browsers and well-thought-out material categories. Navigating these collections and dumping what you need into your mapping project directories is such a simple, fast process that you can get right to work. An example of such a library resource is Autodesk's own Texture Universe collection (see fig. 9.1). This kind of low-cost resource can be an incredible time-saver for people who need to integrate images with high-quality materials, photographic backgrounds, or complex texture maps into their productions. An obvious benefit of this type of a resource is that most of the materials have already been carefully edited to ensure that the bitmaps are perfectly seamless and, if necessary, tileable.

FIGURE 9.1

Texture Universe's Windows Browser utility—the Metals category offers a variety of instantly usable, seamless, and tileable metal TrueColor bitmaps.

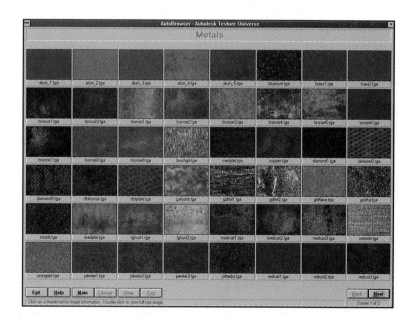

NOTE

A collection that keeps its file resources off your system, whose browser uses a minimum of RAM, and that restores memory after its browser is exited can make a tremendously positive impact on the performance of applications running in the background—such as 3DS MAX.

Key considerations in the purchase of any materials library collection include:

- What is your time worth? Compared to the time and money involved in creating equivalent materials, is the price of the collection reasonable?

- What file formats are used in the collection? Do they have a high enough resolution to be useful for your work?

- Have the images been edited to be seamless and tileable, if necessary?

- Does the collection come with an optimized browsing tool to help you navigate quickly through the collection?

- Are the materials well-organized, with names that make finding what you need easy?

- Does the collection require installation of its own software or drivers? If so, are they compatible with your software?

- Do you have the necessary system resources to accommodate the collection? Does it operate from the CD? Or do you have to spend hard drive space and precious RAM installing and running it while you work in 3DS MAX?

- What is the product support like for the product(s), and how often does the manufacturer update and maintain the library?

An astonishing number of 3D Studio DOS users have never examined either the full World Creating Toolkit that shipped with 3D Studio Release 4 or the full library of materials shipped with 3DS MAX. Also, many Animator Pro users are not aware that the latest version (1.3a) shipped with a CD packed with material images. Before you shop for new material collections, examine *every* material collection you have already purchased. Take the time to go through them all—it is time well-spent—and take notes, if necessary, to remind yourself later where to find what you need.

Paint Programs

Although the detail and believability of many materials depend on raw photorealistic images, the value of a painting program, and the capacity to manually design and edit material images, cannot be stressed enough.

Typical functions reserved for paint programs include the capability to change the level of brightness or darkness in an image; the capability to mirror an image and edit it to create a tileable version of the image; and the capability to change an image's color depth, resolution, gamma correction, colorization, and file format. Although 3DS MAX provides powerful compositing tools in its Video Post dialog, many paint programs are optimized for mixing, matching, and compositing still images and animations with full palette control and file attribute control. These in turn are often used as materials themselves (such as a television screen material that is an animation of a TV show). In addition to the editing tools available for work on preexisting movies and stills, a wide range of painting tools and ink types, image area selection tools, onionskinning tools, and specialized plug-in filters lend invaluable control over the design of materials, texture maps, and background images. Paint programs can often be the ideal environment for creating masks and grid-aligned patterns and for controlling alpha information in an image.

Key considerations in the purchase of any painting program include:

- Does the program run under your current operating system with your current system's resources and drivers? Does it conflict with any previously installed software resources or drivers?

- Does the program offer the types of tools and inks you need for your image or animation editing?

- Does the program have an open-ended architecture to accommodate specialized third-party plug-ins and filter inks?

- Does the program use a minimum of system resources while running so that it can be used as a sidekick to 3DS MAX, if necessary, without significantly degrading MAX's performance?

- Does the program come with adequate tutorial and reference documentation, and product support from the manufacturer?

- Is the program fast? Can it handle a wide variety of file formats, including still image and animation file formats?

- Does it offer control over color depth and image resolution?

- Does it offer batch image processing, if necessary?

- Do the program's features focus on treating animations, still images, or both?

NOTE

Because 3DS MAX does not ship at this time with a powerful 2D-dedicated bitmap browser, you may also want to verify that the paint package you're purchasing comes with one (many do). Test it out on the MAPS directory of 3DS MAX; see how fast the bitmaps load and how much information is reported back for each image. Numerous powerful shareware (and even freeware) utilities are available also on many online forums.

3D Studio MAX and Screen Captures

One of the more obvious sources for creating materials is 3DS MAX itself. Through the use of the program's many tools and features, an unlimited amount of materials can be generated from texture maps, dent maps, noise maps, and geometrical patterns and objects (see Chapter 12, "Designing Special Effects Materials," for examples). You can also create materials from any Windows screen on your computer's monitor by using screen captures. Techniques to do this are outlined in the "Alignment by Screen Capture and Grids" section of this chapter.

Portable Digital Cameras

In recent years, a vast array of portable digital cameras has appeared on the market. Many of them are incredibly affordable. Depending on the number of images you need stored at a time, the file types, the color depths, the resolutions, and the unending accessories that can be added to a camera, these devices can be the "portable scanner" of choice for serious materials designers.

Key considerations on the purchase of any portable digital camera:

- Is it manufactured by a nondigital camera manufacturer? (This often determines the accessories available.)

- What is the camera's battery life, and how expensive are its replacement batteries?

- How many images can the camera store at one time?

- At what resolution and color depths can the images be taken?

- Does the camera have a flash, and does it offer reasonable control and reporting features for addressing lighting considerations?

- Does it require its own specialized software or drivers to interface with your system, and do these conflict with your existing configuration?

- Does the camera come with its own image browser? (A surprising number of them don't.)

- What kind of repair, product support, and warranty are available for the camera? (These pieces of equipment are not cheap to fix.)

Remember that a nondigital camera used with a high-quality scanner or a high-quality scanning service may be a low-cost alternative to a digital camera. A key issue here is how fast of a turnaround you need from the time an image is snapped until you start using it to design your materials. If you can afford to wait for film to be processed, and if the quality, brightness, and resolution of the film are adequate to accommodate the resolution of the images scanned from the photographs, this approach may work fine.

Another key issue is the need for immediate verification and control over an image. Many digital cameras enable you to view an image immediately after it has been taken. There are no surprises. If the image is smudged, unbalanced, off-center, ineffectively lit, obscured by unexpected objects, or for any reason requires retaking, you can immediately replace the unusable shot with a new shot until you are satisfied. Finally, you have far more control over an image at the editing level if the image is originally digital. The graininess, brightness level, and clarity of photo images are highly dependent on the skill of the photo-processing staff and their equipment: You are at the mercy of someone else's work. If you take a superb shot of a material, and the photo-processing business produces a lousy image from it, all the digital scanning and editing tools in the world may not be able to save it. For this reason alone, many MAX users have made the leap to taking complete control over their image acquisitions.

Video Cameras and Video Recorders

From high-end to low-end, video cameras and video recording equipment remain powerful material for background acquisition technology. The considerations for purchasing video equipment vary tremendously with the specific equipment itself. Consulting a multimedia dealership that has experience with the equipment, its installation, and its use is highly recommended. Such a dealership may also have demo units in stock that you can test-drive with real-world examples.

For many people, entering the world of multimedia is also the beginning of a journey into the universe of broadcast technologies. A low-end solution such as the Intel Personal Video Recorder (comprising a single card, cable, and home video camera) may be all that is necessary for some users' applications. It is simple enough to install and use without any training or technical background. By the same token, high-end cameras and recorders that use specialized recording media are rarely plug-and-play. They usually require skilled technical expertise to install properly, and a significant amount of training on the equipment's use, limitations, and industry standards.

One general recommendation can be offered for any video solution: Get your hands on it, or see a real-world demonstration of it before you purchase it! Many users buy equipment that is overkill for their applications, and others buy equipment that doesn't have enough power to do what they need it to do. Some people make a living by installing, tweaking, consulting, and training on video equipment. Generally, an investment in their time is well worth what you pay.

Keep Your Eyes Peeled

Every year new technologies arrive on the scene to make image acquisition simpler, more affordable, and more accessible to the MAX user. Many users attend national conferences to see these solutions in action. By the same token, many users without a budget for expensive hardware have also come up with clever, surprising, and completely accurate schemes to get quality work done.

Here's one example of the way one user managed—on a shoestring budget—to acquire images for designing his materials. First, he used a copy machine to create a hard-copy image of whatever object or material he needed to create. He would then fax this sheet of paper to his own system, which has a fax broadcasting software program. This program would convert the faxed document to a 300 DPI PCX or TIF file that could then be imported into a paint program for cropping or editing, and applied as a material map in MAX. His work was surprisingly impressive at the time, and his first set of projects later paid for more elaborate image-acquiring technologies.

Material Alignment Techniques

One of the first essential techniques that you need to have under your belt for creating any materials accurately is the ability to perfectly align bitmaps and their map modifiers with geometry. No matter what map type you use and no matter how sophisticated it gets, most material maps must have mapping coordinates assigned to them for the objects to which they are applied. Although a great deal of work can be accomplished by eyeballing the fitting of maps to geometry, realistic materials have realistic dimensions: Brick bitmaps accommodate realistic brick sizes, and labels on jars accommodate realistic surface areas of the jars. Should a bitmap have an edge that needs to be perfectly aligned with the edges of geometry, the techniques described here can ensure predictable alignment.

Four methods for aligning bitmaps to geometry are outlined in this section. All four use Paintbrush, a common Windows utility in the Accessories Group, to demonstrate how a bitmap can be manipulated and applied accurately to geometry. Note, however, that any paint package can be used in a similar or more sophisticated manner to accomplish the same types of alignments. The first technique uses the actual bitmap resolution in pixels to control the fitting of a map to geometry with known dimensions. The second technique uses existing bitmaps to create map-accommodating traces for lofted fit-deformed objects. The third uses screen captures of existing objects directly from MAX's viewports to create guides for perfectly fitting painted maps. Finally, the fourth technique uses a nifty freeware utility developed by Peter Watje to create a planar grid representation of any object's texture map coordinates. Perfect alignments are not limited to these four techniques, but these techniques give you several ways to accomplish the task.

Alignment by Pixel and Material ID

Suppose that you have a block of material (any material) whose dimensions are 80 units by 40 units by 20 units, and that each side of this block needs a unique and perfectly matched material. You can do the job by creating three bitmaps with resolutions of 80-by-40, 80-by-20, and 40-by-20 pixels, assuming that 80 pixels, 40 pixels, and 20 pixels are enough to accommodate the necessary resolution of each material on each side of the object.

This unity ratio (1 pixel per unit) can be used as a helpful starting point for any material you design using this technique. After the material is created and aligned with the object, the ratio of pixels per unit can easily be scaled up to create more detailed materials with the same perfect alignment on the object, because bitmaps can be reloaded easily within the Material Editor. Any of the three resolutions used for this tutorial, for example, can be multiplied by any common value if higher or lower resolutions are needed to accommodate the material's detail. The resolutions of all bitmaps could be multiplied by a value of 20.0, so that the bitmap resolutions would be 1600-by-800, 1600-by-400, and 800-by-400, respectively. For this tutorial, values of 80, 40, and 20 are used to control a unity alignment.

1. Start a new session in 3DS MAX. On the Create panel, click on the Geometry button, and create a Box with a length of 80, a width of 40, and a height of 20. Segment values for each dimension can be set to 1. Toggle on Generate Mapping Coordinates. Center the block in the screen, and use the Arc Rotate and Pan tools in the Perspective viewport to get a good look at the block so that your session looks like figure 9.2.

2. Launch Paintbrush (Paint in NT 4.0), and use the Options/Image Attributes (Image, Attributes in NT 4.0) pull-down menu option to set the image attributes. Set the Units to Pels, set the Width to 80, and set the Height to 40. Toggle the Colors to Colors mode. The Image viewport shrinks to an 80-by-40 pixel size.

FIGURE 9.2
*An 80×40×20-unit
block is created.*

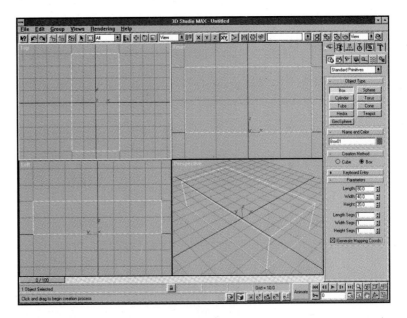

3. Use the View/Zoom In (in NT 4.0 use View, Zoom, Large Size and View, Zoom, Show Grid) pull-down menu option(s), and pick anywhere in the viewport. A large grid of 80-by-40 squares, with each square representing one pixel, appears. Using the mouse pick buttons, create a single pixel border around the entire window and create black squares of 5-by-5 pixels in each corner. Use the View/Zoom Out (in NT 4.0 use View, Zoom, Normal Size) pull-down menu option to return to Full View mode, and use the Text tool to write **80×40** in the center of the bitmap. Zoomed in, your bitmap should look like figure 9.3.

4. Save the file as 80X40.BMP in the \3DSMAX\MAPS directory.

5. Use the Options/Image Attributes pull-down menu option to set the image attributes. Set the Units to Pels, set the Width to 80, and set the Height to 20. Toggle the Colors to Colors mode. The Image viewport shrinks to an 80-by-20-pixel size. Repeat step 3 and save the image as file 80X20.BMP in the \3DSMAX\MAPS directory.

6. Repeat step 5 to create a third bitmap of 40-by-20 units. After all three of these pixel-accurate bitmaps are saved, you are ready to begin creating a perfectly aligned material.

FIGURE 9.3

A pixel-accurate bitmap is created to perfectly fit the 80×40-unit surface of the block.

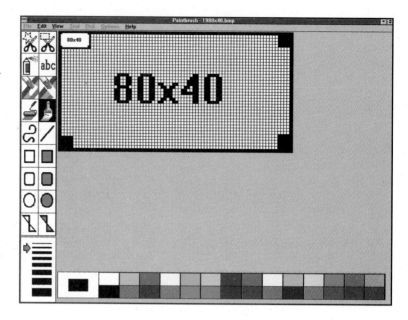

7. Begin material construction by clicking on the Material Editor button on the main toolbar. Select the upper-left sample slot in the Material Editor. Enter **PixelMap** for the name of the material. Click on the Type button, and set the type to Multi/Sub-Object. This material type enables you to apply multiple materials to a single object, with each material corresponding to a material ID assigned to surfaces on the object.

8. In the Basic Parameters rollout menu, click on the Set Number button, set the number of materials to 3, and then click on OK. Three Material buttons appear, with Material #1 corresponding with whatever surfaces are assigned to Material ID #1, Material #2 corresponding with whatever surfaces are assigned to Material ID #2, and so forth. Click on the Standard button to the right of Material #1. Open the Maps rollout menu.

9. Click on the Diffuse button. Select Bitmap from the Material/Map Navigator browser, and click on OK. In the Bitmap Parameters rollout menu, set the Bitmap to \3DSMAX\80X40.BMP. Click on the Show Map in Viewport button beneath the sample slots so that the 80×40 material will eventually be shown in the viewport after Material IDs have been assigned. Also click on the Assign Material to Selection button below the sample slots to assign Pixelmap to the block. Make certain that the block is highlighted when you do this.

10. Click on the Go To Parent button beneath the sample slots to return to the Maps rollout. Enter the name **80×40** in the Material Name edit box. Click on the Go to Sibling button beneath the sample slots to move to the Map parameters for the second material in your Multi/Sub-Object material.

11. Repeat step 9, but select \3DSMAX\80X20.BMP for the Bitmap and name the material **80×20**. Repeat step 9 again, but select \3DSMAX\40X20.BMP for the Bitmap and name the material **40×20**. When you have finished, click on the Material/Map Navigator to see the overall construction of the Pixelmap material. It should look like figure 9.4.

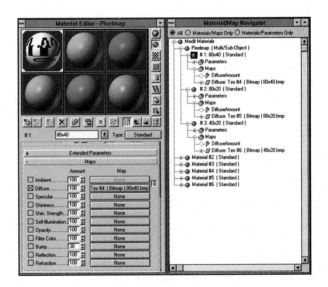

Now that the material is completely defined, begin assigning material IDs to the block surfaces.

12. Close the Material Editor and Material/Map Navigator dialogs. Make certain that the block is selected. Go to the Modify panel and apply an Edit Mesh modifier to the block. Set the selection button at the bottom center of the screen to Window Selection mode. Click on the Select Objects button in the main toolbar. In the Modify panel, set the Selection Level to Face, and click on the Polygon button in the Selection area.

13. In the Front viewport, pick a point to the upper-left of the top of the block, and draw the mouse across the top surface. The top face turns red. Hold down the Ctrl key and drag a window over the bottom surface to add the bottom surface to the currently highlighted set of faces to be treated.

14. In the Modify panel, scroll down until you reach the Edit Surface rollout menu. Type **1** in the ID edit box and press Enter. This assigns the Material ID #1 to the top and bottom surfaces of the block.

15. Right-click over the word *Perspective* in the Perspective viewport, and set the Viewport mode to Smooth+Highlight. Materials now appear on the block in the viewport. They may need to be rotated (this will be done shortly).

16. In the Top viewport, pick a point to the upper-left of the left side of the block and draw the mouse across the left surface. The left face turns red. Hold down the Ctrl key and drag a window over the right surface to add the right surface to the currently highlighted set of faces to be treated.

17. In the Modify panel, type **2** in the ID edit box and press Enter. This assigns the Material ID #2 to the left and right surfaces of the block.

18. In the Top viewport, pick a point to the upper-left of the front side of the block, and draw the mouse across the front surface. The front face turns red. Hold down the Ctrl key and drag a window over the back surface to add it to the currently highlighted set of faces to be treated. In the Modify panel, type **3** in the ID edit box and press Enter. This assigns the Material ID #3 to the front and back surfaces of the block.

Now that all three materials have been assigned correctly to each side of the block, all that remains to be done are rotations of the bitmaps, if necessary. To change the rotation of any of the three bitmaps, click on the Material Editor button in the main toolbar; then, in the Basic Parameters rollout menu, click on one of the three material buttons, and then click on the Diffuse button in the Maps rollout menu. In the Coordinates rollout menu, look for the Angle parameter. Set this to 0, 90, 180, or 270, as appropriate. The bitmap rotates in the viewport. Rotate each diffuse map, as necessary, until your block looks like that shown in figure 9.5.

FIGURE 9.5
Each sub-object material is fitted perfectly to each assigned side of the block.

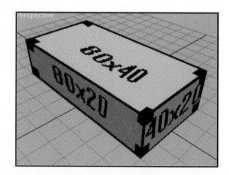

This technique relies on knowing the exact dimensions of the surfaces to which a material will be applied. Figure 9.5 shows the actual pixels in the letters on each material. To make the text appear less pixelated you need a higher resolution for each bitmap, and a smoother font must be used. File 9PIXMAP.MAX can be used as a reference for this technique.

Alignment by Bitmap Traces

In some cases, you may have photographs or bitmaps of something, which need to be used to somehow create an object in 3DS MAX—with the photographs or bitmaps used as a map for the applied material. By setting the viewport background feature to the image, using 2D tracing tools in the Create panel to generate top and side profiles, and generating a fit-deformed Loft object from the profiles, you can crop and apply the same photograph or bitmap to the object as an almost perfectly aligned material.

For this example, a bitmap called 9BIRD.BMP is used (see fig. 9.6). This simple black-and-white, 100-by-60, very low-resolution image is used as a viewport background image to create traced profiles of a bird. The profiles are then used to create a fit-deformed Lofted object of a bird. Finally, the bitmap is used to create a bird material that is applied as a planar map to the side of the bird.

FIGURE 9.6

More elaborate maps can be used in the same way to create traces of profiles.

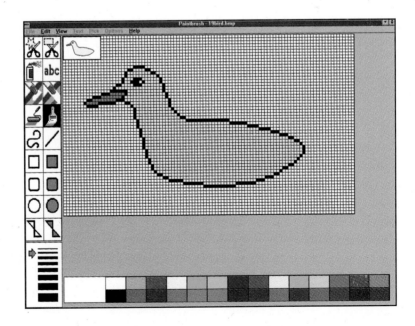

1. Start a new session of 3DS MAX.

2. Right-click in the left viewport. Select the Views, Background Image pull-down menu option. In the Viewport Background dialog, click on the Files button and load 9BIRD.BMP from a legal maps directory to set the Current Background Source (you may need to move this file to \3DSMAX\MAPS). Set the Aspect Ratio to Match Bitmap. Toggle Display Background to On, and then click on OK. Click on the Min/Max Toggle to maximize the Left viewport.

3. In the Create panel, click on the Shapes button, and then click on the Line button. In the Create Method rollout menu, set the Initial Type toggle to Smooth. Pick a point at the tip of the beak in the image background, and then pick points along the edge of the bird's profile until you have traced the entire image. When prompted, close the spline. Use the Views, Background Image pull-down menu option, toggle Display Background to Off, and then click on OK. You can now see the profile you have created from the background image.

4. Using the profile spline as a guide, create a new spline that represents half the top of the bird's profile. Mirror it to produce a perfectly symmetrical other half, and use the spline editing Vertex tools to attach the two shapes and weld together perfectly the vertices at the tip of the beak and tail.

NOTE

If only one bitmap image is available to create a side profile, eyeballing a top profile can take some experimentation. Fortunately, MAX makes it very easy to edit splines and update the resulting Loft objects until you are happy with the results.

5. Create a circle for the Loft object shape and create a straight spline for the Loft object path by using several points to accommodate the curvature of the bird's top and side profiles. The more points you use, the better the fit deformation appears. Use the length of the profiles as a guide for the length of the Loft object path spline. Your profiles, circle, and loft path spline should resemble those shown in figure 9.7.

FIGURE 9.7

Aligning the top profile and the Loft path spline with the side profile makes their construction easier and more accurate.

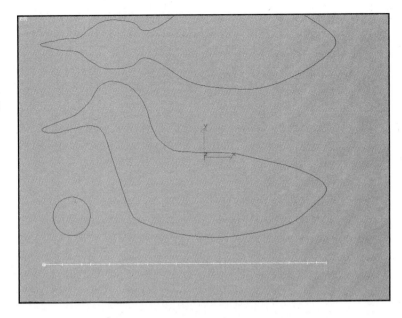

6. Select the Loft object path spline. In the Create panel, click on the Geometry button, and in the combo box click on Loft Object. Click on the Loft button, and then click on the Get Shape button and select the circle. By selecting the loft path spline first and then selecting the Loft object shape, you make the resulting Loft object align itself with the Loft path. In the Skin Parameters rollout menu, toggle Skin to on in the Display area. A cylindrical skin appears in the viewport.

7. In the Modify panel, open the Deformations rollout menu and click on the Fit button. The Fit Deformation dialog appears. Click on the Make Symmetrical button to turn this mode to Off because you will be using different top and side profiles. Click on the Display X Axis button, click on the Get Shape button, and select the original side profile spline you created from the background image. Click on the Fit Deformation dialog's Zoom Extents button, and stretch the dialog to get a good view of the X axis deformation profile. Click on the Display Y Axis button, make certain that the Get Shape button is still active, and select the top profile spline of the bird. Click on the Display XY Axis button to see both deformation profiles (see fig. 9.8).

FIGURE 9.8

The fit deformation profiles immediately update the Loft object in the viewport.

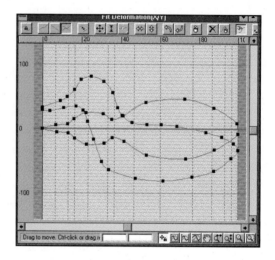

8. Close the Fit Deformation dialog. Use Select and Move to move the Loft object so that it fits perfectly inside the original side profile spline. Click on the Views/Background Image pull-down menu option, and toggle Display Background to On. You are now ready to create the bird material.

9. Click on the Material Editor button in the main toolbar, select the upper-left sample slot, and open the Maps rollout menu. Click on the Diffuse button, click on Bitmap in the Material/Map browser, and click on OK. In the Bitmap Parameters rollout menu, click on the Large Bitmap button and load the file 9BIRD.BMP. Making certain that the Loft object is selected, click on the Assign Material to Selection button under the sample slots. Close the Material Editor dialog.

10. In the Modify panel, apply a UVW Map modifier to the Loft object. Make certain that the Mapping toggle is set to Planar mode. In the Parameters rollout, click on the Bitmap Fit button in the Alignment area and select 9BIRD.BMP as the file to set the dimensions of the modifier's gizmo. Click on Sub-Object to edit the gizmo. Then, using Select and Move and the Select and Uniform Scale transforms, position and scale the gizmo so that it perfectly aligns horizontally with the bitmap shown in the viewport's background image. After this is set, click on the Sub-Object button.

11. Click on the Min/Max Toggle to view all four viewports again. Right-click in the Perspective viewport; then, using the Arc Rotate, Pan, and Zoom buttons, set a good view of the bird Loft object. Right-click over the word *Perspective* in the Perspective viewport, and set the Viewport mode to Smooth+Highlight.

12. Click on the Material Editor button on the main toolbar. You should still be at the Bitmap parameters level of the bird material. Click on the Show Map in Viewport button; the material appears on the bird. You may need to rotate the material by setting the Angle parameter to 180 in the Coordinates rollout menu. (Alternatively, you can do this by rotating the gizmo.) Figure 9.9 shows the material's perfect fit on the bird Loft object.

FIGURE 9.9

By activating the Show Map in Viewport button in the Material Editor, you can experiment in real time with a material's parameters.

Show Map in Viewport

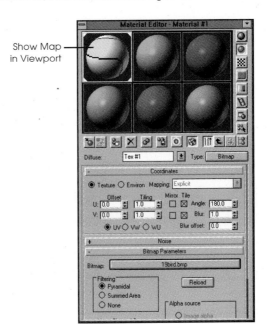

The extremely low resolution of the bitmap is responsible for the chunky black outlines on the bird object's material. This has been done on purpose so that you can see the exact lineup effect of your map with the Loft object. The higher the resolution of the image used for traces and the material, the more cleanly the material aligns itself with the object. The smoothness of the lofted object's geometry also impacts the map's alignment limitations. To ensure that areas of the image outside the object do not appear on the Loft object's material, it is helpful to trace the profiles a short distance "inside" the background image perimeter so that the lofted object is created a fraction smaller than the map image applied to it.

Alignment by Screen Capture and Grids

In some cases, you may have an object in MAX that needs to have bitmaps created from its surfaces to generate its material(s). By using Windows' internal screen-capturing capabilities and by using helpful viewport views and grids, you can create bitmaps that can be used to create perfectly fitted materials. For this example, the file 9BIRD2.MAX (see fig. 9.10) is used as the starting geometry for creating a fitted bird material.

FIGURE 9.10

The geometry for this bird was created through processes outlined in the preceding technique.

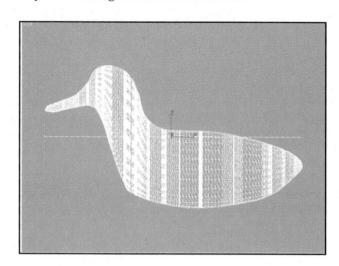

1. Start by opening file 9BIRD2.MAX. The Min/Max Toggle has been used to make the Left viewport fill the screen. The bird has been created from a Loft object whose path is perfectly aligned with the home grid. All other objects in the scene have been hidden, and Zoom Extents has been used to maximize the bird object in the viewport. All work to generate the map relies on not moving the bird and on using Zoom Extents to fit the bird object into the viewport.

2. With the bird maximized in the Left viewport, press the Print Screen button on your keyboard to capture the current screen to the Windows Clipboard. Minimize the 3DS MAX window.

3. Open Paint or Paintbrush from your Accessories group, and maximize its window. Use the Options/Image Attribute (in NT 4.0 use Image, Attributes) pull-down option to set the image pels to your current full-screen resolution. If your screen resolution is set to 1024×768, set the pel values to a width and height of 1024 and 768, respectively. The resolution of the initial bitmap is determined by your full-screen resolution set in Windows.

4. Use the View/Zoom Out pull-down menu option to show the entire graphic area's boundaries. Use the Edit/Paste pull-down menu option to import the image placement, and then use Edit/Paste a second time to paste the contents into the graphic area.

NOTE

In Paintbrush, you must use the Edit/Paste option twice to completely transfer the Clipboard contents to the graphic. In many paint packages, an option enables you to use the current Clipboard contents to create a new image.

Use the View/Zoom In pull-down menu option to verify the integrity of the Clipboard image transfer and to return you to Editing mode (see fig. 9.11).

FIGURE 9.11

After the image has been transferred to the graphic area, you can also control the image's color depth by saving out to any of the permitted file types and then reloading it.

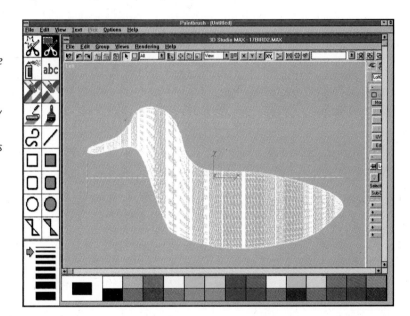

5. Because the next steps make changes to this image, save the image to a file in case you make changes and then decide to start over. Use the available paint tools to paint the image as you want. An example of how you might paint the image is shown in figure 9.12. Having a photograph of the real object nearby can really help when you paint manually. Use the View/Zoom In pull-down menu option, if necessary, to make certain that the borders of the mesh are completely painted.

FIGURE 9.12

A quick way to paint an image like this is to create accurate borders without "leaks," and then use fill tools to fill the interiors quickly.

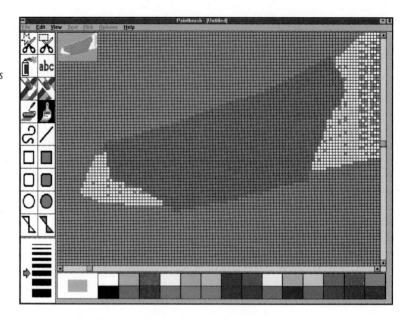

NOTE

Overextending the painted colors beyond the mesh boundaries ensures that all areas of the object's surface receive a nonmesh color when the map is applied. Make one exception to this rule, however: Paint to the exact borders of the topmost, bottommost, leftmost, and rightmost points on the bird so that you can accurately copy the map in later steps.

Figure 9.13 shows one way the bird can be painted. The more time you spend on the detail and blending of colors in the image, the more alive the material appears when applied to the object. Many paint packages also enable you to uniformly scale the image to a higher or lower resolution. If a lower-resolution bitmap will suffice for the material, use it—to reduce rendering times and the use of system resources while you edit. Some paint packages also enable you to use photorealistic images as fill-pattern inks; with this capability, you can hollow out areas of the image and then fill those areas with realistic feather images from real photos.

6. In Paintbrush, use the rectangular Scissors tool to create a cutting border of the bird. If you need to, reselect the borders by repicking the diagonally opposite corners of the rectangle until the bird fits perfectly inside them. Use the View/Cursor Position pull-down menu option to view the pixel X and Y positions of the cursor at the upper-left and bottom-right corners of the scissor rectangle border. Record these numbers and use them to determine the width and height of this area in pixels. In this example, the upper-left corner reports (64,185) and the

bottom-right corner reports (782,582), which means that the image inside the cutting border has a resolution of 718×397. Figure 9.14 shows the cutting boundary.

FIGURE 9.13

This paint job took about five minutes.

FIGURE 9.14

Make certain that your cutting boundary approximates the top and bottom and left and right edges of the mesh as closely as possible.

7. In Paintbrush, use the Edit/Copy pull-down menu option to copy the contents of the border to the clipboard. Use the File/New pull-down menu option to start a new session in Paintbrush. Use the Options/Image Attributes pull-down menu option and set the image pels to the clipboard content's width and height (in this example, set width to 718 and height to 397). Be certain to enable Color mode if your clipboard uses color. Use the Edit/Paste pull-down menu option to paste the clipboard contents into the new graphic area, save the file as \3DSMAX\MAPS\BIRD.BMP, and minimize Paintbrush.

8. Maximize 3DS MAX. Click on the Material Editor from the main toolbar, and select the upper-left sample slot. The Type is already set to Standard. Enter **Duck** as the name of the material. Open the Maps rollout menu and click on the Diffuse button. Select Bitmap from the Material/Map browser and click on OK. In the Bitmap Parameters rollout menu, click on the Bitmap button and load the file \3DSMAX\MAPS\BIRD.BMP. Make certain that the Loft object is selected, and click on the Assign Material to Selection button beneath the sample slots. Click on the Show Map in Viewport button under the sample slots, and close the Material Editor dialog.

9. Right-click over the word *Left* in the viewport, and set the Viewport mode to Smooth+Highlight. In the Modify panel, apply a UVW modifier to the bird object. Make certain that the Mapping mode is set to Planar. The UVW gizmo is already fitted to the Mesh object's boundaries. Flip the U and V tiles as necessary so that the material map is oriented properly to the object. (Alternatively, you could do this by entering an angle value in the Coordinates rollout menu in the Material Editor.) Your bitmap is applied perfectly to the object (see fig. 9.15).

FIGURE 9.15
After a basic bitmap is fitted, you can use it as a guide to create other bitmaps such as bump maps, shininess maps, or opacity maps.

Alignment by Plug-Ins (UNWRAP.DLU)

The technique described in this section demonstrates how to paint literally every surface of an object as you want, with precise control, by using a free plug-in designed by Peter Watje (and available on the accompanying CD-ROM). After you place the plug-in, UNWRAP.DLU, in your \3DSMAX\PLUGINS directory, it can be loaded from the Utilities panel by picking on the Utilities combo box and selecting Unwrap Object Texture.

The plug-in depends on the object to be unwrapped already having its map coordinates assigned. This can be done either by applying a UVW modifier to an object, or by toggling an object's Map Coordinates at the time of creation, or from the Modify panel. This example uses a file called 9WRAP.MAX for reference.

1. Make certain that UNWRAP.DLU has been moved or copied to your \3DSMAX\PLUGINS directory. In the Utilities panel, select Unwrap Object Texture from the Utilities combo box. Set the Width to 640 and the Height to 480. Click on the Pick Object button and then on the Loft object. Save the file out to \3DSMAX\MAPS\UNWRAP.BMP.

2. Start by opening the file 9WRAP.MAX. Three shapes and a lofting path spline have been created to generate a lofted object that transitions (changes) its skin from a circle to a hexagon to a star. In the Control panel, click on the Geometry button and select Loft Object from the combo box. Select the open-ended loft spline path. Click on the Loft button; then, on the Creation Method rollout menu, click on the Get Shape button.

3. Click on the circle. A circle shape appears at the beginning of the loft path spline. In the Path Parameters rollout menu, set the Path value to 50 in Percentage mode, and click on the hexagon. A hexagon shape appears in the middle of the loft path spline. Set the Path value to 100, and pick the star. A star shape appears at the end of the loft path spline. In the Skin Parameters rollout menu, toggle Skin On in the Display area. The loft object skin appears. In the Surface Parameters rollout menu, toggle Apply Mapping On in the Mapping area. This is similar to applying a UVW modifier to the object, except that the mapping coordinates are aligned along the spline path.

NOTE

The higher the resolution you save to, the more precise the texture coordinates represented in the unwrapped bitmap.

4. Minimize 3DS MAX, launch Paintbrush or Paint, and load UNWRAP.BMP. Your image should resemble the one shown in figure 9.16.

   At the top of the image is the unwrapped map near the star, and at the bottom of the image is the unwrapped map near the circle. The horizontal seam running through the exact middle of the image is the unwrapped map at the hexagon. You are now staring at every surface on the object, and you can paint every surface on the object precisely.

5. Using the paint tools in Paintbrush, use the texture grid bitmap to create red stripes perfectly aligned with the alternating sides of the surfaces near the star end of the Loft object, and to create yellow bands of color at the ends and the precise middle of the Loft object (see fig. 9.17).

FIGURE 9.16

Depending on the object's geometry, it may be more advantageous at times to reverse the values in the plug-in for height and width, to better represent the texture surfaces.

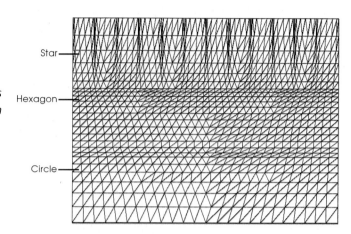

FIGURE 9.17

Remember that many paint packages have fill tools that enable you to use other images as filling inks instead of manually painting each surface.

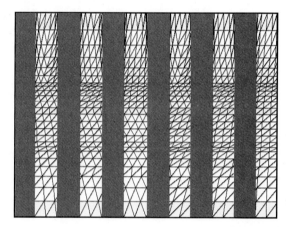

6. Save the file as \3DSMAX\MAPS\UNWRAP.BMP. Minimize Paint-brush and Maximize 3DS MAX. Click on the Material Editor button on the main toolbar and select the upper-left sample slot. Open the Maps rollout menu and click on the Diffuse button. Select Bitmap as the type and click on OK. Click on the Bitmap button in the Bitmap Parameters rollout menu and select \3DSMAX\MAPS\UNWRAP.BMP. Click on the Show Map in Viewport button under the sample slots. The material appears perfectly aligned on the Loft object (see fig. 9.18).

FIGURE 9.18

For crisper, cleaner materials, increase the values used for height and width in the UNWRAP plug-in.

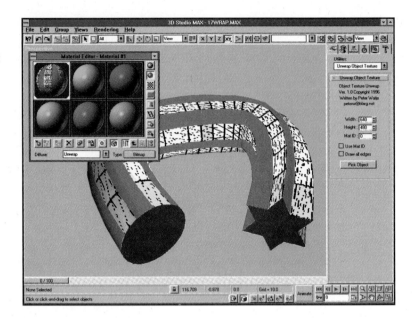

Material Management

Depending on the complexity of the scenes you're creating, a tremendous number of files may be involved in creating and managing your materials. Many users get off to a dangerous start by pooling all the bitmaps for any project into a single support directory. When the next project comes along, searching for and finding the bitmaps they need can take twice as long as it should. If they rely on bitmaps from external sources such as CD collections, their browsing time can increase even more, making the task of building bitmap resources for any project a nightmare. Here are some basic file-management techniques that can keep your material design (and your project) running smoothly and efficiently:

- **Organize all the files you need for a given project into a dedicated project directory structure.** Do not use 3DS MAX's own directories for your work. Doing so can get you into a lot of trouble when you need to start separating out your files from the program's. If a project requires its own meshes, its own bitmaps for materials, its own notes, its own system and MAX configuration files, or any of the resources supplied with 3DS MAX, all of them can be kept together in a separate project directory, isolated from 3DS MAX and other projects. In this way, an entire project can be completely archived or distributed without any missing files, and you always keep 3DS MAX's directories clean.

- **Move external resource files to your project directories.** When you rely on external resources for a project (such as mesh and material file collections off a CD-ROM library), move the necessary resource files to your dedicated project directory so that you know where to find them. Although it may seem redundant and wasteful to have bitmaps common to several projects stored in a unique place for each project, you always know where to find a project's bitmaps regardless of the project you're in. When a project is archived, you won't have to spend time figuring out which maps from a general all-purpose bitmap bin were used.

- **Create intelligent project subdirectories to keep files organized.** In the same way that a project directory can help to manage all the files used and generated in a project, project subdirectories can help to manage the function of the files used in a project. Bitmaps used for materials can be separated from bitmaps used for backgrounds and environment; template meshes (such as floorplans) can be separated from furnishing meshes, in the event that they need to be imported separated into other projects; area lots and streets can be separated from landscaping features, and so forth. Although it may seem a bit cumbersome to organize your files in this manner, it can make life much easier for someone new coming into a project and needing to find something. It can also keep hair on your head if you ever need to revisit an old project and have forgotten how things were organized and used back then.

- **Never abandon anything you have generated until the project is completed.** Clients often change their minds in the middle of a project. It isn't unusual for a client to request that you make modifications to your current work, and then later request that you scratch the modifications and continue with the original plan. This can be devastating if you have overwritten the original work with your modifications. When modifications come into play, do not continue working with the scene by overwriting the prior work. Save the current work at that stage in case you need to come back to it. Create a complete copy of all files in use, and use these to begin working on the modifications. Hard drive space is incredibly cheap these days, and there are numerous large-file–format saving devices you can use to move your current work off your hard disk if you need the space.

- **Use practical file names.** It pays to spend a little time thinking about the names you give to the files you create. Using file names such as WOOD.BMP may work fine for your first and only project, but after a few projects you will not remember whether the wood is maple, ash, cork, or pine. File names such as WOOD01.BMP won't help much either, unless you're using a powerful bitmap browser and don't mind sifting through hundreds of files. One of the great things about today's operating systems is that they enable you to go beyond the eight-character file name limitation. Take advantage of this. The same philosophy can be applied to material library files. LIBRARY.MAT will not remind you of a library's contents unless it is the only library you will ever use. By naming library files after projects or after the types of materials contained in them, you have a far better idea at the File Manager level of where to find what you're looking for.

- **Take advantage of material library files.** It is tempting to keep every material you ever create in 3DSMAX.MAT. After creating your first 100 materials in this file, however, waiting for the Material Browser to display all the materials contained in the file can take a lifetime. There's a reason the program enables you to create your own material library files. Don't hesitate to create a library for each project. In this way, the library file can also travel with the project, if necessary. By keeping library files small and organized, you can sift through their contents faster. It's not unreasonable to use more than one library file for a project either, especially if major changes come along in the middle of the project. Before making modifications to your current materials, save them out to a backup library file in case you need them back some day.

- **Name every level of the material.** 3DS MAX has made it easier than ever to name the materials and their sub-levels. Don't just name the top level of a material. If your material uses several levels of map channels, take a moment to describe the purpose of the material level. This takes some getting used to, but get into the habit of describing what you are doing. This applies not only to material design but to modifiers, objects, selection groups, and coordinate systems. You may know what's going on *today* with a material, but six months down the road you may forget why you designed the material the way you did. Never leave those name fields blank. Explain what you are doing (even if it's only to yourself) as you go along through the material design.

- **Keep notes.** It doesn't take long for a project to get complicated. If you were to try to write out from memory every bitmap file you used in your last project, do you think you could do it? How about from the project before that? Many thumbnail programs have the capability to create hard-copy catalogues of bitmaps in selected directories. If you plan to generate hundreds of custom materials, it can be to your advantage to log everything you use in case you ever need to find it again. This helpful technique can also be applied to any series of techniques you run across, any resource contact information you depended on, any problems that cropped up during the project with your system's hardware, software, drivers, or peripherals—*and how you resolved them.*

Material and Bitmap Navigation

The Material/Map browser in 3DS MAX has come a long way from the material browsing capabilities in 3D Studio DOS. An entire screen of materials in TrueColor can be viewed at one time. Depending on the kind of system you have 3DS MAX running on and the number of materials in your materials libraries, however, it may take some time for all the materials to be calculated and shown in the Material/Map browser's View Large Icons mode. And 3DS MAX has no tool with which to quickly and easily find, report, and graphically show all the information associated with any bitmap on your system. For this reason, it pays to examine some bitmap referencing techniques and utilities.

Image and Material Cardfile

One alternative to waiting for the browser to calculate and show all available materials in a materials library file each time you open the browser to find a material is to create a series of image files from screen captures of all the materials represented in the browser. If the image files are named cleverly to reflect the groups of materials displayed at one time in the browser, the materials in each image can be viewed very quickly by using the File/View File pull-down menu option and selecting the appropriate file. It may take a half hour or so to generate an image for each group of materials, but after they're created, you can reference them with lightning speed.

Even faster than using 3DS MAX's File/View File option is to use a bitmap browser such as PaintShop Pro to view the reference files simultaneously. Screen captures of browser images in other materials collections on external CDs can also be created to help find materials not loaded on your system. It might take you a day to assemble screen captures of all the materials resources you have, but after you create them, all these screen capture images can be opened simultaneously and treated like Rolodex cards. Using minimal system resources, you can view the images instantly without having to load a CD-ROM. Some bitmap browsers can even automate the process of opening all the images for reference, through scripts or batch processing features.

Thumbnail Programs

Finding bitmaps on your system can be a tedious and time-consuming task. When you use a series of still images to create an animated material, or for Video Post editing, converting these files from one file format to another can waste a great deal of time. Fortunately, some powerful bitmap browsers are available to speed along these tasks and make them painless.

Another alternative to navigating materials and the bitmaps associated with them in 3DS MAX is to invest in a dedicated thumbnails program such as ThumbPlus. These types of programs are optimized to search entire directories and report back not only a visual of the bitmaps found, but all the detailed information you might need about each bitmap, including its date of creation, resolution and color depth, DPI, and file size. Figure 9.19 shows an example of the way ThumbPlus reports its findings in the \3DSMAX\MAPS directory.

Thumbnails Plus and other programs like it are graphic file viewers, locators, and organizers that simplify the process of finding and maintaining graphics, clip-art files, fonts, and animations. They display a small image, called a *thumbnail*, of each file in a directory you specify. You can use these types of programs to search, view, edit, or crop images, launch external editors, and copy the images to the Windows Clipboard. They can also organize graphics files by moving them to appropriate directories. Some thumbnail programs can create slide shows from the image files in specified directories, print the files individually, or print bitmap catalogs from all files in a directory. Many can convert images to several formats, either one at a time or in batch mode.

FIGURE 9.19

Programs such as ThumbsPlus can display hundreds of bitmaps in a matter of seconds.

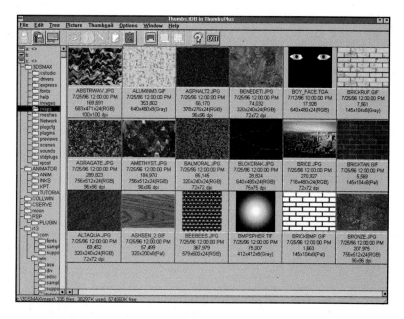

Importing 3D Studio R4 Materials

Recently, an MLI Import plug-in was created and made available to the public. It is not officially supported by Kinetix or the Yost Group, but was supplied as a service to the many users who have asked for a way to import material libraries created in DOS releases of 3D Studio. The file MLIIMP.DLI, provided on the accompanying CD, needs to be placed in the \3DSMAX\PLUGINS directory. Then, on the next session of 3DS MAX, you will be able to import MLI files.

The MLI File Format

The MLI file is the material library format for the DOS releases of 3D Studio. Each material library can store more than 255 material definitions in 3D Studio Release 4 format. The MLIIMP.DLI plug-in translates these earlier libraries directly into 3DS MAX; you don't need to assign them in a 3DS file.

Import Options

After the MLIIMP.DLI file is included on your plug-in path, the MLI extension is listed as a choice from the 3DS MAX File/Import dialog. The MLI Import dialog has two Import Options:

- **Import into Scene.** This option creates an object for every material in the material library (255 maximum). Each object is a single texture-mapped face with a unique material from the library, and shares the name of the assigned material. All objects created by MLI Import are placed in a "fan" configuration, centered at the world origin. To make the fan easier to manipulate, a parental dummy object is placed in the center of the fan with the name of the imported MLI file. The triangles are then attached as children to the dummy object.

- **Import into Material Editor.** This option merges the materials in the material library with the current material library present in the 3DS MAX Material Editor. To see the newly merged materials, enter the Material Editor's Material/Map browser and choose Browse From Material Library.

Converting MLI Files to MAT Files

The Save As function in the Material/Map browser enables you to create a 3DS MAX material library (MAT file) from everything in the scene or from just what is currently selected. When you import an MLI file to the scene by using the MLIIMP plug-in, the fan of material objects is selected. Enter the browser, choose the Browse From: Selected option, and the material definitions that you just imported appear. You can save this list to a MAT file by choosing the Save As option and entering a name for the new library in 3DS MAX format.

NOTE

The MLI Import plug-in does not translate procedural textures (SXPs). To import these materials, you need to assign them to an object in 3D Studio R4, save the 3DS file, and then import the file into 3DS MAX. *3DS MAX does not support the 3D Studio Save Selected option.*

In Practice: Materials Management and Manipulation

- **Minimize the required resources when designing.** One basic truth about 3DS MAX is this: It will never run faster than the moment you start a new session. The fewer objects, lights, and materials in a scene, the faster MAX performs. Therefore, it makes sense that at every level of design, you minimize the number of objects, lights, and materials to only what you need to keep the program running as fast as possible.

- **Keep design elements modular.** By designing materials in dedicated sessions, you enable yourself to subject new materials to a wide range of lighting and geometric mapping tortures without jeopardizing the status of (or being at the rendering mercy of) the final scene in which they will eventually be used. This strategy of modularizing development of materials also makes future development modifications easier to experiment with. Keep track not only of your projects but of your experiments.

- **Stay on top of new design and development resources.** New material development resources are created almost every week, and it can be highly profitable and powerful to regularly explore the Kinetix forums and see what's come out of the oven lately. With the advent of 3DS MAX's capability to use other filters, the same can be said for any compatible manufacturer's resources.

IMAGE BY STEVE BURKE

Chapter 10

by Steve Burke

DESIGNING NATURAL MATERIALS

Natural materials such as grass, water, and rock are often challenging to create on the computer. 3D Studio MAX, however, affords many ways to achieve convincing results. This chapter demonstrates how to build natural materials for a tropical forest scene, replete with pond and tree frog. The materials discussed in this chapter are useful for many types of scenes. In addition, the techniques described are universal and can be used to build any type of natural material.

This chapter describes the creation of several natural materials that are then used to create a realistic tropical forest scene. Further, you build the materials in a logical order, much as an artist would paint a landscape, starting with the sky and ground plane and adding elements one at a time. The primary objective is to present useful techniques for designing natural materials. The secondary objective is to demonstrate a practical method of working that eliminates rework and achieves good results.

The techniques in this chapter include methods to achieve realistic color and texture, and ways to simulate natural variation; these are the two most important considerations when you design natural materials.

This chapter covers the following material types, in order:

- Ground and sky
- Water
- Trees and bamboo
- Stones
- Vegetation
- Plant leaves
- Tree frog

Ground and Sky

Designing the ground and sky materials is the first step because they provide both the backdrop for the scene and a reference for each new material. Many natural materials rely on subtle coloring for their effect. These materials could not be created without first establishing the background of the scene. When finished, if the colors in the scene look natural, and each material looks as though it fits into the scene, the image will be believable.

TIP

When you design natural materials it is often necessary to do test renderings of the scene. Never do test renderings against a black background. A black background makes it very difficult to judge color relationships. Changing the background color to a neutral gray or representative scene color is always a better choice. The best solution is to make test renderings against the actual background you will be using in your scene.

Dirt and Grass

Load file GROUND.MAX from the accompanying CD. The scene in this file consists of a single mesh object that will serve as the ground plane for the scene you are building. A Multi/Sub-Object material containing two sub-materials, Dirt and Grass, has been applied to the object. The Grass material is represented by the green color, and brown represents the Dirt material (see fig. 10.1).

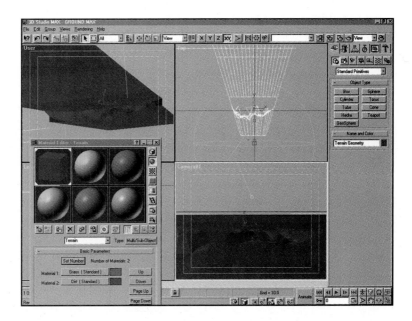

FIGURE 10.1

The terrain mesh with a Multi/Sub-Object material applied.

In the Material Editor, examine the Dirt and Grass materials in Slot #1. Both materials are standard. Neither would be very convincing up close, but because they will be covered with other objects and viewed at a sharp angle, great detail is not needed. As long as the diffuse maps used consist of realistic earth tones and a natural-looking pattern, the effect will be successful.

TIP

When bitmapped materials are viewed at a sharp angle, the bitmaps used should not tile more than a few times across the object; otherwise, obvious patterns are unavoidable. One quick solution is to stretch a small bitmap across the object to provide subtle color fluctuations rather than to create an obvious, unnatural tiling pattern.

Both materials are comprised of a color bitmap used as a diffuse map. Additionally, the dirt material uses a grayscale bitmap instanced for both Bump and Shin. Strength, as well as an RGB Tint to alter the color of the diffuse map (see fig. 10.2). RGB Tint is a great way to fine-tune the appearance of a bitmap in the 3DS MAX environment. It is an important tool because lighting, atmosphere, and geometry all affect the rendered color of a material. Notice also that the diffuse map on the dirt material is not applied at full strength. Lessening the effect of the diffuse map pushes the color of the object toward the diffuse color. This technique can be used to lighten or darken a material. In either case, it always reduces the contrast of a material.

FIGURE 10.2

The definition of the dirt material maps in the Material Editor.

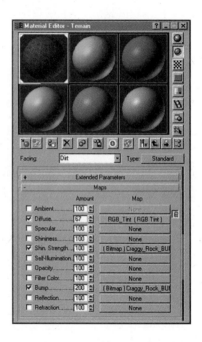

Return to the scene and look at the Terrain object in a shaded viewport. An abrupt break occurs where the dirt and grass materials meet on the Terrain object. This is intentional. The area that is now grass will remain unchanged. The dirt material will be replaced with a Blend material that will form an organic transition from grass to dirt, and then a transition from dirt to mud. The mud material will be placed in the recessed area of the geometry to form the bottom of a pond.

In each Blend material a bitmapped mask will determine how the transition from one material to the other occurs. To define how the mask is applied, the terrain mesh has been given a Planar UVW Mapping modifier (see fig. 10.3). The bitmaps to be used to define the blends that have been built to fit inside the Planar UVW Mapping gizmo. Because the gizmo is smaller than the terrain mesh, the bitmaps used can also be smaller. This saves both memory and rendering time. If you were to apply a blend to the entire object, rather than to just a small portion, you would need an enormous bitmap—and the results would be no better.

FIGURE 10.3

The terrain mesh with a Planar UVW Mapping modifier applied.

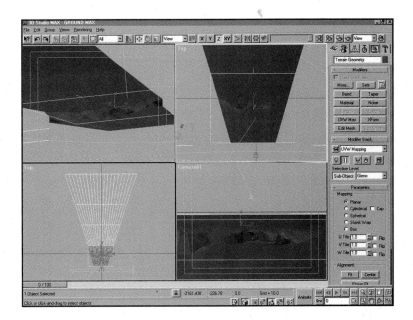

The following tutorials describe how to blend one material into another, using a bitmap as a mask. If you haven't already done so, open file GROUND.MAX from the Chapter 10 Files directory on the accompanying CD.

BLENDING GRASS AND DIRT

1. In the Material Editor, select the Multi/Sub-Object material in Slot #1.

2. Click on the Material 2 button to edit the Dirt material.

3. Click on the Type button to bring up the Material/Map Browser. Choose Browse From New, select material type Blend, and then click on OK.

From the Replace Material dialog, select the Keep Old Material as Submaterial option, and click on OK. This will make the Dirt material the first component of a Blend material.

4. Name this material **Blend_Grass&Dirt**.

5. From the Basic Parameters of the Blend material, click on the Material 2 button to edit the second material.

6. Click on the Type button to bring up the Material/Map Browser. Choose Browse From Material Editor, select the Grass material, and click on OK.

7. Name this material **Grass**.

8. Click on Go to Parent to return to the Blend material. Click on the Mask button to bring up the Material/Map Browser. Choose Browse From New, select material type Bitmap, and click on OK. Load Terrain_Mask_01.TGA from the accompanying CD. Set U and V Offset to 0.1 and −0.07, respectively. Set U and V Tiling to 2 and 0.9, respectively.

The grass and dirt should now blend seamlessly into each other (see fig. 10.4). The next step is to create a smooth transition from dirt to a mud material suitable for the bottom of a pond. The mud material does not need to be detailed because water and reflection will obscure most of it.

FIGURE 10.4
The terrain mesh on the left was done without blend. The mesh in the middle was done with blend. The image on the right is the mask used to create the Blend.

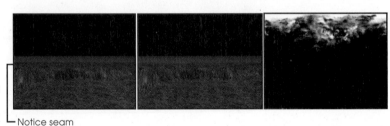

Notice seam

BLENDING DIRT AND MUD

1. In the Material Editor, select the Terrain material in Slot #1.

2. Click on the Material 2 button to edit the first Blend material.

3. Click on the Material 1 button to edit the Dirt material. Click on Type to bring up the Material/Map Browser. Choose Browse From New, select material type Blend, and click on OK (see fig. 10.5). In the Replace Material dialog, choose Keep Old Material as Sub-material and click on OK.

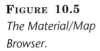

FIGURE 10.5

The Material/Map Browser.

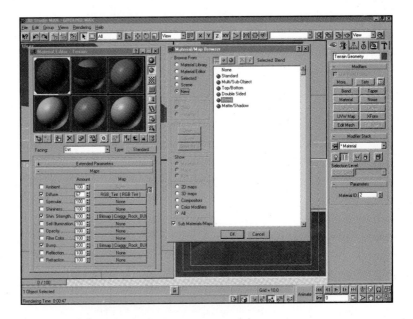

4. Name this material **Blend_Dirt&Mud**.

5. Click on the Material 2 button to edit the second material. Click on the Type button to bring up the Material/Map Browser. Choose Browse From Material Editor. Choose the Dirt (Standard) material and click on OK. The dirt will be the starting point for mud.

6. Rename this material **Mud**.

7. From the Maps rollout of the new Mud material, remove the Bump and Shin. Strength maps by copying one of the empty map slots onto each unwanted map. By removing these maps you make render times faster. Because the mud will be obscured, these maps are not needed.

8. In the Basic Parameters section of the rollout, set the Diffuse color to RGB 62, 53, 42.

9. In the Maps rollout, change the Diffuse amount to 60.

10. In the Maps rollout, click on the Diffuse map to display the RGB Tint applied to the Diffuse map. Set each component of the RGB Tint as follows:

   ■ Set the R component to RGB 141, 0, 0.

   ■ Set the G component to RGB 0, 152, 0.

   ■ Set the B component to RGB 0, 0, 91.

11. Click on the Go to Parent button twice to return to the Blend material.

12. Click on the Mask button to display the Material/Map Browser. Choose Browse From New, select material type Bitmap, and click on OK. Load Water_Line_MASK.TGA from the accompanying CD. Set V Offset to –0,014. This small offset is essential to getting the map into the correct position.

After you complete the preceding steps, the dirt will blend into mud in a very natural way (see fig. 10.6). The mud itself is not a very convincing material, but you don't need to spend a great deal of energy perfecting it because it will not show much in the final scene.

FIGURE 10.6
On the left is the terrain with the transition from dirt to mud; the bitmap used for the Blend is on the right.

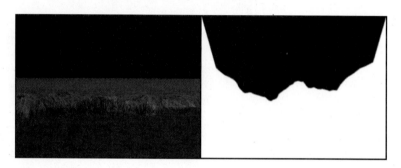

Creating a Sky

A sky does not have to be complicated to be convincing. A realistic sky can be made from a gradient material and assigned as either a background image or a fog map. Because assigning the gradient as a fog map has the added advantage of giving the scene atmosphere, that is the method to use. To create a sky, follow these steps:

USING A GRADIENT TO CREATE A SKY

1. In the Material Editor, select the material in Slot #2.

2. Click on Get Material to display the Material/Map Browser. Choose Browse From New, select material type Gradient, and click on OK.

3. Name the Material **Sky_Gradient**. Set the gradient colors as follows:

   ■ Set Color #1 to RGB 178, 199, 227.

   ■ Set Color #2 to RGB 228, 238, 245.

■ Set Color #3 to RGB 255, 255, 255.

■ Set Color 2 Position to 0.69.

4. Under the Coordinates portion of the command panel, select Environ (Environment) and choose Screen for the Mapping type (see fig. 10.7). This sets the mapping coordinates of the gradient so that it will always appear full-screen; the top of the gradient will appear at the top of the image when rendered, and the bottom of the gradient at the bottom.

The gradient for the sky is completed, but it needs to be assigned in the Rendering Environment dialog for it to appear when rendering.

FIGURE 10.7

The Gradient command panel.

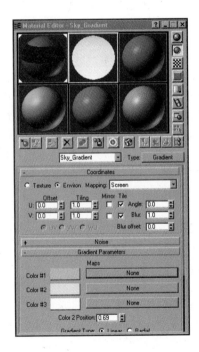

5. Open the Render Environment dialog and click on the Add button in the Atmosphere portion of the dialog. In the Add Atmospheric Effect dialog, select Fog and click on OK. This will add fog to the scene, and you can now assign the gradient to the fog.

6. In the Environment Color Map section of the Fog parameters dialog, click on the Assign button (see fig. 10.8). This displays the Material/Map Browser. Choose Browse From Material Editor, select Sky_Gradient, and click on OK. The gradient will now define the color of the fog.

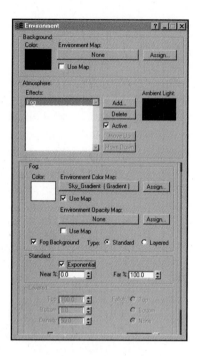

7. Enable the Exponential option. This produces more accurate results when Opacity mapped objects are inside the fog. Many of the objects you will create later depend on opacity mapping for their effect.

8. Render from the Camera viewport to see how the sky gradient affects the scene (see fig. 10.9). The sky is plain but provides a nice backdrop.

Adding atmospheric effects slows down rendering times. If you want to speed up test renderings, you can disable the fog and assign Sky_Gradient as a background image. This will enable you to view your materials against the correct background, but without having to wait for the fog effect to render.

FIGURE 10.9

The terrain with a bitmapped fog effect added.

Water

Water adds a great deal of realism to a scene. The best advice with computer-generated water is probably to keep it simple and understated. You will create a water material from scratch and apply it to a simple plane intersecting the terrain geometry. Reflection and transparency form the basic illusion. A gradient used as a mask can add that extra touch of realism by fading the reflection as the water's surface nears the camera.

Open the file WATER.MAX from the Chapter 10 Files directory on the accompanying CD (see fig. 10.10). This scene contains a planar object intersecting a terrain mesh. This planar object will become the surface of the water.

FIGURE 10.10

A simple plane will form the basis of a water material.

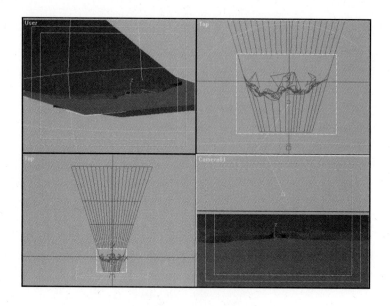

CREATING THE BASIC WATER MATERIAL

1. In the Material Editor, select the material in Slot #1. This material has already been applied to the Water Surface object.

2. Rename the material **Water**.

3. Set the Diffuse color to RGB 81, 73, 60. This is a dark brown color.

4. Drag the Diffuse color onto the Filter color swatch, and select Copy from the Copy or Swap Colors dialog.

5. Set the Ambient color to RGB 26, 26, 26. This is a dark gray color.

6. Set the Opacity amount to 59.

Render the scene to check the new material (see fig. 10.11). Although the effect is still not a convincing one, it is important that you check the color and basic look before proceeding. Remember two important considerations when you create water effects. First, the water is usually darker than the terrain around it. Notice that the water color is similar to the dark colors in the dirt material. Second, the color of the water's surface should be similar to the color of the material under the water. By keeping the colors close in value, the effect of a solid body of water is enhanced. If the water color is too light, it will look like a plastic sheet draped over the terrain.

FIGURE 10.11
The basic water material with no reflection.

NOTE

Dark water colors also provide better reflections. The closer the diffuse color is to black, the more accurate the reflections.

Adding Reflection to the Water

One of the advantages to using a planar object as the water surface is the capability to use a flat mirror reflection on the surface material. This generates an accurate reflection relatively quickly. Follow these steps to add a flat mirror to the water's surface:

1. From the Water material in the Material Editor, open the Maps rollout and click on Reflection map to bring up the Material/Map Browser.

2. Choose Browse From New, select material type Flat Mirror, and click on OK.

3. Click on the Go to Parent button to return to the Maps rollout. Set Reflection Amount to 50 percent.

4. Render the scene to see how the Reflection map has added depth and realism (see fig. 10.12).

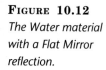

FIGURE 10.12
The Water material with a Flat Mirror reflection.

Fine-Tuning the Reflection with a Gradient

Now, having established the basic look of the water and having added some reflection, it is time to finish the illusion. Next you add a mask to the Reflection map to decrease the amount of reflection as the water nears the camera.

TIP

Fading a reflection as it nears the camera is a subtle touch of realism that adds gobs of credibility to a scene.

1. From the Maps rollout of the Water material, click on the Reflection map button.

2. Click on the Type button to bring up the Material/Map Browser. Choose Browse From New, select material type Mask, and click on OK. In the Replace Map dialog, select Keep old map as sub-map, and click on OK.

3. Click on the Mask button to bring up the Material/Map Browser. Choose Browse From New, select material type Gradient, and click on OK. Adjust the gradient colors as follows:

- Set Color #1 to RGB 255, 255, 255.

- Set Color #2 to RGB 255, 255, 255.

- Set Color #3 to RGB 13, 13, 13.

- Set Color 2 Position to 0.56.

4. Render the Camera viewport so that you can see the impact of the mask (see fig. 10.13). The effect is much more realistic than it was.

FIGURE 10.13
Water with graduated reflection.

Creating Other Water Effects

Bitmaps and masks can be used in other ways to enhance the realism of water effects. A Shininess Strength map could be applied to the water's surface to give the look of particles and debris on the surface. Also, small geometry such as leaves and sticks can be added to the top surface of the water. Gentle currents could be intimated by animating the debris, and moving it across the surface of the water. This would provide a subtle but realistic effect.

In addition, animated bump maps can be used to simulate ripples and movement in the water. As a last resort, the water itself can be animated, although the density of the water mesh would make this a very costly effect.

Trees and Bamboo

The trees are large and prominently positioned in the scene. For this reason, it is important to do them well but not make them overbearing. The tree texture maps use the same colors as the earth around them, which helps them to blend into the scene.

Open the file TREES.MAX from the accompanying CD (see fig. 10.14). This file contains the scene from the first tutorials, with two trees and several bamboo stalks added. The big tree was modeled in 3D Studio MAX and given a cylindrical U/V Mapping modifier and a Bend modifier. The distant tree was made by copying the first tree, rotating it, and then changing the parameters of the Bend modifier. This is a quick way to create two different-looking versions of one object. By placing cylindrical UVW Mapping coordinates on the objects before any of them were deformed, you ensure that the bitmaps stick to the objects and look correct.

TIP

When you build models of natural objects, design them to look different from every angle. Doing so enables you to reuse an object several times in a scene without foregoing a look of natural randomness. One end of a rock could be sharp, for example, and the other rounded; tall at one end, short at the other. When cloned and rotated into different positions in a scene, each clone will look unique and natural.

FIGURE 10.14

The Scene file with the tree and bamboo objects in place.

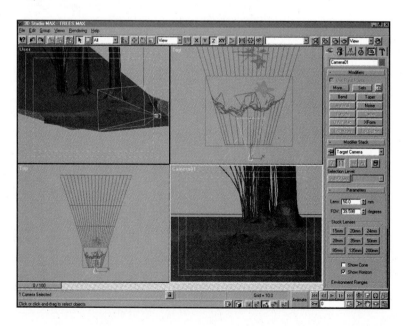

It is important that materials work in combination with models. Creating efficient models gives you the freedom to make better materials. If you create a scene that's overloaded with polygons, waiting for renders may be so laborious that you do not experiment as much as you should to achieve the effect you want.

Sometimes simple geometry can accomplish realism that materials alone cannot. To add credibility to the scene, the bamboo was created as geometry. This bamboo has highlights and depth that Opacity Mapped objects would not have. All shrubbery and foliage for this scene is built with opacity-mapped materials. Combining faked geometry with real geometry makes the faked geometry harder to detect.

The bamboo objects in the scene all started as three-sided cylinders with varying numbers of height segments. The most detailed bamboo pieces appear toward the front of the scene, with the least-detailed ones toward the back. The polygon count of the bamboo was kept to a minimum, and excess faces were deleted to ensure that the objects could be copied several times without greatly increasing rendering times. In addition, each cylinder was given cylindrical U/V Mapping and Bend modifiers. Some of the bamboo objects were assigned material IDs at the face level, others have material modifiers assigned to enable quick changes from one Multi/Sub-Object material to another.

Trees

The most difficult aspect of designing the tree material is keeping the bitmap from smearing across the roots of the tree. The trees are mapped with a cylindrical UVW mapping coordinate, which works well for the trunk, but not for the roots (that project out and are almost perpendicular to the mapping coordinate at certain points). The trees require two separate materials: one for the trunk and one for the roots. A Blend material is used to combine both materials on the Tree objects. This method can be used to blend the tree colors smoothly into the colors of the earth under the tree. This subtle touch of realism adds believability to your scene.

DESIGNING A TREE MATERIAL

1. Load file TREES.MAX from the Chapter 10 Files directory on the accompanying CD.

2. Select Bamboo in the Named Selection Sets pop-up menu. In the Display panel, select Hide Selected.

3. In the Material Editor, examine the Tree_Exotic material in Slot #1. This basic tree material has already been applied to the trees in the scene.

   The material contains a Diffuse map, as well as a grayscale image used as both a Bump and Shininess Strength map. Both maps have been set to 2 and 5 for U and V Tiling, respectively. Note that Shininess is set very low. The Ambient and Specular colors have been tweaked slightly, and the Diffuse color is replaced by the Diffuse map.

4. Click on the Type button to bring up the Material/Map Browser. Choose Browse From New, select material type Blend, and click on OK. In the Replace Material dialog, select the Keep old material as Sub-Material option, and then click on OK. You now have a Blend material with one sub-material already defined. Now for the root material.

5. Click on the Material 2 button to go down in the material hierarchy to the second material.

6. Name this material **Tree_Exotic_Noise**.

7. From the Maps rollout, click on the Diffuse Map button. From the Material/Map Browser, select Browse From New, select material type Noise, and click on OK.

8. Set Noise Type to Turbulence. Set Size to 19.5, and Noise Threshold Low to 0.02. Set Color #1 to RGB 56, 46, 40, a dark brown. Instead of using a second color for the noise, you will use the bitmap from the trunk material, to ensure that the root material blends well with the trunk material (see fig. 10.15).

9. Click on the Color #2 Map button to display the Material/Map Browser. Choose Browse From Material Editor, and select Tree_Exotic_DIFF.

10. Click on the Go to Parent button twice to return to the Blend material. Next you will create the mask bitmap that defines where the two materials appear on the tree objects.

FIGURE 10.15

The Noise material for the tree.

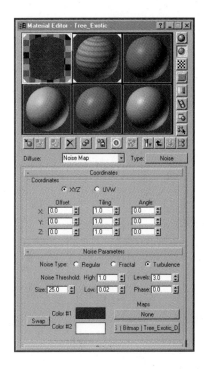

11. Click on the Mask button to bring up the Material/Map Browser. Choose Browse From New, select material type Gradient, and click on OK. Set the gradient colors as follows:

   - Set Color #1 and Color #2 to RGB 0, 0, 0.

   - Set Color #3 to RGB 255, 255, 255.

   - Set Color 2 Position to 0.07.

   - Set Noise to Fractal, Amount to 0.09, and Size to 0.17.

12. Render the Camera viewport to see the finished trees (see fig. 10.16). You may want to experiment with the different Blend, Noise, and Gradient settings to achieve different results.

TIP

Blending between bitmapped and procedural textures is a very powerful technique. Consider using it when you want to map odd-shaped objects with a procedural texture, but also want to use bitmaps for added detail and realism.

FIGURE 10.16
The finished trees.

Bamboo

The bamboo material is simple, but you need to establish variation from one bamboo stalk to another. Two ways to do this are: by altering the objects in the scene so that each looks different, or by creating more than one bamboo material. This scene takes advantage of both methods to make the final image more realistic.

The bamboo stalks in the scene were all created from four original objects, each with a slightly different circumference. They were then cloned and positioned throughout the scene. The copies were rotated, moved, and given unique Bend modifier settings until each stalk faced a different direction, looked unique, and related well to the scene. Then several stalks were grouped, and this group was cloned throughout the scene. By creating the bamboo in this way, you eliminate much of the hard work involved in making each stalk look unique.

Next, you create a Multi/Sub-Object material for the bamboo and apply it to the bamboo objects. Because this material will consist of one light and one dark bamboo material, you can choose whether a bamboo stalk is light or dark by changing the number its Material ID. This makes fine-tuning a scene very easy. The Material IDs for these objects have already been set, but you can change them.

DESIGNING THE FIRST BAMBOO MATERIAL

1. Use the previous file, TREES.MAX, and click on Unhide All from the Display panel.

2. In the Material Editor, examine the Bamboo material in Slot #2. This basic bamboo material contains a Diffuse map and a grayscale image that's used as both a Bump and Shininess Strength map.

   Both maps have been set to 1 and 3 for U and V Tiling, respectively. Also note the Shininess, Ambient, and Specular values. The material looks good as is, but you need to make it brighter, change the material type to Multi/Sub-Object, and then create a second bamboo material, which you will make darker than the first.

3. Navigate to the Diffuse map layer of the Bamboo material. Select the Type button to bring up the Material/Map Browser. Select Browse From New, select material type RGB Tint, and click on OK. In the Replace Map dialog, select Keep Old Map as Sub-map, and click on OK.

4. To brighten the material, you need to add red and green to the bitmap, and decrease the blue. Change each component of the RGB Tint as follows:

   - Set the R component to RGB 255, 73, 0.
   - Set the G component to RGB 113, 255, 20.
   - Set the B component to RGB 0, 0, 209.

   You now have a bright bamboo material. When it's rendered, notice that all the stalks are about the same height and that they are all the same color (see fig. 10.17). Some differentiation still exists because the light is hitting all these objects differently. All the stalks are facing in different directions, and all are placed differently in the scene.

FIGURE 10.17
*A single material,
applied to all bamboo
objects.*

Next, you can add some variety by converting this material to a Multi/Sub-Object material and adding a second bamboo material (by copying the first material and altering some of its parameters).

DESIGNING A SECOND BAMBOO MATERIAL

1. From the top level of the Bamboo material, click on the Type button to bring up the Material/Map Browser. Click on Browse From New, select material type Multi/Sub-Object, and click on OK. In the Replace Material dialog, select Keep Old Material as Sub-material, and click on OK.

2. Rename Material 1 **Bamboo_Yellow**. Now you need to define the second material.

3. Click on the button next to Material 2 to edit its parameters. You are going to replace this material with the first bamboo material.

4. Click on the Type button, select Browse From Material Editor, select the Bamboo_Yellow material, and click on OK.

5. Rename this material **Bamboo_Brown**. At this point, both materials are identical except for their names.

6. Click on the *M* next to the Diffuse color swatch of the new material. This takes you to the RGB Tint map. Change each component of the RGB Tint as follows:

- Set the R component to 255, 0, 0.

- Set the G component to 0, 238, 0.

- Set the B component to 0, 0, 234.

These settings will darken the bitmap.

Finally, you need to make sure that this material tiles differently than the first so that the different stalks don't line up in an ordered, unrealistic way.

7. Select the Map button next to the RGB Tint color swatches. This takes you to the Diffuse map. Change the U and V Offset to 0.2 and 0.3, respectively.

8. Click on the Go to Parent button and then on the Go to Sibling button, to display the Shininess Strength map settings. The offset for this map needs to be the same as for the Diffuse map.

9. Change the U and V Offset to 0.2 and 0.3, respectively. Because the Shininess Strength and Bump maps are instances of each other, this change affects both maps.

10. Render the scene to see the results so far (see fig. 10.18).

FIGURE 10.18
A Multi/Sub-Object material applied to the bamboo objects.

You should see a random assortment of light and dark bamboo stalks growing in different directions. The bamboo is now fairly convincing, but there is one more thing to do. The yellow bamboo looks very nice on top, but is much too bright where it grows out of the earth. It looks unnatural, and not connected to the ground. Also, the bright yellow color is distracting against the dark brown of the tree, focusing attention on a rather unimportant part of the image. You can make the yellow bamboo more convincing by adding a mask to the Diffuse map.

1. Navigate to the Bamboo_Yellow material. From the Bamboo_Yellow material, click on the *M* next to the Diffuse color swatch, to display the RGB Tint map.

2. Select the Type button, select Browse From New, and select material type Mask from the Material/Map Browser. Click on OK. In the Replace Map dialog, select the Keep old map as Sub-map option, and then click on OK.

3. Click on the button next to Mask to add a gradient. From the Material/Map Browser, choose Browse From New, and select material type Gradient. Click on OK. Set the gradient colors as follows:

   ■ Set Color #1 to RGB 255, 255, 255.

   ■ Set Color #2 to RGB 255, 255, 255.

   ■ Set Color #3 to RGB 0, 0, 0.

   ■ Set Color 2 Position to 0.35.

   The mask limits the Diffuse map to only white areas of the gradient. As the gradient fades to black toward the bottom of the bamboo, the Diffuse map becomes less prominent as it is replaced by the Diffuse color.

4. Render the scene again to see the difference (see fig. 10.19).

The yellow bamboo gets darker as it nears the ground. By using a mask, you are able to keep the bamboo color bright and still have it look realistic.

NOTE

Note that the files Foliage.max, Foliage2.max, Plants.max and Plants2.max use the shareware plug-in Grid.DLO.

FIGURE 10.19

The finished bamboo material.

Stones

Load file STONES.MAX from the Chapter 10 Files directory of the accompanying CD. New stone objects have been added to the scene (see fig. 10.20).

FIGURE 10.20

The STONES.MAX file.

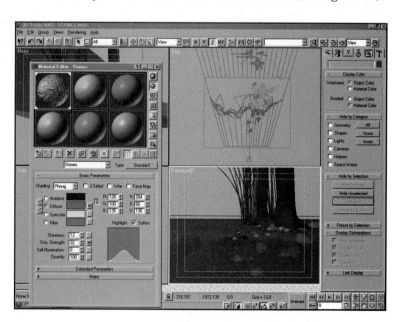

The rocks have all been given spherical or shrink-wrap UVW mapping coordinates. The rocks themselves are clones of about four original rock objects. All were created with as few polygons as possible, and all have had their bottom faces deleted.

The rocks are more than just decoration. They serve three major functions: they provide depth and greater realism to the terrain; they break up the shoreline and hide flaws in the terrain mesh; and they add a small bit of color, texture, and realism to the scene.

The terrain object is not very detailed, compared to a real slice of earth. The Diffuse and Bump maps do provide an illusion of detail, but this effect alone cannot provide true realism. Another way to increase the resolution of the terrain is to use a very high-density mesh, but that requires tremendous rendering time. The solution here is to use low-polygon stone objects that blend seamlessly with the dirt material and add resolution to the terrain.

The second function of the rocks is to break up the shoreline and hide flaws in the terrain mesh. Without the rocks, the shoreline looks too perfect and linear. The rock in the water and the rocks along the edge of the water help to break up this edge and give it a more realistic look. Also, spots appear on the terrain object where the bitmap is smeared or doesn't look quite right. Rather than alter the terrain mesh, it is easier to cover up these spots with rock objects. Generally speaking, hiding imperfections in this way is a bad idea because it often entails cluttering a scene or foregoing aesthetic concerns just to hide sloppy work. In this case, the offense is less egregious because the rocks blend well with the dirt material and also add depth to the ground.

Last, the rocks in the scene add a small bit of color, texture, and realism to the scene without being overbearing. The rock breaking through the surface of the water provides an opportunity to contrast a different texture against both the water and the dirt. The rocks under the water add subtle realism and break up the repetitious pattern of the lake bottom.

DESIGNING A ROCK MATERIAL

1. Load file STONES.MAX from the Chapter 10 Files directory on the accompanying CD.

2. In the Material Editor, examine the Stones material in Slot #1. This, the basic stone material, contains a Diffuse map, and a grayscale image used as both a Bump and Shininess Strength map. Note the Shininess, Ambient, and Specular values in the Basic Parameters section of the rollout.

   An RGB Tint has been applied to the Diffuse map for this material. You will use it to fine-tune the color of the stone material and to ensure that the material blends well with the surrounding terrain. Later, you will change the material type to Multi/Sub-Object and make four versions of the stone material. The first three versions will be used for the rocks on the ground; the fourth, for the stones on the lake bottom.

3. Render the Camera viewport to get an idea of how the stone material looks without the aid of an RGB Tint (see fig. 10.21). The Diffuse map was made from a scanned photo of rock. Although it is a realistic texture, it is much too bright for this scene, and the stones do not blend at all with the surrounding terrain.

FIGURE 10.21
The original stone material, before color correction.

TIP

If rendering the entire scene is too slow on your machine, try turning off Auto Reflect/Refract Maps in the Render Scene dialog. This speeds things up considerably. Rendering by Region or by Selected also saves time.

4. From the Basic Parameters section of the stones material, click on the *M* next to the Diffuse color swatch to display the RGB Tint map. Set each component of the RGB Tint as follows:

■ Set the R component to RGB 144, 0, 0.

■ Set the G component to RGB 0, 154, 0.

■ Set the B component to RGB 0, 0, 154.

Make another test render of the scene to see how the material is affected (see fig. 10.22). Notice that the stones are much more natural now. This example illustrates the paramount importance of color when you design natural materials.

FIGURE 10.22
The stone material after color correction.

DESIGNING MORE ROCK MATERIALS

1. Return to the top level of the Stones material. Click on the Type button to bring up the Material/Map Browser. Click on Browse From New, select material type Multi/Sub-Object, and click on OK. In the Replace Material dialog, select the Keep old material as sub-material option, and then click on OK. Now that you have a Multi/Sub-Object material, you need to create different versions of the original material.

2. Rename Material 1 **Stone_Purple**. Next you need to copy this material; it will serve as a basis for your other rock materials.

3. Click on the Material 2 button. Then click on the Type button and select Browse From Material Editor in the Material/Map Browser. Select the Stone_Purple material and click on OK. Rename this material **Stone_Green**.

4. Click on the *M* next to the Diffuse color swatch to navigate to the RGB Tint map. Set each component of the RGB Tint as follows:

- Set the R component to RGB 122, 0, 0.
- Set the G component to RGB 0, 128, 0.
- Set the B component to RGB 0, 0, 119.

5. Select the Map button next to the RGB Tint color swatches. This displays the texture map being tinted. Change the U and V Tiling to 2 and 2, respectively.

6. Click on the Go to Parent button, and then on the Go to Sibling button to display the Shininess Strength map settings. The tiling for this map needs to be the same as that for the Diffuse map. Change the U and V Tiling to 2 and 2, respectively. Because the Shininess Strength and Bump maps are instances of each other, this change affects both maps.

7. In the Maps rollout of the Stone_Green material, change the Shininess Strength to 100 and the Bump Strength to 400. In the Basic Parameters section, set the Shininess to 30.

   You now have two finished materials. You can retrieve a third material from the scene and place it in the Material 3 Slot.

8. From the top of the Stones Multi/Sub-Object material, click on the Material 3 button. Click on the Type button, select Browse From Scene, select the Stone_Dark_Rough material, and click on OK.

9. Name this material **Stone_Dark_Rough**.

N OTE ───

This material was applied to a hidden object. By Browsing From Scene, it can be retrieved.

This third stone material is similar to the other two but differs in a couple of important ways. First, it uses different Diffuse, Bump, and Shininess Strength maps than the first two stone materials. The bitmaps it uses are the same ones used to create the dirt material. Because these bitmaps are already used elsewhere in the scene, they do not require extra memory at rendering time. Second, the Diffuse map is not applied at full strength. This means that the Diffuse color is used to calculate the final look of the material. This was done because the Diffuse map was overpowering when applied at full strength and detracted from the overall scene. Examine the material parameters and maps used, and compare them to those used for the other two materials.

Render the scene to see how the additional rock materials add to the scene. As you can see from figure 10.23, the scene is much more realistic.

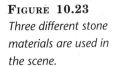

FIGURE 10.23
Three different stone materials are used in the scene.

Finally, you need to create an underwater stone material.

CREATING AN UNDERWATER STONE MATERIAL

1. From the Stones material in Slot #1, click on the Material 4 button to edit the fourth material. Click on Type to open the Material/Map Browser. Choose Browse From Scene, select Stone_Mossy, and click on OK.

2. Name this material **Stone_Mossy**, and examine it to see how it is built.

    Render the scene to see the new rock material with the water (see fig. 10.24). The rocks look rather mossy, but you can achieve a better result by using a Top/Bottom material to blend the two rocks with the mud. Top/Bottom materials are great for static objects, but because they are calculated in world space, they are not well suited to most animation.

3. Make certain that you are at the top of the Stone_Mossy material. Select Type to display the Material/Map Browser, select Browse From New, select material type Top/Bottom, and click on OK. In the Replace Material dialog, select the Keep old Material as Sub-material option, and then click on OK. You now have a Top/Bottom material with Stone_Mossy as the top material.

4. Click on the button next to Bottom Material and select Type to display the Material/Map Browser. Select Browse From Scene, select the Mud material used in the terrain material, and click on OK.

5. Rename this material **Mud**. Click on Go to Parent to return to the Top/Bottom material parameters.

FIGURE 10.24
The underwater rocks do not blend well into the scene.

6. Set the Position to 84 and the Blend to 9. This gives you a nice blend between the mud and rock.

7. Click on Render Last to see how the material has been affected. The stones now blend more naturally into the scene (see fig. 10.25).

FIGURE 10.25
The underwater rocks blend well into the scene.

Vegetation

An important element of any outdoor scene is vegetation. Opacity-mapped plants, weeds, and shrubs not only add realism but also serve to hide and soften the hard edges exhibited by computer-generated objects. Strategically placed plants can add subtle touches of realism. They are not actual 3D objects, however; placed too close to the camera, they can ruin an otherwise good scene. Flat or nearly flat objects such as leaves and palm fronds can be convincing at close range, but objects that are not inherently 2D, such as vines and bushes, do not look good up close.

Bushes and Trees

Bushes and trees are very difficult to model. They also require many polygons, and therefore take a long time to render. Filling a scene with polygonal bush or tree models is impractical. Bushes and trees, viewed from a distance, can be simulated quite easily. The basic method is to apply an opacity map to a set of intersecting planes. If the planes are crossed to form an *X* (viewed from above), the object will appear solid when viewed from most directions. More detail can be achieved by crossing four planes in a double-*X* pattern. You can enhance the realism of this effect by using masks and gradients in addition to opacity maps.

Load the file FOLIAGE.max from the Files directory on the accompanying CD, and examine the geometry used to display the bush material. Four planes intersect to form a double-*X* or asterisk pattern when viewed from the Top viewport (see fig. 10.26). The basic concept is that these four planes act as projection screens. Their only job is to provide a surface for displaying the tree material. The material therefore needs to look as much like a tree or shrubbery as possible. Sometimes this effect is done with noise, but noise will never give you the realism that using a well-drawn bitmap will.

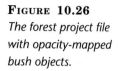

FIGURE 10.26

The forest project file with opacity-mapped bush objects.

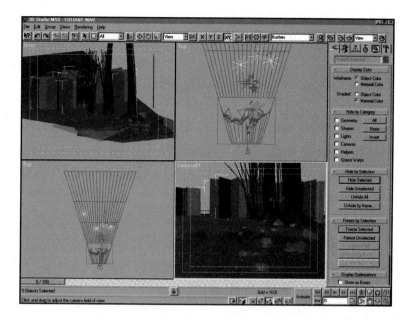

Use the following steps to build an opacity-mapped bush material.

DESIGNING A BUSH MATERIAL

1. With the FOLIAGE.max file loaded, open the Material Editor.

    You will create this material from scratch.

2. Select the material in Slot #1. Click on the Type button to display the Material/Map Browser. Select Browse From New, select material type Multi/Sub-Object, and click on OK. Select Discard Old Material from the Replace Material dialog, and click on OK.

3. Rename the material **Shrubs_and_Plants**. This material has already been applied to the mesh objects in the scene.

4. Click on Material 1 to edit it. Rename this material **Shrubs_01**. Naming materials as you build them will help to keep your project organized.

5. Set the Basic Parameters of the material as follows: set the Ambient color to RGB 9, 23, 11; set the Specular color to RGB 229, 229, 229; set Shininess to 40, and make sure that 2-Sided is checked.

6. Open the Maps rollout and click on the button next to Opacity. This brings you to the Material/Map Browser. Select Browse From New, select material type Bitmap, and click on OK.

7. Select the button next to Bitmap to assign an image. Choose the file Shrub_OPAC02.TGA (from the Chapter 10 Maps directory). Set both U and V Tiling to 1.7.

This gives you the basic Opacity map. The bitmap is a black-and-white painting of indecipherable leaves and twigs. By default, the opacity map will tile across the entire surface of the planar objects to which it is applied. The effect, however, does not look very realistic. The solution is to limit the effect of the Opacity map by adding a mask.

NOTE

View the bitmap Shrub_OPAC02.TGA used in the preceding step 7. This bitmap is tileable in all directions. It is also purposefully ambiguous. This material is meant to provide leafy filler at the back of the scene. If the leaves were too orderly and defined, it might prove distracting. In addition, an orderly pattern, even a well-drawn one, would be easier to recognize and would not look as realistic. The goal is for the viewer not to be able to discern one leaf from another, but to get the impression of a great deal of foliage. Also note that plenty of stems and lines are in the bitmap. The lines are important because they connect the leaves and make the bitmap more realistic.

8. Click on the Type button to display the Material/Map Browser. Select Browse From New, select material type Mask, and click on OK. In the Replace Map dialog, select Keep Old Map as Sub-map, and click on OK.

9. Click on the button next to Mask to assign an image. Select Browse From New, select material type Bitmap from the Material/Map Browser, and then click on OK. Click on the Bitmap button, and assign Shrub_01_MASK.TGA (from the Chapter 10 Maps directory). Set the Blur to .1, the lowest value.

By reducing the Blur value of the mask bitmap you can ensure that parts of the mask do not bleed into other parts of the mask.

NOTE

Combining a mask with different tiling textures and also combining each material with several different masks allows for a great deal of variation without the memory overhead of creating new maps for every situation.

10. Click on the Go to Parent button twice, and return to the Maps rollout. Drag a copy of the Opacity map to the Shininess Strength slot. Select Instance from the Copy Map dialog, and click on OK.

11. Click on the Map slot next to Diffuse. Select Browse From New, select material type Gradient from the Material/Map Browser, and set the gradient colors as follows:

   ■ Set Color #1 and Color #2 to RGB 128, 183, 53.

   ■ Set Color #3 to RGB 82, 109, 69.

   ■ Set the Color 2 Position to 0.76.

These settings create a nice blend from a bright yellow-green to a warm muted green—a nice effect of depth and sunlit foliage.

At present, you have only half a bush material. You still need to create a second bush material. Each bush object requires two materials to keep the objects from looking too symmetrical.

FINISHING THE SHRUB MATERIAL

1. Return to the Basic Parameters section of the Shrubs_and_Plants material. Click on the button next to Material 2 to edit that material. Click on the Type button to display the Material/Map Browser, and select Browse From Material Editor. Select the Shrubs_01 material, and click on OK.

2. Rename the material **Shrubs_02**.

3. Select the Opacity Map button from the Maps rollout, and then select the Map button to edit its parameters. Set both the U and V Offset to 0.4, to ensure that this material and the previous material do not tile in exactly the same way.

4. Click on the Go to Parent button to return to the Mask level, and then select the Mask button to edit the map. Replace the current opacity map with Shrub_02_MASK.TGA.

5. Now that you have finished Material 2, you can render the scene (see fig. 10.27).

FIGURE 10.27
The shape of the bushes was created by combining an opacity map and two different mask bitmaps.

N O T E

The subtlety of the foliage gradient exemplifies why it is important to establish your background imagery first. This effect relies entirely on accurate color choices to be convincing.

This is the basic technique for creating opacity-mapped materials. It can be modified to create a number of different effects. With this method, you could create grass, plants, leaves, and so on. In the next tutorial, you use the technique to create tall grass material.

DESIGNING A TALL GRASS MATERIAL

1. Continuing with the file FOLIAGE.max (from the Chapter 10 files directory). Select Unhide by Name from the Display panel, and click on OK. From the Selection Sets pop-up, choose Grass. Click on Unhide to make all the grass objects visible.

2. In the Material Editor, select the Multi/Sub-Object material in Slot #1. Select Material 4 to edit its parameters.

   Because the grass material is similar to the shrub material, the easiest way to begin is to copy the shrub material and edit it to suit the grass material.

3. Click on the Type button to bring up the Material/Map Browser. Select Browse From Material Editor, select the Shrub_01 material, and click on OK.

4. Name this material **Grass_Clump_Dark**.

5. From the Maps rollout, copy one of the empty map slots onto the Opacity and the Shininess Strength maps. It is easier to recreate these maps than to adjust them.

6. Select the Opacity Map button to bring up the Material/Map Browser. Select Browse From New, select material type Bitmap, and click on OK. Load Grass_OPAC.TGA (from the Chapter 10 Maps directory on the accompanying CD) as the bitmap. Set the Blur to 0.53.

7. Click on Go to Parent to return to the Maps rollout. Copy the Opacity map onto the Shininess Strength map as an instance.

8. Select the Diffuse Map button to edit the gradient. Set the gradient colors as follows:

   ■ Set Color #1 to RGB 117, 172, 53.

   ■ Set Color #2 to RGB 111, 132, 53.

   ■ Set Color #3 to RGB 63, 82, 49.

This new material needs to be applied to the grass objects in the scene.

9. From the Named Selection Sets dialog in the toolbar, select Grass. All the grass objects should now be selected. From the Material Editor, click on the Assign Material to Selection button. The grass objects will now display the Grass material. (The grass objects have already been given the appropriate Material IDs.)

Render the scene to see the new grass material (see fig. 10.28).

FIGURE 10.28
Tall grass created with an Opacity map.

Other Opacity-Mapped Materials

Load the file FOLIAGE2.max from the Chapter 10 Files directory on the accompanying CD. This file contains more bush objects and materials. They were all created in the same way as the shrub and grass materials that you have been building—only the bitmaps have changed.

The rendered scene is starting to look quite natural (see fig. 10.29). You can see how opacity-mapped materials can add depth to a scene that geometry alone cannot provide.

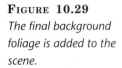

FIGURE 10.29
The final background foliage is added to the scene.

Plant Materials

Plant leaves are not difficult to simulate. To create the plant materials for this scene you combine a simple leaf texture with a bright, mottled plant texture, using Mix, RGB Tint, and Opacity maps to alter the appearance and proportions of each texture. The effects created in this way look very natural and organic.

The mesh for the plant leaves was created from a single plane that was modified into its current shape. Several leaves were then copied, and two of them were created with greater resolution (to hold the bitmap better and also to prevent edges).

Leaves could be made from a simple plane, with the outlines created with opacity maps. This is not a bad method. Your image will be more realistic, however, if you place a texture map on an object that has actual dimension and curves. The leaves in this scene bend and curve, which adds to their realism. A planar mapping coordinate was applied to the objects before they were modified so that the texture would stick to the surface of the leaves without excessive blurring. Because they are foreground objects, it is important that their edges are crisp and that their texture is not blurry.

TIP

Every bitmap in MAX is blurred to a certain degree. The best way to ensure a crisp texture map is to apply a Sharpen filter to your bitmap before you bring it into 3D Studio MAX. This can be done in most paint programs.

DESIGNING A SIMPLE PLANT MATERIAL

1. Load file PLANTS.MAX from the Chapter 10 Files directory on the accompanying CD. Foreground leaves have been added to the scene (see fig. 10.30).

FIGURE 10.30
Plants have been added to the scene's foreground.

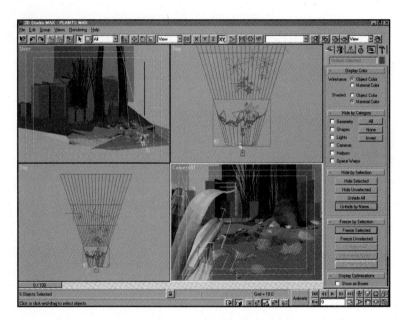

2. In the Material Editor, select the material in Slot #1.

3. Name the material **Leaves**. This material has already been applied to the leaf objects in the foreground of the image.

4. Check 2-Sided.

5. Open the Maps rollout and select the Diffuse Map button. Select Browse From New, and select material type Bitmap from the Material/Map Browser. Load Plant_01_DIFF.TGA as the bitmap file. Set U and V Tiling to 2 and 3, respectively. Set Angle to 25. Click on Go to Parent to return to the Maps rollout.

6. Click on the Bump Map button. Select Browse From New, select material type Bitmap from the Material/Maps Browser, and click on OK. Load Leaf_01_BUMP.TGA as the bitmap. Click on Go to Parent to return to the Maps rollout. Set Bump amount to 61.

7. From the Maps rollout, drag the bump map onto the shininess strength map. Select Instance from the Copy Map dialog, and click on OK.

The first leaf material is complete. Render the scene to view the material. The leaves look realistic, but they are all very similar (see fig. 10.31). Next you will create different versions of the same leaf material and place them on the leaf objects.

FIGURE 10.31
Realistic plants are only seconds away.

NOTE

A spotlight has been added to the scene. The light excludes all objects except the leaves in the foreground. The purpose of the light is to separate the foreground from the background by flooding the leaves with light so that their colors are bright. The spotlight is shadow-casting and also projects a leaf bitmap to create dappled light.

CREATING VARIATIONS OF THE PLANT MATERIAL

1. Select the Leaves material. Click on the Type button to open the Material/Map Browser. Choose Browse From New, select material Multi/Sub-Object, and click on OK. From the Replace Material dialog, select Keep Old Material as Sub-material, and click on OK.

2. Rename Material 1 **Leaf_Green**.

3. Select the Material 2 button.

4. Select the Type button to bring up the Material/Map Browser. Select Browse From Material Editor, select the Leaf_Green material, and click on OK.

5. Name this material **Leaf_Red_Yellow**. You can now edit this material to add variety.

6. In the Maps rollout, select the Diffuse map to edit it. Select the Type button to bring up the Material/Map Browser. Select Browse From New, select map type Mix, and click on OK. In the Replace Map dialog, select Keep Old Map as Sub-map, and click on OK.

7. Click on the Color #2 Map button to bring up the Material/Map Browser. Select Browse From New, select map type Bitmap, and click on OK. Load Plant_Spots_DIFF.TGA from the Chapter 10 Maps directory. Set U and V Tiling to 2 and 4, respectively.

8. Click on the Type button to bring up the Material/Map Browser, select Browse From New, select map type RGB Tint, and click on OK. In the Replace Map dialog, select Keep Old Map as Sub-map, and click on OK. Set each component of the RGB Tint as follows:

   ■ Set the R component to RGB 255, 66, 51.

   ■ Set the G component to RGB 58, 255, 0.

   ■ Set the B component to RGB 0, 0, 255.

9. Click on the Go to Parent button to return to the Mix map parameters.

10. Click on the Mix Amount map button, select Browse From New, select map type Bitmap, and then click on OK. Load Leaf_01_MASK.TGA from the Chapter 10 Maps directory. This map places the brightly colored plant material around the edges of the leaf material.

So far, you're simply varying the leaf material. You can achieve even greater realism by adding an opacity map to the material to simulate the effect of ravenous insects.

11. Return to the top level of material Leaf_Red_Yellow. From the Maps rollout, click on the Opacity Map button to bring up the Material/Map Browser. Select Browse From New, select map type Bitmap, and click on OK. Load Leaf_01_OPAC.TGA from the Chapter 10 Maps directory. Set Blur to 0.1.

This puts a series of holes on one side of the leaf and a ragged edge on the other. The next step is to ensure that no highlights appear on top of the holes. This can be done by applying a mask to the Shininess Strength map. You can use the same bitmap you used to define opacity.

12. Return to the top level of material Leaf_Red_Yellow. From the Maps rollout, click on the Bump Map button to edit its parameters. Click on the Type button to bring up the Material/Map Browser, select Browse From New, and select map type Mask. Click on OK. In the Replace Map dialog, select Keep Old Map as Sub-map, and click on OK.

13. Click on the Mask button, select Browse From New, select map type Bitmap, and click on OK. Load Leaf_01_OPAC.TGA from the Chapter 10 Maps directory. Set Blur to 0.1.

The material for the first two leaves is finished, and you can render the scene to see the extra realism the opacity map has added (see fig. 10.32).

FIGURE 10.32
The final leaf is mapped with two Diffuse maps, a Bump map, an Opacity map, and a Mix Mask.

The final leaf with all mapping applied.

The first Diffuse map is a simple leaf texture.

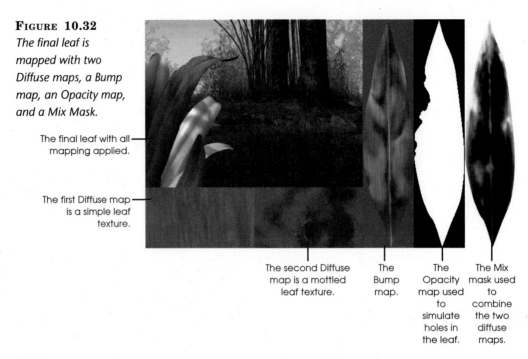

The second Diffuse map is a mottled leaf texture.

The Bump map.

The Opacity map used to simulate holes in the leaf.

The Mix mask used to combine the two diffuse maps.

NOTE

Switching from a Standard material to a Multi/Sub-Object material has caused some of the leaves to lose their textures. This occurs because the Material IDs assigned to those leaves are currently filled with the default texture, and the actual materials have not yet been created.

To see other ways of combining maps to create realistic plant textures, load PLANTS2.MAX from the Chapter 10 Files directory of the accompanying CD (see fig. 10.33). This file contains all the objects with full mapping. The Leaves material in this file contains three additional leaf types. All were created with the same few maps but combined in different ways with different settings. Take some time to examine the materials and maps to get an idea of how they were made.

Most of the materials for the forest scene are now complete. The finishing touch in this scene, however, is an ornery tree frog. The next section describes techniques to texture map a tree frog.

FIGURE 10.33
The finished leaves.

Tree Frog

Mapping oddly shaped objects is difficult in any 3D program. The most important aspect to making texture maps look natural is to apply the correct mapping coordinates. Designing the actual material is the second most important consideration. The texture maps should be designed only after the object has been given appropriate mapping coordinates.

Although most oddly shaped objects can be given spherical, shrink-wrap, or box mapping coordinates, these methods have very distinct disadvantages. First, all these mapping methods will cause distortion and/or seams to appear on your object. Second, these methods are imprecise. They might work fine for rocks and amorphous organic items, but they don't give you the control you need to ensure that each pixel in your texture maps is applied to the appropriate part of an object. Three-dimensional paint programs give you the ability to paint on a mesh, and are one way to apply paint accurately to a mesh. Another effective method is to use Planar and Cylindrical mapping coordinates.

Both cylindrical and planar mapping can be applied without noticeable distortion. Certain caveats apply, however, to using planar mapping on an oddly shaped object. Specifically, smearing occurs when planar mapping is applied to faces perpendicular to the Planar Mapping gizmo.

This streaking can be minimized by reducing the detail of bitmaps where they are likely to hit perpendicular faces and therefore streak through an object.

NOTE

When you create materials for a realistic organic object, the texture maps are critical to the success of the material. Many of the tools and combination map types have little practical impact when maps need to be of the precision necessary for a complicated organic object.

DESIGNING MATERIAL FOR A FROG'S TOPSIDE

1. Load file TFROG.MAX from the Chapter 10 Files directory (see fig. 10.34). This file contains a frog ready to be mapped. Examine the model to become familiar with it.

FIGURE 10.34

The tree frog model, ready for mapping. Notice how the planar mapping coordinate is applied to the object.

NOTE

Both the model and the bitmaps for the frog are of relatively low resolution. The frog will look very good when viewed at a size of no more than one-third that of the screen. Up close, it doesn't hold up well. Both the frog model and the bitmaps were built specifically for this scene and were kept small to conserve memory. How close should one get to a tree frog anyway?

2. In the Material Editor, select the Material in Slot #1. This material has already been assigned to the frog mesh. The next step is to make it a Multi/Sub-Object material. Then you can assign the different materials to the frog mesh by assigning designated faces to an appropriate Material ID.

3. Click on the Type button to bring up the Material/Map Browser, select Browse From New, and select material type Multi/Sub-Object. Click on OK. In the Replace Material dialog, select Discard Old Material, and click on OK.

4. Name the Material **Tree_Frog**.

5. Click on the Material 1 slot to edit the first material. Name this material **TFrog_Top**. Set the Shininess to 31, and check Soften.

6. Open the Maps rollout and click on the Diffuse Map button to bring up the Material/Map Browser. Select Browse From New, select map type Bitmap, and click on OK. Load TFrog_Top_DIFF.TGA (from the Chapter 10 Maps directory). Click on the Go to Parent button.

7. From the Maps rollout, click on the Bump Map button to bring up the Material/Map Browser. Select Browse From New, select map type Bitmap, and click on OK. Load TFrog_Top_BUMP.TGA (from the Chapter 10 Maps directory). Click on the Go to Parent button.

8. Drag the bump map to the Shininess Strength button. In the Copy Map dialog, select Instance, and click on OK.

9. From the Maps rollout, click on the Opacity Map button to bring up the Material/Map Browser. Select Browse From New, select map type Bitmap, and click on OK. Load TFrog_OPAC.TGA (from the Chapter 10 Maps directory). Click on the Go to Parent button.

Next you will render the frog to see how the material is progressing. First, the modifier stack of the frog model needs to be adjusted. Two UVW mapping modifiers are applied to the frog model. The first is a UVW planar mapping coordinate encompassing the whole model and applied from the top viewport. The second UVW planar mapping coordinate is applied from a side view and is used to map the sides of the frog. This UVW map modifier is applied to only a small number of faces. The face selection is defined with an Edit Mesh modifier placed after the first UVW Mapping modifier and left in Sub-Object mode.

10. Return to the scene. Select the Tree_frog mesh by clicking on one of the legs. In the modify command panel, return the modifier stack to the topmost level. The second UVW Mapping modifier, applied to the side faces of the frog, should now be active. Leave all other settings intact.

NOTE

When applying UVW Mapping Coordinates to Sub-Object selections, always apply a UVW Map modifier to the entire object first. Applying a UVW Mapping modifier to only part of an object, without first having given the entire object UVW Mapping Coordinates, can produce unpredictable results.

The material for the top of the frog is finished. Note that many of the presets (such as Blur, Ambient color, and Specular color) were left untouched. It is best to leave the settings as they are until all your maps are in place. Often these items do not have a big impact on the look of your materials and do not need to be altered from their presets.

Render the User view to see the results so far (see fig. 10.35). Notice that the top of the frog already looks finished. Also notice that there is little evidence of the bitmap smearing on the sides of the model. Some streaks are noticeable, but they are minor. If necessary, streaks can be removed by opening the bitmap in a paint program and adding a solid colored border to the outside edge of a bitmap.

Also notice that very little texture is near the edges of the bitmaps. The detail in a bitmap should be decreased in areas where you can reasonably expect the bitmap will hit perpendicular or near perpendicular faces. This takes a bit of guesswork and experimentation, but it is not that difficult to do.

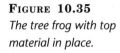
FIGURE 10.35
*The tree frog with top
material in place.*

Several faces on the frog model appear white rather than green. These faces are mapped with the same material as the rest of the object; they look different because they have been given a different mapping coordinate. They are mapped from the side with a planar mapping coordinate.

In the next tutorial, you continue to build the frog material. This time you create the material for the underside of the frog.

DESIGNING THE MATERIAL FOR THE BELLY OF THE FROG

1. Click on the Material 2 slot to edit the second material. Name this material **TFrog_Belly**. Set the Shininess to 4.

2. Open the Maps rollout and click on the Diffuse Map button to bring up the Material/Map Browser. Select Browse From New, select Bitmap, and click on OK. Load TFrog_Belly_DIFF.tga from the Chapter 10 Maps directory. Click on the Go to Parent button.

3. From the Maps rollout, click on the Bump Map button to bring up the Material/Map Browser. Select Browse From New, select Bitmap, and click on OK. Load TFrog_Belly_BUMP.tga from the Chapter 10 Maps directory. Click on the Go to Parent button.

4. Drag the bump map to the Shininess Strength button. In the Copy Map dialog, select Instance and click on OK.

5. From the Maps rollout, click on the Opacity Map button to bring up the Material/Map Browser. Select Browse From New, select Bitmap, and click on OK. Load TFrog_OPAC.tga from the Chapter 10 Maps directory. Click on the Go to Parent button.

That is all it takes to create the material for the underside of the frog. The only task left is to assign Material ID 2 to the bottom faces of the frog.

6. Select the Tree_Frog object in the User window. In the Modify panel, select the Edit Mesh modifier. This modifier is currently defining an active selection. You will also use this Edit Mesh modifier to change the Material IDs of some of the faces of the frog. After you are done assigning Material IDs, you will return the Edit Mesh modifier to its present state.

7. Select TFrog_Belly from the Named Selection Sets drop-down list. This will select all the faces on the underside of the frog that should receive the TFrog_Belly material.

8. Assign these faces Material ID 2 in the Edit Surface portion of the Command panel.

9. Select TFrog_Sides from the Named Selection Sets drop-down list. This returns the selection to its former state. Leave the Edit Mesh modifier in Sub-Object mode.

10. Rotate the User view so that you can see the underside of the frog model, and render the object again (see fig. 10.36).

FIGURE 10.36
Frog model with bottom faces selected and when rendered.

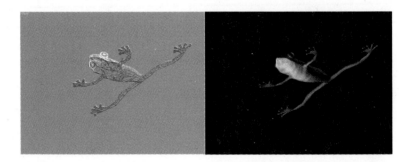

The sides of the frog require a separate material. This material will help to blend both of the top and bottom materials together.

DESIGNING THE MATERIAL FOR THE SIDES OF THE FROG

1. In the Material Editor, click on the Material 3 slot to edit the third material. Name this material **TFrog_Side**.

2. Open the Maps rollout and click on the Diffuse Map button to bring up the Material/Map Browser. Select Browse From New, select material Bitmap, and click on OK. Load TFrog_Side_DIFF.tga from the Chapter 10 Maps directory on the accompanying CD. Set Angle to 90. Click on Go to Parent to return to the Maps rollout.

3. From the Maps rollout, click on the Bump Map button to bring up the Material/Map Browser. Select Browse From New, select material Bitmap, and click on OK. Load TFrog_Side_BUMP.tga from the Chapter 10 Maps directory on the accompanying CD. Click on Go to Parent to return to the Maps rollout. Set Amount to 81.

   This material will provide a nice blend from the top material to the bottom material. First, the side faces that require this material need to be selected and assigned Material ID 3.

4. Make certain that Sub-Object and Face are both still active in the Modify panel and that the side faces of the frog are selected. If not select TFrog_Sides from the Named Selection Sets drop-down list, to select all the faces on the sides of the frog. These faces will receive the TFrog_Side material.

5. Set the Material ID to 3 in the Edit Surface portion of the Modify panel.

6. Rotate the User view to display the sides of the frog model, and render the object again (see fig. 10.37).

You have only three more materials to create. The first is the eye, and the other two materials provide the colored rings around the eye.

FIGURE 10.37

The frog's top, bottom, and sides are mapped.

DESIGNING THE EYE MATERIALS

1. In the Material Editor, click on the Material 4 slot to edit the fourth material. Name this material **TFrog_YellowRings**. Set the Diffuse color to RGB 197, 194, 116. This material provides the cream-colored ring around the eye of the frog.

2. Click on the Material 5 slot to edit the fifth material. Name this material **TFrog_BlackRings**. Set the Diffuse color to RGB 26, 26, 26. This material provides the dark colored ring around the eye of the frog.

3. Click on the Material 6 slot to edit the sixth material. Name this material **TFrog_Eye**. Set Shininess to 48, and Shininess Strength to 91.

4. From the Maps rollout, click on the Diffuse Map button to bring up the Material/Map Browser. Select Browse From New, select material Bitmap, and click on OK. Load TFrog_Eye_DIFF.TGA from the Chapter 10 Maps directory of the accompanying CD.

   This is the last of the frog materials. Next, you assign these three eye materials to the correct faces.

5. Make certain that Sub-Object and Face are both still active in the Modify panel. Select TFrog_Yellow_Rings from the Named Selection Sets drop-down list. This selects a ring of faces around the eye sockets.

6.   Set the Material ID to 4 in the Edit Surface portion of the Modify panel.

7.   Select TFrog_Black_Rings from the Named Selection Sets drop-down list. This selects a ring of faces around the base of the eyeballs.

8.   Set the Material ID to 5 in the Edit Surface portion of the Modify panel.

9.   Exit Sub-object mode.

10. Select Eyeballs from the Named Selection Sets drop-down list. This selects both of the frog's eyeballs. These are separate objects; because they are not attached to the frog, they cannot be selected in Sub-object mode.

11. Apply a Material modifier to both objects. Set the Material ID to 6. This assigns the eyeball material to the two spheres.

That's how to to make materials for a tree frog. When rendered, your image should resemble figure 10.38. The key to success when you create an organic object like a tree frog is to paint the texture maps with care. The entire illusion rests on whether the combination of model and material is convincing. For that reason, as much care should be taken when you design materials for an object as you would take when you model an object.

FIGURE 10.38
The finished tree frog.

The last exercise is to put the tree frog in the scene and animate him—or perhaps her—it's hard to tell with amphibians. A finished version of the scene is shown in figure 10.39. Some new models and materials have been added—all using the techniques described in this chapter. The tree frog is relaxing on a leaf and appreciating all the hard work that went into building his/her pond. There aren't any steps for making the final image, so you are on your own. Good luck!

FIGURE 10.39
Palani's Pond
by Steve Burke.

In Practice: Designing Natural Materials

- **Ground and sky.** These two items often form the foundation of an image or scene. Whenever possible, the background should be established first because it has perhaps the greatest influence on the "look" of a scene.

- **Natural colors and textures.** Perhaps the most important aspect of designing natural materials is the use of realistic colors and textures. RGB Tints are great for perfecting colors and balancing the colors of a scene.

- **Water.** The best, most convincing water effect is sometimes the simplest. Reflection masks can add realism to reflections by fading reflections near the camera.

- **Opacity maps.** Making good use of opacity-mapped materials can add new depth to your work. Opacity maps can achieve results not possible with regular geometry. The best opacity mapping effects are those that are difficult to decipher.

- **Variation.** Natural materials should have imperfections and natural variation. Multi/Sub-Object materials are good for this because they enable you to work with several materials at one time and are quick and easy to use.

IMAGE BY DAVE ESPINOSA-AGUILAR

Chapter 11

by dave espinosa-aguilar

Designing Man-Made Materials

3D Studio MAX makes it possible to create extremely realistic man-made materials if you have an eye for detail and imperfections. Often, the "perfect" man-made material is an "imperfect" man-made material. Look around you. Most man-made objects have noticeable flaws—stains or discolorations; uneven warps, wrinkles or folds along their surfaces; chips, cracks, tears, or dents along their edges; patches of unexpected dullness or shininess; dirty smudges, streaks, dust, or some form of deterioration. Very few things remain unaffected by the elements, handling, or accidents. The key to creating realistic man-made materials is to subject them to entropy.

Man-made materials such as concretes and ceramics, paper and other processed woods, carved or unnaturally shaped stones, plastics and rubbers, glass, metals, and fabrics can all be created with realism if you have effective bitmaps and geometry for each material and if you have material and geometry corruption skills under your belt. This chapter examines essential techniques for creating a wide variety of common man-made materials and corrupting them into believable man-made materials. The following topics are discussed:

- The impact of geometry on realistic materials

- Techniques for corrupting geometry

- Techniques for creating corruption materials such as smears, discolorations, blurry puddles and smudges, scorch marks, dents, dust, and weathering

- Considerations for creating concretes, papers, woods, plastics, rubber, vinyl, glass, metals, wires, fabrics, carpet, and stones (translucent, polished, and dull)

Creating Material Imperfections

Look around the room. Is there a book nearby that you refer to quite often (see fig. 11.1)? Pick it up and look it over for a minute with a careful eye. Don't rush now. Take your time. This kind of close scrutiny is the essence of this chapter. Ask yourself, "How does this book deviate from a box primitive?"

Look for perfectly straight edges and perfectly aligned page grooves. Do they occur? Look for areas of the cover where the paper material shows through. If the cover is shiny, can you see your fingerprints on it? Are the edges of the cover dented, ripped, or worn? Look at the exposed edges of the pages when the book is closed. Are they pure white or do you see dirt along the sides and at the corners? Are there streaks of grime on any of the sides? Set the book down flat on the table or desk and look at its rectilinearity. If you follow the edges of the book, is it a perfect box, or are any of the edges warped? Is the binding of the book perfectly flat, or is it bent and cracked? Does the cover press firmly against the pages when left alone or does it stick up a bit?

FIGURE 11.1
If your 3DS MAX Reference and Tutorial manuals do not make great examples of wear and tear on an object, this may be a bad sign.

It would be easy to create perfect books in 3D Studio MAX. You could create boxes with the dimensions of the books and apply six bitmaps to the sides of each box, representing the cover and pages. But to make a book look realistic, the types of flaws described earlier would have to be incorporated somehow. It would also be easy to create a wooden table by applying a bitmap of wood to the top of a table object. But to give the wood any realism, you would have to consider what can happen to a wooden table after it has been used for a while—discolorations or stains from spilled drinks, chips and dents from things banged against its surfaces, smudges from the oils in people's hands if its surface is polished, dust settled on its surface from lack of use, and perhaps unevenness from years of moisture. All these imperfections have the potential to wage war on your perfect wood bitmap. But these "imperfections" that change "primitives" into "real things" make your scenes look more believable, more "in the world." In many ways, therefore, the study of man-made materials is the study of material and geometry corruption.

The Impact of Geometry on Realistic Materials

No matter how skillfully crafted a material you create in 3DS MAX, its believability is always at the mercy of the geometry it is applied to. If you create a fantastic denim fabric material and you apply it to a box, no one is going to believe that box is a pair of jeans. This chapter does not focus on creating elaborate material-suiting geometries, but it cannot be emphasized enough that your materials are only as realistic as the objects to which they are applied. The following sections provide just a few examples of techniques used to corrupt geometry.

Surfaces and Edge Warps

As figure 11.1 shows, many man-made objects such as books do not have perfectly flat surfaces. On books you might find pen or pencil indentations, scrapes and tears, bends or wrinkles in the paper, warped or frayed edges, and cracked seams from handling. These kinds of geometry imperfections can be created through a variety of techniques. Here are a few:

- **Warped edges.** Separate surfaces that need to be warped from the object, if necessary (for example, to create a separate surface for the top cover of a book) so that they can be treated as separate meshes. Select the vertices along the outer edges of these surfaces and apply subtle Noise modifiers to them.

- **Warped surfaces.** Try applying space warps to, or using Affect Region Edit Mesh modifiers on, different areas of the surface. Vary the values for different areas of the surface. Avoid symmetry to your corruption. Applying subtle Noise modifiers can also do a good job of warping surfaces.

- **Torn or bent edges.** Increase the number of mesh vertices (tessellation) to improve a surface area's capability to be bent, torn, tapered, or warped. Modifiers are only as effective as the density of vertices they treat. You can also edit faces by adding and subtracting vertices to and from a surface to create tears and seams in it.

- **Objects that only need the edges warped.** Create Trim objects around the original objects and apply Noise modifiers, warps, and mesh vertex editing, as necessary, to these much smaller objects, rather than to the larger ones. Figure 11.2 shows an example of the way smaller objects at the perimeter of larger ones can eliminate the need to distort in great detail the high segment values of those larger objects.

FIGURE 11.2

Instead of applying Noise modifiers to large objects with huge vertex counts, use Trim objects to corrupt a large object's edges.

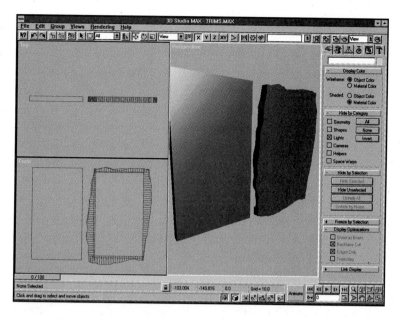

This use of Trim objects can save incredible refresh time and rendering time. Also, instead of increasing segment values for very large objects, you can increase to workable detailed corruption values the length, width, and height segments of Trim objects. This works beautifully as long as the Trim objects and the original objects have perfectly matching seams.

Object Dents and Cracks

Examine figure 11.3. Notice that the bricks are chipped and cracked in several places. Even brand-new materials (such as bricks) may have these types of imperfections. A new material is not necessarily a flawless material. Flaws often lend the desired character to a material.

Here are some techniques to create these types of corruptions at the geometry level:

- **Chips on flat surfaces.** Create objects with high fractal (spiked) noise values and use them as Subtraction objects to take chunks and chips out of flat surfaces. Collapse the stack, if necessary, to keep the resulting object frugal with memory.

- **Splits and seams.** When you're using Loft objects, use open-ended shapes along the path to create splits and seams. On existing Mesh objects, try deleting a few vertices and moving vertices that surround the gap closer together to "almost close the hole."

- **Dents.** After a dent or chip has been carved out of an object, try applying a regional Noise modifier to the dented area by using a Volume Select modifier.

FIGURE 11.3
Brand new bricks for a fireplace often have cracks and chips in them.

Rounded Corners

Two of the most important corruptions you can create in materials are smoothings and rounded edges. Even if an object came with rigid corners, after a time of use its perfect edges may have been worn down to more rounded edges. It is easy to draw loft profile shapes without taking time to create small rounded fillets, but these tiny time-consuming edits are the very things that allow light to dance more realistically off an object and its material. The shower rail in figure 11.4 could easily be drawn with a sharp-cornered profile, but the thin reflective streaks along it are the result of very small rounded edges.

FIGURE 11.4
Although the rounded fillets of this rail are tiny, the reflection they cause is significant.

Shown in figure 11.5 is how the corners of a shower rail loft shape profile were refined to create rounded corners. This type of small refinement can impact even the simplest material's ability to reflect light more realistically.

FIGURE 11.5
Three vertices per corner were used to create these rounded fillets.

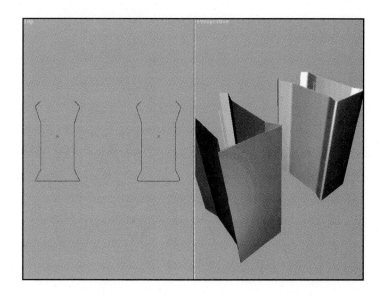

Bulges

Bulges are one of the easiest corruptions you can make to geometry. By applying Bend and Taper modifiers to the surfaces of objects, you can give a surface more character. Grab your favorite thin cardboard tea box or a milk carton and examine to see how the cardboard paper is folded and glued so that the material overlaps and bulges. Notice that the paper material has a visible thickness, and that the lid and the sides cave in or outward to accommodate the folding, leaving gaps everywhere that reveal more of the material maps applied than a "perfect" box primitive would. Figure 11.6 shows how such a tea box might be created with successive Edit Mesh and Bend modifiers applied to the sides of a box-shaped Loft object to bulge its sides. The lid is created with a separate tessellated mesh surface.

FIGURE 11.6
Cartons and packaging rarely look like perfectly orthogonal geometry.

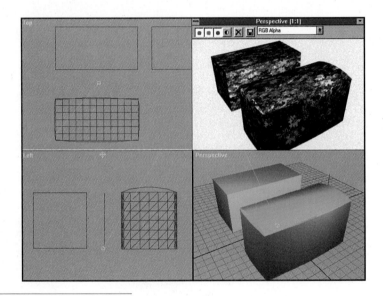

Surface Wrinkles and Folds

Many materials, especially fabrics, get most of their believability from the way the geometry to which they are applied undulates in random directions. Unless you want all your 3DS MAX fabrics to look as though they were soaked in starch for a year, crinkling, wrinkling, and folding geometry are crucial meshworking techniques. Figure 11.7 shows two rectangular meshes to which the same planar acrylic material has been applied. The rectangular mesh on the left was treated with successive applications of Edit Mesh modifiers and Noise modifiers using different Z axis strengths and applied over different areas of the mesh, and by applying a MeshSmooth modifier with "relaxing" over the final mesh.

FIGURE 11.7
Billowy acrylic fabric created from billowy geometry.

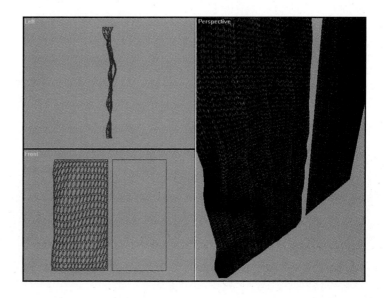

NOTE

The more you look at a material in the real world, the more its imperfect details become apparent. Take a digital camera out to a site where the objects you are trying to create are located. Take close-up photographs of them and view these images as you create the geometry for them. This can have as profound an impact on the resulting image as any bitmap you might apply to the object. When possible, have an example of the material in front of you.

Material Corruption Techniques

This portion of the chapter provides several tutorials to show how to create smears on shiny surfaces, discolorations in a material, puddles of liquid on a material, dusty materials, and dented and warped materials. These techniques can also be modified to create other types of material corruptions such as rot, rust, cracks, and streaks. The tutorials use the two bitmaps shown in figure 11.8 to create all corruptions treated. These types of bitmaps can be generated with any paint program that can export Truevision Targa (.TGA) files with alpha channel.

FIGURE 11.8

FIGURE 11.8
These two corruption bitmaps were generated with an airbrush tool in Animator Studio.

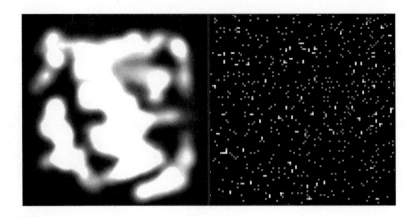

Discolorations

Discolorations in your materials can be the result of prolonged exposure to heat or moisture, defects in the material itself, or other materials resting on it. This technique creates stains, abrasions, spills, and other effects through variations in the RGB levels of bitmaps and the use of masks. Two blocks are used for these tutorials. The vertical wall block has the Kinetix logo on it, and the horizontal floor block is used for the corrupted materials. The floor block starts with a gray material.

CREATING DISCOLORATION

1. Open file 11CORRUP.MAX from the accompanying CD. Right-click on the Camera viewport to make it active. Then, on the main toolbar, click on the Render Scene button and then on the Material Editor button.

2. Make certain that the second sample slot (top middle) is selected. In the Maps rollout menu, click on the Diffuse button, select Composite from the Material/Map Browser, and then click on OK. In the Composite Parameters rollout menu, click on the Set Number button and set the value to 2.

3. Click on the Map 1 button, select Mask from the Material/Map Browser, and then click on OK.

4. In the Parameters rollout menu, click on the Map button; select Bitmap from the Material/Map Browser, and click on OK. In the Bitmap Parameters rollout menu, click on the Bitmap button and select the file \3DSMAX\MAPS\ASHSEN_2.GIF. This is a bitmap supplied with 3DS MAX.

5. Click on the Go To Parent button beneath the sample slots. Click on the Mask button, select Bitmap from the Material/Map Browser, and click on OK. In the Bitmap Parameters rollout menu, click on the Bitmap button and select the file 11IMX08A.BMP from the accompanying CD. Make certain that this file is in a legal Maps directory.

NOTE

You can disable the Show End Result button beneath the sample slots to see how the material is behaving as you construct it, level by level.

6. Click on the Go To Parent button beneath the sample slots. If Show End Result is disabled, an area of the sample slot now displays dark wood. Click on the Go To Parent button again. This takes you back to the Composite Parameters rollout menu, where you define the other half of the material.

7. Click on the Map 2 button, select Mask from the Material/Map Browser, and then click on OK. In the Parameters rollout menu, click on the Map button, select Bitmap from the Material/Map Browser, and then click on OK.

8. In the Bitmap Parameters rollout menu, click on the Bitmap button and select the file \3DSMAX\MAPS\ASHSEN_2.GIF. Open the Output rollout menu beneath the Bitmap Parameters rollout menu and set the RGB Level to a value of 2.0.

9. Click on the Go To Parent button beneath the sample slots. Click on the Mask button, select Bitmap from the Material/Map Browser, and then click on OK.

10. In the Bitmap Parameters rollout menu, click on the Bitmap button and select the file 11IMX08A.BMP. Open the Output rollout menu beneath the Bitmap Parameters rollout menu, and toggle Invert on.

11. Double-click on the Go To Parent button beneath the sample slots. You can now see streaks of brighter wood in the sample slot.

12. Make certain that the floor box is selected. Click on the Assign Material to Selection button beneath the sample slots, and render the Camera viewport. Figure 11.9 shows the discoloration.

FIGURE 11.9

By using masked areas of the same material with different RGB levels of the material, you can create discolorations in the material.

NOTE

For a variation on this technique to create stains, try setting the RGB level to a value between 0.0 and 1.0 instead of increasing the RGB level of the wood bitmap in the Output rollout menu.

Blurry Puddles and Smudges

Whether you are trying to create puddles of water, blurry smudges on polished surfaces, or varying levels of reflectivity in a material, the following technique, which uses a flat mirror and masks, serves a variety of purposes. Because this technique uses a flat mirror for regional reflection control, the entire material must be created not as a Standard material but as a Multi/Sub-Object material.

CREATING PUDDLES

1. Open file 11CORRUP.MAX from the accompanying CD. Right-click on the Camera viewport. Click on the Material Editor button on the main toolbar. Make certain that the second sample slot (top middle) is selected, and click on the Get Material button beneath the sample slots.

2. Select Multi/Sub-Object from the Material/Map Browser, and click on OK. In the basic Parameters rollout menu, click on the Set Number button and set the value to 1.

3. Click on the Material 1 button. In the Maps rollout menu, click on the Diffuse button, click on Mask, and then click on OK in the Material/Map Browser.

NOTE

You can disable the Show End Result button beneath the sample slots to see how the material is behaving as you construct it level by level.

4. In the Parameters rollout menu, click on the Map button, click on Bitmap, and then click on OK in the Material/Map Browser.

5. In the Bitmap Parameters rollout menu, click on the Bitmap button and select the file \3DSMAX\MAPS\CONCGREN.JPG. This is a bitmap supplied with 3DS MAX.

6. Click on the Go To Parent button beneath the sample slots. Click on the Mask button, click on Bitmap, and then click on OK in the Material/Map Browser.

7. In the Bitmap Parameters rollout menu, click on the Bitmap button and select the file 11IMX08A.BMP. In the Output rollout menu beneath the Bitmap Parameters rollout menu, toggle on Invert. Click on the Go To Parent button. If Show End Result is turned off, you can now see where the concrete material will show through.

8. Click on the Go To Parent button again. The main Maps rollout menu is displayed.

9. Click on the Diffuse button; then hold down the Pick button, drag until the boundary of the button is over the Bump Map button, and release. At the prompt, create an Instance of the Diffuse material so that values that change in the Diffuse channel will change also in the Bump channel. Set the value of the bump map to 100.

NOTE ──

Remember that the top limit for a bump map value is 999, not 100.

10. Make certain that the floor block is selected. Click on the Assign Material to Selected button under the sample slots, and render the Camera viewport. The gray areas define the puddles of water.

11. In the Maps rollout menu, click on the Reflection button, then on Mask, and then on OK in the Material/Map Browser.

12. In the Parameters rollout menu, click on the Map button, on Flat Mirror, and then on OK in the Material/Map Browser. The Blur value will be changed later to control the clarity of the reflection.

13. Click on the Go To Parent button. Click on the Mask button, on Bitmap, and then click on OK in the Material/Map Browser. In the Bitmap Parameters rollout menu, click on the Bitmap button and select the file 11IMX08A.BMP.

14. Double-click on the Go To Parent button to display the main Maps rollout menu.

15. Right-click on the Camera viewport, and click on Render Scene on the main toolbar. Now the white puddles on the concrete perfectly reflect the Kinetix logo. To change the color of the water reflecting the logo, decrease the value of the reflection map from 100 to 20. This reveals more of the material's main diffuse color (gray). To change the murkiness of the water, increase the Blur value of the flat mirror. Click on the Reflection Map button, click on the Map button, and change the Blur value to 10.0.

16. Double-click on the Go To Parent button, and render the Camera viewport. Your scene should resemble the one in figure 11.10.

The technique used to create smudges is similar to the puddle technique. The only difference is that the diffuse map uses a bitmap material rather than a masked material. By decreasing the value of the reflection map, therefore, the material bitmap shows through rather than the global diffuse color. To create oil stains on a wooden table, make the following changes to the current material:

FIGURE 11.10

The global diffuse color of the material determines the color of the reflecting material when the reflection map value is decreased.

CREATING OIL STAINS

1. Click on the Diffuse Map button, and then click on the Type button. Select Bitmap and click on OK in the Material/Map Browser. In the Bitmap Parameters rollout menu, select the wood bitmap file you used earlier (named \3DSMAX\MAPS\ASHSEN_2.GIF). Click on the Go To Parent button.

2. Pick on any map button labeled with the word None, and drag the button boundary over the Bump Map button, thereby setting *it* to None. This will make the wooden surface smooth.

3. Set the Reflection Map Value to 30, and render the Camera viewport. The reflective areas of the surface now give the illusion of oily or polished spots on the wood (see fig. 11.11).

FIGURE 11.11

Variations in the flat mirror's blur value and the value of the reflection map can create a wide range of material blemishes.

Scorch Marks and Dents

Chips and dents in the geometry can determine in a crucial manner the believability of some materials, especially when those chips and dents occur along the edges of an object. You can achieve a surprising degree of realism also by taking advantage of the Dent map type.

DENTS

1. Open file 11CORRUP.MAX from the accompanying CD. Right-click on the Camera viewport. Make certain that the second sample slot (top middle) is selected, and click on the Get Material button beneath the sample slots. Select Standard from the Material/Map Browser, and click on OK.

2. In the Maps rollout menu, click on the Diffuse button, click on Dent, and then click on OK in the Material/Map Browser. In the Dent Parameters rollout menu, set Size to a value of 1000, set Strength to a value of 5, and set Iterations to a value of 10.

3. Click on the Swap button to switch the white and black colors of the Dent map. Click on the Color 1 Maps button, click on Bitmap, and then click on OK in the Material/Map Browser. In the Bitmap Parameters rollout menu, select the wood bitmap file you used before (named \3DSMAX\MAPS\ASHSEN_2.GIF).

4. Double-click on the Go To Parent button to return to the main Maps rollout menu. Make certain that the floor box is selected, and then click on the Assign Material to Selection button beneath the sample slots.

5. Click on the Render Scene button of the main toolbar. The Dent map adds "scorch marks" to the wood material. To really get the effect of an indentation, you can recycle the diffuse map as a bump map and take chunks out of the object's edges (see fig. 11.12).

FIGURE 11.12

Actual nonrectilinear dents in the geometry edges and surfaces can be achieved easily by creating subtraction objects from severely deformed Noise-modified spheres.

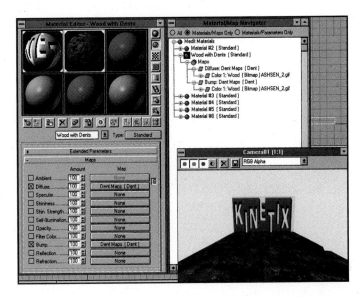

6. Click on the Diffuse button, hold down the Pick button, drag until the boundary of the button is over the bump map button, and then release.

7. At the prompt, create an Instance of the Diffuse material so that values which change in the Diffuse channel change in the Bump channel also. Set the value of the bump map to 100. Render the Camera viewport.

Dust

Creating dust and debris on materials is easy to do with composite materials that use maps with alpha channel information. If a corruption map is a Targa (.TGA) file with alpha information, it can be applied in the same way a decal is applied (but, in this case, to dirty up a surface).

Dust

1. Open file 11CORRUP.MAX from the accompanying CD. Right-click over the Camera viewport. Make certain that the second sample slot (top middle) is selected. Click on the Get Material button beneath the sample slots. Select Standard from the Material/Map Browser, and click on OK.

2. In the Maps rollout menu, click on the Diffuse button, click on Composite, and then click on OK in the Material/Map Browser. In the Composite Parameters rollout menu, click on the Set Number button, and set the value to 2. In Composite maps, higher-numbered maps overlay lower-numbered maps; the dusty material will take the Map 2 slot and the wooden material will take the Map 1 slot.

3. Click on the Map 1 button, select Bitmap from the Material/Map Browser, and click on OK. In the Bitmap Parameters rollout menu, click on the Bitmap button, and select the wooden bitmap file named \3DSMAX\MAPS\ASHSEN_2.GIF.

4. Click on the Go To Parent button beneath the sample slots. Then click on the Map 2 button, select Bitmap from the Material/Map Browser, and click on OK. In the Bitmap Parameters rollout menu, click on the Bitmap button and select the file 11IMX08B.TGA. Make certain that this file is in a legal Maps directory.

Note

To verify the alpha channel data in file 11IMX08B.TGA, use the File, View File pull-down menu option and pick the file 11IMX08B.TGA. When the image is displayed, use the Display Alpha Channel button to show the white-to-black levels of opacity in the image. In purely white areas, nothing will show through. In purely black areas, any materials underneath will show through completely. Gray areas are areas of partial opacity. Close the image window.

5. Make certain that the floor box is selected. Click on the Assign Material to Selection button beneath the sample slots, and render the Camera viewport. This image demonstrates the way basic decals are applied to materials. If the desired effect is a crisp, clean image of the corruption map, the corrupting map must account for areas in the image in which edges meet the underlying material. By softening and anti-aliasing the opaque areas in the corruption map, you can avoid sharp, jagged edges where the overlapping material meets the underlying material. To create the illusion of a thin veil of dust, however, tiling, dimming, and blurring of the corruption map are necessary.

6. In the Coordinates rollout menu, set the U and V tiling values to 3.0, and set the Blur Offset value to 0.1. In the Output rollout menu, set the RGB Level to 0.9. Render the Camera viewport. The specks in the corruption map have been blurred by the expanded tiling, and the RGB Level change has reduced each speck's density (see fig. 11.13). Save this file for use in the weathering tutorial to follow.

FIGURE 11.13

Varying densities in the alpha channel of the corruption map can create very different effects, from dust to large snowflakes.

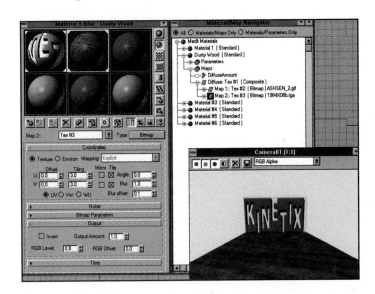

NOTE

The Blur Offset value should be used like Tabasco sauce in cooking: go easy on the amount you use to get the right effect. If you were to change the Blur Offset value from 0.0 to 0.2 rather than 0.1 in this example, the dust effect would be lost.

Weathering

One of the great challenges faced by many 3DS MAX users who want to create realistic scenes is learning how to keep from giving the scenes an overwhelming sense of newness. In the same way you can apply dust and soot (try values between 0.0 and 1.0 for the RGB Level value in the corruption map of the preceding example), you can also make a material look weathered and worn. One such effect is a sort of bleaching out or fading of a material's character. To easily accomplish this effect, take advantage of a Noise map. The next set of steps builds on the preceding tutorial, picking up where it ended.

AGING OBJECTS

1. Click on the Go To Parent button to return to the Composite Parameters rollout menu. Click on the Map 2 button, and then on the Type button. Select Noise, discard the map, and click on OK in the Material/Map Browser. In the Noise Parameters rollout menu, set the Noise Type to Fractal, and set the Size to 50. In the Output rollout menu, set the Output Amount to 0.5.

2. Render the Camera viewport. The effect, shown in figure 11.14, is a bleaching or fading of the material. The two colors specified in the noise map determine the weathering color, and the Output Level determines the severity of the weathering. With values close to 1.0, you can hardly make out wood at all. This also can be a neat corruption. Increasing the size parameter creates larger patches of weathering distortion.

FIGURE 11.14

Values near 1.0 for Noise Levels create wide sweeps of weathering. Values near 5.0 create concentrated splotches of weathering.

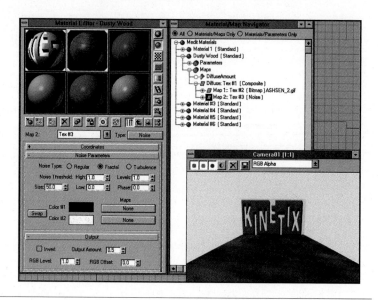

NOTE

For a variation on this technique, try experimenting with different Noise types and Size values. Try a different color for Color #2, or use a bitmap for Color #2. Set global Shininess Strength to 0 to achieve a thoroughly faded material.

These are just a few examples of ways to give your man-made materials some character. Although creating these types of corruptions may seem time-consuming, paying attention to these types of details can have a huge impact on the mood of your scenes. It doesn't take long to build up a library of corruption maps that can be slapped on top of other materials for "instant grime." The real challenge is to keep notes on variable settings. Trying to remember all the possible effects that different numeric values have, applied to a given corruption map, is next to impossible. Experiment with the settings, and when you get the effect you want, take notes!

Creating Man-Made Materials

One very helpful technique for keeping track of the man-made materials you create is to use the material category as the first word of the material's name. By calling a material Concrete Gray rather than Gray Concrete, you can view the entire group of concrete materials in a scene or in a library, if necessary. Users seldom need to look at "all the red stuff" in a library, but often need to look at all the woods, all the concretes, all the glass, or all the plastic materials. Using a consistent set of properties in the material names (such as the material's color and texture) also proves helpful. Having Concrete Gray Grooved, Concrete Gray Smooth, and Concrete Gray Grainy together in a list of materials for a scene or in a library materials can save a great deal of time when you try to find them by color or texture. Some users take this approach to the next level by creating copies of their libraries organized by material category, by color, and by texture. The same material might be named Concrete Gray Grooved in one library, Gray Concrete Grooved in another, and Grooved Concrete Gray in a third. In this way, you can find a material if you know any one of its three main properties.

One of the easiest ways to get your hands dirty with man-made materials is to examine the materials supplied with 3DS MAX in the default materials library. From metals to woods to ceramic tiles, wonderful examples are already assembled on your hard drive. These materials can show you how map types, settings and parameters, and bitmaps can be combined to give surfaces the appearance you want. This section outlines techniques (and variations on those techniques) for creating a variety of man-made materials. Each material category includes examples of diverse material types, a few techniques, and some examples (including corruption considerations) of how to create the material.

NOTE

Frequently, you will need bitmaps of the materials you want to create. For suggestions on how to acquire bitmaps, refer to Chapter 9, "Materials Management and Manipulation."

Concretes

Concretes are one of the quickest man-made materials to create. The 3DS MAX library provides some good examples of concrete, and many architectural material libraries have a collection of different concretes with common textures; Autodesk's Texture Universe (see fig. 11.15) is an example. Some examples of concrete textures include smooth walls, porous CMU block, raked pavement, and sidewalks with tarred seams.

FIGURE 11.15
Concretes come in many different colors. The key consideration for realism is texture, controlled primarily by bump maps.

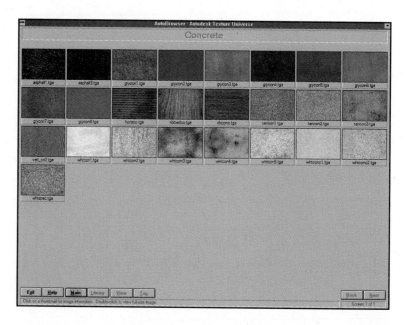

Creation Techniques

Concrete can be created quickly by using a bitmap of the concrete texture for a diffuse map, and recycling it for a bump map to control the texture. Slippery or smooth concrete can be shiny. You can apply a Noise map or a concentrated Dent map for different concrete textures. This works especially well for long strips or wide surfaces of concrete. For CMU and other grainy concrete, a fibrous bitmap used as a bump map works very well and can be generated in minutes with Noise maps of small size values (see fig. 11.16). File CMU.MAX is provided on the accompanying CD for a quick example. For raked driveways, sidewalks, and porches, tileable grooved bump maps work well; seams and cracks can easily be draped over as decal-style materials.

FIGURE 11.16
An example of a fibrous bump map used to create a grainy concrete masonry unit.

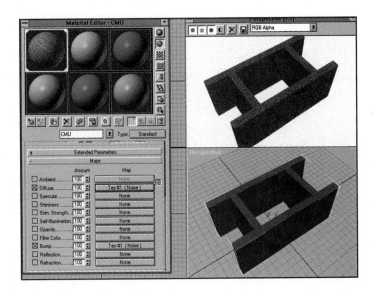

Corruptions

Concrete often has water or oil stains, cracks, chips, or uneven expansion slots. Concrete also collects puddles. It may be covered with debris and have discolorations from heavily used areas. Concrete textures also vary widely from smooth to porous.

Paper and Cardboard

One of the trickiest things about creating paper materials is addressing the material's thickness. For thin paper materials such as bond, a 0.0 height patch grid will usually work with an applied subtle bond texture. For thicker paper materials such as milk cartons and cardboard packaging, however, the geometry gets more complicated.

Creation Techniques

Creating a sheet of paper can be as simple as creating a flat patch grid with a bitmap of what is on the paper. On the other hand, the process is more complicated when you create "sturdier" paper, such as the corrugated packaging cardboard used for heavy shipments. For sheets or reams of paper, use patch grid connected at the seams. This gives you the ability to bend, fold, or bulge edges or areas on the sheet, if necessary. Subtle Noise modifiers can add a hint of realism to sheets sitting on flat surfaces. One way to make cardboard geometry is to create the cardboard profile as a shape and generate a lofted object for the sheet (see fig. 11.17). File CARDBORD.MAX on the accompanying CD provides a simple guide to this method. Widely spaced, subtle dents lend believability to cardboard.

FIGURE 11.17
Cardboard surfaces rarely stay flat. The key to realism in a paper material is the way its geometry sits on truly flat surfaces.

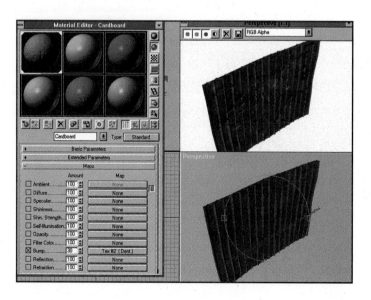

Corruptions

Paper-type materials can be stained, waterlogged, indented, punctured, folded, wrinkled, smudged, and rolled. Surfaces can range from shiny lamination to dull packaging. On some paper objects, especially those used for packaging, rounded corners and subtle bulging can make all the difference in their believability. Try to avoid perfectly orthogonal surfaces; most paper materials are not metal-stiff. Widely spread-out dents and bended edges are classic corruptions.

Woods

Half the challenge of getting a wooden material to look right is having the right bitmap. Wood, being an organic material, can be an extremely difficult pattern to tile seamlessly. Many users will use a high-resolution bitmap to cover an entire object rather than try to use a low-resolution bitmap that is tiled. By purchasing a collection of seamless tileable wooden materials such as those shown in figure 11.18, you can expand significantly your ability to create and work with wooden materials, because creating tileable and seamless wood bitmaps yourself can be very time-consuming.

FIGURE 11.18

If you intend to do much work with woods, a collection of tileable wood bitmaps is an excellent investment.

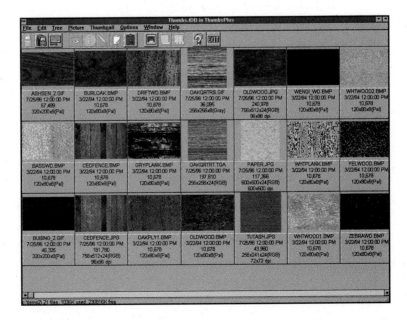

Examples of wood materials include smooth maple desktops, rain-weathered knotted pine fences, punctured cork, patterned floor tiles, dull oak, fake wood laminate, unpolished balsa, chopped logs, sawdust, and grainy plywood.

Creation Techniques

The 3DS MAX default library contains a wide assortment of wooden materials you can look at for examples. If you cannot get a tileable wood bitmap, try to work with wood bitmaps large enough to accommodate the entire object, so as to avoid seams that don't match seams. To apply a wooden planar map to an object with a minimum of streaking, an old trick is to apply the bitmap UVW modifier at an oblique angle to all flat sides of the object. Wood tiling works quite well on floors, walls, and other horizontal surfaces. For unusually shaped wooden objects, use of the Wood map type also can be helpful. To create wood laminates, apply raw wood bitmaps to perfectly flat surfaces; this effect looks intentionally fake.

Corruptions

Woods are easy materials to corrupt. Wood corruptions can include smudges, warps, stains, discolorations, weathering, scratches, chips, dents, scorchings, rough or oily patches, and dust. Examples of these corruptions are discussed in this chapter's tutorials.

Stones

The ability to creating man-made stone materials that have been polished or cut depends in large part on the stone bitmap's detail. For stone types with thin veins of different colors, higher resolutions are a must. Stone materials of stones arranged in patterns pose the same types of challenges that wooden materials do—both materials are difficult to seam and tile realistically. Again, the purchase of a stone materials collection can save you a tremendous amount of time.

Examples of stone materials include translucent and refractive diamonds, metallic and shiny marbles, grainy and dull pebbles, streaked basalts and sharp-cornered crystals, fine sand and sandstones, and petrified wood.

Creation Technique

You can create diamonds of different colors by using lathing diamond profiles and applying reflection or refraction maps (see fig. 11.19). The material requires strong shininess and opacity values, and the filter color determines the color of the "glass." Geometry for believable stones, rocks, and even asteroids can be generated easily by applying strong Noise modifiers along all three axes to a sphere (see fig. 11.20). Grainy stone materials and marbles also can be achieved through the use of Noise and Marble map types. Sand bitmaps work well applied as diffuse maps and bump maps.

FIGURE 11.19

The more facets the diamond geometry has, the more it can play with spectral reflections.

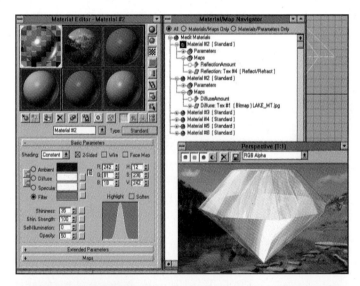

FIGURE 11.20

By using different colors for the Noise diffuse map, you can create very different stone textures.

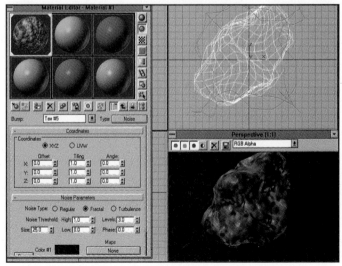

Corruptions

Stones, like woods, are easy materials to corrupt. Corruptions can include smudges, warps, stains, discolorations, weathering, scratches, chips, scorchings, rough or oily patches, and dust. Examples of these corruptions are discussed in this chapter's tutorials.

Plastics

Shininess and opacity play major roles in determining a material's plasticity. The 3DS MAX default library contains several examples of plastics (including shiny, dull, and mottled). Because plastics typically absorb a great deal of light, a hint of ambient light in a scene can dramatically enhance a plastic material's appearance.

Examples of plastic materials include the shiny solid plastic of telephones; the dull, textured, semitransparent plastic of milk jugs; crinkled clear plastic, such as that used for "zippered" storage bags; the tinted plastics used in small accessories for offices; and the mottled, blurry, semitransparent plastic of shower curtains.

Creation Techniques

Solid plastics are fairly easy to create using full opacity. When you create plastic lights, rely on the material's self-illumination settings. Blur values are more important that any other factor in making semitransparent and clear plastics believable, and the plastic's geometry can make or break its realism. Figure 11.21 shows an example of how a Patch grid object, tessellated repeatedly with tri and quad patches and corrupted with Noise and Bend modifiers, can be used with a transparent, highly reflective material to create plastic wrap. Note how crucial the materials and backdrop color behind the wrap are to giving it a sense of transparency. File PLASWRAP.MAX on the accompanying CD can be used as a reference for creating crinkly materials such as plastic wrap and aluminum!

Corruptions

Corruptions can include rips and rough edges, crinkles, cuts and dents, stains, blurred textures, and streaks. The weathering techniques outlined earlier in this chapter can be used very effectively on plastics.

FIGURE 11.21

*If you intend to work
often with plastics,
purchasing a collection
of tileable plastic
bitmaps is a good idea.*

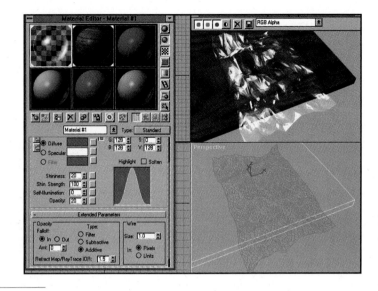

Rubber and Vinyl

Among the easiest types of materials to create are matte materials, such as rubber and vinyl. These can be generated by using small Shininess Strength values with wide spectral areas. Rubber and vinyl objects are more likely to have punctures and tears in them than folds or wrinkles, and rarely are these materials perfectly flat.

Examples of rubber and vinyl materials include tires, furniture coverings, tabletop surfaces, floor stripping, and cartridges.

Creation Techniques

To create a typical rubber material, you can use the default materials in the sample slots with a smaller value for Shininess. Experiment with this value; it can make the difference between a vinyl and a plastic. In the file VINYL.MAX on the accompanying CD, each of the sample slot materials has had its Shininess value set to 20 in the Material Editor. By applying subtle Checker maps, Dent maps, or Noise maps, you can add a grid of graininess or ribbon of wear-and-tear to the surfaces to which the material is applied. Figure 11.22 shows a vinyl shield collar whose rounded edges and bulged surfaces enable the material's dull specular highlights to stand out.

FIGURE 11.22

*By using different
Material IDs assigned
to different faces of
mesh objects, you can
control which areas of
the vinyl are smooth
and which are bumpy.*

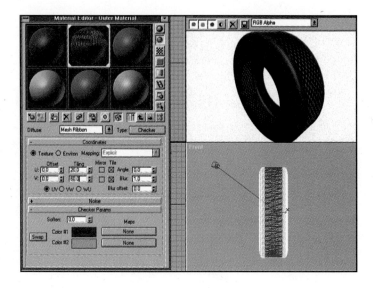

Corruptions

Corruptions include streaks, slashes, punctures, dents, cuts, oily spots, and abrasions. Again, the weathering techniques outlined previously in this chapter work very effectively on vinyls and rubbers.

Glass

Many examples of glass materials are provided in the 3DS MAX default library. The tutorials in the middle of this chapter also treat refraction techniques. Typical challenges a user faces to creating glasswork are obtaining believable refraction of materials behind glass, creating a glass thickness at edges of the object, blurring of images through glass, and glass corruptions.

Examples of glass materials include warped jars, tinted and leaded oven window glass, dot-matrixed textured glass, ceramics, frosted crystal, opaque mixing bowls, textured shower doors, and stained-glass windows.

Creation Techniques

Typical glass materials use mid to low Opacity settings, a two-sided material to create specular highlights through the material, and mid to high levels of Shininess. The Extended Parameters rollout menu has crucial settings that control a glass material's tinting, refraction, and opacity fall-off. A thorough examination of these values is provided in Chapter 21 of *Inside 3D Studio MAX Volume I*, under "Opacity Parameters." Used with subtlety, composite materials (decals) are an easy way to frost, texture, smudge, and blur glass materials. For static scenes, you can get away with murder by using 2D paint programs to create post-processed glass effects. Do not underestimate these types of techniques! They are fast and effective.

One old trick often used to create the illusion of a textured blurry glass material is to render the scene without the glass and use a 2D paint program's brightening, jumbling, tinting, and softening tools in the "glass area" (see fig. 11.23). Autodesk's Animator Studio makes successive applications of different inks to the same areas a cinch with its Repeat Ink application feature. Many refraction and reflection filter inks are also available for these types of raster-editing programs. File CERAMICS.MAX on the accompanying CD shows how the default Glass material can be varied to create a ceramic glass material (see fig. 11.24). IOR values between 0.5 and 1.0 work well for refraction and reflection maps used this way. Loading the default Glass material and experimenting with its values is a great way to discover new types of glass materials.

FIGURE 11.23

Painting glass effects into a static scene can be quick and powerful.

FIGURE 11.24

By using refraction and reflection maps in a glass material, you can create the illusion of textured or opaque glass materials, such as polished ceramics.

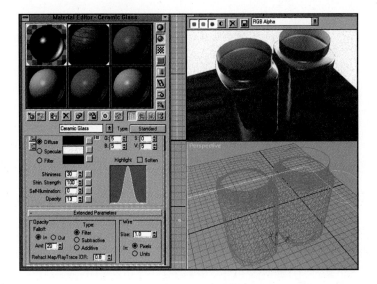

Corruptions

Corruptions include cracks, stains, condensation, oily smears and streaks, dust and rain marks, warping, bulges, and blurs. Bitmaps such as those used to create puddles, dull spots, discolorations, and dust can be applied mildly to glass surfaces to create these types of corruptions.

Metals, Meshes, and Wires

The 3DS MAX default library includes many examples that show how environment and scenery bitmaps can be manipulated to create gold, silver, chromes, and brushed and mottled metallic materials. Crumpling techniques such as the one outlined in the plastics section of this chapter can be used to create foils and crumpled metal sheets. Creating curvilinear metals is relatively easy, but creating believable flat metallic materials can be tricky.

Examples of metal, mesh, and wire materials include tin and aluminum foil, brushed metals, polished brass, dull gold, aluminum siding, stainless steel, woven metallic fabric, chromes, and rusted panels.

Creation Techniques

Materials for many of the metal, mesh, and wire examples exist in the MAX library. Many bitmap material collections contain wide assortments of metallic bitmaps, such as those shown in figure 11.25. When these bitmaps are used as diffuse maps, bump maps, and shininess maps, they make very realistic metals.

FIGURE 11.25

Metals have unlimited textures. By brightening, tinting, or smoothing existing metallic bitmaps, you can create radically new metallic-looking materials.

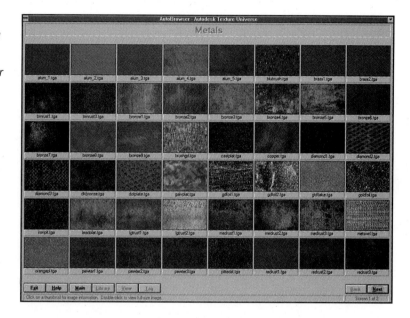

Reflective metals are easiest to create on curved surfaces because those surfaces distort the reflected environment objects and maps more drastically than flat surfaces do. To create reflective flat metals, you need "busy maps" such as the files CHRMWARP.JPG and CHROMIC.JPG in your \3DSMAX\MAPS directory. By themselves, these maps seem like chaotic swirls of black and white. Applied to a flat surface with the right material settings, however, they produce stunning flat metals. To see how this works, follow these steps:

FLAT METALS

1. Open the file 11FLTMET.MAX from the accompanying CD. Two boxes that represent slabs of metal appear. Click on the Material Editor off the main toolbar and examine the materials in sample slots 1 and 2.

2. Notice that a busy map has been applied for the Reflection Map channel. The Coordinate rollout menu uses Spherical Environment mapping mode, double tiling values to spread the bitmap wider across the surface, and a dab of Blur Offset to distort the raw bitmap pattern. Notice also that the Box objects have only one segment in each axis. Render the Perspective viewport to get two very different metallic materials (see fig. 11.26). Concentrated noise maps, dent maps, wood maps, and marble maps can also create these kinds of busy maps.

FIGURE 11.26

"Busy maps," applied with wide tiling and effective blurring, give flat surfaces the appearance of metal.

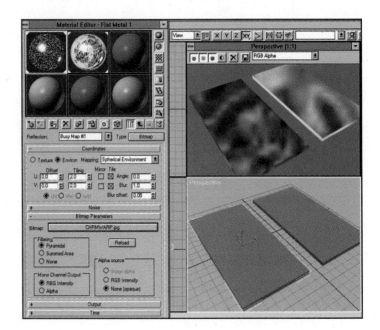

NOTE

For a variation on this technique, change values for the U and V Offsets, change Tiling values, and vary the Blur Offset ever so slightly. The smallest change in this setting has a profound impact on the resulting material.

Woven metal fabric, such as wire screens, can be created in the same way, except that the Wire toggle is activated in the Basic Parameters rollout of the material, the number of segments of the object must be increased to create the wire density of the mesh, the wire thickness must be set in the Extended Parameters rollout, and the thickness of the object needs to be reduced to 0.0. File 11MSHMET.MAX on the accompanying CD can be used as a reference for these settings. In addition, like most fabrics, wire mesh looks more believable when it is wrinkled a bit. This can be achieved by applying a subtle Noise modifier (see fig. 11.27).

FIGURE 11.27

Different Noise modifier seed values can make the wire mesh look very different.

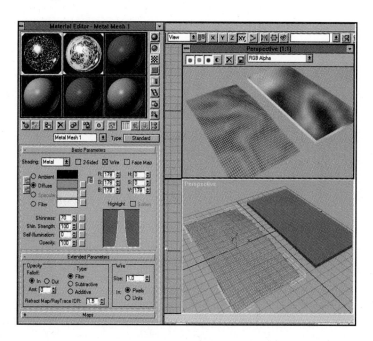

The simplest way to create the geometry for wire is to create a spline for the wire path and use a large circle as a beginning Loft object shape. After the Loft object tube is created and the metallic material has been applied to it, go back to the circle shape; in the Modify panel, decrease the radius value to something very small. To be effective, this value will vary according to the material's distance from the camera. Figure 11.28 shows an example of wire created with this technique. Examine the file 11WIRE.MAX from the accompanying CD for a closer look at the material applied to the Loft object.

FIGURE 11.28
Wire for coat hangers,
for wiring between
circuits, and for
antennae is easy to
create with a splined
Loft object.

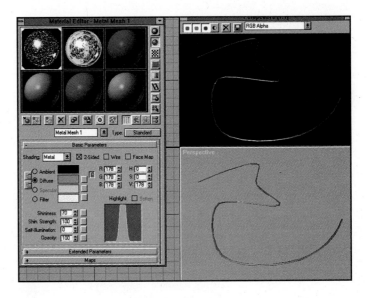

Note

This technique can be used also for creating string and rope. For rope, apply a bump map that recycles the rope bitmap used for the diffuse map.

Corruptions

Corruptions include rust, crumples, dents and bends, smears, abrasions, tears, and corrosion. Rust and corrosions that appear in metallic diffuse maps can be greatly enhanced by applying bump maps that only treat the areas of rust and corrosion. Use a 2D paint program to make a copy of the original metallic diffuse bitmap. Brighten the areas of rust and corrosion in the bitmap, and change all remaining areas to a black color value. Apply the resulting bitmap as a perfectly superimposed bump map.

Fabrics

The realism of fabrics depends almost entirely on the resolution of the fabric bitmap to accommodate the fabric's detail and on the suitability of the geometry onto which the fabric material is mapped. Of all the man-made materials treated in this chapter, fabrics require the greatest attention to detail, for their geometry. Figure 11.29 shows two bolts of fabric, similar to those you might find at a fabric warehouse. The front bolt holds denim, and the one in the rear holds rayon.

FIGURE 11.29
3D Studio MAX's capability to view materials in the viewport saves time when you're setting effective bitmap tiling values. To accelerate the viewport refresh rates of the material currently being worked on, disable the viewing of other objects in a scene.

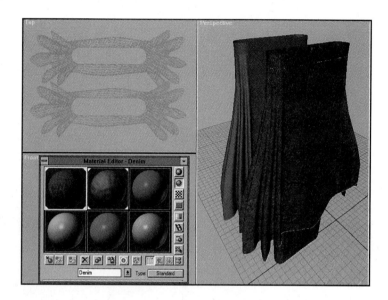

Examples of fabric materials include linens (easily wrinkled fabrics), denim, leather, velvet, corduroy, synthetics (acrylics), terrycloth, flannel, wool, satin, silk, lace, and carpet.

Creation Techniques

The geometry of "folds" of fabric draped over the edges of a horizontal surface can be achieved rather easily through the use of the horizontal surface as a loft shape at 0 percent of the loft path, and a vertical Noise-modified "folds shape" as a loft shape at 100 percent of the loft path. Fabrics with frayed edges can be achieved through the use of fabric bitmaps with alpha channel gaps where the material is frayed, and through the recycling of these bitmaps used for opacity maps. Wrinkling can be achieved through the combined use of space warp transforms and Noise modifiers.

Pay close attention to a fabric's thickness. Silks and satins should be paper thin. Acrylic and wool fabrics, on the other hand, usually have a noticeable thickness when viewed from the side. After using multiple transforms and modifiers to deform an object so that it's the way you want it, you can minimize that object's use of memory by collapsing the stack of the object. Most fabric bitmaps can be used as bump maps to complement their use as diffuse maps, but they can also be used as shininess maps and spectral maps to give highlights to a material.

Creating seamless and tileable fabric materials such as those shown in figure 11.30 can take a great deal of time, and a fabrics bitmap collection is a good investment. One of the greatest challenges for many fabrics is to avoid giving a look of stiffness to the fabric's surfaces and orthogonality to the fabric's boundaries. MeshSmooth and Relax modifiers can help tremendously with abrupt Noise modifiers applied to surfaces. Likewise, by increasing the number of mesh vertices along the perimeter of a fabric object, you are better able to corrupt its unnatural linearity. Metallic materials actually work quite well for satins and silks.

FIGURE 11.30

These fabrics are only as effective as the light cast on them. When fabrics are used in a scene, make certain that Ambient Lighting is set to a value other than zero to brighten their highlights in all areas of the scene.

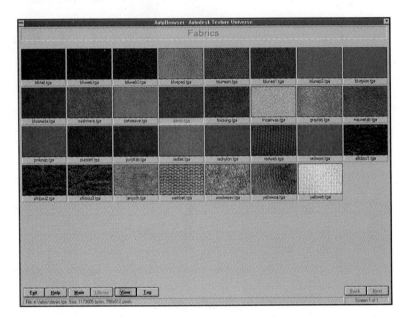

Corruptions

Corruptions include seams, stains, frays, wrinkles, blemishes, and fades. The edges of many fabrics can be corrupted effectively by using flat trim objects, as discussed earlier in this chapter.

Experiment!

The unlimited potential of man-made material bitmaps to create new materials when applied in unorthodox ways is staggering. Fabric materials can create new metals, concretes, and interior wall surfaces—and concretes can create new fabrics. Toy with a bitmap's Tiling and Blur settings to see what other possibilities the bitmap has. Remember that material bitmaps need not be used "as provided" or "as captured." If you have a 2D paint program at your disposal, try corrupting these raw bitmaps with various inks, such as Brightness, Jumble, Soften, and Emboss. Save the new materials with new names.

When possible, place a sample of the material where you can look at it while you are designing the material in MAX. Use a bitmap viewer at full-screen, with photo-captures of the objects or scenes you are reproducing. Toggle back and forth between MAX and the viewer by using Alt+Tab. In this way you can make man-made material design a pleasurable experience.

Many companies that produce man-made materials also provide catalogs and samples. Architectural offices are typically swamped with laminate and tile samples, material catalogs, and color-guides. Trips with a digital camera to your local fabric warehouse or home-building supply warehouse can help you create quick libraries of woods, plastics, glass, and fabric materials in a few days. Balance the cost of a digital camera against the cost of premade material bitmap collections and the value of the time you would have to spend to create seamless and tileable versions of your bitmaps.

Finally, remember to keep a sense of the material's "time and place onstage" when you dedicate hours to material design. It is easy to get caught up in creating masterfully detailed materials, but this is not profitable if your materials will be in front of the camera for only a few seconds or are applied to objects too far in the scene's background to be appreciated.

In Practice: Designing Man-Made Materials

- **Age.** Consider the age of the elements in your scene. Unless everything you intend to visualize is brand-spanking new, you can achieve more dramatic scenes by aging their elements. When you create materials, give thought to how time acts upon them. The white paper pages of an old book fade or yellow. The high-traffic areas of a carpet or wooden floor reveal trails.

- **Lighting.** Consider how imperfect lighting can accentuate imperfect materials in a scene. In the case of a lamp, if the lampshade is tilted or worn, the light emitted from it may be dulled or projected against a nearby wall slightly off-center. The level of brightness above the lamp may be different than the level of brightness below the lamp due to discoloration of the shade. The glow behind the lampshade may have cracks of brightness revealed where an interior plastic lampshade shield has overheated. Imperfect lighting results from imperfect light source materials.

- **Location.** Consider the imperfect locations of elements in your scene. In the case of a house interior scene, tilting one of several chairs at a dining room table, leaving a pen or book resting at a non-symmetrical non-orthogonal angle to the edges of a table surface, leaving curtains half-open, a slightly tilted lampshade, or patches on the rug where more traffic occurs, can all suggest in subtle ways that these places and items are used, and therefore, their materials are real.

IMAGE BY DAVE ESPINOSA-AGUILAR

Chapter 12

by dave espinosa-aguilar

DESIGNING SPECIAL EFFECTS MATERIALS

Many ordinary features in 3D Studio MAX can be used in extraordinary ways to produce wild and unexpected variations in material properties. Through the use of Video Post Filters, Light Objects, Environmental Atmospheres, and unusual geometries, you can generate a vast array of special effects materials. The techniques for designing these materials can vary with static and dynamic images because the believability of a material may or may not be dependent on an object's motion or behavior. This chapter and the following chapter examine several ways to create special effects materials in static and dynamic images, respectively.

Special effects materials can be created in 3D Studio MAX by using tools you may already be familiar with in new ways: by corrupting existing materials with exaggerated settings, by viewing ordinary effects from unusual angles, and by experimenting with some of the program's internal special effects capabilities. This chapter covers the following effects:

- Explosions
- Lighting and Glowing Effects
- Psychedelic Materials

Each of the topics in this chapter outline ways in which these common tools can be combined to produce very different images.

Explosions

The first example shows how two Combustion apparatuses can be combined seamlessly to create the Combustion Atmospheric Effect of a flaming fireball. When Combustion apparatuses overlap, a very noticeable boundary is created by the last apparatus listed in the effects list. It is by tweaking the seed values for the apparatuses and the characteristics of the effect, and by placing the engulfed geometry within the apparatuses that this seam is avoided.

The second example shows how Atmosphere Effect characteristics can be exploited to create explosive shapes other than flames. Through careful placement of the Combustion apparatus, you can limit the concentration of thin flames to create spurts. By using an elongated Combustion apparatus, you can create bands of flames that can be used as tiled materials to produce lava flows and streams of fire.

The third example shows how the combined use of overlapping Particle Systems and Combustion Atmospheric Effects can create shattered glass, blast effects, and smoke. The Combustion Atmospheric Effect has an Explosion capability built right into it. By setting ranges of values for the Phase of the explosion, you an produce smokeless flames, smokey flames, or flameless smoke. Particle Systems can use varying flake or drop sizes to produce a more convincing debris.

NOTE ──

The Combustion Atmospheric Effect was introduced in 3D Studio MAX Release 1.1. If you are using an earlier release, the techniques in this section do not apply.

A Bursting Meteor

Meteors burst into flames when they enter the atmosphere. At the front of the meteor is a superheated flame generated from the air friction, and at the rear of the meteor is a trailing flame. Producing flames with the Combustion Atmospheric Effect and Combustion apparatus is not a difficult thing to do after you know the basic steps, but combining these effects without creating ugly flame boundaries is quite a tricky task.

When two or more apparatuses are positioned close together in a scene, the order in which the effects are listed in the Atmosphere Effects listbox has a profound impact on the final image. If any of the effects have a high enough density to hide effects behind them, a very noticeable seam appears at the flame boundaries.

To dissolve this seam with high-density effects requires two things— tweaking the seed values for each Combustion apparatus so that the flame boundaries match up, and tweaking geometry that can disrupt the seam between the two Combustion apparatuses. Open file 12METEOR.MAX (see fig. 12.1). Use the Rendering/Environment pull-down, and select either of the Combustion items listed in the Effects listbox to examine the shapes and settings of each Combustion Atmospheric Effect. Select the Combustion apparatuses and click on the Modify panel to see the settings for each apparatus.

NOTE ──

The Combustion Atmospheric Effects in this scene have already been linked to the Combustion apparatuses.

The meteor object was created by applying a Noise Modifier with varying strengths in the X, Y, and Z axis to a 16-segment sphere. The Meteor material applied to the meteor is a basic Noise Map applied as a diffuse map and a bump map by using default values. The two Combustion apparatuses have been placed in a way to create the effect of the flames at the front and rear of the meteor.

FIGURE 12.1

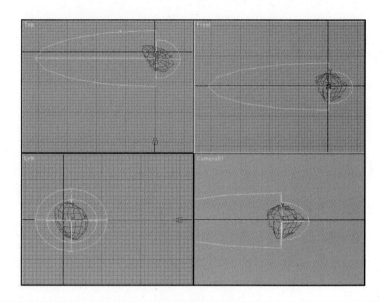

A meteor object with two aligned Combustion apparatuses.

To create a Combustion apparatus, follow these steps:

1. In the Create panel, click on the Helpers button.

2. Click on the object subcategory drop-down and select Atmospheric Apparatus.

3. Click on the Combustion button.

4. Pick a point in a viewscreen and drag to set the radius of the apparatus. A toggle is provided to create spherical or hemispherical boundaries for the object.

You can non-uniformly scale spherical and hemispherical apparatuses to control the shape of the combustion boundary area. After an apparatus is created, you need to attach an Atmospheric Environment Effect to it. To so attach, follow these steps:

1. Choose Rendering, Environment. The Environment dialog appears.

2. In the Atmosphere area of the dialog, click on the Add button. Select Combustion from the Add Atmospheric Effect dialog and click on OK. Combustion now appears in the Effects list.

3. In the Combustion Parameters area, in the Source Apparatus panel, click on the Pick Object button and select the apparatus in the viewscreen. The name of the apparatus now appears in the field to the right of the button.

After an apparatus has been created and attached to an Environment Effect, you can render and view the combustion effect (see fig. 12.2). In this example, a fireball flame type is used at the front of the meteor, and a tendril flame type is used near the rear of the meteor, with a wider apparatus radius to match the flame boundaries of the fireball. By selecting an apparatus and entering the Modify panel, you can vary the shape of the flames by setting different seed values in the Combustion Parameters rollout.

Figure 12.2
The meteor explodes into flames as it enters an atmosphere.

The meteor does not have to be centered on the hemispherical apparatuses. Depending on how much of the object you want revealed through the flames, you can move the object farther from or closer to the camera. You can also move the meteor completely in front of the apparatuses to create a glowing burn that completely reveals the entire meteor rather than a consuming burn that envelopes it.

TIP

Try several different apparatus seeds to get the cleanest flame match at the seam.

Render this scene with the meteor object hidden to get a better idea of how combustion flames match up. The order in which atmospheric effects are listed makes a blatant impact on the appearance of the *seam* between the flame types. In this example, the fireball is rendered after the tendril so that a clean vertical seam is created. It is the geometry of the meteor that destroys the appearance of the seam.

WARNING ————————————————————————————————————

Be aware that fireballs traveling in nonvertical directions can appear to burn *upward* with certain Combustion Parameter settings. You can blur the appearance of fireball flames to avoid giving the flames a direction.

An Erupting Volcano

Volcanoes produce a wide array of different exploding and combusting material effects, from lava spurting from the mouth of the volcano to fiery streams of lava flowing down the side of the volcano. By using tendril flame shapes with thin flame sizes and concealing the core of an attached Combustion apparatus beneath geometry, you can isolate the tips of flame tendrils to produce hot spurts. By using over-elongated apparatuses and rendering a perpendicular view of a Combustion Atmospheric Effect out to a Targa file (which includes alpha information), you can create a lava river material that can be draped over other materials to produce rivers and streams of lava.

Experimenting with the colors, shapes, characteristics, motions, and explosion parameters of the Combustion Atmospheric Effect can be time-consuming, but rewarding; the tool's settings can produce radically different results. Open file 12VOLCANO.MAX (see fig. 12.3). In this model, the landscape is generated with a 0.0 height box that uses a Noise Modifier and an Edit Mesh Modifier's Affect Region function to bulge the object into a volcano.

Examine the settings of the Combustion Atmospheric Effects and the Combustion apparatus to see how the smaller flame sizes and other characteristics create spurts. To create the lava material, open file 12LAVMAP.MAX and render the Camera viewport. After this image is saved out to a Targa file, alpha channel information is saved wherever the flame does not show (see fig. 12.4). An elongated fireball creates a band of fire that can be draped across surfaces. The more elongated the apparatus is, the straighter the band of flames will be.

FIGURE 12.3

Two combustion apparatuses are used to create flames within the volcano and lava splashing against the landscape in the foreground.

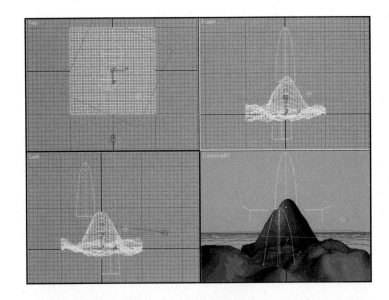

FIGURE 12.4

A band of flames is created from an elongated fireball.

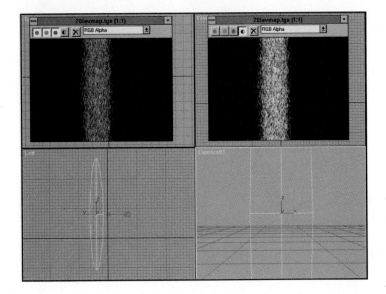

Reopen the file 12VOLCANO.MAX and examine the materials used in the scene to see how the composited maps were tweaked to create a deep-glowing, red-mountainous material with a stream of lava. Notice that the tile settings of the material can have a profound impact on the appearance of the material. You can increase or decrease these settings to change the overall character of the flowing lava.

An Omni light is placed to light the landscape and the lava river material mapped to it. The placement of the Omni light determines the lava's brightness and detail. You can control which areas of the lava flow are brightest by moving the Omni light or adding new Omni lights. As the Omni light is moved forward, the stream of lava flowing down the mountain fades while the stream flowing over land brightens (see fig. 12.5).

FIGURE 12.5
A volcano with a lava flow comes to life.

TIP

By decreasing the smoothness of the geography, applying noise modifiers to the mapping materials, and experimenting with different flame settings, the lava river becomes even more lively. Numerous lava splashes can also be placed along the lava river with varying sizes to simulate rapids and heat pools.

A Shattering Window

Creating realistic explosions can be more difficult in bright scenes than in dark ones. For one thing, the effect of flames is reduced, and motion plays a big part in the believability of an explosion. Looking at still images of real explosions can help tremendously in the modeling of explosions. Depending on the material being exploded, blasts and flames are often shrouded in darker clouds of smoke or debris. The Combustion Atmospheric Effect can create smoke and fog through the uses of its internal Explode capability and by changing the colors of the flames.

Open the file 12WINDOW.MAX. This scene includes a window frame without any glass materials in it (see fig. 12.6). Move the frame slider to about frame 30 to see the Snow Particle Effects objects in the scene. Select each Particle Effect and view its settings in the Modify panel.

Each Particle System uses a different flake size and triangular particles to create the illusion of shattered glass and blast debris.

FIGURE 12.6

Although the window frame has four glass panel areas, only the closest panels are treated with two Particle Systems, each of varying flake sizes.

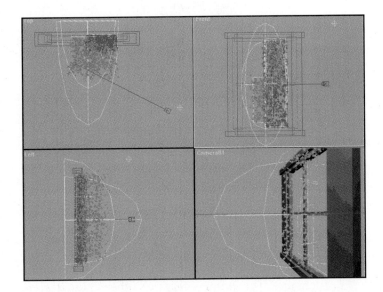

Particle Systems can often render more clearly than Combustion Atmospheric Effects in bright settings. To enable the effects to have a stronger impact at the back of the explosion, no Particle Systems are placed over the farthest glass areas. The Combustion apparatuses have been positioned far behind the window frame to ensure a thicker blast effect at the glass area borders.

Click on the Rendering/Environment pull-down option and examine the two Combustion Atmosphere Effect settings.

The first effect, which uses the larger Combustion apparatus, takes advantage of the Explosion capability built into the effect. By toggling Explosion on in the Explosion area of the Combustion parameters and setting the phase to a value between 100 and 200, smokey flames or flameless smoke can be created (see fig. 12.7).

FIGURE 12.7
A smokey flame bursts from inside the window frame.

Try using various Phase settings between 100 and 200 and re-render the scene. The differences are quite dramatic. The closer you set the Phase value to 100, the more flames you see. The closer you set the Phase to 200, the more smoke you create.

TIP

Finding the right Phase value for a still image is worth taking the time for.

The second effect does not use the internal Explosion capability, but does use a white and black flame color combination to create a blasting *cloud*. The density of the flame is set to a higher value to give the flame a tight fogging effect around the frame area (see fig. 12.8).

Play with the settings of the Combustion Atmosphere Effects and Particle Systems to create very different types of blasts. Particle Systems were used to simulate glass in this example. More sophisticated glass can be generated by applying noise modifiers and bomb space warps to semi-transparent glass objects with high segment values.

FIGURE 12.8
A foggy smoke hugs the window frame.

Light Emitting and Glowing Effects

Numerous ways enable you to create objects and effects that give the illusion of emitting light in your scenes. Video Post filters such as Glow can be applied to self-illuminated materials to create thick or thin ribbons of light that imitate neon, lightning bolts, lasers, and bright filaments. Volumetric lighting can be used from different angles and with different noise levels to create color-banded volumetric lighting. Particle Systems can be used to create an unlimited array of sparkles and highlights.

The first example outlines the basic use of the Glow filter in Video Post to create a neon sign. This includes the use of Object Channels and Material Channels to assign effects to unique objects in your scene or all objects that use a common material.

The second example shows how using different geometry with the Glow filter can produce lightning. A number of lightning-specific utilities are currently in development for 3D Studio MAX, but the technique used in this exercise lends itself to any type of glow that requires streaking or forking.

The third example overcomes a limitation of the Glow filter, namely that it does not behave the same way when the material it is applied to rests behind another semi-transparent material. Through multiple rendering passes in Video Post or through carefully positioned geometry, this problem can be corrected.

The fourth example is an extensive look at how volumetric lights can be superimposed to create gradient and color-banded volumetric lighting, and how surrounding or engulfing auras can be created about objects by viewing volumetric lights from different angles.

The fifth example is a study in the use of mapped Particle Systems to create flares, sparkles, and mixed highlights. The sixth example briefly touches on how Projector Spotlights can be used to create *geometry-independent materials*, *attenuated materials*, and *non-axial materials*.

A Neon Sign

Creating a neon sign is a perfect introduction to the Glow filter in Video Post. After you understand this powerful tool and how it uses Material Channels and Object Channels to create basic glows, you can create new material effects with it which simulate lightning, lasers, and other streams of energy.

Open the file 12NEON.MAX and render the Perspective view. The word NEON has been created using lofting techniques, and a self-illuminated material has been created and applied to each letter boundary (see fig. 12.9).

FIGURE 12.9

The self-illuminated material appears to glow.

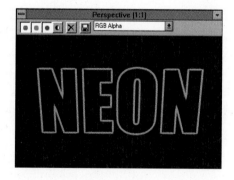

Although self-illumination can create quick and impressive glowing effects on its own, it does not soften or blur the glowing about the edges of the geometry. The glow filter adds a more realistic boundary to the light.

To create and use a glow filter, follow these steps:

1. In the Material Editor, click on the Material Effects Channel button and set it to Channel 5. You can use any one of the channels for this glow effect. Close the Material Editor.

2. Select the Rendering/Video Post pull-down menu option to bring up the Video Post dialog. Click on the Add Scene Event button. Set the View to Perspective, and make certain that the Enabled check box is active in the Video Post Parameters panel. Click on OK. The Queue now displays a scene event.

3. Select the Perspective scene event by clicking on the word Perspective in the Queue. The track to the right turns red.

4. Click on the Add Image Filter Event button. Set the Filter Plug-In to Glow (frame only). Click on the Setup button. In the Glow Control dialog, set the Source to Material Effects Channel mode and set the field to the right of the toggle to a value of 5. Set the Color to User mode and click on the color swatch to the right of the toggle. Set the color to a bright red (around RGB 255, 0, 0). Set the Size to 10 and click on OK. Make certain that the Enabled check box is active in the Video Post Parameters panel, and then click on OK.

5. Click on the Execute Sequence button of the Video Post main toolbar. Set Time Output to Single mode, the Output Size to 640×480, and click on the Render button (see fig. 12.10).

NOTE

When you use the combination of a self-illuminated materials and a glow filter, the colors of the overall neon tubing are a combination of the self-illuminated diffuse color and the Glow filter color.

For a glass-tubing effect, go to the self-illuminated material Basic Parameters rollout and try setting a bright white color for the Specular color swatch, a shininess value of 50, a shininess strength value of 100, and an opacity value of 50. Place one or more Omni lights in front of the neon objects. Experiment with different values for Opacity and Opacity Falloff when varying the Self-Illumination value of the material.

FIGURE 12.10

*A subtle glow gives the
neon material added
realism.*

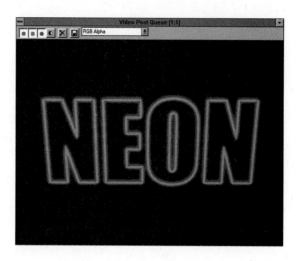

A Lightning Bolt

With effective geometry and a few tweaked settings, similar techniques used to create neon can be used to create sizzling bolts of lightning. This tutorial examines the Glow filter as a function of the Object Channel rather than a Material Effects Channel. Open the file 12BOLT.MAX and render the Perspective viewport. The bolt turns gray from an applied self-illuminated material.

To apply a glow filter by using an Object Channel, follow these steps:

1. Select and right-click on the Bolt object and select Properties to bring up the Object Properties dialog. In the G-Buffer panel, set the value of the Object Channel to 25. Click on OK.

2. Pick the Rendering/Video Post pull-down menu to bring up the Video Post dialog. The Queue still reports a Glow Filter event and the Perspective Scene event. Double-click on the Glow track to bring up the Edit Filter Event dialog. Click on the Setup button. Set the Source to Object Channel rather than Material Effects Channel, and set the Object Channel spinner to 25. Click on OK twice to return to the Video Post dialog.

3. Click on the Execute Sequence button of the Video Post main toolbar. Set Time Output to Single mode, the Output Size to 640×480, and then click on the Render button (see fig. 12.11).

FIGURE 12.11
The smaller the radius of the circle, the cleaner the lightning appears.

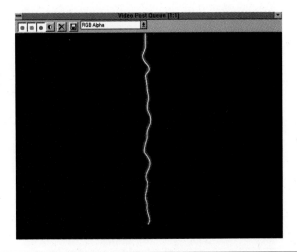

Realistic lightning has many different looks. Forked bolts during a thunderstorm appear very differently than the static discharges of heat lightning softened by clouds. Using the techniques outlined in the previous section on explosions, you can create very thin tendrils of blue-white lightening. Try using multiple lofts of varying radii together for a stringy lightning effect. By using a photo of a lightning bolt as a background in the Front viewport, you can also trace a bolt lofting path easily.

The same techniques for lightning can be used on slender, straight, lofted objects with high values for the Glow size to create sizzling laser bolts and laser bullets. Try using bright greens and reds for the Glow color and vary the size of the Glow filter to achieve the desired effect.

Clear and Soft Lightbulbs

Self-illuminated materials and Glow filters can be used to create lightbulbs. The Glow filter behaves quite differently, however, when it is applied to an object within or behind another object. Open the file 12BULB.MAX and render the Perspective viewport.

To set up Video Post to handle this scene, follow these steps:

1. Pick the Rendering/Video Post pull-down menu to bring up the Video Post dialog.

2. Click on the Add Scene Event button, and set the View to Perspective. Click on OK.

3. Click on the Perspective track. The track turns red.

4. Click on the Add Image Filter Event button. Set the Filter Plug-In to Glow (frame only), and click on the Setup button. Set the Source to Material Effects Channel with a spinner value of 1, set the color to User and the User color swatch to bright white (RBG 255, 255, 255). Set Size to 30. Click on OK twice to return to the Video Post dialog.

For the glow to appear *inside* the glass sphere, the filaments are moved out in front of the glass spheres. You can verify this by moving the filaments inside the spheres and out in front of the spheres.

1. Move the filaments inside the glass spheres.

2. Click on the Execute Sequence button of the Video Post main toolbar. Set Time Output to Single mode, the Output Size to 320×240, and click on the Render button. The glass bulb sphere on the left and the filament inside it render, but without a glow. Select the left bulb glass sphere.

3. In the Display panel, click on the Hide Selected button. Click on the Execute Sequence button of the Video Post main toolbar, and click on the Render button. Without the glass bulb showing, the filament renders with a glow.

4. In the Display control panel, click on the Unhide All button. Click on the Select by Name button from the main toolbar, click on the Loft01 object in the Select Objects dialog, and click on the Select button. Using the Perspective viewport as a guide, move the filament in front of the Sphere.

5. Click on the Execute Sequence button of the Video Post main toolbar and click on the Render button. The glass sphere renders with a glow in front of it, appearing *inside* of it. Figure 12.12 shows two bulbs using this technique. A semi-opaque, self-illuminated, shiny white material is used for the soft white bulb on the right (see fig. 12.12).

The geometry of the lightbulbs can obviously be enhanced, but the example shows the basic workaround to produce glows *within* other materials.

FIGURE 12.12

Placing Glow-filtered objects in front of other objects can give the illusion of glows within objects.

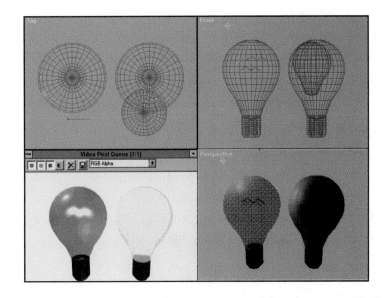

A Radiant Aura

Through the use of superimposed volumetric lights, and by viewing these lights from different angles, you can create a wild assortment of multicolored and multipatterned auras that frame or engulf objects. This can give them the effect of being gaseous, glowing, or radiant. In the examples that follow, techniques to create rays, bursts, auras, and streams of energy are shown. The files 12AURA1.MAX and 12AURA2.MAX can be used as a reference for following these examples.

By setting the camera angle so that it stares directly into a volumetric light, you can create basic ray patterns. The Filter Shadows mode set too high can prevent light banding. The following steps show how this can be done:

1. Use the File/Reset pull-down menu function to start a new session.

2. In the Create panel, click on the Lights button and click on the Target Spot button. Pick a point near the top center of the Front viewport to place the camera, hold the pick button down and drag downward about 200 units, and release the pick button to place the camera target.

3. In the Modify rollout, find the Spotlight Parameters panel and activate the Show Cone check box. In the Shadow Parameters rollout, activate the Cast Shadows check box.

4. Use the Rendering/Environment pull-down menu function to bring up the Environment dialog. In the Atmosphere panel, click on the Add button, select Volume Light, and then click on OK.

5. In the Volume Light Parameters rollout, click on the Pick Light button, move the cursor over the spotlight icon in the Front viewport, and select it. The name Spot01 appears in the Lights edit field. Close the Environment dialog.

6. Use Zoom Extents All. Right-click on an area in the Perspective viewport to make it active. Use Zoom and Pan to zoom in and center in on the spotlight cone.

7. Click on the Render Scene button from the main toolbar. Set Time Output to Single mode, set the Output Size to 320×240, and click on Render. A volumetric light appears, shining past the bottom of the screen.

8. Click on the Modify Panel. In the Attenuation area of the panel, set the Start Range and the End Range to 200, and activate the Use and Show check boxes.

9. Click the Render Last button from the main toolbar. The volumetric light fills only the cone area.

10. In the Create panel, click on the Geometry button, click on the Hedra button, select Star1 from the Parameters Family panel, pick a point in the general center of the spotlight cone shown in the Front viewport, and drag the cursor to create an object that fits entirely inside the cone boundary. Set the Star's radius to 40.

11. Click on the Render Last button from the main toolbar. The spotlight casts shadows from the Star.

12. In the Create panel, click on the Cameras button, click on the Target button in the Object Type panel, and in the same way you created the spotlight, pick points in the Front viewport so that the camera looks directly up from underneath the spotlight cone and the Star. Pick a distance from the Camera to the Camera target of about 100 units, and position the camera's target directly under the spotlight target icon.

13. Right-click on an area in the Left viewport and press C to change the viewport to Camera view. Click on the Render Scene button from the main toolbar, and click on Render.

    Although the banding of the light is a neat effect in itself, it can be dithered by controls in the Environment dialog. Also notice that the Star is completely unlit.

14. Use the Rendering/Environment pull-down menu to bring up the Environment dialog. Pick on Volume Light in the Atmosphere Effects listbox to bring up the Volume Light Parameters rollout. In the Volume panel, pick High mode for Filter Shadows. Close the Environment dialog.

15. In the Create panel, click on the Lights button, click on the Omni button, and pick a point in the Front viewport directly beneath your camera icon. Right-click on an area over the word *Camera* in the Camera01 viewport, and set the viewport mode to Smooth + Highlight.

16. Click on the Render Scene button from the main toolbar, and click on Render. A series of radial streaks shine from behind the lit Star.

T I P

Using High mode for Filter Shadows increases rendering time significantly. Alternate between high and low mode as needed while you work to get the effect you want.

You can assign a projector image to the spotlight to get colored streaks. You can also use other objects between the Star and the spotlight to create streaks that do not fit the Star's geometry.

To create multicolored volumetric lights:

1. Use the Rendering/Environment pull-down menu to bring up the Environment dialog. Pick on Volume Light in the Atmosphere Effects listbox to bring up the Volume Light Parameters rollout. In the Volume panel, set the Volume Fog Color swatch to red (RGB 255, 0, 0). In the Attenuation panel, set the End % to 50.

2. Right-click on an area in the Perspective viewport. Click on the Render Scene button from the main toolbar, and click on Render. Red light only extends halfway from the spotlight source.

3. Click on the Select Move button from the main toolbar. Holding the Shift key, pick on the spotlight icon and release. This brings up the Clone options dialog. Set Copy for the Object mode and click on OK. You now have two spotlights, superimposed on each other.

4. Use the Rendering/Environment pull-down menu to bring up the Environment dialog. In the Atmosphere panel, click on the Add button, select Volume Light, and then click on OK.

You now have two volume lights listed in the Effects listbox.

5. Pick on the second Volume Light entry in the listbox. In the Volume Light Parameters rollout, set the Volume Fog Color swatch to yellow (RGB 255, 255, 0). Click on the Pick Light button. Selecting the second Volume Light by clicking on it can be difficult in this scene. Press the "H" key instead to bring up the Pick Object dialog and select the second Volume Light. The name Spot02 appears in the Lights edit field. Close the Environment dialog.

TIP

If you have difficulty picking Spot02, move one of the spotlights temporarily and select it. Make certain to move the spotlight back to its original position so that both spotlights superimpose.

6. Right-click on an area in the Perspective viewport. Click on the Render Scene button from the main toolbar, and click on Render. The red light from the first spotlight is tinted orange. This is how volumetric lights can be colorbanded. Many volume settings can be used to blend, sharpen, intensify, or thin the blending effect (see fig. 12.13).

FIGURE 12.13
After you know how to overlap attenuated volumetric lights, colorbanding is possible.

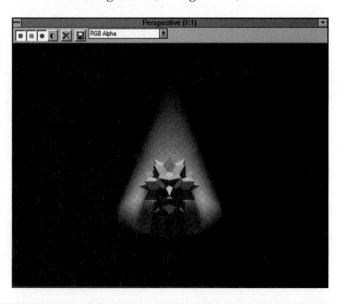

Now that you know how to blend two volumetric spotlights, noise will be added to one, then both, to achieve some remarkable auras around the Star object. The following steps show a possible approach to this technique:

1. Pick on the first Volume Light in the Effects listbox of the Environment dialog. In the Noise panel of the Volume Light Parameters rollout, enable Noise by picking on the Noise On check box. Set Amount to 1.

2. In the Attenuation panel, set End % back to 100. In the Volume Panel, set the Density to 50.

3. Right-click on an area in the Perspective viewport. Click on the Render Scene button from the main toolbar, and click on Render.

   The volumetric lighting appears like a matrix! Variations on this theme can produce some surprising energy fields (see fig. 12.14).

FIGURE 12.14
By combining volumetric lights with noise, you can create multipatterned lighting.

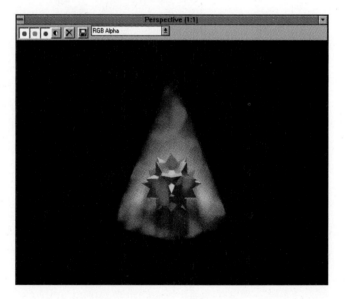

4. Right-click on an area in the Camera viewport. Click on the Render Scene button from the main toolbar, and click on Render. The Star object is surrounded by a misty swirling glow. Try rerendering this scene by setting the Filter Shadows toggle to High mode for the second volume light to see the improved effect.

5. Pick on the second Volume Light in the Effects listbox of the Environment dialog. In the Volume panel, set Density to 20. In the Noise panel, toggle Noise on, set the Amount to 0.8, set Size to 15, and set Phase to 0.5.

In the Modify panel, you can select each spotlight and disable the Cast Shadows check box. This enables the Star object to be engulfed in the aura. If you allow the spotlights to cast shadows, the Star object appears clearly in the camera view, but is surrounded by the aura.

6. Click on the Render Last button from the main toolbar. A sphere of almost gaseous light surrounds the Star object (see fig. 12.15).

FIGURE 12.15

Seen from above or below, volumetric lighting creates unlimited auras.

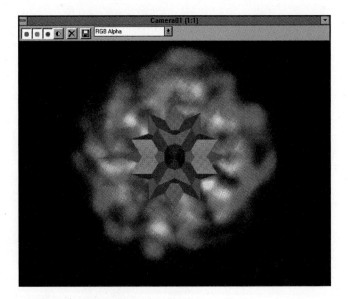

From here on out, things can get downright weird. The number of lights or shapes that can be achieved by combining different light models with different volumetric light settings is limitless. Lights can travel with objects in animations, and wind effects can be applied to animated volumetric light noise values.

You can try to vary these effects in a number of ways, such as:

■ Experiment with different values for the Noise of each spotlight.

■ Try using three or four spotlights together to create four bands of color or four swirls of different densities.

- Remember that volumetric lighting can be applied to other light models. Try using Omni lights or Direct lights. Superimpose Omni lights and Direct lights similar to the way spotlights were used in this tutorial. Streams of volumetric light can be achieved by using Direct lights with small radii.

- Remember that Spotlight cones can be non-uniformly scaled. Limit motion in the X or Y axis and see what happens when you non-uniformly scale one of the two spotlights used in this tutorial.

- Combine projected images with the spotlights.

- Try a camera inside the spotlight cone. Close-up shots from this angle, which fill the screen, can produce some fantastic gaseous materials.

- View the Star object and volumetric spotlight from above or from slightly off-center to the zenith.

Uses of Particle Systems

Particle Systems can be used along with Space Warps, such as Gravity, to generate unlimited sparkles and highlights. Because any particle can have a material mapped to it, clouds of objects can be quickly and easily generated. The one trick that must be played to achieve the follow effects is that the border of each face of each particle must be transparent. This can be accomplished by either mapping a material with transparent (0 opacity) borders or by mapping a material with alpha channel borders. If the material mapped has opaque borders, the square faces of the particles can be seen.

Open file 12SPARK.MAX and move the frames slider to about frame 30. The particles in the Camera01 viewport may not be clearly visible due to the diffuse color being used for them. Select Spray from the modifier stack. In the Parameters rollout the particle models—including drops, dots, and ticks—are shown. Ticks should be selected.

Click on the Materials Editor button in the main toolbar. Six materials appear. These are created by using a Gradient map applied as a diffuse map and an opacity map. When they are applied to a particle system, they generate radically different images (see fig. 12.16).

FIGURE 12.16
The opacity map prevents the square boundaries of the particle faces from being seen.

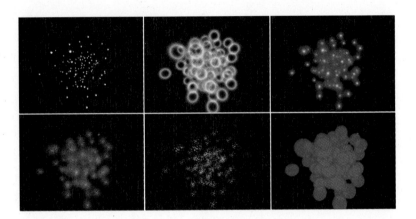

In the same way that opacity maps can be mixed with basic materials to create transparent boundaries, images rendered as Targa files (which include alpha transparency information) can also be used to create clouds and sprays of glowing objects. A basic bubble shape was rendered to a Targa file and applied as a material to the particle system to create this image (see fig. 12.17).

FIGURE 12.17
These bubbles take less time to render as a particle system than they do as objects!

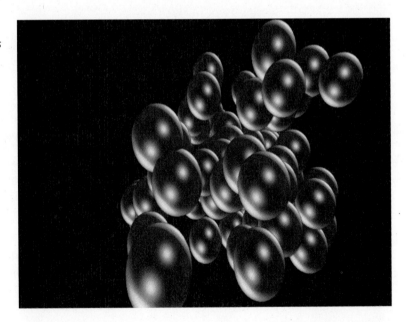

This same technique can generate wisps of bubbles and dust, and swirls of water and fire, with any of the particle system Space Warps: Deflector, Displace, Gravity, and Wind. In this example, a Gravity Space Warp is used to pull particles toward it. Vary the strength of the Gravity Space Warp to see the effect it has on emitted particles. You can get quite a different effect when you stare straight into the particle emitter as well. Render the Camera02 viewport to get a *starburst* effect with any of the materials you map to the particle system.

In a similar way that sparkles can be generated with particle systems, you can also create flares and highlights. Open file 12FLARE1.MAX, move the frame slider to about 30, and select the particle emitter to see how a Gravity Space Warp is being used to create a bended flare.

Three materials are used in this scene: a self-illuminated material is used for the star; a speck material similar to the ones used in the previous spark example is used for the flare; and a gradient material is used for a projector Direct light that shines on the particle system. The appearance of the flare trail is partly controlled by the particle system drop size and the image mapped to each face of the particle system (see fig. 12.18).

FIGURE 12.18
The Direct light helps to control the color and boundary of the flare.

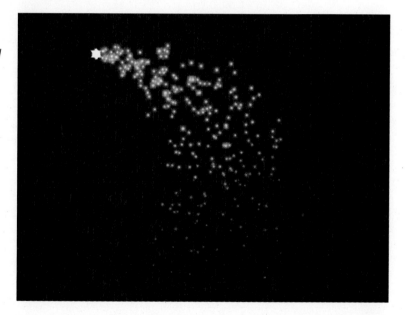

By using different light models, including projector spotlights, you can completely control which areas of a particle system are visible. Attenuated lights can also create a decaying effect on the visibility of particle systems. In the spark example, circular shapes were used as the foundation for most of the particle systems. You can create many different shapes of maps using the spectral profiles of simple geometric objects. Open file 12FLARE2.MAX and render the Front viewport. These are just a few examples of shapes that can be applied as particle system maps (see fig. 12.19).

FIGURE 12.19

The same spectral transparent material is used to create all these shapes.

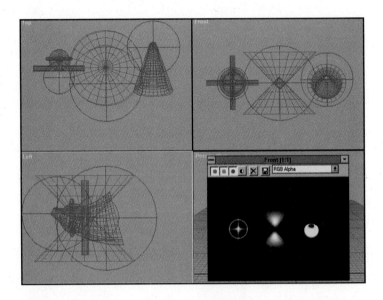

N OTE

These shapes can be used to create highlights, starry skies, starfields, and glares as seen through glass camera lenses. Particle systems use squares, so if you want these shapes to appear undistorted as they are mapped to the particle squares, be certain to render these map shapes by using a uniform resolution. Also, you can control the brightness of the particles by changing the Output Amount in the Output Rollout menu of the Opacity and Diffuse Map.

Open file 12FLARE3.MAX and set the frame slider to about frame 30. In this scene, two particle systems that create two types of stars are being used. One uses the default snow capabilities, the other uses a starburst map material (see fig. 12.20).

T IP

Be certain to set a Shininess strength of 0.0 for these flare materials when using them with particle systems, so that the square edges of the particles do not reflect light sources. These kinds of scenes are also easy to animate so that the particles from both emitters rush at the camera. When white flare materials are used, they also accept colors from light sources effectively.

FIGURE 12.20
*A night sky is
generated.*

Using Lights as Materials

The capability of spotlights to project images onto geometry can also be thought of as projecting *materials* onto geometry. By relying on lights as materials, objects can assume the materials of the lights in front of which they pass, or objects can assume materials based on their location in the scene. This gives rise to the bizarre but powerful concepts of *geometry-independent materials, attenuated materials,* and *non-axial–dependent materials.*

- **Geometry-independent materials.** Materials that can be applied to any object or group of objects in the same manner regardless of their shape.

- **Attentuated materials.** Materials that are a function of the distance from the objects to which they are applied.

- **Non-axial–dependent materials.** Materials that do not require mapping coordinates.

Open the file 12SPOT1.MAX and render the Perspective viewport. In this scene, direct lights are used to project four different materials onto the object word Spotlight. Open the Materials Editor to view the images being used by the lights. From the front view, you can see how the boundaries of three directional lights are *tiled* so that each letter receives whatever *material* it is in front of (see fig. 12.21).

FIGURE 12.21

Three directional spotlights project three different "materials" on to a single text object.

Enabling materials to become a function of an object's location opens up a world of possibilities in creating lighting special effects. Orthographic views provide an easy means of creating *tiles* of directional lights. Because directional spotlights cast the same amount of light on objects regardless of their distance from geometry, you can *cast* materials anywhere in the scene.

Open the file 12SPOT2.MAX and render the Perspective viewport (see fig. 12.22). The *materials* shine through all objects. As new objects move into line, they take on the next materials. Because lights are not limited to being projected in the positive and negative X, Y, and Z axes, you can project any number of materials from any angle and blend them as desired.

NOTE

Using this technique can save a great deal of time when working with vast amounts of different objects that need the same types of materials.

TIP

If Omni lights or target spotlights are used rather than directional lights, attenuation with projected *materials* is also possible. As objects move closer to the light source, the material becomes more apparent.

FIGURE 12.22
Any new object may instantly acquire the "materials" of a specific location in the scene.

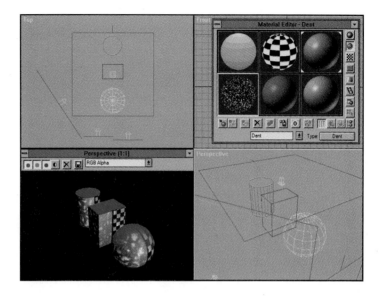

Psychedelic Materials

Through the use of exaggerated settings for geometry, modifiers, and effects, you can produce intentionally unrealistic and bizarre materials. These types of materials can be used stand-alone to create weird images or they can be used as components of other materials to add a touch of the unexpected or unexplainable.

In this first example, a simple box is transformed into a psychedelic materials generator through the use of Noise Modifiers and a top down view. From globular mounds to skin-like streams, the steps show how different values set for the box and modifier can produce different types of effects materials.

In the second example, a single Combustion apparatus is viewed head-on through a camera, and the characteristics of the Combustion Atmosphere Effect are exaggerated to minimum and maximum values, producing visual effects from plasma and fibrous netting to wispy gasses and globular lava.

In the third example, a kaleidoscope object is created through which scenes, objects, and backdrops are viewed. The sides of the kaleidoscope all use flat mirrors so that anything viewed through the object's *opening* can be mirrored. This enhances a material's capability to be mirrored in more than just the U and V directions.

Noise Revisited

Open the file 12NOISE1.MAX. In this scene, a simple box is created, and a Noise Modifier is applied to it. By rendering views in the Top viewport, a multitude of really strange patterns emerges as the Noise Modifier and box settings are exaggerated. Select the box, and click on the Modify panel so that you are able to change the settings of the box and Noise Modifier. Render the top viewport (see fig. 12.23).

FIGURE 12.23
Rectilinear seams resulting from unsmooth surfaces are not a nuisance with this material. They are the effect itself.

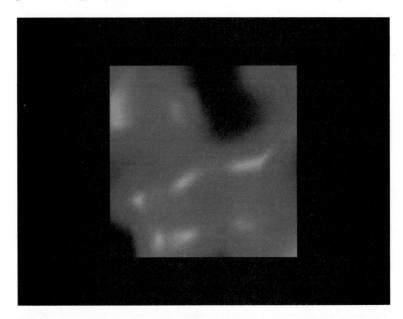

To give you a hint of the wide array of effects materials you can create by experimenting with geometry and modifier values, a series of images is shown here which you will generate in the tutorial that follows (see fig. 12.24).

FIGURE 12.24
Each of these materials can be used by itself or composited with other materials to add a touch of weirdness.

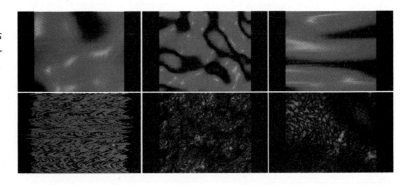

These types of images are difficult to describe. They may or may not occur in the natural world, and may look very awkward. But that's the point! These materials can be mirrored in the U and V directions when applied as a material so that they form strange but seamless tiles, or they can be used without tiling to intentionally produce abrupt and odd patterns. For each step outlined, the top viewport is rendered to see the effect. Some of the steps may not seem to make much of a difference, but the resulting *materials* are striking. An example of this technique is shown in the following steps:

1. Set the Noise Modifier seed value to 1 and render.

2. Click on the Noise Modifier Fractal toggle so that it is active and render.

3. Set the Noise Modifier Seed to 2, the Scale to 50, Roughness to 0, Iterations to 1, and render.

4. Set the Box Length Segments and Width Segments to a value of 30 and render.

5. Set the Box Width Segments to 1 and render.

6. Set the Box Width Segments to 2 and render.

7. Set the Box Length Segments to 50 and the Width Segments to 50. Set the Noise Modifier Scale to 4, Roughness to 0.5, Iterations to 1, X Strength to 50, Z Strength to 400, and render.

8. Set the Box Length and Width Segment values to 20 and render.

All these materials have been generated using the default material. By applying new materials of your own or existing materials with exaggerated settings, you can corrupt the same strange geometry in the preceding steps to create very different materials. An example of this technique is outlined in the following steps:

1. Toggle Generate Mapping Coord active in the Box's Parameters rollout menu. Click on the Materials Editor button from the main toolbar. Select the first (upper-left) sample slot and click on the Get Material button. Select Standard map type, and set the material's Diffuse map to a Noise map. Apply the material to the box by using the Assign Material to Selection button. In the Noise Parameters rollout menu, set the Size to 10 and the Noise type to Turbulence and render.

2. Set the Noise Modifier X Strength to 0, Y Strength to 0, Z Strength to 200, and render.

3. Set the Noise Modifier Scale to 100.0, Roughness to 0, Iterations to 1 and render.

4. Set the Noise Modifier Roughness to 1 and Iterations to 2. Click on the Materials Editor button and select the first sample slot material you created. Click on the Diffuse map to bring up the Noise map parameters. Set the Noise Type to Fractal, Size to 10, and in the Output rollout check the Invert toggle. Close the Material Editor and render (see fig. 12.25).

FIGURE 12.25

A simple box distorted with Noise Modifiers and an inverted Noise Material produces new possibilities for Diffuse, Bump, Opacity, and Shininess maps.

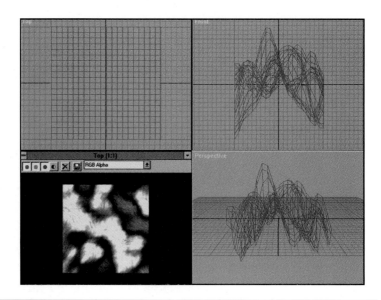

The possibilities are endless when other geometry is used. Experiment using other primitives with the same series of steps outlined for the box; apply materials to the box from the existing library. Use the resulting maps as bump maps or masks on existing materials.

Combustion Revisited

The Combustion Atmosphere Effect tool can also be tweaked to create materials that look nothing like flames or smoke. Through the use of different color schemes, odd flame sizes, and strange values for other characteristics, and through deformation of the Combustion apparatus, you can generate misty and gaseous materials unlike anything the fog tools can produce.

Open the file 12COMB1.MAX. In this scene, a spherical Combustion apparatus is viewed from a camera that uses a lens and FOV value to fill the entire camera viewport. Click on the Modify panel and select either the apparatus or the camera to view and modify its settings. Use the Rendering/Environment pull-down option to bring up the Environment dialog. View the settings for the Combustion Effect by selecting the Combustion item in the Effects list. Render the camera view (see fig. 12.26).

FIGURE 12.26

By using small values for flame size and density, a globular material unlike any flame is created.

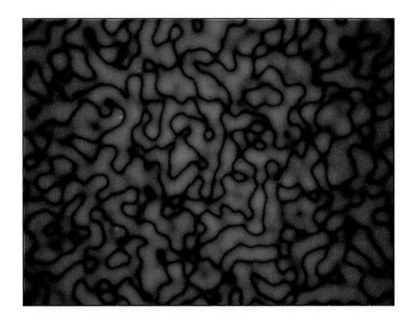

Globular, liquidy, fibrous, gaseous, netted, and spattered materials can all be generated by using the Combustion tool. Shown in the following series of images are a variety of example materials you will generate in the tutorial that follows (see fig. 12.27).

For each step outlined, the camera viewport is rendered to see the effect.

1. In the Combustion Parameters, set the Inner color to a bright green and the Outer color to black. In the Combustion parameters rollout menu for the apparatus, set the seed to 2, and render.

2. In the Combustion Parameters, set the Inner color to white. Set the flame size to 2 and render.

3. In the Combustion Parameters, set the Inner color to yellow. Set the flame size to 1, the Flame Detail to 1, the Density to 10, the Samples to 10 and render.

FIGURE 12.27

*Each of these materials
uses a single
Combustion apparatus
to be created.*

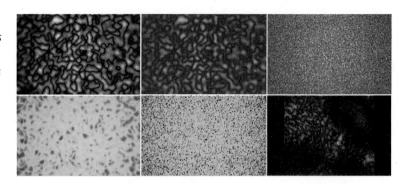

FIGURE 12.27

*Each of these materials
uses a single
Combustion apparatus
to be created.*

4. In the Combustion Parameters, set the Inner color to bright green and the Outer color to bright blue. Set the Flame Type to Tendril. Set the flame size to 5, the Flame Detail to 1, the Density to 5, the Samples to 3 and render.

5. In the Combustion Parameters, set the Outer color to black. Set the flame size to 1, the Flame Detail to 1, the Density to 5, the Samples to 2 and render.

6. In the Combustion Parameters, set the Inner color to cyan. Set the flame size to 20, the Flame Detail to 10, the Density to 5, the Samples to 2 and render.

By using more than one apparatus, you can create intertwining patterns of color and texture. Open the file 12COMB2.MAX and examine the two Combustion Atmosphere Effects in use. Notice that the size of the apparatuses has been varied. By combining the singular effects of each apparatus, you can create plasma, lightning, strange planetary terrains, and a wide assortment of gaseous materials for nebulae and novas (see fig. 12.8).

FIGURE 12.28

*Two apparatuses are
used to create
multicolored plasma.*

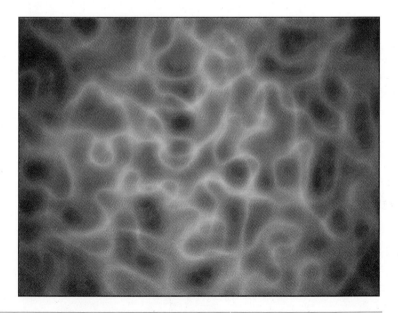

Mirror Tricks

You can extend the mirroring effect of materials from the U and V directions to any number of directions you desire by viewing your materials through kaleidoscope objects. Kaleidoscopes are tubes with three or more flat surfaces through which any scene, material, or object can be viewed.

Open the file 12MIRR1.MAX (see fig. 12.29). A camera is placed *inside* six arrayed flat surfaces which form the kaleidoscope tube. A flat mirror material is applied to each side of the tube so that any object, pattern, light, or effect that can be seen through the hole of the tube reflects on all sides, filling the screen.

FIGURE 12.29

The flat mirror material applied to each tube surface appears as a black area when viewed in the camera viewport.

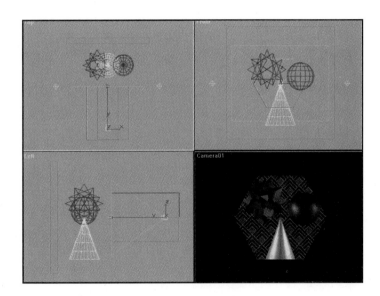

A backdrop with an elaborate pattern shows through the tube opening near the camera's target. If you wish to mirror any material in more than four directions, you can create a number of sides to the kaleidoscope equal to the number of mirroring directions you want and then place the material to be mirrored on the backdrop object. After you have your scene set, render the camera view (see fig. 12.30).

TIP

When using this technique to create new materials, in many cases it can help to set Self-Illumination of the material being mirrored to a high value. By the same token, using scene lights outside the kaleidoscope to highlight areas of the backdrop can also produce neat effects.

FIGURE 12.30
The scene at the opening of the tube creates the entire material.

In Practice: Designing Special Effects Materials

- **Spinner and field values.** Try outrageous values for the spinners and field values when designing special effects materials. Many new effects can be achieved by using values of zero or very high positive or negative values. Revisit the techniques outlined in this chapter using unthinkable values.

- **Camera angles.** Special effects can often be achieved simply through a peculiar placement of the camera. Staring directly into lights, using odd camera lens settings, looking at your scenes through warped surfaces, or projecting your finalized scenes and animations onto warped "movie screens" can take your work one step beyond.

- **Recycling.** There will be times when you accidentally or experimentally create an unexpected effect. Even if you're under the gun, take the time to write down how the effect was accomplished so that it can be recreated if needed later. Don't waste neat accidents!

IMAGE BY LEE STEEL

Chapter 13

by Lee Steel

ANIMATED MATERIALS

It's common knowledge that carefully created materials and mapping far outweigh modeled geometry when the main concern is rendering time or face count. With this in mind, an animator with insight into the materials capabilities of MAX can create very believable scenes using very little geometry. Animated materials can take the place of a large number of applications where you once would have had to do a great deal of modeling to achieve similar effects such as rippling water or clouds in the sky. One aspect of 3D Studio MAX that sets it apart from all other animation packages is the fact that almost everything is animatable—including most parameters in MAX's Material Editor. This capability removes virtually all limitations when you're creating animated materials.

The Material Editor's Make Preview button (see fig. 13.1) is a very important feature. When you tweak animated materials, it is much easier to create material previews by using this function than it is to render the scene itself (even though final adjustments require that you render the geometry to adjust tiling and UVW scaling). The following sections give you greater insight into the capabilities at your fingertips in MAX. Along with the sample MAX files and rendered scene AVIs is a material library that includes all materials used in the exercises in this chapter.

Concepts covered in this chapter include the following:

- Animating color changes and controlling their transition

- Using Blend materials

- Creating the illusion of constant motion by using an AVI file as a map

- Simulating natural phenomena such as water and clouds by using noise

- Using sequential TGA files as an animated environment map

- Using third-party plug-ins to add control and a higher level of realism

FIGURE 13.1

Click on the Make Preview button to generate an AVI file of the current material slot.

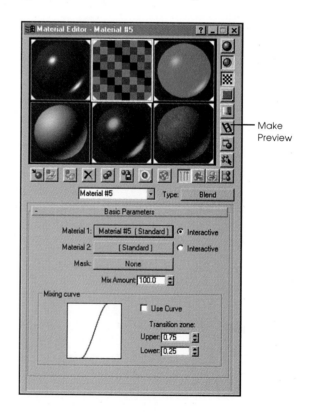

Make Preview

1. Load the sample file 1301.max. The material in slot #1 changes from black at frame 0 to white at frame 20, yellow at frame 40, orange at frame 60, red at frame 80, and back to black at frame 100. In the case of colored particles, this gives you exact control of the particles' color throughout their life span.

2. Open Track View. Click on Medit Materials, Red-Blue (standard), Parameters, and Diffused, opening all these tracks. Keys are located at the exact frame in time of each individual color change in the Diffuse track.

3. Right-click on the key at frame 0 (see fig. 13.3). As you can see, the color swatch represents the color for this key. You also see the function curves for In and Out, which control how the transition is made between the keys. This is where the fun begins. By choosing one of the six preset curves, you have full control over how all the transitions take place.

FIGURE 13.3
Bézier curves display interpolated values between keys.

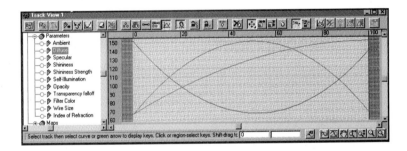

4. Take a few minutes to experiment with the curve settings, and then render material previews by clicking on the Make Preview icon in the Material Editor panel.

5. Render an AVI file of this scene by using Video Post. Most settings have already been made, including a glow effect.

As you can see, you can control an object's color over time with a great deal of precision—a far cry from the R4 days of using an AXP to read a bitmap, pixel by pixel. Don't forget that you can animate other settings in the Material Editor—such as Shininess (Shin), Strength, Self-Illumination, and Opacity—as well. The same techniques of adjusting the keyframes' function curves apply here also. Your final scene should look something like the 1301.avi file located on the accompanying CD.

Blend Materials

Blend is a compound material type that actually enables you to control the way two separate maps are combined. These two maps can be of any map type, including Mix, that would enable you to combine two more maps into each of the Blend's map slots—and so on, and so on. The exercise in this section is a good example of animated opacity coupled with an animated Blend material. In this example, you animate this material mixing to create a dissolve from one material into another.

Load the sample file 1302.max from the accompanying CD. In this scene, you see the transporter room aboard an alien vessel. The task at hand is to create the effect of the alien being teleported into the room. You have been asked to simulate that sparkly *Star Trek* style effect that appears first as static noise and then transitions into the natural skin color. This is the perfect application for a Blend material.

1. Start by setting up the desired skin color for the alien. Name this material **Flesh**.

2. Pick the Type button in the Material Editor interface and select New. A list of material types appears.

3. Select Blend from the list. At the prompt, select Keep Old Material As Sub-Material and click on OK.

4. The original Flesh material is now listed in the Material 1: slot (see fig. 13.4). This is the main control dialog of the new Blend material; all controls that affect how the Blend takes place are located here. Set the initial Mix Amount to 100. In the Material Editor window, rename this material **Skin**.

5. To make any changes to the original skin color, click on the Material 1 button to display the parameter controls for Flesh.

6. Click on the Material 2 button. This is going to be the material that seems to sparkle as the transporter is initialized.

FIGURE 13.4
Main control dialog for Blend.

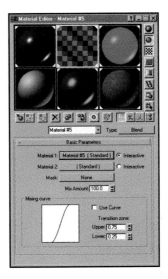

7. Change Shininess, Shin. Strength, and Opacity to 0. This ensures that the material is initially totally transparent.

8. Select Maps and click on the map slot for Diffuse. You are prompted to select a map type. Pick Noise from the list and click on OK.

9. Set the Noise Parameters as follows: Turbulence, High: .5, Low: 0; Size: .5, Levels: 1, and Phase 0. You might want to change some of these parameters later. (Having already gone through the experimentation process, however, the author believes that these parameters work best as a starting point.)

10. Click on the Go to Parent button in the Material Editor interface and drag a copy of the Diffuse Noise down to the Opacity slot. Pick Instance. This ensures that any changes made later to Diffuse Noise are made simultaneously to the Opacity Noise.

11. Set the Amount of Opacity to 0 for now. Add a background to the Material Preview window by clicking on the icon (see fig. 13.5). The material should be completely transparent at this point.

12. Pick Go to Parent, return to the main Blend control window, and change the Mix Amount to 0. The original skin material should now appear.

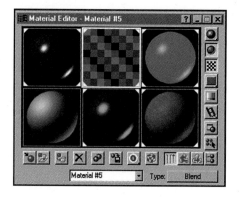

Change Mix Amount back to 100. You are now ready to animate the material.

Start the material animation process by creating some initial keys. You adjust these keys later, using Track View. You make the noise transition from transparent to sparkle take place over 30 frames, sparkle for 30 frames, and transition to the final skin color over 30 frames.

1. Pick the Animate button and move the Frame Slider to 30.

2. In the Material Editor, click on Material 2. Go to Maps, and set Opacity Amount to 100. This creates a fade-in of Noise from completely transparent to sparkle, over the first 30 frames.

3. While you set the parameters for Noise, click on the Diffuse slot. Move the Frame Slider to 100 and set Phase to 10. This causes the Noise to appear to twinkle.

4. Return to the Blend root and (at frame 90) set the Mix Amount to 0. This completes the basic key settings.

5. Now open Track View. Pick the Filters button (see fig. 13.6) and select Show Only: Animated Tracks. Now the keys for Mix Amount and Opacity Amount are visible (see fig. 13.7).

FIGURE 13.6

Click on the Filters icon to keep unnecessary tracks from being visible in Track View.

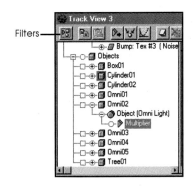

FIGURE 13.7

Mix Amount and Opacity Amount keys are now visible in Track View.

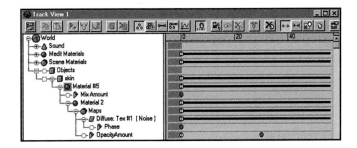

6. Because the transition from Noise to Skin is not scheduled to take place until frame 60, copy the key for Mix Amount at frame 0 and move it. Do this by holding down the Shift key, clicking on the key at frame 0, and dragging the copy over to frame 60. This holds the Mix Amount to a value of 100 from frame 0 through frame 60.

7. Edit these keys by right-clicking on the key at frame 0. Change the In and Out transition curves to Linear style curves. Move between keys by using the arrows in the upper-left corner (see fig. 13.8) of this window, and set all transitions in this manner.

8. Now create a Material Preview. Apply this material to the Skin of the alien (if you haven't already).

FIGURE 13.8
*Click on the left- and
right-arrow icons to
move between keys.*

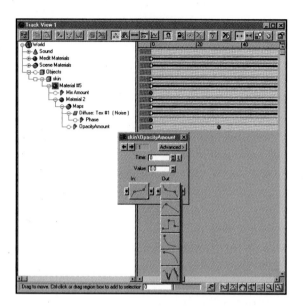

Finally, you need to re-create this process for all remaining mesh objects associated with the alien character. Then your task is complete. Your final scene should look something like the 1302.avi file on the accompanying CD.

Creating the Illusion of Constant Motion

An endless number of things in the world, from tank treads to conveyor belts, display constant motion. This type of motion can be quite easy to approximate in 3D Studio MAX with the use of carefully created animated materials.

An animated material that displays constant motion must loop at some point, and you can accomplish the task in several ways. In this exercise, you create an AVI file that appears to loop because the pattern is moved in such a way that when the next row in the pattern is about to appear, the AVI recycles to frame 1, where this row is visible.

In this next exercise, you create the effect of some clear glass tubes surrounding the transporter platform. Inside these tubes, bubbles rise in an endless flow from bottom to top.

1. Start a new file. Activate the Front view and create a box with the dimensions Length:200, Height:200, and Width:1. Check the Generate Mapping Coords box.

2. Open the Material Editor, create a new Standard material, and name it **Bubbles**.

3. In the Diffuse Map, load the bitmap file, BEEBEES.JPG (a bitmap that ships with 3DS MAX). Apply this material to the box. Click on the Show Map in Viewport icon.

4. From the MAX pull-down menus pick Views, Viewport Configuration, and in the Safe Frames tab, check the box under Application, next to Show Safe Frames in Active View. A series of boxes should appear in the Front viewport. Also make sure you have the viewport set for shaded mode.

5. In the Front viewport, zoom in and move the box until the first full row of beebees down to the second from the last row fills the viewport horizontally and touches the yellow safe frame box from side to side (see fig. 13.9).

FIGURE 13.9
Align the bitmap within the safe frame to ensure proper tiling.

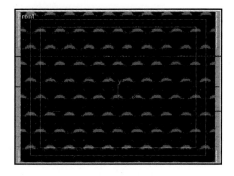

6. Set the animation length to 10 frames. Move the frame slider to frame 10, and click on the Animate button.

7. With the axis constrained to Y, move the box up a distance equal to two rows of beebees, until the row is just above the bottom line of the viewport.

8. Render an AVI of this file, named Bubbles.

Now to apply your newly created animated material to a scene. Open file 1302.max, the scene of the transporter room.

1. Create a new Standard material and name it Post. In the Diffuse map slot, load Bubbles.avi. Set V: Tiling to 2.0. Make an Instance copy of this map to the map slots of both Opacity and Bump. Set Self-Illumination to 100.

2. Apply this material to the four columns in the scene and render the scene. The final outcome should be the illusion of constantly flowing bubble-shaped highlights rising on each of the poles.

This technique can be applied to the creation of any material that needs to appear in constant motion. Your final scene should look something like the 1302.AVI file located on the accompanying CD.

Using Noise to Simulate Water and Sky

Look around the next time you venture into the great outdoors. Many things are always moving around us. Trees and leaves gently move as they are disturbed by wind, even on the calmest of days. A pool of water almost always has slight ripples or swells. Clouds gracefully pass by overhead. All these elements of nature are easily overlooked, yet required for our brain to truly believe that what we are seeing is real.

In 3D Studio MAX, these types of occurrences are easily recreated and help make a much more believable scene. Load the sample file 1303.max—an outdoor scene of a brick well filled with water and surrounded by torches. You enhance the final animated scene by using a Noise material to simulate the ripples in the water without having to model them (which would greatly increase the face count in the scene). You also use a Noise material to create soft puffy clouds as an animated environment map. Finally, you add animated flames to the torches.

Water

Water can be very tricky to simulate. Water is always changing, always moving, and in the real world is very unpredictable. Certain features, however, trigger intuition and assure you of the fact that, "Yes, this is water!"

1. In the Material Editor, pick Get Material, pick New and Standard. Name this material **Water**.

2. Because water is usually very shiny on the surface, set Shininess to 50, and Shin. Strength to 100. And because water has transparency, set Opacity to 80.

NOTE

By activating a material's Background button, you make it easier to visualize just how Opaque the material is.

3. Click on the Diffuse Map slot. Select Noise from the list and click on OK (see fig. 13.10). Under Noise Parameters are two color swatches labeled Color #1 and Color #2. The color of the water is a combination of these two colors.

FIGURE 13.10

The Noise Parameters dialog contains all settings for combining the colors that will be your water.

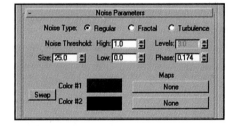

4. Pick the color swatch for Color #1 and make adjustments to create a dark green. A good starting point is Red:0, Green:67, and Blue:57. Now do the same for Color #2 but adjust RGB to create a navy blue. Start by setting Red:7, Green:29, and Blue:49.

5. Because the water's surface must appear to move, activate the Animate button in the main MAX screen, move the frame slider to 100, and change the Phase setting to .6. This animates the intermixing of the two colors throughout the animation. Note that the higher the Phase setting, the faster the colors change over time.

6. Use a similar technique to create the rolling, rippled surface of the water. Click on the Bump Map slot and again select Noise from the list.

7. Change the Angle so that the ripples move in a different direction from the changing color. Note that in nature the surface of water and the waves usually seems to move in opposite directions. To achieve this effect, turn off Animate, and under Coordinates, set X:90 and Y:90.

8. To simulate the water's "rolling" action, be certain that you are still at frame 100, activate MAX's Animate button, and change the Phase setting under Noise Parameters to 5.

9. The settings for your Water material should now be complete. Use the Make Preview button to test-render your material, and apply it to the Water object in the scene.

NOTE

To add one more level of realism to your scene, you can use the Environment Map material that you create in the next section as a reflection map for the water.

Set the Reflection Amount very low—around 10 to 15. Don't forget that because you want to simulate a realistic reflection, the reflection map coordinates need to be rotated 180 degrees.

Now that you have completed the main areas of interest in this scene, let's move on to create the environment these objects will reside in. Note that the tree included in this scene has an animated bend modifier applied to simulate blowing wind and was created with Digimation's Tree Factory Plug-in.

Sky and Space

In this section, you use animated Noise materials to simulate a day and night environment map. Creating photo-realistic environments with plug-ins alone can be anywhere from difficult to near-impossible. Plug-ins, however, can be used to create some very surrealistic effects. The best way to simulate accurate environments is to use time lapse sequences of real images. In the following exercises, you will experiment with both approaches.

1. In the Material Editor, click on Get Material, pick New, and then pick Noise. Name this material **Day Sky**.

2. Select Noise Type: Fractal and Set Size:15.

3. Click on the color swatch for Color #1 and set Red:62, Green:136, and Blue:192. This color represents the sky.

4. Click on the color swatch for Color #2 and set Red:205, Green:205, and Blue:205. This color represents the clouds.

5. Clouds usually appear to be stretched, parallel to the horizon. In the Coordinates section, set Tiling: X:0.2.

NOTE

Appropriate color is always in the eye of the beholder. None of the color values suggested here are set in stone. You, the user, the adventurer, are completely at liberty to experiment with color settings that you feel are most characteristic of sky and clouds.

By decreasing the Tiling:X amount, you make the clouds stretch more along the horizon. By increasing the amount, you make the clouds appear smaller and fluffy.

6. Because you want these clouds to move slightly throughout the animation, activate the Animate button and move the frame slider to frame 100. In the Coordinates section, set Angle X:0.5 and Angle Y:0.5. Now set Phase:0.3. The higher the number in the Phase setting, the faster the clouds move across the sky.

7. Finally, from the main MAX pull-down menu, pick Rendering and then pick Environment. In the Background section, pick Assign and choose Browse From: Material Editor. Select the material Day Sky from the list and pick OK.

8. Render an AVI of your scene. Water and clouds should both appear to be moving.

The sky in your scene should resemble the one in 1303c.avi located on the CD-ROM.

Next turn day into night.

1. In the Material Editor, click on Get Material, pick New, and then pick Noise. Name this material **Night Sky**.

2. Select Noise Type: Turbulence, and Set Size:0.02.

3. Set Noise Threshold: High:0.001, Levels:1.0, and click on the Swap button located next to the swatches for Colors #1 and #2.

This is the star field in your night sky. For one more level of realism, add some night clouds as well.

1. Click on the Maps box just to the right of the color swatch for Color #2, and choose Browse From: Material Editor. Select the material Day Sky from the list and pick OK.

2. Click on the color swatch for Color #1 and set Red:0, Green:0, and Blue:0. This color represents the sky.

3. Click on the color swatch for Color #2 and set Red:60, Green:60, and Blue:60. You want to diminish the whiteness of the clouds because they are not illuminated by the sun.

4. Because this material was a copy of the Day Sky material, all animated parameters are the same.

5. Finally, from the main MAX pull-down menu, pick Rendering and then pick Environment. In the Background section, pick Assign and choose Browse From: Material Editor. Select the material Day Sky from the list and pick OK.

6. Re-render an AVI of the scene. Now you should see a night sky and slowly moving clouds and water.

You can easily animate the transition from day to night by creating a new Blend material and using the material named Day Sky as a Diffuse map for Material 1. Then use Night Sky as a Diffuse map for Material 2. Set Shininess and Shin. Strength to 0 in both instances. Because the animated parameters for the clouds are the same for both day and night, the transition from one to the other should be very smooth. Your final scene should look something like the 1303b.avi file located on the accompanying CD.

Another way to create a realistic daytime environment for the sky is to use a sequence of time-lapse pictures of real clouds. The accompanying CD includes a low-resolution sequence of images from the Image Shoppe's "Colorado Altitudes" CD. Locate these sequential images on the CD-ROM and copy them to your Maps sub-directory.

1. From MAX's pull-down menu select Rendering, Environment, and Assign. From this list, pick Bitmap and click on OK. Now click on the Environment Map button and choose a slot number (see fig. 13.11).

FIGURE 13.11

Choose a slot number from this dialog to begin building your environment map.

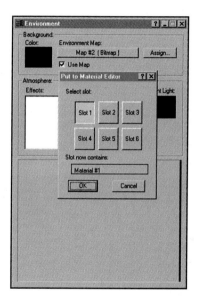

2. In the Material Editor, the slot you have chosen is now black and the controls for Spherical Environment are visible.

3. Because the camera is not moving, use the down-arrow key next to Spherical Environment and pick Screen from the list. This constrains the entire bitmap used as the environment to the viewport.

4. Click on the Bitmap button and locate the path to the Colorado Altitudes subdirectory on the accompanying CD. Under File Name, type **CLDG*.JPG** and click on OK.

5. Now the line next to Bitmap: reads `cldg000a.ifl`. MAX uses each of these images as the environment bitmap in numerical order.

6. If you render a single frame at this point, you can see that the background image is centered in the viewport and partially blocked by the geometry. To fix this problem, set Offset V: to 0.68. This setting raises the image so that the bottom of the bitmap is just below the simulated horizon of the geometry in the scene.

7. Render an AVI of the scene again. Now the moving image of clouds is visible as the animated environment.

With our environment complete, you can now move on to add one more level of realism.

Fire

As a finishing touch to this scene, you add fire to the stacks around the well. You can do this in several ways. One way is to use Combustion, an Atmospheric Effect that ships with 3D Studio MAX. Another method is to map a sequence of time-lapse images of real fire on geometry designed to approximate the shape of the flames. "Pyromania" is a collection of fire sequences created by VCE and available through Trinity Enterprises. The accompanying CD includes a low-resolution sequence of images from VCE's "Pyromania 1" CD.

1. Unhide Sphere01, 02, 03, and 04. Use the Display panel and click on Unhide by Name. These spheres have been deformed to approximate the size of the flames. Cylindrical UVW mapping has been applied. Note that in Sub-Object mode, the height of the mapping gizmo can be nonuniformly scaled to adjust the height of the flames. Locate the Pyromania files located on the CD-ROM and copy them to your Maps sub-directory.

2. In the Material Editor, pick Get Material, and then pick New and Standard. Name this material **Flames**.

3. Change the settings for Shininess and Shin. Strength to 0, and set Self-Illumination to 100.

4. Click on the Diffuse Map button and pick Bitmap from the list.

5. Under Bitmap Parameters, click on the Bitmap button and locate the path to the set of flame images provided on the accompanying CD. Type the name **FR51*.JPG** and click on OK.

6. The Bitmap slot now reads FR510000.ifl. Note that if the files were residing on your hard drive and no IFL file existed, MAX would automatically create an IFL file for you. An IFL file is an ASCII file that includes a list of all image names in the sequence you have specified.

7. Change U: Tiling to 0.8. This scales the image and widens the flames around the diameter of the Sphere object.

8. A total of 79 image files make up the Fire material, and the total animation length is 100 frames. How do you stretch the timing of the flames to match? Go to the Time roll-up at the very bottom of this window and change Playback Rate to 0.7 (see fig. 13.12). This stretches out the sequence over time. If you had entered a value of 2, the sequence would play twice as fast.

FIGURE 13.12

Whenever a sequence of frames is specified as a map, you can use the Time roll-up to scale the rate at which these frames are used to fit the space in which they are needed.

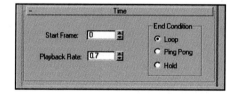

9. Click on the Go to Parent button and make an Instance copy of this map in the Opacity Map slot.

10. Click on the Show Map in Viewport button, select the four spheres, and apply the map.

11. As a final touch, four omni lights are added, one in the center of each flame sphere. Settings in Track View for each light have added Noise Float to the Multiple of each light (see fig. 13.13). Strength has been constrained to 1 and selected the >0 Value constraint to keep the light value from going into negative values.

NOTE ───

The color of the light could also be an animated color map. By adjusting the parameters of the Noise, you are able to simulate the flares of light given off by the flickering flames.

FIGURE 13.13

Noise Float Controller dialog, showing settings for flickering lights.

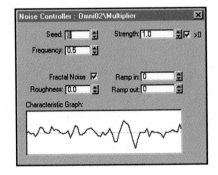

Your final scene should look something like the 1303a.avi file on the accompanying CD. AVI file 1303b demonstrates the night scene, and 1303c demonstrates the day scene, using the Noise settings for sky and Texture Lab (available from Digimation) for the fire.

Third-Party Plug-Ins

Several new routines that are about to hit the market will be a great help in the creation of exciting, realistic animated materials. Because Kinetix and the Yost Group have provided such an open architecture and an extremely user-friendly software development kit (SDK), software developers have begun to flood the market with useful plug-in routines to help speed up the creation of animated effects and, in some cases, create effects that would otherwise be impossible.

In their simplest form, these plug-ins might be nothing more than a programmed macro to help cut down on the time-consuming trial-and-error tweaking of values to achieve a particular task. At the other end of the spectrum is a class of exotic new material types; derived from complex mathematical algorithms, they create otherwise unobtainable material effects. Think of these plug-ins as programs in and of themselves, that are executed from within the MAX environment.

The following list describes four exceptional plug-ins for animating materials:

- **Fractal Flow MAX.** This Video Post plug-in filter, which functions just as its name suggests, is a port from 3D Studio R4 with some added features. The programmers at Digimation have developed elaborate, unique algorithms for creating the smoothest, most believable flowing pixel effects available (to date) for 3DS (see fig. 13.14). By using animated gradients as masks for virtually any or all parameters, gracefully flowing fractals can be used to create a wide variety of believable effects. A few examples are floating, puffy clouds; realistically flowing water; smoke and vapor that bubble up with that "dry ice" look; space dust; whirlpools; predator-style cloaking and uncloaking; heat rising from hot asphalt; and virtually any distortion effect. These effects can be used on an entire scene or masked to affect only a predefined area. Because the effects can be masked, animated maps such as ripples and waves can be used as masks to create the same type of effects previously available in R4 from Mirage. Fractal Flow effects are pixel based, not actual particles, which makes rendering much faster.

FIGURE 13.14

The Fractal Flow MAX interface, showing the Ripples tab. The real-time Preview window provides instant feedback as to how the ripple effect will appear.

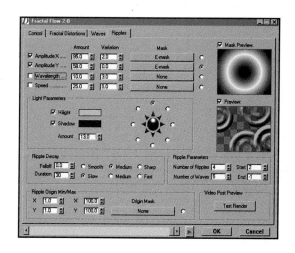

- **Texture Lab.** This plug-in, a collection of procedural textures, will be available soon from Digimation. *Procedural textures* are derived completely from formulas and require no bitmaps. These are very similar to the Marble, Wood, and Dent materials that ship with MAX. Texture Lab includes such materials as Fog, Strata, Electrics, Water, Advanced Noise, and Fire (see fig. 13.15). Also see AVI files 1303b and 1303c located on the accompanying CD. These animations show a good example of the Fire Procedural texture used as the flames.

FIGURE 13.15

*Procedural Fire is just
one of the new textures
in Digimation's Texture
Lab package.*

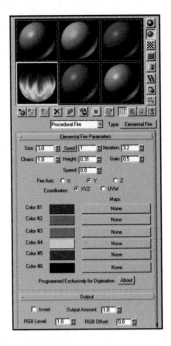

- **Electrolize.** This shareware plug-in, written by Harry Denholm, is included on the accompanying CD. Future upgrades and releases will be available in CompuServe's KINETIX forum. Electrolize creates animated noise barriers between two defined materials that act much like animated wipes. These type effects have been used recently in both the opening logo sequence for *Cable Guy* and the uncloaking effects in *Predator 2*. Electrolize and few other freeware plug-ins for MAX are included on the accompanying CD. Open file 1305.MAX for a closer look at Electrolize.

In this exercise, your alien friend from the earlier transporter room scene has to look down the barrel of what appears to be an ominous freeze-ray. The alien's arms were repositioned using Digimation's Bones Pro, after which a Snapshot was taken of the mesh.

1. Render the scene using Video Post. The result should look somewhat like the file 1305.avi located on the accompanying CD. Around frame 35, the alien's skin turns from tan to white and the edge that appears to grow and take over the mesh has a pixelated edge. This effect was created by using Electrolize.

2. Open the Material Editor and look at the material called Alien. As you can see, this Multi/Sub-Object material includes six different materials. Now click on the button for Material 1: skin (Standard), and click again on the Diffuse Map button. As you can see, Electrolize has been loaded as a material type for this slot (see fig. 13.16).

FIGURE 13.16

Electrolize is a freeware plug-in, written and distributed by Harry Denholm of Ishani Graphics.

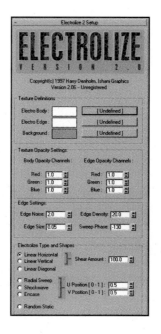

3. Before converting this material slot to Electrolize, the original material color was retained by using MAX's Color Clipboard (see fig. 13.17). Select Color Clipboard from the Utility tab and pick New Floater. A floating color pallet with 12 swatches appears on your desktop. You can now drag and drop the diffuse color from the swatch beside each material slot to the floating clipboard.

4. To add Electrolize, click on the Diffuse Map button and select Electrolize from the Material/Map Browser window.

5. Drag the appropriate color from the floating pallet and drop it on the swatch for Background in Electrolize. The colors for Electro Edge and Electro Body, which in this case are both white to simulate freezing, can be completely different colors.

FIGURE 13.17
Select Color Clipboard from the Utilities tab, and pick New Floater to utilize the floating pallet.

6. Experiment with Edge Size and Edge Density. These controls determine how much of a pixelated edge the wipe effect will have.

7. Sweep Phase is the parameter that causes the edge to move from one location to another. In this case, the effect is set to –130 at frame 0, holds until frame 35, and increases to 100 at frame 70. A few sample renders proved that with Sweep Phase set to –130, the effect is totally hidden from the camera's view until it is increased.

8. Finally, click the Apply WaveForms button. The SINE Waves settings (see fig. 13.18) control the twisted path the edge will have.

FIGURE 13.18
Waveform controls used by Electrolize to bend the edge of the wipe effect.

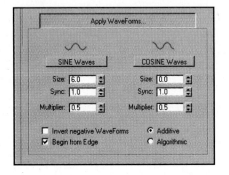

9. Take the time to go through the rest of the materials that make up the Alien and convert these materials to Electrolize.

The animated material features in 3D Studio MAX are among the strongest features that set this animation package apart from the others. With the techniques presented here and a little ingenuity, you should be well on your way to creating some very exciting animated effects.

In Practice: Animated Materials

- You have learned to animate color and use key tangents to control the rate at which colors can be cycled over time.

- You have a better understanding of how to use Blend materials to dissolve from one material to another.

- Creating carefully framed AVI files to create the illusion of constant motion can eliminate the use of unnecessary geometry.

- Using Noise to simulate water, fire, clouds, and stars can be quite effective is some applications.

- The use of sequential files as an IFL can be used to create more realistic scenes.

- You have gained an increased awareness of third-party plug-ins used to generate more appealing animated materials.

INSIDE

3D STUDIO
MAX

VOLUME III:
ANIMATION

Cover art by Raymond Bintz

GEORGE MAESTRI

SANFORD KENNEDY

RALPH FRANTZ

STEVE BURKE

JASON GREENE

ERIC GREENLEIF

JEREMY HUBBELL

PAUL KAKERT

RANDY KREITZMAN

BOB LAMB

DAN O'LEARY

JAROD RUFFO

ADAM SILVERTHORNE

ANDREW VERNON

SERIES EDITOR:
PHILLIP MILLER

Part V

ANIMATION: STATE OF THE ART

IMAGE CREATED BY MECHADEUS

Chapter 14

by Sanford Kennedy

COMPUTER ANIMATION INDUSTRY OVERVIEW

Three-dimensional computer animation has revolutionized the
way motion picture special effects, computer games, television,
multimedia, and even architectural presentations are created.
But the traditional 2D animation industry still remains firmly
entrenched in its own market: 2D animation dominates Satur-
day morning and children's cartoon programming. Disney-style
2D animated motion pictures are blockbuster hits, and a sizable
portion of television commercials use 2D animated characters. So
where is 3D computer animation today? 3D animation has moved
solidly into computer and arcade video games, taken over all

visual effects for television, grabbed a big share of television commercial production, dominates forensic animation, has run away with theme park motion rides and flight simulations, made major inroads into multimedia, and completely eliminated traditional optical film methods in all forms of visual effects and post production for motion pictures.

Both 2D and 3D animation are vying for the available dollars in the media industries. The lion's share of new investment and new technology, however, is being poured into 3D computer animation. 3D animation has generated continuous growth and made a great leap forward in the 1990s.

This chapter introduces you to some of the companies in the 3D computer animation industry through actual interviews, providing insight into the following topics:

- The state of the art in 3D animation

- Who created 3D Studio MAX

- A history of 3D Studio in motion pictures

- Who are the leading game creators using MAX

- What Softimage says about being MAX's competitor

- Who is using MAX in visual effects

- The wide variety of projects currently using MAX

The State of the Art in 3D Animation

The motion picture industry has taken the lead in generating spectacular, groundbreaking 3D computer animation. In the last five years, a series of blockbuster special effects movies have broken all the rules about what is possible with 3D computer graphics. In the early '90s, the first major films with computer animated sequences were released with startling success. First in 1989 came the marvelous computer-animated water snake in Jim Cameron's *The Abyss*, for 20th Century Fox, followed closely in 1991 by the fantastic computer animated liquid metal Terminator 1000 in Cameron's production of *Terminator 2*, for Carolco. Then in 1993, Steven Spielberg and George Lucas's Industrial Light and Magic visual effects studio stunned the world again with *Jurassic Park*, for Universal Studios.

The unbelievable quality of the 3D computer-animated dinosaurs astounded the public worldwide. Even for those who worked every day in the visual effects industry, it was an amazing revelation to see a photorealistic computer-generated Tyrannosaurus Rex rampaging through the rain in the darkness, chasing three helpless victims in a jeep. These images of primal fear were so well done that the film reaped unprecedented profit and caused a ripple of surprise to move through the entire media industry. 3D computer animation had arrived.

Until the mid-'90s, the capability to create photorealistic animation had been the exclusive domain of high-end software such as Alias/Wavefront, SoftImage, Prisms, and Renderman. But Intel changed the rules with its Pentium processor. Around this time, the technology of Intel-based workstations took a giant leap forward. The PC, and the available software such as 3D Studio, improved to the point where the so-called "low-end" PC platform was beginning to be used to generate animation and visual effects for broadcast television and motion pictures.

3D Studio for DOS scored a major breakthrough into high-resolution motion picture visual effects with scenes in the films *Johnny Mnemonic*, *The Craft*, and the titles for the movie *Speed*, all features produced at Sony Pictures. Despite this early success, all off-the-shelf software that ran on the DOS operating system on Intel PCs had serious limitations in color bit depth, memory, and rendering speed. During this period, another "low-end" software package found success in television production—LightWave. It originally ran on the Amiga and was later ported to the PC. Its potential was tapped by Steven Spielberg to create underwater visual effects for his television show *Seaquest*, by Amblin Entertainment. That led to later success in creating special effects for *Hercules* and *Babylon 5*, which are still in production.

By 1994, nearly every major Hollywood motion picture contained at least some computer-manipulated scenes. Digitally generated content ranged from digital compositing using high-end software such as Flame or Wavefront Composer, to special effects such as 3D computer-animated space ships, animated creatures, digitally created environments, or atmospheric visual effects. The majority of these visual effects were done using Alias/Wavefront, Prisms, or Softimage and rendered using Renderman Pro on Silicon Graphics workstations.

When Microsoft purchased SoftImage in 1994 and ported it to Windows NT on the Intel platform (by the end of 1995), the Silicon Graphics–based high-end 3D computer graphics industry got an abrupt wake-up call. To add to their consternation, the new version of 3D Studio MAX for Windows NT was released a few months later. At about the same time, Lightwave, Animation Master, Photoshop, Digital Fusion, and Razor Pro released versions for Windows NT. Suddenly—by the summer of 1996—enough tools were available running on NT on the PC platform to do serious production work. When combined with the new real-time Open GL video display cards and the dual and quad processor Intel PC workstations from Intergraph, the Windows NT platform was finally a force to be taken seriously as a high-end production tool.

The Genesis of 3D Studio MAX

The sudden appearance of all this software for Windows NT was not as miraculous or coincidental as it may seem. Many of these companies had been working on versions for Windows NT for years, and it was generally recognized that Windows NT was the software platform of the future.

Gary Yost realized the possibilities of the Windows NT platform for 3D animation. (Image done in 3D Studio MAX created by Gene Bodio.)

The development of 3D Studio MAX for Windows NT was special because it was not a port of an existing product to a different software platform. MAX was all-new from the ground up.

The story of the creation of 3D Studio MAX is remarkable in both its ground-breaking new technology, and for the way the program was written by a small group of specialists in different parts of the country. Gary Yost was able to gather around him a group of individuals who shared a common vision of creating the first object-oriented 3D animation program for Windows NT.

The birth of MAX took three years and three months. The Yost Group started working on the code in January of 1993. The main problem they had was that they had to "re-invent the wheel." The existing version of 3D Studio ran in DOS and was one of the most un-object–oriented programs available for 3D animation. In writing MAX, they were trying to create the most object-oriented animation program ever written and make it run in Windows NT on regular PC compatibles. They had no prior work on which they could base their new software. Twenty months was spent just working on prototypes.

At the time the 3D Studio MAX project began, the Yost Group was still working to finish 3DS Release 3, so they could not spend full time on MAX's development. They knew that if they didn't get to Windows with an object-oriented program by 1996, however, 3D Studio would be considered archaic.

Gary recalls thinking, "You know, if you are a market leader and you don't obsolete yourself, someone's going to do it for you."

They knew they had a big challenge, and they knew they could not get it all in one jump, so they started writing prototypes.

Building the Team

Gary brought Don Brittain into the Yost Group to begin work on the core code for MAX. Don had been the vice-president of Research and Development at Wavefront. He left because Wavefront decided it did not want to go into NT or Windows and preferred to stay in Unix. Don saw what was coming in the future. Gary explained, "Don was essential to our being able to get this project done because none of us were as deeply involved in Windows as Don was."

Assembling the MAX team. (Image from Westwood Studio's game Lands of Lore, Guardians of Destiny.*)*

Another essential member of the team, who had been working with Gary on 3D Studio since Release 1, was Dan Silva. He had a tremendous amount of object-oriented programming background from his experience at Xerox Park, where they basically invented object-oriented programming. Dan's dream, since he started working on 3D Studio R1 in 1989, was to one day make it object-oriented.

Dan and Don were able to form the nucleus of this new object-oriented seed that would become 3D Studio MAX. Gary described the early stages of the working method of the MAX team:

> They would all fly in to my home every six weeks through 1993 and the first half of 1994. We would have these big marathon sessions where we sat down for four days and looked at Don's prototypes and discussed them. Slowly we zeroed in on how to do something like this.

The Yost Group had a major breakthrough in January of 1994 when they were able to bring in Michael Girard, Susan Amkraut, and John Chadwick of Unreal Pictures. They were responsible for creating the Character Studio Biped plug-in, which was in development on another platform before work started on MAX. Gary recalled:

> They actually had a complete working Biped prototype running in early 1993. When I first saw it, Biped was running on a Silicon Graphics box, but there was nothing available on the SGI platform that they could plug their code into.

When the Unreal folks joined the MAX team, they became an instrumental factor in determining what was needed to make MAX capable of supporting such extensive plug-ins.

> They would come in on one of the days during each one of the marathon sessions, and we would spend the whole day talking to them about what they needed. Having that feedback during the course of the prototype stage gave us the knowledge of what was needed to make sure that the API was as robust as it had to be. They were the API challenge.

By early 1994, the Yost Group had shipped their last IPAS programs, disks 6 and 7, for the DOS version of 3D Studio. Rolf Berteig, who had written many of the most popular IPAS routines, was brought into the MAX team. At 27, he was the youngest member. Gary admitted:

> If it wasn't for his youthful exuberance along with his strong technical background, we couldn't have done the project. We needed that extra bit of energy and drive in the team to keep going with this brutally difficult project. At every critical juncture we'd add another essential person. If you took away any one of these folks, we couldn't have done it.

The last person added to the team who was really critical to the project was Mark Meier. Gary was impressed with the IPAS plug-ins that Meier had written and then given away in the 3D Studio forum. Gary remembered:

> He was a computer artist who got into IPAS programming to create the effects that he needed. He was the first person I discovered who was giving away free plug-ins for 3D Studio. The documentation for his plug-ins was very good, so I asked him if he would like to be a part of the team and develop the SDK.

Gary felt it would be pointless to develop a platform such as MAX and then put it out there without including very good documentation that would enable other people to develop plug-ins for it. He also did not want to farm out the SDK to someone outside the core group.

The third prototype of MAX was finished right before Siggraph of 1994 at Orlando, Florida—Release 4 was launched there as a plug-in upgrade. The reason it was just a plug-in release was that by that time almost all their attention was focused exclusively on developing MAX. Gary said that he was very frustrated at Siggraph because he could not tell anyone about MAX.

Creating the "Virtual" Yost Group

In October 1994, the MAX team actually started writing the shell that was to become MAX. By that point, they had Tom Hudson in Wisconsin, Rolf Berteig in Seattle, Dan Silva and Jack Powell in Marin County, California, Don Brittain in Santa Barbara, and Gary Yost in San Francisco; all were sending data back and forth to each other over modems. But the modems turned out to be a big problem. Gary related:

> We thought we were going to be able to work fast enough by exchanging data over 28.8 modems. We put together a server in Santa Barbara with four incoming lines with source code control software. Then we started sending in code, but we discovered that the source code control software would choke when the line was dropped, so we would get these line hits. The source code would get scrambled and Don had to spend entire days at a time recovering from the line hits.

The isolation of the team brought about data transfer problems. (Image of stingray done in 3D Studio MAX by Marcus Morgan, Kinetix.)

It got so bad that by mid-November they realized that they could not do the project. Because everyone lived in remote locations in different parts of the country, the project was not going to work. It was impossible to relocate everyone.

One day Gary was speaking to Gus Grubba about his frustrations and fears of having to end the project after all the work they had done, and Gus asked whether Gary had thought about using high-speed ISDN modems that are immune to line hits. Gary said:

> I didn't realize that ISDN could be brought into private homes virtually anywhere in the country, but as it turned out, ISDN had just recently become available from each of our regional phone companies.

Gus knew that there had been a recent ruling that said if you were within a few miles of a switch, the phone company was required to make ISDN available to you. In November, all the MAX team members called their local phone companies and requested ISDN. It took five weeks to get connected, but by January 1995 the "Virtual" Yost Group was online and running.

ISDN modems operate at 128 K baud compared with the 28.8 K baud of the consumer modem lines. This was the last key element that fell into place, enabling the creation of MAX to move forward. Gus Grubba then joined the team and took on responsibility for writing the Network Rendering software and the Video Post module.

MAX Meets the Public

By the time of Siggraph 1995 in August, Gary did the first presentation of MAX for the public. One of the greatest problems faced by the Yost Group was how to make a purely object-oriented program run on a regular PC P5-90, which was the target platform. It had to run without performance problems while interactively maintaining real time. The program interface appeared to be finished, and during the demonstrations everything worked well. Considering how far they had come in a relatively short time, this working demonstration was the most amazing feat that the Yost Group had ever accomplished. At that time, there was no renderer, and in terms of the total number of features that shipped with MAX when it was released, only about 20 percent of the total feature set was running. The MAX beta program was started a month later, and the team kept working seven days a week until the program was shipped in April of 1996.

The Yost Group's creation was first seen by the public at SIGGRAPH 1995. (Flower image done in 3D Studio MAX created by Mechadeus.)

After MAX was released, it was very well received, winning awards for its advanced technology and rich feature set. Within the 3D Studio community, a number of people wondered how so few people were able to create such a massive and groundbreaking program. Many rumors were heard that Gary and his cohorts were actually androids like Data on *Star Trek*. Gary smiled and said:

> I know there is that impression out there that we are not built like everyone else because we're so good at writing software. The reality is that we are just regular people working toward our potential. Everyone has that potential. The customers who use 3D Studio have sent back so much positive energy to us over the years that it has helped us achieve our goals.

When asked what made the Yost Group able to work so well together, he stated firmly:

> There are no junk food addicts among us at all. We are all very health-conscious. You can't sustain this kind of work pace unless you take very good care of yourself. The only thing that is perhaps unique about us is that as a team, we are all musicians. We all play at least one, and in many cases, two and three instruments.

The Yost Group functioned like a coalition of experts, with each member of the MAX team responsible for his or her own modules within MAX. The only exception was Dan Silva and Rolf Berteig, who together created the Modifier Stack object pipeline. There was a tremendous amount of specialization. Almost no crossover occurred because the program is so object-oriented and modular. Because of that, any programmer familiar with the SDK could write a plug-in and upload it to the web. Then when it is loaded into MAX, it will look and feel just like it was written by one of the core programmers.

MAX in the Future

When asked what his future goals are for MAX, Gary said:

One of our goals is to create the biggest programming team that has ever been seen on the planet. Because the SDK is shipped for free, and because you are going to see more low-cost educational versions of MAX, you could potentially get 10,000 programmers working on plug-ins by the end of the century. The SDK is a new language and a new way of thinking about graphics and object-oriented programming. It can teach people who never thought they were interested how to do object-oriented programming in 3D graphics. We already have people working on MAX plug-ins all over Europe, in Russia, in Africa, Latin America, Australia, Canada, China, and Japan. In India there is a tremendous amount of work being done on plug-ins. The goal is to make MAX world-wide and to reflect the diversity of the human spirit.

How 3D Studio MAX Is Being Used

Some of the top visual effects and animation studios were interviewed to find out how they were using 3D Studio MAX in production. One of the pioneer users of 3D Studio in Hollywood is Sony Pictures Imageworks of Culver City, California. Sony Pictures is one of the "big seven" Hollywood movie studios, a group that includes Paramount Pictures, Universal Studios, Warner Brothers, 20th Century Fox, Walt Disney Studios, and the newest big studio—which has recently chosen 3D Studio MAX for its Interactive Division—Steven Spielberg's DreamWorks SKG. All these studios now have 3D animation and interactive media divisions employing hundreds of animators and multiple software and hardware platforms.

3D Studio History at Sony Pictures Imageworks

Frank Foster, head of the Multimedia Division of Sony Pictures Imageworks, has been using 3D Studio to create motion picture visual effects for a number of years. In a recent interview, Frank recalled the first time he took an interest in 3D Studio:

> In 1990, I was involved in an R & D project at Tri-Star Pictures (now a division of Sony Pictures). We were looking for a method for doing electronic storyboarding for our pre-visualization work. We looked into a number of different platforms and software applications. We selected 3D Studio to be our pre-visualization software primarily because of how quickly we could place the camera, and how quickly we could render a scene.

Tri-Star's R & D project was one of the first successful uses of 3D Studio in Hollywood. Their first major pre-visualization project was a film called *Striking Distance*. Frank explained how pre-visualization worked:

> We animated about a half hour of the movie in 3D Studio before any film was shot, including boat chases, car chases, train crashes, and some fight scenes. We constructed the location in the computer and then designed the sequence. The scene that got the most focus was a car chase sequence through downtown Pittsburgh. We built accurate models of the city streets based on data from the City Planning Department. We actually had 3D Studio running on computers on location. By doing that project, we learned a lot about what could be done with pre-visualization, and what could be done with 3D Studio and IBM PCs on the road.

During that time, Frank began to expand the activities of his department. It wasn't long before they took on motion picture title design. Frank explained:

> We started looking at doing motion picture title design by incorporating desktop publishing techniques and 3D Studio's ability to take in Adobe Illustrator file format. One of the first title projects we did was a relatively unknown film called *Wilder Napalm*, in 1993. After that, we did a whole string of movie title sequences, including *Manhattan Murder Mystery* and *Thief*. Probably the most well-known titles we have done were in the opening sequence of the movie *Speed*. The elevator sequence was pre-visualized in 3D Studio, and the title sequence itself was designed and rendered at high-resolution in 3D Studio.

Frank pushed the envelope still further by taking on the first actual 3D Studio special effects scene in a Michael Keaton film called *My Life*, for Columbia Pictures. The effects were very bright lighting tricks that created the illusion of going into the "after-life." The effects were rendered in 3D Studio and then handed off for compositing into the film on Wavefront Composer. The visual effects supervisor on that project was John Nelson, who became instrumental in getting further effects shots for 3D Studio.

The next breakthrough came when John Nelson took over as visual effects supervisor on the *Johnny Mnemonic* film project. After doing extensive tests, Frank was able to convince him that 3D Studio could do the cyberspace sequence for the picture. Frank is justifiably proud of his work on *Johnny Mnemonic*. He looked away for a moment, remembering what the project was like, and said:

> We created the telephone call sequence at the beginning of the picture where Keanu Reeves tries to track down the man who wanted to kill him. When the film was almost completed, and in post production, the producer came back to us because they were quite pleased with the work and asked us to do the entire opening of the film. It was a very long sequence that begins with the prologue and goes on for about two and a half minutes of film-resolution work. The prologue is a scene with a scroll moving upward, explaining the story. That is followed by a particle system explosion of the title *Johnny Mnemonic*, and then a trip through the cyberworld of the Internet 20 years in the future. The three scenes lead to the wake-up call scene in the hotel room. The entire sequence was a single render and was our first opportunity to use 3D Studio to create a full film-resolution motion picture effect.

The 3D Studio group moved on to create the stereoscopic 3D titles for the IMAX project *Wings of Courage*, which gave them experience in rendering high-resolution output to large film sizes. Then in 1995, staff graphic designer Brummbaer took on the project of doing the opening for the Siggraph electronic theater using 3D Studio. This was to be a large-format, 70mm Showscan presentation projected at 60 frames per second. Frank said:

> We rendered that out at high resolution. It involved a large number of elements and a sophisticated sound track. It was extremely well received and was shown for five nights at Siggraph.

The next 3D Studio project at Sony was for a film called *The Craft*. Frank explained, very seriously:

> This was a difficult sequence where photorealistic butterflies had to fly around and interact with two live actresses, exhibiting the behavior of real butterflies. Butterflies don't fly like a bird. They have a very erratic kind of floating and jumping movement. It was a key sequence in the film, and we worked very hard doing numerous tests to prove that 3D Studio was capable of doing this kind of high-end animation and rendering. Finally, it came down to a lot of hard work by Dave Schaub, who created the actual animation of the butterflies.

> *The Craft* was the first time that a project used 3D Studio's capability to render in full 16-bit linear colorspace for a motion picture. The way people had used 3D Studio in the past was to dither down the 64-bit 3D Studio colorspace to a TARGA file with 8 bits. Joe Munkaby, our staff plug-in programmer, wrote a custom IPAS that would allow us to input and output RLA file format images directly. Originally, the sequence was to be composited into the movie using the SGI systems, but we were able to get such good results within 3D Studio, that we did the actual final composite for the film and saved significant costs on the production.

Sony Imageworks moved to using 3D Studio MAX in 1996. Imagework's character animation relies heavily on MAX's Character Studio, with its capability to do IK blending. They are also very enthusiastic about the recent developments in using MAX for cartoon rendering. This is done using a plug-in that flattens the image, puts edge lines around the characters, and then does the inking and painting. Imageworks predicts that this will be a very important market area for 3D Studio MAX animation in the future.

The department where 3D Studio MAX is used at Sony is called the Multimedia Department. Frank explained that:

> Pre-visualization, title design, and animation for television and feature effects are just part of the work we do. Our multimedia department is based around both animation and Internet production, including VRML content for the Sony Internet web site is done here with MAX. In character animation, we have recently completed 158 shots using 3D Studio MAX for one of the last episodes in this season's *The Adventures of Johnny Quest*, the television series produced by Hanna-Barbera.

Matt Hausle and Frank Foster (on right) in the video editing suite at Sony Pictures Imageworks Multimedia Division, the facility for laying off MAX images to video.

When asked how they get images from MAX on to motion picture film, Frank replied:

> Sony Imageworks has an input/output department which does both film scanning and film printing. We have multiple cameras so we can do multiple projects at the same time. For any of the film resolution projects that we do, the files will be sent over to the server that supports the film recorders and then output directly to 35mm motion picture film.

3D Studio Has Strength in Computer Games

3D Studio and 3D Studio MAX have a substantial share of the interactive media market and are widely used in computer game production. 3D Studio has been used to create nearly 70 percent of all PC games including *7th Guest, 11th Hour, Area 51, Rebel Assault, Wing Commander II, Crash and Burn, Daedalus Encounter, SimCity 2000, F10-Strike Eagle III,* and *X-Wing.* Major users read like a who's who in Game producers: LucasArts, Turner Interactive, Mechadeus, Electronic Arts Sports, Westwood Studios, Sega, Virgin Interactive, Warner Interactive, Amazing Media, Activision, and DreamWorks Interactive.

DreamWorks Interactive

One of the newest users of 3D Studio MAX is DreamWorks Interactive, in Los Angeles. DreamWorks Interactive is a joint venture between Microsoft Corporation and DreamWorks SKG, owned by Steven Spielberg, Jeffrey Katzenberg, ex-head of production at Disney Studios, and David Geffen, owner of Geffen Records. MAX was chosen by DWI as the main production tool for modeling and animating their characters and building realistic three-dimensional environments for their games.

The DreamWorks Interactive logo.

Currently they are using MAX to produce four new interactive game titles. *Goosebumps II* is a sequel to their successful game *Goosebumps: Escape from Horrorland*, based on R.L. Stine's popular book. *The Lost World*, for the Sony PlayStation, about to be released in August 1997, is based on *The Lost World: Jurassic Park*, the sequel to the original film (released in May 1997). *Trespassers: Jurassic Park* is a whole new kind of game with built-in artificial intelligence, to be released by Christmas 1997. They are also working on *Chaos Island*, a real-time strategy game in which kids can guide expeditions into the heart of *The Lost World's* Dinosaur Island.

*Hunter Deinonychus
Raptors on the prowl in*
Jurassic Park: The Lost
World.

The Lost World is being created under the guidance of Patrick Gilmore, executive producer. One of the game's five animators, Sunil Thankanushy, spoke about how they are using 3D Studio MAX to create the dinosaurs:

> I am building six different deinonychus variations for the game, each of which will attack the player in a slightly different way. They are modeled in MAX at low resolution so they can be moved quickly by the real-time game engine of the Sony PlayStation. Players can encounter deinonychus (which is a cousin to the velociraptor made famous in the first film) while playing one of three different dinosaurs, or two different human player characters. During the game, deinonychus can stalk and attack the player, who has to figure out a strategy to survive.

When Sunil finishes animating a model, it is not exported from MAX into the PlayStation as a MAX file. Instead, the model and its animation are exported as data only. The programming team takes the data and programs the PlayStation game engine to reconstruct and render the dinosaurs moving in real-time during game play. In this way, a library of different moves can be stored. The PlayStation game engine generates both the characters and the environment in real time from data exported from 3D Studio MAX.

When asked how he did the animation of the raptors, Sunil said:

> The models are animated with the Bones Pro plug-in from Digimation, using simple rotations to control the bone skeleton, which in turn deform the character mesh. Philosophically, we chose not to use inverse kinematics because it doesn't accurately capture how creatures really move in nature (nature seems to have a preference for *forward* kinematics). We also experimented with Character Studio, but we ended up going back to using Bones Pro because we got better results.

A Deinonychus ready to attack. (Modeled by Sunil Thankamushy and textured by Matt Hall.)

Another group at DreamWorks Interactive is working on *Trespassers: Jurassic Park*, using a completely different approach under the technical guidance of Executive Producer Seamus Blackley. This game should prove to be a groundbreaking improvement in interactivity with higher resolution models and bump-mapped surfaces. Its unique features will include a built-in artificial intelligence that helps the dinosaurs decide how to react in different situations and a physics engine that makes the animals and their environment react to impacts and move just like animals in real life. This game is due out by Christmas 1997 and is attracting considerable pre-release interest. All the dinosaurs and their environments are being built by an 11-man team working with 3D Studio MAX on Pentium Pro 200s running Windows NT. DWI has 35 3DS MAX seats at the present time.

A Rhamphorhynchus created with 3D Studio MAX at DWI. (Modeled by Scott Hyman and textured by Matt Hall.)

Westwood Studios

Westwood Studios, founded by Louis Castle in Las Vegas, Nevada, has over 65 3DS MAX workstations plus a render farm, making it the largest MAX studio in the country. Mr. Castle was unavailable for an interview, but he did provide a number of exciting images, reprinted here, from Westwood's game *Lands of Lore, Guardians of Destiny*.

Westwood's chief character designer is Elie Arabian, and the creator of the environments is Frank Mendeola. This game contains some very fine examples of modeling and surface texturing done with MAX. Top titles include *Command & Conquer* and *Monopoly*, the world's first game with full Internet support for multiple players.

A gallery of characters and environments created with 3D Studio MAX for Westwood Studio's game Lands of Lore, Guardians of Destiny.

SoftImage and 3D Studio MAX: Respectful Competitors

SoftImage is considered to be the top high-end character animation and modeling software in the industry. When new software such as 3D Studio MAX comes out, it is only natural to make a feature-by-feature comparison with other packages considered the leaders in the industry. SoftImage and MAX both share the Windows NT platform and in many areas have surprisingly similar features. One of the main differences between the two is the fact that SoftImage has had many years in which to mature, adding features in response to market pressures. This author presents the following interview with the head of Special Projects at SoftImage as a way of informing MAX users what their top competitor has to offer, and to try to set up a kind of "reality check" for those of you who don't know what is out there in the marketplace. It is also hoped that some benefit will be derived for all through the cross-pollination of ideas that should occur between the users of the two packages. Remember that it is likely you will be sharing studio space with SoftImage users in the years to come. It is wise, therefore, to know what they can do.

An Interview with SoftImage's David Morin

David Morin is the Director of Special Projects at SoftImage. He regularly commutes between SoftImage in Montreal, Canada, and their movie industry research center near Hollywood in Santa Monica, California.

SoftImage has a strong development team focused on providing leadership in high-end 3D computer graphics and has also invested in creating strong development tools for the clients and third-party market. Through the Software Development Kit (SDK), their third-party developers can work directly with the software to do things like connecting any device to SoftImage, or developing shaders or plug-ins for the 3D interactive interface.

> As the field widens and more and more people do computer graphics, it will be impossible for us to do everything for everybody.

At Siggraph in 1996 we had 19 third-party developers in our booth and this number is booming. We have worked very hard to open a rich development environment to our clients and third-party developers, and as a result we see more enhancements coming to SoftImage.

In the last six years SoftImage has accomplished a great deal in the motion picture industry. It is hoped that by understanding the high level of this accomplishment, everyone who used both MAX and SoftImage will be inspired to do better and greater works.

SoftImage has been essential to the creation of some of the finest 3D-animated special effects that have come out of the Film Industry. David explained their relationship with the top special effects houses in the business:

ILM is one of our big customers. They have been instrumental in breaking new ground and making new special effects, continuously bringing new imagery to the movie screen. SoftImage has been their tool of choice for character animation. They started using SoftImage back in 1992. The first use of SoftImage at ILM was in the movie *Death Becomes Her*, for the "twisting neck" scene. Then they became involved in preparing for *Jurassic Park* where they had some articulated dinosaur figures to do. In the past they had done some figures with other software, such as the liquid man who walks very stiffly in *Terminator 2*. For this project they needed to go beyond that level and to achieve realistic movement. SoftImage 2.5 had just come out at the time which included the first implementation of Inverse Kinematics ever to be offered in any software.

ILM is always looking over the market to see if there is a new tool there to solve their problems and they chose SoftImage to animate the dinosaurs. During that project ILM also developed their own software that works with SoftImage.

After *Jurassic Park*, ILM used SoftImage to do the ghosts in *Casper*, the effects in *The Mask*, and the animals in *Jumanji*. Then they did *Twister*, *Mission Impossible*, and *Mars Attacks*. In all of those productions SoftImage formed a part of their tool set.

SoftImage was used at ILM to generate the 3D Animated tornado for the film Twister.

There are a large number of movie companies using Softimage like Digital Domain, DreamWorks, and Sony Pictures. All of them use it to a different extent for different things. David maintained that:

We have recently introduced a completely new renderer called Mental Ray, which is the best rendering technology available today. It is a fully open, distributed, and configurable raytracer. Developers can add their own effects into it by writing new shaders. Other renderers use shaders very successfully, but they are not ray tracers, and anything that you want to do in terms of reflection or refraction is faked. Over the years Renderman users (for instance) have become very good at developing realistic looking fakes for all their effects. But, it is an old technology. Mental Ray is based more directly on the laws of optics and physics. It reads the scene and allows you to do volumetric rendering like smoke effects and very smooth area lighting. It will even compute caustics for use in animating water.

David explains:

People buy SoftImage sometimes for the character animation, sometimes for rendering, but always because it is a well-rounded tool in all the other areas. In modeling SoftImage has full support for polygonal objects, three types of patches, and complete support of metaballs, and parametric nurbs (non-uniform rational B-splines). SoftImage's modeling attributes are the most complete on the market today.

Caught Their Eye is an Oldsmobile-Aurora commercial done with SoftImage by R/Greenberg Associates © 1996.

Characters created in SoftImage for the game Tekken 2.

Said Morin:

The game industry is very important to us, as well as video, 2D animation, and post production. In games we have been very happy to help Sega who used SoftImage to do the animation for their *Virtua Fighter* games. These were the first fight games done with motion capture and were very demanding on the computer. Because of that, back then, they could only be played on an arcade machine. Today these types of games are running on home game consoles. In the meantime we have developed a whole set of tools for the game industry in general, including PSX converters, Sega Saturn converters, on-target viewing, and playback. We have color reduction and polygon reduction, and a number of polygon selection tools such as raycasting selection.

Sony's Pygnosis game division uses SoftImage to create its characters for its game Tenka.

One of the most visible examples of the ability of SoftImage to do Character Animation is the popular Saturday morning television show *Reboot* produced in Vancouver, Canada. David pointed out that:

> The *Reboot* studio is turning out one episode with 22 minutes of full computer animation every two weeks, a very impressive throughput and quality of work done without motion capture, using only the classical animation approach to maintain the *Reboot* "look."

David's final comment was that:

> One of our ultimate goals at SoftImage is to enable professional artists to create great images and animations and to help them translate what they have in their heads in a way that can be shared by other people.

He encourages all animators to do the best work possible, express their own vision, and learn the tools of the trade.

3D Studio MAX in Visual Effects

Visual effects is the most demanding area of 3D computer animation, and pushes both the software and the hardware to the limits to get the great shots needed to create a special effects sequence for motion pictures or television. A number of independent studios have entered the visual effects field and are finding success by using 3D Studio MAX.

Blur Studio

Pushing MAX to the limit is the normal mode of operation at Blur Studio in Venice, California. Established in 1995 by animators Tim Miller and David Stinnett, with Cat Chapman producer, Blur is a compact, state-of-the-art facility based on Intergraph dual and quad processor workstations. Since they launched the Blur, they have been doing broadcast-quality work for commercials and high-resolution visual effects sequences for motion pictures.

Tom Dillon, a veteran 3D Studio user, was the first animator to join their staff. His background includes 2D animation background painting.

When asked about his use of MAX, he said:

> We have used 3D Studio MAX on movie effects projects, commercial effects projects, Saturday morning cartoon projects, and game work. For the movie *The Crow: City of Angels* we built simulated holographic visual effects that were composited into live action for the film's trailer. One shot was a holographic effect using a round screen with the hologram projected up on to it. It used particle systems and volume lights. Another effect was a morphing shadow of a figure looming up against a wall that morphed from a crow silhouette into a figure.

Blur also generated an intricate effects shot for the trailer for *Hellraiser: Bloodline*, produced by Miramax/Dimension Films. MAX was used to model a close-up section of the cracks in the evil character Pinhead's face. In the sequence, his head explodes. Tom recalls:

> He had little cracks in his face. We built a camera that would fly into the cracks so it looked like a camera flying through a canyon. We added volume lights coming up through all the pinholes in his head. If you have seen any of the *Hellraiser* films, you know that Pinhead has these big nails driven into his head. In the sequence, you see giant nails coming up through the canyon as you are flying through it. When the camera pulls up out of the canyon, his head explodes, and then you cut to a live action shot of him reacting.

Commercials are another area of activity for Blur. For McDonalds, Blur used MAX to create a holographic *Star Trek* transporter effect to animate a shot of a Big Mac hamburger that lands on a space port. For Cadillac, they did a spot called *The Car that Ziggs*. In that commercial, they had to match animation to live action background footage. Tom describes the shot:

> *The Car that Ziggs* is a commercial advertising the new intelligent brake and handling controls. We used MAX's rotoscoping capability to create a line that follows behind the car as it moves along the road. I did the camera tracking in MAX for the shot.

Toy commercials are big business on weekday afternoons and Saturday mornings. Blur did a 30 second 3D-animated *Fruity Pebbles* cereal commercial that involved the use of the Hanna-Barbera *Flintstones* characters. Tom recalls:

> I had fun because I got to work with one of the 2D animators who does the *Flintstones*. We storyboarded out the entire commercial. The scene involved creating a virtual reality background environment where we

built and animated a number of characters like a dinosaur made out of fruit. When our animation was finished, Hanna-Barbera composited their 2D characters into our virtual 3D environment.

The scene of a missile being fired was created in MAX for the television show Pandora's Clock, courtesy of NBC.

Their most recent project is a long animation sequence for the 3D-animated version of *The Real Adventures of Johnny Quest*, produced by Hanna-Barbera, which includes 3D animated segments. One episode required the creation of $9^1/_2$ minutes of 3D character animation and many different environments at broadcast resolution. Eric Pinkel is one of the animators who worked on *Johnny Quest*. Eric talked about his work:

> We put MAX through its paces. I have worked with Electric Image and with Alias, and I find MAX far superior to work with. For me, the strongest points in MAX are its modeling and its texture mapping abilities. The modeling in *Johnny Quest* is very complicated. Patches are used extensively, as well as lofting. What is nice about MAX's lofter is that you can convert a loft into a patch. If you want to use Free Form Deformation to sculpt the model, you can. And when you are done, you can convert it back to an editable mesh, and then back again into a patch, and continue to modify it.

Blur is now working on two more *Johnny Quest* sequences that will be five minutes and three minutes long, respectively.

Blur uses an assortment of MAX's built-in tools and plug-ins. Because Blur is a beta tester for a number of the people who write plug-ins, they get to work with them before the general users do. The plug-ins add tremendously to their ability to create exactly the kind of effects needed for a particular look. Just like the high-end studios, Blur has their own in-house programmers writing plug-ins ranging from simple utilities that optimize MAX for the animator, to elaborate effects to create special explosions. Blur has recently put some of their in-house plug-ins up on the web as freeware plug-ins.

At Blur, they have the capability to do a full range of image output sizes from D1 all the way up to IMAX. They have 12 quad-processor Intergraph workstations in their render farm, and the animators use a mix of dual- and quad-processor Intergraph machines. The quad-processor machines can double the rendering speed when you have a scene with heavy calculations such as volume lighting and atmosphere. Intergraph is working on Render-GL that will enable a frame that normally renders in three minutes to be rendered in 30 seconds. When Intergraph moves from software to hardware-based rendering, they predict a very big increase in rendering speed that is going to give Silicon Graphics serious competition.

Eric Pinkel felt strongly about working at Blur:

> Blur is a really great studio to work in because all of us, including the owners, are animators. Blur was started by animators, so everyone here looks at the work from the viewpoint of an animator. All the way up the chain to Tim Miller, everyone knows what it takes to get the shot done. That makes the pressure go toward quality, instead of toward cranking it out as fast as you can.

Digital Phenomena

Digital Phenomena, located in Corte Madera, California, just north of San Francisco, uses 3D Studio MAX for commercials and film-resolution visual effects. They are the animators responsible for creating the first Character Studio demo animation of dancing figures for the Release 1.0 CD-ROM called *Character Conflict*. The studio is operated by Kevin Olin, who spent many years using AutoCAD, and Jamie Clay, who has been using 3D Studio since its beginnings.

Kevin explained how they got involved in the Character Studio CD:

> Kinetix contacted us mostly because we were a local studio that was familiar with 3D Studio MAX. They needed to produce a Character

Studio demo animation before the release deadline. We wrote the story and started animating. We had to utilize what tools were available in the still un-finished Character Studio beta version. The initial animation was done using pre-release software that was far from stable, but it was powerful enough for us to produce one minute of finished character animation in less than 12 days.

MAX's capability to "solve old problems in new ways," as well as its capability to display full-color, rotoscope-animated backgrounds enabled them to do their latest film project, *Dog's Best Friend*, for the Family Channel on HBO. The production was shot on film and converted to D1 video at 24 frames per second. They did motion tracking and 3D jaw replacement in 3D Studio MAX to make the dog talk.

Kevin explained:

We did 120 shots in about 75 days. MAX enabled us to build an "animation kit" for each of the five barnyard animals. The animation kit consisted of the geometry for the given jaw that was going to be replaced, and the jaw controls. The kits gave the animators high-level controls that enabled them to move a jaw, curl the lower lip, pull the tongue forward, or curl the tongue to simulate speech. They moved the controls and synchronized the jaw movements with MAX's sound track.

John Wainwright, creator of MaxScript, contributed to the project by writing software for tracking objects in MAX. Building the jaw and locating it in the correct position in a background plate is very time-consuming. Through John's plug-in for MAX, the animator could position the jaw automatically in each plate. When in the correct location, it was automatically tracked and maintained in position by the plug-in. Jamie Clay recalled, "With our network, we were able to render a large number of shots for *Dog's Best Friend* very quickly because we were only rendering the animal's jaw as it moved."

Jamie and Kevin did an interesting group of visual effects shots using MAX for the independent film called *Conceiving Ada*, produced by Hot Wire Productions of San Francisco. It was produced and directed by Lynn Hershman. Jamie explained:

It stars Tilda Swinton, Karen Black, and Timothy Leary. Leary's character dies in this movie. Coincidentally, Timothy Leary died about two weeks after he finished the film. 3D Studio MAX was used extensively to embellish his final scene as he passes on.

The exteriors were all shot on 35mm film. Then we came in and shot the interiors on a digital betacam. We stitched together scenes to create a virtual set by combining modified photographs and actors. Using MAX and our network rendering ability we were able to build animations on the fly for use during the actual shoot. The director would ask for some cloud effects, or maybe some rain to go on outside the windows, or maybe some fire in the fireplace, and we would build those on the fly and cue those up during the shooting. We stitched together many images in real time using Digital Ultimatte.

With innovators such as Kevin and Jamie at Digital Phenomena, the versatility of 3D Studio MAX is just beginning to be explored.

A Wide Variety of Media for MAX

Even though 3DS MAX is known as a 3D animation software package, it is the MAX users who determine how it will be applied in the real world. The range of imagery that can be created with MAX covers a broad spectrum from flying logos for a television news hour, to photorealistic growing bacteria for a science-fiction movie thriller. Even a 2D cartoon with lip sync sound, a cover for a fashion magazine, or an industrial product presentation could easily be done using only a portion of MAX's capabilities.

Part of what makes MAX a great software product is its flexibility. Part of what makes 3D Studio MAX fun to work with is the community of creative computer artists that make up the bulk of the MAX users. Unlike the high-end software packages that cost thousands and thousands of dollars, MAX is affordable even on a modest budget. This means that a much wider variety of creative individuals can become MAX users. The major studios and the big media corporations that insist on using Silicon Graphics-based mega-buck software have little room for flexibility and even less imagination in their headlong pursuit of profits at all costs. It is in the domain of the smaller independent animation studios where you find the small groups of dedicated animators with great depth of talent, adaptability, and creativity.

As a realistic but somewhat tongue-in-cheek example of the talent and adaptability of a typical independent animation studio, the following anecdote describes the exotic kinds of job opportunities that are often presented to the independent 3D Studio animation houses. This scene could take place at any studio, anywhere from Hollywood to the Lower East Side of New York City: A producer has just received a large sum of money from an eccentric software billionaire, and he is searching frantically for a studio to do his revolutionary multimedia film and graphics project. The producer meets with the creative director of an independent 3D Studio MAX–based production company and proposes the following project that has never been done before.

Waving his arms he explains:

It will be the greatest multimedia project ever produced! It will be shot on 35mm film with a cast of hundreds, and then digitized as a background plate for computer animation. You will be expected to create fantastic visual effects, with two monsters that fight a battle. Then you will synchronize a sound track with a video screen that plays interactive cartoons during a love scene between the prince and the fair maiden in the castle tower, just before the explosion of the extinct volcano. During the explosion, the Castle will tumble down with lightning and flames belching up through the cracked earth, and the lovers will fall into the boiling lava. You will end the sequence as a tidal wave of water rushes in to drown the flames, and the lovers emerge as winged angels rising up with the steam that morphs into a stairway to heaven as the camera flies into the clouds and we fade to black! Can you do it?

The owner/animator of the studio glances at his partner, who is a programmer for MAX plug-ins. They smile at each other. The owner/animator says, "We can do *that*. That will only use a small part of 3D Studio MAX's capabilities."

Pyros Pictures

Greg Pyros is well known within the 3D Studio community for his ability to wear many hats. Like many independent studios in the field, Pyros Pictures has a small, but very talented staff of ten animators. With the programming expertise of his associate Gus Grubba, who was part of the team that wrote 3D Studio MAX, there are few tasks that Greg and his staff at Pyros Pictures could not take on. They have done a variety of work that covers the animation field from games, to commercials and visual effects for TV and feature films, to forensic animation.

When you enter the Pyros Pictures studio located high atop a modern glass and steel high rise edifice in Orange County, California, you are immediately impressed with the warm, yet businesslike atmosphere that resembles an architectect's office that suddenly discovered it was fun to do animation and play music. As a matter of fact, that is exactly what Pyros Pictures is. Greg

Pyros was destined from an early age to be an architect, following in his father's footsteps. But right in the middle of a budding career, he contracted the dreaded 3D Studio animator's bug and has never recovered.

Greg, who is still an architect, but prefers to animate, explains:

> I started out in 1981 as an architectural firm. I became a dealer for AutoCAD because there weren't any dealers who could answer my questions, and later for 3D Studio when I realized I could do fly-through animations of my buildings. My architectural firm was busy designing commercial industrial buildings, so our first 3D Studio projects were doing fly-through renderings first for ourselves, and then for other architects. The experiences we had there made me realize that once you have done a number of fly-through animations of entire buildings, it is relatively easy to do flying logos. About three years ago I sold the software dealership, and I have been doing nothing but computer animation since then.

Pyros Pictures is using 3D Studio MAX exclusively on a number of different kinds of jobs. Some of their animators are working on a game, another group is doing visual effects for a feature film, and two more are doing a television commercial. They have a forensic animation division called TrialVision that is booked solid with forensic animation work for lawyers. And finally, a programming group works on projects with Gus Grubba. Greg explained that his team:

> [H]as probably written and sold more IPAS plug-in routines for 3D Studio than any other group. The difference between us and other companies, who only distribute plug-ins written by other people, is that we write them and test them right here under production conditions. We are currently shipping a plug-in for MAX that allows you to output YUV images to the Abekas, Accom, and other digital disk recorders, in both PAL and NTSC. MAX ships with a YUV reader, which we wrote, but without this plug-in, there is no way to output files.

Their current feature film project is a sequel to *Oh God,* the hit film that starred George Burns back in the 1970s. Pyros is bringing him back for this one. They have scanned a portrait sculpture of George Burns and created a very detailed model in MAX. They also modeled George's famous El Producto cigar and his trademark round glasses. Rich Little is going to do the voice for the film. They are currently doing facial animation tests with dialogue. The animated model was shown on television on the first anniversary of George Burns' death.

Greg recalled a few more film projects they have worked on over the past three years:

On *Fair Game,* with William Baldwin and Cindy Crawford, we did the animated images for all of the computer monitors and the Sun laptop that they used. We also worked on a pilot for Francis Ford Coppola based on his film *The Conversation*, and we created visual effects for a film called *Lightspeed* that still is not finished.

Game work has kept Pyros Pictures busy, including a baseball game for Virgin Interactive called *Grand Slam* in which they modeled all 28 North American baseball stadiums for a real-time rendered game. The first large game project that Pyros Pictures did was *Zork Nemesis* for Activision. Greg's studio was chosen because Activision wanted to create a number of realistic architectural-animated interiors for their game. His expertise as an architect proved to be the deciding factor that got him the job.

The whole game was built around a number of interior environments with wrap-around walls. Activision wrote their own version of QuickTime VR. In the game, the players have the ability to spin completely around 360 degrees and look at any part of the environment or the room they are in. The spin is completely seamless.

We did 1,800 frame renderings of all the environments, and from those images, we took a one pixel wide strip out of the center of each one. When we put them all together, they formed a 360 degree circular image of the room. The game engine was programmed to paste the image strips on to the left or right side of the game viewport in real time if the player decided to spin left or right. You never notice a gap or a seam in the wall. Activision even figured out how to do animations during a spin. For example, they have flickering torches on the wall that are animated as the room spins. *Zork Nemesis* runs on Windows 95 and Macintosh.

The resourcefulness and flexibility of Pyros Pictures, and other independent production studios using 3D Studio MAX, is filling an important function in finding and developing new markets for 3D animation created with MAX. The size of the studio in no way limits the size of the project you can do. Greg would agree that the motto of his company could be "We can do that."

Evolution of MAX in 3D Animation

It has been a year since the first version of 3D Studio MAX was released, and many changes have taken place in both MAX and in the market for 3D Animation. A very significant number of 3D animation production studios have embraced 3DS MAX as one of their main production tools, and there are now over 25,000 licensed MAX systems out of 70,000 3D Studio systems now operating worldwide. With its open architecture and powerful new operating system, 3D Studio MAX is being accepted rapidly throughout the 3D Animation Industry, and is on its was toward becoming the most widely used, flexible, and feature-rich 3D animation software package in the industry.

In Practice: Computer Animation Industry Overview

The versatility of 3D Studio MAX is constantly being extended by third-party plug-ins. This has enabled a talented group of 3D animation studios to enter into new areas of high-end animation production. The improvements in MAX over 3D Studio R4 in the areas of character animation, modeling, lighting, and visual effects have established MAX as a professional-level production tool. Special effects animation for motion pictures was formerly the exclusive domain of expensive Unix-based software systems. But MAX, running on the Windows NT platform, has revolutionized the way motion picture special effects studios think about the most cost-effective ways to create their computer games, television commercials, and special effects. Softimage has recently ported its professional software from Unix to take advantage of the widely used Windows NT platform, and many studios now use both 3D Studio MAX and SoftImage in production.

Studios such as Sony Pictures Imageworks, Digital Phenomena, Blur, and Pyros Pictures have been instrumental in the development and testing of MAX under rigorous production conditions. Kinetix and the Yost Group development team have been extremely responsive to the needs of the 3D Studio animation community. It is their open and helpful relationship with the MAX users that has driven the rapid development of MAX into what could become the most versatile, powerful, and widely used 3D animation software available. The quality of the work presented in this chapter is just the tip of the iceberg, and a hint of what can be done with the advanced animation tools in 3D Studio MAX.

IMAGE CREATED BY SANFORD KENNEDY

by Sanford Kennedy

USING 3D STUDIO MAX IN PRODUCTION

You are probably comfortable by now with 3D Studio MAX, and you have worked with all the tools. The next step is to integrate these tools into effective systems for solving a variety of advanced real-world animation problems. However, working effectively in the real world of production computer animation goes beyond simply knowing how to use software and computers. On a daily basis, you deal with clients, directors, producers, animation supervisors, network system administrators, your fellow animators, and the ever-present deadlines. In nearly every animation project, a similar sequence of events must be followed to bring the project to completion. As an animator using MAX in a production studio, you function as part of a team that may create hundreds of different visual elements over a period of months. At the end of the production, all these different elements must come together perfectly to integrate into the final product.

This chapter provides an overview of how a large production computer animation studio operates in the motion picture industry, and what kinds of opportunities and problems exist in this fast-paced, creative world. This chapter covers the following concepts:

■ Organization of a production studio

■ Production flow from concept to completion

■ Working with producers and directors

■ Windows NT and UNIX on one network

■ MAX sharing files with other production software

Computer Graphics Production Studio

One of the most rewarding jobs in computer graphics is the creation of digital visual effects for film and video productions. The greatest benefit that digital effects can provide to movie production is the capability to manipulate the source imagery so that the digital effects fill in all the gaps between the different kinds of mechanical and practical special effects. Good digital effects can create a smoothly flowing visual experience, with transitions and elements otherwise impossible to obtain by using traditional sets, props, and miniature photography.

In the past ten years, it has been repeatedly predicted that computer graphics will take the place of traditional special effects and will make miniature photography obsolete. But, digital visual effects still comprise less than half of the special effects seen each year on the movie screen. It appears that a stable balance has been achieved in the struggle between digital and traditional special effects. Rather than taking over the effects industry, digital effects have joined with traditional special effects to enhance the director's ability to tell a story.

Many of the major motion picture studios have physical effects departments that work in concert with their digital effects departments. Digital effects directors now work with traditional special effects directors sharing storyboards and information, for example. Because much of the film effects footage is shot for use by the digital effects division, this kind of collaboration guarantees that the footage falls well within acceptable color, lighting, and camera steadiness parameters. This practice ensures that no unpleasant surprises arise when the digital and physical effects shots are composited together during the final stages of the production.

Figure 15.1 shows the physical organization of a typical high-end digital animation studio. All large computer graphics studios have similar equipment and departmental divisions. Until recently, if you walked into any of the well-established computer animation studios in Hollywood, you would find nothing but rows of Silicon Graphics workstations running extremely expensive 2D and 3D software packages. But, since the introduction of Adobe Photoshop running on the Macintosh computer, studios have gradually opened their doors to other software and hardware combinations, including 3D Studio MAX running on the IBM Pentium Pro.

FIGURE 15.1

The physical layout of a large computer animation studio in the motion picture industry.

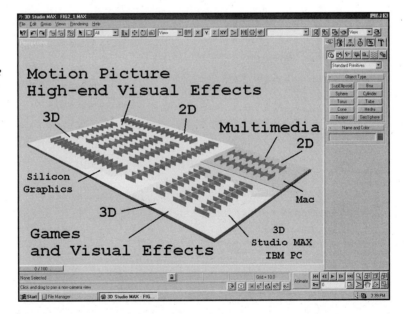

Figure 15.1 shows how a large computer animation studio in the motion picture industry is divided into different areas of activity. The upper half is the high-resolution motion picture visual effects division. The lower half is the game and multimedia division. In practice, both divisions share the workload, passing parts of projects back and forth according to what needs

to be done. At any time, a studio may be working on one or more motion pictures, a game, a multimedia CD-ROM, and a music video. The digital effects business is diversified, always with a wide variety of projects in production.

The top half of figure 15.1 is a large area labeled Motion Picture High-end Visual Effects. It is split into two sections, 3D Animation and 2D Compositing.

The following list identifies the departments in the 3D Animation section:

- Modeling

- Animation

- Character Animation

- Color and Lighting

- Particle and Atmospheric Effects

- Character Animation

- Textures and 3D Paint

- Programming (which includes Renderman)

This next list identifies the departments in the 2D and Compositing section:

- Compositing

- Rotoscope

- 2D Paintbox and Stunt Wire Removal

- Flame Compositing and Image Stabilization

- Image Processing and 2D Morphing

These department titles may vary in different studios, but the division of work is generally the same everywhere. A number of the studios in Holly-wood also use the Silicon Graphics machines for games, commercials, television station logos, music videos, and motion capture. The separation of all these different functions into departments is necessary because it helps divvy up the massive workload and frees the individual animator from the tedium and stress of having to do every process on every shot by himself.

The lower half of figure 15.1 is labeled Games and Visual Effects. 3D Studio MAX can usually be found here. The "Games" label does not mean that MAX is only used in Hollywood for game production. Substantial work overlap occurs between divisions in the visual effects, game, and multimedia production studios. 3DS MAX is used for a wide variety of animation work, including animation and special effects for commercials, special effects and character animation for television productions, station breaks and logos, music videos, motion picture pre-visualization, games, and some visual effects for motion pictures.

MAX in the Working Environment

As figure 15.1 shows, the Games and Multimedia division is smaller than the Silicon Graphics-based Visual Effects division.

The Games division is not so obviously divided into separate departments. But, during a project, the same functional divisions in labor will appear, as animators are assigned in groups to perform different jobs. One group of animators, for example, might be asked to do modeling, another group the Character Studio animation, and another the particle systems. The following list indicates how MAX animators are grouped by function. This list looks almost the same as the previous list of Visual Effects department names.

The division of labor in 3D Studio MAX productions follows here:

- Modeling
- Animation
- 3D Morphing
- Character Animation with Bones Pro
- Color and Lighting
- Camera Tracking
- Particle and Atmospheric Effects
- Character Studio Animation
- Texture Mapping and 3D Paint
- Image Processing and LenzFX
- Video Post Compositing
- Pre-visualization and Video Animatics

This list makes it clear that 3D Studio MAX has the capability to do many of the 3D functions performed by the Silicon Graphics Visual Effects division. Most large studios that have purchased 3DS MAX have set up their MAX workstations in an area separate from the main visual effects production area because MAX is still primarily perceived as a strong game and character animation software package.

3D Studio MAX has not taken over a larger part of the visual effects work in the motion picture industry for two important reasons. The first reason is its lack of file compatibility with UNIX-based 3D Animation software. Almost all motion picture visual effects are rendered using Renderman Pro, which requires a new type of RIB file format that can only be written based on a Nurbs surface model. A NURBS (non-uniform rational B-spline) surface model is built from curved splines. The surface that is generated behaves like a quad patch in MAX, but it is not converted to polygons before it is exported for rendering, so it is resolution independent and very smooth. You cannot output this kind of a RIB file from a polygon-based software package, and MAX is a polygon-based package.

The second reason is that 3D Studio MAX cannot run on anything but an IBM PC. The current version of MAX is limited to the processor speed and databus throughput of the Pentium Pro microprocessor. The dual and quad multiple processor machines will render atmospheric scenes faster, but a straight geometry animation renders the same speed no matter how many processors are used. Geometry rendering is not multithreaded. The SGI rendering driver that allowed 3DS R4 .3DS files to render on multiprocessor SGI machines was released in 1995, but has never been updated to work for MAX files. In production, 3DS MAX files cannot be rendered on any of the big production render servers. IBM PC desktop workstations do not have the data throughput to deal directly with the massive frame sizes typical of visual effects work on digitized film footage. Here are the typical digitized image memory requirements: in the 70mm format, one individual 4 K film frame, which is over 4,000 pixels wide, requires 40 MB to store. A shot of 2,400 frames, which is just over 1 1/2 minutes long at 24 frames per second film speed, would require 96 GB! Even a single digitized frame of 35mm film is 2,048 pixels wide and requires 10 to 12 MB of RAM per frame to store. It is known as 2 K image. With images this size, the currently available Pentium Pro workstations are not powerful enough to render the thousands of images needed in the production of a typical effects film with 150 to 200 effects shots. Even a large rendering farm built from IBM Dual Pentium Pro workstations would not have the massive file handling capability and multi-megabyte data throughput necessary to keep up with the Silicon Graphics Render Servers in motion picture production today. At the larger studios it is not uncommon to have image storage capacities of 250 GB or more.

So how does an animation studio use 3DS MAX to do visual effects for motion pictures? Even though you cannot display a 2,048-pixel-wide image in the MAX viewport, you can render your output at that size. MAX can output finished images in the RLA, Targa, and TIF file formats, which can be read by high-end compositing programs, such as Flame, after translation by a file conversion program. It is not necessary to work directly on the film images themselves. Instead, animated effects sequences are done in MAX at film resolution, and then later composited into the film as animated elements. Figure 15.2 shows a number of the film and animated elements composited together to create one frame of a motion picture visual effects shot.

Figure 15.2

Film and digital image elements are combined to create one frame of a typical visual effects shot for a motion picture.

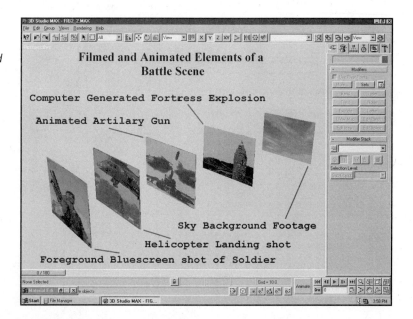

Any of the computer-generated image elements shown in Figure 15.2 could be created with MAX by translating MAX's output images to Unix-compatible 24-bit color TIF or TGA files, and then loading them, along with their alpha channel files, into Flame for compositing. MAX cannot do some of the fine subtle vapor effects that Alias can, but many films don't need vapor effects. The real trick is to correctly match the perspective of the original image with the inserted image, and then get the resolution, color, and lighting to match. After the images are color balanced and color matched, they can be composited seamlessly into the motion picture visual effects sequence, and will be undetectable from the images created by the SGI high-end software. As a result, MAX is being used increasingly for low- and medium-budget visual effects shots where economy, modeling, lighting, and animation capabilities are more important than the issues of brute strength rendering speed, subtle vapors, and file incompatibility with Renderman.

Finding Your Strengths

As you find yourself drawn to a particular area of interest in MAX, it is important to realize that after you are identified as having a special skill in a particular area, a studio is unlikely to move you to any other specialty. That particular skill may become what you do for your entire career as an animator. This is a common practice for people who are good at character animation, modeling, or compositing. Fitting yourself into a company usually means that you fit your skills to the needs of the team, and then everyone counts on you to continue doing that specific job.

But what do you do if you lose interest in modeling and are drawn toward compositing? Telling your supervisor that you no longer want to be a modeler and would like to switch jobs will very likely result in him telling you that the company thinks of you as a modeler only, and that the company cannot afford to retrain you. In simple terms, that means if you want to switch jobs, you must also switch studios.

If you are determined to make a change, you need to be able to present yourself as a compositor, not a model builder. To do this, you need a show reel that only contains examples of compositing you have done. The new company must see you as a compositing specialist, not a modeler. You can prepare a "compositing" show reel by using Video Post in MAX, and then look for a new job while continuing to build models for your present employer.

Importance of Specialization

The demand for specialists in the animation industry is very high, especially for people good at modeling, texture mapping, or lighting. A generalist animator who has learned a little about everything in MAX cannot compete on the same level as someone who has spent years on computers doing lighting only. The reality of the business is that specialists at every level fill the vast majority of the jobs.

Learning complicated animation procedures, such as the sequence of steps for setting up all the rotation limits on a skeleton, would be very useful if you wanted to specialize in character animation. Of course it is important to know all the tools in MAX, but after you are on the job, most of the work you are asked to do will be tailored to match your specialty. In this way, the company is best served, and your skills always remain in demand.

Concept to Delivery

The long journey from storyboard to finished visual effects can take anywhere from six weeks to more than a year. Even animated video game productions last for many months. No matter what kind of production you find yourself involved in, you still need to go through the same careful steps to turn a storyboard's line drawings into smooth, professional animations, filled with color, action, and excitement. In a production containing only computer animation, the storyboard depicts every important moment in the finished project. You can get a sense of the flow of the story, which helps you understand how everything fits together.

In motion picture visual effects or even in commercial work, however, rarely do the computer animators see the complete storyboards for the production. Instead, you are given a bundle of storyboard pages showing miscellaneous disconnected visual effects shots (which make little sense). You may never be given a script to read, so you may never know how those shots fit into the production until it is shown in the theater. You have to trust the art director's instructions and come as close to the storyboard images as you can.

At the initial production meeting, the producer and art director discuss the shots assigned to the individual animators. The animators hear about how the storyboards should be interpreted from the viewpoint of the client, and they ask questions to clarify what the final project should look like. The entire project is examined in detail and the final look of the project is agreed upon. At this point the storyboards become the guiding force behind the project. From then on, the animators refer to them as the final authority for how each shot should be done. But, even though they are the main reference that you go by, they are subject to constant revision, sometimes two or three times a day. A good assistant producer stays on top of all the changes and comes by your desk with new boards and the director's latest notes while you work.

Problems often arise, especially if the storyboards have been drawn incorrectly. Poor storyboards can be a constant source of damaging trouble to a project. Many times you will see wild distortions of perspective, impossible to re-create in the computer. The artists seem to have a subconscious need to cheat the laws of perspective to give their boards drama, and in their enthusiasm, they draw objects in impossible situations. This causes the client and the producer endless hours of discussion to try to work out a compromise between the dynamic appearance they see in the storyboards and what can be done in real life. Figure 15.3 shows a frame from an exciting storyboard, but one that violates the laws of perspective and scale to achieve an exciting image.

FIGURE 15.3

A storyboard with incorrect perspective, object scale, and in the angle at which the plane is approaching the ground, which in the real world would crash traveling at supersonic speeds.

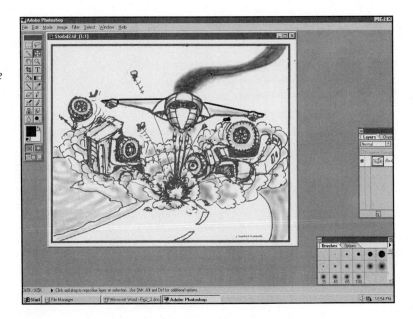

It is always important to point out any errors you see in the storyboards as early in the production as possible. This gives your producer time to get the boards corrected early, and protects the production from needless trouble as it nears completion.

Estimating Time of Completion

Time estimation in most industries is based on the tracking and measuring of repetitive tasks that are the same, year after year. In this way, most industries have compiled extensive lists of data about the costs of production and the length of time it takes to perform a specific task. If computer graphics were as simple and straightforward as traditional cel animation production, each action could be added up by a secretary who could prepare an accurate time estimate from years of previous data.

But you are working with 3D Studio MAX, which did not even exist as a production tool a short time ago. The process of animation can still be measured, but the tremendous increase in the number of variables associated with the computer animation production process makes it difficult to estimate the actual cost of production per frame.

Yet you will be asked to provide this information to your supervisor and producer at a moment's notice, even if you are doing something you have never done before. It makes business sense for them to want to know how long it will take, but it is very difficult to estimate something that has not been done before. In reality, this expectation is placed on every animator in the business, and they are often asked to meet a deadline set by making an educated guess.

The basic dilemma inherent in the business is that the people estimating the time and costs of a job are often not the ones doing the job. An interesting problem also occurs when producers used to working with Silicon Graphics machines come in to supervise a job in the PC/MAX department. They fail to ask what can and cannot be done in 3DS MAX and go ahead and start the job assuming that you can do anything an SGI machine can do. Even though MAX is tremendously powerful and versatile, it cannot do everything. They simply pass out the storyboards and start telling you when your part of the job has to be done. Because they do not understand MAX, it is important to tell them where the area of difficulty will be and then negotiate an adjusted deadline based on reality, not assumption. Remember, you are responsible for finishing the shot on their deadline, no matter how incorrect their time estimate might be.

Keeping a log book in a situation where the estimating of time and the capability of the system to do the job come into question helps you to cover your back. A log book is the best job insurance an animator can have. This proves especially true when problems with the machine or your work load prevent you from delivering your work by deadline. Toward the end of any project, the progress of the work undergoes constant re-examination, and the producer often calls so many meetings to ask for information on what you are doing, that you spend a great deal of time away from your machine, causing you to be later still.

Figure 15.4 shows a page from a dated sequential log book, with a list of every instruction change that you receive.

FIGURE 15.4

A page of an animator's log book showing dates when instructions were given and when they were changed, along with the time and date when all problems or delays occurred.

Animator's Log Book

Shot No.	Revision No.	Production:

Date of this page:	Date Due:
Approved by?:	

Storyboard Revision No.   Date.
Change Requested:

Notes:

By Who?:	Supervisor:	Director:

Problem:	Bad Machine:	Bad Art Work:	Bad Instructions:
Description:

Solution:

Fixed:?	Time Lost:
Witness:	Person Notified:

It is simple to make up a notebook of these pages and then add more if needed. This effort is not wasted if you are working on many different shots or animation sequences at the same time. It is not unusual to be told to change something, and then be told to change it back to the way you were doing it originally, and then to be given slightly different directions by the art director, and then to have to change it again when the storyboard artist gives you a new version of her updated boards. The log helps you keep it all straight, which comes in handy when someone tells you, "that's not what I told you to do." It is impossible to try to keep track of all details in your head, especially when you run into problems. Record the exact time when you discovered the problems, what the problems were, and how they were resolved. Finally, note how much time you lost. It may not seem important until the producer asks you why you are late finishing your work and tells you that you are responsible for holding up production.

Deadlines Written in Stone

Deadlines can be a positive force in an animation studio. They can get everyone pulling together and help get your work organized quickly. Where deadlines cease working is when technical or artistic difficulties arise that stop you. Often you need more information or a *buy off*, which means that your work is approved and your progress is accepted. On most jobs, that can only come from one or two people (such as the director or the art director). On a motion picture, the art director is on the set, and you rarely get to see or talk to him because he is too busy. Many times during a project, you find yourself sitting at your computer for days trying to work on other parts of a project, without being able to go forward because the director is shooting on location and has not approved what you have done so far.

In every production studio, the deadline is treated by management as the most important event in your life. When a project gets close to the completion deadline, and shots are not yet finished, the producer goes into panic mode, which usually means that you don't go home until you have finished your work for the day and have it rendering on the network. Some companies expect you to camp out for 24 hours a day, seven days a week if necessary, and they compensate you by bringing in catered food and crackers.

Producer's assistants and animation supervisors have a tough job because they are the people in the middle. They are expected by management to get the work out by the deadline, but they can do little more than watch you work. Gung-ho assistant producers often slow the animation process by calling numerous pep-talk meetings where all the animators have to explain why their work is not yet finished. Big studios have two or three meetings a day with different people involved in supervising different portions of the project, and then the animators find themselves staying late to make up the time lost sitting in the meetings.

When production is behind, there is no best way to reduce the tension. The best strategy is to encourage everybody to be open about mistakes and problems as soon as they happen. Many animators become virtual hermits in their cubicles, buried under a pair of headphones and surrounded by trinkets they brought from home. Hiding under headphones is a mistake. An open, communicative group is always more efficient.

Working with Producers

The producer can be your best friend because he or she is directly responsible for keeping the animation studio running and keeping you employed. You can benefit by knowing as much as possible about the kinds of problems that can arise between producers, clients, and the animators who do the work.

The producer's main functions include searching for animation jobs, preparing estimated budgets, bidding against other companies to get the jobs, dealing with clients, and staying on top of every production problem and process along the way until the job is finished. They are the ones who take the final product of your labors to the client to ask them to sign off on the project. Half the time, the client does not approve the work on its first submission. The producer must then return to the studio for *re-dos*, which could mean anything from redoing a simple animation scene, to doing the entire job over again. Producers cope with a great deal of stress, but at the same time they get tremendous satisfaction from seeing a job they brought in turn out well.

Dealing with Client's Source Materials

One of the most critical contributing factors to problems in a production is the quality—or more often the lack of quality—of the source image materials. This one factor has been a major cause of losses for computer graphics companies for years. The image providers don't understand what level of quality must be maintained in the source material to make it usable for compositing and computer animation. Figure 15.5 shows the different types of source images that an animator must be expected to work with, and lists some of the problems that occur.

The animation supervisor is responsible for ensuring that the source images are placed on the network so that the animators can start reviewing the source material. It is important to familiarize yourself with what must be done and to check all the source material as soon as possible for image instability and color flaws.

In many cases, you must start the job before all your materials are available. Sometimes the digital scanning of the source material is delayed. Or, if you are working on a film or a commercial, the scene you are supposed to work on may not even be filmed yet (hence, no source images). This prevents you from checking the footage for omissions or bad frames.

FIGURE 15.5

Chart showing the different kinds of source imagery with associated problems.

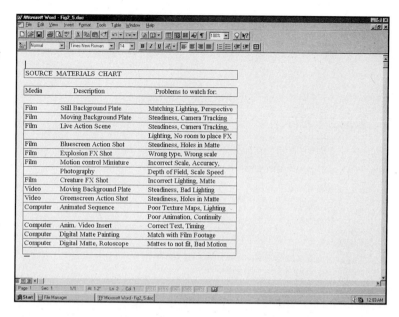

The following is the source materials chart shown in the figure:

Media	Description	Problems to watch for:
Film	Still Background Plate	Matching Lighting, Perspective
Film	Moving Background Plate	Steadiness, Camera Tracking
Film	Live Action Scene	Steadiness, Camera Tracking, Lighting, No room to place FX
Film	Bluescreen Action Shot	Steadiness, Holes in Matte
Film	Explosion FX Shot	Wrong type, Wrong scale
Film	Motion control Miniature Photography	Incorrect Scale, Accuracy, Depth of Field, Scale Speed
Film	Creature FX Shot	Incorrect Lighting, Matte
Video	Moving Background Plate	Steadiness, Bad Lighting
Video	Greenscreen Action Shot	Steadiness, Holes in Matte
Computer	Animated Sequence	Poor Texture Maps, Lighting, Poor Animation, Continuity
Computer	Anim. Video Insert	Correct Text, Timing
Computer	Digital Matte Painting	Match with Film Footage
Computer	Digital Matte, Rotoscope	Mattes to not fit, Bad Motion

As soon as the visual effects job is awarded to the Digital Animation Studio, all the source images on film negative are delivered to the Digital Film Scanning department. They begin scanning the film immediately, testing for color matching and performing the necessary corrections to the digital files they are generating. In practice, studios often reject part or all of the source footage, usually because the developing process has badly modified the color, the source image is scratched, a shaking or wobbling image appears, or there are missing frames in a shot.

Normally, a motion picture is photographed with special curved lenses in the 35mm Anamorphic Wide Screen Format, which is a horizontally squeezed image. It appears distorted when you look at the film negative. Many digital effects companies can work with squeezed images just as easily as unsqueezed. It is not unusual to be asked to work directly with Anamorphic squeezed footage when doing digital effects. This request is popular with low-budget filmmakers who need to save the extra cost of getting an unsqueezed *dupe* or negative copy made. After working with squeezed images for a few days, you get used to it.

Bluescreen footage must also be tested to determine whether there are any blue areas on the actor, caused by *blue spill*—blue light that reflects back on to the actor from the blue background. Wherever there is blue spill, the matte is incomplete, and there is a hole that must be repaired before the image is acceptable.

If you work on any project that has elements shot on video or film, whether for commercials or an action movie, you are likely to have some of the previously mentioned problems.

Visualizing the Flow of Work

A production schedule bar chart is used by most studios to track the progress of each shot or animation sequence. Using the chart as a reference, the producer lets everyone involved see the flow of work. This works as a useful visual yardstick by which to measure your own progress and to remind yourself of forgotten details and upcoming deadlines. It is easy to get so bogged down in a barrage of details that a deadline seems to sneak up. Figure 15.6 shows a sample production schedule bar chart for one animator doing camera tracking.

FIGURE 15.6

A typical production schedule bar chart.

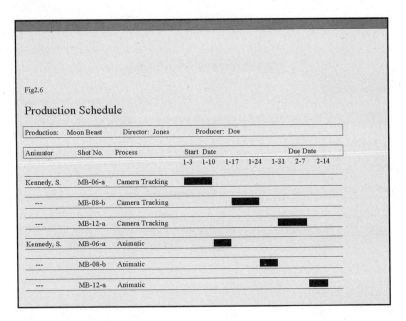

Fig2.6

Production Schedule

| Production: | Moon Beast | | Director: Jones | | Producer: Doe | | | |

Animator	Shot No.	Process	Start Date				Due Date		
			1-3	1-10	1-17	1-24	1-31	2-7	2-14
Kennedy, S.	MB-06-a	Camera Tracking	■■■						
---	MB-08-b	Camera Tracking		■■					
---	MB-12-a	Camera Tracking					■■		
Kennedy, S.	MB-06-a	Animatic		■					
---	MB-08-b	Animatic				■			
---	MB-12-a	Animatic							■

An updated, printed copy of the production schedule chart is handed out to each animator, usually every Monday morning as a reminder of how much time remains for the completion of each shot. Referring to this chart often makes it easy to plan your work.

Learning to See Through the Camera

Chapter 20 from *Inside 3D Studio MAX Volume I*, "Cameras and Setting the Shot," provides a conceptual overview of proper camera movement, but learning to see through the computer's camera is a skill that can best be perfected by shooting film or video. Physically moving around the room while peering through a camera viewfinder teaches you to see what the computer's camera should see and helps you understand lens angles. In this way, you soon accumulate and recall many different alternative kinds of camera moves. Sadly, exercise with a real camera does not free you from the awkwardness of having to use the computer's mouse interface to drag the Camera icon around, but it gives you some great camera move ideas.

Networking Windows NT and Unix

On a studio network where Silicon Graphics machines are running Unix, IBM PCs are running Windows NT, and Macintosh Power PCs are running System 7.5, the machines are invisible to each other. Special software must be installed that enables all machines to be recognized and files to be read and stored on the main network file server. This can be accomplished by using a Silicon Graphics workstation as the Network File Server, and installing the KA Share software package. After installation, it enables the SGI server to recognize IBM and Mac machines on the network if they are NFS mounted. Each machine then shows up on the SGI Server as just another accessible hard drive.

For a detailed explanation of how to set up and run a rendering network with Windows NT and 3D Studio MAX, refer to Chapter 29, "Network Rendering," in *Inside 3D Studio MAX Volume I*.

MAX in Production with Other Software

Very few studios run only one software package or computer platform. Most studios combine many different programs to come up with a set of tools that best satisfies the demands of the work they do. Even game companies and architectural firms employ other software in addition to 3D Studio MAX to get work finished. The motion picture visual effects industry uses a tremendous variety of different software in the course of a motion picture production. No single package can do it all.

File Translation Programs

File Translation programs fall into two categories: consumer and professional. These programs convert both model and image files from one format to another to make them readable by different software platforms.

Many studios use Kodak's digital scanning services to scan their film footage. The patented Kodak Cineon digital image format is 10-bit color. It can be stored on DLT digital tape, on a large Metrum, or on an Exabite tape. The files can then be uploaded and read by most compositing software on a Silicon Graphics workstation, or it can be uploaded to a Macintosh Power PC and read by software packages such as DeBabelizer or Missing Link. No software is currently available on Windows NT that reads the Kodak Cineon format in the full 10 bits of color depth. To be used in MAX, the files must be converted to 8 bits per color channel TGA or TIF files. Then they can be loaded into 3D Studio MAX for use as background images for modeling or animation.

MAX with Matador and Flame

Matador and Flame are industry-standard, compositing and matte creation software packages that run on the Silicon Graphics Irix (UNIX) platform. 3D Studio MAX can output 24-bit TIF and TGA image files that can be read by both programs after translation. Matador is the real workhorse of the visual effects industry.

Matador is the software in which most of the matting, rotoscope, paintbox wire removal, and a major portion of the compositing is performed. Other packages, such as Prism's ICE and Wavefront Composer are used, but they are not quite as versatile. Flame is the high end of the compositing programs made for image stabilization and equipped with an extensive set of color and automated interactive compositing tools. Most of the final visual effects shots in a motion picture are finished in Flame. In Flame, images created by Alias, Wavefront, SoftImage, and Lightwave can be mixed together seamlessly with images generated by 3DS MAX.

MAX and SoftImage

The main competition for MAX in character animation is SoftImage running in Windows NT with its spline-based modeler, excellent inverse kinematics, and built-in motion capture data interface. It also has very advanced particle system capability and raytracing. SoftImage can read standard 3D Studio files, but at present it cannot read 3D Studio MAX files. It can be found in both large studio game divisions and in smaller, independent computer animation studios. SoftImage can output MAX-readable DXF files.

MAX and Alias

Alias is well-known as one of the best spline-based NURBS surface modeling programs available. It can also generate and work with polygonal models. This enables you to import models into Alias created in MAX as DXF files. This works well on models that are not too complex. If you try to import a model with a high number of faces, however, the resulting file in Alias can be very large, slowing redraw speed. Polygonal models cannot be converted to spline models, but MAX can read properly translated DXF output files from Alias.

MAX and Wavefront

An .OBJ file export plug-in now exists for MAX, which outputs a .MAX file and a polygonal .OBJ file with no spline or NURBS surface information. It can be read and animated in Wavefront Kinemation, but it cannot be output from Wavefront to Renderman Pro because it is not a NURBS surface model. Some game companies have written in-house conversion programs to change MAX triangular polygonal models to Wavefront-style quad polygonal models so that MAX models can be used in standard game authoring software that require quad polygons.

Working with a Service Bureau

Most studios must send all film scanning or film printing work out to a service bureau. Only the largest studios have their own digital film scanners and printers. The scanner stores digital output from a super high-resolution nitrogen-cooled LCD photo array, which converts light projected through the film into digital information. After the scanning is complete, the digital images are transferred to the studio on digital tape and then stored on the main network server's hard drive where all the animators have access to them.

Digital data to film image conversion, called *film printing*, is also available. A film printer is a combination of a motion picture camera and an enclosed high-resolution CRT (cathode ray tube) screen, which the camera photographs. One digital frame can be displayed on the unit's CRT screen at a time as a full-color image, or as three separate color separation images. The camera automatically photographs the CRT screen and then steps forward to the next frame.

Other services available at service bureaus include digital-to-video output, video editing, audio editing, and video tape duplication.

In Practice: Using 3D Studio MAX in Production

- **Model Building and Character Animation.** 3D Studio MAX workstations are proving to be very capable, powerful, and extremely cost-effective per investment dollar when compared with Alias/Wavefront UNIX-based workstations.

- **Game Production.** At the present time in the computer animation industry, the game and multimedia departments are where most of the 3D Studio MAX animators can be found.

- **Visual Effects.** Producers and directors in the motion picture and television production studios are beginning to recognize that real savings can be obtained by using 3D Studio MAX for music videos, television commercials, and motion picture visual effects.

- **Animation.** MAX is fully capable of creating high-end, professional quality animation for any media.

Part VI

ANIMATION TECHNIQUES

IMAGE CREATED BY SANFORD KENNEDY

Chapter 16

by Sanford Kennedy

ADVANCED TRANSFORMATION ANIMATION

Since doing your first MAX tutorial, you have been building and animating objects by using move, rotate, and scale transforms. In almost all animation projects, you will find constant uses for transform animation. In this chapter, you work with transformations to solve advanced animation problems in a real-world project. Transformation techniques are applicable to all forms of animation, including games, multimedia, television commercials, and animation for motion pictures.

This chapter demonstrates the following advanced transformation methods:

- Transform animation with Out-of-Range Type Curves

- Using Helper objects to link complex objects for transform animation

- Using grouped objects and linked dummies to create complex animations

- Using XForm and Linked XForm modifiers to animate selected portions of objects at the sub-object vertex level

- Performing pick transformations along surfaces by using Grid objects

- Transform instances

Using Combinations of Basic Tools

Advanced transform animation is actually a collection of strategies for combining a wide variety of animation tools and tricks, which enables you to use basic tools in complex ways. Transform animations are the most commonly used techniques in 3D Studio MAX's set of animation tools. With them, you can open the power of MAX's modifiers and controllers and create nested layers of motion. The challenge is to figure out new ways to do sophisticated types of motions with the existing set of tools. Every animator's goal is to bring objects and characters to life and to create the kind of entertaining professional animations driving the current success of the animation industry.

In this chapter, you use advanced transform animation techniques to animate a television commercial about one of mankind's most familiar and constant companions: the cockroach.

Before you begin a real-world project such as this television commercial, you need to study the action needed for the characters. In most cases, you will be given a storyboard that illustrates the important actions in the animation. If you are handling the art direction yourself, however, you start with a script and then generate your own storyboards. In this chapter, the script for the R.E.A. Exterminators animation project is reprinted to give you an idea of the sequence of events and what the characters should be doing. The following tutorials are based on the script in which a sophisticated voice-over narrator speaks the dialogue in the pompous manner of an English lord. All the action you will animate is timed to synchronize to the words as the narrator speaks them.

The R.E.A. Exterminators Script

Opening Scene: *An interior shot of a small table on which is a plate with a slice of cheese. The camera begins with a close-up of Rocky the Roach sitting on the plate quietly eating the corner of the cheese. A "sophisticated" British voice begins speaking:*

Voice-over Narration:

Narrator:

Since the Garden of Eden, mankind has tried to rid himself of the cockroach. In the beginning, there were primitive implements such as:

Cut to: *Wide shot of the kitchen table.*

Narrator:

A rock...

A huge rock falls on the table, hitting the edge of the plate and sending Rocky and the cheese flying into the air and onto the floor.

Cut to: *Close-up dolly shot that follows the action closely for the rest of the commercial as Rocky falls to the floor, flips over, and runs across the floor trying to escape a series of weapons. Each one narrowly misses him.*

Voice-over continues along with the action as Rocky runs:

Narrator:

A club...

A club swings in from the side causing Rocky to veer to one side.

Darts...

Three feathered darts sock into the floor around him and he jinks left.

Narrator:

When mankind became civilized, he turned to more advanced weapons, such as:

Traps...

A box "roach hotel" looms up ahead and Rocky leaps through it and out the other side without being caught.

Spray...

A spray can of poison appears over his head, and the stream of poison just misses him as he runs by.

Shoe…

A big shoe stomps down on him, and it looks like he is crushed, but miraculously he runs, unhurt, out from under the instep.

Magic charms…

A crude cloth cockroach voodoo doll looms up in his path stuck with long pins and he runs between its legs.

Demons…

An irregular ball of dirt suddenly unfolds into a spiny demon with two big angry eyes. Rocky veers around it.

And brooms…

A broom slaps the floor right behind him as Rocky reaches the wall and dives into a hole in the baseboard before the broom can smash him.

End Dolly Shot in Close-Up: Hole in the baseboard. The camera stops moving and zooms into the hole in the baseboard. Rocky's head peeks out for a moment and then ducks back out of sight.

Narrator (still serious):

Wouldn't it be easier to call R.E.A. Exterminators? Pick up the phone now and call: ROACH EATERS ANONYMOUS, the exterminators with an appetite.

Fade to Black

In this script, an undertone of ironic humor must be translated to the screen through your animation. In all comedic animations, the timing, the pace, and the follow-through of the action are very important. First, however, you must prepare your cockroach model and set the scene.

Transform Animation with Out-of-Range Type Curves

To establish a foundation of related techniques used in advanced transform animation, you will begin with a simple example of a series of boxes linked together with dummies similar in shape to an insect's leg. The boxes are arranged to resemble the leg segments with Dummy helper objects placed at every joint. After the leg is constructed and animated, you will learn to create a looping animation that simulates the walking motion of an insect's leg by setting the Parameter Curve Out-of-Range Type to Ping Pong in Track View. Figure 16.1 shows the simple chain of boxes that will simulate the motion of a cockroach's leg.

NOTE

For a detailed explanation of Parameter Curve Out-of-Range Types, review Chapter 23 of *Inside 3D Studio MAX, Volume I,* "Animation Control Tools."

FIGURE 16.1

View of the box leg with the Helpers rollout menu open.

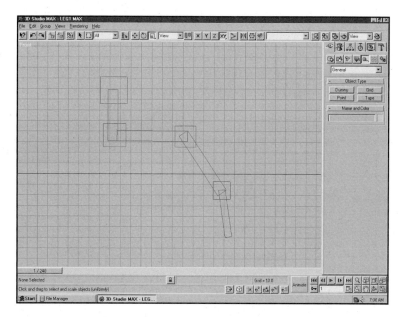

To set up the box leg for animation, you will use the leg1.max file from the book's accompanying CD. The boxes have already been created. You will create and place the dummies and link the leg together.

PLACING THE DUMMIES AND LINKING THE LEG TOGETHER

1. Load leg1.max from the accompanying CD.

2. In the Create command panel, click on the Helpers icon to display the Helper object types. In the Object Type rollout, click on Dummy.

3. Create four dummies in the Front view, starting at the upper-left end of the upper-left box (refer to fig.16.1).

4. Click on the Select and Link icon and then click and drag a link from the lower-right box, Box04, to the lower-right dummy, Dummy04.

5. Click and drag a link from Dummy04 to the next higher box, Box03. Move up the leg and link Box03 to Dummy03, then link Dummy 03 to Box 02, and so on. Repeat this process, linking all the boxes and their dummies together in a hierarchy to the parent Dummy01.

6. Save the scene as **cleg01.max**.

You have now established a parent-child hierarchical relationship between the leg segments. The nature of hierarchies dictates that the parent will pass on its transformations to the child. The child adds its transformation to the parent's and passes the total on to the next child in the chain. To simulate the motion of an insect's leg, each box in the chain will be rotated slightly farther than the box higher up in the hierarchical chain. The last box, called the Leaf, will rotate the farthest. In the next exercise, you apply a rotation transform to each dummy to create the motion of the leg. The boxes will be moved as passive objects controlled by the transformations of the linked dummies.

APPLYING A ROTATION TRANSFORM

1. Click on the Time Configuration icon and in the dialog, set the Animation Frame Range to 30.

2. Close the dialog and click on the Go To End icon to move the Time Slider to frame 30.

3. Click on the Animate button to turn on Animation mode.

4. Click on the Select and Rotate icon. To apply the first rotate transform, click on Dummy01 and drag upward so that the entire leg rotates clockwise 15 degrees.

5. Click on Dummy02 and rotate it counterclockwise 20 degrees.

6. Click on Dummy03 and rotate it clockwise 30 degrees.

7. Click on Dummy04 and rotate it clockwise 40 degrees, and then turn off Animate.

8. Play the animation. The leg pulls in and moves like an insect's leg.

9. Save the scene as **cleg02.max**.

This animation does not cycle correctly. If played in a loop, it would jerk each time it made the transition from frame 30 back to frame 0 as the animation repeats. To create a smooth repeating cycle of motion, you can change the Out-of-Range Type Curve to Ping Pong to make the leg move in and out smoothly.

CHANGING THE OUT OF RANGE CURVE

1. Click on the Min/Max Toggle icon and then click on the Track View icon.

2. In the Track View window, click on the Filter icon. In the menu, click on Animated Tracks and then click on OK.

3. All the Dummy animation tracks will be displayed with their range bars. Now change the length of the animation by opening the Time Configuration dialog and changing the animation length to 240.

4. In the lower toolbar of the Track View, click on the Zoom Horizontal Extents icon. This enables you to see the new length of the animation.

5. In the Hierarchy window of the Track View, click on the name of the Rotation track for Dummy01. It will be surrounded by a blue box.

6. In the upper Track View toolbar, click on the Parameter Curve Out-of-Range Types icon. A Param Curve dialog opens (see fig.16.2).

7. In the Param Curve dialog, click on Ping Pong. This causes MAX to smoothly cycle the motion of the leg over the length of the animation.

8. Repeat step steps 5–8 to change to a Ping Pong curve for each of the four Rotation tracks.

9. Minimize the Track View and play the animation. The leg will move in and out smoothly four times.

10. Save the scene as **cleg03.max**.

FIGURE 16.2

View of the Track View showing the Parameter Curve Out-of-Range Types menu.

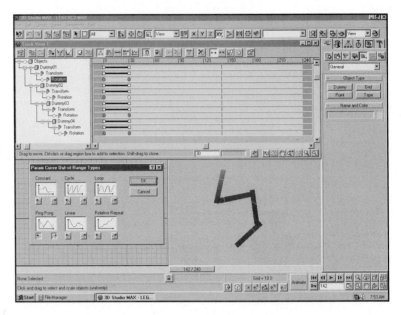

To examine a finished version of this animation load legcyc2.max from the Ch16 directory on the accompanying CD. The looping animation you have just created is identical to the way you will set up and animate the run cycle motion of the legs of the cockroach. This is one of many ways to apply advanced transforms to complex models for character animation without the need for Inverse Kinematics.

Of course, you can use IK because the hierarchy is already set up. You can try to animate the leg with IK by clicking on the Inverse Kinematics On-Off toggle, turning on Select and Move, and then dragging Dummy04 around. But without going through the process of applying axis constraints, the leg will twist on every axis and be totally uncontrollable in the IK interactive mode. IK is not needed for transform animation, therefore no further discussion of it appears in this chapter.

Using Helper Objects to Link Complex Objects

In the first tutorial of this section, you prepare the main character, Rocky the Roach, for animation by setting up the linkages in his head and legs. You use Rotate transformations to animate Rocky's frantic run through the gauntlet of weapons that rain down on him during the commercial. You use helper objects to aid in the animation of his head movements in the opening eating scene and his leg movements for his running scenes.

Helper objects in 3DS MAX are extremely flexible and useful in transformation animations. By using dummy and grid objects, simple transformations can be made to produce complicated multiple motions.

NOTE

For a general discussion of Grid and dummy helper objects, see Chapter 6, "Selections, Transforms, and Precision," of *Inside 3D Studio MAX Volume I.*

You will begin the tutorial by using a grid object to quickly place Dummy objects in the correct location for linking together the different parts of the insect's head. In animating any model, you can find axes that are not in the correct location or orientation. Moving the pivot point with the Place Pivot command can be effective for your current transformations, but does not permanently fix the problem. The use of Dummy objects will permanently solve these problems by enabling you to build the parts in any orientation you want. Then you place a dummy where you want the object's pivot located, and link the object to the dummy. This enables you to place the axis exactly where you want it.

The use of a Grid Object as a temporary construction plane speeds up the process of adding dummies to a complex model. Normally, you would create a dummy in a front or side view. It will look correct, but in fact it is only correct in two of the three axes because the dummy's origin is always on the active construction plane for the viewport in which it was created. In a 3D model, the joints are seldom located on the same flat construction plane. That means that if the dummy is placed correctly in the front view, the X and Y axes, you must then go to the side or top view to select and move the dummy in the Z axis. If the model has a dense overlapping mesh structure, or has many overlapping dummies, you may have difficulty selecting and placing it correctly. It is important to give a logical name to each of the dummies as you create them. That way, when you want to translate a particular dummy, you can quickly select it in the Select By Name dialog.

You will create and position six dummies in the cockroach's head to act as pivots for the feelers, palps (mouth appendages), and the jaws (see the following exercise). After the dummies are placed on the head, you link the parts to the dummies and then the dummies to the head. Then you link the head to the forward body shell. To prepare the model correctly, you need to place dummies at all the joints and link all the leg parts to the abdomen. The reason for using so many dummies is twofold. The first reason is to correct any of the X, Y, and Z axes orientations that are incorrectly located or flipped in the wrong direction on one side of the model. Many times the axes are rotated at the wrong angle for correct leg movement. The second reason to use dummies is that each joint should have its own specific name so that they can be easily located and selected for translation. Figure 16.3 shows the Grid Object creation rollout in the Helpers menu. Figure 16.4 shows how to position the grid object.

FIGURE 16.3
The Grid Object rollout menu in the Create/ Helper Object panel.

FIGURE 16.4
View of the model cockroach's head showing a Grid object temporary construction plane bisecting the head of the cockroach with dummies in place to link to feelers, palps (mouth appendages), and jaws.

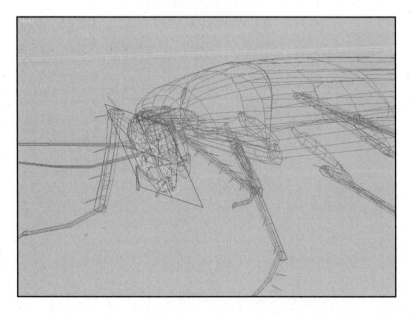

NOTE

All of the following exercise files can be found in the CHAP16 directory on the accompanying CD. You will also need the roach.mat material library file, and the bitmaps found on the CD-ROM in the Chap16\Maps directory. You can temporarily add the CD-ROM to MAX's Bitmap file path so MAX can find all the bitmaps for the materials. For example, if your CD-ROM is drive E:, the entry in the Configure Paths/Bitmaps dialog would look like this: E:\CHAP16\Maps. The room.tif background image for the rendering screen background is also in the Maps directory. If you need to review how to set up the bitmap in background for rendering, review Chapters 26 and 27 in *Inside 3D Studio MAX Volume I*, or your 3D Studio MAX manual.

CREATING A GRID OBJECT AND PLACING DUMMY HELPER OBJECTS

1. Load croach01.max from the accompanying CD. The scene includes a cockroach, a kitchen table, and a plate with a piece of cheese sitting in the middle of it.

2. In the toolbar, click on the Select By Name icon, and in the Select Object menu that opens up, select the Head, Antennae, Palps, and Jaws, and then click on Select. When the menu closes, click on the Zoom Extents All Selected button.

3. It is important to freeze all the parts except the Head, Antennas, Palps, and Jaws to prevent incorrect linkages from being made. Click on Display, and then click on the Freeze by Selection bar to open the rollout. Click on Freeze Unselected.

4. To create a Grid helper object, click on the Create tab and then click on the Helpers icon. In the Object Type rollout menu, select Grid.

5. In the Left viewport, click and drag a rectangle around the Head object to create a grid object (refer to fig.16.4 for the approximate size).

6. In the Front viewport, zoom out until you can see the new grid and the head of the cockroach. The grid is currently located on the Home construction plane, but the roach's head is some distance away.

7. Select and move the grid in the Front viewport in the X axis until it is centered in the head, and then rotate it until it passes through the base of the feelers and the palps as shown in figure 16.4.

8. With the Grid selected you will Activate the Grid object by clicking Views in the menu bar, and from the pull-down menu, click on Grids. From the pop-out menu select Activate Grid Object.

9. Again in the Helpers, Object Type rollout menu, click on Dummy. In the Left viewport, click and drag to create a small dummy at the base of the feeler on the right.

10. In the Name and Color window in the Command panel, rename the dummy **DummyLFeel** for Dummy Left Feeler. This enables you to identify exactly which dummy is linked to which feeler. Repeat the process to create identical dummies for the feelers, palps, and jaws as shown in figure 16.4. Be certain to give them all names that identify them, such as **DummyRJaw**.

11. Now you link all the parts to their respective dummies. Click on the Select and Link icon and select the first feeler. Click and drag from the feeler to DummyLFeel to link the feeler to its dummy. Then click on that same dummy, and drag a link from the dummy to the head.

12. Repeat the process with the right feeler and its DummyRFeel, and then do the left and right jaw, and the left and right palp.

13. To link the head to the cockroach shell and place the pivot under the shell behind the head, you create another dummy. But first you must unfreeze the body of the roach. Click on the Display tab, and in the Freeze by Selection rollout, click on Unfreeze by Name. Select RoachBody and click on Unfreeze.

14. Before creating the neck dummy, turn off the Grid Object by clicking on Views, and then in the drop-down menu, click on grid, then on Activate Home Grid.

15. To create the dummy for the neck as shown in figure 16.5, click on the Create/Helpers icon, and then click on Dummy. Click and drag in the front view to create a neck dummy at the back of the roach's head.

16. Click on the Name and Color window in the Command panel, and then change the name of the dummy to **DummyNeck**. Lock the selection and use Select and Move to position the dummy near the top of the head, under the front lip of the forward body shell.

17. Activate the top viewport, click Zoom Extents and drag the dummy downward until it is centered on the centerline of the roach's head. Click on the spacebar to unlock the selection.

18. In the right, link the roach's head to the DummyNeck object and link the DummyNeck to the RoachBody object.

19. When finished, make certain that all the parts of the head (including the DummyNeck) are unfrozen. Then select all the parts of the roach's head. Click on Group in the menu bar, and then click on Group in the pull-down menu. In the Group dialog, type the name **RHead** and then click on OK.

20. Be certain to save your scene file as **rocky01.max** to make sure that you don't lose your work.

FIGURE 16.5

This is view of the DummyNeck object that links the head to the roach's shell and acts as the new pivot point for the head.

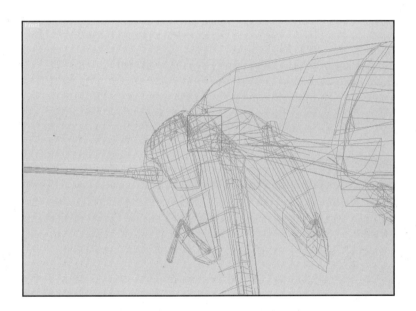

Using Grouped Objects to Create Complex Animations

The technique of animating objects within groups of objects that are themselves part of larger groups of objects is a very powerful technique. It is similar in concept to nesting one software program within another. This is a way to link together many different animated objects in different parts of a scene without actually creating hierarchies. This technique is used in combinations with various animation tools throughout the rest of this chapter. The animated objects within a group can have any number of different modifiers, controllers, and other animations applied to them; the group itself can be treated as a single object and linked to a parent dummy. Then that parent dummy is linked to a larger animated system of grouped objects, to be animated in additional ways.

Here is where the complexity of overlapping objects can move beyond the capability to the mouse to be an effective selection and animation tool. You will switch to using direct data entry through the Transform Type-in to animate many of the more complex portions of this project. The next exercise explains the sequence of steps required to open a group, in this case the cockroach's RHead group, to animate the objects within the group by using the Transform Type-in dialog, and then to close the group.

Using the Transform Type-In

The model is now ready for animation. Figure 16.6 shows the opening shot as described in the script. It is a close-up of the cockroach poised in the correct position to take a bite from the corner of a piece of cheese. Rather than use the mouse to try to select the dummies linked to the feeler and jaws, and then move these small parts with the clumsy mouse, you will use type-in commands. The Select by Name dialog will be used to choose the object to move, and then the Transform Type-in will be used to animate the rotations of the head, feeler, and mouth parts. This method enables you to work on very densely packed models in complex scenes without fear of transforming the wrong object or going too far with your mouse.

As you work in Animation mode, the Transform Type-in dialog stays open as you move the Time Slider along with the mouse. This enables you to type entries into the Absolute and Relative numeric entry fields to set animation keys while you are selecting objects and moving through the animation. In this way, you can create very accurate transform animations without ever using the mouse.

In the next tutorial, you animate the head and antenna moving over the cheese to make it appear that the roach has bitten into the cheese. The action in this part of the animation is subdued, and requires subtle movements, in direct contrast to the frantic motion of the rest of the animation after the rock hits the table. This shot will be called **Scene 1**. The animation has been divided into four scenes that coincide with each major change in camera position.

FIGURE 16.6

Close-up view of the cockroach with all the Dummy objects in place, sitting on the plate just behind the piece of cheese.

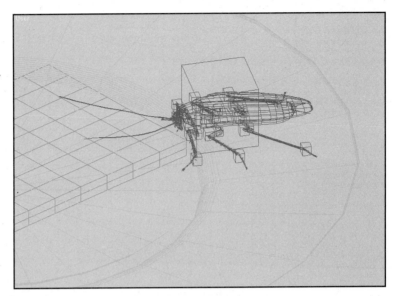

ANIMATE THE HEAD AND ANTENNA OVER THE CHEESE

1. Load croach02.max from the accompanying CD, which includes Camera01 in the correct position. Make certain that the Frame Range is set to 900 frames.

2. Click the Select by Name icon, and in the object list, click on the cockroach's head group, called Rhead, and click Select.

3. To animate the left antenna, you must first open the cockroach's head group. To open the RHead group, click on Group. In the pull-down menu, click on Group, and then click on Open. Now all the objects inside the head group will be accessible, and will be listed in the Select by Name menu.

4. To use Zoom Extents All Selected to bring the cockroach's face into a close-up view, click Select by Name and from the object list click on head. Click select, then click the Zoom Extents All Selected icon.

5. Animate Rocky's left feeler by rotating its parent dummy. Use the Select by Name dialog to select DummyLFeel, and lock the selection.

6. Right-click in the front viewport to activate it, then turn on the Animate button, and move the Time Slider to frame 20.

7. In the Edit menu, click on Transform Type-in.

8. The Rotate Transform Type-in dialog opens. To move the antenna, place the cursor over the Offset Screen Z axis spinner. Drag the spinner up and down to watch the antenna rotate up and down.

9. Rotate the feeler down until it touches the top of the cheese.

10. Use the Select by Name dialog and select DummyRFeel for the right feeler, and then repeat steps 8 and 9.

11. To animate the feelers, click the Animate button and move the Time Slider to frame 40. Using the previous rotation techniques, rotate the feeler dummies so that both feelers move upward to their original frame 0 angles.

12. Click the Time Configuration icon and turn off Real-time playback, then Click on Play to watch the animation of the feelers going down and up.

13. Now animate the head rotating toward the camera. With the Animate button on, move the Time Slider to frame 35. Select DummyNeck in the Select by Name dialog and lock the selection.

14. With the Front viewport active, click on the Offset Screen Y axis spinner in the Rotate Transform Type-in dialog. Drag the spinner up until the head rotates to face the camera at frame 35.

15. Move the Time Slider to frame 50 and rotate the Y spinner in the opposite direction so that the head returns halfway to its original position at frame 50.

16. Turn off Animate, and preview the animation.

Because the head is positioned with its jaws almost in contact with the corner of the cheese, this is all the motion necessary to suggest that Rocky is taking a bite of cheese. You may want to animate the palps wiggling, and the jaws actually taking a bite of the cheese on your own.

17. The first scene ends with a cut. Save your file as **rocky02.max**.

NOTE

From this point on, you will no longer be given detailed instructions about how to perform any operation that has already been described in previous exercises. An example of this is the use of the Group command. In the rest of this chapter, the instructions will say "group the object" without describing the steps needed to group something. Also Hide and Freeze will no longer be detailed step by step. You should already be very familiar with how to use these commands.

Animating Rocky's Legs for the Run Cycle

In this exercise, you use linked rotation transforms to animate the leg movement for Rocky the Roach's run through the gauntlet of the exterminator's weapons. This will be a simple 30-frame exercise to demonstrate the alternate "reach forward and reach back" insect leg movements necessary to make Rocky run. All of the leg dummies move from the start position at frame 0 to the end position at frame 5. This enables the keys of the animation to "hook up" perfectly for a smooth run cycle using the Out-of-Range Type function curve. Figure 16.7 shows the "starting" position for the legs, and figure 16.8 shows the "ending" position.

When finished, Rocky's short run cycle can be turned into repeat cycles and multiplied in length by applying Out-of-Range Cycle types to each rotation transform track of the leg dummies. Rocky runs continuously.

To move on with the exploration of other methods of advanced transform animation, the Out-of-Range animation technique explanation will not be repeated in this exercise. If you do not recall how to apply it, please return to the first two exercises in this chapter to review.

Only a simple walk or run cycle is needed to get convincing insect run animation for this commercial because much of the viewer's attention is drawn away from Rocky by the rain of weapons attacking him in the final animation.

FIGURE 16.7

The legs of the cockroach are shown rotated into their starting positions at frame 0, the starting frame of the run cycle animation.

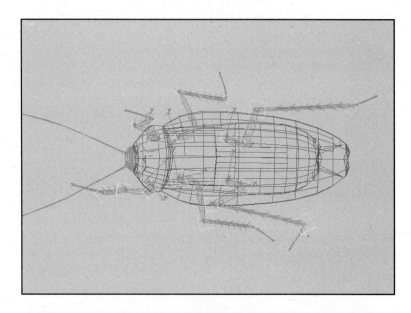

FIGURE 16.8

The opposite or "ending" leg position for the cockroach at frame 5, the opposite of figure 16.7.

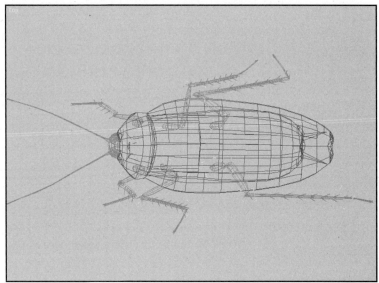

ANIMATING A SIMPLE RUN CYCLE

1. Load croach03.max from the accompanying CD so that you can use the finished cockroach model with linked dummies at each leg joint.

2. In the Top viewport click on Select Object, and then hold down the Ctrl key and select the cockroach's wing, abdomen, and prothorax (front shell).

3. Freeze the objects by clicking on the Display tab and then clicking Freeze Selected.

4. Expand the Top viewport by clicking on the Min/Max Toggle. The legs are at the neutral middle position. To animate the run cycle they need to be rotated into the more extreme starting position as shown in figure 16.7 at frame 0.

5. The leg dummies are easily seen, and can be selected with the mouse in the Top viewport if you are careful. Zoom in on the right front leg. The innermost dummy is named LegRF01, meaning: Leg, Right Front, joint01. Each leg has four Dummies 01 to 04 numbered from the innermost Parent, to the outermost child 04.

6. Click Select and Rotate, restricted to Z. Carefully click one corner of Dummy LegRF01, and drag the mouse downward to rotate the entire leg 15 degrees CCW, or counterclockwise.

7. Go to the next farther out dummy, LegRF02. Repeat step 6, except you will rotate this dummy 20 degrees CCW. Continue working, repeating this same procedure until all the legs match the starting position as shown in figure 16.7.

TIP

It is often hard to select a Dummy object overlapped by another object, such as a leg segment. MAX enables you to click once or twice more to shift MAX's Selection tool back along the Z axis to the dummy. You can then lock the selection and rotate it safely.

8. After the legs are at their starting positions at frame 0, move the Time Slider to frame 5.

9. The next operation at frame 5 is almost the exact opposite of what you just did at frame 0, as shown in figure 16.8. Now click on the Animate button to turn on Animation mode.

10. At frame 5 reverse all the leg positions and create the second half of the run cycle.

11. That completes the setup for the run cycle. Now go to the Track View, click the Filter icon and select Animated tracks only. Then apply the Out-of-Range Type curve to each of the leg dummy rotation keys at frame 5. For every key, select Ping-Pong type in the Out-of-Range dialog box.

I use a Dry Erase Marker pen to trace guide lines over the legs to record their starting angles. I draw these lines right on my computer screen. They rub off easily with a cloth or fingers.

The basic trick I use in creating an insect's walk with transform animation is to think of the legs as two sets of counter-rotating tripods. The insect shifts its weight from one tripod to the other as it walks. Try to keep the legs tucked in close to the sides of the cockroach's body as they move to ensure greater realism.

12. Play the animation in the Top viewport to test the motion. The animation should have no visible jump or hesitation.

13. When you have successfully created the 30-frame run cycle, save the scene file to your MAX directory as **rocky03.max**.

The next step would normally be to apply this animation to the entire project. Because, however, there are areas where you don't want Rocky to run in the final animation, you do not actually animate the run cycle until all the other animation operations are complete. Then you save two copies of the final file— one where Rocky doesn't run and the other where you apply the run cycle animation. By selecting different cameras, you assemble the final animation by rendering cameras 1 and 2 from the non-run cycle file and cameras 3 and 4 from the run cycle file. See the New Riders web site (www.newriders.com) for more detailed instructions on assembling the final animation.

It is important to first establish the movement path of Rocky's body through the gauntlet of weapons before applying the run cycle to its legs. For this reason you will see Rocky sliding along without moving his legs during the following exercises.

Use Nested Groups of Objects to Create Complex Animations

The *nested groups* term used here is borrowed from programming language, meaning objects contained within objects. Even though these nested groups are not linked together in a parent/child hierarchy, they do pass on motion from the master group to the sub-group. The transform animation of nested groups require you to open the master group, called FlipObjects, and then apply rotate transform animations to the objects within the group. This can get complicated in big projects, but it is a very powerful and straightforward technique for creating complex motion.

Transforming Groups by Using Offset Dummies

On many occasions, you will want to create animated objects that are part of a larger group of objects. In this animation, you animate an object group that rotates around an offset dummy used as a pivot point. In Scene 2 of the R.E.A. Exterminators commercial, which is called "Flip," the objects on the tabletop stay together as they are flipped into the air.

The script calls for a large rock to drop onto the table from above frame, just after the narrator says the words, "A rock...." The script calls for a cut to a medium camera shot showing the tabletop and some of the space above it. Rather than trying to animate Camera01 to move up to this new location, it is more practical to create a second camera, Camera02, for Scene 2. Figure 16.9 shows the four cameras in place for the four different camera angles. Camera04 is linked to the cockroach and follows it during Scene 4, the big running scene.

FIGURE 16.9

View of four cameras in their starting positions for the four scenes requiring different camera angles.

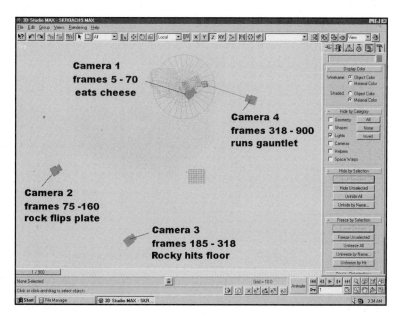

NOTE

To animate this commercial, you will use four cameras in all. You will not completely finish the commercial in this chapter because Video Post procedures will be covered elsewhere. Instead, you will render .AVI movies to see the results of your exercises. If you want to finish the project as it was originally designed, render and output each of the four scenes as individual targa or jpeg frames. Then, in Video Post, create .IFL files for the images, set up the render Queue to assemble them together, and re-render the project as an AVI movie.

In Scene 2, the plate, cheese, and roach should remain visible within the Camera viewport during the arc of their flight. Figure 16.10 is a portion of the storyboard that illustrates the camera angle and the action for the Flip sequence. Figure 16.11 shows the 3DS MAX models built to match the storyboard drawing.

FIGURE 16.10
A storyboard panel showing the main elements of the Flip scene.

FIGURE 16.11
A view of the 3DS MAX models in a position matching the storyboard drawing.

In the following exercise, a number of dummies have been created to provide different offset rotational pivot points for the grouped objects in the plate Flip scene. Because of the difficulty of explaining in words where each object and dummy should be placed and how their links should be set up, the entire scene has been set up to demonstrate how you could create this scene. This is only one way to accomplish the effect of flipping the plate up into the air. You can easily modify this scene to change the way each object moves.

ANIMATING THE PLATE FLIP

1. Load croach04.max from the accompanying CD, which includes the animated falling rock and Camera02 in the correct position for the Flip scene.

2. Zoom into a close-up of the plate in the top viewport. You will notice a number of dummy objects. The scene is constructed as a combination of groups of objects that are linked to dummies. The cockroach is a group of objects called Roach, linked to its own dummy called RoachRoll.

3. To see how the different dummies are linked, and what they are designed to do, you will select and rotate each one, starting with the RoachRoll dummy located in front of the Roach's head. Use Region Zoom in the top viewport to zoom into a close-up of the cockroach and its associated dummies. Click the Min/Max toggle to enlarge the viewport.

NOTE

You will be testing the way each dummy affects its linked object, but remember to hit the Undo button each time after you move something. All the animation keys are already set, and if you disturb the relationships of the various objects at this point, you may end up seeing the roach pass through the plate during the animation. If you mess up the scene, re-load croach04.max and continue with the exercise.

4. Click on Select by Name and, from the object list, select RoachRoll. Click and drag the selected dummy. Notice that the entire roach moves around the dummy's Z axis in a circle with the dummy as the central pivot point. Be sure to click Undo immediately after rotating the dummy.

5. Try switching the axis from Z to X or Y, then rotate the RoachRoll dummy again. Click Undo.

6. To see how the rotation of this dummy was set up for the animation, move the time slider to frame 108 where the movement of the RoachRoll dummy begins. To see what is moving, zoom the viewport out until you can see the entire plate.

7. Click the Next Frame button and step through the animation to frame 113. Notice how in only five frames the plate, the cheese, and the cockroach are all beginning to move in different directions.

8. The RoachRoll dummy has begun to rotate on its X axis to flip the roach upside down.

9. Click the Min/Max Toggle to restore four views. Continue stepping forward until you reach frame 128. The Roach is a child of the RoachRoll dummy which is, in turn, linked to the Plate. That means that the roach will maintain its position relative to the plate's motion no matter where the plate goes, unless you choose to move it.

10. In the front viewport you can see that the rock has already hit the table and that the plate, the roach, and the cheese are now up in the air above the table (see fig.16.12). This elevation is controlled by the large dummy below the table, DummyFlip.

11. DummyFlip provides the main offset center of rotation that will lift all the grouped objects off the table and send them up into the air and eventually over and down to impact the floor. Click and rotate the DummyFlip dummy in the front viewport to see how it moves the plate, cheese, and roach in a long arc. Click Undo to restore the correct relationships.

12. Try running the animation back and forth and rotating all the different dummies to see how they affect the movement of the objects. They include PlateRoll, and of course, CheeseRoll. Remember to click Undo each time. Also remember that in an animation of this type, the effect is ruined if any of the objects can be seen passing through each other.

13. To experiment with increasing the rate and violence of the movements, you can modify the existing animation keys. Click the Animation button to enter Animation mode, then use the Select by Name dialog to select an object. Try modifying the rotation of the CheeseRoll dummy.

14. Lock the selection. You can use the Key Mode toggle to quickly move between the selected object's keys by clicking the Next Frame and Previous Frame buttons. Use the Select and Rotate tool to change the position and rotation of the dummy at its keyframe. Then turn off the animation mode and render a preview to see how your changes affect the animation.

15. When you are satisfied, save the file as **rocky04.max**. Activate the Camera02 viewport and Render an AVI movie of the sequence from frame 80 to frame 160, to see your own version of the Flip sequence.

FIGURE 16.12
View of the table, the cockroach, the plate, and the cheese, after the rock has hit the plate and flipped it into the air.

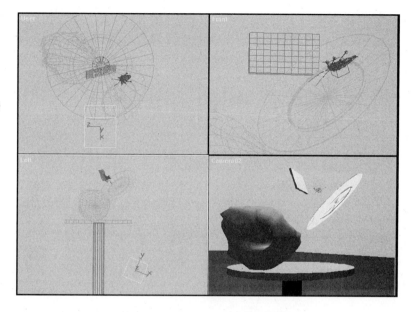

Using XForm and Linked XForm Modifiers

One of the most advanced features of 3D Studio MAX is its capability to animate individual vertices, or sets of vertices, by using the XForm and the Linked XForm modifiers. After the vertices are selected on the sub-object level by an Edit Mesh modifier or a Volume Select modifier, the transform tools can be applied to the vertices. After you have animated the vertices, you can still animate the original object with transform tools. You could rotate a selected set of vertices in an object in one direction, for example, and add a Rotate transform to turn the whole object in another direction. The animated sub-object transform modifies the surface shape in reference to its own axis, ignoring the axis of the object. By experimentation, a number of exotic animated forms can quickly be made from primitive shapes. Doing detailed animated surface modification, however, takes careful planning.

Distorting Objects with XForm

Simulating Squash and Stretch animation can be done by using Volume Select to select the entire object, and then applying XForm. The object's local axis is then scaled by scaling the XForm modifier gizmo in two of the axes.

In the R.E.A. Exterminators animation, the Club object is transformed with an XForm modifier to create a Squash deformation as it hits the floor right behind Rocky the Roach.

In this exercise, you will only apply a Volume Select modifier to the end of the club and then use an XForm modifier to squash only the immediate area of the club that contacts the floor, leaving the rest of the club unchanged (see fig.16.13).

FIGURE 16.13

The end of the club with a Volume Select gizmo scaled down to select the portion that contacts the floor.

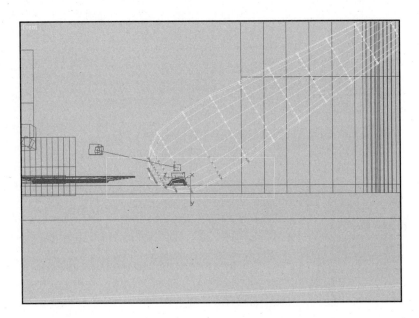

THE "ROCKY ROACH CLUB" INITIATION

1. Load croach06.max from the accompanying CD, select Club in the Select by Name dialog and click on Zoom Extents All Selected. The camera viewport should show the scene through Camera04, which is linked to Rocky and follows right behind him during the rest of the animation.

2. The movement of the club is already animated so that it rotates downward and strikes the floor at frame 334, just after Rocky the Roach runs by. Move the Time Slider to frame 334, where the club hits the floor.

3. Click on Modify/More. From the Additional Modifiers menu, select the Volume Select modifier, and then click on Vertex under Selection Level in the Parameters rollout menu.

4. Click on Sub-object and then scale and rotate the yellow Volume Select gizmo so that it only surrounds the lower half of the tip of the club where it contacts the floor at frame 334. Rotate the gizmo so that it is parallel to the floor as shown in figure 16.13.

5. Next add a XForm modifier to the stack. Click More, and from the Additional Modifiers list, select XForm. An XForm gizmo will replace the Volume Select gizmo. The XForm modifier is animatable.

6. You will now animate the scale of the XForm modifier gizmo. Click Lock Selection. The business end of the Club should expand out horizontally in the X and Z axis just as it hits the floor, giving the appearance that the club is made of semi-hard rubber.

7. Move the Time Slider to frame 325. Turn on Animation mode. You will set a "null" key at this point to prevent the XForm distortion from being passed back to earlier frames. Click and drag upward a small amount on the XForm gizmo at the end of the club. Without releasing the mouse, drag it back downward so that the end of the club looks unchanged. This sets a key that holds the vertices in their original size.

8. Move to frame 331, and repeat the creation of another null key at this point to control the scale of the club. Then move to frame 335 where you will now scale up the end of the club to create a Squash and stretch by scaling up the XForm gizmo. In the left viewport, click on the red selected vertices at the end of the club and drag the mouse upward to scale them up 20 to 30 percent. The selected region of the Club will spread horizontally.

9. Turn off Animation mode. Scroll the time slider to observe the effect of the animaiton. Click the Sub-object button to turn off the XForm modifier, then click the Create icon to close the Modifier panel. This deselects the vertices.

10. Render a preview and save your scene as **rocky06.max**.

In the R.E.A. Exterminators animation, XForm and Linked XForm modifiers are applied to many of the weapons to make them react to the heavy impact as they hit the floor next to the cockroach. The Demon Sphere model uses an XForm modifier to create pseudo-morphing shapes, where selected vertices are animated extruding out of a smooth surface to form threatening points as the roach comes within striking distance.

Use XForm to Animate Portions of Objects

The XForm modifier works in conjunction with other modifiers to animate vertices and modify surfaces. It cannot select vertices by itself, but must inherit the selection set from other modifiers in the stack. It works by generating a gizmo around a selected set of vertices when you open the XForm modifier. In practice, you would select vertices with Edit Mesh, Edit Spline, or Volume Select.

In the next exercise, you animate the shape change of a Demon. It is actually a modified torus that expands and extrudes spiny appendages with two big angry eyes, and then attempts to impale Rocky the Roach by rolling over him. Rocky is barely able to slip by. Figure 16.14 shows the spines created by applying the XForm modifier to the sphere at the vertex level. The eyes are separate objects linked to the sphere and then animated to scale-up by using an animated Uniform Scale transform.

FIGURE 16.14

View of the Demon torus after it has been morphed with the XForm modifier to form the spines.

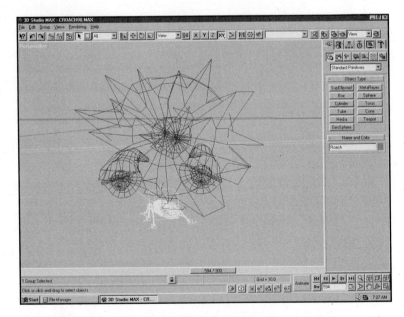

ANIMATING THE SHAPE CHANGE OF A DEMON

1. Load croach07.max and move the Time Slider to frame 600 where Rocky approaches a lumpy ball that will turn into a spiked rolling Demon.

2. Select Demon from the Select by Name object list and click on Zoom Extents All Selected.

3. Click on the Min/Max toggle to expand the Front viewport, and then Click on Modify. From the rollout, select Edit Mesh.

4. Click on Sub-object on the vertex level. You will select small groups of vertices from all over the surface of the Demon torus.

5. Click on Select Object, hold down the Ctrl key, and select every third individual vertex. Spread them out across the underside of the torus. These points will become spines. When you have a number of them, lock the selection.

6. Add XForm to the stack by clicking on the More button in the Modifiers rollout and selecting it from the additional modifiers menu. When it opens, the XForm modifier will create an animatable gizmo around the selected vertices.

7. Make certain that the Sub-object button is yellow. You can now manipulate the gizmo with any of the transform tools.

8. To animate the growth of the selected points into long spines, move the Time Slider back to frame 560. Click the animation button to turn on Animation mode, then click on Select and Uniform Scale. You will set a "null" Scale key, which prevents the vertices from scaling up before frame 560. Click and drag a tiny amount in the Front viewport, then release the mouse—this establishes the null starting key for the scale animation.

9. Move to frame 600 then click and drag upward to scale up the selected points, turning them into long spines. Turn off Animate.

10. Render a preview from frame 560 to 600 in the Camera viewport. You can continue to animate different modifications to the shape of the Demon torus by adding additional XForm modifiers to the stack, which act on different selected vertices.

11. After the Demon grows spines, it should roll forward rapidly, attacking Rocky as he passes. Save your scene as **rocky07.max**.

N OTE

The XForm gizmo's center acts as the gizmo's pivot point. When you're manipulating the gizmo, you don't have access to the object's pivot point.

Use Linked XForm to Modify a Lofted Object

When working with a Lofted object, you can animate its shape by inserting a Linked XForm modifier in the stack just above an Edit Mesh or Edit Spline modifier. The Linked XForm enables you to animate the selected vertices to create changes in the shape of the model. This is a very useful technique for bringing organic models to life by making them move and breathe. The Linked XForm controller can effectively animate small or even large parts of a one-piece mesh model, reducing your dependence on plug-in skeletal deformation programs such as Bones Pro or morph targets.

In the following exercise, you animate a change in the shape of the voodoo doll. To animate the doll, you will animate the movement of a Dummy object, which is linked to the vertices of the doll's loft path and which will deform and bend the model forward to lunge downward. The selected and linked vertices of the loft path appear as red crosses (see fig.16.15).

FIGURE 16.15

This shows the impaled Voodoo Doll Roach with the selected vertices, which are linked to a dummy by the Link XForm modifier, shown here as red tick marks on the loft path.

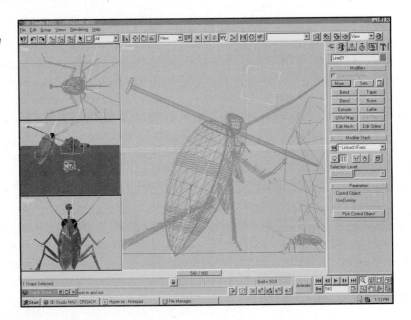

CHANGING THE SHAPE OF THE VOODOO DOLL

1. Load the croach08.max file from the accompanying CD, and then select the Voodoo Doll in the Select by Name dialog.

2. Click on Zoom Extents All Selected, and then move the Time Slider to frame 540, which will place Rocky the Roach near the voodoo doll.

3. Click on Create, Helpers, and then Dummy. Click on the Top viewport to make a dummy a short distance to the right of the Voodoo doll's head. Switch to the Left viewport, zoom out, and move the dummy down to place just above the Doll's head. Rename the dummy **VooDummy**.

4. Select Line01, the doll's loft path spline, from the Select by Name dialog.

5. Click on Modify. The Modifiers rollout will open, showing Edit Spline Modifier in the modifier Stack window.

6. Click on the Sub-object button and then on Select Object, and in the Front viewport, drag a selection box around the top half of the white spline that runs up through the center of the doll's body. The top two vertices will turn red to show they are selected. These are the vertices that you will control with a Linked XForm modifier to distort the doll's body.

7. In the Modifiers rollout, click on the More button. From the Additional Modifiers menu, select Linked XForm.

8. Linked XForm will pick up the selected vertices and open its rollout menu. Click on the Pick Control Object button, then in the Top viewport where it is easy to see, click on VooDummy to link the selected vertices to the VooDummy Helper object. The dummy will now be listed as the control object.

9. You will now be able to use Rotate and Move transform to animate the position of the VooDummy and the spline's vertices. This will now automatically pass its parameter changes back down the stack to the lofter to modify the body mesh.

10. Before you animate the VooDoo doll, you must link the pin, head, and legs of the doll to the VooDummy so they will move as the body mesh deforms. These parts are all grouped in the VooDooPin object. Select the pin through the doll's head, and all the parts will turn white. Click on the Select and Link icon and drag a link from the pin to the VooDummy.

11. To test the dummy to see if it works correctly, click on Select and Move and drag the dummy up and down a short distance. Then click Undo. The Pin and the legs will move with the expanding and contracting body mesh. With the VooDummy still selected, lock the Selection.

12. To animate the VooDoo doll, turn on the Animate button and move the Time Slider to frame 535.

13. Set "null" transform keys at frame 535 by right-clicking on the Time Slider and in the Create Keys dialog, click on OK—this establishes a key to hold the VooDummy where it is.

14. Move the Time Slider to frame 545 and click on Select and Move. Click on VooDummy and move it a short distance forward and down, closer to Rocky the Roach. This causes the doll's head and shoulders to jut forward at an awkward angle. Next, you will rotate the dummy to correct the body angle.

15. Now click Select and Rotate, and drag the mouse downward to rotate the VooDummy object so that the doll's body twists downward, making the pin almost plunge into Rocky's back as he runs by.

16. Render a preview of the animation from frame 525 to 560 to see the action. This section of the animation is all rendered from the Camera04 viewport.

17. Save the scene file as **rocky08.max**.

NOTE

You cannot select and modify vertex and lattice control handles and vertex region curves with an XForm modifier because they are not part of the object's geometry.

Perform Pick Transformations Along Surfaces

This transform animation technique takes advantage of the capability of the Pick Reference coordinate to enable you to transform an object along one axis of another object. Helper objects are especially useful for this purpose because they are easily created and they do not render. Moving objects along a Grid or a helper object that has been aligned to a surface gives you the capability to easily create an effect such as a morphing drop of rain running down an inclined window. The local axis of a tape measure helper object can also be picked as a path of motion for any object.

Using Tape Measure Objects as a Motion Axis

In the R.E.A. Exterminators animation, three Tape Measure objects are used as axes of motion or path for the darts thrown at Rocky the Roach.

In this exercise, you use a Tape Measure helper object as a pick transform Path object to aim and animate the flight of a dart hitting the floor right next to Rocky's legs (see fig.16.16).

FIGURE 16.16

View of the dart in position aligned to the axis of the tape measure with the Pick command.

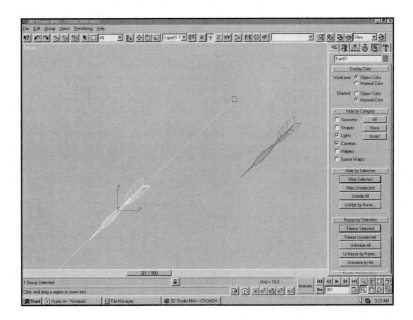

ANIMATING THE DART'S FLIGHT

1. Load the croach09.max scene file and click on Zoom Extents All.

2. Move the Time Slider to frame 380. Click on Select by Name and select the Roach group from the list. Click on Zoom Extents All icon so that you can see where the dart hits the floor next to Rocky as he runs for his life.

3. In the left viewport, zoom out to see the Dart01 object and the yellow tape measure line. You can see that a Tape Measure object is in place and is being used as the axis of travel for the dart.

4. Create two more tape Helper objects for darts 2 and 3. Move the time slider to frame 400. Notice that there is a dummy indicating where the dart will hit the floor as Rocky runs by. You will now make a tape axis to guide Dart02. Zoom out in the Left viewport until you can see both the dummy and Dart02 positioned above it.

5. Click on Create, then on the Helpers icon. From the rollout menu, select Tape. Create a tape by clicking on the tip of the dart and dragging the mouse downward to the dummy beside the cockroach. Lock the selection.

6. Right-click to switch to the Top viewport. Zoom out until you can see the darts, the roach, and the new tape, which is still selected. Click Select by Name and select Tape02 and Tape02target from the list. Select and lock the selection.

7. Click on Select and Move, and drag the tape over until it is directly below Dart02. Switch to the Front viewport and click on Zoom Extents Selected. You will see the tape extending straight down. Zoom out until you can see Dart02 and the dummy beside Rocky the Roach.

8. Click the spacebar to turn off Lock Selection. Click in an empty area of the viewport to deselect the tape and then click and drag the bottom end of Tape02 over to the dummy sitting beside Rocky the Roach. The tape will now be on a 45-degree angle, in alignment with the axis of Dart02.

9. You are now ready to align the dart's local axis with the tape to create a travel path for the dart.

10. Click on Select Object and select Dart02. Open the Reference Coordinate System pull-down menu in the menu bar and click on Pick.

11. Now click on the top end (not the target) of the yellow tape measure to pick it as the local Pick Transform axis for the dart. Tape02 should be displayed in the Reference Coordinate window.

12. The dart can now be animated along the tape by clicking Select and Move, Restrict to Z axis. It will track smoothly along the local axis of the tape measure Helper object.

13. Select Dart02, and lock the Selection. Move the Time Slider to frame 380. The dart should impact the floor at frame 400. Click on the Animate button and drag Dart02 a very short distance down the tape to establish a starting key at 380. Move the time slider to frame 400.

14. Click and drag the dart down along the Z axis until its point is stuck in the floor at the dummy. Rocky should be right next to the dart. The point

should just miss Rocky's head. The third dart should hit the floor at frame 420. Animate it on your own.

15. Turn off Animation mode and render a preview. That's it.

16. Save the scene as **rocky09.max**.

The final animation can be viewed from the New Riders web site at www.newriders.com. The roach.txt file explains how the animation was completed.

Using Grid Objects as Transform Paths

To move an object along a surface (as you may occasionally want to do), the simplest way is to first create a grid helper object. Then you use the Align tool to place the grid object coincident to the surface you want to move along (see fig.16.17). Select your object. After the grid is in place, you can use the Pick Reference Coordinate command to pick the grid as the surface on which you want your object to move. In practice, you would constrain the axis of movement to the axis on which you want to move.

FIGURE 16.17

View of a polyhedron showing a grid aligned to one face of the polyhedron, and a small sphere set to move along the object's surface.

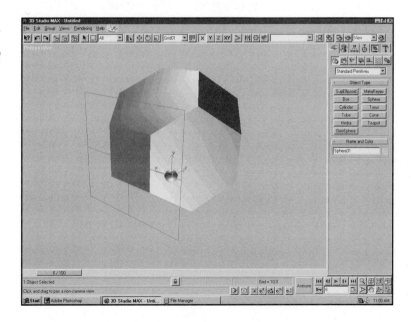

Animating Multiple Object Instances

The Shift key used with any transform will enable you to create multiple instance clones that can be animated with transforms. The convenient feature of this technique is that you only need to animate the first object. All the others will copy the motion exactly. In addition, the instances can be moved, and their keys can be adjusted in the Track View to make them appear to be unique. And if you decide you want one of them to be unique and animatable on its own, you need only click on the Make Unique button in the Track View.

In the R.E.A. Exterminators animation, the second and third darts are instances of this type. Only the first dart is animated. The animation track ranges for the second and third dart have been slid down to create a time lag between the first, second, and third dart.

Instance animation is useful for re-creating natural phenomena such as flocks of birds, schools of fish, and blades of grass. But it can also be used to create a "herd" of cockroaches to simulate an infestation (see fig.16.18).

FIGURE 16.18

An infestation of instanced cockroaches animated with transform animation.

Transforming Lights

Creating good lighting is a difficult problem for many animators. It is an easy task to use a spot and two omni lights to light a scene, but it is very difficult to equal the real light in a room, a building, or in nature. Many animations contain boring, flat lighting that does not change at all and takes no advantage of MAX's capability to animate lights with transforms. In real life, light changes as you move through an environment. Lights are modified either by being blocked by objects such as walls or trees, or by changing angles of reflection from surfaces of objects that vary as you move past them.

No matter how good an animator you are, your scenes will look lackluster if you do not devote considerable time to lighting. There is no room in this chapter to expand on the definition of what makes good lighting. This topic of lighting is brought up only to remind you to explore some of the special kinds of transformation techniques that can move tiny accent lights along and over surfaces to give them a touch of realism that can never be attained with static key and fill lights. Use your ingenuity and experiment. It is the small details that can turn a good animation into a great one. For more information, read Chapter 28, "Animating Lights and Atmospheres."

Finishing the R.E.A. Exterminators Animation

This chapter does not take you through the entire animation of this project step by step. If you want to continue working on it, however, you can work with croach09.max and try setting up all the different weapon gags. Remember, four cameras are used and the project should be rendered as four separate parts and then assembled. The roach.txt file on the New Riders web site contains instructions for finishing all the weapons animations, the frame number at which the weapon should impact the floor, notes about setting up your camera frame ranges, and the Video Post Queue setup for finishing this animation. Have fun with it!

In Practice: Advanced Transformation Animation

- **Linked transforms.** When you don't want to take the time to set up Inverse Kinematics to create complex motion, linked transforms can do the job simply and quickly.

- **Out-of-Range Type Curves.** Out-of-Range animation will enable you to extend a short animation into a repetitive cycle loop and save having to enter additional keys.

- **Helper objects.** Helper objects are valuable for linking complex objects, for acting as temporary transform movement axes, and for creating offset pivot points.

- **Grouped objects.** Using Nested Grouped objects enables you to treat a group of animated objects as if it were a single part of a larger object, enabling you to create very complex layered animations.

- **XForm and Linked XForm.** Use the power of XForm and Linked XForm modifiers to animate selected portions of your models at the vertex level.

IMAGE CREATED BY DAN O'LEARY

Models courtesy of Viewpoint DataLabs International, Inc.

Chapter 17

by Randy Kreitzman
and Dan O'Leary
with Ted Neuman

ANIMATING WITH CONTROLLERS

3D Studio MAX provides users with an amazing set of tools for animating their scenes. Central to this task are controllers—*a group of plug-ins that handle the creation and manipulation of all animation data in 3D Studio MAX.*

Controllers handle the user data for any and all animated tracks, storing keyframe information and procedural animation settings. Any time you create a keyframe or adjust a function curve in Track View, data is sent to the animation controller assigned to that track. Controllers also generate all interpolated animation, calculating the value of animated parameters for each frame based on keyframe data.

All animation tracks, including object transformations, creation parameters, and modifier parameters, are assigned a default controller. For most tracks, this assignment is made when the track is first animated. Transform controllers are assigned when the track is first created.

This chapter explores the following topics:

- Path controller

- Euler Rotation controller

- Look-At controller

- List and Noise controller

- Expression controllers

Project: WWII Air Combat

To illustrate the proper use of and applications for animation controllers in 3D Studio MAX, you will use a sample project. Your goal is to animate a WWII air combat scene in which an American B-17 bomber is attacked by a German FW-190 fighter (see fig.17.1). You will build on this one example throughout the chapter to emphasize the power and flexibility provided by animation controllers. This example will give you a feel for how an animator might approach this kind of assignment.

Before you begin, open bomber.avi on the accompanying CD-ROM to watch the final animation.

Throughout this project, you will be using two 3D models provided by Viewpoint DataLabs. Both the B-17 bomber and FW-190 fighter pictured in figure 17.2 are from their outstanding catalog and are included on the accompanying CD.

FIGURE 17.1
WWII air combat.

FIGURE 17.2
3D models by Viewpoint DataLabs International, Inc.

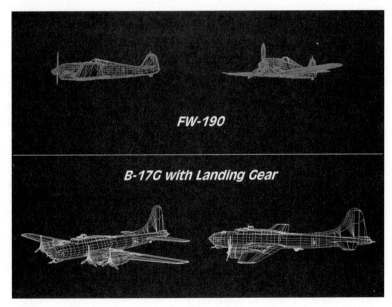

Animating with Path Controllers

The project begins with a static shot of the B-17 with some background clouds. You will keep the camera and bomber stationary, and use other tricks to give the impression of forward motion and relative velocities. This approach helps to keep the action focused on and around the Bomber.

You will make extensive use of Path controllers to animate this scene. The *Path controller* is a compound controller created as an alternative position controller. It receives the output of a subordinate Percent controller that specifies the path position, expressed as a percentage of total path length. This data is combined with the path data itself to determine the X, Y, Z position in time of an object following the specified spline.

First you will make the clouds fly past the bomber by applying a Path controller. Then, you will assign a Path controller to the attacking fighter. Finally, you will add more realism to your animation by adjusting the relative velocity of the plane.

Background Cloud Motion

The clouds in this scene have been created as Combustion objects. Combustion is a MAX atmospheric effect for creating realistic fire, smoke, and explosion effects. Without the animated clouds, this scene would feel extremely static and unconvincing. They create the illusion of forward motion and add a great deal of depth to the scene.

BACKGROUND CLOUD MOTION

1. Load bomber.max from the accompanying CD. Select Combustion01 and open the Motion panel.

2. Under Assign Controller, expand the Transform controller hierarchy and highlight Position.

3. Click on Assign Controller, choose Path, and click on OK.

4. Under Path Parameters, click on Pick Path and select Cloud Path 01 in the viewport.

The Combustion object jumps to the start of the path. If you scroll through the animation, you will see the combustion travel from the beginning to the end of the path.

NOTE

When a Path controller is first assigned, two keys are automatically created at the first and last frame of the active time segment. By default, the value of the first key is 0, the second key has a value of 100.

Now for the second set of clouds, follow these steps.

5. Select Combustion02 and open the Motion panel.

6. Under Assign Controller, expand the Transform controller hierarchy and highlight Position.

7. Click on Assign Controller, choose Path, and click on OK.

8. Under Path Parameters, click on Pick Path and select Cloud Path 02 in the viewport.

Combustion 02 has a slightly longer path and therefore a greater distance to travel in the same amount of time as Combustion 01. The difference in speed between the two cloud objects should give a better sense of depth to the scene. Figure 17.3 illustrates the correct Path controller assignment.

FIGURE 17.3

Animating clouds with the Path controller.

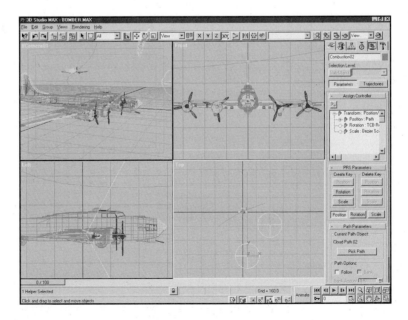

Fighter Attack

Here again, you use the Path controller to animate the attack of the German fighter. The Path controller is truly one of the most useful new controllers included with MAX. Working with keys is often frustrating when it is easy to visualize exactly the path you want an object to follow. In those cases, working directly with the path splines is a very natural way of molding the animation.

FIGHTER ATTACK

In this exercise, you assign a Path controller to the attacking fighter.

1. Open the Select by Name dialog and choose the Fighter Body object. Open the Motion panel.

2. Under Assign Controller, expand the Transform controller hierarchy and highlight Position.

3. Click on Assign Controller, choose Path, and click on OK.

4. Under Path Parameters, click on Pick Path and select Fighter Path in the Top viewport.

5. Switch to the Camera view and slide the playback bar slowly toward frame 100. Compare your results to figure 17.4.

FIGURE 17.4
Creating the fighter flight path.

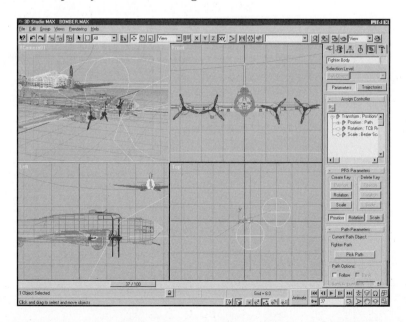

The fighter flies into frame along the path, but something is not quite right. For one thing, the fighter is not banking with the turn and, more importantly, it is flying away from the camera—not a very dramatic effect at all. This is because the Fighter Path spline vertices were mistakenly created in reverse order. You can easily remedy this problem by reversing the key values of the Percent track.

6. Open Track View and expand the Object hierarchy.

7. Select Fighter Body. Right-click and select Expand Tracks from the pop-up list.

8. Find the animated Percent track and right-click on the first key. Change the default value of 0.0 to 100.0.

9. Click on the Next Key button to jump to the key at frame 100. Change the value of this key to 0.0.

TIP

An alternative fix for this problem is to reverse the direction of the spline itself. Apply an Edit Spline modifier to the path, select the last vertex in the spline, and click on Make First. This method does not work for closed spline shapes.

With that minor crisis behind you, look into improving the look and feel of the Fighter's attack run by adding some banking.

10. Select Fighter Body and open the Motion panel.

11. Under Path Parameters, click on Follow and Bank for Path Options.

12. Slide the playback bar slowly from frame 0 to 100.

Now the fighter is moving toward the camera, but it is flying backward! To fix this, you must change its default orientation before adding follow and bank.

13. Uncheck Follow and Bank for the Fighter Body object. Choose the Select and Rotate tool and make the Top viewport active. Verify that the View coordinate system is selected.

14. In the Top viewport, rotate the Fighter Body 180 degrees about the Z axis. It now faces the opposite direction.

15. Again, check the Follow and Bank options for the path controller. The fighter should snap in line with the path, facing the direction of travel as seen in figure 17.5. Verify the results by playing the animation in the Camera viewport.

FIGURE 17.5

Correcting the fighter orientation.

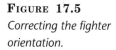

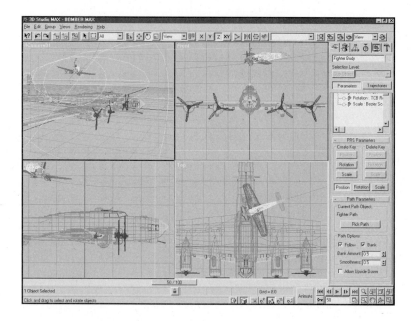

That is better, but the banking of the fighter is very subtle. Go to a good reference frame (about frame 60) and adjust the Bank Amount. A value of 3 gives a very dramatic feel to the attack run. You may want to raise the smoothness to around 1, which will take out some of the jerkiness in the angle correction.

Relative Velocities

Because you are dealing with a locked-down camera and you are simulating objects flying by, you must take into account that the attacking fighter should drift back some during its flight.

Because the path controls the fighter, animating that path sliding backward should do the trick. The fighter will inherit the motion of the path and slide across the screen.

RELATIVE VELOCITIES

1. Switch to your Top view and select the Fighter Path.

2. Go to frame 0 and activate the Animate button.

3. Move the path forward so that it is just in front of the bomber (about −40 units).

4. Go to frame 100 and move the path back until it is at the tail of the Bomber (about 70 units).

5. Turn off the Animate button.

6. Switch to the Camera view and slide the playback bar to view the animation. Compare to figure 17.6.

FIGURE 17.6

Bandits at 8 o'clock!

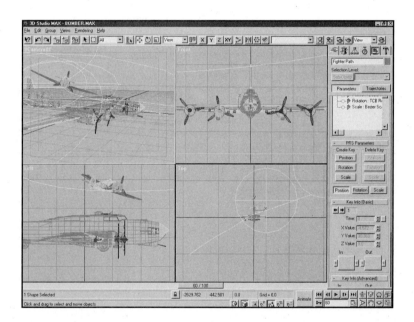

The fighter drifts back as it attacks and scrapes past the camera. Already you have the core of an exciting animation. Next you will add some wobble to the bomber to give it a more realistic feel.

Animating with Euler XYZ Rotation Controllers

There are a couple of ways to rotate the bomber. One of the easiest and most adjustable methods makes use of another powerful 3D Studio MAX animation controller: the Euler XYZ Rotation controller.

The Euler XYZ controller is provided as an alternative to the standard TCB Rotation controller. Anyone familiar with the DOS version of 3D Studio is quite aware of the problems and limitations presented by the TCB controller because it was the only option for controlling rotations in that package. The Euler XYZ controller is superior to the TCB controller in several ways, most notably in that it enables the user to view and adjust rotation values in the Function Curves mode of Track View.

This controller works by decomposing the orientation of an object into discrete X, Y, and Z rotations. A unique track is created subordinate to the Euler XYZ controller for each of these components. This approach provides the user with very precise rotational control, enabling him or her to individually animate the rotation about each of the object's local axes. With a TCB controller, you cannot adjust the interpolation values about one axis without affecting the others.

Unfortunately, the Euler XYZ controller comes with its own set of problems. Key among these is a phenomena known as *gimbal lock*. In any system of Euler angles, orientations exist for which two Euler angles are undefined. When a mechanism is rotated into such a singularity, it locks up—rigid to any rotation about the two undefined axes.

Bomber Wobble

With the Euler XYZ Rotation controller, animating wobble in the bomber is as simple as assigning the controller to the body and creating an appropriate curve for the X rotation.

BOMBER WOBBLE

1. Switch to the Camera view and select the B17 body.
2. Open the Track View.
3. Right-click on the Filters button and select Selected Objects Only and Transforms Only. These filters are very useful in keeping your workspace uncluttered and focused only on what you need.

4. Expand the Transform controller hierarchy for B17 Body and highlight Rotation.

5. Click on Assign Controller from the Track View toolbar, select Euler XYZ, and click on OK.

6. Expand the Rotation controller hierarchy. Beneath the parent Euler XYZ controller are individual X, Y, and Z rotation tracks. Each of these tracks has been assigned a Bézier Float controller as seen in figure 17.7. Highlight the X Rotation.

FIGURE 17.7

Assigning the Euler XYZ Rotation controller.

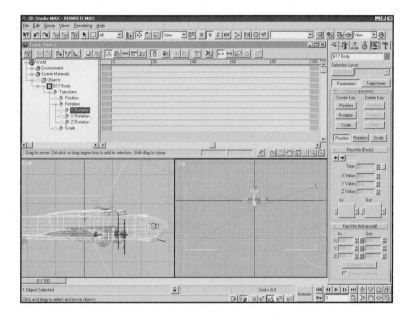

7. Click on Function Curves from the toolbar.

8. Click on Move Keys and select the dotted line that lies at value 0 (right now there are no keyframes laid out).

9. Click on Add Keys and create a keyframe around every 20 frames or so, increasing and decreasing the value and adding a few random keys here and there (see fig.17.8). Because you want the effect to be subtle, try not to let the values go higher than 0.5 degrees or lower than −0.5.

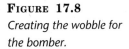
FIGURE 17.8
*Creating the wobble for
the bomber.*

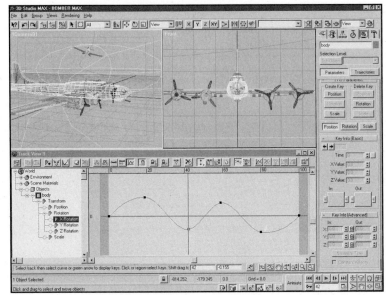

10. Save your scene as **mybomber01.max** and render out a Smooth + Highlights preview of the Camera01 viewport, frames 0–100.

If the motion looks unnatural, try lowering the values of the keyframes or the frequency at which they occur (maybe a key every 30 frames). One advantage of working with Euler controllers is that the function curves enable quick and easy adjustment of your animation. They also provide a better picture of what each key is doing.

NOTE

You may find yourself wondering why you would ever want to use TCB Rotation controllers again. If so, save yourself the trouble of assigning Euler XYZ controllers to every rotation you animate by choosing Make Default in the Replace Controller dialog. This sets Euler XYZ as the default controller for all future rotation parameters.

Another place to try a Euler Rotation controller is the Y Rotation of the Fighter Body. The Banking option for the Path controller takes care of this to an extent, but you may want to try adding some of your own keyframes to spice up the attack a bit. Perhaps a barrel roll in the beginning of the pass or at the end as it flies by the camera? Feel free to experiment before moving on to the next section.

Animating with the Look-At Controller

Another useful controller included with 3DS MAX is the Look At controller. The Look At controller is a compound controller that combines the output of an object's position, roll, and scale controllers. It completely replaces the standard PRS (Position/Rotation/Scale) controller and outputs the transformation matrix of associated objects.

The Look-At controller takes the negative Z axis of an object and points it toward a selected target. The most graphic example is that of a character's head staring at an object, following it automatically as it moves through the scene. Look-At controllers are used by Target Spots and Target Cameras to keep them directed at their point of interest.

Tracking Turrets

In this example, you use a Look-At controller to make the turret on top of the bomber track the fighter as it flies by.

First you link the turret and its guns to a dummy object. You then apply the Look-At controller to the dummy, which in turn affects the turret and guns.

TRACKING TURRETS

1. Before getting started, choose Edit, Hold.

2. In the Top viewport, zoom in on the turret just behind the cockpit of the bomber.

3. Select the Top Turret object and link it to the surrounding Top Turret dummy.

4. Select the Turret Guns and also link them to Top Turret dummy.

5. Select Top Turret dummy, open the Motion panel, and highlight Transform under Assign Controller.

6. Click on Assign Controller, select Look At, and click on OK.

7. In the Motion panel, click on Pick Target and select Fighter Body.

8. Switch to the Camera view and slide the playback bar to view the animation.

So what went wrong? The dummy and turret follow the fighter, but as you can see from figure 17.9, the turret is turned on its side and the guns are pointing straight up. That is because the negative Z axis of the dummy object was pointing in the default world orientation, which is straight down. When the Look-At controller was applied, the dummy rotated itself back (along with the linked turret and guns) so that the negative Z points to the passing fighter. A quick way of fixing this is to adjust the pivot of the dummy so that it and its children face the right direction.

FIGURE 17.9
Creating the turret hierarchy.

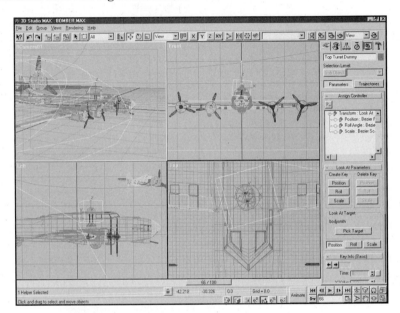

ADJUSTING THE TURRET

1. Select the Top Turret dummy and open up the Hierarchy panel.

2. Click on Pivot and select Affect Pivot Only.

3. With the Local coordinate system active, rotate the pivot –90 degrees along the X axis in the Top viewport.

You won't actually see the pivot rotate, but the turret and guns now face the right way. By scrolling through the animation, however, you might notice a new problem. The rotating turret tilts up and down as it follows the fighter. In reality the turret would only spin and the guns themselves would angle up and down. A little preplanning could have prevented this, but because you performed a hold not too long ago, you can go back and prevent all these problems from occurring.

4. Choose Edit, Fetch and click on Yes.

5. Select Top Turret dummy and open the Hierarchy panel.

6. Click on Pivot and Affect Pivot only.

7. Verify that the View coordinate system is currently selected in the Reference Coordinate System drop-down. Rotate the pivot for Dummy01 90 degrees along the X axis in the Top view as before. The blue Z axis now points toward the rear of the aircraft.

That will save the correction step later. To lock down the turret so that it only inherits Z rotations from its Dummy parent, follow these steps.

8. Select Top Turret and click on Link Info in the Hierarchy panel.

9. Under Inherit, uncheck the X and Y for Rotate.

10. Link the Turret and Turret Guns to the Top Turret dummy.

11. With the Top Turret dummy selected, open the Motion panel and highlight Transform under Assign Controller.

12. Click on Assign Controller, select Look At, and click on OK.

13. In the Motion panel, click on Pick Target and select the Fighter Body.

14. Switch to the Camera view and slide the playback bar to view the animation.

The turret stays level and the guns tilt as they follow the fighter (see fig. 17.10).

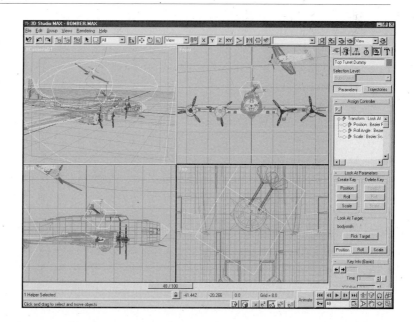

FIGURE 17.10

The Look-At controller at work.

Animating with Noise and List Controllers

The Noise controller is one of two parametric controllers included with 3D Studio MAX. A *parametric controller* is unique in that it automatically creates animation data for an object based on user-specified data values. No keyframes are ever set for a parametric controller, as the user data totally defines the behavior of the animation. Instead, range bars appear in Track View for tracks animated with parametric controllers.

The Noise controller is useful for creating an amazing variety of irregular animated effects. Buzzing wings, rustling leaves, flashing lights, and many, many other effects can be handled quickly and effectively with a Noise controller.

NOTE

The other parametric controller that comes with MAX is the Expression controller. It is significantly different from any other controller and is addressed later in this chapter and more fully in Chapter 18, "Animating with Expressions."

The List controller is a user-defined compound controller used to combine the effects of multiple controllers. It is frequently used to add noise to a predefined motion. The effect can be subtle or drastic, adding natural irregularities to a motion, simulating rough terrain, or similar effects. This combination of parametric and key-based animation is indeed a powerful and efficient technique.

Gunfire Effects

For the gunfire of the bomber turret and fighter plane, you will try a simple but effective approach. You will apply a Noise controller under a List controller for the XYZ scale of the cones, causing them to shrink and expand rapidly during the flyby, giving the illusion of flashing gunfire. A Visibility track can then be used to make the fire sporadic.

CREATING GUNFIRE

1. Zoom in on the Turret object in the Top viewport and select Flash02.

2. Open the Track View. Right-click on the Filters button and select Selected Objects Only and Transforms Only.

3. Expand the hierarchy until you get to Flash02 and its parameters.

4. Highlight Scale and click on Assign Controller. Select Scale List and click on OK.

5. Expand the Scale hierarchy and select Available.

6. Click on Assign Controller, select Noise Scale, and click on OK (see fig.17.11).

7. Click on Properties from the Track View toolbar. Change the X, Y, and Z strengths to 300. Close the Properties dialog and minimize the Track View.

8. Slide the playback bar to view the animation.

FIGURE 17.11

Creating the List Scale controller hierarchy.

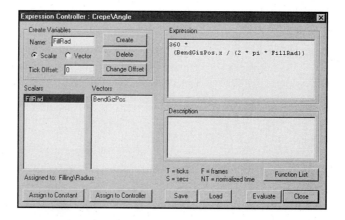

The Flash02 cone scales randomly in all directions. Now copy that same effect to the other gun flashes.

9. Click on Select By Name and select Flash01, Flash02, Flash03, and Flash04.

10. Maximize your Track View. Highlight Objects at the top of the hierarchy and right-click, selecting Expand All.

11. Select Scale for Flash02 and click on Copy Controller from the toolbar.

12. Select Scale for Flash01 and click on Paste Controller, making certain to select Paste As Instance in the dialog.

13. Repeat step 12 for Flash03 and Flash04, making them instances as well.

14. Minimize your Track View and switch to the Camera viewport. Slide the playback bar to view the animation.

Both the turret on the bomber and the guns on the fighter emit throbbing cones.

15. Select Flash03 and Flash04 of the fighter. Maximize your Track View.

16. Right-click on Filters and select Show All (this is necessary to work with Visibility tracks).

17. Locate and select Flash04.

18. From the toolbar, click on Add Visibility Track. Click on Add Keys and place a key at frame 0.

19. Right-click on keyframe 0, choose Step Tangent for both the In and Out, and close the Properties dialog.

20. Click on Move Keys and Shift-drag a copy of keyframe 0 to frame 1.

21. Right-click on keyframe 1 and change the value to 0. Shift-drag a copy of keyframe 0 to frame 2.

22. Click on the Parameter Curve Out-of-Range Type from the toolbar and select Loop.

23. Open the Function Curve for the Visibility track. Compare your results to figure 17.12.

FIGURE 17.12

Animating the Visibility function curve.

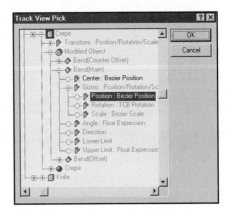

The curve for visibility shifts from 1 to 0 every other frame, causing the gunfire to appear and disappear. Now layer another curve to control when the firing starts and stops.

24. Click on Assign Controller from the Track View toolbar and select Float List.

25. Expand the Visibility hierarchy and select Available. Click on Assign Controller and select Bézier Float.

26. Select Add Key and place a keyframe at frame 0 and frame 60.

27. Click on Move Keys, select frame 0 and 60, and open their Properties dialog.

28. Right-click on keyframe and choose Step Tangent for both the In and Out.

29. Change the value of frame 0 to 0 and frame 60 to –1.

The original Looping Bézier Curve, created in steps 18 through 22, will be unaffected by this second curve from frame 0 to frame 60 (where the value is 0). Beginning at frame 61, the value drops to –1. The gunfire flashes on and off for sixty frames, and then turns off entirely. The combined output of the list controller is best seen by selecting the parent Visibility track in the function curve mode of Track View (see fig.17.13).

FIGURE 17.13

The combined output of the Visibility List controller.

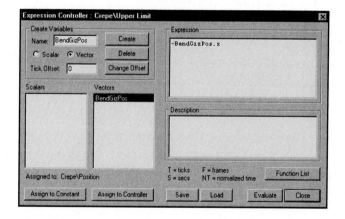

Now to copy this set of curves to the other Flash objects and offset them accordingly, follow these steps:

30. Select Visibility for Flash04 and click on Copy Controller. Find and select Flash03 and add a Visibility track.

TIP

If the Add Visibility Track button is not on the toolbar, remember that you must be in Edit Keys mode to access it.

31. Select Visibility for Flash03 and click on Paste Controller, pasting as an Instance.

Finish up by copying your newly animated Visibility tracks to the guns in the turret of the bomber. Because you want to make a few subtle changes to the firing of those guns, you will paste the controllers as copies.

32. Minimize your Track View and select Flash01 and Flash02.

33. Maximize your Track View and add a Visibility track to both Flash01 and Flash02.

34. Select Visibility for Flash01 and click on Paste Controller, pasting as a Copy, not an Instance this time.

35. Repeat step 34 for Flash02.

36. For both Flash01 and Flash02, move frame 60 of the second Bézier Float to frame 90.

37. Select the first Bézier Float for Flash 01 and offset the three keyframes by one (this alternates the firing of the barrels).

Expression Controllers

The latter half of this chapter introduces Expression controllers as a means to reference and manipulate animation data output by other controllers in the scene. Expression controllers contain a fairly comprehensive set of functions that can be used to create enormously complex equations, if necessary. This advanced level of functionality is discussed in greater detail in Chapter 5.

Project: Making Crepes

The next project uses a few relatively simple expressions to communicate animation data between two separate objects: a crepe and its filling. The goal is to configure the objects to reference specific characteristics of each other so that the crepe can be made to roll up, wrapping the filling as it goes. You will use expressions to affect the following aspects of the scene:

- Controlling the crepe's roll with its Bend(Main) modifier.

- Controlling the crepe's outer radius with the Bend(Offset) and Bend(Counter Offset) modifiers

- Controlling the filling's transforms with the crepe's Bend modifiers

Load the file ch17_1.max from the accompanying CD. Open Track View and expand the objects to display the Crepe and Filling objects' modifiers (see fig.17.14).

FIGURE 17.14

Track View layout displaying Crepe and Filling objects.

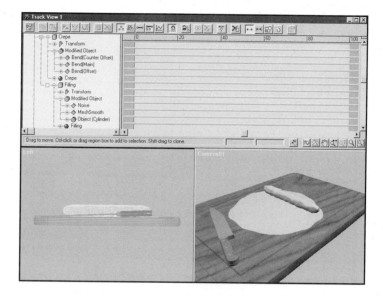

This scene shows four objects: a knife, a conveniently precooked crepe sitting on a cutting board, complete with a filling of your choice. The crepe was once a squashed geosphere with a Noise modifier, but has since been collapsed into an Editable (and edible) Mesh object containing three Bend modifiers. Used in conjunction with one another, the Bend modifiers will precisely control the behavior of the crepe as it is rolled. The filling is a cylinder with MeshSmooth and Noise modifiers. The filling's radius will control how tightly the crepe is wound up. The Bend modifiers will control the filling's position and rotation.

Controlling the Crepe's Roll with the Bend(Main) Modifier

The Bend(Main) modifier will be responsible for the crepe's primary roll component. As the bend's Angle value increases, the crepe winds up tighter onto itself. Moving the modifier's gizmo along its local X-axis causes the wound-up crepe to roll along that axis. Adjusting the Angle value, gizmo position, and Upper Limit simultaneously enables the crepe to start out flat and roll up onto itself. Now take a closer look at these components.

PREPARING THE CREPE

1. Select and hide the Cutting Board, Knife, and Filling objects for the time being while you work with the crepe.

2. Select the Crepe object and go to the Bend(Main) modifier in the Modifier Stack.

3. Use the spinner to adjust the Angle value between 0 and –270.0 degrees.

The bend pivots about the gizmo center positioned at the far-right end of the crepe (see fig.17.15).

FIGURE 17.15

Adjusting the Crepe object's Bend(Main) Angle value.

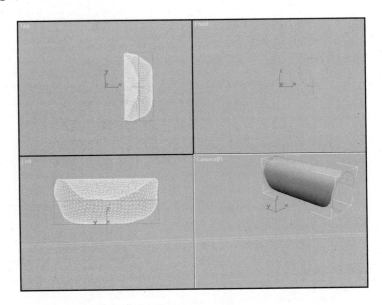

4. Go to the Sub-Object gizmo level. In the camera viewport, select and move the gizmo along the crepe's local X-axis only.

TIP

Turn on the Snap Toggle prior to transforming the gizmo; this will simplify placing it back in its original position when necessary.

The crepe appears to roll through the bend as the Bend(Main) gizmo is moved (see fig.17.16).

FIGURE 17.16
Moving the Crepe object's Bend(Main) gizmo along its local X-axis.

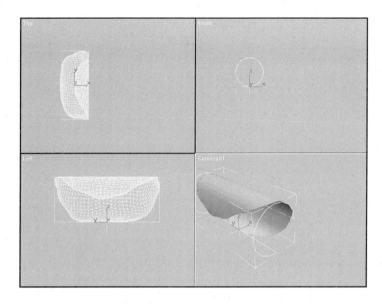

5. Check the Limit Effect check box to activate the modifier's limits.

6. Change the Upper Limit value to 100.0.

7. In the camera viewport, select and move the gizmo along the crepe's local X-axis only.

The crepe appears to curl up and roll over onto itself (see fig.17.17).

FIGURE 17.17
Moving the Crepe object's Bend(Main) gizmo with Limits enabled.

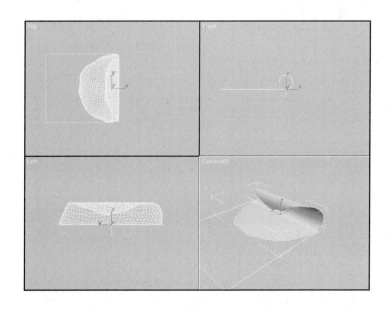

Notice that the roll effect stops working after the right edge of the crepe has passed the Upper Limit value. If you increase the Upper Limit value, you need to also increase the Angle value to maintain a constant radius. For the roll to work properly, the Angle and Upper Limit values must change as the gizmo is moved. You can either manually keyframe these values to keep pace with the gizmo's changing position or you can let expression controllers handle the tasks for you and update the results procedurally.

Using Expressions to Control the Angle and Upper Limit Values

Expression controllers are incredibly powerful, enabling you to represent any parameter with a complex mathematical expression that can include data referenced from other controllers in the scene. Expressions do not have to be complex to take advantage of this capability to relate and interpret values from other controllers. The following exercise uses expressions to update the Bend(Main) modifier's Angle and Upper Limit values, by:

■ Converting the gizmo's position into a rotational equivalent

■ Moving the Upper Limit value in the opposite direction as the gizmo's position

ASSIGNING EXPRESSION CONTROLLERS TO THE ANGLE AND UPPER LIMIT TRACKS

1. Open Track View and expand the tracks to display the Crepe object's Bend(Main) modifier's tracks (see fig.17.18).

TIP

Turn on Track View's Controller Types filter when preparing to assign or manipulate controllers (see fig.17.19).

2. Select the Angle and Upper Limit tracks and click on Assign Controller in the Track View toolbar.

3. Select Float Expression and click on OK (see fig.17.20).

FIGURE 17.18

Track View layout displaying Crepe object's Bend(Main) modifier's tracks.

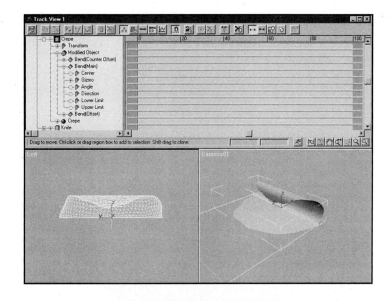

FIGURE 17.19

The Track View's Filters dialog.

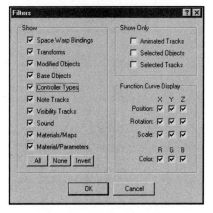

FIGURE 17.20

The Track View's Replace Float Controller dialog.

4. Select the Angle track only and click on Properties in the Track View toolbar. The Expression Controller dialog appears (see fig.17.21).

FIGURE 17.21

Track View's Expression Controller dialog.

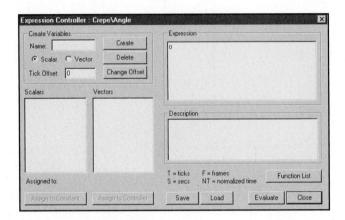

You need two variables to control the angle of the Bend(Main) modifier as its gizmo moves along the local X-axis. One variable will reference the position of the gizmo itself; the other will reference the radius of the Filling object. With this information, the expression can calculate the position and radius of the crepe's curl as it rolls.

5. In the Expression Controller dialog, enter **BendGizPos** in the Name field, select the Vector radio button (if it is not already selected), and click on Create.

Vector variables are used to reference data containing three separate components, such as the gizmo's X, Y, and Z position data.

6. With the newly created BendGizPos variable selected, click on Assign to Controller.

7. In the Track View Pick dialog, expand the tracks to display the Crepe object's Bend(Main) modifier and select the gizmo's Position track (see fig.17.22). Click on OK.

Expression controller variables can be assigned either to a constant value or to a value output by another controller in the scene. A variable assigned to a controller will update dynamically as that controller changes state.

FIGURE 17.22

Track View Pick dialog with the Bend(Main) gizmo's Position track selected.

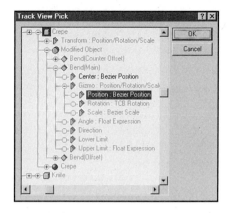

8. In the Expression Controller dialog, enter **FillRad** in the Name field, select the Scalar radio button, and click on Create.

Scalar variables are used to reference data containing only one component, such as the Filling's radius data.

9. With the FillRad variable selected, click on Assign to Controller.

10. In the Track View Pick dialog, expand the objects and tracks to display the Filling object's Radius track. Select the Radius track (see fig.17.23). Click on OK.

FIGURE 17.23

The Track View's Pick dialog with the Filling object's Radius track selected.

WARNING

The Expression Controller's "Assigned to" field is designed to display the name of the controller assigned to the selected variable. Although this is usually accurate, it is a good idea always to name your variables so that they remind you which object they are assigned to. Do not rely on the "Assigned to" field.

Now that you have the two variables assigned to their respective controllers, it is time to create the expression. Although expressions can be intimidating, the following simple equation converts the Bend(Main) gizmo's position along its local X-axis into a rotational equivalent with respect to the Filling object's radius.

11. In the Expression field, replace 0 with the expression **360 * (BendGizPos.x / (2 * pi * FillRad))** (see fig.17.24). Close the Expression Controller dialog.

FIGURE 17.24

The Track View's Expression Controller dialog with new expression.

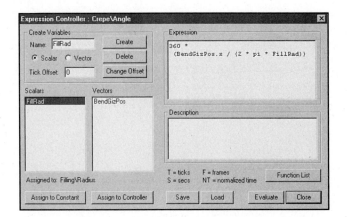

To complete this exercise you now need to configure the Upper Limit's Expression controller. You need only one variable to control the Upper Limit of the Bend(Main) modifier as its Gizmo moves along the local X-axis.

12. Select the Upper Limit track only and click on Properties in the Track View toolbar.

13. In the Expression Controller dialog, enter **BendGizPos** in the Name field, select the Vector radio button, and click on Create.

14. With the BendGizPos variable selected, click on Assign to Controller.

15. In the Track View Pick dialog, expand the tracks to display the Crepe object's Bend(Main) modifier and select the gizmo's Position track (see fig.17.25). Click on OK.

FIGURE 17.25

The Track View Pick dialog with the Bend(Main) gizmo's Position track selected.

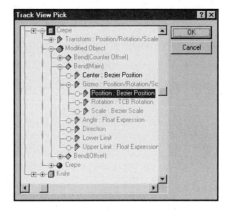

The following expression references the Bend(Main) gizmo's position along the local X-axis and communicates its negative value to the Upper Limit.

16. In the Expression field, replace 0 with the expression **–BendGizPos.x** (see fig.17.26). Close the Expression Controller dialog.

FIGURE 17.26

The Track View's Expression Controller dialog with new expression.

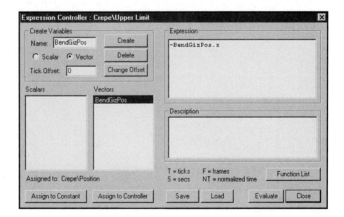

17. In the camera viewport, select and move the Bend(Main) modifier's gizmo along the crepe's local X-axis only. Watch the Angle and Upper Limit values change as the gizmo moves.

The Bend(Main)'s Angle and Upper Limit values now update dynamically as you move the gizmo along its local X-axis. On close examination of the roll, however, you will notice that the crepe's outer radius does not increase as the roll is wound up (see fig.17.27). To control the outer radius offset, use the crepe's Bend(Offset) and Bend(Counter Offset) modifiers. Because you will be diverting your attention away from the Bend(Main) modifier for a while, first animate its Gizmo's position along the local X-axis to automate its movement.

FIGURE 17.27

Rolled up crepe with constant radius.

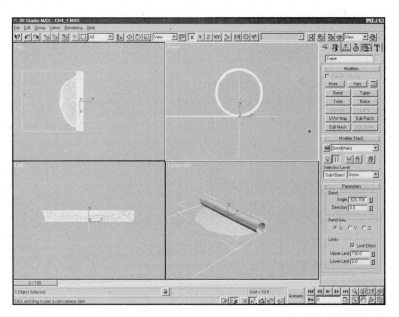

Load ch17_1_1.max from the accompanying CD if you would like to start where the previous exercise left off.

ANIMATING THE GIZMO

1. Select and move the Bend(Main) modifier's gizmo back to its original position so that the crepe lies flat (see fig.17.28).

2. Go to frame 100. Turn on the Animate button. In the camera viewport, select and move the Bend(Main) modifier's gizmo −200.0 units along its local X-axis (see fig.17.29).

FIGURE 17.28

Bend(Main) modifier's gizmo returned to its original position.

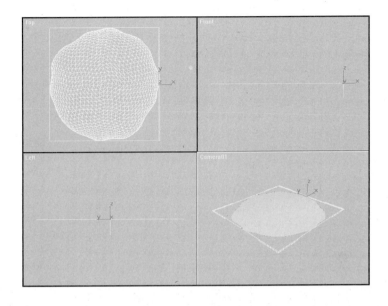

FIGURE 17.29

Bend(Main) modifier's animated gizmo.

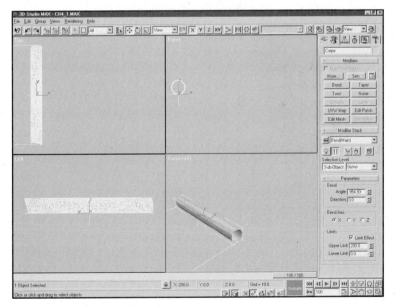

3. Turn off Animate and play back the animation.

Now that you have animated the roll, it is time to take a closer look at the crepe's Bend(Offset) and Bend(Counter Offset) modifiers.

Controlling the Crepe's Outer Radius

To make the crepe look more natural, it needs to grow slightly larger as it rolls up to compensate for its thickness. To achieve this, you will use the crepe's Bend(Offset) and Bend(Counter Offset) modifiers to increase its outside radius by a constant amount. The Bend(Offset) modifier sits below the Bend(Main) modifier in the stack; the Bend(Counter Offset) is above. If the Bend(Offset)'s Angle value is greater than zero, the Bend(Main)'s effect is compounded and the roll radiates outward. The Bend(Counter Offset) modifier is used to correct unwanted sloping that results from the initial offset.

ROLLING UP THE CREPE

Load ch17_1_2.max from the accompanying CD if you would like to start where the previous exercise left off.

1. Go to frame 75 so that the crepe is three-quarters of the way rolled up.

2. Select the Crepe object and go to the Bend(Offset) modifier in the Modifier Stack.

3. Use the spinner to adjust the Angle value between 0 and 15.0 degrees.

The crepe's outer radius increases as the Bend(Offset)'s Angle value moves positively away from zero (see fig.17.30).

FIGURE 17.30
Bend(Offset) modifier's positive Angle value increases the crepe's outer radius.

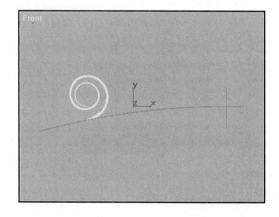

4. Change the Angle value to 8.0 degrees. Play back the animation.

A side effect of the increasing outer radius is that the entire crepe now slopes down by the Bend(Offset)'s angle amount (see fig.17.31). An examination of the crepe's Bend(Counter Offset) modifier should help you see how to remedy this.

FIGURE 17.31
Side-effect of the increasing outer radius.

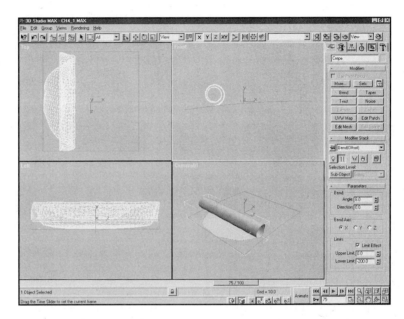

5. Go to the Bend(Counter Offset) modifier in the Modifier Stack.

6. Change the Angle value to 8.0 degrees, matching that of the Bend(Offset) modifier.

7. Play back the animation.

The sloping side-effect has been eliminated (see fig.17.32). The Bend(Counter Offset) modifier's Direction value is set to 180.0 degrees; this applies the bend effect in the opposite direction to that of the Bend(Offset) modifier. This counters the overall slope, but leaves the crepe's increasing radius intact.

Because the bend offset is only used to compensate for the thickness of the crepe, you can use a much smaller amount.

8. Reduce the Bend(Offset) and Bend(Counter Offset) Angle values to 1.2.

FIGURE 17.32

Rolled-up crepe with increasing outer radius minus sloping side effect.

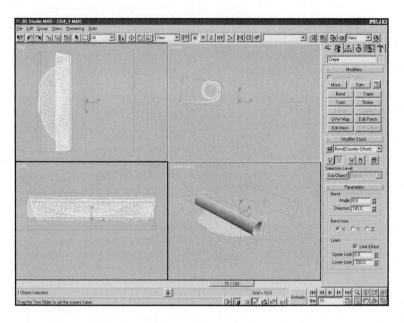

Because the Angle value of both Offset modifiers should always be equal, it makes sense to use two instances of the same animation controller for these parameters. Chapter 24 of *Inside 3D Studio MAX Volume I* discusses copying and pasting of controllers. If you copy either Bézier Float controller to the other Angle track and paste it as an instance, adjusting either the Bend(Offset) or Bend(Counter Offset) Angle parameter will identically affect the other.

Controlling the Filling's Transforms with the Crepe's Bend Modifiers

Your crepe is well on its way to becoming part of a delicious entree (or dessert). Now it is time to reintroduce the Filling object and prepare it for its journey into the culinary arts. Your task is to enable the filling to precisely match the movement and rotation of the crepe as it is rolled up. To control its position, you will use a Position Expression to reference several components of the crepe, including the Bend(Main) gizmo's position, the Bend(Main) and Bend(Offset) Angle values, as well as the filling's own radius. To control its rotation, you use a Euler XYZ compound controller with a Float Expression referencing the crepe's Bend(Main) angle.

PREPARING THE FILLING

Load ch17_1_3.max from the accompanying CD if you would like to start where the previous exercise left off.

1. Unhide the Filling object.

2. Open Track View and expand tracks to display the Filling object's Position track.

3. Select the Position track and click on Assign Controller in the Track View toolbar.

4. Select the Position Expression controller and click on OK (see fig.17.33).

FIGURE 17.33

Replacing the Filling object's Position Expression controller.

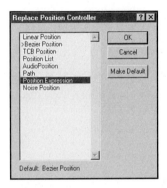

5. With the Position track selected, bring up the Expression Controller dialog by clicking on the Properties button in the Track View toolbar.

For this expression, you will create four variables that will enable the filling to remain centered in the crepe's curl as it is rolled up. The first variable references the Bend(Main) gizmo's position, the second variable references the Bend(Offset)'s Angle value, the third variable references the filling's own height, and the fourth variable references the filling's own radius.

6. In the Expression Controller dialog, enter **BendGizPos** in the Name field, select the Vector radio button, and click on Create.

7. With the newly created BendGizPos variable selected, click on Assign to Controller.

8. In the Track View Pick dialog, expand the tracks to display the Crepe object's Bend(Main) modifier and select the gizmo's Position track (see fig.17.34). Click on OK.

FIGURE 17.34

The Track View Pick dialog with the Bend(Main) gizmo's Position track selected.

9. In the Expression Controller dialog, enter **BendOffAng** in the Name field, select the Scalar radio button, and click on Create.

10. With the newly created BendOffAng variable selected, click on Assign to Controller.

11. In the Track View Pick dialog, expand the tracks to display the Crepe object's Bend(Offset) modifier and select the Angle track (see fig.17.35). Click on OK.

FIGURE 17.35

The Track View Pick dialog with the Bend(Offset) Angle track selected.

12. In the Expression Controller dialog, enter **FillHeight** in the Name field, select the Scalar radio button, and click on Create.

13. With the FillHeight variable selected, click on Assign to Controller.

14. In the Track View Pick dialog, expand the objects and tracks to display the Filling object's Height track. Select the Height track (see fig.17.36). Click on OK.

FIGURE **17.36**

The Track View Pick dialog with the Filling object's Height track selected.

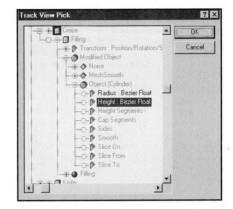

15. In the Expression Controller dialog, enter **FillRad** in the Name field, select the Scalar radio button, and click on Create.

16. With the FillRad variable selected, click on Assign to Controller.

17. In the Track View Pick dialog, expand the objects and tracks to display the Filling object's Radius track. Select the Radius track (see fig.17.37). Click on OK.

FIGURE **17.37**

The Track View Pick dialog with the Filling object's Radius track selected.

The Position Expression controller uses a vector expression containing three components to determine the location of an object in space. The following expression (in step 18) uses the four variables to control the precise position of the Filling object as the crepe rolls up.

- The expression's X-axis component references the Bend(Main) Gizmo's position to control the filling's position along the crepe's local X-axis.

- The expression's Y-axis component references the filling's height to keep it centered in the crepe along the crepe's local Y-axis.

- The expression's Z-axis component references the filling's radius along with the crepe's Bend(Offset) Angle value and Bend(Main) Gizmo's position to control the filling's position along the crepe's local Z-axis.

18. In the Expression field, replace the existing values with the expression **[BendGizPos.x + 100, FillHeight / 2, FillRad + tan((BendOffAng/360) * BendGizPos.x) * BendGizPos.x]** (see fig.17.38). Close the Expression Controller dialog.

FIGURE 17.38
The Track View's Expression Controller dialog with the new expression.

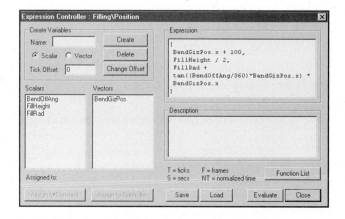

This expression will dynamically compensate for changes to both the filling's shape and the crepe's increasing outer radius. You can test this by altering the filling's radius and height or by changing the crepe's Bend(Offset) Angle.

The last step to controlling the Filling object's motion is to convert the Bend(Main)'s changing Angle into the filling's rotation. You will use a Euler XYZ compound controller in the filling's Rotation track and then assign a simple expression controller referencing the Angle value to its Y-axis component.

NOTE

It would be very convenient to simply copy and paste an instance of the Bend(Main) Angle's Bézier Float controller into the Y-axis component of the Euler XYZ rotation. However, pasting into sub-track controllers (such as Eulers, Lists, Ease, and Multiplier curves) is not supported in MAX 1.x.

ASSIGNING AN EXPRESSION CONTROLLER (VIA EULER XYZ) TO THE ROTATION TRACK

Load ch17_1_4.max from the accompanying CD if you would like to start where the previous exercise left off.

1. Open Track View and expand tracks to display the Filling object's Rotation track.

2. Select the Rotation track and click on Assign Controller in the Track View toolbar.

3. Select the Euler XYZ controller and click on OK (see fig.17.39).

FIGURE 17.39

Replacing the Filling object's Rotation controller.

4. Expand the Rotation track to display the Euler's X, Y, and Z components.

5. Select the Y Rotation track and click on Assign Controller in the Track View toolbar.

6. Select the Float Expression controller and click on OK

7. Click on Properties to bring up the Expression Controller dialog. Enter **BendMainAng** in the Name field, select the Scalar radio button, and click on Create.

8. With the BendMainAng variable selected, click on Assign to Controller.

9. In the Track View Pick dialog, expand the objects and tracks to display the Crepe object's Bend(Main) Angle track. Select the Angle track (see fig.17.40). Click on OK.

FIGURE 17.40

The Track View Pick dialog with the Crepe object's Bend(Main) Angle track selected.

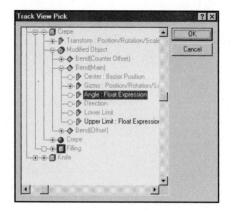

The following expression references the Bend(Main)'s Angle value and converts it from degrees to radians. This conversion is necessary when channeling nonrotation angle values (such as bends or twists) into rotation expressions.

10. In the Expression field, replace the existing value with the expression **degToRad(BendMainAng)** (see fig.17.41).

FIGURE 17.41

The Track View's Expression Controller dialog with new expression.

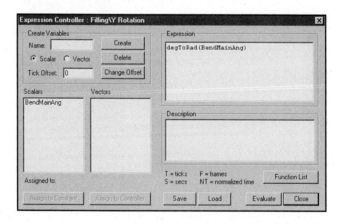

When you play back the animation, you will see that the filling now moves and rotates precisely with the rolling crepe. Load ch17_1.avi or ch17_2.max from the accompanying CD to see the finished scene.

In Practice: Animating with Controllers

- **Controllers.** Understanding how controllers can be made to communicate with each other is an important step toward mastering your animated scenes.

- **Path controllers.** The Path controller is a compound controller created as an alternative position controller. It receives the output of a subordinate Percent controller that specifies the path position, expressed as a percentage of total path length.

- **Euler XYZ Rotation controller.** The Euler XYZ controller is provided as an alternative to the standard TCB Rotation controller. The Euler XYZ controller enables the user to view and adjust rotation values in the Function Curves mode of Track View.

- **Look-At controller.** This controller is a compound controller that combines the output of an object's position, roll, and scale controllers. It completely replaces the standard PRS (Position/Rotation/Scale) controller and outputs the transformation matrix of associated objects.

- **Parametric controller.** A parametric controller is unique in that it automatically creates animation data for an object based on user-specified data values.

- **Noise controller.** One of two parametric controllers, the Noise controller is useful for creating an amazing variety of irregular animated effects, such as buzzing wings, rustling leaves, flashing lights, and other effects.

- **List controller.** The other parametric controller, the List controller is a user-defined compound controller used to combine the effects of multiple controllers.

- **Expression controllers.** Expression controllers contain a fairly comprehensive set of functions that can be used to create enormously complex equations, if necessary. However, they do not have to be complex for you to take advantage of their capability to relate and interpret values from other controllers.

- **Instancing.** Instancing controllers across multiple tracks is a powerful way to simplify complex procedures.

- **Naming Strategy.** Use a sound naming strategy for variables so that you never lose track of your controller assignments.

IMAGE CREATED BY DAN O'LEARY

Chapter 18

by Dan O'Leary

ANIMATING WITH EXPRESSIONS

Expression controllers provide a level of animation control just short of that afforded by scripting plug-ins or the SDK. Without learning a programming language, any MAX user familiar with Expression controllers can mathematically define animations for the transforms and numeric creation, modifier, or material parameters of an object.

Additionally, expressions enable astute users to define relationships between the animation controllers of objects. A wheel's rate of rotation, for example, can be defined as a function of its radius.

This kind of precise control has applications in many animation markets. Forensic animation and scientific visualization are obvious examples because simulation is often the goal. Beyond these niche markets, expressions are a very useful tool for creating behaviors that enhance the primary animation.

This chapter explores the following topics:

- Transform animation with Expression controllers
- Control objects
- Modifier animation

Expression Controllers Overview

Expression controllers are not for everyone. They require the user to take on a different level of understanding than any other tool in the MAX interface. This is largely due to the fact that, by itself, the Expression controller does absolutely nothing. It is a do-it-yourself controller kit that requires the user to do the following:

1. Recognize effects that could be implemented more efficiently or effectively using procedural techniques than by using other key-based controllers.

2. Create an equation or group of equations that produce the required results. Those of you comfortable with math, especially algebra and trigonometry, are at an advantage here.

The time invested in understanding the applications of this unique and powerful tool in your daily work will pay off in increased efficiency and improved effects. The results are limited only by your creativity, ingenuity, and determination.

As powerful as they are, keep in mind that expressions do not work magic. They give users new ways to control the animation of existing parameters only. Anything beyond that requires you to spend some quality time with the MAX SDK or scripting application.

Transform Animation with Expression Controllers

Expression controllers are very useful for creating motion or effects to supplement the primary action in a scene. The work process for most animators begins with a simple representation of the scene to establish the basic motion and timing for the shot. The final animation is arrived at through a series of refinements in which increasing detail is added to the motion. Each iteration improves the look and feel of the animation without making drastic departures from the original timing and composition.

The following series of examples demonstrates the application of Expression controllers to create a complex natural behavior. This discussion approaches this in a way that enables you to layer the effects of each Expression on top of a base animation to create the final effect. In this example, Expression controllers will be used to control the position and rotation transforms of a tornado object.

Tornado Project

This project begins with a tornado animated with a simple Path controller. Some additional keys have been set so that it pauses along the way.

1. Load the file twister.max.

2. Play the animation in the Camera viewport (see fig. 18.1).

FIGURE 18.1

Tornado motion animated with a Path controller.

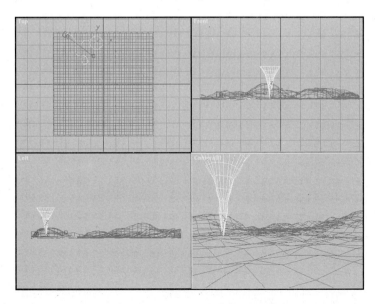

Not terribly exciting stuff, but it is enough to define timing and basic motion for the scene. Open twister.avi on the accompanying CD to see how expressions bring the scene to life.

The goal of this exercise is to create a collection of position and rotation expressions that work together to define a natural tornado behavior. You will use List controllers to add this behavior to the predefined path. Each step along the way refines the original animation, making it more lifelike than before.

Start with the basics. The most obvious problem with twister.max is that the tornado does not spin!

ANIMATING ROTATION

1. Open Track View and expand the Transform tracks for the Twister object.

2. Right-click on the Filters button in the upper-left corner of Track View and select Controller Types on the resulting menu. Verify that the Rotation Transform has been assigned a TCB controller.

To assign an Expression controller to the tornado's Z Rotation, you must first replace this TCB controller with a Euler XYZ controller. If a Euler controller was assigned by default (many users prefer it to the TCB controller), skip the following step.

3. Select the TCB Rotation and click on Assign Controller. Select Euler XYZ in the Replace Controller dialog.

4. Expand the Rotation track to reveal unique Bézier controllers on X, Y, and Z.

5. Select the Z Rotation track and assign a Float Expression controller. A range bar appears in the track to indicate the active controller.

WARNING

Assigning an Expression controller to an animated track overwrites the existing key information. If you wish to use Expressions and keyframe data together, both controllers must be subordinate to a List controller. An example of this is provided in the "Position Expressions" section later in the chapter.

6. Bring up the Expression Controller Properties dialog by right-clicking on the range bar.

7. Click on Load to import a previously defined expression. Using the resulting file requester, load zrot.xpr.

8. Click on Evaluate to apply the new expression (see fig. 18.2).

9. Without closing the Expression Controller dialog, play the animation in the Camera viewport. The tornado makes one complete rotation as it moves along the path.

FIGURE 18.2

Setting up the Tornado Rotation Expression.

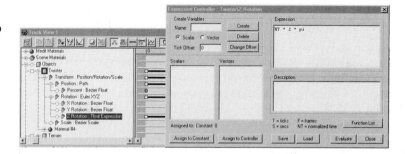

Take a moment to review the mechanics of this simple expression: NT*2*pi.

pi is a static function predefined in MAX. Its value is 3.14159, the number of radians in 180 degrees. 2*pi is the radian equivalent of 360 degrees, a complete circle. When creating expressions that control the rotation of an object, the output must be in radians to match the range of values expected by the parent Transform PRS controller.

NT is a reserved variable for Normalized Time. The value of NT increases linearly from 0.0 to 1.0 as a function of the current frame and active time segment. It is frequently used in expressions to match the timing of an animated effect to the active time segment. In this example, it serves to increase the value of your expression from 0 at the beginning of the animation (when NT=0) to 2*pi at the end (when NT=1). Table 18.1 illustrates how NT and the expression change with time.

TABLE **18.1**

Using Normalized Time (NT) to Drive an Animated Expression

Frame	NT	Expression (in radians)	Expression (in degrees)
0	0	0	0
25	0.25	1.5708	90
50	0.50	3.1415	180
100	1.0	6.2832	360

Now that you have the Rotation controller up and running, it is time to make some improvements. After viewing the animation, it seems clear that a single rotation just is not enough. It would be nice to have control over the number of revolutions that the tornado makes during the course of the animation. This can be done simply enough by adding a multiplier to your current expression.

10. In the Name field of the Expression Controller Properties dialog, enter the word **Repeat**.

11. Select the Scalar option and click on Create to create a new scalar variable.

12. Click on Assign to Constant and enter a value of 5.0.

13. Click on the Expression Edit window. Edit the expression to include the Repeat multiplier: Repeat*NT*2*pi.

14. Click on Evaluate to confirm your changes and update the controller. Play the animation in the Camera viewport. The tornado now makes five complete rotations as it moves along the path.

15. Save the new expression as **zrot-r.xpr**.

Expressions were purposely, and with much effort, used in this example as an introduction to their usage—it would have been a trivial matter to keyframe this effect.

Rules of the Road

Next you move on to some more complicated behaviors not so easily animated with traditional methods. But first, take a minute to review some important rules to remember while working with expressions.

- Above all, expressions must be mathematically valid statements. Although this should be obvious, it is often easier said than done. A good way to help make your expressions clean, neat, and error-free is to use "white space." Spaces, tabs, or returns can be used freely when composing your expressions to improve readability. Clean code is bug-free code—or at least easier to make that way.

- Expressions must evaluate to a compatible variable type. Float expressions must output float data; Vector expressions must output vectors.

- Variable names are case sensitive and cannot contain spaces. Variable names may contain numbers, but must begin with a letter.

- Variables are local to the controller—its name and value apply only to the track that it is used in. An Expression controller has no knowledge of variables defined in other tracks.

- Braces and parenthesis must be balanced; open vectors or subexpressions are illegal.

Position Expressions

The Path controller animation for your tornado is too simplistic for the needs of almost any animator. Real tornadoes wander along their way, directed yet chaotic. You want to create an Expression controller that simulates that behavior automatically. Ideally its action would be independent of the path data so that it could be reused—just point the Path controller at a new spline and go!

To pull it off, make use of a List controller and some not-too fancy math.

ANIMATING THE TORNADO'S POSITION

1. Continue from the previous exercise. Close the Z Rotation Expression Properties box and stop the animation playback.

2. In the Track View, select the Path Position controller.

3. Use Assign Controller to replace the Path controller with a Position List controller.

4. Expand the List controller. Note that the old Path controller has been retained as the primary child of the List.

5. Assign a Position Expression controller to the Available slot and open the Properties box (see fig. 18.3).

FIGURE 18.3

Creating the Position List controller hierarchy.

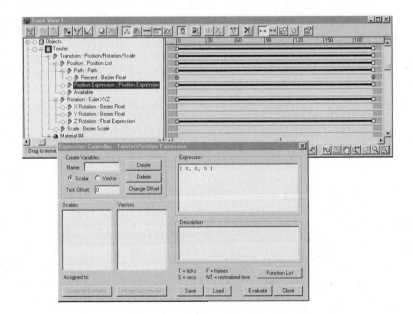

All Position Expression data must be output as vectors. This is indicated by the format of the default [0, 0, 0] expression. With a single controller, you calculate the X, Y, and Z position of the object, output in [X, Y, Z] format. Contrast this with the scalar output of the Rotation controller in the preceding example, where only the Z orientation was output.

The data output by your Position expression is then passed up to the List controller, where it is added as an offset to the output of the Path controller.

6. Load the expression 18leaf.xpr from the accompanying CD.

7. Assign a value of **10.0** to the Radius variable.

8. Assign a value of **2.0** to the Repeat variable.

NOTE

Saved expressions do not include assignments. Any constant or controller assignments must be redefined after loading. It is a good idea to include usage notes and suggested values for user-defined variables in the Description field of saved expressions.

9. Click on Evaluate to update your changes and update the controller.

10. Without closing the Expression Controller dialog, play the animation in the Camera viewport. The tornado now meanders lazily along its path of destruction.

With one expression, you have added significantly to the believability of the animation. You should now examine the components of this motion more carefully.

11. Make certain that the tornado is selected. In the Display panel, check Trajectory under Display Optimizations. The output of the Position List controller and the original spline path are now clearly visible in the Top viewport (see fig. 18.4).

FIGURE 18.4

Comparing the List controller trajectory and spline path.

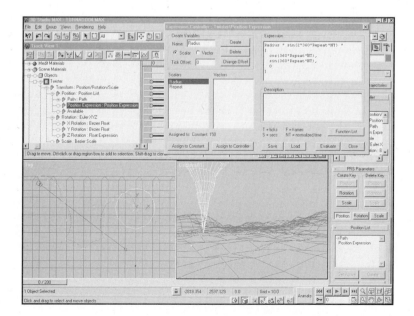

TIP

Trajectories are an excellent visualization tool when working with Position expressions; they provide instant visual feedback to the changes you make.

12. Take a few minutes to experiment with different values for Radius and Repeat, observing the effect of your changes on the trajectory. Remember that you must click on Evaluate after each new assignment to apply your changes.

13. When you are finished experimenting, reset the values of Radius and Repeat to something that creates a natural look.

As the value of Radius increases, the effect of the Position Expression controller becomes much more pronounced, visually overpowering the effects of the Path controller. With very large Radius values, the curves of the expression output are obvious. Large Repeat values tend to make the animation very jittery and knotted.

For the purposes of studying, debugging, and modifying an expression such as this, it would be nice to have a method for isolating its output in the List. Unfortunately, MAX does not provide a mechanism for making the various components of a List controller active or inactive. Here is a quick work-around—not pretty, but perfectly functional.

14. In Track View, find the keyframes for the tornado Path controller. Right-click on the key dot at frame 100 to bring up the keyframe information.

15. Change the value for that key to 0. This simple trick effectively disables the Path controller, enabling you to study the output of the Expression controller in isolation (see fig. 18.5).

FIGURE 18.5

The output of the four-leaved Rose curve Position Expression.

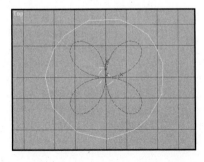

The expression used to create the meandering behavior in this example is a curve known to mathematicians as the Four-leaved Rose curve. In the polar coordinate system (r, theta), it is described by the equation r = a*sin(2*theta). Conversion to the Cartesian coordinate system (x, y, z) is achieved by substituting this for r in the following equations for x and y:

x = r*cos(theta) = a*sin(2*theta)*cos(theta)

y = r*sin(theta) = a*sin(2*theta)*sin(theta)

These equations provide an easy mechanism for determining both x and y position given an angle, theta. Spinning the value of theta from 0 around to 360 traces out the curve in x and y. To vary theta in this manner, borrow from the lessons of the first example, replacing theta with 360*Repeat*NT, to create the following equations:

x = a*sin(2*360*Repeat*NT) *cos(360*Repeat*NT)

y = a*sin(2*360*Repeat*NT)*sin(360*Repeat*NT)

Notice that the first two terms of each expression are the same. Put this into vector format for the Position expression, collecting those shared terms and replacing the variable name *a* with *Radius*, a more fitting description:

Radius*sin(2*360*Repeat*NT)*

[

    cos(360*Repeat*NT),

    sin(360*Repeat*NT),

    0

]

You can pull shared terms outside of the vector without error because of the distributive property of multiplication. In evaluating this expression, MAX multiplies each term of the position vector by the scalar.

As a final experiment, you might want to try replacing the 2 in the first sin() function with other values to vary the number of leaves in the pattern. Any even integer value *n* produces a rose with *2n* leaves. Odd values create roses with *n* leaves. Non-integer values have unpredictable results. Also, try changing that entire sin() function with a cos() to rotate the pattern 45 degrees. See figure 18.6 for an example of an alternate Rose Curve.

FIGURE 18.6
The output of an eight-leaved cosine Rose curve.

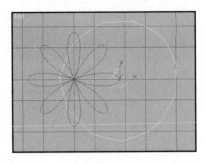

The equation for this and other useful curves can be found in most Analytic Geometry texts and mathematical handbooks.

Adding Wobble

The animation is looking much better now, but it still lacks some character. You need to add some wobbling and teetering action to give it that out-of-control look. This requires a pair of expressions for the X and Y rotation that are similar in nature, yet out of sync enough to complement the crisscrossing pattern of the Position Expression.

WOBBLING AND TEETERING

1. If you have not already done so, close the Position Expression Properties dialog and change the Path Position percentage key back to 100 percent.

2. Assign Float Expression controllers to the X and Y Rotation tracks of the tornado model.

3. In the X Rotation Expression Properties dialog, load xrot.xpr from the accompanying CD. Assign a value of 5 to MaxXAngle and a value of 2 to Repeat.

The scalar expression defined by xrot.xpr is similar in some ways to the others used in this example, with a few new twists:

degToRad(sin(Repeat*360*NT)*MaxXAngle)

Again, you are using NT to drive the animation through a repeating sine wave. This time the variable MaxXAngle is your goal and the maximum value for the expression. *degToRad* is a function that MAX supports for converting from degrees to radians as required by the Euler XYZ controller. It is the equivalent of multiplying the value by pi/180.

4. In the Y Rotation Expression Properties dialog, load yrot.xpr from the accompanying CD. Assign a value of 8 to MaxYAngle and a value of 1 to Repeat.

The yrot.xpr expression is the cosine version of xrot.xpr to make its rotation out of sync:

degToRad(cos(Repeat*360*NT)*MaxXAngle)+pi

pi is added to keep the tornado upright.

Before you play the animation, take a minute to view the function curve output of these expressions.

5. Click on the Function Curves icon in the Track View toolbar.

6. Select the X Rotation: Float Expression track label to show its output in the Function Curve display.

7. With the Shift key depressed, select the Y Rotation: Float Expression track label to add its output to the Function Curve display (see fig. 18.7).

FIGURE 18.7

Using Function Curves with Rotation Expressions.

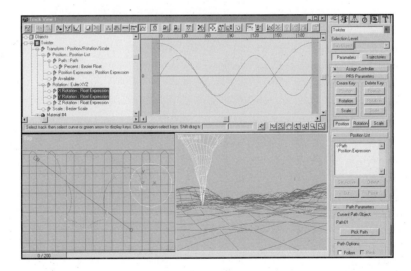

TIP

The Function Curves display is another excellent tool for visualizing your work as you develop, modify, and debug expressions.

The various properties of the X and Y rotation expressions are clearly visible in the Function Curve display, including MaxAngle, Repeat, and the phase difference between sine and cosine functions.

   8. Play the animation in the Camera viewport.

You have come a long way from the original scene. With a group of four relatively simple expressions, you created a convincing behavior that can be used with any path- or key-based animation. As a test of that claim, make one last change to this animation.

   9. Save the project.

   10. Unhide Line02.

   11. Select the tornado object and go to the Motion Panel.

   12. Click on Pick Path and select Line02.

   13. Play the new animation.

FIGURE 18.8
The finished twister.

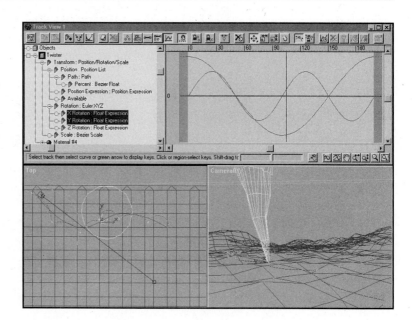

NOTE

Internally, all 3DS MAX Rotation controllers represent the orientation of an object with quaternion math. Developed in the 1840s by Sir William Hamilton, *quaternions* allow for smooth interpolation of rotation values that is impossible with the separate X, Y, and Z rotations required by a matrix solution. Additionally, quaternion interpolation schemes result in more direct, natural, and predictable motions. The output of these controllers consists of four components: a three-component unit vector and a scalar rotation value. Together these describe the orientation of the object in quaternion format for the parent PRS Compound controller.

Remember that expressions recognize (and therefore output) only scalar and vector data types. Because they do not support quaternion data types, you are forced to use Float Expressions in the Rotation tracks of a Euler XYZ controller.

The Euler XYZ controller is a List controller that converts the output of three unique Float controllers into their quaternion equivalent. This approach enables users to work with familiar X, Y, and Z rotations individually without losing the many hidden benefits of quaternion math.

Although it is easy to comprehend the physical significance of the X, Y, and Z float components of a Euler controller, the four-dimensional output of a Quaternion controller is extremely difficult to visualize. Because of this, most of the Rotation controllers that ship with MAX do not support the Function Curves display of Track View. This makes the Euler XYZ controller unique and powerful.

It is not hard to imagine the applications for this kind of flexibility in a production environment. Imagine yourself tasked with animating a tornado in several different shots for a blockbuster feature film with tight deadlines. After making the initial time investment to develop these controllers, a lot of the work is done for you. You finish on time with better effects (because you had more time to focus on them), and you are really looking forward to working on the sequel!

Control Objects and Modifier Animation

In addition to their proven utility in controlling transform animations, expressions are a very powerful tool for animating the parameters of all imaginable modifiers. Imagine creating a simple expression to relate the mix amount of a blush texture map to the bend angle of a smile. How about decreasing the density of a mesh as it moves away from the camera by automatically varying the parameters of an Optimize modifier?

Any effect that can be achieved by animating the parameters of a MAX modifier can be controlled mathematically with an Expression controller. Many secondary motion effects such as bouncing bellies and bending hair can be realistically achieved with a well-placed modifier and a few simple expressions. You can make the belly of a jovial character jiggle by animating the strength of a Displace modifier with an expression tied to Position track of his center of mass.

Another, often overlooked application of expressions is the creation of Controller objects. A *Controller object* is an object created to provide the user a physical input mechanism to an expression or system of expressions. By creating groups of virtual knobs, levers, and sliders and assigning their transformations to expression variables, users can tackle complicated gestures with relative ease.

Imagine creating a virtual lighting panel for controlling complicated systems of animated lights. How about animating the gestures of your next character with a few sliders with labels such as smile and frown? This is the kind of approach that Pixar animators used when creating and controlling AVARS (Animation Variables) for *Toy Story*.

The Whirlygig Project

In the following series of examples, you create a set of expressions controlled by the position of a Control object. By moving that object in the scene, you control the animation of the Fantastic Whirlygig carnival ride.

Start by loading the project and having a look around. Load the file whirl.max and play the animation in the shaded Camera viewport (see fig. 18.9).

FIGURE 18.9

The Fantastic Whirlygig project.

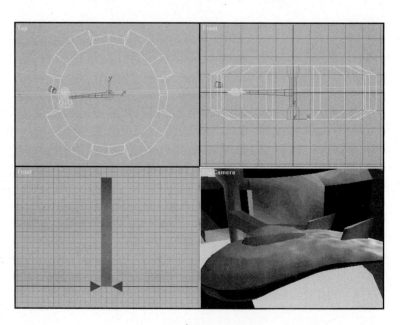

Creating a Control Object

First, you need to create the expression and assignments necessary to control the vehicle's rotation with another object in the scene.

CONTROLLING VEHICLE ROTATION

1. With the whirl.max file open, open Track View.

2. Right-click on Objects and select Expand Objects. Right-click again to expand Tracks.

3. Click on Filters in the toolbar and activate Show Only Animated Tracks and Show Controller Types.

TIP

This combination of filters is a quick way to isolate the animation data in complex or unfamiliar scenes.

4. Right-click on the Z Rotation range bar and bring up the Properties dialog for that Float Expression.

As you can see, you are using the standard expression for object rotation, as developed in the previous set of examples. What you need to do is alter it so that Repeat can be driven by the position of another object in the scene. Because variables can only be assigned to controllers of the same data type, you must create a new vector variable.

5. Select Repeat in the list of scalar variables and click on Delete.

6. Type **Repeat** in the Variable Name edit box, choose Vector, and click on Create to define the new, improved vector variable.

7. Assign Repeat to the Position controller of Pointer.

8. Edit the Expression, changing –Repeat to –Repeat.z.

By appending ".z" to the Repeat variable, you specify that only the z component of the vector should be used in the expression. To correspond with the MAX World coordinate system, z was chosen.

9. Click on Evaluate and play the animation in the Camera view.

Nothing happens! This is because the default position of the Controller object is on the Z axis, so –Repeat.z = 0 and the entire rotation expression zeros out.

10. Change the bottom-left viewport to a Front view. Select Pointer and Bar and perform a Zoom Extents Selected.

11. Deselect the bar, and activate Select and Move. With Snap on, move Pointer up in Y by three snaps (30 units). Check your results with figure 18.10.

12. Play the animation in the Camera view.

Even at this low setting, the car is spinning too quickly. You need to find some way to scale the input of the expression.

FIGURE 18.10

Animating the Pointer Control object.

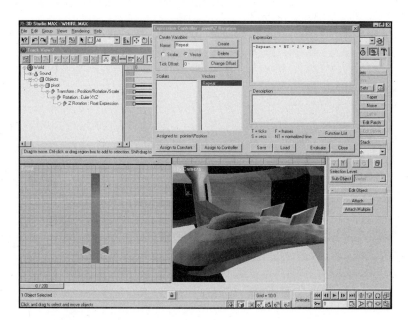

13. Edit the expression to include a scale factor on the Z component of Repeat: –Repeat.z/50*NT*2*pi. Click on Evaluate and play the animation in the Camera viewport. Close the Properties dialog.

Take a moment to think about what is going on here. In this expression, the term –Repeat.z/50 again determines the number of complete rotations or "laps" that your car will make during the course of the animation. At the pointer's current position, Repeat.z has the value of 30—3 snaps on a 10 unit grid. The car will therefore spin 30÷50 or 60 percent of one full lap in the 200 frame animation.

Before adding the scale factor, each click of the pointer increased the vehicle speed by three complete revolutions per second! By dividing –Repeat.z by 50, you desensitized the controls, providing the user much smoother input and cleaner control of the animation.

Animating with Control Objects

Now that you have a means of controlling the rotation of the vehicle, try setting some position keys for the Pointer object to animate the spin-up of the ride.

ANIMATING THE SPIN

1. With the Pointer object at its minimum position on the bar, click on Animate. Go to frame 70 and move the pointer up 3 clicks to 30.

2. Jump to frame 100 and slide the pointer up 3 more clicks to 60.

3. Add another key at frame 130 by sliding the pointer up 6 more clicks to 120.

4. Add one last key at frame 200 with a value of 120. Turn off Animate.

5. Play the animation in the Camera viewport.

The car smoothly accelerates until around frame 160, when it reverses direction for the final second of animation. What is going on here? The keyframes you defined for the animation of the Pointer Control object would not seem to account for any deceleration, let alone backward travel. Take a look at the function curves to get a better idea of what is going on.

6. Bring up Track View and find the pointer position keys you just created. Click on the Function Curves icon and select the pointer Position track to display its profile.

7. Pan up in the Track View list panel to find the arm Z Rotation track. With the Ctrl key depressed, click on the Z Rotation track to add its output to the function curve display.

8. Zoom Horizontal and Value Extents to see the entire animation (see fig. 18.11).

FIGURE 18.11

Troubleshooting with function curves.

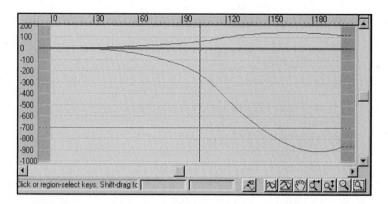

The top blue curve is the position of the Pointer Object, the lower green curve is the rotation of the arm. As you can see, the green rotation curve is decreasing throughout the animation until a point near frame 180, where it clearly reverses direction.

Looking at the blue pointer position curve, you can see the problem. Because of the nature of Bézier controllers, the Pointer Control object does not immediately level off following the key at frame 130. Instead, it overshoots that key and smoothly turns to the final key at frame 200.

Although it may be very comfortable to think of the Pointer object as a gas pedal that directly controls the angular velocity of the arm, it does not actually work that way. Changes in the position of the Pointer object are directly proportional to changes in the position of the arm at any frame.

By animating the position of the pointer upward, you create the impression of acceleration by forcing the arm to catch up with an ever-increasing "total twist" factor.

9. Click on the blue pointer position curve to display its key information dots.

10. Select the key at frame 200 and right-click to display its key information dialog. Change the Z value to 160.

11. Open the In tangent flyout and select the Slow tangent type.

12. Add a key at frame 170 with a Z value of 160. Set the In and Out tangents to Slow. The position curve should now slope smoothly up to this key and flatten out (see fig. 18.12). Play the animation in the Camera viewport.

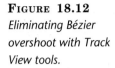

FIGURE 18.12

Eliminating Bézier overshoot with Track View tools.

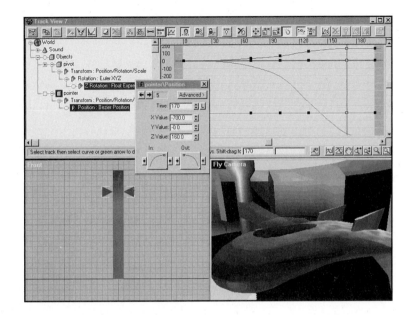

Parametric Modifier Animation

In all the previous examples, you have seen how expressions can be used to create object transform animations. Expressions can also be used to define the numeric creation parameters of an object as well as any modifiers applied to it. This gives users a very unique and powerful tool for animating the geometry in their projects.

In your example, it would be nice to see the support arm bend as the vehicle accelerates. With Expression controllers, it is simple enough to relate that bend angle to the position of the Control object defined in the preceding example.

BENDING THE SUPPORT ARM

1. Select the Arm and Car objects in the Top view. Maximize the Top view and go to frame zero of the animation.

2. Go to the Modify Command panel and apply a Bend modifier to the two selected objects.

3. Activate Sub-Object Selection mode and choose Center to edit the position of the Bend Gizmo Center. Activate the Snap mode.

4. In the Top view, move the Gizmo Center –190 in X to near the World Coordinate Center (0,0,0). This centers the Bend effect at the pivot point of the support arm.

5. Set the Bend Axis to X and the Direction to 270. Spin the Bend Angle up and down to see the effect. The arm bends back and forth about the center of rotation. Unfortunately, the bend is deforming the car as well. Limit the Bend effect to avoid this undesirable effect.

6. Click on Limit Effect at the bottom of the Bend rollup and set the Upper Limit to 268, the length of the arm (see fig. 18.13). Test the Bend effect to see that the car is no longer distorted. Click on Min/Max Toggle to restore the viewports.

FIGURE 18.13
Setting up the bend modifier.

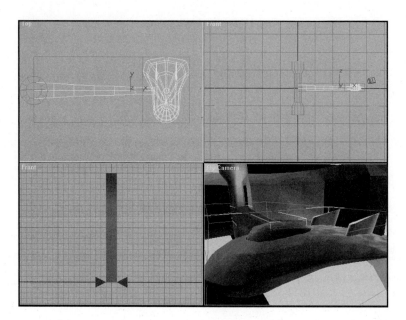

7. Open Track View and expand the arm hierarchy for the Bend modifier. Select the Bend Angle track.

NOTE

The Bend Angle track is one of many that begins life in MAX with no assigned controller. Unlike the Gizmo Position track above it, which has been assigned a standard PRS controller, the Angle track shows no assigned controller type.

To reduce memory usage in MAX, many tracks that can be animated do not have a controller assigned at the time of their creation. This normally has no impact on the animator because an appropriate controller automatically attaches whenever keys for the track are generated.

The main opportunity for this to cause confusion is when assigning Expression controller variables to the output of a track that is not animated. If you wanted to create an expression for the rotation of a wheel based on its radius, for example, you might create a Scalar Variable named Radius and attempt to assign it to the Radius track of the Wheel object. Because the Wheel object radius is unlikely to be animated, that track will be ghosted (grayed out) in the Track View Pick dialog when you try to create the assignment. MAX allows only variables to be tied to tracks that have been assigned controllers. Tracks such as Bend Angle have to be manually assigned a controller in Track View before they can be attached to an expression variable.

8. Assign a Float Expression to the Bend Angle, open the Expression Properties dialog, and create a vector variable named Repeat.

9. Assign Repeat to the Position track of the Control object Pointer.

10. Enter the following equation: **Repeat.z/10**. This causes the arm to bend one degree with each snap (10 units) of the Control object.

11. Find the Car object in Track View. Click on the square plus box to the right of the arm object to show the objects linked to it, including the car.

12. Expand the Car object hierarchy and locate the Angle track of its Bend modifier. As you can see, the Float Expression you just created for the arm Bend Angle track has been assigned here as well. Magic? No. Recall that when you first applied the Bend modifier, both arm and car were selected. Whenever modifiers are applied to multiple selected objects in MAX, the result is instanced for all objects. Any changes that you make to the Bend Float Expression therefore automatically affect both objects!

13. Test the new expression by moving the Pointer Control object up and down in the Front view. If all is well, play the animation in the Camera viewport (see fig. 18.14).

Now add one last expression to keep the camera pointed at the action.

14. Expand the camera hierarchy. Assign a Euler XYZ controller to the camera rotation.

15. Assign a Float Expression controller to the Z Rotation track of the Euler XYZ controller.

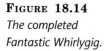

FIGURE 18.14
*The completed
Fantastic Whirlygig.*

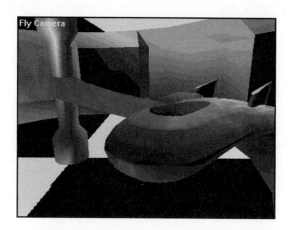

16. Open the new Expression Controller dialog and create a vector variable named Repeat.

17. Edit the expression to take into account the arm bend: $1.17302 - (Repeat.z/1500)$.

18. Play the animation in the Camera viewport.

For one last trick, unhide the Counter group in the Whirlygig scene and play the animation in the Front viewport. A pair of expressions has been used to provide a real-time readout of the pointer position.

The Counter group is made up of four objects: one object for each digit and a controller object. A unique Material modifier has been applied to each of the objects, and a Multi/Sub-Object Material called *Digits* has been assigned to the group. The Digits material is comprised of 10 standard materials, one material for each digit bitmap 0–9. By animating the Material ID track of the Material modifier on each Counter object, the digits animate, creating the effect of a numeric counter.

The Material ID track of the Counter Controller object holds the Z component of the pointer position controller. The expression used by each Counter object references that value, which is decomposed with floor and mod functions to provide the appropriate digit. Take some time to study this simple but well-designed set of expressions—it points to yet another powerful area of application for this impressive tool.

In this example you have used Expressions to animate object transforms (rotation in this case), the parameters of an object modifier, and the Material ID assigned to an object. It isn't difficult to appreciate the power of Expressions. With careful planning, they can be used to help you work more efficiently and generate better results.

In Practice: Animating with Expressions

- **Animated Variables.** Before a variable can be assigned to the output of other tracks in a scene, those tracks must have an Animation controller assigned.

- **Rotation Expressions.** Euler XYZ controllers must be used on objects whose rotations will be animated with expressions. A Float Expression controller is then assigned as desired to each of the independent X, Y, and Z tracks.

- **Animated Expressions.** For an expression to produce an animated effect, it must be driven by the output of another animated track or by one of the animated MAX reserved variables (T, S, F, or NT). Additionally, animated expressions can be created using the noise (p,q,r) function.

- **Clean Code.** Use white-space in your expressions to keep things clear and legible. Also, make use of the Description field to keep usage notes and suggested values for user-defined variables in your expressions, because variable assignments are not saved with the expression.

- **Trajectories and Function Curves.** These two visualization tools are invaluable to Expression controller users. Both provide direct and very useful visual feedback of the output of your functions for verification and troubleshooting.

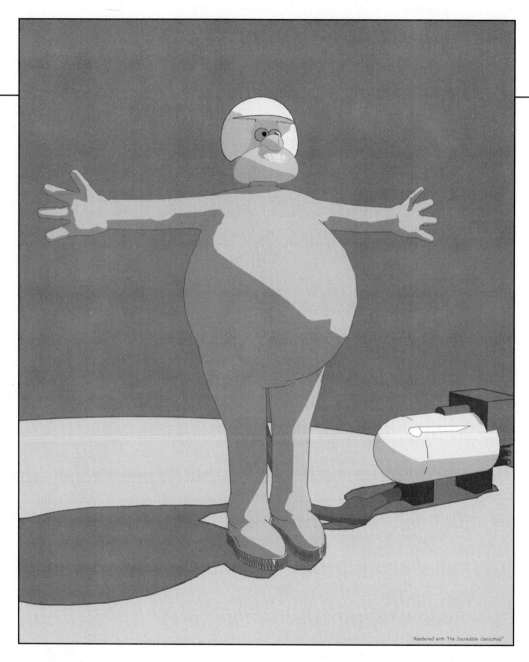

Rendered with The Incredible Comicshop™

IMAGE CREATED BY DAN O'LEARY

Chapter 19

by Dan O'Leary

ANIMATING WITH MULTIPLE MODIFIERS

Modifiers in 3D Studio MAX give users the ability to deform and enhance geometry without these alterations being carved in stone. Changes in a model's appearance can be broken up into any number of separate "modifiers" that can be deactivated, deleted, or have their parameters changed at any time. These parameters can also be animated. Apply a Taper modifier and animate the object going to a point. Apply on top of that a Bend modifier and animate the object bending as it points. Days could be spent creating abstract animations where every available parameter of an object and its deforms are animated.

Modifiers can be used in this way—where the changes they make to your geometry are the focus of your animation. But more often, they are useful for more subtle effects, enhancing the action taking place rather than directing it. This chapter uses modifiers both as a means to perform broad changes to your geometry as well as a tool for embellishing your scene. This chapter explores the following topics:

- Animating Object modifier parameters

- Using Object modifiers for global animated effects

- Using Object modifiers for subtle animated effects

- Using objects to affect sub-object selections (linked XForm)

Animating Object Modifier Parameters

Modifier animation can start at the most elementary level—the basic parameters that make up an object. A cylinder can have its measurements change over time or have its number of sides and segments increase or decrease as the view gets closer or farther away.

Beyond animation of a primitive object's creation parameters are the Standard modifiers. Bends, Twists, Skews, and so on can have their respective angles, strengths, directions, and so forth, animated, as well as animating the gizmo that controls where and how the modification is made.

To illustrate some examples of using multiple modifiers in animation, you will experiment on a simple character affectionately named Henry. For the purpose of these animations, Henry is basically like a test pilot of old. A model such as Henry should make an interesting and enjoyable subject on which to try out some modifications. Initially, some tortuous ideas came to mind, some of which you'll explore. But also keep in mind the power of using modifiers for less extreme examples.

Air Pump Project

This first scene contains the Henry Editable Mesh, an air hose made up of a Loft object, and a simple pump model (see fig. 19.1). You will start by performing some modifications to the character model.

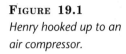

FIGURE 19.1

Henry hooked up to an air compressor.

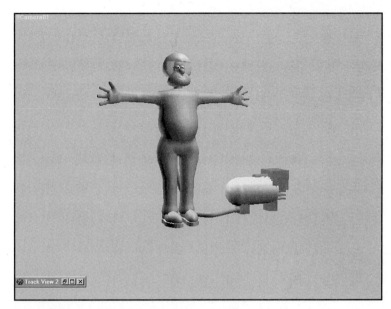

Before you start, open wpumpedcomic.avi from the accompanying CD-ROM to view the final animation to get an idea of what you are going to do.

Pumped Up—Using Displace

Displace, both as a modifier and as a space warp, is commonly used in conjunction with a bitmap, where the luminance values in the image determine the severity of the displacement. In this way, it is an excellent tool for creating effects such as surface detail and terrain. Displace can also be used alone as a force that acts on the geometry. The Displace gizmo can be animated, and so can the settings of Strength and Decay that control it. The effect can be as gentle as a dent or bulge on the surface of an object or as extreme as the inflating of a character with an air compressor.

1. From the accompanying CD-ROM, load wpumped.max.

2. Select Henry Body and open the Modify panel.

3. Add a Displace modifier to the stack. You may have to click on More under modifiers to locate Displace.

4. Open the Edit Stack dialog and click on Displace.

5. In the Name field, add the word **Body** at the end of Displace and click on OK.

6. Change the Mapping parameter from Planar to Spherical.

7. Select the Displace gizmo as your sub-object.

8. Uniform Scale the gizmo 60 percent.

9. Move the gizmo to the center of the torso, just below the chest and above the stomach, making certain to check other views to see whether it is centered (see fig. 19.2).

FIGURE 19.2

Centering the Displace gizmo for the torso-swelling effect.

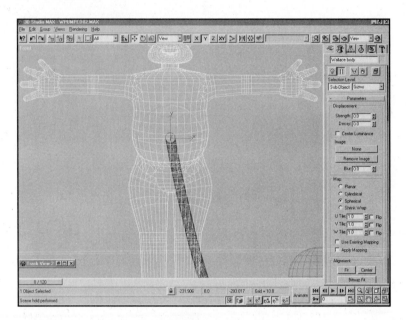

The size of the gizmo ultimately affects the shape to which the stomach will balloon. For the nice round ball effect, it is best to make the gizmo fit just inside the stomach area. A smaller gizmo would result in an oddly elongated displacement; a larger one would carry the displacement too far into the legs and chest. With the gizmo at the proper size, see how things look by performing the following steps:

1. Slide the Strength slider up and down to see the effect, stopping around 5.

The Displace is spreading out too much and scaling the entire body. You want to localize the effect more so that there is less stretching overall.

2. Slide the Decay slider slowly up, stopping around 0.8.

The feet and head stay about where they are; the stomach and chest balloon outward. That's more like it (see fig. 19.3).

FIGURE 19.3

Adjusting the Displace.

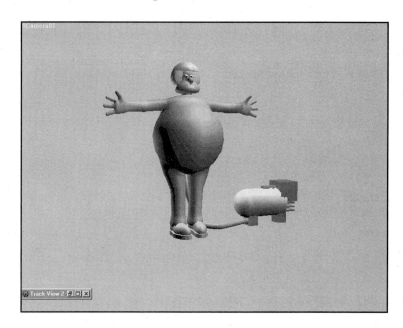

Animating Stomach Pump

Now that you have your first modifier in place, you need to set some keyframes for the inflation. To set the keyframes, perform the following steps:

1. Return the Strength slider to 0, keeping Decay at 0.8.

2. Turn on the Animate button and go to frame 30.

3. Slide the Strength slider to around 8.

4. Go to frame 60.

5. Slide the Strength slider to around 15.

6. Go to frame 90.

7. Slide the Strength slider to around 20. Now you have the beginnings of the pump effect.

8. Save your scene as **mypump01.max** and render out a Smooth + Highlights preview of the Camera01 viewport, frames 0–90.

Not bad, but instead of a steady inflation, make it look more like the pumping is happening in three stages. To do this, set a lag time in between frames, so the effect swells, pauses, swells again, and so on.

9. Open the Track View.

10. Right-click on the Filters button and filter out everything but Animated Tracks, Transforms, Modified Objects, and Base Objects.

TIP

Because these track types are all that you will be animating in this tutorial, you can hide things such as Materials and Maps tracks so that they don't clutter your view. In a scene with as few objects as this, it doesn't matter much, but later on it can make a big difference, and you can save yourself a lot of time scrolling through hierarchies.

Now, add some easing in and out to the pumping keys.

1. Find the Displace Strength controller from the hierarchy list.

2. Select the Strength controller (by clicking on the name in the hierarchy) and open its function curve.

3. Select the spline. The four keys from 0–90 appear at a steady slope.

4. Select Edit Keys from the toolbar to go back to the Range and Animation tracks.

5. Holding the Shift key, select the key at frame 30 and drag a copy to frame 35.

6. Do the same for frames 60 and 90, offsetting a copy of each five frames.

This creates a lag between each phase of pumping. To smooth things out, perform the following steps:

7. Open the function curve for Strength.

The curve now has a slight stair-stepping effect (see fig. 19.4).

8. Open the Properties dialog for keyframe 30 by right-clicking on the key.

9. Select the Custom Tangent type (last one in the pull down) for the In (this automatically changes the Out to a Custom Tangent as well).

10. Repeat steps 8 and 9 for frames 60 and 90.

FIGURE 19.4

*The function curve now
has extra frames,
creating a pause each
time the curve levels off.*

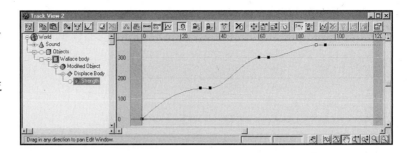

11. Now go back and region-zoom in on frames 30 and 35.

12. Adjust the custom tangent handle, pulling it down to make a shallow dip
    (see fig. 19.5).

FIGURE 19.5

*Easing around the
swelling keyframes.*

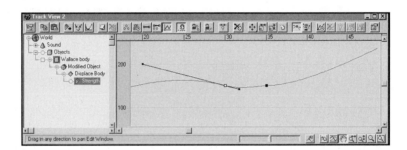

NOTE

If you can't see the tangent handles, make certain that the Show Tangents button on the toolbar
is on.

13. Repeat steps 11 and 12 for frames 60 and 90, adjusting the tangent for
    each so that the In rises gently while the Out slopes down.

14. Minimize the Track View and make another preview of the Camera01
    viewport, frames 0–90, saving your scene before you do.

TIP

To avoid having to set the filters every time, try minimizing the Track View rather than closing
it completely. Sometimes it is easy to forget that you have a Track View already open (especially
when it is tucked away at the bottom of the screen), and you will end up opening a new one even
though the other one is still minimized. I like to move the minimized Track View up into the
corner of the viewport while animating, so it is less easy to forget about it.

The body swells and pauses as if being inflated by multiple pushes of a bicycle pump. This effect may not be entirely accurate when taking into consideration that the character is being inflated by a mechanical compressor that would supply an even flow. For something this "cartoony" in nature, however, it is sometimes best to illustrate the stereotypical effect rather than the physical reality. Open wpumped.avi from the accompanying CD to see this effect.

Now keeping in the cartoony scheme of things, inflate Henry's head in a similar fashion.

1. Go to frame 0.

2. Select Henry Body and open the Modify panel.

3. Add a second Displace modifier to the stack.

4. This time rename Displace to **Displace Head** in the Edit Stack dialog.

5. Change the Mapping parameter from Planar to Spherical.

6. Select the Displace gizmo as your sub-object.

7. Uniform Scale the gizmo 60 percent.

8. Move the gizmo to the middle of the head (check to make certain that it is centered).

9. Maximize your Track View and select Edit Keys from the toolbar.

To save some steps, copy the Strength keys from Displace Body and paste them onto Displace Head. Then you will adjust the keys so that the majority of the head ballooning happens at the end.

1. Turn off the Animated Objects Only filter so that you can see the tracks for Displace Head (because it currently has no keyframes).

2. Expand your window and scroll down until you can see the tracks for both Displace Body and Displace Head (you may need to expand the Displace Head tracks).

3. Select the Strength controller and click on Copy Controller.

4. Select the Strength controller for Displace Head and click on Paste Controller.

5. Make certain that Paste as Copy is selected rather than Instance (because you will be making changes to the head inflation that you don't want on the body displace).

You now have keys for Henry's head. If you render a preview now, you will see the head inflating to about the same size as the body, giving it a snowman look (see fig. 19.6). A preferred and suggested approach, however, sees the body inflate first, and then, when it almost reaches its capacity, the head swells up. To do this, you need to lower the values of the strength keys for the head.

FIGURE 19.6

The head swells as much as the body and looks a little too extreme.

1. Select the Strength controller for Displace Head in the Track View and look at its function curve. You see the stair-stepping slope from before.

2. Region select frames 30 and 35 and change the value in the Key Value field to 0.5.

3. Region-select frames 60 and 65 and change the value in the Key Value field to 1.5.

4. Region-select frames 90 and 95 and change the value in the Key Value field to 3.

5. Finally, flatten out the custom tangent curves by leveling off the handles for frames 30, 60, and 90 (see fig. 19.7). After all, you don't want as much shrinking and swelling of the head in between pumps.

FIGURE 19.7

Leveling off the ease curves for the Displace Head strength.

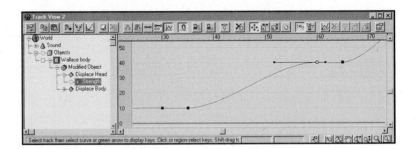

6. Save your scene and render out a Smooth + Highlights preview of the Camera01 viewport, frames 0–90.

Floating Henry—Using Linked XForm

Somewhere during this process, it would be nice to have Henry start to rise off the ground. This can be done simply enough by setting move keys, but Henry has an air hose attached to his back. Realistically this should stretch and follow any vertical movement you give him. This can again be done with modifiers.

The air hose is a Loft object, which means that its basic components (the loft shape and its path) can still be edited and, in this case, animated. For this example, you need the hose to remain connected to his back as he rises off the ground. You do this by selecting the end vertex of the spline that makes up the path for the Loft object and apply a Linked XForm modifier.

Linked XForm allows a sub-object selection (in this case a vertex of a spline) to be linked to another object in this scene. What you do is create a dummy object where the hose meets Henry's back, link the dummy to Henry, and link the end vertex to the dummy. The reason you link the hose to the dummy object and not directly to Henry himself is so that as he swells up, you can move the dummy back so that the hose doesn't pass through him.

1. Create a dummy at the point where the hose meets Henry's back (see fig. 19.8).

FIGURE 19.8

Creating a dummy object to help control the air hose spline.

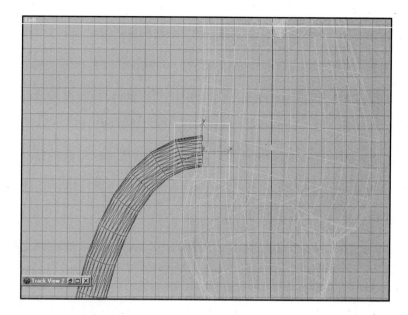

2. Link the dummy to Henry.

TIP

When using the various Select icons (select and move, link, rotate, and scale) it's easy to forget that these remain active until you select another, which is usually harmless. However when you're simply selecting objects to edit their parameters or tracks, having move, link, or rotate selected can cause you to perform an unwanted transform when you simply want to select something. It is a good habit to go back to the basic Select Object icon when you have finished your transforming or linking.

3. Select the Spline object at the center of the air hose loft (Line01).

4. In the Modify panel, apply an Edit Spline modifier to the spline.

5. Activate Sub-Object and select the end vertex where the hose meets the back.

6. Apply a Linked XForm modifier to the vertex sub-object.

7. Click on Pick Control Object and select Dummy01.

All set. Try selecting Henry and moving him around the viewport, undoing any moves you make by right-clicking before letting go of the mouse button or by pressing Undo. You will see the hose stretching to follow him. If you try the same thing from the top view, however, it looks like the hose should move more, especially in the middle where it curves. Because there happens to be a vertex in your path spline there, you can repeat the same Linked XForm technique to give it a little stretch.

1. Select the air hose spline (Line01) again.

2. Add another Edit Spline to the stack.

3. Find and select the middle vertex.

4. Apply a Linked XForm.

5. Create another dummy object centered on the middle vertex (see fig. 19.9).

FIGURE 19.9

Creating a second dummy object to affect the middle of the air hose loft.

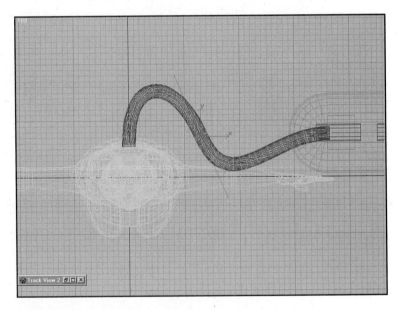

6. Click on Pick Control Object and select Dummy02.

By moving Dummy02 around, the middle of the air hose follows. Now you link Dummy02 to Dummy01.

7. Select Dummy02 and link it to Dummy01.

Moving Henry now moves both parts of the air hose as well, but the middle section doesn't look natural when it rises off the ground with him. You fix this by locking down the inherited links of Dummy02 so that it only slides along the ground.

8. Select Dummy02.

9. Open the Hierarchy panel and click on Link Info.

10. Deselect all the transforms except for Move along the Y axis.

This causes Dummy02 to inherit only translations along the Y axis from its parent, Dummy01. Try moving Henry around and you will see the middle slide along with him. Rotating him (your next step), however, is a different story. Before you do this, you disable the rotational inheritance for Dummy01.

1. Select Dummy01.

2. Open the Hierarchy panel and click on Link Info.

3. Deselect the X, Y, Z options for Rotation.

Now you can move and rotate Henry safely.

4. Go to frame 90 and turn on the Animate button.

5. Move Henry up and to the left about 20 units each.

6. Go to frame 120 and move Henry up and to the right about 15 units each (see fig. 19.10).

FIGURE 19.10
Only the inflated Henry floats upward.

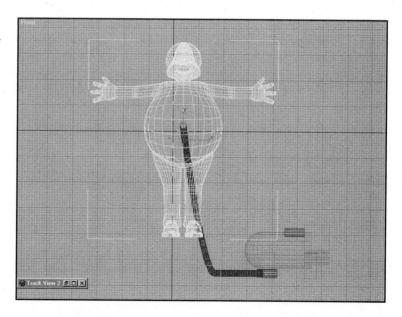

7. Maximize your Track View and find the position keys for Henry.

8. Move the key at frame 0 to frame 40.

9. Repeat step 6 for his X rotation key.

10. Minimize Track View and go to frame 70.

11. Rotate Henry 5 degrees.

12. Go to frame 100 and rotate Henry –20 degrees.

13. Go to frame 120 and rotate Henry –5 degrees.

14. Maximize your Track View and apply Ease Out controller curves to your first position and rotation keyframes and Ease In controller curves to your last.

15. Save your scene and render a Smooth + Highlights preview of the Camera01 viewport, frames 0–90.

That should do it for Henry.

Animating the Hose

You could add another touch to make things a bit more cartoony. How about some bulges pumping through the air hose? You could do this with more Displace modifiers, animating the gizmos along the path of the air hose, but a few steps in between would slow you down. Basically, a secondary object such as a dummy would have to be animated along the path and then that Position track copied to the Displace gizmo in the track view. Because the Displace space warp gives you the same effect and can be assigned a Path controller in one step, you can take the easy way out.

1. Create a Displace space warp from the Create panel about twice the width of the air hose at its base near the pump (see fig. 19.11).

2. Change the Strength to 1.0, the Decay to 0.8, and the Map to Spherical.

3. Bind the air hose to the Displace space warp.

Now to animate the bulge along the path of the hose, follow these steps:

4. Select the Displace space warp and open the Motion panel.

5. Under Parameters, open the Assign Controller rollout and select Position.

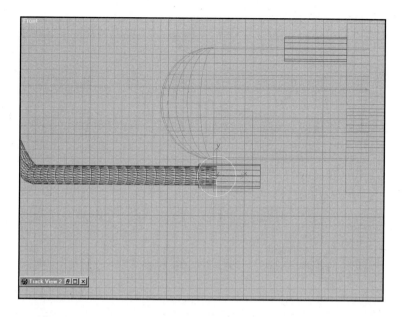

6. Click on the Assign Controller button and select Path. A new rollout entitled Path Parameters appears.

7. Click on Pick Path and choose the spline for the air hose Loft object.

8. Move the Time Slider back and forth to see the bulge's effect.

Now you set up the timing for the bulge. You will also animate the strength so that the effect builds as it comes from the pump and fades as it approaches the character.

9. Maximize your Track View.

10. Move the last Percent keyframe for the Displace space warp from 120 to 45 and click on the Percent heading in the Track Hierarchy.

11. Click on Parameter Curve Out-of-Range Type and select Constant for before the animated range (left arrow) and Loop for after the animated range (right arrow).

12. Minimize your Track View and select the Displace space warp.

13. Turn on the Animate button.

14. At frame 0, set the Displace space warp Strength to 0.

15. At frame 15 and frame 30, set the Strength to about 5.7.

16. Finally at frame 45, set the Strength back to 0.

17. Maximize your Track View.

18. Select Strength from the Displace hierarchy and open the function curve.

19. Apply Ease In and Ease Outs to your four keyframes.

20. Click on Parameter Curve Out-of-Range Type and select Constant for before the animated range (left arrow) and Loop for after the animated range (right arrow).

This creates one looping bulge pumping through the hose. To create a second trailing bulge, copy the first space warp and offset the keys.

1. Minimize your Track View and make a copy of the Displace space warp directly on top of the other.

2. Maximize your Track View and select Edit Keys and Slide Keys from the toolbar.

3. Offset the Percent and Strength keys for Displace02 forward 20 frames (see fig. 19.12).

FIGURE 19.12

Offsetting the timing for the second Displace space warp.

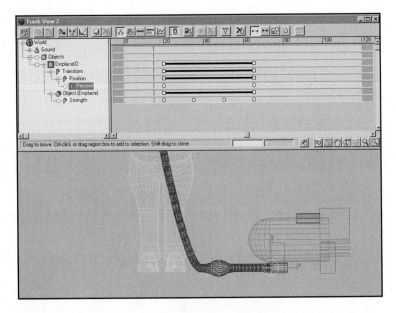

4. Minimize your Track View, save your scene, and render a Smooth + Highlights preview of the Camera01 viewport, frames 0–90.

That's about it. You can add some finishing touches such as moving the hose back as Henry's body swells. For the camera angle you're rendering, however, things work pretty well. A noise controller applied to the position or rotation path of the air pump could add that extra bit of detail. Or if you really want to get carried away, you could try detaching the hose and have Henry wiggle and deflate like a pierced balloon. Perhaps an animated Wave, Ripple, or Noise modifier alone or in conjunction would do the trick?

Magnetic Boots Project

The last test was a bit hard on Henry, so for this next scene you will be a little more easy on him. This time he will be trying out a pair of magnetic boots in a wind tunnel experiment.

FIGURE 19.13
Henry ready for the next test.

Open wbootscomic.avi from the accompanying CD and view the final animation.

Starting the Reaction

In the AVI, Henry appears in his latest predicament. A blowing fan blows in his face, his eyes squint, his mouth closes, and his clothes ripple in the wind. Eventually the force becomes too strong, and he bends over backward. To make things somewhat more exaggerated, he begins to stretch off into the distance.

For a final production animation, you would ideally have some arm and head motion added for extra character, but that would involve a skin deformation program, such as Physique, which might not be available to everyone. Instead, everything you see here was done with simple transforms and modifier animation.

First you start with Henry's basic reaction to the fan. The wind is just starting to pick up in the first 30 frames, so start by squinting his eyes. Henry has what might be referred to as "cheap" eyelids. They are basically a pair of squashed torii that have a slightly larger radius than the eye itself. The closing of the lids is performed by changing the Slice From and Slice To values in the basic parameters of the object. These parameters can also be animated.

1. Load wboots.max from the CD-ROM. Switch to the Left viewport and zoom in on Henry's eyes.

2. Select either eyelid object (W Eye L or W Eye R, which are instances of each other and will animate in tandem).

3. Activate the Animate button and go to frame 30.

4. In the Modify Panel, change the Slice From value to 270 degrees and the Slice To value to –90 (see fig. 19.14).

Now that the eyelids are set to close from frame 0 to frame 30, add a quick blink in the beginning for a more natural feel.

1. Select one of the eyelids and open the Track View.

2. Set the filters to Animated Tracks Selected Objects Only.

3. Expand the eyelid tracks and open the Function Curve for Slice To.

4. While holding the shift key, drag a copy of the keyframe at frame 30 to frame 10, making sure the value remains at –90 degrees.

The Slice To and From is touchy because crossing over 360 degrees will cause the object to fold back in on itself and start the slicing from scratch.

5. Select all keys in the Function Curve for Slice To and change the Tangent Type for In and Out to Linear.

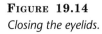

FIGURE 19.14

Closing the eyelids.

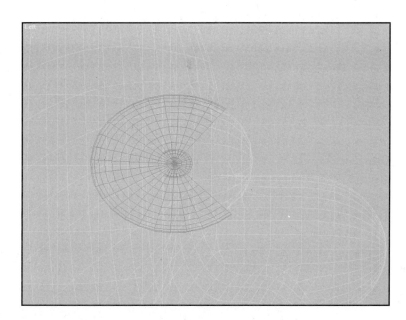

6. Copy the keyframe for frame 0 to frame 8, making certain that the value remains at –37.50.

7. Copy that same key (frame 8) to frame 11, again making certain that the value doesn't change.

8. Switch to the Function Curve for Step From.

9. Copy the keyframe for frame 30 to frame 10, making certain that the value remains at 270.

10. Select all keys in the Function Curve and change the Tangent Type for In and Out to Linear.

11. Copy the keyframe for frame 0 to frame 8, making certain that the value remains at 222.50.

12. Copy that same key (frame 8) to frame 11, again making certain that the value doesn't change.

13. Minimize the Track View and slowly scroll through the first 30 frames.

14. Save your scene as **myboot01.max**.

Simple enough. If you want to add a little flutter to the eyelids as they close, go ahead and copy around the extra keyframes in the function curves. Next you add a Free Form Deformation lattice to the mouth for some extra effect.

Free Form deformations were new to 3D Studio MAX R1.1. They enable you to affect an entire object or a sub-selection of vertices. The deformation is controlled by a set of control points that form a lattice around the object or selection. The selected geometry within the volume of the lattice is influenced by the changing positions of the control points. The effect is similar to that of deforming a spline object. This is great for regular Mesh objects because moving vertices around can often have very jagged and undesirable results. For Henry, you select the vertices of the mouth and apply a Free Form Deformation modifier to this sub-selection.

1. Select Henry Body and zoom in on the mouth in the left window.

2. In the Modify panel, set the selection level to Sub-Object Vertex.

3. Select the vertices of the teeth and the general area surrounding the mouth (see fig. 19.15).

FIGURE 19.15
Selecting the vertices surrounding the mouth.

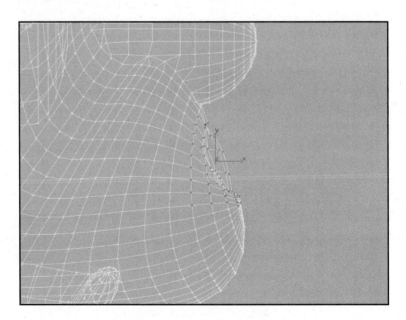

You don't have to worry about being too exact at this point because you can always change the sub-selection later.

4. Add a 4×4×4 Free Form Deformation modifier.

5. Switch to a Front viewport and zoom in on the mouth.

6. Activate Sub-Object Control Points in the Modify panel and region-select the two inside rows of control points (see fig. 19.16).

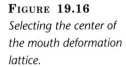

FIGURE 19.16
Selecting the center of the mouth deformation lattice.

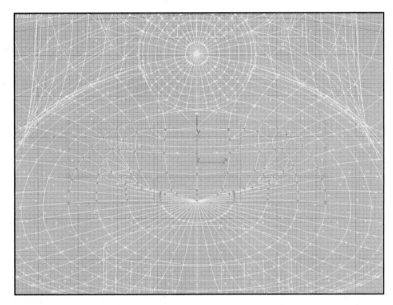

Select Non-uniform Scale and try sizing the center control points up and down, right-clicking at the end to undo the changes. Change your axis to Y and see how the effect is spread throughout the lattice—full intensity in the center and tapering off to the unselected edges. For this exercise, you scale the mouth down to give Henry a bit of a grimace as the wind picks up. True, his teeth are being squashed unnaturally, but the camera is far enough away and, after all, this is a cartoon.

Now set a single keyframe for the mouth at frame 30.

1. Turn on the Animate button and move to frame 30.

2. With the Y axis selected, non-uniform scale the two inside rows of control points about 40 percent. Too little will be unnoticeable and too much will stretch the surroundings too much.

3. Save your scene as myboot01.max and render a Smooth + Highlights preview of the Camera01 viewport, frames 0–30.

Previews are somewhat sketchy, so you might have to render at a higher resolution to make out what's going on. So far you have only animated basic nuances, but don't worry. Things will get a bit more interesting.

Windy City—Using the Noise Modifier

Now that you have Henry's facial reaction set, what about the rest of his body? Ideally his jumpsuit would ripple from the effects of the fan. A simple Noise modifier provides just that sort of chaotic feel.

The Noise modifier is often used to create basic terrain models or enhance existing topography. It is also handy for adding a subtle roughness to surfaces where a bump map just isn't enough. In this case, you apply an animated noise to Henry's suit. It is a more random effect than ripple or wave, which is just what is needed for this example.

1. Switch to the Front viewport and zoom out to view the entire body.

2. Apply an Edit Mesh modifier to the Henry Body object.

3. Select Sub-Object Vertex and region-select all vertices except for the hands, head, and boots (see fig. 19.17).

FIGURE 19.17

Isolating the noise effect.

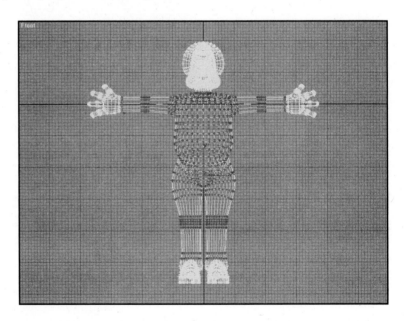

4. Apply a Noise modifier.

5. Set the Scale to 10 and Y Strength to 10.

6. Click on Animated Noise and render a Smooth + Highlights preview of the Camera01 viewport, frames 0–30.

Well, it is doing something. Rather than a wind tunnel, however, it looks as if he's more underwater than anything. This slow crawl of noise results from the low frequency setting.

7.   Raise the frequency to 4 and re-render the preview.

That's better. Notice that you did not touch some options, such as the X and Z strengths and fractal noise. Displacing the geometry in Y was sufficient to achieve the desired effect. Adding X and/or Z on top of that would be overdoing things. Also fractal noise (which produces more jagged results) seems inappropriate. Feel free to play with some of these settings before moving on to see whether you agree.

Weak at the Knees—Using Edit Mesh, Bend, and Skew

So far you have been pretty easy on Henry, so it's time to turn things up a notch. What you have so far indicates a windy environment, but you need some additional modifier help to make things more extreme.

1.   Save your scene as **myboot01.max**.

2.   Apply an Edit Mesh modifier to the Henry Body object and deselect Sub-Object.

3.   Select Henry Body and both eyelid objects.

TIP

At this point, you might want to make a named selection set of Henry and his eyelid objects. Selection sets are a great tool for keeping track of groups of objects. It is easy to forget which objects go together without resorting to groups (which can cause problems later on) or attaching elements (which limits the amount of in-depth animation you can do). Selection sets are a nice alternative to these other, more "permanent" methods.

4.   Apply a Bend modifier.

5.   Switch to the Left viewport and zoom out to view the entire body.

6.   Select Sub-Object Center for the Bend modifier and move the center down in Y to the base of the feet (about 380 units).

7.   Change the Direction to 90 and the Bend axis to Z.

8.   Slide the Angle spinner up and down to view the effect.

Henry rocks back and forth while his boots stay locked in place. Now it is time to set some keyframes. You will make Henry resist the wind for the first second or so, and then he will bend back uncomfortably and flap in the breeze. You do this by setting a single key that times out when he bends, and then alter the time curve to add a wobbling effect.

1. Go to frame 75 and turn on the Animate button.

2. Drag the Bend Angle spinner down to about –150 degrees (see fig. 19.18).

FIGURE 19.18
Henry bending over backward.

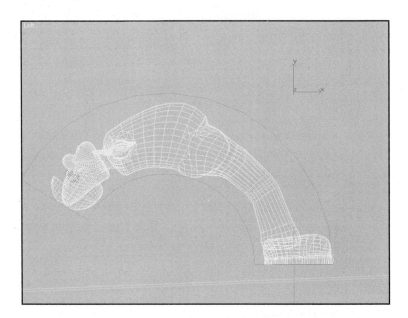

3. Open the Track View and expand the tracks for Henry body.

Notice that there is a ton of tracks for the Free Form deformation 4×4×4 (one for each control point), so you might want to collapse those tracks to avoid cluttering your window.

4. Open the Function Curve for the Bend Angle and select the key at frame 0.

5. Move the keyframe from frame 0 to frame 30, keeping the angle value at 0.

6. Select both keys and change the tangent type to Slow on the In and Out.

Henry will hold steady for the first second, and then ease into his bend. Now you create some wobble frames.

7. Select the key at frame 30 and while holding the Shift button, drag it back to make a copy around frame 25, lowering the angle value to about −15.

8. Repeat this step a few more times, creating a sine wave of sorts that decreases in intensity as it approaches frame 0. Make a key about every three or four frames until you reach 0 (see fig. 19.19).

FIGURE 19.19

Wobbling in the bend.

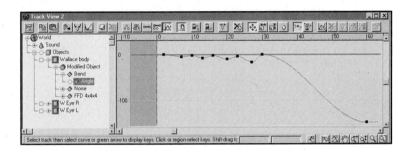

9. Save your scene as myboot01.max and render a Smooth + Highlights preview of the Camera01 viewport, frames 0–75.

The wobble might be a little too extreme. Try softening the effect by zooming in on the Function Curve for the first 30 frames and make the highs of your wave around 0 degrees and the lows starting around −2 degrees and increasing to about −5 before finally bending over all the way (see fig. 19.20).

FIGURE 19.20

Softening the wobble.

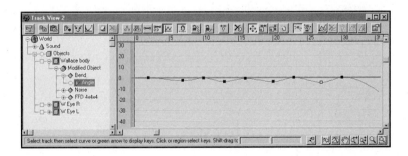

Another problem could be that the final bend seems too smooth in comparison to the wobbly beginning. Try adding a slight stair-step effect to the curve from 30 to 75. Be careful not to level off between keys; this would cause an unwanted delay in the bend (see fig. 19.21).

FIGURE 19.21

Roughening the back bend.

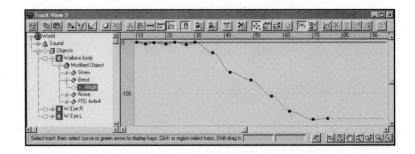

10. Save your scene as myboot01.max and render a Smooth + Highlights preview of the Camera01 viewport, frames 0–75.

Not bad, but is the bend modifier enough, or should another modifier be layered on top? How about a Skew?

Adding a Skew modifier is just like adding a bend. Just change your center and animate the strength. You could also give it the same treatment you gave the bend by wobbling the direction a bit.

1. Minimize any other windows and switch to the Left viewport.

2. Zoom out and select Henry Body and both eyelid objects.

3. Go to frame 0 and apply a Skew modifier.

4. Select Sub-Object Center for the Skew modifier and move the center down in Y to the base of the feet (about 380 units).

5. Change the Skew axis to Z and the Direction to 90.

6. Go to frame 100 and activate the Animate button.

7. While pressing the Ctrl key, drag the Amount spinner up and down to view the effect, stopping around –300.

TIP

The spinner for Skew Amount is slower than most, providing accuracy up to three decimal places. Holding down the Ctrl key increases the rate at which the value changes.

8. Open the Track View and find the keyframes for Skew Amount.

9. Move the key at frame 0 to frame 30.

10. Save your scene as myboot01.max and render a Smooth + Highlights preview of the Camera01 viewport, frames 0–100.

Henry wobbles, bends, and then stretches backward.

1. Go to frame 100 and activate the Animate button.

2. Slide the Skew Direction spinner up and down to view the effect, stopping around 95.

3. In the Track View, open the Function Curve for the Skew Direction and select the key at frame 0.

4. Move the keyframe from frame 0 to frame 60, keeping the angle value at 90 degrees.

5. Select both keys and change the tangent type to Slow on the In and Out.

6. Add a few more frames between frame 60 and 100 by shift-dragging the existing frames to create copies, and make a sine wave similar to the bend wobble. This time, increase the effect by having the strength start off mild and increase in value and frequency as you approach frame 100, dipping to 80 at the valleys and 100 at the peaks (see fig. 19.22).

FIGURE 19.22

Increasing the effect of the back bend.

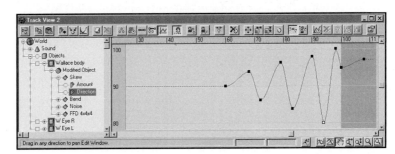

7. Save your scene as **myboot01.max** and render a Smooth + Highlights preview of the Camera01 viewport, frames 0–100.

One object that has been hidden all this time is the source of Henry's trouble, the fan. Next you add a simple oscillation to the body of the fan for a finishing touch.

1. Unhide the object called Fan Body.

2. Select Fan Body and open the Track View.

3. Expand the tracks for Fan Body and find Radius 1 and Radius 2 under Modified Object/Object.

4. Select Radius 1 and assign a Float List controller.

A List controller enables you to layer multiple controllers that combine their own effects into one. The controllers are calculated in the order you specify in the Properties dialog box.

In this case, you want to oscillate the fan body by changing its radius. A Noise controller would do this, but applied alone would cause the radius to jump from one extreme to the next (try it to see what happens). By applying a Noise float below the existing Linear Float, the Linear takes precedence and the Noise is merely an enhancement.

5. Expand the Float List for Radius 1 and select Available.

6. Click on Assign Control and assign a Noise Float.

7. Click on the Properties button and change the noise frequency to 4 and the strength to 10.

8. Minimize the Track View window and move the Time Slider slowly from frame 0 to frame 100.

The outer radius of the fan body shrinks and expands randomly. Now do the same to Radius 2 by repeating steps 4 through 7. Copying the controller from Radius 1 to Radius 2 is not an option because the initial values for each need to be different (Radius 2 being smaller than Radius 1).

After you have added the Noise Float and adjusted its parameters for Radius 2, unhide the Fan Blade object and render your final preview animation, saving your scene beforehand.

Alright, maybe it is time to leave Henry alone. There *are* other modifiers, not touched on here, that would work well with him. What about a torture rack animation using Stretch and Twist? Maybe combine some of these with the modifying power of Free Form Deformations for some distorting results? Feel free to play around with different combinations and effects, not just on a character model such as Henry, but on any object.

As you work with 3DS MAX, you will discover ways of enhancing your projects by adding an Animated modifier to an element in your scene or setting keyframes for a standard primitive's creation parameters.

One effect I needed to create along the way was an energy sphere encircled by arcs of lightning. I created the sphere itself with an animated material, but I was uncertain as to the approach to take for the lightning effect. Lightning plug-ins were available, but didn't have the look I was after. The solution turned out to be right here in MAX.

Open lsphere.avi from the accompanying CD-ROM and view the final animation.

The arcs that shoot out and surround the sphere are torus primitives with animated Slice values and a Noise modifier on top. Try a quick example.

1. Save any scene you have open and reset MAX.

2. Create a sphere in the center with a radius around 70 units.

3. Create a thin torus encircling the sphere with a radius around 100 (see fig. 19.23).

FIGURE 19.23

Creating a thin torus.

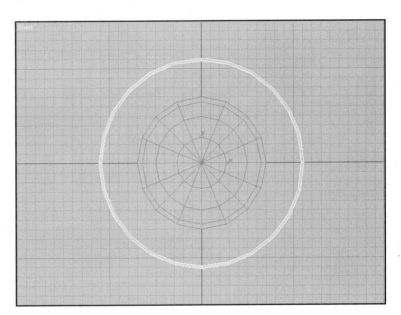

4. Activate the Animate button and move to frame 100.

5. Rotate the torus about 120 degrees in Y and then 120 degrees in X.

6. Slide the playback bar around to get a feel for what you have.

7. Go to frame 0 and click on Slice On under the torus parameters in the Modify panel.

8. At frame 0, set the Slice To value to –0.5.

9. Go to frame 25 and change the Slice To value to –360.

10. Go to frame 50 and change the Slice To value to –600 and the Slice From value to –360.

11. Go to frame 75 and change the Slice To value to –720 and the Slice From value to –600.

12. Finally, go to frame 100 and change the Slice From value to –719.5.

13. Play the animation in wireframe or render a preview.

Now you have a torus chasing its tail around a sphere. Next you apply some noise.

1. Turn off the Animate button and go to around frame 50.

2. Apply a Noise modifier to the torus.

3. Set the Noise Scale to 20, the X, Y, and Z strengths to 20, activate Animate Noise, and change the Frequency to 5.

4. Play the animation in wireframe or render a preview.

That's the basis for the lightning arcs. Try turning off Animated Noise and double the Frequency for a smoother effect. You could also enhance things by adding a Noise Float controller underneath a Linear Float for the Radius 2 of the torus. With a low frequency and strength setting, the torus will randomly change its thickness as it travels around the sphere.

Another quick solution I needed for a project was to animate a cloth banner on a wall being affected by an object flying by.

The banner is a patch grid with an animated Ripple modifier moving through it at the right moment. The extra fold of the corner of the cloth was achieved by applying a Linked Transform to the corner vertex of the patch. A dummy object then takes that vertex and folds over the end. Patch grids are an excellent subject for Linked Transforms because they work with a minimum of control vertices, deforming the object smoothly between them.

In Practice: Animating with Multiple Modifiers

- **Geometry modifiers.** Geometry modifiers are useful tools for broad animation of the dimensions of an object or for subtle changes over time.

- **Linked XForm.** Objects can be controlled on the sub-object level by linking selected pieces to any other object.

- **Function curves.** Adding and adjusting keys directly on the function curve of a controller is a quick and powerful way of animating transforms and parameters.

- **List controllers.** Controller types can be layered much in the same way that modifiers are layered to mix multiple effects.

- **Object parameters.** Keeping a primitive object open to Object Parameter animation (by not collapsing it into a mesh) enables adjustment of the basic parameters of an object and animation later on.

IMAGE CREATED BY PAUL KAKERT

Chapter 20

ANIMATING ACCURACY FOR FORENSICS

The use of multimedia in the courtroom is becoming common-place. So much so that the courtroom of the future will be wired for multimedia. High-tech trials are where the legal industry is heading. Besides the widely recognized vehicular accident recon-struction, animations play a key role in dramatizing crime scenes, personal injury, product liability, fire damage, faulty construc-tion, workers' compensation, and many other situations. Even though admissibility in court should be the basis for all your work, animation also takes part in pretrial settlement discussions. After all, settling out of court is what most attorneys would like to do. Animation can be a "big stick" in negotiations, showing the attorney is prepared to go to great lengths to persuade the jury.

Regardless of the kind of animation you are working on, accuracy is key. MAX aides in your accuracy by offering great support for DXF files, and helpful third-party plug-ins. Because most of the experts working with animators on cases are engineers or reconstructionists with engineering skills, you can often use their DXF files as the basis of your layout. Aside from that, you will discover in this chapter's tutorials that MAX does not do things automatically for you. You will have to figure out speeds of vehicles and pedestrians and keyframe them manually over time. When a car skids to a stop, you must use a third-party program to create the skid marks. If you want to have scratches, gouges, and dents appear on objects throughout the course of the animation, it is easiest to work with yet another plug-in for those effects. These are not downfalls of MAX. They are good points, illustrating the advantage of using a program open for developers to create specialized plug-in tools. This chapter shows how to achieve an accurate level of detail within MAX with the help of some important plug-ins along the way.

This chapter covers the following topics:

- Forensic animation industry overview

- Timing

- Advanced character studio motion

- Details

Forensic Animation Industry Overview

A few key factors affect an animation's admissibility. The following list identifies some of the areas you should be concerned with as you start production:

- **The animation must be based on facts.** A forensic animator takes the role of a visualization expert in a case. The party hiring you, whether an attorney or otherwise, is not like a commercial business client. They cannot direct you to re-create a vehicular accident, for example, in a manner that defies physics or is inaccurate in any way just to suit the needs of their client. To be admitted in court, your animation must be based on facts supplied by experts involved in the case or some other known circumstances, such as eyewitness testimony.

- **The animation must be unbiased.** In criminal trials, for example, the use of low-detail, faceless human figures makes the subjects of your animation unidentifiable. The purpose of the trial is not to prove whether the defendant was or was not the subject portrayed in the animation. The animation should just show the actions of the subject.

- **Only include details relevant to the case.** There is a fine line between making it look realistic and including things just for aesthetic reasons. Bottom line is, if there were not five other cars on the road when it happened, don't put them in.

Regardless of the amount of time you spend working on the details of these admissibility factors, admissibility is out of your control. The judge is the ultimate gatekeeper of the courtroom. If a judge is unfamiliar with what the animator is doing, that may be enough to keep the animation out of the courtroom.

Accuracy—Make It Obvious in Your Animation

Where did you get your information, and how did it become an animation? These key questions come up in almost every trial. A good place to start any animation, therefore, is with diagrams, blueprints, layouts, and photos supplied by experts. Every case you work on will involve an expert in the field of accident reconstruction, engineering, medicine, or some other relevant field. In accident reconstructions, for example, many reconstructionists can supply you with DXF files direct from their reconstruction program, making it easy to establish the accuracy of your work.

It is a good idea to start your animated presentation by setting up a reference to any technical diagrams or material you were supplied. Figure 20.1 shows the diagram of a vehicular accident scene as supplied by the accident reconstructionist in a DXF file. This type of technical drawing provides a great foundation for your work. Transition from this image to the same reference view in your animation. Figure 20.2 shows the first frame in an animation that used the preceding DXF layout. It shows the degree of accuracy in translating data from the expert's reports or diagrams to your animation and the realism of the animation you created.

FIGURE 20.1

Include a DXF wireframe reference viewed from above the scene and identify it as a technical drawing supplied by the expert reconstructionist.

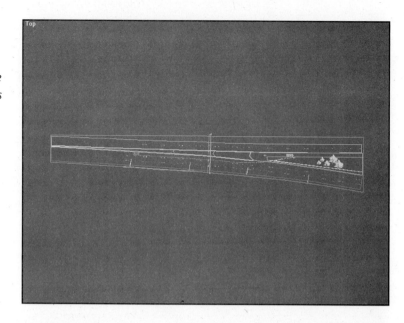

FIGURE 20.2

Transition between the DXF wireframe and a rendered MAX reference view from the same vantage point of the scene.

If you have the advantage of using an aerial photograph, use it in conjunction with your reference rendering to show how accurately the scene is depicted (see fig. 20.3).

FIGURE 20.3

An aerial photo reference view makes for a great comparison to the actual layout of the scene.

It is a good idea to document the basis for the different aspects in the animation. If one expert gave you the dimensions of a vehicle and another gave you dimensions of pedestrians, make a note of each source. In commercial animation, and even in other technical applications for animation, you are rarely pressed to provide verification of your every keystroke. The courts may not look for a video documentary of how you created the animation, but it is a good idea to document your sources. You will likely be asked where you received the details and how you can prove they are shown accurately in the final product. Overlaying animations over still photographs and wireframe DXF files, as outlined previously, is a great way to show accuracy.

Animation Proves Nothing

Your animation proves nothing more than the fact that you are a competent animator and can accurately portray the facts provided to you. Even high-tech simulations using animation fall into this category. The picture proves nothing; it is always the numbers behind the scenes that are the proof in a case. The pictures just tell the story. Keep this in mind as you accept work from attorneys. Make certain that they are clear on the fact that unless expert findings back up your work, the animation will just be an illustration with no foundation. Attorneys who misunderstand your role may ask you to animate different scenarios of an accident without thinking about involving an expert in crash scene analysis. For an animator to run scenarios after changing starting position of vehicles or pedestrians, for example, would be pure speculation and would not be admissible.

A special case exists when animating eyewitness testimony—which itself, proves nothing. You can validate your work with a reference to the eyewitness testimony. What a witness claims to have seen, however, does not prove or disprove whether it was actually the case or whether it was even possible.

The rest of this chapter focuses on the main differences between a commercial animation and one created for use in the courtroom. The following issues are covered:

- Timing

- Advanced character studio motion

- Details—humans, vehicles, and skid marks

Accurate Timing

Where in MAX do you input that the car was traveling 55 miles per hour or that the pedestrian was walking 3 feet per second? Well, you don't. Not exactly. MAX does have some built-in features, such as constant velocity, that will aide in accurately portraying speeds in your animation. In the following tutorial, you will work with a basic two-car collision scene. You will figure out where to start each vehicle in order to re-create the scene as it happened. You will also create an alternate scenario with the vehicles moving at different speeds.

NOTE

All information in this case was supplied by the accident reconstructionist who worked on the case with the animator.

In this timing tutorial, a passenger vehicle failed to stop at a pedestrian crosswalk due to an obstructed view caused by another vehicle. The speed of the striking vehicle was determined by the reconstructionist. The placement of the obstructing vehicle was determined by eyewitness testimony. The objective in this case was to visualize the obstructed view of the driver and the limited reaction time it created, resulting in the accident.

To create this animation, you need the following details:

- The prebraking speed of the car was 26 mph.
- The car's speed at impact was 24 mph.
- Based on the age of the pedestrian, you will use a walking speed of 3 feet per second (slightly slower than a standard walk of 4 feet per second).
- The position of the view-obstructing vehicle based on witness statements.
- The skid marks for the car start 15 feet north of the crosswalk.
- The point of impact was 3.5 feet south of the north edge of the crosswalk and 17 feet east of the west curb.

NOTE

Walking speed is a variable you will never be able to re-create precisely. The average of 4 feet per second is what is used by civil engineers who design devices such as walk signals at stop lights. The standard has been set by the National Advisory Committee on Uniform Traffic Control Devices and the American Association of State Highway and Transportation Officials (AASHTO). Manuals and books by either group discuss the standards for walking speeds in more detail.

TIMING

1. Load the file fmtiming.max from the accompanying CD-ROM. Save it to your hard drive as **mytiming.max**.

2. Click on Unit Setup from the View menu and set units to Decimal Feet.

3. Maximize the Top viewport to fill the screen and Region Zoom until you see only the crosswalk area. You will do all your measurements with the tape measure from this view.

4. Start with the point of impact and work backward to determine where to set starting points for movement. You know exactly where the car strikes the pedestrian. Select Create-Tape and specify a length of 3.5 feet (see fig. 20.4).

FIGURE 20.4

By using the Tape Measure, you can input your exact measurements.

5. Click on the north edge of the crosswalk and drag the tape south. When you release the mouse, you will have your north-south reference to the point of impact. Name this tape **north-south impact**.

6. Click on the Tape button again and specify a new tape length of 17 feet.

Warning

Before specifying your second tape length, you must deselect the current tape by either right-clicking or clicking on the Tape button. If you don't, you will be adjusting your current tape rather than creating a new one.

7. Click on the west curb in the middle of the crosswalk and drag toward the east curb. Name this tape **west-east impact**.

8. Before deselecting the west-east tape you just created, select the Move tool, constrain movement to the Y axis, and move the tape until it touches the end of your north-south tape. Figure 20.5 shows the point of impact you just defined.

FIGURE 20.5
The point where the west-east and north-south tape measures meet represents the point of impact.

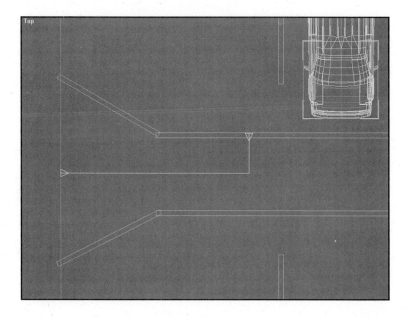

To select and adjust the position of a tape, make certain that you select both the Tape Measure object (yellow triangle) and its target (blue box). If you select one without the other, you will be adjusting the angle of the tape measure only.

In this case, there is a view-obstructing second vehicle that is stationary and that makes a great reference. It has been placed in the scene for you. There also is an arbitrary starting position for the car. It left the town public square 392 feet north of the north crosswalk line.

9. Click on Create-Tape and specify a length of 392 feet. Click on the center of the north crosswalk line and drag north. Name this tape **392 feet car path**.

10. The car is currently in the wrong position. Click on Named Selection Sets and select Caddy and Dummy.

11. Position the front of the car at the end of the 392 feet car path tape measure in the outside (west) lane, facing the crosswalk.

You need to figure out how long it takes for the car to travel to the point of impact. This will involve two speed translation because the car travels one speed prebraking and another speed after braking is applied. MAX does not support miles per hour (mph), so you must do the translation to feet per second (fps). There are 5,280 feet in one mile. Work with the prebrake speed first, which is 26 mph, and multiply it by 5,280. Divide that number by 60. Take that result and divide it by 60. The resulting number is your fps. The equation looks like this:

26 mph×5,280 = 137,280÷60 = 2288÷60 = 38.13 fps.

Round this to 38 fps. This is the speed of the car from the starting position to the point of braking. You'll have to apply the same equation to the speed after the brakes are applied, which is 24 mph. That result is 35 fps and will be used later.

12. The point of braking (measured from the center of the north crosswalk line to the rear tires) is 15 feet north of the crosswalk.

13. Click on Create-Tape and specify a length of 15 feet. Click on the center
     of the north crosswalk line and drag north. Name this tape **15 foot skid**.
     Now you are ready to keyframe the position of your car at the point of
     braking.

The front of the car is now 392 feet from the center of the north crosswalk
line. The brakes are applied 15 feet north from the same reference
point. The distance from the front of the car to the rear tires is 14 feet, which
means that the front of the car is one foot north of the north crosswalk line
when the brakes are applied. Divide the 391 feet the car travels by the
prebraking speed of 38 fps, and you get 10.3 seconds. You will use 309 frames
(10.3×30 fps).

TIP

The Road Safety and Motor Vehicle Regulation Directorate of Canada has a database of
manufacturer's vehicle specs available on disk. The program contains most makes and models.
Make requests for copies to

Dr. Alan German
Collision Investigation, Transport Canada
P.O. Box 8880
Ottawa Postal Terminal
Ottawa, Ontario, K1G 3J2
Tel: 613-993-9851
E-Mail: GermanA@tc.gc.ca

14. Click on Zoom Extents to see the entire scene.

15. Click on Select By Name and select dummy caddy front; the dummy
     aligned with the front of the car. Click on Lock Selection Set.

16. Click on Animate and go to frame 309. Using the Move tool, constrained
     to the Y axis, drag the dummy toward the crosswalk until the back tires
     line up with the 15 foot skid tape measure (see fig. 20.6).

The point of impact is now just 4.5 feet away. In that distance, the car slows
to 24 mph or 35 fps. That translates to .13 seconds to travel 4.5 feet. That is
only 4 frames in this animation.

17. Go to frame 313 and move the front of the car to the impact point. Turn
     off Animate.

FIGURE 20.6
The car's rear wheels are now aligned with the point where the skid marks started.

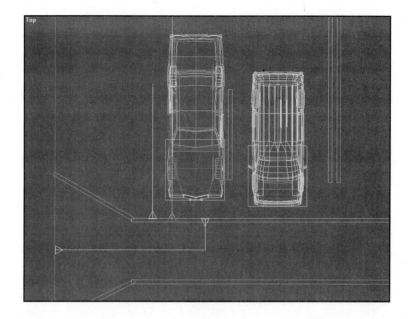

Now you set the starting position of the pedestrian. You want the walking time equal to the car's traveling time, which is 10.4 seconds (313 frames divided by 30 frames per second). At 3 fps, determined by the reconstructionist, the pedestrian will travel 31.2 feet.

18. Unhide the pedestrian. Click on Display-UnhideAll. This unhides Bip01 and all its child objects. Bip01 is a Character Studio Biped already placed 31.2 feet from the point of impact.

19. With the biped selected, click on the Footstep Track in the Motion Control panel.

20. Using the Default Walking Gait, click on the Create Multiple Footsteps button (see fig. 20.7).

21. The only settings you need to adjust are the Stride Length and the Number of Steps. Set the Actual Stride Length to 1.5 feet. This length is an arbitrary setting you can play with to get the effect you want. Leaving the time to the next footstep at 15 frames, the pedestrian will travel 3 feet per second and will take 2 steps per second. This below-average setting is appropriate because the pedestrian is older.

FIGURE 20.7

Character Studio has only one dialog box where you make all of your adjustments for the footsteps of the pedestrian.

Create Multiple Footsteps: Walk

General

Start Left ○   Number of Footsteps [21]
Start Right ●   Parametric Stride Width [1.0]
Alternate ☑   Actual Stride Width [0.579']
                 Total Distance [378.00]

OK
Cancel

Timing

Auto Timing ☑   Start after last footstep ●
Interpolate ☐   Start at current frame ○

First Step

Parametric Stride Length [0.518]
Actual Stride Length [1.5']
Actual Stride Height [0.0']
Time to next Footstep [15]
Speed (units per frame) [0.01]
Walk Footstep [ ]
Double Support [ ]

Last Step

Parametric Stride Length [ ]
Actual Stride Length [ ]
Actual Stride Height [ ]
Time to next Footstep [15]
Speed (units per frame) [0.01]
Walk Footstep [ ]
Double Support [ ]

22. Set the Number of Footsteps at 21 (10.4 seconds×2 steps per second).

23. Click on OK. Your footsteps are generated, leading the pedestrian to the point of impact.

24. Click on Create Keys for Inactive Footsteps and preview your pedestrian's motion (see fig. 20.8).

FIGURE 20.8

This represents the point of impact in the final animation, complete with Character Studio footprints.

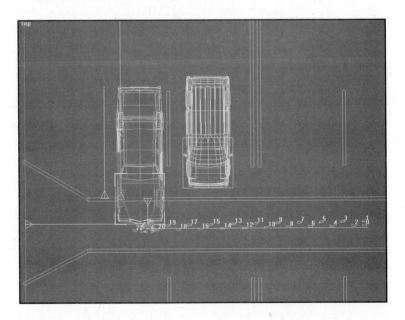

25. Save your file. Load fmtiming.avi from the accompanying CD-ROM to see the final rendered animation. You can load the final animation file in MAX by loading the fmtiming finished.max file from the CD.

Now that you have learned how to set up accurate timing in MAX, the next step is to accurately portray bipedal motion that is suddenly disrupted. One of the most effective and easiest ways to accomplish this is through the Character Studio plug-in.

Advanced Character Studio Motion

The Character Studio plug-in is a great time saver for any animator, not just those interested in forensics. Forensic animations, however, may offer the greatest deviation from normal bipedal motion that you will ever encounter. After all, how many other situations have a walking, running, or jumping person suddenly hit and rolled over by a car? It is a gruesome thought, but animating such incidents is a common necessity in many forensic cases involving personal injury.

Where do you draw the line between using a product such as Bones Pro with inverse kinematics and using Character Studio (CS)? You will have to decide for yourself, but consider this: CS motion is very easy to set up, and it enables quick edits to your motion. One possible drawback is that you cannot place any keys after the last footstep. If you use CS to animate a biped running across the street and being hit by a car, therefore, your last footstep cannot be at the point of impact. If you want the biped to move after impact, you will need additional footsteps. You will also need to utilize free-form editing between footsteps. Free-form editing enables you to turn off the biped's vertical dynamics. In other words, the force of gravity will not affect your biped's motion.

Before looking at how to create unique CS motion, take a quick look at how CS normally constructs a scene's vertical dynamics.

1. Load the file flip.max from the Character Studio folder. This file was installed with Character Studio in the c:\3dsmax\cstudio\scenes folder. Save it to your hard drive as **myflip.max**.

The character in this scene does two backflips. The flip would have to be added by the user, but the height of each jump is determined by CS and is user definable. Play the animation, or drag the Timeline Slider to see the height of each jump and the motion of the character prior to and immediately after each jump. The character crouches and squats for a realistic appearance according to the height of the jump. Both attributes are set by the Gravitational Acceleration spinner in the biped's motion panel (see fig. 20.9).

FIGURE 20.9

Character Studio uses the Gravitational Acceleration setting to automatically determine the height of vertical motion.

2. Maximize the Front viewport. Click on Select By Name and choose the Bip01 object.

3. Enter the Motion panel. In the General section, set the GravAccel spinner to 369.032.

4. Drag the Timeline Slider to see the height of the jump and the pre- and post-landing motion of the character.

5. Adjust the GravAccel spinner to .01.

6. Drag the Timeline Slider again and notice the difference in the vertical motion. Basically, there is no vertical motion. In the real world equivalent of this example, this type of motion would be impossible.

The limitation of the GravAccel setting is that it is a universal setting for the biped for the entire animation and cannot be animated, which is why free-form editing is the best method to change from motion affected primarily by gravity and motion that is unnatural and caused by a force such as an impacting vehicle. Free-form editing enables editing of the vertical dynamics of each airborne interval, independent of the other motion of the character. In simpler terms, it enables you to temporarily turn off the GravAccel setting you adjusted in the preceding tutorial.

You will use the same file as used in the Timing tutorial. In that tutorial, you dealt only with motion up to the point of impact. You will now look at how to keyframe the positions of the pedestrian post-impact. The objective is strictly to work with Character Studio free-form editing.

1. Load the file fmcstudio.max from the accompanying CD and save it to your hard drive as **mycstudio.max**.

2. Start by identifying the ending position for the biped in the animation. The animation already has motion for the vehicle ending at frame 359, so use that frame for your last footstep placement.

3. Go to frame 359 and maximize the Top viewport. Region zoom the area showing the point of impact and the final rest position of the vehicle (see fig. 20.10).

FIGURE 20.10

Use the final rest of the vehicle to set the final footsteps for your biped's final rest position.

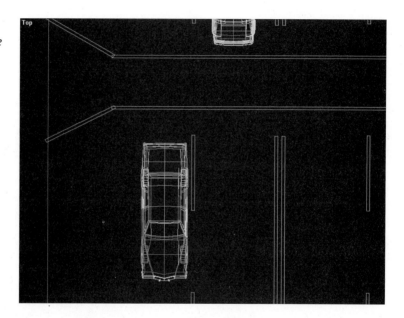

NOTE

From this point forward, you will be adjusting the rotation and position of the biped post-impact. The degrees and amounts of movement are not meant to be precise. You may have to adjust slightly to get the correct positioning in your scene. This tutorial will run through the basics of animating the biped through to its final rest. For a more realistic motion, you could add more upper body rotation, arm movements, and so on.

4. Click on Select By Name and choose the Bip01 object.

5. Click on the Motion panel. Under Track Selection, click on Footstep Track.

6. Because you already have footsteps generated for the biped, add new footsteps starting at the end of the existing ones. Under Footstep Creation, click on the Create Footsteps (append) button (see fig. 20.11).

FIGURE 20.11

Character Studio
enables you to append
new footsteps to the
end of existing ones.

7. This will enable you to manually place alternating left and right footsteps. Notice that your cursor is now an arrow and a footprint. Click on an area in the viewport at a location just to the right of the front tire of the car.

8. Click a second time on an area next to that footstep to generate the second footstep (see fig. 20.12).

FIGURE 20.12

This shows the position
of the final rest
footsteps of the
character.

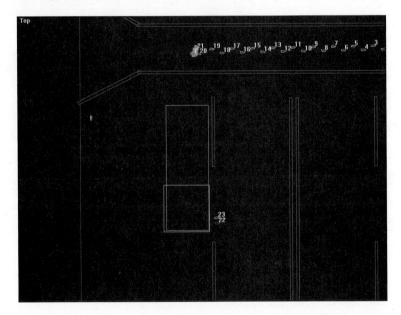

9. In the Footstep Operations section, click on Create Keys for Inactive Footsteps.

10. Drag the Timeline Slider to see the effect on the character's motion. The character takes a huge sideways leap to the final rest footsteps. Not what we need it to look like, but that's the way to get the character to the final rest position.

Now you will do the free-form editing for the airborne period between the impact and final rest to make the character react appropriately. You want to adjust a time period that starts at impact and ends at the final rest. Because the free-form edit is of airborne time only, you have to make certain that the character leaves its feet at impact, around frame 314. You make this adjustment in Track View.

1. Click on the Track View button. Position the Track View window in the lower half of the screen so that you can see the top and front view above it.

2. Click on the Filters button in the Track View menu bar (see fig. 20.13).

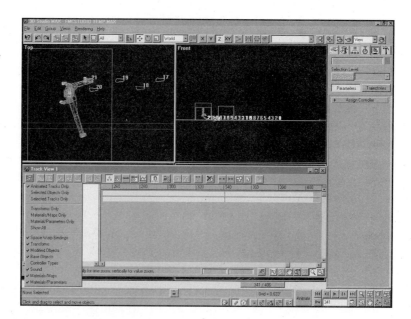

FIGURE 20.13

Avoid cluttering your screen by viewing only the animated tracks.

3. Select Animated Tracks Only.

4. Right-click on Objects and click Expand Objects from the pop-up menu. Then click on the plus sign next to Bip01 Footsteps to reveal the footstep tracks (see fig. 20.14).

5. Use the Zoom Region tool within Track View so that you can see footsteps 20 through 23 only. You want to zoom in far enough to see the starting and ending frame for each footstep, especially footstep 21. Depending on the resolution of your monitor, you may at different times throughout this tutorial have to zoom in to see the detail described.

FIGURE 20.14

These are the biped's footsteps as seen in the Track View.

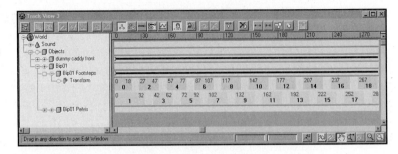

6. Adjust footstep 21 by clicking on the middle of the footstep and dragging it toward footstep 20.

7. Watch the numbers on the left side of the footstep; they indicate the starting frame of that footstep. Stop dragging when it reads 307.

8. Right-click on the footstep to open the Footstep Track window for the biped.

9. Under Footstep Edge Selection, click on the right button. This enables you to scale the footstep.

10. Click and drag the right edge of the footstep until the far right number in the footstep reads 313. Now the last footstep ends at the point of impact (see fig. 20.15).

FIGURE 20.15

The last pre-impact footstep now aligns with the impact.

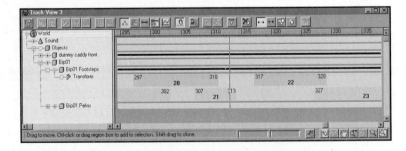

11. Pan to the right until you can see footsteps 22 and 23, the final rest footsteps. You will keep these footsteps together, and want them to occur at the same frame. Click on footstep 22 and drag toward footstep 23. Make certain that each footstep starts on frame 359.

12. Click on the right edge of footstep 22 and drag the duration to be equal to footstep 23 (see fig. 20.16).

13. Zoom out to see footsteps 20 through 23 again.

FIGURE 20.16

By clicking and dragging on the end of the footstep, you make adjustments to the last two footsteps.

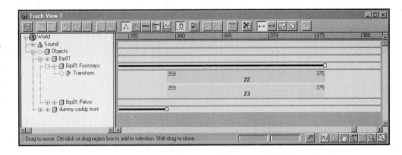

14. The area between footsteps 21 and 22 is the airborne time post-impact. To designate it as a free-form area, right-click on any footstep.

15. In the Footstep Track window that opens, click on Edit Free-form (no physics).

16. The areas between the footsteps are now outlined in yellow. Click on the yellow outlined area between footsteps 21 and 22. The area turns solid yellow, indicating it is a free-form area (see fig. 20.17).

FIGURE 20.17

Free-form editing areas are indicated by the solid yellow boxes.

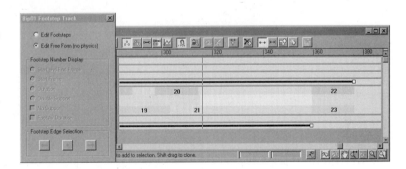

17. Close the Track View window and maximize the Left viewport.

18. Now start adjusting the position of the biped from impact to final rest. Start by going to the final rest position at frame 359.

19. Click on Select By Name and choose Bip01.

20. Adjust the final rest position so that the character is lying flat on its back.

21. Click on the Footstep Track button in the Track Selection section.

22. Because you placed the final two footsteps from the Top viewport, they are not aligned correctly. Click on Select and Rotate and select footsteps 22 and 23.

23. Select the Local Coordinate System and rotate the two footsteps about their Z axis –90 degrees and then rotate the two footsteps about their Y axis –90 degrees. Both feet should be pointing up.

24. Click on Select and Move.

25. Constrain movement to the Z axis and move the footsteps above ground level (see fig. 20.18).

FIGURE 20.18
Place the final footsteps above ground level.

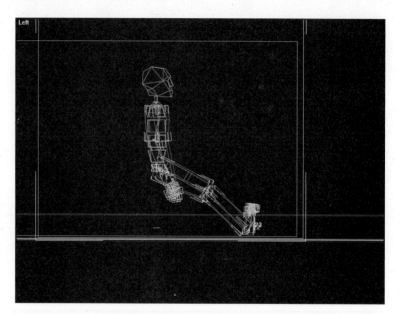

26. Click on Footstep Track in the Track Selection section to leave Footstep mode.

27. With the Bip01 still selected, click on the Select and Rotate tool.

28. Click on Lock Selection set.

29. Constrain movement to the Y axis and rotate –80 degrees.

30. Under Track Operations, click on the Set Key button. This creates a key for the current position.

WARNING

Remember to click on the Set Key button after every move, or your actions will be lost as soon as you move to another frame. This is the same effect as not turning on the Animate button when keyframing motion in MAX.

31. Click on the Select and Move tool.

32. Move down until the biped is on the ground. Click on the Set Key button. This is the final rest position (see fig. 20.19).

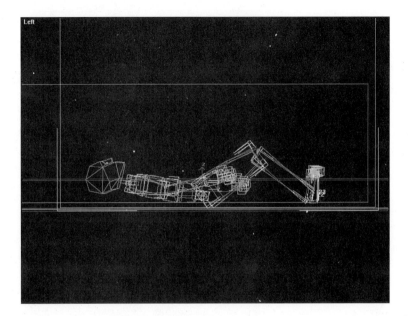

33. Go to frame 316, the frame immediately after impact. With the Bip01 still selected, click on Select and Rotate and constrain movement to the X axis.

34. Rotate –75 degrees and click on Set Key.

35. Click on Select and Move and move the biped up along the Z axis to clear the top of the car. Click on Set Key (see fig. 20.20).

36. Go to frame 340, just about halfway to the final rest.

37. Move the biped up along the Z axis again until it clears the top of the car. Click on Set Key.

38. Rotate about the Y axis –80 degrees and click on Set Key (see fig. 20.21).

39. Go to frame 349 and switch to the Top viewport.

40. Move the biped along its X axis until it clears the car. Click on Set Key (see fig. 20.22).

FIGURE 20.20
Adjustments are made at the point of impact.

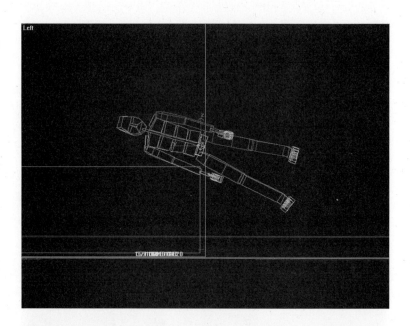

FIGURE 20.21
Rotate the position of the biped along its airborne path as it bounces atop the car hood.

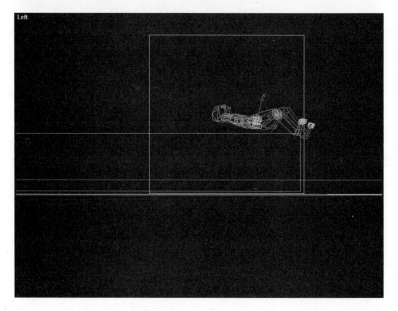

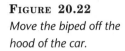

Figure 20.22

Move the biped off the hood of the car.

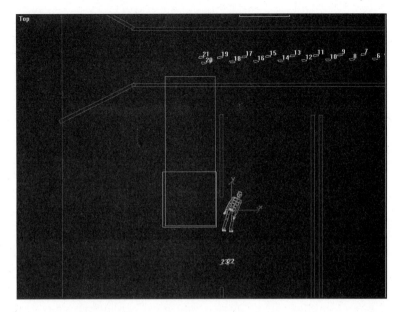

41. Switch back to the Left viewport and rotate the biped along its Y axis −60 degrees, until it is again parallel to the ground. Click on Set Key.

42. Move the biped up along the Z axis to a point about halfway up the car height. Click on Set Key.

43. The biped should now fall into position at frame 359, the end of the animation.

NOTE

Remember that at frame 360, footsteps 22 and 23 begin, ending the free-form editing. Character Studio will again gain control of the vertical dynamics of the character, which is why, in this example, you would end the animation at 359 and only render to that frame.

44. Save your file. Load fmcstudio.avi from the accompanying CD-ROM to see the final rendered animation. You can load the final animation file in MAX by loading the fmcstudio finished.max file from the CD.

The first two tutorials have shown you how to make accurate animations, including speed for objects and movements and interactions between different objects, including people. What's left are the details of those objects that will be accurately moving about in your animation. In forensic animation, the texture maps you use can not only make your animation look more convincing, but they can also play a significant role in the admissibility of your work.

Details

As any attorney will tell you, when they go up against an animation, they look for any inaccuracy to discredit the work of the animator. Ignoring details or including innacurate details opens the door for the "perception" of inaccuracy in the minds of the jury and the judge. When you are making the decision of which details to include, think in terms of relevance to the events that occurred or the subjects involved. Using this as a rule of thumb will enable you to answer questions about why certain things appear in the animation and why others are left out.

Leaving the details off human figures is a good idea. If you make a subject appear as a black person when there is no evidence suggesting this (other than perhaps the accused being a black person), for example, the animation is going to cause trouble. Use a generic mannequin shaded in a neutral tone such as a dull grey color.

It is also best to err on the side of conservatism. Don't speculate or include details based on averages unless expert opinion will be used in testimony to back up the images. In other words, even though the average traffic flow is a certain number of cars every 30 seconds, that average might not be appropriate or relevant to this event; the particular day of the accident might not have been an average day.

You can usually get away with low-resolution models for human subjects and vehicles. The two exceptions to this are when you are working with an injury or surgical animation, or in a vehicular case where some aspect of the vehicle may have contributed to the accident.

In the same way that Character Studio, as a plug-in, gives added abilities to animate bipedal motion in MAX, other plug-ins help you add just the right detail. The following section describes some of the most helpful applications and plug-ins that will save you time and add to your capabilities. The following topics are covered:

- Human Models

- Vehicular Models

- Skid Marks, Tracks, and Trails

Human Models

The ever famous mannequin will do just fine for many reenactments. When you need more detail, however, it becomes a more complex task. Two new programs help produce incredible detail with reduced effort. Poser 2 and Detailer from Fractal Design make a great combination.

Poser 2 enables easy creation of predefined figures. You can adjust the body specifics, such as weight, height, and age. It makes for a great motion and pose study program for your animations. It also directly supports the exporting of 3DS files for use in MAX.

Detailer enables painting directly on your 3D models. The program creates all your texture and bump maps for you as you draw and paint on the mesh. Detailer also directly exports 3DS files for use in MAX. Detailer is great for human figures, especially faces. It also comes in handy when trying to paint gouges and scratches on vehicles and other surfaces.

Detailer works directly on your exported 3DS or DXF files from MAX, but a plug-in called Unwrap is a time-saving tool that literally unwraps the mapping coordinates of your model and saves the flat map as a graphic file. When you open the file in Photoshop, you see the form of the model represented as a flat outline. You can then paint on the map using the lines as a reference for positioning on the mesh in MAX.

N O T E

Each of these programs is highlighted in *Inside 3D Studio MAX Volume II*.

Vehicle Models

A majority of the time, the vehicle does not cause, or even contribute to the cause of, a vehicular accident. Therefore, do not spend a fortune buying highly detailed models, or hours of your time modeling vehicles yourself. Companies such as Viewpoint have growing libraries of vehicles with varying degrees of complexity that will suit most of your needs. If you must have a model custom made, make that decision early. It is not cheap!

The realism of your models will play a large part in how real the scene will appear to the jury. Many programs are now available that enable you to create models based on photographs taken from two different angles. These programs, such as Wireframe Express, create a relatively simple mesh file with the photo serving as a texture map. What you get is a quick rendering, very realistic model. These programs can be great for modeling before and after models of vehicles in collisions where you need to show the details of the damage. The downside is that, as in any modeling task, it takes quite a bit of time. This also is not a good choice if you have to interact with the models. Your car door will look like it is there, for example, but it only exists in the texture map. If you want to open the door, you will need to do some model modification.

Skid Marks, Tracks, and Trails

When did the vehicle start braking? When did it drive off the road? These events are often evident from tire marks, skids, or skuff marks.

One plug-in offers an easy way to create these effects: the MAXTrax plug-in from Sisyphus. It enables you to automate the process of creating procedural tracks and trails. It combines both a geometry-based application and a particle system to create everything from wake patterns in water to trails behind airplanes. The program is a big time saver, especially in forensic work. The key issue in skid marks is the location and duration. Their function is to point out things such as when brakes were applied or when tires left contact with the road as the car skidded across uneven terrain.

The use of MAXTrax is not limited to skid marks, although that is a common application. It is just as easy to set up the plug-in to create odd markings. Use it to create a gouge or paint mark on the side of a car as two cars bump against each other, or to place a skuff or gouge in the ground as a car tumbles across the side of a road after a collision.

Skid Marks

This first tutorial sets up skid marks from a tire in a simple head-on vehicular collision. This is a basic tutorial on how to apply tire tracks in your scene. You will take it one step further to show areas where the tire loses contact with the ground and the tracks stop and then start again when the tire lands back on the ground. Within the program's parameters, you have control over just about everything except designating multiple starting and stopping points for the same track. An easy workaround enables forensic animators to meet this common need. The following tutorial shows the workaround you will need to use.

1. Load the file trax1.max from the accompanying CD and save it to your hard drive as **mytrax1.max**.

The animation in this scene is simple and completed for you. The truck realizes that the car is not going to clear its path and applies its brakes. But it is too late, and the collision takes place. The goal in such a case may be to show one of two things. It may show that the car turned in front of the truck when it should have yielded, or it may show the truck was going too fast to react in time. This tutorial does not deal with these issues.

The basis of MAXTrax is to place an emitter (skidmark or track) between the object leaving the skidmark or track and the object on top of which the skidmark or track should appear—in this case, between the tire and the road. In MAXTrax terminology, the tire is the reference object, and the road is the target object.

2. Maximize the Top viewport and Region Zoom the area that includes the back tires of the truck and the right side of the road (see fig. 20.23).

FIGURE 20.23
Isolate the tires that will produce the tracks, but make certain that you can see a selectable edge of the road.

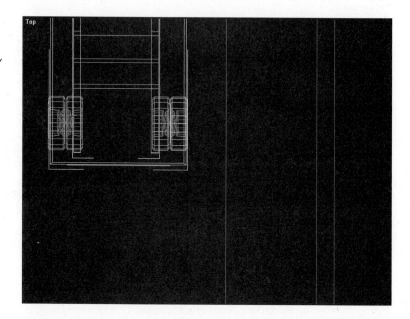

3. Because the roadside is a separate object from the road, it would be easy to select the roadside object when you go to click on your reference object. To avoid this, click on Select By Name and select Shoulder of Road.

4. Click on Display and Freeze By Selection, and Freeze Selected, to make the shoulder of the road unselectable.

5. Click on Create, Geometry, Particle Systems (see fig. 20.24).

FIGURE 20.24
The particle systems selection as it appears in the Create Geometry module in MAX.

6. Click on the MTrack button to enter MAXTrax. Figure 20.25 shows the layout of MAXTrax parameters.

FIGURE 20.25

The MAXTrax

parameters.

7. Enter a start frame of 80 and an end frame of 130 for your first track.

8. Enter the end frame of 157 in the Display Until setting to make certain that the tracks stay visible after they are generated. Accept the rest of the default settings.

9. Click on the PICK button. This process has two steps: clicking on the reference object and then the target object.

10. In the Top viewport, click on the far left tire as the reference object. The emitter, which generates the track, will be made to fit the width of this object.

11. In the Top viewport, click on the edge of the road, making it the target object. The emitter will be aligned by face with your selection. It will be placed just above the road's surface to give the illusion of the tracks being painted on the road itself.

12. If it is not aligned with the tire, select and move the patch in the Top viewport until it is centered on the tire. Make certain that you do not move the patch vertically. Figure 20.26 shows the properly aligned emitter patch.

13. Click on the Select and Link button.

FIGURE 20.26

The emitter, which generates the skidmark or track, is aligned with the tire object.
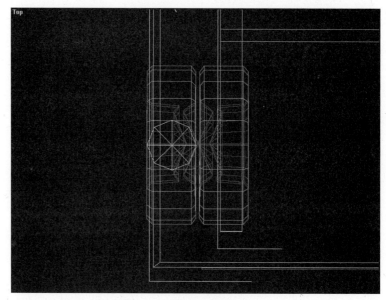

14. Click and hold the mouse button on the emitter and drag the cursor until it is over the tire. When you see the Link Boxes icon, release the mouse. The emitter patch will now follow your tire.

15. Change your viewport to the Shortbird camera and scroll the timeline to see the animation. The track is generated starting at frame 80.

16. With the emitter patch selected, take a few minutes to adjust the settings in the MTrack parameters to see your changes in real time. By adjusting the starting and stopping frame, you can see the track adjusted in the Camera viewport.

17. The only thing missing is the skid mark. Open the Material Editor and start a new material by clicking on the Standard button and choosing a New-Standard material. You will use both a Diffuse and Opacity map to create the tire tracks.

18. Click on Maps and the check boxes next to Diffuse and Opacity.

19. Click on the Map button for the Diffuse map and select Bitmap from the list.

20. Click on the blank button next to Bitmap and select the tireblak.tif file from the accompanying CD.

21. In the Mapping Coordinates section, adjust the UV mapping by setting the tiling factor for U to 24. You must play with this setting for each track you set to get the look you want (see fig. 20.27).

FIGURE 20.27

Adjusting the UV mapping coordinates is critical to get the correct aspect ratio along the length of track.

22. Click on the Map button for the Opacity map and select Bitmap from the list.

23. Click on the blank button next to Bitmap and select the tiretrak.tif file from the accompanying CD.

24. In the Mapping Coordinates section, adjust the UV mapping by setting the tiling factor for U to 24.

TIP

In most cases, unless you want a distorted map for your path, remember to make the exact same settings for mapping coordinates for the diffuse and the opacity maps.

25. Save the material as **tiretrax** and save it to your material library.

26. With the emitter selected, click on Assign Material to Selected and close the Material Editor.

27. Make certain that the shortbird view is displayed and go to frame 130.

28. Render a single frame of the animation, and you will see the tire track left behind the far left wheel.

29. Add a wrinkle to this basic track by making it stop and then start again. The only way to do this is to add a second emitter.

30. Go to frame 0 and Region Zoom to see the far left tire.

31. Click on the Select and Move button and constrain to the X axis.

32. Hold the left Shift key down and click on the emitter object without moving it. When you release the mouse, the Clone Options dialog box appears.

33. Click on OK to make a copy of the emitter.

34. Note that the first emitter is named Mtrack01 and the copy is Mtrack02.

35. Click on Select By Name and select Mtrack01.

36. Adjust the start frame to 30 and the end frame to 60. Leave the other settings the same.

37. Click on Select By Name and select Mtrack02.

38. Adjust the start frame to 90 and the end frame to 130. Leave the other settings the same.

39. Make certain that the shortbird view is displayed and go to frame 130.

40. Render a single frame of the animation. Figure 20.28 shows the broken track effect you just created.

FIGURE 20.28
A broken track effect is achieved by creating two emitters for the same tire.

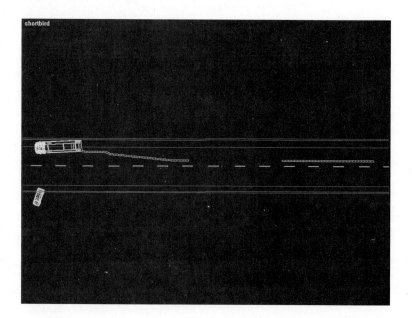

41. Save your file and load trax1.avi from the accompanying CD to see the final rendered animation. You can load the final animation file in MAX by loading the trax1fin.max file from the CD.

TIP

Make certain that you assign the same material to each track. You may have to adjust the UV tiling for each track separately to compensate for any difference in track length.

Footprints

This second tutorial uses MAXTrax to add footprints behind a Character Studio biped. Placement of the footprints is not an exact science in this method, but it will generate a footstep path for your character. The results look great from a distance and good from close up. If your perspective is a tight shot centered on the feet as the character walks, don't use this method because you will see inaccuracies. Similarly, if you are interested in the exact placement of the footprints, this method will not work.

In forensic animation, you quite often need to show footprints because a victim or defendant left some physical evidence showing the path he or she took. Perhaps a pedestrian claims to have been stuck by a car on the side of the road, but she left footprints in the mud or snow that show she was actually in the street when hit. In criminal cases, you may want to show how a burglar entered a building or how a murder suspect stalked a victim. In these situations, you could use footprints solely to identify the path taken. Using footprints enables the jury to see the path as the character walks and to refer back to it even after the walking sequence is complete. When these or similar situations arise, MAXTrax can help.

For short sequences of steps, it is easier to create a ground-level planar object at the point of each footstep and apply an opacity-mapped footprint manually. For longer runs or walks, the MAXTrax solution may be the best option. The main advantage would come if you had to change the path your character takes. If you use MAXTrax to create the footprints, any changes in your character motion would be automatically reflected in the footprints.

TIP

Sisyphus, the creators of MAXTrax, has commented that it would be very difficult to align the footprints with the footsteps precisely. This tutorial comes very close to being accurate by way of some extra steps to create texture maps that closely match the walking distance of each step. You may find that through making modifications to the MAXTrax settings, texture maps, or the walking gait of your character, your animations can be more accurate. If you discover a way to use the program to precisely place the footsteps, call Sisyphus; they would be very interested in hearing your technique.

As you set up your own animations to create footprints behind bipeds, refer to the following list of key areas to make adjustments that affect where the footprints are generated:

- The placement of the emitter patch from MAXTrax

- The size and scale of the emitter patch

- The UV tiling of the footprint texture and opacity maps

- The dimensions of the image files used in the footprint texture and opacity maps

- The footstep pattern of your character

Load the file walktrax.max from the accompanying CD and save it to your hard drive as **mytrax2.max**. The scene contains a hunched over biped character created with CS that takes a basic walk across the screen.

1. Maximize the Top viewport and Region Zoom until the character takes up most of your screen. Make certain that you can see a selectable edge of the floor object. You will need to select it as MAXTrax's target object.

2. Click on Create, Geometry, Particle Systems.

3. Click on the MTrack button to enter MAXTrax.

4. Leave the start frame of 0 and enter a stop frame of 306.

5. Enter the end frame of 306 in the Display Until setting to make certain that the tracks stay visible after they are generated. Accept the rest of the default settings.

6. Click on the PICK button to select the reference and target objects.

WARNING

You must select the reference object first. MAXTrax reminds you of the order in which you are choosing objects; just watch the MAX display bar for the prompts.

7. Click on the character as your reference object.

8. Click on the floor as your target object.

9. Click on My Choice in the Position Relative section of the MAXTrax panel. You should see the emitter patch appear aligned to the Top viewport.

10. Size the emitter patch to match the width of the character's feet by clicking on the Size and Uniform Scale tool and resizing the XY coordinates of the patch. Don't worry about the Z coordinate of the patch; MAXTrax aligned it directly above the floor when you picked the target object.

11. Click on Select and Move and move the patch directly under the character (see fig. 20.29).

FIGURE 20.29

This shows the correct size and location of the emitter patch relative to the character's feet.

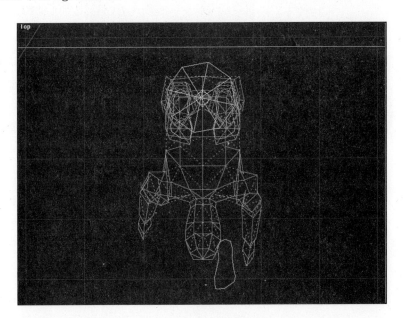

12. Switch views to show the Left viewport and Region Zoom to close in on the character, leaving room to show the first few footsteps.

13. Create a dummy for the character by clicking on Create, Helpers, Dummy. Draw a dummy of any size aligned near the front of the feet of the character. You will link this dummy to the character and the emitter to this dummy (see fig. 20.30).

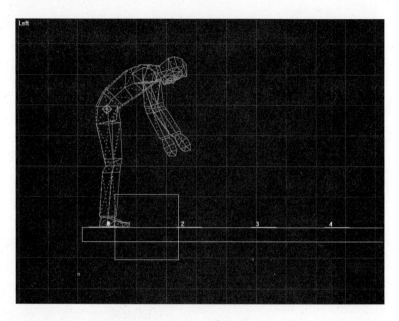

14. Because you need the footprints to stay on the ground, you want the dummy to follow only the horizontal motion of the character. You will do this by limiting the inherited links to only the Y axis by using the World coordinate system. Click on Hierarchy, Link Info, and uncheck everything but the Y check box under Inherit (see fig. 20.31).

FIGURE 20.31

The dummy object needs to inherit only the Y axis data from the character.

15. Click on Select and Link.

16. Select the dummy, drag the cursor over the character, and release the mouse. This links the dummy to the character.

17. Now link the emitter to the dummy. With Select and Link still the active tool, click on Select by Name and select the emitter (Mtrack01).

18. Click on Select by Name again to select the parent object, which is the dummy.

19. Switch views to the top view and drag the timeline to see the dummy and emitter move with the character (see fig. 20.32).

FIGURE 20.32

The emitter and dummy now move with the character. The emitter generates the footprints as it moves.

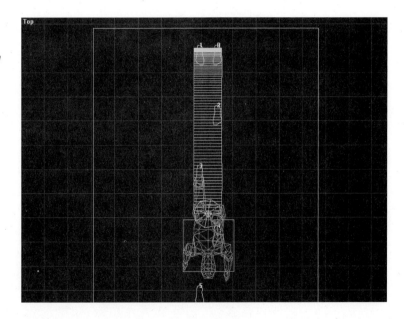

The only thing left to do is to assign the footprint material to the emitter. Use a paint program such as Photoshop to create the maps. To make the best attempt at an accurate map, you will need the following measurements:

- The distance from heel to heel in the walking pattern

- The length and width of each foot

- The distance from the outside edge of the left foot to the outside edge of the right foot

NOTE

These measurements will aid in the creation of the Diffuse and Opacity maps. They will not guarantee easy success in lining up the footsteps with the footprints generated by MAXTrax, but they should reduce the amount of playing around with settings it takes to get the amount of alignment you need.

1. Because you need the measurements in inches, click on Views, Units Setup and make certain that Decimal Inches is selected.

2. Using the Left viewport, drag the timeline to a point where the left and right foot are farthest apart.

3. Click on Create, Helpers, Tape.

4. Click on the viewport at the left heel and drag forward to the right heel. Because you will not use this tape measure again, you don't need to create it. When you reach the right heel, make note of the distance listed in the Parameters section for the length of the tape. In this example, it is roughly 22 inches (see fig. 20.33).

FIGURE 20.33
Gathering measurements from the character will help create an image map more easily aligned with the footsteps.

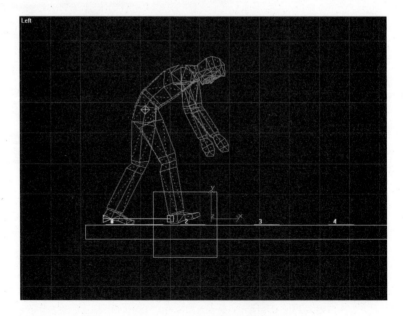

5. Right-click to cancel the creation of the tape measure.

6. Repeat this technique to gather the measurements listed in step 4.

7. With those measurements, create your footprint pattern in Photoshop, consisting of one left and one right footprint. Make the left foot the first print you create, followed by the right (see fig. 20.34).

FIGURE 20.34
This is the image created for the diffuse map of the footprints.

8. After you have created your footprint diffuse map, you will need an opacity map to drop out the surrounding area so that the footprints will appear on top of whatever surface your character is walking on in the animation. In Photoshop, do this by inverting the colors, changing to greyscale, and finally changing to a bitmap using diffusion dithering (see fig. 20.35).

FIGURE 20.35

This is the image created for the opacity map of the footprints.

NOTE

Remember that in the opacity map, everything black will be transparent and will let the underlying elements (in this case, the floor) show through.

9. Back in MAX, open the Material Editor and start a new material by clicking on the Standard button.

10. On the next screen, select Standard and click on OK.

11. Click on Maps and then on the check boxes next to Diffuse and Opacity.

12. Click on the Map button for the Diffuse map and select Bitmap from the list.

13. Click on the blank button next to Bitmap and select the 2steps.jpg file from the accompanying CD.

14. In the Mapping Coordinates section, adjust the UV mapping by setting the tiling factor for U to 1.0 and for V to 6.8. You also have to adjust the angle to get the footprints facing the same direction as the character. You must play with these settings to get the look you want (see fig. 20.36).

TIP

The settings for the UV tiling at 1.0 and 6.8 respectively are not exact. They came from numerous attempts at aligning the footprints. A good place to start is to take the total distance that your character walks and divide it by the distance covered by a left-right footstep sequence (the length of your image map) and to enter that number. If your character travels 21 feet and the length of your map is 3 feet, for example, enter a number of 7.0 for the V tiling and adjust from there.

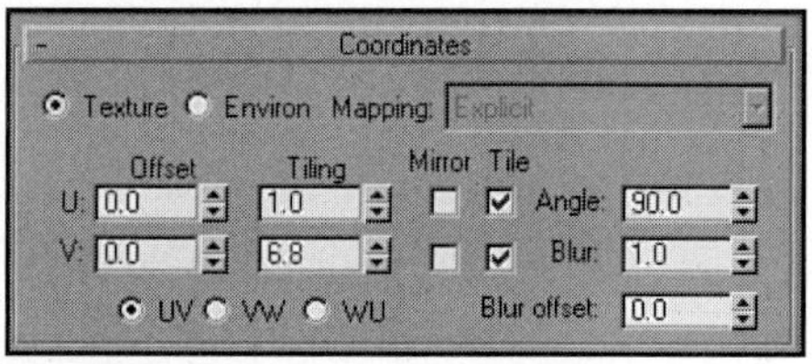

FIGURE 20.36

To align the footprints, adjust the UV mapping coordinates and the angle of the map.

15. Click on the Map button for the Opacity map and select Bitmap from the list.

16. Click on the blank button next to Bitmap and select the 2stepsop.tif file from the accompanying CD.

17. In the Mapping Coordinates section, adjust the UV mapping and angle setting to the same settings that you used for the diffuse map.

18. Save the material as **walking footsteps** and save it to your material library.

19. With the Mtrack01 emitter selected, click on Assign Material to Selected and close the Material Editor.

20. Click on Display and uncheck Cameras in the Hide by Category section.

21. Click on Select by Name and select both Camera01 and Camera01.target.

22. Click on Select and Link and drag the cursor to the dummy object and release the mouse button. The Camera and its target will now follow the character's dummy so that you can follow the walk and see all the footsteps MAXTrax will generate.

23. Activate the Camera viewport and slide the timeline to various frames along the walking path. Render a single frame at each frame to see how realistic the footprints appear (see fig. 20.37).

FIGURE 20.37
A rendered frame showing the footprints generated by MAXTrax.

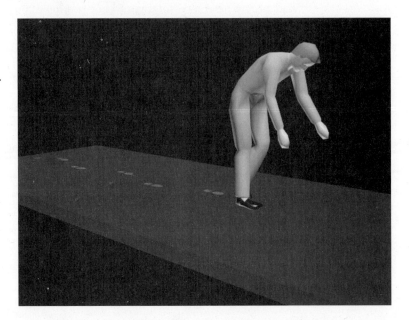

24. Save your file and load walktrax.avi from the accompanying CD to see the final rendered animation. You can load the final animation file in MAX by loading the walktrax.max file from the accompanying CD.

3DS MAX is a valuable tool for the forensic animator, and plug-ins are an essential part of the complete toolbox. One of the biggest production advantages you should realize from using Character Studio and MAXTrax is the time they save. The nature of the forensic industry is to create exhibits, such as animation, as a last thought. Attorneys tend to focus on current trial dates, depositions, and similar events. Not a lot of thought is put into exhibits for a trial nine months away. It is not uncommon, therefore, to be producing forensic animations in a very short time. Any tool that speeds up the process is worth its weight in gold. Because of the complexity of scenes and the necessity for accuracy, animators must focus on details, not methods of creation.

There are other means of creating effects such as skid marks and footprints besides the ones mentioned in this chapter. The methods introduced in this chapter were outlined because of their simplicity and automation. New plug-ins are being developed that will aid in the details of real-world physics that may play a large role in further automation of collisions. The main point is that MAX is an intentionally incomplete program. As new plug-ins are announced, the usefulness of MAX will increase, and the animator will benefit even more.

In Practice: Animating Accuracy for Forensics

- Go back to the timing.max file and add a camera in the driver's seat of the car to see what the driver's view would have been in this case. Based on the time the pedestrian is visible from behind the car, an expert could determine whether there was sufficient time to react and apply the brakes.

- To add more realistic movements, use Character Studio's biped in the fmsctudio.max file to adjust the body movements post-impact for the character. Subtle adjustments to the flailing of arms or the abrupt snap of the head at impact can make a more dramatic visual of the force of the impact.

- MAXTrax may be even better suited for group or herd foot- or hoofprints. Try setting up a scene where a large group of people or animals travels across the sand or snow—something that would show tracks. Create your image maps of randomly placed prints at different angles and positions. Make the map a long rectangular shape, filled with the prints, and attach it to a dummy object in the center of the rushing crowd.

- When designing tire tracks in MAXTrax, try making a map that looks more like a skid than a perfect tire track. It will look more realistic because the tires are not turning during the skid. You could do this by creating a distorted image map, or adjusting the UV tiling for the map in the Material Editor.

- There are a number of ways to place distinctive markings in your forensic animations. Scratches in paint where two cars impacted, for example, can be made by painting on the mesh's image maps with a program such as Detailer, or by using Unwrap to make a flat image map with the outline of the mesh visible for painting in Photoshop. For times when there is a dent or gouge (something that penetrates a flat surface), try making a clone of the object to be damaged, linking it to its original/parent object, and hiding it in the scene until the impact occurs. At impact, unhide the damaged clone, and hide its original.

Part VII

CHARACTER ANIMATION

IMAGE CREATED BY GEORGE MAESTRI

Chapter 21

by George Maestri

Setting Up Characters for Animation

Setup is one of the most important tasks a character animator faces. It involves not only building the character so that it looks nice, but also tweaking the models and adding elements such as skeletons and expressions to help the animation process along. If a character is built solidly and is easy to animate, the process goes faster, and the animator's creative flow isn't interrupted by frustrating problems and system delays.

Setup includes deciding how to build your characters and how to manipulate them. Characters can be built in segments so that they are animated at the object level, or they can be built as one solid object and animated at the sub-object level. Characters that are one solid mesh are usually deformed with a skeleton, which also needs to be set up so that it can be manipulated with IK. Characters created out of separate objects also can be manipulated with IK. This chapter covers the following topics:

- Types of characters
- Creating skeletons that deform meshes
- Building a skeleton from scratch
- Skeletons for hands

Types of Characters

3D Studio MAX offers a number of strategies for creating characters. Many of these methods are the same used for creating any object within MAX; the previous volume discussed many of these techniques. How the character is animated depends on how it is built.

Characters can be animated at the object level. Object level animation requires that the character be split up into discrete segments that are linked together in a hierarchy. Object level animation is how most characters in video games are animated.

Characters that need to have a smooth, seamless skin should be animated at the sub-object level, which means that the vertices of the mesh or the patch are affected by using any number of techniques, described in later chapters. These techniques include Physique, Bones Pro, FFDs, and linked XForms, to name a few.

Object Level Animation—Segmented Characters

The easiest way to animate a character is to separate the body into segments and animate the individual objects. Picture a segmented character as the classic artist's mannequin, constructed of wood and fitted together with pins at the joints. An armored knight or a jointed robot would be other examples of a segmented character (see figs. 21.1 and 21.2).

FIGURE 21.1
A good example of a segmented character.

FIGURE 21.2
This exploded view shows that his body is composed of multiple objects.

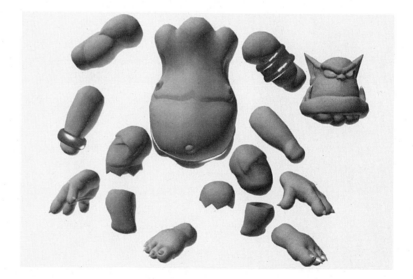

Segmented characters are pretty much required for applications such as video games. Most game machines require that objects be segmented because deforming a mesh requires too much overhead. The same is true for MAX. It animates segments faster because deforming a mesh requires extra calculations.

The many parts of a segmented character are joined together via a hierarchy, which can then be animated using forward kinematics or inverse kinematics (IK).

There are, of course, drawbacks to creating segmented characters. First, the seams always find a way to show themselves—no matter how hard you try to hide them. You can always turn this pitfall to your advantage by purposely designing your character with exposed seams. Pixar's Buzz Lightyear is a good example of such a design.

Solid Mesh Characters

A solid mesh character is built as one solid object and animated at the sub-object level. This character can be built out of any supported MAX geometry, from polygons to patches. Animating such a character requires use of a mesh deformation system (see fig. 21.3). MAX has two such systems, sold as plug-ins: Physique and Bones Pro. Physique is sold as one part of Character Studio by Kinetix, and Bones Pro is a product from Digimation. Operation of these plug-ins is described in Chapters 24, "Mesh Deformation" and 25, "Physique." For now, however, it is important to know that both plug-ins require a skeleton of bones to deform the mesh.

FIGURE 21.3

A solid mesh character can be constructed out of spline patches or polygons, but must be deformed using a mesh deformation plug-in, such as Physique or Bones Pro.

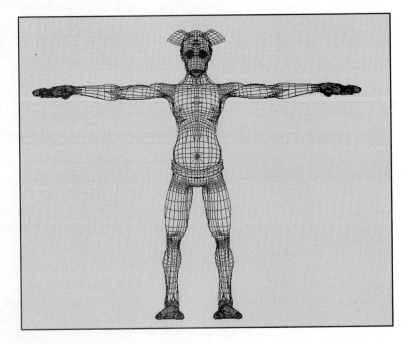

Building Solid Meshes out of Polygons

Historically, polygons have typically been the modeling method of choice for many 3D Studio and MAX animators. One reason to animate with polygonal meshes is because MAX's mesh modeling tools are very robust. This wealth of tools allows for much more control over the modeling process, but the end result of that process is a mesh.

Polygonal meshes definitely have the advantage of a wealth of tools, and this may make them a good choice for characters animated within MAX. The disadvantage of creating polygonal mesh models is that they can be difficult to control when animated at the sub-object level with a mesh deformation tool:

- The first reason is speed. Polygonal meshes require significantly more vertices to create a smooth skin than a patch object does. A larger number of vertices means that the CPU needs to perform more calculations, slowing down the process and hampering interactivity.

- Second, and more importantly, the increased density of a polygonal mesh means that the vertices are closer together, which gives the character a much higher probability of tearing, crimping, or bulging in the wrong places. Deciding which vertex belongs to which skeletal bone can prove to be an exercise in hair splitting.

Still, MAX does have tools such as MeshSmooth, which can allow for a low-polygonal count model to behave in much the same way that a spline model would. This is discussed in detail in Chapter 24.

Building Solid Meshes from Spline Patches

As was mentioned previously, patches are much better for organic characters, particularly in solid mesh characters deformed by a skeleton. The reason for this is that patches cover a much larger area with fewer vertices and remain smooth over a wider range of motion. The fewer things you need to animate, the less you have to worry about. Although MAX's patch modeling tools can be a bit tough to master, models built this way can perform much better at animation time.

The introduction of Digimation's Surface Tools has given animators an easy to use and serious tool for animating patch surfaces. As described earlier in this volume, the plug-in gives animators a much better way of creating a patch surface by defining the outline with simple Bézier curves.

Surface Tools contains a number of modifiers, most important of which are Cross Section and Surface. Cross Section is similar to a skinning tool in that it takes a series of spline outlines and connects them together. Surface completes the process by turning the splines into a flexible patch surface. Bodies can be built using Surface Tools by creating a "cage" out of splines and using the Cross Section tool to stitch them together. The objects created within Surface Tools resolve to patches, which, in turn, resolve to meshes.

Placement of Detail Within a Solid Mesh

Whether you build out of splines or polygons, you should always pay attention to where the detail is in a character. A character needs extra detail at the joints, such as the knees and elbows. This extra detail enables the joints to bend smoothly and realistically. Areas that don't flex, such as the part of the thigh and shin outside the knee, can be spared extra detail. In figure 21.4 the hand is very flexible, so it requires more detail. The forearm is relatively rigid and requires less. More detail is added at the elbow because it also flexes. More vertices in the middle part of the joints only add weight to a character, but doesn't help add detail to the outline of the character.

FIGURE 21.4
This close-up of the alien's arm shows the varying degrees of detail.

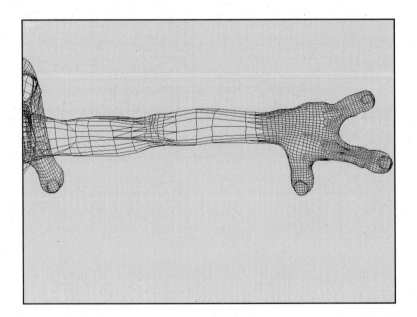

Two other areas that require attention to detail and the placement of it are the groin and shoulder areas. These areas are also flexible, but along a much wider range than the knees or elbows. When constructing the intersection of the legs and the hips at the groin area, try to model extra detail along the "bikini line," roughly a 45-degree line that runs from the inside of the crotch to the top of the hips (see fig. 21.5).

FIGURE 21.5

This close-up of the hip area shows the extra detail along the intersection of the thighs and hips.

The shoulders are probably the most flexible joints in the body and thus need to be modeled properly to allow for proper deformation. Think of the shoulders as a slight funnel shape that leads from the arms to the torso, with extra detail in the upper arm that broadens out into the chest area (see fig. 21.6)

FIGURE 21.6
This close-up of the shoulder area shows how the extra detail is added to the upper arm as it transitions to the chest area.

Metaball Characters

Metaballs can also be used for creating characters. MAX has a number of metaball plug-ins (some of the most innovative on the market). Two of the most notable are Infografica's Meta-Reyes (see fig. 21.7), which can create dynamic muscle-shaped metaballs, and Digimation's Clay Studio, which allows for spherical, ellipsoidal, and rectangular primitives. The simple capability to create non-spherical objects significantly reduces the number of objects needed to construct a character. Animating fewer objects makes for fewer headaches when animation time comes around. MetaReyes is discussed in detail in Chapter 24.

Mapping was a problem with earlier metaball implementations. Both Digimation and Infografica have addressed this with *sticky mapping*, which allows the underlying metaball objects to be animated. The map, however, remains glued to the surface, enabling some very natural and organic animation.

The metaballs created by these programs can be linked among themselves to build a blobby, segmented character without seams. They can also be attached to skeletons, such as those created by Biped. As with a solid mesh character, the skeleton can be animated fairly easily like a segmented character, with the metaballs fusing only at render time.

FIGURE 21.7
This character was created using Info-grafica's MetaReyes plug-in by Jose Maria de Espona. Notice how the metaball primitives follow the natural lines that muscles normally would.

Hybrid Characters

Because MAX can mix and match geometry types on the fly, there is no reason you cannot mix and match any of the previously discussed methods when building your character. Facial animation, which is covered in Chapter 26, "Facial Animation and Lip Sync," can be accomplished quite effectively with Surface Tools. The entire character can be constructed out of Surface Tools–generated geometry.

Building a hand using Surface Tools, however, might prove to be too much effort, and metaballs can be used to make simple hands quite easily. Metaballs also work well for bodies, but facial animation using metaballs can be difficult to achieve.

Polygons can also be used in any of these situations, from heads to bodies to hands. The choice of tools depends on the individual character and the animation tasks it needs to perform. It might be a good idea to use a Surface Tools–generated head on a polygonal body with metaball-generated hands. Any number of combinations is possible, so it is always a good idea to consider all possibilities and tools at your disposal.

Creating Skeletons that Deform Meshes

If you build a seamless mesh character, you will need to deform that mesh in one way or another. For very simple characters, modifiers such as Bend, Twist, or an FFD might work. Typically, however, this is not enough. In most cases, you must create a skeleton and use a plug-in such as Physique or Bones Pro.

The skeletons required by these plug-ins are very similar to the bones in a human body. Most digital characters built in this way have thigh bones, shin bones, spines, necks, shoulders, and hips (to name a few). Of course, digital skeletons are merely a simplified approximation of the real thing. The human body has dozens of vertebrae in the spine. A digital skeleton may have only three.

Skeletons are put together in much the same way as segmented characters. They are merely objects linked together into a hierarchy. You can build your own skeletons out of MAX's bones or out of simple geometry, such as boxes. If you are building a two-legged creature, you can use the prebuilt skeletons supplied with Biped—the other half of Character Studio (see fig. 21.8).

FIGURE 21.8

Biped provides a good example of a skeleton, though there are many ways of building skeletons in MAX.

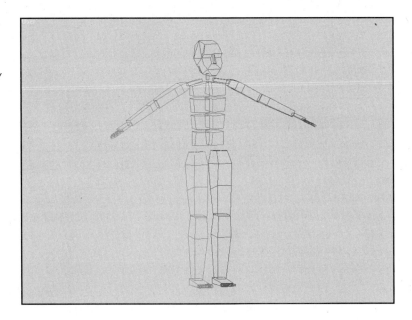

MAX Bones

MAX has the capability to create a system of bones. In the simplest sense, bones are helper objects linked hierarchically. Bones can be found in the Create panel under the systems glyph.

MAX Bones work with jointed characters, but to be used with a solid mesh character, they must be coupled with a mesh deformation plug-in, such as Physique or Bones Pro. Vertex animation can be accomplished through a linked XForm modifier so that the vertices of the mesh are actually controlled and moved by the bones system. All of these methods are discussed in detail in Chapter 10, "Animating with Biped."

The nice thing about bones is that creating them automatically generates a hierarchy. If you look in Track View, you can see that a two-bone chain actually consists of a base object (bone01) plus the two bones.

The bones can be animated and manipulated by clicking on the bones and translating the objects. The bones behave in two ways, depending on whether IK is turned on or off.

- When IK is off, only the end effectors of each bone move, enabling you to reposition and change the length of the bone on the fly (see fig. 21.9).

- When IK is turned on, the bone's length remains fixed. The bone will automatically flex and bend much like the bones in a skeleton. As you will see, the IK rotations of these bones can be constrained in a number of ways (see fig. 21.10).

Bones can also be rotated manually to accomplish forward kinematic-type motions. The trick here is knowing which object to rotate. You must rotate the bone at its base—the joint where the bone begins. The forearm, for example, is rotated at the elbow. This is the same for MAX bones.

When IK is on, the bones are always rigid. This can cause headaches because your skeletons can change shape if you forget to switch on IK. Some animators consider this a detriment; others use this to get stretchy cartoon-like effects because—in both Physique and Bones Pro—stretching the bone stretches the underlying mesh. If you want to move the chain as a whole, you can always select the entire bone structure and move it with IK turned off without affecting the shape.

FIGURE 21.9
Moving a bone with IK off resizes the bone.

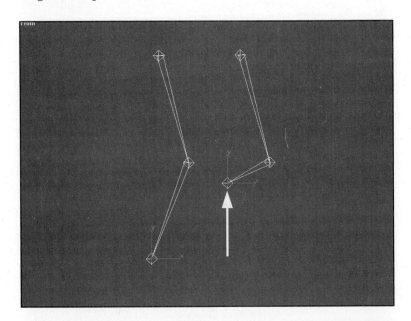

FIGURE 21.10
Moving a bone with IK on, however, keeps the bone rigid and forces the chain to bend.

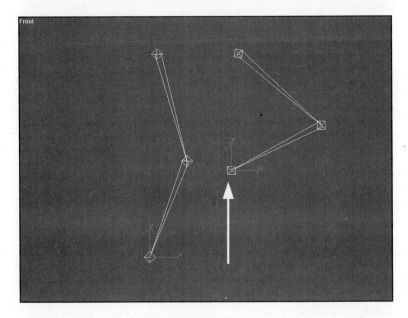

Boxes as Bones

In addition to bones, MAX users are fortunate that both Physique and Bones Pro can use any type of object as a bone. Most animators use simple boxes, though any geometry works. The bones created by Character Studio's Biped module are box-like and are a very good example of how to construct an effective skeleton out of simple objects.

The advantages of using box bones over MAX bones is that the boxes are easier to visualize; you can watch them in Shaded mode and render simple tests. Another advantage is that box bones retain their shape regardless of whether IK is flipped on; their shape must be changed by scaling.

Box bones are a bit harder to model and set up, and the extra geometry adds a bit to the weight of the scene. Boxes must also be hidden before rendering, which adds a step to the rendering process.

Digimation's Skeleton plug-in, provided with Bones Pro, can turn MAX bones into box bones. The plug-in retains the linking from the original bones and enables you to sketch out a skeleton quite easily, changing the bones into boxes after the skeleton is set (see fig. 21.11).

FIGURE 21.11

Two skeletons. The one on the right is made of MAX Bones, and the left is made of box bones.

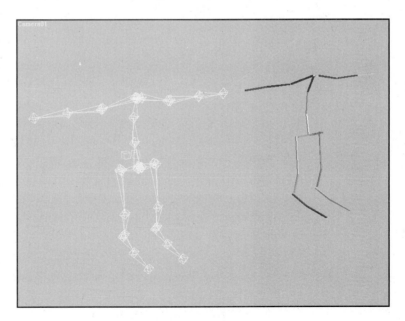

Building a Skeleton from Scratch

If you have Biped, building a skeleton is as easy as clicking and dragging. Still, building your own will give you insight into the entire process of how a skeleton works. Creating a skeleton is similar to creating a segmented character, only the geometry is much simpler. Likewise, setting up IK for a segmented character is the same as for a generic skeleton. This basic skeleton can be used in conjunction with either Physique or Bones Pro.

Creating Bones

Creating a skeleton can be intimidating, but it is simply a matter of creating bones that mimic the bones of your character's body. Your skeleton will have arm bones, leg bones, and a spinal column, to name a few. Typically, it is a good idea to load your target mesh and freeze it, using it as a guide for creating, fitting, and sizing the bones of the skeleton. The following exercise strips away the mesh so that you can see exactly how the bones are built and tied together.

The first step is to build two basic bones: one vertical, one horizontal. Create the vertical bone first.

STRIPPING AWAY THE MESH TO SEE THE STRUCTURE

1. Go to the Creation panel and create a simple box to use as a bone. For demonstration purposes, make a box of 10×10×40 units. (Of course, the size of the box depends a great deal on the size of your mesh object being deformed.)

2. Go to the Hierarchy panel and click on the Pivot button. Under Move/Rotate/Scale, click on Affect Pivot Only. Move the pivot so that it rests neatly along the top of the box and the Z axis of the pivot is aligned with the length of the box. This will be the basic bone.

3. Now create a horizontal box with dimensions of 40×10×10, which will become the basis of your skeleton's hips and shoulders.

4. Again, go to the Hierarchy panel and click on the Pivot button. Under the Move/Rotate/Scale rollout, click Affect Pivot Only. Next, under Alignment, press Center to Object. Check your results against figure 21.12.

FIGURE 21.12

The two basic bones. The horizontal bone has its pivot centered, while the vertical one's pivot is at the base.

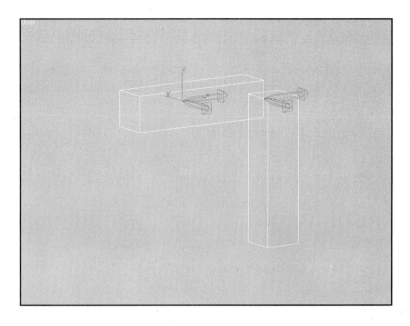

5. If you plan to use IK, it is best to change the default rotation controller to Euler XYZ for both bones. As is explained in *Inside 3D Studio MAX Volume I*, this is the best controller to use with IK. With this default, when you copy the bone, the controller will go with it. You set this controller as the default by clicking on the Make Default button in the Replace Rotation Controller dialog box (see fig. 21.13).

FIGURE 21.13

Select Euler XYZ as the rotation controller for use with IK.

Creating a Skeleton

The next task is to copy and arrange these bones into a skeleton. It may be a skeleton for a human, as is constructed here, or it can vary as widely as your characters.

ARRANGING THE SKELETON

1. Give the first bone a descriptive name. This will be a shin bone in this particular skeleton, so name the bone **R-Shin**.

2. Copy this bone and drag the copy upward so that it rests immediately above the first. Name this bone **R-Thigh**.

3. Copy R-Shin and R-Thigh, and drag these new bones approximately 45 units to the left. Name these **L-Shin** and **L-Thigh**.

4. Copy the horizontal box and place it between the two legs to create the hips. Name this bone **Hips**. Compare what you have to figure 21.14.

FIGURE 21.14
The hips and legs of the skeleton.

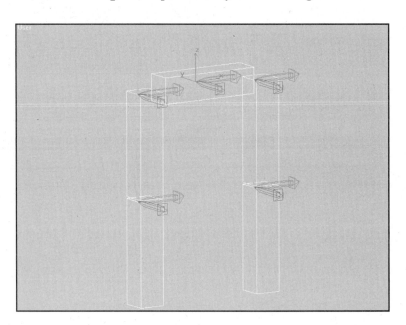

5. Copy one of the leg bones and resize it so that it is 20 units high. This will be the base of the spine.

6. Rotate this bone 180 degrees so that the pivot is located at the bottom of the box. Place this bone directly above the center of the hips. Name the bone **Spine-01**.

7. Copy this bone twice to create the rest of the spinal column. Name these **Spine-02** and **Spine-03**. Typically, three bones are just enough to give the illusion of a full spine, though you can add more if your character needs more flexibility. Check figure 21.15.

FIGURE 21.15

The spine. Notice how the pivots for these bones are located along the lower part of the joint.

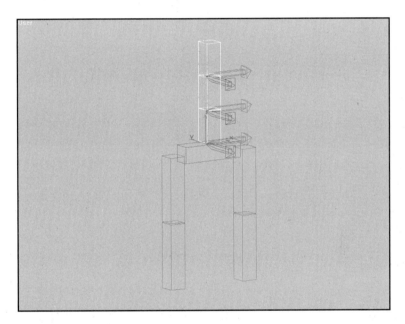

8. Copy the hips and drag the box upward to make the shoulders. Resize this box so that it is 30 units wide. Copy this again and name the two bones **L-Shoulder** and **R-Shoulder**, respectively. Copy it again and make a smaller bone the width of the spine (10 units). Name this bone **Collar**. Reposition the pivots of these bones so that they lie on the end of the spine (see fig. 21.16).

FIGURE 21.16

Positioning of the shoulder and collar bones. The shoulders should pivot along the edge of the bone closest to the collar bone.

Having two separate bones will help your character shrug its shoulders and such, and will also help you create more natural arm motions. One long shoulder bone can work for simple characters who do not need to perform these types of actions. If all your character does is walk, the extra bone may not be necessary.

9. Copy the leg bones and rotate them 180 degrees to make the right arm. Position these just outside the shoulders. Name these two bones **R-Bicep** and **R-Forearm**. Copy these two to the left side of the body and name those bones **L-Bicep** and **L-Forearm**.

10. You now can link the hand hierarchy to the ends of the arms. If your hands are separate objects, link those in. In this case, use a dummy object as a stand-in for a hand that can be added in later. Name these objects **L-HandDummy** and **R-HandDummy**. Compare your results to figure 21.17.

11. Copy a spine bone and use it to create a neck. Name this bone **Neck**.

12. Many animators like to keep the head as a separate object. If this is the case, just link the head to the neck. In this example, a sphere will stand in for the head. Name this object **Head**.

FIGURE 21.17

The arms. Notice how the pivots are located along the top edge of each bone.

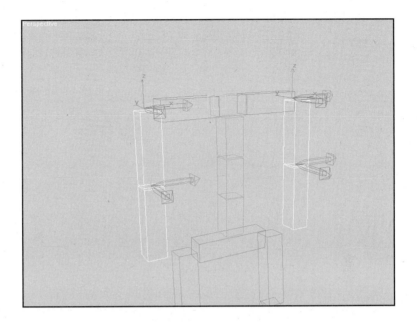

If your body and head are one seamless mesh, the facial animation method must be considered. If you are using bones to animate the face, these bones can be linked into the hierarchy for the rest of the body. If you are using direct manipulation tools such as linked XForms, you will need to link the XForms to the body in some fashion—usually by linking them hierarchically to a dummy, which in turn is linked to the neck.

With some facial animation methods you actually use two heads, one of which is actually attached to the body. The first head contains Bones or linked XForms used to actually animate the shape of the face. The second head is simply a referenced clone of the first and is the one actually attached to the body. Animation performed on the first head is reflected on the second. This allows you to attach a head to the body that is free of helper objects, such as bones, that also need to be attached. The first head can then be placed out of camera range and animated.

13. Finally, create the feet. If your character is barefoot and needs to wiggle its toes, you may need to construct a complete skeleton for the feet, but this hardly ever happens. Most characters wear shoes and toe wiggling is not a common action, so you can simplify the feet with two bones—one for the foot and one for the toes. Name these bones **R-Heel** and **R-Toe**. Copy these two to the left leg and rename the copies **L-Heel** and **L-Toe**. Compare your final result against figure 21.18.

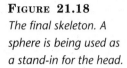

FIGURE 21.18

The final skeleton. A sphere is being used as a stand-in for the head.

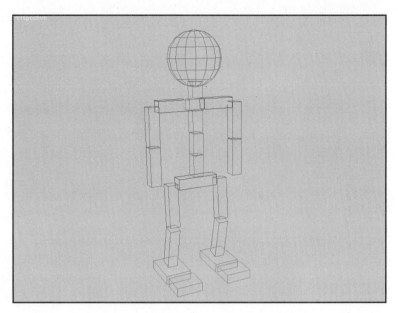

Methods for Linking the Bones Together

After the skeleton is in place, the bones must be linked together into a hierarchy. This speeds animation and enables you to use IK. How the hierarchy is constructed depends on the character and the requirements of the animation.

For a two-legged character, the hierarchy is always centered around the hips in some manner. The hips are the center of the body's weight distribution, and they are where the upper body, supported by the spine, connects to the legs. How the hips are connected to the legs is one of the central questions that you must ask. The hip-centric places the hips at the top of the hierarchy with the legs and spine as children. Other methods break the hierarchy at the hips and keep each of the legs as separate hierarchies.

Hip Centric

By far the most common is a simple hierarchical linkage that uses the hips as the base of the hierarchy.

A hip-centric hierarchy (see fig. 21.19) is the best way to keep the body so that it moves as one. It is also the best method to set up a skeleton for IK.

SETTING UP A HIERARCHY FOR A HIP-CENTRIC HUMAN BODY

1. To link the legs to the hips: On the right side of the body, link the toes to the feet, the feet to the shins, the shins to the thighs, and the thighs to the hips. Repeat for the left side.

2. To link the spinal column together: Link the head to the neck, and the neck to the top of the spine. Link all the spinal joints, top to bottom, and finally the base of the spine to the hips.

3. Link the forearm to the bicep, the bicep to the shoulder, and the shoulder to the top of the spine. Repeat for the left side.

4. Save the model.

FIGURE 21.19

The hip-centric hierarchy has the hips as the parent with the legs and spine as children.

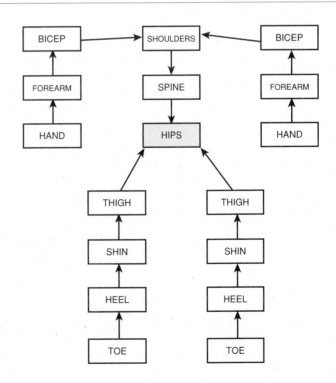

Broken Hierarchies

Using the broken hierarchies method typically turns the hierarchy of the legs upside down, making the toes the parents of the feet, which parent the legs (see fig. 21.20). Because an object can't have two parents, the hierarchy must be broken at the hips. This gives you a total of three chains to work with: one for each leg and one for the upper body, starting with the hips.

FIGURE 21.20

The broken hierarchy has three separate chains, one for the hips and spine, and one each for the legs.

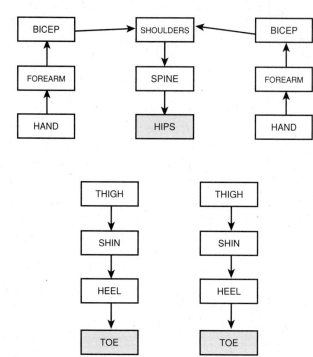

Another thing you need to do when setting up this type of hierarchy is to reverse the pivots of all the leg bones. In a hip-centric hierarchy, the thigh pivots at the hip. In a broken hierarchy, the thigh pivots at the knee, the shin at the ankle, and so on.

The broken hierarchy method is certainly the exception rather than the rule, but it works great if you want to avoid setting up IK for a skeleton. Because the hips are not connected, they must be animated so that they "float" above the legs, which invariably causes some gaps between the joints, and it is best used for skeletons that deform a mesh (because those skeletons are ultimately hidden). It can also be used for characters where the hips are hidden—a character in a dress, for example. Another caveat is that a broken hierarchy may cause problems with single mesh characters and Physique because that plug-in relies on the hierarchy to determine how the mesh is deformed.

TIP

One easy way to get the hips to line up in a broken hierarchy is to create a dummy object linked to the tops of each thigh and add two more to each end of the hips. The dummies on the hips can then be linked to the ones on the thighs by using Bind Position in the IK rollout. This will enable you to move the legs, and the hips will automatically float between them.

Setting Up and Controlling IK

After the hierarchy is in place, you can actually turn on IK and manipulate the skeleton. Doing so, however, invariably makes the skeleton go haywire because, by default, all the joints are completely unconstrained. Without constraints, the IK system comes up with multiple solutions for each joint's position, making the model very hard to control.

To keep the model under control, you first need to limit the actions of the joints so that they rotate naturally and that the solutions generated by the IK system are regular and predictable. The elbow only bends along one axis, for example, so limiting the other two axes so that they don't move will give you a more predictable motion. This is done by setting the rotational limits for each joint.

WARNING

One strong warning needs to be given at this point. MAX's IK does not like any objects created or modified using non-uniform scale at the object level, or mirror, or mirrored clones. Be sure to avoid these religiously when modeling objects intended to be used in IK chains.

TIP

By default all objects are free to rotate in all three axes. If you set an axis constraint for the first bone at the start of the skeleton building process (say x-only) before you start cloning all the bones, IK can be much faster to set up.

Setting Rotational Limits

Rotational limits are found on the IK panel under Rotational Limits. Each axis (X, Y, and Z) has parameters that can be set. Most of these are discussed in *Inside 3D Studio MAX Volume I*. Table 21.1 lists suggested joint parameters for this skeleton. In the table, it is assumed that the Y axis of each joint runs along the length of the bone. Joints with limits of zero can be set inactive.

TABLE 21.1

Rotational Limits for a Generic Hip-Centric Human Skeleton

Joint	X	Y	Z
Hips	0–0	0–0	0–0
L-Thigh	-90–20	0–30	0–15
L-Shin	0–125	0–0	0–0
L-Heel	-115– -60	0–0	0–0
L-Toe	-40–10	0–0	0–0
R-Thigh	-90–20	0–30	0–15
R-Shin	0–125	0–0	0–0
R-Heel	-115– -60	0–0	0–0
R-Toe	-40–10	0–0	0–0
L-Shoulder	0–0	-6–12	-20–10
L-Bicep	-140–45	0–0	0–180
L-Forearm	-135–0	0–0	0–0
R-Shoulder	0–0	-6–12	-20–10
R-Bicep	-140–45	0–0	0–180
R-Forearm	-135–0	0–0	0–0
Spine-01	-5–10	0–0	0–0
Spine-02	-5–10	0–0	0–0
Spine-03	-5–10	0–0	0–0
Collar	0–0	0–0	0–0

Terminating IK Chains

Rotational limits, however, are only the first step. You also need to terminate some of the chains to further refine the motion. If you pull on the hand, for example, it is usually to position the arm only. The hierarchy of the arm, however, runs through the shoulder to the spine and down to the hips. Without terminating the chain at the shoulder, moving the hand would invoke an IK solution in every joint between the hand and the hips. This would likely cause your skeleton to go haywire again.

The Terminator button can help prevent this from happening. This button enables you to dictate which joints are calculated in an IK chain. The arm, for example, should be terminated at the shoulder to prevent hand motion from affecting the spine (see fig. 21.21). Terminating each chain in the skeleton makes it much easier to control the behavior of the skeleton. The joint that terminates the chain is the one immediately above the chain you want to constrain. The arm is terminated at the shoulder; the legs are terminated at the hips. See figure 21.22.

FIGURE 21.21

Positioning an arm without termination affects the entire upper body.

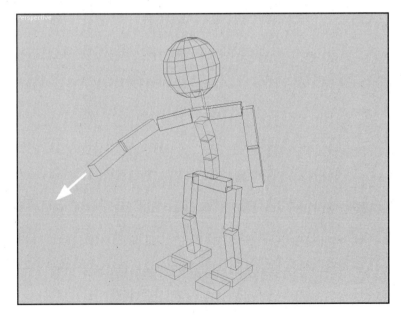

FIGURE 21.22
With the shoulder set as the terminator, only the arm itself is affected, giving you more control over how it is posed.

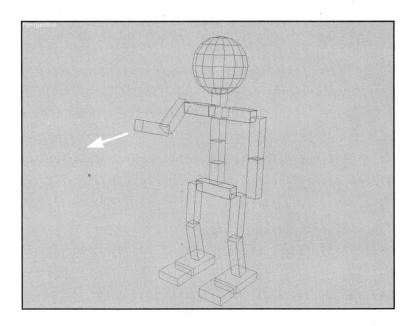

To set termination, simply select the joint you would like to affect, in this case the shoulder; go to the IK panel and toggle the Terminate button on. Once toggled, all IK calculations will stop at the chosen joint. In a hip-centric hierarchy, the spine and legs are naturally terminated at the hips, which, as the top of the hierarchy, are also the end of the chain. This makes the hip bone a natural terminator.

Creating Handles

Handles are an aid to help you simplify the task of animating a skeleton. Typically, they are dummy objects linked into the skeleton at critical points, such as the ends of the toes, fingers, ankles, and so on. The most important place to put these is at the ends of a chain (at the toe, for example). If the toe itself is dragged, IK will not change its angle (to be specific, the toe itself is a handle) (see fig. 21.23). For the toe to be included in the solution, a dummy object must be placed beyond the end of the toe and used as an effector, or, more generically, a handle (see fig. 21.24).

FIGURE 21.23

Pulling the toe flexes the leg, but does not enable the toe itself to flex.

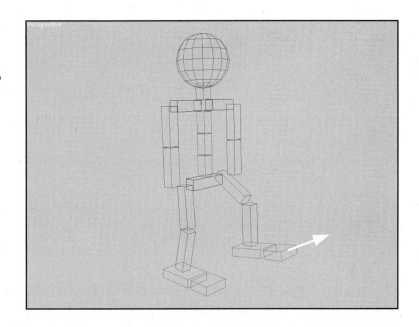

FIGURE 21.24

A dummy object placed at the end of the toe (shown in white) becomes a handle, enabling the toe to flex.

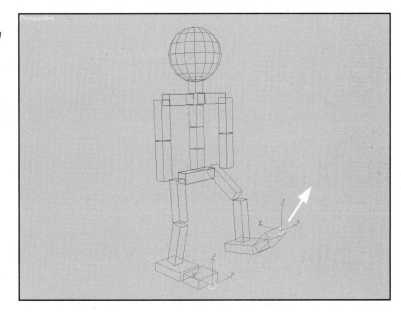

Effectors placed beyond the end of the chain are also very important when using Physique because this plug-in relies on the hierarchy to determine how a mesh is affected. Physique requires that the hierarchy extend one joint beyond the end of the mesh. If the hierarchy stops at the toe, Physique only affects vertices up to, but not including, the toe area.

To further refine the skeleton, you can insert a handle inside the hierarchy to act both as a terminator and as a handle. Again, a good example is the foot. The hips, being the root of the hierarchy, act as a terminator for the leg chain. If a handle at the end of the toe is moved, IK will have to solve for the toe, the heel, the shin, and the thigh. Four joints in the chain increase the possibility of multiple solutions and reduce the amount of control you have over the leg. Using extra dummies in the hierarchy can also allow more complex ranges of motion (the shoulder for example) so that limits can change when certain angles are met.

Introducing a second dummy into the hierarchy between the ankle and the shin (see fig. 21.25) enables it to act as a terminator for the foot. This way, pulling the toe now only affects the toe and the heel. This second dummy can also be used as a handle to manipulate the shin and the thigh. Breaking the leg into discrete IK segments with handles gives you more control. The only objects that need to be animated are the handles, not the actual geometry of the skeleton itself (though this is certainly possible). You can also add such handles at the shoulders and at the spine.

FIGURE 21.25

A handle (shown in white) inserted into the hierarchy between the foot and the leg.

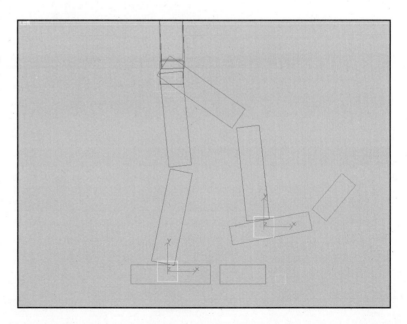

TIP

When placing a handle inside a hierarchy, it is important to set all IK rotation limits to zero (or deactivate them). This way, the dummy will remain fixed in relation to its parent. If it is allowed to rotate, the rotation limits for the lower joint (in this case, the heel) will become skewed.

Testing a Skeleton

The easiest way to test a skeleton is to manipulate it through a wide range of motion. If you have created handles for all the major points of the skeleton, these should be the only objects that need to be animated (see fig. 21.26). To make it easier to select a handle, freeze the bones of the skeleton, leaving only the handles active.

FIGURE 21.26

Typical placement of handles for a human skeleton.

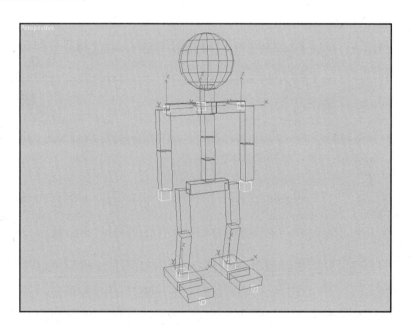

After this is done, manipulating the skeleton is a simple matter of turning on IK, selecting the appropriate handle, and moving it. To fine tune an animation, however, you may need to go back to some joints, such as the hands or feet, and fine tune joint rotations as needed.

The finished skeleton is located in a file named ik-skel.max on the accompanying CD.

Skeletons for Hands

Hands are one of the most complex parts of the human body. A hand has dozens of bones, muscles, and tendons covered with a pliable skin that bends and flexes. Modeling and setting up a skeleton for a hand so that it animates well presents a daunting task.

Construction of the Skeleton

Placement of the bones for the fingers is fairly obvious. Each finger has three joints, and each joint requires a bone. If you want to set up IK for a finger, you need to add a dummy object as the end effector for each finger chain. The upper two joints of the fingers should have their rotations constrained to one axis only. The lowest joint of the finger, however, can also move along a second axis, enabling the fingers to spread.

The palm and the thumb are another matter. The palm of the hand contains many bones, enabling the hand to flex enough so that the thumb can touch the pinky. (If the palm were rigid, this couldn't occur.)

One way to allow for this motion is to model a separate bone through the palm for each finger. If such flexibility is not needed, the palm can be represented by a single bone (perhaps a box).

Another situation involves the knuckle, over which the skin stretches when the fingers curl under the palm. Accurately simulating this stretching motion can be difficult, even with advanced tools such as Physique. Adding knuckle bones to the hand hierarchy can help the situation by giving Physique (and Bones Pro) an extra bone to help define the outline of the hand (see figs. 21.27 and 21.28).

Though only two joints are visible on the thumb, a third joint exists within the body of the palm. This joint enables the thumb to move above and below the plane of the hand, giving humans their opposable thumbs.

Figure 21.27
A simple skeleton for the hand uses a box as the basis for the palm.

Figure 21.28
Adding separate palm bones for each finger gives the hand more flexibility.

Attaching a Hand to the Arm

To attach a hand to the skeleton, the hand hierarchy can be linked to the wrist. One good tactic is to place a dummy inside the hierarchy between the palm and the wrist. This dummy can act as a handle to manipulate the arm and also as a terminator for the hand hierarchy.

Using Reference Objects to Animate a Hand

One problem when manipulating a hand is getting a good view of the hand and its exact pose. Posing a hand can require some very delicate fine tuning, requiring a clear, close-up view of it. Unfortunately, the hand itself can move over a large range if the arms are in motion, which makes it difficult to maintain a clear view of what your character's hands are doing. There are a number of way to keep an eye on the hands, so to speak.

One method is to make a referenced clone of the entire hand, with an instancing of the controller so that both the clone and the original animate in perfect sync (see figs. 21.29 and 21.30). This means that changes to hand #1 are mirrored on the other. The copy can then be placed in front of a camera and posed quite easily. You can find an example of these hands in the file refhand.max on the accompanying CD.

FIGURE 21.29

Make a clone of the hand by setting Object Reference and Controller Instance on.

FIGURE 21.30

When created in this manner, changes to one hand skeleton affect the other.

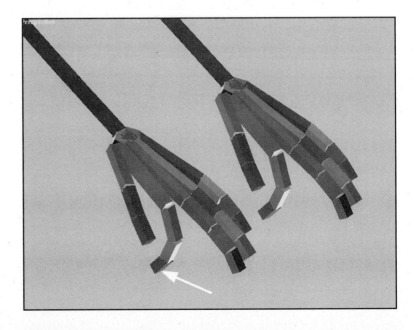

Unfortunately, this form of manipulation does not work on the hands attached to a biped because cloning the hand of the biped clones the entire skeleton. In this case, it is probably best to lock a camera directly on each of the biped's hands.

Create a target camera slightly above the biped's hand, with the target residing on the hand itself. Hierarchically link both the camera and target to the palm (see fig. 21.31). When the hand moves, the camera moves as well, keeping the hand centered in the camera's viewport. Because the camera's target is centered on the palm, the camera can be orbited around the hand at will to get a bird's eye view wherever the hand may be. This method not only works for bipeds, but for any type of character. It works quite well for facial animation, too.

FIGURE 21.31

The camera is locked to the biped's hand by linking it and the target to the biped's palm.

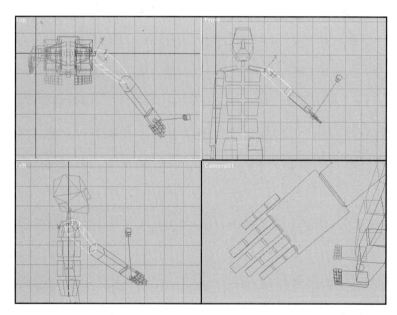

To see a biped with a camera locked to the hand, open camlock.max on the accompanying CD.

In Practice: Setting Up Characters for Animation

- **Building Solid Mesh Characters.** A character needs extra detail at the joints, such as the knees and elbows. This extra detail enables the joints to bend smoothly and realistically. Areas that don't flex, such as the part of the thigh and shin outside the knee, can be spared extra detail.

- **Using MAX Bones.** Remember to turn on IK when manipulating bones; otherwise, they will change their length. If you want to move the chain as a whole, you can always select the entire bone structure and, with IK off, move it without affecting the shape.

- **Fitting Skeletons.** When building a skeleton, it is a good idea to load your target mesh and freeze it. This allows you to use it as a guide for creating and fitting the bones of the skeleton so they match up with the mesh.

- **Limiting Joints.** The key to limiting joints is keeping the chain short enough so that the chain follows a predictable motion. This can be accomplished not only through setting joint limits, but also by using dummy objects as terminators and handles.

IMAGE CREATED BY GEORGE MAESTRI

Chapter 22

by George Maestri

ANIMATING WALKING

A character's walk conveys a great deal about its personality. The next time you are in a crowded place, notice all the different types of walks that people have. Some people waddle, others saunter, and some drag their feet. It is amazing how almost everyone you see has a unique walk. Mae West, Groucho Marx, John Wayne, and Charlie Chaplin were all characters who had very distinctive walks. If you want to know who a character is, figure out how that character walks.

This chapter covers the following topics:

- The mechanics of walking

- Animating a two-legged walk

- Creating a four-legged walk

- Creating a six-legged walk

The Mechanics of Walking

Walking has been described as controlled falling. Every time someone takes a step, he or she actually leans forward and falls slightly, only to be caught by his or her outstretched foot. After a foot touches the ground, the body's weight is transferred to it, and the knee bends to absorb the shock. The leg then lifts the body and propels it forward as the opposite leg swings up to catch the body again, and the cycle repeats.

Walks are very complex. Not only do the feet have to move across the ground, but the hips, spine, arms, shoulders, and head all move in sync to maintain balance in the system. Though complex, if you break down each of these movements joint by joint, the mechanics of walking become clear.

The Feet and Legs

The feet and legs propel the body forward. To keep your character looking natural, you should always keep the joints bent slightly, even at full leg extension. An animated walk usually starts where the feet are fully extended and farthest apart—this is the point where the character's weight shifts to the forward foot (see fig. 22.1).

As the weight of the body is transferred to the forward foot, the knee bends to absorb the shock. This is called the *recoil* position and is the lowest point in the walk (see fig. 22.2).

FIGURE 22.1
The walk usually starts with the feet at the extended position— where the feet are farthest apart.

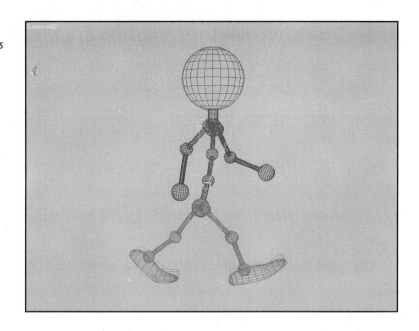

FIGURE 22.2
When the foot plants, the knee bends to absorb the shock.

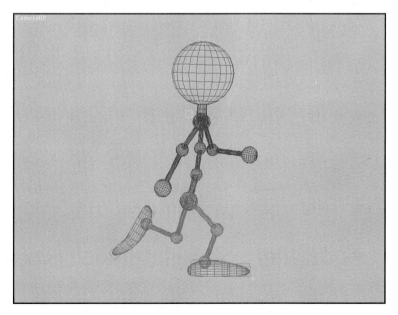

This is halfway through the first step. As the character moves forward, the knee straightens and lifts the body to its highest point. This is called the *passing* position because this is where the free foot passes the supporting leg (see fig. 22.3).

FIGURE 22.3

As one foot passes the other, the knee straightens to full extension, lifting the body.

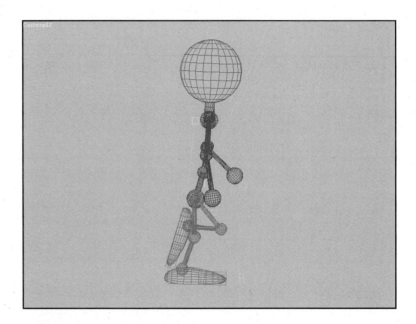

As the character moves forward, the weight-bearing foot lifts off the ground at the heel, transmitting the force to the ball of the foot. The body starts to fall forward now. The free foot swings forward like a pendulum to catch the ground (see fig. 22.4).

The free leg makes contact. Half the cycle has been completed (see fig. 22.5). The second half is an exact mirror of the first. If it differs, the character may appear to limp.

FIGURE 22.4
As the weight is transferred from one foot to the other, the body falls forward as the free leg swings forward to catch it.

FIGURE 22.5
As the weight is transferred from one foot to the other, the body falls forward a bit.

The Hips, Spine, and Shoulders

The body's center of gravity is at the hips—all balance starts there, as does the rest of the body's motion. During a walk, it is best to think of the hips' motion as two separate, overlapping rotations. First, the hips rotate along the axis of the spine, forward and back with the legs. If the right leg is forward, the right hip is rotated forward as well. Second, at the passing position, the free leg pulls the hip out of center, forcing the hips to rock from side to side. These two motions are then transmitted through the spine to the shoulders, which mirror the hips to maintain balance.

When the feet are fully extended, the hips must rotate along the axis of the spine. To keep balance, the shoulders swing in the opposite direction. From the front, the spine is relatively straight. From the top, however, you can see how the hips and shoulders twist in opposite directions to maintain balance (see fig. 22.6).

FIGURE 22.6

From the top, the rotation of the hips and shoulders are apparent.

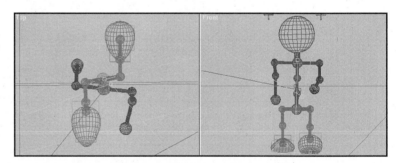

At the passing position, the front view shows the hip being pulled out of center by the weight of the free leg, which causes a counter-rotation in the shoulders. From the top, however, the hips and shoulders are nearly equal angles (see fig. 22.7).

FIGURE 22.7

As one leg passes the other, the hips are even when viewed from above, skewed when viewed from the front.

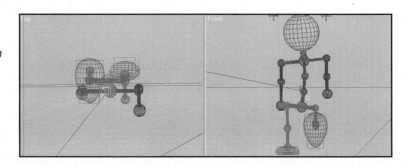

At the extension of the second leg, the hips and shoulders again are flat when viewed from the front. From the top, however, you can see the rotation of the hips and shoulders has completed (see fig. 22.8).

FIGURE 22.8
When the weight shifts from one foot to the other, the hips are again twisted when viewed from above, even when viewed from the front.

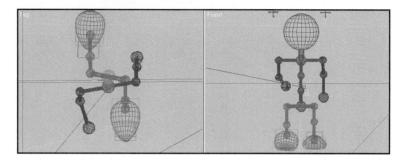

The Arms

Unless the character is using its arms, they generally hang loose at the sides. In this case, they tend to act like pendulums, dragging a few frames behind the hips and shoulders. If the character is running, the arms may pump quite a bit and lead the action by a few frames. Even at full extension, the arms should be slightly bent at the elbows. This keeps them looking natural.

The Head

In a standard walk, the head generally tries to stay level, with the eyes focused on where the character is going. It will then bob around slightly to stay balanced. If a character is excited, this bobbing will be more pronounced. The head may also hang low for a sad character or may look around if the scene requires it.

Body Posture and Emotion

The character's body posture changes, depending on the character's mood. A happy character arches his back and juts out his chest proudly and swings the arms jauntily (see fig. 22.9), whereas a sad character slumps over, barely swings his arms, and hangs his head low (see fig. 22.10). If a character is running scared, he may lean forward quite a bit and push his arms out in

front of him, trying to escape the danger (see fig. 22.11). A character who is
sneaking around may walk on tiptoe while keeping his hands at the ready
(see fig. 22.12). These postures translate beyond walking and should also be
used as examples for portraying emotion in non-locomotive scenes.

FIGURE 22.9
A happy character arches his back and sticks out his chest proudly.

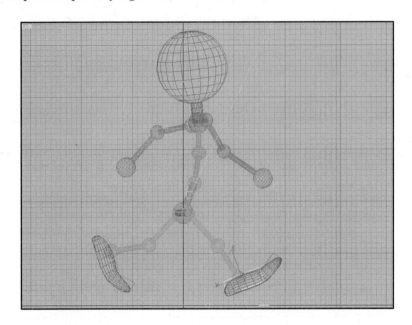

FIGURE 22.10
A sad character hangs his head low and slumps over.

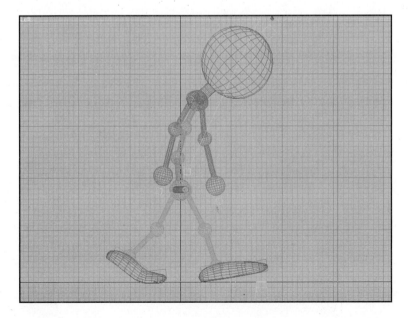

FIGURE 22.11
A character who is running scared leans forward to get away from the danger.

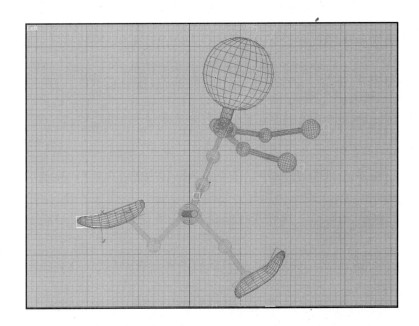

FIGURE 22.12
A sneaky character may walk on tiptoes.

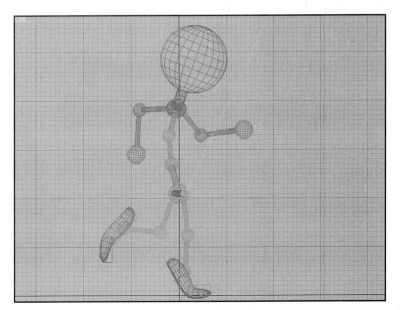

Walk Cycles

Because walking is a cyclical motion, it may behoove the animator to create walking motion as a cycle rather than as straight ahead-animation. If done properly, a cycle can save an inordinate amount of animation time. It can also be applied to a number of different environments, creating a library of motions (perfect for video games).

The use of cycles does, however, have its downside. First, because the cycle is repetitive, it can seem sterile and homogenous, particularly when viewed for an extended period of time. Second, cycles work best on flat terrain. If your character has to walk around a corner or over a hill, the cycle might not match up properly.

Animating a cycle is similar to making your character walk on a treadmill. The body does not move forward—the feet just move beneath it. To maintain the illusion of walking, the entire character must be moved across the ground (or the ground moved past the character) at the exact same rate as the feet are moving. Otherwise, the character's feet will appear to slip. Also, the foot on the ground needs to move the exact same distance on each frame. Not doing this will again cause the feet to slip.

Animating a Walk

With the introduction of Biped, animating a basic walk in 3DS MAX has been reduced to a few simple mouse clicks. Although Biped has become a preferred method for animating walks, it is still entirely possible to animate convincing walks by using basic MAX tools. Also, to truly understand a walk, it is a very good exercise to animate several walks from scratch.

An Animated Walk Cycle

A cycled walk is one of the easier walks to construct. Because walks are repetitive, the first two steps are all that need to be animated; the rest can be duplicated from there. The cycle can also be used as the basis for the cycles and actions used in video game environments. Of course, no two steps are exactly alike, so if possible, make the cycle several steps long and adjust the keys on each step to give the walk a subtle bit of variety, as well as added life.

The following exercise is a good method for producing an animated walk cycle.

Creating an Animated Walk Cycle

1. Load the skeleton you created in Chapter 21. A version of this appears on the accompanying CD-ROM in the file called ik-skel.max in the Chapter 22 folder.

2. This walk cycle is timed at 16 frames per step. At 30 fps, this averages out to approximately one half second per step. Go to the Time Configuration dialog box and set the Animation Length to 32 frames, plus one extra frame for the first frame of the next cycle (see fig. 22.13). This extra frame is not rendered, but helps the cycle repeat smoothly.

FIGURE 22.13

The Time Configuration dialog box.

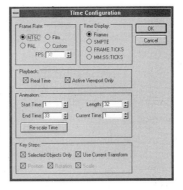

It is best to start such a walk with the hips because all other motions derive from the hips. The hips have two separate, overlapping rotations mirrored by the shoulders. The first rotation is along the vertical axis of the spine and follows the position of the legs and feet.

3. Start the walk with the right foot. This means the right hip must go forward as well. On frame 1, rotate the hips around the axis of the spine so that the right side of the hip bone is forward by 10 degrees. From the top view, rotate the collar bone so the shoulders mirror this rotation in the opposite direction (see fig. 22.14).

FIGURE 22.14

In the Top viewport, you can see the rotation of the hips and shoulders match the back and forth motion of the legs.

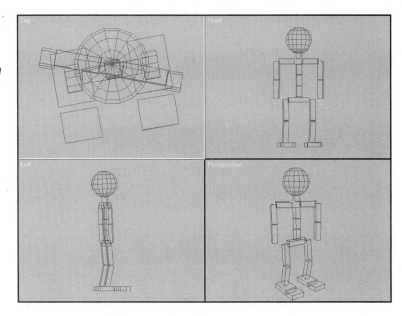

4. Go to the halfway point (frame 17) in the cycle and rotate the hips and collar bones in the opposite direction.

5. Open Track View. Find the rotation keys for the hips and collar. Copy the keys on frame 1 to frame 33 by shift-clicking and dragging. Scrub the animation to make certain that the motions are even.

6. Create the sway of the hips. Go to the frame in the middle of the first step (frame 9). If your rotations are correct, the hips and shoulders should be parallel when viewed from the top. This is the passing position, or the highest leg extension. At this point, the body rests on the right leg, whereas the left pulls the hips out of center. From the Front viewport, rotate the hips 5 degrees around the Z axis so that the right hip is higher (see fig. 22.15). Adjust the spine and shoulders so that you get a smooth line of action and the shoulders mirror the hips.

7. Go to the middle frame of the second step (frame 25) and reverse the rotations. The body rests on the left leg at this point, and the spine curves in the opposite direction.

FIGURE 22.15

From the Front viewport, the sway of the hips can be adjusted.

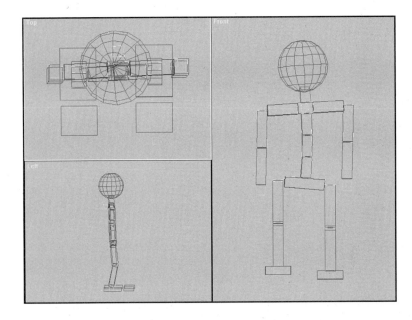

8. At this point, the spinal bones (Spine01–Spine03) will have keys only at frames 9 and 25. Go to frame 1 and, within the Motion tab, create a rotation key for each of the spinal bones. From within Track View, locate these rotation keys located on frame 1 and copy them to frame 33 to complete the cycle. Scrub the animation to check it for smoothness.

9. Go back to each keyframe and add rotation keys to the legs and arms so that they hang vertically and the toes point forward throughout the cycle.

10. The hips also bob up and down during a walk. The lowest point in the walk occurs at the recoil position. In this animation, this is at frame 5. Go to frame 5 and move the hips down slightly (about 4 units in this case). The highest point occurs at the passing position. In this animation, it is at frame 9. Go to that frame and move the hips up (about 6 units above the position at frame 5). Within Track View, copy the keys for frames 1, 5, and 9 to frame 17, 21, and 25, respectively. Copy the key at frame 11 to frame 33 to complete the cycle. Scrub the animation to check it for smoothness.

On the accompanying CD, the file hips-sho.max shows the motion of just the hips and shoulders.

Animating the Legs

How the legs are animated depends to some degree on personal preference. MAX's Inverse Kinematics is one good solution, but Forward Kinematics is often overlooked and is also a valid method. MAX's IK solves the joint motion as rotations and actually places rotation keys into Track View, much like keyframing by hand with Forward Kinematics. This makes it entirely possible to block in the character's broad motions by using IK and then going back over the scene, tweaking the joint rotations with Forward Kinematics.

Using IK to Lock the Ankles to an Elliptical Path

For a cycle, the first method is to lock the ankles to an elliptical path, which enables you to let MAX's IK control the rotation of the legs. The feet, however, remain free and able to rotate.

LOCKING THE ANKLES TO THE ELLIPTICAL PATH

1. First, draw a spline curve similar to that shown in figure 22.16. The curve should start at the front bottom, run back along the ground, and arch over on the return. The section along the ground should be completely flat and the curve needs to have an equal number of segments along the flat part of the path as the curved part. Duplicate this curve. Place one curve over each foot.

2. Create a dummy object. Go to the Motion panel and assign a Path Controller to the dummy. Within the Path Parameters rollout, click on Pick Path. Select the right path. Create another dummy and assign it to the left path in the same way.

3. Select the handle at the skeleton's right ankle. In the IK panel, select Bind Position. Under Bind to Follow Object, press the Bind button. Click on the right ankle's handle and bind the handle to the dummy object. Repeat the procedure for the left side.

4. Select both of the handles at the ankles. In the IK panel, press the Apply IK button. This solves the rotations for the leg joints and places rotation keys within Track View for every frame of the cycle. Go into Track View and observe the tracks for the thighs and shins.

FIGURE 22.16

Create two spline paths, such as this (highlighted in white), and place them over the feet.

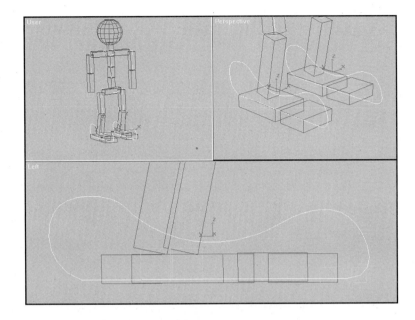

5. Play the animation. The legs will now follow the path. Unfortunately, both legs move in sync, making the skeleton look like it is hopping. This occurs because both paths start at the same point.

6. Select the left path. Under the Modify panel, select the Edit Spline modifier. Under Sub-Object, select Vertex. This shows the vertices that comprise the spline, with the first vertex indicated by a small box. This needs to be offset by exactly 180 degrees. Select the vertex exactly opposite the first vertex and press the Make First button under the Edit Vertex rollout.

7. Select both of the handles at the ankles again and press the Apply IK button. Play the animation. The legs will now appear to walk. If the legs lock or are not quite fully extended, you may use the Edit Spline modifier to adjust the shape or positioning of the paths.

8. Go through the animation and adjust the feet so that they remain flat against the ground while planted and the toes don't scrape the ground while passing.

9. After this is done, the paths are no longer needed. Pressing the Apply IK button in step 7 resolved all the IK tasks to explicit joint rotations. If you so desire, delete the paths and the dummies.

An example of the elliptical path method is found in the file pathwalk.max on the accompanying CD.

Using Guides to Keyframe a Walk Cycle

The path method as previously outlined is a very easy method, but the walk can be keyframed manually by using Inverse Kinematics, Forward Kinematics, or a combination of both. The entire process can be simplified by using a simple box as a guide to help place the feet. In addition to animating a cycle, IK and Forward Kinematics can also be used to keyframe a straight-ahead walk that does not cycle—just move the hips forward at the same constant rate as the feet.

KEYFRAMING A WALK CYCLE

1. First, create the first extreme pose. Turn on IK. Using the Left viewport, go to frame 1 and make the first pose by dragging the handles on the feet into place. You do this by turning on IK and pulling the handle into place, which creates rotation keys for the joints in the chain. If you so desire, you can rotate the joints manually to achieve the same effect, or use a combination of the two methods.

Regardless of the way in which the pose is achieved, the legs are now at maximum extension (see fig. 22.17). Copy these keys to the end of the cycle (frame 33). Next, go to the middle of the cycle (frame 17) and mirror this pose with the left leg forward.

2. To aid in the animation process, create a guide to help position the feet (see fig. 22.18). To create the guide, model a simple box the length of the stride and place it directly beneath the feet, with the edges of the box at the balls of the toes. This box acts as a guide for the stride length.

FIGURE 22.17
The first frame of the animation has the legs at full extension.

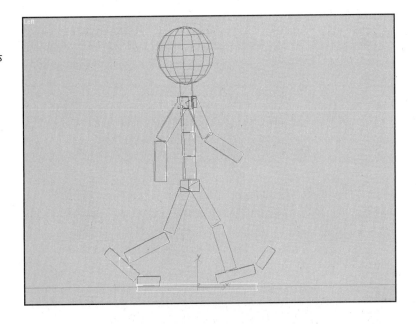

FIGURE 22.18
This guide (highlighted in white) is aligned on its leading edge with the character's forward foot and also indicates the stride length.

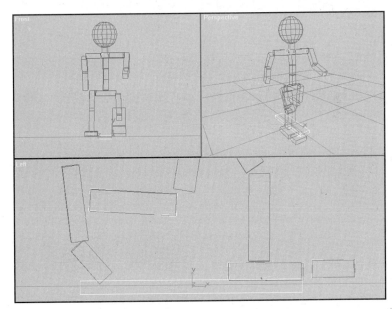

3. Go to the middle of the cycle (frame 17) and position the guide to the exact same place on the toe as in frame 1. Set the guide so that it inbetweens these two positions at a linear rate. This is done within the Key Info rollout within the Motion panel. With a linear inbetween, the guide will now tell you exactly where the toe needs be at any point in the first step.

4. One quarter of the way through the first step on frame 5 is the recoil position—where the leg absorbs the shock and the hips reach their lowest point. Adjust the foot so that it remains even with the guide.

5. Halfway through the first step, at frame 9, the body recoils upward into the passing position. The hips are at the highest point, meaning that the planted foot is fairly well extended. Again, adjust this leg so that the foot rests even with the guide. It is very important to keep the knee bent slightly to make the action look natural.

6. Three quarters of the way through the first step, at frame 13, the weight of the body is on the ball of the foot. The heel lifts off the floor as the body falls forward. The hips are moving down at this point. There can also be problems with the free foot as it swings forward. If the character has extra-big shoes, they will hit the floor unless you bend the toes slightly.

This completes the first step. Create a second guide and repeat these procedures for the left foot on the second half of the cycle. Be careful to make the second half as close to the first as possible. Render a test and go back to tweak any inconsistencies.

Animating the Arms

No matter how the legs were animated, it is still necessary to create the motion of the arms and head. In the simplest case, the arms swing back and forth to maintain balance in opposition to the legs. The arms also drag behind the action a bit, making the arm's extreme poses a few frames behind the legs.

1. Using the same ik-skel.max model, grab the handles on the arms and pull them into the position on frame 1 (see fig. 22.19). Because the right leg is forward on this frame, the right arm will be back, the left arm forward. This is not an extreme pose, but it's close.

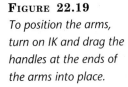

FIGURE 22.19

To position the arms, turn on IK and drag the handles at the ends of the arms into place.

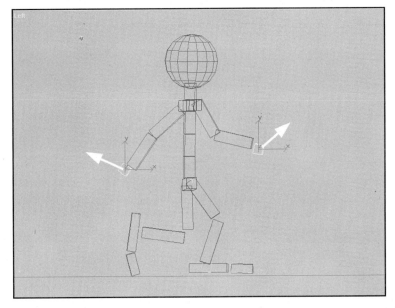

2. Go to frame 5 and set the arm's extreme pose. On the left arm, pull the handle or rotate the forearm back to a nice extension. On the right, pull the forearm up slightly.

3. Go to frame 21 and mirror the extreme from the previous step (on frame 5). Finally, copy the keys on frame 1 to the last frame so the arm will swing through to the end of the cycle. Scrub the cycle and check for smoothness, or render a test.

An example of this walk is on the accompanying CD as walkcycle.max.

Moving the Cycled Character

Now that the cycle is animated convincingly, it is time to get the character off the treadmill and out into the world. This may be as simple as rendering the animation as a sprite for a video game or passing the rotational data to a 3D game engine. You can also move the character by creating an environment within 3DS MAX.

You can move the skeleton through the environment in two ways: by moving the character past the ground, or by moving the ground past the character. Moving the ground is best when you want to use a panning camera locked on the character. Because the character is still, the camera can remain still as well. Moving the character is best in cases when you want the camera stable and the character to walk past.

Calculating the Stride Length

In either example, the character or ground needs to move at a constant rate. This rate can be calculated quite easily. Load the file walkcycle.max and follow along.

walkcycle.max is used as a guide to assist in the animation. Find the absolute position of the guide (Box01) on frame 1, and then again when it stops in the middle of the cycle (frame 16). This is done by opening Track View and looking at the keyframe data for Box01 and doing a little math.

In this case, the guide moves along Y from −10.8 to 82.0 over 16 frames, which works out to 92.8 units for one stride. Dividing by the number of frames gives $92.8 \div 16 = 5.8$ units per frame.

TIP

If an elliptical path is used to drive the legs, the stride length can be calculated by using the Tape object, found under the helper buttons in the Create panel. Set the Time Slider to frame 1 and measure the distance from toe tip to toe tip. Divide this by the number of frames for a stride (16 in this case) to get the same figure.

This number (5.8 units÷frame) is exactly how far the character or the ground needs to move on each frame. If the cycle is replicated four times for a 128 frame animation, this means the character travels 5.8 units÷frame×128 frames = 742.4 units.

Duplicating the Cycle in Track View

To cycle the animation four times, it is just a matter of increasing the length of the animation to 128 frames and copying all the keys for each joint four times. This will create explicit keys for the animation. If you want a strict repeat, with no modification of the keys, you could use the Cycle or Loop function in Out of Range parameters to get a nice repetition. Copying the keys is more flexible because it allows them to be edited individually, should the need arise.

CYCLE DUPLICATION

1. Activate the Time Configuration dialog box and change the length of the animation so that it runs from frame 1 to 129.

2. Activate Track View. Press the Filters button and check Animated Tracks Only. Right-click on the Hips object and select Expand All to bring up all the keys (quite a large number).

3. Select all the keys from frame 1 to 33, which is done by holding down the Ctrl key while clicking and dragging over the keys to select them.

4. After the keys are selected, hold down the Shift key and click on one of the keys. Drag the mouse to the right and the keys will clone themselves. Place the clones from frame 1 at frame 33 and release the mouse. The frames have been copied. Repeat this twice more to create four full cycles.

Play back the animation and watch for any glitches in the transitions between steps.

Moving the Ground to Match

After the cycle has been duplicated, the ground can now be moved to match the footstep rate. To do so, follow these steps:

1. Select the object named Ground, which is a simple patch grid that needs to be moved at a constant rate to match the calculated rate of the character. In the preceding section, this rate was calculated at 5.8 units per frame, or 742.4 units for 128 frames.

2. Set the Time Slider to frame 1. Open the Motion panel and press Create Key/Position. Move to the last frame and press Create Key/Position again.

3. Go back to frame 1. In the Key Info rollout, set the In and Out ramps to linear. In the Y-Value spinner, set the position to –371.2 units. (This number is half of the required distance of 742.4 units.)

4. Go to the last frame and repeat this procedure. Set the In and Out ramps to linear, and in the Y-Value spinner, set the position to 371.2 units. (Along with the 371.2 units in the negative direction, this makes the total distance 742.2 units.)

Play back the animation. The character should now appear to take four steps with the feet locked exactly to the ground. A rendered version of this walk is located on the accompanying CD as walkcycle.avi.

Creating Four-Legged Walks

Four-legged creatures are quite common in animation. Unfortunately, a package such as Biped does not help much with this task. Laying down footsteps for two feet is quite straightforward, but the overlapping footsteps required of a four-legged creature can be difficult for an algorithmic package such as Biped to handle.

A four-legged walk is very similar to the two-legged variety, but multiplied by two. The creature's legs still rock back and forth at the hips, but the upper-body motion happens parallel to the ground rather than perpendicular to it. Whereas human shoulders rock back and forth in the vertical axis, a dog's "shoulders" will rock back and forth horizontal to the ground as the front paws move back and forth.

The center of gravity is also slightly different for a four-legged beast. Instead of being located at the hips, it is further up on the body, roughly centered between the front and back legs. This may cause you to set up the hierarchy of a quadrupedal skeleton slightly differently. Because both the front and back legs move equally, the hierarchy can be set up with the center of the spine as the parent.

The location of the root of the hierarchy is important because it represents the *center of gravity*. If the animal were to leap, for example, the entire body's rotation would center around this point, so it is important to place it properly. The center joint of the spinal column makes a good candidate because many four-legged creatures have a center of gravity that is evenly located between the front and rear legs (see fig. 22.20). If the creature has its center of gravity closer to the chest (a cheetah or a greyhound, perhaps) then the shoulders or the first spinal joint may make a better center of gravity (see fig. 22.21). The head also plays a role in determination of center of gravity. A giraffe's long neck will place it further up the spinal column, near the shoulders.

FIGURE 22.20

The center of gravity of a dog is centered between the front and rear legs.

FIGURE 22.21

The center of gravity of a cheetah, however, is closer to the shoulders.

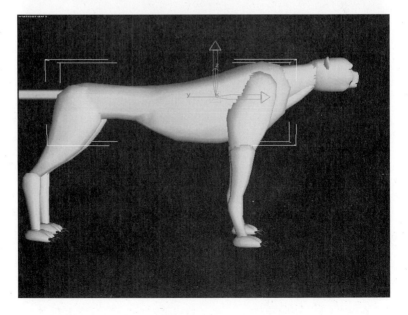

Creating a Quadruped Skeleton

One easy way to set up a skeleton for a four-legged creature is to modify a bipedal skeleton. To do so, follow these steps:

1. Load ik-skel.max from the accompanying CD-ROM. This is the skeleton created in the preceding chapter. If IK is on, turn it off.

2. Select the foot bones and delete them.

3. Select the bone at the base of the spine (Spine01). Using the Unlink Selection button, unlink this bone from the hips.

4. Rotate Spine01 90 degrees so that the spine is now parallel to the ground.

5. While Spine01 is still selected, adjust the bone's pivot so that it is at the top rather than the bottom of the bone. From the Hierarchy panel, press Affect Pivot Only. Move the pivot forward so that it lies even with the top of the bone (see fig. 22.22).

FIGURE 22.22

If the center spine bone is the center of the hierarchy, the pivots of the children should be located next to it.

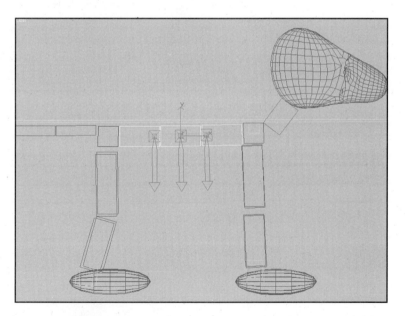

6. Link the skeleton back together. Select Spine02 and press the Unlink Selection. Next, press the Link Selection button and select the hips. Link these to Spine01. Link Spine01 to Spine02, the parent of the hierarchy.

7. Rotate the arms down 90 degrees so that they hang down like legs. If you notice, these new legs bend forward like bird legs, which is exactly how most four-legged creatures' front legs are jointed.

8. Tilt the head up, adjust the lengths of the legs and shoulders as you see fit. A dachshund will have much shorter legs than a greyhound, for example. Also adjust the width of the shoulders so that they match the hips more closely. Finally, add a tail if needed.

Although elementary, this is a basic four-legged skeleton. Building this from a human skeleton shows you just how close our skeletons are to our fellow mammals (see fig. 22.23).

FIGURE 22.23
A bipedal and quadrupedal skeleton are surprisingly similar.

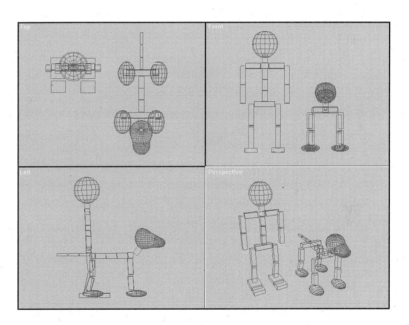

For reference, a version of this skeleton has been placed on the accompanying CD-ROM in the file fourskel.max.

Analysis of a Four-Legged Walk

A four-legged walk is very similar to a two-legged walk in that the hips and shoulders have rotations that mirror each other. When the right hip is forward, the left shoulder is back, and vice versa. This action usually varies a bit in that the front and back legs might be offset by a few frames (see fig. 22.24). Notice how the spine curves much like a human and that the left shoulder and leg are back, mirroring the hip pose. This means that the left front leg, too, is about to plant.

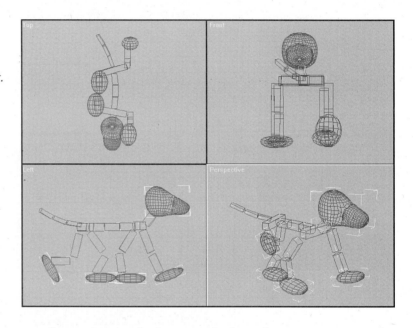

As the legs move forward through the step, the legs that are not currently planted on the ground (the free legs) move forward. The rear legs are fairly similar to a human's, bending at the knee in much the same fashion. The front legs, however, are actually jointed so that they bend forward, much like a bird's (see fig. 22.25). This dictates a slightly different lift motion for the front legs. At this point, the spine is straight when viewed from the top, but it may bow or arch a bit more when viewed from the side. This will be character dependent. A dilapidated horse's back may sag quite a bit.

FIGURE 22.25

Halfway through the step, the free legs are moving forward. Notice how the front leg's joint causes a different bend in the leg.

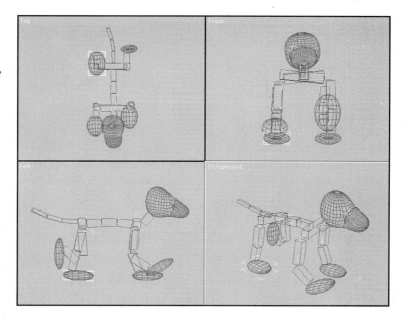

The legs then move through the step and plant the free feet, repeating the first step. In addition to this, a four-legged animal can have several different gaits: the walk, the trot, the canter, and the gallop. The animal will vary the timing and rhythm of its steps as it moves faster and faster. In the walk, the animal's legs behave very much like the arms and legs of a human—if the right rear leg is back, the right front leg is forward, with the opposite happening on the left. This changes as the strides change, however. By the time the creature has reached full gallop, the front legs are in sync—going forward and back nearly in unison, with the back legs operating as a mirror to the front.

Animating a Four-Legged Walk Cycle

This skeleton can be made to walk quite easily. It is a simple matter of getting the back legs to walk much like a two-legged character's and then adding in the front leg motions. A cycle is a good way to create such a walk because keyframing four legs over a large number of frames can be quite tedious.

1. Get the hips and shoulders moving. Like in a two-legged walk, the hips and shoulders mirror each other.

2. Move the feet. This can be done by attaching each ankle to an elliptical path, much like in a two-legged walk. The legs can also be keyframed manually using either forward or inverse kinematics.

TIP

When animating a four-legged walk, it is important that both pairs of legs move the same distance with each step. If the back legs have a larger stride than the front, for example, one set of feet will appear to slip.

3. Make certain that the feet remain planted by rotating them at the ankles.

4. For a cycle, again move the ground in relation to the character, or the character in relation to the ground. Like in the two-legged walk, this rate can be calculated by using a Helper object, such as a tape, to measure out the stride over a series of frames and then dividing this by the number of frames.

You can find on the accompanying CD-ROM an example of a four-legged walk using the supplied skeleton. The file is called fourwalk.max, and it is also rendered to the AVI file fourwalk.avi.

Animating Six-Legged Walks

If four-legged walks seem complex, then six legs might seem intolerably difficult. This, fortunately, is not the case. An insect walk actually follows a definite, repeatable pattern that can be animated on a cycle. A six-legged walk is very similar to the four-legged walk—the front two legs move back and forth, while the second set of legs mirror this motion (see fig. 22.26). The insect's third set of legs simply mirrors the second again, closely matching the motion of the front legs. Generally, insects keep at least three legs on the ground, forming a stable tripod at all times.

FIGURE 22.26

Insect legs and body parts are naturally segmented, making direct animation of the joints possible.

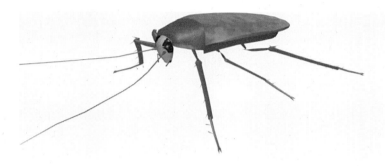

Because insects are the quintessential segmented creatures, their parts can be put together in a simple hierarchy. Shape animation or spinal bones are not needed for such a creature because an insect's exoskeleton does not change shape. The one exception may be antennae on the insect, which can be animated with bones, or more directly, by using a simple bend modifier.

Animating the walk of an insect is simply a matter of getting the front legs to walk, mirroring this motion on the second set of legs, and then mirroring the second set of leg motion on the third. The legs of an insect have three main segments, with the first segment, the one closest to the body, acting like a suspension bridge that holds the body of the bug aloft (see fig. 22.27).

FIGURE 22.27

Insect legs suspend the insect's body like a bridge.

The accompanying CD-ROM contains a file called roach.max, which contains a roach model that has been set up in a hierarchy and is ready to animate. Load this file into MAX and follow along.

Body

Like the body of a two- or four-legged creature, the body of an insect bounces up and down as the creature walks. This rate of bounce is directly proportional to the rate of the walk, which means that the body bounces up and down once per step—the insect bounces twice for a full cycle of right and left leg steps. The bug is highest when the legs are in the middle of the stride.

The rate of an insect walk will depend on the species of bug and its demeanor. Generally, bugs move pretty fast compared to mammals, and a quarter or eighth second per step is not out of the question. When walks get this fast, the frame rate of the animation becomes a limiting factor. At 24 fps, an eighth second stride would only take three frames per step. This is about as fast as a walk could be animated, with one frame each for the forward, middle, and back portions of the step. For this animation, 6 fps gives you a good pace for the insect walk.

1. At frame 0, the insect will be at the bottom of the stride. Move the abdomen object down along Y about 12 units.

2. At frame 6, the insect will be at the top of it's stride. Move the abdomen up 12 units to get it back to center, plus another 12 units to make it the top of his stride, for a total upward movement of 24 units.

3. At frame 12, the cycle repeats. Copy the abdomen position key from frame 0 to this frame.

4. To get enough up and down motion for a full cycle of steps, copy these keys once again to make a second cycle, for a total of 24 frames.

The Legs

The legs are best dealt with a set at a time. The front legs are always a good guide, so these are best animated first. Once the front legs are moving, the rear sets can be keyframed in the same manner (see fig. 22.28).

Front Legs

As mentioned previously, the front legs are a good guide to animating each set of legs. These will be animated in the next exercise.

FIGURE 22.28
One extreme of an insect walk. When the right leg is forward the left is back and vice versa.

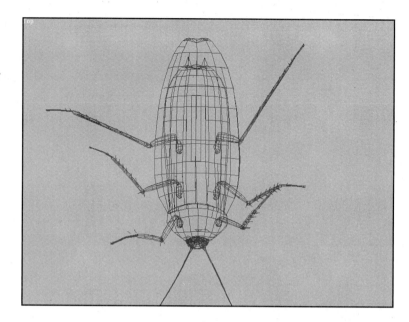

ANIMATING THE FRONT LEGS

1. At Frame 0, the right front leg should be rotated forward about 15 degrees, the left front leg rotated back approximately the same amount. Both legs should be touching the ground.

2. At Frame 6, both legs should be roughly centered. The left front leg is moving forward, so it should be raised off the ground. The right front leg is firmly planted. The body at this point is also at its highest point.

3. At Frame 12, the legs switch—the left leg plants and the right leg lifts. The left front leg should be approximately 15 degrees forward, while the right front is 15 degrees back.

4. Repeat the same positions outlined in the previous steps for the opposite legs on frames 12 through 24. The left leg should be planted, while the right leg lifts and moves forward.

5. Scrub the animation and adjust the rotations of the front legs to make sure they remain planted on the ground throughout their respective steps.

Middle and Rear Legs

The middle and rear legs move in an identical manner as the front, but are simply mirrored. This makes creating the animation as simple as repeating the exact same steps for the front legs—creating a key for the beginning, middle, and end of each step, then adjusting the inbetweens as required.

One tactic to take while animating the rear legs would be to copy and paste the controllers from the front legs to the corresponding rear legs. In order for this to work, the pivots of all the joints of the respective legs need to be aligned along the same axis. If they are not, the rotations will not translate properly, and the legs will not mirror exactly the rotations of the front. This is easily done by aligning all of the pivots on the legs to the world before animation begins.

Another problem with copying the controllers may be one of scale. The cockroach, for example, has rear legs that are quite a bit longer than the front legs. Copied rotations from the front leg may not match up exactly. Still, it may prove to be a good starting point, but the effectiveness of this tactic depends on the anatomy of the insect being animated.

Another factor to consider is timing. If all of the legs move at the exact same time, the animation may look unnatural. To compensate for this, it is simply a matter of sliding the keys for each set of legs back a frame or two so that they touch slightly behind the leading legs. This will add an extra touch of realism.

One final thing to consider with insects is their antennae. These act as feelers for the insect, constantly searching out a path for the bug to follow. Antennae can be animated using a number of methods, such as bones with a mesh deformation system, such as Biped or Physique. A simple bend modifier can also be quite effective for this effect, as the angle and direction of the bend can be keyframed to give a nice effect.

To view how a walk cycle such as the one created can be worked into a full animation look at the file roachwalk.max, which is also rendered out to the file roachwalk.avi.

Using Expressions to Automate an Insect Walk

Keyframing six legs can be quite tedious, so the procedure can be sped up quite significantly using MAX's expressions. Expressions enable you to create mathematical relationships between objects. In the case of insect legs, the rotation of one leg can easily control the actions of the other five.

The key to making an expression-driven insect work is that insect legs follow a predictable pattern. As was described previously, the rotations on each row of legs simply mirrors the rotations of the row in front of it. Additionally, the left side of legs mirrors the rotations on the right. These simple rules make it quite easy to set up a series of expressions that can make one leg drive many.

Load the file bugexp01.max. This file contains a simple bug. The body is a simple box, as are the legs. This particular bug only has one leg, which needs to be duplicated to create the other five. Before the leg is duplicated, however, it needs to be properly positioned and aligned to the world.

Position the leg so that it is slightly bent, with the "knee" slightly above the body of the insect. A bent knee gives the insect a more relaxed and realistic pose (see fig. 22.29). In the Hierarchy panel, select Affect Pivot Only and click on Align to World. This simply puts the pivots in world space, which makes each leg movement work along the same axis as the body. Rotations around the leg's local Z axis move the leg forward and back. Rotations along the local Y axis lift the leg off the ground and also plant it. Local X rotations will twist the leg. The two primary rotations used in walking are the Y and Z rotations. The legs must move back and forth along Z to propel the insect forward. Additionally, legs must rotate along Y to lift and plant the feet.

Because Y and Z rotations of the leg need to be isolated to create the expressions, the leg must be assigned the Euler XYZ rotation controller, which is the only controller that separates the X, Y, and Z components of the rotation. To assign this, simply select the object Leg01, the upper part of the first leg, open the assign controller rollout within the motion panel, and assign the Euler XYZ controller to the leg.

FIGURE 22.29

The proper positioning of the leg and the pivots.

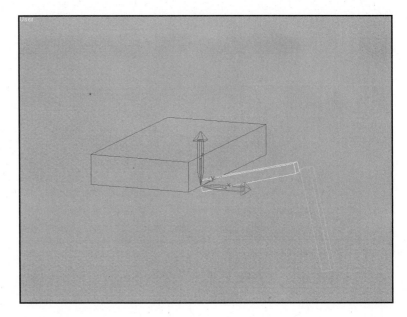

To make the expressions easier to construct, all six of the insect's legs will need to have their X, Y, and Z axes aligned in the same fashion. The easiest way to make sure the legs are aligned properly is simply to clone the first leg to create the others.

ALIGNING THE LEGS

1. From the Top viewport, select both leg joints (Leg01 and Leg02) and clone them to create the two other legs on the right side.

2. Now create the left legs from the right. Select all of the legs on the right side and click the Mirror Selected Objects button. Select the X axis as the mirror axis and create copies of the right legs.

3. Position the left legs along the left side of the insect's body. When they are finished, they should look like figure 22.30.

FIGURE 22.30

After all of the legs have been copied and properly placed, their pivots should be aligned.

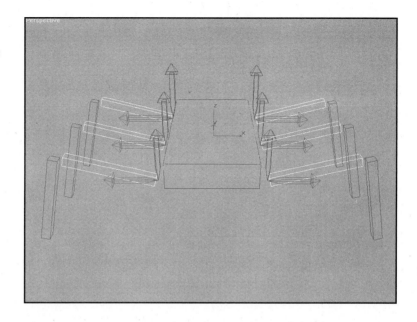

Now that the legs are in position and properly aligned with the Euler XYZ controllers assigned, they can be assigned individual expressions. Select the upper joint of the second right leg. This joint will mirror the rotations of the front right leg. When the front right leg rotates forward along Z, the second right will rotate back. When the front right leg plants itself on the ground, the second right will lift. This is simply accomplished by multiplying the controlling leg's rotation by –1.

4. Open TrackView. Select the track for the second right leg's (Leg04) Z rotation. Change the controller type to Float Expression. Open the properties panel to get the Expression controller dialog.

5. Within the Expression Controller dialog, create a scalar variable named **Leg01Z** and assign this to the Z rotation controller for the front right leg (Leg01).

6. Enter the expression **–Leg01Z**. This will make the second right leg's Z rotation exactly opposite the front right (see fig. 22.31).

FIGURE 22.31

The Expression Controller dialog box with the expression for the leg rotation entered.

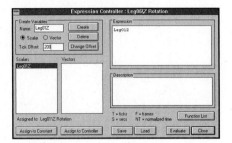

Evaluate the expression and close the dialog.

7. Select the front right leg and rotate it around its local Z axis. The second right leg should mirror it exactly.

Repeat this procedure for the Y rotation of the second right leg. Create a scalar variable named "Leg01Y" and assign this variable to the Z rotation controller for the front right leg (Leg01). Create the expression **–Leg01Z** in the Expression box and evaluate it. The leg's Y rotation will now follow the front right leg.

Work your way around the body, creating expressions for every leg. Each set of legs mirrors the one in front of it, and the left side mirrors the right. Remember that the left legs were created by mirroring the right legs, so their rotations will automatically be mirrored as well, making their expressions the same as their corresponding right leg. The expressions are listed in table 22.1.

TABLE 22.1

Mirrored Leg Expressions

LEG	EXPRESSIONS
Second Right	–Leg01Z ; –Leg01Y
Third Right	Leg01Z ; Leg01Y
Front Left	Leg01Z ; Leg01Y
Second Left	–Leg01Z ; –Leg01Y
Third Left	Leg01Z ; Leg01Y

After all 10 expressions are written, moving the front right leg will move all of the rest in perfect sync. The file bugexp02.max is included on the accompanying CD as a reference. It has all of these expressions in place.

Of course, no living creatures, including insects, are perfect, so this method has its limitations when compared to purely keyframing the animation by hand. The limitations are that the legs may seem too perfect because they move in lockstep. One way to get around this limitation is to add a Tick Offset for each succeeding row of legs to make them move with a slight delay for each step, adding a touch of realism. The Tick Offset is found along with each expression in the Expression controller dialog, accessed by clicking on the Properties panel within Track View. Each variable in the expression created within the dialog can have its own offset.

Recall that each tick is exactly 1/4800 of a second, so a good tick offset would be in the range of 1–3 frames, or approximately 200–600 ticks, depending on the frame rate. Because the tick value is time driven, the effects will only show up when animated. After the expressions have been set up, animating a walk cycle is quite easy. The front leg simply needs to be moved forward and back in a walking motion, as in the previous section, and the other legs will follow.

Another way to create a similar insect walk is to write the expressions so that both front legs are involved. The front left leg would control the second right and the third left, whereas the front right leg would control the second left and the third right. This forces animation to be created for two legs, but the front legs can have slightly varying motions, which can add to the shot's realism. Adding a tick offset to each succeeding row of legs adds even more realism. As can be surmised, using expressions to help drive walks has quite a few other possibilities, so the rest is left up to your imagination.

In Practice: Animating Walking

- **Walking.** The two-legged walk is like a controlled fall, with the legs catching the body on each step. Each step has several major components: the plant, the lift, and the passing position. The spine twists and bends along with the shoulders and hips to maintain balance. Different character attitudes manifest themselves in different body postures.

- **Walk cycles.** Walk cycles are good for environments such as games where cyclical motions are a requirement. An elliptically shaped path can be used quite effectively along with MAX's IK to get the legs moving in a walking motion. After the Apply IK button has been clicked, rotation keys are generated, and the path can be dispensed.

■ **Four-legged skeletons.** Four-legged skeletons are very much like the two-legged variety. All of the bones are in similar places, but the spine is parallel to the ground and the size relationships of the bones are different.

■ **Four-legged walks.** The key to this is the spine, which moves much like the spine of a two-legged walk, with the shoulders and hips still flexing and bending. Be sure to keep both sets of legs moving at the same rate. If one set of legs is longer than the other, there may be a temptation to move it further, but this causes an apparent slip of the creature's feet.

■ **Six-legged walks.** The sheer number of legs makes these a bit vexing, but they follow regular, repetitive motions that makes them easy to set up. This regular motion lends itself to the use of expressions to help animate the many legs.

IMAGE CREATED BY GEORGE MAESTRI

Chapter 23

by George Maestri

ANIMATING WITH BIPED

Although creating and animating your own biped skeletons gives you freedom to customize how they are built, these skeletons can typically fall short when it comes to animation. These skeletons typically use inverse kinematics to position the limbs of the skeleton based on the position of their extremities. The position of the arm, therefore, is controlled by the position of the hand. To approach life-like motion of the limbs, the animator must configure the constraints on each skeleton joint to restrict the rotation to the appropriate axis (knees bend but do not twist) and set the appropriate limits for each axis (knees bend backward, but not forward). Even with these constraints properly configured, the resulting motion is still not life-like. The motion of the limbs in-between keyframes uses a spline-based interpolation which, while smooth, does not match the kinematic motion of a biped.

Even more important for bipeds, inverse kinematics knows nothing about the skeleton other than it is a collection of joints. As such, it is easy to have the skeleton in a pose that causes a bipedal animal to fall on its face. An example of this is the forward rotation of the spine. Unless the hips move backward as the spine is rotated, a bipedal animal quickly reaches an unstable position where it would fall forward.

Biped is exactly one half of the Character Studio plug-in. It not only enables automatic construction of "smart" humanoid skeletons with a built-in IK system, it also enables extensive customization of those skeletons' structural details such as the number of fingers and toes, and whether the biped has a tail. Biped is primarily a footstep-driven animation tool, where the position of the biped is controlled by the timing and placement of footsteps. The IK system used in Biped was designed specifically for animating bipeds and takes into account the mechanics and restrictions of how bipedal animals move. Integral to Biped is the handling of gravity and the biped's center-of-mass. This enables Biped to interpolate the position of the biped properly when both feet are off the ground, and to dynamically balance the biped about the center-of-mass to achieve life-like motions.

This chapter covers the following topics:

- Creating a biped

- Manipulating a biped

- Animating a biped with footsteps

- Performing free-form animation of a biped

- Using animatable IK attachments

- Using libraries of biped animation

Creating a Biped

The Biped creation button is located under the Systems button in the Create panel. To create a biped, click on the button and then on a viewport, and drag. A box appears indicating the size of the biped. Releasing the mouse generates the Biped skeleton.

After the mouse is released, the Biped Creation panel appears (see fig. 23.1). From within this panel, you can configure the skeleton exactly to your needs, including details such as how many segments are in the spine and neck, whether the character has a tail, how many links are in that tail, how many fingers and toes, and whether the character has arms. (A bird, for example, has no arms.) Another important parameter to consider is the Leg Links spinner, which determines how the legs are configured. This has two settings: 3 and 4. A human has a setting of 3 (thigh, calf, and foot), and some birds or dinosaurs have a setting of 4 (thigh, calf, shin, and foot).

FIGURE 23.1

From within the Biped Creation panel, you can change the structure of the biped.

Once created, the biped can be controlled through the Motion panel (see fig. 23.2). Select any part of the biped, and all the controls for manipulating and animating the biped appear. Because Biped is essentially a very sophisticated animation controller, its controls appear on the motion panel rather than on the Modify panel.

FIGURE 23.2

Selecting the Motion
tab brings up the Biped
Control panel.

Manipulating a Biped

Bipeds have their own built-in IK, completely separate from MAX's native IK. This system has been configured to give smooth, controllable, predictable motion. Biped's IK always works in real time, and there is no need to apply IK as you would within MAX's native IK. The joints of a biped can be manipulated through translation, rotation, and by using footsteps.

With Biped's IK, if you are adjusting a biped's arm by moving the hand, the position of the arm and hand returns to the exact starting position if you return the hand to its original position. This is impossible in MAX's, and most other, IK systems. The typical result with those systems is that, although the hand returns to its original position, the arm's position is different. An additional feature of Biped is the use of IK Blend to blend between forward and inverse kinematics. This feature enables you to link a hand or foot to another object and have that hand or foot follow the object. The amount of IK blending is animatable, so the hand or foot can effectively be attached and detached from the object over time, enabling you to easily animate the biped catching and throwing a ball, dancing with a partner, or performing other actions where the biped interacts with other objects in the scene. The "Attaching the Hands and Feet to MAX Objects" section of this chapter describes IK Blend further.

Translating a biped's joints is straightforward—grab the joint and move it. Unlike MAX's IK, the joints moved need not be constrained with end effectors or terminators for the joint to move properly. All that intelligence is built into the biped. You can just as easily move the biceps as the pinky and still retain a single, predictable solution for the limb, no matter how many joints the move affects.

To move the biped himself, the Center of Mass object needs to be selected and moved (see fig. 23.3). Rather than a hip-centric model, Biped uses the center-of-mass as the top of the hierarchy. As such, the pelvis itself is not translatable. The tetrahedral-shaped object found near the center of the pelvis represents the biped's center-of-mass. Translating this object accomplishes the same effect as moving the pelvis on a hip-centric skeleton.

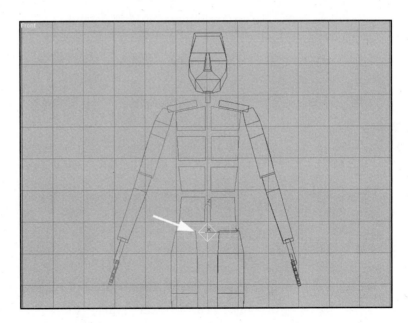

FIGURE 23.3

To move the biped's body, the Center of Mass object (arrow) must be moved, not the pelvis. The Center of Mass object is represented by a tetrahedron.

Rotating joints is also possible, giving the animator the flexibility of positioning a skeleton by using any combination of forward or inverse kinematics. Translating joints on the fingers, for example, normally causes a translation of the entire arm. For motions such as hand gestures, rotations are required.

Another thing to be aware of is that not all biped joints can be translated, and not every joint can rotate around every axis. The restrictions on translating joints are that only the Center of Mass object and the leg and arm joints (except for the clavicles) can be translated. The restrictions on rotating joints are more involved. In general, if you cannot rotate a joint in your body about an axis, you cannot rotate the same joint in the biped about that axis. The following are special rotations or restrictions:

- **Elbows and Knees.** The elbow and knee joints can be rotated both on their local Z axis (like a hinge) and along their local X axis (along their length). When rotated along their local X axis, the rotation does not occur at that joint. Instead, the upper and lower leg/arm are rotated together along an axis formed by the hip/shoulder and ankle/wrist.

- **Feet.** If the foot is planted on a footstep, the foot can be rotated on its local Y and Z axes. The foot remains in contact with the footstep, and the leg joints are rotated to maintain the position of the pelvis. A foot cannot be rotated on its local X axis if the foot is planted.

- **Legs.** If a foot is planted and a leg is rotated, the rotation may be limited to ensure that the foot remains in contact with the footstep.

When a joint is selected, the disallowed motions are grayed out on the menu bar, which can prove a bit frustrating for the novice. After the restrictions are understood, however, nearly any pose can be effectively attained.

Other Biped Selection and Manipulation Tools

In addition to the standard MAX translation and rotation tools, the Biped Motion panel contains a number of Biped-specific tools to assist in manipulating your skeletons:

- **Center of Mass.** Found under the Track Selection rollout, it selects the biped's Center of Mass object. Sometimes this object can be hard to locate in a complex scene; this button speeds the process.

- **Symmetrical Tracks.** Found under the Track Selection rollout, clicking on this button mirrors the current selection on the opposite side of the body. If the left leg is selected, pressing Symmetrical Tracks adds the right leg to the selection.

- **Opposite Tracks.** Found under the Track Selection rollout, clicking on this button selects the identical limbs on the opposite side of the body. If the right arm is selected, pressing the Opposite Tracks button selects the left arm and deselects the right.

- **Copy Posture.** Found on the Track Operations rollout, this is a very handy tool that enables you to copy the position of any joint or group of joints.

- **Paste Posture.** Enables you to paste copied postures to another point in the animation or to another biped. Copy and paste posture is also handy for saving the state of a biped if you want to experiment with a pose. If the new pose does not work out, pasting the original pose returns the biped to normal.

- **Paste Posture Opposite.** This is identical to Paste Posture, but this button mirrors the pose to the opposite side of the body, enabling you to take a pose on the right leg, for example, and paste it on the left.

- **Bend Links.** Found on the Track Operations rollout, this tool evenly bends linked joints, such as the spine, tail, or a multi-jointed neck (see fig. 23.4). Activating the Bend Links button causes all joints in the section (the joints in the spine, for example) to be evenly adjusted by adjusting a single joint.

FIGURE 23.4

Bipeds with a single spine joint rotated without and with Bend Links enacted. Bend Links mode makes possible even rotations of the spine.

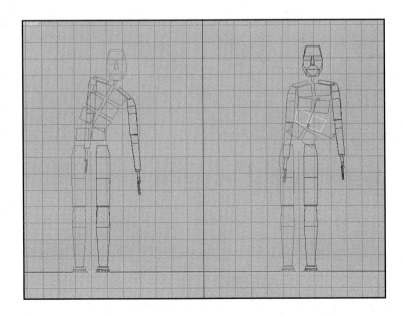

Animating a Biped

There are many ways to animate a biped. Creating and adjusting footsteps are the obvious method. With version 1.1, however, you can also free-form animate bipeds without footsteps. This, however, is a one way street—after keys have been added to a free-form animation, footsteps may not be added to that biped's animation later. If you are in doubt as to whether footsteps will be used in an animation, it is best to assume that they will be and create a free-form area between footsteps. This section takes you through the process of animating with footsteps and free-form animation.

Animating with Footsteps

Footsteps enable you to take advantage of Biped's built-in dynamics to create quasi-realistic motion. The walks, runs, and jumps created by Biped are purposely generic because Biped is a tool that tries not to force a specific style on the animator. The keys automatically generated from footsteps are the minimum required to achieve the motion. This enables the animator to add the desired characteristics without having to delete the many keys that would have to be generated to achieve a realistic default motion. Instead, these keys should be thought of as a motion "sketch" that can be easily modified.

To create footsteps, click on the Footstep Track button within the Track Selection rollout to activate the Footstep Creation rollouts; additionally, Sub-Object Footsteps is enabled for the biped. This means that only footsteps may be selected, created, or manipulated while the Footstep Track button is toggled. After this button has been toggled on, you are free to create footsteps.

Creating Footsteps

There are two methods of creation (footstep creation and adjustment) along with three types of footsteps: walk, run, and jump. The different types of footsteps represent the different timings for the footsteps. Again, you should think of the footstep timing and placement as an easily modified motion "sketch."

- **Walk.** One foot always remains planted, while the other swings forward. At least one foot is always on the ground. There can also be a section in the walk motion—called Double Support—where both feet are on the ground. Both the number of frames that each footstep remains on the ground (Walk Footstep) and the number of frames in a double support period (Double Support) are defined by spinners that activate when the Footstep Track button is toggled on.

- **Run.** One foot is on the ground at a time with no double support. There is also a point in the cycle where both feet are airborne. Both the number of frames that each footstep remains on the ground (Run Footstep) and the number of frames that the biped is airborne (Airborne) are defined by spinners that activate when the Footstep Track button is toggled on.

- **Jump.** Both feet are on the ground equally and are airborne equally. The number of frames that both feet are on the ground (2 Feet Down) and the number of frames that the biped is airborne (Airborne) are defined by spinners that activate when Footstep Track is toggled on.

Biped footsteps can be created singly or in multiples. When creating a set of single footsteps, the footstep can be appended in time to the current footsteps, or created starting at the current frame. Each method has its own button, as follows:

- **Create Footsteps (append).** This button enables you to lay down footsteps by clicking on a viewport—a good method for creating footsteps over tricky terrain or for complex motions such as dance steps. Footsteps are appended to any current footsteps.

- **Create Footsteps (at current frame).** Same as Create Footsteps (append), except that footsteps are added starting at the current frame. If the footstep being added overlaps in time with an existing footstep, an alert appears, and the footstep is not created.

- **Create Multiple Footsteps.** This button creates a user-defined number of footsteps with user-specified spacing and timing. Footsteps created in this manner run along a straight line and are best for walking a character through a scene.

TIP

Using the Interpolate option in the Create Multiple Footsteps dialog, you can change the stride length, stride height, and timing of the footsteps over the footsteps being created.

Activating Footsteps

After a series of footsteps has been laid down, the footsteps need to be activated. To activate footsteps, click on the Create Keys for Inactive Footsteps button in the Footstep Operations rollout. Activation computes dynamics for the biped for any footsteps that have been created, but not yet activated, and creates keys within Track View for the biped. Once activated, you can still modify the walk by manipulating the footsteps or keys. If new footsteps are added after activation, those footsteps must also be activated.

Creating a Simple Walk

You can always get instant gratification from Biped by creating a few footsteps and activating them. The following simple task makes a biped walk and gives you a supply of footsteps with which to work.

CREATING A SIMPLE WALK

1. Load biped01.max from the accompanying CD. This file contains a biped and a ground plane.

2. Select any portion of the biped. Select the Motion tab to bring up the Biped Motion panel.

3. Footsteps are created and modified from within Footstep mode. Click on the Footstep Track button under Track Selection to enter Footstep mode. When this button is toggled on, it enables Sub-Object Footsteps selection on the biped. While in Footstep mode, only footsteps may be selected and modified.

4. There are two ways to create footsteps: single footsteps manually placed with the mouse, or multiple footsteps automatically placed. Footsteps can be one of three types: walk, run, or jump. Click on the Walk button in the Footstep Creation rollout.

5. The fastest way to create footsteps is with the Create Multiple Footsteps button. This creates a number of footsteps with user-specified spacing and timing that can be modified and manipulated later. Press this button to display the Create Multiple Footsteps dialog. Enter **10** for the number of footsteps, make certain that the Start Left option is chosen in the General section, and click on OK.

6. Ten numbered footsteps appear, which need to be activated for the biped to follow them. To do this, press the Create Keys for Inactive Footsteps button in the Footstep Operations rollout (see fig. 23.5).

7. Activate the Left viewport with a right-click and play the animation. The biped now follows these footsteps. Instant gratification!

FIGURE 23.5
Activating the footsteps causes the biped to walk.

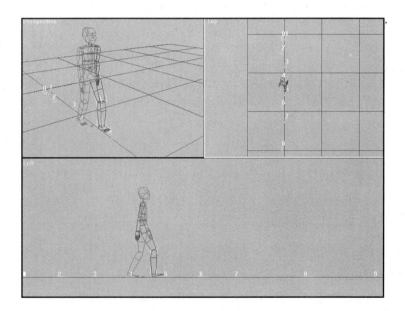

Appending to an Animation

You can append to Biped-created animations quite easily. It is simply a matter of creating additional footsteps and activating them.

APPENDING BIPED ANIMATIONS

1. Click on the Run button and then on the Create Multiple Footsteps button. Type in **4** for the number of footsteps, choose the Start after last footstep option in the Timing section, and click on OK. This appends four footsteps to the end of the animation. Activate the new footsteps.

2. Zoom extents the Left viewport and play back the animation. As you might notice, the biped changes from a walking to a running gait for the new footsteps.

3. Press the Jump button and then the Create Multiple Footsteps button. For the number of footsteps, type in **2**. Activate the footsteps.

4. Zoom extents the Left viewport and play back the animation. The biped now ends the run with a small jump.

An example of this animation is stored on the accompanying CD in the file named biped02.max.

Modifying Footsteps

Once activated, the footsteps can be moved and modified on the fly, with Biped adjusting the biped to match the footsteps automatically.

MODIFYING FOOTSTEPS

1. Using the animation just created, go to the Display panel and click on Unhide All. A small platform with a staircase appears. Play back the animation. The biped should walk right through the stairs because Biped just follows the footsteps, which are laid in a straight line across the ground. Biped does not perform collision detection with other objects in the scene.

2. This obstacle can be overcome quite easily by adjusting the footsteps. Zoom in the platform in the Left viewport. Select any part of the biped and, in Motion panel, toggle the Footstep Track button on. Using the standard MAX selection tools, select footsteps 3 through 15. Move these up so that footstep 3 resides on the first step of the platform. Select footsteps 4 through 15 and move these up so that footstep 4 lies on the second step. Repeat until all the footsteps are properly positioned on the stairs.

3. Play the animation. The biped now walks up the stairs and then runs off the edge of the platform.

4. This can also be adjusted quite easily. Select the biped, go to the Motion panel, and enter Footstep mode. Select footsteps 6 through 8. In the Footstep Operations rollout, adjust the Bend spinner up to 30. The selected footsteps automatically bend. Footsteps prior to footstep 6 are not affected, and footsteps after footstep 8 are rotated to maintain their alignment with footstep 8.

5. Play the animation. Notice how the biped automatically banks as it goes through the turn. A problem still exists, however. The biped still runs off the end of the platform and jumps from and lands in mid-air.

6. In the Front viewport, select footsteps 9 through 13. In the Footstep Operations rollout, uncheck the Width option and adjust the Scale spinner so that footstep 13 resides precisely on the edge of the platform. By unchecking the Width option, the width between footsteps remains the same as the footsteps are scaled downward.

7. Now select footsteps 14 and 15, which are still in mid-air off the edge of the platform. Move these down so that they lie level with the ground plane (see fig. 23.6).

8. Play the animation. The biped now walks up the stairs, rounds a corner, runs, and jumps off the edge. Not bad for a few minutes worth of work.

FIGURE 23.6

Obstacles such as stairs can be overcome quite easily by repositioning the footsteps.

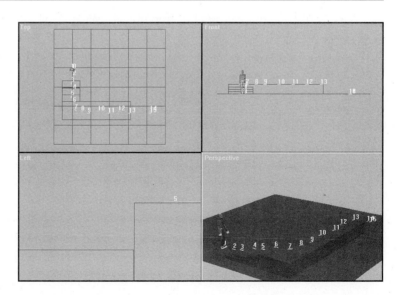

What has this demonstrated? First, by moving the footsteps up the stairs, you saw that footsteps are sub-objects that can be manipulated either individually or in groups. The footsteps can be moved and rotated anywhere in the scene to account for uneven terrain. Also, groups of footsteps can be scaled and bent quite easily by using the Bend and Scale spinners in the Footstep Operations rollout.

The final animation is on the accompanying CD in a file called biped03.max.

Individual footsteps or a selection set of footsteps can also be rotated using Select and Rotate. Rotating the footsteps this way is different than using the Bend spinner in that the unselected footsteps are not moved or rotated. When a selection set of footsteps is rotated in this way, the rotation pivot point is the pivot point of the footstep that the mouse cursor is over when you click and drag. If you change the transform coordinate center from Use Pivot Point Center to Use Selection Center, each footstep is rotated about its local pivot point. Go figure.

Copying and Pasting Footsteps

Biped enables you to select a set of footsteps, copy those footsteps to a buffer, and splice the footsteps into either the middle or end of the footstep sequence. You can even copy and splice a set of footsteps from one biped to another. The section "Saving and Loading Canned Motions" later in this chapter provides an example of this.

In this example, you copy and splice footsteps on a single biped.

COPYING FOOTSTEPS

1. Load cswalk.max from the accompanying CD. This file contains a biped walking forward, turning left, and walking a bit farther. For this exercise, you want the biped to turn left again near the end of the animation.

2. Select any portion of the biped. Select the Motion tab to bring up the Biped Motion panel. Click on the Footstep Track button in the Track Selection rollout.

3. Maximize the Top viewport and select footsteps 4 through 8. To be able to splice a set of footsteps into the middle of a sequence, the first and last footsteps selected need to be for the same leg.

4. Click on the Copy Selected Footsteps button in the Footstep Operations rollout to place the selected footsteps into the Footstep buffer.

5. Click on the Insert Footstep Buffer Onto Footsteps button in the Footstep Operations rollout. A copy of the footsteps in the buffer appears in the viewport.

6. Rotate the footsteps 90° about the Z axis.

7. Using the Move tool, click and drag the footsteps so that the first footstep is over the biped's footstep number 12. This target footstep turns red to signify that a splice is possible (see fig. 23.7). Release the mouse button.

   The first buffer footstep replaces the target footstep, and remaining buffer footsteps follow. The original footsteps after the target footstep are automatically copied into the footstep buffer and are now available to paste.

FIGURE 23.7

When you move the first pasted footstep over a valid target footstep, the target footstep turns red.

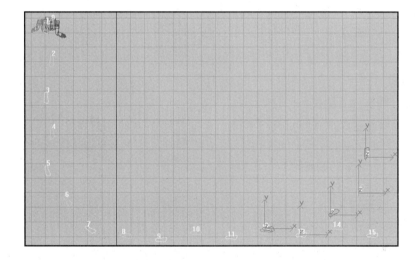

8. Rotate the footsteps 90° about the Z axis.

9. Using the Move tool, click and drag the footsteps so that the first footstep is over the biped's footstep number 16. Release the mouse button. The buffer footsteps are now spliced on to the end of the animation.

10. Minimize the Top viewport. Click on the Perspective viewport to activate it and play back the animation.

After copying the footsteps into the Footstep buffer and before pasting them into the scene, you can edit the footsteps and associated keys that are in the buffer. To do this, click on the Buffer Mode button in the General rollout to toggle on the Buffer mode. The footsteps in the buffer appear in the viewport, applied to the biped. In Track View, the footsteps are shown as the footsteps for the biped, and the associated keys are shown for the biped. These footsteps and keys can be edited just like the normal biped footsteps and keys. To return to the actual footsteps and keys for the biped, toggle off the Buffer Mode button.

Dynamics of Motion

As a biped walks, runs, or jumps, several factors affect the biped's motion: Gravitational Acceleration, Dynamics Blend, Ballistic Tension, and Balance Factor. Each of these factors affects the motion of the biped between keyframes.

NOTE

In the Samples directory of the Character Studio CD-ROM, you can find examples of different settings for the parameters described in this section. You can experiment with the set of AVI and MAX files provided.

A walk cycle is the act of falling forward and then catching yourself. To start walking, you extend one leg forward, which shifts your center of mass forward. As your center of mass moves forward past your planted foot, you start to fall forward. The back of your planted foot lifts off the ground, whereas the ball and toes of the foot remain planted. You continue to fall forward until the heel of the moving foot hits the ground. At this point, the momentum of your body pulls the back leg forward, and as the back foot leaves the ground, it also pushes you forward. This back leg continues forward until it passes the front leg, and you begin to fall forward again. While one of your feet is off the ground, your entire weight is being supported by the other foot. To maintain balance, the body arcs over the moving foot (the hip shifts toward the planted foot). Biped properly animates the hip to provide this motion (see fig. 23.8).

FIGURE 23.8

While only supported on one foot, the hip swings over the planted foot.

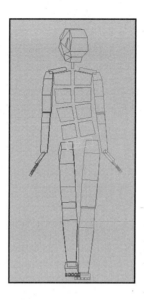

As you walk, the height of your pelvis (and center of mass) from the ground varies. It is at a minimum right after the front foot hits the ground, and at a maximum as the back leg passes the front leg.

A run cycle is similar to a walk cycle, except that instead of falling forward, you throw yourself forward. In a walk cycle, at least one foot is always on the ground. During a run cycle, however, there are split seconds when both feet are off the ground. During these periods, you are either airborne or ballistic. You move forward at a constant velocity during this airborne period, and the vertical height of your center of mass is based on how hard you "push off" and gravity. Leading up to this push off, your legs are typically bent more than during a walk cycle to generate more power with which to push. As the legs are bent, the center of mass also is lowered.

A jump cycle, in turn, is similar to a run cycle. The only difference is that both feet are in the air at the same time, and both hit the ground at the same time. Again, you move forward at a constant velocity during this airborne period, and the vertical height of your center of mass is based on how hard you push off and on gravity.

When you land in a run or jump cycle, your center of mass continues downward and forward due to momentum. Your legs act like springs, absorbing this momentum.

Dynamics Blend

Biped stores both Vertical and Horizontal keys for the biped's Center of Mass object. The Horizontal keys are generated at the middle of each footstep's support period and provide the forward motion of the biped. The Vertical keys are generated at the start, middle, and end of each footstep. The Vertical keys store the extension of the legs and the actual vertical height of the Center of Mass object.

During walking motions, the height is interpolated based on the extension of the legs recorded at each vertical key. This ensures that the supporting leg's knee angle does not change direction between two vertical keys. In effect, when walking, the leg extensions (and rising and falling foot pivots on the ground) control the height of the body in a natural way.

You can defeat this approach (or selectively blend it) with an interpolation of the actual vertical height by setting Dynamics Blend at each vertical key. At a Dynamics Blend setting of zero, Biped performs a spline interpolation of the vertical heights and ignores the leg extension information at each key. At a Dynamics Blend setting of one, Biped interpolates the leg extension distances and ignores the vertical heights at each key. You can change the Dynamics Blend value only while the Center of Mass object is selected, Move is active, and Restrict to Z is active.

During running and jumping motions, or transitions between them, the height is always determined by the vertical heights at each key because running and jumping are governed by the requirements of gravity, the heights of the body at liftoff and touchdown, and the duration of each airborne period. For running and jumping vertical keys, therefore, Dynamics Blend is grayed-out because it is not applicable.

Gravitational Acceleration

While the biped is airborne during a run or jump cycle, the vertical dynamics are controlled by Gravitational Acceleration (GravAccel in the General rollout of the Biped Motion panel) and the length of time between the lift and landing footsteps. If the length of time between these footsteps is shortened, or the Gravitational Acceleration value is decreased, the maximum height during the airborne period is decreased (on the moon, you don't need to jump very high to cover a lot of ground). The Gravitational Acceleration value is not animatable.

Ballistic Tension

The Ballistic Tension value controls how "springy" the legs are before lift-off and after touchdown in run and jump cycles (see fig. 23.9). The higher the value, the stiffer the legs are, resulting in less leg bending. You can change the Ballistic Tension value only while the Center of Mass object is selected, Move is active, and Restrict to Z is active. This value can only be set at the touchdown keyframe, unless three or more Vertical keys are set during the footprint support cycle. In this case, a Ballistic Tension value can also be set at the lift-off keyframe.

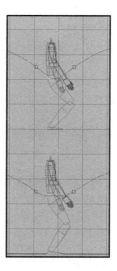

FIGURE 23.9

The follow-through of a landing for bipeds with a low (top biped) and high (bottom biped) Ballistic Tension value.

Balance Factor

The Balance Factor value specifies the biped's weight distribution by positioning the biped weight anywhere along a line extending from the center of mass to the head. A value of 0 places the biped's weight in the feet. A value of 1 places the biped's weight over the center of mass. A value of 2 places the biped's weight in the head. The Balance Factor value has no effect on the walk, run, and jump cycle motions; however, it can be used to your advantage when adjusting the rotation of the spine.

Assume, for example, a biped is sitting on a chair, and you are animating it so that it leans over a table. With the default value for Balance Factor (1.0), as you rotate the spine forward, the pelvis moves backward to maintain a constant position for the Center of Mass object. If you set the Balance Factor to 0, as you rotate the spine forward the pelvis remains at the same location. If you attempt to do this while the biped is standing, however, the biped looks very unnatural—like it should be falling over but isn't (see fig. 23.10). The Balance Factor value is set in the Structure rollout while in Figure mode. The Balance Factor value is not animatable.

FIGURE 23.10

The movement of the pelvis back from the center of mass when the spine is bent forward for bipeds with a normal Balance Factor (left) and a low Balance Factor (right).

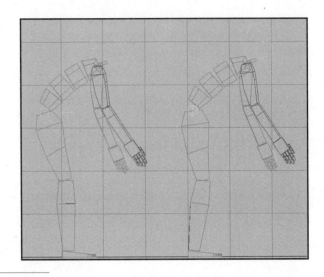

Bipeds in Track View

Although manipulating the footsteps themselves can change the walk quite a bit, the timing of a walk is also very important. A biped's timing can be changed quite radically from within Track View. When viewed as keys within Track View (see figs. 23.10 and 23.11), a Biped animation looks slightly different from ordinary MAX animation. When viewing a Biped animation, notice that the legs, arms, and spine do not have separate keys for each joint—Biped keys span all joints in the limb (arms, legs, spine, tail). A leg does not have separate keys for the thigh and shin, for example; instead, it has only one key that comprises the position of all the limb's joints. This enables Biped to transfer animation between disparate skeletons quite easily.

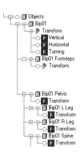

FIGURE 23.11

Biped tracks in Track View. The footstep keys are represented as blocks rather than dots, and locked Biped keys are highlighted in red.

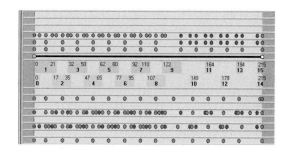

Footstep Tracks

One of the more important tracks is the footsteps track, which has a distinct appearance of alternating green and blue blocks—green are right footsteps, blue are left. The colored blocks indicate exactly when the feet are on the ground. Space between the footsteps for a foot indicates that the foot is airborne. If neither foot has a footstep at a given frame, both feet are airborne, such as in a run or a jump. Walks, by definition, always keep at least one foot on the ground. Places where the blocks overlap means both feet are on the ground. Displaying the footsteps this way enables you to know exactly what the feet are doing.

A footstep key actually spans several frames and has a number of components. By default, each footstep is labeled in its center with the footstep number, and each footstep indicates the start and stop frame in the top corners.

To modify a footstep, click on the center of the footstep near the footstep number and drag. Clicking on the start or stop frame in the corners of the footstep enables you to modify these positions as well, affecting the duration of the footstep. Like with any other key, you can also select, move, and resize groups of keys.

Right-clicking on a footstep key brings up the Footstep Track dialog (see fig. 23.12), which gives you control over how the footsteps are displayed, as well as some additional selection tools. The top portion of this dialog is for turning off vertical dynamics in free-form areas and is discussed in this chapter's "Free-Form Animation" section. The Footstep Number Display section provides options on the frame information shown for each footstep. The

Footstep Edge Selection section enables you to change which portion of previously selected footsteps remain chosen. If you have chosen three footsteps and click on the Left button, for example, only the left edges of these three footsteps remain selected. You can then move these edges to increase or decrease the duration for the footsteps.

NOTE

Release 1.1 of Character Studio enables you to select any combination of left and right edges, and generally improves footstep editing in Track View.

FIGURE 23.12

Right-clicking on the footstep track displays the Footstep Track dialog.

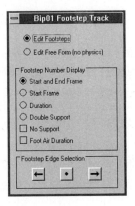

Other Tracks

In addition to the footstep tracks, the Biped also has another class of keys not normally found within MAX. These are keys for skeletal objects, such as the legs, and are calculated by Biped and are shown in red. Called *locked keys*, these are keys that Biped requires for it to perform its calculations. The locked keys cannot be moved or deleted except by changing the footsteps themselves. If you edit a footstep track, the locked keys appear and disappear as the track changes. Finally, Biped also creates normal MAX keys (shown in gray). These are for skeletal elements, such as the arms, spine, and head. These keys can be edited, moved, or deleted, like any other MAX key.

Right-clicking on a Biped track other than the Footstep track displays the Change Multiple Keys dialog (see fig. 23.13). This dialog enables you to select keys based on a number of user-defined filters defined as Tracks and State filters, and to apply the last transform performed on a portion of the biped to a selected set of keys.

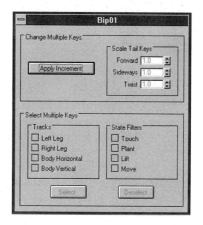

The Tracks section defines which tracks in the animation are marked for selection. These can be the Left Leg, Right Leg, Body Horizontal, and Body Vertical tracks. If you want a character's walking body to bounce up and down more, for example, check the Body Vertical box.

State filters define which portion of the step is selected. Biped defines four states that correlate to the major states of a footstep. These are not to be confused with the major poses of a walk described in the previous chapters— contact, recoil, and passing. States define where the foot contacts and leaves the ground, not the pose of the body.

- **Touch.** The point in the step where the forward foot first touches the ground.

- **Plant.** Any keys where the leg is planted on the ground. This includes the recoil and passing position.

- **Lift.** Where the planted leg lifts off the ground.

- **Move.** Any keys where the leg is off the ground. This includes the recoil and passing position.

By using a combination of Track and State selections, you can select and modify multiple keys. This can change the character of an entire walk quite easily while keeping the walk consistent.

Biped records the last mouse movement and moved body part whenever you do anything with a biped. When you click on Apply Increment, Biped applies that mouse move and updates the key for each selected key in Track View that matches the same moved body part type. If you have keys selected on both arms and legs, and you move or rotate an arm and perform an Apply Increment, only the selected keys on the arms are modified.

If you actually set a key when performing the move that is going to be applied to the entire set, the increment of that key happens twice: once for the Set Key and again for the Apply Increment. In general, you should never be in Animate mode or use Set Key if you are attempting to just modify a selected set of keys in a uniform way. The normal sequence of events is to select a set of keys, perform some interactive transform on the body part in question, and click on Apply Increment. If you do set a key when the interactive move is performed (either via Set Key or if Animate is on), the key should not be selected in Track View when performing the Apply Increment.

The frame number or keyframe for this "last recorded mouse move + body part" makes no difference because Biped is really just recording the "increment," not the actual posture. It is usually convenient, however, to adjust the increment relative to a particular keyframe.

NOTE

A bug is present in release 1.1 of Character Studio where, if you have keys selected for opposing body limbs (for example, both legs), and you perform more than one Apply Increment, the first key on the limb opposing the one transformed is not properly modified. If you perform the transform with Animate on (and deselect in Track View the modified key), Apply Increment properly updates the keys.

You may have noticed in the last example that the biped's feet were passing through the steps as the biped walked up the stairs. In the following exercise, you use the Change Multiple Keys dialog to correct this.

PLANTING THE FOOT ON THE STAIRS

1. Load the file biped03.max, which is the platform animation created previously.

2. Maximize the Left viewport and zoom in to the area of the footsteps 2 through 6. Advance to frame 40.

3. Open Track View and right-click on the Filters button. Choose Animated Tracks Only. Right-click on Objects and choose Expand All. Scroll the Track View windows to display the Footsteps track and the left and right leg transform tracks.

4. Select the right foot. Note that in Track View that a key is already present on the left leg track at this frame. Because the foot is off the ground, this is a Move state key.

5. In Track View, right-click on one of the leg transform tracks to display the Change Multiple Keys dialog. In the Select Multiple Keys section, check Left Leg and Right Leg under Tracks, and Move under State Filters. Click on the Select button. The Move keys on the right and left legs are selected in Track View.

6. The set of keys selected contains more keys than you want to adjust. Deselect the keys at and before frame 40. Deselect the keys after frame 108 (the right edge of footstep 6 is at frame 108). Deselect the last key currently selected on the right leg (see fig. 23.14).

FIGURE 23.14

The keys on the left and right leg selected when performing the first Apply Increment.

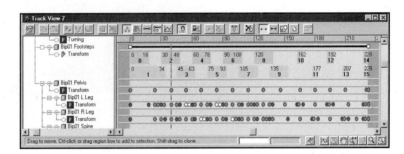

7. Click on the Animate button to turn on Animate mode. Move the right foot up 2 units on the world Z axis.

8. Click on Apply Increment in the Change Multiple Keys dialog.

9. Advance to frame 54 and select the left foot. Move the left foot back 10 units on the world Y axis, and up 1 unit on the world Z axis.

10. In Track View, deselect the second key in each pair of keys currently selected. Deselect the left leg key at frame 54 (see fig. 23.15).

FIGURE 23.15

FIGURE 23.15

The keys on the left and right leg selected when performing the second Apply Increment.

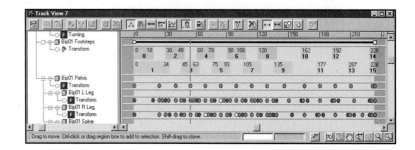

11. Click on Apply Increment in the Change Multiple Keys dialog.

12. Play the animation. As the biped walks up the stairs, his feet no longer pass through the stairs.

The final animation is on the accompanying CD in the file biped04.max.

Manipulating Biped Animation Within Track View

Manipulating a biped within Track View is an easy way to change the character of an animation quite quickly. The timing of the footsteps can be affected just by moving or resizing the footstep blocks.

Walks can also be made into runs or jumps, and vice versa. If the footstep keys are placed so that they overlap, the footsteps are *walk* footsteps (see fig. 23.16). If the footstep keys are moved so that they don't overlap, the double support is eliminated and the walk footstep becomes a *run* footstep (see fig. 23.17). If the run footstep is then moved so that both the left and right foot are airborne at the same time, and both are in contact with the ground at the same time, it becomes a *jump* (see fig. 23.18).

FIGURE 23.16

Footstep 9 is a walk footstep because it overlaps footstep 8 by three frames, giving it double support.

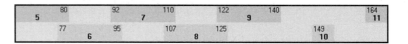

FIGURE 23.17

Moving the edge of footstep 9 so that it doesn't overlap footstep 8 turns the step into a run because double support is eliminated.

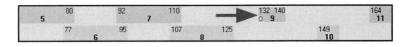

FIGURE 23.18

Moving footstep 9 so that it overlaps footstep 10 turns it from a run into a jump, because both feet are airborne before the step.

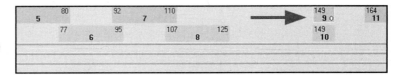

Directly Animating a Biped

Besides animating with footsteps, a biped can also be keyframed directly. The only limits are for a walking biped, because footsteps introduce calculated keys that cannot be deleted or moved outside of changing the footsteps. Outside of this handful of keys, the biped can be keyframed to give a walk more character and life. This animation can be as simple as bobbing the body up and down by animating the center of mass or as involved as introducing complex leg and arm motions—for a dance sequence or gymnastics, perhaps.

Animating a Flip

In this exercise, a gymnastic flip is added to an existing biped animation.

FLIPPING

1. Load the file biped04.max, which is the platform animation created previously. You are going to make the biped do a flip as it jumps off the platform between frames 213 and 233.

2. To make viewing this action easier, maximize the Front viewport and zoom in to the area of the jump.

3. The biped himself can be flipped 360 degrees by rotating his Center of Mass object. Select any portion of the biped and open the Motion panel. To select the Center of Mass object, click on the Center of Mass Object button in the Track Selection rollout.

4. Move the Slider to frame 219. Click on Angle Snap and rotate the Center of Mass object 140 degrees about the Y axis (see fig. 23.19). Press the Set Key button on the Biped panel.

TIP

The Set Key button sets a key for the selected limb(s). If a limb is transformed while the Animate button is toggled on, a key is automatically generated.

FIGURE 23.19
Rotating the body is a simple matter of rotating the Center of Mass object.

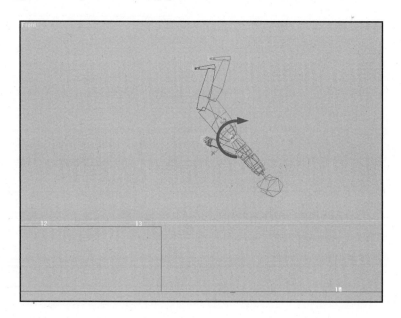

5. Move the Slider to frame 225. As you may notice, the biped tries to reverse his rotation to complete the animation because this is the shortest way to interpolate between the rotation key set at frame 219 and the key at 233. This can be fixed by further rotating the body back in the desired direction and setting another key. With Angle Snap still toggled on, rotate the biped's Center of Mass object an additional 200 degrees. Set a key.

6. Notice how the biped automatically extends his legs because the plug-in automatically computes the dynamics of the biped. As you will see later, dynamics can be turned off. For this animation, it is perfectly acceptable.

7. Play the animation. The biped does the flip. Still, the animation looks rather stiff. This animation can be given a bit more liveliness in many ways. These methods also employ the various Biped tools.

8. The takeoff step (step 13) is 6 frames long. To make the takeoff slightly quicker, this can be shortened to 4 frames. From Track View, locate the footstep block for step 13 and click on its right edge. Drag the edge to shorten the step so that it runs from frame 207 to 211.

9. The biped also seems a little light when it takes off. To give it the illusion of weight, the body needs to move lower before taking off because the legs need to absorb the shock of the body and also anticipate the leap. On frame 207, when the foot makes contact, select the Center of Mass object and move it down approximately 5 units in Z. Set a key.

10. During the flip, the left leg moves forward and kicks backward to make the body flip. Anticipate the kick motion by bringing the left foot forward at frame 207 (see fig. 23.20). Set a key.

FIGURE 23.20
Move the right leg forward by dragging the foot. This helps to anticipate the flip.

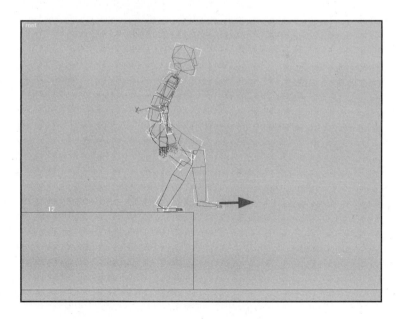

11. Animate the kick of the left foot. Go to frame 200 and drag the left foot back behind the right leg. Set a key.

12. The body should bend forward a bit more before it takes off. This can be done by rotating the spine around the Z axis. The easiest way to do this is by using the Bend Links mode. Toggle the Bend Links button on and then select a spine segment. Go to frame 207 and rotate the segment about 40 degrees around the Z axis. Set a key.

13. Scrub the animation. Notice that the spine motion pops at frame 209. When Biped created the original jump, it placed a key for the spine at frame 209. With the key just set at frame 207, this key is now extraneous. Delete this key either in Track View, or by advancing to frame 209 and clicking on the Delete Key button in the Track Operations rollout with a spine segment selected.

14. Scrub the animation. At the end of the jump, the spine straightens out—which is fine for a standing pose—but the spine straightens out too early. Go to frame 207, where the spine key was set. Select the spinal segments. Click on Copy Posture. Move to frame 223, slightly before the landing, and press Paste Posture. The spine bends. Set a key.

15. To anticipate the jump, the arms swing forward quite a bit. Go to frame 205. Select the right hand and move it forward and up so that it is even with the chest and the arm is slightly bent (see fig. 23.21). Set a key. Do the same with the left arm.

FIGURE 23.21

The arms swing forward before the flip.

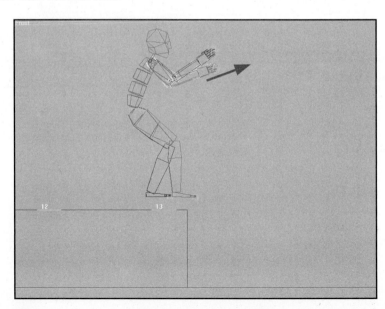

16. When the flip begins, the arms pull in toward the body to help give it rotation. On frame 213, move both the right and left hands so that they are roughly even with the hips and the arms are slightly bent. Set keys for both limbs.

17. The head needs to be tucked toward the chest as the body rotates. Go to frame 223 and rotate the head in to the chest. Set a key.

18. Finally, the biped should absorb the impact of the landing a bit more. Go to frame 230 and move the Center of Mass object down about 6 or 7 units (see fig. 23.22). Set a key.

FIGURE 23.22

Upon impact, the body continues moving down to absorb the shock before the character stands.

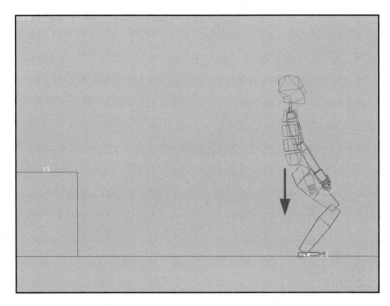

Play the animation. These little tweaks go a long way toward making the flip more realistic and natural. The lesson here is that Biped gives you basic motion only; it is the animator who makes the skeleton come alive. Biped is a very nice tool, but it still needs to be driven by an animator.

This animation can be found on the accompanying CD as biped05.max.

Free-Form Animation

Not every action in every animation requires footsteps. People also stand still, sit, swim, and sometimes fly. As stated previously, with version 1.1, footsteps are no longer a requirement to animate a biped—making the previously mentioned actions easier to animate. If footsteps are in the scene, the free-form animation must be set up in an area between footsteps. Free-form keys cannot be set before the first footstep, nor after the last.

Free-Form Animation Without Footsteps

Free-form animation without footsteps is an all or nothing proposition. After keys have been set, footsteps cannot be added to the shot. If footsteps are required in addition to free-form animation, you can accomplish this by suspending dynamics. This is discussed in the next section.

Animating a biped in free-form mode without footsteps gives you many advantages, most important of which is that the biped's IK remains active, making it very easy to pose the character. Biped keys are still calculated in the same way, with the keys being assigned to limbs rather than individual joints. The only exception is that vertical dynamics is suspended while in free-form mode without footsteps. The vertical and horizontal position of the biped's Center of Mass object between keyframes is based on a spline interpolation of the keyframes. Because there are no footsteps, there will also be no calculated or restricted keys.

Free-Form Animation with Footsteps

Free-form animation with footsteps is very similar to animating a biped without them. The task requires a few extra keystrokes to enable. The free section must be free of any footsteps. Normally, Biped's dynamics want to control the trajectory of the biped, as in a jump. To animate the character completely unencumbered, these dynamics need to be suspended.

FREE-FORM FOOTSTEPS

1. Open Track View and right-click on the Footsteps track to open the Footstep Track dialog.

2. In the Footstep Track dialog, choose the Edit Free Form (no physics) option.

3. The areas between footsteps are highlighted with a yellow box. These are areas where vertical dynamics are being calculated. Clicking on a box turns it solid yellow, causing vertical dynamics to be suspended (see fig. 23.23).

FIGURE 23.23

*Free-form areas with
vertical dynamics
turned off are shown
as solid yellow boxes in
the Footstep track in
Track View.*

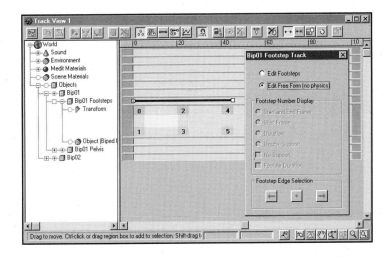

FIGURE 23.23

*Free-form areas with
vertical dynamics
turned off are shown
as solid yellow boxes in
the Footstep track in
Track View.*

After vertical dynamics is suspended, the biped can be animated in any manner desired—to fly it around the world, for instance, or to mount and ride a bicycle. The only caveat is that the free-form animation must occur between two sets of footsteps, which means that the biped's feet automatically attach themselves to footprints when the free-form section ends.

If the free-form section is at the end of the animation, the end footsteps must be placed a few frames past the end of the animation. The converse goes for free-form animation at the beginning of a scene. In that situation, the footsteps preceding the free-form section are placed before the first rendered frame.

If the character is to resume walking, the free-form animation needs to match up to the footprints at the end of the free-form section, otherwise the biped seems to pop into place.

Standing Still

If your character's feet are firmly planted throughout the animation, you can place only two footsteps in the scene and extend their lengths from within Track View to match the length of the scene. This locks the feet down and gives you the freedom to animate the upper body as desired.

Attaching the Hands and Feet to MAX Objects

Biped has the capability to attach or lock a biped's hands and feet to any object in the scene, which enables Biped skeletons to grip and hold onto things, as well as to keep their feet firmly locked to moving objects (an escalator, perhaps). The object it is attached to may be a point in the world space or a point relative to another object (the Object Space object).

These attachments can be animated through the use of the IK Blend spinner in the Track Operations rollout (see fig. 23.24). This spinner is the heart of Biped's animatable IK attachments. With it, you can make a biped's hand or foot gradually release his lock. When the IK Blend is set to 1.0, the hand or foot is firmly locked relative to the object space object or at a point in space. If the rest of the biped is moved, the hand or foot remains at the same location. At an IK Blend of 0.0, the motion of the hand or foot is based on the motion of the biped. If the rest of the biped is moved, the hand or foot moves along with it.

Each key for a hand or foot can be set in the Body or Object coordinate space. If two consecutive keys are set in Body space, and the IK Blend value for each is set to 1.0, the location of the hand or foot is interpolated between these keys based on the motion of the object space object. If the object space object is moving, therefore, the hand or foot moves along with that object. To attach a hand or foot to an object or a point in space, use the following steps.

ATTACHING HANDS OR FEET

1. Select the hand or foot.

2. Position the hand or foot in its desired position relative to the object to follow.

3. Click on the Select Object Space Object button.

4. Click on the object to follow. Not selecting an object binds the hand or foot to a fixed position in world space.

5. In the Kinematics section, choose the Object option.

6. Set the IK Blend spinner at 1.0

7. Click on Set Key.

To release an object, spin IK Blend to 0.0 and set another key. As the spinner animates to zero, the lock is gradually broken. If you want to keep a hand or foot locked for a period of time and then release the lock, a second IK Blend key of 1.0 is needed to keep it locked for the time up until the release begins. To maintain the position of the hand or foot relative to the object space object, toggle on the appropriate Anchor button in the Track Operations rollout. This action holds the hand or foot in place regardless of the keys set for the hand or foot. Anchors are not permanent, rather they are interactive tools to enable you to set keys with the hand or foot in a fixed position relative to the object space object (or fixed in world space if no object space object has been chosen).

One new feature with version 1.1 is the capability to attach portions of a biped to himself by using the IK Blend function. This enables you to work with closed loops of biped linkages and objects. A sword may be linked to a biped's left hand, for example, and the right hand may be linked via IK Blend to the sword, creating a closed loop of links that can be animated together. As a result, movement of the left hand controls both the sword and the movement of the entire right arm. In addition, you can animate the IK Blend spinner for the right hand to release its grip on the sword during motion.

Using IK Attachments to Dribble a Ball

In this exercise, you experiment with IK attachments, and see how changing the IK attachment parameters affects the biped's motion.

DRIBBLING A BALL

1. From the accompanying CD, load dribble.max, which contains a biped and a ball. Activate the Left viewport and play the animation.

The left hand has been positioned to be on top of the ball at frame 0. It then moves down to the biped's side at frame 16. The ball moves up, and then down to hit the ground, and bounces back up.

2. Select the biped's left hand and open the Motion panel.

3. Go to frame 0. Click on the Select Object Space Object button and then click on the ball. Object Ball appears as the object space object. Select Object in the Kinematics section of the Track Operations rollout. Set the IK Blend value to 1.0, and click on Set Key.

    Based on the height of the ball, you want the hand to remain locked to the ball until frame 10. If we just advance to frame 10 though, the hand is no longer in its proper position relative to the ball.

4. At frame 0, click on the Anchor Left Hand button to toggle it on. Advance to frame 10, select Object in the Kinematics section of the Track Operations rollout, set the IK Blend value to 1.0, and click on Set Key. Click on the Anchor Left Hand button to toggle it off and play the animation.

    The hand now remains in a fixed position relative to the ball on frames 0 to 10, and then drops away from the ball and moves to the side of the biped. Now you want to catch the ball on its rise.

5. At frame 0, click on the Anchor Left Hand button to toggle it on. Advance to frame 33, select Object in the Kinematics section of the Track Operations rollout, set the IK Blend value to 1.0, and click on Set Key. Click on the Anchor Left Hand button to toggle it off and play the animation. The hand now meets the ball as it is rising.

6. Perform an Edit/Hold to save the file and start playing with the IK attachment parameters, particularly on frames 0 and 10. Note that if Body space is selected or the IK Blend value is 0, the motion of the ball has no affect on the motion of the hand.

The final animation can be found on the accompanying CD as dribble2.max.

Using IK Attachments to Ride a Bicycle

In this exercise, you see how Biped's animatable attachments can help with difficult animation tasks. Locking objects to a bicycle, such as both hands to the handlebars, can easily cause dependency loops in MAX's native IK.

Biped provides a very elegant solution and enables you to lock different parts of the biped's hierarchy to any object or combination of objects.

RIDING A BICYCLE

1. From the accompanying CD, load bipbike.max, which contains a biped and a simple bicycle (see fig. 23.25).

2. Select the biped's Center of Mass object and open the Motion panel. Drag the biped so that his pelvis is over the seat. Go to frame 0 and set a key for both the Vertical and Horizontal tracks. This can be done by selecting the Restrict to X or the Restrict to Y button and clicking on Set Key, and selecting the Restrict to Z button and clicking on Set Key. Alternatively, you can select the Restrict to XZ or Restrict to YZ button and click Set Key. This will create keys on both the Vertical and Horizontal tracks. When you set the first key, a warning stating that you are about to create a Biped animation without footsteps appears. This is fine, so press OK.

3. Link the biped to the bicycle. Press the Select and Link button on the toolbar. Drag a line from the Center of Mass object to the bicycle seat to make the biped a child of the bicycle, enabling him to move wherever the bicycle moves.

4. Bend the biped over a bit so that the arms can reach the handlebars. Select one spine segment and, using Bend Links, rotate the spine approximately 32° about his Z axis so that the chest is over the pedals (see fig. 23.26). Set a key.

5. Select the biped's right foot. Drag this up and forward so that it rests directly over the right pedal. Select the left foot and drag it to the left pedal in the same manner (see fig. 23.27).

6. Link the right foot to the right pedal. Select the right foot. In the Kinematics section of the Track Operations rollout, choose the option marked Object. Press the Select Object Space Object button. Click on the right pedal to select this as the object space object. Set the IK Blend spinner at 1.0. With the Time Slider on frame 0, set a key for the foot.

7. Repeat this procedure for the left foot and left pedal.

   Both feet are now locked to the pedals. They will move wherever the pedals move. The pedals have already been linked to the crank, so they will rotate as the crank rotates.

8. Scrub the animation. The feet now follow the pedals. Next, you need to attach the hands to the handlebars.

9. Select the hands and position them over the handlebars. To get a more natural pose, you should also rotate the arms so that the elbows are slightly out from the body. At frame 0, set a key for each arm to lock in the angle of the elbows.

10. Using the same procedure in step 6, lock each hand to the Bike-Handle object and set a key for each hand's IK Blend at frame 0.

11. Rotate the handle bars. The hands and arms should follow.

12. Adjust the biped's Center of Mass object so that the pelvis rests firmly on the seat. Set a key at frame 0. Figure 23.28 shows the final position of the biped.

FIGURE 23.28
With the hands and feet locked to bike, the biped's animation is driven by the animation of the bike.

13. Experiment with the animation. Because the links are bound on frame 0, any motion of the bike past that point is reflected in the biped. You can extend the animation by copying the cycle of the pedals, and can make the bicycle move by translating it. Rotations to the handlebars are reflected, and if you want to make the biped stand up on the pedals, translate the Center of Mass object up so that the biped stands.

This final animation is on the accompanying CD in a file called bikefin.max.

Saving and Loading Canned Motions

Biped enables you to save motions from one biped and apply them to another. The motions apply regardless of the differences in size and structure of the two bipeds. This is very powerful in that it enables you to create canned libraries of motions that can be applied anywhere. Biped has two types of motion files: Biped (.BIP) files store the footsteps and associated keyframes of a biped character; and step files (.STP) store just the footsteps.

The STP file format is rarely used because it merely generates the default Biped motions when loaded. This file format was mainly provided for programmers who might wish to write software that parametrically creates STP footstep patterns (crowds of bipeds walking in a building, for example).

A major feature of Biped is its capability to adapt any BIP file to your character without changing its kinematic structure, dimensions, distribution of weight, and so on. Furthermore, any Physique mapping is also completely independent from the motions. You may load any BIP file on to a biped without changing his Physiqued skin, or his pose, kinematic structure, and center-of-gravity in Biped's Figure Mode. The only animation type data not stored in a BIP file are IK attachments to scene-specific objects—because these are, by nature, scene specific. This data is best stored in scenes in the normal MAX file format.

To save a STP or BIP file, select any portion of the biped and, in the Biped Motion panel, click on the Save File button in the General rollout. Select the type of file to save and its path and file name, and click on OK. All footsteps (and keys for BIP files) associated with the biped are saved.

To replace the entire animation currently applied to a biped with that defined in a BIP file, select any portion of the biped and, in the Biped Motion panel, click on the Load File button. Select the BIP file to load and click on OK.

A BIP file can also be read into the Footstep buffer and spliced into the current animation. To do this, you need to be in Buffer mode and then load the BIP file. To enter Buffer mode, however, footsteps need to be present in the Footstep buffer. To do this, you need to go into Footstep Track mode, select one or more footsteps, and click on Copy Selected Footsteps in the Footstep Operations rollout. This action copies the selected footsteps into the Footstep buffer and enables the Buffer Mode button.

Frequently, you will not want to apply the entire animation defined in a BIP file, but only a section of it. Currently, there is no way to do this directly. Although you can load the animation defined by the BIP file into the Footstep buffer and delete the undesired footsteps, this causes the animation keys to be regenerated. This can cause a loss of the very animation data you are trying to splice in. The easiest way to get around this is to place another biped in the scene, apply the animation in the BIP to that biped, and copy and paste motions from this biped to the desired biped.

SPLICING MOTIONS

1. Load cswalk.max from the accompanying CD. This file contains a biped walking forward, turning left, and walking a bit farther. You want to splice in a motion where the biped walks on tiptoes.

2. Create another biped in the Perspective viewport. This biped will be used as an intermediary, holding the animation imported from the BIP file for application to the original biped.

   Because Biped can properly adjust the animation data while moving between dissimilar bipeds, the details of this biped do not need to match those of the original biped. To prevent the loss of data, however, if the original biped has arms or a tail, this biped also should have arms or a tail. As a practical matter, this biped should be roughly the same height as the original biped.

3. With this new biped selected, in the Biped motion panel click on the Load File button in the General rollout. Load creep.bip from the accompanying CD.

4. Play the animation. As the original biped walks along, the new biped creeps along.

5. With the new biped selected, click on the Footstep Track button. Select footsteps 3 through 5, and click on the Copy Selected Footsteps button in the Footstep Operations rollout. Click on the Footstep Track button to exit Footstep mode.

6. Select any portion of the original biped and click on the Footstep Track button. Click on the Insert Footstep Buffer onto Footsteps button to display the footsteps in the Footstep buffer.

7. Drag the first buffer footstep over the biped's footstep number 10 and release the mouse. The remaining original footsteps are now shown in their saturated colors. Drag these footsteps so that the first one is over the new footstep number 12 and release the mouse.

8. Click on the Footstep Track button to exit Footstep mode, activate the Perspective viewport, and play the animation. At this point, you can delete or hide the biped added to the scene.

When you splice in a set of footsteps, sometimes the leg rotation near the end of the splice is very visibly incorrect—the upper leg is pointing toward the biped's head. A single key has been improperly set in these cases. To correct this, perform the remaining steps:

9. Select the leg with the incorrect rotation.

10. Toggle the Key Mode Toggle button on (the Key Mode Toggle is located at the bottom on the MAX window, with the Time controls).

11. Click on the Select and Move or Select and Rotate button.

12. Click on the Next Frame or Previous Frame button to advance to the keyframe where the leg rotation is incorrect. Note the frame number and the pose of the biped.

13. Click on the Next Frame or Previous Frame button to advance to a keyframe where the biped is in a similar pose.

14. Click on the Copy Posture button to copy the leg's rotation to a buffer.

15. Return to the keyframe where the leg rotation is incorrect. Click on the Paste Posture button to set the leg's rotation from the buffer. Click on Set Key.

By using BIP files, you can set up libraries of motion that can easily be applied to any biped. The capability to share animations between bipeds, regardless of their size or structure, is not found in any other application.

In Practice: Animating with Biped

- **Manipulating bipeds.** Using Biped's manipulation tools, such as Select Opposite, can help streamline your work. It is also possible to freeze or hide parts of a biped while working on others.

- **Footstep driven animation.** Although footsteps certainly take a lot of the drudgery out of creating locomotive sequences, they are only the first step. To truly bring your characters to life, you need to go back over the Biped-generated motions and bring them to life by adding animation.

- **Bipeds in hierarchies.** If your biped is a child of another object, the biped and his footsteps move in relation to the parent. This makes scenes that require moving footsteps—such as ice-skating or walking up a moving escalator—possible by parenting the escalator's stairs to the biped.

- **Free-form animation.** Free-form animation between footsteps defaults to having dynamics turned on, which causes the biped to simulate a jump motion. Typically, it is best to turn dynamics off when starting a free-form animation.

- **Animatable locks.** This is a very powerful feature, so be certain to practice its use, and be familiar with the keystrokes. In addition to locking hands and feet to objects or world space, they can be locked in relation to the body itself.

- **Splicing motions.** This is a feature unique to Biped that enables you to apply animation data to bipeds with dissimilar structures. By building and using libraries of canned motions, you can quickly build complex animations for your characters.

IMAGE CREATED BY GEORGE MAESTRI

Chapter 24

by George Maestri

MESH DEFORMATION

In real life, most characters are made out of a single skin. In MAX, this skin can be a single polygonal or patch mesh. This mesh, however, will look like a rigid statue unless you find a way to deform it. In real life, skin is very flexible, and the actions of muscles and bones beneath the skin are all that is needed to bend and flex the skin. In MAX, a number of tools do exactly the same thing. These are known as skeletal deformation tools *because they take a skeleton—a biped or a custom-built skeleton—and use that skeleton to deform a mesh much like it would appear in real life.*

MAX's open architecture allows for any number of methods for deforming meshes, and several plug-ins are on the market. Most popular are Character Studio's Physique and Digimation's Bones Pro. Additionally, several methods for deforming MAX geometry use native MAX tools—most notably the Linked XForm tool.

This chapter covers the following topics:

- Getting meshes to behave

- Basic mesh deformation

- Fitting a skeleton to a mesh

- Bones Pro

- MetaReyes

Getting Meshes to Behave

Although deforming a character with a mesh deformation tool may look easy, getting your mesh to deform smoothly can sometimes be a real problem. No matter which plug-in you decide to use, your joints will find ways to crimp, bulge, tear, or flatten at the wrong places, making your character look worse than when you started. Every animator runs into these problems, but you can use several techniques to help your meshes behave:

- Choose patches over polygons

- Build the mesh with the character's arms outstretched

- Add extra detail at the bends

Patches over Polygons

Spline patches control far more surface area with fewer vertices than a polygonal model does. As such, a patch-based model will be easier to control for two reasons. First, because there are fewer vertices, it will be easier to assign those vertices to the proper bone in the skeleton. Second, and more importantly, patches always keep a smooth surface between the vertices. A polygonal model, on the other hand, has many more vertices, and has flat areas between the vertices. Currently, the best and easiest way to build spline patch-based models is by using Digimation's Surface Tools.

Surface Tools enables the user to generate patch surfaces from interwoven splines. Any segments that form a three- or four-sided closed polygon create a surface that will be patched. Currently, it is one of the best ways to create seamless surfaces within MAX (see fig. 24.1). The surfaces created are also completely compatible with both Character Studio and Bones Pro MAX.

FIGURE 24.1

A cylinder constructed out of a spline patch deforms much more smoothly than the same cylinder constructed out of polygons. The same goes for characters.

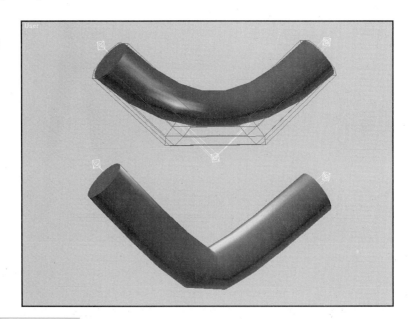

Arms Outstretched

The best argument for building a character this way is that the arms are exactly halfway between the extremes that the arm can take. It is tempting to build a character with its arms at its side. This is one of the more common poses a human takes. Unfortunately, if a character built that way needs to put his arms above his head, the skin around the underarms will have to stretch twice as much as if it were built with the arms outstretched. Centering the arms helps prevent crimping, tearing, and unwanted bulging later on when the character is deformed (see fig. 24.2).

Because the legs don't have nearly the range of motion the arms have, keeping them outstretched is not as critical, particularly for characters that only walk and sit. If the characters are supposed to be performing gymnastics, it might give you a bit more control if the legs were slightly apart when built.

FIGURE 24.2

*Building a character
with the arms
outstretched allows for
a much wider range of
motion.*

Extra Detail at the Bends

Adding detail only where it is needed will keep your models light and easy to control. Many places on the body don't flex as much as others. The elbow and the skin around it flexes quite a bit, for example, but the forearm itself remains fairly rigid. Therefore, the forearm does not need nearly as much detail to retain its shape as the area around the elbow joint. Extra detail also needs to be placed at the knees, the shoulder, the crotch area, and the areas around the wrists and the many joints of the hand. One good reference is the Viewpoint models supplied with MAX and Character Studio, which are built with detail in the proper places.

Eliminating the detail from rigid areas such as the forearm significantly reduces the number of vertices in the model and also reduces the total weight of the model (see fig. 24.3). A lighter model will animate easier, will deform more quickly, and will render faster.

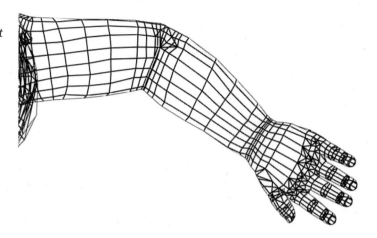

Fitting a Skeleton to a Mesh

After the solid mesh model is built, a skeleton of bones needs to be fit into it for the solid mesh to be deformed. Construction of skeletons was discussed in detail in the previous three chapters. The skeleton can be a biped, a skeleton of MAX bones, or be made from geometry such as boxes. The skeleton is usually tied together in a hierarchy and set up for animation using forward or inverse kinematics.

If you are not using Biped and are building a custom skeleton from scratch, it is best to construct the skeleton with the mesh in mind—even going to the point where you are actually loading the mesh model, freezing it, then building the skeleton within it, and finally linking the skeleton together in a hierarchy and setting up IK last.

However it is done, the key to fitting a skeleton to a mesh is lining up the joints correctly. Typically, the extra detail that was modeled in the joints is the guide to use. Line up the joints of the skeleton so that they match up with the joints of the mesh. The key areas to focus on are

- The elbow and knee
- The hip and pelvis
- The shoulders

The Elbow and Knee Areas

Placement of bones in the elbow and knee areas is fairly straightforward (see fig. 24.4). Center the joint of the bones within the area defined by the joint. If it was modeled properly, the mesh should have a bit of extra detail in this area to help guide the positioning of the bones.

FIGURE 24.4
Placement of bones in an elbow or knee joint.

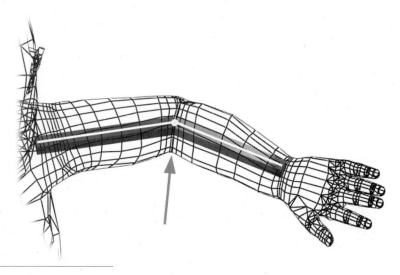

The Hip and Pelvis Area

The hips and pelvis can prove a bit problematic. The hip bone needs to be centered within the hip area, with the leg bones proceeding down through the center of the leg. The detail in the crotch usually flows along an approximately 45-degree angle along the so-called bikini line. Place the joint of the hips and the legs along this line, resizing the hips if necessary (see fig. 24.5).

The Shoulder Areas

The shoulder areas can also be problematic. A flexible shoulder joint aids in placement, particularly if the character is normally sloop shouldered. If this is the case, the shoulder can be rotated downward to match the sloop of the shoulders. The joint between the shoulder and the upper arm should be placed immediately above the armpit (see fig. 24.6).

FIGURE 24.5
Placement of joints in the pelvis area.

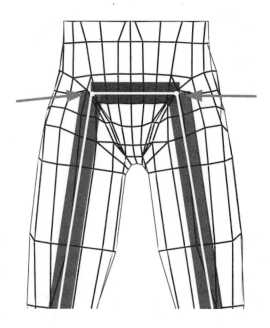

FIGURE 24.6
Placement of joints in the shoulder areas.

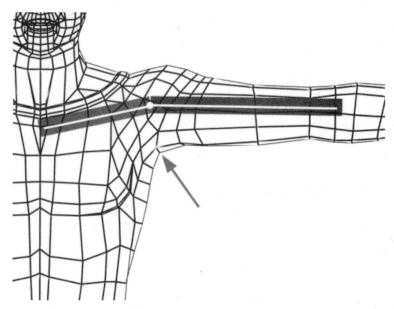

Basic Mesh Deformation

After the model has been built, it will look like a very attractive statue. To animate it so it will spring to life, the model will need to be deformed, much like the bones and muscles deform and shape our skin. Several methods can be employed to accomplish this. The most popular methods are Linked XForms, Bones Pro, and Physique. Each method requires a different procedure. To get a comparative overview, therefore, it is best to show the fundamentals of each procedure on a simple object such as a cylinder, which is very similar to an arm or leg joint.

Deforming a Cylinder with Linked XForms

Using Linked XForms is one method that can be employed without additional plug-ins. The Linked XForm is a very direct manipulation tool that can be used in a variety of situations. It enables you to link a set of vertices to a control object, such as a dummy, a box, or in this case, a MAX bone. This technique leverages on the flexibility of this modifier to attach specific vertices of the model directly to the skeleton.

XFORM DEFORMATION

1. Load the file bone-cyl.max from the accompanying CD. This file contains a simple cylinder with a set of MAX bones inside.

2. Apply an Edit Mesh modifier to the cylinder.

3. From the front or top viewport select the vertices on the right side of the cylinder (see fig. 24.7).

4. Select the Linked XForm modifier.

5. Within the Linked XForm rollout, press the Pick Control Object button.

FIGURE 24.7

Select the vertices on either side of the cylinder and apply a Linked XForm modifier to them.

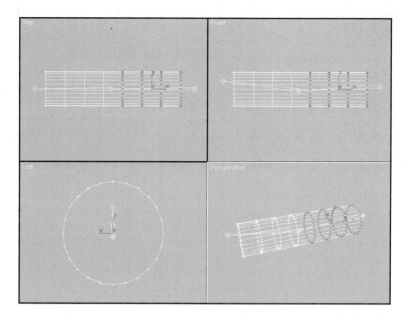

6. Select Bone01 as the Control object. Select by name to avoid mistakes.

7. Select the cylinder once again. Add another Edit Mesh modifier to the stack.

8. Select the vertices on the left side of the cylinder.

9. Select the Linked XForm modifier.

10. Within the Linked XForm rollout, press the Pick Control Object button.

11. Select Bone03 as the Control object.

The mesh of the cylinder will now be deformed by the bones. Turn on IK and translate the end of the bone chain. Because the vertices of the mesh are directly connected to the bones, they move along with them. The one problem with this method is that there is no weighting of vertices, so you can get flat spots in the area between the neighboring Linked XForm modifiers (see fig. 24.8).

FIGURE 24.8

The cylinder's mesh deformed with Linked XForm modifiers. Notice the flat spots at the joint's "elbow."

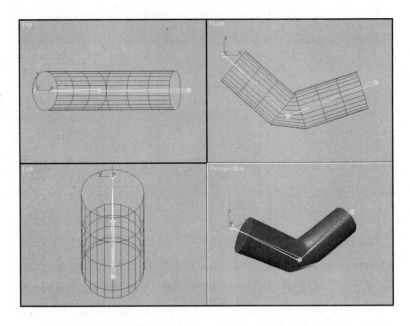

If the cylinder object were created out of spline patches, the flat spots would smooth themselves over automatically. Not all characters are made of splines, however. One way to sneak around this is to introduce a Mesh Smooth modifier in the stack after the Linked XForms. MeshSmooth will actually add vertices and smooth out the flat spots in the mesh.

1. To further smooth the mesh, add an Edit Mesh modifier to the top of the stack.

2. Select those vertices immediately surrounding the joint area.

3. Apply the MeshSmooth modifier.

The file bonexfor.max on the accompanying CD shows an example of this technique.

This procedure adds vertices in the problem area and smooths out the joint (see fig. 24.9). Mesh Smooth could be applied to the entire cylinder, but this is not necessary because it would just add extra vertices where they are not needed. Applying the modifier to only the problem area helps keep the vertex count down and keeps the model as light as possible.

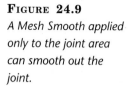

FIGURE 24.9

A Mesh Smooth applied only to the joint area can smooth out the joint.

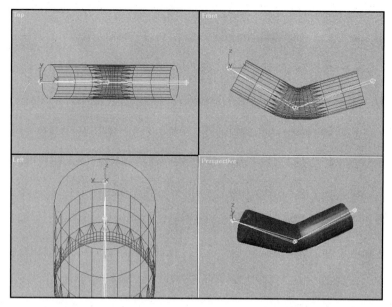

The one problem with the Mesh Smooth modifier is that it adds vertices to the model and can adversely affect topology-dependent modifiers, such as texture mapping. All UVW mapping must be placed on the object after the MeshSmooth modifier has been applied.

Deforming a Cylinder with Bones Pro

Bones Pro is a plug-in sold by Digimation. It enables much more discrete control over the mesh than the previous method. As you will see later in this chapter, Bones Pro enables vertex-by-vertex control over the deformation of a mesh, along with weighting of vertices between bones. A demo version of Bones Pro is on the accompanying CD.

BONES PRO DEFORMATION

1. Load bone-cyl.max from the accomanying CD-ROM.

2. The Bones Pro modifier is a space warp. To create a modifier, go to the space warp Creation panel and press Bones Pro.

3. Click in a viewport. A six-sided object appears that resembles a jack. This is the Bones Pro object and will not render.

4. Space warps need to be bound to the object they affect. Press the Bind to Space Warp button on the toolbar. Select the cylinder and drag a line to the Bones Pro object.

5. After the cylinder has been bound, you may select the Bones Pro object and go to the Modify panel. This is where specific bones are applied to the cylinder.

6. Assign some bones. In the box marked Bones, select Assign. A dialog appears with the names of the objects in the scene. Highlight Bone02 and Bone03 and then press Select.

7. Assign the bound node. In the box marked Bound Node, select Assign. A dialog appears with the names of the objects in the scene. Highlight Cylinder01 and then press Select.

8. Bones Pro deforms objects that are animated only and references a "Master" frame (defaulted to frame 0) that indicates the starting position of the deformation (see fig. 24.10). To make the mesh deform, turn Animate on and move the Time Slider a few frames into the scene. Manipulating the bones will cause the mesh to deform.

FIGURE 24.10

The cylinder deformed using Bones Pro.

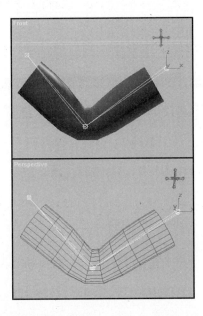

Deforming a Cylinder with Physique

Physique is part of Character Studio. It is a direct modifier and, as you will see in the next chapter, it has a number of features that closely tie it to Biped. The package also supports a number of advanced features, such as the capability to accurately define bulging and crimping of joints.

PHYSIQUE DEFORMATION

1. Load bone-cyl.max.

2. Select the cylinder.

3. From the Modify panel, select the Physique modifier and apply it to the stack.

4. Press Attach to Node. The cursor will change to resemble a stick figure.

5. In the Front viewport, position the cursor over the root node of the bone hierarchy all the way to the right. The cursor turns into a skeleton. This is Bone01. Click on the bone.

The modifier is now attached. Turn on IK and select the end node of the bone chain. Translating the bone will deform the mesh (see fig. 24.11).

FIGURE 24.11

The cylinder deformed using Physique.

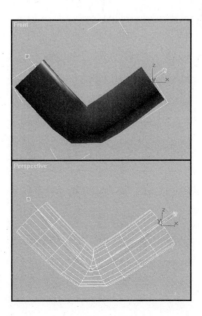

Differences Between Bones Pro and Physique

Although Bones Pro and Physique accomplish the same task, they go about it in two completely different ways. No plug-in is ideal for all tasks, and the plethora of MAX plug-ins gives you more freedom in deciding which plug-in will work for a specific task. Because the mesh deformation plug-ins are so different, it is a good idea to outline these differences.

- Bones Pro is a space warp. Physique is an Object modifier.

- Bones Pro references the pose of the skeleton at a specific frame (usually frame 0). Physique references the pose of the skeleton when the Physique modifier is applied.

- Bones Pro requires that the Animation button be set active and keyframes be set to deform the mesh. Once attached to the default pose, Physique always deforms the mesh.

- Physique requires that all bones be connected via a hierarchy. Bones Pro can use any combination of bones, linked or not.

- Bones Pro enables vertex-by-vertex assignment and weighting to any bone in the skeleton. Physique can allocate to a bone only those vertices located within a cylinder defined by the edges that bone.

- Physique enables user-defined bulging and crimping, as well as tendons for maintaining an object's overall shape. To control bulging and crimping in Bones Pro, extra bones may need to be added.

Deformations Using FFD Lattices

Free Form Deformations (FFDs), or lattices, are another way to deform meshes without resorting to third party plug-ins. Lattices are good overall tools for modeling, and their control vertices can be animated, which makes them a good option for performing mesh deformations. The best way to use lattices is for local deformations. Because FFDs cannot be linked together, or the control vertices of the lattice manipulated by Linked XForms, it is not feasible to use lattices as the sole tool used to deform entire bodies. Lattices, however, can help out quite a bit with other tasks, such as creating bulging biceps or making fat bellies jiggle.

To accomplish these sorts of effects, the FFD is best applied as a sub-object modifier, usually in conjunction with edit mesh. The best FFD to use in this context is the 4×4×4 modifier, which enables you to keep one row of vertices stable on each end of the modifier to keep the transition into the lattice deformed area smooth. Once inside, two rows of vertices are available to deform the mesh inside the area.

Creating a Bulging Muscle by Using FFDs

Combined with Linked XForm and MeshSmooth, FFDs can help the plug-in–challenged MAX animator create bulging muscles. For those with Character Studio, the following method can also be used to create deformations that are difficult for Physique to conquer, such as the jiggling of a fat man's belly.

BULGING MUSCLES

Load the file ffdbulge.max, which contains a simple cylinder attached to a set of bones using Linked XForm and MeshSmooth.

1. Scrub the animation to see how the arm bends.

2. Select the cylinder. Apply an edit Mesh modifier to the stack.

3. Select the vertices at the far right side of the Cylinder, from the end of the cylinder to where the MeshSmooth modifier is applied.

4. Apply the 4×4×4 FFD modifier to these vertices.

5. Enable Animation and scrub the animation to frame 30. At this point, the arm is bent, and the Bicep can bulge. Unfortunately, the lattice remains oriented the wrong way. It will need to be rotated.

6. With the FFD modifier active, select sub-object/lattice. Select the lattice and rotate it so that it is oriented in the same direction as the upper part of the cylinder.

7. Select Sub Object/Control points. Select the points along the top side of the bicep. Move these points upward to create a nice bulge (see fig. 24.12).

Because the animation button was enabled, the bulge should grow as the time slider is scrubbed. This file has been saved as ffdbulg2.max.

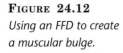

FIGURE 24.12
Using an FFD to create a muscular bulge.

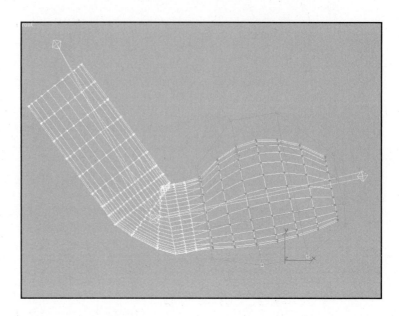

Bones Pro

Digimation's Bones Pro is classified as a space warp. As the previous example illustrated, a space warp needs to be bound to the object it affects. Bones Pro also needs Animation to be active when the body is manipulated for the effect to work.

Bones Pro may use any object as a bone, but it only looks at the bounding boxes of those objects when deciding which vertices to affect. This means that complex geometry used as bones is not necessary. A sphere will still be seen by Bones Pro as a cube because that is the shape of the sphere's bounding box. Because a box's outline is also its bounding box, boxes make for light and easy-to-visualize bones.

Bones Pro Rollout

The Bones Pro rollout is where the bones themselves are selected and assigned to the mesh. You should be aware of certain controls in this rollout (see fig. 24.13):

- Master Frame

- Bones and Bound Node boxes

- Falloff and Strength spinners

FIGURE 24.13

The Bones Pro rollout.

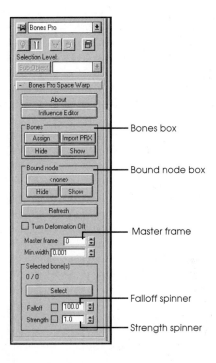

Bones box

Bound node box

Master frame

Falloff spinner

Strength spinner

Master Frame

The Master Frame spinner determines on which frame the vertices are assigned to the mesh. Usually, this is frame 0, but any frame can be selected. What is essential is that the skeleton be fitted properly to the mesh on the selected frame.

The fact that Bones Pro requires a Master Frame may make it a bit tricky to get it working with a biped. Bones Pro does not reference Biped's Figure Mode information, so getting the biped into a stable pose so that it can be fit to the mesh may be a bit tricky. If a biped's animation involves footsteps, the best way to get around this is to create a Freeform section in the animation outside the rendering range, and then pose and fit the biped to the mesh within the Freeform section.

Bones and Bound Node Boxes

Within these boxes are buttons for assigning both the bones and the bound node (that is, the mesh) to Bones Pro. Bones and meshes may also be hidden or revealed by using the Hide and Show buttons. This is handy for switching off the mesh while animating. On all but the fastest systems, the calculations required to deform the mesh can slow down the system considerably. Hiding the mesh will prevent these calculations from taking place and speed up real-time playback. Conversely, the skeleton should be hidden before rendering, and the Hide and Show buttons enable this.

Falloff and Strength Spinners

Bones may be selected from the rollout and assigned to Falloff and Strength spinners individually or in groups. The Falloff spinner determines how much of the mesh is affected by the bone. A larger number means that the bone affects a larger area and more vertices. The Strength spinner determines how heavily these vertices are affected. A larger number will pull the affected vertices closer to the bone.

Influence Editor

This is where vertices are assigned to the skeleton. The Influence Editor has a viewport for viewing the skeleton and the mesh, along with a number of tools for selecting, modifying, and visualizing the effects of bones on vertices (see fig. 24.14). Because the Influence Editor has a viewport, there are the standard navigation controls, along with a pull-down menu to select the standard views (Front, Top, Left, and so on).

FIGURE 24.14
The Influence Editor.

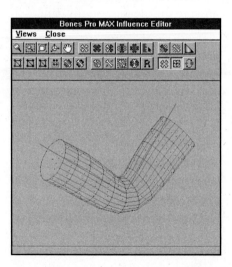

Bone Selection Tools

By default, the Influence Editor is in Bone Selection mode. Clicking on any bone selects and highlights it. Clicking again deselects it. In addition, a number of selection controls are provided to assist in filtering the selection. They enable you to select All, None, or Invert the Current Selection. In addition to this are two buttons named Select Unlinked and Deselect Unlinked. These buttons highlight all bones that are not direct parents or children of the selected bone.

In addition to bone-selection controls, tools are provided for assigning falloff and strength values to any bone or group of bones. These replicate the controls found in the Space Warp Control panel.

Visualization Tools

The Visualize button enables you to see exactly how a selected bone is influencing the mesh. Pressing this button and selecting a single bone will produce a rendered image of the mesh. Highlighted on the mesh will be a gradient that represents the selected bone's strength and falloff. Colors closer to blue are unaffected vertices, and colors closer to red are more strongly affected.

Vertex Selection Tools

Vertex Selection buttons enable you to select groups of vertices so that they can be assigned or excluded from the influence of specific bones. These tools enable you to select or deselect all vertices, select them by region, or select and deselect vertices in the range of a specific bone or groups of bones.

Assigning and Excluding Bones to Vertices

By far the most important group of buttons are the Bone & Vertex Exclusion buttons. These buttons are the heart of the Influence Editor window, because they control the assignation and exclusion of specific vertices to specific bones. This is accomplished by selecting a group of vertices and a group of bones, and then including or excluding the vertices from the bones.

By default, all Bones Pro vertices are influenced by all bones. The Bone & Vertex Exclusion buttons enable you to alter this. One obvious example might be the head. It should not be affected by bones in the hands or feet. If the character were to scratch his head, for instance, the vertices in the head, by default, would tend to be attracted to the bones in the hand. These buttons enable you to exclude the specific vertices in the head from being influenced by the bones in the hand.

One of the more handy buttons is the Exclude Unlinked button. This enables you to quickly exclude bones that should have no direct influence. A good example of where this might be used is the feet and legs. The right leg should be immune from the effects of the left. Exclude Unlinked assigns vertices between bones that neighbor each other in the hierarchical scheme only. This way, the bones in the right shin are affected by the right thigh and the right foot, but not any other bones.

T IP

Assigning vertices with the Select Vertices by Region tool should only be done as a last resort for packets of stray vertices. It is usually better to select vertices by bone influence rather than by regions, because selection by region will invariably produce stray vertices.

Deforming a Body with Bones Pro

One of the more challenging tasks that Bones Pro can be used for is to deform an entire body. This is also a good way to understand the basic tools and procedures contained within the Influence Editor.

DEFORMING THE BODY

1. Load the file bonepro.max.

2. This file has a simple mesh character with a skeleton fitted to it. The skeleton also has a simple animation. This has been added so that it moves the character through a wide range of motions.

3. Create the Bones Pro space warp and bind it to the object named Body.

4. Select the Bones Pro space warp and open the Modify panel. Click on Display Subtree from the selection panel. All of the bones are parented by the hips. Select these objects.

5. From the Bones Pro rollout, open the Influence Editor.

6. Move the Time Slider to frame 30. Notice how the feet are influenced by each other, causing the shoes to distort (see fig. 24.15). Select the bones in the shin, feet, and toes for the right and left side of the body. Press Exclude Unlinked from Selected Bones. The feet should snap into place.

FIGURE 24.15

This situation with the feet can be corrected by selecting the lower leg bones and using the Exclude Unlinked from Selected Bones function from within the Influence Editor.

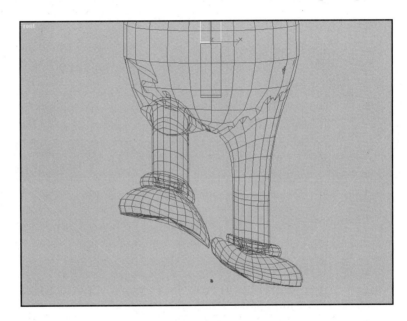

7. Move the Time Slider to frame 10. On this frame, the arms are above the head, and there is a significant bulge underneath the arms (see fig. 24.16). This is a common problem. To visualize this, select one of the upper arm bones and press Visualize Bone's Influence. This will show a bright area around the upper arm and extending down to the rib cage. Selecting the Spine03 bone and performing the same function will show that the spine has little or no influence over this area.

FIGURE 24.16

*The Visualize tool
indicates that the
arm's influence over
the rib cage is large,
causing a bulge.*

FIGURE 24.16

*The Visualize tool
indicates that the
arm's influence over
the rib cage is large,
causing a bulge.*

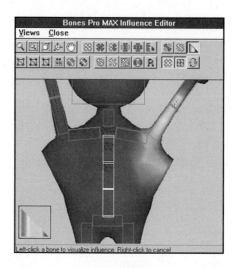

This is because the spinal bones in this particular skeleton are rather small, and their bounding boxes don't extend to the rib cage. Rather than rebuilding the skeleton, you can amplify their influence by increasing the falloff—the volume affected. For the three bones in the spinal column, set falloffs at Spine01 = 150, Spine02 = 200, Spine03 = 250. As these are set, notice how the model begins to snap into place. You can further amplify the effect of these bones by increasing their strength to 2.0. This should pull the model further into place.

8. The arms, however, are still affecting the rib cage area (see fig. 24.17). Because these bones are supposed to affect the area immediately around the arm only, these bones' influences can be reduced. Set the bones in the upper arm to a falloff of 75.

FIGURE 24.17

*Adding more strength
and influence to the
spine pulls the bulge
into place.*

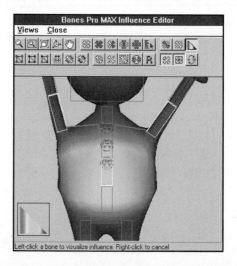

9. Move the Time Slider to frame 30. At this frame, you will see the legs distort the lower belly. To eliminate this, reduce the influence of both thigh bones so that they have a falloff of 60. Increase the strength of the hip bone from 1.0 to 1.5.

10. You will see a single vertex being pulled off of the right shoe by the left (see fig. 24.18). From the Front view, zoom into this vertex. Using the Select by Region tool, select this lone vertex.

FIGURE 24.18

This stray vertex can be fixed by selecting it and including it into the proper foot.

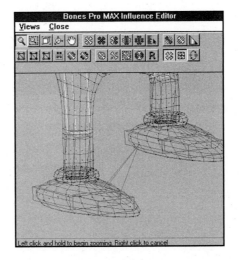

11. Zoom out slightly and use the Bone Selection tools to select both bones in the right foot. Press the Include Selected Vertices into Selected Bones button. The vertex will snap halfway between the two feet. This is because the left foot is still affecting this vertex.

12. Press the Invert Bone Selection button. Now press the Exclude Selected Vertices from Selected Bones button. This frees the stray vertex from any influences, except for those of the right foot. It will snap into place.

The basic setup is now complete. You can continue to work through the model and fine-tune the parameters within the Influence Editor.

Getting the mesh to deform properly over a wide range of motion may give you some headaches. If you are diligent and test every conceivable body position, however, you should have a rock-solid character. Hopefully, you will only have to set up the skeleton one time; after it is set up, you will have a character that you can use again and again. Even if it takes a day or two to set up the skeleton properly, it is worth it. The time you spend tweaking the skeleton pales in comparison to the time you will spend animating your character. Also, having to go back and fix things is never pleasant, so test thoroughly.

MetaReyes

Unlike mesh deformation routines, MetaReyes, and metaball plug-ins in general, work in the opposite way that a mesh deformation plug-in works. There is never a fixed mesh that needs to be deformed. Instead of the mesh being completely fixed and rigid, a metaball-created object generates its own mesh on the fly. This always makes for a smooth surface without any stray vertex-induced crimping and bulging. The one downfall of a metaball-generated character may be that the skin sometimes seems too smooth because it can be difficult to get a good hard crease when you need it.

MetaReyes originated as a plug-in for 3D Studio Release 4. The 3.0 plug-in for 3D Studio MAX takes the metaball modeling process to a new level, allowing for the creation of metamuscles, which operate in much the same way that real muscles do. A metamuscle can be attached to a bone in a skeleton, or a biped, and it will bend and flex the same way that real muscles do. Add to that the smooth surfacing created by metaball-style fusion of the metamuscle objects, and you have the basis of a very complete way to create smooth, deformable surfaces. These surfaces can also be textured using dynamic texture mapping, which allows for sticky placement of maps on metaball objects for textures that move with the skin. MetaReyes is covered more thoroughly in Chapter 8, "Character Modeling with Plug-Ins."

Metaball Concepts

The "balls" in metaballs derive their name from simple spheres, which are the building blocks of metaball objects. By assigning each sphere a weight and a sphere of influence, the metaballs modeler fuses many spheres into a single blob. How much the spheres fuse really depends on the weights, influences, and the distances between the spheres. In plug-ins such as MetaReyes, other shapes may also be used in addition to spheres.

Consider two spheres of equal size. The sphere of influence surrounds each of the spheres like a shell. Any other sphere coming within this range will try to fuse with the balls. The weight determines exactly how much fusion actually occurs. In figure 24.19, there are two balls of equal size. They'll fuse together at the intersection of their spheres of influence (see fig. 24.20). The amount that they fuse depends on their weights. As weights and the spheres of influence change, you get different effects. A higher sphere of influence will make an object softer and more willing to fuse with another. On the other hand, if one sphere is given more weight than another, it would appear more stable and solid.

FIGURE 24.19

Each metaball has its own sphere of influence. Where these two spheres of influence cross determines how the two objects fuse.

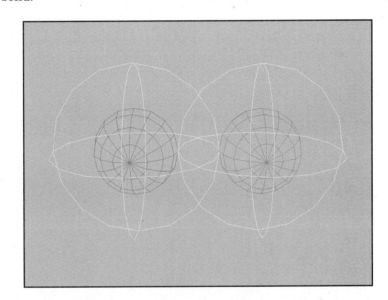

FIGURE 24.20

When they become metaballs, they will blob together.

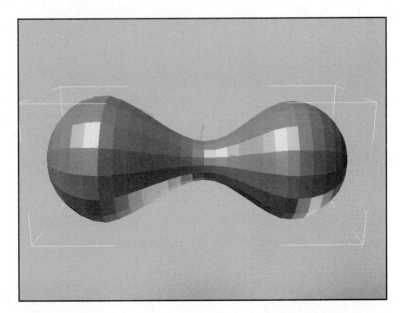

Using MetaReyes

A metamuscle is the standard primitive of MetaReyes. The metamuscle has two main components: control points and radii. *Control points* determine the linear path of the muscle, and the *radii* determine the outline of the muscle at any given point (see fig. 24.21). This metaphor is an outgrowth of the modeling methods used for MetaReyes 2.0 for 3D Studio R4. In that release, metaballs were aligned along a spline path to make complex surfaces in the Keyframer, sometimes making surfaces with dozens of individual balls. This method dispenses with the need for dozens of metaballs, and only requires a radial outline where the surface changes.

FIGURE 24.21
Basic components of a metamuscle are the path and the radii, as seen on the top object. From this, the surface is derived.

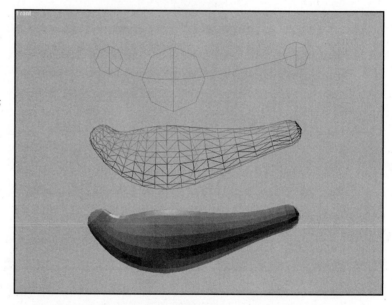

If you still wanted a sphere, you could simply create a surface with only one radius. Two radii would make a pill-shaped surface, while three, four, and more radii can make some very complex primitives (see fig. 24.22). By keeping the primitives simple, manipulation becomes easier as well. Instead of dealing with dozens of primitive spheres, you can work with a handful of spherical primitives and achieve the same results much more quickly.

FIGURE 24.22
With a handful of primitives, you can create anything from a simple sphere to some very complex shapes.

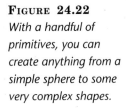

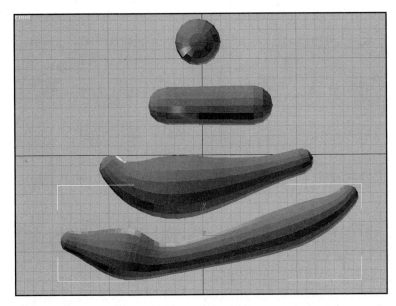

The metamuscles fall into two main categories. *Static muscles* are essentially rigid, but can flex and vibrate dynamically. *Dynamic muscles* can be attached to a skeleton so that they flex and bend much like the biceps and triceps of a human arm.

Static Muscles

Static muscles make excellent modeling tools. They can have any number of radii and can be of any shape. Static muscles can also have a dynamics component, so if a character were to stop or accelerate suddenly, the muscles would flex and vibrate much like real skin.

CREATING A STATIC MUSCLE

1. Click on the Geometry button in the Create menu.

2. Select MetaReyes as the geomtery type.

3. The MetaReyes rollout will appear. In the Muscle Types box, click on the button marked Static.

4. Click in a viewport to start making a metamuscle.

5. The first click determines the first control point of the muscle. After this is set, the radius can be set simply by dragging the mouse. A second left click sets the radius.

6. Clicking again sets another control point and allows another radius to be set. This sequence can be repeated until the muscle is defined. Left-clicking at any point in the procedure terminates the process.

After the muscle is created, you can turn the mesh generated by the muscle on and off by toggling the mesh box in the muscle's Modify panel. The resolution of the muscle's mesh can also be adjusted by using the Fast and Seg. Density spinners.

Dynamic Muscles

Dynamic muscles add a new dimension to modeling and animating with metaballs. Dynamic muscles act much like the muscles of the body in that they can vary their thickness dynamically, much like the bulging muscles of a bicep.

Dynamic muscles are structurally more restricted than static muscles. Dynamic muscles can only have four control points, no more, no less. Two of these points are designated as anchors, which affix the muscle to a skeleton much like a biological muscle is connected via tendons at either end. Moving the skeleton stretches and bulges the muscle by moving the end points of the muscle.

CREATING A DYNAMIC MUSCLE

1. Click on the Geometry button in the Create menu.

2. Select MetaReyes as the geomtery type.

3. The MetaReyes rollout will appear. In the Muscle Types box, click on the button marked Dynamic.

4. Click in a viewport to start making a metamuscle.

5. As with static muscles, the first click determines the first control point of the muscle. This point should be positioned close to the object that will be used to deform it (a skeletal bone, perhaps). Once this is set, the radius can be set simply by dragging the mouse.

6. Next the end point of the muscle needs to be set. Position the mouse near the second anchor point and click. This will make a second radius with the same diameter as the first.

7. A third click sets the default radius for the muscle. This can be adjusted later.

8. After the radius is set, the cursor changes to a question mark. The muscle will now be linked to the skeleton. As the cursor moves over an appropriate object, the cursor changes to read "link 1." The first object to select is where the first anchor point will be affixed.

9. The second anchor point needs to be chosen next. Again, the cursor changes as it passes over an appropriate object. Select the second anchor point.

After the muscles are anchored, moving the control points moves the ends of the muscles. This causes a squash and stretch effect on the metamuscle. The closer the ends are, the more the muscles will bulge, the further apart, the thinner it will get (see fig. 24.23).

FIGURE 24.23

The dynamic muscle follows the joint and stretches as the joint rotates.

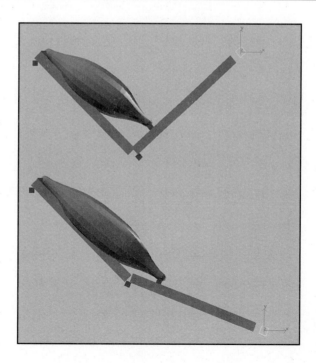

T I P

After the muscle is anchored, you will not be able to move it in relation to the object it is attached to. It is a good idea to attach the muscles to dummy objects, which are, in turn, linked hierarchically to the skeleton or controlling object. This way, the dummies can be repositioned to fine-tune the attach points of the muscle.

With a combination of dynamic and static muscles, you can construct a very realistic skeleton. The dynamic muscles should be placed at the places where muscles bulge and flex, where the static muscles are used to fill in the space between the dynamic muscles, and also to even out the profile of the character (see fig. 24.24).

An example of an arm created using metamuscles has been added to the CD as the file muscles.avi.

FIGURE 24.24
Adding a combination of static and dynamic muscles helps even out the profile while keeping the joint flexible.

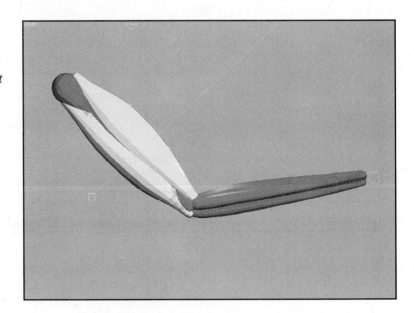

Hierarchies and Linking Metamuscles

In order for metamuscles to fuse, they need to be joined in a hierarchy. Only muscles that are hierachically linked will fuse. The hierarchy may be one built entirely of metamuscles, or it can contain metamuscles and a combination of other objects.

A good hierarchy to attach a family of metamuscles to is a simple skeleton. This could be a custom-built skeleton made of MAX bones or boxes, or it could be a biped, which takes the muscle analogy to the logical conclusion, as the virtual bones of the skeleton will thus have virtual muscles attached to it.

The *master* object is the metamuscle that contains all of the information about the grouping of the test of the muscles in the tree. This metamuscle is simply the highest one in the hierarchy. If this muscle is deleted, all of the grouping information will be lost.

TIP

If you are connecting the metamuscles to a skeleton, it is a good idea to parent one tiny metamuscle to the skeleton and hide this metamuscle within the body of the character. This muscle will then be easily accessed and be the parent of the entire group. As the parent, the metamuscle will contain all of the grouping information for the entire model.

Fusion

Metamuscle fusion happens very much like the previous version of MetaReyes. Each muscle is assigned a color that indicates how hard or soft the degree of fusion is. Red indicates the softest, and most "blobby" of the fusion settings, whereas blue represents a hard negative value (to subtract matter out of a space). Fusion is applied to each individual muscle either at creation time or through the Modify panel for the individual muscle.

Grouping

After the muscles have been created, assigned fusion values, and linked into a hierarchy, they can be grouped. Grouping simply excludes some muscles from fusing with others. Think of the legs. If they were not excluded from each other, the skin of one leg would tend to fuse with the other every time they got close. By excluding the muscles in one leg from the other, this situation is prevented, preserving the illusion.

Grouping is accomplished through the MetaReyes utility panel, found under Utilities. This panel enables you to select a *model* (a hierarchically attached organization of metamuscles) and select individual muscles to be added to or deleted from various groups.

Muscles can also be included in more than one group. This is done to preserve the continuity of the skin. The arm muscles would be excluded from the torso muscles, but both would include a shoulder metamuscle, which provides a seamless bridge between them.

The Muscle Edit Modifier

The Muscle Edit modifier is an object modifier that can only be applied to the metamuscle primitives. Muscle Edit enables you to edit the muscles and the components held within. This is accomplished through sub-object editing of the vertices of the control point radii, as well as the capability to add or delete control points. When performing vertex-level editing of dynamic muscles, be sure to avoid the Insert and Delete buttons because these will convert the dynamic muscle to a static one.

The Muscle Edit modifier also allows for dynamics. This is not to be confused with a dynamic muscle. Dynamics allows both static and dynamic muscles to react to motion and vibrate like rubber as they change speed and direction. This adds considerably to the realism of the muscle. The dynamics has several options:

- **Oscillation Amplitude.** This is the level of amplification. The lower the value, the more rigid the muscle.

- **Contraction Level.** This parameter affects only dynamic metamuscles. Higher numbers increase the thickness of the muscle as it contracts. Lower numbers reduce this effect.

- **Inertia Level.** How the muscle is affected by inertia, or changes in speed. This ranges from VL (very low) to VH (very high).

In Practice: Mesh Deformation

- **Building the Mesh.** Patches work better than polygonal meshes, add extra detail at the joints, and model the character with the arms outstretched.

- **Fitting the Skeleton to the Mesh.** Use the extra detail modeled into the mesh as a guide for placing the bones. If you are creating a custom skeleton, freeze the mesh and use it as a guide.

- **Linked XForms.** These are a handy way to perform skeletal deformations right out of the box. Although they don't give you as much control as more sophisticated plug-ins, Linked XForms can work perfectly well on simple objects needing deformation.

- **Bones Pro.** This program gives you more control over mesh deformation than linked XForms does because it can assign weight vertices to bones in any combination. When animating with Bones Pro, remember to keep the Animate button toggled on at all times, because manipulating a skeleton without this button on will change the Master Frame and affect the way the bones are assigned to the vertices.

IMAGE CREATED BY GEORGE MAESTRI

Chapter 25

by George Maestri

ANIMATING WITH PHYSIQUE

Physique is the second half of Character Studio. It enables some very sophisticated and controllable deformations of MAX objects. Physique gives MAX users the ability to define specific bulging and crimping over a wide range of joint and body types. Combined with Biped, Physique gives MAX users a very robust environment for animating characters. Although Biped is the preferred method for creating skeletons, Physique may be used with any type of MAX skeleton, including custom-built skeletons or, as seen in the previous chapter, simple chains of bones.

This chapter covers the following topics:

- Physique overview
- Using Physique
- Physique and Biped
- Tendons

One of the more vexing problems digital animators face is simulating the realistic flexing and bending of muscles underneath skin. Moving the vertices of an object so that they deform along with the skeletal bones is only the first step. In real life, the bones are actually driven by muscles and tendons under the skin. These muscles relax and contract to pull the bones in the skeleton around. As anyone who has witnessed a Mr. Universe pageant can attest, contracting muscles can change the shape of the skin significantly.

Although not every character animated in MAX needs to be a Mr. Universe contestant, the capability to effectively control and manipulate the shape and appearance of the skin is very important to all characters. Accurate control of the shape of a character enables you to not only bulge muscles, but also to eliminate nasty crimping and tearing of vertices that can be so common in any mesh deformation package.

Physique enables you to store the outlines and bulge angles of any portion of a character's geometry and apply these to the character according to the joint angle. In theory, it works exactly the opposite of nature. In nature, the bulging muscle pulls on the joint and causes it to bend. In Physique, bending the joint causes the muscle to bulge. Although opposite in procedure, visually, the effect is identical.

In addition to bulge angles, Physique's tendons feature gives you the ability to maintain a character's shape over many links, to simulate details such as the small web between the thumb and forefinger, or the stretching of the skin around the shoulders as the arm rotates.

Using Physique

As was demonstrated in the previous chapter, Physique is an object modifier. It is applied like any other object modifier to the object's stack. To be activated, the Attach to Node button must be toggled and the root node of the skeleton must be selected. After this occurs, Physique takes a snapshot of the positions and orientations of all the bones on the skeleton and uses it to assign specific vertices to specific bones.

The Physique modifier has two types of sub-objects: Link and Vertex. Link sub-objects are just the bones themselves; Vertex sub-objects are the vertices of the mesh.

TIP

Physique is an object modifier. As such, it should be placed in the stack above any UVW mapping or sub-object mapping applied to the object because the texture needs to be applied before the mesh is deformed.

Hierarchies and Physique

Physique determines its vertex assignments based on the hierarchy of the skeleton. Bones Pro uses the bounding boxes of the bones themselves to determine vertex assignation, whereas Physique simply looks at the pivot points of the bones and uses that information to create its default vertex assignments.

Physique assigns vertices by placing an imaginary plane at each pivot in the hierarchy and then making a cylindrical projection through the mesh. The imaginary plane is aligned perpendicular to the axis of the joint. Vertices that lie between the two planes are assigned to the joint; vertices residing outside these boundaries are not (see fig. 25.1). The assignment of vertices is strictly controlled by their location in relation to the joints. This makes joint placement of the skeleton of paramount importance.

In the case where these imaginary planes do intersect and overlap, vertices can be assigned to one joint or the other, but not both. A common case would be the vertices surrounding the pelvis area. Because the pelvic bone and the thigh bones are oriented along different axes, significant overlap occurs in the assignment of the vertices. Vertices in these areas typically need to be reassigned during the course of Physique setup. This procedure is discussed in detail in the section "Vertex Control," later in the chapter.

FIGURE 25.1
Physique assigns
vertices by placing an
imaginary plane at the
end of each joint.

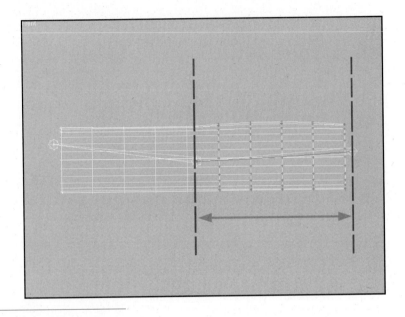

Creating Realistic Bulges

The easiest way to visualize exactly how Physique creates and manages bulges is to use a simple, predictable object, such as a cylinder. This also introduces a number of fundamental concepts, and by using a regularly shaped cylinder, the effects of Physique are made perfectly clear.

APPLYING PHYSIQUE TO THE CYLINDER

1. Load the file bulge.max from the accompanying CD.

2. Select the Cylinder.

3. From the Modify panel, select the Physique modifier and apply it to the stack.

4. Press Attach to Node. The cursor changes to resemble a stick figure.

5. Position the cursor over the root node of the bone hierarchy. This is Bone01. Click on the bone.

This is the same procedure that was discussed in Chapter 23, "Animating with Biped," but now that the Physique modifier has been added, it can be taken further by adding a realistic bulge to the cylinder. The file contains a short animation where the bone in the forearm flexes 90 degrees and then relaxes. Scrubbing the Time Slider reveals how the cylinder is currently affected—the joint rotates, but the cylinder retains its outline as it deforms with the joints. The joint rotation can be used to create a nice bulge.

The Cross Section Editor

The Cross Section Editor is the heart of many Physique operations, and it is one you will become quite familiar with when using the plug-in. The Cross Section Editor is a floating dialog that enables you to create bulge angles, their cross sections, and, as you will see later, tendons. The Cross Section Editor dialog is shown in figure 25.2. There are two ways to bring up this window, first by clicking on the Cross Section Editor button from within the main Physique rollout, and second, by clicking on a specific joint's rollout when Physique is in joint Sub-object mode.

The Cross Section Editor is modeless, meaning you can use it along with the standard MAX viewports to select and modify parameters on the fly. The window has a toolbar with two windows along the bottom—on the lower left is the cross section view, on the lower right is the link view. In combination, these can be used to create and manage the bulge of the skin around the joint.

FIGURE 25.2

The Cross Section Editor. The circular graph on the left is the outline editor, the one on the right is the link editor.

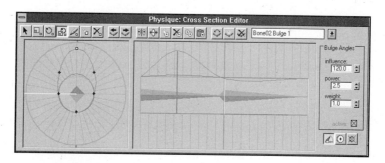

EDITING THE LINK'S CROSS SECTION

To select a specific joint, you need to go into Physique's Sub-object Selection mode.

1. Using the same cylinder as before, press the Sub-Object button and select the sub-object type as Link.

2. From within the MAX viewport, select Bone02. The bone's link parameters appear.

3. To enable the Cross Section Editor, click on the Cross Section Editor button in the Physique Link Parameters rollout.

4. To create a bulge, you first need to tell Physique at what angle the bulge will be defined. The default angle is the angle at which the bone was positioned when Physique was applied. The second angle should be where the joint is rotated the most. In this animation, the maximum rotation is at frame 30. Move the Time Slider to frame 30.

5. To add a bulge, press the Insert Bulge Angle button. A new bulge angle is created and automatically named Bulge 1.

6. Next, you need to tell Physique exactly where the bulge occurs. This is known as a cross section. Press the Insert CS Slice button. The cursor changes. Click on the Link view portion of the Cross Section Editor dialog near the center of the leftmost link. A red line appears, indicating the cross section has been added.

7. You can now use the Cross Section Editor to resize the bulge at that angle. Press Select and Scale Ctl Points and, within the Cross Section View, click on the topmost control point and drag it upward. This movement is reflected in both the Link view and also within the normal MAX viewports.

8. Scrub the Time Slider. The muscle now bulges, as shown in figure 25.3. When the joint is flat, there is no bulge, when the joint is flexed, the bulge appears.

FIGURE 25.3

A cylinder bulges according to the angle of the joint.

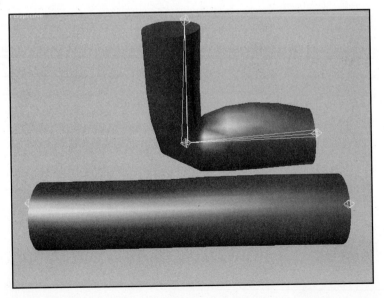

9. You can further modify the shape of the bulge by adding more cross sections or by adding more control points.

Physique Link Parameters

The bulge can be even further modified by using the Physique Link Parameters in the Link Sub-Object panel. These parameters give you additional control over how the skin stretches and compresses as the joint bends, twists, and scales.

Bend

Bend parameters control the flow of skin over a bending joint, such as a knee or elbow. They apply to hinge-like movement perpendicular to the axis of the bend.

Tension determines the tightness of the crimp at the bend. A higher number produces a more arc-shaped bend, and a lower number causes the joint to crimp more.

Bias determines the angle of the crimp. At 0.5 it is evenly centered between the joints. When it moves higher, the crimp is angled toward the link's child; when it is lower, it is angled toward the link (see figs. 25.4 and 25.5).

FIGURE 25.4
Cylinder bent with different Bias settings.

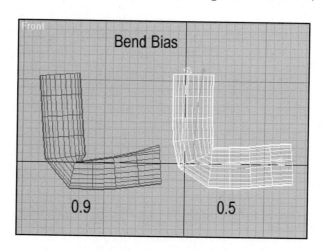

FIGURE 25.5

*The figure on the
bottom has a high
bend tension, the one
on the top has a low
bend tension.*

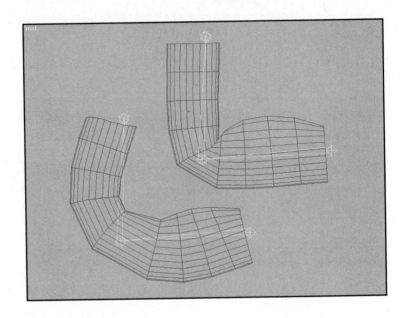

Twist

Twist parameters determine how the mesh is affected when the joint is twisted along its length, such as when a hand turns a screwdriver.

Tension determines how much the skin rotates around the length of the joint. A value of 1.0 causes all skin along the length of the joint to rotate evenly. Lower values emphasize the twist closer to the rotating link, and higher values add extra twisting to the skin farther away from the point of rotation. The effects of Twist are shown in figure 25.6.

Bias shifts the twist effect toward or away from the link. A value lower than 0.5 puts more of the twist on the skin covering the child link, and a higher value puts more of the twist on the selected link.

Scale

The scale parameters affect how the skin and any underlying cross sections are affected by the scaling of the links. Because Physique looks at the hierarchy, not the physical bones themselves, the links can be scaled by turning off IK and translating the bones to increase or decrease the distance between the links.

FIGURE 25.6
Checkerboard indicates how twist works.

Activating the Stretch and Breathe buttons is one easy way to get squash and stretch effects when using Physique. Stretch and Breathe enable you to create this effect automatically by moving or scaling the bone. Stretch pulls out the mesh along the length of the link, whereas Breathe expands the mesh radially (see fig. 25.7). You cannot use this technique with Biped bones, however, because they cannot scale over time.

FIGURE 25.7
Bone scaled with and without Breathe option.

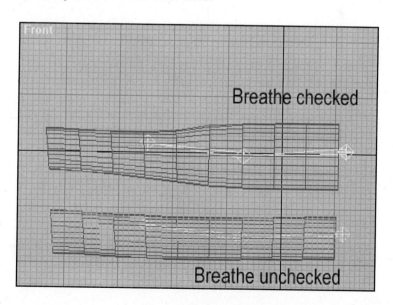

Physique Joint Intersections

Joint intersections determine how and where the joint creases. Physique tries very hard not to have skin vertices cross over each other because this would cause one part of the skin to penetrate another—not something that would happen in real life.

To prevent this, Physique places an imaginary plane between the joints and restricts vertices on either side from crossing over. This keeps the skin seamless and can cause a natural crease. A good example is the skin around the fingers. It tends to crease along a nice, flat plane. Sometimes, however, you may want the joint intersections to be less planar, to create a dimple, perhaps.

Typically, the default planar joint intersections are fine, but they can sometimes "go flat" before the skin actually touches, particularly when the skin bulges dramatically. This can be tweaked using the Joint Intersections dialog. This determines how the plane affects the crease. A bias value of 1.0 means that the plane is fully active, causing a planar crease; a lower value reduces the planarity of the effect. The From and To spinners determine how much of the skin around the joint is affected by the plane.

Physique and Biped

Although Physique can be used with MAX's native bones or any hierarchy of objects, marrying the two halves of Character Studio enables Physique to be affected by a Biped skeleton. This gives you a very good solution for creating a lifelike character.

Any class of geometry works with Physique, but it is much easier to deform a spline-based surface because this kind of mesh has fewer vertices. Digimation's Surface Tools provides a very good solution because you can animate just the spline cage while turning off the surface, making manipulation much faster.

TIP

If you are using prebuilt polygonal models, you can use optimize modifiers to reduce the face count and help improve manipulation performance. When you are ready to render the model, delete the Optimize modifiers from the stack.

Fitting a Biped to a Mesh

For Physique to work correctly, the Biped must be properly fitted to the mesh. The joints of the Biped must line up with the joints of the mesh. The most critical area is the area where one joint intersects the other. Because Physique uses the intersection of the joints to define vertex assignment, a misplacement can cause vertices to go astray.

Figure Mode

To facilitate the fitting of a Biped to a mesh, you need to place the Biped in Figure mode, which is a special pose that Biped remembers and can always be returned to at the press of a button. Figure mode also allows for resizing and positioning a Biped freely.

NOTE

You must have an authorized copy of Character Studio installed on your computer to do the exercises in this chapter.

FITTING A BIPED TO A MESH

1. Load your character's mesh file, which is a file on the accompanying CD entitled meshman.max that can be used for practice.

2. Create a Biped roughly the same height as the mesh. In the Biped's Structure rollout, set the number of fingers and toes to match the character. If your character is wearing shoes, one toe will suffice.

3. Select the mesh. Go to the Display panel and press Freeze Selected. This way, the mesh will not accidentally get selected while the Biped is being manipulated.

4. Select the Biped. Go to the Motion panel and place the Biped in Figure mode. In Figure mode, you are free to rotate and scale every joint of the Biped.

5. Select the Center of Mass object, and position the Biped over the body so the hips rest inside the Pelvis area. One thing to remember is that manipulating a Biped in Figure mode puts the navigation tools in world space. This means that, from the front, the Biped moves along the XZ axis (see fig. 25.8).

FIGURE 25.8

Proper placement of biped inside mesh (note that ZX is the front plane).

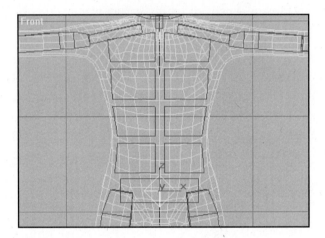

6. Non-uniform scale the PELVIS in Z so that the joint between the hips and thighs rests along the V-shaped area that defines the crease between the tops of the thighs and the crotch (refer to fig. 25.8).

7. Scale the spinal segments so that the shoulders are slightly beneath the shoulders of the mesh, and so the joint between the shoulder and the upper arm resides above the mesh's armpit.

8. Scale the legs in X so that the biped's knees are properly aligned within the joint area of the mesh. Rotate the legs to align them with the mesh. The Symmetrical tracks button can be used to easily select both legs for manipulation. Do the same for the arms and scale them so the elbows of the Biped line up with the elbow area of the mesh. Rotate the arms to fit into the mesh (use the Top viewport to do this).

9. If your character has fingers that move, adjust the bones in the hand to match the fingers. The Biped's fingers can not only be resized and rotated, but they can also be moved along the edge of the palm bone to get an exact fit.

10. When positioning joints at the end of a chain, such as the head or toes, be certain to place the ends of the bones slightly beyond the edge of the mesh. Because Physique uses the bounding planes of the joints to determine vertex assignment, any vertices not included within these planes will be left behind (see fig. 25.9). In this example figure, the head is too small, so when it tilts forward, the top of the skull remains stationary.

FIGURE 25.9

If the vertices of the mesh do not lie inside the bounding planes of the joints, the vertices will get left behind.

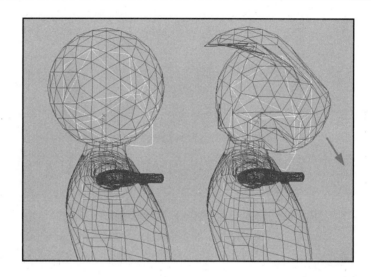

Applying Physique to a Biped

After the mesh has been fitted, you can link the skin to the Biped. The important thing to remember is that the Physique modifier needs to be attached to the pelvis of the Biped, not the Center of Mass object. The Center of Mass object moves on every frame to reflect the changing mass distribution of the Biped. This means that the joint between the center of mass and the rest of the Biped will stretch and change shape, causing all sorts of problems.

If parts of the body or clothing are modeled as separate objects, such as a head or a hat, select all the objects and apply a single Physique modifier to them all. Later, you'll need to make some of the vertices rigid so that they do not deform (see the next section for a description of how to do this).

Refining How Physique Affects the Mesh

If the character is being used for a wide variety of shots, the model needs to be tested over a wide range of motion to ensure that the skin behaves the way that it should. To test this, it is a good idea to have a test animation that puts the character through its paces. This animation should have the character move its arms and legs through the extremes of motion.

The file phystest.max on the accompanying CD is a good example of a test animation to put a Biped and its attached mesh through a wide range of motion. The animation is also saved as a biped file (phystest.bip) so that you can easily apply it to other models.

Conversely, if the character is only being used for a very specific set of actions, those actions are the only ones that need to be tested. In this case, it might be faster to animate a rough version of the action and then correct any deficiencies in the vertex assignment for those actions only.

Regardless of how you test the motion, if the joint placement of the Biped is correct, most of the vertices in the mesh will follow along with the Biped's joints. Unfortunately, nothing is perfect, and there will almost always be stray vertices that cause unwanted bulges.

Vertex Control

If a joint affects an unwanted area of the mesh, the vertices in those areas may need to be reassigned to another joint. To do this, select the Vertex Sub-Object rollout from the Physique panel and reassign the vertices or change their behavior. In Physique, vertices are assigned colors, either red, green, or blue. The specific color of the vertex defines the way the individual vertex behaves. The Vertex Sub-Object rollout is shown in figure 25.10.

The following list describes the three different types of vertex assignments.

- **Red Vertices.** These vertices are deformable. They flex, bend, and move with the joint to which they have been assigned.

- **Green Vertices.** These vertices are rigid. They move along with the joint, but they do not flex or change shape. This is good for areas such as the head and skull, which remain relatively rigid.

- **Blue Vertices.** These vertices are not assigned to any specific joint and are known as root vertices. They will not move with the skeleton.

FIGURE 25.10

The Vertex Sub-Object rollout.

By default, each vertex is assigned as deformable, so every vertex in the body should be red. If a vertex is defaulted as root (blue), it means that the vertex did not lie within the bounding planes of any joint within the skeleton and could not be assigned. This is often caused by joints at the end of the chain, such as the top of the head or the ends of the fingers, which did not protrude through the ends of the mesh when Physique was applied. In this case, the Biped needs to be refitted and the Physique modifier reapplied.

One of the most common situations encountered is when the joints in the upper arm affect the area under the arm along the side of the rib cage, causing the skin to bulge as the arm lifts above the head. This happens because the vertically oriented bounding planes of the upper arm intersect the horizontally oriented bounding planes of the spinal bones. In cases when a vertex can be assigned to more than one joint, Physique assigns the vertex to the closest joint. Unfortunately, the closest joint is not always the correct joint. One common situation is bulging along the ribcage (shown by the arrows in figure 25.11), which happens because the vertically oriented bounding planes of the upper arm intersect the horizontally oriented bounding planes of the spinal column.

The Physique Vertex Assignment rollout contains the tools for selecting and assigning (or reassigning) vertices to the correct links.

- ■ **Vertex Type.** This set of three buttons gives you control of which vertices are selected and assigned. These buttons affect the selection set that you create with the Select, Select by Link, and Assign to Link buttons (described on the following page). For example, if the red button is depressed, only deformable (red) vertices will be selected or assigned.

- **Select.** This button enables you to use the standard MAX selection tools, such as the box or fence, to select groups of vertices.

- **Select by Link.** This button enables you to select all the vertices currently assigned to a single joint. The type of vertices selected depends on the settings of the Vertex Type buttons.

- **Assign to Link.** This button assigns the currently selected vertices to the selected link. The setting of the Vertex Type button determines how these are assigned. If the button is red, the vertices are assigned as deformable, green assigns them as rigid, and blue as root.

FIGURE 25.11
Incorrect vertex assignment causes the mesh to deform incorrectly around the chest.

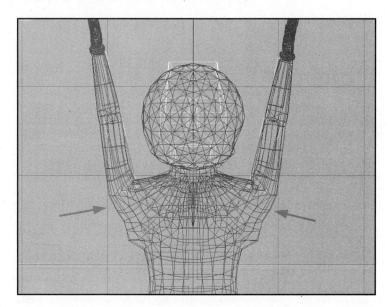

TIP

In Character Studio Release 1.1, there is a new checkbox labeled Initial Skeletal Pose in the Vertex Assignment rollout. This checkbox enables you to toggle between the initial pose (typically with arms outstretched) and whatever pose the figure happens to be in when you enter Physique Vertex Sub-Object level.

MODIFYING THE VERTICES

1. Load the file meshbipd.max from the accompanying CD. This file contains the same character contained in meshman.max, but with a Biped fitted to it. The Biped also has a short animation to help test the mesh attachment.

2. Select the Biped. From the Motion panel, place the biped in Figure mode.

3. Select the object MeshMan. From the Modify panel, add the Physique modifier to the stack.

4. From the Physique panel, press Attach to Node. Select the pelvis of the Biped as the root node. Be sure not to select the Center of Mass object. Zoom in so you are sure to hit the right object. By default, the Pelvis object is a yellow-colored rectangular box.

5. Reselect the Biped. Go to the Modify panel and turn off Figure mode.

6. Move the Time Slider to frame 10. This is where the Biped moves its arms above its head. Notice the bulge under the arm. This must be fixed by reassigning the vertices within Physique's Vertex Sub-Object mode.

7. Select the mesh. In the Modifier Panel, with the mesh selected under Sub-Object Vertex, press Select by Link and select the shoulder link. This action highlights all the vertices affected by the shoulder. Notice how the vertices extend down to the underarm area and up into the head.

8. Click on the Select button and, while holding down the Alt key and using the Fence Selection tool, deselect the vertices along the upper half of the shoulder, leaving only those along the underarm highlighted (see fig. 25.12).

FIGURE 25.12

The vertices in the bulge are best assigned to the spinal column.

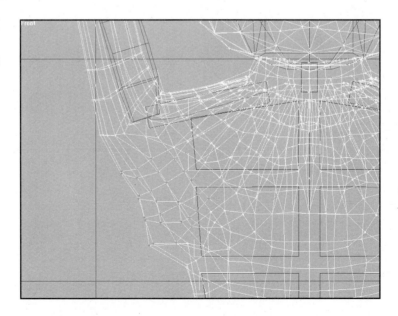

9. Click on Assign to Link, select the joint Bip01_Spine3. Most of the vertices pop into place and remain red. A few turn blue, meaning these are out of the bounding plane of the selected joint.

10. To select only the blue vertices, click on Select by Link. Within the Vertex Type box, turn off the Red and Green vertex type buttons, leaving only the Blue button depressed. Select the joint Bip01_Spine3. Only the blue vertices are selected.

11. Assign these vertices to the spine link immediately below the clavicles. The vertices change color to red.

TIP

Steps 10 and 11 show the "long way" to get the results. In step 10, you can simply Ctrl+click on the desired link to assign the root vertices to that link.

The head is another area affected by the shoulders. On this character, the head should be rigid. To accomplish this, make the vertices comprising the head green, or rigid.

12. Set Vertex type to all three (red, green, and blue). Click on the Select button and, using the Box Selection tool, select the vertices in the head.

13. Set the vertex type to rigid (green) and click on the Assign to Link button. Select the head joint. The vertices turn green.

14. Continue through the rest of the body, modifying and reassigning vertices as needed.

15. Save the file as meshphys.max (note that this file is also provided on the CD-ROM).

TIP

If it is difficult to get vertex assignments exactly right in critical areas such as the pelvis, linking a dummy object to the offending joint can give you an extra joint to assist in assigning vertices. If this is done, the Physique modifier's default pose must be reapplied.

T I P

In Character Studio Release 1.1, you can save the vertex assignments that you've made to one figure and then apply them to another figure, using a new file format called .VPH. This can be a great time-saver, assuming that the two models are very similar and start from more or less the same pose. You can use this feature, for example, to replace a low-resolution model with a high-resolution version of the same model.

You can use the Cross Section Editor not only for creating bulging muscles, but also to fix problem areas of the mesh, such as bulges or creases. This is not an obvious use of the Cross Section Editor, and it is not described in the Character Studio manual. However, it is such a useful technique that an exercise is included to show you how to do it.

As previously described, a particularly common problem occurs when the arms raise above the head and the underside of the arm bulges out, and the vertices under the arm tear or cause creases in the body. The Cross Section Editor can be used to further refine the behavior of these joints.

USING THE CROSS SECTION EDITOR TO FIX PROBLEM SPOTS

1. Open the file meshbip2.max (this file already has the Physique modifier applied to the mesh). Within the Physique panel, go to Link Sub-Object mode.

2. Select the shoulder joint and open the Cross Section Editor from the Physique Link Parameters rollout.

3. Move the Time Slider to frame 10 and insert a new bulge angle from within the Cross Section Editor. Name this bulge **Frame 10 Bulge** by using the text box at the top right. Move the slider to frame 20 and insert a second bulge angle. Name this bulge **Frame 20 Bulge**.

4. Move the Time Slider back to frame 10 and select the appropriate bulge angle (Frame 10 Bulge). Select default CS slice on the joint between the shoulder and the upper arm. Within the Section view, scale down the part of the outline representing the underside of the arm to reduce the size of the bulge (see fig. 25.13).

FIGURE 25.13

Adjusting the bulge angle by scaling the cross section.

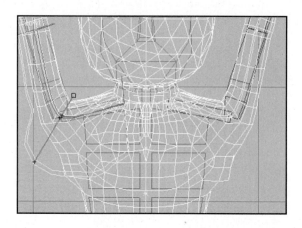

5. Move the Time Slider to frame 20 and select the second bulge angle created (Frame 20 Bulge). Select default CS slice on the joint between the shoulder and the upper arm. Within the Section view, scale the part of the outline representing the underside of the arm. This also reduces the size of the crease. Adjusting this bulge angle also reduces the bulge at frame 10.

6. If you need more control, you may add a second CS slice on each arm and scale those appropriately as well.

Figure 25.14 shows the meshman model after modification. Even though the vertices have been reassigned, when the arm is raised above the head, a slight bulge still exists. This is fixed by adding a cross section to the Bulge angle on the joint between the shoulder and arm. A second bulge angle on the same joint can also help prevent crimping when the arm is at its side (see fig. 25.15).

Tendons

Tendons are used to further refine the way the character's skin behaves across many joints when cross sections and bulge angles aren't enough. They enable you to make one joint affect the outline of another joint's vertices over many links. They can be best used in areas such as the shoulder and pelvic areas, where T-shaped branching exists. They can also be used in skinning hands, particularly the fleshy webbing between the thumb and forefinger. A tendon has three main components:

■ **Base.** The base is where one or more tendon cross sections originate. A base may be applied to any link in the skeleton. Usually the base resides in the torso.

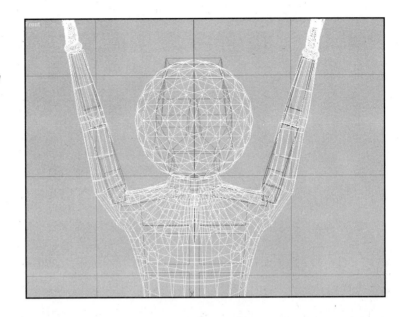

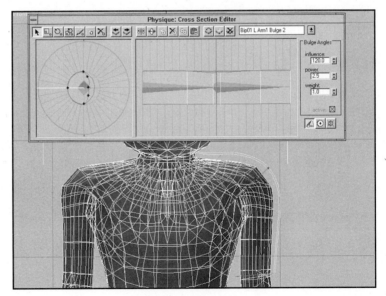

- **Cross sections.** These are much like the cross sections used to create bulges; attach points are located at radial subdivisions of the outline of the cross section.

- **Attach points.** These are the points on the cross sections that can be tied to another link. The attached link is usually a shoulder or pelvic bone. Each attach point may be tied to a different link.

How Tendons Work

For a good example of how tendons affect the skin across multiple joints, use a simple T-shaped mesh and attach a few tendons between the joints as it flexes.

HOW TENDONS WORK

1. Load the file tbone.max. This file contains a T-shaped mesh and a set of tendons attached to it. The tendons run from the middle joint of the vertical branch to the middle joint of the right horizontal branch (see fig. 25.16).

FIGURE 25.16
This T-shaped object can be used to demonstrate how tendons affect the skin across multiple joints.

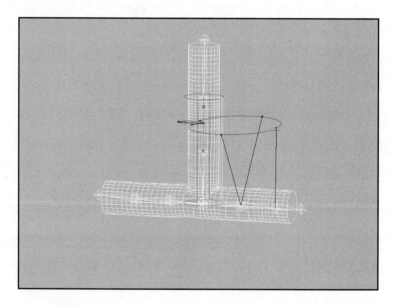

2. Move the Time Slider to frame 25. Notice how the middle joint on the right limb affects the vertical joint. This is due to the action of a tendon (see fig. 25.17).

3. Move the Time Slider to frame 50. As the middle-right joint flexes down, it affects the skin on the vertical joint.

FIGURE 25.17

FIGURE 25.17

As the far joints rotate, the skin on the vertical shaft is affected, even though the two joints are not adjacent.

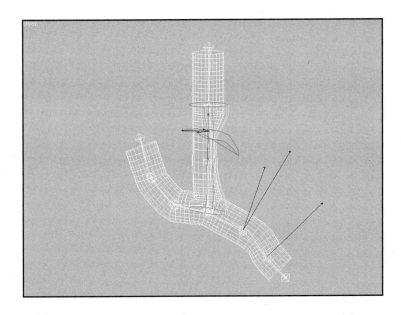

4. Move the Time Slider to frame 75. Again, the skin on the middle joint bulges, even though many other joints are active.

This shows that tendons can give a more globalized effect than just bulge angles, enabling skin to flow across many joints. The T-shaped branch is very similar to the branches that occur in the human body—between the spine, shoulders, and arms; between the spine, pelvis, and legs; and even between the thumb and forefinger. Tendons can be used to the same effect with a biped or with other types of skeletons, such as 3DS MAX bones.

Creating Tendons

Tendons are created in the Link Sub-Object mode from the Physique panel. You just need to select the link that will become the base and press the Create button on the Physique Tendons rollout. This panel has a number of parameters.

- **Sections.** This is the number of cross section bases created for the link.

- **Attach Points.** This is the number of radial attach points around each of the cross sections.

- **Resolution.** The radial resolution of the cross sections.

A pair of tendons can be used to help maintain the outline of the belly where it meets the pelvic area. Many times creasing occurs in this area. Tendons can help maintain the shape of the character.

ATTACHING TENDONS

1. Open the file meshphys.max. This file has an animation to test the flexibility of the character. Move the Time Slider to frame 50.

2. Select the mesh and go to the Physique Modifier panel. Select Link Sub-Object mode.

3. Select the central spinal joint (Bip01 Spine 2), scroll down to the Physique Tendons rollout, and set the default sections parameter to 1. These must be set before the tendon's base is created.

4. Click on the Create button. This action creates a base for tendons originating from this joint.

5. Open the Cross Section Editor by clicking on Cross Section Editor. Activate the Tendon panel within the Cross Section Editor. Select the attach point along the front right of the torso, as shown in figure 25.18.

6. Attach this point to the right clavicle joint. To do this, click on the Attach button within the Tendon panel of the Cross Section Editor, and then click on the right clavicle joint from within the Front viewport.

7. Repeat the same procedure for the front-left attach point and the left clavicle joint. The tendons are now attached. The tendon, however, does not yet pull the mesh correctly (see fig. 25.19).

8. Save the file. You will modify the tendons in the last exercise.

Modifying Tendons

After being attached, the tendons may need to be modified so that they affect the way the skin behaves across the joints. A number of parameters within the tendon panel of the Cross Section Editor enable you to modify the tendons as needed. These parameters are described in the following list.

FIGURE 25.18

The tendon is in place on the spine link and is ready for attachment.

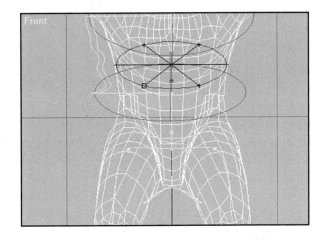

FIGURE 25.19

After the tendons are properly attached, they look like this.

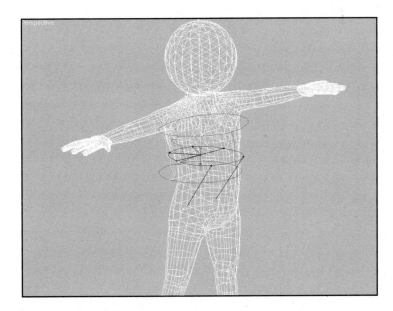

- **Radial Distance.** This is how far out the attach points lie from the body. If you look at the tendons from within a MAX viewport, you see a purple outline that roughly matches that of the character's skin. Increasing or decreasing this amount affects the size of the outline.

- **Pull.** This determines how much the skin is pulled by the attached joint. A good example is the chest and shoulder area. As the arms move outward, the skin of the chest is pulled outward along the surface of the skin as well.

- **Pinch.** This determines how much the skin is pushed inward by the action of the tendon attached joint. A good example is the crease that forms in the web of the hand as the thumb moves next to the forefinger.

- **Stretch.** This determines how much the skin is stretched by the tendon attached joint. This gives the skin more or less pliability.

Normally, the values for all these joints are set at 1.0 to give a good skin behavior when the tendons are attached to a nearby link. If the tendons span multiple links, these numbers should probably be reduced somewhat because the effect of a change on a link normally decreases the further away from the link you are. For example, the clavicle should have more of an effect on the upper spine than on the lower spine.

Tendon Boundary conditions are also important for tendons that span multiple links. These determine exactly how far the skin is affected. If these are off, only the joint with the tendon is affected. When the upper bound value is high, the skin on the spanned joints is also affected by the tendon. This is very important for getting a smooth behavior across the skin.

If you enable boundary conditions, it is a good idea to turn off the joint intersection parameters for each of the spanned joints. This action prevents the two features from trying to create different outlines at the joint intersections, and causing unpredictable results.

MODIFYING TENDONS

1. Continue with meshphys.max.

2. In the Cross Section Editor, select the two front attach points. Change Radial Distance to 16, Pull to –0.25, and Pinch to 0.0.

3. In the Tendons rollout, change upper bound to 2.0 and pull bias to 0.0, and then change the lower bound to –1.

4. Unhide the biped skeleton turn on Animate, and, at frame 10, rotate the clavicles up 30 degrees in the Y axis.

These modifications have the effect of lifting the skin evenly over the front of the chest as the clavicles raise. The file meshtend.max on the accompanying CD contains the completed tendons. The figure has a texture map applied so that the effect of the tendons is more visible.

5. Make a preview of frames 0–20 to see the effect.

In Practice: Animating with Physique

- **Bulge Angles.** Bulges can be used not only to create bulging muscles, but also to help prevent unwanted effects such as crimping and tearing of the skin.

- **Vertex Reassignment.** Vertices can only be assigned to one joint, and thus must be reassigned to the proper joint from time to time.

- **Using Biped.** Always assign the Physique modifier to the pelvis, not the Center of Mass object. If you need additional control, you may link dummy objects to the Biped skeleton to get additional joints to help control the skin.

- **Tendons.** Tendons affect the skin across multiple joints and are very helpful in branching areas of the body, such as the shoulder and pelvis areas.

IMAGE CREATED BY GEORGE MAESTRI

Chapter 26

by George Maestri

FACIAL ANIMATION AND LIP SYNC

Animating the face is one of the most challenging and rewarding tasks that animators encounter. People are all experts in the subtleties of expression and emotion. A bad actor elicits instinctively negative reactions, typically because his emotions seem forced rather than genuine. The same goes for animation—great facial animation looks seamless and does not draw attention to itself. Bad animation seems curiously off for some unknown reason.

Within MAX, there are many ways to accomplish the shape deformations necessary to animate the face, each method approaching the problem from a slightly different angle. The vertices of the face can be directly manipulated, either by attaching them to a control object via a Linked XForm, or through morphing to one or many targets. Bones can also be used for facial animation, and the mesh of the face deformed by using either Physique or Bones Pro.

Anatomy of the Face

Animating the face requires a good eye and a strong knowledge of acting and emotion. You also need to understand the underlying anatomy of the human head and face to understand exactly how it moves. The face is by far the most important part of the equation because this is where emotion is shown. The face is the most flexible area of the head. It is driven by approximately a dozen muscles that connect the skin to the skull. As with muscles in the body, these muscles affect the shape of the skin by bulging, stretching, and pulling it.

The trick is to understand how these muscles pull and shape the face to create expressions. The groups of muscles fall into two categories: lower face muscles, which control the mouth and jaw (see fig. 26.1); and upper face muscles, which control the eyes and brows (see fig. 26.2).

FIGURE 26.1

The muscles surrounding the mouth pull the lips outward radially. Another set of muscles compress and purse the lips.

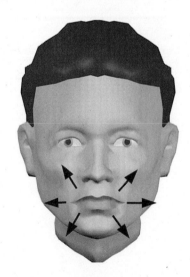

FIGURE 26.2

In addition to opening and closing the eyelids, muscles on the upper half of the face raise, lower, and furrow the brow.

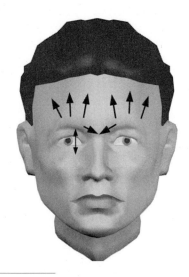

How Muscles Move the Face

At the mouth, the muscles make the following three major types of movements:

- The muscles that lie across the cheeks and jaw pull the lips outward radially from eight major anchor points.

- The muscles surrounding the lips contract to purse the lips, forcing them together and forward.

- The jaw can drop.

At the eyes, the muscles make the following three major movements:

- They open and close the eyelids.

- The Frontalis muscles on the brow raise and lower the eyebrows.

- The Currogator pulls the eyebrows in toward the bridge of the nose, furrowing the brow.

Human anatomy, especially an understanding of muscle action and reaction, provides an exceptionally useful model when you are constructing a face. Human anatomy can also be used as a model for the construction of the face. If the face you create within MAX moves easily along the same lines that these muscles are pulling, you have a much better chance at animating the face.

Modeling and Setting Up Faces for Animation

Before the face is animated, however, it must be modeled and set up for proper animation. How a face is modeled relates intimately to the way that it is animated. A face made from Surface Tools has very few vertices controlling a large surface. It may be animated quite easily using Linked XForms. This method is not useful on denser polygonal models, however, which may be more effectively animated by using a single or multiple target morphing package.

As with bodies and their associated skeletons, faces need to be set up properly and tested over a wide range of motions. Thorough testing prevents difficult problems that can interrupt the creative flow when animating.

Surface Tools

Digimation's Surface Tools has quickly become one of the preferred methods for performing facial animation within MAX. This suite of tools enables you to create very flexible and easy to manipulate mouths and faces. Anyone attempting facial animation should consider Surface Tools to be a standard plug-in. It should be in every MAX animator's toolkit.

Surface Tools contains a number of modifiers, most important of which are Cross Section and Surface. Cross Section is similar to a skinning tool in that it takes a series of spline outlines and connects them together. Surface completes the process by turning the splines into a flexible patch surface.

Modeling a Simple Face with Surface Tools

When building a facial model, a simple and effective way is to build the mouth by using a radial topology—the splines created for the face are oriented so that they stretch out from the mouth radially, in much the same way that the muscles of the face affect the underlying skin. A radial face can also be modeled purely from quadratic patches, so you can avoid tangency problems that crop up when triangular patches are added to the mix.

To picture such a face, think of a cylinder with one end folded inside itself. A face like this can be easily constructed by taking a number of circular splines as outlines, attaching them together, and using the Cross-Section modifier to create a cage of splines that can be surfaced.

CREATING A RADIAL FACE

1. From the Create/Shapes panel, select Line.

2. Draw an egg-shaped outline with eight vertices (for a complex face, more detail may be required).

3. Copy this simple outline three or four times (see fig. 26.3). Using the Edit Spline tool, reshape these outlines so that they taper toward the mouth.

FIGURE 26.3

A simple outline copied four times to create the front part of the face.

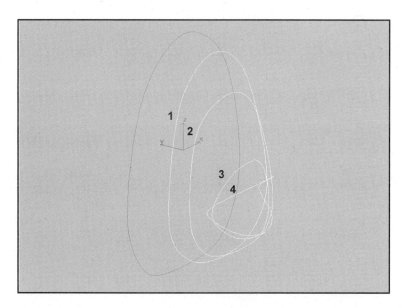

4. Copy the original outline three or four more times. Use these outlines to shape the back portion of the head. The last outline needs to be scaled to zero because it will be the back of the head. If you want, the outlines can also be rotated and tapered so that they become the neck of the character (see fig. 26.4).

FIGURE 26.4

Copying the original outline to create the back of the head.

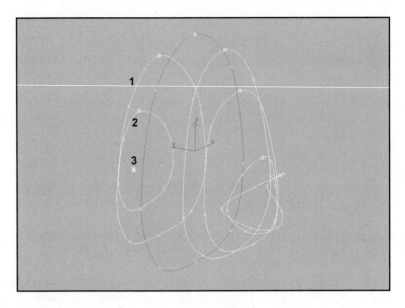

5. Select the outlines near the mouth. Copy these three more times and reshape them to make the throat. Rotate the last outline so that it angles the throat downward into a trachea-like tube (see fig. 26.5).

FIGURE 26.5

The trachea is also created from the same outline.

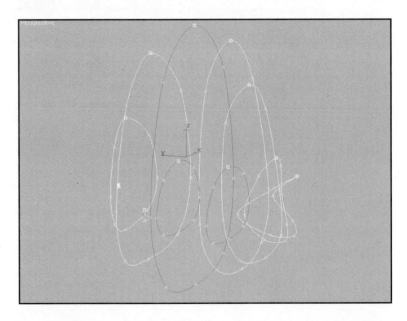

6. Select this spline. Using the Attach tool on the Edit Spline modifier, attach the other splines in order, up the throat, across the face, to the back of the head.

7. Apply the Cross Section Modifier to this spline (see fig. 26.6).

8. Apply the Surface modifier to the stack.

FIGURE 26.6

The original splines, the splines with Cross Section applied, and the final Surface.

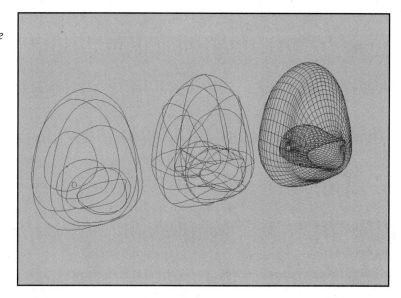

9. Reshape the splines as necessary to create the proper shape. For additional reference, it is a good idea to create a referenced clone of the surfaced face. This can then be used as a live reference of the face while the original splines are being modified.

You can view a simple head created by using Surface Tools. Take a look at the file named splinehd.max on the accompanying CD. A more complex head using the same topology is also on the CD, and is in a file named splineh2.max.

Another important thing to remember is that too much detail in the splines themselves is self-defeating when it comes time to animate. Creating an easily animatable face is an exercise in minimalism. The goal is to get the most detail out of the fewest number of vertices. Typically, 8 or 12 radial subdivisions should be enough to create a usable face.

Because Surface Tools supports triangular patches, it is also possible to use these to help add detail only in those areas that need them, such as around the nose and eyes (see fig. 26.7).

FIGURE 26.7
*This face is more
realistic and was
created using the same
basic topology, but
with slightly more detail
to help define the nose.*

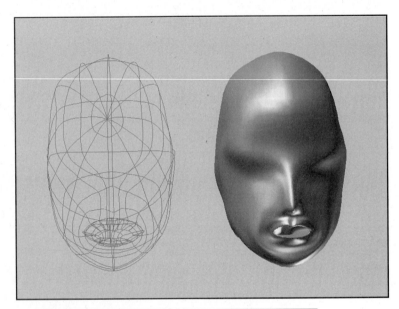

Setting Up a Surface Tools Face for Animation

One very direct method of animating a Surface Tools created face is to use MAX's Linked XForm modifier to attach parts of the spline cage to objects that become handles for the vertices held within. The handle objects, typically dummy objects, can be freely manipulated and keyframed to give the face a wide range of motion.

The face can then be surfaced and textured, while the Linked XForm attached handles give the animator control over the underlying structure. It also enables you to manipulate the underlying vertices while the face is surfaced, giving you a visual cue as to how the skin is behaving. In a typical radial face, eight handles for the mouth and one for the jaw are all that are needed to create convincing mouth animation.

The procedure for creating the handles is very straightforward. The Linked XForms need to be applied to the vertices of the splines used to create the face. On the accompanying CD is a simple, but effective head. It is in the file named xformhd.max. Load this file and follow these steps:

CREATING THE HANDLES

1. Create eight small objects to be used as handles. Any geometry may be used, but dummy objects work best because they don't render. Place

these handles near the vertices of the face you wish to control. In the example head, there will be a total of eight objects arrayed radially around the mouth, each distanced approximately 45 degrees apart.

TIP

Some people use text objects for facial animation because they do not render handles (see fig. 26.8). The text itself serves as a label for the associated handle.

FIGURE 26.8
Arrangement of the handles around the mouth. The white cubes are the handles.

2. Select the spline that represents the head and apply an Edit Spline modifier to it.

3. Activate Sub-Object/Vertex, and select the vertices that comprise the top center of the lip.

4. With Vertex Sub-Object mode still active, add a Linked XForm modifier to the stack. Because this was applied while Sub-Object mode was active, it only affects the selected vertices.

5. Within the Linked XForm rollout, click on Pick Control Object and select the handle object nearest the top center of the lip. The handle now controls these vertices.

6. Add another Edit Spline to the stack, and select the next set of vertices— those on the top left of the lip. Add a Linked XForm modifier to this and attach it to the handle.

7. Repeat this procedure for the remaining handles.

8. Now use a dummy object or a simple piece of geometry to create a handle for the jaw. Place this handle underneath the chin.

9. After all the XForms are in place, apply the Surface modifier. This action creates the skin as the last step in the procedure. Because the Surface modifier is computationally intensive, it slows down manipulation times considerably. It is very easy to switch this modifier off to get additional speed while animating.

The one catch with this method is that the handles themselves are not attached to the head. This means that when the surface of the head is moved, the handles do not follow along. The handles also cannot be bound to the head in a hierarchy because a dependency loop will result.

The easiest way around this problem is to make a referenced clone of the head (see fig. 26.9). The clone can then be attached to the body quite easily, and the original tucked safely away in a separate viewport, so the face can be viewed directly as it is manipulated.

FIGURE 26.9

Creating a referenced clone of the original head.

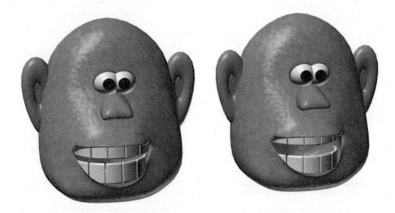

An additional problem concerns the bottom teeth. Because the bottom teeth are attached to the jaw bone, they need to move along with the skin of the jaw—controlled by the jaw handle. On the master model, this can be accomplished by binding the lower teeth to the jaw handle.

The clone, however, has no handles with which to attach the teeth, forcing other solutions to be considered. One way is to use Digimation's Object Glider space warp, which will constrain any object to a surface. This can be used to attach a dummy to the bottom of the chin, which can then be used to parent the lower teeth, forcing them to move along with the skin.

Another sly way to do this without using a third-party plug-in is to apply an Edit Mesh modifier to the objects representing the lower teeth. Select all the vertices in the object and add a Linked XForm modifier to the selection, linking these vertices to the Jaw handle. Because all the vertices are being affected by the Linked XForm, the teeth appear to move as if linked. Technically, however, the teeth are changing shape relative to their pivot. They can be cloned and placed inside the cloned head. They will appear to move just like in the master.

To attach the cloned head to the body, just create a dummy to parent all the objects in the head—the skin of the head, the teeth, tongue, eyes, and so on.

This dummy can then be attached as a child to the body and used to rotate and manipulate the position of the head. If you are using a biped for the body's skeleton, the skull of the biped could be used in place of the dummy object.

You can view the final version of this head by loading the file named xformhdf.max from the accompanying CD.

Morphing

One way to animate faces is with shape animation, also known as morphing. In its simplest sense, morphing just changes the shape of one object into another. MAX has a number of methods for morphing objects, including third-party plug-ins such as MorphMagic, which is discussed later. Included in the base package is a single target morphing function, which is implemented as an animation controller.

Single Target Morphing

Single target morphing changes the shape of one object into another over time. The controller in MAX is of the TCB variety, which gives adequate control over how the morph takes place.

Modeling Morph Targets

To set up your model for animation, you just have to model a library of the appropriate poses. This method works for both spline and polygonal models. MAX requires that the models being morphed have the same number of vertices in the exact same order. This is easily accomplished by modeling a single stock, expressionless face, copying it, and reworking the one face into the many expressions and facial poses required.

Morphs can be created under the Compound Objects Creation panel (see fig. 26.10). The morphs are selected and added to a scrolling list of objects. The trick here is to keep the Instance button toggled as the morph targets are selected, thereby keeping the overhead of the shot lower. After the targets have been selected and the animation has been authored, the geometry for the morph targets are no longer needed, and can be safely deleted from the shot. This deletion keeps geometry counts lower when rendering.

FIGURE 26.10

The Compound Objects Creation panel.

One downfall of this method (and any single target method, for that matter) is that it seems as though you never have enough poses (see fig. 26.11). The number of expressions a human face can make is essentially infinite, so you need to pick your battles and model the broad expressions needed most. Many of the delicate subtleties can get lost when using such stock poses. Strictly morphing between poses can also look mechanical. Having a few different versions of the same pose, therefore, can be one way to avoid this problem. This, of course, adds more geometry to the scene.

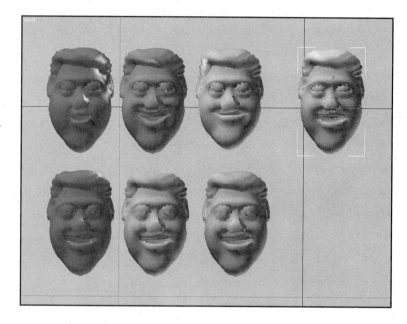

FIGURE 26.11

For MAX's morph manager and for MorphMagic, the models need to be constructed from a master, neutral face so that the vertex counts and vertex order is identical.

Multiple Target Morphing

MorphMagic, a plug-in available through Platinum Pictures, gives MAX the capability to accomplish morphing with multiple targets, along with a number of other features. MorphMagic operates as an object modifier in the standard 3D Studio MAX interface. Because MorphMagic allows for multiple targets, the targets will be much more specific than those used for MAX's single target controller. You may model a single target for a left eye blink and another for a right eye blink, for example, as well as individual extremes for the right and left sides of the face.

MorphMagic enables you to load up to 100 different shapes into a Channel Control menu, and then morph between any number of those shapes at any ratio, or "weight." You can overshoot by using negative values or values greater than 100 percent to amplify the distortion of your objects. You can also limit the effects of the morph to certain areas of your individual objects by first making a selection of vertices in individual targets by using the Edit Mesh modifier.

Morph Magic Interface

The interface is centered around the concept of channels. A *channel* contains a shape, which can be an individual model, a combination of models, or selected vertices within a model. For best use, the MorphMagic modifier should be applied to a neutral, relaxed face, with the extremes applied to the channels. MorphMagic has 10 pages of 10 channels each, for a total of 100 channels (see fig. 26.12). Each channel may be labeled, and each may contain any one of the following three types of targets:

- **Morph Target.** This enables you to select an entire object as a channel.

- **Compound Target.** Compound Target enables you to take a snapshot of any shape you have created by combining channels and inserting them into another channel as a new morph target without remodeling. Then you can just drag one slider to make the "compound" facial expression, rather than remixing the original channels.

- **Selected Vertices.** Using selected vertices enables you to save modeling time and memory by isolating parts of a model as channels. A good example is blinking. Rather than creating two separate models with the right and left eyes closed, you can create a single model with both eyes closed and select the vertices representing the right and left eyes.

FIGURE 26.12
The Morph Magic interface.

Weighted Channel Morphing

After the targets have been selected, you must animate the spinners that represent the individual channels. By combining and mixing multiple channels, you can get any number of combinations. You could model individual shapes for expressions such as anger, fear, joy, surprise, disgust, and so forth, and then combine them so that a pose is 30 percent surprise and 70 percent joy, for example. If you want to transition that to 100 percent joy, animate the surprise channel down to zero, while moving joy up to 100 percent. You can combine two, three, four, or as many channels as you want; all you really need to animate is the relative weights. This makes it much easier to create the exact right pose for the given moment, and also requires that fewer poses be modeled.

The accompanying CD contains a demo version of the MorphMagic plug-in. This demo can be used only with the supplied file mmdemo.max. It gives you a good overview of how this plug-in can be used.

Setting Up a Face with Bones

Using bones to animate the face is another method that can be employed. This method is similar to using the Linked XForm method that can be used with Surface Tools. The similarities lie in the placement of the bones.

Digimation's Bones Pro is a good tool to use for the mesh deformation portion of the process, because this plug-in allows for overlapping influences of bones and allows multiple bones to affect a single vertex. The deformations created with Bones Pro work well on a face.

Bones can also work on a Surface Tools generated face. In this case, however, Physique is the preferred mesh deformation tool to use. One problem with using Bones Pro with a Surface Tools face is that the modifier always floats to the top of the stack, disallowing bones to directly manipulate the underlying splines themselves.

Boning a face is very similar to creating the Linked XForm handles described previously with Surface Tools. The placement of the bones follows the same radial pattern with eight or more bones arrayed approximately 45 degrees apart around the mouth.

If you use bones to animate a face, proper placement of those bones is essential. This face is made out of polygons, but the principles apply equally as well to a patch face. For this exercise, Bones Pro is used. Bones Pro uses the bounding boxes of the bones for initial vertex assignment, so the bones should roughly match the volume of the area of the head they are affecting.

BONING A FACE FOR ANIMATION

1. Load the file head.max. Place a large bone in the center of the head to define the skull.

2. Add a jaw bone. This is a simple box that fills the volume from slightly in front of the ear to the tip of the chin.

3. The jaw bone needs to be pivoted somewhere near the bottom front corner of the ear. Link this bone to the skull bone.

4. Like with the Surface Tools face, create a radial array of eight bones around the mouth.

5. Link the bones along the upper part of the lip to the skull.

6. The bones in the lower part of the face move with the jaw bone. Link or constrain these bones to the jaw bone so that when the jaw pivots down, the bones and the vertices they affect move with it.

7. Placement of the bones around the eyes is very similar to the mouth, but one or two bones per lid is sufficient. Be certain to pivot the bones along the center of the eyeball, so the lid moves along its surface. Link these bones to the skull bone.

8. Add a bone for the nose to help keep it rigid, and add bones for the eyebrows, and maybe even a bone or two to help puff out the cheeks during a smile. See figure 26.13 for a rendering of a basic face.

After the bones are in place, you can continue the exercise and create a Bones Pro space warp to apply to the head. From within the Bones Pro rollout, assign the bones that were just created and the head as the bound node.

Turn on the Animation button and create a simple test animation for the face. Rotate the jaw to open the mouth, move the lip bones to test the range of motion of the mouth, and blink the eyes. Do not worry too much about stray vertices; this animation helps to find them. After this is done, enter the Influence Editor.

FIGURE 26.13

The arrangement of bones for a simple face.

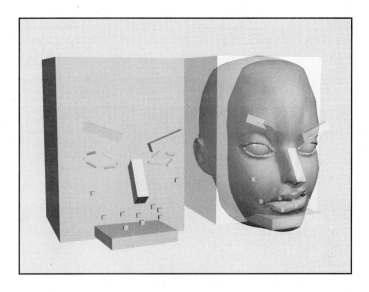

1. Assign the vertices representing the solid portions of the head to the skull bone. These vertices remain rigid, so exclude them from other bones.

2. Assign the vertices of the chin and lower face to the jaw bone (see fig. 26.14).

FIGURE 26.14

The vertices in the lower face need to be assigned to the jaw.

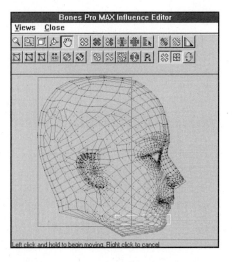

3. You will probably notice some tearing in the lips, where stray vertices from the top lip are influenced by the bottom and vice versa. Go to the mouth and select the vertices representing the upper lip and exclude them from the lower lip bones.

4. Do the same for the lower lip vertices (see fig. 26.15). Exclude them from the upper lip bones.

FIGURE 26.15

The vertices in the top lip need to be excluded from the bones in the bottom lip.

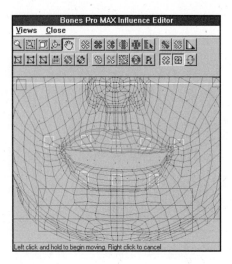

5. To get a smoother transition of vertices, it is a good idea to increase the influences of the bones surrounding the mouth so that they overlap significantly with their neighbors.

6. Locate and reassign any stray vertices in the eye area. The eyes are very similar to the lips in that the upper lid vertices need to be excluded from the lower lid bones and vice versa.

Continue to test and reassign stray vertices as required. A version of this file is located on the accompanying CD as bonehead.max.

Setting Up Eyes and Other Facial Features

Setting up the skin of the face so that it deforms properly is only half the process. Other components of the face need to be set up for animation, such as the eyes, eyebrows, teeth, and tongue, which is heavily involved in speech and lip-sync.

The eyes are by far the most important of these components. Eyes not only need to blink but also need to express emotion. Many emotions and moods are expressed through subtle changes in the eyes, and stiff, unnatural eyes make your character look like a doll rather than a living creature. Eye motions as simple as a blink can add a tremendous amount of life to a character, and more subtle changes in eye shape can add significantly more dimension to the character. On a broad scale, a shifty character may squint his eyes, a surprised character would open his eyes wide, and sad character would furrow his brow. With this in mind, it is essential to have eyes that are controllable in every respect. The lids of the eyes need to follow the surface of the eyeball, and eyebrows need to be able to lift and furrow themselves.

Internal Eyes

Internal eyes are akin to realistic eyes. The eyelids are part of the facial surface with the eyeball inside the skull. If your character design dictates internal eyes, you need to plan for this by modeling eye sockets when constructing the head. This can add a lot of detail, however, particularly when using Surface Tools.

The eyeball itself can be either a sphere or a hemisphere because only the front part of the eye ever shows through the skin (see fig. 26.16). The pupil can be made with a simple texture map, or second hemisphere sitting on the first.

FIGURE 26.16
Eyes inside the head can be constructed out of simple spheres or hemispheres.

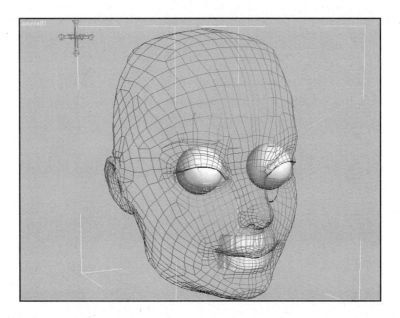

The big problem with internal eyes is that you need to keep the eyeballs locked in the socket while the head moves. This is usually accomplished with a hierarchy—the head being the parent of the eyes. Another issue is the movement of the eyelids. They must move along an arc that is the same radius as the eye.

One way to do this is to place a bone or Linked XForm on the eyelid to close it. To make certain that the skin of the lid follows the arc of the eyeball, place the pivot point of the bone at the center of the eyeball. That way, rotating the bone automatically makes it track the surface of the eye. In this case, a tool-like MorphMagic becomes very useful because the eyelids can be selected out as groups of vertices and morphed into a blink.

Another way to go about this is to create a second lid that animates and remains hidden until the eyes close. For fast eye closures, such as blinks, this can be fine. If the lid is closed too long, however, the audience may pick up the seam where the second lid pokes through the skin.

External Eyes

External eyes have a more cartoon-like appearance, and are easier to control than internal eyes. These eyes are separate objects made from spheres or cylinders that sit on the surface of the face. Because they do not have to line up exactly with the eye sockets on the face, you have much greater control over how they are placed. They are great for Tex-Avery style eye popping, and afford the animator a variety of stylistic choices.

The following are very simply constructed eyes that can be used in many situations. The lids of these eyes are not directly attached to the surface of the face, but rather are separate objects linked to the eyeball itself. This allows for simple construction and gives the lids the capability to change shape along with the eyes, the lids following the surface exactly, even when the eyes are scaled to an oblong shape.

MODELING EXTERNAL EYES

1. From the Geometry Creation panel, create a standard sphere that is 30 units in diameter and has 32 radial subdivisions. Name this sphere **R-Eye**.

2. Select the sphere and then Shift-click on the sphere to clone it as a copy. Name this object **R-Eyelid**.

3. Select the copy, being careful not to move it. (If you accidentally jog it, you might want to use grid snap to align the two pivots exactly.) Within the Modify panel, increase the diameter to 31 units.

4. Remaining in the Modify panel, set the hemisphere spinner to 0.5. This makes the eyelid half a sphere.

5. Clone the object R-Eye again to make the pupil. Name this object **R-EyePupil**.

6. Set the diameter of this object to 30.5 units, and the hemisphere to 0.9.

7. Select R-Eyelid and R-EyePupil and link them to R-Eye.

8. Duplicate these three objects to make the left eye.

Because the objects all rotate around the same center, eye rotation is as simple as rotating the pupil, and blinking is as simple as rotating the lid.

Cartoon Eyes

The method just described produces spherical eyeballs. Not all characters, however, have perfectly round eyes. Sometimes, it is nice to place oblong or asymmetrical eyes on a character to get a cartoony effect.

This can be accomplished quite handily by making certain the Inherit Scale boxes under the Hierarchy/Link Info panel are checked. Because the eyelid and the pupil are children of the eye, the eye's scaling information is inherited. This enables you to scale the eyes in any manner possible, including non-proportional scale to make the eyes oblong (see fig. 26.17).

FIGURE 26.17

A non-proportional scale stretches the eye, yet still allows the lid to follow its surface.

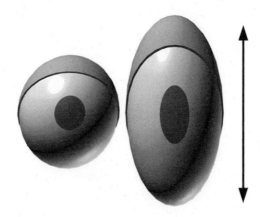

Furthermore, the scaling can be animated to give the eyes a very flexible squash and stretch effect. This enables you to use the eyes far more expressively on the character. Some examples of this expressive behavior might include the following situations:

- During a blink, the eyes can be scaled along the horizontal axis for two or three frames to help give the blink itself more snap.

- When a character is surprised, his eyebrows raise up. Scaling the eyes along the vertical axis accentuates this even further.

- If a character is loopy or has been knocked senseless, the eyes can be scaled along different axes to give a crazy or mixed-up look.

- Shifty-eyed characters would have their eyes elongated along a horizontal axis.

Blinks happen all the time, and they are a very useful tool for the animator. Blinks can be used to help shift the direction of the eyes or to convey emotion. They also help keep your characters alive—blinking the eyes every few seconds gives your characters believability. In a squash and stretch cartoon environment, animators emphasize motions, such as blinks, by animating the shape of the objects as they move in order to help exaggerate the differences and to help add contrast to the animation.

ANIMATING A CARTOON BLINK

1. Using the eyes just created, turn on the animation button and use the Non-Proportional Scale tool to make the eyes slightly elongated along the vertical axis.

2. Move the Time Slider to frame 6. This is the start of the blink. Within the Motion panel, set keyframes for the scale of the eyes and rotation of the eyelids.

3. Move the Time Slider to frame 9. This is the middle of the blink. Rotate the eyelids 90 degrees so that they cover the eyes. Notice that, even though the eyes are scaled, the lids still follow the surface of the eyes.

4. Select the Squash Scaling tool and squash the eyes down so that they are elongated along the horizontal axis (see fig. 26.18).

FIGURE 26.18
*To get a more
"cartoony" effect,
squash the eyes as
they blink.*

5. Move the Time Slider to frame 12. Rotate the lids open and use the Squash Scaling tool to put the scaling of the eyes back to normal (for complete accuracy, the keys on frame 6 can also be copied to frame 12 from within Track View).

TIP

Eyes never blink at exactly the same time. Offsetting the blink of one eye by a single frame can add more life to your shot.

Run the animation. Notice how the extra squash added to the blink helps make it look more cartoony. Also notice how the lids stay along the surface of the eye no matter what the shape. For reference, a file is located on the accompanying CD—eyes.avi.

Eyebrows

Depending on the design of your face, the eyebrows can be on the surface of the face or separate. Eyebrows go a long way toward indicating emotion, so be certain to plan for them when designing your characters. If the eyebrows are on the surface of the face, they can be painted on as a texture. For a more complex effect, you can use a displacement or bump map to further define the illusion of hair. Moving these eyebrows requires moving and animating the surface of the face.

MorphMagic makes a good tool for creating surfaced eyebrow motion. Because bitmap textures and displacement maps can be morphed from within the plug-in, the eyebrows can be created as a bump or displacement map that morphs from within MorphMagic.

Eyebrows separate from the face are less realistic, but can take a wider variety of shapes and positions. These can be constructed from a variety of shapes and can float free or ride along the surface of the forehead. Bones Pro or Physique can be used to change the shape of the eyebrow and also help keep it attached to the surface of the face.

Tongues

The tongue is particularly important when animating speech. The tongue is a very flexible object and needs to be animated with bones or some form of shape animation. The tongue is invariably a separate object that just floats in the mouth cavity. The back of the tongue is rarely seen. Directors, after all, rarely fly digital cameras down characters' throats.

The easiest way to build a tongue is by squashing a sphere and putting a dent down its length. Texture and bump maps can also be used to make a more detailed surface. It is a good idea to fade this texture to black at the back of the tongue so that the back of the tongue remains hidden.

The tongue is easily animated using either morphing or a chain of bones and a package such as Physique or Bones Pro. Using MAX's bones with IK turned off makes a particularly good tongue controller, because the mesh stretches along with the bones as they themselves stretch.

Animation and Lip Sync

After the face is properly set up for animation, the actual process of animation becomes easier. Faces set up well can be controlled easily and new expressions can be created on the fly. This can be done by manipulating the bones or Linked XForms, or manipulating and reshaping the morph targets.

Creating a Library of Poses

No matter which animation method you choose, it is a good idea to build up a stock library of expressions that you can draw from when creating your animation. If you use Linked XForms, bones, or single target morphs, the library will actually be keyframes sitting within Track View.

If you animate a Surface Tools face, for example, the positions of the handles at each keyframe determine the individual expression. By copying these keys to other parts of the timeline, you can make animation easy. You can separate the components of each expression and copy them where needed. The keyframes of the handles that control the eyes, for example, can be manipulated and copied separately from those controlling the mouth.

One easy way to create a library is to create keyframes or groups of keyframes on the timeline that can be copied (see fig. 26.19). The negative frame numbers before frame zero serve as one convenient place to store these keys. That way, you do not have to worry about offsetting your animation.

FIGURE 26.19

Store groups of keyframes in the timeline before frame 0 (grayed) to create a library of stock poses.

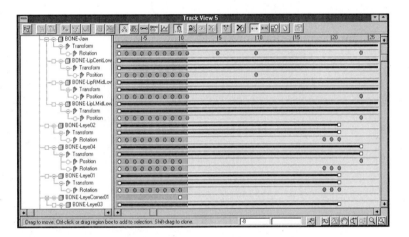

When creating a library, which sort of expressions do you want to model? For a plug-in such as MorphMagic, these are not keyframes, but most likely are the extremes of each of the major muscles of the face. This way, you can have a slider for each extreme, theoretically being able to create all expressions from a handful of sliders. Added to this could be mouths used for lip sync and a number of stock expressions.

The muscle-based method also translates to keyframe-based methods, such as Bones and Linked XForms. These methods, however, lend themselves to groups of keys to create stock or novel poses that your character's face may make. These could be as simple as the mouths used to animate dialogue. Also, as you animate a character, you may create new expressions that strike you as ones that you may need to use again.

The Eight Basic Mouth Positions

The mouths used to create lip sync are a good start to creating a library of poses. Because many characters that do facial animation also perform lip-sync, these poses always come in handy.

Position 1 is the closed mouth, used for consonants made by the lips, specifically, the M, B, and P sounds (see fig. 26.20). In this position, the lips may usually be the normal width. For added realism, you can add an additional position with the lips slightly pursed, for sounds following an "ooo" sound, such as in the word "room."

Position 2 has the mouth open with the teeth closed (see fig. 26.21). It is a very common shape and is used for consonants made within the mouth, specifically those made by C, D, G, K, N, R, S, TH, Y, and Z. All these sounds can also be made with the teeth slightly open, particularly in fast speech.

FIGURE 26.20
Position 1 is the closed mouth.

FIGURE 26.21
Position 2 has the mouth open with the teeth closed.

Position 3 is used for the wide open vowels such as *A* and *I* (see fig. 26.22). The tongue should be visible at the bottom of the mouth, and the jaw relatively slack.

Position 4 is used primarily for the vowel *E* (see fig. 26.23). It can also be used on occasion for *C*, *K*, or *N* during fast speech.

FIGURE **26.22**

Position 3 is used for the wide open vowels such as A and I.

FIGURE **26.23**

Position 4 is used primarily for the vowel E.

Position 5 has the mouth wide open in an elliptical shape (see fig. 26.24). It is used for the vowel *O*, as in the word "flow." Sometimes, particularly when the sound is at the end of a word, you can follow this shape with the one in position 6 to close down the mouth.

Position 6 has the mouth smaller, but more pursed (see fig. 26.25). It is used for the "oooo" sound, as in "food." This can also be used for the vowel *U*.

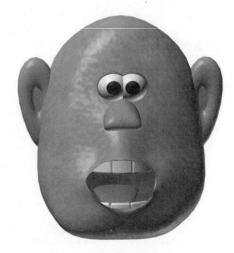

Position 7 has the mouth wide open with the tongue against the teeth (see fig. 26.26). This is reserved for the letter L. It can also sometimes be used for *D* or *TH* sounds, particularly when preceded by *A* or *I*. If the speech is particularly rapid, this shape may not be necessary, and position 2 might be substituted.

Position 8 has the bottom lip tucked under the teeth to make the sound of the letters *F* or *V* (see fig. 26.27). In highly pronounced speech, this shape is necessary, but the shape can also be replaced with position 2 for more casual or rapid speech.

FIGURE 26.26
Position 7 has the mouth wide open with the tongue against the teeth.

FIGURE 26.27
Position 8 has the bottom lip tucked under the teeth to make the sound of the letters F or V.

Loading Sound into MAX

MAX has the capability to load sound directly into Track View, which makes it excellent for lip sync applications. Sound is loaded by right-clicking on the Sound Track object and selecting Properties from the pull-down menu that appears.

MAX then displays the audio waveform from within Track View, giving you the ability to read the track directly in MAX. Simply sliding the time slider audibly scrubs the audio, allowing you to read the phonemes of the dialog frame by frame. This is best done before animation begins because a properly read track serves as a good roadmap when animating.

Also, reading the track after animation has been added to the shot may prove troublesome due to machine speed and animation complexity issues. If shape animation is being used, the calculations required to perform this can tax even the most powerful systems, so real time playback may not be possible.

Using an Audio Controller for Automatic Lip Sync

One of the easier ways to do lip sync is to use MAX's audio controllers. These controllers enable you to translate, rotate, and scale objects based on the volume of a standard Windows .WAV file. The lip sync produced by this method is not exceptionally accurate; it produces a simple lip flapping effect, which is not particularly convincing. Still, for stylized characters, the method may prove more than adequate.

The Rotation controller is the one chosen most often because it can be used to rotate and flap the lower jaw (though the Translate and Scale controllers can also be put to similar use). These controllers can be applied from within Track View or within the Motion panel.

Once applied, the Rotation controller is accessed from within Track View. The controller's dialog has a number of parameters (see fig. 26.28). First is the name of the sound file to be loaded. It must be noted that the sound file does not have to match the sound file used for Audio sync. This allows for multiple sound files to be used as controllers—perhaps to flap the lips of a dozen people in a crowded room.

FIGURE 26.28

The Audio Controller Rotation controller dialog.

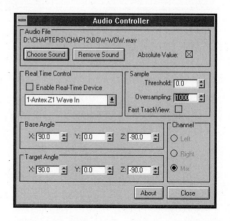

A sound file does not even have to be used because the controller has a check box to enable a live audio source to be used as the controller. This can be useful for real-time or performance-animation applications.

The oversampling spinner is the most critical for smooth operation. A CD-Quality audio waveform changes 44,100 times per second, rising and falling constantly. The audio controller takes the value of the waveform on the given frame and uses that number to calculate the rotation. This can cause jittery behavior because the waveform could coincidentally be at zero, maximum, or somewhere in between when it is sampled.

Oversampling prevents this jittering movement, by smoothing out the waveform seen by MAX. The procedure averages the waveform over a large number of samples (maximum 1,000), giving the effect of a much smoother motion (see fig. 26.29).

FIGURE 26.29

The Waveform display within MAX. The top waveform is the audio itself, and the bottom two are controllers.

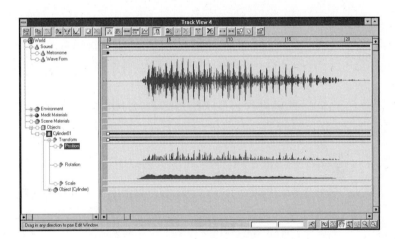

TIP

Sometimes if your audio sample rate is high (44,100 kHz), you may still see some unwanted jitter, even though oversampling spinner is cranked to 1,000. To eliminate this, load the audio file into a sound editing program and convert it to a lower sample rate (11,025 kHz, for example). Fewer samples force the controller to oversample over a wider range of time, effectively doubling or quadrupling the oversample effect.

Along the bottom of the dialog are the limits for the rotation controller. This enables you to set a Base angle, which is the position when the sound is silent, and a Target angle, which is the position when the waveform is at 100 percent.

The following exercise demonstrates the oversampling principle using a barking dog.

MAKING THE DOG BARK

1. Load the file toondog.max. It has a simple cartoon dog with a very simple skeleton inside. The skeleton is configured for use with Bones Pro, although Physique works just as well. The skeleton is set up so that the lips flap when the bones in the mouth and nose rotate around their Y-axis.

2. Select the bone named BONE-Mouth. From within Track View, apply the Audio Rotation controller. Open the controller's dialog.

3. Select the sound. On the accompanying CD is an audio file named bow-wow.wav.

4. Set the Oversampling spinner to a high number between 250 and 1,000. Notice how the waveform shown in Track View smooths out as this number increases.

5. The bone is set to rotate along its local Y-axis. Set the Target angle to 30.0 degrees.

6. Repeat the preceding procedure for the bone named BINE-Nose. Set its Target angle to –70.0 degrees.

Scrub the Time Slider. The skeleton moves and the lips flap along with the sound. On most systems, it may be necessary to render a test to see the effect in real time.

Using a Third-Party Sound Editor

Third-party sound editors can provide more flexibility when reading a track. Some packages enable you to scrub the audio quite accurately in real time, and also to label the tracks as they are read for further reference.

Several third-party lip-sync applications also run under Windows. One popular application is Magpie, distributed over the World Wide Web at http://www.cinenet.net/users/rickmay/CGCHAR/magpie.htm.

Magpie enables you to load a series of bitmap files that represent the key mouth poses as found in your library of poses. These bitmaps can then be timed to the track on a frame-by-frame basis; the final result output is a text file that looks very much like an animator's dope sheet.

Reading the Track

Now that you understand the basic mouth positions, it is time to break down the track. If you have animator's exposure sheet paper, use it. Otherwise, get a pad of lined paper to read your track on, using one line per frame. If you want, you can also create a spreadsheet for this purpose and do it all digitally. There is an example Excel spreadsheet on the CD entitled xsheet.xls. You may use this or print it if you so desire. Load the dialog in a sound editing program.

The first thing you should do is match your sound editing program's timebase to the timebase you are animating—30, 25, or 24 frames per second, for example. After your timebase is set, selecting out a snippet of dialogue should enable you to listen to the snippet and read its exact length on the editor's data window. The visual readout of the dialogue gives you clues as to where the words start and stop. Work your way through the track, and write down each sound as it occurs on your exposure sheet, frame by frame. It is a tedious, but necessary chore.

3DS MAX enables you to play back audio in sync with the animation. This is particularly helpful because you might be able to skip the step of reading the track and instead just eyeball the sync. Still, it is always a good idea to have read the track methodically before animating so that you know exactly where all the sounds occur.

TIP

In MAX, Realtime Play Back must be checked in the Time Configuration dialog for sound to play back.

When reading the track, be certain to represent the sounds accurately. In human speech, most consonants are short, and usually won't take up more than one or two frames. Vowels, however, can be of any length. If a person is shouting, for instance, you may have vowels that top 30 frames in length.

In these cases, it is important that you don't just hold the mouth in the exact same position for over a second; it would look unnatural. Instead, create two slightly different mouth positions and keep the mouth moving between them so that the character looks alive.

READING A TRACK

1. On the accompanying CD, there is an audio file called dial.wav. Load this into your favorite sound editing program. The dialogue says, "Hello, how are you?" At 30 fps, the dialogue measures 46 frames.

2. Highlight the first 14 frames of the sound file. This is the word "Hello." Play this section back. Highlighting smaller sections to get the individual phonemes HE - L - OOO. Notice how vowels are usually taller and louder than the consonants.

3. Work through the entire track, writing down the positions of each phoneme. Here is a graphic representation of where the phonemes fall.

4. On paper, you should have something similar to table 26.1.

TABLE 26.1

Corresponding Frame, Phoneme, and Mouth Positions for this Exercise

Frame	Phoneme	Mouth Position
1	H	4
2	E	
3	L	7
4	L	
5	OH	5
6	OH	
7	OH	
8	OH	
9	OH	
10	OH	
11	OH	

Frame	Phoneme	Mouth Position
12	OH	6
13	OH	
14	OH	
15	OH	
16	OH	
17	OH	
18		
19		
20		
21		
22		
23		
24		
25		
26	H	4
27	H	
28	OW	5
29	OW	6
30	OW	
31	AH	3
32	AH	
33	AH	
34	Y	6
35	OO	
36	OO	
37	OO	
38	OO	
39	OO	

After the track is read, it is just a matter of copying the appropriate keys to the appropriate places in the timeline.

1. The *H* and the *E* sounds are really one vocalization. This can be best represented by mouth position D.

2. Next, you have the *L* sound at frame 3. Again, copy the appropriate keys for position 7 to frame 3.

3. Finally, the *OH* sound. Because this sound is fairly long, it is probably best to close down the mouth from position 5 to position 6 over the course of the sound.

As you can see, it is really just a matter of placing the keyframes at the right position on the timeline. Go through the rest of the dialogue and finish animating the mouth positions.

In Practice: Facial Animation and Lip Sync

- **Surface tools/Linked XForms.** Surface tools enables you to construct a simple surface with a few vertices, controlled by Linked XForms. This method produces a huge stack, however, which can become memory intensive. Keeping the geometry as light and as efficient as possible prevents the memory hit from becoming too large.

- **Morphing.** The facial poses required for a good morph need to be modeled from the same basic head so that vertex order is maintained. One way of manipulating the morph targets is by using bones, Linked XForms, or any of the other methods as modeling tools. The models created can then be reworked with additional tools to get a perfectly smooth surface.

- **Eyes.** It cannot be stressed enough how important the eyes are to facial expression. This is one of the major spots where animation can fall flat. Characters should blink every few seconds, and the position of the lids and brows should change as the mood changes.

- **Creating a library of poses.** Track View does not have any way of identifying which frame number of the library contains which facial animation pose. To help keep track of the poses in your library, it might be a good idea to render out the frames containing the library to a small AVI file and insert the frame numbers. That way, you can scrub through the AVI from within MAX and find the pose you want, simply by indexing the frame number.

Part VIII

ANIMATING THE ENVIRONMENT

IMAGE CREATED BY ERIC GREENLIEF

Chapter 27

by Eric Greenlief

ANIMATING CAMERAS

In today's world, people are used to seeing through the eye of a camera. Television, movie theaters, and VCRs have become everyday elements of peoples' lives. Because of this, people are very aware of how their "electronic eye on the world" should behave. The capability to animate cameras in 3D Studio MAX enables production of animations to have the look and feel audiences expect.

As an animator, you have the ability to involve the audience through camera motion. Viewers want to feel as though they are participating. How do you accomplish this? You must uphold the suspension of disbelief. That is, do not allow the audience to realize they are watching still images moving by at 30 frames per second on a flat screen. Create your animation so that they believe they are looking at this other world directly.

One element of 3DS MAX that gives you the capability to suspend disbelief is camera animation. It gives you capabilities that can make a director of photography or a cinematographer of any major movie jealous. These tools enable you to increase the professionalism of your animations enormously. This chapter covers how to achieve success in camera animation, including examples and details on the following topics:

- Traditional film camera techniques and history

- Creating an architectural walkthrough

- Camera work for a moving character

- Special camera motion styles

- Creating camera special effects

Traditional Film Cameras

Virtually any film or television show you have seen has been produced by a professional, experienced staff. One of the primary and integral people involved in the production of films is the cinematographer. The cinematographer is responsible for setting the camera shot and deciding what movement is necessary to tell the story. Cinematographers have typically been trained in film school, studied camera motion, and worked around film for many years before being given the responsibility of capturing the film sequences that you take for granted.

As a CG animator operating a "virtual camera," you have probably not been trained in film school, studied camera motion, or even been on the set of a film in production. But you are suddenly given the same responsibility as the cinematographer—to involve the audience in the scene through the use of a camera. Camera placement and movement is an art that is not easily mastered and should be studied and practiced. All the methods of cinematography that are taught in film school are also valid in CG animation. If possible, take some classes in filmmaking and study the ways of the master cinematographers and directors.

Computer animation often suffers from the obtrusiveness of the camera. This can happen when the freedom of using a virtual camera in a virtual world tempts the animator to get away from the constraints a real-world camera operator faces. When you push the envelope of what is expected, whether it is by moving through a scene at supernatural speed or by being able to fly above, below, and through anything, the audience is more likely to notice the camera work rather than the message of the work itself.

You can avoid the obtrusive camera by using it in ways that people understand. Nearly everyone in today's world has viewed thousands of hours of moving pictures on television and in theaters. Mimicking real-world camera techniques in computer animation gives viewers visual cues they already understand.

One characteristic of computer-generated animation, for example, is the machine-driven precision of the virtual camera. This precision can make the presence of the camera obvious. Computer-animated camera moves often tend to be very uniform in pacing and direction. Working to simulate a human camera operator adds a quality to the animation that brings it closer to the type of camera work people are used to seeing.

A good way to learn about refined camera work is to step back and take an objective look at motion picture and television footage. Ignore the content and focus on what the camera actually is doing. Try turning down the sound while watching TV and analyzing what you see. You are likely to be surprised by the complexity.

The following elements are what cinematographers must consider when recording moving images:

- Field of view
- Transitions
- Camera angle
- Camera moves
- Panning
- Dolly shot
- Crane shot
- Lenses

Field of View

Field of view is the angle described by an imaginary cone, the vertex of which is at the camera's location. This angle is determined by the focal length of the lens being used.

Short focal length lenses (28mm or 35mm on a 35mm SLR) give a very wide angle of view. Objects in the scene tend to appear far apart from one another. Something appearing on the horizon is nearly invisible, although an object near the camera looks huge. If you take a close-up portrait of someone with a wide angle lens, he or she will appear to have a huge nose and tiny ears. See figure 27.1 for an example of different lens sizes.

FIGURE 27.1

The same scene shot with 20, 50, and 200mm lenses.

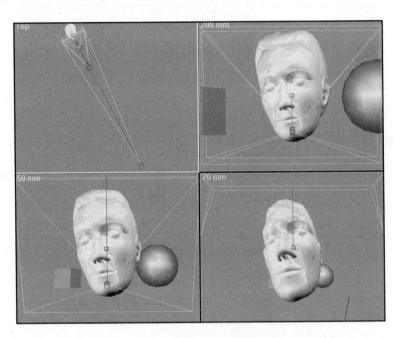

Wide angles of view are useful for showing many objects in a scene simultaneously, for establishing shots of buildings and other large subjects, for building interiors, and to show emphasis by exaggerating perspective.

Medium focal length lenses ("normal" or 50mm on a 35mm SLR) cover a moderate angle of view. The perspective in the resulting display seems to be about what people "normally" perceive with their own vision. The spatial relationships of objects in the scene look normal.

Long focal length, or telephoto, lenses (135mm to 500mm on a 35mm SLR) cover narrow angles of view. Because only objects at the very center of a scene fill the frame, those objects appear to be very close to the camera. Spacing of objects in the scene appears to be compressed.

Narrow angles of view are useful when you want to show objects both near to and far from the camera in the same shot, or when you just cannot get close enough to the object to view it with a normal or wide-angle lens.

Because the computer camera can go anywhere and do anything, you won't need a long focal length to get near something, but because people are used to seeing shots using long lenses, you may want to use them anyway. Refer to table 27.1 for standard lens lengths.

TABLE 27.1

Standard Lens Lengths, FOV, and Names

Lens	Field of View	Type of Lens
15mm	115.0°	Extreme wide-angle
20mm	94.29°	Very wide-angle
28mm	76.36°	Wide-angle
35mm	63.0°	Moderate wide-angle
50mm	46.0°	Normal
85mm	28.0°	Moderate long/portrait
135mm	18.0°	Long
200mm	12.0°	Very long

NOTE

In 3DS MAX R1.0, as well as 3DS DOS, the method used to calculate FOV is different from real-world lenses. In these programs, the FOV is measured along the *width* of the frame. If you are using these programs and attempting to match the angle of view between your computer-generated images and live-action scenes, it is always best to refer to the focal length of the lens instead of the FOV.

In 3DS MAX R1.1 and later, as well as real-world lenses, the FOV is measured *diagonally* across the frame. This eliminates the discrepancy between the CG lenses and real-world lenses concerning FOV.

When you observe a scene on film or television, you will notice that it consists of a series of shots, each made from a different perspective, joined together. Even though the shots are distinct and separate, the way they are joined makes each sequence appear seamless. This joining of the individual scenes is accomplished through a technique known as *transitions*.

Table 27.2 shows the basic types of shots and their uses.

TABLE 27.2

Standard Camera Shots and Their Traditional Uses

Shot Name	Visual Composition	Use
Extreme Long Shot	Characters small in frame, all or major part of buildings appear.	Establish physical context of action. Show landscape, architectural exteriors.
Long Shot	All or nearly all of a standing person shows. Large parts, but not all, of a building show.	Show large scale action (athletics, and so on). Show whole groups of people. Display large architectural details.
Medium Shot	Character shown from waist up. Medium size architectural details show.	Face plays important role. Two or three people shown in conversation. Moderate sized architectural detail.
Close-up	Head and neck of character shown. Small architectural details. Objects about the size of a desktop computer fill the frame.	Focus on one character. Facial expression very important. Small architectural details.
Extreme Close-up	Frame filled with just part of a character's face. Very small objects fill the frame.	Show small objects entirely. Very small architectural details. Emphasize facial features in character.

Transitions

Effective transitions are an art form and some gesture to that fact should be made. In a cross-fade, for example, the editor often tries to align the compositions in such a way that the fade is not overly abrupt (looking for a strong vertical contrast, and so on).

The transition from one camera to another determines the overall effect of an edited sequence. Again, as a CG animator, you are taking the place of someone on a professional film crew. This time it is the editor. And again, film editors have typically been through film school to study the art of filmmaking. One of the techniques editors learn is to focus on a specific element that is consistent between the two shots. This element is often a physical object in the scene, such as a door. Imagine approaching the outside of a door, then seeing the inside of the door in the next shot.

The focus element, however, does not have to be an object. It can just as effectively be a compositional element, such as a specific motion, color, direction (such as looking down a long row of starkly vertical telephone poles, then transitioning to a low shot in a cornfield looking down a row of tall corn stalks), and even contrast or balance. Remember, filmmaking is an art, and the artistic relationship between shots must be taken into consideration to achieve an effective transition.

The easiest transition in traditional filmmaking, as well as computer animation, is a straight cut. A straight cut is an abrupt transition between shots. It is the most common edit and, depending on the nature of the adjacent shots, can either be nearly unnoticeable or very obvious.

Another family of transitions depends on an effect called *fade*, in which the overall value of the scene increases or decreases until the entire frame is just one color. When one scene fades out as another fades in, the result is a *dissolve*.

Generally, fades from or to a black frame indicate the beginning or end of a sequence. It is appropriate to fade out and then fade in again when two sequences are different in location or time. Fades in animated sequences fill much the same purpose as chapter divisions in writing. A fade is accomplished in 3DS MAX with a fade image filter event in Video Post.

Dissolves, in which one scene fades out while the next fades in so that the images overlap, most often indicate passage of time. In an animated walkthrough of a building, for example, you may choose to compress part of the journey by dissolving from a shot at the base of a long staircase to a shot of the room at the top of the stairs. The dissolve can be accomplished in 3DS MAX through Video Post using a cross fade transition image filter event.

There are other transitions in which a scene *wipes* across the frame, displacing the previous scene. These wipes can move in any direction or start in the center or edges of a frame and move out or in. Wipes call attention to themselves and are best used conservatively when necessary for the telling of your story. An example of a wipe would be to show the passage of time. Imagine the exterior of a country barn during the day. A wipe begins at the right side of the screen to reveal the same shot, but this view is at night. Wipes are accomplished in Video Post using a simple wipe image filter event. To achieve more complex wipes, you can use image alpha or pseudo alpha filter event, and animate a bitmap in whatever wipe you want.

Another transition effect is the *swish pan*, in which the camera suddenly pans (rotates horizontally on its axis) so fast that the image becomes a blur. This is cut into another swish pan at the beginning of the next shot. The effect is of the camera jumping a great distance instantaneously, as if to say, "Meanwhile, back at the ranch...." A swish pan can be accomplished with the combination of scene motion blur and video post.

Camera Angle

Determining the point of view of the camera is very important in setting up scenes in an animation. Years of exposure to film and television have conditioned viewers to interpret the camera's "eye level" as conveying meaning.

Generally, viewers expect the camera to show a level horizon. If the camera is rolled sideways from the horizontal, thus tilting the horizon—as was often done in the 1960s TV series *Batman*—viewers expect something sinister to happen.

In terms of the camera's height above ground level and its angle in relation to the ground, expectations reflect real life. A "bird's eye" or "worm's eye" view is not part of a viewer's natural experience, and so draws attention to itself. These "unnatural" views are appropriate if the effect matches the message. When the camera is outside the normal range of experience, however, it may detract from the content of the animation. The ease of placing a virtual camera anywhere often leads to excessive use of inappropriate camera angles in computer animations.

It is good practice to observe existing footage and try to determine how far above ground level the camera is, and then use that information when placing cameras for animated scenes. When surveying a scene in a wide-angle shot, the camera's lens is usually where your eyes would be if you were sitting in a comfortable lawn chair. In close-ups of characters, males are usually shown from just below eye level, females from just above.

NOTE

Placing a camera at eye level of a standing person actually looks too high under most circumstances. You should determine whether placing your camera above or below the subject is appropriate in each situation.

Camera Moves

Not long after the invention of motion picture cameras, several basic moves evolved, forming the backbone of camera movement technique today. The same techniques apply to the use of virtual cameras in computer animation. You are by no means restricted to these basic moves because cameras are not constrained by time and space. Knowing real-world camera techniques, however, is essential because audiences have learned to read moving images through these basic moves.

The fundamental moves are as follows:

- Pan
- Tilt
- Dolly
- Track
- Crane

All these moves create motion by moving the camera itself. Pan and tilt are rotations around the camera's axis. The others are translations of the camera's location in space. Another category of moves involves changing the focal length of the camera lens during a shoot. It is not really a move, however, in that the camera remains stationary. A move is simulated because the changing angle of view makes objects appear to move closer to or farther away from the screen.

Panning and Tilting

Panning is used to follow a moving object or character, to show more than can fit into the frame at one time (such as when panning across a landscape), and as a transition between one camera position and another.

Inexperienced camera operators often make the mistake of panning too fast. You have probably seen home videos that cause motion sickness. When looking from one thing to another, you are panning with your eyes. Panning a camera as fast as you move your eyes just does not work.

Video is played at 30 frames per second. Computer animation is often played back at slower speeds, such as 15 or even 8 frames per second. Panning too quickly causes the difference between one frame and the next to be so great that the illusion of motion is broken. In cinematography, that effect is called *strobing*. In computer animation, it can also be referred to as *tearing*.

There are two ways of dealing with strobing in computer animation. One is to make certain that pans are not too fast. The following table gives some safe pan speeds for various conditions. Again, observe film and television footage to see just how slow most pan moves are. Refer to table 27.3 for recommended pan speeds.

TABLE 27.3

Number of Frames Needed for a 45° Pan

Type	15 fps	24 fps	30 fps
Quick turn	11	18	22
Comfortable turn	15	24	30
Casual turn	33	54	66

Another way of correcting strobing is to use motion blur when rendering. Two kinds of motion blur are available in 3DS MAX: scene and object. *Scene* motion blur shares information between frames. Most of the information comes from the current frame, but some is from the previous and following frames. The effect is to have less difference between frames, expanding the acceptable limits of camera motion. *Object* motion blur produces motion blur for individual objects in a scene, not the entire scene itself like scene motion blur. For this reason, it is not used to prevent strobing.

In addition to preventing strobing, motion blur allows the computer animator to simulate the effects of real-world cameras. In the real world, the shutter of the camera is open for a specific amount of time. If, during the time the shutter is open, the camera moves quickly, the scene moves a significant distance in relation to the camera, and appears to blur, or streak. Because virtual cameras do not have a shutter to open and close, this streaking or blurring does not occur automatically. Instead, you must explicitly tell the camera to add motion blur. In 3DS MAX, scene motion blur is done in Video Post. This small extra step can be invaluable in simulating the realism of real-world cameras.

To see the unrealistic effects of not having motion blur, animate the rotation of a propeller on an airplane or the rotor of a helicopter at a very high speed. When you play the animation back, the propeller or rotor appears to jump around, but does not look like it is rotating. Apply object motion blur to the propeller or rotor and re-render. With motion blur, you get a much more realistic motion that simulates the mechanics of a real camera. Although this example uses object motion blur, the concept is exactly the same for scene motion blur.

NOTE

One of the other ways to simulate real-world optics in a computer-generated scene is with depth of field. Depth of field is covered later in this chapter.

Tilting is functionally similar to panning, except that the camera rotates vertically. The same precautions should be followed when tilting as when panning.

Dolly and Tracking Shots

A *dolly* is a small wheeled vehicle used to move a motion picture camera and its operators about in a scene. It is piloted by a *dolly grip* whose job is to smoothly start and stop the dolly and synchronize its motion with the pans and tilts of the camera operator. When you design camera paths, you take on the role of dolly grip. The most challenging part of the job is achieving smooth, subtle starts and stops. As a virtual dolly grip, you need to re-create the human touch in your camera paths.

When the camera moves in and out of a scene (generally on the same axis as the lens), it is referred to as a *dolly move*. When the move is perpendicular to the lens axis, it is called a *tracking shot*. The same precautions must be observed when tracking as when panning. Because you do not have the ability to get inside your virtual scene, you do not have a very good frame of reference to judge the speed at which you should dolly your camera. The speed of dolly and tracking moves are usually based upon how fast a person moves. Refer to tables 27.4 and 27.5 for recommended speed tables.

TABLE 27.4

Pedestrian Gaits

Type	Miles per Hour	Feet per Second	Inches per Second
Casual stroll	1.5–2.0	2.2–3.0	26–36
Average walk	2.5–3.5	3.6–5.0	43–60
Brisk walk	4–5	6–8	72–96
Average jog	6–8	9–12	108–144
Average run	8–10	12–15	144–180
All out sprint	12–16	18–24	216–288

TABLE 27.5

Number of Frames Needed to Move 10 Feet

Type	15 fps	24 fps	30 fps
Casual stroll	50–68	80–109	100–136
Average walk	30–42	48–67	60–83
Brisk walk	19–25	30–40	38–50
Average jog	12–17	20–27	25–33
Average run	10–12	16–20	20–25
All out sprint	6–8	10–13	13–17

Crane Shot

When the camera moves up or down, the shot is traditionally called a *crane shot*. It may also be referred to as a *boom shot*. Observe the same timing and rendering practices with a crane shot as you would with a tilt.

Zoom Lenses

The invention of zoom (variable focal length) lenses made it possible for camera "moves" to be made without actually moving the camera. Orthodox cinematographers use the zoom lens only to change the angle of view between shots and prefer to move the camera itself when a move is called for. (Home videographers love to zoom in and out while making fast pans and tilts to enhance the nauseating effect.)

It is as easy (or easier) to move the camera itself rather than to zoom when creating a computer animation. The zoom, however, can be a very effective tool. Because people are accustomed to seeing zoom effects in films and on television, you can use it to accomplish the same effects in computer space. On the surface, zooming appears to move the camera closer to or farther from objects in the scene. In reality, the angle of view is changing, so perceived spatial relationships also change.

The "Vertigo" Effect

Vertigo is a technique made famous in the Alfred Hitchcock film of the same name. It takes advantage of the zoom lens's capability to change the angle of view dynamically during a shot.

In this effect, the subject moves toward or away from the camera (or the camera moves and the subject is stationary). As the distance between the two changes, the zoom lens' focal length is changed to keep the size of the subject constant in relation to the frame. The effect is that the background appears to "zoom" in or out while the subject stays the same size.

Achieving vertigo in 3DS MAX has been a very tricky proposition. With the release of 3D Studio MAX 1.2, however, the process became much simpler. The 1.2 upgrade contains two MAX sample files that demonstrate how to achieve vertigo. For you to be able to complete the next exercise, you must have at least version 1.2 installed. This upgrade can be found on the Kinetix web site at `www.ktx.com`. If you need to install the upgrade, be certain to read the readme file that comes with it.

VERTIGO

1. Open the vertigo.max file installed by the 1.2 upgrade (you can find it on the accompanying CD-ROM).

2. Select camera01 and open Assign Controller in the Motion Control panel.

3. Right-click on the Position Expression Controller and select Properties. This expression controller contains the formula for creating the vertigo effect. Save this expression as **Vertigo.XPR**.

TIP

Choose Summary Info from the File menu to read more information about this sample file.

4. Load vertigo2.max from the accompanying CD.

5. Create a target camera as shown in figure 27.2. Change the camera lens to 85mm.

FIGURE 27.2
The position of camera
for the vertigo effect.

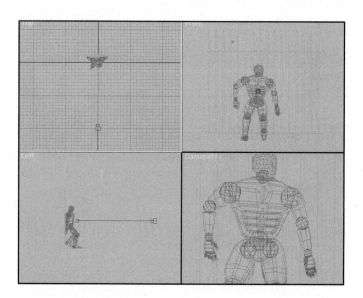

6. Link the camera to its target.

7. Turn on the Animate button and move to frame 150. Change the lens length to 24mm. Turn off the Animate button.

8. Open Track View, copy the FOV key at frame 0 to frame 30, and change the Bézier tangent to slow in and slow out for each of the three keys.

9. Assign a Position Expression Controller to the camera. Select and right-click on the controller and choose Properties. Load the vertigo.xpr created in step 3.

10. Select W in the Scalars box and assign it a constant of 200.

11. Select FOV in the Scalars box, click on Assign to Controller. Expand the tracks if necessary and select the FOV: Bézier Float under Camera01. Close the Expression Controller box.

12. Unlink the camera from its target. Move to frame 150. With the Animate button off, move the target directly upward until you can see the top of the fence in the Camera viewport.

NOTE

The Expression Controller evaluated the position of the camera while it was linked to the target. During this evaluation, the motion of the camera was set. After the motion of the camera is set, you can unlink the camera and move the target to a position where the vertigo is enhanced by the viewer seeing the top of the fence come into view. This approach enables you to have the camera move in a horizontal line, while not moving directly toward the target.

13. Play the animation in the Camera viewport and render the animation to a flic or AVI.

The vertigo.avi included on the accompanying CD shows the completed animation for this exercise.

Architectural Walkthrough

Architectural walkthroughs have been a major selling point for computer animation from the beginning. Imagine the possibility of being able to walk through your dream home before it has been built. Imagine choosing the color of the carpet, walls, all the furniture, and experiencing them in your home before the plans are even finalized. Unfortunately, this has hardly become the norm for building a new home, or even for expensive commercial buildings. As an animator, you know all the time and effort that goes into creating an architectural animation on the computer. You also know how much more time and effort goes into creating an environment that enables the audience to believe that what they are seeing is real.

After the architectural model has been built, materials applied, and lighting created, your next job is to put the audience into the scene. The camera enables the audience to believe they are moving through the building. They are observers taking part in the animation.

All too often, camera motion in walkthroughs has the objective of showing off everything that the animator has built in one lengthy shot. The animator chooses specific points of interest in the building, chooses a point outside the building to enter from, and then proceeds to draw a spline path that connects all these points. The results are similar to what early movie makers attempted before the subtleties of editing were discovered. A brilliant 3D model that may have taken weeks or months of work is cheapened by unrefined camera work.

A good example of consistently bad camera moves is in the show *Cops*. Each time the camera is inside the car and the police are chasing a vehicle, the camera typically points directly out of the front of the car. How many times is the suspect's car lost from the frame, and you are disoriented because you can't see the car? Unfortunately, this is the exact same motion that occurs when the camera and target are put on the same path thoughout the building with no concern for the composition of the scene.

As you work through the next exercises, and as you are composing your architectural animations, keep the following points in mind:

- Analyze sequences created by professional cinematographers for ideas on timing, composition, camera motion, and transitions.

- Don't waste time getting from one point of interest to another. Use transitions to eliminate boring or insignificant material.

- Avoid moves that draw attention to the camera at the expense of the subject.

- Compose and evaluate your camera moves by using the camera viewport as a viewfinder, not by looking at the top view of the floor plan.

- Avoid camera moves that would not be possible with traditional cameras. Don't do the "death dive" over a railing just to get to the next floor.

- Give the audience time to observe significant objects and points of interest, then move on.

- Do not move the camera too quickly just because you want to save time rendering or animating. Move at a comfortable pace.

TIP

Use a stopwatch to time yourself walking through a building or other interesting space to give yourself a feeling for how long it should take for certain sequences in a walkthrough. A stopwatch is also useful when examining live-action film sequences and transitions.

NOTE

When you visit a space, you remember the important features of that space. You don't waste memory on the uninteresting walks down the hall or across the parking lot. As an animator, you are responsible for the same selective memory when creating a walkthrough.

Creating the Establishing Shot

The first step in many film sequences is to create an establishing shot. The *establishing shot* shows the exterior of a building or area in which the action will be taking place. The establishing shot serves many purposes, including the following:

- It associates the building with the environment.

- It enables the viewer to identify with the character of the building. Architects strive to achieve harmony between the interior and exterior of a building. This harmony is essential to the building's character. The establishing shot serves as the audience's introduction to the building.

- It gives the audience a frame of reference to begin their journey. After experiencing the introduction, they feel more comfortable exploring the interior of the building. The audience understands where their journey will be taking place.

THE ESTABLISHING AND OPENING SHOTS

1. Load church-e.max from the accompanying CD. The scene consists of the exterior of a church in a simulated environment.

2. Choose Configure Paths from the File menu. Click on the Bitmaps tab and add the path to the CD Maps directory. You may optionally copy the necessary map files to your local hard drive.

3. Create a target camera at the position and angle shown in figure 27.3. Name the camera **es-cam1**. While still in the Create panel, change the lens length to 24mm.

FIGURE 27.3

The placement of camera es-cam1.

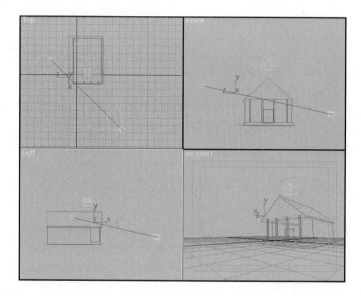

TIP

In a walkthrough, you generally want to create a camera that sees more than the standard 48° seen by the human eye. This can help simulate peripheral vision, and also enable the audience to feel more involved in the animation.

4. Activate the Perspective viewport and press C to change the view to the current Camera view.

NOTE

It is important to adjust the camera position and rotation while observing the Camera viewport. This is the "viewfinder" that enables you to see what the camera sees. Do not simply place the camera in the Top viewport and aim it at something you want to show. Throughout this chapter, pay particular attention to what is shown in the Camera viewport, and try to match the composition shown in the figures.

5. Move to frame 90. Use the Motion Control panel to create a position key for the camera and target. Change the Bézier tangents to slow in and slow out for the target and camera. This setting enables the camera to be motionless for the first 90 frames, enabling the audience to become stable and comfortable in the shot before moving.

6. Turn on the Animate button, and change to frame 360. Move the camera and target to match figure 27.4. After you have established the camera, turn off the Animate button.

FIGURE 27.4

Position of es-cam1 at frame 360.

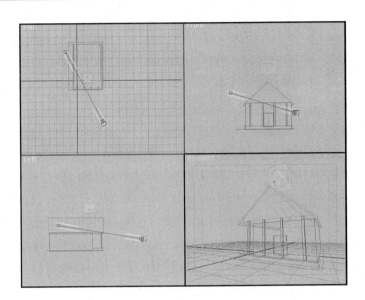

NOTE

It is important to keep the audience moving slowly throughout the animation, avoiding any sudden movements that might detract from the suspension of disbelief. Keep in mind that you are taking the audience on a pleasant trip, not a roller coaster ride.

You do not need to show the entire building at this point. The motion in the camera is needed only to enhance the three-dimensionality of the scene and make it come alive to the audience.

TIP ————————————————————————————————

If you need to show the entire exterior, create a second animation that follows the walkthrough. A good technique is to introduce facts about the building in this second animation. Facts could include square feet, number of rooms, interior and exterior finishes, and so on. It will also enable you to create a more technically oriented animation using simpler geometry that can release you from the necessity of creating a fully realistic 360° environment.

Exterior Detail Shot

The next shot enables you to transition from the initial exterior establishing shot to the inside of the building. You should not just appear inside the building. Each camera shot you create must be a logical progression from the previous one. This progression is called a *transition*. Often, a director focuses on a particular object at the end of a camera shot. This object is then seen at the beginning of the next camera shot, but from a different perspective, enabling the audience to remain oriented throughout the sequence.

For the transition to the interior of a building, it is common to use the main entrance as the transition focus area. Again, you want to add motion to the scene as you did with the last camera. The motion in this case should progress toward the entrance to communicate the feeling of entering the building. After this, the audience knows the next logical place to be is inside.

THE EXTERIOR DETAIL SHOT

1. Continue from the previous exercise. Create a free camera at the position and angle shown in figure 27.5. Name the camera **es-cam2**. While still in the Create panel, change the lens length to 24mm and change the Camera viewport to this camera.

2. Move to frame 315 and create a position and rotation key.

TIP ————————————————————————————————

When using multiple cameras in a scene, animate them at the same time coordinates at which they will be presented in the final animation. Resist the temptation to create all the camera motions at the beginning of the scene. This enables you to compose the timing of your scene more logically, without having to remember exactly how many frames and in what order each camera is to be shown. This also keeps the frame numbers correct when rendering to individual files in the final rendering. Create a Note track in the Track Editor for each camera that shows exactly in which frames this camera will be rendered. Place the note key at the first frame in which the camera will be rendered.

FIGURE 27.5
The position of camera es-cam2.

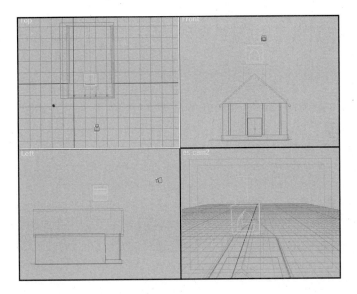

3. Turn on the Animate button and change to frame 530. Move and rotate the camera to match figure 27.6. After you have established the camera, turn off the Animate button.

FIGURE 27.6
The position of es-cam2 at frame 530.

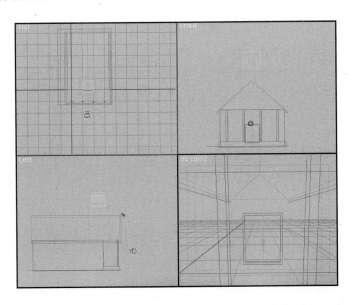

It is important to determine at this point what kind of Video Post transition will be made between cameras. Will it be a fade to/fade from black, or a dissolve from one camera to another? The length of the transition needs to be incorporated into the beginning and ending of each camera move so that the motion does not stop.

For the transition between es-cam1 and es-cam2, you have a 1.5 second (45 frame) dissolve from one camera to the other. In other types of animation, this transition time might be too long, but in the case of an architectural walkthrough, you want to ease the audience from one camera to the other and keep them moving comfortably.

For the transition between es-cam2 and the first interior camera, have the audience pause at the entrance, fade to black, and then fade from black to a motionless camera. This transition helps the audience relate more easily to the change from interior to exterior.

4. Change the in position tangent for the camera to slow in at frame 530.

5. Save your MAX file.

Creating the Interior Shot

Before you begin creating cameras for the interior shots, take a few moments to preview the cameras you have animated and save them as flic files. Keep these files so that they can be examined later as well.

The interior of the chapel is created by using a separate MAX file. Using separate files can help you in the following ways:

- Lowers polygon count for rendering because you do not have exterior geometry for interior shots, and interior geometry for exterior shots.

- There are fewer objects to sort through in object lists.

- The file size is smaller and more manageable.

WARNING

If changes are made to one file that will affect the other, you must be certain to change both files simultaneously. This can be done easily by making the changes in one file, temporarily merging it into the other, making changes, and then deleting the objects from the merged file.

THE INTERIOR SHOT

1. Load the file church-i.max from the CD. This scene consists of the interior of the church.

2. Create a free camera at the position and angle shown in figure 27.7. Name the camera **int-cam01**. While still in the Create panel, change the lens length to 24mm and change the Camera viewport to this camera.

FIGURE 27.7

The position of camera int-cam01.

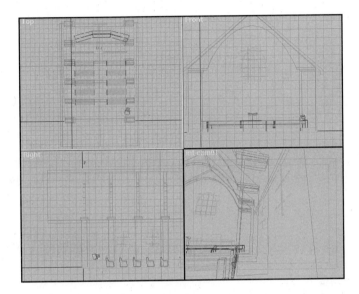

3. Turn on the Animate button, and change to frame 305. Move and rotate the camera to match figure 27.8.

The transition between the three interior cameras uses a 1.5 second (45 frame) moving dissolve. This overlap needs to be incorporated into the timing of the cameras as it was in the establishing shots. Also keep in mind that during the dissolve, neither of the camera views will be clearly visible.

Because the composition of each camera shot is critical to the success of the animation, be certain to compose the beginning and ending shots through the Camera viewport, and then adjust the path between them.

4. Select the camera and click on the Trajectories button in the Motion Control panel. At this point, you can see the path your camera will take.

5. Change the end time to 305 in the Spline Conversion section, and the samples to 2. Click on the Convert To button.

FIGURE 27.8

Position of camera int-cam1 at frame 305.

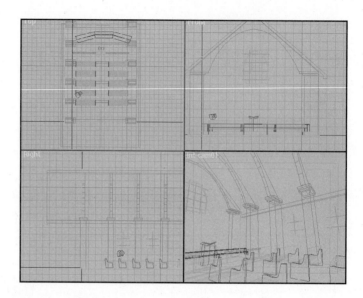

6. Access the Modify panel and select the spline just created. Change the name to **spline int-cam01** and add an Edit Spline modifier. Change the endpoints of the spline to Bézier and modify the spline to approximate the one shown in figure 27.9.

FIGURE 27.9

Shape of path spline for int-cam01 after modification.

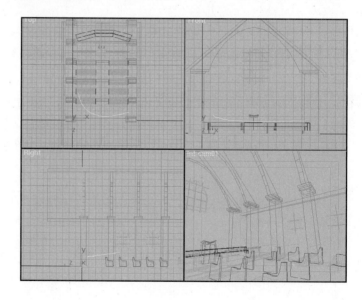

7. Select the camera and access the Motion Control panel.

8. Change the samples to 10 in the Spline Conversion section. Click on Convert From and select spline int-cam01.

9. Play the animation in the Camera view.

By using this technique, you can maneuver the camera path around walls, furniture, and other objects while still maintaining the beginning and ending frame composition. If necessary, add a few vertices to the spline. You may also adjust the timing of the camera by adjusting the start and end times in the Spline Conversion section of the Motion Control panel.

If you add vertices, keep in mind that the more vertices in the spline used for a path, the more radical the camera movement will tend to be. It will also become increasingly difficult to edit the spline and keep it smooth. Keep the fewest possible number of vertices in the spline to ensure smooth motion.

TIP

If you need to edit the path more, do not convert the camera path to the spline again. Simply edit the existing spline and then convert the camera trajectory from that spline.

Because camera timing is critical, try to view the animation in as close to real time as possible with a minimum of strobing. To aid in this, keep the camera view set to wireframe. If needed, you can also hide unnecessary objects and change the viewport to Box mode. You may also want to pause at this point and create a preview animation. To keep the animation close to real time, keep the resolution low. You are only evaluating camera motion, which can usually still be distinguished sufficiently at low resolution.

10. Create a free camera as shown in figure 27.10. Name the camera **int-cam02** and change the lens length as before. Change the Camera view to this camera.

NOTE

If one camera is selected from multiple cameras in the scene, and you change a viewport to a Camera view using the C shortcut, the view automatically changes to the currently selected camera. If you want to select a different camera, either deselect the camera and press C again, or select the desired camera by right-clicking on the viewport title.

FIGURE 27.10

The position of int-cam02.

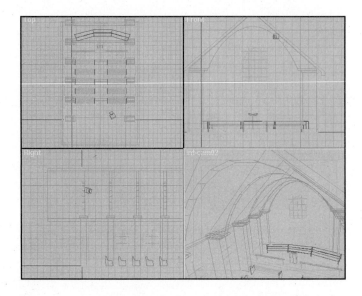

11. Move to frame 261 and create a position and rotation key for the camera. Activate the Animate button, move to frame 670, and modify the camera and camera path by using the technique shown earlier (see fig. 27.11).

FIGURE 27.11

The position of int-cam02 at frame 670 and its spline path.

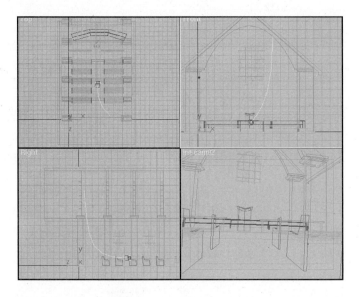

12. Create a preview for the camera.

Closing Shot

The closing camera shot can be the most important one. It is the last picture of the interior of the building that the audience will see. To aid in determining the final shot, think of the impression with which you want to leave the audience. You may choose to show a wide view of the lobby of the building, or the view of a beautiful sunset from the penthouse. Whatever you choose, be certain that you compose the last frame carefully. Use your knowledge of color, composition, balance, and so forth to help you.

After you have determined the last frame of the closing shot, use the animation of the camera to lead up to it. Swing the camera around the room to enable the audience to discover other interesting details. As they are focusing on the smaller details, they will soon discover the sunset out the window, and realize they have come to the end of their journey. As the camera comes to the end of its move, be certain to allow the audience to settle into their last glimpse by using a slow in on the last key, and then pause. After the audience has had a chance to enjoy the last frame, use a slow (45–60 frame) fade to black.

THE CLOSING SHOT

1. Create a free camera as shown in figure 27.12. Name the camera **int-cam03** and change the lens length as before. Change the Camera view to this camera.

FIGURE 27.12

Position of int-cam03.

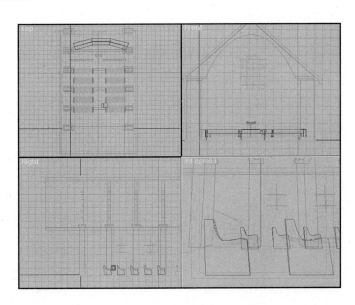

2. Create a rotation and position key on frame 626.

3. Move to frame 945, activate the Animate button, and modify the camera as shown in figure 27.13. Change the position Bézier tangent to slow in, the rotation TCB continuity to 0, and ease in to 25.

FIGURE 27.13

Position of int-cam03 at frame 945.

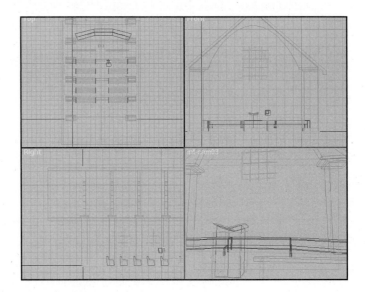

4. Preview the last camera for motion.

Previews

As you completed animating your cameras, you created a preview for each one. These previews can help you determine proper timing for your animation. They also enable you to determine whether the length of the entire animation is correct. To view your preview animations in sequence, it is best to use a viewer outside of 3D Studio MAX. This enables you to script your animations together and view them sequentially. One of the standard viewers, AAPlay for Windows, is available at the Kinetix web site (www.ktx.com).

Unfortunately these previews do not enable you to examine the fades and dissolves that are important to the animation just completed. To accomplish this, use Video Post. When creating these files, keep the resolution as small as needed to keep the animation playing near real time. If you are using two separate MAX files for your animation, and the transition between them is a fade to/from black, just script them together in your animation player. If the transition is a cross fade (dissolve), render the first MAX file out to individual files rather than a flic, and then add them as an Image Input event in the second file's Video Post.

TIP

Using separate image files rather than flics for the individual camera shots makes the creation of the final rendering run more quickly because Video Post must examine each preceding frame to obtain all the color information for a frame in the middle of a flic. This is not necessary when individual image files are used.

A copy of the Video Post VPX file is included on the CD for your reference. You may load this file while in Video Post to render your preview animation.

NOTE

AVIs could also be used for your preview. AVIs tend to have a larger number of colors, many different possible codecs, and drop frames to keep the animation playing at the desired speed. They also tend to be more portable to other systems because they are more popular at this time.

Flics are limited to 256 colors and are compressed with a delta compression scheme. They play back every frame and, if necessary, slow the frame rate of the animation to accomplish this. Although there are fewer colors when using a flic, as long as the resolution is kept low, flic playback is generally superior to AVI playback.

Camera Animation for Characters

Study almost any movie or television sequence showing people and you will see the basic camera techniques involved for animating characters. Most sequences can be built from basic shots: long, medium, and close-up.

The "long" or full shot, shows all or most of the character's body. This is used to show the context in which the character appears, or to show large body actions such as running or tumbling. In a full shot, the body is the most important visual element of the character (see fig. 27.14).

When framing a character in full shot, try to avoid centering in the frame. Use the "rule of thirds" to place the character on one of the two axes that divide the frame in thirds. When tracking or panning with a character in full shot, make certain that there is plenty of "nose room" between the character and the edge of the frame he is facing.

A "medium" shot generally shows a character from the waist up. It shows more facial expression. Most conversations in which both speakers appear together in one frame are shot in medium format. The same rules apply regarding nose room. If a character in a medium shot is facing the side of the frame, allow more space on that side of the frame (see fig. 27.15).

A "close-up" focuses on the character's face. A medium close-up shows the head and neck, where an extreme close-up closes in on the face itself and lets hair and so on go out of frame. It is especially important in close-ups to make certain that the framing is comfortable. Keep an eye on that nose room (see fig. 27.16).

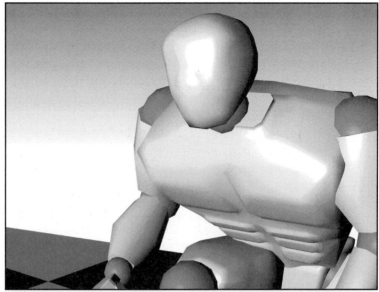

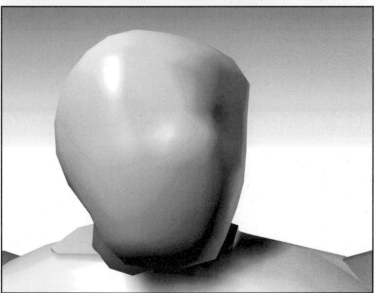

Real people have a very difficult time sitting or standing still—only television news anchors have mastered the technique. Most people also move their hands and body a great deal to add meaning to verbal communication. One of the challenges a real-world camera operator faces is maintaining a pleasing composition in a frame in which the subject is constantly moving. A skillful operator "floats" with the person, always maintaining appropriate visual relationships in the frame. When studying live action footage, notice that the camera is very seldom locked down when a person appears in the frame. There are constant subtle moves. For computer animation to simulate real life effectively, the same techniques should be adopted. As a character moves from left to right, or turns and faces a different direction in the frame, adjust the framing to compensate.

Use the established live action camera techniques when animating characters, and thereby move your animation into the realm of "film grammar" your audience understands.

The following exercise shows you successful camera placement and animation for a moving character.

CAMERA PLACEMENT FOR A MOVING CHARACTER

1. Load robot.max from the CD.

Similar to the establishing shot of the walkthrough, you will have an establishing shot of your character. In this case, however, the character suddenly enters from above. You want to establish the audience's attention on the scene before the character enters.

2. Move to frame 50 and create a free camera as shown in figure 27.17. Change the lens length to 35mm.

The ominous shot is often used in establishing a character's attitude. See whether you recognize this shot from virtually any action movie you have seen. When you see this shot, you know something exciting is going to happen.

3. Create a dummy object and center it on the character's head using the Align button on the main toolbar. Name the dummy object **camera02**.

4. Move to frame 150 and create a target camera as shown in figure 27.18. Align the camera's target to the center of the dummy object. Use this camera for the active Camera view. Link the camera to the dummy object.

FIGURE 27.17

*Position of camera01
using frame 50 as a
reference frame.*

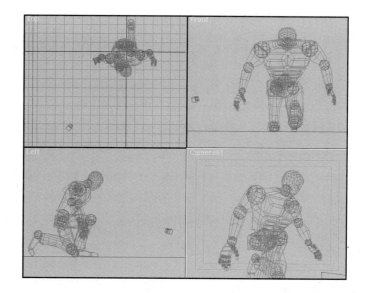

FIGURE 27.18

*The dummy object and
camera02 at frame
150.*

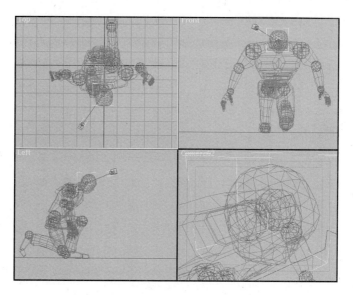

5. Select the dummy object and create a rotation key at frame 150. Move to frame 310, turn on the Animate button, and then rotate the dummy 67 degrees on its local Z axis. Change the continuity to 0 for both frames.

6. While still on frame 310, move the camera approximately 28 units straight down (see fig. 27.19). Turn the Animate button off.

FIGURE 27.19**

*Camera02 at frame
310 after dummy
rotation and camera
movement.*

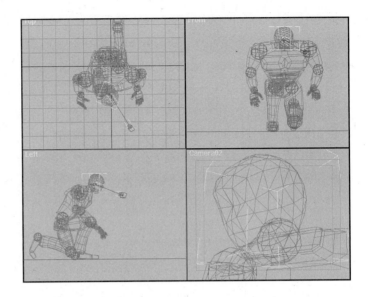

7. Change the camera's position controller to linear position.

8. Change to frame 505 and create a target camera as shown in figure 27.20. This is camera03.

FIGURE 27.20

*Camera03 at frame
505.*

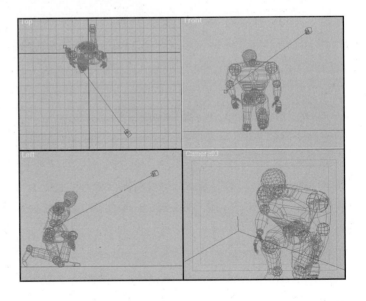

9. Change to frame 570 and create camera04, a target camera (see fig. 27.21). Create a position key at this frame for the target of camera04.

FIGURE 27.21

Camera04 at frame 570.

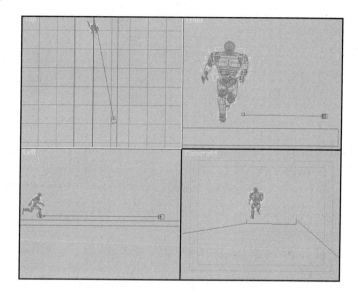

10. Turn on the Animate button and move to frame 600. Move camera04's target straight along the path of the robot so that the robot is approximately centered in the view. You will be modifying this key, so its exact location is not important now.

11. Change to frame 650 and move the camera's target to put the robot right of center in the view.

12. Turn off the Animate button and play the Camera viewport from frame 570 until the end. Determine whether the camera movement as the robot goes by will keep the robot sufficiently in the frame. The entire figure will not be in the frame; you are just looking at the timing of the movement. Do not allow the robot to move completely out of the frame at either side during the move. Also keep in mind the nose room principle mentioned earlier (see fig. 27.22).

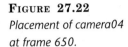

FIGURE 27.22

Placement of camera04 at frame 650.

Preview and Video Post

As with the last exercise, many cameras are being used, and they must be composited in Video Post. Unlike the walkthrough, however, this exercise is used to show action. Straight cuts from one camera to another on the same subject tend to raise the audience's excitement level, so you will not use any dissolves or fades except at the end.

Preview each camera for the frames shown in table 27.6. As before, save the individual files out and script them together to get an idea of the timing of the final rendered animation. After you have verified the timing and made any corrections, render to a flic or AVI.

TABLE 27.6

Video Post Setup for Robot

Camera	Beginning Frame	Ending Frame
camera01	0	120
camera02	121	505
camera03	506	560
camera04	561	690
camera04 fade out	660	690

"MTV" Camera Style

In computer animation work, you will likely be asked to generate material for use in what might be described as "MTV-style" footage. Music videos have developed a visual style related to their musical content and youth culture audience. This style has been around long enough to have spread well beyond just music videos.

The music video style is characterized by camera and editing techniques often just outside the boundaries of the normal and expected. Thus you find unusual camera angles, extreme field of view, unorthodox camera motion, and fast, sometimes jarring, cutting from one scene to another. This style has become a staple in television commercials and other non-music areas (for an excellent example, watch *Bill Nye the Science Guy* on your local Public Broadcasting Station).

The best way to adopt the music video style in your animations is to objectively observe the type of footage you are trying to emulate. Visualize how the camera was used, in terms of lens focal length, placement, motion, and so on, and decide what must be done in 3DS MAX to duplicate the effect. Most of the techniques needed can be derived from information and examples given in this chapter.

Shaky Cam

For many years, cinematographers have faced the challenge of keeping the camera steady while moving it through rough terrain. At first, this problem was overcome by building tracks, using cranes and cherry pickers, and using other engineered solutions that generally cost a great deal and chewed up a lot of time.

Of course, a camera operator could just grab the camera and run overland with it on her shoulder. The resulting images would have an unsteady, jerky action that we have come to associate with documentary and television news footage. The implication to the viewer when they see shaky camera images is that the footage is immediate, spontaneous, and somehow more "real" than carefully locked-down and smooth studio shots.

Even though a device was invented several years ago (the Steadicam) that can eliminate undesirable motion in hand-held shots, many contemporary directors and cinematographers deliberately hand-hold the camera to imply spontaneity. You see this most often in television commercials and music videos.

In the real world, achieving a steady image is not easy. In the computer realm, however, perfect steadiness is the default. You may want to use random camera motion to add a "documentary" effect to an animation, in which case you will need to corrupt that perfection with a virtual "shaky-cam."

The concept behind creating a shaky cam in 3DS MAX is fairly simple. You will assign a noise controller to the position controller of the camera (see "Earthquake!" later in the chapter).

One of the challenges is creating a shaky cam combined with live action footage. Luckily, this can also be solved easily in 3DS MAX. Film your live-action with a stationary camera. In your MAX scene, create a flat plane object or box in the background of the scene. Create a material for this object that includes the live-action footage as a diffuse map and adjust the mapping so it appears as a "movie screen" to project the live footage onto.

NOTE

The mapping can be accomplished best through a camera mapping plug-in. One is available on the Kinetix web site in the Yost Group "Fun Stuff" plug-ins.

This setup enables you to have the live footage appear as a background, similar to what you would accomplish in Video Post, but the camera movement is independent of the background. If you shake your computer camera in the scene, the "movie screen" is stationary and achieves the proper illusion. Another valuable benefit of this setup is that it allows scene motion blur to be applied to the virtual movie screen, and you can add motion blur to your live footage *after* it has been filmed!

Earthquake Cam

Another effect seen in film and TV is the "earthquake cam." This is where the camera shakes to simulate ground motion. This effect can be easily duplicated in 3DS MAX.

Earthquake!

1. Load earthqua.max from the CD.

2. Select camera01 and open the Motion Control panel. Apply a Position List Controller to camera01. A List Controller enables you to use multiple controllers on an object at the same time.

3. Apply a Noise Position Controller to the available controller slot in the Motion Control panel. The Noise Position Controller gives the camera a random position simulating the earth shaking.

4. Open Track View and expand the camera01 tracks. Select Noise position, right-click, and select Properties. This action opens the Noise Controller settings. Here you can control specifics about the randomness of the position.

5. In this camera effect, you want to have the camera move suddenly at the beginning. This is shown on the characteristic graph as a spike at the left side. You may scan through the seed possibilities to find a suitable graph. This exercise will be using seed 1.

6. Change the X, Y, and Z strength values to 20, and ramp out to 90. The ramp makes the camera motion settle down as time passes. Close the Noise Controller box.

7. Drag the Noise Position range bar to begin at 96 and end at 150. Minimize Track View.

Tip

Because there is no way to type in frame numbers to set the range for this kind of controller, it can be helpful to set the current frame to where you want the beginning or ending of the range. The current frame is represented by a thin vertical line in Track View and can help in the alignment of ranges.

Play the animation in the Camera viewport to see the effect. Play the animation in the Right viewport as well. Notice that the camera position in the Right viewport changes as the animation cycles to the beginning. Generally, you will want specific, predictable control of the camera position before and after the shaking. As you can see, the randomness of the Noise Controller placed the camera at a different position at the end of the shaking than at the beginning. The Position List Controller assigned earlier will enable you to compensate for this difference in position.

8. In the Motion Control Panel, change the Bézier Position Controller to Linear Position Controller.

9. Move to frame 96 and create a position key.

The dummy object around the camera has been aligned with the pivot point of the camera at its original position. This positioning enables you to realign the pivot point of the camera to the center of the dummy after the Noise Controller has placed it out of position.

10. Be certain that the camera is still selected, move to frame 150, and turn on the Animate button. Align the X, Y, and Z coordinates of the camera pivot point to the center of the dummy object by using the Align button on the main toolbar. Turn off the Animate button.

11. Hold your MAX file. You will be coming back to this point.

To make the effect a little more realistic, you will also want to add a little random rotation to the camera.

12. Open the Motion Control Panel, and assign a Rotation Noise Controller to the camera.

Notice that the camera has oriented its Local coordinate system to the World coordinate system and the camera is pointing at the ground. To avoid this, assign the Noise Rotation Controller to the dummy object, and then link the camera to the dummy.

13. Undo the Noise Rotation Controller or perform a fetch. Assign a Noise Rotation Controller to the dummy.

14. Open Track View, select the Noise Rotation, right-click, and select Properties. Set the seed to 22, the X, Y, and Z strength to 5.0, and ramp out to 40. Close the Noise Controller box.

15. Drag the range bar to begin at 96 and end at 150.

16. Link the camera to the dummy object and play the animation.

17. To add a little more to the effect, animate the camera to move and rotate as the ground ripple hits.

18. Render to a flic or AVI.

NOTE

You can also render the scene in Video Post and turn on Scene Motion Blur to increase the realism in the camera motion.

To view a version of the final animation with the final camera motion, play quake.avi from the CD.

Depth of Field

One of the problems faced by users of real-life camera optics is that depth of field is limited. When an object in the foreground of a shot is in focus, the background is out of focus. This characteristic is a problem in some circumstances, but it can also be very useful when trying to emphasize an element of the visual composition. Virtual cameras have unlimited depth of field. This leads to computer-generated images that are sharply focused from foreground to background.

You may want to introduce limited depth of field to re-create the "realism" people are used to seeing in film and television. Shallow depth of field enables you to isolate specific objects in a scene. You can also shift the plane of focus during a shot to move emphasis from one object to another. That effect was used to great advantage in *Jurassic Park* when the game warden is surprised by a velociraptor emerging from the undergrowth.

Included on the accompanying CD is a shareware version of a depth of field plug-in. Other excellent depth of field plug-ins are available on the market today. The two popular ones are Cebas' Real Lens Flare and Digimation's LenzFX MAX (not yet released at this writing). Each of them has specific advantages and features. The one included on the accompanying CD has the advantage of low price, while still creating a very realistic effect. At the time of this writing, however, it does not have the capability to animate the focus plane independently of geometry in the scene. The next exercise is designed to simulate this effect with the included plug-in.

TIP

Although this exercise is designed for a plug-in without an object-independent, animatable plane of focus, the same technique can be used to save large amounts of rendering time on plug-ins that do have this feature as well.

ANIMATING DEPTH OF FIELD

1. Install the plug-in and read the accompanying documentation.

2. Load the demoscen2.max from the plug-in installation.

3. Select geosphere06, right-click, and select Properties. Change the G-buffer object channel to 1. Follow the same procedure to assign geosphere02 to object channel 2, and geosphere05 to object channel 3.

Because the plug-in is a Video Post filter, all the rendering is done in Video Post. In this animation, you create three separate images, each focusing on a different sphere. You then composite the three images to simulate the animated focus plane.

4. Open Video Post and clear the entries by selecting New.

5. Add a Scene event of camera01 with a range from 0 to 0.

6. Highlight the Scene event and add an Image Filter event. Select the Fields of Depth filter plug-in. Select Setup, set the Object Focus object ID to 1, and set aperture size to 14.

7. Add two more Scene and Image Filter events as previously described—one with a range of 1 to 1 and an object ID of 2, and the other with a range of 2 to 2 and an object ID of 3 (see fig. 27.23).

FIGURE 27.23

*Use Video Post to
create the three images
to be composited.*

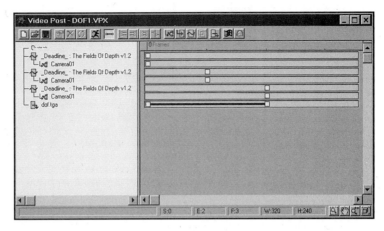

8. Add an Image Output event from frame 0 to 2. Type **dof.tga** for the output file name.

TIP

It is always a good idea to save the Video Post VPX files as you complete them. Save this file to DOFI.VPX.

9. Execute the sequence to render the three TGA images and clear Video Post again. It is not necessary to include the alpha channel for this exercise; 24 bit is sufficient.

10. Add an Image Input event from frame 0 to 30 with the file DOF000.TGA.

11. Add an Image Input event from 31 to 45 with DOF000.TGA and another with DOF001.TGA for the same frames. Select these two entries and add a cross fade transition between them.

12. Use the same cross fade technique for frames 46 to 60 using DOF001.TGA and DOF002.TGA.

13. Add an Image Input event for frames 61 to 90 with DOF002.TGA.

14. Add an Image Output event from frame 0 to 90 to a FLIC or AVI (see fig. 27.24).

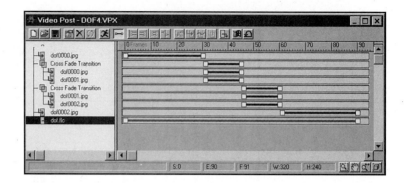

15. Save the VPX file and execute the sequence.

NOTE

For most applications, only two different focus planes are needed, not three as were used in this exercise.

As you can see, just doing a cross fade transition between different image files achieves a fairly realistic effect and suits most circumstances. If examined closely, however, the technique is apparent.

If the animated focus plane needs to happen while the camera is moving, you must render out the entire camera move to sequential images for each different focus plane. This takes considerably longer because the computer not only calculates the entire range of frames for depth of field, but also must calculate it again for the second focus plane.

A workaround for this can be achieved with the included plug-in with the use of an object that has a completely invisible material applied to it. Use the object focus option, set the object ID for the invisible object, and then animate the position of the invisible object. The focus plane then follows the object as it moves. To achieve the desired effect, you will probably need to experiment with the shape and size of the object as well as use a lower aperture setting.

Another less automatic workaround is to use the manual focus option and change the distance one frame at a time.

In Practice: Animating Cameras

- **Study established camera technique.** Viewers understand an established camera "grammar" derived from years of watching television and film. Using the same techniques in computer animation helps the artist communicate effectively.

- **Architectural walkthroughs.** Effective walkthroughs depend on using multiple cameras and creative transitions between shots. Make the camera's presence as unobtrusive as possible so that the viewer can be drawn into the scene. Use motion blur where appropriate and pace camera moves, such as pans and tilts, to avoid strobing.

- **Character animation.** "Float" the frame so that there is always a comfortable composition as characters move. Use multiple shots in a scene. Observing existing live footage will help you learn effective camera technique.

- **"Shaky cam" and "earthquake cam."** Adding random motion to the camera path can duplicate the kind of motion that disturbs cameras in real life. The effect can be used to dramatically emphasize the force and impact, or to simulate a hand-held camera for a documentary effect.

- **Vertigo.** Dynamically altering angle of view during a shot creates a captivating effect. Use it to dramatize the relationship of a character or object to its background.

- **Depth of field.** Simulating real-world optics is possible by using a depth of field plug-in. Controlling depth of field enables selective emphasis on different objects in the field of view.

"SUNNYVALE OPEN HOUSE" BY STEVE BURKE

Chapter 28

by Steve Burke

ANIMATING LIGHTS AND ATMOSPHERES

Animated lights and atmospheres can add texture and character to a scene. With these tools, you can add drama to an otherwise simple animation. They also help to establish mood, because most animated light and environment effects evoke some type of emotion. The tranquillity of a candlelit room is one example. Compare this to the tension and foreboding created by a powerful lightning storm. A good way to use these tools is to suggest an effect—to provide strong visual clues and invite the viewer to imagine what he or she cannot see. This chapter uses animated lights and environments to create a range of rich lighting and atmospheric effects. The focus—always—is on achieving an aesthetic result as efficiently as possible, using all the tools 3D Studio MAX has to offer.

The tutorials in this chapter cover animated light effects and touch on animated environmental effects. Further, the tutorials describe modeling, material, and other considerations necessary to create these effects. When describing the techniques in this chapter, the most pertinent steps are presented first, followed by additional steps that complete or refine the techniques. Often, this type of comprehensive approach is necessary for an effect to look convincing.

The following tutorials all use a variation of the same basic scene file, a cozy living room. By varying the lighting and animation, a number of effects and moods can be obtained.

This chapter covers the following general topics:

- Candlelight

- Moonlight

- Lightning storm

- Volumetric light

To get the most out of this chapter, follow the tutorials in order because each tutorial builds on the previous one. The end results of these tutorials comprise some very intricate effects.

The first scene presented is a candlelit room. Aside from the flame effect, candlelight presents a lighting problem you will encounter in many situations—too little light. Nighttime, cave, and underwater scenes fall into this category. The techniques discussed are as applicable to these situations as they are to candlelight.

As a course of habit, a scene should be built, texture-mapped, and lit before beginning any animation. Establishing the scene in this way provides a solid foundation for animating lights and environments. Examine the next scene and complete it before beginning to animate.

Using Candlelight to Create Ambience

The concepts and techniques presented in this section of the chapter are quite extensive, covering every element of lighting a candlelit room. This includes special materials, creating and animating lights, some aspects of Video Post, and much emphasis on aesthetic concerns. Later in the chapter, you build on these techniques to create some great variations on the simple candlelight theme.

Candlelight produces a warm, low-intensity, flickering light. 3DS MAX makes creating this effect simple. Low-light scenes, however, can be difficult for the viewer to read. These scenes must have enough illumination to make the composition clear without being overly bright. Too much light spoils the candlelight effect; too little light produces a dim incomprehensible image.

Examining the Lighting

Load candle.max from the Chapter 28 directory of the accompanying CD. This file contains a pleasant living room scene illuminated with several low-intensity lights (see fig. 28.1). In the foreground of the scene is a TV tray and candle. At present, only the background of the scene is lit. Later, you will create the candle flame effect, and create the illumination from the candle. First, take a moment to examine how the scene is lit.

FIGURE 28.1

The candle.max scene as seen from the Camera viewport.

The scene contains several spotlights and one omni light. Each affects a different part of the scene. It may seem unnecessary to have so many lights for such a dimly lit room, but actually the opposite is true. Because the scene is very low-key, every bit of light is important and needs to be precisely directed. One or two lights could not adequately do this.

Some lights affect several objects, but most are focused on a specific object or an edge or corner of an object. Combined, the lights hit every part of the scene. Using several lights in this way enables you to brighten or darken any area by changing the multiplier of one or more lights. Using lights in this way enables you to fine-tune a scene with relative ease.

NOTE

If you are getting missing bitmap file errors when rendering, copy the bitmaps from the Chapter 28 Maps directory on the accompanying CD to the 3DSMAX maps directory on your hard drive.

Render the scene from the Camera viewport. Although it is dimly lit, notice that the background of the scene is clearly visible and that the foreground is very dark (see fig. 28.2). If too much background light hits the foreground objects, the foreground objects appear washed-out when more lights are added to the scene. Remember, the foreground lighting still needs to be created and the darker the foreground objects are now, the deeper their shadows will be after these additional lights are added.

By adding a relatively strong light source to the foreground and retaining the deep shadow color already present, the foreground will have strong contrast. This contrast helps to separate the foreground items from the background. When working with a dimly lit scene, proper contrast can make the difference between a clean, readable image or a murky, indecipherable one.

Select some of the lights in the scene and examine their parameters. Notice that all the lights are gray or blue and have very low multiplier settings (see fig. 28.3). This setup helps create the illusion of diffused and reflected night-time light. Further, these lights are kept minimal so that they will not overpower the candlelight in the foreground. The candle flame is the focal point of the scene, and the background should be lit only enough to make the background visible; it needs to be much less intense than the candlelight.

Now that you are familiar with the background lighting, it is time to add some foreground light to the scene. The foreground light in this scene is emanating from a single source, the candle flame. You will, however, need to add more than one light to the scene to create the foreground lighting. This is a common practice in computer graphics where lights don't behave quite as they would in real life.

FIGURE 28.2

The candle.max scene as seen from the Camera viewport.

FIGURE 28.3

To create a subdued light effect, each of the many lights has a very low multiplier setting.

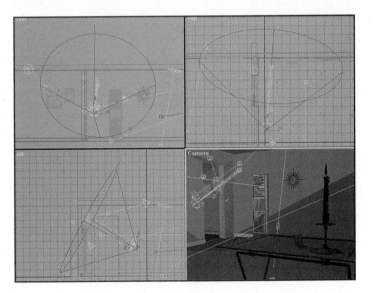

CREATING THE PRIMARY FOREGROUND LIGHT

The first light you add to this scene simulates the light of the candle flame shining down on the foreground objects. To create this effect, place a spotlight above the candle aimed downward toward the floor.

1. If it is not already loaded, load candle.max from the accompanying CD. All of the bitmaps for this file are located in the Chapter 28 Maps directory on the CD; you may want to copy them to your 3DSMAX maps directory.

2. From the Viewport Controls section of the interface, Click on the Min/Max Toggle button. This action minimizes the Camera viewport and makes the three orthogonal views visible.

3. Create a new Target Spotlight in the Front viewport. Name this light **Spot_Candlelight**. It does not matter where you place it; you will type in the exact coordinates next.

4. With the light selected, choose Transform Type-In from the Edit menu. This dialog can be used to enter exact coordinates for any object (see fig. 28.4). You use it to precisely place each new light.

FIGURE 28.4

A new spotlight is added to the scene and precisely placed with the Move Transform Type-In dialog.

5. Make certain that the Select and Move tool is active. Place the light up and to the right of the wall (at about X: 180, Y: –50, Z: 75).

6. Select the target of the new spotlight. Set the Absolute:World coordinates as follows: X: 159.992, Y: –115.266, Z: –13.727.

NOTE

The Transform Type-In dialog affects objects based on the currently active transform tool: Move, Rotate, or Scale. If you type coordinates into the dialog and nothing happens, check to make certain that one of these tools is active. When the Select tool is active, the Transform Type-In dialog has no effect on these parameters.

Entering the previously designated coordinates places the new spotlight directly over the candle. The next step is to enter the spotlights parameters.

7. Select Spot_Candlelight and open the Modify panel. Set General Parameters as follows (see fig. 28.5):
   Set Color to RGB 216, 194, 126.
   Set Multiplier to 0.65.
   Under Attenuation, check Use.
   Set Attenuation Start Range to 97.
   Set End Range to 187.

   Set Spotlight Parameters as follows:
   Set Hotspot to 98.
   Set Falloff to 147.2.

   Set Shadow Parameters as follows:
   Check Cast Shadows.
   Set Map Bias to 2.5.
   Set Size to 320.

The preceding settings create a soft, yellow-orange light that casts shadows and fades over distance.

FIGURE **28.5**

The Modify panel for Spot_Candlelight.

8. Render the scene to see how this single light has changed the scene (see fig. 28.6).

FIGURE 28.6

The foreground cleanly separates from the background with the addition of a well-placed spotlight.

The foreground, except for the candle and flame, is now well-lit and separated nicely from the background. You still need to add candlelight shining on the walls. Later you will create special materials for the candlestick and flame and then animate the scene.

The illumination from a candle flame can be simulated with a single omni light or a single spotlight with overshoot enabled. This method, however, is not as flexible as using several lights. When using multiple lights, each light can have a different multiplier, shadow setting, attenuation, and so on.

You have already built the first spotlight for the candle illumination. Next you continue with the scene, adding two more lights to enhance the candle-light effect. You will merge these lights into the scene.

ADDING SECOND AND THIRD FOREGROUND LIGHT

1. Choose Merge from the File menu. Choose the file candle_2.max from the accompanying CD and click on OK. From the Merge dialog, scroll to the bottom of the list and select the last two items: Spot_Candle-Sidewall and Spot Candle-Wall. Click on OK.

2. Click on Select by Name in the menu bar. Click on None to deselect any objects. Now select Spot_Candle-Sidewall and click on OK. With the first light selected, you can examine its parameters in the Modify command panel.

    This light has a very low multiplier and is aimed at the wall toward the left of the image. It provides a very subtle effect. Note that the light itself is not positioned anywhere near the actual candle flame. The light could have been positioned near the flame and angled to hit the wall in the same place. Lights that are nearly perpendicular to the surfaces they are illuminating, however, are easier to control.

3. Click on the Exclude button in the Modify panel to see which items have been excluded from the light's illumination. The Exclude/Include dialog should look like that shown in figure 28.7. Including only the aforementioned objects minimizes the effect the light has on the room, ensuring that this additional light does not destroy the lighting already created for the background.

FIGURE 28.7

The Exclude/Include dialog is used to limit the effect of the spotlight Spot_Candle_Wall.

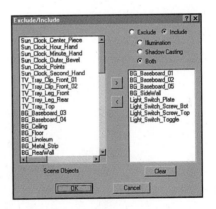

4. Examine the second new spotlight Spot_Candle_Wall. This is the light aimed from the candle toward the rear of the room (see fig. 28.8). It creates a nice yellow glow on the back wall.

FIGURE 28.8

Only the new spotlights you added to this scene are visible; the other lights have been hidden to reduce clutter. Spot_Candle_Wall is selected.

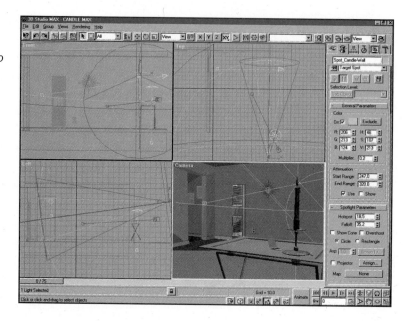

5. Render the scene to see the combined effect of the new spotlights (see fig. 28.9).

FIGURE 28.9

The candlelight scene as rendered, with final lighting arrangement. The candle and flame still require special materials.

The rendered scene now looks complete except for the candle and flame, which at present, look quite dreadful. You will create the flame material first.

Creating the Flame Material

You can use various means to create fire and flame effects: particles, combustion, compositing, and so forth. They all have their strengths. Often you will find the simplest solution is also the most effective. The flame effect described in this tutorial is a combination of modified geometry, materials, and a Video Post Glow filter.

The flame itself is a sphere that has been elongated and tapered with an FFD 3×3×3 (Free Form Deformation) modifier. It was then given a Cylindrical UVW Mapping modifier and a Material modifier. Last, it was assigned a Multi/Sub-Object candle material (see fig. 28.10). Next, you create the material for this object.

FIGURE 28.10

The flame object is a sphere, tapered and elongated with an FFD 3×3×3 modifier. It has been given a Cylindrical UVW Mapping modifier.

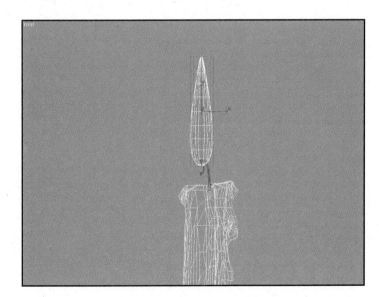

NOTE

The FFD modifier plug-in is an indispensable modeling and animation tool. You can download it free from the Kinetix web site. This modifier enables you to manipulate object surfaces by manipulating a lattice object.

CREATING A CANDLE FLAME MATERIAL

1. Load candle_2.max from the accompanying CD. This file contains the candle scene with the final lighting setup in place. If you have been following along during the last few tutorials, you do not need to load this file.

2. From the Display Command panel, choose Hide by Category Lights to make the screen less cluttered (see fig. 28.11).

FIGURE 28.11

The candle_2.max scene file. Lights are hidden to reduce screen clutter.

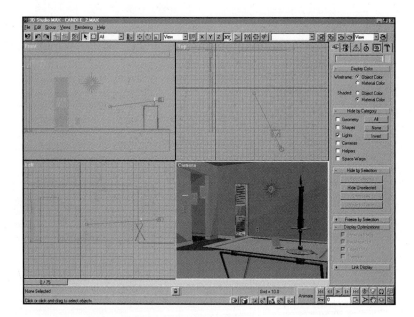

With the lighting in place, it is time to create special materials for the candlestick and flame. Because these objects exhibit some self-illumination, they cannot be lit with lights alone. The material for the flame needs to be created first. The brightness of the flame determines how bright the candlestick needs to be. There is already a Multi/Sub-Object material applied to the flame and candle, but it needs to be adjusted.

3. In the Material Editor, select the Multi/Sub-Object material in Slot #1.

4. Click on the Material 2 button to edit the flame material.

5. From Basic Parameters, Set Shininess and Shin. Strength to 0. Set Self-Illumination to 100.

6. From Extended Parameters, set Opacity Amt to 10. Leave Opacity Falloff at In. Set Type to Additive. These settings make the flame material slightly transparent and behave more like a natural light source. Next you add a diffuse map.

7. From the Maps rollout, click on the Diffuse Map button. From the Material/Map Browser, select Browse From New, select material type Gradient, and click on OK. Set the Gradient settings as follows (see fig. 28.12):

   Set Color #1 to RGB 255, 205, 77.
   Set Color #2 to RGB 62, 20, 0.
   Set Color #3 to RGB 14, 32, 69.
   Set Color 2 Position to 0.16.

FIGURE 28.12

Defining a gradient diffuse map for the candle flame material. The colors are kept dark because they will brighten considerably when applied to the scene and a glow effect is added.

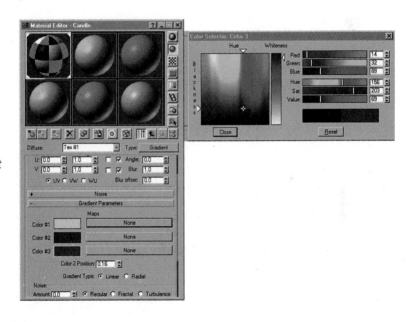

TIP

When defining more than one color, it is helpful to keep the Color Selector dialog open until all colors have been defined. After defining the first color, click on the next color swatch you want to edit. There is no need to close and reopen the dialog each time.

These flames' color settings are subjective and have been tailored to fit this particular scene; they will not fit every situation. The colors previously specified have been kept very dark because they will not be used directly.

Rather, because Transparency Type is set to Additive, the flame colors will be added to the colors behind them, making them appear much brighter in the scene. In addition, you will add a glow to the flame through Video Post. This step also brightens the flame color. If you start with too bright a flame color, the flame turns white. If the settings are kept low, the flame retains some of its color.

The next step is to add an opacity map to the flame material. The purpose of the opacity map is to fade the flame toward its bottom, much like a real flame.

8. Click on Go to Parent and return to the Maps rollout. Drag a copy of the diffuse map to the Opacity Map slot. Select Copy from the Copy Map dialog and click on OK.

9. Click on the new opacity map to edit it. Set the Gradient settings as follows:
   Set Color #1 to RGB 255, 255, 255.
   Set Color #2 to RGB 131, 131, 131.
   Set Color #3 to RGB 128, 128, 128.
   Set Color 2 Position to 0.02.

You are almost finished. In the last few steps, you set the material effects channel for the material and set up Video Post for rendering. Setting the material effects channel is necessary when using some filters, such as glow, in Video Post.

10. Click on Go to Parent to return to the top level of the flame material. Click on the Material Effects Channel pop-up, located just above the material name, and select channel 1.

11. Choose Video Post from the Rendering menu. To use the Glow filter in 3DS MAX, it is necessary to render from Video Post. It makes rendering slightly more tedious, but is definitely worth the added effect.

12. From Video Post, click on the Add Scene Event button, choose View Camera, and click on OK.

WARNING

For tutorials in this chapter, it is important not to add new events with any item in the queue selected. Doing so affects the way events are handled and prevents you from getting proper results.

13. Click on the Add Image Filter Event button, choose Filter Plug-in, Glow (frame only). Click on the Setup button. Set the Size to 7. Leave the other settings intact. By default, this filter affects all materials assigned material ID 1. Double-click on OK to return to Video Post.

NOTE

Glow (frame only) has a rather odd name. "Frame only" signifies that the filter can only render full-frames and does not support field rendering.

Your Video Post queue should like that shown in figure 28.13. Note that the queue is organized into a hierarchy and that both the Camera and Glow events are indented by the same amount.

FIGURE 28.13

The Video Post queue includes a Glow filter for the candle flame effect.

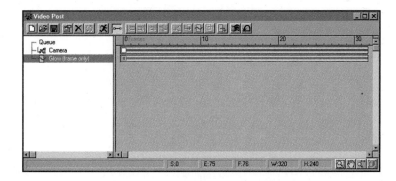

14. Click on the Execute Sequence button, set Time Output to Single and Output Size to 640×480, and click on the Render button.

You now have a decent candle flame material (see fig. 28.14). Next you will create the candlestick material by using the same scene file.

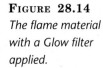

FIGURE 28.14
The flame material with a Glow filter applied.

CREATING A CANDLESTICK MATERIAL

1. In the Material Editor, select the Multi/Sub-Object material in Slot #1. Navigate to the top of the material hierarchy.

2. Click on the Material 1 button to edit the candle material.

3. From Basic Parameters, set Shininess to 55 and Shin. Strength to 52. Check Soften to enable.

4. From the Maps rollout, click on the Diffuse Map button. From the Material/Map Browser, select Browse From New, select material type Gradient, and click on OK. Set the Gradient settings as follows:
   Set Color #1 to RGB 255, 220, 136.
   Set Color #2 to RGB 255, 255, 234.
   Set Color #3 to RGB 255, 255, 255.
   Set Color 2 Position to 0.65.

5. Click on Go to Parent and return to the Maps rollout. Drag a copy of the diffuse map to the Self-Illumination slot. Select Copy from the Copy Map dialog, and click on OK.

6. Click on the new Self-Illumination Map to edit it. Set the Gradient settings as follows:
   Set Color #1 to RGB 200, 200, 200.
   Set Color #2 to RGB 99, 99, 99.

Set Color #3 to RGB 55, 55, 55.
Set Color 2 Position to 0.52.

7. Render the scene from Video Post (see fig. 28.15). The still image is complete. The gradient maps applied to the candle produce a realistic light effect. You can load the final scene file, candle_4.max, from the accompanying CD. The next step is to animate the scene.

FIGURE 28.15

The scene with final lighting and materials. The next step is to animate the flame effect.

Animating the Scene

Animating the scene brings the illusion to life. In the next tutorials, you create a five-second, looping animation. The flame effect will be animated in three different ways:

- The flame itself will gently sway with unseen air currents.

- The shadow-casting spotlight centered above the candle will move with in time with the flame.

- All three spotlights that comprise the candle's illumination will flicker slightly.

The flame object will be animated with two Bend modifiers. The first animates the flame very quickly back and forth over a very small distance, creating a jittery motion. The second Bend modifier animates more slowly and gracefully. The combined effect of both types of movement creates a realistic flame.

NOTE

Before you begin animating any scene, you should consider carefully the requirements of the animation. For this chapter, each animation is five seconds in length, at 15 fps, for a total of 75 frames. Each is rendered as an AVI file at 320×200 pixels and each is scored afterward. Establishing the parameters up front can prevent rework and obviate confusion.

For this chapter, knowing the exact frame count is critical to making the first and last frames of the animation synchronize properly. For smooth looping, each animated parameter needs to have the same value at frame 0 as on frame 75. To meet this requirement, all animation cycles need to multiply evenly into 75. Animation cycles of 5, 15, 25, and 75 frames, for example, would all loop properly.

ANIMATING THE CANDLE FLAME

1. Load candle_3.max from the accompanying CD (see fig. 28.16). If you have been following along during the last several tutorials, you do not need to load this file.

2. From the Front viewport, select the flame object and open the Modify panel.

3. Add a Bend modifier to the flame object. Click Selection Level Sub-Object and choose Center from the drop-down list.

4. From the Front viewport, move the center of the Bend modifier downward so that it aligns to the top of the candlewick (see fig. 28.17). Turn off Sub-Object mode.

5. Turn on Animate and set keyframes for the Bend modifier as follows:
Frame 0: Set Bend Angle to 8.
Set Bend Direction to 0.
Frame 6: Set Bend Angle to 0.
Frame 10: Set Bend Angle to 9.5.
Set Bend Direction to 237.5.

FIGURE 28.16
The flame object is
ready for animating.

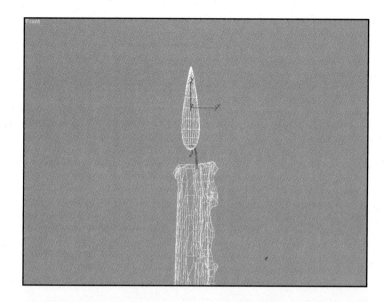

FIGURE 28.17
The center of the Bend
modifier is aligned
vertically to meet the
candlewick.

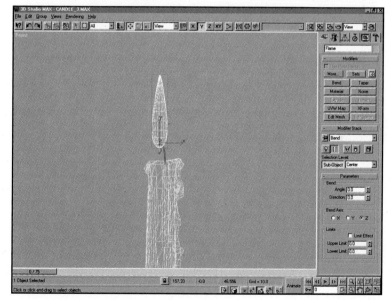

6. Turn off Animate. You will Ping-Pong this animation in Track View.

7. Open Track View. Right-click on the Filters button, and choose Selected Objects Only. Navigate down the Objects hierarchy to the Bend modifier. Select both Angle and Direction in the hierarchy window, and then click on the Parameter Curve Out-of-Range button. Set the Out Type to Ping Pong (see fig. 28.18).

FIGURE 28.18

The Track View and Parameter Curve Out-of-Range windows for the first Bend modifier.

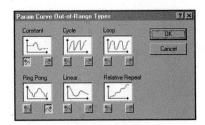

Preview the animation in the Front viewport. The flame now has a jittery movement. Next you add a gentle swaying movement.

8. With the flame still selected, add a second Bend modifier. As with the first Bend modifier, align the Bend Center with the top of the wick. Set Bend Direction to 90.

9. Turn on Animate and set keyframes for the Bend modifier as follows:
   Frame 20: Set Bend Angle to 31.
   Frame 40: Set Bend Angle to –49.5.
   Frame 60: Set Bend Angle to 26.

   Turn off Animate. The animation needs to be completed in Track View.

10. From Track View, navigate to the Angle parameters of the new Bend modifier. Click and drag to select all the keys for Angle. Without deselecting anything, right-click on one of the Angle keys. Set the tangency In and Out types to Linear (see fig. 28.19).

FIGURE 28.19

The tangency In and Out types for the second Bend modifier are set to Linear.

11. Select the Angle key at frame 0. Shift-click and drag to copy this key to frames 30, 50, and 70.

12. The flame animation is now complete. Make a preview of the animation from the Camera viewport to see the result.

The flame animation has been kept simple and understated and the animation is well-suited to most purposes. The next step is to animate the lights in the scene.

TIP

Keep movements subtle and flowing when making a looping animation. Because the motion will be viewed many times in sequence, any harsh or drastic movement will become obvious and the looping more noticeable.

ANIMATING A SHADOW-CASTING SPOTLIGHT

1. Create a dummy object in the Front viewport. Name it **Dummy_Candlelight**. Use the Align tool to center it to the flame object. Move the dummy upward so that it lies above the flame (see fig. 28.20).

NOTE

Often, the best way to animate the movement of lights is to link them to one or more dummy objects. The primary advantage is that any number of objects can share the same animation—a spotlight and target can both be animated simultaneously, for example, by linking each to the same dummy. In addition, any animation can be removed just by unlinking the object in question.

FIGURE 28.20

A dummy object is created and positioned over the flame.

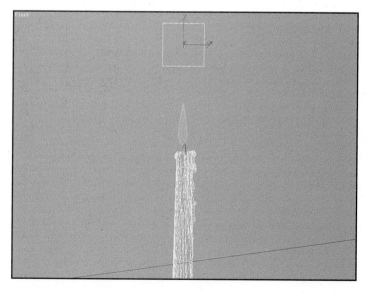

2. From the Display panel, uncheck Hide by Category Lights, making the lights visible again.

3. Link Spot_Candlelight and Spot_Candlelight.Target to the dummy object. The dummy will be used to control the movement of both the light and target objects.

4. Select the dummy object and open Track View. Right-click on the Filters button, and choose Selected Objects Only. Navigate down the Objects hierarchy to the Dummy_Candlelight Position track. Click on the Add Keys button and add a new keyframe at frame 0.

5. Right-click on the new position key at frame 0. Set tangency In and Out to Linear. Enter a new X Value of 160.02. This moves the dummy to the right slightly.

6. Ensure that the Move Keys tool is active. Copy the key at frame 0 to the following frames, adjusting each key's X Value as listed:
    Frame 20: Set X Value to 160.21.
    Frame 28: Set X Value to 159.99.
    Frame 37: Set X Value to 159.75.
    Frame 42: Set X Value to 159.84.
    Frame 62: Set X Value to 160.08.
    Frame 71: Set X Value to 159.95.
    Frame 75: Set X Value to 160.02.

After entering the preceding values, the Dummy_Candlelight object and the attached spotlight and target move left and right in-time with the flame movement. The synchronization of this movement is purposefully imprecise so that the effect is not too rigid. Before you render the scene, complete the animation by adding some variation to the strength of the lights.

ANIMATING THE INTENSITY OF CANDLE ILLUMINATION

1. Select Spot_Candlelight from the scene. Open Track View. Right-click on the Filters button, and choose Selected Objects Only. Navigate down the Objects hierarchy to the Multiplier track for Spot_Candlelight. Click on the Add Keys button and add a new keyframe at frame 0.

2. Right-click on the new key at frame 0. Set tangency In and Out to Linear.

Note that the multiplier is currently set to 0.65. You will animate the multiplier to create a flickering effect. Keep in mind, however, that the flicker needs to be very subtle and that the variation in the multiplier will be minimal.

3. Ensure that the Move Keys tool is active. Copy the key at frame 0 to the following frames, adjusting the multiplier value as specified:
   Frame 0: Set Value to 0.65.
   Frame 6: Set Value to 0.69, Tangency to Fast In, Fast Out.
   Frame 12: Set Value to 0.65.
   Frame 16: Set Value to 0.66.
   Frame 21: Set Value to 0.63.
   Frame 25: Set Value to 0.65.

NOTE

Bézier tangent types are described in Volume II of the *3D Studio Max User Guide* on page 32-13. Familiarity with the different tangent types is critical to creating good animation.

4. Select Multiplier in the hierarchy window, and then click on the Parameter Curve Out-of-Range button. Set the Out Type to Loop. The animation will loop every 25 frames.

5. With Multiplier still selected, click on the Copy Controller button. You will paste the multiplier settings into two other lights.

6. Select Spot_Candle-Wall from the scene. Look at the Modify panel and make a note of the current multiplier setting for this light. It should read 0.2.

7. In Track View, navigate down the Objects hierarchy and select the Multiplier track for Spot_Candle-Wall. Click on the Paste button, select Copy, and then click on OK (see fig. 28.21).

FIGURE 28.21

The animation from one light is copied to another.

Copying the multiplier animation from one light to another is a useful shortcut. There is a downside to this method, however. By pasting one light's multiplier into another, the second light is sometimes adversely affected. In this case, your second light is now much too bright. As you noted, the second light's original multiplier was 0.2. By pasting a new multiplier track into the light, it has become over three times brighter. The solution is to use a Multiplier Curve to restore the brightness level of the second light while retaining the pasted multiplier animation.

TIP

Copying animated multiplier tracks from one light to another often causes an unwanted change in the recipient light's intensity. This can be corrected with a Multiplier Curve. The setting for the Multiplier Curve can be calculated by dividing the Multiplier setting of the recipient light at frame 0 by the Multiplier setting of the copied light at frame 0.

If you copy an animated multiplier track with a value of 0.65 at frame 0 into a light with a multiplier of 0.2 at frame 0, the correct Multiplier Curve setting will be 0.2 divided by 0.65 or 0.31.

8. With Multiplier still selected, click on the Function Curves button and then click on the Apply Multiplier Curve button. Return to Edit Keys mode.

The Multiplier Curve is placed beneath the Multiplier track in the Track hierarchy and will contain a key at frame 0 and frame 75 (see fig. 28.22).

TIP

If you can't find the multiplier curve, it's a flyoff from the ease curve.

9. In the Multiplier Curve track, delete the key at frame 75. Right-click on the key at frame 0 and set the Value to .31. This action restores the light to its original intensity. Only one more light to go.

10. Select Spot_Candle-Sidewall from the scene. Look at the Modify panel and make a note of the current Multiplier setting for this light. It should read .07.

FIGURE 28.22

A Multiplier Curve is used to decrease the value of a multiplier track without compromising the animation keyframes.

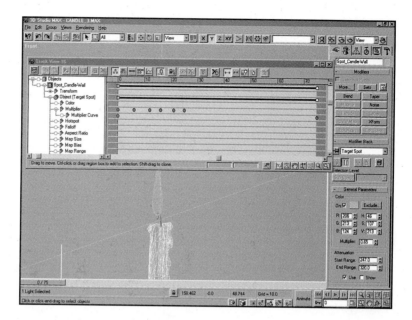

11. In Track View, navigate down the Objects hierarchy and select the Multiplier track for Spot_Candle-Sidewall. Click on the Paste button, select Copy, and then click on OK.

12. With Multiplier still selected, click on the Function Curves button and then click on the Apply Multiplier Curve button. Return to Edit Keys mode.

13. In the Multiplier Curve track, delete the key at frame 75. Right-click on the key at frame 0 and set the Value to 0.1077. The scene is complete.

14. Render frames 1 to 75 from Video Post to see the final result. Make certain to add an Output Event first or your file will not be saved. You can also view the file candle.avi from the ch28_avi directory of the accompanying CD.

The finished candle animation is very subtle but makes good use of several animation and lighting techniques. Next you add moonlight streaming into the scene from a pair of off-camera windows.

Using Moonlight for Effect

Like candlelight, moonlight produces a low-intensity, diffuse light. Unlike the warm yellow-orange hue of candle light, moonlight illuminates with a cool, bluish color. Because orange and blue are complementary, placing the candle in front of the moonlit wall makes both their colors appear brighter and more vibrant. In addition, this makes the scene more legible by clearly separating the foreground, lit with candlelight, from the background, bathed in moonlight. Using color theory is especially helpful in this scene because both candlelight and moonlight are low-intensity and therefore do not allow for a great deal of contrast.

TIP

When defining colored lights, such as blue lights to simulate moonlight, keep the light color as close to white as possible. Reduce the necessary RGB components only enough to arrive at the correct hue.

White light, or any shade of gray light, is very predictable; it lights all colors evenly. Saturated light, such as a deep blue, has a strong impact on like-colored objects (blue objects in this example) and little impact on anything else. The end result of over-saturated lights can be strange—uneven lighting and objects that appear to glow.

Realistic Moonlight

You will create a realistic moonlight effect by using almost the exact same setup as the previous file. To give the impression of light beaming in from unseen windows, two additional spotlights will be added to the scene, each projecting a bitmap of a paned-window onto the far wall. You complete the effect by adding a swaying tree in front of the two windows. The tree is not visible in the animation. The shadow from the tree, however, falls onto the far wall, framed by the two windows.

CREATING A MOONLIT WINDOW EFFECT

1. Load moonlit.max from the accompanying CD. This file contains the familiar candle scene (see fig. 28.23).

2. Create a new Target Spotlight in the Front viewport. Name this light **Spot_Window_Right**. The exact placement of the light is not important.

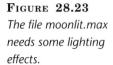

FIGURE 28.23

The file moonlit.max needs some lighting effects.

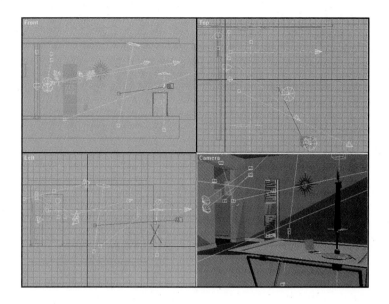

3. With the light selected, choose Transform Type-In from the Edit menu. Make certain that the Select and Move tool is active.

4. Set the Absolute:World coordinates for the light as follows: X: 53.397, Y: –130.203, Z: 57.12.

5. Select the target of the new spotlight. Set the Absolute:World coordinates as follows: X: 106.955, Y: 79.517, Z: 52.512.

6. Select Spot_Window_Right and open the Modify panel.

   Set General Parameters as follows:
   Set Color to RGB 51, 121, 226.
   Set Multiplier to 0.9.
   Set Attenuation Start Range to 191.
   Set Attenuation End Range to 251.
   Check Use to enable attenuation.

   Set Spotlight Parameters as follows:
   Set Hotspot to 11.3.
   Set Falloff to 13.7.
   Enable Rectangle and set Asp:(Aspect Ratio) to 0.57.

   Set Shadow Parameters as follows:
   Check Cast Shadows.
   Set Size to 110.

These settings create blue rectangular light that casts blurry shadows. The blurry shadows help make the tree effect, delineated in the next tutorial, more believable.

The next step is to add the pane effect for the windows. To accomplish this, turn on the projection option for this light and assign a black and white bitmap of window panes.

7. Check the Projector option and click on the Assign button to bring up the Material/Map Browser. Choose Browse From New, select material type Bitmap, and click on OK. The light now has a bitmap assigned but you still need to tell MAX which bitmap to use.

8. Click on the Map button and put the bitmap to slot #2 of the Material Editor. Click on OK.

9. Open the Material Editor and select the new Bitmap in Slot #2. Load window_m.tga from the CD. Leave the other settings intact.

The spotlight is finished. You will make a clone of it to create the second window.

10. From the Top viewport, select Spot_Window_Right and its target object.

11. Press the Shift key and drag a clone of the spotlight 53 units to the left. From the Clone/Copy dialog, select Instance and click on OK.

12. Your scene should like figure that shown in figure 28.24. If it doesn't, load moonlit2.max from the accompanying CD.

13. Render the scene from Video Post to see the result of adding the new spotlights. The window effect adds a nice touch of color to the scene (see fig. 28.25).

FIGURE 28.24
The two projection spotlights will create a convincing moonlight effect.

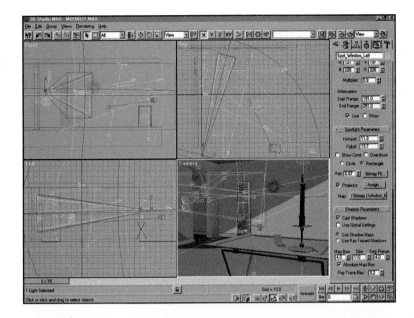

FIGURE 28.25
The rendered scene shows the effect of the two additional spotlights.

Casting the Tree Shadow

Looking at the rendered image, you may be wondering where the tree came from. The tree is a collection of flat, leaf-like geometry sitting in front of the two new spotlights. The shapes that comprise the tree have very low detail. This is one reason why you lowered the Size parameter of the spotlight shadows. The second advantage to a blurry shadow is that it lightens the shadows and helps distinguish the tree from the window panes.

The next step is to animate the tree leaves using dummy objects and Bend modifiers.

ANIMATING THE TREE GOBO

1. Maximize the Front viewport. Select Tree_Gobo from the Named Selection Sets pull-down. This action selects the tree objects. Click on Zoom Extents to select it, giving you a better view of the gobo objects (see fig. 28.26).

FIGURE 28.26

The tree gobo is comprised of several small leaf objects. These will be animated with dummy objects and Bend modifiers.

NOTE

A *gobo* is a cutout used to reduce light. In this case, the gobo is shaped like a tree and is comprised of flat geometry.

The tree gobo objects are split into two groups, one for the left window and one for the right. This split is necessary because your window effect is created with two separate lights that do not overlap or touch. The windows would have to be touching or overlapping for them to hit a single group of objects.

Between the two groups of gobo objects are four dummy objects. These have already been assigned a wavelike motion. Preview the animation in the Front viewport. The motion of the dummy objects increases in magnitude with the dummy object on the left being the most dramatic; the dummy on the right is the least dramatic. The dummy on the left is most appropriately assigned to the leaves most distant from the trunk and vice-versa.

By assigning groups of leaves to the dummy objects in this way, the tree leaves can be animated with relative ease. Note also that the leaves overlap other leaves and create subtle new shapes with every frame.

2. Select Gobo_1_Leaves from the Named Selection Sets pull-down list. Click on the Select and Link button and link the leaves to the rightmost dummy object. When linking the leaves to the dummy, it may help to lock the selection with the toolbar and to limit the Selection Filter to Helpers to avoid linking the objects to the background objects.

3. Select Gobo_2_Leaves from the Named Selection Sets pull-down. Link these leaves to Dum_Gobo_02, the dummy second from the right.

4. Select Gobo_3_Leaves from the Named Selection Sets pull-down. Link these leaves to Dum_Gobo_03, the dummy second from the left.

5. Select Gobo_4_Leaves from the Named Selection Sets pull-down. Link these leaves to Dum_Gobo_04, the dummy to the far left.

Preview the animation. The leaves should be moving up and down with a certain rhythm. Now add the Bend modifiers to complete the illusion.

6. Select Gobo_Trunk_Left from the Named Selection Sets pull-down. Apply a Bend modifier to this object. Set Bend Axis to Y. Choose Selection Level Sub-Object and select Center. Move the center to the right 3 units and down 13 units (see fig. 28.27). Exit Sub-Object mode.

FIGURE 28.27

A Bend modifier is applied to the first tree trunk gobo object and the center is moved to the bottom right of the object.

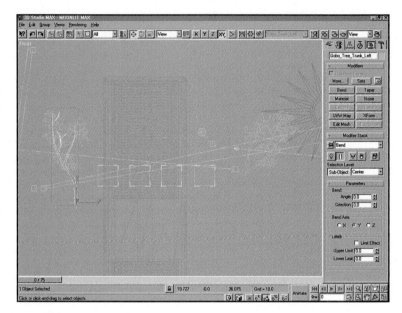

7. Turn on Animate. Set Angle to 1.33 at frame 52. Set Angle to 0 at frame 75. Turn off Animate.

8. Select Gobo_Trunk_Right from the Named Selection Sets pull-down. Apply a Bend modifier to this object. Set Bend Axis to Y. Choose Selection Level Sub-Object and select Center. Move the center to the left 7 units and down 12 units (see fig. 28.28). Exit Sub-Object mode.

9. Turn on Animate. Set Angle to 1.33 at frame 52. Set Angle to 0 at frame 75. Turn off Animate.

The purpose of the Bend modifiers in this example is just to add a little motion to the tree trunks. Next you apply a second bend to each group of gobo objects to enhance the movement.

10. Select Tree_on_Left from the Named Selection Sets pull-down. Apply a Bend modifier to this object. Set Bend Axis to Z. Choose Selection Level Sub-Object and select Center. Move the center to the right 3 units and down 10 units. Exit Sub-Object mode.

FIGURE 28.28

A Bend modifier is applied to the second tree trunk gobo object and the center is moved to the left and below the object.

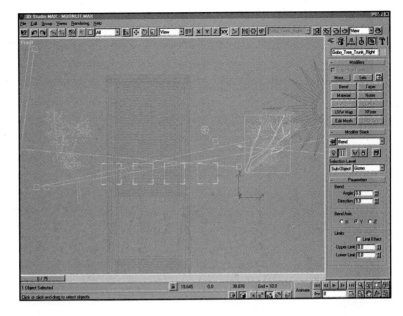

11. Turn on Animate. Set Angle to –3 at frame 38. Set Angle to 0 at frame 75. Turn off Animate.

12. Select Tree_on_Right from the Named Selection Sets pull-down. Apply a Bend modifier to this object. Set Bend Axis to Z. Choose Selection Level Sub-Object and select Center. Move the center to the left 8 units and down 12 units. Exit Sub-Object mode.

13. Turn on Animate. Set Angle to –3 at frame 38. Set Angle to 0 at frame 75. Turn off Animate.

The trees are now animated and you can preview the animation in the front window before doing a final rendering.

14. Render frames 1 to 75 from Video Post to see the final result. You can also view the file moonlit.avi from the CD. You can load the final scene file, moonlit3.max, from the accompanying CD.

The scene is starting to come to life. How about adding some rain and lightning?

Creating a Lightning Storm Effect

Animated lights can be used to create some great lightning storm effects. Following is a discussion of how to create a realistic lightning and storm effect. Lightning requires animating a scene's lights between two states: with lightning and without. These lighting techniques can also be applied to other situations, such as explosions, X-rays, bug-zappers, or any lighting situation that requires two distinct states. You will be navigating through a finished scene file to learn how this effect was created. You can view the animation by loading storm.avi from the CD.

Note

Sound is very important in animation. Neglecting this element can rob your work of much of its potential. The soundtracks for the animations in this chapter were scored by Maurice Jackson, of Strategic Simulations, Inc.

The animation is an extension of the last scene. It portrays the same burning candle in a moonlit room but with the addition of rain streaking down the windows and flashes of lightning illuminating the scene. You will add some new spotlights and materials to the scene, and examine how the effect was created from start to finish.

Load storm.max from of the CD. You use this file for the rest of this tutorial.

Examining the Basic Lightning Effect

A basic lightning effect is created by establishing two different lighting conditions. The first lighting condition is the scene in normal light. In this case, normal light is warm candlelight in the foreground and cool bluish moonlight filling the background. The second lighting condition is the scene illuminated by lightning. Compare the two lighting conditions (see fig. 28.29). At this point, the lightning effect is almost full-force.

Creating the second lighting condition was troublesome because it essentially required relighting the scene. To do this, several existing lights had to be animated and new lights were added to the scene.

FIGURE 28.29

The image on the left shows the scene at frame 1 under normal lighting conditions; the right shows the animation at frame 38.

To facilitate the light animation, the timing of the lightning was established first. You can more clearly see the pattern of the lighting by viewing the Multiplier Curve of a typical light in the scene.

1. Select Spot_Window_Left and open a Track View window. Right-click on the Filters button and choose Selected Objects Only. Navigate to Spot_Window_Left and select Multiplier. Click on Function Curves.

A very large spike appears, followed quickly by a very small one (see fig. 28.30). This light was used as the basis for animating the other lights in the scene. The multiplier track for this light was copied and pasted into the existing scene lights that needed to animate with the lightning. Using the techniques described earlier in the chapter, a Multiplier Curve was then added to most of the lights to scale down the strength of the light.

FIGURE 28.30

The Multiplier for a typical light in the scene shows the rhythm of the lightning flashes.

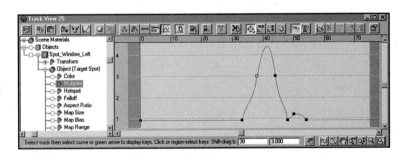

Other elements needed to be adjusted for the lightning effect to work. The color of the windows shining on the wall, for example, needed to be whiter. The animation keys for this were created in the Track Editor and matched to the animation of the Multiplier.

2. Select Edit Keys in the Track window and examine the keys for both Color and Multiplier. Notice that the color of the light is animated in time with the Multiplier (see fig. 28.31).

FIGURE 28.31
*The Color and
Multiplier settings for
this light are animated
in the same manner.*

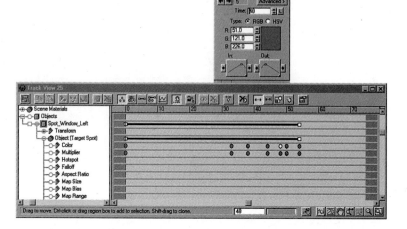

Additionally, the material created for the candlestick also needed to be animated. The candlestick was mapped with a self-illuminated material. The material was well-suited to the normal lighting conditions of a dark room, but did not look good when illuminated by the lightning. The self-illumination of the material overpowered the lightning. Animation keys were added to eliminate the self-illumination during lightning flashes.

The last effect to be added to the scene was the illusion of water running down the window panes. This effect was accomplished by modifying the bitmap the projector spotlights use.

3. Open the Material Editor and examine the Window_&_Rain material in Slot #2. This bitmap contains a noise map and a bitmap of window panes used as a mask.

4. Click on the Map button to view the Slow_Rain map. This map is a standard noise map. The Y offset has been animated to give the map movement.

The animation was looped by animating the Y offset from 0 to 20 over the first 38 frames and animating the Y value from –20 to 0 over the remaining frames. This created an abrupt break in the animation at frame 39, but the lightning hides the switch.

That covers the basics of creating a lightning effect. You may want to examine this file further on your own to learn more about the effect.

Animating Volumetric Light

Volumetric light is a combination of a light and an atmospheric effect. For this tutorial, you create a small living room illuminated by a television set. The TV screen is not visible in the animation because the set faces away from the camera. The light from the television will be provided by a volumetric spotlight.

The volume light for this tutorial appears as one light, but is actually a combination of three different lights. The first is the actual volumetric light. This is the foggy cone of light visible in the scene. You place the second light in a similar fashion to the volumetric light and provide the illumination for the light. To achieve the right effect, it is often necessary to give a volumetric light a high multiplier or a short falloff region. Both of these make illuminating surfaces with volumetric lights difficult. The best solution is to create two separate lights: one for the volume effect and one to simulate the lighting effect. In this way, the volume light can be fine-tuned for appearance without consideration for how it actually disperses light.

The third light simulates light reflecting from the volumetric light back toward the light source. Together, the three lights create a very nice effect.

TIP

When creating artificial light sources, give each light character by assigning a unique color, intensity, or animation. Doing this adds believability to your scene and comes at almost no cost to rendering times or file size.

CREATING A VOLUMETRIC LIGHT

1. Load tv.max from the accompanying CD (see fig. 28.32).

This file contains some new objects and similar lighting to the previous tutorials. Render the Camera viewport to see how the new scene looks rendered (see fig. 28.33).

2. Create a new Target Spotlight in the Top viewport. Name this light **Volume_Light_TV**. The exact placement of the light is not important.

FIGURE 28.32
The tv.max file demonstrates volumetric lighting.

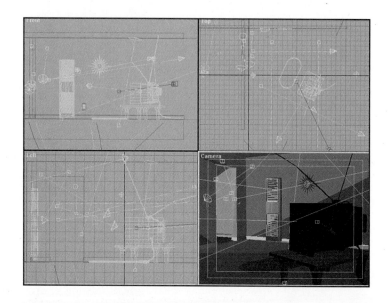

FIGURE 28.33
A rendering of the tv.max file prior to adding the volume light effect.

3. With the light selected, choose Transform Type-In from the Edit menu. Make certain that the Select and Move tool is active.

4. Set the Absolute:World coordinates for the light as follows: X: 148.465, Y: –32.274, Z: 32.582.

5. Select the target of the new spotlight. Set the Absolute:World coordinates as follows: X: 58.258, Y: 12.126, Z: 33.4.

6. Select Volume_Light_TV and open the Modify panel.
Set General Parameters as follows:
Set Color to RGB 210, 211, 208.
Set Multiplier to 2.
Set Attenuation Start Range to 68.
Set Attenuation End Range to 105.
Check Use to enable attenuation.

Set Spotlight Parameters as follows:
Set Hotspot to 57.
Set Falloff to 59.6.
Enable Rectangle and set Asp:(Aspect Ratio) to 1.38.

Set Shadow Parameters as follows:
Check Cast Shadows.
Leave Size to 256.

These settings create the foundation for the light. A bitmap assigned to the light as a Projector image enhances the final look of the light.

7. Check the Projector option and click on the Assign button to bring up the Material/Map Browser. Choose Browse From Material Editor, select the bitmap TV_Projection and click on OK.

Assigning this bitmap to the volume light rounds the edges of the volume light cone, removing the sharp, unrealistic edges created by using a rectangular shaped light.

The basic spotlight is finished. You still need to create a new volume light, however, in the Environment dialog and assign the Volume_Light_TV.

8. Choose Environment from the Rendering menu. Under Atmosphere, click on the Add button and choose Volume Light, and then click on OK.

9. Click on the Pick Lights button and select the spotlight Volume_Light_TV.

10. Edit the parameters of the volume light as follows:
Set Fog Color to RGB 225, 232, 255.
Set Density to 2.5.
Check Noise to enable it.
Set Noise Amount to 0.14.
Set Noise Uniformity to 0.06.
Set Noise Size to 0.9.

Next you add a spotlight to provide the illumination for the volume light.

CREATING A SECOND SPOTLIGHT FOR ILLUMINATION

1. Create a new Target Spotlight anywhere in the Top viewport. Name this light **TV_Illumination**.

2. With the light selected, choose Transform Type-In from the Edit menu. Make certain that the Select and Move tool is active.

3. Set the Absolute:World coordinates for the light as follows: X: 132.369, Y: −20.612, Z: 33.645.

4. Select the target of the new spotlight. Set the Absolute:World coordinates as follows: X: 17.072, Y: 34.202, Z: 33.645.

5. Select TV_Illumination and open the Modify panel. Set General Parameters as follows:
    Set Color to RGB 172, 203, 210.
    Set Multiplier to 0 (you animate this later).
    Set Attenuation Start Range to 107.
    Set Attenuation End Range to 180.
    Check Use to enable attenuation.

    Set Spotlight Parameters as follows:
    Set Hotspot to 38.8.
    Set Falloff to 77.2.

These settings create a bluish light aimed in the same direction as the volume light.

CREATING A THIRD SPOTLIGHT FOR REFLECTED LIGHT

1. Create a new Target Spotlight anywhere in the Top viewport. Name this light **VL_Reflected_Light**.

2. With the light selected, choose Transform Type-In from the Edit menu. Make certain that the Select and Move tool is active.

3. Set the Absolute:World coordinates for the light as follows: X: 29.579, Y: 36.67, Z: 89.046.

4. Select the target of the new spotlight. Set the Absolute:World coordinates as follows: X: 117.039, Y: −7.609, Z: −12.988.

5. Select VL_Reflected_Light and open the Modify panel.
   Set General Parameters as follows:
   Set Color to RGB 156, 190, 216.
   Set Multiplier to 1.
   Set Attenuation Start Range to 109.
   Set Attenuation End Range to 146.
   Check Use to enable attenuation.

   Set Spotlight Parameters as follows:
   Set Hotspot to 37.9.
   Set Falloff to 73.5.

   Set Shadow Parameters as follows:
   Check Cast Shadows.
   Set Map Bias to 1.

After adding this last light, your scene should look like that shown in figure 28.34. If your scene doesn't match the one shown, you can load tv2.max from the accompanying CD.

The last step is to animate each of the lights. You animate the Multiplier to create a flickering pulsing television effect.

FIGURE 28.34

The tv.max file with the three new spotlights added. The other scene lights have been hidden.

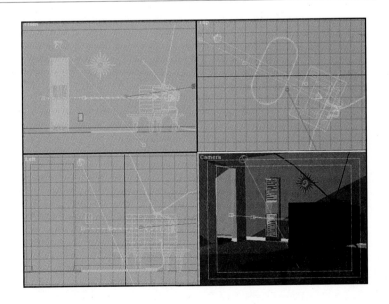

ANIMATING THE VOLUME LIGHT EFFECT

1. With the VL_Reflected_Light spotlight still selected, open Track View. Right-click on the Filter button and choose Selected Objects Only. Navigate to the light's Multiplier track and add keyframes as specified below:
   Frame 0: Set Multiplier to .2 Linear In, Out.
   Frame 10: Set Multiplier to .22 Linear In, Out.
   Frame 16: Set Multiplier to .2 Linear In, Out.
   Frame 33: Set Multiplier to .24 Slow In, Smooth Out.
   Frame 39: Set Multiplier to .2 Smooth In, Smooth Out.
   Frame 44: Set Multiplier to .21 Smooth In, Smooth Out.
   Frame 58: Set Multiplier to .18 Smooth In, Smooth Out.
   Frame 75: Set Multiplier to .2 Linear In, Out.

2. Select the TV_Illumination spotlight and navigate to the light's Multiplier track. Add keyframes as specified below:
   Frame 0: Set Multiplier to 0 Linear In, Out.
   Frame 10: Set Multiplier to .22 Linear In, Out.
   Frame 16: Set Multiplier to 0 Linear In, Out.
   Frame 33: Set Multiplier to .24 Slow In, Smooth Out.
   Frame 39: Set Multiplier to 0 Smooth In, Smooth Out.
   Frame 44: Set Multiplier to .21 Smooth In, Smooth Out.
   Frame 58: Set Multiplier to .18 Smooth In, Smooth Out.
   Frame 75: Set Multiplier to 0 Linear In, Out.

3. Select the Volume_Light_TV spotlight and navigate to the light's Multiplier track. Add keyframes as specified below:
   Frame 0: Set Multiplier to 2 Linear In, Out.
   Frame 10: Set Multiplier to 2.4 Linear In, Out.
   Frame 16: Set Multiplier to 2 Linear In, Out.
   Frame 33: Set Multiplier to 2.8 Slow In, Smooth Out.
   Frame 39: Set Multiplier to 2 Smooth In, Smooth Out.
   Frame 44: Set Multiplier to 2.2 Smooth In, Smooth Out.
   Frame 58: Set Multiplier to 1.6 Smooth In, Smooth Out.
   Frame 75: Set Multiplier to 2 Linear In, Out.

4. You are finished. Render the animation to see the results of all your hard work (see fig. 28.35). You can also view the animation by loading tv.avi from the accompanying CD. You can load the completed scene file, tv3.max, from the CD.

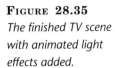

FIGURE 28.35
The finished TV scene with animated light effects added.

In Practice: Animating Lights and Atmospheres

- **Animation Requirements.** Establish the requirements of your animation in advance. How long is your animation going to be? How many frames per second? And so on…. Ask yourself these questions before beginning a project.

- **Value and Contrast.** Proper value and contrast are necessary for foreground objects to separate from background objects. Good lighting can mean the difference between a great-looking animation and something quite atrocious. Color theory should also be used to enhance your imagery.

- **Lighting Control.** Using many low-intensity lights can provide great control over a scene's lighting because each light can be minutely adjusted to get subtle effects.

- **Simple Effects.** Simple geometry placed in front of lights can produce very nice effects. The swaying tree in this chapter was comprised of flat, low-polygon objects.

- **Simple Approach.** The simplest approach to a problem is often the best. Creating a candle flame from a modified sphere is an example of a practical technique.

- **Dummy objects.** Dummy objects are great for animating lights. They enable you to create complex animation effects that would be difficult to do any other way.

- **A quality soundtrack.** A quality soundtrack can greatly improve the appeal of an animation.

- **Volume lights.** Volume lights work best when combined with other lights. In this chapter, two additional spotlights were used to create the illumination from the volume light.

IMAGE CREATED BY RALPH FRANTZ

Chapter 29

by Ralph Frantz

PARTICLES, SPACE WARPS, AND PHYSICS

This chapter attempts to help you get a firm grasp on the wonderful world of 3D Studio MAX particles and space warps. Particles are a great way to simulate a myriad of objects, such as rain, snow, bubbles, or blowing dust. They simulate real-world effects that just can't be represented efficiently by modeling in MAX. As you go about everyday life, you will soon recognize many objects in nature (or even imaginary objects) that can be represented this way. A single particle system can represent hundreds or even thousands of tiny objects that all act similarly but are still slightly different from one another.

Space warps are a great way to affect and deform your MAX objects and particles in world space. This should not be confused with modifiers that affect objects in Object Space.

- **World Space.** The universal coordinate system used by MAX to keep track of objects in the scene. Represented by the Home Grid.

- **Object Space.** The coordinate system used by MAX to keep track of everything that is applied to an object.

Space warps automatically alter objects after they are set up and bound to the object. In this chapter, you use particle systems and space warps together to create several different natural and man-made effects. The following topics are covered:

- Snow particle system

- All Purpose Particles plug-in by Sisyphus Software

- Sand Blaster Particle plug-in by Digimation

- Spray particle system

- Deflector space warp

- Path Deform space warp

- Bomb space warp

Particles and Their Space Warps

The first three exercises in this section have been set up to further teach you about using particle systems and their associated space warps. In these exercises, you use the following systems and space warps:

- **Particles.** You use particles to simulate confetti falling from the sky. Snow particle systems are used because of their natural tumbling capability.

- **The All Purpose Emitter from Sisyphus.** You use the All Purpose Emitter (APE) to create smoke coming from a train. APE particles react very well to the train's starting and stopping motions on the tracks.

- **Sand Blaster by Digimation.** You use Sand Blaster for a unique number countdown. It has a wonderful feature called target simulation that enables you to dissemble objects particle by particle and then reassemble them into a new object.

The next two exercises, as described in the following list, explore the Spray particle system with different space warps. A particle system has yet to be developed that allows particles to follow a path after being emitted, so a series of wind space warps is used to coax them along. Note that Digimation's Sand Blaster comes close to achieving this through its use of multiple targets.

■ The first exercise uses Spray and a series of Wind space warps to cause the particles to flow aerodynamically over a sports car, as if in a wind tunnel.

■ The final Spray exercise utilizes a Gravity space warp and a couple of Deflectors to simulate the sparks emitted from a welding head. Spray is pretty versatile in this respect, and along with the judicious use of space warps, can be made to simulate all kinds of natural phenomena.

The Snow Particle System with Deflector Space Warp

In the following exercise, you create a ticker-tape parade down a New York City street. To simulate thousands of small colorful pieces of confetti falling from the buildings, you use the second MAX core particle system, Snow. Consistent with its name, Snow produces 2D flakes that can spiral and tumble as they fall. Think creatively: This particle system has many uses other than simple snow. The falling confetti created in this exercise is but one example.

TIP

Snow is created as a coplanar set of faces. A snow "flake" thus has only one orientation and can be seen in only one direction. If you want to see both sides of the flake as it tumbles, use a 2-Sided material.

TICKER-TAPE PARADE

Go ahead and load imx29f.max from the accompanying CD and check out the scene. The scene represents a typical New York City street and is just the type on which you would expect to see a ticker-tape parade.

1. In the Particle Systems drop-down list of the Create panel, click on Snow.

2. In the top viewport, click and drag to create an emitter just longer than the street and the length of the five city blocks. A width of about 50,000 and a length of about 3,000 should do. Name it **Snow_OH**.

3. Center the emitter down the middle of the street and move it above the street surface about 7,000 units (see fig. 29.1). With the front viewport active, you can right-click on the Move icon and type **7000** in the Type in Transforms Offset: screen Y field.

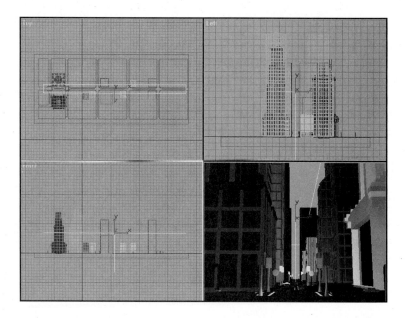

FIGURE 29.1

Place the snow emitter down the center of the street and off the ground about 7,000 units.

Notice that the emitter's direction vector is pointing away from you in the orthographic viewport. Notice also that because the scene is in such a large scale, most of the Snow parameters need to be adjusted.

4. With the emitter active, go to the Modifier panel and set the Viewport Count at 500 and the Render Count at 10,000. Raise the Flake Size to 40 and the Speed to 20. Also, choose to Render Triangle Faces.

Play the scene. Even with these parameters raised, the lazy way snow particles fall keeps them too close to the emitter before they die. It takes a major adjustment in the timing section to get them to reach the ground.

5. Set the Start Frame to –1000 and the Life to 900.

6. In the Named Selection Set drop-down list, choose NYC Street to select all the geometry in the scene except the snow particles. Click on the Display tab, and under Hide by Selection, choose Hide Selected. Then play the scene.

TIP

It is a good idea to create selection sets for the sole purpose of the hiding and unhiding of geometry to speed up your work. This is especially true when working with thousands of particles. It takes only two steps to select all geometry and to use your hot key to hide selected geometry. When you want to unhide the geometry, select it from the Named Selection set and answer Yes to the alert dialog that asks whether you want the objects unhidden.

Naturally, pieces of paper tumble as they fall, and the MAX Snow particle system gives you two parameters to get just the tumble you need. *Tumble* is the amount of random rotation; *tumble rate* is the speed of rotation. MAX provides built-in rotation chaos by randomly generating a different axis of rotation for each particle.

7. Set Tumble to .5 and Tumble Rate to .5. This setting gives you medium tumble at a slow speed. Set Variation to 3, which will vary the initial speed and direction of the particles.

8. Open the Material Editor and assign the multi-sub-object material from slot 5 Red/Wht/Blue Multi to the snow particles.

When multi-sub-object materials are assigned to particle systems such as Snow, each particle receives a different material ID number according to the number of material IDs in the multi-sub-object material assigned to it. Thus each particle as it is emitted gets a different material and will cycle through these different materials in a continuous loop.

NOTE

There is currently an anomaly in using two-sided multi-sub-object materials on snow particles. Using a standard material maps one side only, clicking on 2-Sided maps both sides. It seems that using multi-sub-object materials, whether two-sided or not, does not map both sides of the flakes. The same thing applies to a double-sided material type.

Use the "Force 2-Sided" option in the Render dialog if you really must have both sides of the particle rendered and want to use a multi-sub-object or blend material.

9. Render a frame to the Video Frame Buffer. Then assign the double-sided material Red/Blue Double from slot 6 in the Material Editor and render last.

Notice that the scene appears to have twice as many particles because both the facing and back sides of each particle are now mapped—one side red, the other blue.

Because you should always think about efficiency, use the double-sided material—you get two for one: Each flake does not disappear as it turns its normal away from the camera. This also gives you the opportunity to use more and varied particles. As the flakes rotate to show the color on the other side, the particle confetti seems to sparkle in the sunlight.

10. Set the Render Count to 5000. In the toolbar, select Edit, Clone, and make a copy with the name **Snow_OH2**. Because Snow has no "seed" parameter, you should set the Variation parameter to 4 so that each particle of the copy is not in the same position as the original particles.

11. In the Material Editor, assign the double-sided material in slot 3 Wht/ Yelo Double to the copy.

TIP

If you're not planning to animate the camera down the street, you could create your emitter smaller and farther from the camera, enabling the use of fewer particles. Then by borrowing a gag from the movie industry, you could place a small snow emitter close to the camera to give added depth.

12. In the Create panel, click on the Space Warp icon and pick Deflector. Drag in the top viewport to define the Space Warp about twice as wide as the particle emitter (see fig. 29.2).

13. Select both Snow systems, click on the Select and Bind icon, and drag from the Snow systems to the Deflector space warp.

NOTE

You can bind any number of particle systems to a space warp simultaneously by selecting them all and dragging to the space warp.

FIGURE 29.2

Create a deflector large enough to catch all the particles as they hit the ground.

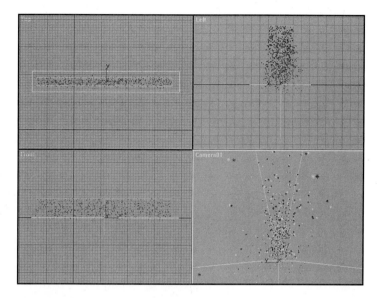

14. Select the Deflector. In the Modifier panel, set the deflector's Bounce parameter to 0.1. This setting provides a collision as the confetti reaches the ground and gives it just a slight movement as it hits.

15. In the toolbar's Named Selection Sets drop-down list, choose NYC Street. This usually would just select the geometry, but because it is hidden, answer yes at the alert to unhide.

To give the scene added depth, you want to add a few small individual snow particle systems emanating from the individual buildings. These individual systems represent people throwing the confetti into the street from a balcony or window. Because you should have a good understanding of snow by now, you can either experiment with this yourself or go ahead and merge the file "more confetti" from the accompanying CD.

This merged file contains four smaller snow emitters streaming confetti from the closest buildings.

16. Choose File Merge from the top menu and pick moreconf.max from the accompanying CD. Select all but the camera from the Merge dialog and click on OK.

17. Hold down the Ctrl key and click on the Gravity space warp to deselect it, leaving the merged Snow systems selected (snow sml1 through snow sml4). Now bind them to the Deflector space warp.

The particles are not affected correctly because they seem to move too far away from the deflector. The particles should not react this way, but it seems to be a viewport refresh thing as witnessed by the following step.

18. Press the Next Frame button and then the Previous Frame button. Then the binding to the deflector will be as you expect (see fig. 29.3).

Notice that these snow particles are assigned a multi-sub-object material with 64 sub-object materials. This shows that a maximum of 64 sub-object materials can be assigned to a particle system, and that the particles cycle through these 64 materials.

Feel free to experiment with this file by changing the materials or animating the camera down the street. It would be really interesting if you animated the camera and placed a windshield up front (as if you were in a car, for example). By using your knowledge of the Wind space warps that you will gain later in this chapter, you could simulate the effect of wind turbulence. A Wind space warp used with a bit of Decay would push the confetti out of the way of the windshield as the confetti came into close proximity of the windshield.

19. Save your scene. Take a look at the rendered file nycparade.avi on the accompanying CD.

All Purpose Particles Plug-In

You will use the following exercise to create smoke pouring from the smoke-stack of a train. Creating smoke or vapor can add realism to a scene. In this exercise, you will use the third-party particle system All Purpose Particles from Sisyphus Software.

NOTE

This is the only particle system that provides sub-frame launching of particles. These routines from Sisyphus are very inexpensive. In my opinion, everyone in the MAX community should encourage and support companies that provide quality affordable plug-ins.

All Purpose Particles includes the following particle systems and space warps:

- **The All Purpose Emitter.** A general particle system with many options and built-in presets.

- **Halo.** A particle system with generalized circular motion about an axis.

- **Phasor.** A particle system that creates and animates particles along the long dimension of a box emitter object.

- **Molasses.** A space warp that provides the viscous damping of particles.

- **Vortex.** A space warp that binds particles into a vortex-like swirling mass.

SMOKIN'

Start by loading the file 29himx.max from the accompanying CD. This is a simple scene of a train building up steam and then traveling down the tracks. Put the viewport in Wireframe and play.

Make things easier for the next few steps by clearing the scene of all but the train by hiding the tracks and ground plane, changing to four viewports, and then performing a Zoom Extents All.

1. Hide the tracks and ground and perform a Zoom Extents All. In the Create panel, choose Particles from the drop-down list and pick APE (All Purpose Emitter). In the top viewport, click and drag to create an emitter with a width of 20, a length of 20, and a depth of 35. (Check size in the Display rollup.)

2. Move the emitter to position it directly over the train's smokestack with barely less than half of the emitter overlapping the stack (see fig. 29.4), and then link it to the Train Dummy object.

FIGURE 29.4

Place the All Purpose Emitter just above the smokestack as the particles emit from the center.

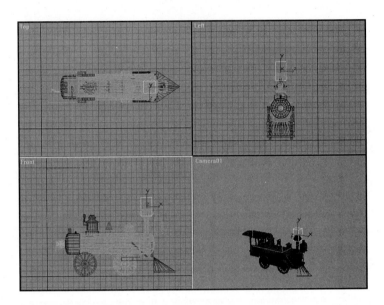

APE has six discrete rollups, each pertaining to a different set of particle parameters. It may seem a bit daunting at first, but the rollups are organized logically. To make life a little easier, they have included the following six presets and a return to default to get you started:

- Bubbles
- Fireworks
- Hose
- Shockwave
- Trail
- Weldsparks
- Default

APE presets can be used as is, or they can be used as the basis for your own custom particle effects.

3. Choose the Hose preset and move the Frame Slider to see that you are emitting particles that are somewhat close to the effect you are trying to achieve.

The first rollup section enables you to set up Particle Count, Size, Life, and Timing.

4. Open the Particle Generation rollup. Increase the Viewport Count to 500, change the Size to 14, and raise the Variation parameter to vary the particle size by 80 percent.

5. Change the End Frame to 400 to match the length of the scene. Also change the Life to 45 and add a variation of 50 percent. Close the rollup.

Next is the Velocity Settings rollup, which is an important part of this routine because it sets up the speed and direction of the particles.

6. Go to frame 50 and open the Velocity Settings rollup. Set both Vertical Velocity Angle and Horizontal Velocity Angle to 0—straight up. To spread the particles out a bit from straight up, set the Vertical Variation to 25 and the Horizontal Variation to 45.

7. To speed up the particles coming up from the emitter, set Vertical Speed to 2.8 and its variation to 50 percent.

The emitter velocity section of this rollup controls the particles' secondary motion data, which controls the amount of influence the emitter's speed has in relation to the particles' own velocity. As you can see, the Hose preset has set up 100 percent influence because the water leaving a hose takes on quite a bit of secondary influence as the hose is whipped around. You can experiment with this later. For now, however, turn this off because you do not want the particles flung forward as the train stops.

8. Set Emitter Velocity Influence to 0 percent. This effectively turns off secondary motion data and renders null the Multiplier and Variation parameters. Close the Velocity Settings rollup.

The following rollup, Gravity/Bounce, carries over the parameters from their original IPAS routine. Because you have better control and flexibility by using built-in gravity and deflector, you can turn these off.

9. Open the Gravity/Bounce rollup and turn off Gravity's Z influence. Bounce is off, so go ahead and close this rollup.

Skip down to the last rollup, which contains the Display settings. Here you set the Viewport Display of dots or ticks, ticks being preferred. Display also contains the Emitter Size parameters and the option to hide the emitter box.

NOTE

Changing the emitter size has no bearing on any parameter and will not affect the appearance at all. All APE parameters are based on the emitter's local coordinate system.

The last part to set up is particle Type/Mapping. This, along with the material assigned in the editor, is what controls the final appearance of the rendered particles. This control is important when trying to create a smoke effect.

In terms of particle type, you will see the familiar types of Triangle and Facing. A few new types are presented:

- Cube renders cube-shape particles.

- Special is the old Yost group IPAS type, which renders particles as three intersecting square planes.

- Pixel renders rangeless anti-aliased pixels.

Cube, Facing, and Special have been specifically set up to accept face-mapped materials. Face mapping enables you to use a graduated radial opacity map to hide the geometric shape of the particles that would ruin a smoke effect. Smoke is, of course, a series of soft-edged, semitransparent, somewhat rounded shapes.

10. Open the particle Type/Mapping rollup and choose Facing as the particle type. Because you are using a face-mapped material, the Mapping section becomes moot.

NOTE

It seems that the Cube particle type—used with a larger particle size (about 40) and a two-sided material—also shows promise as smoke.

11. Open the Material Editor and assign the material Smoke from slot number 1. Examine this closely; it is key to the smoke's appearance. The following text provides an explanation.

TIP

The use of a face-mapped radial gradient or radial gradient bitmap with Facing type particles effectively smooths out and hides the abrupt edges of the Quad Face particles. This also works well with Cube and Special type particles.

Because it is so important to this exercise, some time must be taken here to explain this Smoke material.

Notice that the Smoke material is a face map. This enables the mapping of the material to individual particles. In the map section, a graduated radial dot bitmap—white inside, black outside—is used in both the diffuse and opacity slots (see fig. 29.5). The use in the opacity slot effectively hides the edges of the Quad Facing particles. Notice that the opacity channel has been cranked way down to 6 to provide semitransparency throughout the particle, even in the whitest (most opaque) part of the bitmap. The dot bitmap in the diffuse slot tints the edges of the visible texture gray. Note that the tiling has been adjusted to give just the right amount of edge opacity and grayness. Noise has also been added to give more randomness to the smoke puffs. This could even be animated.

FIGURE **29.5**
This soft white dot bitmap used as an opacity map provides great transparency falloff to the Quad Facing particles.

12. Lastly, right-click to get at the particle properties and turn off Cast and Receive Shadows. You can also turn on Motion Blur.

13. Unhide the tracks and ground objects.

WARNING

Motion Blurred particles can sometimes add quite a bit to the final effect, but can be very costly in terms of processor time as the particle count goes up. Be certain to do a few test renders to ensure that motion blurring is not only necessary, but also worth the extra CPU cycles.

Save your scene and take a look at the final rendered file smokin.avi on the accompanying CD.

Sand Blaster Particle Plug-In

In the following exercise, you will work with the third-party particle plug-in Sand Blaster from Digimation. Sand Blaster is quite a particle package that does much more than just simple particle emitting, although it can be used that way. Sand Blaster's strengths include its capability to use an arbitrary object as an emitter and its ingenious way of using a series of target objects to guide the particles. Don't worry if you do not own Sand Blaster; a demo of the plug-in has been supplied on the accompanying CD. This demo enables you to follow through this exercise, but it does not enable you to render, which is okay because you are also supplied with the rendered animation.

COUNTDOWN

In this exercise, you will create an animation suitable for the intro of a demo tape. You will create a five-second countdown by using a series of numbers that blow apart into particles that rebuild themselves into the next number exactly one second (30 frames) later.

Load 29iimx.max from the accompanying CD and take a look at the scene. It is composed of the numbers 1 through 5 and a sphere. The sphere will be your emitter and the numbers will be the targets.

1. In the Create panel, Particle System drop-down, click on Sand Blaster. In the top viewport, click and drag to create a Sand Blaster icon about 12 units in size.

2. Go to the Modifier panel, in the Sand Blaster Setup section, and click on Set Emitter. Then use Select By Name to pick the hidden Sphere01 object.

3. Click on the check box to turn on particle activation.

Notice that the Sphere01 name is placed as the emitter in the rollup and also that a new rollout panel has been created called Emitter: Sphere01. Particle ticks are seen covering the sphere ready to go. If you make the front viewport active and maximized, you can scrub the frame bar to see that the particles are drawn off the sphere in the direction of the Sand Blaster icon arrow, which was created pointing down in the top viewport.

4. Open the Particle Parameters section, raise the Particle Render Count to 1000 and leave the default particle, Pyramid, chosen.

5. Open the Emitter: Sphere01 section which is at the bottom. The only change you will make here is under the Speed and Direction section, where you will choose From Icon Out. Notice that the Sand Blaster icon changes to point in all six directions. It does so because you have instructed the particles to move away from the icon in all directions. Go ahead and use the Align tool in the toolbar to center the icon to the numbers.

You are not adjusting the emitter parameters much because you are only using this emitter to get set up for the numbers. It is easier to get the movement of the particles to behave consistently between numbers, as is needed here, by adjusting them all as targets.

6. Close the Emitter rollup and scroll back up to the Setup section and click on Set Target. Use the H key select-by-name shortcut to choose the object 5 Text.

Notice how its name is placed as the target and that a new rollup has been created called Target: 5 Text—just as the emitter name was placed and a rollup created for the emitter earlier.

7. Scroll down to the bottom and open the rollout Target: 5 Text. In the Timing section, set the Begin Assembly to 30 and the End Assembly to 40. Set Chaos to 10 and Influence Time to 15. Because you want the particle simulation to hold for a bit at the numbers instead of just using them as a path, check the Transition Delay box and set Delay to 10 frames.

8. In the Assembly Direction section, check Center. In the Speed After Transition Delay section, set Speed to 5. Also click on From Icon Out.

9. In the Particle Location section, click on Target Simulation to present a great feature: As the particles leave the target, they appear to disassemble the object face by face.

The number objects have all been given a different-colored metal material. This enables you to change colors as you build the new numbers. Sand Blaster enables you a wide range of options over how to use materials and how change will be timed.

Sand Blaster uses a master/slave method for changing materials, whereby the resultant particle material and mapping can be inherited by the master object. You can elect to use the emitter's or particle's own material instead. In this exercise, you change the particle's color at each number by using the Master option from the targets.

10. In the Material and Mapping section, click to assign this target as a Master and then check Use Target Material. Set Stable Before and Stable After to 5. Set Transform Time to 20. Select and hide all objects except the Sand Blaster itself (Sphere01, 5 Text, 4 Text, 3 Text, 2 Text, and 1 Text).

TIP

In this author's opinion, the following functions are worthy of F key shortcuts.

F2   Unhide by name

F3   Hide unselected

F4   Hide selected

These have become second nature to me and are used often during production. In step 10 of this exercise, it would be more efficient to select the Sand Blaster icon and select F3 to hide everything unselected.

11. Because you are going to start the countdown animation from here, go into the Time Configuration dialog by clicking on the Time Configuration button and set Start Time to 40.

This finishes the set up of the number 5 object as the first target. Notice that the 5 Text object's outline shows up telling you that the particles are assembled into this configuration at this frame as part of the target simulation.

From here on out, it is just a matter of calculating the begin and end assembly times for the remaining targets and setting the other parameters identical to the first target. First, get all your targets assigned, remembering that this is a seconds countdown that is played at 30 fps.

12. In the Setup section, just above the Set Target button, click on the up spinner next to the target # field to set it to 2. Then click on the Set Target button and press the Select by Name button (or H key) and select object 4 Text as target 2. Notice that hidden objects appear in the Pick Object dialog.

13. Repeat this for target #3 as 3 Text, target #4 for 2 Text, target #5 for 1 Text, and finally set target #6 as Inside 3D Text.

NOTE

During the preceding steps, you had Particle Activation on to see the effect along the way. You get a much quicker response in production, however, if you turn Particle Activation off. This proves especially effective when you want to set a series of Sand Blaster parameters quickly.

14. Turn off Particle Activation in the Setup section.

15. Expand the target: 4 Text roll-out section and set Begin Assembly to 60 and End Assembly to 70.

16. Expand the target: 3 Text roll-out section and set Begin Assembly to 90 and End Assembly to 100.

17. Expand the target: 2 Text roll-out section and set Begin Assembly to 120 and End Assembly to 130.

18. Expand the target: 1 Text roll-out section and set Begin Assembly to 150 and End Assembly to 160.

19. Expand the target: Inside 3D Text roll-out section and set Begin Assembly to 180 and End Assembly to 190.

20. Then in each of these roll-ups, set the following parameters to match that of the first target, object 5 Text:

    Chaos—10
    Influence Time—15
    Check Transition and Set Delay—10
    Set Assembly Direction to Center
    Start Speed 5, Variation 2
    Check From Icon Out
    Check Target Simulation
    Check Master and Use Target material
    Set Stable Before and After to 5 and set Transition Time to 20

21. Close all the roll-outs. In the Setup section, turn on Particle Activation and Render Activation. Make a preview of the scene to test the movement of this particle simulation.

22. Turn on the Sand Blaster particle's Motion Blur property and save your scene.

Render the scene if you like or load the rendered file countdwn.avi from the accompanying CD.

Spray Particle System with Wind Space Warps

In this section, you explore the use of the Spray particle system in combination with the Wind space warp. You use Spray to act as the visible air flow to check the aerodynamics of a sports car in a wind tunnel. You use numerous Wind space warps to make the particles conform to the aerodynamics of the sports car. Because a particle system has yet to be created to implicitly cause particles to follow a path, you use a series of four Wind space warps to persuade them to follow the path over the sports car's contour. The Wind space warp, as well as most of the other particle space warps, have a feature called Decay, which allows the use of a series of space warps to modify the path of particles by setting them up with a fall-off to the space warp effect. Thus, each Wind space warp only affects a specific portion of the particles.

WIND TUNNEL AERODYNAMICS

Before you start, load 29aimx.max from the accompanying CD. This is the sports car model from the World Creating Toolkit.

1. From the Create panel, choose Particle Systems from the drop-down list. Then choose Spray from the list.

2. In the front viewport, click directly in front of the sports car.

3. Drag the mouse and click to create an emitter with a width and length of about 5 (see fig. 29.6).

Notice that the emitter is placed on the home grid with its vector pointing away from you. This is typical of creating particle systems in an orthographic viewport.

Note also that no particles are showing yet because the default timing starts the generation of particles at frame 1. If you move the Frame Slider, they are generated at the default sustainable rate of 3.3 particles per frame.

4. Now, you are going to increase the number of particles. With the Spray Emitter selected, go to the Modifier panel.

5. Increase the Viewport Count to 200 and the Render Count to 1000.

6. Open the Material Editor and apply the White Self Illuminated material from material slot 1 to better see the rendered particles.

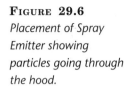

FIGURE 29.6

Placement of Spray Emitter showing particles going through the hood.

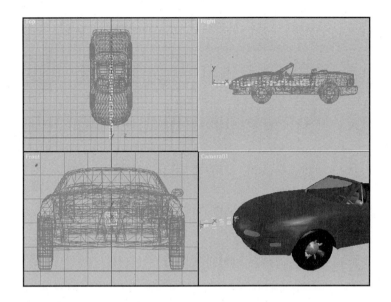

Now you have your first Spray particles. Obviously, however, it does not look right—the flow of particles goes through the roadster (see fig. 29.6). This is where Wind space warps come in.

7. From the Create panel, select the Space Warps icon, and then choose Wind from the list of space warps.

8. In the front viewport, click on an area just under the body of the sports car and drag to an icon size of about 10, and center it in front of the sports car.

Notice that the default Wind is planar (you will get into spherical in a moment), and the Wind space warp is created with its vector pointing toward you in orthographic viewports.

9. Rotate the Wind in the right viewport –135 degrees around the Z axis (pointing upward and toward the back of the sports car).

10. Click on Bind to Space Warp in the toolbar.

11. Select the Spray emitter (notice the cursor changes to the bind cursor) and drag to the Wind and release.

The cursor changes to the green ready bind cursor when over an appropriate space warp. You can use the hit key (Select By Name) and select the space warp from there. MAX conveniently filters the list to show only space warps.

Now you see the effects of the Wind space warp on the flow of particles.

WARNING

It is possible to Bind in reverse by selecting the space warp and binding to the particle system. This is easy to do because you usually bind directly after creating the space warp. Be careful though: In this way, the bind cursor changes to enable you to bind a space warp to geometric objects, even though a space warp can only affect particles.

12. Pick Select and Move from the toolbar.

13. Select the Wind and move it. Notice that no matter where you move the Wind, the particle effect is unchanged.

Remember that space warps influence world space. It is the vector coming off the space warp that tells the particles which direction to turn toward. Without a Decay setting (or effect from another space warp), moving this wind has no affect in the scene.

Seeing the effect the wind space warp has had in figure 29.7, you realize the particles are being coerced in the correct direction but they are not exactly right yet. The particles need to be sent over the hood by this wind. What you need is a stronger wind effect and a way to cause a fall off of the effect. You will use the Decay setting to give a fall off to the wind space warp effect.

FIGURE 29.7

Placement of the first wind space warp gets the particles moving in the correct direction, but not over the hood yet.

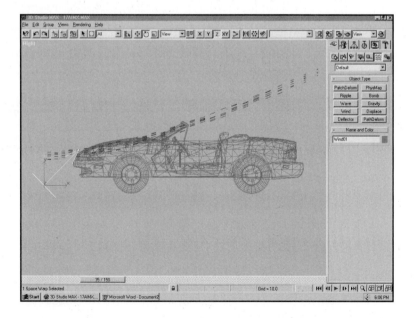

14. Go to the Modifier panel. With the Wind selected, set the Strength to 2.1 and Decay to 0.04.

Now adjust the Spray.

15. Select the Spray object.

16. Click on the drop-down list in the Modifier stack and select Spray.

17. Adjust the Speed to 6.5 (which also shortens their travel) and raise the Life to 40 to compensate for the shortening of distance that the particles will travel with this reduced speed.

Now you have coerced the particles over the hood as seen in figure 29.8.

FIGURE 29.8

By raising the wind strength, adding decay, and slowing the speed of the particles, they now go over the hood.

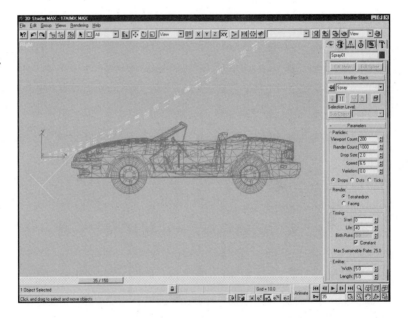

Notice that if you move the Wind space warp now, it makes a difference in the effect because of the fall-off effect of the Decay setting.

Now that the particles are starting to push over the hood, it is time to create another Wind space warp to keep the particles hugging the hood.

18. From the Create panel, choose Wind again.

19. Under the Force section, click on spherical and create a Spherical Wind space warp with an icon size of about 10.

20. Place the new Wind space warp about a third of the way up the hood, just above it (see fig. 29.9).

21. Select and Bind the Spray to this space warp.

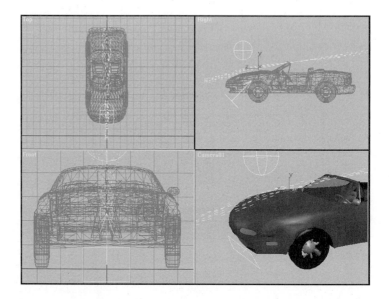

Because a spherical Wind space warp has a vector pointing directly out from the center in all directions, it needs at least some Decay to create the effect you need.

22. Change from Select & Bind to the Select icon, then select the spherical Wind object that MAX has named Wind02 by default.

23. In the Modifier panel, set the Decay at 0.055 and set the Strength at 3.1.

Now you need to do some position adjusting to get the particles to follow the contours of the sports car.

24. Drag the Frame Slider to frame 80 or so and position the two warps so that the particles appear to be flowing over the hood.

25. Move the planar space warp horizontally until it is directly under the spherical Wind space warp.

26. You might have to move the Spray emitter up or back a bit to prevent the particles from going into the hood (refer to figure 29.9).

Now you can make a third Wind space warp that will be used to push the particles up and over the windshield.

27. Shift+Clone (copy) the spherical Wind02 space warp to just below the intersection of the hood and windshield.

28. Set its Strength to 1.9 and its Decay to 0.045.

29. Bind to space warp as before.

30. Position this warp to get the particles to flow over the top of the windshield (see fig. 29.10).

FIGURE 29.10

Positioning third Wind space warp to coax particles to flow over windshield

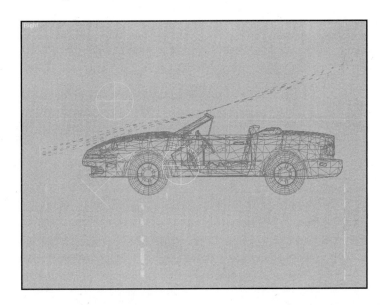

Now you just need one more Wind space warp to push the particles back horizontal after they flow over the windshield.

31. Shift+Clone (copy) Wind03 and place it just past the windshield.

NOTE

All the existing files have a net render directory default in Save File/Render. Change to your local drive before rendering.

32. Set its Strength to 18 and its Decay to 0.09.

33. Bind to space warp as before.

34. Position the Wind04 to push the particles back into a horizontal direction after passing over the windshield (see fig. 29.11).

35. Save your scene. (You may have to adjust these space warps a bit differently than outlined here, depending on exactly where they were placed.)

FIGURE 29.11
Positioning the fourth Wind space warp to coax the particles horizontally.

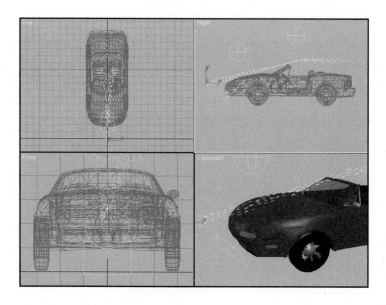

Load wtunnel.max from the accompanying CD to see the final version of the scene. Make a preview of the Camera View. Notice how the particles flow nicely over the roadster.

Notice that all the Spray particles seem to be aligned as they leave the emitter. This is one of the biggest caveats of using Spray. The problem is that the Spray particles are generated from the emitter on a per-frame basis. You would much prefer sub-frame generation of particles. When particles are generated per frame, a particle ends up being in the same position as the last particle in the next frame, which is very apparent as they leave the emitter, but is somewhat hidden as they are affected by the space warps. The best way to lessen this problem is to assign Motion Blur to the Spray particle system.

You can take a look at the renderings with and without Motion Blur by loading and viewing wtunnel.avi (without Motion Blur) and wtunnelm.avi (with Motion Blur).

Spray with Deflector and Gravity Space Warps

In the last exercise, you saw how you could affect Spray particles through the use of multiple Wind space warps. In the next exercise, you use the Spray particle system again, but this time you affect them by using the Gravity space warp and multiple Deflector space warps. Gravity, just as it sounds, adds a gravitational pull to the particles and a Deflector in a 2D plane that acts as collision detection.

In this exercise, you add Spray particles to a robotic welder to simulate the welding arc and flying sparks. You then explore the Deflector space warp that is used to bounce the sparks off the sled as it's welding. A second Deflector is used to bounce some of the sparks along the conveyer table. A Gravity space warp is used to add gravitational force to bring the particles back down to Earth.

ROBOTIC WELDER

Get started by loading 29bimx.max from the accompanying CD. This file consists of a robotic welding arm and a conveyor table with metal rails of a sled waiting to be welded together.

Slide the Frame Slider, and you see that the robotic arm has already been hierarchically linked, and interactive IK was used to place the welding head at a few weld spots. Go ahead and put the first weld together.

1. From the Create panel, choose Particle Systems from the drop-down list, then choose Spray.

2. In the top viewport, create a Spray Emitter at the tip of the weld head with an icon size of 4.

Notice that the emitter is created with its vector pointing down, away from you in the view. In the Front viewport, place the emitter at the end of the weld head and link it to the weld head.

3. Move and rotate the emitter as necessary to place it at the tip of the weld head with the vector pointing out from it (see fig. 29.12).

4. When it is in position, link the emitter to the weld head.

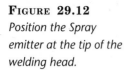

FIGURE 29.12

Position the Spray emitter at the tip of the welding head.

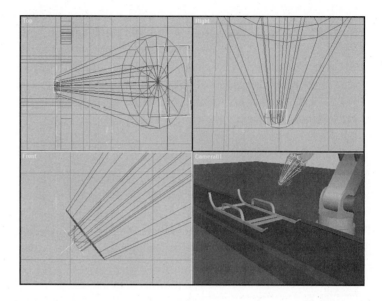

Scrub the Frame Slider and notice how the particles behave now that the emitter is animated. The particles seem to have a secondary motion to them because after a particle is emitted, it travels in that direction until acted on by another force. This happens as subsequent particles are emitted in a new direction, which gives you a nice "water out the end of a moving hose" effect. File that thought away for future use.

In the preceding exercise, you let the particles be emitted in a continuous stream starting at frame 0. Here, this will not work. You need to start emitting the particles when the weld head comes to a stop.

5. Move to frame 25 when the weld head is in position.

6. Be certain that the Spray emitter is selected and go the Modifier panel and set Viewport Count at 200 and Render Count at 1000.

7. In the Timing section, set the Start to 23, a couple frames before the weld head stops.

You'll see the particles on the frame after this start frame. You'll leave the start frame here to get a jump on the particle creation just before the weld head stops.

Now as you scrub the Frame Slider, the particles appear to be emitted as the head comes to position. You need to stop the particles as the weld head lifts up. A bit of calculation is called for here.

The weld head begins to lift off the mark at frame 40. You could probably stand to overshoot this a bit. Assume, for example, that you want to spray for 20 frames, from frame 23 to frame 43. If you want to exhaust all 1,000 particles over 20 frames, you need to birth the particles at 50 particles per frame because 1,000 particles/20 frames = 50 particles per frame.

8. Turn off the Constant button and set the Birth Rate at 50.

NOTE ———

You don't have to do the calculation here. You can do it interactively.

9. Set the Birth Rate back to about 15.

10. Go to frame 43, the frame at which you want to stop emitting particles.

11. Click on and drag the Birth Rate slider and drag to increase its value.

While you are raising this value, watch the emitter, and you will see the particles slowly stop being emitted. This should be around frame 50.

You will want the particles to last longer than 30 frames.

12. Make certain that the Birth Rate is set to 50.

13. Set the Life to 50.

Scrub the Frame Slider and see that the particles do indeed appear to start as the Spray head comes to rest, and end as the Spray head moves again.

The problem now is that Spray particles, once destroyed, are always regenerated again. This regeneration would be okay if the next stop of the weld head were to pause to coincide with the next release of particles, but this is unlikely—although it almost happens here.

To stop particles from being emitted altogether, you'll have to animate its Birth Rate to 0.

You can do this at any frame after frame 44 (when they stop being emitted) and before frame 74 (when they start after being reborn).

14. Go to frame 60.

15. Turn on the Animate button.

16. Set Birth Rate to 0.

17. Turn off the Animate button.

Doing this, you know that a Bézier float key is created at frame 60. You also know that another key is created automatically at frame 0, resulting in the particle birth rate animating from 50 at frame 0 to 0 at frame 60. Nice effect if you want a tapering off of the effect, but it is not what you want here. As good animators though, you should file this information away for another time.

Now, drop the Birth Rate from 50 to 0 over just 1 frame.

18. Go into Track View, scroll down to Spray01, and get to the Birth Rate track. Right-click on the first key and change the Out Tangent to Steps. This automatically changes the next keys in Tangent to Step. (As an alternative, you could just move the key at frame 0 to frame 59.)

During welding, the sparks usually bounce around a bit—so use your Deflector space warp to create this effect. Remember, a Deflector is a 2D plane that causes particles that come in contact with the deflector plane to bounce off of it. A Deflector provides collision detection for particles.

19. In the Create panel, click on the Space Warp icon.

20. Click on Deflector and, in the Top View, drag to create a Deflector with a width and height of 20.

21. Move the Deflector to the height of the top of the cross bar to be welded, centered on the weld head (see fig. 29.13).

22. Select the Spray object and bind it to the Deflector space warp.

FIGURE 29.13

Position the Deflector directly under weld head, just above the cross bar.

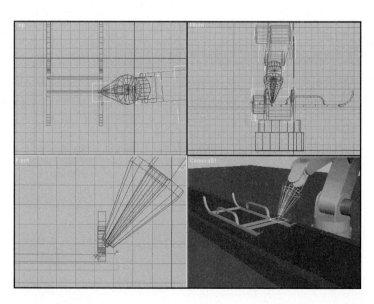

As you scrub the Frame Bar, you see the particles bounce off the Deflector.

Because you left the default Bounce parameter at 1, the particles bounce off the Deflector at the same speed that they collide with it.

NOTE ——

It does not matter which way the Deflector is facing. Particles bounce off either side of a Deflector. You can witness this by rotating the Deflector 180 degrees.

The effect does not look quite right because the particles bounce off at a predictable angle. Add some randomness to help the effect.

23. Select the Deflector and open Track View.

24. Select the Transform Rotation Track and click on Assign Controller.

25. Assign the Noise Rotation Controller and open its Properties.

26. Because there is no need to rotate on that axis, drop the Z Strength to 0.

27. Set Frequency to 0.35.

28. Set Fractal Noise Roughness to 0.4.

Go back to the Spray to give the particles a longer drop size. You should also add a bit of variation for even more randomness. Variation varies the speed and direction of particles, spreading them out. You should also slow the speed.

29. Select the Spray, go to the Modifier panel, Modifier Stack, and select Spray from the drop-down list.

30. Set Drop Size to 4 and Variation to 1.

31. Set Speed at 7.

Scrub the Frame Slider. You are starting to get the effect that you want now. Notice the randomness of the sparks as they hit the sled's frame and bounce about.

WARNING ——————————————————————————————————————

Notice as you scrub the Frame Slider that it is possible to upset the Spray to Deflector collision detection when animating the Deflector in certain situations. A few of the particles can get by the Deflector (see fig. 29.14).

FIGURE 29.14

*Some particles may go
through a Deflector
when the Deflector is
animated.*

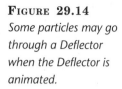
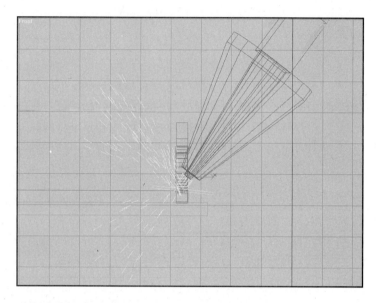

Don't think of the particles going through this Deflector as a problem. Think of it as a feature. Do what any good animator would do: Use it to your advantage! These non-deflected particles give you a great opportunity to place a second Deflector at the table height to bounce the missed particles across the table. Besides, in real life, not all the welding sparks would bounce away anyway; some would hit the table.

32. Create a Deflector with the same width (114) as the table and a length of about 120.

33. Set Bounce to .5.

34. Move the Deflector to the top of the table (see fig. 29.15).

35. Bind the Spray to this Deflector.

For realism, you can add one more thing. Make the particles fall under gravity. To do so, use a Gravity space warp.

36. Go to Create panel, choose the Space Warp icon, then pick Gravity.

37. Click on an area in the top viewport and drag to create a Gravity space warp with an icon size of about 50.

Notice that the default Gravity space warp is planar and that it is created with its vector pointing away from you in an orthographic viewport. The force of gravity is in the direction of the vector.

38. Bind the Spray to this Gravity space warp.

FIGURE 29.15

Placing a second Deflector to bounce some particles across the table.

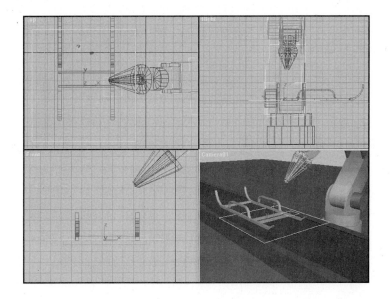

Instantly, the particles are affected by gravity. Note that it does not yet matter where the icon is placed in the scene. Gravity is simply a force in the scene in the direction of the vector. Because Decay controls the falloff of the effect from the icon, it matters where the icon is placed when used with Decay.

39. Move the icon above the scene until its vector arrow touches the table as seen in figure 29.16.

FIGURE 29.16

Place the Gravity space warp here so the vector arrow just touches the table.

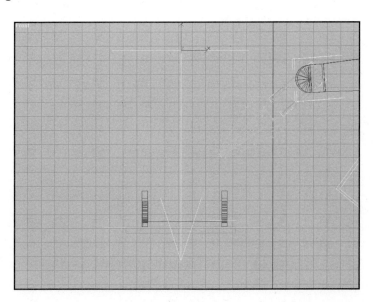

40. Set the Decay to 0.01

Now assign a better material to get the particles to stand out better.

41. Select the Spray emitter, open the Material Editor and assign the Red Hot Particle material from slot number 5 to the emitter.

You now have some nice spark action going on. You may want to play with a few of these settings to get an effect you like. You might want to have the particles last longer. To make them last longer, raise the life of the Spray to 75. You might want to see the particles dance a bit more as they scoot across the table. In that case, increase the Deflector Bounce parameter to 0.8.

42. Save your file.

Load up welder.max from the accompanying CD. Take at look at the rendered version welder.avi.

Object Space Warps

The next two exercises deal with object space warps. As the name implies, these are space warps that are meant to be used to deform objects (as opposed to particles). Note that the Displace space warp is a universal space warp in that it can be used to deform particles as well as to deform objects.

- **Displace Space Warp.** This is a two-part exercise that delves into the use of Displace to deform a tire on a surface. The first part causes the tire to deform on a flat road; the second has the tire deform on a bumpy road. The bumpy road exercise uses the bitmap mapping option that is available for the Displace.

- **Path Deform Space Warp.** This is a new space warp that the Yost Group included with the MAX 1.1 upgrade CD. The Path Deform has many uses, such as flying text along a path, deforming to the path as it goes. In this exercise you use Path Deform in two ways. One way is to use it strictly for modeling as you will do to create piping; the other is to use the same Path Deform as an animation path for objects to travel inside of the pipe.

- **Bomb Space Warp.** Here you blow up the sun for a bit of Big-Bang fun. The Bomb space warp is used to explode an object into its individual faces. The importance in this exercise is to minimize the effect of seeing the individual faces as they blow apart.

The Displace Space Warp

The following exercise presents you with the task of creating the illusion of a car tire as it rolls down the road. How about creating a car tire that doesn't just rotate, but also bounces a bit? That would be great, but what would you do to solve the tire contact with the road? In real life, the air-filled rubber tire deforms a bit against the road as it rolls along.

This is a great job for a MAX space warp. In particular, look at Displace— the only MAX space warp that works with both particles and geometry.

ROUGH ROAD AHEAD (PART 1)

Before you begin, load 29cimx-1.max from the accompanying CD. This file consists of a tire rotating down the road with a bit of bounce happening. The camera is linked in such a way as to keep the tire in view and not bounce with the tire. Unfortunately, as the tire goes down the road, it goes right through the road. The following steps take care of that.

1. In the Create panel, choose the Space Warp icon and pick Displace.

2. Create a Displace space warp in the top viewport about the same size as the ground surface (see fig. 29.17).

3. Select the tire. Using the Bind to Space Warp icon, bind it to the Displace space warp. Make certain that you bind the Geometric object to the space warp. This way the bind cursor only allows binding to space warps.

FIGURE 29.17
The Displace space warp in relation to the ground plane.

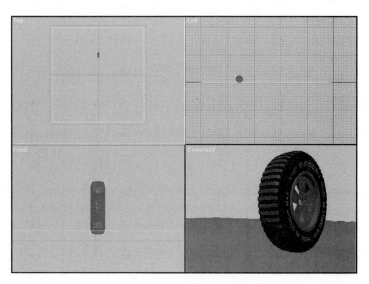

TIP

Use the H key to assign the Bind object.

There currently seems to be an anomaly in the Tire object that flips the normals of the tire after it is bound to the Displace space warp. The problem can be traced back to a mirrored spline before the tire was lathed, which can mess with the object's data flow. The cause of this is reviewed a bit later in the second part of this Rough Road Ahead exercise. For now, it is easy enough to fix.

4. Go to the Modifier panel and, with the tire selected, apply a Normal modifier and check Flip to reverse the normals.

5. Nothing is deforming yet because the Displace space warp has no strength. Therefore, select the Displace space warp, go to the Modifier panel, and set Strength at 2.

Notice that the whole tire object, which is the parent of the rim, moves away from the rim object. Because they are separate objects, albeit linked objects, the tire is affected by the space warp but the rim is not. This is not yet the effect we are looking for anyway because a space warp is applied in world space and goes on forever, which has moved the entire tire off of the rim. The Decay setting, which acts as a falloff for the effect, takes care of this by deforming only a small portion of the tire at a point where the tire meets the road surface. This will leave the parts of the tire surrounding the rim unaffected, and the effect will look correct.

6. Still in the Modifier panel, grab the Decay Spinner. While holding Ctrl for acceleration, drag the spinner up.

You see the effect interactively begin to fall off. The tire returns to the rim and the effect is concentrated at the bottom.

7. Set Decay to 100.

Take a look at figures 29.18 and 29.19 to see the difference between No Decay and Decay at 100.

You must do some tweaking to get the tire to meet the road surface. As it is now, the tire's deformation happens, but not exactly at the road surface. Also, as the tire bounces along, it goes above the road surface at certain frames. The following steps correct this.

FIGURE 29.18

Displace with No Decay causes the whole tire to move off the rim.

FIGURE 29.19

Displace with Decay of 100 concentrates the space warp at the bottom of the tire.

8. In the Front View, zoom in to the bottom of the tire.

9. Drag the Time Slider to frame 3, where the tire is at a low position.

10. Select the Displace space warp and move it along the Y axis until the tire meets the surface (see fig. 29.20).

11. Move to frame 12, where the tire is a bit in the air.

12. Select and move the tire to meet the surface (see fig. 29.21).

FIGURE 29.20
Move the space warp down until the tire meets the surface.

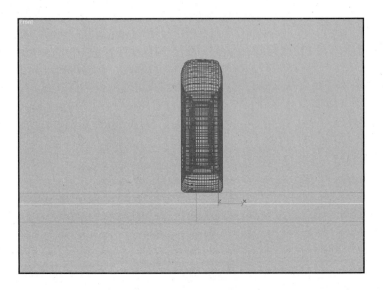

FIGURE 29.21
Move the tire down to meet the surface.

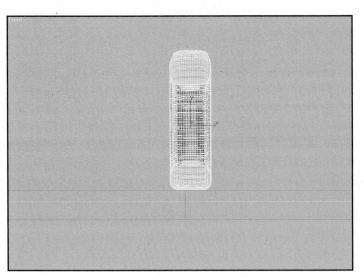

Play the animation in the front viewport or play the bounce.avi file from the accompanying CD. Notice how niccly the rubber meets the road as it bounces along.

Save your scene and load bounce.max. Take a look at the rendered file bounce.avi on the accompanying CD.

ROUGH ROAD AHEAD (PART 2)

Now, take this exercise a bit further. What if the road surface you're traveling is not flat? How could you solve the illusion of the tire riding on a bumpy surface?

You know there are different types of Mapping parameters: Planer, Cylindrical, Spherical, and Shrink Wrap. If you had a rock in the road, you could use Spherical mapping to deform the tire going over the rock. If you had an obstacle such as a pipe, you may be able to use Cylindrical mapping. But a bumpy surface does not lend itself to these types of mappings. In such cases, use a bitmap to adjust the strength of your planar mapping.

Take a look at the next scene.

Load 29cimx-2.max from the accompanying CD. This file shows the tire riding over a bumpy surface. Animation keys cause the tire to go up and down according to the bumps.

You could tweak the keys to cause the tire to ride perfectly over the bumps, but that would be very tedious—especially if the surface you're traveling over is randomly bumpy. The bumps here are somewhat repeatable to help you see the effect you will try to create. The tire was also purposely animated not to go completely over the bumps, but goes through the top of them.

The MAX Displace space warp helps you correct the tire's ride over the bumps. In particular, you can use the Luminance Value of a bitmap to influence the amount of displacement.

Now is the time to create a Displace space warp.

1. In the Create panel, choose the Space Warp icon and pick Displace.

2. Maximize the top viewport. In that view, click and drag, starting in the center of the ground surface. Try to make this the same size as the ground surface

Because of how the ground surface was created, it is important for this exercise that the Displace space warp be the same size and in the same position as the ground surface. It is pertinent to this exercise to know how it was done, but you will not go through the steps.

The ground surface started out as a 500-by-500-by-5 box. Because a Displace modifier was to be used to shape the surface, it was given 100 segments in the X and Y. An Edit Mesh modifier was then applied. Next, all the faces not on the top plane were selected and deleted. Note that there is now a parametric object plug-in called Grid, created by Peter Watje, that was uploaded to the CompuServe Kinetix forum libraries that will create a 2D planar grid object. Had this been available earlier, it would have greatly reduced the amount of steps and time needed to create this preceding ground surface. The remaining faces were then tessellated. Next, the Displace modifier was applied using a bitmap (2bump.tga) to deform the surface of the box, which transformed it into the bumpy ground surface you see.

Lastly, an Optimize modifier was applied to lower the number of faces. The stack was then collapsed to an editable mesh for memory and viewport speed reasons.

Remember that the Displace modifier is like the Displace space warp. Modifiers, however, work in Object Space; space warps work in World Space.

T I P

Always save a copy of an object before collapsing the stack. You may have to come back and adjust the object later. In which case, you will be glad you saved it.

3. With the space warp still selected, click on the Align icon.

4. Click on the ground surface and then Align in the X and Y axes.

There are no Width and Length parameters, so you must scale the Displace space warp by using the Select and Scale icon in the toolbar. If you had a Width and Height parameters, you could just set them to the same measurements as the ground surface.

5. Select Scale from the toolbar.

6. Scale the space warp to a size very close to the size of the ground surface (see fig. 29.22).

Back to your scene, bind the tire to the displace space warp.

7. Select the tire.

8. Bind it to the space warp.

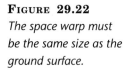

FIGURE 29.22
The space warp must be the same size as the ground surface.

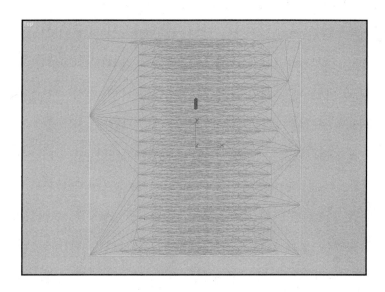

WARNING

Strange things seem to happen to an object when, during its creation, Transform Scale or Mirroring (Negative Scale) has been used. The tire was created from a line that was mirrored to make both sides symmetrical before lathing. This is a result of Object Data Flow; because MAX transforms are evaluated at the end of the stack and modifiers are evaluated earlier, there is no "mirror" occuring for the modifier stack to affect. The result here is that the face normals get flipped. Basically, mirror and non-uniform scale should only be performed in conjunction with the Xform modifier. It is easily enough fixed with a Normal modifier though.

9. Go back to the four viewports, apply a Normal modifier to the tire, and flip the normals.

Notice that when you apply a modifier to the stack after you have applied a space warp, the modifier is placed *before* the space warp. It is very important for MAX users to understand this. 3DS MAX has a very specific order in which it calculates object data. The following list shows the order in which objects are evaluated.

- Master object (creation parameters)
- Object modifiers (Bend, Normal, Lathe, and so on)
- Transforms (Position, Rotate, and Scale changes)
- Space Warps
- Object properties (Name, Material, and so on)

This is not the place to get heavily into this. You must, however, understand object data flow to understand why the normal modifier was placed where it was in the stack and why space warps are always evaluated after transforms. For more information about Object dataflow, refer to *Inside 3D Studio Volume I* (pages 20–26) and the *MAX User Guide* (pages 1–14 through 1–17).

Now, to get back to setting up your Displace space warp. The trick is to set up and vary the strength of the Planar space warp by using the Luminance Value of a bitmap image. You use the same image in your Displace space warp as was used in the ground surface Displace modifier.

10. Select the Displace space warp and go to the Modifier panel.

11. In the Image section, click on None and select 2bump.tga from the accompanying CD.

12. Before clicking on OK, click on View to take a look at the image.

The image is but a single white radial gradient dot on a middle gray background (refer to figure 29.5).

13. Click on OK to select this bitmap.

14. Set Strength to 4 and Decay to 100. Set Blur to 2.

The ground surface modifier was tiled in the V direction to create long bumps. Your Displace space warp must also be tiled.

15. Set the Map V Tile Setting to 20.

16. Maximize the left viewport and play the scene.

Notice how the tire now deforms according to the Luminance Value of the bitmap. The same bitmap was used to deform the ground surface and influence the strength of the Displace space warp (both were lined up and the same size). The result is that the tire appears to deform as a result of the bumps of the surface.

The illusion is completed by making a few adjustments to the tire and space warp to bring the tire into better contact with this surface.

17. As necessary, move the Displace space warp down to effect a better contact between the tire and ground surface (see fig. 29.23).

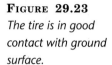

FIGURE 29.23
The tire is in good contact with ground surface.

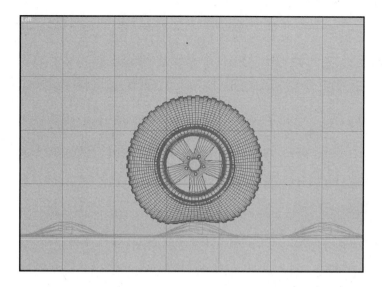

18. Save your scene.

Load bumps.max and see how the illusion has been completed. View the rendered animation bumps.avi on the accompanying CD.

Path Deform Space Warp

In the following exercise, you use the Path Deform space warp, which was not included in the original shipping of MAX 1.0, but was one of the new features added with the 1.1 update. This space warp enables you to deform an object along a spline path. You use that capability in this project of the new and improved Flexible Head Roto-Rooter. This space warp is quite unique compared to the other space warps. For one thing, it deforms in Object Space rather than World Space.

THE ROTO-ROOTER

1. Load imx29e.max from the accompanying CD. This file consists of a Tube object, a Roto-Head, and a spline. This spline serves as the basis for both your modeling and animation.

2. In the Create panel, choose the Space Warp icon, then pick Path Deform.

The only parameter is a Pick Path button. All object deformation is controlled through the Binding parameters in the Modifier Stack—another difference from the other space warps.

3. Click on the Pick Path Button.

4. Click on the spline.

The name of the referenced spline is placed above the Pick Path button and a space warp gizmo is shown in the viewport. Notice that the splines first vertex is used as a start for the gizmo.

Note

The spline's Step settings have no effect on the space warp. You can crank the line steps down to 0 and, although the line will be linear from vertex to vertex, the Path Deform gizmo is not affected. It uses true spline interpolation. If you go to the Edit Spline level of the modified line and move the vertices, however, the gizmo conforms.

5. Select the Tube Pipe object and Bind it to the Path Deform space warp

6. Go to the Modifier panel and click on Move Object to Path.

Notice that the length of the tube is shorter than the path. This was done purposely to show that the object is deformed along the path and not modified to fit the path. No problem though, just adjust the height of the tube.

7. Go to the Tubes Creation parameters and increase its height interactively until it matches the length of the path (or type **475**).

The process of binding to the space warp effectively deforms the tube to the gizmo, and the Move to Path places the object directly on the path. Your Tube Pipe should resemble that shown in figure 29.24.

Note that it is important to have a sufficient number of segments to get a good deform around the bends.

Tip

The Path Deform space warp is not just an animation tool; it is also a great modeling tool. Used in place of lofts in some instances, it takes care of the problem of a shape being scaled non-uniformly as it gets lofted around bends.

FIGURE 29.24

Deforming the Tube Pipe to the Path Deform space warp.

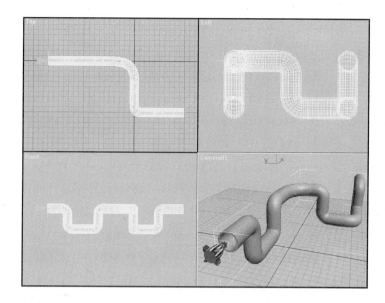

8. Select the Roto-Head object and Bind it to the Path Deform space warp.

9. Click on Move Object to Path.

Now, explore the animation capabilities of the Deform space warp.

10. Go to frame 200 and turn on the Animate button.

11. Set the Percent parameter to 100.

12. Turn off the Animate button.

13. Select the Tube, and open the Material Editor and apply the Glass Piping material.

Play the scene and notice how animating the Path Deforms percent value animated the Roto-Head object from the path start (0 percent) at frame 1 to the path end (100 percent) at frame 200.

NOTE

See how the object deforms according to the gizmo as it goes around the bends. Notice that as the Roto-Head rounds the bends, certain parts deform more smoothly than others. When the Roto-Head was created, it was created to have enough faces where the object was to bend freely. Other parts were kept face simple to simulate the semi-rigid scraping extrusions. There will always be some deformation though, especially closest to and opposite of the apex of the bends. Figure 29.25 shows a close-up view of the Roto-Head object.

FIGURE 29.25

Controlling the Deform by using various face densities.

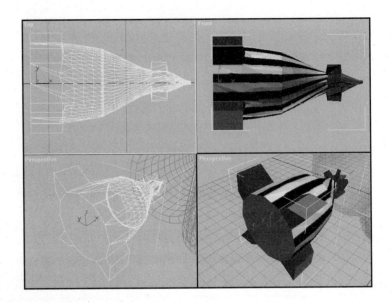

The Roto-Head must now rotate because it's scraping the pipe.

14. Click on Rotate and try to rotate the Roto-Head.

Another difference from other space warps is that animation of an object bound to a Path Deform space warp is fully controlled by that space warp's parameters. The bound object does not respond to Transform Move, Rotate, or Scale. To rotate the head, you must use the space warp's parameters.

15. Go to frame 200 and turn on the Animate button.

16. Set the Rotation parameter to 2,000.

17. Turn off the Animate button.

Play the scene. Now you have a rotating Roto-Head. Now, have a cable follow the Roto-Head.

18. Unhide the Cylinder Cable.

19. Select and Bind it to the space warp.

20. Click on Move object to path.

The cable has a Striped material running down its length. Use your Path Deform parameters to simulate the twist of the cable.

Remember the Twist parameter twists the end of the object while the start of the object is held still. This parameter is also animatable, but is not animated here.

21. Set the Twist parameter to 20,000.

As the Roto-Head travels along the path, you need to have the cable appear along the path, with these steps.

22. Turn on the Animate button.

23. Set Stretch to 0.

24. Go to frame 200.

25. Set the Stretch parameter to 1.

And then you need to rotate to match the Roto-Head animated rotation by using the following steps.

26. Set the Rotate parameter to 2,000.

27. Turn off the Animate button.

WARNING

Track View displays some Path Deform space warp parameters at 1/100th of their actual parameters, including the Stretch and Twist parameters. So be careful when doing work in Track View with Path Deform. If you open Track View and look at the key info for stretch at frame 200, you see it displayed at a value of 100, and yet the display shows 1.0.

28. Unhide the Tube Dirt object.

29. Select and Bind it to the Path Deform space warp.

30. Click on Move object to path.

Now animate to simulate the dirt being scraped away, a reverse of the cable animation.

31. Go to frame 200 and turn on the Animate button.

32. Set the Stretch parameter to 0.

33. Set the Percent parameter to 100.

34. Turn off the Animate button.

Play the scene. The Tube Dirt object seems to be scraped away by the Roto-Head. Animating the Stretch parameter from 1 to 0 shrinks the Tube Dirt to 0 height, and animating the Percent from 0 to 100 makes the shrinking begin from the opposite end.

35. Save your scene.

Load rooter.max. Take a look at the rendered animation file rooter.avi on the accompanying CD-ROM.

The Bomb Space Warp

In the following exercise, you work with the Bomb space warp. The Bomb space warp explodes objects into their individual faces. You use it in this exercise to create a sun exploding for a big-bang explosion effect.

THE BIG BANG THEORY

To begin, load 29gimx.max.

1. In the Create panel, pick GeoSphere, click in the Camera View, and drag to create a geosphere in the center of the home grid with a radius of 12. Leave it at the default isoca type and raise the segments to 5. Turn on Generate Mapping coordinates.

2. Open the Material Editor and assign the material Sun from slot 1.

Notice that the Sun material is composed of an orange and red noise map for the diffuse map channel, and that UVW is checked so that it maps to object coordinates rather than world coordinates. Modified versions of this noise map are also used for the self illumination and bump map slots. Render to see the effect.

3. In the Create panel, Space Warps icon, pick Bomb. Click in the Camera View to place it inside the geosphere.

Because the Bomb effect originates from the position of the Bomb object, go ahead and align it to the geosphere.

4. Pick Align from the top menu and click on the geosphere. Then click on the X, Y, and Z positions.

5. Select the geosphere, pick Select and Bind from the toolbar, and bind the geosphere to the bomb.

6. Select the Bomb space warp, go to the Modifier panel, and set Detonation to 25. This is the frame at which the bomb begins to explode the sun.

Scrub the frame slider past frame 25 a couple times to see the effect. Notice how symmetrical the explosion looks—not very realistic (see fig. 29.26). Go to frame 27 so that you can see the effect of changing the following parameters.

7. Set the Strength at .4 to slow the exploding faces, and set Gravity at 0— after all, there would be no gravity in space to pull the pieces downward.

8. Turn on the Animate button, go to frame 100, and set Chaos to 2.5. Turn off the Animate button.

9. Open Track View and filter down to selected objects only. Expand Bomb01 and Object (bomb) to get to the Chaos track. Select the key at frame 0 and slide it to frame 25. Minimize Track View. Notice the difference in the apparent randomness (see fig. 29.27).

FIGURE 29.26

Default bomb parameters showing a very symmetrical explosion.

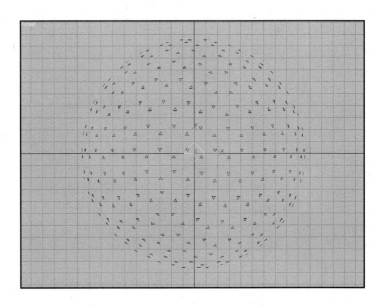

FIGURE 29.27
*Adding chaos to the
Bomb space warp can
add a bit of
randomness.*

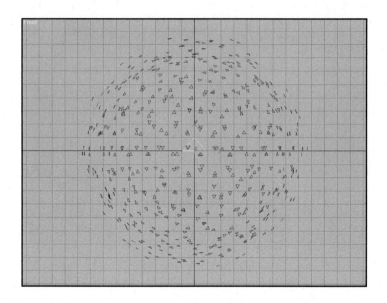

WARNING

The Bomb Detonation parameter does not update in the viewport if it has been animated. It shows the setting of the current frame at the time that the panel is opened. Always check in the Track View, Track Info dialog for the true setting.

The following two parameters were included in the original Yost Group explode IPAS for 3DS DOS and are sorely missing in this space warp.

- More control over the fragmenting of faces. It would be nice to be able to set a min/max fragmentation range instead of exploding every face.

- Capability to assign a rotation or tumbling amount to the exploding faces.

TIP

The following shows workarounds for the missing parameters.

You can animate an increase in the number of faces (segments) as the explosion happens to simulate larger pieces of the object being broken up into smaller pieces. Motion Blur also helps, if appropriate.

You can fake the tumbling of faces by animating the Chaos parameter.

10. Select the geosphere and open the Modifier Stack to get to the geosphere Creation parameters. Go to frame 35, turn on the Animate button, and set Segments to 14. Turn off the Animate button.

11. Restore Track View that is still filtered to selected objects only. Expand the GeoSphere01, Object (GeoSphere) track to get to the Segments track. Select and move the key at frame 0 to frame 26. Minimize Track View.

Scrub the frame bar to see the effect. Between frames 27 and 35, the number of segments is increased by one per frame until frame 35. Also, the animated chaos from step 8 creates a nice scattering of these faces. Notice the difference in the number and size of faces (see fig. 29.28).

FIGURE 29.28

The sun after animating its segments to increase their number and make them smaller.

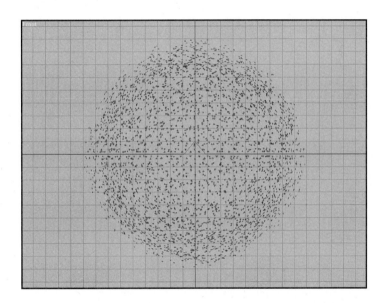

The explosion is so sudden that it seems to need some anticipatory characteristics before the actual big bang—the sun should shudder a bit before blowing apart.

12. Restore Track View, get to the geosphere Position track. Highlight position, click on the Assign Controller button, and pick Position List. Expand the tracks to get to the "available" track. Click on the Assign Controller button again and pick Noise Position.

13. Open the Noise Controller properties, set Seed to 13 and set X, Y, and Z Strength to 2. Raise ramp-in to 25 and Fractal Roughness to .5. Drag the right end of the range bar to coincide with the start of the explosion at frame 26.

Scrub the frame slider to see that the sun now starts to shudder in anticipation of the big bang.

14. Unhide the combustion apparatus that is already set up. Select and link it to the sun.

The big bang is just about ready to render, but to help make it as realistic as possible, you should lessen the look of the triangular faces during the explosion. These can ruin this effect.

15. Right-click on the Sun and turn on its Motion Blur parameter in the Properties dialog. Also set the G-buffer channel to 1. The Render dialog's Motion Blur parameter has already been set.

16. Open the Video Post dialog and notice that Glow has been added to the sun pieces after the explosion. This has the dual purpose of adding a nice glow to the exploding faces and helps blur the triangle face edges.

Notice also that Tom Hudson's starfield generator has been added to the queue. This freeware plug-in has been provided on the accompanying CD-ROM for your convenience.

17. Minimize Track View and change the Camera View to the *Cam-shake* Camera View. This camera is animated to add to the realism of being affected by the shockwave of the explosion. This camera dollies out to show more of the explosion and has a noise controller added at the time of the explosion to simulate the impact of the shockwave.

18. Save your scene.

View the rendered file bigbang.avi on the accompanying CD-ROM.

NOTE

After this chapter was written, a new freeware plug-in called Bomb2 was released to the CompuServe forum by Johnny Ow. This plug-in can be installed in your 3DS MAX plug-in directory and will appear under the Space Warps icon in a new listing in the drop-down list called Johnny Ow. Bomb2 adds the Fragmentation Min/Max parameters (for chunks) and Spin parameters mentioned in the preceding exercise, as needed by an Explosion space warp. It also adds a Scale parameter for scaling the chunks over time. Bomb2 is included on the accompanying CD, please send a note thanking Johnny Ow (Johnny@ywd.com) for this fine contribution to your MAX toolbox and for his support of the MAX community at large.

Feel free to repeat this exercise, using his Bomb2 space warp to create chunks of the sun exploding, rather than just faces.

In Practice: Particles, Space Warps, and Physics

- **Particle systems can simulate many objects.** As these exercises show, particle systems are very versatile and can be used to create the illusion of all sorts of natural and unnatural phenomena. Smoke, dust, jet exhaust, rain, laser blasts, and welding sparks are all possible with particles. As you explore them further, you will find many more uses. How about a little dust kicked up by the tire as it rolls down the street? How about a ring of space dust particles as the sun explodes?

- **Each of the particle systems has similarities, but each also carries its own particular strengths for a given effect.** Each particle system has some similar parameters, but it is the differences between them that make them versatile. Use each particle's differences to your advantage.

- **Particle systems can be used alone, but are often used in combination with Particle space warps.** Depending on what is called for in the shot, a space warp can usually be added to change their original path or to give the particles a more professional look. Particles that behave more believably result in a better-looking scene. The welding sparks bouncing along the table top is a good example of this.

- **Space warps are a great way to coax particles to move according to your plans.** The speed and direction particles take is solely dependent on the particle parameters and emitter orientation at the time of birth for that frame in time. The only way to change that is for the particles to be affected by a space warp. A little bit of Gravity or a Deflector plane can go a long way.

- **All space warps influence world space.** Whether you are using an Object space warp or a Particle space warp, remember that they affect the scene in world space.

- **Space warps are always evaluated last in the stack.** 3DS MAX uses a predefined data flow to evaluate objects in your scene. Space warps are at the end, after Object modifiers and transforms.

IMAGE CREATED BY RALPH FRANTZ

Chapter 30

by Ralph Frantz

HYPERMATTER

HyperMatter is a physically based animation system being developed by Second Nature Industries as a plug-in for 3D Studio MAX. It should be shipping by the time this book is published. HyperMatter enables you to apply real-world material properties, according to physical and dynamic laws, to MAX objects. These properties include elasticity, dampening, incompressibility, friction, and gravity. Objects can stretch and wobble according to the values you give these parameters. HyperMatter objects are capable of collision detection with infinite plane walls and with each other.

Because HyperMatter is a soft body system, objects can also be bounced around and off each other with full deformational collision detection.

Although HyperMatter excels at representing highly deformable, soft-bodied objects and it is in this manner that the majority of work will be done, it can also be made to represent rigid objects. One of the exercises in this book, which deals with tossing dice, covers rigid HyperMatter objects. This chapter covers the following topics about HyperMatter:

- Doing its own thing

- Rigid objects, dynamics, and one-way collisions

- Fully deformable collision detection between two objects

- Inheriting the keyframed momentum

- Sub-object solidification of a HyperMatter control object

- Animating substance parameters and the follow constraint

Doing Its Own Thing

After an object is turned into a HyperMatter Control object, the whole object or only parts of the object may be acted upon by HyperMatter. The object, or part thereof, is then said to be *solidified*—or *cladded*, if you will— in a cubic volume element. This cubic volume element is what the HyperMatter effect is applied to. This cladding, in turn, then influences the underlying geometry and is referred to as a HyperMatter *solid*. Each whole object or sub-object solid is then able to be controlled to behave like a real object according to the laws of physics and dynamics. HyperMatter is controlling the object according to these laws, and, as such, the HyperMatter Solid reacts as any real object would. The HyperMatter Solid falls and accelerates according to gravity, and squashes, wobbles, and spins when involved in a collision. The HyperMatter Solids are allowed to "do their own thing" according to these physical and dynamic laws.

Because HyperMatter objects do their own thing, constraints can be set up to act upon the HyperMatter cladding, to constrain selected points (the corner of each cube in the cubic volume element) to a place in the scene where you need them to be and when in time you need them to be. The rest of the cladding will react accordingly. The points can be positioned anywhere in the scene through the use of numerous constraints, such as Fix and Follow. (See figure 30.1 for a view of different types of the Constraints rollout.) These point constraints can be given a lifespan, and their parameter values can also be animated. There is also a Forces panel for adjusting gravity (-Z force) or adjusting the force in the X or Y.

FIGURE 30.1

The Constraints rollout.

HyperMatter may at first seem to be a complicated plug-in, and there is no argument that it can do some incredible things. Some of the cause and effect deformation can truly amaze. You will soon learn that HyperMatter Solid deformations can be easily and quickly achieved. This chapter will help you achieve them and further your understanding at the same time.

NOTE

This author has had some of the most enjoyable times "playing" with the dynamics and physics of HyperMatter. It has been truly enjoyable to participate (in a small way) with the developers on this plug-in. Hopefully, you will receive the same enjoyment I did as you begin learning what HyperMatter can do for you and your scenes.

In this chapter, you will witness a MAX object turned into a deformable object, receiving a sudden impact and observing the rest of the object react. This physical process adds greatly to the realism of motion in your scenes. The illusion of real-world properties and cause and effect are what HyperMatter is all about.

Keep the following rules in mind while going through this chapter:

- When working with HyperMatter, you should try to avoid jumping around between frames as much as possible because of the time-stepping concern discussed previously. It is important, therefore, to turn off Real Time in the Time Configuration dialog box during these exercises. This is very important when you are asked to play the scene.

- It is okay to experiment with the stated parameters, but please return to the stated parameters before proceeding.

- All steps that do not explicitly call for you to be at a specific step should *always* be performed at frame 0. This is important with HyperMatter because it will set certain parameters automatically for you depending on the current frame—most importantly, when applying constraints.

Processing and Time Stepping

You may notice at times in the following exercises that MAX has to wait while a *HyperMatter Processing* progress bar comes up. Attempts have been made to minimize this wait time in the exercises, but maybe an explanation is in order.

MAX can procedurally calculate objects at any time. Given a certain frame number, all objects can calculate their shape and position/orientation at any other random frame number. HyperMatter objects cannot. To calculate a HyperMatter object at a certain frame, it has to time step sequentially through each frame, one by one, to arrive at its new shape and position/ orientation. In fact, this is done on a much finer scale than frames, as HyperMatter time steps according to a "sampling rate" or sub-frame calculation. *Sampling rate* refers to the number of internal calculations performed per MAX frame. This is the reason the progress bar comes up. HyperMatter is stepping sequentially through the frames. Generally speaking, you should get to a particular frame by typing in the frame number rather than scrubbing the frame bar.

Substances

The way a HyperMatter Solid reacts and is made to simulate many different real world materials is by means of the Substance Editor rollout. In this rollout you will find the different properties that define how rubbery or soft an object is. The properties you adjust here not only dictate the softness or hardness of the HyperMatter Solid, but also set its friction attributes and mass. The following explains each of these substance parameters.

The following are the substance properties associated with HyperMatter:

- **Elasticity.** The capability of an object once deformed, to try to return to its natural state. An elastic object maintains internal forces that try to make the object return to its natural shape. The higher the elasticity (more rigid), the harder and more bouncy the object is. The lower the elasticity (less rigid), the softer and more stretchy the object is.

- **Damping.** The force within a deformable object that tries to prevent its changing shape. Damping reduces the elastic wobble of an object and fights its momentum.

- **Incompressibility.** A HyperMatter object's attempt at maintaining volume throughout a deformation.

- **Friction.** The degree of slipping when objects collide with each other or when objects slide along the ground or bounce off walls. With less friction, objects slide more freely. With more friction, no relative motion occurs between colliding surfaces.

- **Density.** The mass per unit volume. Remember from your physics lessons that force equals mass times acceleration. The heavier (more dense) an object is, the less inclined it is to react to an implied force. Heavy objects will dominate lighter objects in collisions and move more lethargically. The lighter (less dense) an object is, the faster an object will respond and the higher it will bounce.

Rigid Objects, Dynamics, and One-Way Collisions

In the following exercise, you solve the task of animating a dice roll. This is extremely difficult to animate by traditional keyframing methods, but by using HyperMatter's built-in dynamics, it becomes an easily attainable prospect and can look very natural, as well as more dynamically accurate. Just how would you keyframe the intricate movements of a dice toss?

You will be rolling the dice across a craps table with multiple collision detection against the table surface and sides. Because the title of this exercise is "Snake Eyes," you will have to ensure that both dice end up rolling a number 1. Note that a demo version of HyperMatter was not available at the time of this printing

NOTE

The following exercise assumes that you have a copy of HyperMatter installed on your system. If you do not, install the demo version included for your convenience on the accompanying CD. This demo version enables you to go through the steps, but does not enable you to render the deformed HyperMatter objects.

S NAKE E YES

Load 30aimx.max from the accompanying CD-ROM and examine the scene. It is a simple craps table and a pair of dice. The camera has been animated to enable you to see a large part of the table for the initial toss, but animates a zoom-in that enables you to see the intricate collision with the sides of the table. This also facilitates the close-up view as HyperMatter does the subtle movements of the dice coming to rest.

1. Select Dice #1. In the Create panel, select Second Nature from the drop-down list. Then click on HyperMatter to make Dice #1 a HyperMatter Control object named **H_Dice#1**.

NOTE

When you create a HyperMatter Control object, HyperMatter automatically hides the original object and builds a new copy of the geometry as it is at that frame with all the modifiers collapsed. This is an important feature because it always enables you to go back to this original object if you need to. Do an Unhide by Name to see that the original Dice #1 is there.

2. In the HyperMatter rollout, click on Solidify Object to make all of the dice a HyperMatter Solid object. You can leave the default resolution of the HyperMatter Solid at 2.

What you have now is a copy of Dice #1, solidified in a cubic volume element. Default substance properties, Elasticity of 1 and Damping of 1, have been applied to this H_Dice #1. Knowing that a HyperMatter object "does its own thing" by acting according to physical laws, you will see that playing the scene from the Left viewport shows the object falling pursuant to gravity's effect.

The first thing you will want to do is set up one-way collision detection—one-way because HyperMatter has two ways to do collisions.

■ **HyperMatter Walls.** One-way collision detection can be set up with HyperMatter Walls, which are represented like a Box object in the scene. A HyperMatter Solid, once set up, senses a HyperMatter Wall for collision detection and animates/deforms accordingly. This is very CPU-efficient.

■ **Collide Constraint.** Full deformational collision detection between two HyperMatter objects can be set up. Each object senses collisions between each other by sensing when the selected solid cladding points surrounding the object collide and thus animates/deforms accordingly. This is much more CPU-intensive.

You should use HyperMatter Walls in this case because you need the dice to sense the tabletop and sides only, but don't need or want the tabletop to deform.

3. In the Create panel, while still under the Second Nature drop-down, click on Walls. In the Top viewport, drag to define the walls to the same size as the inside of the craps table (see fig. 30.2). The following values should define the length, width, and height of the walls to fit the inside of the table.

    Length = 590
    Width = 1480
    Height = 500

4. In the viewports, move the Wall object to coincide with the surface of the table, as well as with the inner sides. Play close attention to the table surface and upper-right corner of the table because this is where you will be throwing the dice and doing the collisions (again, see fig. 30.2).

If you play the scene in the Left viewport, you will see that the dice still drops according to gravity and does not collide with the walls yet. To have the walls be "seen" by H_Dice #1, you must set up a constraint (in this case, a Walls constraint). Because HyperMatter Solids "do their own thing," you need and will use constraints to get them to behave according to your script in the scene.

FIGURE 30.2

Create and position the HyperMatter Walls object to fit the inside of the craps table.

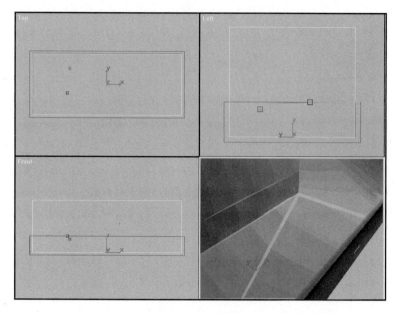

5. Select H_Dice #1 and go to the Modify panel. This is where most of your tweaking will be done to a HyperMatter Solid. Click on Sub-Object and select HyperMatter from the drop-down list. This will enable the Substance, Constraints, and Forces icons. Click on the Constraints icon (see fig. 30.3).

FIGURE 30.3

A shot of the HyperMatter Control panels, showing the Substance, Constraints, and Forces icons with the Constraints icon selected.

Notice that the various constraints are greyed out and are not ready to be used because all constraints need to be set up to affect a certain set of points in the cubic volume element. Constraints can then be set up to act on the whole object or only a sub-object selection. These *named selection sets* (of points) are created and can be selected from the top toolbar. When a HyperMatter Control object is solidified, three named selection sets of points are automatically created and named for you. These auto assigned points are the Exterior points, Interior points, and All points. Remember, the constraints act on the cladding points, and the deformation of the cladding points causes a deformation of the underlying geometry.

6.   Choose the Exterior set of points from the Named Selection Set dropdown list. The Exterior points in the clad will turn red, which immediately enables the various constraints. You are now able to constrain these selected points.

7.   Click on the Walls constraint and click in the viewport on the H_Wall01 object you created in step 3. The Constraints drop-down list will note "WAL [Exterior]->H_Wall01," showing you that all was done correctly.

8.   Get out of Sub-Object mode, and select and hide the H_Walls01 object. It is no longer necessary to see it in the scene because you will not need to see the walls for the collision to happen.

Play the scene in the Left or Front viewport and observe the collision. You have now successfully set up collision detection between the H_Dice #1 HyperMatter Solid and the HyperMatter Walls, which will appear to look like collision detection against the tabletop. Also notice how fast the display playback is; one-way collision detection is very CPU-efficient.

TIP

HyperMatter works on the basis of *time stepping*. In other words, HyperMatter Solids are calculated a frame at a time starting from the first frame and every frame sequentially thereafter. You should get in the habit of moving through frames by playing the scene or typing the frame number. Scrubbing the frame bar may cause unnecessary processing and cause your display to wait. This is evident by a *HyperMatter: Processing* progress bar while it is calculating, frame by frame, the HyperMatter effect. This will be more apparent as your scene gets more complicated.

As you may have noticed during playback, the die is kind of soft and squishy—because the default substance property given to all HyperMatter objects is soft and squishy. HyperMatter is by definition a soft-body dynamics system. It is capable of representing rigid objects as well, and this is the purpose of the Substance parameter rollout. Go ahead and make the die a bit harder.

9. Select H_Dice#1, go to the Modify panel, select Sub-Object HyperMatter, and click on the Substance Editor icon. Set Elasticity to 10, Damping to 30, Incompressibility (Incompress.) to 0, Friction to 0.75, and Density to 2.

Now play the scene in the Left viewport and notice how rigid the die appears. The lists provided in the "Throwing the Dice" exercise give a quick reference of Substance parameters.

See the HyperMatter manual for more information about substance properties. Now is a good time to hold your scene.

Using the HyperMatter Velocity Constraint

Now that you have been successful in creating rigid die and causing it to collide with the table, examine the ways that you can toss the die down the table. As is true for most operations in MAX, you can accomplish this task in many different ways, including the following:

■ Keyframe the die to move down the table and have HyperMatter take over the velocity at the first key.

■ Apply HyperMatter forces to push the die down the table. You are already using default forces in the negative Z (–100) for gravity.

■ Use the HyperMatter Velocity constraint.

All of these are viable choices, but you will use the last option in the following steps. You may want to experiment on your own with the other two later. You will also be working with HyperMatter's capability to inherit an object's momentum in an exercise later in this chapter.

THROWING THE DICE

1. While still in the Modify panel, select All points from the Named Selection Set drop-down list. Choose the Constraints icon, and then click on the Velocity constraint. VEL[All] appears in the Constraints list.

2. Click on VEL[All] from the constraints list (below the various constraints buttons) to highlight it and bring up the Velocity panel controls. Click on the Enable check box to the right of X in the Velocity rollout and type **250**.

Most constraints are animatable, and they all have a lifespan during which the constraints are enabled. Lifespans can be set separately for each constraint. What you have to do here is give the die some initial velocity to get it moving and then turn off the velocity at a latter frame. If you were to keep the velocity constraint active throughout the entire animation, the die would try to push through the Walls object collision and strange behavior might occur.

Warning

As was mentioned at the beginning of this chapter, it is important always to be at frame 0 when applying constraints. If you are at a frame other than frame 0, say frame 50 when you apply a constraint, HyperMatter will automatically set its lifespan to start at the current frame, frame 50 in this case.

3. Just above the Velocity rollout is the Start and End Lifespan for this Velocity constraint. Leave the Start at 0 and set the End of its lifespan to frame 60. This should give the die enough momentum to create the toss.

4. Click on the Refresh button in the HyperMatter Control section of the rollout.

You have done quite a bit of tweaking to the Substance and Constraints of this die, so it is advisable to manually refresh the dynamics of the scene now and then when dynamics are as important as they are here. HyperMatter automatically refreshes itself under most conditions.

Play the scene from the Camera view and notice how the velocity of the die rolls it down the craps table. Look at how nicely the collision is with the surface and how the die tumbles as it collides. Notice the collision at the end of the table and the subtlety as the die comes to rest. Smile because you appreciate how difficult this would have been to keyframe so naturally.

Velocity in the X is okay, but a bit of Y velocity is in order to make the action of the die and its collisions more interesting.

5. While still in the Modify panel, Velocity rollout, and VEL[All] still highlighted, click on the Y Enable check box and set this to 30.

Play the scene again from the Camera viewport. Notice that the animation has changed, providing better action with the die as it also is striking the other side wall of the table.

How about rolling snake eyes? How do you roll the die to end up with a 1 rather than a 6 (as it does now)?

NOTE

Your animated roll of the die may end up slightly different depending on a couple of different criteria. Your Wall object may be placed in a slightly different spot than that of the author. This might change your outcome. Also, the author is creating these exercises during the beta period of HyperMatter, and sometimes the dynamics vary slightly from build to build.

Do not be alarmed or concerned that you did something wrong. If your roll of the die ends up being a number different than 6, however, just substitute your number roll with the 6 mentioned in the next few steps.

You'd hate to retweak the animation and dynamics to try to find a toss that ended up rolling a 1. The numbers on the sides of the dice are maps in a Multi-Sub-Object material. The best way to accomplish this is just to swap the maps between the 1 map and the 6 map.

6. Open the Material Editor. Select the Dice #1 Multi-Sub-Object material from slot 1 and click on the Material 1 Dice 6 material. Change the Diffuse texture map Dice 6.tga to the Dice 1.tga bitmap. This replaces the 6 on the die at rest with 1. You must also replace the Dice 1.tga bitmap for Sub-object material 6 Dice 1 to Dice 6.tga, so as not to be cheating with non-standard dice.

Play the scene and notice that H_Dice#1 now rolls a 1.

When satisfied with your HyperMatter dynamics setup—and especially if you are about to go further with the scene by adding more HyperMatter objects—it is advisable and highly recommended to lock in the dynamics by making the object a Record object.

A Record object is basically that: a recorder. A HyperMatter object turned into a Record object behaves the same way as the original HyperMatter object did, but is no longer a HyperMatter Solid as its actions become set. It does not change when influenced by other HyperMatter objects, constraints, or walls, and you will not be able to change any of its HyperMatter attributes. Think of a Record object as a sort of Morph object set up to behave like the original object did at the time it was made a Record object.

Basically, Record makes a new copy of the HyperMatter Control object (with an R_ prefix) and uses a special HyperMatter Record Controller with associated keyframes to match the original position, rotation, and deformation.

7. Select the HyperMatter H_Dice #1 object, go to the Create panel, Second Nature drop-down, and choose Record. In the HyperMatter Record rollout, choose Auto Create Keys. In the Create Record Keys dialog box, change the Key Creation Timing to every 2 frames and then click on OK. Select and hide H_Dice #1.

Now that you are somewhat familiar with the setup of the first die, go ahead and experiment with the second die or use the following settings to set Dice #2. Don't be afraid to change any of these settings. Observe the difference in action after each change.

8. For Dice #2, make it a HyperMatter object, and Solidify Object.

9. In the Modify panel, Substances Editor set:
   Elasticity 10
   Damping 30
   Incompress 0
   Friction .75
   Density 2

10. In the Constraints rollout set a Velocity constraint to All constraint points:
    VEL [All]
    Lifespan: Start 20
    Lifespan: End 100
    X: 220
    Y: 50

11. In the Constraints rollout, set up a Walls constraint using Exterior as the selected set of points. Then pick the H_Walls01 object by using Select By Name. Using the Pick Object dialog box enables you to select the Walls object without first unhiding it.

    WAL[Exterior]->H_Wall01 appears in the drop-down list.

12. If you used these settings and all went well, this die should roll a 1. If your die rolls anything besides a 1, assign the Dice #2 material from the Material Editor and swap bitmaps for the actual number rolled with the Material 6 Dice 1 bitmap DICE1.tga (see fig. 30.4).

FIGURE 30.4

This is the Camera view of the dice after they have come to rest with a roll of snake eyes.

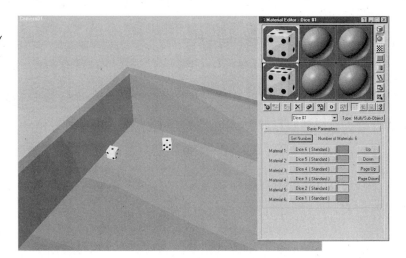

13. Make this H_Dice #2 HyperMatter Solid into a Record object as you did in step 7 for H_Dice #1.

Play the scene and notice how well HyperMatter has dynamically rolled the dice. Also note how well the subtleties of the dice, as they come to rest, have been represented.

View the rendered animation snakeyes.avi from the accompanying CD.

Fully Deformable Collision Detection Between Two Objects

In the following exercise, you use HyperMatter to create a silly carnival duck shoot animation. Silly because it will not be a plain old wooden duck that just falls down when hit. Not that HyperMatter would have a problem with this, but it would be more interesting if the duck were not so rigid. What would be the reaction if a ball hit a rubber duck?

In the last exercise, you did simple one-way collision detection with HyperMatter Walls. In this exercise, you will use the Collide constraint to do fully deformational collision detection between two MAX objects. You will also explore the Fix constraint and see how HyperMatter deals with the velocity of a keyframed ball.

DUCK SHOOT

Go ahead and load 30bimx.max. The scene consists of a dual duck target set up on a shaft. You will be tossing a ball at the upper duck to win the prize. Set that up now.

1. In the Create panel, select Second Nature from the drop-down list. Select the duck. Then turn it into a HyperMatter Control object by clicking on HyperMatter, and then solidify it by clicking on the Solidify Object button.

TIP

Keep the solidify resolution down to the lowest setting you can use and still be able to get the job done. This saves CPU cycles and speeds up the interaction of your scene.

Notice that the default resolution setup for the duck is 2. You have the ability to change this default by clicking on the Options button at the bottom of this rollout. Remember, it is the clad surface itself that will do the checking for collisions, so you should examine the fit direction. Because you will be tossing the ball at the duck from the front, you should make a change from the default fit in the X direction.

2. Go to the Modify panel and try cladding in the different fit directions X, Y, and Z (see fig. 30.5).

FIGURE 30.5

The result of "fitting" the solid cladding in the different X, Y, and Z directions.

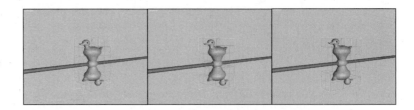

The difference in the fit directions may seem subtle at first and they are in fact very similar. The important point here is that the duck is being set up to swing around the pole when hit, so you will need to hold in place a row of points in the very center (of the duck and the pole) for the duck to swing around, which will have a result of looking like the duck is indeed held to the pole. Not choosing the correct fit direction in this step is important enough to make the difference between whether the gag will work or not.

Although the Fit Y direction seems to give the best fit for a collision from the front, a compromise will have to be made to make the duck swing around the pole. Therefore, you will need a set of clad points in the very center for the constraint and a Fit Z seems to be best.

3. Because the Fit Y has no point in the center, the next best fit would be in the Z direction. Choose Fit Z. Note that this may seem to go against the intended use of fit direction, but it should not impact your collision accuracy enough to be a problem.

Next you need to set up a couple of constraints. Remember that HyperMatter objects "do their own thing" according to physical and dynamic laws. You use constraints to place any point in the solidify clad anywhere in the scene you want it, at any time you want it. The order in which you set up constraints will have no bearing on the outcome, but you will set up the collision constraint first.

4. Select Sub-Object HyperMatter mode. From the Named Selection Sets drop-down list, select the auto assigned Exterior points.

Notice how many points will be collision tested. You can minimize this by using the MAX selection tools.

5. Click in a viewport to unselect the Exterior points. Then from the Left viewport, select just the top front points of the duck cladding (see fig. 30.6). Name this selection **Duck front** in the Named Selection Set drop-down list.

TIP

Doing collisions between two HyperMatter objects can get very CPU-intensive so you should always be thinking of ways to minimize the number of points being examined for collision.

6. Click on the Constraints icon and click on Collide. COL[Duck front] appears in the *constraints* list.

FIGURE 30.6

Select the top front set of points on the Duck clad for use with the Collide constraint and name them Duck front.

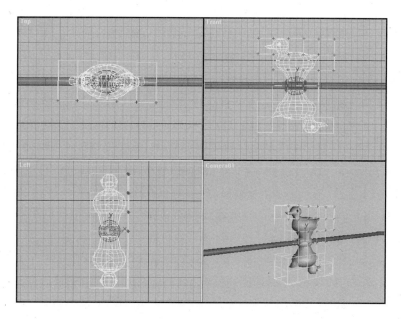

Besides the use of Exterior, Interior, and All Named Selection Sets that are automatically assigned, you are free to select your own as you have just seen. You can save and constrain any number of Named Selection Sets. Because the action required here is to have the duck spin around the pole after the ball hits it, you will need a way to hold the duck to that pole.

Examine the Fix Constraint

A "fixed" point may not move in the scene, but it can rotate around itself. The fixed point can rotate in place, but it is not allowed to rotate around any selection center because this would "move" the point in the scene. This was the reason you selected the Fit Z in step 3 to get the row of points in the center of the duck.

1. In the Left viewport, select just the row of points in the center of the duck (see fig. 30.7). Call this Named Selection Set **Center** and click on Enter to enable the Constraints buttons. Click on the Fix constraint. FIX[Center] appears in the constraints list.

FIGURE 30.7

Select the center row of points for the Fix constraint and name the selection set Center.

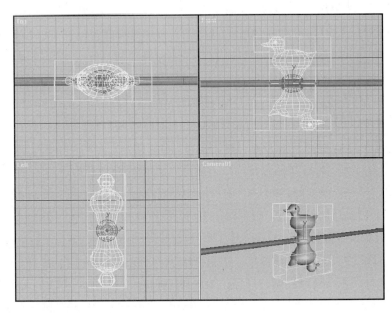

Play the scene from the Camera view and notice that even with the default gravity, the center points stay fixed in space. The rest of the duck can wobble about slightly, all within the constraint of the fixed points and the default substance properties.

The duck is a bit too wobbly, so you should tighten it up a bit.

2. Still in the Modify panel, click on the Substance icon. Open the Library roll-up, click on Use Library and pick Slow Wobble from the drop-down Library list of pre-assigned substances.

This is a great HyperMatter feature. It enables you to quickly set up a substance in terms that you can quickly grasp and identify with. It is often advantageous to use a Library material to get close to the substance you want. From there you can easily tweak it to fit your needs by means of the Copy Library Substance to Local icon. This enables the adjustment of Elasticity, Damping, and the rest of the Substance properties as usual starting from the settings of the Library Substance.

Now that the Duck is set up, go ahead and throw the ball at it.

3. Play the scene and notice that it is already keyframed to be thrown at the duck through frame 40.

4. Make certain that you are at frame 0. Go to the Create panel and make the sphere a HyperMatter Control object and Solidify object.

Play the scene and notice that the object keeps the keyframed info and HyperMatter makes it fall under its own gravity. More important is the fact that HyperMatter calculated the speed of the sphere from frame 0 and maintained that velocity from there. HyperMatter then ignores the keyframed stop at frame 40, because this keyframe was only used to set up the velocity for HyperMatter to assume.

NOTE

HyperMatter is capable of precisely interpreting the keyframed velocity of an object. This provides a transparent transition from keyframed animation to real-world physics.

It seems the ball's gravity may be a bit much for your scene; your ball is moving in slow-motion. HyperMatter even enables you to play with the effects of gravity. Actually, you can set forces in any direction. You could even use a force of Y to throw the ball, although it would accelerate much differently than it does now.

5. In the Modify panel, Sub-Object HyperMatter, select the Forces icon. Set the Z force to –50.

6. Click on the Constraints icon, select the Exterior set of points from the Named Selection Set drop-down in the toolbar, and click on Collide.

7. Click on the Substances icon and open the Library rollout. Select the library substance Power Ball from the drop-down.

Play the scene and notice that the ball just doesn't have enough *oomph* to knock over the duck. Going back to your memory of physics, you remember that force equals mass times acceleration. Therefore, heavy objects will dominate lighter objects in collisions. The duck has a density (mass) of 1 and the sphere also has a density of 1. You should increase the density of the sphere so that it will dominate in the resultant collision.

8. While still in the Modify panel, H_Sphere01 selected, and in Sub-Object HyperMatter mode, select the Substance icon. Under the Library Substance rollout, click on the Copy Library Substance to Local icon. Then under the Properties rollout, Attributes section, raise the Density to 4.

Play the scene in the Camera viewport now and notice the difference. The heavier, or denser, ball knocks the duck pretty good. In fact it hits it hard enough to spin the duck completely around the pole.

View the rendered animation duck_col.avi from the accompanying CD.

This is a very interesting file to experiment with, especially the Density settings of both the duck and ball. Also notice the effect different substance settings such as Elasticity and Damping have when applied to the duck. You can get some wild effects from a little experimentation here. You may even be able to get a double collision as the ball stops its forward momentum just enough to bring it into contact with the duck a second time. Note here that you would have to redo the Collide constraint to use the Exterior set of points, not just the Duck Front selection set that was originally set up for efficiency's sake.

There are a couple of extra rendered versions on the accompanying CD, created during experimentation for this exercise. Feel free to view them, and maybe come up with a few cool duck shot animations of your own.

Inheriting the Keyframed Momentum

In the following exercise, you work with HyperMatter to help with animating the game of curling. If you are not familiar with the sport of curling, it has to do with bowling a "stone" with a handle toward a target laid out on ice. It is kind of like shuffleboard. Perhaps you remember the Beatles in the movie *Help* playing a game of curling? (Although you would think that Ringo would surely have noticed that one of the stones was actually a bomb.)

HyperMatter will help you in the exercise because you will be using HyperMatter's Friction parameter to take care of the deceleration of the stones as they come to rest on the ice. You will also set up one of the stones to knock another out of the target, which HyperMatter's Collide constraint will solve for you. You will use another constraint not previously covered in these exercises called Fix Orientation. The Fix Orientation constraint prevents a HyperMatter from tumbling or rotating. This file also shows how wonderfully easy it is to have HyperMatter inherit the momentum from traditional keyframed objects.

CURLING

Begin by loading 30cIMX.max from the accompanying CD. Examine the scene to see that the rink and targets have been set up, and that a single stone has been placed at one end. Notice that there are also three dummy objects and that these dummies have already been keyframed.

1. Select the object STONE rubber. In the Create panel, choose Second Nature from the drop-down list and click on HyperMatter to turn it into a HyperMatter Control object. Then solidify it by picking Solidify Object.

To keep the object from falling and to give it a surface to travel across and sense friction from, you will create a HyperMatter Wall object.

2. In the Create panel, Second Nature drop-down, click on Walls. Drag in the Top Viewport to create a Walls object totally surrounding the curling target layout (see fig. 30.8).

FIGURE 30.8
Create the Walls object to totally surround the curling target layout.

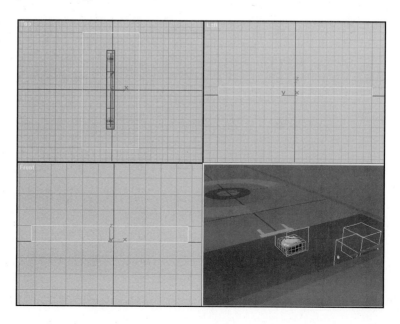

3. Unhide the ICE Plane object. Zoom in enough to the stone, in the Front or Left Viewports, to enable you to see that the Walls object is a bit above the ICE plane. Move the Walls so that they are level with the ICE plane and be certain that the stone is sitting on the ICE plane and Walls object (see fig. 30.9.).

4. Hide the Walls object.

FIGURE 30.9

Be certain to move the HyperMatter Walls object so that it is on the same Z plane as the second ICE plane object.

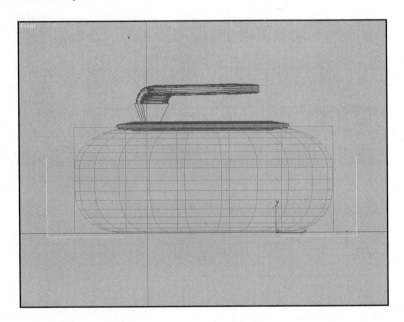

5. Select the Stone and go to the Modify panel. Go into Sub-Object HyperMatter mode and click on the Constraints icon. In the Named Selection Set drop-down, choose All the HyperMatter points and then choose the Walls constraint. Choose Select by Name from the toolbar or press the H key, and then pick the H_Wall01 object. The constraint list should read Wal[All]->H_Wall01.

Play the scene. The stone now rests on the ice but is a bit more rubbery than needed.

6. While still in the Modify panel, Sub-Object HyperMatter mode, click on the Substance Editor icon. In the Attributes section, click on the Elasticity/Damping lock and set the Elasticity to 4 (which also sets Damping to 4).

Playing the scene shows that the stone is a harder rubber and about right for the scene's needs. This would be a good time to Hold your scene.

Now for the task of throwing the stone toward the target. As mentioned previously, there are numerous ways to accomplish this task. In this instance, dummy objects have already been created for the initial throw of the stone, and thus the movement will be nicely created with HyperMatter inheriting that momentum.

7. Release Sub-Object mode. Link H_STONE rubber to the dummy surrounding it. Link the Stone Handle to the H_STONE rubber. In the Dispay panel, turn off Hide by Category, Cameras. Select the Camera (linked) and the Camera (linked) Target and link them to the stone.

8. Maximize the Camera (linked) view and play the scene.

NOTE

HyperMatter is quite heavy in terms of a plug-in. It may even be stretching the limits of the MAX 1.x SDK (Software Developers Kit). It may be necessary and advisable at times to click on the Refresh button located in the HyperMatter rollout of the Modify panel. If your scene is not responding to the link in step 7, this may be one of those Refresh times.

At this point, you should take notice of the following:

- Notice how well the stone has inherited the motion from the keyframed dummy object.

- Notice that although the dummy object has a keyframe at frame 59 to stop, a HyperMatter object ignores this. Only the initial velocity at the time of HyperMatter initialization is assumed by the HM object.

- Notice that the default friction creates such a drag on the stone that the stone actually flips and tumbles after a few frames.

9. In the Modify panel, Sub-Object HyperMatter mode, Substances icon, set Friction to 0.45.

Play the scene. Now the motion is starting to look good. Congratulations, you have thrown the stone inside the red outer circle.

Perhaps you could calm down the slow wobble of the stone as it glides. The substances seem fine for this stone rubber, so you will go elsewhere to solve this tweak.

10. Still in Sub-Object HyperMatter mode, select the Constraints icon. Select All set of points from the Named Selection Sets drop-down list. Select the Fix Orientation button. Notice NOS[All] appears in the Constraints list indicating that the HyperMatter object is not allowed to spin. (NOS = No Spin)

Play the scene. The stone no longer spins or wobbles but still maintains its substance characteristics. It may not be apparent while playing the scene, but if you create a preview (or view 30c-pre.avi from the accompanying CD), you will see the wonderfully subtle secondary motion as the stone comes to rest. The camera link enables you to *feel* this effect. This overshadows the dynamically correct deceleration caused by friction that was automatically computed by HyperMatter.

11. Select the H_STONE rubber and STONE Handle objects. Hold down the Shift key and, from the Top viewport, drag (copy) them into the lowest dummy object, Dummy02. While they are still selected, click on the Unlink icon on the toolbar to release their link from the first dummy.

12. Link H_STONE rubber01 to Dummy02, and then link STONE handle01 to the H_STONE rubber01.

Play the scene. Notice that the link is apparently not working; this stone does not move with the dummy to which it is linked when you play the scene. If you select and move the dummy, however, you will see that the link is working. Why isn't the HyperMatter object moving with the animated dummy?

NOTE

If you remember, it was explained earlier in this exercise that "only the initial velocity at the time of HyperMatter initialization is assumed by the HyperMatter object." HyperMatter initialization starts at frame 0 by default and this dummy object starts moving at frame 50. Therefore HyperMatter does not see the velocity at frame 50. It has inherited the dummy's velocity at frame 0, which is, of course, a velocity of zero.

13. With Dummy02 and H_STONE rubber01 selected, go into Track View and filter for selected objects only. Expand the H_STONE rubber01 track, and the Object (HyperMatter Control) track to get to the Lifespan track. Grab the left end of the range bar and drag that end to line up with frame 50. This will correspond with the dummy's first key, and thus HyperMatter will initialize at frame 50 to "see" the momentum of the dummy to which it is linked.

Play the scene and see that the HyperMatter initialization has correctly linked the stone to the dummy.

14. Change the Camera (linked) view to the Camera02 view. Play the scene now to see that the stone decelerates and ends up in the inner blue target.

Now throw one more stone.

15. In the Top viewport, select the second stone and handle and shift copy them into the third dummy. With the two objects still selected, unlink these objects. As before, link the H_STONE rubber02 to the dummy and the STONE handle02 to the H_STONE rubber02.

16. Go into Track View and move the start of the Range bar for the Lifespan of H_STONE rubber02 to frame 100 (as you did before). This now matches the start keyframe for the dummy to which it is linked.

Play the scene and see that you have thrown this stone through the last stone throw. Click on the Refresh button if necessary. This path is lain on purpose because you can now set up a collision to push the second stone out of the way.

17. Go to frame 275, which is just before the two stones collide. Zoom in to these stones in the Top viewport and Maximize the view.

18. Select H_STONE rubber01 and go into the Modify panel, Sub-Object HyperMatter mode. Click on the Constraint icon. Select the front row of points and call this Named Selection Set **Front** in the Named Selection Sets drop-down list, and then press Enter (see fig. 30.10).

FIGURE 30.10

Select these points in the clad, call the selection set Front, and set up a Collide constraint to start at frame 275 for the second stone.

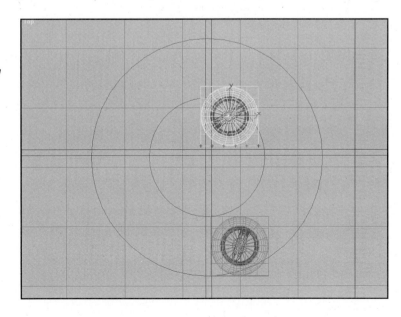

19. Click on the Collide constraint. COL [Front] appears in the Constraint drop-down list. Highlight this COL [Front] and notice that HyperMatter has automatically set up the Lifespan for the Collide constraint to start at frame 275, the current frame.

20. Click on the Select Next HyperMatter Object button to quickly change to the third stone. Select the back row of points, call this Named Selection Set **Back**, and then press Enter (see fig. 30.11). Click on the Collide constraint.

FIGURE 30.11

Select these points, call the selection set Back, and set up a Collide constraint to start at frame 275 for the third stone.

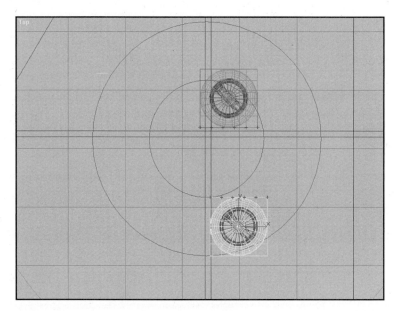

Play the scene from this top view. Remember that you may have to click on the Refresh button. A great collision has been created, and you have been successful in knocking the second stone out of the target and replacing it with this last stone throw.

View the rendered animation included on the accompanying CD as Curling.avi.

Sub-Object Solidification of a HyperMatter Control Object

You should now be familiar with most of HyperMatter's command panels and parameters. You have touched on most of them in the last few exercises and should be somewhat comfortable moving around in them. The one thing common to the previous exercises is that all the HyperMatter Control objects were solidified using the whole object. This may be acceptable in quite a few instances, but sooner or later you will want to have HyperMatter influence only a portion of an object, or influence different portions of an object in different ways. For this reason, you are given the separate Sub-Object mode of Geometry.

In this exercise, you add a bit of motion to a running mouse. Perhaps you remember watching the Olympics and observing how radically the faces of the sprinting runners were affected by the motion of the run itself. You will try to duplicate some of that here. Specifically, you will be using HyperMatter to sub-object solidify portions of the head of a running mouse, using the motion of the mouse head to affect the different parts of the head geometry with different substance attributes.

RUNNING MOUSE

Load 30dIMX.max from the accompanying CD and meet Mortimer Mouse courtesy of Viewpoint Datalabs. Play the scene and observe that Mortimer has already been keyframed with a basic running motion, and that his head has a good movement from which HyperMatter can work.

1. From the Create panel, choose Second Nature from the drop-down list. Select Mortimer's head and click on HyperMatter. Do not click on Solidify Object. (Sub-object solidify is done in the modify panel.)

2. Go to the Modify panel and click on Sub-Object to get into Sub-Object Geometry mode. Change the viewport to the Front view. In the top toolbar, change the Rectangular Selection Region icon to Fence Selection Region. Zoom in so the head fills the viewport.

Now you are ready to select the faces from the mouse head from which you will sub-object solidify. You will be creating a few separate selections including the ears, snoot, nose, and eyebrows.

3. Drag a fence selection in the Front viewport to select just the ear on your left (Mortimer's right ear) (see fig. 30.12). Make certain that you select all the ear. Perform an Arc Rotate Selected and spin the viewport around to make certain. Name this selection set **Ear Right** in the Named Selection Sets drop-down list.

FIGURE 30.12

Select all the faces of Mortimer's right ear for the first sub-object solidification. (3D models by Viewpoint Datalabs International, Inc.)

4. Scroll the HyperMatter Control panel down to get to the Automatic Solids rollout. Notice that in this mode of sub-object geometry, the Solidify button reads Solidify Sub-Object. Click on this Solidify Sub-Object button. Rename the Sub-Object HyperMatter Solid from SO_face_1 to **SO_Ear Right**.

You have now made a HyperMatter sub-object solid out of Mortimer's right ear. Notice that the cladding at sub-object level has a default resolution of 6 as opposed to the default for object level solidify of 2. Generally speaking, a higher resolution is needed for sub-objects.

NOTE

The default resolution for both solidify whole and solidify sub-object is an option you can set. If you take a look at the bottom of this Automatic Solids rollout, you will see an Options button. Click on this button to set the default resolutions. Of note here is that these settings (and other HyperMatter preferences set elsewhere) are saved in the Windows Registry, making them configurable per user. Therefore, if another user were to log on after you and change your preferences, he would still be working with the default preferences.

Note the following two differences when working with sub-object solids:

■ There is a separate default resolution set up for whole object solidify and sub-object solidify when performing an automatic solidification.

■ HyperMatter automatically creates a Named Selection Set of points called Join. Furthermore, a Fix constraint is automatically set up to use these points to hold it to the HyperMatter Control.

Play the scene to see how the sub-object solidified ear reacts to Mortimer's head movements. Notice that it is a bit too soft.

5. Go into Sub-Object HyperMatter mode, click on the Substance Editor icon to get to the Substance panel, and set Elasticity to 2.5 and Damping to 2.0.

Go ahead and sub-object solidify Mortimer's left ear.

6. Change to the Front viewport, go into Sub-Object Geometry mode and select the faces of Mortimer's left ear (see fig. 30.13). Name this selection set **Ear Left**. Click on the Automatic Solidify icon and then click on the Solidify Sub-Object button. Rename this sub-object HyperMatter Solid to **SO_Ear Left**.

FIGURE 30.13
Select the faces of Mortimer's left ear for the second sub-object solid. (3D models by Viewpoint Datalabs International, Inc.)

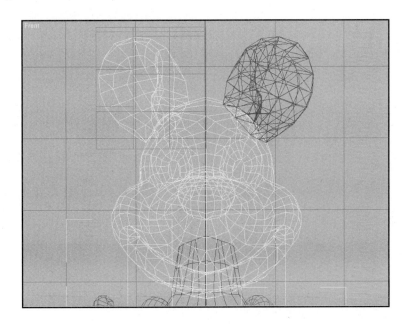

7. Go into Sub-Object HyperMatter mode, click on the Substance Editor icon to get to the Substance panel, and change Elasticity to 2.5 and Damping to 2.0.

Now go ahead and create a HyperMatter sub-object solid out of Mortimer's snout. This is a good time to Hold your scene.

8. Change the viewport to the Left view and zoom in close to the snout. Go into Sub-Object Geometry mode, and with Fence Selection mode still active, select the faces making up the snout (see fig. 30.14). Name this selection set **Snout** in the Named Selection Set drop-down.

FIGURE 30.14
Select these faces of the snout in preparation of sub-object solidification. (3D models by Viewpoint Datalabs International, Inc.)

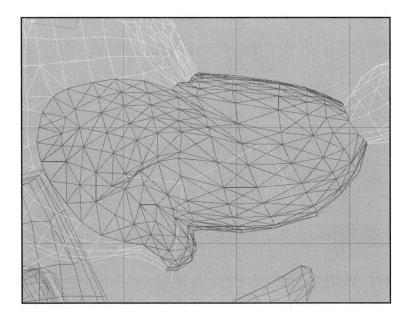

9. Select the Automatic Solidify icon and choose Solidify Sub-Object. Rename the Sub-Object solid to **SO_snout**.

10. Go into Sub-Object HyperMatter mode and click on the Substance Editor icon, set Elasticity to 5 and Damping to 4. Change the viewport to Camera view and play the scene.

Notice that with these substance settings, the snout appears to react well to the running motion and jiggles as if the face were actually reacting to the force of the footsteps. Now go ahead and create a HyperMatter sub-object solid out of Mortimer's nose.

11. Change the viewport to the Left view. Go into Sub-Object Geometry mode and use the Fence Selection tool to select just the faces of the nose (see fig. 30.15). Name this selection set **Nose**.

FIGURE 30.15

Select these faces of the nose for sub-object solidification. (3D models by Viewpoint Datalabs International, Inc.)

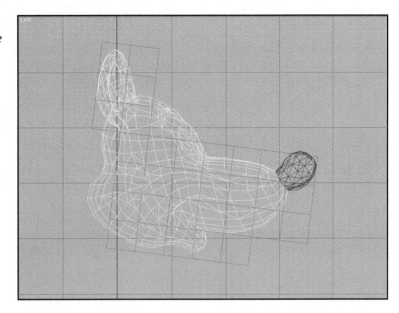

12. Select the Automatic Solidify icon and choose Solidify Sub-Object to rubberize his nose. Rename this sub-object **SO_Nose**. Change the viewport to the Camera view. Get into Sub-Object HyperMatter mode, Substance panel, and change the Damping to 4.

Play the scene and notice how Mortimer's nose is now reacting to the movement of the head and also to the HyperMatter deformation of the snout. Mortimer Mouse is getting very cartoon-like.

NOTE

Feel free to experiment with these substance parameters. These exercises, after all, were created so that you could gain insight into HyperMatter's parameters. And like any other project, experimentation can lead to wonderful new insight.

Just be certain to return to the parameters mentioned here before going on with the exercise; otherwise unexpected behavior may result and cause confusion in later steps.

The great thing about sub-object solidifying a HyperMatter Control object such as this is that you can continue to the sub-object solidify portions until the object has just the dynamic motion you like. Remember how different parts of the Olympic runners' faces were affected by the force and power of the sprint? Mortimer's eyebrows seem to be crying out for a bit of this reaction, don't you think?

The faces of the eyebrows are going to be a bit trickier to select. It would be advantageous to simplify the scene as much as possible before proceeding.

13. With Mortimer's head selected, go into the Display panel and Hide Unselected (or use your keyboard shortcut). Back in the Modify panel, go into Sub-Object HyperMatter mode and click on the Display Preferences icon.

In this rollout, you can turn on or off much of HyperMatter's display attributes. Not only can you show or hide the solidify cladding, you can also adjust how you would like it displayed. The default is to show all faces of the clad, but you also have the choice of showing just the edges or points.

You also have the choice of showing just the solidify cladding and hiding the geometry. Taking that a step further, you can also highlight the geometry of the selected sub-object solidify.

One more button at the bottom of this panel enables you to set the options for the color used to display Solids, Sub-Object selections, and so forth. Remember that these are saved in the Windows Registry, and thus are configurable by each user.

14. In the Display Preferences rollout, click on Hide All to hide all of the sub-object solidify claddings. Change the viewport to the Front view, then perform an Arc Rotate Selected and spin the view so that Mortimer's right eyebrow is isolated with no other geometry behind it. Make certain that you are in Sub-Object Geometry mode and Fence select the eyebrow faces (see fig. 30.16).

15. Arc Rotate again to get a straight-on view of the selected eyebrow, and while holding down the Ctrl key, add to the existing selection set by selecting the faces immediately adjacent to the eyebrow faces. Name this selection set **Eyebrow Right** (see fig. 30.17).

FIGURE 30.16
Arc Rotate the view to select these faces of the eyebrow. (3D models by Viewpoint Datalabs International, Inc.)

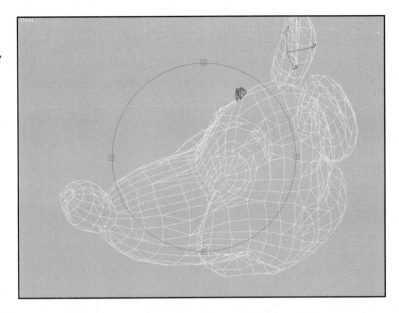

FIGURE 30.17
Arc Rotate again to select these faces surrounding the eyebrow, adding the faces to the last selection. (3D models by Viewpoint Datalabs International, Inc.)

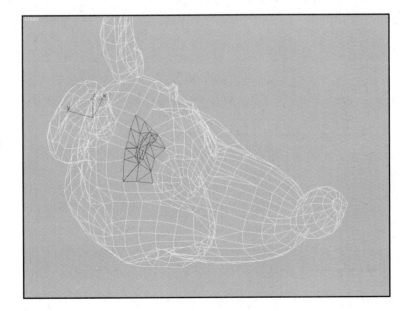

16. Select the Automatic Solidify icon and Solidify Sub-Object. Rename this sub-object selection **SO_Eyebrow Right**. Get into Sub-Object HyperMatter mode, Substance panel, and change Elasticity and Damping to .7. Change the viewport to the Camera view.

Play the scene. This character is starting to get some real personality. You can finish by doing a HyperMatter sub-object solidify to the other eyebrow.

17. Repeat steps 14, 15, and 16 for Mortimer's left eyebrow. Select the same area of faces around this eyebrow (see fig. 30.18). Use the same substance values and substitute the name **Eyebrow Left** in both the Named Selection Set drop down and the sub-object solidify solid name.

FIGURE 30.18

Select these faces for Sub-Object Solidification of Mortimer's left eyebrow. (3D models by Viewpoint Datalabs International, Inc.)

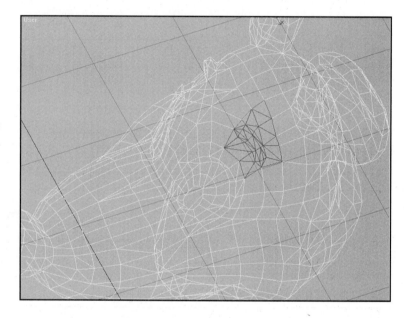

18. Change to the Camera view. Unhide all the objects except for the original Face object that was copied by HyperMatter and then hidden.

Play the scene. Notice the sub-object solids reacting, all in their own substance ways, to the keyframed motion of Mortimer Mouse running.

View the rendered scene. It is included on the accompanying CD as mouserun.avi. The same file rendered without HyperMatter is included for comparison as nohm.avi.

Animating Substance Parameters and the Follow Constraint

In this exercise, you will work again with Mortimer Mouse. You will actually be working with a manufacturing line of rubber mice on a conveyor. This part of the manufacturing line is testing the mice for the consistency of the rubber material. As the conveyor starts and stops, any inconsistency in the rubber material is detected. When an overly soft mouse is found, it is taken (or rather thrown) off the line.

In the following exercise, you are introduced to a new HyperMatter parameter, Follow. The Follow constraint is a very useful constraint, one that enables you to have any point in the HyperMatter Solid follow any other object in the scene. This constraint, like the other constraints, has an adjustable lifespan, which enables you to follow the particular object during the frames you deem necessary only.

NOTE

The Follow constraint, in certain regards, can be thought of as a specialized type of link. This link would have two big differences from what you normally think of as a Hierarchy link. One is that the link can be used with the whole HyperMatter Solid or with any sub-object portion of the HyperMatter Solid using point selection sets. The other difference is that you can set up as many Follow constraints as needed, making it possible to give each Follow a different lifespan—thus having multiple links to different objects within the same animation.

You will set up multiple follow constraints in this exercise and will even go so far as to overlap the lifetime of the Follow constraints for an interesting stretching effect.

Although you have been told that HyperMatter substances can be animated, you have not animated any Substance parameters in the exercises yet. You will animate both the Elasticity and Damping parameters in this exercise, causing a very nice tightening of the substance over time, which can be useful if you want a very elastic object, and yet want to control how long it continues to wobble.

This exercise is quite involved, so it has been broken up into two parts. In the first part, you set up the mice as HyperMatter Solids and move them on the conveyor. The second part includes a mechanism that picks up the mouse and throws it off the conveyor.

MOUSE REJECT, PART 1

Load 30eimx.max from the accompanying CD and check out the scene. Notice that three mice are on the conveyor and that a dummy object is animated below. This dummy will be the impetus that moves the mice down the line.

1. Select the first mouse named Mouse 1. In the Create panel, choose Second Nature from the drop-down list and click on HyperMatter to turn the first mouse into a HyperMatter Control object. Click on Solidify Object. Make Z the Fit Direction so that the solid cladding is tight against the feet.

2. In the Modify panel, go into Sub-Object HyperMatter mode and select the Substance Editor icon. Set Elasticity to 18 and Damping to 15. This will be the normal mouse substance property.

3. Go back to the Create panel, select the third mouse, named Mouse 3. Choose Second Nature from the drop-down list and click on HyperMatter. Click on Solidify Object. Set Fit Direction in the Z direction if necessary, although the Fit Direction choice should be sticky within the MAX session.

4. Go to the Modify panel, Sub-Object HyperMatter mode, and select the Substance Editor icon. Set Elasticity to 18 and Damping to 15 (just as you did for Mouse 1).

5. Go to the Create panel, select the mouse named Mouse 2, Choose Second Nature from the drop-down list, and click on HyperMatter. Click on Solidify Object and raise the Resolution to 3. Be certain that Fit Z is active.

You have raised the resolution of the solid clad on Mouse 2 because this mouse will be defective and as such will be acting differently than the others. You will be having some real fun with this mouse, so more detail will give you better action. By the way, this creates the perfect solid cladding resolution for the tail. With a resolution of 2, the solid cladding holds the tip of the tail rather rigidly to the body as witnessed by the continuous cladding across the bottom, from front to tail tip. With a resolution of 3, the tail is separated from the body much better.

6. In the Modify panel, with H_Mouse 2 still selected, get into Sub-Object HyperMatter mode, and choose the Substance Editor icon. Set Elasticity to 5 and Damping to 2.

If you play the scene, you will notice the typical HyperMatter Gravity affecting the mice and making them fall.

(Be certain that Real Time is off in the Time configuration dialog box.) You have used HyperMatter Walls before to keep this from happening, but walls and their associated collision and friction is not what is needed here. You need to keep the mice from falling and move them effortlessly forward. This is where the Follow constraint comes in.

7. Select the first HyperMatter mouse H_Mouse 1 (use the Select Next HyperMatter Object button). Click on the Constraints icon. Change the view to the maximized Left viewport and zoom in closer to the first mouse.

TIP

Use the Select Next HyperMatter Object and Select Previous HyperMatter Object icons if you need to go from working on one HyperMatter object to the next. This saves a few steps because you will not have to get out of Sub-Object mode, select the next HyperMatter object, and get back into Sub-Object HyperMatter mode.

8. Select the bottom front four points of the solid clad (see fig. 30.19). Name this point selection set **Bottom4**.

FIGURE 30.19

Select these points for use with the Follow constraint. (3D models by Viewpoint Datalabs International, Inc.)

9. Zoom out a bit so that the dummy is partly in the viewport. Click on the Follow button; it presses in and turns green while putting you into an Object Pick mode. Place the arrow cursor over the viewport to see the pick cursor as it passes over objects. Pick the Dummy object. Change to the Camera view.

FOL[Bottom4]->Dummy01 appears in the Constraint list. Play the scene and notice that this first mouse no longer falls from gravity because the Bottom4 points will not allow it; they can only follow the dummy. Notice that the rest of the mouse is still affected by gravity though, and that the mouse moves forward, dragged by his feet.

The Bottom4 points, moved by the Follow constraint, have created in the rest of the mouse what HyperMatter is best at—Cause and Effect motion according to soft body dynamics. This is the kind of motion you would not want to keyframe/morph, and now you don't have to.

10. Go to frame 0. Repeat steps 7, 8, and 9 on the third mouse. Use the same selection set name **Bottom4** and pick the same Dummy01 as the follow object. Change to the Camera view.

Now that these two mice have been set up, you can concentrate on the rubbery reject H_Mouse 2. First you can get these two mice out of the way and clear up the scene a bit to speed up your interaction with the scene and to speed up playback.

11. Get out of Sub-Object mode. Select the first and third mouse in preparation of hiding them. From the Display panel, click on the Hide Selected button (or use your keyboard shortcut). Also select and hide the Floor, Conveyor, and Conveyor Belt objects.

12. Maximize the Left viewport and do a zoom extents.

13. Select the mouse (H_Mouse 2) and go to the Modify panel. Go into Sub-Object HyperMatter mode and select the bottom three points directly below the feet (see fig. 30.20). Name this point selection **Bottom3**.

14. Click on the Follow constraint and then pick the dummy. Change this viewport to Camera.

FIGURE 30.20

Select these points for use with the Follow constraint. (3D models by Viewpoint Datalabs International, Inc.)

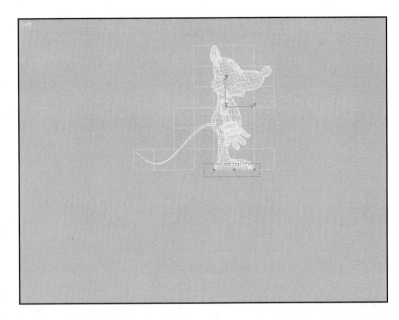

Play the scene. You should see some great cause and effect motion to this rubbery mouse. Notice the tail and how well it reacts. Okay, the tail goes below the conveyor, so you should take care of this now.

15. Go to frame 0 and put the viewport into 4 View mode. Go to the Create panel and choose Second Nature from the drop-down list. Click on Walls. In the Top viewport, drag to create HyperMatter Walls surrounding the mouse and its travels. Make the wall 600 in Length, 150 in Width, and 150 in Height. Position the wall bottom halfway between the dummy and the bottom of the mouse feet. This will position it just below the conveyor (see fig. 30.21).

You are moving the Wall object down below the top of the conveyor for an important reason. A collision occurs between the wall and the solid cladding, not the actual geometry. Because the illusion you need is that of the tail colliding with the conveyor, and the tail's solid cladding is a bit away from the actual tail, you can compensate for this by moving the wall below the conveyor top—about the same distance below the conveyor as the solid cladding is from the bottom of the tail (see fig. 30.22).

FIGURE 30.21

Position the Wall object surrounding the entire path of the mouse with the bottom halfway between the dummy and mouse feet. (3D models by Viewpoint Datalabs International, Inc.)

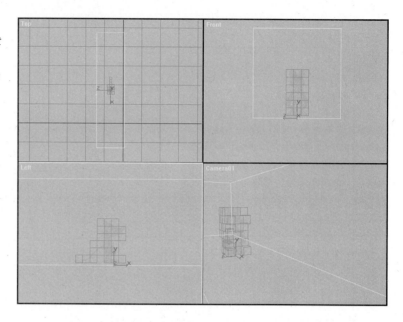

FIGURE 30.22

Position the Wall object below the conveyor belt top to compensate for the difference between the tail geometry and the solid cladding surrounding the tail. (3D models by Viewpoint Datalabs International, Inc.)

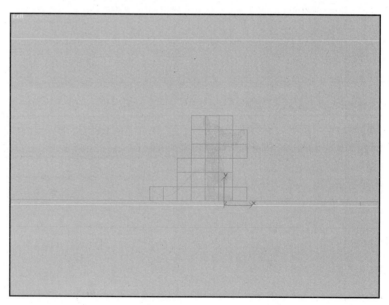

16. Select the mouse, go to the Modify panel, and get into Sub-Object HyperMatter mode. Maximize the Left viewport and select the two points directly under the tail, but do not include the tip of the tail (see fig. 30.23). Name this point selection **Tail**. Click on the Walls constraint and click on the H_Wall01 object. Hide the Wall object. Unhide the conveyor and conveyor belt.

FIGURE 30.23

Select these points under the tail for use with the Walls constraint. (3D models by Viewpoint Datalabs International, Inc.)

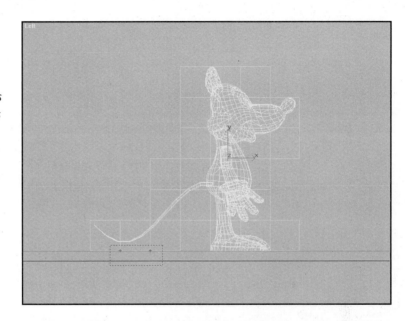

Play the scene and observe that the tail no longer goes through the conveyor but bounces nicely against it. Notice also that the tip of the tail actually unwinds as it slaps against the conveyor in a few spots. See the file 30e-pre.avi on the accompanying CD for a preview of the Left viewport. Adjust the wall in your scene if necessary.

A new camera was set up and linked to the mouse just for rendering. Check out the rendered file Ch30e-1.avi. You may notice a minor irregularity in the tail. It seems that on certain frames the tail appears to stick to the conveyor. This seems to be caused by the friction of the tail selection set points as they collide with the wall.

17. Select the mouse, go to the Modify panel, Sub-Object HyperMatter, and choose the Substance Editor icon. Set Friction to 0 to eliminate any friction of the solid clad points as the tail whips across the HyperMatter Walls (conveyor).

Check out ch30e-2.avi from the accompanying CD and compare the new tail action—a minor change, but a big improvement. No other points in the solid cladding will be affected by changing the friction parameter.

This exercise is getting a bit long, and because there is a lot more to be done to this mouse, now would be a good time to save your work and take a break. When you come back, you will finish up the scene as well as throw the mouse off the conveyor belt.

MOUSE REJECT, PART 2

Load your saved scene from part 1 of the preceding exercise or load 30e-hold.max from the accompanying CD. The mice are all set up and the first and third mice are still hidden. The conveyor and floor are also hidden. Now it is time to remove this defective mouse from the conveyor line.

1. Unhide the Clamp assembly and Clamp 1 through 4. Do a Zoom Extents All. This is the mechanism that will take care of the defective mouse. Also unhide Strap 2a and Strap 2b. These keep the mouse in place as it travels along the conveyor. Select these straps and link them both to the dummy. Return to the Select icon from the toolbar.

Play the scene from a maximized Left viewport. You will notice that this Clamp assembly starts moving toward the mouse at frame 175. The individual clamps tighten up and the mechanism stops at frame 200. Only problem is that the mouse is so rubbery that it has not stopped wobbling enough to be picked up yet. Sure, you could change the substance properties of the mouse, but what if you really like these parameters and want to keep them?

You can have the best of both worlds with HyperMatter because all the substance parameters are animatable. What is called for here, therefore, is an animated tightening of the Elasticity and Damping parameters.

2. Select the mouse. Open Track View and filter for selected objects only. Expand the H_Mouse 2 track, Object track, SO_Mouse 2_1 track, and finally the Substance track.

3. Click on the Add Keys icon and add 3 keys for both the Elasticity and Damping tracks somewhere between frames 100 and 200.

4. Right-click on the keys to use the Key Info dialog.
    Set Elasticity keys:
    Time 100 Value 5 Slow-Out Tangent
    Time 175 Value 35 Fast-In / Step-Out Tangent
    Time 200 Value 8 Step-In Tangent
    Set Damping keys:
    Time 100 Value 2 Slow-Out Tangent
    Time 175 Value 35 Fast-in / Step-Out Tangent
    Time 200 Value 4 Step-In Tangent

What you have done is animate the Elasticity and Damping parameters to become more rigid from frames 100 through 175. Then at frame 200, coinciding with the grasping of the Clamp Assembly, the mouse will instantly soften back up. You could just as well have turned on the animate button and adjusted these values in the user interface. It is better and faster (in this author's opinion) to use Track View because you don't need to have HyperMatter process frames as you set up the keyframes.

Play the scene again in the Left viewport to see the mouse turn more rigid between frame 100 and 200. In fact, if you have the Substance Properties rollup visible, you will see the values animate.

5. Go to frame 200 by typing it in the Current Frame Number field and pressing Enter. With the mouse still selected and being in Sub-Object HyperMatter mode, choose the Constraints icon. Select the two rows of points in the solid cladding directly through the ear (see fig. 30.24). Name this selection set **Ears**.

6. Click on the Follow constraint and then pick the Clamp assembly from the scene.

FOL[Ears]->Clamp assembly is added to the constraints list. Highlight this entry and notice that HyperMatter has automatically set the start frame (lifespan) to coincide with the current frame, frame 200.

Play the scene in the Camera view until the clamp assembly stops. Notice that the Clamp is further animated to rise up, resulting in a stretching of the mouse. The mouse is still stuck to the conveyor because of the Follow constraint to the dummy.

Notice also that because the Clamp assembly is still at frame 200, the Follow points will also be still. This results in quick stopping of ear motion and a resultant shudder of motion through the rest of the mouse: Cause and Effect at its finest! Remember that Elasticity and Damping has been animated with a step tangent to be more rubbery at precisely this frame to emphasize this shudder.

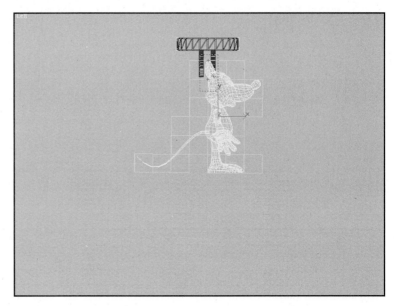

7. Go to frame 260 by typing the Current Frame field. This is the frame at which the Cable assembly reaches the top of its travel and the frame at which you should release the feet.

8. With the mouse selected and still in Sub-Object HyperMatter mode, click on the Constraint icon. Highlight the first Follow constraint from the Constraint list FOL[Bottom3]->Dummy01 and make the current frame the end frame by clicking on the Set End To Current Frame icon next to the End Frame parameter. It will change to 260.

9. Get out of Sub-Object mode and unhide space warps Bomb01 and Bomb02. Bind Strap 2a to Bomb02 and Bind Strap 2b to Bomb01. Hide the Bomb space warps. They have already been set up to detonate at frame 260, completing the release of the mouse feet.

Play the scene for a few frames and stop. Notice that at frame 260, when the Follow constraint to the dummy is released, the stretched mouse springs about as it tries to get back to its original shape.

If you continue playing the scene, you will see the Clamp assembly rotate back and forth, during which time the clamps open up to release the mouse. That is fine except that the mouse does not release. The Follow constraint to the Clamp is not letting the mouse be released from the Clamp assembly for the throw.

10. Go to frame 395, the frame at which the Clamp assembly reaches the end of its travel. Select the mouse, go to the Modify panel, Sub-Object HyperMatter, and choose the Constraints icon. Choose the Ears Follow constraint, FOL[Ears] -> Clamp assembly, from the Constraint list and change the end frame to 392. This is 3 frames before the current frame.

Play the scene starting from frame 0 and check your work. Although it may be fun to see the mouse bounce off the wall object at the end, there is no object there and it doesn't make any sense.

11. While still in the Constraints drop-down list, select the Walls constraint WAL[Tail] ->H_Walls01. Change the end frame to 275 as the walls are no longer needed after the mouse is lifted off the conveyor.

12. Unhide objects Conveyor, Conveyor Belt, H_Mouse 1, H_Mouse 2, Strap 1a, Strap 1b, Strap 3a, and Strap 3b.

Play the scene again in its entirety and admire your handiwork. This has been a lengthy exercise, and you have made it through. Save your scene and make a preview if you would like. Load Mreject.avi from the accompanying CD to see the final rendered animation.

In Practice: HyperMatter

- **HyperMatter Solids react according to the laws of physics and dynamics.** Use HyperMatter whenever you need a MAX object to act as if it were a real-world object. Whether you need a realistic bounce or a deformable collision, HyperMatter is there to help you get it right.

- **When you need to take control of a HyperMatter Solid "doing its own thing," use the available constraints.** You have full control over your HyperMatter Solid through the use of the various constraints. Whether you need to have HyperMatter Solids follow another object, collide with another object, or you just want to prevent it from spinning/tumbling, the HyperMatter's Constraints panel is available.

- **HyperMatter gives you complete control over your objects substance attributes.** HyperMatter's Substance panel gives you full control over your objects' elasticity requirements. HyperMatter objects can represent a highly elastic rubbery substance that deforms easily or a rigid object, such as a pair of dice.

■ **HyperMatter can be used on the whole object or selected parts of the object.** The versatility of using HyperMatter on the geometry as a whole or on a sub-object selection level gives you much freedom. Use HyperMatter dynamics to influence just one part of your object or many parts of the same object with varied substance attributes.

■ **Have fun.** HyperMatter can be a blast and turn a complicated keyframing task into a smooth and realistic joy to behold.

Part IX

VIDEO POST

IMAGE CREATED BY ADAM SILVERTHORNE

Chapter 31

by Adam Silverthorne
and Jarod Ruffo

COMPOSITING AND EDITING

This chapter familiarizes you with some of the powerful and exciting elements of 3D Studio MAX's Video Post module. For many, the words "exciting" and "powerful" don't come to mind when they think of Video Post. Instead, when people think Video Post, they conjure up negative connotations of confusing icons and range bars. Others think of Video Post as just a utility used to splice animations together. Many animators even work productively without ever touching Video Post.

This chapter shows you, however, that Video Post is indeed a very powerful and exciting aspect of 3D Studio MAX. Video Post enables you to composite and edit your animations, which ushers in a whole new world of 3D possibilities. After you realize what MAX Video Post can do for you, you may entirely change the way you animate in MAX.

This chapter covers the following topics:

- Compositing basics
- Using the Alpha Compositor
- Understanding shadows and compositing
- Screen mapping and compositing
- Camera mapping and compositing
- Shadow/Matte and Matte/Shadow
- Masking
- Bluescreening
- Other methods of compositing
- Editing your animations

Compositing Basics

Compositing refers to the act of combining two or more images to make one image. Video Post enables you to perform this action and also to extend it by performing a composite of two images a multitude of times. Because an animation is just a string of images, Video Post enables you to composite animations. Video Post also enables you to composite a single image with an animation.

System Performance

One of the strongest arguments for compositing is system performance. You might find that when you animate a small scene, it is nice to have all your objects in the scene simultaneously. This way you can animate them and see them in relation to one another. As your scenes become larger and you begin to tax your system resources, however, you might find yourself yearning for a faster machine (or taking a lot of coffee breaks). Even if you have the fastest machine money can buy, a serious face count coupled with some special effects can make it extremely painful to animate with everything in the same scene. The more complex your scene, the slower MAX responds to your commands. Even fast 3D acceleration hardware does little to help out when you have extremely complex scenes. If you use motion blur, volumetric lighting, or render at a high resolution, you also gobble up a lot of RAM. If you use up all your RAM, your computer is forced to use Virtual Memory, which is not good. Compositing enables you to break up your animation into pieces. Because each piece is a fraction of the total face count, the computer handles the file much more efficiently. You might find that an animation you create through compositing might otherwise be impossible.

NOTE

Virtual Memory is memory allocated on your hard drive to store information that your computer cannot fit into its RAM. Because hard disk drives access data much more slowly than RAM does, using virtual memory in a scene can dramatically slow down render times. In many cases, buying more RAM can be a more effective upgrade than a faster processor for 3D work.

Modular Design Approach

Splitting up your animation also facilitates a modular design approach. Working with the pieces frees you to concentrate on individual areas. If you are working on character animation and have an elaborate 3D background, compositing enables you to concentrate on your character animation exclusively. You can get the motion you want for your characters, and then composite on top of a background prepared separately. This approach also enables you to use that same background for any other animation while simultaneously freeing you from the headache of merging the MAX files together and re-rendering. Furthermore, many animators find that approaching animation from a modular point of view works well because it enables them to focus on one element of the animation without getting confused or distracted by other elements. Compositing also enables multiple animators to tackle the same scene without stumbling over one another. After you get used to compositing, you might find yourself using it even when memory and hardware constraints are not an issue. Despite these benefits, compositing does have a few pitfalls. If objects are not rendered together, they are not picked up in reflections or shadow casting. Ways to get around the shadow problem exist, however, and are discussed later in this chapter.

This modularity also forces the animator to be a little bit more organized. It is important to create subdirectories for your file renders, for example, to avoid cluttering up one directory with long lists of sequential files.

Using the Alpha Compositor

Because of the tools MAX provides, the Alpha Compositor is arguably the best way to composite your animations. The *Alpha Compositor* is an Image Layer event that composites two images based on an image alpha channel. The images are combined based on the alpha data present in the second image. This means that to see the top child, the bottom child of a layer event must contain alpha data (see fig. 31.1). Layer events are like plates that cover one another. The alpha data provides a method for seeing through one plate and on to another. If the bottom child of your Layer event is a Scene event, MAX renders that image and automatically provides transparency data wherever nothing obstructs the background in your scene. If the last layer in the Video Post queue is a Scene event such as a Camera viewport, for example, that viewport is rendered as if it had an alpha channel, and the blank areas become transparent automatically.

FIGURE 31.1

The bottom child covers the event above it.

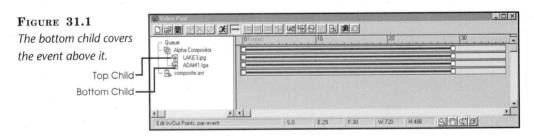

NOTE

You should be aware that transparency data adds an extra 8 bits of information to an image. Consequently, when you need transparency data in an image, the file needs to be 32 bit instead of the default 24 bit. When you composite, you might need this transparency data to see through one layer and on to another. You need to be aware of when you need which type of file, however, so that you don't needlessly waste disk space on 32-bit files if you only need 24-bit files.

For this chapter, you need to understand certain aspects of MAX directly related to compositing, but not necessarily part of the Video Post module. Therefore, image setup parameters, the virtual frame buffer window, the graphics buffer (G-Buffer), and the Image File List (IFL) are explained prior to diving into some compositing examples. If you already know some of these concepts, you may want to skim the familiar parts.

Image Setup Parameters

When you have your scene ready to render, and you specify a file in the Render Scene dialog, you are given options specific to a particular file type. If you render a JPG file, for example, you can specify the level of compression versus the quality of the image. With TGA files, you can specify whether you want the rendered file to have an alpha channel. You do this by setting the Bits-Per-Pixel to 32 in the Image Setup dialog (see fig. 31.2). The parameters that you set for an image file type stay that way until you change them again. If you set the Bits-Per-Pixel for TGA images to 32, for example, all TGA images you render from now on are automatically saved with alpha data even if you close and reopen MAX. With this in mind, be certain to check the Image Setup dialog to make certain that you set up the image properly. This dialog also gives you an option called Alpha Split. An *Alpha Split* creates a separate 8-bit image, in addition to the 24-bit rendering. This 8-bit separate image contains the alpha data only. Alpha Split is useful because you could then use this 8-bit Alpha Split image or image sequence in masking operations (see the section on masking later in this chapter).

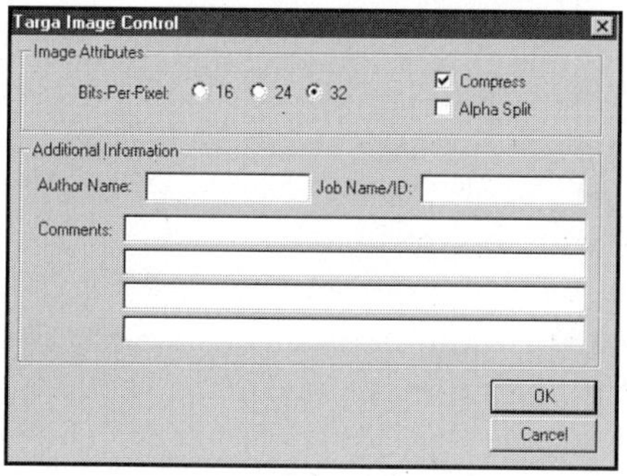

FIGURE 31.2

By setting the Bits-Per-Pixel to 32, you tell MAX that you want to include an alpha channel in the rendered image.

The Virtual Frame Buffer Window

Figure 31.3 shows an image of the Virtual Frame Buffer window. Notice the buttons at the top of the window. On the left, buttons labeled with red, green, and blue circles are followed by a button with a half black, half white circle. Each button represents one of the four channels in an RGBA image. RGBA stands for red, green, blue, and alpha—the four standard channels in a 32-bit image.

FIGURE 31.3

The Virtual Frame Buffer window.

The half-black, half-white button is the Display Alpha Channel button. If you press this button, the image in the window changes and reveals the alpha channel (see fig. 31.4). The white areas represent opaque sections of the image, and the black areas are transparent. Notice that the alpha channel for this image provides an area of transparency where no geometry is present. In this image, the transparent area is present in the area revealed by the opening door. The space beyond the door can be a background that you composite in later. The Display Alpha Channel button proves particularly useful when doing compositing because it enables you to visualize your areas of transparency. The buttons with the red, green, and blue circles toggle the corresponding channel in the image. If you press the Red button, for example, the red channel of the image no longer displays in the Virtual Frame Buffer window. By clicking on the various buttons, you can toggle the corresponding channel on and off. Visualizing the individual channels that use these buttons is useful when you want to perform masking operations (see the section on masking later in this chapter). Notice the two other buttons next to the RGBA channel buttons. The button labeled with an X clears the current frame buffer. The button with the disk icon enables you to save the image to a file—useful when you do test renders and don't necessarily want to specify an output file in the Render Scene dialog. The pull-down menu shows what G-Buffer information is available in that particular file.

FIGURE 31.4
The Display Alpha Channel button enables you to visualize your areas of transparency.

The G-Buffer

The term *G-Buffer* (graphics buffer) refers to a method of storing geometric information about objects in 3D images. The geometric information is stored so that it may later be calculated and used by image-processing programs. The information is stored in various channels similar to the way an alpha channel is stored. Within a G-Buffered image, for example, there might be data that describes how far a pixel is from the camera. This information can then be used to calculate fog or distance blur effects. 3D Studio MAX implements G-Buffer technology. If you specify a material effects channel or an object channel, for example, you set data within the G-Buffer. The Virtual Frame Buffer window enables you to view this data by selecting the appropriate channel from the pull-down list. If no G-Buffer data is available, no channels are listed in the pull-down menu. MAX supports 10 total possible channels, but not all are added automatically. Not all image types support G-Buffer information. The G-Buffer information recorded by MAX is in a format unique to MAX's renderer. This format is public, but it is not extensible. For this reason, MAX uses Silicon Graphics' popular RLA image format for saving images with G-Buffer information.

The Image File List

IFL stands for Image File List. An *IFL file* is a standard text-only file that contains a list of images. Each image in the list corresponds to a 3D Studio MAX frame. MAX reads the file line by line and loads each listed file for a particular frame of animation. Creating IFL files is easy. You must first have a sequence of images. If you rendered an animation to sequential TGA files and called the output file Homey.tga, for example, the sequence of files would look like the following:

Homey0001.tga

Homey0002.tga

Homey0003.tga

And so on…

To create this particular IFL, in the File Selection dialog, navigate to the directory that contains the sequential images and type **Homey*.tga** as the input file. The list continues until it reaches the number of rendered frames. MAX automatically creates a file with an IFL extension. The file contains the list of sequential files that matches the Homey*.tga wild card.

MAX creates the IFL file in the directory that contains the list of images. You cannot, therefore, create an IFL file if the images you intend to use are on CD-ROM. Because CD-ROM is read-only media, MAX cannot create the IFL file because MAX will try to write the file to the CD-ROM.

WARNING

If you are on a network or if you plan to network render, IFL files can slow down your renders significantly. This slowdown occurs because the network needs to send each file specified in the IFL over the network for every frame being processed by Manager. 100BaseT networks seem to handle this increased traffic without too much difficulty. 10BaseT or coaxial networks bottleneck, however, if they must send large TGA files on very limited bandwidth.

Now that you are familiar with some of the core concepts important to compositing, you should discover the power of Video Post's Alpha Compositor. The following exercise illustrates how to perform a composite by using the Alpha Compositor. In this example, a door swings open and reveals an image that you composite behind it. The door is one layer of your composite, and the background revealed as the door swings open is the other layer.

USING THE ALPHA COMPOSITOR

1. From the accompanying CD, load ch31ex1.max.

2. Activate the Camera viewport and scroll the Time Slider.

Notice the animation of the door opening. This scene presents a good scenario for compositing. The file does not contain complex geometry, but remember that when you have an animation that can be broken up into elementary pieces, that animation makes a good candidate for a composite. If you want, you can now render this animation as a set of sequential images. The images are included on the accompanying CD, however, so this is not a necessary step. With the rendered images ready and waiting, you have what you need to perform a composite.

3. From the Rendering pull-down list on the MAX main screen, select Video Post.

Notice the buttons along the top of the window. Some of the buttons are grayed out, meaning they are inaccessible. Certain buttons are only accessible when events upon which they can perform an action are within the Video Post queue.

4. Click on the Add Image Input Event button.

The Add Image Input Event dialog appears (see fig. 31.5). This dialog enables you to specify a file, a sequence of files, or a device. An example of a device you might use is the Accom WSD Digital Recorder. For this exercise, it is assumed that you are using standard images.

FIGURE 31.5

The Add Image Input Event dialog.

5. In the Image Input section of the dialog, click on the Files button.

6. Navigate to the CD-ROM and highlight back1.tga.

7. Click on the View button.

The View button is a useful button included in the MAX File Selection dialog. The same dialog appears whenever you are called upon to choose an image file regardless of whether you are in Video Post, the Material Editor, or any other section of MAX. While viewing the image, notice that the buttons available to you while viewing rendered images in the virtual frame buffer are available to you now.

8. Click on the Show/Hide Alpha button.

Notice that this file has no alpha channel. Because you use this file as your background, it is essentially the ultimate layer of your composite. It is not necessary to see past it because it is the last one. Remember that you only need alpha data if you need transparency. Because there is no need to see through the background, no alpha channel is necessary in the image.

9. Close the Image Display window.

10. Click on the Cache check box to enable the cache.

11. Click on OK to accept the file and return to the Video Post window.

TIP

The Cache check box instructs Video Post to load the image into RAM and then to use that same information throughout the sequence. This should always be checked if you are using a single image in an Image Input event. By loading the image information into RAM, MAX does not reload or scale the image for every frame. Reloading and scaling takes time and that makes the render take longer. If you are using a single image, checking the Cache check box saves a lot of time. Do not use this option if you are using a sequence of images. It is necessary to load each image for each frame if you want your background animation to correspond with your foreground animation.

You now have the background ready and waiting in the Video Post Event queue. Because compositing requires two images, you need to add another Image Input event.

1. Deselect the current event in the Video Post queue by clicking on a blank area in the Video Post window.

2. Click on the Image Input button to select another Image Input event.

3. Navigate to the CD-ROM and select dooro.ifl in the Dooropen folder.

4. Click on OK to accept the image and return to the Video Post window.

You should now have two Image Input events listed in the Video Post queue. One event is a single image and another event is a list of images. Make certain that the range bars for the two events both span 60 frames. By stretching the range bar for the background image over 60 frames, you are instructing Video Post to use the same image for all 60 frames of your animation.

5. Click on the back1.tga event to highlight it.

6. Hold down the Ctrl key while simultaneously clicking on the dooro.ifl event.

Both events should now be highlighted. Notice that when both events became highlighted, some of the buttons in the Video Post window became active. Notice also that the range bars turned red when events were selected, indicating that the event was active. When both events become active, the Add Image Layer Event button becomes available.

7. Click on the Add Image Layer Event button.

8. Select Alpha Compositor from the pull-down menu and accept it as the Image Layer event.

After creating an Image Layer event, both of your Image Input events lined themselves up below the Alpha Compositor Layer event. This arrangement graphically illustrates that the Input events are now children of the Layer event. The Alpha Compositor is ready to combine these two images.

Warning

Make sure that the background image is listed above the animation sequence in the Alpha Compositor hierarchy (see fig. 31.6). If it is not, the opaque background will be rendered on top of the animation sequence. The result will be an animation of the background only. Thus, the order of children is very important. If you need to switch the order, you can highlight both children and click on the Swap Events button.

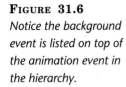

FIGURE 31.6

Notice the background event is listed on top of the animation event in the hierarchy.

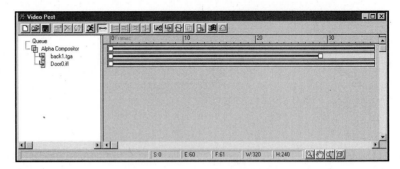

9. Deselect any events in the Video Post queue by clicking on empty space within the Video Post window.

10. Click on the Add Image Output Event button.

11. Navigate to the \3dsmax\images directory on the accompanying CD, specify ch31ex1.avi as an output file, and then click on OK.

12. If you want, you can specify parameters for the AVI file by clicking on the Setup button for the Image Output event. Then click on OK to return to the Video Post window.

13. Click on the Execute Sequence button (the running man) and render frames 0–60 at any resolution you want. If you prefer not to render the animation, you can skip this step.

14. From the 3D Studio MAX file pull-down menu, select View File, navigate to the \3dsmax\images directory and double-click on ch31ex1.avi to view the composited animation. If you chose not to render the animation, you can view it from the accompanying CD.

Congratulations! You just performed a composite entirely within 3D Studio MAX. Using the Alpha Compositor will prove to be a valuable tool to add to your 3D Studio MAX arsenal. In the previous example, you composited a single image with an animation. You could also have specified an animation as the background Scene event. You could use an AVI file, for example, or you could create an IFL from sequential images to use as the background. You should now be beginning to realize the power of the Alpha Compositor.

Multi-Layer Compositing

One great thing about Layer events is that they can be children of other Layer events. Earlier you learned that the Alpha Compositor must have two scene events to perform a composite. This is true only at the bottom of each branch in the hierarchy. The term *branch* refers to a subset of the hierarchical list of parents and children. You could have an Alpha Compositor event with two more Alpha Compositor events as each of its children, for example. The children of the children could be Scene events, or they could be other Alpha Compositor events (see fig. 31.7). This kind of setup is referred to as a *multi-layer composite*. Consider the previous example of the door swinging open. Suppose that you want the door to begin its motion in the open position and then swing closed, blocking out the background temporarily. Suppose further that when it swings back into position, it reveals a different background. This kind of scenario is made possible with a multi-layer composite.

FIGURE 31.7

The children of an Alpha Compositor Layer event can be Alpha Compositor Layer events themselves.

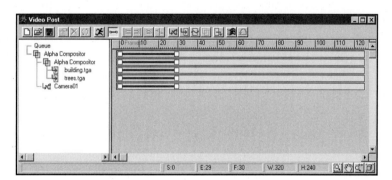

1. From the CD, load ch31ex2.max.

2. Drag the Frame Slider and notice the animation of the door closing over frames 0–60 and then swinging back open over frames 60–120 (see fig. 31.8).

3. Select Rendering from the MAX pull-down menu and choose Video Post.

FIGURE 31.8

*You can use the Alpha
Compositor to separate
the background into as
many layers as you
want.*

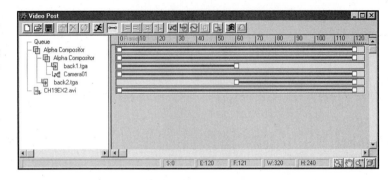

Here you have a Video Post layout that contains multiple Alpha Compositor Layer events. One child of the root of the hierarchy is an Alpha Compositor event. The root of the hierarchy itself is also an Alpha Compositor event. The child Alpha Compositor Event has an Image Input event and a Camera Scene event as its own children. Notice that the range bars in the Video Post window for each event correspond to the frames that you want the image to be viewed in the scene. Because you want back1.tga to be present over frames 0–60, the range bar for that event covers frames 0–60. The back2.tga event picks up where the back1.tga event ends, and covers frames 60–120. The Output event range bar spans the total animation of 120 frames. You can execute this sequence and render the files, or you can view the pre-rendered ch31ex2.avi file from the accompanying CD.

In this instance, a multi-layer composite was used because you wanted to change a background image during an animation. The range bars do the work here. At a specified time, one Image Layer event ends and another event picks up where the first event left off. You might also want to perform a multi-layer composite during one specific time frame. You might need to do this if you want to separate a complex background into various different layers. You can have, for example, some buildings on a bottom layer, some trees on a middle layer, and a character on a foreground layer. To accomplish this task, you might set up the Video Post queue like that shown in figure 31.7.

Notice the first child of the main Alpha Compositor event is another Alpha Compositor event with two Image Input events as children. The building.tga image on top is the background layer. If you think of the events like plates that cover one another, you can see that this Image Input event will be covered up by the trees.tga Image Input event. It is necessary, therefore, that the trees.tga Input event be an event that contains a 32-bit image or images.

If this event did not contain 32-bit files with alpha data, the image would have no transparency and consequently it would completely cover the buildings. The second child of the main Alpha Compositor event is a Camera Scene event. In this instance, the camera would be pointed at a character in the scene. Remember that Scene events in the Video Post queue are rendered as if they had alpha data automatically. The result of this Video Post sequence would be the trees and buildings composited together, and then the character in the scene composited on top of the buildings and trees.

Understanding Shadows and Compositing

Sometimes an animation requires certain elements that make compositing a little more difficult than just laying images on top of one another. If you use the Alpha Compositor to composite a character on a background, for example, it might look like the character is floating in space while the background is pinned up behind her. In other words, it might look like a composite. A good composite should not give away the fact that it is composited. To avoid this dilemma, you need to "ground" your composited objects in their backgrounds. You need to make an object feel like it is a part of its environment, and that it could interact with the background if it wanted to. To make an object feel like it is part of the scene, the object should cast a shadow. Shadows give the illusion that an object is present in its environment. For a long time, a strong argument against compositing in many animation studios was the fact that it has been difficult (if not impossible) to achieve realistic shadows in a composite. While compositing in MAX, however, techniques enable you to achieve realistic shadows. These techniques are outlined here. Furthermore, lights that might be present in your foreground should affect the background and vice versa, and there is a method for achieving this effect as well.

Screen Mapping and Compositing

Using screen mapping to achieve realistic shadow effects in a composite is considered by many to be a "hack" or a workaround. It is only useful in certain situations. It is worth discussing and understanding because it does work for particular situations, and it can work in conjunction with other compositing methods. The main limitation of the screen mapping method is that the camera in the scene must be static. The general term *screen mapping* might sound familiar if you have ever used a background image for an environment map. Essentially, a screen-mapped background remains in a direct-facing orientation to the camera and fills the screen. If you are using a background and you use screen mapping, you would not want to animate camera movement because the background would move exactly with the camera. If you moved the camera 45 degrees, for example, it would still be looking at the same background scene. The result would be a foreground that moved against an unchanging background. This is quite an unrealistic and unwanted effect. For this reason, if you use an environment map and you have camera movement, you want to use one of the other mapping types, such as spherical. If you use the screen mapping method to perform a composite, you encounter the same problem with camera movement. If you have a stationary camera, however, screen mapping can be used to fake shadow and light effects.

The screen mapping method entails setting up a background image in your Camera viewport. You then create geometry and move it so that it matches the perspective of the part of the background image on which you want to cast a shadow. By applying a material that contains the same image as the background in the diffuse channel and specifying screen mapping as the mapping type, the object is mapped with the background image. Because the mapping type is screen, the object has only a section of the map visible. The section of the map visible on the object is exactly the part that the object obstructs from the background. The effect is that the geometry disappears into the background. The geometry, however, is still present and can receive shadows and lighting. Confused? The following example illustrates exactly how this works.

1. From the CD, load ch31ex3.max.

2. Make certain that the Camera viewport is active, select Views from the MAX pull-down menu, and then select Background Image.

The background image feature can be useful for referencing what is happening in a composite. A shaded viewport with a background image displayed can give you a good idea of what to expect from your final render. The background image can be a single image or an animation. You can specify an IFL file (discussed previously in this chapter), or you can specify an AVI file. When using screen mapping for compositing, it is important to display the background image or animation because you need to match the image's perspective with geometry you create in the viewport.

3. Click on the Files button and select back3.jpg from the accompanying CD.

4. Under Aspect Ratio in the lower-left corner, check the box titled Match Rendering Output.

5. Click on the Display Background button in the lower-right corner to enable it, and click on OK to dismiss the dialog (see fig. 31.9).

FIGURE 31.9

The Viewport Background dialog enables you to display a background in the viewport.

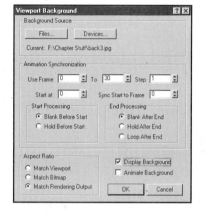

You should also turn off the viewport grid by right-clicking on the viewport label and selecting Show Grid to toggle it off. The grid can obstruct your view of the background image and consequently make perspective matching more difficult. Notice the object in the scene named Ground. This geometry is a simple box that has been aligned to match up with the ground plane in the image. By applying a material with screen mapping, you can make the object seem to disappear into the background image.

6. Open the Material Editor, select a material slot, and name it Screen Map 1.

7. Set Shininess and Shininess Strength to 0.

8. Click on the gray button next to the Diffuse color selector. From the ensuing dialog, double-click on Bitmap.

9. Under Bitmap Parameters, click on the long gray box next to the Bitmap label and select the same file that you selected for your background image, back3.jpg from the accompanying CD.

10. Under the Coordinates rollout, change Texture to Environ, and then from the list box, change Mapping to Screen.

11. Make the object named Ground in the scene the currently selected object, and then click on the Assign Material to Selection button from the Material Editor toolbar.

12. Render the scene to the Virtual Frame Buffer window (see fig. 31.10).

FIGURE 31.10

By using Screen Mapping in the Material Editor, you can make the object seemingly disappear into the background.

You should now see an object in the scene with a material applied that matches the background image. Notice, however, that the background image didn't show up. Setting the background image in the viewport is not the same as setting a background image for rendering. To set up the background image for rendering, follow this procedure:

1. From MAX's Rendering pull-down menu, choose Environment. Click on the Assign button and change the Browse From section of the Material/ Map browser to Scene.

2. Find back3.jpg in the list and double-click on it. Make certain that the Use Map check box is checked and click on the X in the upper-right corner to dismiss the Environment window.

Now when you render the scene, you should see the background image and the CG telephone pole. The Ground Plane object has almost disappeared into the background image. One problem you might notice is that the ground plane is not lit correctly to match the lighting in the background image.

1. Select the Spot01 spotlight that is above the telephone pole, open the Modify panel and adjust the multiplier to approximately 1.5 to correctly match the lighting.

2. Check the Cast Shadows check box in the Shadow Parameters section.

3. Make certain that the Camera viewport is active and re-render the scene.

You should now see that the telephone pole is seemingly casting a shadow on the background image. The shadow makes the object feel as if it is present in the scene. You can also use this method for lighting effects.

4.   Select the Spot02 spotlight, open the Modify panel, and check the On check box that is next to the color selector. You might also adjust the color of the spotlight to match the color of your typical pale yellow street light.

5.   Render the scene.

Notice that the light appears to affect the ground in the background image as well. To add to the realism of the scene, you might create some telephone wires connecting the CG telephone pole with the real one in the image. Using screen mapping in this manner can be quite useful for creating shadow and light effects over real images or CG backgrounds. This effect is not limited to ground planes. You can cast shadows over buildings or other objects by making simple boxes and perspective matching them to the objects. The backgrounds that you use can be animated, but remember that screen mapping is not the way to go if there is camera movement. If there is camera movement and you need shadow effects, you should use the Shadow/Matte material (discussed in the Shadow Matte/Matte Shadow section later in this chapter). The Display Background feature proves very useful for all types of compositing because it gives you an idea of what to expect from the background and enables you to place foreground objects in relation to the background.

Camera Mapping

The Camera Mapping plug-in works similarly to the way the screen mapping method does. Camera mapping maps the background image on to an object by using a modified planar projection from the camera's point of view. The result is that the object with camera mapping applied disappears into the background image the same way that it did with screen mapping. You could use camera mapping to achieve shadows in a composite. The plug-in contains two parts: a modifier and a space warp.

The *modifier* sets the objects mapping to the background image for a specified frame. The modifier doesn't work properly if there is camera movement for the same reason that screen mapping doesn't. If you use the modifier, the background image is mapped properly only for the current frame you are on when you choose a camera to use for the mapping. If the camera moves, the other frames disorient the mapping from the background.

Essentially, the Camera Mapping modifier is another way to do screen mapping. Screen mapping has some advantages because camera mapping relates to the tessellation of the geometry. For the mapping to be accurate, the object needs to have a high number of faces. Screen mapping works with the minimum number of faces. The second part of the plug-in, the space warp, recalculates the mapping for every frame of animation. The result is that the object is mapped with the correct background perspective for each frame, enabling you to move the camera. You could use this to composite an animation that has a moving camera with a static or moving background. It can be difficult, however, to match the background camera movement with the foreground camera movement. Typically, you must merge the same camera you use in the background MAX file into the foreground MAX file. Furthermore, using this method to match the lighting in a file that has camera movement can be tough. If you want to composite an animation that has a moving camera with shadows, it is easier to use the Shadow/Matte Material described in the next section. This plug-in is quite useful, however, if you are doing special effects. You can blend an object into the background with the space warp, for example. You can then animate the self illumination of the material, or do a morph material and make the object "cloak" in and out of the background. The Camera Mapping plug-in is included on the accompanying CD.

Shadow/Matte and Matte/Shadow

There are ways to composite with shadows that get around the static camera problem that limits Screen Mapping and the Camera Map modifier's functionality. Shadow Matting is one such method. Shadow Matte is a plug-in for 3D Studio MAX written by an invaluable member of the MAX development community, Peter Watje. The Shadow/Matte plug-in is a material that doesn't visually render, but instead functions by receiving shadows. The received shadow is stored in the alpha channel of the rendered image. Then, when you use the Alpha Compositor, the alpha channel darkens the area that the shadow occupies.

Shadow/Matte is essentially an extension of the built-in Matte/Shadow. Matte/Shadow is a material that doesn't render either, but it does not store the shadow in the alpha channel. Matte/Shadow, in essence, functions by poking a hole in your rendering wherever the material is present in the scene. This hole lets the background image through. The object to which Matte/

Shadow is applied can receive shadows. By allowing the background image through, it can give the illusion that something in the background image is casting the shadow. Although Matte/Shadow works, using Shadow/Matte and saving the shadow in the alpha channel is generally the superior method because it is easier and more accurate. For a more complete description of Matte/Shadow, refer to *Inside 3D Studio MAX, Volume I*, pg. 821.

The following example illustrates how to use Shadow/Matte in conjunction with the Alpha Compositor to create realistic shadows within a composite. Before doing this example, you need to copy the smatte.dlt file from the accompanying CD into your \3DSMAX\PLUGINS directory and reload MAX.

1. Open the ch31ex4.max file from the accompanying CD and activate the Camera viewport.

2. Render a single frame to the virtual frame buffer.

3. You should see an image of the IK walking man on a ground plane. Click on the Show Alpha button to display the alpha channel. Notice that the opaque areas of the alpha channel completely cover the ground plane and the character.

4. Close the Virtual Frame Buffer window, right-click on the label for the Camera viewport, and click on Show Background. If you composited this file over the background, the ground plane covers the ground plane in the image.

5. Open the Material Editor. Activate a material slot and click on the gray button labeled Standard, which defines the material type. Make certain that New is selected in the Browse From section and double-click on Shadow Matte to change the material type. Notice that the material preview in the material slot disappeared. This indicates that the material will not render visually.

6. Under Shadow Matte parameters, there are a few options (see fig. 31.11). Beneath Matte, a check box called Don't Effect Alpha toggles whether the material will save the shadow in the alpha channel. This option is what Peter Watje added to the Matte/Shadow material. If you disable this feature by clicking on this check box, the material functions exactly like Matte/Shadow. Leave this button unchecked. You can also make atmospheric effects such as fog affect the Matte object by checking the Apply Atmosphere button.

FIGURE 31.11

The Shadow Matte
material options.

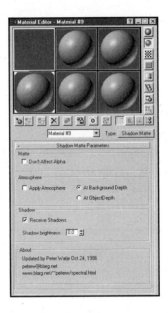

7. Under Shadow is an option called Receive Shadows. Make certain that this box is checked. The Shadow Brightness spin box enables you to adjust the brightness of the shadow. Because the background image is dark, set the shadow brightness to 0.

8. Make certain that the ground plane is selected, and then apply the Shadow Matte material to the selection.

9. Render the scene to the Virtual Frame Buffer window. Notice that the ground plane has disappeared from the rendering. Click on the Show Alpha button to view the new alpha channel. The Shadow Matte material has created an accurate representation of the shadow within the alpha channel.

10. Open Video Post. The Video Post window is set up for a simple composite using the Alpha Compositor. You can execute the sequence and render it on your hard disk, or you can view the ch31ex4a.avi from the accompanying CD. Notice that the shadow is accurately represented and appears to fall on the image in the background.

Using Shadow Matte for shadow effects is usually the best way to go. If you are compositing because of rendering time considerations, you can create a "dummy" scene composed of simple primitives that represent your complicated background. Suppose, for example, you have a scene that calls for characters to chase each other through the aisles of an intricate junkyard. Stacking up bunches of junked up car meshes, barrels, and other miscellaneous objects could create an incredibly complex scene quickly. Trying to concentrate on character animation within this scene would be futile. You should therefore create the complex background and render it on its own. Then you can animate your characters and use simple geometry to stand in for the complex background. Apply the Shadow Matte material to these simple primitives, render, and then composite your character animation over the complex background that you rendered previously. Shadow Matte offers the best choice here because you would likely have lots of camera movement in a chase scene. As long as the dummy background and the real background are laid out in the same manner, the shadow effects should be accurate enough to fool the eye.

You can also combine the different methods outlined so far. Although Shadow Matte enables you to move the camera, you cannot use it to receive lighting. Therefore, certain scenes might call for a combination of Screen Mapping and Shadow Matte. ch31ex4b.avi on the accompanying CD shows a combination of Screen Mapping and Shadow Matte.

Masking

Sometimes the images you need to composite are 24 bit and have no alpha channel. If you hope to composite such images, you need some way of creating areas of transparency. You can use a program such as Adobe Photoshop to create an alpha channel in your source images. This can be difficult, however, if the colors in the image are not distinctive. In certain situations, you may need to use a mask to obtain good results in a composite. A mask enables you to use a separate file to get your transparency data and create your areas of transparency. You can use a separate file's alpha channel for your transparency data, for example. Commonly, the alpha channel is used to create the mask. MAX, however, enables you to use any of the image channels, as well as G-Buffer information to create a mask. You can use G-Buffer channels such as Material Effects or Object channels to mask out certain objects. If you intend to use G-Buffer information for masking, be certain to use the RLA image format to save your files (see previous section in this chapter on G-Buffer). If you have one object in an animation that you want to mask out, for example, you can set the object to have an object channel and then render out to RLA. You can then specify object as the mask type and wherever that object is present in the scene shows up transparent or opaque. It would be opaque by default and transparent if you checked the Inverted button next to the mask type.

Using the Red, Green, or Blue channel to create a mask is often useful and functions similarly to the way an opacity map works. When you use these color channels to create your mask, the intensity of each pixel (0–255) controls the level of transparency. Because different channels have different intensities in different images, you can pick and choose which color channel you want to use for your particular needs. The following example illustrates how you might use one of the color channels to composite flames over an animation. The flames used come from the Pyromania CD-ROM available from Trinity Enterprises (http:\\www.trinity3d.com). These flames make a good illustration for masking because they ship without an alpha channel. Furthermore, you can experiment with which channel to use to get varying levels of transparency.

1. Open MAX or save and reset. Open Video Post.

2. Add back1.tga from the accompanying CD as an Image Input event. Be certain to check the Cache check box so that MAX doesn't load and rescale the same file for every frame of animation. This is going to be the background that you will be compositing flames over.

3. Add another Image Input event and navigate to flames.tga from the accompanying CD. With the image highlighted in the directory list, click on View to view the image. Click on the Display Alpha button and notice that the file has no alpha channel. Click on the Red, Green, and Blue buttons in turn to see the different channels of the image. Accept the image and return to the Video Post window.

4. Select both Image Input events by holding down Ctrl and clicking on both events. Add the Alpha Compositor Layer event. The Flames event should be listed below the Engine Room event in the hierarchy. Because flames.tga does not have an alpha channel, a straight alpha composite will not work. If you render this sequence, only the flames appear because they have no transparency information yet.

5. Double-click on the Alpha Compositor event to bring up the Layer Event window (see fig. 31.12). Under the Mask section, click on the Files button, navigate to the CD, and select flames.tga. Notice that the Enabled check box became checked automatically. Check the Inverted check box to invert the mask.

FIGURE 31.12

The Mask feature enables you to use the different channels in an image to create custom areas of transparency.

6. In the pull-down list box, select Blue Channel from the list. You use the blue channel of the flames.tga image as a mask for your composite. Areas containing information other than black in the blue channel represent varying levels of opacity.

7. Render a single image to the Virtual Frame Buffer window.

You should see the flames over the image of the engine room. You can view the rendered sequence, ch31ex5.avi with animated flames, from the accompanying CD. You might experiment with using different channels in the image for the mask. You can render the image by using the red channel instead of the blue, for example. Fire makes for a particularly tricky composite because the flames need to be semi-transparent themselves. For this example, the blue channel seems to work best, but you should experiment depending on each particular project. Masking is a powerful way to composite animations because it enables greater flexibility than the standard alpha channel.

Bluescreening

Bluescreening is a widely used method for compositing. Bluescreening is a chromakey technique. *Chromakeying* is a process whereby a foreground image is shot against a monocolored screen. The monocolored screen represents a background that can be replaced by film, video, or computer graphics. Chromakey techniques such as bluescreening are commonly used in film and television to composite different layers of action together. An actor filmed against a bluescreen in a small studio, for example, could seemingly be placed anywhere on earth or beyond. The method involves shrouding the background in a particular color, commonly blue or green, and then keying the area filled with that color in the image to be the transparent area. To successfully bluescreen, you need to use a material with little or no shininess or luster. Special blue or green screen material is available from certain mail-order outlets and specialty stores, but you can also use standard color board available at any art store if you are careful with how you set up and light it. The background must be solid and consistently lit for the computer to successfully find every instance of the color. Inconsistencies such as shadows or crumples can cause the computer to miscalculate the areas you intend to be transparent.

Probably the most difficult part of setting up a successful bluescreen is lighting. You need to place high-powered lights behind your subject and point them at the bluescreen material. You should be careful not to create a hotspot on one part of the bluescreen material. The light you use to illuminate your subject cannot be brighter than the lights used to illuminate the bluescreen material, or you will create a shadow. The color you choose for the bluescreen material should also be a color that doesn't conflict with what you intend to be the foreground. You do not want to key a color close to the color of skin, for example, if you want to have an actor in your foreground. This is why a bright solid blue color is normally used. You can, however, theoretically use whatever color you desire.

3D Studio MAX itself does not provide tools necessary to perform chromakey operations. A company called Photron (`http:\\www.photron.com`), however, makes a plug-in for MAX called Primatte, which performs this function. A demo version of Primatte is on the CD. The following example illustrates how you might use Primatte to perform a simple chromakey composite of a person shot against a bluescreen background over a background that comes with MAX. Before doing this example, you need to install the demo version of Primatte into MAX. Copy the primatte.flt file from the accompanying CD to your \3dsmax\plugins directory and then restart MAX.

1. Reset or load MAX. Open Video Post.

2. Add lake3.jpg from your \3dsmax\maps directory as an Image Input event in the Video Post queue.

3. Add adam1.tga from the accompanying CD as an Image Input event. This image was shot with a Kodak DC40 digital camera against a bluescreen background using Savage Widetone bluescreen material from the Savage Universe Corporation.

4. Highlight both Image Input events and add the Primatte Chromakey Compositor as an Image Layer event. Click on OK to return to the Video Post window. You must have the Layer event set in Video Post before you can change the setup for the filter.

5. Double-click on the Primatte Chromakey Compositor Layer event, and then click on Setup. In a few moments, the Primatte plug-in window appears.

6. Click-drag the mouse cursor from the left side of the background area to the right side without dragging over the person. This function tells Primatte what area you intend to be transparent. Notice that part of the person has also become transparent. You need to give Primatte some more information.

7. Click on the button labeled FG (Select Foreground Pixels) on the button bar and click-drag around the torso of the person. You may also need to click-drag around the head area or any area that is transparent that shouldn't be.

8. Click on the button labeled with the black/white man (View Matte) to see the matte. You can now activate the FG and BG buttons, and then click-drag within the matte display to modify your chromakey settings with this view active. This view can help you visualize what your final Matte object will look like (see fig. 31.13).

FIGURE 31.13
Primatte shows the Matte object only.

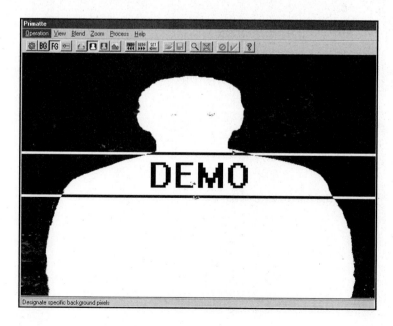

9. Click on the View Composite button to return to the Composite Preview
    window. You have now set up Primatte to chromakey accurately. The
    result of this composite is Adam standing in front of a beautiful lake
    rather than in front of a bluescreen (see fig. 31.14). By choosing OK from
    the Operation menu, you can accept this composite and render. The
    demo version, however, is functionally crippled, so select Cancel. Feel
    free to play with the various settings within the Primatte plug-in.

FIGURE 31.14

*The final chromakeyed
image.*

Other Methods of Compositing

So far in this chapter, you have used the Alpha Compositor exclusively when
using the tools MAX provides to perform compositing. The reason for this is
a simple one. The Alpha Compositor is the best tool that MAX provides for
compositing purposes. You should be aware, however, that the following
compositing functions are available in MAX, as well:

■ Pseudo Alpha

■ Simple Additive Compositor

Pseudo Alpha

Pseudo Alpha is a method of compositing that obtains the color value of the first pixel of the image and uses it to make all other pixels with the same value in the image transparent. The first pixel in the image is the pixel in the upper-left corner. This method has limited functionality. You might use it if you want to use a particular image for transparency, but the image has no alpha channel. In practice, however, you can only use images that you render with MAX or some other computer program. The reason for this is that the exact value of the first pixel is used to locate all other transparent pixels throughout the image. If you tried to use Pseudo Alpha to do chromokeying, for example, all the blue would not have the same value (even with great bluescreen material). The tiny variations in the color that occur as a result of film or video transfer and compression render Pseudo Alpha useless. You end up with many random holes where the values happen to have the same value as the first pixel. If you use computer-generated images, however, this is not as much of a problem because you can set the background color to be exactly one solid color, and one consistent HSV value. You can use Pseudo Alpha as either a Layer event or a Filter event, and it performs the same function in either instance. A useful plug-in would be to rewrite Pseudo Alpha so that you could pick the color you want and then set a threshold to determine the tolerance of the HSV value.

Simple Additive Compositor

The *Simple Additive Compositor* composites the two images by using the second image's intensity or HSV value to determine transparency. Areas of full intensity 255 are opaque, areas of 0 intensity are transparent, and areas of intermediate transparency are translucent. This method also has limited functionality. In practice, the only time you would want to use it is if you want to do a funky blend of two images.

Editing Your Animations

You have now seen how you can composite different images and animations within Video Post. You have your composited animations rendered, and they are ready to impress your clients and friends. You might find that you could really knock the socks off some people, however, if you could add some nice transitions and turn all your individual animations into one cohesive unit. You just took out a second mortgage to buy that nifty new dual Pentium Pro, and there's not much left in the coffers for video editing software. What do you do?

Fortunately, Video Post enables you to edit your animations as well as composite them. MAX ships with a few filters that enable you to do fades and wipes, and third-party plug-ins are certain to follow, enabling you to extend MAX's functionality as an editing system. In addition to using the Filter events that ship with MAX, you can use the Alpha Compositor with animated masks to create great transitions. The accompanying CD comes with 50 FLC files that can be used as luminance masks to create great transition effects. The following examples show how you can use Filter and Layer events as well as masks to edit your animations and create transitions.

Video Post Event Transitions

This example illustrates how you might arrange a Video Post queue by using layers, filters, and range bars to string together some of the animations used in previous examples in this chapter and do transitions between them.

1. Load MAX or save and reset.

2. Add ch31ex2.avi, ch31ex4b.avi, and ch31ex5.avi as Image Input events in the Video Post queue.

3. Select ch31ex2.avi to highlight it and then click on the Add Filter Event button. Select Fade from the list of filters, click on the Setup button, and make certain that In is currently checked active.

4. Select ch31ex2.avi to highlight it, hold down the Ctrl key and click on ch31ex4b.avi, highlighting both events. Align the animations from the end of one to the beginning of the other by clicking on the Abut button on the toolbar. The ch31ex4b.avi event's range bar should now begin where the ch31ex2.avi event's range bar ends, which is at frame 120.

5. With both events still highlighted, click on the Add Image Layer Event button and select Simple Wipe from the pull-down list box. Click on the Setup button to bring up the Setup dialog for Simple Wipe (see fig. 31.15). Set the direction and mode to whatever you wish. When you have a setup you like, click on OK and specify frames 110–120 in the VP Post parameters as a start and end time for the event. Click on OK to return to the Video Post window.

FIGURE 31.15

Simple Wipe enables you to create wipe transitions between animations.

6. Use the Ctrl key to highlight both the ch31ex4b.avi event and then the Wipe event. It is important that you highlight the ch31ex4b.avi event first so that Video Post knows that you want to align the AVI file to the beginning of the Wipe and not align the Wipe to the beginning of the AVI. Click on the Align Selected Left button to align the beginning of ch31ex4b.avi to the beginning of the wipe. You just set up a simple wipe between ch31ex2.avi and ch31ex4b.avi.

7. Now highlight ch31ex5.avi and Abut, and align it to ch31ex4b.avi to align the two animations back to front.

8. Click on the Zoom Extents button in the lower-right corner to make the range bars fit within the Video Post window.

9. Use the Ctrl key to highlight ch31ex5.avi and the Simple Wipe. Add a Cross Fade Transition Image Layer event. In the Video Post parameters, set the VP start time to 200 and the end time to 210.

10. Control highlight ch31ex5.avi and the Cross Fade Transition event, and then click on the Align left button to align them properly.

11. Highlight ch31ex5.avi and add a Fade Filter event (see fig. 31.16). Set the VP start time to 279 and the end time to 289. Click on Setup and make certain that Out is specified. Click on OK to accept this event.

12. Click on blank space within the Video Post window to deselect everything. Add an Image Output event and specify the range from 0–289.

FIGURE 31.16

Video Post can be used to provide transitions between your animations.

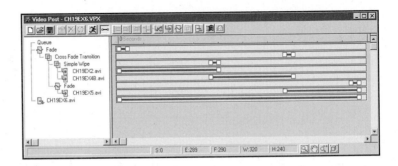

You can render this sequence to your hard disk or view the final rendered ch31ex6.avi from the accompanying CD. If you're uncertain whether you set up the Video Post queue correctly, you can load the ch31ex6.vpx into Video Post from the accompanying CD.

Video Post Masking Transitions

You can use masks (see section on masking in this chapter) within the Alpha Compositor to do transition effects as well. The accompanying CD comes with many useful images and texture maps. There is a directory of 2D black-and-white animated FLC files that serve very well as masks. The following example illustrates how you might set this up.

1. Load or reset MAX and open Video Post. Load the ch31ex7.vpx Video Post file.

2. Double-click on the Alpha Compositor Layer event. In the Masking section, click on the Files button to bring up the file selector. Navigate to the accompanying CD, highlight TIDE.FLC, and click on the View button to view the animated mask.

3. The TIDE.FLC file is one of 50 files in the \samples\maps\wipes directory on the accompanying CD. Because this file is made up of either absolute black (0) or white (255), you can use the luminance of the image for the mask. Luminance indicates that a value of 0 is transparent, 255 is opaque, and intermediary values are translucent. Because the FLC is only solid black or white, it works well for transitions. In the list box for the mask, select Luminance.

4. Add an Image Output event and render the sequence, or view the rendered, ch31ex7.avi file from the accompanying CD.

Feel free to experiment with the other FLC wipes that come on the accompanying CD to achieve other interesting transition effects.

In Practice: Compositing and Editing

- **Alpha Compositor.** You can use MAX's Alpha Compositor to combine images or animation. The ordering of Image Input events is important because it relates to which files need to contain alpha channels. Alpha channels provide a way to create areas of transparency, which are necessary for seeing through one layer event and on to another. Multilayer compositing enables you to combine as many layers of background and foreground images as you want.

- **Shadow and Light.** You can composite and retain shadow and light effects by using the screen mapping method, the Camera Map plug-in, and Peter Watje's Shadow/Matte material.

- **Masking.** You can achieve complex compositing effects by using MAX's powerful masking feature. With masking, you can use any channel in the image to create a custom area of transparency. This includes using alpha data or even using any of the channels specific to 3D (G-Buffer).

- **Chromakey.** You can use chromakey techniques to composite live action with CG. The Primatte plug-in provides a method of doing chromakeying within MAX.

- **Other Methods.** MAX provides methods other than the Alpha Compositor for doing compositing. Pseudo Alpha and Simple Additive Compositor are both limited in their functionality. They do, however, provide an opportunity for a creative programmer to expand and improve upon them. Thanks to MAX's open architecture, this is a likely possibility.

- **Editing.** You can edit your animations in Video Post by using the range bars and Filter and Layer events. You can also use masking to create transitions and achieve new effects that add impact to your animations.

IMAGE CREATED BY ADAM SILVERTHORNE

Chapter 32

by Jarod Ruffo

VIDEO POST EFFECTS

This chapter introduces you to producing specialized effects with MAX's Video Post module. Video Post enables you to produce some amazing effects within your animations. Most effects are used as standard Video Post filters that you add to the Video Post queue. MAX ships with only a few Video Post effects as part of the standard package. Despite the lack of included special effect-oriented Video Post filters, plug-in developers are producing some fantastic software geared toward special effects. For this reason, the bulk of this chapter focuses on plug-ins. Some of the plug-ins discussed are freeware, and the fully working versions are included on the accompanying CD-ROM. Other plug-ins are commercially available from their respective vendors for various prices.

The sheer number of plug-ins available today is phenomenal, especially considering the relatively short time that MAX has been out. Furthermore, new plug-ins are becoming available on a daily basis. Consequently, many more effect-oriented plug-ins are likely to be available by the time this book goes to print. The best way to keep track of the new plug-ins is to regularly check the Kinetix forum on CompuServe and the Kinetix web page (www.ktx.com). You may also find many other MAX-oriented web pages while browsing the web.

Even though many more effects plug-ins are on the horizon, what is available now is enough to make some eyes bulge. Therefore, the overall goal of this chapter is to get you excited about MAX's special effects capabilities. Hopefully, this chapter's examples will inspire you to integrate some of these Video Post effects into your own animations.

This chapter covers the following topics:

- Glows
- Lens flares
- RealLensFlare
- LenzFX MAX
- Blurs
- Adobe Photoshop plug-in filters
- Fractal flow
- Miscellaneous Video Post effects

Glows

Glows are achieved with MAX's Video Post filter events. Glows are useful for heat effects, such as glowing coals or exhaust, surrounding lights in a soft halo, planetary space scenes, lasers, and just about anything else you can think of. MAX ships with a Glow filter that adds glowing luminosity to objects in your scene. The effect is that the objects in your scene that are intended to appear like they give off light will glow near the source as they would in reality. The glow effect is based on G-Buffer information (see Chapter 31, "Compositing and Editing"). The effect is applied to either a Material ID channel or an object channel. Some Glow filter plug-ins enable you to choose either Material ID or Object channel, and some enable use of one or the other without giving you a choice.

You have a few different options when choosing a Glow filter. The standard Glow filter that comes with MAX is simple, but is very useful; in many situations, it is all you will need. A freeware plug-in that is an extension of the standard Glow is available. This plug-in is called Animated Glow, and it enables you to cycle the glow to produce interesting animated effects. Another freeware plug-in, called Super Glow, adds some different features and is designed to function with the freeware lightning plug-in. Arguably the most powerful and flexible glow utilities are available in the commercial packages: RealLensFlare and LensFX MAX. The following sections outline and use the various Glow filters to illustrate how they are similar and how they differ. The last section outlines some glow tips to help you achieve more realistic glow effects.

Glow (Frame Only)

The Glow (frame only) filter is the one that ships with the MAX standard package. This glow affects only the current frame, and therefore cannot be animated. Hereafter in this chapter, Glow (frame only) is referred to as standard glow.

Standard glow functions similarly to the other Glow filters. You can affect objects in your scene in two ways. You can choose the material you want to affect by setting the Material Effects channel to a particular value, or you can specify Object channel in the Video Post filter setup.

The Material Effects channel value is adjusted in the Material Editor, and you must adjust it for the materials you want to be affected by glow (see fig. 32.1). The Video Post filter then finds instances of that Material Effects channel in your scene and glows the corresponding material, or sub-material (in a multi-material).

FIGURE 32.1

The Glow (frame only)
dialog.

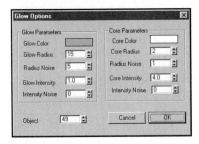

If you choose to apply the glow based on the Object channel, the glow effect will be associated with a particular object or set of objects. You set the ID value for the Object channel in the Properties dialog for the corresponding object. (The properties dialog is accessed by right-clicking on an object and choosing Properties from the list of options.)

In the Properties dialog, the G-Buffer section enables you to set the Object channel to any positive value. The Video Post filter finds instances of corresponding Object channels in your scene and glows the matching object. The color section determines the color of the glow. You can make the glow color the same as your material by selecting the Material radio button, or you can choose the color of the glow by selecting User and choosing a color from the color picker. The size spinner determines how much glow to apply. The higher the value, the more intense the glow is inside the object.

TIP

You should be careful not to set this number too high. Otherwise, the intensity inside the object will wash out the material, and all you will see in your render will be a washed-out blob. Generally, the closer the glowed object is to the camera, the lower the glow size should be and vice versa.

The following example provides a scene containing a construction area stand. These objects usually have a flashing warning light attached to them. In the following example, you use the Glow Video Post filter to re-create how, in reality, the flashing object would glow when lit.

RE-CREATING FLASHING OBJECT GLOW

1. Load or Reset MAX and open the ch32ex1.max file from the accompanying CD.

2. Open the Material Editor. The first material slot in the Material Editor contains the material for the warning light's bulb. Change the Material Effect ID from 0 to 1 (see fig. 32.2). This material is already applied to the Light object, so you do not need to apply it.

FIGURE 32.2

You set the Material Effect ID on materials you want Glow to affect.

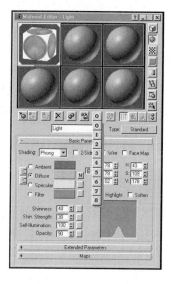

3. Open Video Post. Add a Camera01 scene event. Highlight the Camera01 scene event and add the Glow (frame only) filter.

4. Click on the Setup button to set the Glow parameters. Notice that the default source value is a Material Effects channel value of 1. You can set this to any positive integer. In the Material Editor, you leave this value at 1. Because the Glow filter is set at 1 also, the filter will glow the corresponding material.

5. Set the Glow size to 6. Accept the Glow Control values and return to the Video Post window. Execute the sequence to render a single frame to the Virtual Frame Buffer window.

6. With the Virtual Frame Buffer window displayed, click on the G-Buffer pull-down and change the value from RGB Alpha to Material Effects. The Virtual Frame Buffer window displays a representation of the Material Effects channel that you activated in your scene. This representation displays the area on which the Glow acted. Figure 32.3 shows the final scene.

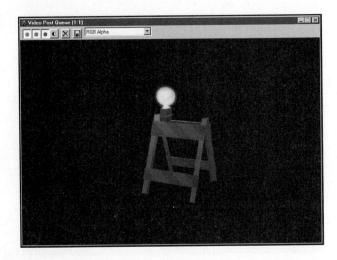

The image looks realistic. The standard glow filter, however, works on every frame the same way. Consequently, you cannot animate the blinking of the light. The Animated Glow plug-in described next enables you to realistically create the flashing light.

Animated Glow

Animated Glow is an extension of the standard glow (see fig. 32.4 and refer to fig. 32.2). Animated Glow functions by cycling the glow effect based on a mathematical equation. You can choose to have the glow cycle based on a Sine wave, a Square wave, an Exponential wave, or a Sine(x)/x wave. With the standard Glow filter, you set a single size parameter. With the Animated Glow plug-in, you must set two size parameters, which determine the maximum and minimum values that the equation will use to determine its cycle. If you are using a Sine wave, for example, the maximum and minimum values determine the crest and the trough of the wave.

FIGURE 32.4

Animated Glow enables you to cycle the glow effect over time.

In the previous example, the glow effect that you applied to the construction area stand worked only for a still frame. With Animated Glow, you can cycle the glow of the light to achieve a realistic flashing effect. The procedure is essentially the same as that of the standard glow, except you must set the additional options that Animated Glow provides. The files ch32agl1.avi, ch32agl2.avi, ch32agl3.avi, and ch32agl4.avi show the geometry from the standard Glow exercise rendered with Animated Glow using each of its four equation options. View each file with the graph of the mathematical equations in mind. The maximum and minimum size values for these examples were left at the default values, but it is possible to change these values to achieve more or less intense flashes.

Did you notice the flaw in the four Animated Glow renderings? If the bulb were flashing the way it does in the renderings, the light emanating from the bulb would illuminate the stand in sync with the flashing of the bulb. It is possible to achieve this effect with the Animated Glow filter by animating the multiplier with Track View to match the Animated Glow cycle. This can be difficult to do manually, however, because you cannot directly visualize where the glow cycle will be at a particular frame aside from doing test renders. You could get around this problem by using the Waveform Controller plug-in.

Waveform Controller

The Waveform Controller is a plug-in animation controller that sets animation values based on a mathematical waveform. You can use the Waveform Controller on the multiplier track of an omni light, and it will sync with the

Animated Glow filter parameters. The following example shows this. Before you can do this example, you need to copy the wavectrl.dlc file from the accompanying CD to your \3DSMAX\PLUG-INS directory.

1. Open or Reset MAX. Load the ch32ex2.max file from the accompanying CD.

2. Open Video Post. Double-click on the Animated Glow filter event. Click on Setup. Notice that the equation is set to Sine and the cycle is set to 20 frames. Accept the settings and close the Video Post window.

3. Open Track View. Expand the omni light named Omni Hazard. Expand the Object parameters. Highlight multiplier by clicking on the text.

4. Click on the Assign Controller button on the Track View toolbar. Select Waveform Float from the list and click on OK.

5. With Multiplier still highlighted, right-click and select Properties from the list to bring up the Waveform Controller dialog (see fig. 32.5).

FIGURE 32.5
The Waveform Controller enables you to control parameters based upon a mathematical waveform.

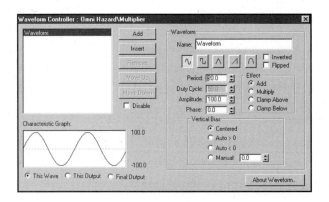

6. Notice that the first button in the row of equation options is the Sine wave. Keep this option selected because it corresponds with the equation set in Video Post for the animated glow filter. Because the period was set to 20 for the Animated Glow filter, you also need to set the period to 20. Increase the period spinner until it reads 20.

7. Close the Waveform Controller dialog and close Track View. You can now open Video Post and render a sequence, or you can view the rendered result in the file ch32ex2.avi from the CD.

You can use the other equations as well. Note that the two plug-ins name the functions differently. Animated Glow's Exponential equation corresponds with Wave Controller's sawtooth. Animated Glow's Sine (x)/x corresponds with Wave Controller's triangle. Make certain that the periods coincide, and you can sync secondary lighting to glow with this combination of plug-ins.

Super Glow

Super Glow is a little different from standard glow or Animated Glow. The advantage that Super Glow has over the standard Glow is that you can specify two different settings for the glow. One setting affects the inside portions of the glow, or the *core*. The other setting affects the falloff of the glow. The core is very close to the object being glowed, and the *falloff* is the rest of the glow. This effect is useful if you need to have two different colors for your glow.

Super Glow works on an Object channel. Both the glow and the core have the same options. The color determines the tint of the glow and partially affects the intensity. Brighter colors result in a brighter glow. The Radius parameter measures a distance in pixels from the edge of the object toward the center. The distance determined by the radius parameter affects the intensity of the glow. The Radius Noise parameter creates variations in the size of the radius. The Intensity determines how much glow will be applied. The Intensity Noise parameter creates variations in the intensity of the glow.

T I P

Super Glow works well with another plug-in, Lightning, which generates a randomly jagged mesh in the shape of a lightning bolt. By applying Super Glow with an intense core and a slightly less intense falloff, you can get something that looks like a lightning bolt (see fig. 32.6). Lightning is available for free download from 3D Café (http://www.3dcafe.com).

FIGURE 32.6

*The Super Glow plug-in
works well for effects
such as lightning.*

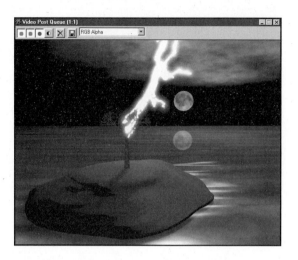

Real Lens Glow

The RealLensFlare plug-in (see the "Lens Flares" section in this chapter) contains its own glow module. Real Lens Glow is a highly optimized glow procedure that processes extremely quickly. Real Lens' glow procedure is roughly three times faster than the standard glow procedure. Real Lens Glow adds flexibility as well. In addition to being able to control the size of the glow and animate it, you can also adjust the density and luminance and animate those aspects of the glow. You can choose to glow the edges if you want. These additional options give you finer control than the other glow plug-ins. You might, for example, want a really subtle glow around an object. With standard Glow, you might find that a size setting of 6 is too little, and a setting of 7 is too high. The additional controls that Real Lens Glow provides enable you to make subtle changes to different aspects of your glow.

Real Lens Glow works as a Helper object, which is another advantage. Because the glow effect is a Helper object, the parameters you set for the glow are fully animatable. Furthermore, you have access to the parameters in Track View. In the sample AVI files you viewed in the "Animated Glow" section, you saw that the glowing bulb did not illuminate the stand. Because Animated Glow cycles its glow effect based on an equation, it is difficult to sync the light with the glow. With Real Lens, however, you can animate the values in Track View and make them correspond with the multiplier of an omni light in the scene. The ch32rlg1.avi file on the accompanying CD shows the construction stand and light glowed by using Real Lens Glow synced with the animated multiplier of the omni light.

LensFX Glow

Glow packages typically enable you to choose a user-defined color, or they automatically base the glow color on the material assigned to the specified object. Although LensFX Glow is still in beta, early indications are that the LensFX Glow module of LensFX MAX will add significant flexibility and power to MAX glow effects. Perhaps its strongest attribute is the implementation of gradients for all aspects of glow color. With LensFX Glow, you can choose a single color or a rainbow of colors to use for both the radial and circular glow colors.

Additionally, with LensFX Glow you can use greyscale gradients to determine different amounts of transparency for various portions of the glow. You can also load and save gradients you or others create. A large preview window enables you to preview your glow settings interactively. You can adjust the position and the color of gradients over time to create animated glow effects. A special scroll bar in the Preview window enables you to preview what the final animation will look like. Almost all the glow parameters are available for editing in Track View. An Inferno tab enables you to use a fractal noise procedure (Fractal Noise is discussed in the section on lens flares later in this chapter) to distort various regions of the glow effect.

Glow Tips

Many animators live for subtlety. Some have found that glow effects go a long way toward improving the visual impact of images and animation. This is especially true when glows are coupled with good lighting. Consequently, you may spend many hours tweaking with glow settings and trying different methods to achieve specific glow effects. Consider the following tips when you use glow in a scene.

Glowing Behind Objects

In certain instances, you may want the glow effect to come from behind your object. One way to achieve this effect is to render the scene with glow applied to the whole object, saving the file or files to disk. Then render the same scene with no glow applied, saving the file or files with Alpha data. You can then composite (see Chapter 31) the no-glow rendering over the glow rendering. This results in a glow behind object effect. The glowcomp.tga file on the accompanying CD is an image rendered using this technique.

Using Glow with Animated Parameters

You can achieve certain animated effects by using any of the glow procedures outlined in this section (including standard Glow) by applying the glow to a material that has animated parameters. If a material uses an animated map or procedural texture such as noise, for example, the glow effect will change based on the state of the material. You can also animate a material's self illumination, and the glow effect will change based on the self illumination value. This technique works well for flashing lights or objects. The technique is also useful for creating effects such as the back of an engine on a spacecraft. The NOISEGLW.AVI file on the accompanying CD is an example of what you might get by using standard Glow on a material that has animated noise in the Diffuse channel.

Glowing Text

Sometimes it is better not to glow an entire object. If you want to create a glowing logo and you apply the glow to the entire object, for example, you might find that the glow appears to slightly shroud and fade out your text. This happens because the glow is being applied to every surface in the text. The surfaces on the inside of the text are glowing inward, slightly obstructing the geometry. In this case, it is usually best to apply the glow only to the faces normal to the camera. This way only the surfaces facing the camera are glowed. The following exercise illustrates this:

1. Load the ch32ex3.max file from the accompanying CD.

2. Select the Extruded Text object and apply an Edit Mesh.

3. In the Sub-Object list box, change Vertex to Face, click on the Window Selection button at the bottom of the screen under the Time Slider, and select only the faces facing toward the camera. This is easily done from the Left or Top viewports.

4. With the faces selected, go to the Edit Surface section of the Edit Mesh modifier rollout and change the Material ID spinner to 2.

5. Open the Material Editor. The first slot in the Material Editor contains a Multi/Sub-Object material. Because you just activated Material ID 2 for the front faces, material number 2 will be assigned to those faces. Therefore, material number 2 is the one you want to glow. Notice that material 2 is a slightly different color than material 1. Another advantage to glowing only certain faces in an object is that you can change the color or texture of those faces to obtain different glow results. Set Material 2 to Effects channel 1 to enable Glow to act on it. Assign this material to the selected text.

6. Open Video Post. The glow size is currently set at 11, but you can adjust this value if you wish. Execute the sequence and render a frame to the Virtual Frame Buffer window. The text appears to glow like neon (see fig. 32.7).

FIGURE 32.7
Using the Glow filter adds realism to a neon sign.

Animating Glow Location

You can also animate the location of the glow on an object to achieve interesting special effects. You can have a ring of glow travel down the arm of a magician character, for example. To achieve this effect, you use the Volume Select modifier. The Volume Select modifier selects a volume of vertices or faces without using the Edit Mesh modifier. The key aspect of Volume Select is that it enables you to animate the movement of the gizmo. You can, therefore, animate a selection volume moving around an object. After you apply the Volume Select modifier, you apply a Material modifier and set the Material ID value to 2. This results in an animated selection volume that changes the Material ID value of the faces it selects while moving around on an object. If you then assign a multi-material that has glow turned on for Material ID 2, that which the selection volume is currently selecting will glow. The following example illustrates this procedure:

1. Reset or load MAX.

2. Create a cylinder of Radius 10 and Height 60. Change the Height Segments value to 50.

3. Apply a Volume Select modifier.

4. Under Stack Selection level, click on the radio button labeled Faces. Activate sub-object selection by clicking on the Sub-Object button. From the Front viewport, non-uniform scale the gizmo down to 10 percent along the Y axis.

5. Move the gizmo so that it is just above the cylinder. Click on the Animate button to activate it. Move the Time Slider to frame 100. Move the gizmo so that it is just below the cylinder. Click on the Animate button to deactivate it.

6. The gizmo should now be animated moving down the faces of the cylinder and selecting the faces that fall within its volume. Add a Material modifier. Change the Value Next to the Material ID spinner to 2.

7. Open the Material Editor. Create a Multi/Sub Object material. Set the number of sub-materials to 2. Click on the color selector for material number 1 and set the color value to Red: 12, Green: 0, Blue: 255. Accept the settings and click and drag the color swatch from material 1 to material 2 to copy the color values. Click on the button for material 2 and change the material's Material Effects channel from 0 to 1.

8. Open Video Post. Add a Perspective or Camera Scene event, highlight it and add a Glow Filter event. Set the value for the Glow to 12. Add an Image Output event and render an AVI to see the results. You can also view the pre-rendered ch32volg.avi file from the accompanying CD.

Lens Flares

Lens flares are optical effects that occur in the lenses of real cameras, but not in MAX's virtual cameras. The effect occurs when light bounces around inside the glass material of a camera's lens. The image is captured while the light beams are in this state of flux, resulting in a photograph containing a bright star-like flare. The term *lens flare* is often used when referring to blemished photographs taken with low-quality camera lenses. If you see a light source through glass in daily life, or if you squint at a bright light source, you should also see a lens flare. If you look at oncoming traffic through the windshield of your car at night, for example, you will see a lens flare.

In 3D animation, lens flares are often used to create added realism in a scene. Furthermore, if you are creative with how you use a lens flare, you can use it to simulate many other interesting special effects. You can use a lens flare to simulate the bursting of a bright star in the galaxy, for example. You can also use it to create more realism for car headlights or streetlights. If you have an object in your scene that gives off light, adding a slight lens flare to it can go a long way toward adding visual impact and realism. Essentially, any time the effect you desire is to make the viewers of an animation know that a specific light is particularly bright, you should consider using a lens flare.

The only Lens Flare package currently available for 3D Studio MAX is a commercial product called RealLensFlare from Cebas software. Another commercial product, LenzFX MAX from Digimation, is in the works. This product is currently in beta and may be available by the time this book is in print. Both plug-ins extend the notion of the lens flare significantly. They enable you to create many special effects beyond the bright star flare traditionally associated with lens flares. You might use RealLensFlare (RLF) to create the sparks of a welders torch, for example. You could also use it to create an animated space nebula or an electrical explosion (see fig. 32.8).

FIGURE 32.8
*RealLensFlare 1.5
Fractal Fury.*

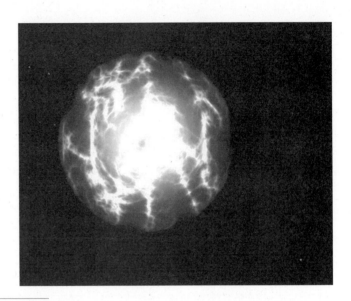

RealLensFlare (RLF)

Release 1.0 of RLF has brought fast and accurate optical effects based on the physics of real-world glass lenses to 3D Studio MAX. Nearly every aspect of RLF is animatable and expression-controllable. In the lenses of real cameras, four types of optical effects occur: lens flares, glows, highlights, and focal blur. RFL uses four distinct modules to re-create these effects as accurately as possible. RFL's corresponding modules are called Flare, Glow, Starfilter, and Depth of Field.

- **Flare.** This module re-creates about every possible optical lens flare that could be brought about by shining different light sources directly into the glass lens of a real camera.

- **Glow.** This module adds powerful and fast glow effects to your MAX renderings.

- **Starfilter.** This module re-creates the star-shaped sparkle that might appear close to extremely shiny materials such as chrome. You can also add twinkling highlights to objects or particle systems to create sparkly fireworks and other special effects.

- **Depth of Field.** This module enables MAX's virtual camera to blur objects that are a specified distance from the location of the camera. This effect can give your animations the cinematic realism of a real camera by focusing the viewer's attention on the foreground action. The module is optimized to handle the borderline between foreground and background objects seamlessly and without jagged lines.

RLFs as Helper Objects

RealLensFlares are added to your scene as Helper objects. You access RLF settings in two places. You can open the Modify panel and access all of RLF's parameters from the standard MAX rollouts. With the Modify panel open, you can also right-click on the Helper object and select Properties. This action brings up the RLF graphical user interface. This GUI is where RealLensFlare's biggest strength lies. The interface is intuitive and fun to use. It provides a preview window where you can see a fully rendered image of the lens flare (see fig. 32.9). When you change the settings in RLF, the preview window updates to show the result of the change. The update rendering is extremely fast.

FIGURE 32.9

RealLensFlare has a fast lens flare preview window.

When you work with lens flares, it is often useful to attach, or *bind*, the lens flare to an object or a light. If you have a light with a lens flare in your scene and you want to animate it, for example, you need the lens flare to move with the light. One of RLF's coolest features does this. This feature is called the Automatic Analytical Binding System (AABS). Despite its complicated name, AABS is extremely simple to use and is extremely powerful. AABS is seamless and invisible to the user. To activate AABS, you need only create the lens flare helper on the object, light, or particle system you want to bind it to. The RLF helper detects and attaches itself automatically.

Binding RLFs to Particle Systems

Binding lens flares to particle systems is great for creating all kinds of special effects. You can bind an RLF Helper object to MAX's standard Spray and Snow particle modules. RLF also binds to Sisyphus's All Purpose Particles and Digimation's SandBlaster particle system. When you bind a lens flare helper to a particle system, each particle becomes an individual lens flare (see fig. 32.10). If you are interested in doing special effects, this feature should cause your imagination to run wild. Sparks from a welder's torch or pulses from a laser rifle are just the beginning. Release 1.5 will extend the power of AABS and particle systems with an added system called Particle Magic. This system will enable you to generate variation on each particle. The result is a particle system that generates different looking light particles. Particle Magic is also capable of analyzing the rotational position of each particle in 3D space, enabling you to make your highlights rotate with the spin of the particle.

FIGURE 32.10
RealLensFlare enables you to make each particle of a particle system a lens flare.

RLF 1.5

At the time of this writing, version 1.5 of RLF is still in beta. It should be publicly available by the time this book is in print. Release 1.5 is a free upgrade to registered owners of 1.0. Version 1.5 greatly extends the functionality of RLF, as the following list illustrates:

■ **RLF Files.** A drawback of release 1.0 was that you could not save lens flare settings, which meant that if you had a lens flare looking just the way you wanted, and you wanted to use the same flare in another scene, you would need to write down all of your settings. Now you can save an RLF file and load the settings into your new scene. You can also build a library of effects, download other settings, or share settings with coworkers.

- **Gradients.** RLF 1.5 enables you to adjust the lens flare effect by using gradients. You create a gradient that determines the transparency of the lens flare area, which is useful if you want to soften or feather the lens flare in your scene. Another new feature is the added support of motion blur. You can use motion blur to simulate realistic special effects. One way to create interesting smoke is to apply motion blur to a particle system made up of lens flares. This might sound scary if you have used motion blur in the past. RLF, however, handles motion blur very quickly. Adding motion blur to lens flares with RLF only adds approximately 30 percent to your render time. Motion blur with lens flares is also useful for doing trailers. You can give your 3D animation the *Akira* look, for example, by trailing fast moving objects with motion blurred lens flares.

- **Fog.** RLF is now fog aware. As you move the lens flare into the fog, the lens flare fades and eventually dies out. This proves useful for underwater scenes where an object, such as a submarine, slowly disappears into murky water. The lens flare also inherits the color set for your fog.

- **Alpha channel blur.** RLF 1.5 adds the capability to blur the alpha channel. This is useful for compositing glowing or focal blurred objects.

- **Glow Edges.** The Glow Edges function gives you greater control over where the glow appears on an object. This is particularly useful for glowing text and logos because it saves you from needing to set the glow for certain faces only.

Fractal Fury

One very cool addition to RLF is a module called Fractal Fury. Fractal Fury is a procedure that distorts the lens flare and the glow halo that RLF generates. The procedure uses fractal noise, which is a mathematical procedure that produces random perturbations based on fractal mathematics. The distortion results in gaseous clouds of intense color and variety, wispy electrical arcs, and fire tendrils. Fractal Fury can generate realistic looking space nebula, science-fiction–type explosions, and other special effects.

Like the other modules in RLF, Fractal Fury renders very quickly and its parameters are fully animatable. Because Fractal Fury is a distortion, the setup of your original flare affects your result. You can, therefore, get a different Fractal Fury result by adjusting the basic lens flare parameters. The Fractal Fury module contains three basic types of effects: electrical, glowing clouds, and burning flames. Electrical randomly generates thin electrical arcs. The glowing clouds effect creates globular and swirling gaseous systems. The burning flames effect creates twirling, threadlike flames. Figure 32.11 illustrates some of the effects you can generate with Fractal Fury.

FIGURE 32.11
Some of the possibilities you might achieve with Fractal Fury.

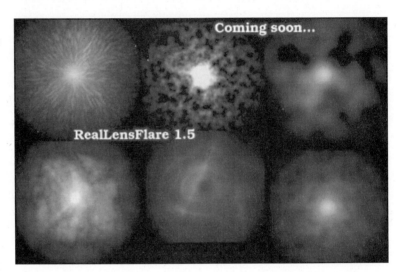

LensFX MAX

LensFX was the best selling special effects package ever for 3D Studio DOS (for good reason). It enabled 3D Studio animators to add beautiful special effects to their animations while providing great flexibility. The LensFX legacy has migrated out of the DOS world and into the world of 3D Studio MAX with a new lens flare package called LensFX MAX. At the time of this writing, LensFX MAX is undergoing beta testing and is not currently publicly available. By the time this book is in print, however, it will likely be shipping. Although LensFX MAX inherits most of the features of its DOS predecessor, it is not simply a direct port of the DOS software. LensFX MAX is completely redesigned to follow 3D Studio MAX's 32-bit object-oriented architecture.

The new interface contains four distinct modules: Lens Flare, Glow, Hilight, and Depth of Field.

- **Lens Flare.** This module re-creates optical lens flares brought about by shining different light sources into the glass lens of a real camera.

- **Glow.** This module adds glow effects to your MAX renderings.

- **Hilight.** This module adds brilliant, photorealistic effects to shiny metals and glass. Hilight simulates a photographic cross star effect and comes with dozens of user-definable settings.

- **Depth of Field.** This module blurs objects based on their distance to the camera. LensFX MAX module enables you to easily create rack focus effects to add an extra touch of realism to your work.

The lens flare module enables you to select from pre-built flare effects, load and save .LZF LensFX MAX lens flare settings, or set your own settings manually. You can create your flares by combining any combination of glows, rays, rings, and secondary reflections. Figure 32.12 diagrams these various lens flare parts.

FIGURE 32.12

The parts of the LensFX lens flare.

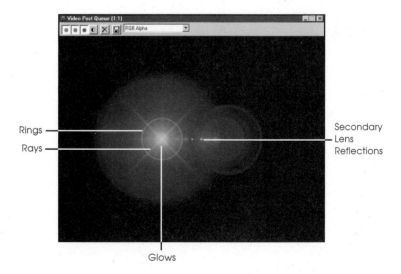

LensFX MAX enables the user to control the color, transparency, intensity, shape, and size of the lens flare effect. Custom animation parameters allow effects to be animated as well. LensFX MAX is accessed as a Filter event in the Video Post queue. Lens flares are created by choosing a source object in the Filter Setup dialog. Anything selectable from within 3D Studio MAX is a valid source object. A large preview window enables you to preview your lens flare, and a special Time Slider enables you to cycle the preview window to see how your parameters affect your lens flare over time.

Another new feature is called Auto Secondaries, which automatically creates any number of secondary lens reflections. For specialized flash effects, LensFX MAX provides a feature that enables the user to control the amount that the flare will brighten the entire scene. This feature proves useful when creating explosions and other effects that require a bright burst of light. LensFX MAX also has special commands that enable you to control the positioning of secondary flares in your scene, enabling you to have secondary lens reflections that follow different paths and change size based on the camera's field of view. LensFX MAX also has a channel soften feature that enables you to blur your scene based on G-Buffer channel information.

One of the neatest features of LensFX MAX is its extensive use of gradients. Every section within the flare module has at least one color selector for the corresponding part of the lens flare. Each color selector can be set to a solid color or a gradient range of colors. The range for the gradient can contain an unlimited number of flags. The flags set the color for the gradient at the location of the flag (see fig. 32.13). The result of these gradient selectors is unparalleled control when choosing a color combination for your lens flare. You can have, for example, a gradient that cycles from blue to red to green for the glow radial color of the lens flare. LensFX MAX also has a special new feature called Inferno, which is a fractal noise procedure similar to RealLensFlare's Fractal Fury module. Inferno adds realistic fire and smoke effects to LensFX MAX. Although LensFX MAX is still currently in beta, the indications are that it will be a solid lens flare package when it ships.

FIGURE 32.13

LensFX MAX makes extensive use of gradients.

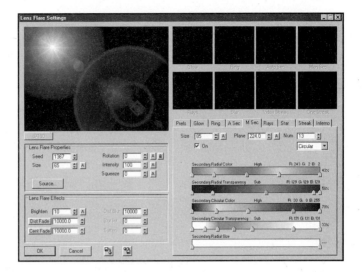

Blurs

Blur effects are useful in a number of situations. Blur effects are commonly used to create a depth of field. When your eyes focus on an object, that object comes into focus and objects on the periphery of your field of vision become slightly blurred. The effect occurs in real cameras and is often exaggerated in motion pictures. When viewing a scene, the effect serves to focus the viewer's attention on a particular spot. By using fields of depth in your MAX scenes, you can force your viewers to focus their attention on the action. This technique can also save modeling time. Because certain areas of your scene are blurred, you don't need to spend a lot of time detailing those areas. The effect can give your animations the cinematic realism of a real camera. Blurs are also used for special effects, such as the atmospheric distortion created by heat. By using blurs, for example, you can re-create a jet engine's exhaust system and be faithful to reality. This section outlines four methods you might choose for depth of field or other blur effects.

Blur (Frame Only)

The Blur (frame only) plug-in is a freeware plug-in written by Johnny Ow. The plug-in blurs the scene based on a Material ID channel or an Object channel. Because the plug-in blurs the scene based on G-Buffer information and not on computational physics, it is better suited for special effects than it is for depth of field. The Blur plug-in is accessed as a Video Post filter event. Figure 32.14 shows the Blur Control dialog.

FIGURE 32.14

You can blur a scene based on the Material ID or Object channel.

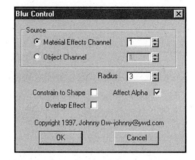

The Source section enables you to specify the particular Material Effects or Object channel you want to use. The Radius parameter controls the level of the blur. A higher radius results in a blurrier area. The Radius parameter also controls the size of the soft edge that surrounds the blurred portions of the image. The Constrain to Shape check box instructs the blur to limit its effect to the exact pixels occupied by the specified Material Effects or Object channel. If Constrain to Shape is checked, the Radius parameter no longer controls the size of the soft edge because the soft edge is eliminated. The Affect Alpha check box instructs the blur filter to blur the alpha channel, which allows for seamless compositing of blurred images. The Overlap Effect check box instructs the blur filter to computationally overlap the pixel sections that it blurs. The effect is usually an increased blurriness, but it also tends to distort and smear the affected regions. The following example illustrates how you might use the blur plug-in to create heat distortion effects. Before you do this example, you need to copy the Blur.flt file from the accompanying CD to your \3dsmax\plug-ins directory.

1. Reset or load 3DS MAX and load ch32ex4.max from the accompanying CD.

2. Select the Exhaust01 object, right-click on it, and choose Properties. Set the Object channel to 1. The Exhaust01 geometry already has a material applied that has Opacity, Shininess, and Shininess Strength all set to 0.

3. Create a Ripple space warp with amplitude 1 set to 5.0, amplitude 2 set to 6.0, and wave length set to 50. Bind the Exhaust01 object to the space warp. For the heat effect to appear realistic, you need it to animate. Because the Blur filter works on each frame the same way, you need to change the form of your Exhaust object to get the effect you want.

4. Click on the Animate button, go to frame 100, and set the phase for the Ripple space warp to 15.

5. Open Video Post. Double-click on the Blur filter to edit the Filter event, and click on Setup to bring up the Blur Setup dialog. Activate the Object radio button and be certain that the value is set to 1. Set the Radius to 4 and leave everything else unchecked. Click on OK to exit the Blur dialog and click on OK again to return to the Video Post window.

6. Execute the sequence and render a single frame to the Virtual Frame Buffer window. You can add an Image Output event to the Video Post queue and render an animation, or you can view the pre-rendered ch32ex4.avi file from the accompanying CD.

TIP

You can also use the Blur filter to create a faux depth of field effect. Essentially, you leave your foreground object focused and blur your background. By setting the object channel to 0 in the Filter Setup dialog, everything in your scene will blur unless you change the default value on your objects to a number other than 0. You can blur everything except specific objects, or you can blur everything and then composite a focused foreground.

Fields Of Depth

The Fields Of Depth plug-in is an inexpensive utility written by Andrew Cross. A demo version is provided on the accompanying CD—if you send the author $15, he will e-mail (or snail mail) you a fully registered version. The shareware registration form is in the fodreg.txt file on the CD. Fields Of Depth is a Video Post filter. The plug-in uses computational physics to simulate a real camera lens, and thus enables you to simulate camera focus (see fig. 32.15). The Fields Of Depth plug-in provides broadcast-quality depth blur in an easy and understandable interface. The plug-in renders relatively quickly and supports alpha channel processing for seamless compositing. The Fields Of Depth plug-in has an elegant interface with understandable icons that illustrate the various options available (see fig. 32.16).

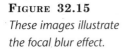

FIGURE 32.15
These images illustrate the focal blur effect.

FIGURE 32.16
The Fields Of Depth plug-in enables you to blur areas of your image based on real camera lens physics.

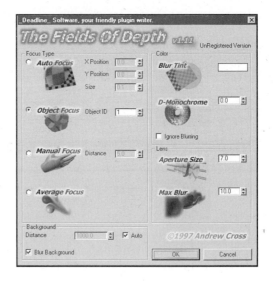

The various options of Fields Of Depth that follow enable you to specify and adjust the focus region:

- **Auto Focus.** This optional mode enables you to position an area of focus in your scene. The X and Y values correspond to the horizontal and vertical positioning of the focus area. The values for these settings range from –1 to 1, with 0 being the center of the screen and –1 and 1 being the antipodes. The size parameter determines the size of the focus area. The value ranges from 0 to 1, and the value determines the size relative to the size of the screen to keep in focus. A value of .1, for example, means that the focus area will occupy a circle 1/10 the size of the screen.

- **Object Focus.** This option enables you to specify an Object channel. Objects with the corresponding value set for their property direct the camera's area of focus. This is different than the Blur (frame only) method because it is based on the camera, and consequently the focused area extends beyond the proximity of the object. Object Focus is the easiest and most useful of the focus types that Fields Of Depth offers and is probably the method you should use in most situations. The area of focus follows the object specified if it is animated. The ch32ex6.avi file on the accompanying CD shows an example of Object Focus in action.

- **Manual Focus.** This option works somewhat like a standard camera's manual focus feature. You specify the distance from the camera, and Fields Of Depth adjusts its area of focus on the specified distance.

- **Average Focus.** Average focus calculates the average of all distances in the scene and creates its area of focus at the average point. This is useful if you want the area of focus to be in the center of your scene. Average focus requires no user-definable parameters.

The color section of the Fields Of Depth plug-in enables you to tint the out-of-focus objects. The D-Monochrome parameter works in conjunction with the Blur Tint Color picker. If you adjust the D-Monochrome value without choosing a blur tint color, the most blurred objects become monochrome. You must set a value in D-Monochrome if you want the Blur Tint Color picker to function. The value ranges from 0.0 to 1.0. A 1.0 value fully tints the most out-of-focus areas to the specified color. If no color is specified, the most out-of-focus areas are turned completely monochrome. If you check the Ignore Blurring check box, the color section affects the image but no blurring occurs.

The Aperture Size setting determines the size of the area to be blurred. A higher number results in a smaller blur area and vice versa. The MAX Blur spinner adjusts the maximum amount of blur. The higher the number, the more the blur, and the longer it will take to render.

The Background section enables you to adjust how Fields Of Depth will blur the background image if there is one. Auto Blur, however, works fine for most purposes. If you uncheck Auto, you can specify a distance to the background. The further the distance, the blurrier the background image will be. You may want to uncheck the Blur Background check box if the image you are using for your background is already blurred.

RealLensFlare: Distance Blur

One of RealLensFlare's modules is a depth of field plug-in. Like the other modules of RealLensFlare, Distance Blur is created as a Helper object. You place Distance Blur helpers in your scene, which allows for easy placement of focus points. Distance Blur can blur the background, adjust focal depths, and has an auto focus feature for quick and easy blur effects. You can access the Blur parameters in Track View, and you can animate the position of the Helper object. This is useful for creating rack focus effects, where blurred objects in the background suddenly come into focus and vice versa. In version 1.5 of RLF, the Distance Blur module has been enhanced. It now supports alpha channel processing so that you can composite focal blurred images seamlessly. Another added feature, 3D Space Blur Radius, enables you to set near and far ranges for the Distance Blur helper. You can then animate the helper moving smoothly through your scene to create realistic fly through and other effects. A Fancy Blur option enables you to blur specified objects only, based on their distance from the camera. This feature enables you to create object-based distance blurs.

LensFX Focus

The LensFX Focus module of LensFX MAX enables you to do depth of field effects as well. Like the other modules in LensFX MAX, LensFX Focus is a modeless window. This means that with the LensFX Focus module open, you can still access other parts of MAX. When you bring up the Setup dialog for LensFX Focus, a phantom Control object is automatically created. You can set or edit the parameters of the Control object in Track View. LensFX Focus enables you to set values for horizontal and vertical focal loss, which adjusts the overall level of the blurriness. You can lock these values so that they adjust symmetrically, or you can create streaking blurriness and other effects by making the horizontal and vertical blurriness values different.

- A *Scene Blur* option blurs the entire scene based on the values set for horizontal and vertical focal loss.

- A *Radial Blur* option creates a circular target area that remains in focus. You change the focal area with focal range and focal limit spinners. The focal range sets the distance for the cameras focus, and the focal limit sets the distance at which the scene will become completely out of focus.

- A *Focal Object* option enables you to use a selectable item in your scene to create your focus area.

Alpha channel support is available for seamless compositing of focal blurred scenes and a Preview button enables you to generate a preview of how your settings will affect the Video Post queue.

Adobe Photoshop Plug-In Filters

Release 1.1 and later of 3D Studio MAX includes a Video Post filter that enables you to run Adobe Photoshop-compatible filters on images and renderings from within Video Post. Hundred of filters are currently available for Photoshop and other image processing, editing, and enhancement programs. You can create all kinds of interesting effects by using Photoshop-compatible filters with your MAX renderings. Most any image processing effect you can think of probably has a corresponding Photoshop-compatible filter. You can use Photoshop-compatible filters, for example, to make your rendering look like a painted fresco, to add a film grain look, or to tweak out the colors in creative ways.

The MAX Photoshop Plug-in Filter event will work only with 32-bit Photoshop-compatible filters. Consequently, not all the available Photoshop filters will work with MAX. Older 16-bit filters will not be recognized. Furthermore, some of the plug-ins that ship with Adobe Photoshop are programmed to work only with Photoshop. Figuring out which ones will work and which won't is a matter of trial and error. If you attempt to use a Photoshop filter designed to work only with Photoshop, MAX will crash. You should save or hold your file, therefore, if you intend to experiment in this manner. Photoshop-compatible filters have an .8BF file name extension. You can find many 32-bit Photoshop-compatible filters available for free download on the web.

TIP

The following is a list of fun and useful filters you might try applying to some of your animations. You are likely get some extremely psychedelic results. All of the filters in this list are included with Adobe Photoshop 4.0 and have tested well with the Adobe Photoshop MAX plug-in.

- Diffuse Glow
- Glass
- Ocean Ripple
- Film Grain
- Smudge Stick
- Watercolor
- Plastic Wrap
- Rough Pastels
- Paint Daubs
- Sponge

The MAX plug-in uses the native interface of the Photoshop filter to give you an interactive preview of the effect. In most cases, the parameters you set for the filter are saved with the .MAX file and the Video Post .VPX file. This feature enables you to return to the filter to make modifications of the parameters. Some plug-in filters do not allow MAX to access the settings, and therefore MAX cannot save them. The Kai's Power Tools third-party Photoshop plug-in utility pack does not allow MAX to save settings. If you intend to use filters from this product, you should make certain that they are set correctly before exiting the setup, or you should write down the settings for use in future sessions. The Adobe Photoshop Plug-in Filter event can be nested, enabling you to use multiple filters on one image or rendering. You cannot animate the effect, however. If you apply the filter to animation, for example, the filter is applied with the same settings to every frame. When the Filter event is applied to an Image or Scene event, the Image or Scene event appears as the child of the Filter event in the queue. The Filter event then applies to the Image event that is a Child event of it.

Figure 32.17 shows the Photoshop Plug-In Setup dialog. You must first add the filter to the Video Post queue. You can then double-click on the event to bring up the Edit Filter Event dialog and then click on Setup to bring up the Setup dialog for the filter.

FIGURE 32.17

The Photoshop Plug-In Setup dialog.

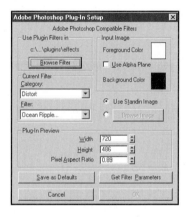

The Use Plugin Filters in section is where you specify the directory where the Photoshop-compatible plug-in filters reside on your hard disk. Click on the Browse Filter button and navigate to the directory to select it. After a directory containing filters is specified, select the category you want from the Category list box in the Current Filter section. The category is encoded in the plug-in file and typically is the name of the developer or the name of the filter package.

Beneath the Category list box is the Filter list box, where you specify the filter you want to use. The Input Image section enables you to specify a foreground and background color, which is needed for some Photoshop filters to function correctly. The KPT Page Curl filter, for example, curls the corner of the image like a turning page. To work properly, this filter needs to know the background color because it places the background color into the area revealed by the upturned page.

The Use Alpha Plane check box determines how the filter handles the alpha channel in an image. Typically, if an alpha channel is available, the Photoshop filter affects only the opaque areas of the image. If the Use Alpha Plane check box is unchecked, the alpha channel information is discarded and the filter affects the entire image. If you are using a mask for the filter (see the section on masking in Chapter 31), for example, the mask is still used and serves to replace the alpha channel. If the Use Alpha Plane check box is checked, only pixels designated as opaque in the alpha channel and pixels that are not masked are affected by the filter.

The Use Standin Image radio button sets the background for the preview window to a standard checker pattern. You can specify an image to use instead by activating the Browse Image radio button and clicking on the Browse Image button to select an image.

The Plug-In Preview section sets the size of the image that you want to use in the preview window. These settings determine how faithfully the preview window will represent what you will see in your final rendering. You should set these parameters to correspond with the image you are using for the preview. Clicking on the Get Filter Parameters button brings up the Interactive Preview window and enables you to adjust the settings to use for the selected Photoshop-compatible filter. Figure 32.18 illustrates an example of the Ocean Ripple Distortion Photoshop-compatible filter applied to the Tutvally.tga file that ships with MAX.

FIGURE 32.18

The Adobe Photoshop Plug-in Filter enables you to use Photoshop-compatible plug-in filters from within Video Post.

Fractal Flow MAX

Fractal Flow, the popular 3D Studio DOS image processing IPAS routine, is currently making its way into the world of 3D Studio MAX. Currently, Fractal Flow MAX is in beta, but it should be available by the time this book is in print. Fractal Flow uses fractal mathematics to distort an image or specific parts of an image in various ways. Fractal Flow is useful for simulating cloaking spaceships, creating heat distortion, or creating realistic fire, smoke, clouds, water, and other special effects.

Although Fractal Flow is a Video Post filter, the Setup dialog is modeless. Modeless dialogs enable you to access other parts of the program while they are open. Because it is modeless, when you bring up the Setup dialog for Fractal Flow, the Video Post window vanishes. You can minimize or move the Fractal Flow Setup dialog and continue to work in MAX. When you hit the Setup button for the first time, Fractal Flow places a phantom Control object in your scene. The Control object enables you to edit and modify the animatable parameters within Track View. The Setup dialog also has its own Time Slider and preview window, which is linked to the MAX Time Slider. By pressing the Time Slider's play button, you can view your Fractal Flow effect in the preview window interactively. Fractal Flow is divided into four main panels: Control, Fractal Distortions, Waves, and Ripples.

Within the Control tab, the *Settings* section enables you to load and save your Fractal Flow settings (see fig. 32.19). One of the most powerful aspects of Fractal Flow is that it contains the capability to use the saved Fractal Flow setting as a standard bitmap. This means that you can use your Fractal Flow settings as bitmaps in the Material Editor.

- **Preview Size.** Enables you to set the image size that Fractal Flow will use for its preview window.

- **Render Preview.** Determines how much of the Video Post queue will be used for the preview.

- **Up To Filter Only.** Creates a preview image containing the Video Post image as it appears in the queue up to the point of the Fractal Flow filter.

- **Whole Queue.** Makes the preview contain the image as it would appear if the entire queue is processed.

- **Bitmap Background.** Enables you to use a background image for the preview.

FIGURE 32.19

The Fractal Flow Control tab.

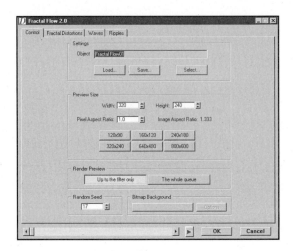

TIP

If you intend to save your Fractal Flow settings and use the corresponding .FLO file in the Material Editor, you need to specify a background image. Using the background image is necessary for Fractal Flow to export the settings correctly for use as a material.

The Fractal Distortion tab is where you set the general Fractal Noise parameters that distort your images (see fig. 32.20). The check boxes on the left activate the corresponding parameter. After you activate a parameter, you can adjust the value and view the results in the preview window. You can also animate the parameters by moving the Time Slider at the bottom of the dialog and set checked parameters to different values at different frames. MAX's Animate button does not need to be activated to set keyframes.

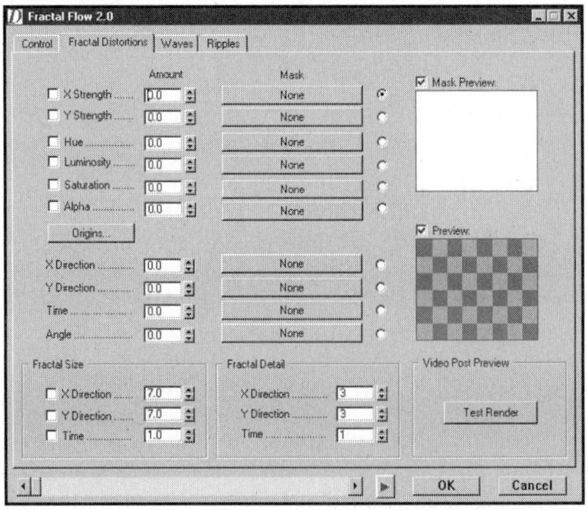

FIGURE 32.20

The Fractal Distortion tab is where you set your general Fractal Noise parameters.

WARNING

Because you can set frames without the Animate button being active, you may end up setting keyframes inadvertently. If your results seem erroneous, you should open Track View and make certain that you have not accidentally set extra keyframes.

The preview window at the bottom right corner gives you a preview of the effect against a checkered background. If you click on the Test Render button, Fractal Flow renders the Video Post queue and shows you a rendered preview of your settings. The mask buttons next to the various animatable parameters enable you to create a mask for the effect. Clicking on the radio button next to the mask buttons activate the corresponding mask. After you select a mask, the Mask Preview window updates to show what your mask looks like. Fractal Flow has very powerful masking features. You can mask using linear or radial gradients. You can create a mask by using bitmaps as well. Seven buttons enable you to specify the alpha channel, the RGB color channels, the M channel (Maximum luminance) or the Y channel (Chrominance value) to use as your mask. You can also specify a specific Material ID or Object channel, and you can limit the mask to a depth range or face normals. A Blur parameter softens the edges of your mask.

The Waves tab enables you to create a wave distortion across an image. You can set the number of waves, the height of the wave, the angle at which the waves cross the image, and the speed at which they move across the image (see fig. 32.21). You can animate and mask these parameters in the same manner as those in the Fractal Distortions tab. The Waves tab also enables you to specify the highlight and shadow color and the direction and intensity of the light that will accentuate the waves.

FIGURE 32.21

The Waves tab enables you to create a wave distortion on your images.

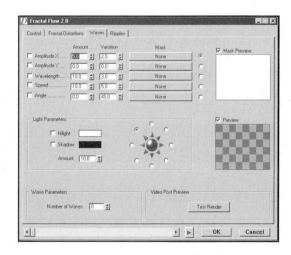

The Ripples tab enables you to create circular ripples across an image. The options for ripples are similar to those of Waves (see fig. 32.22). You can, however, also control how the ripples will decay as they move away from their origin. You can set the origin of the ripples and use a mask for the origin.

FIGURE 32.22

The Ripples tab enables you to create a ripple effect on your images.

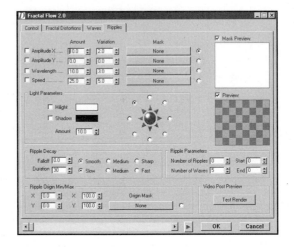

Miscellaneous Effect Plug-Ins

Many miscellaneous plug-ins are available in addition to the ones discussed so far. Some are quite useful, and because of MAX's open architecture, many more are sure to follow. This section outlines a few miscellaneous plug-ins that have proven most useful.

Negative

The Negative filter ships with MAX. This filter inverts the colors of an image. The result looks like the negative of a color photograph. You might use this filter if you need to model a film reel. You can render a frame through the Negative filter and use that image as a tiled map on some celluloid film geometry. You might also use this filter in an abstract or psychedelic animation. Negative requires no setup parameters.

Outline

The Outline plug-in is a Video Post filter written by Harry Denholm. This plug-in creates an outline around specified objects or materials. The outline can be a user-definable color. This plug-in is particularly useful for creating reference frames and examining motion. By surrounding specific objects with an outline, it is easier to dissect subtle animated movement. It is also useful for *rotoscoping*, the process of compositing computer graphics over live action. In certain situations, the computer graphics match the background closely, and it is useful to have a mechanism whereby you can easily discern the CG and the live action as separate elements. By outlining certain objects, you can achieve this goal. The plug-in works on a Material ID or an Object channel.

Stamper

Stamper is a nifty Video Post filter written by Andrey Zmievski. It takes an embossed image and stamps it into a background image. Stamper is a charityware plug-in, meaning if you find it useful, the author asks that you make an appropriate contribution to your favorite charity. The stamp looks like an inverse imprint (see fig. 32.23). This utility is useful for placing logos and copyright information on images and animations. Stamper also supports .IFL files to use as the input image, so you can animate the movement of a stamped image around the screen. This effect is similar to the identification tag that T.V. stations sometimes place over their shows. If you use Adobe Photoshop, you just take your logo, make it black and white if it is not already, and then run the Stylize/Emboss filter on it. After you have an embossed image, you are ready to stamp it. The Stamper interface has a few options. Browse to select the embossed image you want to stamp. After you have an image selected, the four buttons in the Location section determine where the embossed image will appear in the final image. After you choose a location, you can offset the stamp from that location by adjusting the X and Y value spinners. The Stamper plug-in (stamper.flt) is included on the accompanying CD.

FIGURE 32.23

The Stamper plug-in enables you to stamp an embossed image on to your MAX renderings.

Starfield Generator

Starfield Generator is a Video Post filter written by Tom Hudson. It is useful for creating realistic space scene backgrounds. The plug-in is included on the accompanying CD. There are many ways to create star fields in MAX. You can create them with environment maps by using bitmaps or procedurals such as noise. Starfield Generator's advantage over other methods, however, is motion blur. If your scene requires camera movement, the Star Field generator enables you to control the amount that the stars will blur in relation to the movement of the camera. Motion blur is great for creating added impact in space scenes. Motion blur can also be useful for creating special effects such as warp speed star streaks and other effects. Starfield Generator works off of a camera in your scene. You should apply the filter to a Camera Scene event. Access the Setup parameters (see fig. 32.24) by clicking on the Setup button in the Edit Filter Event dialog.

Figure 32.24

*Starfield Generator
Setup parameters.*

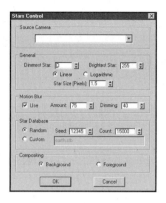

Figure 32.24

*Starfield Generator
Setup parameters.*

The Source Camera section enables you to select a camera for Starfield Generator on which to base its calculations. If you have multiple cameras in your scene, you should specify the same camera that you add to the Video Post queue. If you specify another camera, the stars will not match the motion of the camera that you render.

The General section enables you to specify the general parameters that determine how your starfield will look. The Dimmest Star and Brightest Star spinners range from 0–255, with 0 being completely black and 255 being solid white. If you want your starfield to be composed completely of dim stars, for example, you can lower the value of the Brightest Star spinner.

The Linear and Logarithmic radio buttons mathematically determine how the brightness changes from dim to bright. The Star Size spinner determines the size of the star dots in pixels.

The Motion Blur parameters determine how the streaking effect occurs when the camera moves. The Use check box turns Motion Blur for the stars on or off. The Amount spinner determines how much motion blur to use and ranges from 0–100. The Dimming spinner sets the amount that the motion streaks will dim as their trails get longer. This value also ranges from 0–100. The default values for Amount and Dimming work fine in most cases.

The Star Database section determines how many stars appear and where they are generated. The Random button uses the number in the Seed spinner to generate a random number of stars and to place them. The Custom radio button enables you to read in a star layout from a specified file. There is currently no way to save your own star layouts.

Finally, the Compositing section determines whether the stars are placed behind your rendering or in front of it.

In Practice: Video Post Effects

- **Special effects.** Special effects go a long way toward adding visual impact to a scene. By using Video Post filters, you can include a variety of effects in your images and animations. Most of the special-effects–oriented filters available today are plug-ins. Keeping track of all the new plug-ins can be both a daunting and exciting task. The Internet and CompuServe are both great resources for obtaining new MAX plug-ins.

- **Glow.** Glow effects are useful in many situations. Currently, a number of glow plug-ins are available. You should experiment with the various free plug-ins to determine whether they will suit your needs. If not, the commercial plug-ins RealLensFlare and LensFX MAX contain more powerful and flexible Glow modules.

- **Lens flares.** Lens flares can be a striking addition to any scene. The most common criticism of lens flares has been their gratuitous overuse. You should make certain that your scene warrants using a lens flare before you start tossing them into scenes. Subtle use of lens flares will take your images further. Slight or barely noticeable flares around light sources give extra realism to your scenes. Remember that lens flares can also be used for special light effects. The Fractal Fury module of RealLensFlare 1.5 and the Inferno module of LensFX MAX both add the capability to create realistic special effect phenomenon.

- **Blur.** Blur effects are useful for creating special effects and reproducing camera focal blur. You can use blur effects to reproduce atmospheric heat distortion, for example. You can use depth of field blur to more faithfully reproduce the look of a real camera.

- **Adobe Photoshop Plug-in filters.** These filters enable you to modify your images and animation in a great variety of ways. The Internet is a great resource for obtaining Adobe Photoshop compatible 32-bit filters, and a variety of third-party commercial collections are available.

- **Fractal Flow MAX.** This makes special image processing effects possible from within Video Post. You can create general fractal distortions, waves, and ripples within your images and animations.

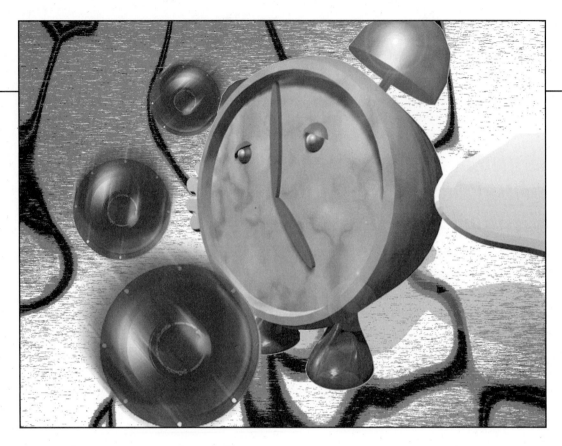

IMAGE CREATED BY JEREMY HUBBELL

Chapter 33

by Jeremy Hubbell

SOUND IN MAX

Over the past few years, multimedia has become an explosion of sight and sound. Sound has always been a part of computers, but really nothing more than blips and bleeps from a four-inch speaker. Today, sound in computers has changed the way we communicate, the way we are entertained, and the way we are informed.

This chapter introduces you to what sound is all about as it relates to your PC and 3DS MAX. The following topics are among those covered in this chapter:

- The basics of sound
- Sound technologies
- Sound hardware
- Sound mixer controls for NT
- Using sound in MAX
- The Audio Controller plug-in

The Basics

Sound on a PC comes in various *flavors,* which means that there are varying levels of quality and file size to suit your needs. A review of the basic concepts of digital sound is a good place to start this discussion.

Digitizing

When your computer records sound, it takes electrical signals from an analog source, such as recording from a microphone, and turns them into digital information—essentially ones and zeros. The computer interprets the digital information and displays it to you as a two-dimensional representation—a waveform.

The waveform displays a great deal of information, such as the given amplitude and the length of the sound. It does not display, however, the third dimension—the medium in which the sound travels. This medium is normally air, but it could be water or even rock.

If you look closely at the waveform, you will see where it derives its name. The waveform is really a graph of peaks and troughs (see fig. 33.1). The distance from the peak to the trough is known as *amplitude,* and the lateral distance from one peak to the next is a *cycle*.

Figure 33.1

A display of a waveform.

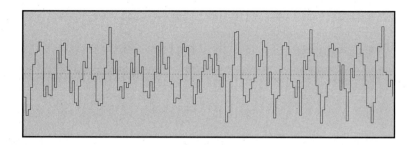

The best way to think of how cycles and amplitude relate to what you hear is that amplitude is usually associated with how loud a sound is, and cycles are governed by the pitch (how high or low).

Note

A WAV file in Windows contains all cycle and pitch information of a digital sound.

Sampling Rates

When the computer records a sound, it must do so by taking several samples of that sound and piecing them together to represent that sound digitally. This technique, known as *sampling*, can greatly affect sound quality and file size. Recording at a sampling rate of 44,100 Hz, for instance, is comparable to CD quality; half that is more akin to "radio" quality.

Waveforms of identical sounds recorded at different sampling rates differ noticeably in appearance (see fig. 33.2). Notice that the steps are very visible on the 8,000 Hz example. The 44,100 Hz sample, on the other hand, is much more smooth. You are essentially just looking at the resolution of the waveform. Much like an image, the more "chunky" it appears, the more information has been lost from the original.

FIGURE 33.2

The same sound file at 8 kHz, 22 kHz, and 44.1 kHz. Notice the amount of "stair-stepping" in the 8 kHz sample.

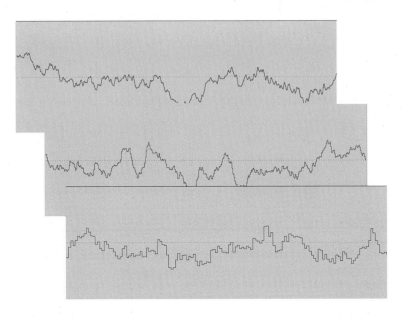

Bit Depth

Much like your display has different bit depths for the number of colors you can have in an image, sound on your PC possesses the same quality. Most sounds have one of two bit depths: 8 or 16.

As with sampling rates, as bit depth increases, so does sound quality. The bit depth setting is controlling the number of levels of amplitude per sample you can have for a digital sound. A wider amplitude range reproduces better high frequencies such as a cymbal and much deeper low frequencies such as rumblings from a kettle drum in the same sample.

An 8-bit sample can have a maximum of 256 levels of amplitude. A 16-bit sample can go as high as 65,536 levels of amplitude. The differing end results are quite dramatic both in sound quality and file size. You can expect a doubling in file size by choosing a 16-bit sample over an 8-bit sample. If sound quality is important, however, then you will need to work with 16-bit samples.

A 16-bit sound recorded at 44,100 Hz (CD-quality) is a standard referred to as *Redbook Audio.*

3D Studio MAX is designed to use any size or type of waveform that your PC supports. Before you start animating your WAV recordings of your favorite CDs, make certain that you take the following into account.

Higher sampling rates produce higher quality recordings but can take up enormous amounts of storage space. This is especially true of lengthy recordings. You must weigh what is critical when using sound in MAX.

It is often better to work with sound in a lower quality form. There is really no need to load a 60 MB WAV file into MAX and sacrifice interactivity when you can use a scaled-down version in sampling rate and bit depth that maybe only uses 10 percent of that. Programs such as SoundLab, part of Autodesk Animator Studio, have this type of conversion functionality. Save the high-quality sound for final output.

PC Sound Technologies

The important thing to remember is that 3D Studio MAX only reads WAV files, by default. Therefore, if you only plan to synchronize your animation to an already existing sound, all you need to have is a sound card capable of digital audio playback. Basically, any standard sound card you buy these days will have digital audio playback and recording capabilities. The following are the "must haves" for sound cards in MAX:

- 16-bit digital audio playback
- Stereo sound

With MAX's release 1.2, you can now use WAV files to control an object's animation. This new feature is called the Animation Controller. The audio controller animates objects based on the amplitude of a WAV file. For that to be possible, the sound card must have some kind of input. This could be a Line-In, Mic-In, or CD-In, or all three. The following sections describe some of the other technologies that you may want in a sound card.

MIDI

A set of instructions called MIDI is the key to the computer talking to the sound card. MIDI stands for Musical Instrument Digital Interface, a standard that has been around for many years in the music industry. A MIDI signal contains all the necessary information to play a sound for a specific length of time at a certain pitch. Because the file contains only instructions and not the actual digital sound, MIDI files (.MID) are much smaller in size than their WAV counterparts. With a plug-in, MAX could easily animate objects based on MIDI instructions. Both FM and Wavetable technologies, discussed in the next few sections, use MIDI for playback and recording.

FM Sound Chips

The FM (frequency modulation) sound chip has been around since PC sound cards were first produced. FM chips work off the principle that they can create duplications of real sounds by using the chip's circuitry. The result is that sounds from a drum to an environmental sound such as wind can be re-created by the FM chip.

The main downside of the FM chip is that the re-created sounds don't often sound like the real life counterpart, resulting in very computer-generated sounding music.

Wavetable Synthesis

FM chips still have their uses but are being quickly replaced by a newer technology called *Wavetable synthesis*. Wavetable synthesis on a PC is equivalent to what transistors were for the computer. Instead of having a computer play wimpy, tinny sounds out of your speaker system, you can now have an orchestra!

Here's how it works. Wavetable technology incorporates a lookup table of digital samples of real instruments or real sounds. An entire table is referred to as a *bank*. A bank of sounds can be various samples of different instruments or sounds, or it can be one specific type of sound. When the computer requests to play a sound, the Wavetable chip determines which type of sound needs to be played, the length of playback, and the pitch. It then makes the necessary modifications to the digital sample stored in the table and plays the modified sample through your sound card—all in about a millisecond. This technology will make your projects, presentations, games, and anything that uses music seem more real.

Wavetable synthesis uses compact MIDI information to play back real sounds that would normally be too large if used in a file. In the past, MIDI information only sounded good when played back on a PC if you had expensive hardware. Today more and more sound card manufacturers are using Wavetable synthesis combined with 16-bit digital audio to provide consumers with the complete sound experience.

Digital Signal Processing (DSP) and 3D Sound

Digital signal processing is a technology that allows a sound being created or played back by the sound card to be modified to change the way the sound is heard. The most common forms of DSP are changing the acoustical properties of a sound, making you feel like you are sitting in a different space. A sound that was recorded in a studio, for instance, sounds like it was recorded in a studio when played back. A DSP chip could add the effect of *reverberation* (basically an echo), however, to make it sound like you are sitting in a concert hall.

DSP is at the heart of 3D sound, the latest technology to hit the PC airwaves. With 3D sound, not only can you get an effect of being somewhere else, but you can also hear sound coming from different locations other than your speakers! The amazing thing about 3D sound is that you really don't need extra hardware. You can use your existing sound card with your speaker system and still get many of the benefits.

More and more sound cards are implementing DSP. Both DSP and 3D sound play perfectly into the MAX production environment because that environment is simulating a different 3D space. That 3D space could be the one you are designing in the viewports! Best of all, DSP works with both MIDI and digital sound playback.

Speakers

Speakers are the remaining link in your PC sound system and are probably the most critical. Consider that you could have bought a $500 sound card only to realize its capabilties on a pair of $30 speakers. You have come this far, now is not the time to skimp.

When considering what type of speakers you might like, ask yourself the following questions:

- What will be the primary use?

- Where will I be listening?

- How much space do I have for speakers?

- Will the speakers need to be portable?

These are probably not the only questions you could ask yourself, but you should at least consider them before making a speaker purchase.

You have many brands and types of manufacturers to choose from when buying speakers. Obviously, the best test of all is to listen for yourself. Don't buy speakers before you have listened to them. When shopping around, you should follow a few guidelines:

- Make certain that the speakers are magnetically shielded.

- Make certain that the speakers contain the necessary cabling to hook up to your sound card.

- Make certain the speakers can be returned if they're no good.

If you are serious about speakers, plan to spend some time shopping. Sometimes your best selection and deal might be where you least expect it. You might be wondering how much speakers will cost you. On average, a good set of speakers sells for about $100. The price ranges from $20 to $700, however, depending on the setup.

The next few sections review what is available in speaker technology and attempt to demystify how speakers work.

Traditional Desktop Speakers

Almost every computer store you go to now has some form of "multimedia" speakers that you can add on to your PC or purchase with an "upgrade kit." Unfortunately, most of these stand-alone speaker types are of poor quality and deliver relatively little in terms of sound.

The Ranks of the Non-Amplified

Perhaps at the bottom of the speaker food chain, besides your internal PC speaker, is the unamplified (passive) four-inch multimedia speaker set. These speakers usually sell for less than $20 and don't do much except produce small sound amplified only by the two watts coming from your sound card.

Although small, non-amplified speakers normally are not used for production, they do have some good uses—especially when portability is an issue. For a small presentation that needs to be portable, these speakers are a great solution. They are light because there are no batteries or power transformers to lug along, and they can be placed anywhere around the computer. You do not, after all, usually need a massive speaker system when giving a presentation in a small boardroom.

Getting Powered

The next level up in the traditional system is a powered (active) speaker—powered in the sense that it can amplify the signal coming from the sound card. Even the slightest bit of power amplification in your speakers can make them sound much bigger than they really are. You can pick up some powered speakers for only a little more than the non-powered. You will be glad you did. Even if portability is an issue, you might be able to get some speakers that require small batteries and don't necessarily need to be hooked up to a power socket.

Amplified speakers tend to have a few more features than non-amplified ones. If you are trying to get the best bang for the buck, make certain that the speakers have at least the following:

- Bass control
- Treble control
- Balance
- Separate A/C or battery power options

You could substitute tone control for a separate bass/treble control, but this limits you. A tone control acts as sort of a fulcrum. When tone is balanced, there is an even ratio of bass to treble. If the tone leans toward bass, however, bass increases while treble decreases. The result is a heavy bass, but it sounds rather muffled because the treble is gone. The reverse happens if tone is altered in the opposite direction.

Having separate bass and treble control gives you the flexibility to boost both levels or raise one while the other remains normal. It is to your advantage to spend a little extra to get this functionality.

The Satellite/Subwoofer Combination

Perhaps the most popular speaker combination in the marketplace, the satellite and subwoofer combination, can produce an enormous amount of high-quality sound.

The combination works very well in small- to medium-sized spaces. The addition of the subwoofer breathes a whole new life into your computer's sound system. You can now experience the low to lower mid-range frequencies most traditional speakers can't reproduce.

The satellite speakers—smaller speakers that handle mid- to high-range frequencies—can be purchased separately, but you will usually find that most are sold in conjunction with the subwoofer. The satellite speaker's placement is fairly crucial. You may not want the speakers to be sitting immediately to the left and right of your monitor, but you certainly don't want them sitting three or four feet from either side. Left and right speakers in a computer system handle 90 percent of the sounds that come from your sound card. They should be placed in such a way that a monaural sound appears to be coming directly from the center of your screen.

The subwoofer is the next step in this combination. The subwoofer can really go anywhere in a room, but is best placed near the computer in a corner somewhere. Corners provide some of the best bass response but can also produce what are known as *standing waves*—bass that hangs around longer than it should. If you find that occurring, just move the subwoofer farther away from the walls. Your hearing cannot really perceive where a low frequency (such as a rumble) is emanating from, so placement is not as critical. Subwoofers are also usually monaural. They will combine left and right low frequencies and produce one sound. Again, this is okay because you really can't hear the difference at such a low frequency.

This combination of satellite speakers with a subwoofer is what most people will get because they produce great sound at an affordable cost.

Other Speaker Types

There are other speaker combinations for you to choose from besides the standard computer speakers. As a matter of fact, you might find that an alternate solution is better for your needs.

Three-Dimensional Sound Speakers

Three-dimensional sound speakers rely on licensed 3D sound technology to modify the sound coming from your sound card and to add 3D spatialization effects. Usually these speakers are designed to work with any sound coming from your computer, and make it sound as if it is all around you—making your speakers seem as if they are everywhere.

When used in conjunction with software, 3D sound speakers can place sounds in certain locations. A good example of this is a jet flying straight at you and passing overhead. Normal speakers would just treat this as a sound starting softer and then getting louder as the jet passes. 3D speakers would actually make adjustments in the acoustics of the sound so that your ears perceive something to be flying overhead and behind you.

3D sound speaker systems usually look just like a satellite/subwoofer combination, but they have special circuitry to handle the 3D effects.

Proper placement of 3D speakers is as crucial, if not more so, as a traditional speaker setup. Usually, you want the speakers to be immediately to the left and right of your monitor. The manufacturer will usually provide you with the optimum placement settings.

Surround Sound Speakers

Surround Sound (Dolby Pro-Logic) speakers might sound like a frivolity at this point. After all, when would you have a usage for surround sound from your computer? If you are involved in any production work designed for broadcast, you know why. Surround sound is used by hundreds of television stations and every network utilizes it somehow. Almost every household that has purchased a home-entertainment system in the past five years has some type of surround sound unit. Only recently, however, has the PC industry adopted surround sound.

Dolby Pro-Logic uses what is known as *matrix* technology to encode all four channels of sound into just two (left and right). This makes WAV files a perfect technology for playing back surround sound on your computer, because they only incorporate left and right channels.

The technology incorporates a six-speaker system: three front speakers, two surrounds, and usually one subwoofer. Here is how the decoding process works:

1. Left and right audio is fed from your VCR, LaserDisc player, or computer to your Dolby Pro-Logic receiver/decoder.

2. The Dolby Surround matrix is decoded by the Pro-Logic circuitry. The two channels are broken into four.

3. The four channels (Left, Center, Right, and Surround) are then sent to the appropriate speakers. The subwoofer usually just takes the front channel information and uses an electronic crossover to cut out all the high frequencies.

Although you don't have the ability to directly access these individual channels by default in MAX, you can play a WAV file recorded in surround sound. You can then edit your animation not only based on the sound heard, but also the sound's location in 3D space!

There are several ways to get this technology for your PC. Manufacturers produce multimedia speakers with the Pro-Logic circuitry built in. This is a compact solution that gives you great results, especially when you are strapped for desktop space. If you have a little more room, you can purchase a "traditional" home system and just hook it up directly to the PC. Magnetic shielding for the speakers is the only important thing here, because the magnets in your speakers can produce some rather colorful patterns on your monitor if they get too close.

After sorting out your hardware, it is time to get your computer talking to it. Software configurations vary from computer to computer. Make certain that you follow the manufacturer's installation instructions for both hardware and any drivers that need to be set up.

Windows NT and Sound

Windows NT 4 brings a level of sound functionality in high-end PC operating systems not previously found before. In a nutshell, Microsoft has now provided many of the sound board mixing and configuration controls previously only available on actual physical sounds mixing consoles.

Volume Control

When your sound card is installed and configured properly, a little picture of a speaker appears on the Taskbar. Click on it to adjust the main volume of the sound card with the Volume Control slider that appears (see fig. 33.3). There is also an option to mute. This controls the overall volume of all inputs of your sound card. If you want to control those outputs individually, double-click on the speaker icon to bring up the Mixer.

FIGURE 33.3

The Windows Volume Control slider. Single-click the speaker on the Taskbar to get this dialog.

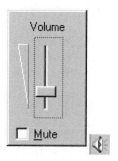

The Windows NT Mixer

After double-clicking on the speaker icon, you will be presented with the main Volume Control panel, which is very similar to many mixer utilities that come with most sound cards (see fig. 33.4).

FIGURE 33.4

The Volume Control panel is used to mix the sound as you might with an "analog" soundboard.

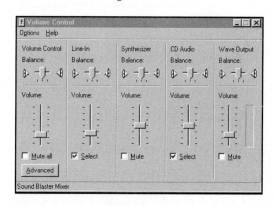

This panel is comprised of the following components:

■ **Main Volume Control.** This is a duplicate of the volume control available by single-clicking on the speaker icon. The main difference is the balance control available for all outputs.

- **Line-In.** This volume control enables you to specify the volume output of whatever source is plugged in to your line-in input of the sound card. This is the volume control you use if you have an external CD-ROM drive.

- **Synthesizer.** Next to that is the Synthesizer output control, which controls the MIDI output volume from either your sound card's MIDI device (OPL chip or Wavetable synthesis) or a dedicated MIDI interface connected to an external MIDI instrument.

- **CD Audio.** The CD volume control sets the input level of the digital audio tracks coming from your CD player. Note that it does not control the volume of a program running from a CD. In that case, you would use the Wave Output control. The CD volume control is only useful if you have your internal CD playing through your sound card. Most sound cards have internal hookups to connect the audio-out of the CD so that you can use this feature. You can also use the line-out of your external CD player to connect to the line-in on your sound card.

- **Wave Output.** Next to that is the Wave volume control. This enables you to adjust digital audio volume control. Notice also that it has an empty box next to it; that is the output level meter—a critical component when making recordings because it can tell you whether your settings are too high and might result in distortion. The level meter will come on when you are playing back WAV files in Windows.

- **Advanced.** If you select Advanced Controls from the Options pull-down menu, an Advanced button appears underneath the main Volume control. Clicking on this button brings up a panel to control the Bass and Treble settings during playback (see fig. 33.5). Adjust these as necessary to produce the best sounding playback possible.

FIGURE 33.5

The Windows Advanced Controls dialog. You can control bass and treble amounts for your sound card here.

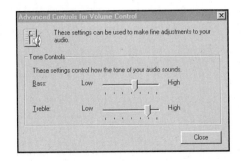

- **Recording.** If you click on the Options pull-down menu and choose Properties, you are presented with a dialog to choose a Mixer panel for various controls, one of which is Recording. Click on Recording and then on OK. A new panel that has many of the same controls as the playback Volume Control panel appears. These settings enable you to adjust how sounds are recorded.

Animating to Recorded Sounds

One of the best parts of animating in 3DS MAX is using its sound features. Out of the box, MAX can play back WAV files through a sound card as well as a metronome played through your PC internal speaker. This is useful when you are animating objects based on pre-recorded sounds. You can load up any length WAV file and position it in Track View. Figure 33.6 shows a WAV file loaded into the Sound Track of Track View.

FIGURE 33.6

The Track View with a WAV file assigned.

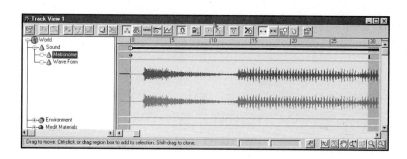

WARNING

Large WAV files consume precious amounts of RAM and may lead to hard disk paging. Use caution when working with long or high-resolution WAV files. Chop up your sound into smaller pieces so MAX can eat it.

Using WAV Files in Track View

To add WAV files in Track View, first click on the Track View icon in the MAX toolbar or choose Track View from the Edit pull-down menu. Click on the Sound entry in the Track hierarchy list, and then either click on the Properties button in the Track View toolbar or right-click and choose Properties (see fig. 33.7).

FIGURE 33.7

Track View with the Properties dialog for sound track.

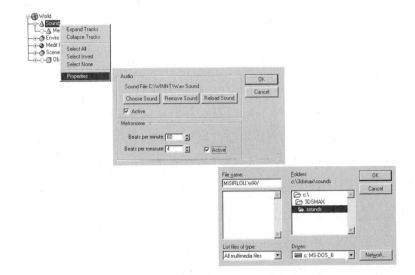

To add a sound, click on the Choose Sound button. By default, MAX looks in its Sounds directory or whichever directory is chosen for sound in the Preferences section. You can choose any file that has an audio stream attached to it. This is typically an AVI file or a WAV file. Click on OK to add your sound.

Once loaded, the sound's waveform appears in the Track View track display. By default, the beginning of the sound is aligned with frame 0 of your animation. You can use the Range Bar to position the sound anywhere in time. If the sound is shorter than the length of your animation, it is repeated as many times as necessary to reach the end. Otherwise, the sound is terminated at the end of your animation. MAX does not enable you to modify the sound in any way except altering its starting position in your scene.

To hear your sound, just click on the Play button in the MAX interface. You can also *scrub* the sound—that is, play it from the Frame Slider by dragging the slider back and forth along the Timeline. Sound can be scrubbed forward, but not backward.

NOTE

To hear sound during playback or scrubbing, the Real Time box must be checked in the Time Configuration Panel. Access this with a right-click on the Time Icon in the lower-right corner.

Sounds loaded in Track View can be attached to an AVI rendering. By default, when you have a sound active in Track View, it will automatically be attached to AVI output. This includes previews and full renderings. If you want to use the sound merely as a guide and not to be included with the final output, you must uncheck the Active option beneath the file assignment buttons within Track View.

If you are editing the sound file in a sound editing package, you can use the Reload Sound button to load the newly saved version. That way, you can just Alt+Tab between MAX and your sound editing tool. To remove a sound, click on the Remove Sound button.

Using the Metronome

The metronome is designed to provide a rhythmic, repeating beat with which to synchronize your animation. It consists of two parameters and an Active check box (see fig. 33.8).

The Beats per minute value specifies how many beats the metronome will play every minute of animation. The default, 60, means that your PC speaker will beep every second with a "low" tone. The minimum is one beat per minute.

The Beats per measure value specifies which beat of the Beats per measure value is played in a high tone. This places emphasis on that beat. The default is four, and the minimum is two. With a value of two, every other beat is emphasized.

Both values are dynamically displayed in Track View's Track display. As you adjust the Beats per minute variable, small vertical lines appear to move farther apart or closer together depending on the values you are selecting. Beats per measure are displayed graphically by black dots in the Metronome track.

NOTE

You cannot scrub the Metronome track. It can only be heard when using MAX's Playback button with the Real Time option checked on.

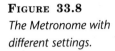

FIGURE 33.8
The Metronome with different settings.

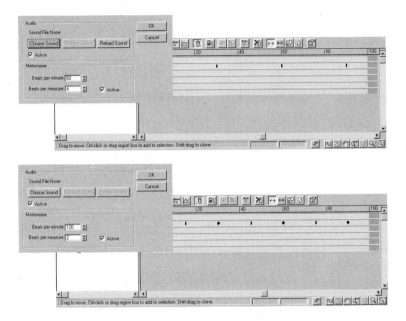

The Audio Controller Plug-In

Developers have taken it upon themselves to take advantage of the extensibility of MAX and add new sound capabilities. One of these is the Audio Controller from Kinetix. Like any other animation controller in MAX, it is used to control the behavior of an animatable property over time. In this case, instead of using math functions like the other controllers, Audio Controller uses sound. The sound can be a WAV file or recorded in real time from a microphone or CD source.

Setting Up the Audio Controller

First, make certain that the file auctl.dlc is in your Plug-ins directory or in a directory where MAX knows to find them. After that's done, all access to the Audio Controller's parameters will be in Track View. Apply the controller as you would any other controller from within Track View. After you have applied it, you can access its properties by selecting the Track name from the hierarchy display and then clicking on the Properties button. Figure 33.9 demonstrates assignment of the Audio Controller to the Rotation track.

NOTE

You cannot control the plug-in from within the Motion panel. You can, however, apply it to any of the Transform tracks there.

FIGURE 33.9

Assigning the Audio Controller to the Rotation track.

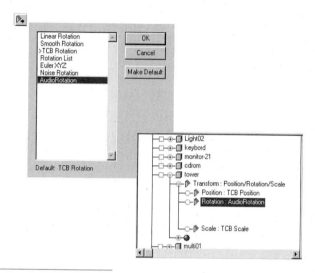

Audio Controller Parameters

As demonstrated in figure 33.10, the Audio Controller has several functions that you can edit. This section presents what those parameters are and how they can affect your overall animation. The following tutorial shows how to apply the controller and use its functions.

Choosing and removing sounds works just like assigning a sound to the sound track. The Absolute function, however, is new. Use the Absolute option when you want a sound to utilize all 256 possible levels of amplitude when working with the audio controller—even if it does not use it. This function works best when you have a recorded sound of something quiet. Because the Audio Controller works from amplitude, the resulting animation would be minor. Using the Absolute option causes the sound to be stretched out across the entire possible amplitude range, however, sending more dramatic changes in amplitude to the controller and therefore resulting in better animation.

The real-time control enables you to use an input device hooked up to your sound card to animate your objects. The devices displayed in the drop-down list are what NT knows are valid recording sources. This is typically a function of the sound card and its drivers.

FIGURE 33.10

The components of the Audio Controller window.

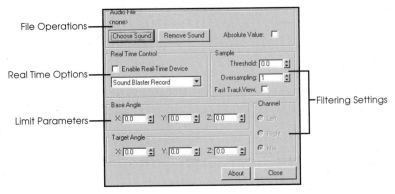

To use the Real Time option, just choose the input device from the pop-down list and then check Enabled. Animating with the Real Time option can be one of the easiest ways to do lip-sync animation. All you have to do is talk into a microphone, and you can make a character's mouth jaw flap. Mouth morph targets or animating bones or other control devices will give a more professional lip-sync, but this method is perfectly acceptable in more limited animation productions. The following paragraphs describe how to control the various animation parameters for an object.

The Sample section is for fine-tuning the values sent by the controller to the track you have assigned it. This works for both sound files as well as real-time recording. The best way to think of the Sample parameters is as a filter from the sound to the values input to the track itself. When you look at a WAV file, for example, you can usually see sharp peaks and troughs. This can cause the Audio Controller to send rather sharp values and result in "jumpy" animation. The Oversample value enables you to smooth out those peaks and troughs. The higher the Oversample value, the smoother the waveform becomes. The other value, Threshold, acts like a faucet. Based on values between 0 and 1, you specify what the cutoff point is for a sound. The higher the number, the less of a sound that actually comes through. You would use this value only if you have serious amounts of noise in the sound.

NOTE

A value of 1 for Threshold will effectively cancel out the sound's effect on that track because it filters out everything.

Another Filtering option is which channel of the sound to use: left, right, or both. If you are using a monaural WAV file or a microphone input, these options are grayed out because both channels are equal. With stereo sounds, however, you can isolate the left or right channels to suit your needs. Normally, you will leave this set to both, but sometimes one channel is louder than the other or has more distortion. In that case, choose the channel that best animates your objects.

Beyond the Filtering parameters and channel selection, you also have the ability to specify what range of movement, rotation, scaling, or values will pass from the sound to the track itself. The Audio Controller actually exists in five forms. As a result, the animating parameters or limits differ based on which type of track you have assigned them to. The five types of Audio Controllers are:

- Audio Position

- Audio Rotation

- Audio Scale

- Audio Float

- Audio Point

The three audio transforms obviously map to the respective Transform track. The Float version works with other types of animatable parameter that wouldn't use audio for position, rotation, or scaling. The Point version works with tracks where multiple limits are used (the RGB values for a diffuse color on a material, for example). Figure 33.11 shows the versions of the limits section for each type of controller.

If you are interested in seeing what the Audio Controller is capable of, the next exercise explores the application of the controller to bells of an alarm clock to cause them to vibrate wildly to an alarm clock sound.

FIGURE 33.11
*The limit values for
each of the different
types of Audio
Controllers. Note that
depending on which
controller you use, you
may have several
values to work with.*

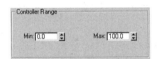

Making an Alarm Clock Ring with Audio Controller

In this exercise, you will take a look at how to use the Audio Controller to animate alarm bells on a clock character by using a WAV file. First start by opening the file of the model.

TIME TO WAKE UP

1. Select File, Open. Choose clock.max and click on OK.

The next step is to bring up Track View and expand the display so that you can see the left Bell object's Rotation tracks.

2. Click on the Track View button in the toolbar and expand the hierarchy to Clock/Left Bell/Transform/Rotation. This displays the Clock object's hierarchical structure.

The Audio Controller is assignable to any type of track. In this case, apply it to the Rotation track.

3. Click on the Rotation label to highlight it.

4. Click on the Assign to Controller button (see fig. 33.12). This brings up the Controller Assignment dialog.

FIGURE 33.12

Click on this button to assign the Audio Controller to the Rotation track.

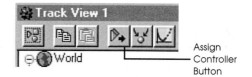

Assign Controller Button

5. Choose Audio Rotation and click on OK. This exits the dialog and assigns the new controller to the Rotation track (see fig. 33.13).

FIGURE 33.13

The Audio Controller is now assigned to the Rotation track. Note that a blank area now exists in the main track display.

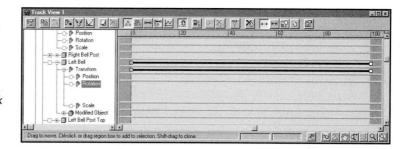

After you have applied the controller, the Rotation track's display changes a bit to make room for the WAV file you will use. As it stands right now, there are no parameters for the controller, so there is no animation. You will assign the sound file of an alarm clock's alarm going off in the Audio Controller's Control panel.

6. Right-click on the Rotation label and choose Properties.

7. Click on the Choose Sound button.

8. Select alarm.wav and click on OK. This loads the alarm clock sound and displays it in the Track display.

As soon as you assign the sound, its waveform display appears in the Rotation track. Right now, it is a bit small. You will change that through various settings in the Control panel. The first thing is to turn on the Absolute parameter.

9. Check on Absolute Value (see fig. 33.14). The displayed peaks of the alarm waveform are increased.

FIGURE 33.14

The Audio Controller
configuration
parameters for the
Rotation track.

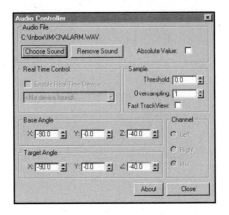

The next step is to use the Oversampling feature. With it, you can smooth out a waveform—they are generally rough. Rough sounds can make an object animate rather strangely, so it is best to use this feature most of the time.

10. Set 10 for Oversampling to smooth out the waveform.

The next set of parameters to define are the Start and End ranges for an object's animation when it uses the sound. The Base value represents an object's rotation state when the sound is at an amplitude of 0. The target value is the maximum rotation an object will have at an amplitude of 255.

11. Set the Base angle value for Y to 60.

12. Set the Target angle value for Y to 20. This changes the target angle for when the WAV file is at maximum amplitude.

13. Click on the Close button of the Audio Controller's Control panel to exit.

NOTE

Currently, there can only be one Audio Controller per scene. You can have multiple *instances* of the controller in the scene, however, to control various parameters for the object.

14. Expand the hierarchy to Clock/Right Bell/Transform/Rotation.

15. Click on the Assign to Controller button. This brings up the Replace Controller button.

16. Choose Audio Rotation and click on OK. This exits the dialog and assigns the new controller to the Rotation track.

17. Right-click and hold on the Rotation label and choose Properties to bring up the Audio Controller's Control panel.

18. Click on the Choose Sound button to bring up the Select File dialog.

19. Click on OK to load alarm.wav and display it in the Track display.

TIP

Because the Audio Controller can only work with one sound at a time, the last sound loaded is stored in any Audio Controller you apply. All you have to do is click on OK after you have clicked on Choose Sound.

20. Turn on Absolute and set Oversampling to 10 to assign the same parameters to the new controller.

21. Set the Base angle value for Y to –60. This changes the base angle so that there is no sound from the WAV file.

22. Set the Target angle value for Y to –20. This changes the target angle for when the WAV file is at maximum amplitude.

23. Click on the Close button of the Audio Controller's Control panel to exit the Control panel.

NOTE

The reason why you didn't instance the Audio Controller from the left bell to the right was that all values, including base and target angles, would be instanced. Because the bells are rotated at different angles, instancing would have produced the wrong result.

You are done! All that's left is to make a preview. If you like the preview, you can do a complete rendering afterward.

24. Make certain that the Perspective view is active and choose Rendering/Make Preview. This brings up the Make Preview dialog.

25. Click on Create to create the preview.

NOTE

The Audio Controller does not play back the audio in MAX. If you want to create a preview with the sound attached, assign the alarm.wav file to the Sound track in Track View.

Remember, the Audio Controller is assignable to any track. The main difference to you is what you see in the dialog. Applying the Audio Controller to the Rotation track, for instance, uses the Audio Rotation controller. That controller has parameters specific to rotation when using sound. On the other hand, applying it to the Angle track of a Bend modifier will use the Audio Float controller, which has slightly different settings.

The Absolute parameter makes the sound file use a complete range of 256 levels of amplitude, even if it doesn't have it originally. This parameter helps when you have a relatively minor sound by making the highest amplitude be a value of 255 and the lowest 0. Think of it as scaling the sound file's amplitude to fit the entire range possible for digital sound.

By changing the Oversampling, you can see a visible difference in the waveform display. If the object's animation is too smooth or "watered" down, lower the value. If it is still too "jumpy" or rough, increase the value. Displaying a large oversampled sound file can tax the Track View display and cause slow redraws. If this is happening to you, check on the Fast Track View parameter. This returns the display to the original waveform, but still uses the oversampled sound file for animation purposes.

If you want to enhance the animation a bit, you can assign the Noise modifier to the clock's body for both scale and position. That way, when the bells go off, the clock's whole body shakes. See the file clockcmp.max on the accompanying CD to get a better idea of how to set this up.

In Practice: Sound in MAX

- **Sound in the 3D world:** Traditionally, audio has never been part of the world of 3D modeling and animation packages. Today, with sight and sound merging more and more through multimedia, companies such as Kinetix and the Yost Group realize the need to implement sound into a visual software package. In the future, you will see even better integration. MAX's sound features are a testament to that fact.

- **Out-of-box capabilities:** Audio capabilities in MAX are quite extensive out of the box. You can completely animate a scene based on a WAV file or to a metronome.

- **Sound plug-ins:** With the extensibility of MAX, it is now possible to add your own types of sound features through plug-ins such as the Audio Controller. Expect to see more of this in the future.

INSIDE

3D STUDIO MAX

BONUS MATERIAL

JASON GRAY

JASON GREENE

WILLIAM HARBISON

SERIES EDITOR:
PHILLIP MILLER

JESSE K. MIGUEL, AIA

MICHAEL TODD PETERSON

Part X

BONUS MATERIAL

IMAGE BY JASON GREENE

by Jason Greene

COMPOSITING, RETOUCHING, AND POST-PROCESSING WITH PHOTOSHOP

For anyone working with computer graphics, Adobe Photoshop is an indispensable, powerful, and wondrous tool. It is rare to find a 3D artist who hasn't spent time with Photoshop's extensive tool set; it has proven to be a top-notch tool for creating rich, tactile textures and a necessity for preparing still renderings for printing. Additionally, Photoshop can serve as a powerful post-processing tool for your 3D Studio MAX renderings, including both still images and animation.

When 3D artists use 3DS MAX for the first time, there are two things that they see: all the new features and an entirely new methodology for generating 3D graphics. The release of Photoshop 4.0 has culled similar feelings from its users, simultaneously causing excitement and frustration. Be assured, however, that this update of Photoshop moves in the same direction as the update of the 3D Studio series—toward providing the artist with the most advanced controls and the best tools for exploring their creativity.

This chapter covers compositing, retouching, and post-processing work as well as this following topics with regards to Photoshop 4.0 use. Many of the techniques this chapter covers, however, can be applied to earlier versions of Photoshop as well as other image-editing applications:

- Compositing: Video Post (automatic) versus Photoshop (manual)
- Working with Photoshop layers
- Creating and using masks
- Adjustment layers and blending modes
- Using the Actions palette for batch processing

Compositing: Video Post (Automatic) Versus Photoshop (Manual)

3DS MAX contains a powerful post-processing tool of its own, known simply as Video Post. In addition to providing an additional channel to produce special effects (such as lens flares), Video Post provides strong compositing features as well. Many of these features are so well implemented that at times Photoshop can be avoided altogether, and stunning output can be developed without ever leaving 3DS MAX.

You will find, however, that as your production needs grow, so does your need for external post-processing. Although Video Post can do a superb job of combining a rendered 3DS MAX object with external bitmap images (whether they be photographs or other already-rendered images), it falls short in a few key areas.

One shortcoming of Video Post is that it cannot be used interactively; once executed, Video Post runs its predefined series of instructions until it's done. If a compositing process doesn't turn out the way you planned in Video Post, you must go back through your hierarchical instruction list debugging, checking settings, and re-executing—a tedious, technical process that isn't friendly to artistically driven folk with a particular look and feel in mind for their final image.

Performing these same operations in Photoshop—although requiring manual, hands-on work—provides much more satisfying results and gives the user greater control. Soft edges are applied between layers of objects and backgrounds, field-of-view and focus are altered with ease, color balance is instantly tweaked back and forth, and light and shadows affect all objects and layers in a composition. Best of all, with Photoshop 4.0, this is all endlessly tweaked without ever affecting the source images. The addition of the Actions palette makes it possible for many of these post-processing features to be applied to thousands of frames of animation at the click of a mouse.

If your project demands rendering an animated object moving across or around a stationary background, however, you are definitely better off rendering your entire animation and compositing onto the background in Video Post. Your instruction set will be simple (four steps) and can be performed in conjunction with the rendering operation.

It's a project-by-project decision that you must make, and it's best if you make it early. Determining post-processing time and requirements is a necessary and major step in the timing and budgeting of projects, not to mention in the simple capability to deliver on what you've set out to do.

Working with Photoshop Layers

Before delving into the details of editing and post-processing, the following is a brief overview of the heart of Photoshop's compositing power: the Layers feature.

Navigating and Manipulating Layers

How does Photoshop define layers? Think of it this way: Each layer is a completely transparent sheet that is stacked above or below another layer. If something is filled in or painted onto one of these sheets, it is seen through any other sheet that is transparent in that same area. Only one layer, the "background" layer, is not fully transparent. As is demonstrated in figure 34.1, the circle and square layers overlap against the "background" layer.

FIGURE 34.1

The use of the Layers feature complete with user-created Background, Text, Circle, and Square layers.

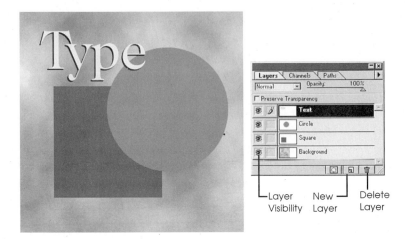

One of the first things you must learn about layer manipulation is how to move the image content of a layer. Imagine sliding panes of colored glass, creating different image and color combinations with each movement, almost like a kaleidoscope. Photoshop does a remarkable job of maintaining the transparency values among layers, which makes for spectacular control when compositing a 3D rendered object with a non-3D element such as a photographic background or 2D type.

To move a layer's contents, first select the layer by clicking on the layer name or thumbnail. Once the layer is highlighted, click on the Move tool in the toolbar (see fig. 34.2) or hold down the Ctrl key. Your mouse cursor should now look like the Move tool icon. Click and drag in the image window to move the layer's contents in any direction. For precise movement, use the arrow keys with the Move tool selected or while holding down the Ctrl key. Each click of an arrow key moves the layer one pixel, and holding down the Shift key while pressing an arrow key moves the layer in 10 pixel increments.

TIP

With any tool in Photoshop (including brushes), you can constrain movement to horizontal (X axis) or vertical (Y axis) by holding down the Shift key while you drag with the mouse.

Another type of layer movement has to do with movement within the vertical space of the Layers palette—you can restack them in any way you like, making certain objects and images appear in front or behind others. To move a layer vertically in the Layers palette, click either the layer name or its thumbnail and drag the layer up or down through the Layers palette. A solid black line appears between the layers as you drag it, showing where the layer will be inserted when the mouse button is released.

FIGURE 34.2

The Photoshop tool palette and icons for its various tools.

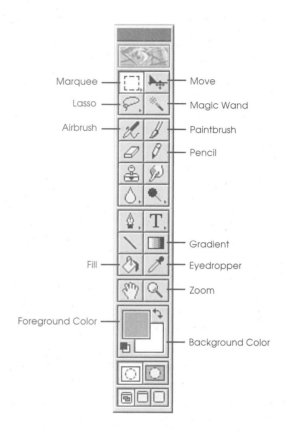

In figure 34.1, moving the layer named Square to the top brings the square to the foreground in the image. Likewise, moving the layer named Background to just above another layer places the background in front, obscuring the layer beneath. This is one of the key advantages to compositing and post-processing in Photoshop as compared to Video Post; for example, by rendering separate elements of your scene out to Photoshop and placing them on their own layers, you'll have infinite, precise control of the placement of each element. Imagine having four separate 3D objects that need to be composited against a photographic background. Simply render each individual object by itself onto a solid color, bring each rendered graphic and background into Photoshop, and you can begin to assemble your scene. You'll notice that by simply moving the layers your objects are on, you can place those objects in front of and behind each other.

The following is a brief list of other layer controls:

- **Hiding layers.** To hide a layer from view, click the eye icon in the Layers palette, which is located to the left of the layer, as in figure 34.1. Click on the same space to make it visible again.

- **Creating new layers.** To create a new layer, click on the New Layer icon at the bottom of the palette. To create a copy of a layer, drag any layer on top of the New Layer icon (refer to fig. 34.1). To delete a layer, click on the Trash Can icon with the layer selected.

With Photoshop 4.0, whenever you paste something into your file, Photoshop automatically creates a new layer to hold the contents of what you've just pasted. This is seen as both a blessing and a curse. When you bring in multiple elements for composition against a background, this is a great feature to have. As you paste each element into your file, a layer is assigned to each, making it much easier to move layers. The "curse" is that many times you don't want to have different layers for everything, and Photoshop doesn't make it easy to paste directly into a layer; you first need to paste (which creates a new layer for the stuff you've pasted) and then merge those two layers, which can possibly trash Layer Masks, Adjustment Layers, and any blending modes in one click.

WARNING

Be aware that if you delete the background layer that is created by Photoshop with every new image, you may no longer have a solid background—only do this if you're going to be compositing a full-frame background into your image.

To rename a layer, double-click on the layer name or its thumbnail image. The other options in the Layer Options pop-up box, Opacity, Blending Mode, and Blend If… are reviewed later in the chapter in the section, "Adjustment Layers and Blending Modes."

TIP

Most of these commands, as well as most menu commands in Photoshop, can be accessed by clicking the right mouse button over a selected layer (or any object or tool). Experiment freely with right mouse-clicking throughout Photoshop. It changes greatly for every tool and every function, and it can speed your production time greatly.

Creating and Using Layer Masks

Okay, so you've opened your background image and all the rendered objects that you want to composite. You've also pasted those objects into your Photoshop image as separate layers, with your background image as the bottom layer in the Layers palette. The problem is that the only thing visible is the top layer. It's time to look at Photoshop's Layer Mask features.

Two methods define a layer's transparency: image content and mask definition.

TIP

When working on individual layers, especially with masks and transparencies, it's best to disable the visibility of all other layers, including your background layer. This enables you to see exactly how Photoshop views the transparency of each layer. Any transparent areas of the layer show through to the Transparency Grid, which as a default is a gray-and-white checkerboard.

Image content with regards to transparency is quite simple. On any layer, where there is no image content, the layer is transparent. Don't confuse the color white with no image content. As far as Photoshop is concerned, white pixels are the same as red, green, and blue pixels in layer transparencies. To create areas of your layer that are empty of image content, delete areas of the image from your layer. To do so, select a portion of your image with either the Marquee tool or the Lasso tool (refer to fig. 34.2) and press Delete. This removes the selected portion entirely and from the selected layer only. By using a combination of the various Marquee, Lasso, and Path tools you can gradually work around your image, deleting parts that should be transparent. This process, however, is quite tedious and is often irreversible. This is why using Layer Masks is good for most compositing work.

A Layer Mask can best be described as a type of modifier for a layer: It defines the areas of a particular layer that are visible, as well as the transparency or opaqueness in certain areas of a layer. By using the grayscale range from white to black, the Layer Mask can act much like a part of the modifier stack in 3DS MAX. It can always be altered, without affecting the original image or any other layers in the file.

The general principle behind a Layer Mask is that whatever is masked from visibility on a particular layer will be transparent on other layers. To illustrate what this means, a basic example of compositing is given.

Pretend that you want to composite two pieces: a 3D-rendered apple and a photograph of a wooden table. The first step is to open the photograph image into Photoshop, crop it to whatever image borders you prefer, and resize it if necessary. This photograph serves as your background, or bottom-most layer. Figure 34.3 is an image brought into Adobe Photoshop by scanning an original photograph. By using layers and adjustment layers, you will soon notice a difference in the composition of the photograph.

The next step is to bring the 3D apple into the same file. If the apple has not been rendered onto a solid, constant-color background, that's fine. One of the great bonuses of working with a Layer Mask in Photoshop is that working without solid or consistent backgrounds is not nearly the hassle it can be with other composition programs. A solid color background, however, can make the masking process slightly faster, so be sure to render with a solid background whenever possible (see fig. 34.4).

FIGURE 34.4

The picture of a 3D rendered apple before being added via layers to the table.

Tip

When rendering a solid background, it's best to choose a color with an RGB value that is the most different from that of the rendered object. An apple with a dark, reddish tone, for example, may have a predominant RGB value of 150, 20, 20. Flip those values around (this can be done by subtracting them from 255) and you'll get a value of 105, 235, 235, which translates into a bright blue. In this case, the sky blue color clearly offsets the dark red; but the important factor here is in the RGB values, because that's how Photoshop views its colors. Often, using just your eyes to pick an opposite color will actually result in choosing a color that is more similar, at least according to Photoshop. This can result in extra work during the compositing process.

To bring the 3D apple image into the same file as the photograph, open the rendered file, then copy and paste the entire contents into the photograph image. Photoshop automatically creates a layer for the 3D apple. The apple layer should be the highlighted layer (see fig. 34.5).

FIGURE 34.5
The 3D apple rendered with a solid color background.

The next step is to create a Quick Mask. You have two options, both dependent on how your source file was rendered. The next exercise takes you through the steps.

Creating a Quick Mask from a File with a Solid Background

1. If the file has a solid background, a good starting point for the Quick Mask is to mask out the solid color. The quickest way to do this is to use the Magic Wand tool. Double-click on the Magic Wand tool to access the

tool's options while making sure the tolerance is set fairly low. The tolerance determines the range of colors surrounding the solid color that the Magic Wand selects. A value of 1 selects only that exact color; a value of 255 selects everything on the layer. A value less than 32 is generally recommended when masking a solid color.

2. After setting the tolerance, click once on the background color. If the apple were rendered with a light blue background, this would make a moving dotted-line selection (also known as *marching ants*) that encloses all the blue.

3. Because you want to use the apple for composition onto the table (and not the blue background), invert the selection (choose Select, Inverse from the Menu bar or press Ctrl+Shift+I). This creates a selection that encloses only the apple.

4. Now that you've defined the area that will remain visible (and opaque), create the Quick Mask by clicking on the Create Mask icon. This adds the mask "modifier" to the layer. Looking at the Layers palette, the Layer Mask appears just to the right of the Layer thumbnail, looking like a black-and-white cutout of your selection. The apple's layer should now look like figure 34.6.

Layer Mask applied (and linked to layer)

FIGURE 34.6

The 3D apple with a layer mask applied. Note the black-and-white thumbnail of the apple's layer mask.

Create Mask

Looking at the thumbnail of the layer mask in figure 34.6, you see that anything represented in white remains visible, and anything in black is now invisible. Additionally, anything covered by the black area is now transparent, enabling any layers beneath it to show through, which in this case is the table.

If your rendered file doesn't have a solid background, extra touch-up is required. Many artists prefer the method outlined in the following tutorial even when they are given an image with a solid background because every method requires touch-up at some point. No method is right or wrong, or better or worse—it's whatever feels best to the user.

CREATING A QUICK MASK FROM A FILE WITHOUT A SOLID BACKGROUND

1. Outline the object. The quickest method of doing this is to select the Lasso tool and trace around the outside of the object. Don't worry if you cut into the object or stray far from the edges. This can all be adjusted in the mask after it is created.

   For skilled Photoshop users, it is recommended that selections be defined either by using the Polygon Lasso tool or by using the Path tool. The Path tool offers the greatest control because paths can be saved and the control points re-edited. The Path tool works much like the Bézier line creation tools used in Adobe Illustrator, Macromedia FreeHand, and CorelDRAW. See the Photoshop manual for more information on using the Path tool and converting a path into a selection.

2. After your traced selection is made (and the ants are marching around your object), click on the Create Mask icon at the bottom of the Layers palette. A thumbnail of the mask should appear to the right of the image layer thumbnail; anything represented in black is no longer visible (and transparent, enabling other layers to show through), and everything in white is visible and opaque (refer to fig. 34.6).

Before scaling down the composited object to the necessary size and placing it on the table, it's best to get your Layer Mask perfectly set. This involves editing and painting into the Layer Mask. The next exercise shows you how to fine-tune your mask.

FINE-TUNING YOUR MASK

1. Click once on the Layer Mask thumbnail to select it. You'll notice that your color palette is now switched to a grayscale palette because you'll work directly in the mask. As long as the mask is selected, all selections, deletions, painting, and filters you apply pertain to the Layer Mask only.

2. Zoom in on the object to view it close-up. This enables you to see the pixels that define the edges of your object. In the case of the apple, a few blue pixels might be scattered here and there. Additionally, portions of your object might not be visible that should be (perhaps a shadowed or highlighted edge, for example).

3. Clean up the areas that need it. Cleanup of these areas is quite simple and is accomplished in a variety of methods. The basic concept is to fill in the areas that you want to be seen with white, and to black out the areas that you want to be invisible and transparent. The Airbrush tool works great in this situation, using both hard-edged (for a defined edge) and soft-edged (for a shadowed or highlighted edge) brushes to make corrections. The closer you zoom in, the better you can adjust the mask.

   Additionally, by painting with some of the grays that fall in the spectrum between black and white, you can gain various levels of transparency. Many times a darker gray tone is better suited for some of the finer edges of an object, because it requires less precision to accurately mask the edge and also blur the edge a bit, making for a smoother composition.

NOTE

This is a major reason why so many 2D artists swear by pressure-sensitive tablets; personally, I don't know how I could live without mine. By using the Airbrush tool and varying stylus pressures, I can work with the entire range of black to white, as well as the size of brushes, providing the ultimate control when masking edges of objects for compositing work.

The best thing about using a mask is that you're not truly deleting anything—just painting back and forth between visible and invisible. You're never risking or compromising the original image, and anything you do in a mask can always be undone.

After you're satisfied with your mask, you can proceed to other tasks such as scaling, rotating, and positioning your object to appear in just the right spot.

One of Photoshop's greatest strengths is its capability to apply all such image operations to both the image and the mask simultaneously—this enables you to start working with one mask and keep the mask for the duration of the project, requiring only slight alterations as your image requirements change.

WARNING

Whenever you transform (move, scale, or rotate) your object layer, ensure that both the image layer and the layer mask are linked (refer to "apple" layer in fig. 34.6). If they're not linked, the operation will only be performed in either the image layer or the layer mask (whichever you've got selected), but not both.

Adjustment Layers and Blending Modes

In most cases, compositing won't end with masking objects and layers together. Often, the lighting between objects and background is different, the color saturation is off, shadows appear with inconsistent length and depth; you name it. Once again, however, Photoshop can make all of these operations to correct these problems virtually painless and infinitely adjustable, all without compromising your original image. Groovy.

Managing Color, Levels, Brightness/Contrast, and Curves with Adjustment Layers

Perhaps the most anticipated and useful new feature set of Photoshop 4.0 is the addition of Adjustment Layers. Adjustment Layers work in a similar manner to Layer Masks in that they act as layer Modifiers that can always be adjusted without changing the source image, and can be set to adjust only the layers the user wants.

Adjustment Layers can be used to make the following modifications to a layer (or set of layers):

- **Levels.** Adjust amounts of light and dark, median luminosity; extremely useful for brightening lighter areas and darkening shadows, wonderful for creating bump maps.

- **Curves.** Adjust individual RGB or CMYK color ranges without affecting the other values; for example, to make grass greener without adding noticeable green to anything else.

- **Brightness/Contrast.** Adjust the overall brightness and contrast of a level; an option with limited uses due to its global approach.

- **Color Balance.** Shift the balance of color in three ranges: shadows, midtones, and highlights. Can often be used to fix color imbalances instead of Curves, due largely to a simpler interface with less room for error; great for experimenting.

- **Hue/Saturation.** At times klunky, but a powerful tool for changing base color as well as saturation; for example, handy for changing a predominantly red image to a predominantly blue image.

- **Selective Color.** This is another alternative to Curves. Enables you to pick a range of colors (reds, yellows, greens, cyans, blues, magentas, whites, neutrals, blacks) and modify them based on CMYK values. Not as advanced as Curves, but more powerful than Color Balance. Excellent for novice color correction when producing an image for print.

- **Invert.** Inverts the color values of the entire image; usually used for creating background effects rather than modifying a particular object. No usable options, but handy to have as an adjustment layer.

- **Threshold.** On its own, looks purely at a range of colors and converts them to black or white (the median is adjustable). Used in combination with masks and Blending Modes (see the later section, "Adding That "Special Touch": Blending Modes") can produce some stunning results.

- **Posterize.** Similar to Threshold, except that it will generate a range of solid colors. Can produce similarly wondrous results when used with masks and Blending Modes.

Determining which adjustment level to use for which purpose depends mostly on two factors: whatever you feel comfortable using (most important) and the end result you're trying to achieve. Experienced Photoshop artists and retouchers often add multiple adjustment layers to an image layer, each adjustment layer building off the previous one.

This is where ordering can become important. This is much like using the modifier stack; for example, each Adjustment Layer affects all the layers beneath it but not the layers above it. Applying both Color Balance and Posterize adjustment layers to an image can return two entirely different results, depending on the order in which they're stacked. Applying a Color Balance first followed by a Posterize generally results in a much more color-splashed, saturated image, similar to Warhol's famous portrait of Marilyn

Monroe. By applying a Posterize first, however, Color Balance then is used to give a softer, less-saturated image, with wider swaths of solid color as seen in a late nineteenth century Toulouse-Lautrec poster.

Unlike MAX, Photoshop enables much more freedom moving around both Image Layers and Adjustment Layers—you'll never have a problem with losing certain parameters of a modifier stack or rearranging the stack; and better yet, you can *always* Undo.

To apply an Adjustment Layer, first select the Image Layer that you would like to adjust, add an Adjustment Layer, and link the Adjustment Layer to the image layer by holding down the Alt key and clicking on the dividing line between the two layers (this is assuming you don't want to adjust all of the layers in your image). After that, anytime you want to change the settings for the adjustment, you can double-click on its layer and tweak away. By linking the adjustment layer, you ensure that any settings you change affect only a single layer, rather than the entire image. To see how a linked Adjustment Layer appears in the Layers palette see figure 34.7.

FIGURE 34.7
An Adjustment Layer added and linked to the apple layer.

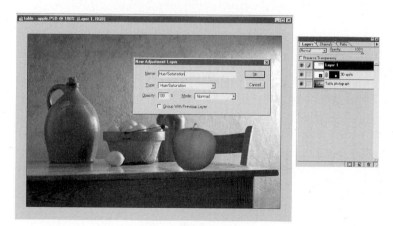

You've now learned half of the features available to image layers. The second half, Blending Modes, can both replace or complement Adjustment Layers.

Adding That "Special Touch": Blending Modes

Blending Modes are of just as much importance to adjusting the appearance of your image as Adjustment Layers, because they provide many features that enhance the overall design and composition of your work. Whereas

Adjustment Layers serve primarily to fix problems such as lighting inconsistencies and under/over saturation for individual pieces. Blending Modes tend to work on a more relational basis, combining the colors that define each layer in a complementary way to produce the desired effect or look.

Blending Modes can be used to filter images, giving images the appearance of being photographed or filmed with a particular camera or lens. They can also be used to bring texture into a piece. Many 3D artists began as traditional artists, and sometimes feel disappointed in the flat appearance of a rendered scene. Blending Modes, especially when combined with Adjustment Layers, can bring a traditional artistic feel to computer graphics, whether it means simulating a canvas-like texture, emphasizing and de-emphasizing edge definition, or simply by providing a finishing polish to the image, adding to its color depth and definition.

The Blending Mode for a particular layer can be specified by selecting it from the menu at the top of the Layers palette. Unlike Adjustment Layers, Blending Modes have no direct settings because the results are defined by the content of the actual layers. A Blending Mode for a layer can be changed at any time without ever affecting the content of the layer. Additionally, the order in which you stack layers makes a great deal of difference when it comes to Blending Modes.

N OTE

Blending Modes do have a small amount of adjustability. You can specify to what degree the blending mode works based on grayscale values. Double-click on the layer to access the Layer Options pop-up; by adjusting the Blend If... values for "this layer" and "underlying layer" you can tweak the amount of blending that occurs between layers. See the Photoshop manual for more information on this feature.

In the following list of Blending Modes, Original Colors refers to the appearance of all visible colors contained in layers *below* the selected layer; Blending Colors refers to the colors on the selected layer (the layer to which you're applying a Blending Mode); and Final Colors refers to the appearance of colors in the final image.

The following is a list of all the Blending Modes:

- **Normal.** This is the default mode, in which each pixel on a layer covers up any pixels on layers below it, regardless of color.

- **Dissolve.** Briefly, this mode replaces the pixels of the blending colors in a random fashion, in what can best be described as a spattering pattern. The appearance of the final colors depends largely on the opacity setting of the layer. The more transparent a layer, the more pixelated the colors become. This is a great tool for creating texture and bump maps, but has little use as a tool for compositing an image. The pixelated blending is akin to generating a noise-like result—generating and controlling noise within Photoshop can be done in much better ways.

- **Multiply.** This mode produces darker, more saturated colors by multiplying the original colors with the blending colors. If one of the multiplied colors is white, the final colors wind up unchanged. Multiplying any color with black always produces black. This mode has two strong uses:

  In dealing with black-and-white images (b/w looks great in 3D), stacking identical layers on top of one another and applying the Multiply mode produces a sharper, more contrasted image. This is great for compositing pieces that may not utilize the same spectrum of light and dark, because it equalizes them. This is similar to utilizing the Levels Adjustment Layer, but accepts the values of the original colors instead of manually input values.

  When compositing layers of other colors, however, Multiply serves a different purpose. Rather than being used as a tool to composite one object or layer with another, Multiply can be used to alter the layer's appearance. One way to think of this is to imagine drawing over the original colors with Magic Markers—repeated strokes turn the colors underneath the ink darker and darker. Another way to think of this is to imagine placing an acetate of color over an image: a sheet of red acetate adds a red tint to all lighted areas, as it darkens and de-emphasizes the shadowed areas. This effect is great for FX work because this is the exact look you want if your scene or animation requires that infrared look.

- **Screen.** This is basically an opposite of Multiply. This multiplies the *inverse* of the original and blending colors. Screening anything with black leaves the original colors unchanged, whereas screening with white produces white. Think of this effect as bleaching your image. This effect can be used to simulate an area of film that has been overexposed or when a camera focuses on an overlit area (a great alternative for those of us tired of lens flares).

- **Overlay.** This combines both Multiply and Screen into one blend, preserving both highlights and shadows of the original colors. Overlay acts as if you're mixing (rather than replacing) original colors with blending colors. This is the best mode to use if you want to apply a tint to your image (for example, if an object is rendered out with a flat, yellowish hued light but the image it needs to be composited with contains a strong amount of bluish light). If the object drives the scene, the background image can be overlaid with the image's yellow light; if the object needs to fit within the scene, overlay the object with a bluish hue picked up from the background image.

- **Soft Light.** Both darkens and lightens original colors based on the luminosity of the blending colors. If the luminosity of the blending color is above middle gray (51 percent or greater), the image appears to be lightened by the blending colors, producing a soft hue of the blending color. Conversely, if the luminosity is below middle gray, the image appears darkened, increasing color saturation and darkening shadows.

  The Soft Light effect is most similar to lighting an object or area with a diffused light and a colored gel; it can serve direct purposes to 3D compositors. Volumetric lights and glows, for example, can be better simulated by using a lighter color, such as airbrushing a bright yellow over a light source. As the light generated by the rendering falls off, so does the amount of yellow.

  When using darker colors, the results are similar to that of using an Overlay. Rather than tint the entire image with an Overlay, Soft Light performs much better with a scene where lighting is important. Overlaying a scene with a slight orange or brown tint gives it an orange or brown appearance, often producing clashing, unacceptable color ranges, applying the color to the entire scene. Using Soft Light and an orange or brown tint, however—especially with a scene utilizing volumetric lighting—appears to affect only the lighting. This is perfect for giving a scene a dusty, dry appearance without losing any of your original color.

- **Hard Light.** Runs the opposite direction of Soft Light, multiplying or screening the original colors depending on the luminosity of the blending color. A luminosity higher than middle gray lightens the entire image, much in the way a Screen Blend mode does, but by adding more of the blending color. Likewise, a luminosity lower than middle gray (49 percent or less) darkens the image as a Multiply blend would, but again with a tint more akin to the original colors.

Whereas Soft Light is useful for affecting an entire image, Hard Light is invaluable for touching up areas of an image. Highlights can be enhanced or created by using a lighter color. Used over light sources, a diffused, foggy appearance can be simulated. Using a darker color can add depth to existing shadows or create new shadows, while still retaining the properties of the image. If shadows in the original image contain a blue cast, for example, painting shadows into a layer using a Hard Light blending create shadows with the same blue cast. This certainly makes touching up light and shadow much easier!

- **Color Dodge and Color Burn.** Depending on the original colors, this mode either brightens (Dodge) or darkens (Burn) the appearance of the image to approximate the blending color. For compositors, both of these blending modes are useful for touching up areas of an image rather than affecting the entire image. A Color Burn can be used to de-emphasize highlights, such as a visible light source (an exposed bulb, for example). Painting with the same color of light from the original image and using Color Burn is much like turning down the dimmer switch, but without affecting the ambient light in the entire scene. Likewise, painting with Color Dodge can create areas of light color saturation, perfect for softening or lightening areas of backgrounds such as the sky or for toning down the detail in a overpowering texture.

  For FX artists, both Color Dodge and Color Burn can produce wild results. Affecting an entire image of Color Dodge when using a gradient fill of colors can produce a wild, glowing, neon-like environment in which only the color black remains unaffected—similar to the effect used when looking through a Heat Sensor. Using a Solid (or Gradient) Fill on top of a Color Burn can create a great effect for simulating drastically changing light conditions—such as the setting sun—especially when animating a Gradient Fill that ranges from white to yellow to dark red.

- **Darken and Lighten.** These functions demonstrate how straightforward Blending Modes can be. Lighten and Darken compare original and blending colors and use either the darker or lighter of the two to define the final colors. With Darken, colors lighter than the blending color are replaced; with Lighten, colors darker than the blending color are replaced. Darken and Lighten is a simple tool with simple results. Better results might be achieved with Multiply and Screen.

- **Difference.** In a nutshell, Difference reverses your color values, producing unique color combinations. This mode subtracts both the blending and original colors from the other, depending on which has a greater luminance. The unpredictability of this mode combined with the often-bizarre results makes you wonder why it's even here at all—after all, if you wanted these types of results in your finished product, you would probably design it this way from the beginning. Has immense use for print designers (especially poster makers) in the 2D world, and limited use for FX artists. Can be fun to play with late at night!

■ **Exclusion.** Nearly identical to Difference, although Exclusion produces a softer, more usable result. Still, this Blending Mode tends to take away from the depth of your 3D image, rather than add to it, giving a flat, untextured look.

■ **Hue.** Combines the hue of the blending color with the saturation and luminance of the original colors. For a quick change of colors, this is the best solution—your lights and shadows remain, along with all texture details, only changing the predominant color of the affected area. Best use here is for taking an entire scene or composited image and changing the color cast (for example, changing a predominantly blue scene to a predominantly green scene). Also an excellent tool for taking a series of objects or images and uniting to a common color cast.

■ **Saturation.** Combines the saturation of the blending color with the hue and luminance of the original colors. An excellent mode when you want to increase color saturation of an entire image or just bring out a few particular colors or areas of an image, such as enhance a red glow from a burning furnace.

■ **Color.** Combines the hue and saturation of the blending color with the luminance of the original colors. For applying slight tints to color images or coloring select areas of black-and-white images, this mode can't be beat because it keeps the gray levels of the image constant. An excellent tool for touching up texture maps and parts of objects, such as applying a heat-sourced glow to the hot spot of an object. Also a great mode to use when creating and modifying texture maps; it enables you to edit colors of the texture map without affecting the underlying (grayscale) bump map.

■ **Luminosity.** Combines the luminance of the blending color with the hue and saturation of the original colors. Luminosity mode is basically the opposite of the Color mode and can serve to Blur or Detexturize areas of an image. A handy tool for creating quick post-production fog or clouded areas—any areas affected by the Luminosity mode are fogged over without needing to have the fog itself be visible. Luminosity can often be used as a good alternative to rendering with Environment Settings and their incremental additions to rendering time.

Blending Modes are used best when they are placed on their own layers rather than on the layer you're modifying; just create a new layer directly above the layer you want to modify, choose the Blending Mode for the layer (these can be selected and changed at any time), and paint away. If you are working with a variety of layers and images, it's recommended that you bind this new Blending Mode layer to only the layer you want by holding down the Alt key and clicking on the dividing line between your source layer and your layer containing the Blending Mode. See figure 34.8 to see a blending mode linked to a single layer.

FIGURE 34.8

Modifying the color for the apple by painting into a layer with a Color Blending mode applied. Note the layer is linked to the apple.

These Blending Modes are not just limited to Layer use; brushes can also utilize Blending Modes. Be aware however, that choosing a Soft Light mode for your Airbrush and painting into a new layer produces a different effect from painting a Normal mode into a new layer with Soft Light applied to the layer; this is because Airbrush mode does not calculate the other layers in the image—only the content of the layer itself. Painting onto a new blank layer means that the blending color of the brush is combined with the original color of the layer only—white.

To use the Blending mode of a brush, paint directly onto the image layer. If you want to color a portion of a black-and-white image but not work in separate layers, for example, select the layer containing the source image, choose the appropriate brush, double-click on the brush to access its options, and select the Color Blending mode. Then you can work directly on the image and receive the same end results you would by working in separate layers. Be aware however, that you gain nothing in this manner aside from using fewer layers (and therefore less memory), but you lose all the ability to modify, change, and undo your Image Editing.

Stick with Layers.

Bringing It All Together: Polishing Your Composition

Let's return to the example of compositing the 3D rendered apple onto the photograph of a table. You already brought both images into the same file as separate layers, and created a layer mask for the apple to separate its background color and composite it with the table. Now it's time to balance the color and contrast of the composition.

Balancing the Color and Contrast of the Composition

The next task ahead—one that's just as important as properly compositing a 3D image—is balancing the color and contrast of both the apple and table, and then adjusting lighting and shadow on the apple to make it part of the scene.

Assume that the background photo of the table has been photographed with soft lighting, long shadows, and has been developed with a strong sepia tone. It seems that a single light source is coming from high above and to the right of the table. As a 3D artist, many of the skills you employ while using 3DS MAX in setting up a scene can be employed similarly to analyze an existing scene, in this case a photograph. While compositing any image, it's a good idea to have the original photo visible in a separate location from the one you're compositing. If you have the original photo, tape it to your monitor. If not, open up a second image window of the photo. Try to keep both the compositing window and the original window open at all times, so that you can always compare both images.

The next step is to determine your plan of attack in finalizing your composition. Although many of Photoshop 4.0's tools have been designed to facilitate frequent change at any time in the project, some steps, such as adding shadows, are accomplished best only after more general steps, like matching color saturation and tone have been accomplished.

With that in mind, the first step is to match the colors of the apple (deep, saturated red) to that of the background table photograph (soft, unsaturated browns and tans). The first thing you must do is compare the apple to the background. Ask yourself a few questions. Are the edges of the apple soft like the edges of the table in the background? Does the apple have any highlights or shiny areas? Because the apple was rendered in 3D, it most definitely has sharp edges, and although specular highlights were not part of the texture map during rendering, the lighting was positioned differently on the apple than on the background table.

Because the lighting is controlled by the 3D designer, the best results are usually produced by rerendering the object (the apple). Although many artists can reproduce lighting falloff and the subtleties that appear deep in highlights, remember that this is one thing that 3DS MAX was designed to do for you. If a rerendering is not possible or feasible, however, you're not entirely stuck.

You can do a number of things to even out the lighting on the apple. This example uses a Color Blending mode (refer to figure 34.8). After creating a new layer just above the apple, bind it to the apple (hold down Alt and click between the two layers) so that nothing you do affects the bottom layer of the table.

To begin fixing the lighting, use the Eyedropper tool to pick up the color of the apple that looks best, and begin painting with a slight soft-edged airbrush. Rather than attempt to paint variations in color of the apple itself, however, first paint a constant color over the entire apple. After the wrongly lit areas of the apple have been painted over, choose the Color blending mode for the layer in which you are airbrushing; this way, the texture of the apple comes through the new color.

Applying Shading to the Composition

Now that the entire apple's color looks good, you need to apply the proper shading for lighting. To do so, create another new layer, and bind it to the layer in which you just airbrushed. This layer is used to apply the highlight to the right side of the apple, and a bit of shadow to the left side of the apple, but not to the table. First, stick with the Airbrush, but then choose a large brush with a soft edge. For this layer, use the Hard Light Blending Mode—you get the benefits of both light and shadow simultaneously (see fig. 34.9).

Because the lighting of the apple is being worked on, you want to Paint with light and dark, rather than color. For this reason, choose to paint in shades of gray. Because the background photo appears to be somewhat dimly lit, start by darkening the apple as a whole. Choose to paint with a slightly dark gray, roughly 60 percent. By painting with a shade darker than the middle, you are able to darken the areas of the apple that are painted over. After a few smooth passes over the apple it begins to darken, and you can stop when you've achieved the desired luminosity of the color.

Now it's time to add the highlight on the right and the shadow on the left. Starting with the highlight, choose a much lighter gray (around 20 percent), and choose a smaller, yet soft-edged brush. Using such a soft edge enables the light gray with which you are currently painting to blend smoothly with the darker gray that has been painted across the apple; it will enable the area where the two tones meet to blend seamlessly, with no sharp line but a gradual falloff of light.

After a few light strokes on the right side of the apple, the highlight begins to take form, so switch to a much darker gray (80 percent) for the shadow. Working with the same brush and the same technique, the shadow on the apple takes form as well.

FIGURE 34.9

Adjusting the lighting on the apple by painting into a new layer with a Hard Light Blending Mode applied and linking it to the apple.

At this stage look at the Layers palette. At the bottom is the background image of the table. Next comes the 3D apple with two layers linked to it—the first layer for the color, the second layer for the light. Moving down the "lighting" layer to sit just above the apple drastically changes the appearance of the apple. The reddish color added to the apple is still evident, but the texture doesn't seem to show through as well anymore, and the lighting appears to be opposite from the way it needs to be. This is why stacking order can be important; because we relied on visual feedback building each step, changing their order likewise changes the way the layers work together.

The final major step in finishing the apple comes in slightly softening its edges. The best method is to modify the existing layer mask, which is currently made up of hard, solid edges. You can select the layer mask and paint with a soft airbrush around the edges of the mask; by using a soft brush, a simple gradient running from black to white can be painted along the edge, enabling the edge to blur somewhat. However, this method is slightly time-consuming and not terribly accurate. Because you want to blur the edges, you can use the Gaussian Blur filter (see fig. 34.10).

FIGURE 34.10
*Layer Mask with
Gaussian Blur being
applied to edges (by
Alt+clicking on the
layer mask thumbnail
you can view only the
layer mask as shown
here).*

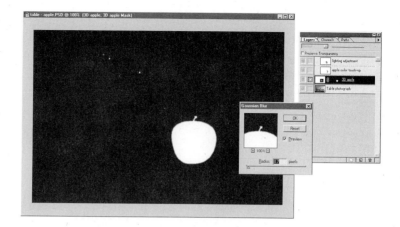

Because the layer mask is composed of solid black and white at this point, Gaussian Blur has no trouble blurring the hard edge between the two colors. If the mask contained other areas you did not want to blur or was not contained solely of solid blacks and whites, however, you would want to select only the area of the mask. This can be accomplished by using the Magic Wand, the Lasso tool, or by loading the mask selection.

Another wonderful implementation in Photoshop is the capability to save a selection. You can create a variety of selections and save them manually, or have Photoshop load a selection based on various criteria for you. Because the Layer Mask has been defined for the apple, you can load the selection of the apple simply by holding down the Ctrl key and clicking on the thumbnail of either the apple or the apple's mask. This creates the selection of marching ants.

After doing so, Gaussian Blur can be applied (again, this method need only be used if your mask contains more than one masked area). Under the Filters menu, choose Blur, Gaussian Blur. For creating a slight falloff in the edge, use a value of 2. After executing the blur (make sure the mask is selected, not the apple), you see that the edges of the apple now blend nicely with the background of the table and match the edge definition of the entire photograph.

Now for the next stage, which is matching up the overall tone and color to produce a clean sepia-toned apple that fits in with the background. To do so, a new layer is created and positioned at the top of the apple's stack of linked layers. This layer is also linked to the apple. You wouldn't want to recolor the background photo.

To achieve the overall color, use the Eyedropper tool on the background image to pick up on the predominant color: a slightly dark brown. With the newly created, topmost layer selected fill the entire layer with this color and then choose the Color Blending mode. (Hue makes the apple too sharp; in this case, Color uses better saturation values.) Because this layer is bound to the apple, the only visible area affected by the filled brown is the apple itself, which now appears no longer red, but with a brown cast. If the apple appears too dark, fill the layer with a lighter brown, and vice-versa if the apple appears too light. As a final measure of color matching, adjust the opacity of the layer slightly, enabling a tiny amount of the red to sneak into the brown to achieve just the right tone (see fig. 34.11).

FIGURE 34.11

The tone of the apple modified to match the background photograph by using a solid layer of color with the Color Blending mode, and linked to the apple.

Casting a Shadow in Your Composition

The only thing that remains at this point is to add the shadow that the apple casts onto the table. Although one method of adding this shadow is to return to 3DS MAX and rerender the scene with a surface at the same angle as the table, complete with a shadow cast just so, doing so is a far less interactive manner than just painting directly onto the image. In the time it takes you to set up the lighting and shadow properties and align them to the bitmap background, you could airbrush your shadow in Photoshop, print a color copy, and e-mail it to the entire planet.

Adding shadows within Photoshop can be done in two ways. The first apparently simple way is to use the Airbrush tool to approximate the shadow, which results in a somewhat inaccurate representation. The second, seemingly detailed method is to use the shape of the apple, transform its shape, apply color, blur it, and allow the underlying texture to show through.

The great thing is that both will take about the same amount of time when done in Photoshop—seconds.

T I P

Although it does appear that I have a strong affinity for the Airbrush tool, when creating shadows I prefer to stick with a fairly technical method, as you'll see in the following paragraphs.

Naturally, the first thing you do is to create another new layer that contains the image of the shadow. Place this layer just below the apple layer. After all, the shadow appears underneath the apple, not above it, right?

Here's the fun part: With the empty shadow layer selected, load the selection of the apple from its layer by holding down the Ctrl key and clicking on the thumbnail of the apple. This places the selection of marching ants right into the new layer that has been created. Now all you need to do is fill this selection with the same color that is used for other shadows in the original photo, picked up with the Eyedropper tool. After filling the selection, turn the selection off (Select, None or press Ctrl+D).

Now to rotate and stretch the shadow into proper position (right now it's basically invisible because it's directly behind the apple). Activate the Free Transform function within Photoshop by pressing Ctrl+T; this gives you an eight-handled selection box (see fig. 34.12). Now, simply rotate, squash, and stretch the box until the shadow is the right length and at the right angle (see the Photoshop manual for instructions on using the Free Transform tool; it's similar to using the FFD modifier in 3DS MAX).

FIGURE 34.12

The Free Transform tool is used to rotate and squash the shadow layer. Note the shadow is now visible behind and beneath the apple, and the layer's opacity is set to 51%.

Double-click on the Free Transform tool to apply the transformation, then turn down the opacity of the layer to match the opacity of the other shadows in the scene and voilà! Perfect shadow. Elapsed time: 25 seconds. No need for adjustments or blends.

Now the scene is complete, and best of all, fully editable (see fig. 34.13). If the texture on the apple seems to be too prominent, you can add another layer into the apple's stack using the Luminance blending mode and paint lightly over the areas where the texture is too strong. If the background image changes to a black-and-white image, change the color of the apple's Color Blending layer from brown to gray. Should you decide you want to make an artistic statement with a red apple composited into a sepia-toned photograph, you need only remove that layer of brown.

FIGURE 34.13

The finished, composited image of apple and table. Note the additional layer of reflection added (created the same way as the shadow but with different opacity).

With only a little bit of practice and a willingness to have a lot of fun, you'll find that you can perform these kinds of compositing actions in a matter of minutes. Best of all, you don't have to wait for rendering!

Using the Actions Palette for Batch Processing

Another huge advancement made with Photoshop 4.0 was the addition of the Actions palette. With the Actions palette, many of the tasks described in this chapter can be entirely automated and used on a series of images. This can prove to be a valuable tool for animation purposes, because many special effects can be created by using the Actions palette in a loop, even on a single image.

It was mentioned earlier that using a Color Burn in conjunction with a white, yellow, and red gradient could simulate a setting sun. To create this simulation, you need not render an entire animation with an animated light that changes position and color. Rather, you can use the Actions palette and a single rendered image.

Assume that you've got a single rendered image of a room in a building or house, with the sky visible outside the windows, and you want to animate the sun setting. Doing so is a fairly basic process when facilitated by the Actions palette in the manner outlined in the following exercise.

SETTING THE SUN USING THE ACTIONS PALETTE

1. Open the rendered file of the room. Create a layer mask for the room to make all of the windows fully transparent (see fig. 34.14).

FIGURE 34.14

A 3D-generated room with layer mask applied to create transparent windows. (Note the checkerboard transparency pattern.)

2. Create a new layer and position it below the layer with the room. Using the Gradient tool (see the Photoshop manual for more information on this), create a custom gradient using the colors found in a beautiful sunset. A drastic change shows the most, so use a gradient that starts at an off-white and runs through yellow, then orange, then dark red, ending at a nearly black maroon. Apply the gradient to the new layer horizontally, with the off-white at the bottom, parallel to the bottom edge of your image. Create the gradient so that the off-white area begins just above the top level of the windows (only a slight hint of yellow is at the top), and the near-black maroon finishes near (but not right at) the top of the image (see fig. 34.15).

FIGURE 34.15

The room with the white portion of the sunset gradient layer visible through the windows.

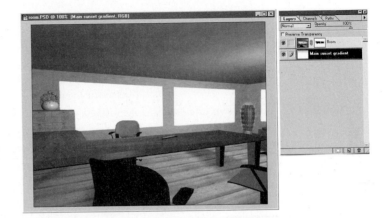

3. The gradient should now be visible only through the windows of the room. By using the Move tool and sliding the gradient layer up and down, you will see how the sunset looks through the windows. If the colors do not look right, it's best to fix the colors now, before you begin to work on interior lighting.

4. Because you want the light of the sunset to affect the inside of the room, you must perform two major operations. The first is separating the major light-reflecting elements of the room—the walls. Because the walls, ceiling, and floor will each be affected differently by the colors of the sunset, you need to make sure they work independently of each other. After all, Photoshop doesn't see the room you've created in three dimensions. You need to separate the single room layer into three different layers: one for the ceiling, the walls, and the floor. To do so, you will use the Cut To New Layer feature.

Taking the ceiling as an example, choose the Polygonal Lasso tool and mark a selection that encloses the entire ceiling of the room (see fig. 34.16). With the ceiling selected, right-click your mouse and choose Layer Via Cut. This will cut the contents of the ceiling from the room layer, placing them on a new layer. Double-click on the new layer and name it Ceiling. Repeat the same process for the floor, and you should have three layers: the ceiling, the original room layer (now only the walls), and the floor. In the Layers palette, be sure that the gradient layer remains at the bottom (see fig. 34.17).

FIGURE 34.16
The ceiling is selected, as indicated by the marching ants.

FIGURE 34.17
The ceiling, floor, and room (walls) now separated onto three layers. Note that because the ceiling and floor have no windows they require no mask.

And now for the real fun!

5. Duplicate the gradient layer by dragging it onto the Create Layer icon, and position the new gradient layer just above the room (walls) layer. Name this layer Room Lighting and link it to the room layer. Repeat this process for both the floor and ceiling layers. Each of the three room layers should now have their own gradient layer linked to them, as shown in figure 34.18.

FIGURE 34.18

Each of the room's layers (ceiling, floor, and room) linked to their own gradient layers, with Color Burn and 70% opacity applied.

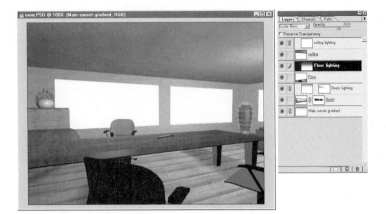

6. Because you want the colors of the sunset to bounce off the ceiling, splash off the walls, and spill onto the floor, you need to choose a Blending Mode. Because sunset is a darkening of the sky, the best choice here is Color Burn, because it will darken the tones and textures within the room with the colors of the gradient. While assigning the Color Burn Blending mode to each of the room's gradient layers (don't modify the main gradient at the bottom), you want to be sure that the sunset effect won't be overwhelming, so set each of these gradient layer's opacity to about 70 percent (refer to fig. 34.18).

7. The final step in setting up the sunset is to position each of the gradients in their "final" positions—that is, the position at which the sunset animation will end. Using the Move tool and the Shift key (to constrain movement to a vertical axis), adjust each layer, including the main gradient layer, until the colors are where you want them. It's best to start with the main gradient layer, because that defines your sunset. Then, follow with the gradient linked to the room layer so that you can see how the colored light fills the room. Finish up with the floor and the ceiling. You should have something that looks like the setup displayed in figure 34.19.

8. Now sit back and look at your image. The lighting all around should work in tandem to bathe the room in a beautiful orange, red, or dark maroon glow—perhaps a deep red-orange sunset, with just a hint of yellow on the horizon. You may see a few spots within the architecture of the room where either too much color spills through (it's rare that not enough color would spill through). In this case, create a Layer Mask on the gradient layer causing the spill, and begin airbrushing sparingly with a light gray and a soft-edged brush. If your mask blocks out too much color, go back over the same area in white. An example of this can be seen in the Room Lighting layer in figure 34.19.

FIGURE 34.19

The "final" position of the sunset, with each gradient layer adjusted for proper lighting. Note the layer mask applied to the Room Lighting gradient layer.

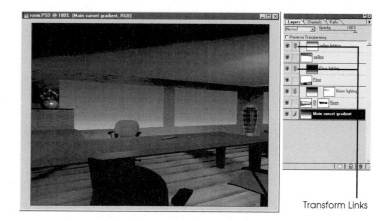

Transform Links

9. After all the gradients are set in place and necessary masks are touched up, it's time to test the setting of the sun. Select any of the gradient layers and link their transform functions. The transform link icons appear in the column between the eye (visibility) icons and the thumbnail images. Click the space in this column next to each gradient layer to create the transform link—and make sure that no other layers are linked. Your Layers palette should now look like the one in figure 34.19.

10. The transform link enables the linked layers to be moved in conjunction with each other, completely independent of any other layers that they may have modification links to. With the Move tool selected and while holding down the Shift key, slowly move the layers up and down to see the sun both rise and set. Feel free to look at the various positions; you won't lose content from layers by moving them around. If you're happy with the way everything looks, position the sunset so that it's mid-afternoon again, where only the slightest hint of color is visible near the tops of the windows.

11. The final step in this process is to automate the task of moving down the sunset a few degrees and saving the file. By creating a Photoshop Action you can do just that. Additionally, if you had another rendered sequence of images, such as a dog that scoots by, you could composite the dog images into the scene through the Actions palette, also having the dog images affected by the light of the setting sun. A basic setting sun however, simply requires use of the Offset and Select features. Figure 34.20 shows just that—frames of an animation created entirely through the steps outlined previously and with the Actions palette. (For information on setting up a Photoshop Action, see your Photoshop manual.)

FIGURE 34.20

Frames of an animation created with Photoshop Actions. Note how the color on the ceiling changes inversely to the color of the sunset.

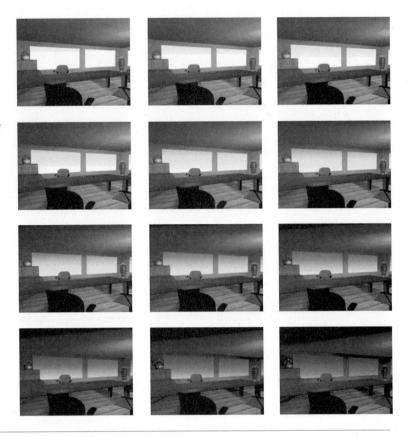

This method doesn't necessarily produce better results than a carefully layed out animation using colored volumetric lights and atmospheric settings. For producing such effects, nothing can produce better output than 3DS MAX. However, if you're working in a crunch, the method in the tutorial can be accomplished in as little as half an hour from setup to final batch processing. Rendering with volumetric lights could never go that smoothly or quickly.

After Effects, Premiere, DeBabelizer

In addition to working within Photoshop, the majority of what has been described can be used in Adobe's After Effects, which should be available for Windows NT by the time you read this. If you're not familiar with After Effects, it is an indispensable tool for any animator or film or video maker.

After Effects enables you to animate post-effects with exceptional control, from moving image Layer Masks up to animated Blending Modes and Adjustment Layers. Additionally, After Effects can animate Photoshop plug-ins and filters.

T I P

Working with corporate film and video, one of my favorite uses involves combining Posterize (adjustment) and Screen (blending) with a moving Layer Mask to simulate the overexposing of film—a fantastic transition, especially if it's brought on by the presence of an animated 3D object.

While not on the level of After Effects, Adobe Premiere can also animate many of the features previously described, with less control than After Effects but in some cases, with more control than the Actions palette.

Last, Equilibrium's DeBabelizer can also batch-process files. It can utilize an advanced scripting function to facilitate batch processing of even the most complex compositing functions. Although DeBabelizer cannot handle soft-edged masks, blending modes, and Adjustment Layers in the same method as Photoshop, DeBabelizer clearly stands on its own when it comes to *filter interpolation* (animating Photoshop filters over time) and preparing files for production to a variety of destinations from digital video to multimedia delivery.

All three tools are necessities for the serious animator, although many functions of all three can also be performed simply by intelligent use of Photoshop and the Actions palette.

In Practice: Compositing, Retouching, and Post-Processing with Photoshop

- **Plan your attack.** Whether you use Video Post or Photoshop for your compositing and post-processing work, it is essential that you plan your attack. Before jumping straight to Video Post to batch process an animation, see if using Actions within Photoshop is a better alternative. Before spending precious processing time with Photoshop, run some tests to see what you can do in Video Post. The key here is careful planning.

- **Layers.** By keeping your objects and images on separate layers, you maintain adjustability. You can move, rotate, restack, adjust color, and blend to your heart's content—all without sacrificing the integrity of your original image.

- **Layer Masks.** By using Layer Masks cleverly and effectively, you can composite a variety of images and objects with the greatest control with a few quick strokes of the Airbrush.

- **Actions.** Anything you create or manipulate in Photoshop can be programmed into an Action, allowing for batch post-processing and compositing of animation and utilizing features otherwise unavailable through Video Post.

- **Experiment.** The best way to learn Photoshop's vast capabilities is to experiment with them. Play. Try using odd color combinations in conjunction with various Blending Modes; paint back and forth with the Airbrush using a Difference Blending setting to achieve an otherworldly graffiti effect; use the Actions palette to gradually adjust the Luminosity and Posterize settings throughout an animation. You'll never know what you can do until you try.

IMAGE BY TODD PETERSON

by Todd Peterson

TROUBLESHOOTING 3D STUDIO MAX UNDER WINDOWS NT

Windows NT is a large, complex, and powerful operating system packaged in an easy-to-use Windows interface. But you are bound to run into problems with the system every once in a while, just like you would in any other operating system. This is especially true if you are working with a complex program such as 3D Studio MAX. This chapter explores what you can do if you run into problems with 3D Studio MAX under Windows NT.

3D Studio MAX does run under Windows 95, which presents a whole different set of problems when it comes to troubleshooting. Since most users will run MAX under NT, 95 is not covered in this chapter. If you need help with MAX problems under 95, consult your 95 documentation or your 3D Studio MAX dealer.

Thanks to a strong suite of diagnostic and system tracking tools, troubleshooting NT is easier than troubleshooting other systems. What makes it easier is the immediate availability of more tools to help you find and solve problems.

NT can crash or "hiccup" in a number of different ways. This chapter focuses on the following topics:

- Troubleshooting basics

- Handling system crashes

- Types of conflicts

- Identifying conflicts

- Detecting a conflict

- Using Windows NT Diagnostics to detect conflicts

- Troubleshooting 3D Studio MAX

After finishing this chapter, you might not be an expert at troubleshooting Windows NT and all the various problems that can arise, but you should have a fundamental grasp of how to diagnose and cure such problems.

N O T E

This chapter assumes a basic level of familiarity with NT. If you have never used NT before, you should not try to troubleshoot the system, because you may cause more damage than good. If you are not comfortable with NT, this chapter may seem a little daunting at first. Read your NT documentation and make sure that you are familiar with NT before trying some of the things prescribed in this chapter.

Troubleshooting Basics

Troubleshooting your NT system can be a long, difficult task until you have the appropriate skills. Therefore, this chapter gives you a solid introduction to troubleshooting Windows NT, beginning with the basics. The following steps are helpful for troubleshooting your Windows NT machine:

1. Recognize that there is a problem. Generally, under NT this comes in the form of a warning message or erratic system performance.

2. Always try to eliminate the most basic solutions first. Problems are usually fairly simple.

3. Check the Event Log to see if the problem is listed there. (See the section "The Event Log" later in this chapter.) If so, use the information provided in the Event Log to determine which piece of hardware or software is causing the problem.

4. Use NT Diagnostics to determine hardware conflicts. (See the section "Using Windows NT Diagnostics to Detect Conflicts" later in this chapter.)

5. Most conflicts can be solved by making a few adjustments in the Control Panel; check your hardware documentation for more information. An IRQ conflict with a sound card, for example, can be fixed in a couple of seconds by adjusting the IRQ in the Drivers Control Panel applet.

6. If nothing else works, and you cannot resolve the problem, call for help. In general, your system manufacturer should be able to support NT. If they cannot, call Microsoft or your 3D Studio MAX dealer for help. But do so armed with the correct information. Have available to you the NT error message—if one exists—and your current NT configuration. The support technician will have a much easier time helping you solve your problem.

7. Finally, if the support technician cannot help, verify that the hardware or software works under NT. If it does and you cannot resolve the problem, you must replace the software or hardware.

Now that you are armed with an outline of the basics, you should be able to read the rest of this chapter and become fairly proficient at troubleshooting Windows NT problems. Even with this knowledge, however, you can expect some problems during your troubleshooting experiences. Be prepared for the following scenarios:

- Some frustration and confusion. This is normal. Try not to let it get the best of you. Getting mad only makes solving the problem more difficult.

- Long waits for technical support. You are not the only person having trouble with your system. Almost everyone has some type of problem with his computer at one point or another. Make sure that you have your information ready. This makes solving the problem much easier.

- The possibility that a solution does not exist for your problem. This is rare, but NT does not support all software and hardware options. A CD-ROM drive with a proprietary interface, for example, might not work with NT either now or in the future.

Fortunately, the odds are you will not run into any problems with your NT system, especially if the manufacturer or a qualified consultant installed it. But if you do, the rest of this chapter is devoted to methods of solving NT problems.

With the basics out of the way, you are ready to delve into the specifics of troubleshooting Windows NT. Take the first step by understanding how to handle system crashes.

Handling System Crashes

A *crash* is defined as an error generated by an application or the operating system causing the application or operating system to become unstable or unusable. With Windows NT's crash protection, programs are protected from one another in memory, so when one program crashes, it does not bring down other running programs. But occasionally you encounter a crash that brings down the whole system. This is appropriately called a *system crash*.

A system crash is evidenced in one of two ways. Either NT locks up to the point where nothing else works, or you receive a blue screen with a system dump. A lock appears as a frozen system with no warning messages. The only solution is to reboot the system. A blue screen crash, however, provides you with a *system dump*, which is a print of the contents of the registers on the

CPU at the time of the crash. A system dump gives valuable information for troubleshooting to NT technicians. In general, a *blue screen crash* is indicative of some sort of hardware problem. Both types of crashes require NT and the system to be rebooted; however, the first crash is much less serious than the latter type of crash.

In the first case, a simple lockup can be caused by a number of things. The most common cause of a lockup is when an executing thread within a program gets caught in an infinite loop. When this happens, the program ceases to respond, and in a lot of cases, so does the NT system. What you can do to diagnose the problem is to reboot the machine and see if the problem goes away. Nine out of ten times it does. If it does not, record what you were doing when the system crashed.

When you record this information, be as accurate as possible. For example, you might record: "I was running AutoCAD with Photoshop and Word was running in the background. When I placed the mouse cursor on the OK button in the File dialog and clicked, the system locked up."

After being as specific as possible when writing down this information, read through this chapter and garner as much information as you can from the tutorials and examples. Then determine whether you can isolate the problem.

The second type of system crash is a blue screen crash (commonly called a "Blue Screen of Death"). It is much worse than a simple lockup and indicates a serious problem. The only times you see a blue screen crash under NT are generally hardware-related issues. If you misconfigured your SCSI controller, for example, you might get a blue screen crash.

There are two things you can do when you encounter a blue screen crash: first, reboot the machine and see if the blue screen reappears. If it does, you will probably need to use the crash recovery disk you made during the installation of the NT software (see the section "Using a Recovery Disk" later in this chapter). If the blue screen does not reappear, it was probably an isolated incident and can be ignored. Second, repeat the steps you performed previously to see if the blue screen crash appears again. If it does, you must troubleshoot the system as outlined later in this chapter.

Both a blue screen crash and a simple lockup have one solution in common for the user: you (the user) must record all the information you can to fix the problem.

Recording Crash Information

Whenever you receive a blue screen crash, NT provides you with all the information it knows as to why the system crashed. You will see half a page of register dumps from NT on the blue screen: always record all this information. If you ever have to call tech support for help, this information can help your support person define and solve the problem.

As mentioned earlier, the same procedure applies to any type of crash you receive anywhere in the system. When this happens, record as much information about the crash as you can off the screen. Do not wait a couple of minutes; instead, record the information when the system crashes. To be on the safe side, record all of the information available. In some instances, this may seem like a lot of information to record, but it will come in handy when you call tech support. This makes it easier for you or someone else to solve the problem if it occurs again.

Using a Recovery Disk

In the case of a blue screen crash, you should probably use the recovery disk you created to put the system back in order. After putting the system back in proper order, analyze what you did or what happened in NT to cause the system crash in the first place. By retracing your steps, you should be able to find the problem. The following steps show you how to restore the system with the recovery disk. Please note that you must have created the recovery disk when NT was loaded. If not, see the note at the end of this section after the tutorial for restoring the system using the recovery disk.

TIP

Make sure that you create the repair disk from a clean, stable, working installation of Windows NT. If you are having problems with NT, it is not a good idea to create a repair disk from a bad installation. If you create a repair disk from a bad installation, you can possibly transfer the problems to the repair disk.

1. When resetting the system with a recovery disk, you must first reboot the system with original system disks. Insert the Windows NT system disk 1. If you do not have disk 1 and are using the CD, re-create the disk.

2. Load disk 2 when requested. NT then asks if you are doing a new install, or if you want to use the recovery disk. Press R for the recovery disk.

3. Insert the recovery disk and follow the directions on-screen.

After inserting the recovery disk and following the commands on-screen, NT copies that information from the recovery disk. This information includes critical device drivers and other necessary devices. When the process is finished, you must reboot the machine.

NT should then be in the state it was directly after you created the recovery disk. Recovery disks only contain the information on the system at the time you make the disk. Any software, hardware, service packs, and so on, installed after the disk was made may not work correctly after recovery. In that case, you will have to reinstall the hardware or software. If the system crashes again, try re-installing NT. If that does not work, you might have a faulty or incompatible piece of hardware.

If you do not have a recovery disk (because you either lost the disk or did not create one when NT was installed), perform the following steps to create a recovery disk. You might want to update your recovery disk every time you install new hardware or software as well.

1. Go to the Main program group and double-click on the DOS prompt icon to start a DOS session. Under Windows NT 4.0, you can start the DOS session from the Start, Programs, Command Prompt.

2. At the command prompt, type RDISK. This displays a dialog that enables you to update or create a repair disk. Figure 35.1 shows this dialog.

FIGURE 35.1

The RDISK Utility in Windows NT 4.0 for creating repair disks.

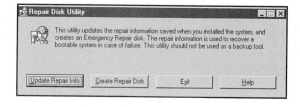

3. Choose Create Repair Disk to create a disk or Update Repair Info to update a disk. You are then prompted to place a disk in the drive for the information to be copied onto.

4. Choose OK, and the repair disk is created. Repair disks are used in the most serious of problems that you can run across in NT or in any case where you cannot get the system back up and running. Fortunately, most problems in NT do not disable the system; rather, they disable just a portion of the system. These types of problems are classified as conflicts.

Identifying Types of Conflicts

A conflict can occur at two levels: hardware and software. A hardware error generally occurs when the operation of one piece of hardware interferes with another. Usually, these errors occur because you have misconfigured the hardware's IRQ or base address. Hardware conflicts are generally easy to resolve, after you find out which piece of hardware is causing the conflict.

Detecting a Conflict

Now that you know what a conflict is, how do you detect one? Conflicts can be detected in several ways under Windows NT, as shown in the following list:

- The most common way to detect a conflict is to let NT tell you of the existence of one. To do this, NT uses an Event Log to record all system functions that occur. This Event Log (covered in the next section, "The Event Log") makes it easy to detect the devices that are causing the conflicts. When an event is recorded to the Event Log, a warning message appears notifying you of this fact. You can then use the Event Viewer to view the log entry.

- Software conflicts usually generate an error message. Depending on how you have NT configured, this error message might be recorded in the Event Viewer.

- Sometimes your only indication of a problem in your system is inconsistent behavior by NT or programs running under NT. This type of conflict is the most difficult to track down. When a program behaves inconsistently, no error messages or Event Logs are created. The program just doesn't work like it should. Sometimes this is caused by a software conflict, while other times it is a bug in the program.

The Event Log

To begin detecting conflicts, use NT's Event Viewer to take a look at the Event Log that lists events. An event in NT is an action by the NT system that needs to be recorded for information purposes, such as an access violation by a program. The Event Viewer is located in the Administrative Tools program group. To access it, double-click on the Event Viewer icon to start the program and it displays the screen shown in figure 35.2. For users of Windows NT 4.0, the Event Viewer is found under Start, Programs, Administrative Tools.

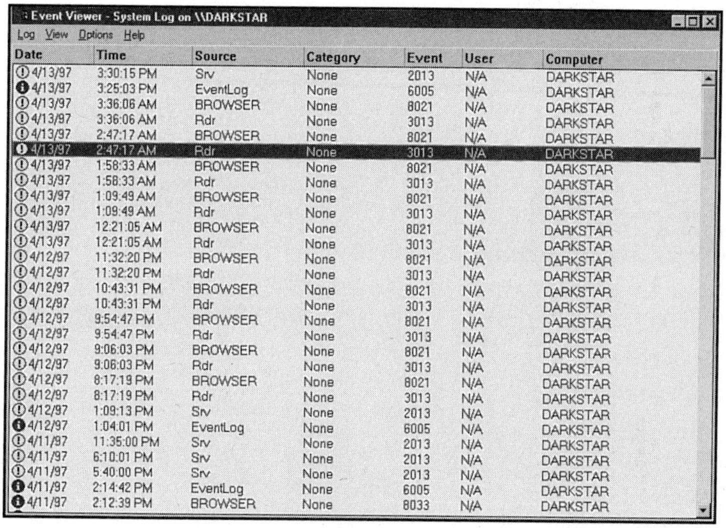

FIGURE 35.2

The Windows NT 4.0 Event Viewer where you can find out about system problems.

Date	Time	Source	Category	Event	User	Computer
4/13/97	3:30:15 PM	Srv	None	2013	N/A	DARKSTAR
4/13/97	3:25:03 PM	EventLog	None	6005	N/A	DARKSTAR
4/13/97	3:36:06 AM	BROWSER	None	8021	N/A	DARKSTAR
4/13/97	3:36:06 AM	Rdr	None	3013	N/A	DARKSTAR
4/13/97	2:47:17 AM	BROWSER	None	8021	N/A	DARKSTAR
4/13/97	2:47:17 AM	Rdr	None	3013	N/A	DARKSTAR
4/13/97	1:58:33 AM	BROWSER	None	8021	N/A	DARKSTAR
4/13/97	1:58:33 AM	Rdr	None	3013	N/A	DARKSTAR
4/13/97	1:09:49 AM	BROWSER	None	8021	N/A	DARKSTAR
4/13/97	1:09:49 AM	Rdr	None	3013	N/A	DARKSTAR
4/13/97	12:21:05 AM	BROWSER	None	8021	N/A	DARKSTAR
4/13/97	12:21:05 AM	Rdr	None	3013	N/A	DARKSTAR
4/12/97	11:32:20 PM	BROWSER	None	8021	N/A	DARKSTAR
4/12/97	11:32:20 PM	Rdr	None	3013	N/A	DARKSTAR
4/12/97	10:43:31 PM	BROWSER	None	8021	N/A	DARKSTAR
4/12/97	10:43:31 PM	Rdr	None	3013	N/A	DARKSTAR
4/12/97	9:54:47 PM	BROWSER	None	8021	N/A	DARKSTAR
4/12/97	9:54:47 PM	Rdr	None	3013	N/A	DARKSTAR
4/12/97	9:06:03 PM	BROWSER	None	8021	N/A	DARKSTAR
4/12/97	9:06:03 PM	Rdr	None	3013	N/A	DARKSTAR
4/12/97	8:17:19 PM	BROWSER	None	8021	N/A	DARKSTAR
4/12/97	8:17:19 PM	Rdr	None	3013	N/A	DARKSTAR
4/12/97	1:09:13 PM	Srv	None	2013	N/A	DARKSTAR
4/12/97	1:04:01 PM	EventLog	None	6005	N/A	DARKSTAR
4/11/97	11:35:00 PM	Srv	None	2013	N/A	DARKSTAR
4/11/97	6:10:01 PM	Srv	None	2013	N/A	DARKSTAR
4/11/97	5:40:00 PM	Srv	None	2013	N/A	DARKSTAR
4/11/97	2:14:42 PM	EventLog	None	6005	N/A	DARKSTAR
4/11/97	2:12:39 PM	BROWSER	None	8033	N/A	DARKSTAR

In the Event Viewer, you see a list of events that have already occurred. Windows NT tracks three types of events. Each type is briefly described in the following list:

- **System events.** These are events that affect the NT system and can range from IRQ conflicts to network and printer problems. System events also include regular recorded information, such as the startup of the event log.

- **Application events.** These are events that occur when an application is installed or crashes. If you have set up the system recovery options in the System Control Panel applet to write application events to the system log, all application errors are automatically recorded to the Event Log.

- **Security events.** Examples of these events include attempts to illegally delete a file that is security-protected, or print to a printer you are not allowed to access. This type of event only occurs if you are using an NTFS file and have set up the appropriate security measures.

TIP

You can switch between the event lists by choosing Log from the pull-down menu and then selecting the type of event you want to view.

By far, the most common events in NT are system events. Security events only occur if you have an NTFS file system and have security set up. Application events only occur when a specific application has a problem. System events, on the other hand, occur every time you run NT and are the events you track to detect hardware conflicts. When a conflict occurs, NT generates a warning message and records the event in the log. The warning message appears as an information box, as shown in figure 35.3. Each event listed in the Event Log has a colored icon at the far left, followed by the date, time, and source of the event.

FIGURE 35.3

An information box for

a system event.

If the icon on the left is blue and an error was not recorded, the event occurred naturally and is recorded for information purposes only. Notice that the icon actually looks like the international symbol for information. When you start up the system, for example, the Event Log records each time you load and unload the system.

If the icon is yellow, an event or error occurred that is not critical, but needs attention. An example of this type of error might be that your printer has run out of paper and returned a Printer Out of Paper error message to the system. This is then recorded in the Event Log.

If the icon at the left is red, a serious system event has occurred. In a correctly set up NT system, you should not see any red icons at all. An example of a serious system event is an IRQ conflict of a device with another device in the system.

To view the details of an event, double-click on that event. Figure 35.4 shows a sample system event, recorded as an entry in the Event Log.

FIGURE 35.4

The Event Log for a specific system event.

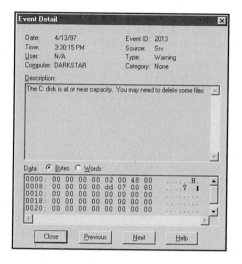

At the top of this dialog, you see all the general information about the entry, such as the date and time when the entry occurred. The Description box gives a brief description of what happened in the entry. In this case, the description tells you that the C drive is nearly full and that you should delete some files.

The next window in the Event Detail dialog gives you the hexadecimal dump of the entry. This information is generally given in hexadecimal numbers and contains the register and memory information about the entry. This is of little use to you, but can come in handy when you call a support technician.

The buttons at the bottom of the dialog enable you to move up and down through the Event list. The Close button enables you to return to the Event Viewer, as seen in figure 35.4.

The Event Viewer is a powerful method of tracking and locating errors in NT. The Event Viewer lets you know when and where errors occur, but it is still up to you to find out the exact error and how to fix it. To repair your problem, you must use your own problem-solving resources along with Windows NT Diagnostics.

Before looking at the NT Diagnostics, it's a good idea to practice reading and understanding recorded events. The following sections attempt to give you that practice by presenting several possible event problems and one or more solutions to those problems. The detailed view of the event is shown, followed by a quick description of what is occurring. Finally, the solution is given—if one exists.

Recognizing System Events

This section shows you several examples of problems recorded in the system event log that you might encounter. Of course, system events come in hundreds of types. The events presented in this section are given as examples of how to reason your way through the information given.

Problem 1: Network Card Error

Figure 35.5 shows a possible event problem that might occur in a given NT system configuration. You can see a brief description of the problem in the Description box. In this case, NT tells you the server could not bind to the transport:

```
\Device\NetBT_Elnk31.
```

As you can see in the figure, a 3Com Etherlink III Ethernet card is being used on the network in this system configuration.

FIGURE 35.5

The Event Detail dialog tells you the server cannot bind to the transport.

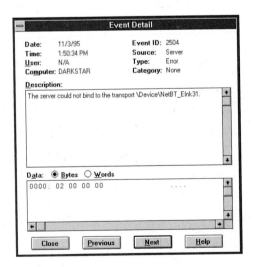

Due to the nature of the description, you can probably see that the error is related to the network card. In many instances, when an error is related to the network card, you might see a series of errors instead of just one. If the network card is misconfigured, for example, how can the remaining network services under NT run? They can't, which means that you will get other errors. In this case, the other errors that occur need to be explored to understand the problem more fully. Figure 35.6 shows the next error in the Event Log.

FIGURE 35.6

The description in the Event Detail dialog tells you that the driver device could not be initialized.

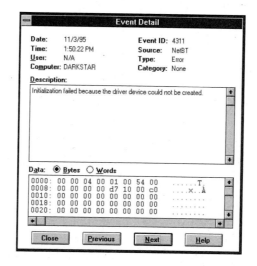

The description in the Event Detail dialog tells you that the driver device could not be initialized. But you still do not know exactly what driver failed to start properly. Move on to the next Event Detail dialog (see fig. 35.7).

The Event Detail dialog tells you NT was not able to initialize the IP interface for the adapter. In figure 35.7, the Event Viewer tells you that NT was not able to initialize the IP address for the adapter. This is the critical piece of information. IP stands for Internet Protocol and is related to the TCP/IP network drivers installed on the system. The best solution in this situation is to do one of the following:

- Check your TCP/IP network configuration. More than likely, you have not recorded the IP address for your machine or have an incorrect address listed. If you do not know your address, contact your network administrator.

■ In some cases, you might get this error message when nothing is wrong. Use NT's Remote Access Service to create a Point-to-Point Protocol connection to an Internet provider or a phone link to your network, for example, and you might choose to leave the TCP/IP not configured, but installed in the system. This situation is okay because every time you log in to the service provider, the TCP/IP is reconfigured.

FIGURE 35.7

The Event Detail dialog tells you NT was not able to initialize the IP Interface for the adapter.

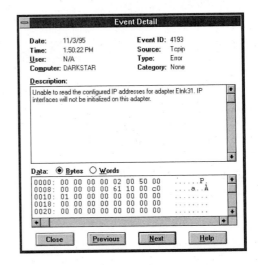

As you can see from this example, it might take more than one event detail to localize and solve the problem. You also need to be familiar with what hardware is installed in the system to be able to determine what the error is referring to in the system. For example, if you did not know the system had a 3Com Etherlink III card, you might have missed the Elink3 notation and not understood what it meant. By the same token, terminology is important. If you didn't know what IP meant, you would have a tough time understanding that this was a TCP/IP error.

NOTE

Don't worry if you don't know the jargon of your system yet. Experience helps a lot with problems such as these. You'll learn about your system as you go through the process of solving problems with it. You might experience frustration, but eventually, you will know how to solve most problems as they occur.

Problem 2: Sound Card Problem

Figure 35.8 shows the Event Detail dialog for a problem that might occur on an NT system. In the Description box, you see a notice telling you a boot-start or system-start driver failed to load. This indicates that a hardware driver is not functioning correctly. This information is followed by the driver name:

```
multisnd
```

FIGURE 35.8

The Event Detail dialog showing a hardware device that failed to load correctly.

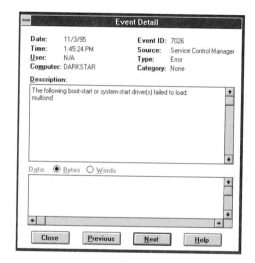

As with the first problem, knowing the system configuration helps to solve this problem. In this case, the driver refers to a Turtle Beach Multisound Monterey card driver.

The driver failed to load, and you can do several things to determine why. The following is a list of things to try:

1. Go to the Control Panel and verify that the driver is loaded in the Drivers Control Panel applet.

2. If the driver is loaded, verify its configuration.

3. If the driver is not loaded, reload the driver from disk.

4. If none of the above items solves your problem, you will probably have to do a little more snooping around using the NT Diagnostics. (See the section "Using Windows NT Diagnostics to Detect Conflicts" later in this chapter.)

Problem 3: A Problem with the Mouse

In the Event Detail dialog shown in figure 35.9, the description is fairly straightforward. NT cannot detect the device object for one or more pointer port devices. The key here is *pointer*. This refers to the mouse on the system. In other words, NT is telling you it cannot find the mouse.

FIGURE 35.9

The Event Detail dialog showing a problem with the system pointer.

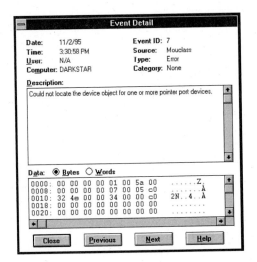

The following are some possible solutions to this problem:

1. Check to make sure that a mouse is connected to the correct port on the system.

2. If the mouse is connected to the correct port, verify that the mouse is not damaged by plugging it into another system.

3. If the mouse is not damaged, reboot your NT system and see if the error occurs again. If it does, this probably indicates a problem with the port. This could be an IRQ conflict or a bad piece of hardware. Use NT Diagnostics to further troubleshoot the problem.

Again, another simple problem—but this one can be rather nasty to solve. Without a mouse, getting to the Event Viewer could pose a problem! In this case, it helps to know how to move around in NT using the keyboard only. If you do not know how to use the keyboard to navigate in NT, consult your NT documentation.

Problem 4: A Printer Time Out Error

Figure 35.10 shows a different type of event. First, notice that this event is a warning and not an actual error. The description informs you that a document being printed on the system has timed out, and tells you the amount of time NT waited before generating this error.

FIGURE 35.10

The Event Detail dialog shows a simple printer problem.

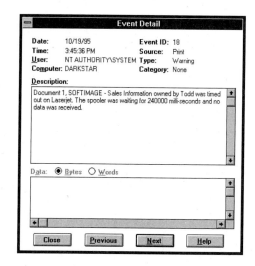

This is a simple printer problem. The following are a few basic solutions to the problem:

- Make sure the printer is online.

- Make sure the printer does not have a paper jam.

- Make sure the printer has paper.

- If the error is still there after verifying the preceding information, turn the printer off and back on, then try to print the document again. When you turn off the printer, make sure that you leave it off for a minute or so before you turn it back on.

- If none of the preceding methods work, make sure that you have good connections on the printer cable.

- If the cabling is well-secured, you might need to verify that you do not have an IRQ conflict with the parallel port or a bad cable. The IRQ conflict can be solved with NT Diagnostics. The cable, however, must be checked by using the cable on another system.

This simple problem has many solutions that might work. Always start with the simplest solution and work your way toward more complex solutions. In this case, the problem was ultimately a paper jam.

Problem 5: A SCSI Card Problem

In the problem shown in figure 35.11, NT indicates that the \Device\ScsiPort0 timed out. This refers to the first SCSI card in the system. NT made a request of a device connected to the SCSI card, and because the device did not return a value within the timeout period, an error occurred.

FIGURE 35.11

The Event Detail dialog showing a SCSI timeout error.

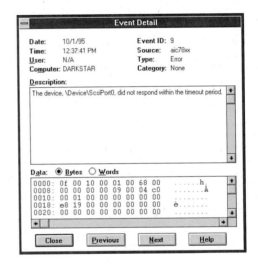

The SCSI timeout error may be caused by one of the following:

- The SCSI controller was too busy to respond to the request at the time. This is unusual and very rarely is the case.

- The Device connected to the SCSI controller is not turned on.

- The Device connected to the SCSI controller generated the error and is now locked up. In this case, you must reboot the system.

- The SCSI drivers are not well written and are causing this problem. Try to find the latest drivers or contact the manufacturer of the SCSI card to see if they can solve the problem.

- The SCSI controller has gone bad and needs to be replaced. Contact your manufacturer.

In this particular case, the problem was partially caused by the drivers used on the system. The error occurred when NT tried to read information from an ISO9660 CD-ROM in a quad speed SCSI CD player. The CD-ROM drive was constantly trying to read information, but never found the correct information. The error was corrected, for the most part, with updated SCSI drivers.

Problem 6: A More Serious Network Error

In the error shown in figure 35.12, the description tells you that the Computer Browser service failed to start because it depends on the Server service, which in turn, failed to start as well. Then NT informs you that the dependency group failed to start. As you might guess, this is another network error because it involves the Browser and the Server services.

FIGURE 35.12

The Event Detail dialog showing a vague network error.

This error is sometimes called a *cascade failure*, which occurs when one error causes another, which in turn causes another, and so on. In this particular case, a total of seven errors occurred. You must explore each error to find the resulting cause. Figures 35.13 through 35.17 show the rest of the associated error messages.

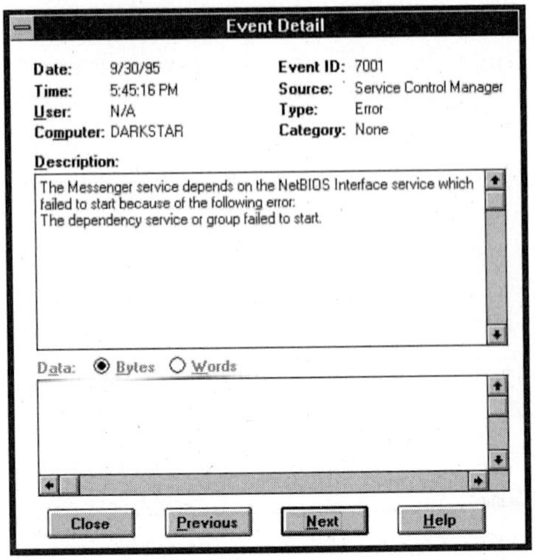

FIGURE 35.13

The Event Detail dialog showing a failure of a dependency service or group to start.

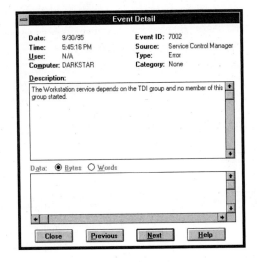

FIGURE 35.14

The Event Detail dialog showing a Workstation service error.

FIGURE 35.15

The Event Detail dialog showing a NetBIOS Interface error.

FIGURE 35.16

The Event Detail dialog showing a NetBEUI Protocol error.

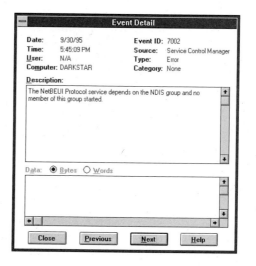

FIGURE 35.17

The Event Detail dialog
showing an Ethernet
adapter error.

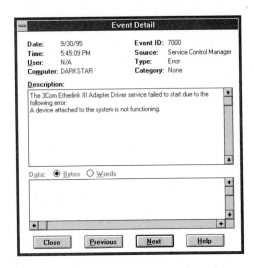

The last Event Detail dialog gives you the cause of all the previously mentioned errors. The error tells you that the 3Com Etherlink III service failed to start. Unlike the earlier network problem in which the card was misconfigured, this time the card failed to start at all.

The following list presents possible problems:

■ The network services are installed, but there isn't a network card in the system. The solution is to install an Etherlink III card or remove the network services from the system.

■ The card is installed in the system, but not sitting securely in the bus slot. Check the card to ensure that it is seated firmly in the slot.

■ The card is installed, but not working. More than likely, the network card is bad and must be replaced.

■ An IRQ conflict is causing an error so severe that NT cannot see the network card. Use NT Diagnostics to track down this error.

As you can see, each of the previously mentioned errors has one or more possible solutions. It is difficult to tell which solution is correct. Remember, troubleshooting a system can be a painstaking process because a single error can have multiple causes.

Recognizing Application Events

Now that you have a feel for what system events are and how you can solve conflicts involving them, it is time to look at some application events. Application events are recorded every time a specific application crashes. Under Windows NT 3.51 and 4.0, a program called DrWatson usually records the error to the system log and tells you what the errors are. 3D Studio MAX-specific errors are covered at the end of this chapter.

Most application errors are warnings because most application errors affect only the running of that application, not the rest of the system. Also, application events are not generated unless you set the recovery options in the System Control Panel to write to the Event Log.

A General Protection Fault Error

A general protection fault is an error that occurs when an application tries to read data from memory and reads the wrong area or the data no longer exists. General protection faults can be caused by any of a large variety of problems from program bugs to hardware or software conflicts. Figure 35.18 shows a possible Event Detail dialog for a given application under Windows NT.

NOTE

The terminology, General Protection Fault applies to Windows NT 3.51 and earlier when running 16-bit programs. 32-bit programs and programs running under Windows NT 4.0 use the terminology "Access Violation" to refer to the same type of problem. Access violations are recorded by a utility called DrWatson under Windows NT 4.0. If you are using NT 4.0, an Access violation is similar to a GPF under NT 3.51.

First, notice the fact that this Event Detail comes under an information category! In this Event Detail, an application generated a general protection fault (GPF). The date and time that the error occurred are given, along with the hexadecimal location. This type of error indicates that a program has crashed.

FIGURE 35.18

The Event Detail dialog showing a general protection fault (GPF).

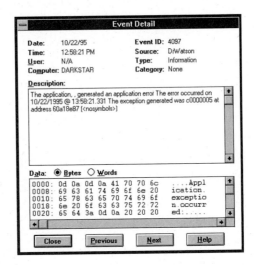

General protection faults are difficult to diagnose. Sometimes it is just a memory allocation error that occurs only once. The only time you should worry about a general protection fault is when it occurs every time you reach a certain point in an application. When a GPF or access violation occurs, you can try one of the following solutions:

1. Try rebooting NT and see if it happens again. If this is a Windows 3.1 or a 16-bit application, look at the program properties and turn on the Run in Separate Memory Space option to help crash-protect the program. This ends up taking up a little more memory than normal because all the critical DLL (Dynamic Link Library) files are loaded into separate memory spaces, but it can help you to isolate the problem.

2. It is possible that as a result of a crash, one of the modules or files of the application has become corrupted. Try reinstalling the software.

3. If reinstalling the software doesn't correct the problem, make sure that no other applications are running. Set your video to VGA mode and try again. If the error does not occur this time, it is probably the video driver. In this case, get the latest video driver from your video card manufacturer.

4. Check with your manufacturer to ensure that the software will run under Windows NT. Applications that cannot run under NT might generate a GPF. Generally speaking, NT also generates GPFs for poorly written applications.

5. If none of the preceding solutions work, record exactly what you do that causes the error, and then call tech support for that application. The Event Detail dialog should give them enough information to help you solve the problem.

NOTE

The previously mentioned problem report is recorded by a diagnostic program with Windows NT called DrWatson. It is only recorded when you set the recovery options in the System Control Panel under Windows NT 3.51. When the error occurs, NT gives you an error message and notifies you that it is recording the event in the system log. Under NT 4.0, DrWatson is enabled by default.

Event Log Information Entries

Figure 35.19 shows a possible event detail for a Windows NT configuration. This Event Detail dialog presents information and is called an Autochk Event Detail. Whenever you boot into another operating system and make changes to the hard drive, when you return to NT, NT checks the hard drive for errors using the NT version of CHKDSK/F. The information is automatically recorded to the application log.

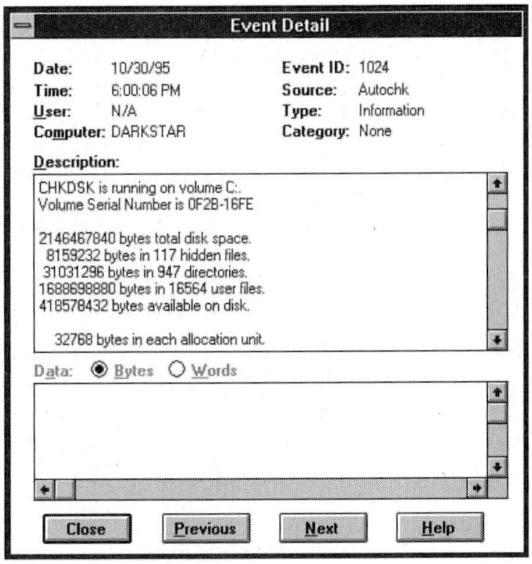

FIGURE 35.19

The Event Detail dialog showing the results of a CHKDSK run.

If you see that CHKDSK has found errors—such as lost chains—NT automatically converts these lost chains to files. This conversion has taken place if you notice a directory titled FOUND.000 in your system. Generally, you can delete this directory and all files in it because they are junk. As you can see, many problems can occur in an NT system, although this discussion presented only a small percentage. As mentioned before, some problems have obvious answers; others do not. The Event Detail dialog tells you the location and the nature of the error, but not the exact details. For this, you will use Windows NT Diagnostics.

Using Windows NT Diagnostics to Detect Conflicts

Windows NT's diagnostics programs are used to find out information about your current hardware and software configurations. The information is presented in a straightforward and easy-to-read manner, making it simple to detect configuration errors.

To start the diagnostics program, go to the Administrative control group and double-click on the Windows NT Diagnostics program item. This launches the Windows NT Diagnostics dialog, shown in figure 35.20. For users of Windows NT 4.0, the diagnostics are found under Start, Programs, Administrative Tools. These diagnostic tools only provide information about the system and are only necessary when you need that information.

FIGURE 35.20

The Windows NT 4.0 Diagnostics Program.

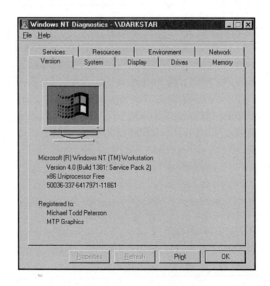

The first thing you will notice is a series of buttons representing each of the diagnostic areas. NT Diagnostics does not perform physical diagnostic testing, but it does provide a wealth of information for you to use. The following sections describe each diagnostic area in detail.

Note

Under NT 3.51, each of the sections of NT Diagnostics displays a separate dialog of information. NT 4.0 shows you the same information in one dialog with tabbed sections. The layout and locations of the information is slightly different in NT 4.0; nonetheless, all the same information is displayed. You cannot change any of this information. It is there for your use and knowledge.

The Version Option

Choosing the OS Version button in the Windows NT Diagnostics dialog displays the OS Version window, shown in figure 35.21. When you choose OS Version, you are given all the important information about the current version of NT that you are running.

Figure 35.21

The OS Version window.

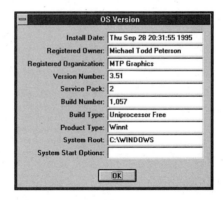

The OS Version window presents some important information:

- **Install Date.** The date you installed the system.

- **Version Number.** The version of NT that you are running.

- **Service Pack.** The service pack level that you are running. Service Packs are bug fixes for NT provided by Microsoft. Service pack 0 means no service packs are installed.

- **Build Number.** This is Microsoft's internal build number for NT. This represents the number of times they have rebuilt the base kernel of the NT operating system.

- **Build Type.** This tells you whether you are running a multiprocessor version of NT or a uniprocessor version. The other information in this window is self-explanatory. Please note that you cannot change any of the information presented in this dialog. Choose OK to return to the Windows NT Diagnostics dialog.

The Hardware Option

Choosing Hardware in the Windows NT Diagnostics dialog leads to the display of the Hardware dialog shown in figure 35.22. This dialog tells you the system's important hardware information.

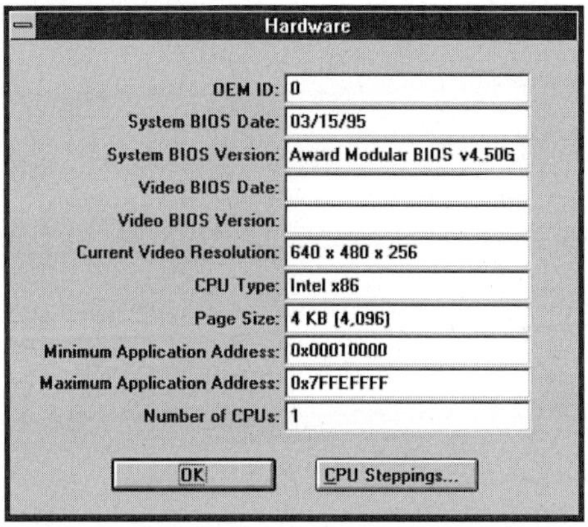

FIGURE 35.22

The Hardware dialog.

The following list explains the items in the Hardware dialog:

- **OEM ID.** This is the ID number that identifies the manufacturer of NT. If NT was installed by your hardware manufacturer, you might see a different OEM number here.

- **System BIOS Date.** The date of your computer's BIOS chips. This is useful when you call tech support with hardware or installation problems.

- **System BIOS Version.** The version of your computer's BIOS. As with the date, this is useful information.

- **Video BIOS Date.** The date of the BIOS for your video card. If this field is blank, NT cannot get this information directly from the video card.

- **Video BIOS Version.** The version of the BIOS for your video card. Like the date, this field might be blank.

- **Current Video Resolution.** Where NT is currently running.

- **CPU Type.** The type of CPU on which NT is running.

- **Page Size.** This is the size of a "page" or chunk of memory. Generally, this size is determined by the type of CPU you are running. For Intel CPUs, it is 4 KB. It might vary with RISC CPUs.

- **Minimum Application Address.** This is the location of the lowest memory address that an application can use.

- **Maximum Application Address.** This is the largest memory address that an application can use.

- **Number of CPUs.** The number of CPUs installed in the system that NT is using.

At the bottom of the dialog is a CPU Steppings button. This button enables you to see the version number of each processor you are using. Choosing this button displays the CPU Stepping window, shown in figure 35.23.

The stepping is the latest revision of a particular processor. This is given as a letter followed by a number. This can be useful for detecting the revision of your chip when errors such as the Intel Pentium floating point error occur. Also notice that CPT Stepping dialog gives you this information for up to 32 processors supported in the machine.

Choose OK twice to return to the main Diagnostics window.

FIGURE 35.23

The CPU Stepping window.

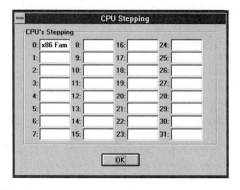

The Memory Option

Choosing Memory in the Windows NT Diagnostics dialog displays the Memory window shown in figure 35.24. This window presents information about your system's current memory configuration.

FIGURE 35.24

The Memory window.

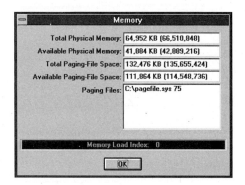

As a graphics professional, you are probably aware of the fact that the amount of memory in a system directly affects the performance of an application. But you have probably never been able to see how the memory in the system is being used. The Memory window provides this information. The following list explains the items in the Memory window:

- **Total Physical Memory.** The amount of memory installed in your machine.

- **Available Physical Memory.** The amount of memory available to applications at this time. This number takes into account all other applications currently running.

- **Total Paging-File Space.** The size of your swap file.

- **Available Paging-File Space.** The amount of swap file space you have left. Adding this number and the free physical memory number gives you the total memory available to you before NT will crash.

- **Memory Load Index.** An interactive bar that warns you when the system should have more memory. If you have an application running, such as a rendering application, you can pull up the Memory dialog and watch how the system memory is used. The memory load index is a graph of the system memory use. When the index bar goes all the way to the right and the index gets fairly high, you have used all the memory in the system. If this occurs often, you might want to install more memory in your system for better performance. When the index is high, the graph changes from green to yellow to red, with red being a critically high index number.

Choose OK to return to the main Diagnostics window.

The Drivers Option

When you choose the Drivers button in the Windows NT Diagnostics dialog, you are given a list of currently active and running device drivers on your NT system (see fig. 35.25).

FIGURE 35.25
The Driver List dialog.

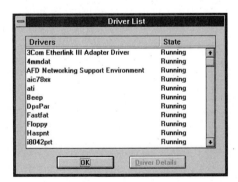

The Driver List is helpful to know when you call tech support because it tells you the drivers that you are currently running. You can see individual driver details by choosing a driver and then clicking on the Driver Details button. A secondary window appears, as shown in figure 35.26.

FIGURE 35.26

The Driver Detail window showing the critical information for TCP/IP.

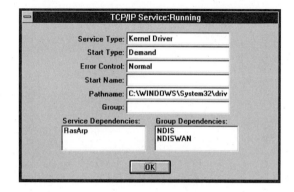

The TCP/IP Service:Running window displays all the critical information about the driver you selected in the Driver List, including any dependent services. If this driver fails to load correctly, the dependencies also fail. Choose OK twice to return to the main Diagnostics dialog.

The Services Option

When you choose the Services button, Windows NT displays a list of all the services currently running in the NT system (see fig. 35.27).

FIGURE 35.27

The Service List dialog.

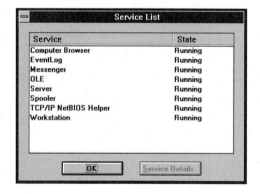

A service is a primary part of the system. As figure 35.27 shows, several services are running at this time, including the Workstation, Spooler, Server, and Event Log services. To see the details of a service, click on that service, then choose the Service Details button at the lower-right portion of the dialog. Figure 35.28 shows this window.

FIGURE 35.28

The Detail window for
the Workstation
service.

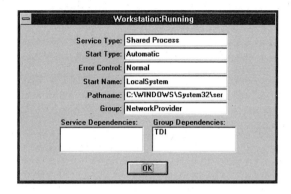

FIGURE 35.28

The Detail window for
the Workstation
service.

The Workstation:Running window provides the same information as the Driver Detail window except that the information in the Workstation: Running window is related to services. Choose OK twice to return to the main Diagnostics dialog.

The Drives Option

Choosing the Drives button enables you to see the exact configuration of each of the drives in your system, including hard drives, floppy drives, CD-ROMs, and so on (see fig. 35.29).

FIGURE 35.29

The Drive Information
window.

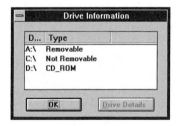

To see the details of a drive, click on the drive, and select the Drive Details button. Figure 35.30 shows the resulting dialog.

The Drive Information window is a simple list of the drives, their types, and their assigned drive letters. The Drive Details dialog tells you all the details about the drive.

Some of the important information in this dialog includes the following:

- **Free Space.** The total amount of free space (in bytes) on the drive.

- **Used Space.** The space on the drive being used by programs and data.

- **Total Space.** The overall size of the drive.

- **File System Name.** The type of file system for which the drive is formatted.

- **Maximum Component Length.** The maximum length for a file name on the drive.

FIGURE 35.30

The Drive Details dialog.

Again, this information is useful if a tech support person asks for it. Choose OK twice to return to the main diagnostics dialog.

The Devices Option

Choosing the Devices button displays a Devices dialog, as shown in figure 35.31, which lists all the current and active devices in the system.

The Devices dialog is important because it lists all the devices on the system. By selecting a device and choosing the Device Details button, you can see the configuration of that device. Figure 35.32 shows this dialog.

The Details dialog breaks down information into five areas:

- **DMA.** This lists the Direct Memory Access channel and port. This value is important for sound and MIDI cards.

- **Interrupt.** This is the IRQ of the device. The important number here is the Level. The Level gives you the IRQ number for the device. Each device that uses an IRQ number must use a different IRQ.

- **Memory.** If the device driver takes up memory, it is listed here, along with its address and the amount of memory it takes.

- **Port.** This is the location of the driver in memory. The physical offset address and then the length of the driver are given. No two devices should share the same port address space. The numbers here are given in hexadecimal. Finding the port address of a device is not difficult in most operating systems, but finding the length of the address to ensure that you do not overlap address spaces is challenging.

- **Share Disposition.** This field gives you the share information about the device and who has access to it.

FIGURE 35.31

The Devices dialog showing all the devices on the system.

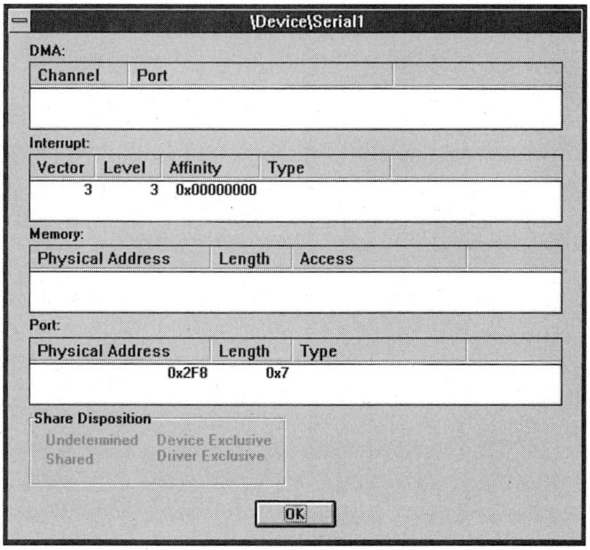

FIGURE 35.32

The configuration for a serial device.

By far, the most important aspects of this dialog are the IRQ and Port address fields where you can begin to track down IRQ conflicts. If you have an IRQ conflict, you can begin here or look at the next diagnostic tool. Choose OK twice to return to the main Diagnostics dialog.

The IRQ/Port Status Option

By choosing the IRQ/Port Status button, you can get a list of the currently assigned and active IRQs and Port address values. Figure 35.33 shows you this window.

FIGURE 35.33

The Interrupts/Ports window.

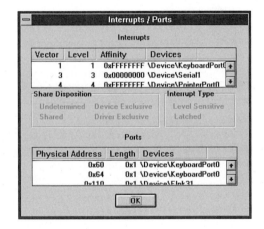

The first thing you will notice is a list of the currently assigned IRQ or interrupt values. If you scroll up and down through this list, you see the IRQs as they are currently assigned. To the right of the list, you see the devices that are assigned to the IRQ. Any unassigned IRQs are either available for use or reserved by the system. In general, IRQs 5, 11, 12, 13, and 15 are available for you to use.

The Ports section displays the physical location in memory of the driver for each device, and its size. The important thing is to make sure that no drivers' addresses are overlapping. Overlapping causes an error when you try to access the device. The Interrupts/Ports dialog is one of the most important dialogs in the diagnostics set because you can immediately see the IRQ and Port relationships. Most hardware problems are a result of IRQ or Port conflicts. As far as adjusting a device that does have a conflict, you must read the device's documentation. Some can be changed and some cannot. Some devices can be changed using software, whereas others must have jumpers changed on the device. Choose OK to return to the main Diagnostics dialog.

The DMA/Memory Option

By choosing the DMA/Memory button in the Windows NT Diagnostics dialog, you can see what devices are using Direct Memory Access (DMA) channels and where your video card is using memory (see fig. 35.34).

FIGURE 35.34

The DMA/Memory window.

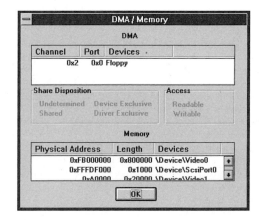

The DMA section shows you the devices that are currently using a DMA channel. A DMA channel enables a device to directly access the main memory of the system without going through the CPU. This greatly increases the performance of the device. Sound cards use this feature a great deal since they transmit data at high rates. The channel is given, followed by the port or address and the device using the channel. The Memory section tells you the addresses in physical memory that your video card is using. Generally, this information is not changeable. Choose OK to return to the main Diagnostics dialog.

The Environment Option

Choosing the Environment button displays an Environment window (see fig. 35.35), in which you can see all the environment variables that NT is currently working with.

FIGURE 35.35

The Environment window.

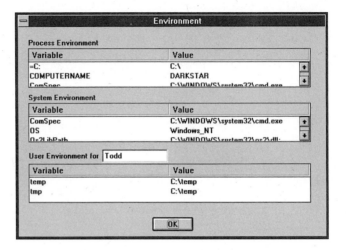

In this window, you can see each of the three available types of environment variables. These include Process, System, and User variables. These variables are set in the System Control Panel applet and can be viewed there as well. Choose OK to return to the main Diagnostics dialog.

The Network Option

Choosing the Network button displays a Network window (see fig. 35.36), in which you can view the current network configuration of your machine.

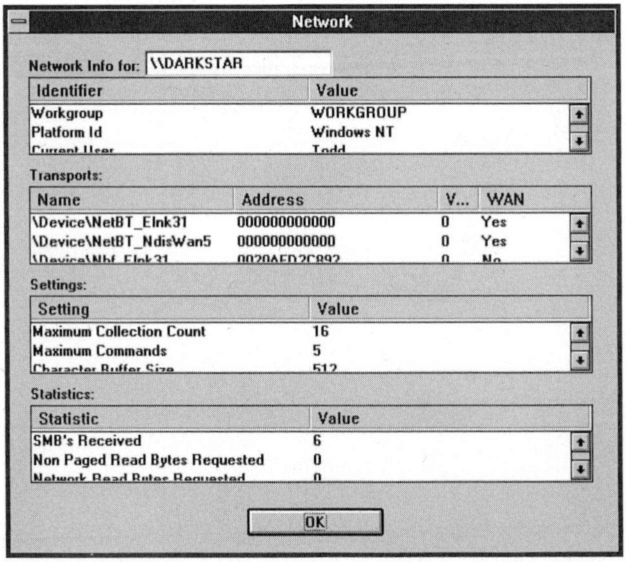

FIGURE 35.36

The Network window.

The Network window is broken into four sections. Each is presented and briefly described in the following list:

- **Network Info.** This section contains the base networking information such as the computer name, workgroup membership, and so on.

- **Transports.** This section contains a list of all the active network transport protocols such as TCP/IP or NetBEUI.

- **Settings.** This section contains all the network device and protocol settings.

- **Statistics.** This section lists all the network statistics such as amount of bytes transmitted and received during the current session.

If you have to talk to a technical support representative about your network, all the information they should need is given in this one dialog. Otherwise, you would have to hunt through several other programs under NT to find this information. When you are finished, choose OK to return to the main Diagnostics dialog.

The Windows NT Registry

The final thing that the Windows NT Diagnostics program can do is enable you to view and edit the Windows NT Registry. The Registry is what NT uses to keep track of program, system, and hardware initialization values. Under Windows 3.1, you had the WIN.INI and SYSTEM.INI files that contained this information. NT still has these two files, but they are used only for 16-bit applications. All other applications register themselves and their default values in the Registry.

WARNING

The Registry is a complex and confusing aspect of NT. Don't edit the Registry unless you have to. Changing the wrong variable can cause the whole system to crash. This book introduces the Registry but doesn't fully explore it; however, if you are interested in more information on the Registry, pick up *Windows NT Server Professional Reference* by New Riders Publishing.

To view the Windows NT Registry, choose Tools, Registry Editor from the Windows NT Diagnostics dialog. You can also access this program from the command prompt by typing **REGEDT32**. When the program loads, you see four windows, as shown in figure 35.37.

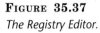

FIGURE 35.37

The Registry Editor.

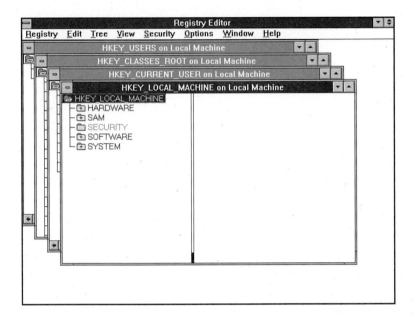

The Registry is divided into four sections; each represents a unique aspect of the Registry values. The sections are described in the following list:

- **HKEY_USERS on Local Machine.** This contains the default values for each user on the local machine. One example of something contained here might be an environment variable, while another example might be each user's password.

- **HKEY_CLASSES_ROOT on Local Machine.** This section of the Registry Editor contains all the file extensions on the system and the programs with which they are associated. When a file extension is associated with a program, you can double-click on that file in the File Manager, and the creating program will load and load up the file.

- **HKEY_CURRENT_USER on Local Machine.** This contains the same information as HKEY_USERS, but for the currently logged in user of the system.

- **HKEY_LOCAL_MACHINE on Local Machine.** This section contains all the hardware and software configuration information for this machine.

- **HKEY_CURRENT_CONFIG on Local Machine.** This is an NT 4.0–only registry that contains all the current configuration information for the system. This registry is not in 3.51, due to system enhancements in 4.0.

Figure 35.38 gives you an example of an expanded display of the Registry and how complex it really is.

FIGURE 35.38

The Expanded Registry.

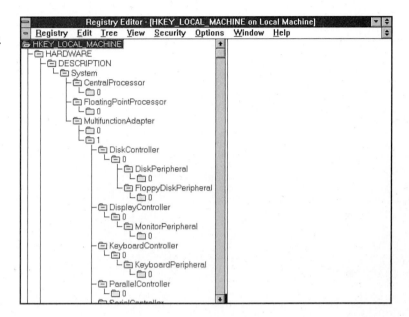

Fully exploring the Registry is well beyond the scope of this book; the best you will get is a basic outline of the Registry. You should only edit the Registry if you are an experienced user, or if you are following the directions of a technician.

More often than not, you will not need to edit the Registry. The Registry contains many values that can actually be adjusted through the Control Panel. The Registry should be used as a last resort option only. Choose Registry, Exit to exit the Registry Editor, and return to the main Diagnostics window. Choose File, Exit to exit the Windows NT Diagnostics.

Troubleshooting 3D Studio MAX

3D Studio MAX is a large and complex piece of software with a highly extensible plug-in architecture. Because of these two factors, you may occasionally run into system problems.

Almost always, an error in MAX under Windows NT 3.51 or 4.0 will appear as an Access Violation and you will be exited from the program. When an access violation occurs under NT, a program called DrWatson records the access violation to the application event log. When diagnosing access violations, you must take a close look at the access violation. Access violations appear as two sets of numbers such as the following:

```
Access Violation (0xc00000037), Address: 0x77f85019
```

What you want to look for are repeating access violations. If you get an access violation once, you probably don't need to worry about it. But, if you get the same access violation at the same address by repeating the same steps inside of 3DS MAX, you have a problem.

The majority of access violations are (0xc00000005), at an address. You may get the same access violation at different addresses, however, which indicates two distinct problems that need to be solved. Some access violations are identified by Kinetix and already have solutions. If you have access to Compuserve or Kinetix's web site at

```
www.ktx.com
```

you can download tech support documents that describe the specifically identified problems.

In other cases, you may have to solve the violation error yourself. The following are some general steps, rules, and descriptions for solving access violation errors:

■ Try to isolate the nature of the error. Did you make changes to your system before you started having the access violation? If so, undo the changes you made.

■ Many times, a plug-in, especially some shareware plug-ins, are the cause of access violations. If you have any plug-ins installed besides the standard 3DS MAX plug-ins, remove them from the plug-in search path. This can easily be accomplished by copying all the files out of the \3DSMAX\PLUGINS directory to another directory and deleting all the files in PLUGINS. Then retry. If the error occurs again, it is not plug-in related. If not, then return each plug-in to the system one by one and try each one. When you find the offending plug-in, you may either remove it or contact the manufacturer or author of the plug-in to get the situation resolved.

NOTE

An incorrect documentation of a programming technique in the SDK resulted in problems with some early plug-ins written with the 1.0 MAX SDK. Since then, Kinetix has released a test version of the CORE.DLL part of 3DS MAX, which can be downloaded from the Kinetix web site or CompuServe. When this version of CORE.DLL is loaded, it checks for offending plug-ins and tells you if it finds any. This version of CORE.DLL is intended for plug-in checking only and not for production use. Please read the instructions contained with the add-on, if you decide to use it.

- Sometimes a corrupted 3D Studio MAX configuration can result in an access violation. To solve this type of problem, delete the 3Dsmax.ini file from the \3DSMAX directory and restart 3DS MAX. This reconfigures 3DS MAX to default settings. Also, if you are using a MAXSTART.MAX file as a default for new scenes, you may try removing that file, in case it is corrupted as well.

- Verify your build of NT. If you are a developer, you may be running a "checked" version of NT, which can cause problems. Make sure you are running the retail version of NT at all times.

- Clean boot your system. Remove any sort of memory caching from your system BIOS and see if that solves the problem. You may find you have a bad Cache module or some other type of error.

- Your video card can also be a source of access violations. If you are running a Software Z-Buffer configuration of 3DS MAX, restart your system in VGA mode to disable the high-end video driver for your card. Then try 3DS MAX and see if you get the error. If you do, then the video card is probably not the error. If you do not get an error under VGA mode, it is probably a poorly written or improperly configured video driver, in which case, you should try to obtain the latest drivers for your board. (It is always a good idea to get the latest drivers anyway.)

- For Glint cards or other high accelerators, you can also see access violations. The easiest method of testing is to restart 3DS MAX with a software Z-buffer. You can accomplish this by adding an "–h" to the command line of 3DS MAX in the program Icon or desktop shortcut. When you start 3DS MAX, you will be asked to reconfigure the video display. If the problem still occurs, boot into VGA and follow the previous steps. Alternatively, if you are running Glint, you can delete the Wglint.ini file in \3DSMAX which will force a reconfiguration the next time you launch 3DS MAX.

- Occasionaly, Microsoft releases updates to the NT operating system, called *service packs*. Sometimes Microsoft makes large changes to the way NT works in these service packs that can cause problems with a program such as 3DS MAX. As for NT 4.0 Service Pack 2, Microsoft now provides an uninstall utility for the service pack, making it easier to install and try a new service pack. In general, new service packs rarely cause problems with 3DS, but you never know—it depends upon your hardware configuration. If you feel a service pack is causing a problem, try upgrading to a newer pack or reinstalling NT with an older service pack.

N O T E

Service Packs for NT may be downloaded from Microsoft's web site at `www.microsoft.com` or from their FTP server at `ftp.microsoft.com`.

- Sometimes a network problem can also cause an access violation. If you use the command-line option "–N", you can disable network support in 3DS MAX and see if that solves your problem. If it does, something is wrong with the networking under NT.

- If you are running a system with an AWARD BIOS, you may get random access violations. If you do, try getting a BIOS update or a completely different BIOS for your motherboard. If neither option is available, you may just have to live with random violations every once in a while.

- If you are running a multiprocessor system, you should make sure the CPUs are identical, including their revision numbers. You can see CPU revision number through NT diagnostics. If you are getting access violations, especially when rendering—which is highly multithreaded—try setting your machine to Uniprocessor mode by removing one of the processors. If the problem goes away, you either have processors with different revisions, a bad processor, or a bad motherboard.

■ Sometimes the memory in your system can cause Access violations or performance problems. Make sure all your SIMMS or DIMMS are securely and properly seated. Also make sure all of the memory modules are the same speed and that your BIOS is configured for that speed memory. If you have memory modules of different sizes, place the largest ones in the first memory bank. Last, you may try removing or shuffling your memory modules to see if that helps.

■ Under NT, you also need a large amount of memory to ensure that 3DS MAX can run smoothly. This includes a large swap file. If your swap file is not large enough, this can cause problems in 3DS MAX. Swap file sizes of 200 or more MB are not uncommon in 3DS MAX. Try setting your swap file to a larger size, and all you will sacrifice is a little hard drive space.

■ As a last resort, remove any unnecessary components from your system, such as sound cards, video capture boards, extra SCSI devices, and so on. Then try running 3DS MAX again. If the problem is gone, replace each component one at a time and try again until you find the problem component. If you find it is a hardware component, try getting new drivers or reconfiguring the component to other settings to resolve the problem.

NOTE

To further help you solve access violations, pick up the NT 4.0 or 3.51 Workstation Resource Kit, which contains help files that list all of the known types of errrors in NT. You can pick these up from most computer and book stores.

■ If you are running Windows 95, you may have an entirely new set of issues. In general, many plug-ins for 3D Studio MAX may or may not be compliant with Windows 95 and may be a problem. If at all possible, do not run 3DS MAX under Windows 95, rather operate it under NT. Outside of plug-ins, 3DS MAX should run fine under Windows 95, but may be as much as 10 to 20 percent slower because of how Windows 95 handles memory and video issues.

- Make sure you are running the latest version of 3DS MAX. Currently, this is 3D Studio MAX 1.2. (Newer versions may be available by the time you read this.)

- If all else fails, you may have found a bug in 3DS MAX. You can always try the Kinetix support lines to get a resolution to these types of problems.

As you can see, many things can cause access violations in 3DS MAX. Hopefully, you will not have any. If you do, try to solve software problems first, before moving to hardware problems. As always, if the problem is not repeatable, you will probably not be able to solve it, so make sure the problem is repeatable.

Another type of error that creeps up occasionally is an assertion failed error, which causes 3DS MAX to crash. *Assertions* are a programming technique used to verify that variables in a program are correct at certain points in the process of the program. If they are not, you get an error. These generally point to a specific line, such as line 20 in sphere.cpp. This indicates the exact location of the assert command in the source code of the program. An assertion is more than likely a bug in the program. If it occurs in 3DS MAX, report it to Kinetix. If it happens in a plug-in, report it to the plug-in manufacturer. Assertion errors are rare.

The last type of error that you might run across in 3D Studio MAX is a simple program dump. You can be working in 3DS MAX and all of the sudden, you will be dumped back to the NT desktop without warning. You will receive no error messages at all. In general, these types of crashes are bugs in the program or plug-ins. If you receive this frequently, try some of the trouble-shooting methods previously mentioned; otherwise, contact the manufacturer of the software to see if they can solve it. Remember, you must have a recurring problem!

As always, try to have patience while troubleshooting—it is a time-consuming and aggravating process. But, with a little patience and a lot of work, you will probably be able to isolate most of the problems yourself.

In Practice: Troubleshooting 3D Studio MAX Under Windows NT

This chapter introduced you to many complex topics related to troubleshooting NT and 3D Studio MAX. When it comes to troubleshooting, you have many options that you can pursue to solve your problem. For troubleshooting, you must remember the following mental processes:

- **Troubleshooting Basics.** Identify that there is a problem with your system. By eliminating simple solutions using Windows NT Diagnostics, checking the Event Log, and (as a last resort) the support technician, you should be able to find and eliminate the problem.

- **Handling System Crashes.** Windows NT's crash protection guards programs from one another in memory, but occasionally a crash will bring down the whole system. This scenario is classified as a system crash. Meanwhile, NT has other types of crashes such as a blue screen crash that provide the user with a system dump to identify and solve the problem.

- **Resolving the Problem.** With the aid of Windows NT Diagnostics and the Event Log you should be able to find and solve problems.

- **Troubleshooting 3D Studio MAX.** Errors in 3D Studio MAX generally appear as access violations. These can be resolved by isolating errors, checking plug-ins, contacting Kinetix through the Internet, and scanning hardware and service packs.

Troubleshooting is likely to give you a headache—hopefully, you will not have to do it too much. But if you do decide to troubleshoot your system, be patient and be intuitive, and you should be able to resolve the problem. If not, call someone for help!

CREATED BY JESSE K. MIGUEL, AIA (COURTESY HNTB SPORTS ARCHITECTURE)

Chapter 36

by Jesse K. Miguel, AIA

ARCHITECTURAL RENDERING: EXTERIOR DRIVE-THROUGHS AND FLY-BYS

This chapter takes a look at exterior, architectural, and highway 3D models used in creating photorealistic still images and computer animation. These consist of drive-throughs and fly-bys for video output. Animation of the 3D models allows the viewer of the design to experience what the 3D model looks like while walking through the building, driving through a proposed roadway, or flying by the proposed site.

3D Studio MAX enables 3D architectural designers the ability to build 3D models in the computer. This gives realism to their designs by using mapped materials that operate with bitmaps which can duplicate the look of actual materials. The realism in 3D Studio MAX additionally gives designers the ability to experience and view their design as if the building actually exists. This chapter is an overview of creating the 3D architectural models, and the use of the camera as the animation tool to record the experience of the models.

These topics are covered in this chapter:

- Constructing exterior 3D models

- Choosing and creating materials for exterior models

- Naming conventions of the objects to enable quick selecting and hiding.

- Using cameras for photorealistic still images

- Rendering high-resolution images; printer types

- Positioning sunlight in the model

- Understanding the moving camera

- Developing a storyboard

- Developing the background for the fly-by

- Animating the model with drive-throughs and fly-bys

- Transitioning from interior shots to exterior fly-bys

Exteriors of 3D Studio MAX Meshes

Exterior models refer to 3DS MAX meshes or models for exterior viewing, such as architectural buildings, roads and highways, airports, or even entire cities. As such, these models are intended to serve the same role as the traditional physical scaled-down constructed model. The computer model, however, offers an advantage over the physically built model; the computer model has the capability to realistically visualize the way that proposed structures look as static images and the ability of walking-through or flying-by proposed structures.

When you construct these exterior models, you must decide what to include in the model, and more importantly, how detailed it needs to be for the purposes of your design. Traditionally, architects and engineers work in a CAD system—like AutoCAD—that can set the units with a high degree of precision (down to decimals or fractions of an inch) that the program demands. Architects and engineers require that precision in their construction drawings; thus, when they construct 3D models, they tend to create every object in great detail.

For a 3D model that is used for manufacturing parts in a CAD/CAM system, such as automotive parts, precision in modeling every part correctly is required. Yet, for a typical perspective camera view of an entire building taken many hundreds of feet away, you never see the detailed texture or pattern of an exterior material unless you happen to zoom in for a close-up shot.

Examples of intricate details and their views from different distances are seen in figures 36.1 and 36.2. Figure 36.1 is a 3D model of a single bay for the new terminal building at T. F. Green Airport in Warwick, RI. The model simulates a "mock up" model usually built at the construction site, and is studying the appearance of the custom frit pattern in the glazing system.

Frit is the use of a silk-screened pattern on the inside layer of insulating glass, or sandwiched between two pieces of glass, that is used to reduce the amount of light transmission and create an intriguing appearance of architectural glass. This custom frit pattern consists of tiny 1" squares spaced about 1/2" apart, with a selected custom color. The rendered view of the bay in figure 36.1 shows the bay at eye level on the departure (2nd floor) level. Depending on the type of resolution on the final rendered image, the frit pattern may or may not be visible.

Not until you zoom in closely at the glazing (see fig. 36.2) can you tell that the frit is composed of tiny squares.

The model was built in AutoCAD and brought into 3DS MAX for rendering. The frit pattern shown was also drawn in AutoCAD, with each 1" square frit drawn as a closed polygon, arrayed accordingly, and brought into 3DS MAX where the single frits became a face. The glazing was assigned a green/blue glass material that was created in the Material Editor, and the frit was assigned the custom color. All other objects (the column enclosures, the steel columns, and the mullions) are a white matte material.

If this frit pattern created in AutoCAD was used for the glazing in the entire airport terminal building (see fig. 36.3), the file size would be tremendous due to the number of elements in the frit pattern's composition. Using mapped materials will reduce the file size and the total number of elements in the frit's pattern. You can create a substance in the Material Editor that uses a bitmap image of the frit pattern created in Adobe Photoshop, and use the bitmap as a diffuse map for the created material. This is covered later in the chapter in the section, "Creating Signs and Lettering."

FIGURE 36.1
Rendered view of single bay, T. F. Green Airport (courtesy HNTB Corp.).

FIGURE 36.2
Close-up of frit pattern on glazing (courtesy HNTB Corp.).

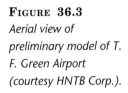

FIGURE 36.3
Aerial view of preliminary model of T. F. Green Airport (courtesy HNTB Corp.).

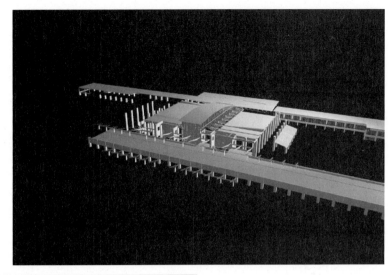

Constructing Exterior 3D Models

Architects generally build 3D representations of their design by first building physical scaled-down models. The types of models built range from inexpensive, simple-but-solid blocks that architects call "massing models" to intricate and highly detailed, realistic-looking presentation models used for client and public presentation. These physical presentation models can be quite elaborate, showing minute details to represent the types of materials the building is constructed of and can be wired for lighting to add to the realism of the model. The cost of these presentation models can be expensive based on certain criteria: the detail involved, the method constructed (some architects have used CAM with lasers to create parts of their presentation models), whether there are moving parts such as the retractable roofs in sports complexes, and the overall physical size of the model.

Building a 3D model in the computer is similar. For instance, the types of models can range from low-detail massing models to high-detail presentation models. The differences between various computer models is in the amount of detail created in the objects. The more details that are created in the scene and the larger the number of objects, the bigger the file sizes become. Just as the need to determine cost and complexity is a major concern in physical modeling, you need to use discretion with computer modeling when determining what needs to be built, and you also must consider the amount of detailing that will appear in the final images or animation.

Despite the similarities between these two different kinds of model creation mediums, differences do exist. Creating realistic 3D models in the computer can cost less than the traditional physical presentation model mentioned earlier. The time required to create a model in the computer is usually less than creating a physical presentation model, depending on the amount of detail required. One advantage in the computer model is its capability to make changes and revisions easier, such as altering materials and colors. But the biggest advantage of the computer model is its capability to enable viewers the chance to see what a building looks like while walking through it, what a driver sees while driving down a highway, and what it looks like to fly around a site. Physical models, however, are scaled-down representations of the proposed design, and cannot portray the actual visualization of the design like the computer model can.

An example of a low-detail massing model of buildings is shown in figure 36.4, which shows a model of a proposed elevated bridge over an existing highway in downtown San Juan, Puerto Rico. The focus of the project is the elevated bridge structure, for which a fly-by animation and a drive-through were illustrated in the final video. Due to its urban location, most of the building masses were needed to show the bridge in context of the site. Time constraints, however, prevented creating a more realistic set of buildings. Figure 36.5 shows the bridge. The photo matches and the picture results in a still image.

FIGURE 36.4
Aerial view of PR-181.

FIGURE **36.5**

(Top) An existing photo of PR-181. (Bottom) The proposed new elevated roadway, San Juan, Puerto Rico (courtesy HNTB Corp.).

Figure 36.6 illustrates a highly detailed presentation 3D model. HNTB's design for a multipurpose stadium, the TranStadia, focuses on the design concept. The 3D model's exterior elements are more defined for the purpose of conveying the overall design concept and the transformation of a multipurpose stadium. Because the idea behind the animation is to illustrate the conversion from a football stadium to a baseball park—as well as a fly-by of the stadia—most of the views were constructed from an aerial viewpoint. This outlook on the stadia is similar to the view from a blimp during a televised game. Later in the section, "Flying Through a Model—TranStadia," we will use this stadia as an example of the fly-by animation created for the video.

FIGURE 36.6
(Top) TranStadia football configuration. (Bottom) TranStadia baseball configuration, (courtesy HNTB Sports Architecture).

Most 3D architectural designers have been trained to use a CAD package such as AutoCAD to create their 3D models. They import the models from AutoCAD into 3D Studio MAX through DXF, 3DS, or DWG import features. Still others have become proficient in creating 3D architectural models strictly in 3D Studio and 3D Studio MAX. Experience tells computer graphics experts that no modeling method is more correct than any other as long as the end result is a model that illustrates the design's intent effectively.

NOTE

As a designer whose work comes primarily from designs generated in a CAD package such as AutoCAD for architectural projects and Microstation and Inroads for bridges and highway design, I have relied on CAD data to help generate the 3D models either in AutoCAD R13 or R14. I have done this by creating the 3D models in AutoCAD using their Solid Modeling commands and importing them into 3DS MAX, or by importing the lines created in AutoCAD as shapes and paths into 3DS MAX for lofting and extruding into 3D models.

TIP

Flipped faces in which the normals are facing the wrong way are always a problem when importing 3D files from CAD systems. If several random faces need to be flipped to render correctly, use the forced two-sided option in the Rendering dialog. You must weigh the time involved in correcting every face that appears in your renderings to rendering that is not as fast.

Choosing Materials for Exterior Models

Choosing the materials for your model is the most critical aspect for creating a realistic impression of the proposed design. Models made of stone, glass, plastic, or steel materials must convey the visual characteristics of those given physical materials. Understanding the properties of certain materials is critical for mastering the ability to create photorealistic images. The Material Editor enables you to obtain materials from the default 3DS MAX library or manipulate them to create new materials. In addition, thousands of textures are available in 3D Studio's World Creating Toolkit, Texture Universe (included in the Designer Utility Pack from Kinetix), and after-market texture CD-ROMs.

TIP

Autodesk has a Browser available to view their materials and textures. Certain aftermarket texture CD-ROMs come with illustrations of the texture images for a quick reference. The German book, *Autodesk 3D Studio -World Creating Toolkit,* published by permission of Autodesk Germany, also has all the images and textures in 3D Studio's World Creating Toolkit, making it easier to view and locate images quickly.

The Material Editor can create some special effects morphing, transformations, and even animation of characters for physical movement, hence enabling them to dance. In the construction industry, however, materials are normally not special-effects oriented. Architects and engineers rely on showing their design; consequently, their needs are showing various materials' design realistically.

Two basic material types can be used to model buildings:

- **Solid materials.** This classification includes brick, stone, concrete, and steel; with matte or shiny finishes that have no transparency.

- **Transparent materials.** This classification includes glass for windows and glazed curtain wall systems. All are clear, colored, shiny, and reflective.

Most materials you need for a given 3D model can be taken directly from the 3D Studio MAX Materials Library, the World Creating Toolkit, or other CD-ROMs with textures. For the most part and especially for architectural projects, you will end up creating custom materials not found anywhere else. You can revise characteristics of existing brick materials (such as color and texture) from the 3DS MAX Materials Library to create variations of custom brick materials. For each project, it is wise to create a separate Materials Library file (*.MAT) rather than load new materials into the existing default 3DSMAX.MAT Library file.

One way of creating unique materials is to scan the actual sample of the material. To accomplish this, it is preferable to take a photograph of the material. In this case, take a picture of the mockup sample wall to use as mapping.

Figure 36.7 shows a photograph of an actual mockup wall of the Arriscraft material, a precast concrete block system that simulates a stone finish, built for the Northeastern University Marino Recreation Center. Several types of mockup walls were built, using various exterior materials such as brown brick, white brick, concrete block, and Arriscraft (chosen material). These walls were built to study and determine the material to use for the actual building. The sample wall was not available during the design phase, so the materials were created using some of the default materials. The properties were then changed by using different texture maps, adjusting colors, or adjusting lighting properties.

Figure 36.7
Photograph of Arriscraft from sample mockup wall, Northeastern University.

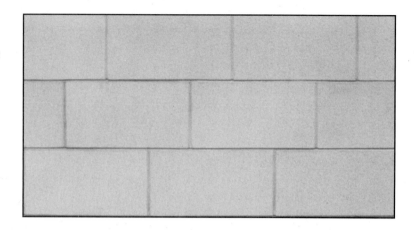

Note

Photographs of materials can be revised in an image-editing program, such as Adobe Photoshop, to correct contrast, adjust brightness, or correct positions of masonry joints due to parallax created when the camera is tilted upward. Problems with tiling may occur when you use images as maps for materials. *Inside 3D Studio MAX Volume I* by New Rider's Publishing also contains an excellent section on tiling maps.

Often, no sample wall is created because the 3D models for visualization studies occur early in the design stage instead of in the construction document stage. Figure 36.8 shows the bitmap used to create a new material in the Material Editor. The pattern was drawn originally in AutoCAD as closed polylines, imported as a DXF into 3DS MAX (which creates a surface on a closed polyline from AutoCAD), rendered in 3DS MAX as an image, and refined in Adobe Photoshop to create a tileable bitmap. This could have been built as actual geometry, but the time savings to create the actual surfaces in addition to the capability to revise and change surface materials, makes using the mapped method more efficient.

This new material was used for the exterior finishes for the new Oakland Coliseum Arena, home of the Golden State Warriors (see fig. 36.9). HNTB has redesigned the interior bowl section and added outer structures housing the new entrance lobbies, fire stairs, retail and office areas to the existing exterior glass wall, x-bracing, and roof. The exterior treatment called for the diamond scoring in the upper panels (to parallel the x-bracing, which is the new material used in the bitmap in figure 36.9).

FIGURE 36.8
Bitmap image for exterior panel, Oakland Coliseum Arena.

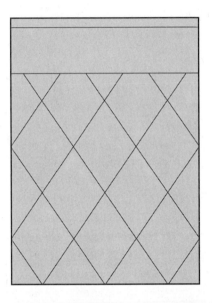

FIGURE 36.9
Exterior perspective view of Oakland Coliseum Arena, Oakland, CA (courtesy HNTB Sports Architecture).

Simulating Masonry in 3D Designs

Creating brick buildings could be as simple as assigning the default brick material from the Material Library in the Material Editor. In the real world, there are literally thousands of variations of brick and masonry products that architects select for their buildings. With architectural design in 3DS

MAX, use the Material Editor, because new masonry materials are created by using bitmaps that can be tiled, adjusting the color parameters, and varying the bump map to create a textured appearance.

Figure 36.10 shows the across-the-street view of the Northeastern University Marino Recreation Center. This camera view shows the entire recreation center in addition to the fence and trees surrounding the complex, and distant buildings in the background. The primary attribute of the masonry from this distance is its color. The texture enrichment becomes more apparent in the close-up view shown in figure 36.11. If you study photographs of architectural buildings, you notice that textures are difficult to see from a distant shot unless the masonry is heavily rusticated.

FIGURE 36.10

Perspective view of Northeastern University Marino Recreation Center (courtesy HNTB Corp.).

Subtle textures of the masonry are not as apparent in this far-away view as they are in the close-up view shown in figure 36.11.

Creating Glass Surfaces

Creating glass material could be simple if all you needed to do was to use the default materials. Unfortunately, in the real architectural world, there are a myriad of glass types, consisting of colors, tints, reflective coatings, and ceramic frit patterns within the glazing.

FIGURE 36.11
*Close-up view of east
wall (courtesy HNTB
Corp.).*

For an interior view of the building, using default glass types such as clear glass may be adequate to show a background; for instance, an interior view of the sky through the glass. For an exterior shot, however, the parameters are difficult. When seeing a daytime view of the building, the color of the glazing is difficult to see due to the reflection of the blue sky off the glass. Reflections of surrounding elements such as trees or neighboring buildings also cast a reflection. The final effects you must take into consideration are sunlight and creating highlights, shadows, and reflections.

Figure 36.12 shows a close-up detail of the glazing system used for the Northeastern University Recreation Center. The glass material was created in the Material Editor using the default glass, adjusted to a blue-green tint in the Diffuse and Ambient button under Basic Parameters, with the reflection map in the Map pullout changed to Flat Mirror in the Material/Maps Browser. Reflections of the steel columns are visible in the glazing.

These glass materials with the flat mirror created in 3DS4 or earlier 3D Studio programs cross-over effectively into 3DS MAX.

You can change the characteristics of color, shine, and glass materials from the Material Editor library to create diverse glass materials. To create a reflective curtain wall with a mirror finish, for example, you must create a glass material with the flat mirror texture in the reflection map Note that any type of reflective properties, such as reflective glass, increase the rendering time. This is because of the extensive computations that 3DS MAX or AutoCAD must perform to mirror the image, as well as calculations of lights turned on and shadows cast.

FIGURE 36.12
View of glazing and steel column, Northeastern University (courtesy HNTB Corp.).

Creating Signs and Lettering

Signs and lettering give buildings and their environment additional realism. An airport terminal without the different airline logos would look less real compared to a terminal showing the logos. Lettering and text created in 3DS MAX using the Create, Shapes, Text command and applying the Extrude Modifier is the mainstay for commercial logos. For a majority of signs that are flat, the use of a bitmap image of the sign is effective in creating signs and lettering.

Figures 36.13 and 36.14 illustrate two other options that were studied for the east wall of the recreation center. These studies were done for the design options of identifying the building with the university as well as for showing the name and seal of the university. One proposal was for a metal seal, and the other was for a carved stone seal.

FIGURE 36.13
Metal university seal at the east wall (courtesy HNTB Corp.).

FIGURE 36.14
Cast stone seal at the east wall (courtesy HNTB Corp.).

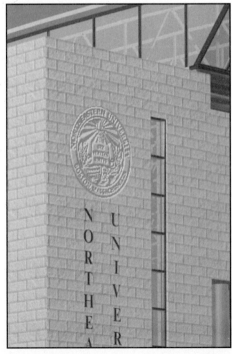

A scanned image of the Northeastern University logo was used as a map for both seals. In the Material Editor of 3DS MAX, the metal logo used an opacity map to enable transparency in the open areas. The cast stone look was achieved by using the Bump map and setting it to Invert. It is possible to actually build the model of the metal logo. On the other hand, using this mapped method reduces the object to a single element as opposed to using an object comprised of thousands of faces and elements to make up the metal logo.

The lettering is created as a shape using Create, Shape, Text and applying the Extrude modifier to give thickness to the letters. It is inserted into place at the east wall as well as at the top row of glazing at the curved curtain wall (see fig. 36.24 for the front view of the recreation center).

Creating 3D roadway signs, billboards, and posters from objects that are usually flat 2D objects is typically resolved by using an image-editing software program such as Adobe Photoshop. Figure 36.15 shows a tollbooth with the express toll lane sign. The sign was created by scanning a black-and-white drawing from a set of construction drawings, and touching up the image in Photoshop with the correct colors. The image was saved as a JPG file and placed in the 3DSMAX\maps directory. A new material was created with the JPG image as a texture map, with the decal option on.

FIGURE 36.15
KTAG express toll lane sign, East Topeka Interchange. Topeka, KS (courtesy HNTB Corp.).

Creating Variations in Paint Color

The ability to change the appearance of the materials assigned to the objects in 3DS MAX is an advantage over the physical model. An example is the color of the model. In a physical model, to show different color options, the modeler has to either create separate models with the different colors, or create several parts of the model that has to be physically inserted into and removed from the building model. In 3DS MAX, the color changes quickly by simply modifying the Ambient and Diffuse color in the Basic Parameters of the Material Editor.

Using the Material Editor to assign different types of colored material to a 3D object provides the architect with an opportunity to study various color schemes. Figure 36.16 shows four color studies for the roadway canopies for the aforementioned T. F. Green Airport.

FIGURE 36.16

Four color studies for the roadway canopies, T. F. Green Airport (courtesy HNTB Corp.).

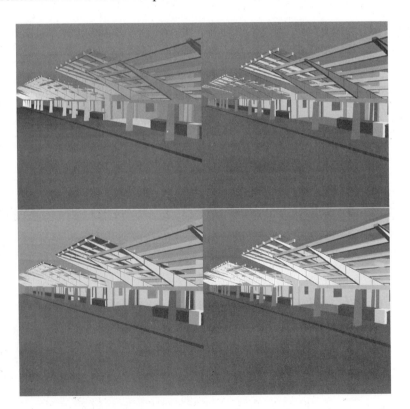

Hiding 3D Objects in Exterior Views

To decrease rendering time, hide objects that aren't visible for a particular image. If you have a model constructed of interior and exterior objects but you need to render only the exterior for a daytime scene, for example, select the objects and choose the Display button. Then do a Hide Selected command to hide interior objects that don't need to be seen.

TIP

Due to the large number of interior objects for a building and to avoid time-consuming selection of the objects, you might want to use wildcards in the Select Objects dialog to save time.

Figure 36.17 shows an example of objects starting with the letters BAR (for parts for a bar). Using the Select Objects dialog, type **BAR*** in the top box and press Enter; all the objects beginning with the letters BAR are selected. This saves considerable time versus having to select each object to hide or not hide the selection. Naming objects appropriately to allow for hiding objects assumes great importance.

FIGURE 36.17

Select Objects dialog.

Refer back to figure 36.10 for a daytime view of the building. The interiors of the recreation center—including the roof trusses, walls, and columns—are slightly visible. Yet, the interior view of the building contains even more objects. Figure 36.18 shows an interior view of the atrium of the Oakland Coliseum Arena, with all the interior elements visible. Select the majority of the interior elements, such as the floor, carpet, base trim, doors, and some railing. Use the Display, Hide Selected button to hide objects not visible in an exterior daytime shot.

FIGURE 36.18

Interior atrium of club lounge, Oakland Coliseum Arena (courtesy HNTB Sports Architecture).

You might need to leave the interior objects on for a nighttime view, because with the lights turned on inside the building, the interiors often are visible from the outside. Figure 36.19 illustrates a night view of a student recreation center whose interiors are visible as a result of the light source within the building.

Always keep in mind that sometimes you can get carried away building every part of the 3D model, from the most minute detail visible in the interiors to the smallest blade of grass. Unless you do heavy Hollywood-type animation and your storyboard shows a minute detail of the texture of the brick material zooming out to an aerial view of a particular building, you really don't need to try to show every invisible part throughout the duration of the animation.

FIGURE 36.19
Night view of Northeastern University Marino Recreation Center (courtesy HNTB Corp.).

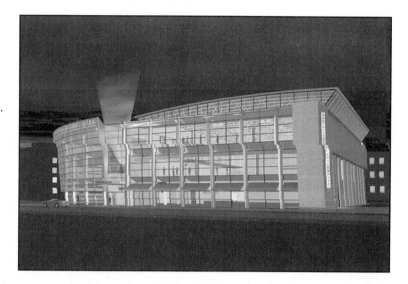

The opposite rule applies to still images. You need to show every detail pertaining to the particular view created for a high-resolution image. A client might not notice certain subtleties while viewing an animation on the monitor or through a videotape, yet if that client has a hard copy still image like an 8×10 color photograph, for example, he would notice every finite detail of the image. Architects dealing with material choices and color selections especially must consider this issue. The models they construct usually require a high degree of detail.

Figures 36.20–36.22 show a proposed pavilion at T. F. Green Airport in Warwick, Rhode Island. The pavilion is designed to enable departing passengers to get from the ground level parking lot to the departure level on the second floor. Inside is an escalator, a stairway, and an elevator for access to the departure level. The intricate guardrails consist of stainless steel rods spaced 2 1/2" apart. For the still image, small detailing like the guardrail is visible. If you are viewing the animation figure through the pavilion, however, the guardrail appears only as a blur in the background. The guardrail could have been replaced by a material with a map applied, such as the signs mentioned in the "Creating Signs and Lettering" section.

FIGURE 36.20
Exterior view of stair pavilion, T. F. Green Airport (courtesy HNTB Corp.).

FIGURE 36.21
Interior view of stair pavilion, T. F. Green Airport (courtesy HNTB Corp.).

FIGURE 36.22

Interior view of stair pavilion, T. F. Green Airport (courtesy HNTB Corp.).

Using Appropriate Materials for Different Distances

Depending on the distance of the camera views and the path of the animation, you might have to use different materials for the same object, depending on the view of the building. Still images might require that you use a material produced by texture-mapped photographic images to show realism. If the entire sequence of an animation is an aerial view from a certain distance, you really don't need to use the same detailed material when a similar material of the same color would suffice. If the animation passes the material quickly, the resulting animation might appear to be a blur, as mentioned previously. If you don't have time to change materials back and forth between the fine detailed material and the simpler material, stick with the detailed material. If your goal is to save time because you need to generate several animation renderings without sufficient rendering time, go for the appropriate models for the required rendering purpose.

T I P

Keep a single master model as the base, and copy several models with various material types from the close-up, detailed version to the model used for long-range shots. Imagine Hollywood movie setups that create various sets for different scenes.

An example of using both an interior-detailed model and an exterior model for an animation sequence is discussed later in the section "Moving From an Interior View to an Exterior Fly-By, Oakland Coliseum Arena." The script calls for a panning view within the interior of the arena. Then it asks for dollying backward from the basketball court moving up toward the upper deck seating, through the exterior wall and ending as a fly-by of the arena for the final ending of the video.

Cameras in 3D Studio MAX

The camera is the key animation element for creating walk-throughs of buildings, drive-bys in roadways, and fly-bys of exterior models. As mentioned previously, most buildings do not have parts that move and therefore do not need to be animated to show motion. Yet, the ability to visualize the experience of going inside a building or driving a new highway is what most laypersons want to see to understand the intented design. It is imperative in creating a convincing animation of an exterior mesh that you have essential knowledge of the camera controls.

3D Studio MAX offers a powerful, easy-to-use camera feature that behaves similarly to an actual 35 mm single lens reflex camera, yet has the capability to act like a video camera with its option to record over time. The 3DS MAX camera is also similar to the AutoCAD camera, except that it operates at a higher level in the following ways:

■ Offers far greater control over the distance and type of lens

■ Offers more powerful capability to calculate field of vision

■ Offers better dollying capabilities

■ More clearly illustrates the location of the camera and its target on-screen

To generate realistic camera views, you need to understand basic photography principles. You don't have to be a professional photographer to use 3D

Studio MAX's camera, but understanding types of lenses, field of vision, effects using wide angle and zoom lens, and target viewpoint help you create photorealistic images without coming off as an amateur. 3DS MAX has camera controls that allow stock lenses (15 mm, 28 mm, 50 mm, 85 mm, and so on) or manual lenses that you adjust (like a zoom lens). This automatically adjusts the field of view and the range (depth of field), just like a 35 mm camera. No need for f-stops adjustment, since lighting needs to be placed to create the ideal lighting condition for the camera. All these camera controls are animatable, which means if you want to zoom in over time, it's a matter of changing the zoom lens with the Animate button on.

Recording Photographs of the Existing Site

When you take photographs of an existing site to use as backgrounds for 3D Studio MAX models, note the date and time of the photographs, in addition to the type of camera and lens you use (for example, 35 mm versus a 4×5, 28 mm versus a 50 mm). Location on the site is also beneficial for creating camera views in AutoCAD using the DVIEW command, and imported to 3DS MAX. Noting the date enables you to use the Sun Locator from the Designer Utility Pack to create the light source for importing into 3DS MAX.

Matching Camera View from AutoCAD DVIEW Perspective Views

AutoCAD R12 and earlier didn't enable you to export camera perspective views created with the DVIEW command into 3D Studio MAX using the DXFOUT command. To re-create camera views, you first had to jot down the location of the target and the camera, the camera zoom lens used, and the height, or Z coordinate. Next, you had to create a line with a thickness or a 3D face from the target point to the camera point. Finally, you had to try to create the camera using this line or face imported into 3DS MAX as a guide for camera and target placement.

AutoCAD R13's 3DSOUT command eliminates this problem. With perspective views, the DVIEW command is used to create and save, especially as views convert to 3D Studio MAX cameras with the same corresponding view and camera names. 3D Studio MAX R1.1 and later versions can read DWG files from AutoCAD, and can also bring in the cameras created in the AutoCAD R13 and later versions.

Using 3D Studio MAX Camera Controls

Using the Camera feature in 3D Studio MAX is fairly straightforward. The camera simulates a standard 35 mm SLR camera. In 3D Studio MAX, you now have the option of creating a camera with targets, or creating a free camera. The target camera is the same camera used in 3D Studio and AutoCAD. You choose Create, Camera to create a camera, and then set the camera to a target point to set the camera's location. Then select the appropriate settings under the Parameters rollout or under the Modify command panel with the camera selected at the same time you are creating the camera (lens type, field of view, range). The free camera has no target to create, and its use is geared toward following a complex path with several banks and vertical orientation—such as a roller coaster ride or flying in an F-14. The type of animation you are using determines the type of camera that is used for a fly-by or drive-through.

One important feature in the camera control parameters is clipping planes. By setting the amount to a range that the camera sees, the view can be *clipped*, or cut off. To generate cross-sections through a model, you can slice the model to see its sections, in the same way that architects and engineers draw their structures. For animation that shows walk-throughs and drive-throughs, the clipping plane feature helps reduce the completion time by rendering only the portion of the scene that the camera is viewing when a particular frame is being rendered.

TIP

Knowing the camera type, lens type, approximate camera location, height, and target helps when you try to match the background to the 3D model.

When you want to create photorealistic camera views, consider your use of the 3D Studio MAX camera as you would a real 35 mm camera. You don't need to study photojournalism or know darkroom techniques. Having a basic understanding of using a real 35 mm camera will help you in using the 3D Studio MAX camera. This includes understanding how using super-wide angle lenses or telephoto or zoom lenses affects your scene. In addition, it's important to know how the field of vision affects the appearance of the view and to realize how views outside the cone of vision become severely distorted.

Perspective Matching: 3D Studio MAX

Creating images of the 3D model superimposed over a photographic background is what most architects have used in presentations to illustrate how the proposed model looks in a given existing site. Using the perspective match, architects can show the proposed building without having to model all the existing background, and clients have a method of visualizing the design in their setting.

3D Studio MAX includes a feature that enables you to do perspective matching easily and more accurately using the photographic image as a background for the 3D model or mesh. Chapter 21, "Using Cameras," of the *3D Studio MAX User's Guide Volume II: Rendering and Animation*, offers a good explanation for learning and using this perspective matching feature; it also explains the improvements made in 3D Studio MAX over 3D Studio. Camera moving and background moving controls are now easier due to these enhancements, such as the ability to see a fully colored background, and the moving controls that retains the model image in the viewports that 3D Studio did not offer.

Two examples of 3D models superimposed with a photographic background are shown in figures 36.23 and 36.24. Figure 36.23 shows an aerial view of Boston, with an exterior model of the recreation center near the center of the image (see fig. 36.23). Figure 36.24 shows the view of the recreation center at street level, with the model of the building set on the site. The images in figures 36.23 and 36.24 used an image-editing software program such as Aldus Photostyler for correcting foreground figures; for example, the buildings to the front in the aerial views (see fig. 36.23) and the cars in the street-level view (see fig. 36.24) used an image-editing program.

FIGURE 36.23
(Top) Aerial view of Boston. (Bottom) Close-up of Northeastern University Marino Recreation Center (courtesy HNTB Corp.).

FIGURE 36.24

Street-level view of Northeastern University Marino Recreation Center (courtesy HNTB Corp.).

TIP
_____

For many projects, I opt to match the 3D model with the photographic background, but render the image without the background and merge the rendered 3D image with the photographic background in Adobe Photoshop 3.0 and higher-powered Photoshop programs. With Photoshop's extensive layering capabilities, the image of existing background and foreground together with the 3D rendered model is quickly edited, revised, and removed. The image can be removed by editing each part of the layer, or by shutting the layer that shows several phases of the project.

The images in figure 36.25 show the beginning and completed use of the photomatching process, merged in Photoshop. The project is a proposal for a new bridge over an existing public natural parkland with a bike trail running adjacent to the Poudre River in Fort Collins, CO. The bridge and landscape have multiple design changes and the bike path is relocated. It made sense to create one rendered image of the bridge and use the layering of Photoshop to show the modifications of the site after the bridge's completion (showing the existing trees in background and foreground of the bridge), and the view after additional trees are planted and have matured years later.

FIGURE 36.25

(Top) Existing photo of Timberline bridge location. (Middle) Timberline bridge view after completion. (Bottom) Timberline Bridge view after added landscaping.

Photoshop is also helpful when creating a photographic background that does not exist. An on-bridge view is shown in figure 36.26. No photos were taken of the background—the view for the position above the river could not be created because existing trees would have blocked the view if the picture was taken from a position that used a zoom lens to simulate the view on top of the proposed bridge. Additionally, new landscaping on the side of the new roadway and the banks of the river would need to be shown. Showing the bridge without any background would not have conveyed to the public what the bridge would look like in its true context; thus, Photoshop was used to create a background.

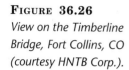

FIGURE 36.26
View on the Timberline Bridge, Fort Collins, CO (courtesy HNTB Corp.).

Rendering High-Resolution Images

After you create the views, the cameras, and the light setups, final output to a hard copy requires some additional steps. Experts are asked how to generate remarkably high-resolution, color hard copies—usually 8×10 photographic images—for presentation or distribution to clients. Many types of color printers exist in today's market, ranging from affordable bubble jet printers and dye-sublimation printers to expensive offset color printers used for high-end publications. Technology is changing rapidly in the color printing process, so it's important to see what latest methods for color printers are available through service bureaus.

Judge the following criteria when you are looking for a high-resolution color printer:

- **Resolution.** The dots or pixels per inch it generates.

- **Calibration.** The color calibration required to match the color seen in your monitor to the final output.

- **Cost.** The cost of printing—printer, paper, ink costs.

- **Quality.** Quality of printer output—color laser copies, bubble-jet, photographic dye-sublimation.

- **Network capabilities.** Cross-platform (PC and Mac).

Color images on your video monitor appear to be high-resolution, with images typically shown in 640×480 or 1024×768, depending on your monitor size. Yet, when you output these same images, their on-screen crispness disappears. In the past, you had to render the images at a higher number of pixels than the typical computer monitor resolution, with the belief that screen resolutions matching process resolutions yielded better results. This is no longer true. Process resolutions like 1600×1200 now provide excellent results in 8×10 glossies. Additionally, 1024×768 or 1280×1024 (common render resolutions) produce nice results in modern processes that anti-alias non-integral dpi counts, such as most current dyesub and photoimager processes. Furthermore, a service bureau who insists on using TIFs or TGAs with imbedded dpi counts is no better than a service bureau that can't read a standard TIF *without* embedded dpi information. Photoshop and other programs will interpret this as being in inches across a figure equal to the resolution.

Positioning the Sunlight in the Model

A particularly useful type of animation is the creation of time-lapse photography, in which a still camera records a view of the exterior 3D model and shows the light and shadows cast by the building during the course of a particular day.

The Sunlight plug-in from Kinetix's Designer Utility Pack enables you to create the direction of the sunlight for any location. Using the Create, Systems Sunlight, the roll-out for the Sun Locator appears. Clicking on the "Get Location" button enables the Geographic Locator dialog box (see fig. 36.27). The geographic locator enables you to pinpoint locations of major cities throughout the world. You can do this by selecting the listed cities, clicking on the maps of all the continents, or even entering the latitude and longitude of a particular location The path of the sun for any particular day can be animated, enabling shadow studies for buildings.

Figure 36.27
Geographic Location from the Sunlight plug-in in the Designer Utility Pack by Kinetix.

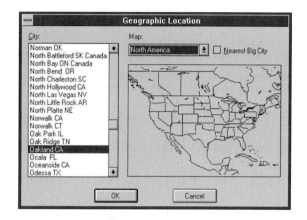

Animating the Model with Drive-Throughs and Fly-Bys

Constructing the model is by far the most time-consuming part of the design process. When time is a factor, creating still images and animating the completed exterior model is much faster than creating a 3D model to final rendered animation.

Models of buildings, cities, bridges, or landscape usually don't involve moving objects. The medium by which drive-throughs and fly-bys are used to animate these exterior views is the moving camera rendered over time. Animating 3D exterior models—because of their size—is usually associated with views from a moving automobile or from a flying structure such as a helicopter or a plane.

Understanding the Moving "Motion" Camera

The moving camera used in animation is more like a motion picture camera. Think of a moving camera as a flying object—such as a plane—that flies through the model and records the flight through its camera; think of yourself as the pilot of that plane. You have to navigate or create the flight path for the camera to fly, and you want to make that path as fluid as the flight path of a plane. Any sharp, quick turn of the camera results in a blurring effect. Like a camcorder left on Record while the user turns rapidly and shoots from side-to-side, the moving camera produces the same erratic motions. Fortunately, 3D Studio MAX has made creating the moving cameras simpler through the Move command, the Animate button, and smooth Bézier movement along the path, as well as enabling different camera controls to be changed or animated over time.

Developing a Storyboard

If you want to produce effective computer animation, you must begin with a storyboard. A *storyboard* is a series of rough sketches that illustrate the key scenes in a movie or animation. (Figure 36.28 shows an example of storyboarding.) 3DS MAX users can create an animation while playing with 3DS MAX, but to effectively convey your message and intentions to others and create a truly successful animation requires you to put down your strong ideas into sketch form.

FIGURE 36.28

Storybook sketch of animation for Northeastern University.

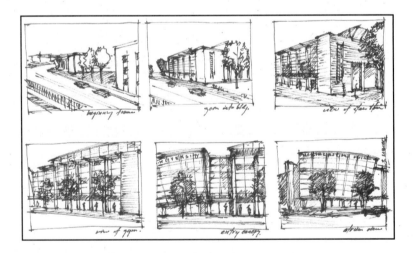

For good examples of storyboarding, you might study books on cartoon animation and film making. These books show you that artists draw rough sketches illustrating scenes throughout a movie, and this is called *storyboarding*. You also might study movies and film. As you watch a movie, pretend you're the director and imagine composing the shots, panning the views, and timing the sequences. The ultimate goal is to tell a good story, because all the special effects are wasted if they don't contribute effectively to telling the story.

Computer animation as a final product manifests itself in many ways, such as videotapes for public and client presentation, marketing, or public hearings. Creating a video usually involves not only computer animation, but also a script, additional video footage, music, and voice-overs to create an effective video that conveys a message. Figure 36.29 illustrates the storyboard sketches created in conjunction with the script written by the New Media group at HNTB who specialize in creating video and multimedia projects. It was presented to the clients for their review and approval before going ahead with the final video (see fig. 36.29).

FIGURE 36.29

Storybook sketch and script for the Oakland Coliseum Arena, Golden State Warriors (courtesy HNTB Technology Group).

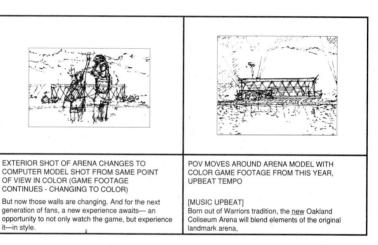

EXTERIOR SHOT OF ARENA CHANGES TO COMPUTER MODEL SHOT FROM SAME POINT OF VIEW IN COLOR (GAME FOOTAGE CONTINUES - CHANGING TO COLOR)

But now those walls are changing. And for the next generation of fans, a new experience awaits— an opportunity to not only watch the game, but experience it—in style.

POV MOVES AROUND ARENA MODEL WITH COLOR GAME FOOTAGE FROM THIS YEAR, UPBEAT TEMPO

[MUSIC UPBEAT]
Born out of Warriors tradition, the new Oakland Coliseum Arena will blend elements of the original landmark arena,

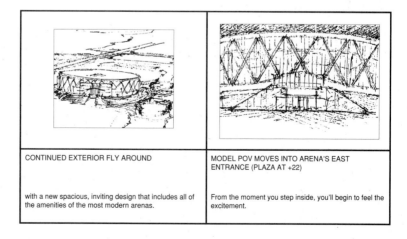

CONTINUED EXTERIOR FLY AROUND

with a new spacious, inviting design that includes all of the amenities of the most modern arenas.

MODEL POV MOVES INTO ARENA'S EAST ENTRANCE (PLAZA AT +22)

From the moment you step inside, you'll begin to feel the excitement.

Creating the Background for the Fly-By

You have to use the sky as a background for daytime exterior animation—you can't just use the background method used for still image renderings. Because the camera moves through the site, the sky remains unchanged while the building viewpoint changes, and this gives your animation an artificial appearance. You can approach this sky background problem from a couple different directions:

- Build a planetarium or a dome over the entire building or site. (If the animation requires a moving camera, you want to build a mega dome over the building (or preferably the city) to serve as the sky. You then want to add the material sky texture or any other sky or clouds material to the inside surface of the dome.)

    1. Choose Create, Geometry, Sphere to build the sky dome or planetarium over the building or city.

    2. Increase the number of segments to make the sphere smoother, then set the Hemisphere to .5 (50 percent of the sphere) and check Generate Mapping Coordinates.

    3. Apply an Edit Mesh Modifier, click on Sub-Object, select Face, then select all the faces of the hemisphere. Next click on Flip in the Normal area of the Edit Surface rollout to make sure that the inside rather than the outside of the dome is visible (see fig. 36.30).

WARNING

Be sure to delete or detach the bottom of the hemisphere; otherwise, the sky appears on the ground. See figure 36.31 for a rendered view of the dome.

- Create a background environment for the animation.

    1. Use the Rendering, Environment setup to create a background environment for the animation.

    2. Use the spherical or cylindrical environment in the Material Editor, and apply a sky or cloud bitmap.

FIGURE 36.30
The planetarium or dome over the city for creating a sky background.

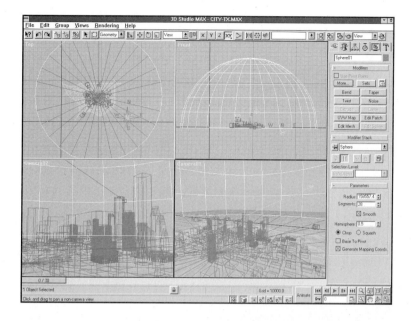

FIGURE 36.31
Rendered view of sky dome from an aerial view.

WARNING

Refer to the User's Guide or to *Inside 3D Studio MAX Vol. I* for a more detailed description of using the environmental maps.

Driving Through a Model—East Topeka Interchange

Using 3D CAD in highway design software has created a method for understanding the design clearly. Rather than creating flat 2D plans, by creating vertical elevation (or heights) of the roadways, 3D data has the capability to generate correct cross-sections of the highway, as well as provide the capability to create 3D views of the proposed highway design. One of the differences between architecture design and highway design is that in buildings, the floors are flat, set to a constant elevation, and construction components of the buildings are based on certain set elevations for every given floor. Roadway design, on the other hand, does not have a given fixed elevation, because for the most part, roadway elevation (verticals) changes constantly as it goes up and down hills. Another feature of roadway design is that it has slope banks at exit and entrance ramps, and it is typically placed in a site with various contours (with the exception of a flat plain area).

Visualization of the proposed roadway is the public's primary handicap. Viewing plans of a proposed interchange in plan view, or even in an aerial perspective view, may be too intimidating for the general public, stemming from their concern about its impact to their community (see fig. 39.32). By showing the public what their driving experience could be, they are given a greater understanding of the proposed design.

FIGURE 36.32
Aerial view of proposed Interstate 70 Interchange, Topeka, KS (courtesy HNTB Corp.).

As mentioned earlier in the chapter, using 3D highway design software means you must import that data into 3D Studio MAX to create a rendered model and to create animation. For the East Topeka Interchange, the original 3D CAD files were generated in Microstation using Inroads, a 3D highway design software. 3D data was brought into AutoCAD Release 13 and *then* brought into 3D Studio MAX; this extra step was required because Microstation's DWG and DXF export was to an AutoCAD R12 or earlier file format, and only AutoCAD R13 files could be imported into 3D Studio MAX. Figure 36.33 shows the highway design in AutoCAD.

FIGURE 36.33

AutoCAD file of East Topeka Interchange (courtesy HNTB Corp.).

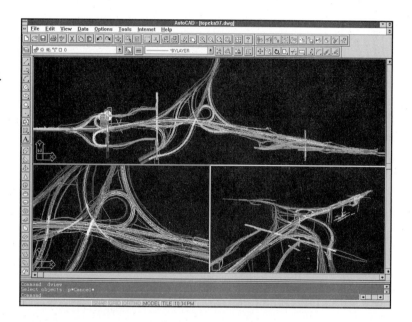

The 3D lines (penlines) generated in Inroads were used to generate the profiles of the proposed roadway, showing the centerline of the roadway, edge of the pavement, and edge of the shoulders. These lines were used as a base for creating the camera path needed for the drive-through animation. Figure 36.34 shows the imported interstate, indicating the trajectory of the imported path. This drive-through shows Interstate 70 heading westbound for 3 1/2 miles, starting before the tollbooths (refer to fig. 36.15), under the flyover ramps (see fig. 36.35), and exiting at the circular ramp to the intersection. Creating this path in 3D Studio MAX could be possible, but with the adjustments—tweaking and matching the height of the path above the roadway constantly—it is better to bring in the path from the CAD data and adjust the variables, such as changing the speed and banking adjacent in TrackView.

FIGURE 36.34

*Top view of East
Topeka Interchange
showing trajectory of
Camera01 for drive-
through (courtesy
HNTB Corp.).*

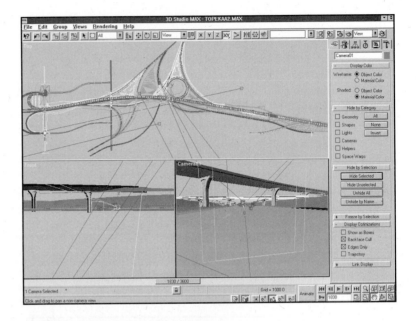

FIGURE 36.35

*East Topeka
Interchange at frame
1840 (courtesy HNTB
Corp.).*

Flying Through a Model—TranStadia

Creating fly-through animation has become simpler in 3D Studio MAX. Rather than having to generate a path first and then link the cameras to it, 3D Studio MAX's capability to move the target camera's position and target, while changing the frame numbers makes it simpler to create quick fly-through animation. Most fly-by paths are not restricted to an actual flight pattern (with the exception of some planes) like the roadway is, resulting in greater freedom for the animator in creating camera movement.

For HNTB's TranStadia, the multipurpose football to baseball stadium, the script calls for a shot that starts in the inside of the football stadium, according to figure 36.36. The shot slowly rises and circles while the voice-over describes the football stadium and its amenities (see fig. 36.37). After that, the camera careens out of the bowl between the light standards and the rising scoreboard (see fig. 36.38), and finally stops with an aerial view (see fig. 36.39) as a point to show the conversion from a 70,000 football stadium to a 45,000 baseball park (see fig. 36.40).

FIGURE 36.36

TranStadia in football configuration, frame 0000 (courtesy HNTB Sports Architecture).

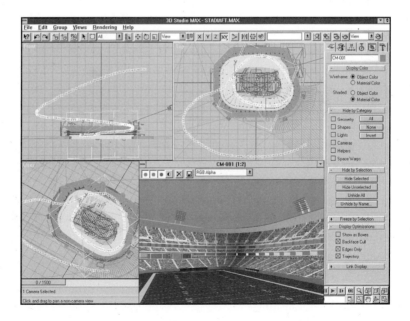

FIGURE 36.37
TranStadia in football configuration, frame 0400 (courtesy HNTB Sports Architecture).

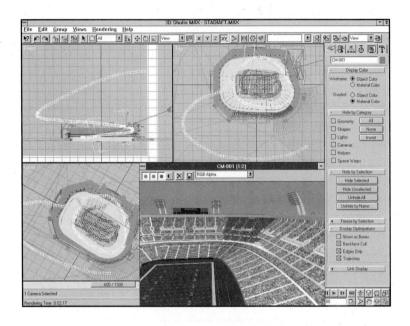

FIGURE 36.38
TranStadia in football configuration, frame 0880 (courtesy HNTB Sports Architecture).

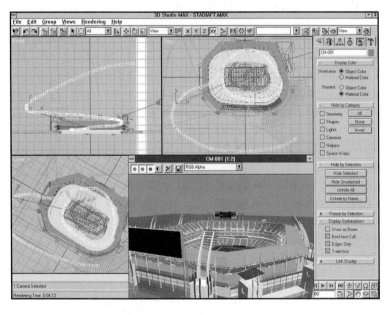

FIGURE 36.39
TranStadia in football configuration, frame 1500 (courtesy HNTB Sports Architecture).

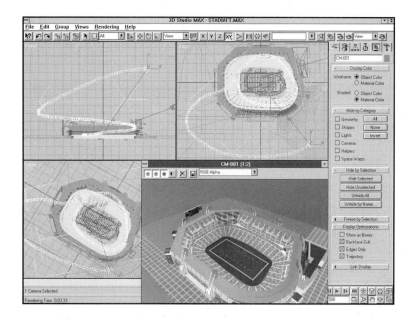

FIGURE 36.40
TranStadia converted to baseball configuration, frame 1800 (courtesy HNTB Sports Architecture.).

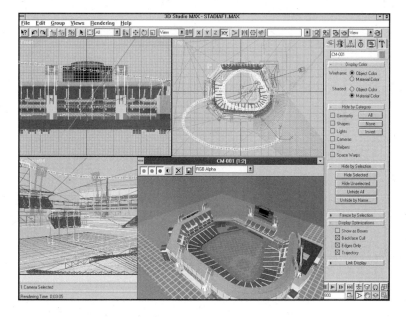

The camera position was placed in certain locations in the stadium and then moved around with the Animate button on from frames 0000–1500 at regular intervals of 100 frames. The camera target was also moved at regular intervals of 100 frames to correspond to the camera position while the camera was still inside the stadium bowl, but was not moved after frame 800 at midfield. This is where the target position remained stationary while the camera continued its flight toward the exterior and finally to the fixed aerial position at frame 1500.

3D Studio MAX creates the path or trajectory of the movement of the camera position and target into a smooth curve between the keyframe positions using the default Bézier Position controller. It does this by interpolating between keyframe positions using the default Bézier Position controller, which allows for a smooth gliding path of the moving camera. Editing the changes to the path are possible using the Track View and adjusting various controllers.

TIP

Refer to the *3D Studio MAX User's Guide* for more general uses of Track Info. For more in-depth information, see *Inside 3D Studio MAX Volume I*, Chapter 23, "Animation Control Tools" and Chapter 24, "Using Controllers and Expressions." Both are published by New Riders Publishing.

Moving from an Interior View to an Exterior Fly-By—Oakland Coliseum Arena

The TranStadia stadium was more of an exterior 3D model, because the inside seating is still visible viewed from the air. As mentioned earlier, it might be a good idea to create an exterior model of a building, then create a separate interior model showing more of the interior features. It is possible to have a single model for all the exterior and interior features. The time spent in selecting and hiding various objects for the various camera views, in addition to the cost in rendering time, however, could make using a single model more difficult than using several models.

For the Oakland Coliseum Arena, the ending animation script called for the camera to fly around the inside of the arena, showing the seating, suites, basketball floor, and scoreboard. The camera dollys back quickly toward the upper deck, crashing through the exterior curtain wall, and continues to fly backward and rises up, away from the building (see fig. 36.41 for storyboard).

FIGURE 36.41

Storyboard sketch of final sequence, Oakland Coliseum Arena (courtesy HNTB Technology Group).

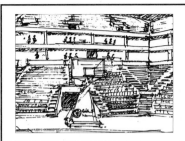

MODEL POV MOVES UP FROM COURT SHOWING A BAR AREA ON SUITE LEVEL AND ROTATES TO SHOW COURT

And to top off your arena experience, a bar area at the end of the court serves Club Members, Suite Patrons, other select guests, and offers a spectacular view of the action below.

CONTINUE MOVE AROUND INTERIOR ARENA BLENDING IN A (B/W) SHOT OF PAST PLAYER WITH MATCHING COLOR SHOT OF CURRENT PLAYER

...Building on strong traditions, it's clear that the NEW Oakland Arena will reward you with a totally new atmosphere for a totally awesome experience.

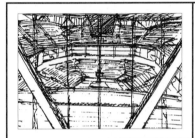

CONTINUE SHOT - POV MOVES BACKWARD THROUGH ARENA WINDOWS SHOWING EXTERIOR

For tickets or more information about Club seats, Club membership, or Suites for the '97-'98 season...

PHONE NUMBER ON SCREEN - POV SPIRALS UP SHOWING EXTERIOR

...call: XXX-XXX-XXXX...and take the first step toward enjoying exciting Golden State Warriors basketball, in style.

This animation sequence began by creating the camera movement for the entire animation sequence, using the interior model as the starting point of the camera path, then copying the camera and its target to the exterior model by using the Merge command. After determining the transition point from the interior view prior to crashing through the windows toward the exterior (approximately frames 428–450), a cross-fade effect is created using frames 428–450 from the interior camera. The cross-fade effect was created after it was merged with frames 428–450 of the exterior camera. The Cross-Fade feature in the Perception Video Recorder was used to create a cross-fade transition (see fig. 36.42). Note that other video-editing programs such as Adobe Premiere, Insync Speed Razor, or the Media 100 have features to create other types of transitions.

FIGURE 36.42

Perception Video Recorder with the cross-fade effects.

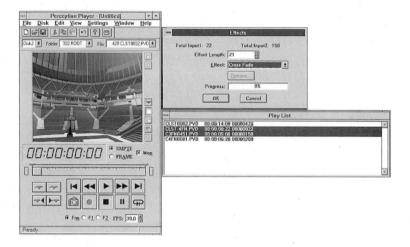

Figure 36.43 shows a view of the interior, prior to the camera swooning toward the upper deck via the exterior curtain wall. Figure 36.44 is the image created from the cross-fade effects, while the interior view fades out over 22 frames The exterior view has a fade-in effect. Figure 36.45 shows the image after the camera has flown past the glass and headed outward and upward. Video footage provided by the Golden State Warriors was added for the closing of this animation and the video. The resulting animation shows a smooth transition in which final viewing appeared to the viewer as one single animation from the inside to the outside.

FIGURE 36.43

Interior view of Oakland Coliseum Arena (courtesy HNTB Sports Architecture).

FIGURE 36.44
View created using the Cross-Fade effects for transitioning from interior to exterior (courtesy HNTB Sports Architecture).

FIGURE 36.45
Exterior view of Oakland Coliseum Arena, merged with video footage (courtesy HNTB Sports Architecture, HNTB Technology Group).

In Practice: Architectural Rendering: Exterior Drive-Throughs and Fly-Bys

- **3D Exterior Models.** Creating successful exterior computer architectural and engineering models depends on your skill in 3D design and the particular CAD system you operate in conjunction with 3D Studio MAX. Remember that the amount of detail necessary for viewing the model as a high-resolution still image varies from viewing the model as part of an animation. Animation is the end product to create the image of realism, but this chapter has shown that without realistic models, the animation is ineffective.

- **Use of Materials for Realism.** Material selection and lighting effects are the keys to making the object materials look real. Use of bitmaps from existing libraries of material images, and the mastery of knowing how to create custom materials is the key in creating a realistic appearance of your design. Understand the different properties of architectural materials (glass, stone, steel) to create "realistic" looking materials.

- **3D MAX Camera Use for Still Images.** Camera usage correctly finalizes the "real" image. Understand the use of the camera controls to achieve photorealism versus creating a snapshot. Perspective matching of an existing background photo to a 3D model needs to convey a "real" building at the proposed site.

- **Understanding the Moving "Motion" Camera.** Architectural animation of walk-throughs, drive-throughs, and fly-bys means the use of the 3DS MAX camera moving through the design over time.

- **Use of Naming Objects to Allow for Wildcard Selection.** Name the objects in a manner to allow for fast selection to select and either hide or not hide objects. With literally hundreds of objects within an architectural 3D model, an organized naming convention will be a time-saver.

- **Developing a Storyboard.** In creating animation, remember to use storyboarding while thinking about what the drive-through and fly-by animation looks like. A quick sketch of your vision of the animation is necessary for preliminary animation studies. Some of my storyboard sketches will consist of one sketch of a plan, with scribbled lines showing the camera and target positions over a time segment. For an animation set to video for a public presentation, the sketches need to be coordinated with the script. Remember that the animation you create must effectively tell a story.

- **Creating Drive-Throughs and Fly-Bys.** With the moving motion camera, understand the methods of using the cameras to generate drive-throughs and fly-bys. Use the free camera for following a specific path such as a drive-through. Use the target camera when the animation calls for a moving camera that changes its view or target, such as in filming a fly-around.

Index

If you need 3D Models Then... You Need VIEWPOINT

With enough time, you can probably create any 3D computer model imaginable...a sport utility vehicle, a pelican, even the Statue of Liberty.

But we think you can make better use of your time. Instead of creating models that already exist, get them instantly from Viewpoint. Put the world's largest and fastest growing archive of 3D models for animation and visualization to work for you. Convenient access and flexible licensing options make it easy for you to get exactly the models you need, when you need them.

Order your Viewpoint catalog and DataShop CD-ROM today, and give your 3D projects a jumpstart.

VIEWPOINT
D A T A L A B S

Call today, and learn how easy it is to get the finest 3D models available.

Toll Free	▼	1.800.DATASET
Telephone	▼	1.801.229.3000
Fax	▼	1.801.229.3300

www.viewpoint.com

Inside 3D Studio MAX Volume I

ISBN: 1-56205-427-9, $59.99 USA/$84.95 CAN, CD
by Steven Elliott and Phillip Miller
Accomplished-Expert

The definitive resource for 3D Studio MAX users! This industry favorite will take you beyond the documentation to explain professional concepts, behind-the-scenes information, and advanced techniques that will enable you to master this powerful program. A must-have for your 3D Studio MAX library!

Available Now

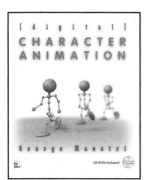

Digital Character Animation

ISBN: 1-56205-559-3, $55.00 USA/$77.95 CAN, CD
by George Maestri
All User Levels

Add the spark of life to your computer-generated animations! Animation expert George Maestri provides you with all the essential information needed to create convincing CG characters in 2D and 3D. The full color presentation and step-by-step tutorials make this nonsoftware-specific book a must for every animator library.

Available Now

Inside Adobe Photoshop 4

ISBN: 1-56205-681-6, $44.99 USA/$63.95 CAN, CD
by Gary David Bouton, Barbara Mancuso Bouton, Gary Kubicek
Intermediate-Expert

You can master the power of the world's most popular computer graphics program. Easy-to-follow tutorials, in Gary's famous style, teach you the full spectrum of Photoshop's powerful capabilities. The most comprehensive book available on Photoshop 4!

Available Now

Inside AutoCAD 14

ISBN: 1-56205-755-3, $49.99 USA/70.95 CAN, CD
by Dave Pitzer, Michael Beall, Bill Burchard, et al.
Accomplished

Completely redesigned and rewritten for today's AutoCAD user, this best-selling guide takes you to the next level—beyond the documentation. This book is packed with practical tutorials, hundreds of tips and techniques, and advice from leading AutoCAD experts.

Available Now

MACMILLAN COMPUTER PUBLISHING USA

A VIACOM COMPANY

Technical ---- Support:

If you cannot get the CD/Disk to install properly, or you need
assistance with a particular situation in the book, please feel
free to check out the Knowledge Base on our Web site at
http://www.superlibrary.com/general/support. We have
answers to our most Frequently Asked Questions listed there.
If you do not find your specific question answered, please
contact Macmillan Technical Support at **(317) 581-3833**.
We can also be reached by email at **support@mcp.com**.